# Encyclopedia
# of Sociology

# Encyclopedia of Sociology

## VOLUME 1

**Edgar F. Borgatta**
*Editor-in-Chief*
University of Washington, Seattle

**Marie L. Borgatta**
*Managing Editor*
University of Washington, Seattle

**MACMILLAN PUBLISHING COMPANY**
New York

**MAXWELL MACMILLAN CANADA**
Toronto

**MAXWELL MACMILLAN INTERNATIONAL**
New York · Oxford · Singapore · Sydney

Macmillan Publishing Company
866 Third Avenue, New York, NY 10022

Maxwell Macmillan Canada, Inc.
1200 Eglinton Avenue East, Suite 200
Don Mills, Ontario M3C 3N1

Printed in the United States of America

Library of Congress Catalog Card No.: 91-37827

printing number
3  4  5  6  7  8  9  10

Macmillan, Inc., is part of the Maxwell Communication
Group of Companies.

**Library of Congress Catalog in Publication Data**
Encyclopedia of sociology / Edgar F. Borgatta, editor-in-chief, Marie
  L. Borgatta, managing editor.
      p.      cm.
    Includes bibliographical references and index.
    ISBN 0-02-897051-9 (set).—ISBN 0-02-897052-7 (v. 1) : $90.00
    1. Sociology—Encyclopedias.      I. Borgatta, Marie L.
  HM17.E5   1991
  301'.03—dc20                                              91-37827
                                                                CIP

**EDITORIAL AND PRODUCTION STAFF**

Philip Friedman, *Publisher*

Elly Dickason, *Editor in Chief*

Martha Goldstein, *Senior Project Editor*

Lynn Constantinou, *Production Manager*

Karin K. Vanderveer, *Assistant Editor*

  The paper used in this publication meets the minimum requirements
of American National Standard for Information Sciences—Permanence of
Paper for Printed Library Materials. ANSI Z39.48–1984.

# Contents

# Preface

The idea for this *Encyclopedia of Sociology* was in gestation for a long time. Probably the notion arose when, as Sociology Advisory Editor for Rand McNally and Company, I arranged for a series of handbooks that were published in the 1960s and 1970s. This influential group of volumes covered most of sociology, especially with the *Handbook of Modern Sociology* (Robert E. L. Faris, 1964) as a key volume. Other titles in the list included: *Handbook of Marriage and the Family* (Harold T. Christensen, 1964); *Handbook of Organizations* (James G. March, 1965); *Handbook of Socialization Theory and Research* (David A. Goslin, 1968); *Handbook of Personality Theory and Research* (Edgar F. Borgatta & William W. Lambert, 1968); *Handbook on the Study of Social Problems* (Erwin O. Smigel, 1971); and *Handbook of Criminology* (Daniel Glaser, 1974). Effectively, the series functioned as an encyclopedia, especially since there was additional related coverage already provided by the *Handbook of Social Psychology* (Gardner Lindzey and Elliot Aronson, 1968). At that time Macmillan's *International Encyclopedia of the Social Sciences* (David L. Sills, ed., 1968) was also available, and a separate encyclopedia for sociology seemed superfluous.

With time, however, as social-science research and professional involvement grew, along with the proliferation of subfields, each of the social and behavioral sciences and, indeed, other specialties, such as statistics, area studies, and applied areas, developed useful encyclopedias. In the late 1970s I talked about an encyclopedia of sociology with F. E. (Ted) Peacock (F. E. Peacock Publishers, Inc.), who encouraged the development of the project. However, since it takes time for these things, it was not until the early 1980s that I actually started reflecting actively on what would need to be done, and I sought advice on what actually would be involved in such a project. Fortunately, Raymond J. Corsini, a good friend with whom I had worked on other matters, invited me to be an Associate Editor for the *Encyclopedia of Psychology* (Corsini, 1984). I got a close look at what was involved in undertaking a project of this magnitude and I was persuaded that the task would be a feasible one for sociology.

The field of sociology had been growing and evolving rapidly in the post–World War II period. Possibly the decades of the 1960s and 1970s will be seen in retrospect as one of the periods of great change for the discipline. Of course, different people will judge past developments differently, but some of the changes that have to be recognized as important include the following:

*First.* Sociology, which August Comte had blessed with the title of the "Queen of the Social Sciences," seemed to be losing much of the empire. In particular, applied fields dealing with social behavior blossomed, but as they did so, sociology seemed indifferent, uninvolved. The field of social work developed its advanced degree programs and established research interests that sociology relinquished as uninteresting because they were "applied." The field of industrial sociology virtually disappeared as the interest in research flourished in several specialties in psychology and in schools of business and management. Interest in the key institution, the family, was largely lost to the special applied organizations in that area. And so it went in a number of other fields. The "Queen" appeared indifferent, possibly with the exception of the field of medical sociology, in which there was considerable development.

*Second.* Technical training in sociology became increasingly more demanding. When I taught the first graduate course in statistics for sociology at the New York University Graduate School in 1954, it included regression analysis and factor analysis. The reception and reputation was a bit like that greeting the arrival of extraterrestrials. The title (or epithet) "Factor Analyst" was definitely not meant to be complimentary. Nevertheless, in the 1950s, the Social Science Research Council (SSRC) and others supported the idea that the formal theory and technical bases of the social sciences required attention, and programs were initiated to foster a greater appreciation of mathematics and statistics. Particularly with the support of the National Institutes of Mental Health (NIMH) graduate training grants, the University of Wisconsin, the University of Michigan, and other centers concentrated on "research methods" during and following the 1960s. The discipline reflected this focus in its journals. Sociology also became known as the leader in research training in the social sciences, with the new generation of scholars becoming conversant with statisticians, econometricians, and psychometricians, and providing service to history, political science, and anthropology. The "Queen" again had some empire.

*Third.* The 1960s experienced the civil-rights movement, the student movement, the feminist movement, and, implicitly or explicitly, sociologists reacted to and sometimes participated actively in these social movements. Challenges arose to the "traditional" values of objective and "value free" science in sociology. These challenges ranged from positions asserting knowledge by intuition to the posing of more serious epistemological questions. Attention was drawn to the fact that sociology apparently had little utility in solving social problems, aside from assisting in exposing them, but, further, sociologists were often accused of not studying complex problems because they were limited and hampered by their methodologies. A resurgence of interest in "qualitative" approaches developed, which also provided a stimulus for a reexamination of existing research approaches.

*Fourth.* At the same time, the scope of what sociologists could accomplish more generally expanded with technical development. Two of the more prohibitive cost factors in research and scholarship have progressively been reduced, since the development of computing packages made possible the elimination of computing clerks at the same time that it made possible complex numerical and statistical analyses. Additionally, this development eliminated time losses as the labor intensive aspects were eliminated. Also, the availability of word processing packages made it possible for even the most helpless scholar to by-pass the secretary or typing pool and get materials into a readable and revisable format. As these earlier "barriers" to productivity were removed, presumably the social sciences responded accordingly. In any event, there has been a proliferation of journals, and increasing collateral publication continues in various media.

*Fifth.* The continued development of the field of sociology can be marked by the increase of special subfields. Aside from the increases in publication, the number of specialization sections in the American Sociological Association (ASA) continues to grow, as do the Research Committees in the International Sociological Association (ISA). A reflection of this may be seen by glancing at the topical coverage of *Contemporary Sociology*, the ASA journal of book reviews.

This broadening of the field of sociology affected the way topics were chosen for the *Encyclopedia of Sociology*. In the early stages, a broad set of topics was used to accumulate the important concepts and subfields included in sociology. Initially, the objective was to be as inclusive as possible and to avoid errors of omission. A constant problem in the process was that topics did not fit neatly into only one broad category. Often they could fit as easily into two, three, or four. In fact, the number of broad categories became increasingly elastic, but eventually these were reduced to seventeen, corresponding to no known system of organization other than expedience. The broad categories did not have any obvious theoretical basis of division, which was disconcerting, but represented the pragmatic result of many revisions. Our

Advisory and Associate Editors participated in reviews of the total set of categories or of selected subsets for a few of the broad categories. It is fair to report that while we often saw consensus in the process, sometimes we felt that there was no effective way to manage the procedure for selection of topics or to satisfy every piece of advice, sound as it might seem. At one point we had more than 1,700 potential entry titles. These eventually were consolidated into about 400 titles with notations of how overlapping concepts were handled, how related concepts were to be combined, and so forth. In making the arrangements with authors, further consolidation brought the final number of entries to the 370 in this 4-volume set.

The process of defining topics, thus, while driven by theoretical interests and strategic representations of the field, ultimately resulted in a pragmatic and eclectic product. Thus some topics became very comprehensive while others have more specific content. In areas where there is intensive attention by sociologists, such as social stratification, race and ethnic studies, gender, medical sociology, and aging, coverage by authors may overlap in a way that provides emphasis.

Other factors that guided the formulation of entry topics included defining the audience for whom the encyclopedia was intended. It was expected that sociologists would read about areas with which they were not familiar, but we wanted the materials to be useful to other scholars and professionals who need information about topics in sociology. Further, encyclopedias are gold mines for students, and so a central concern was that articles could be read and understood by younger and uninitiated persons looking for a first introduction to a sociological topic. This latter message was communicated to authors, and in large part it has been possible to provide presentations that will reach a broad range of literate audiences. There are some obvious exceptions. In some technical areas the presentations, while self-contained and elegantly presented, do require a preexisting knowledge base in order to be fully understood by the readers.

*October 1991*

EDGAR F. BORGATTA
*Editor-in-Chief*

## REFERENCES

Borgatta, Edgar F., and William W. Lambert 1968 (eds.) *Handbook of Personality Theory and Research.* Chicago: Rand McNally and Company.

Christensen, Harold T. 1964 (ed.) *Handbook of Marriage and the Family.* Chicago: Rand McNally and Company.

Corsini, Raymond J. 1984 (ed.) *Encyclopedia of Psychology.* New York: John Wiley & Company.

Faris, Robert E. L. 1964 (ed.) *Handbook of Modern Sociology.* Chicago: Rand McNally and Company.

Glaser, Daniel 1974 (ed.) *Handbook of Criminology.* Chicago: Rand McNally and Company.

Goslin, David A. 1968 (ed.) *Handbook of Socialization Theory and Research.* Chicago: Rand McNally and Company.

Lindzey, Gardner, and Elliot Aronson 1968 (eds.) *Handbook of Social Psychology,* 2nd ed. Boston: Addison-Wesley Publishing Company.

March, James G. 1965 (ed.) *Handbook of Organizations.* Chicago: Rand McNally and Company.

Sills, David L. 1968 (ed.) *International Encyclopedia of the Social Sciences.* New York: Macmillan Company and Free Press.

Smigel, Erwin O. 1971 (ed.) *Handbook on the Study of Social Problems.* Chicago: Rand McNally and Company.

# Acknowledgments

The process of inviting scholars involved many phone calls and letters, and we depended on our Advisory and Associate Editors in the selection of authors. We needed not only to locate experts but also contributors who would be dependable and willing to make themselves available for the several years of the project. Our debt and gratitude to our Advisory and Associate Editors cannot be emphasized enough. It is to them that we owe the fact that there were so few refusals. Virtually all who accepted the invitation to participate not only did so graciously but actually delivered their manuscripts within a reasonable time frame. Obviously, we are also grateful to the authors of the articles, who are truly those responsible for writing this Encyclopedia.

Finally, the Macmillan Publishing Company, particularly in the persons of Publisher Philip Friedman, Editor in Chief Elly Dickason, and Senior Project Editor Martha Goldstein, was helpful in every way possible, including the provision of extraordinary copy editors and proofreaders, whose work has been much appreciated by the authors. The division of work between Ed and Marie was reasonably as described by their titles: As usual, Ed was the big chief, did the talking, persuading, stomping, and stalling; Marie kept the work progressing, handled the problems, did all the worrying, and effectively brought the task to completion.

# List of Articles

# List of Authors

**Alan C. Acock**
*Department of Human Development
and Family Science*
*Oregon State University*
STATISTICAL INFERENCE

**Patricia A. Adler**
*Department of Sociology*
*University of Colorado*
COUNTERCULTURES

**Peter Adler**
*Department of Sociology*
*University of Denver*
COUNTERCULTURES

**Ronald L. Akers**
*Department of Sociology*
*University of Florida, Gainesville*
ALCOHOL

**Richard D. Alba**
*Department of Sociology*
*SUNY/Albany*
ETHNICITY

**Martin Albrow**
*Department of Sociology and Social
Administration*
*Roehampton Institute*
*Froebel Institute College, London*
BRITISH SOCIOLOGY

**Howard E. Aldrich**
*Department of Sociology*
*University of North Carolina*
COMPLEX
ORGANIZATIONS

**Walter R. Allen**
*Department of Sociology*
*University of California, Los Angeles*
AFRICAN STUDIES

**Paul D. Allison**
*Department of Sociology*
*University of Pennsylvania*
EVENT HISTORY ANALYSIS

**Gunnar Almgren**
*NORC and The University of Chicago*
COMMUNITY
DEMOGRAPHIC
TRANSITION

**Rodolfo Alvarez**
*Department of Sociology*
*University of California, Los Angeles*
ORGANIZATIONAL
STRUCTURE

**Duane F. Alwin**
*Department of Sociology*
*University of Michigan*
EQUITY THEORY
FACTOR ANALYSIS

**Paolo Ammassari**
*Facoltà di Scienze Politiche*
*Università di Roma "La Sapienza"*
EPISTEMOLOGY

**Ronald E. Anderson**
*Department of Sociology*
*University of Minnesota*
COMPUTER APPLICATIONS
TO SOCIAL RESEARCH

**Robert J. Antonio**
*Department of Sociology*
*University of Kansas*
MATERIALISM

**Sharon K. Araji**
*Department of Sociology*
*University of Alaska, Anchorage*
SEXUAL VIOLENCE AND
ABUSE

**J. Michael Armer**
*Department of Sociology*
*Florida State University*
EDUCATION AND
MOBILITY
MODERNIZATION THEORY

**David J. Armor**
*Rutgers University, and*
*Former Acting Assistant Secretary of*
*Defense for Force Management*
*and Personnel*
*Washington, D.C.*
MILITARY SOCIOLOGY

**Cathleen Armstead**
*School of Social Science*
*University of California, Irvine*
PARTICIPATORY RESEARCH

**Carol Austin**
*College of Social Work*
*Ohio State University*
SOCIAL WORK

**Ginna M. Babcock**
*Department of Sociology*
*Washington State University*
FAMILY POLICY IN
WESTERN SOCIETIES

**Kenneth D. Bailey**
*Department of Sociology*
*University of California, Los Angeles*
TYPOLOGIES

**Paul Morgan Baker**
*Department of Sociology*
*University of Victoria, Canada*
LEADERSHIP

**S. J. Ball-Rokeach**
*The Annenberg School for*
*Communication*
VALUE THEORY AND
RESEARCH

**Robert D. Benford**
*Department of Sociology*
*University of Nebraska*
SOCIAL MOVEMENTS

**Neil G. Bennett**
*Department of Sociology*
*Yale University*
DEMOGRAPHIC METHODS

**Felix M. Berardo**
*Department of Sociology*
*University of Florida, Gainesville*
LOVE
WIDOWHOOD

**Ivar Berg**
*School of Arts and Sciences*
*University of Pennsylvania*
INDUSTRIAL SOCIOLOGY

**Richard A. Berk**
*Department of Sociology*
*University of California, Los Angeles*
TIME SERIES ANALYSIS

**Lakshmi K. Bharadwaj**
*Department of Sociology*
*University of Wisconsin*
HUMAN ECOLOGY AND
THE ENVIRONMENT

**Bruce J. Biddle**
*Center for Research in Social*
*Behavior*
*University of Missouri*
ROLE THEORY

**Dwight B. Billings**
*Department of Sociology*
*University of Kentucky*
CRITICAL THEORY

**Albert W. Black, Jr.**
*Afro-American Studies*
*University of Washington*
APARTHEID
SEGREGATION AND
DESEGREGATION

**Hubert M. Blalock, Jr.**
*Department of Sociology*
*University of Washington*
CAUSAL INFERENCE
MODELS

**Fred L. Block**
*Department of Sociology*
*University of California, Davis*
ECONOMIC INSTITUTIONS

**Robert Boguslaw**
*Department of Sociology*
*Washington University, St. Louis*
LIBERALISM/
CONSERVATISM
SYSTEMS THEORY
UTOPIAN ANALYSIS AND
DESIGN

**George W. Bohrnstedt**
*American Institutes for Research*
REALIABILITY
VALIDITY

**Edna Bonacich**
*Department of Sociology*
*University of California, Riverside*
CLASS AND RACE

**Edgar F. Borgatta**
*Department of Sociology*
*University of Washington*
DESCRIPTIVE STATISTICS
MEASUREMENT
SOCIOLOGICAL
ORGANIZATIONS

**Jomills H. Braddock II**
*Center for Research on Effective*
*Schooling for Disadvantaged*
*Students*
*The Johns Hopkins University*
EQUALITY OF
OPPORTUNITY

**Augustine Brannigan**
*Department of Sociology*
*University of Calgary*
LEGISLATION OF
MORALITY
POSTMODERNISM

**George S. Bridges**
*Department of Sociology*
*University of Washington*
DEVIANCE THEORIES

**David Britt**
*Department of Sociology*
*Wayne State University*
APPLIED SOCIOLOGY

**Sarajane Brittis**
*Department of Sociology*
*Case Western Reserve University*
NURSING HOMES

**Kris Bulcroft**
*Department of Sociology*
*Western Washington University*
MATE SELECTION
THEORIES

**Richard A. Bulcroft**
*Department of Sociology*
*Western Washington University*
ANALYSIS OF VARIANCE
AND COVARIANCE
GENERAL LINEAR MODEL

**Peter J. Burke**
*Department of Sociology*
*Washington State University*
FEMININITY/
MASCULINITY

**Craig Calhoun**
*Department of Sociology*
*University of North Carolina*
SOCIAL CHANGE

**Richard T. Campbell**
*Department of Sociology*
*University of Illinois at Chicago*
LONGITUDINAL
RESEARCH

**Francesca M. Cancian**
*School of Social Science*
*University of California, Irvine*
PARTICIPATORY RESEARCH

**Theodore Caplow**
*Commonwealth Professor of Sociology*
*University of Virginia*
COALITIONS

**Philippe Cibois**
*Groupe Méthodologie Sociologique,*
*Paris*
FRENCH SOCIOLOGY

**Lee Clarke**
*Department of Sociology*
*Rutgers University*
TECHNOLOGICAL RISKS
AND SOCIETY

**Bernard P. Cohen**
*Department of Sociology*
*Stanford University*
PARADIGMS AND MODELS

**James S. Coleman**
*Department of Sociology*
*University of Chicago*
RATIONAL CHOICE
THEORY

**Randall Collins**
*Department of Sociology*
*University of California, Riverside*
CONFLICT THEORY

**Carol Conell**
*Department of Sociology*
*Stanford University*
LEGITIMACY

**Karen S. Cook**
*Department of Sociology*
*University of Washington*
EXCHANGE THEORY

**William A. Corsaro**
*Department of Sociology*
*Indiana University*
CROSS-CULTURAL
ANALYSIS

**Raymond J. Corsini, PhD**
*Honolulu, Hawaii*
PERSONALITY THEORIES

**Herbert L. Costner**
*Department of Sociology*
*University of Washington*
CORRELATION AND
REGRESSION ANALYSIS
MEASURES OF
ASSOCIATION

**Richard M. Coughlin**
*Department of Sociology*
*University of New Mexico*
CONVERGENCE THEORIES

**Andrew L. Creighton**
*Department of Sociology*
*University of Washington*
DEMOCRACY
ORGANIZATIONAL
EFFECTIVENESS

**Eileen M. Crimmins**
*Andrus Gerontology Center*
*University of Southern California,*
*Los Angeles*
LIFE EXPECTANCY

**Robert Crutchfield**
*Department of Sociology*
*University of Washington*
ANOMIE AND
ALIENATION

**Solomon Davis**
*Department of Sociology*
*Hampton University*
MEDICAL–INDUSTRIAL
COMPLEX

**William D'Antonio**
*American Sociological Association*
*Washington, D.C.*
AMERICAN
SOCIOLOGICAL
ASSOCIATION
VOLUNTARY
ASSOCIATIONS

**Kay Deaux**
*Department of Personality and Social*
*Psychology*
*CUNY Graduate Center*
SEX DIFFERENCES

**John D. DeLamater**
*Department of Sociology*
*University of Wisconsin*
ATTITUDES

**Linda Derksen**
*Department of Sociology*
*University of Alberta*
SCIENTIFIC
EXPLANATION

**William DiFazio**
*Department of Sociology*
*St. John's University*
ECONOMIC DETERMINISM

**Don A. Dillman**
*Director, Social and Economic*
*Sciences Research Center*
*Washington State University*
INFORMATION SOCIETY

**Joseph E. DiSanto**
*Department of Sociology*
*University of Calgary*
ENVIRONMENTAL IMPACT
ASSESSMENT

**Kevin Dougherty**
*Department of Sociology*
*Manhattan College*
EDUCATIONAL
ORGANIZATION

**Nancy E. Durbin**
*Battelle Institute, Seattle*
COMPARABLE WORTH
ORGANIZATIONAL
EFFECTIVENESS

**Alex Durig**
*Department of Sociology*
*Indiana University*
QUALITATIVE MODELS

**Glen H. Elder, Jr.**
*Carolina Population Center*
*University of North Carolina*
LIFE COURSE

**Hyman A. Enzer**
*Professor Emeritus, Department*
*of Sociology*
*Hofstra University*
LITERATURE

**Carroll L. Estes**
*Department of Social and Behavioral*
*Sciences*
*University of California,*
*San Francisco*
HEALTH POLICY
ANALYSIS
MEDICAL–INDUSTRIAL
COMPLEX

**K. Peter Etzkorn**
*Department of Sociology*
*University of Missouri, St. Louis*
MUSIC

**Henry Etzkowitz**
*Department of Sociology*
*SUNY/Purchase*
INVENTIONS
TECHNOLOGY AND
SOCIETY

**William M. Evan**
*Department of Sociology*
*University of Pennsylvania*
LAW AND SOCIETY

**Peter B. Evans**
*Department of Sociology*
*University of California, Berkeley*
GLOBAL SYSTEMS
ANALYSIS

**Bernard Farber**
*Department of Sociology*
*Arizona State University*
KINSHIP SYSTEMS AND
FAMILY TYPES

**Yvette Farmer**
*Department of Sociology*
*University of Washington*
REFERENCE GROUP
THEORY
ROLE MODELS

**Joe R. Feagin**
*Department of Sociology*
*University of Florida, Gainesville*
AFRICAN-AMERICAN
STUDIES

**David L. Featherman**
*Social Science Research Council,*
*New York City*
SOCIAL SCIENCE
RESEARCH COUNCIL

**Richard B. Felson**
*Department of Sociology*
*SUNY/Albany*
SELF-CONCEPT

**Robert A. Fiala**
*Department of Sociology*
*University of New Mexico*
POSTINDUSTRIAL
SOCIETY

**Thomas J. Figurski**
*Institute of Gerontology*
*Wayne State University*
MORAL DEVELOPMENT

**William Form**
*Professor Emeritus, Department of*
*Sociology*
*Ohio State University*
LABOR MOVEMENTS AND
UNIONS

**Jacqueline Darroch Forrest**
*The Alan Guttmacher Institute,*
*New York City*
FAMILY PLANNING

**Martha Foschi**
*Department of Anthropology and*
*Sociology*
*University of British Columbia*
EXPECTATION STATES
THEORY

**John Fox**
*Department of Sociology*
*York University, Canada*
STATISTICAL GRAPHICS

**Howard E. Freeman**
*Department of Sociology*
*University of California, Los Angeles*
EVALUATION RESEARCH
HEALTH SERVICES
UTILIZATION

**Frank F. Furstenberg, Jr.**
*Department of Sociology*
*University of Pennsylvania*
ILLEGITIMACY

**Rosemary I. Gartner**
*Faculty of Law*
*University of Toronto*
CRIME DETERRENCE
VIOLENT CRIME

**John Gartrell**
*Department of Sociology*
*University of Alberta*
AGRICULTURAL
INNOVATION
SCIENTIFIC EXPLANATION

**David Gartrell**
*Department of Sociology*
*University of Victoria, Canada*
AGRICULTURAL
INNOVATION

**Alberto Gasparini**
*Departimento di Scienze dell'Uomo*
*Università degli Studi di Trieste*
ITALIAN SOCIOLOGY

**Viktor Gecas**
*Department of Sociology*
*Washington State University*
SOCIALIZATION

**Linda K. George**
*Department of Sociology*
*Duke University Medical Center*
SOCIAL GERONTOLOGY

**Don C. Gibbons**
*Department of Sociology*
*Portland State University*
CRIME, THEORIES OF

**Samuel L. Gilmore**
*School of Social Science*
*University of California, Irvine*
CULTURE

**Nathan Glazer**
*Graduate School of Education*
*Harvard University*
AFFIRMATIVE ACTION

**Paul C. Glick**
*Department of Sociology*
*Arizona State University*
MARRIAGE AND DIVORCE
RATES

**Leonard Gordon**
*Department of Sociology*
*Arizona State University*
PROTEST MOVEMENTS
STUDENT MOVEMENTS

**Howard P. Greenwald**
*School of Public Administration*
*University of Southern California*
ETHICS IN SOCIAL
RESEARCH

**Larry J. Griffin**
*Departments of Sociology and*
*Political Science*
*Vanderbilt University*
COMPARATIVE-
HISTORICAL ANALYSIS

**Allen D. Grimshaw**
*Department of Sociology*
*Indiana University*
SOCIOLINGUISTICS

**David B. Grusky**
*Department of Sociology*
*Stanford University*
SOCIAL STRATIFICATION

**Oscar Grusky**
*Department of Sociology*
*University of California, Los Angeles*
INTERGROUP AND
INTERORGANIZATIONAL
RELATIONS

**Jaber F. Gubrium**
*Department of Sociology*
*University of Florida, Gainesville*
FIELD RESEARCH
METHODS
QUALITATIVE METHODS

**Jeffrey K. Hadden**
*Department of Sociology*
*University of Virginia*
RELIGIOUS
FUNDAMENTALISM
RELIGIOUS MOVEMENTS

**John Hagan**
*Faculty of Law*
*University of Toronto*
JUVENILE DELINQUENCY,
THEORIES OF

**Lee J. Haggerty**
*Department of Sociology*
*Portland State University*
URBANIZATION
URBAN SOCIOLOGY

**Warren O. Hagstrom**
*Department of Sociology*
*University of Wisconsin*
SCIENCE

**Archibald O. Haller**
*Brazil Projects, Department of Rural*
*Sociology*
*University of Wisconsin*
SOCIETAL
STRATIFICATION

**Floyd M. Hammack**
*Program in Educational Sociology*
*New York University*
EDUCATIONAL
ORGANIZATION

**Janet Hankin**
*Department of Sociology*
*Wayne State University*
LIFE-STYLES AND
HEALTH
MENTAL HEALTH

**Melissa Hardy**
*Department of Sociology*
*Florida State University*
RETIREMENT

**A. Paul Hare**
*Department of Behavioral Sciences*
*Ben-Gurion University of the Negev*
GROUP PROBLEM SOLVING
GROUP SIZE EFFECTS

**Lowell L. Hargens**
*Department of Sociology*
*University of Illinois*
REPLICATION
SAMPLING PROCEDURES

**Charlene Harrington**
*Department of Social and Behavioral*
*Sciences*
*University of California,*
*San Francisco*
HEALTH-CARE
FINANCING
MEDICAL–INDUSTRIAL
COMPLEX

**Laurie Russell Hatch**
*Department of Sociology*
*University of Kentucky*
AMERICAN FAMILIES

**Marie R. Haug**
*Department of Sociology*
*Case Western Reserve University*
COMPARATIVE
HEALTH-CARE
SYSTEMS

**Lawrence E. Hazelrigg**
*Department of Sociology*
*Florida State University*
INDIVIDUALISM

**R. Alan Hedley**
*Department of Sociology*
*University of Victoria, Canada*
INDUSTRIALIZATION IN
LESS DEVELOPED
COUNTRIES
TRANSNATIONAL
CORPORATIONS

**David M. Heer**
*Population Research Laboratory*
*University of Southern California,*
*Los Angeles*
INTERNATIONAL
MIGRATION

**Karen A. Hegtvedt**
*Department of Sociology*
*Emory University*
SOCIAL COMPARISON
THEORY

**David R. Heise**
*Department of Sociology*
*Indiana University*
AFFECT CONTROL
THEORY AND
IMPRESSION
FORMATION
QUALITATIVE MODELS

**Jon Hendricks**
*Department of Sociology*
*Oregon State University*
DEPENDENCY THEORY

**John Heritage**
*Department of Sociology*
*University of California, Los Angeles*
ETHNOMETHODOLOGY

**Beth B. Hess**
*Department of Sociology*
*County College of Morris, N.J.*
INCOME DISTRIBUTION IN
THE UNITED STATES

**Charles Hirschman**
*Department of Sociology*
*University of Washington*
SOUTHEAST ASIA STUDIES

**Barbara Hirshorn**
*Institute of Gerontology*
*Wayne State University*
INTERGENERATIONAL
RESOURCE
TRANSFERS

**James A. Holstein**
*Department of Social and Cultural*
*Sciences*
*Marquette University*
FIELD RESEARCH
METHODS
QUALITATIVE METHODS

**Judith A. Howard**
*Department of Sociology*
*University of Washington*
ALTRUISM
ATTRIBUTION THEORY

**Laurence R. Iannaccone**
*Department of Economics*
*Santa Clara University*
SOCIOLOGY OF RELIGION

**Marilyn Ihinger-Tallman**
*Department of Sociology*
*Washington State University*
MARRIAGE

**James Inverarity**
*Department of Sociology*
*Western Washington University*
CRIMINAL SANCTIONS
SOCIOLOGY OF LAW

**Rita Jalali, PhD**
*Falls Church, Virginia*
CASTE AND CLASS

**David R. James**
*Department of Sociology*
*Indiana University*
SLAVERY AND
INVOLUNTARY
SERVITUDE

**Carl-Gunnar Janson**
*Department of Sociology*
*University of Stockholm*
SCANDINAVIAN
SOCIOLOGY

**Brian Michael Jenkins, PhD**
*Kroll Associates, Los Angeles*
TERRORISM

**J. Randal Johnson**
*Department of Sociology*
*University of Washington*
SOCIAL SUPPORT

**Eva Kahana**
*Department of Sociology*
*Case Western Reserve University*
NURSING HOMES

**Yoshinori Kamo**
*Department of Sociology*
*Louisiana State University*
FAMILY ROLES
MARITAL ADJUSTMENT

**Howard B. Kaplan**
*Department of Sociology*
*Texas A and M University*
SOCIAL PSYCHOLOGY

**John D. Kasarda**
*Director, Kenan Institute*
*University of North Carolina*
URBAN ECONOMIC
TRANSITIONS
URBAN UNDERCLASS

**John Katsillis**
*Department of Sociology*
*Florida State University*
EDUCATION AND
MOBILITY
MODERNIZATION THEORY

**John R. Kelly**
*Department of Sociology*
*University of Illinois*
LEISURE

**Stephen A. Kent**
*Department of Sociology*
*University of Alberta*
CULTS
HISTORICAL SOCIOLOGY

**Kyle Kercher**
*Department of Sociology*
*Case Western Reserve University*
MULTIPLE INDICATOR
MODELS
QUASI-EXPERIMENTAL
RESEARCH DESIGNS

**Jae-On Kim**
*Department of Sociology*
*University of Iowa*
TABULAR ANALYSIS

**Paul W. Kingston**
*Department of Sociology*
*University of Virginia*
SOCIOLOGY OF
EDUCATION

**Edgar Kiser**
*Department of Sociology*
*University of Washington*
WAR

**Carl B. Klockars**
*Department of Sociology*
*University of Delaware*
POLICE

**David Knoke**
Chair, Department of Sociology
University of Minnesota
POLITICAL
ORGANIZATIONS

**Igor S. Kon**
Institute of Ethnography
USSR Academy of Sciences, Moscow
SOVIET SOCIOLOGY

**Karl Kosloski**
Institute of Gerontology
Wayne State University
AGGRESSION
COGNITIVE CONSISTENCY
THEORIES
DECISION-MAKING
THEORY AND
RESEARCH
SOCIAL IMITATION

**Louis Kriesberg**
Department of Sociology
Syracuse University
PEACE

**Maria Krysan**
Department of Sociology
University of Michigan
AMERICAN
SOCIOLOGICAL
ASSOCIATION
VOLUNTARY
ASSOCIATIONS

**Manfred Kuechler**
Department of Sociology
Hunter College/CUNY
VOTING BEHAVIOR

**Leo Kuper**
Department of Sociology
University of California, Los Angeles
GENOCIDE

**Kenneth C. Land**
Chairman, Department of Sociology
Duke University
SOCIAL INDICATORS

**Mary Riege Laner**
Department of Sociology
Arizona State University
COURTSHIP

**Eric Lang**
American Institutes for Research
HAWTHORNE EFFECT
ROLE CONFLICT

**Gladys Engel Lang**
School of Communications
University of Washington
ART AND SOCIETY
MASS MEDIA RESEARCH

**Kurt Lang**
School of Communications
University of Washington
MASS MEDIA RESEARCH
PUBLIC OPINION

**Otto N. Larsen**
Department of Sociology
University of Washington
SOCIOLOGY AND
FEDERAL RESEARCH

**Barrett A. Lee**
Department of Sociology
Pennsylvania State University
HOMELESSNESS

**Gary R. Lee**
Department of Sociology
University of Florida, Gainesville
FAMILY AND HOUSEHOLD
STRUCTURE

**Robert K. Leik**
Department of Sociology
University of Minnesota
MATHEMATICAL
SOCIOLOGY

**Janet Lever**
Behavioral Science Department
The RAND Corporation
SPORTS

**Sol Levine**
*The Institute for the Improvement of*
*Medical Care & Health*
*New England Medical Center*
*Hospitals, Boston*
HEALTH STATUS
MEASUREMENT
MEDICAL SOCIOLOGY

**Robert C. Liebman**
*Department of Sociology*
*Portland State University*
REVOLUTION

**Nan Lin**
*Department of Sociology*
*Duke University*
SOCIAL RESOURCES
THEORY
STRESS

**Seymour Martin Lipset**
*Department of Sociology*
*Stanford University*
INTELLECTUALS

**Allen E. Liska**
*Department of Sociology*
*SUNY/Albany*
SOCIAL CONTROL

**William T. Liu**
*Department of Sociology*
*University of Illinois at Chicago*
ASIAN-AMERICAN
STUDIES

**Clarence Y. H. Lo**
*Department of Sociology*
*University of Missouri*
ALIENATION

**John R. Logan**
*Department of Sociology*
*SUNY/Albany*
SUBURBANIZATION

**William E. Loges**
*The Annenberg School for*
*Communication, Los Angeles*
VALUE THEORY AND
RESEARCH

**J. Scott Long**
*Department of Sociology*
*Indiana University*
STATISTICAL METHODS

**Charles F. Longino, Jr.**
*Department of Sociology*
*Wake Forest University*
INTERNAL MIGRATION

**Joseph Lopreato**
*Department of Sociology*
*University of Texas at Austin*
SOCIOBIOLOGY

**Judith Lorber**
*Department of Sociology*
*CUNY/Graduate School and*
*University Center*
GENDER

**Diane N. Lye**
*Department of Sociology*
*University of Washington*
STANDARDIZATION

**David R. Maines**
*Department of Sociology*
*Wayne State University*
LIFE HISTORIES
PRAGMATISM

**Nicolas D. Mansfield**
*Washington, D.C.*
COURT SYSTEMS OF THE
UNITED STATES

**Margaret Mooney Marini**
*Department of Sociology*
*University of Minnesota*
OCCUPATIONAL AND
CAREER MOBILITY

**Ronald W. Maris**
*Department of Sociology*
*University of South Carolina*
SUICIDE

**Kyriakos S. Markides**
*Division of Sociomedical Sciences*
*Department of Preventive Medicine*
*and Community Health*
*University of Texas Medical Branch,*
*Galveston*
QUALITY OF LIFE

**Barry Markovsky**
*Department of Sociology*
*University of Iowa*
SOCIAL PERCEPTION

**Cora B. Marrett**
*Department of Sociology*
*University of Wisconsin*
CORPORATE
ORGANIZATIONS

**Peter V. Marsden**
*Department of Sociology*
*Harvard University*
COMPLEX
ORGANIZATIONS
SOCIAL NETWORK
THEORY

**William Marsiglio**
*Department of Sociology*
*University of Florida, Gainesville*
HETEROSEXUAL
BEHAVIOR PATTERNS
SEXUAL BEHAVIOR AND
MARRIAGE

**Gerald Marwell**
*Department of Sociology*
*University of Wisconsin*
EXPERIMENTS

**Alexandra Maryanski**
*Department of Sociology*
*University of California, Riverside*
FUNCTIONALISM

**Karen Oppenheim Mason**
*East-West Population Institute,*
*Honolulu*
FAMILY AND POPULATION
POLICY IN LESS
DEVELOPED
COUNTRIES

**Douglas S. Massey**
*Department of Sociology*
*University of Chicago*
SEGREGATION INDICES

**Armand L. Mauss**
*Department of Sociology*
*Washington State University*
SOCIAL PROBLEMS

**Lisa J. McIntyre**
*Department of Sociology*
*Washington State University*
FAMILY LAW

**Susan McWilliams**
*Department of Sociology*
*University of Washington*
PERSUASION

**David Mechanic**
*Institute for Health, Health Care*
*Policy, and Aging Research*
*Rutgers University*
HEALTH AND ILLNESS
BEHAVIOR

**H. Andrew Michener**
*Department of Sociology*
*University of Wisconsin*
GAME THEORY AND
STRATEGIC
INTERACTION

**Gale E. Miller**
*Department of Social and Cultural*
*Sciences*
*Marquette University*
CASE STUDIES

**Rhonda J. V. Montgomery**
*Institute of Gerontology*
*Wayne State University*
FILIAL RESPONSIBILITY
IN-LAW RELATIONSHIPS
LONG-TERM CARE

**Patrick H. Mooney**
*Department of Sociology*
*University of Kentucky*
CAPITALISM

**Raymond A. Morrow**
*Department of Sociology*
*University of Alberta*
MARXIST SOCIOLOGY

**Jeylan T. Mortimer**
*Life Course Center*
*University of Minnesota*
ADULTHOOD

**Lise Mounier**
*Groupe Méthodologie Sociologique,*
*Paris*
FRENCH SOCIOLOGY

**Charles Mueller**
*Department of Sociology*
*University of Iowa*
WORK ORIENTATION

**Chandra Mukerji**
*Department of Communication*
*University of California, San Diego*
POPULAR CULTURE

**Ilene Nagel**
*U.S. Sentencing Commission*
*Washington, D.C.*
COURT SYSTEMS OF THE
UNITED STATES

**Saad Z. Nagi**
*Department of Sociology*
*Ohio State University*
NATIONALISM

**Keiko Nakao**
*Department of Sociology*
*University of Southern California*
OCCUPATIONAL PRESTIGE

**David G. Nickinovich**
*Department of Sociology*
*University of Washington*
BUREAUCRACY

**Steven L. Nock**
*Department of Sociology*
*University of Virginia*
DIVORCE

**Robert M. O'Brien**
*Department of Sociology*
*University of Oregon*
LEVELS OF ANALYSES

**Mary Ellen O'Connell**
*Law School*
*Indiana University*
INTERNATIONAL LAW

**Richard Ofshe**
*Department of Sociology*
*University of California, Berkeley*
COERCIVE PERSUASION
AND ATTITUDE
CHANGE

**Valerie K. Oppenheimer**
*Department of Sociology*
*University of California, Los Angeles*
LABOR FORCE

**Angela M. O'Rand**
*Department of Sociology*
*Duke University*
SOCIAL INEQUALITY

**Myron Orleans**
*Department of Sociology*
*California State University, Fullerton*
PHENOMENOLOGY

**Suzanne T. Ortega**
*Department of Sociology*
*University of Nebraska*
MENTAL ILLNESS AND
MENTAL DISORDER

**Fred C. Pampel**
*Population Program*
*University of Colorado at Boulder*
SOCIAL SECURITY
SYSTEMS

**Toby L. Parcel**
*Department of Sociology*
*Ohio State University*
SECONDARY DATA
ANALYSIS AND
DATA ARCHIVES

**Ronnelle Paulsen**
*Department of Sociology*
*The University of Texas, Austin*
CROWDS AND RIOTS

**Ronald W. Perry**
*School of Public Affairs*
*Arizona State University*
DIFFUSION THEORIES

**Thomas F. Pettigrew**
*Stevenson College*
*University of California, Santa Cruz*
DISCRIMINATION
PREJUDICE

**W. David Pierce**
*Department of Sociology*
*University of Alberta*
BEHAVIORISM

**Karl Pillemer**
*Department of Sociology*
*University of New Hampshire*
DISENGAGEMENT THEORY
INTERGENERATIONAL
RELATIONS

**Susan R Pitchford**
*Department of Sociology*
*University of Washington*
RACE

**Richard Brian Polley**
*Business Administration*
*Lewis and Clark College*
FIELD THEORY
OBSERVATION SYSTEMS

**Samuel H. Preston**
*Department of Sociology*
*University of Pennsylvania*
INFANT AND CHILD
MORTALITY

**Thomas W. Pullum**
*Department of Sociology*
*University of Texas, Austin*
POPULATION

**Enrico L. Quarantelli**
*Disaster Research Center*
*University of Delaware*
DISASTER RESEARCH

**Barbara F. Reskin**
*Department of Sociology*
*University of Illinois*
WORK AND OCCUPATIONS

**Maurice N. Richter, Jr.**
*Department of Sociology*
*SUNY/Albany*
EVOLUTION: BIOLOGICAL,
SOCIAL, CULTURAL
TECHNOLOGY AND
SOCIETY

**Cecilia L. Ridgeway**
*Department of Sociology*
*University of Iowa*
COMPLIANCE AND
CONFORMITY

**Lynn M. Ries**
*Department of Sociology*
*University of Washington*
NEW STRUCTURALISM
SOCIAL MOBILITY

**John W. Riley, Jr.**
*Chevy Chase, Maryland*
DEATH AND DYING

**Matilda White Riley**
*National Institute on Aging,*
*Bethesda*
COHORT PERSPECTIVES

**Bryan R. Roberts**
*Department of Sociology*
*University of Texas, Austin*
MEXICAN STUDIES

**Leah Robin**
*Department of Sociology*
*University of California,*
*Los Angeles*
ORGANIZATIONAL
STRUCTURE

**Richard C. Rockwell**
*Social Science Research Council,*
*New York City*
SOCIAL SCIENCE
RESEARCH COUNCIL

**Patricia A. Roos**
*Department of Sociology*
*Rutgers University*
PROFESSIONS

**Norman B. Ryder**
*Office of Population Research*
*Princeton University*
COHORT
ANALYSIS

**Steven L. Rytina**
*Department of Sociology*
*McGill University*
SOCIAL STRUCTURE

**Georges Sabagh**
*Department of Sociology*
*University of California, Los Angeles*
MIDDLE EASTERN
STUDIES

**Nancy E. Sacks**
*Department of Sociology*
*SUNY/Stony Brook*
REMARRIAGE

**Joseph Sanders**
*Law School*
*University of Houston*
LAW AND LEGAL SYSTEMS

**Masamichi Sasaki**
*Department of Social Sciences and*
*Bureau of Sociological Research*
*Hyogo Kyoiku University, Japan*
JAPANESE SOCIOLOGY

**John H. Scanzoni**
*Department of Sociology*
*University of Florida, Gainesville*
HETEROSEXUAL
BEHAVIOR PATTERNS
SEXUAL BEHAVIOR AND
MARRIAGE

**Erwin K. Scheuch**
*Institut fur Angewandte*
*Sozialforschung*
*Universitat zu Köln*
GERMAN SOCIOLOGY

**Marie-Ange Schiltz**
*Groupe Méthodologie Sociologique,*
*Paris*
FRENCH SOCIOLOGY

**Ronald J. Schoenberg**
*Aptech Systems*
*Kent, Washington*
PROBABILITY THEORY

**Howard Schuman**
*Institute for Social Research,*
*Ann Arbor*
SURVEY RESEARCH

**Pepper Schwartz**
*Department of Sociology*
*University of Washington*
SEXUALLY TRANSMITTED
DISEASES

**Karen Seccombe**
*Department of Sociology*
*University of Florida, Gainesville*
ALTERNATIVE
LIFE-STYLES

**Vimal P. Shah**
*School of Social Sciences*
*Gujarat University, India*
INDIAN SOCIOLOGY

**Constance L. Shehan**
*Department of Sociology*
*University of Florida, Gainesville*
PARENTAL ROLES

**Larry Dwight Shinn**
*Vice President for Academic Affairs*
*Bucknell University*
WORLD RELIGIONS

**James F. Short, Jr.**
*Social and Economic Sciences*
*Research Center*
*Washington State University*
CRIMINAL AND
DELINQUENT
SUBCULTURES

**Robert W. Shotola**
*Department of Sociology*
*Portland State University*
SMALL GROUPS

**Robert A. Silverman**
*Department of Sociology*
*University of Alberta*
CRIME RATES

**William Simon**
*Department of Sociology*
*University of Houston*
SEXUAL ORIENTATION

**John H. Simpson**
*Department of Sociology*
*University of Toronto*
RELIGION, POLITICS, AND
WAR

**C. Matthew Snipp**
*Department of Rural Sociology*
*University of Wisconsin*
AMERICAN INDIAN
STUDIES

**David A. Snow**
*Department of Sociology*
*University of Arizona*
CROWDS AND RIOTS

**Subhash R. Sonnad**
*Department of Sociology*
*Western Michigan University*
NONPARAMETRIC
STATISTICS

**Kenneth I. Spenner**
*Department of Sociology*
*Duke University*
PERSONALITY AND
SOCIAL STRUCTURE

**Robert E. Staples**
*Department of Sociology*
*University of California,*
*San Francisco*
INTERMARRIAGE

**Rodney Stark**
*Department of Sociology*
*University of Washington*
SOCIOLOGY OF RELIGION

**Robert A. Stebbins**
*Department of Sociology*
*University of Calgary*
DEVIANCE

**Lauri Steel**
*American Institutes for Research*
FAMILY SIZE

**Ardyth Stimson**
*Department of Sociology*
*Kean College*
INTERPERSONAL
ATTRACTION

**John Stimson**
*Department of Sociology*
*William Patterson College*
SOCIAL FORECASTING

**Philip J. Stone**
*Department of Sociology*
*Harvard University*
CONTENT ANALYSIS

**David Strang**
*Department of Sociology*
*University of Iowa*
DECOLONIZATION
IMPERIALISM AND
COLONIALISM

**Murray A. Straus**
*Director, Family Research Laboratory*
*Department of Sociology*
*University of New Hampshire*
FAMILY VIOLENCE
MEASUREMENT
INSTRUMENTS

**Robin Stryker**
*Department of Sociology*
*University of Iowa*
GOVERNMENT
REGULATION

**Sheldon Stryker**
*Department of Sociology*
*Indiana University*
IDENTITY THEORY
SYMBOLIC INTERACTION
THEORY

**Donald E. Stull**
*Department of Sociology*
*University of Akron*
HEALTH AND THE LIFE
COURSE

**J. Jill Suitor**
*Department of Sociology*
*Louisiana State University*
INTERGENERATIONAL
RELATIONS
REMARRIAGE

**Deborah A. Sullivan**
*Department of Sociology*
*Arizona State University*
BIRTH AND DEATH RATES

**Gene F. Summers**
*Department of Rural Sociology*
*University of Wisconsin*
RURAL SOCIOLOGY

**Marvin B. Sussman**
*Professor Emeritus, Department of*
*Sociology*
*University of Delaware*
INHERITANCE

**Richard Swedberg**
*Department of Sociology*
*Stockholm University, Sweden*
ECONOMIC SOCIOLOGY

**Szonja Szelényi**
*Department of Sociology*
*Stanford University*
SOCIALISM

**Jacek Szmatka**
*Institute of Sociology*
*Jageiellonian University, Poland*
POLISH SOCIOLOGY

**Karl E. Taeuber**
*Department of Sociology*
*University of Wisconsin*
CENSUS

**Azumi Ann Takata**
*Department of Sociology*
*Stanford University*
SOCIAL STRATIFICATION

**Irving Tallman**
*Department of Sociology*
*Washington State University*
FAMILY POLICY IN
WESTERN SOCIETIES

**Howard F. Taylor**
*Department of Sociology*
*Princeton University*
INTELLIGENCE

**Marylee C. Taylor**
*Department of Sociology*
*Pennsylvania State University*
DISCRIMINATION
PREJUDICE

**James E. Teele**
*Department of Sociology*
*Boston University*
CRIMINOLOGY
JUVENILE DELINQUENCY
AND JUVENILE CRIME

**Ann R. Tickamyer**
*Department of Sociology*
*University of Kentucky*
MACROSOCIOLOGY

**Marta Tienda**
*Population Research Center*
*University of Chicago*
HISPANIC-AMERICAN
STUDIES

**Jackson Toby**
*Institute for Criminological Research*
*Department of Sociology*
*The State University of New Jersey,*
  *Rutgers*
CRIMINALIZATION OF
DEVIANCE

**Judith Treas**
*Department of Sociology*
*University of California, Irvine*
SOCIAL HONOR

**Donald Treiman**
*Department of Sociology*
*University of California, Los Angeles*
STATUS ATTAINMENT

**Gaye Tuchman**
*Department of Sociology*
*University of Connecticut*
FEMINIST THEORY

**Nancy Brandon Tuma**
*Department of Sociology*
*Stanford University*
SOCIAL DYNAMICS

**Austin T. Turk**
*Department of Sociology*
*University of California, Riverside*
POLITICAL CRIME

**Herman Turk**
*Department of Sociology*
*University of Southern California*
SOCIAL ORGANIZATION

**Jonathan H. Turner**
*Department of Sociology*
*University of California, Riverside*
FUNCTIONALISM
POSITIVISM

**Ralph H. Turner**
*Department of Sociology*
*University of California, Los Angeles*
COLLECTIVE BEHAVIOR

**Maurice D. Van Arsdol, Jr.**
*Population Research Laboratory*
*University of Southern California*
CITIES

**Karl M. van Meter**
*Groupe Méthodologie*
*Sociologique, Paris*
FRENCH SOCIOLOGY

**Brenda J. Vander Mey**
*Department of Sociology*
*Clemson University*
INCEST

**Wayne J. Villemez**
*Department of Sociology*
*Louisiana State University*
POVERTY

**Carlos H. Waisman**
*Department of Sociology*
*University of California, San Diego*
LATIN AMERICAN
STUDIES

**Walter L. Wallace**
*Department of Sociology*
*Princeton University*
METATHEORY

**Marilyn E. Walsh**
*Society and Justice Program*
*University of Washington*
ORGANIZED CRIME

**Kathleen A. Warner**
*Department of Sociology*
*University of Washington*
DRAMATURGY
PERSONAL
RELATIONSHIPS

**Susan Cotts Watkins**
*Department of Sociology*
*University of Pennsylvania*
FERTILITY
DETERMINANTS

**Barbara Wauchope**
*Family Research Laboratory*
*University of New Hampshire*
MEASUREMENT
INSTRUMENTS

**Robert Philip Weber**
*Northeast Consulting Resources, Inc.,*
*Boston*
CONTENT ANALYSIS

**Frederick D. Weil**
*Department of Sociology*
*Louisiana State University*
POLITICAL PARTY
SYSTEMS

**Joseph Weis**
*Department of Sociology*
*University of Washington*
PROBATION AND PAROLE

**Jack Whalen**
*Department of Sociology*
*University of Oregon*
CONVERSATION ANALYSIS

**Donald Whyte**
*Department of Sociology and*
*Anthropology*
*Carleton University, Canada*
CANADIAN SOCIOLOGY

**Martin King Whyte**
*Department of Sociology*
*University of Michigan*
CHINA STUDIES

**Robin M. Williams, Jr.**
*Department of Sociology*
*Cornell University*
AMERICAN SOCIETY

**Charles Winick**
*Department of Sociology*
*CUNY/Graduate School and*
*University Center*
DRUG ABUSE
PORNOGRAPHY
PROSTITUTION

**Halliman H. Winsborough**
*Department of Sociology*
*University of Wisconsin*
DEMOGRAPHY

**Alan Wolfe**
*Graduate Faculty of Political and*
*Social Science*
*New School for Social Research*
HUMAN NATURE
SOCIAL PHILOSOPHY

**James R. Wood**
*Department of Sociology*
*Indiana University*
RELIGIOUS
ORGANIZATIONS

**James D. Wright**
*Department of Sociology*
*Tulane University*
PUBLIC POLICY ANALYSIS

**Robert Wuthnow**
*Department of Sociology*
*Princeton University*
RELIGIOUS ORIENTATIONS

**Peter Xenos**
*East-West Population Institute,*
*Honolulu*
FAMILY AND POPULATION
POLICY IN LESS
DEVELOPED
COUNTRIES

**Lewis Yablonsky**
*Department of Sociology*
*California State University,*
*Northridge*
WHITE-COLLAR CRIME

**Rosalie F. Young**
*Department of Community Medicine*
*School of Medicine*
*Wayne State University*
COMMUNITY HEALTH
HEALTH PROMOTION

**Elena S. H. Yu**
*Graduate School of Public Health*
*San Diego State University*
ASIAN-AMERICAN
STUDIES

**Morris Zelditch, Jr.**
*Department of Sociology*
*Stanford University*
INTERPERSONAL POWER

**Viviana Zelizer**
*Department of Sociology*
*Princeton University*
MONEY

# Encyclopedia
# of Sociology

**ABORTION**   *See* Family Planning.

**ACCULTURATION**   *See* Ethnicity.

**ADDICTION**   *See* Alcohol; Drug Abuse.

**ADOLESCENCE**   *See* Adulthood; Juvenile Delinquency and Juvenile Crime; Socialization.

**ADULTHOOD**   Becoming an adult is a life-cycle transition signified not by a single event but by a series of markers or activities designating adult status. The diversity of the more formal markers (completion of education, independent residence, economic self-sufficiency, marriage, parenthood, voting, military service, and entry into full-time work) and the variability in the ages at which they typically occur make the timing of this transition rather ambiguous (Buchmann 1989). There has been a trend in the United States and Western Europe toward earlier assumption of full adult civil rights (e.g., permission to vote or to marry without parental consent), from age twenty-one to age eighteen (Coleman and Husen 1985). However, with the extension of formal education,

youth are remaining economically dependent on their parents for longer periods of time. Adolescents are sometimes restrained from "growing up" when assuming adult-like statuses threatens adult interests and values. For example, the extension of required schooling has been seen as motivated, at least in part, by a desire to curb youth unemployment and to allay older workers' fears of job competition (Osterman 1980).

In addition to the more visible, formal markers, there are informal but nonetheless clearly recognized prerogatives of adult status (e.g., smoking, alcohol use, and sexuality) that are widely frowned upon or legally prohibited when engaged in by minors. Youth's engagement in these "problem behaviors" can represent attempts to affirm maturity or to negotiate adult status. Jessor and Jessor (1977, p. 206) view them as "transition behaviors . . . a syndrome of activities oriented toward accession to a developmentally later status." Finally, there are even more subtle indicators—differences in psychological orientation considered appropriate for preadult and adult persons. Young adults are expected to give up the dependent, playful, experimental, carefree, even reckless stances of adolescence and youth and become financially and emotionally independent, productive, hard-working, and responsible (Klein 1990). Whereas it is sometimes alleged that the timing of transition to adulthood is especially unclear in contemporary Western societies, Foner and Kertzer (1978) describe similar ambiguity in premodern contexts, where elders and the rising adult generation struggle over the timing of age-set transitions and corresponding transfers of power, wealth, and privilege.

## HISTORICAL CHANGE IN THE TRANSITION TO ADULTHOOD

Historical studies demonstrate that both the timing and the process of becoming adult are in no way universalistic or biologically determined. Through the centuries in Western societies, there has been increasing differentiation of early life stages, postponement of entry to adulthood, and changes in the status positions from which adulthood is launched (Klein 1990). In medieval times persons moved directly from infancy, when small size and limited strength precluded productive work, to adulthood, at which time younger persons worked alongside their elders (Aries 1962). A new stage of childhood, intermediate between infancy and adulthood, arose with the emergence of formal schooling. As economic production shifted from agriculture to trade and industry, persons increasingly entered adulthood after a stage of apprenticeship or "child labor." By the beginning of the twentieth century, with schooling extended and child labor curtailed, a new stage of adolescence was recognized (Hall 1904). The adolescent came to be seen as free of adult responsibilities; oriented to fun, sports, popular music, and peers; receptive to change; and ready to experiment with alternative identities and, sometimes, mood-altering substances.

With the majority of young people now obtaining some form of higher education (or entering military service) in the United States, a new stage of "youth" or "postadolescence" has emerged, extending into the twenties and characterized by limited autonomy but continued economic dependence and concern with the establishment of adult identity (Keniston 1970; Coleman and Husen 1985; Buchmann 1989). Youth's residence in dormitories or military barracks provides independence from familial monitoring, while a formal institution assumes a greater or lesser degree of control (Klein 1990). It has been suggested that societal wealth encourages postponement of adulthood and the extension of "youthful" values and life-styles to older ages. Japanese young people, traditionally oriented to the extended family, obedience, educational achievement, and hard work, are apparently becoming more rebellious and are seeking immediate enjoyment as delayed gratification becomes more difficult to sustain in an increasingly affluent society (Connor and De Vos 1989).

For those who enter the labor force after high school, there is also a continued "moratorium" period (Osterman 1989) lasting several years, in which youth hold jobs in the secondary sector of the economy and experience high unemployment and job instability. Such youth lack career orientation and instead emphasize peer relationships, travel, adventure, and short-term jobs to satisfy immediate consumption needs. At the same time, employers express preference for low-wage workers who do not require fringe benefits and are not likely to unionize. When filling adult-like "primary" jobs, such employers seek evidence of stability or "settling down." Comparative research in the United States and West Germany indicates that youth "irresponsibility" and employer reluctance to fill primary jobs with youthful recruits are not universal in modern societies. Instead, they are functions of particular institutional arrangements, specifically, the absence of clear channels of mobility from education to the industrial sector in the United States. According to Hamilton (1990), the highly developed institution of apprenticeship in West Germany effectively provides such linkage.

Whereas the onset of adulthood has been increasingly delayed through historical time, during the past century in the United States the various changes marking the transition have come to take place first in quicker, then in more lengthy, succession. Movement into adulthood (as indicated by school exit, work entry, departure from the family, marriage, and the establishment of an independent household) took place over a longer period of time in 1880 than in 1970 (Modell, Furstenberg, and Hershberg 1976). Historical census records show that while the age of departure from school and entry to the work force rose, leaving home, marriage, and the establishment of a separate household occurred at younger ages in the mid-twentieth century (a similar pattern of cohort change occurred in Norway; see Featherman and Sorensen 1983).

However, this trend toward accelerated timing of family events and more uniform passages to adulthood has reversed in recent decades, as evidenced by later marriage, delayed childbearing (Rindfuss, Morgan, and Swicegood 1988), increasing variability in the ages of first marriage and initial childbearing, increasing divorce rates, and other demographic changes (Buchmann 1989, p. 52). There is also some indication that youth are returning to their parental homes, after leaving for college or other destinations, more frequently today than in the past. Largely as a result of technological change and increasing educational requirements, the entry to adulthood has been extended, diversified, and individualized; and it has become less well defined (Buchmann 1989). Increasing diversity of the sequencing and combination of transitional life events and activities (schooling and work, parenting and women's employment) have promoted more autonomous courses of action. The greater individualization of the adult transition and early life course in recent times may have increased the potential for freedom as well as stress.

Modell's (1989) social history of the transition to adulthood in twentieth-century America finds youth increasingly taking charge of their heterosexual relationships and the formation of new families, becoming ever freer of adult surveillance and control. At the turn of the century, parents closely supervised the practices of "calling," "keeping company," "courtship," and "engagement" and retained veto power over developing relationships. With the emergence of the comprehensive high school came a new autonomous meeting ground for socializing away from parents' watchful eyes. By the 1920s, new patterns of dating, thrill-seeking, music, and dancing were fueled by technological advances (the car, telephone, motion picture) as well as by economic affluence.

Thus, each new generation's experience of transition to adulthood may be somewhat unique and depend on the particular economic, political, and social currents of the time (Mannheim 1952). Historical events and broad macroprocesses clearly influence the process of family formation, an important marker of the adult transition (Modell 1989). When the Great Depression limited material support for new families, engagement was extended. Subsequent mobilization for war, economic growth, and support for returning servicemen promoted earlier marriage. Familistic values during the baby boom were reflected in a gender-asymmetric youth dating system and in the practice of "going steady." Those who moved through adolescence in the 1950s married and became parents earlier than both earlier and later cohorts (Marini 1984a; 1987). By the mid-1960s, the feminist movement, criticism of contemporary life-styles, and weakening restrictions on sexual expression contributed to the erosion of the dating system, declining marriage rates, and growing interest on the part of young women in careers (Modell 1989). Inflation and slower economic growth at the same time lessened the availability of resources for early marriage and parenthood. By the 1970s, young people were no longer as interested in dating, and youth were negotiating their sexual relationships in an even more individualistic fashion. Cohabitation, slow movement into parenthood, and divorce became more prevalent.

It is pertinent to note the changing symbolic meanings of the institutions and experiences that structure the early life course (Modell 1989). In the 1950s, independence and the rejection of adult authority were expressed in dating, going steady, and early marriage. Disenchanted youth, alienated from school, moved directly into marriage and parenthood. But by the 1970s, youthful independence was expressed by immersion in the youth subculture. Many young people saw dating, still linked to marriage, as a conservative, even anachronistic, institution.

## THE TIMING AND SEQUENCING OF EVENTS IN THE ADULT TRANSITION

It is widely believed that age norms, specifying the timing of key life events, structure passage through the life course (Neugarten, Moore, and Lowe 1965; Neugarten and Datan 1973). Those who are "off-time" (too early or too late) are thought to be the target of negative social sanctions and to experience strain (Rossi 1980). Divergence from normative timing or sequencing sometimes generates public alarm and comes to be seen as a social problem. Thus, teenage pregnancy and childbearing mark a too early transition to adulthood, and youth unemployment signifies unacceptable delay in entering adult roles. However, the extent to which the timing of transition to adulthood is normatively driven has been questioned. Marini (1984b) notes that there is little direct evidence regarding the existence or content of social norms governing the timing of life events signifying adult status. National polls asking about the ideal age to marry and to become a parent yield age distributions that cluster around the modal ages at which these changes actually occur. Evidence that age preferences ("ideal" ages) lag behind behavioral change (Modell 1980) contradicts the notion that norms actually control timing behavior (for evidence that expectations about life-course activities follow aggregate behavioral change, see McLaughlin et al. 1988, Chapter 9).

Marini (1984b) draws a clear distinction between norms—involving a sense of "ought" or "should" and linked to sanctions for transgression—and behavioral preferences arising through socialization and observation of typical patterns. Teenage childbearing is clearly linked to school dropout, difficulties in the job market, restricted income, and marital instability (Furstenberg, Brooks-Gunn, and Morgan 1987), but these consequences may have little to do with the operation of social sanctions. Moreover, Furstenberg, Brooks-Gunn, and Morgan's (1987) study of a panel of black adolescent mothers sixteen to seventeen years after their children were born showed considerable diversity in maternal socio-economic outcomes. Marini (1984b) notes that if norms (and associated sanctions) do exist, they probably vary by population subgroup (e.g., by socioeconomic status, gender, and ethnicity) and may designate such a wide range of acceptable ages for given transitions that they lack causal significance.

Demographers have charted changes in the linkages among transition events (Hogan and Astone 1986). There is considerable variability in the United States in their sequencing; many people, for example, experience the atypical pattern of entering full-time employment before completing schooling (Marini 1984a). The sequencing and the amount of time spent in various combinations of role activities during the adult transition vary by gender, as do the socioeconomic consequences of these transitional patterns (Marini, Shin, and Raymond 1989). In a cohort of young people born in the early 1940s, males ages sixteen to twenty-nine were found to spend more time in school and in simultaneous schooling and employment (Marini 1987). Higher educational attainment predicted labor-force entry prior to finishing full-time schooling, especially for males (Marini 1984a). Males were also more likely to experience familial role changes before finishing school (Marini 1987). Primarily because of earlier marriage and parenthood, women moved through the transition to adulthood at a faster rate than males (Marini 1987, p. 24). But females who attained high levels of education were more likely to delay family roles (marriage, parenthood) until they completed school. Marini (1987, p. 28) explains these patterns as follows: "Males are more likely to continue their educations after entry into adult family roles because education contributes to fulfillment of the traditional male roles of husband and father by improving a man's ability to provide for the family financially. Education bears a less important relationship to fulfillment of the traditional roles of wife and mother."

Cross-national comparison of Britain and the United States reveals considerable differences in transitional patterns (Kerckhoff 1990). British youth (of the cohort born in 1958) leave school and enter the full-time work force earlier than their American peers but leave the parental home and marry later. They are also more likely to reenter the educational system on a part-time basis to gain credentials after leaving full-time schooling. The period of transition to adulthood is shorter in the United States, and it is also characterized by greater diversity in event sequences.

## FACTORS INFLUENCING ADULT STATUS PLACEMENT AND ADJUSTMENT

The U.S. school assigns children to grades based on age and, with some exceptions, allows movement to the next level each year. Since it is customary for the completion of education to precede other transitional events (Marini 1984b), individual educational attainment largely determines the timing and portal of entry to adult occupational positions and other roles marking entry to adulthood. Critics of contemporary high schools argue that their internal structure—the division into college preparatory, vocational, and commercial "tracks"—perpetuates inequality intergenerationally (Bowles and Gintis 1976; Rosenbaum 1976). The cognitive learning, occupational preferences, and career expectations fostered by formal schooling are most useful as preparation for white-collar and, especially, professional or managerial employment (Coleman and Husen 1985). While vocational education programs in secondary schools are designed for noncollege youth, their effectiveness may be limited given their detachment from actual employment settings (Grubb 1989).

As Hogan and Astone (1986, p. 115) remark, "the organizational structures of schools, military service, and labor markets differ across societies, producing unique institutional bases of age-grading, and societal variability in age-stratification systems." But there is considerable variation within societies in such age-grading and status allocation processes. While in the United States the timing of passage through the various institutional pathways to adulthood is to some extent legally regulated (e.g., by age criteria for compulsory

schooling, marriage, employment, military entry, etc.), such rules set only minimum standards. Moreover, there may be asynchronies in the age-grading systems of different societal institutions, and these asynchronies generate status inconsistencies (Buchmann 1989). Adult identities confirmed in some contexts may not be confirmed in others, and this situation can generate strain. It is widely believed that adolescence and youth are stressful life stages and that problems diminish with successful acquisition of adult roles (Modell, Furstenberg, and Hershberg 1976). Consistent with this supposition, men's self-perceptions of personal well-being and competence were found to decline during college and to rise during the following decade (Mortimer, Finch, and Kumka 1982).

Several factors facilitate adult socialization and adjustment (Mortimer and Simmons 1978). For example, the degree of institutionalization of the transition has implications for adaptation, as it influences recognition of the newcomer (by the self and others) as having a new status and identity, carrying with it new rights and obligations. Rituals such as marriage and graduation allow public recognition of successful passage to adulthood.

The availability of opportunities for anticipatory socialization or practice of adult roles may also affect adjustment. It is sometimes said that youth are isolated in schools, cut off from meaningful contact with adult workers (excepting their teachers), and prevented from engaging in processes of anticipatory socialization to adulthood (Panel on Youth of the President's Science Advisory Committee 1974). Many parents encourage adolescent children to work, believing that this experience will help them to become responsible and independent, to learn to handle money, and to manage their time effectively (Phillips and Sandstrom 1990). However, "youth jobs" are quite different from adult work, as they generally involve rather simple, repetitive tasks requiring little training or skills. Greenberger and Steinberg (1986), doubting the benefits of such work experience, report that employed adolescents have more cynical attitudes toward work than those who are not employed. While the full impact of employment in adolescence on the transition to adulthood is not known, there is evidence that investment in adolescent work is related to restricted educational aspirations and attainment, which would limit adult career options (Mortimer and Finch 1986). However, several studies have shown that employment during high school predicts more stable work histories and higher earnings in the years immediately following (Freeman and Wise 1979; Meyer and Wise 1982; Mortimer and Finch 1986). Stern and Nakata (1989), using data from noncollege youth in the National Longitudinal Survey of Youth, report that more complex work activity in adolescence is associated with lower incidence of unemployment and higher earnings three years after high school.

There is further evidence that the quality of adolescent work experience matters for psychological outcomes that influence adult attainment (Mortimer, et al. forthcoming). An ongoing longitudinal study of working in adolescence shows that adolescent boys who feel that they are obtaining useful skills and who perceive opportunities for advancement in their jobs increased in their sense of mastery (internal control) over a one-year period. Girls who thought that they were being paid well for their work similarly manifested increasing levels of self-efficacy over time (Finch et al. 1990).

The character and outcomes of the transition to adulthood clearly depend on diverse resources that are differentially distributed among young people. Socioeconomic differences can affect the age at which individuals acquire adult roles, the character of marking events, and even the availability of opportunities to assume adult status positions. The socioeconomic level of the family of origin sets the level of available resources that can facilitate or lessen the likelihood of a successful adult transition, fostering intergenerational continuities in attainment (Blau and Duncan 1967; Sewell and Hauser 1976). Postsecondary education and the purchase of a home may depend, at least in part, on the financial status of the family of origin. Moreover, there is growing recognition that the socioeconomic context of the family of origin may change over time and that this change could affect young people's developing aspirations and plans (Featherman and Spenner 1988). Relative advantage or disadvantage can also derive from placement in familial and other networks that provide information (Granovetter 1974; Osterman 1989), for example, about higher educational opportunities, jobs, or even prospective marital partners.

Personal resources facilitating the educational and occupational attainment process have been linked to social class background. Adolescents' educational and occupational aspirations are important mediators of the effects of occupational origins on destinations (Featherman 1980). The transmission of self-directed values may also constitute a mechanism through which socioeconomic status is perpetuated across generations. The more self-directed values of men in higher occupational positions can be attributed largely to the complexity and autonomy of their work tasks (Kohn and Schooler 1983). Importantly, self-directed values influence the qualities that parents seek to instill in their children, and parental self-directed values influence adolescent and young-adult children's own values as well (Kohn, Slomczynski, and Schoenbach 1986).

Parents of higher socioeconomic level typically engage in more supportive child-rearing behavior (Gecas 1979), which fosters the development of personality traits that are conducive to adult attainment. In a panel of highly educated youth, closer, more supportive relationships with fathers fostered a sense of competence, work involvement, and positive work values, which facilitated early adult socioeconomic attainments (Mortimer, Lorence, and Kumka 1986). Social support from parents became a less important source of these psychological traits as sons moved from late adolescence to early adulthood. (A similar pattern of diminishing effects of parents' views on daughters' political orientations has been observed; see Alwin, Cohen, and Newcomb forthcoming). Close father–son relationships in late adolescence also engender similarity in paternal occupations and sons' early adult occupational destinations (Mortimer and Kumka 1982).

Of course, parents may not provide role models of successful adult functioning, and, as a result of social learning or inadequate resources, a problematic transition to adulthood may result. If the family is an important institutional context for the acquisition of economic and other resources for the adult transition, family poverty or disintegration may be expected to have negative consequences. Experiences in youth may thus set in motion a train of events that have profound impact on the early life course. Quinton (1988) finds that institutionally reared girls from disrupted homes were more likely to become pregnant before age nineteen, to marry deviant men, and to experience disturbed family relationships in early adulthood, irrespective of their level of functioning in early adolescence. Moreover, when these women were beset with marital and economic problems similar to those experienced earlier in life, difficulties arose in early parenting.

Disruption and single parenthood in the family of origin, and the economic loss and emotional turmoil that frequently ensue, may clearly jeopardize investment in children and youth. However, Coleman and Husen (1985) argue that declining investments in the next generation may occur even in more favorable and affluent circumstances. As the functions of the family are transferred to other agencies in welfare states (e.g., as the government takes over education, welfare, support of the aged, and other functions), there is a declining economic dependence of family members on one another. As the multigenerational organization and functions of the family weaken, parental motivation to invest attention, time, and effort in the younger generation may also decrease throughout the population.

While psychological resources (e.g., a sense of mastery or internal control, self-esteem) are influenced by formative experiences in the contexts of family, school, peer group, and workplace, once formed they constitute important assets in the transition to adulthood. Increasingly it is recognized that early orientations toward and expectancies about competent action are critical for later adult success (Mainquist and Eichorn 1989). Jordaan and Super (1974) report that adolescents' planfulness, responsibility, and future orientation

predicted their level of occupational attainment at the age of twenty-five. The more explorative adolescents, who actively engaged the environment, had more positive early adult outcomes. "Planful competence," denoting self-confidence, intellectual investment, and dependability in adolescence, has also been linked to men's adult occupational status (Clausen 1991). These attributes imply planfulness, delayed gratification, and a sense of control over goal attainment. The propensity to plan early in life is also related to positive adult outcomes among institution-reared girls (Quinton and Rutter 1988).

Ogbu (1989) implicates beliefs about success as critical to understanding the paradox of high black adolescent aspirations coupled with low subsequent achievement. The "folk culture of success," fostered by a history of discrimination and reinforced by everyday experience (e.g., the observation of black career ceilings, inflated job qualifications, housing discrimination, and poor occupational achievement despite success in school), convinces many young blacks that desired occupational outcomes will not be assured by educational attainment. Given the belief that external forces controlled by whites determine success, alternative strategies for achievement are endorsed—hustling, collective action, or dependence on a more powerful white person. These, in turn, diminish the effort in school that is necessary to obtain good grades and educational credentials. The "What's the use of trying?" stance of young blacks contrasts sharply with the "effort optimism" characteristic of middle-class whites and some immigrant groups.

For the most disadvantaged segments of society there is concern that poor educational opportunities and a rapidly deteriorating economic base in the inner cities preclude access to viable adult roles (Wilson 1987), irrespective of personal efficacy, ambition, or other traits. Black males' lack of stable employment limits their ability to assume the adult family role (as male provider) and fosters the increasing prevalence and legitimacy of female-headed families. This concern about the availability of adult work roles and high youth unemployment extends beyond U.S. inner cities.

With increasing technological complexity of occupations in advanced industrial economies, and the exportation of low-skill work to less developed countries, there are declining work opportunities for youth who lack formal educational qualifications and technical skills (Coleman and Husen 1985). Further exacerbating the problems of unskilled youth, increasing postsecondary education inflates educational requirements for job entry well beyond task requirements.

## THE TRANSITION TO ADULTHOOD AS A CRITICAL PERIOD OF HUMAN DEVELOPMENT

The transition to adulthood is recognized as a critical period for the crystallization of certain psychological orientations that tend to remain stable throughout the adult life course. Evidence for such "aging stability," or increasing attitudinal stability following the adult transition, is fairly substantial in the realm of political attitudes and preferences (Glenn 1980). Alwin, Cohen, and Newcomb's (forthcoming) study of a panel of Bennington college women from the 1930s to the 1980s reports extraordinary persistence of political attitudes formed while in college over an approximately fifty-year period (a stability coefficient of 0.781). There is also evidence that work orientations become more stable following early adulthood (Lorence and Mortimer 1985; Mortimer, Finch, and Maruyama 1988). Three explanations have been put forward to account for this pattern. The first implicates the environment; the second, features of the person; and the third combines both elements.

According to the first line of reasoning, the relatively dense spacing of major life events during the transition to adulthood (completion of education, marriage, parenthood, entry into the work force or the military) generates external pressures to form new attitudes or to change previous views (Glenn 1980). While the same kinds of events sometimes occur later in life, they are usually spaced more widely and involve a revision of previous experiences rather than wholly new circumstances requiring adaptation (e.g., a job or career change, remarriage, or entry into an adult education program). Similarly, experiences at work generally assume greater constancy after an initial period of job instability (Osterman 1980). Primary relationships, which provide support for attitudes, are often in flux during the transition to adulthood; thereafter, stable primary groups may provide continuing support for previously crystallized attitudinal positions (Sears 1981; Backman 1981). According to this perspective, there may be continuing capacity to change throughout life (Baltes, Reese, and Lipsitt 1980), but if environments become more stable after the adult transition, there will be less impetus for such change over time (Moss and Susman 1980).

Another set of explanations links the "aging stability" pattern to individual attributes that foster growing resistance to change. Mannheim's (1952) classic concept of generation implies that the young are especially receptive to influences generated by the important historical changes of their time (economic upheaval, war, or political revolution). Alwin, Cohen, and Newcomb (forthcoming) find evidence for a "generational/persistence model," which similarly combines notions of vulnerability in youth and persistence thereafter. Before role and character identities are formed, a person may be quite malleable. However, preserving a consistent, stable sense of self is a major motivational goal (Rosenberg 1979); and once self-identities are linked to key attitudes and values, a person's self may become inextricably tied to those views (Sears 1981). Moreover, feelings of dissonance (Festinger 1957) arise when attitudes and beliefs that provide a sense of understanding are threatened (Glenn 1980). Consistent with the notion that young adults may be more ready to change, occupational experiences (i.e., experiences related to autonomy) have been found to have stronger influences on the work orientations of younger workers, ages sixteen to twenty-nine, than on those who are older (Lorence and Mortimer 1985; Mortimer, Finch, and Maruyama 1988).

According to a third point of view, an interaction between a young person and the environment fosters a process of "accentuation" of preexisting traits. While early experiences provide initial impetus for personal development, attitudes and values formed in childhood or adolescence are later strengthened through the individual's active selection, production, or maintenance of environmental circumstances that support earlier dispositions. According to this view, youth making the transition to adulthood are not passive recipients of environmental forces; instead they select or mold their environments (Lerner and Busch-Rossnagel 1981) so as to maintain or reinforce initial psychological states. As a result, there may be an "increase in emphasis of already prominent characteristics during social transitions in the life course" (Elder and Caspi 1990, p. 218).

Illustrations of such processes abound in the literature. For example, students choosing particular college majors become increasingly similar in interests and values over time (Feldman and Weiler 1976). Mortimer, Lorence, and Kumka's (1986) study of a panel of young men showed that competence measured in the senior year of college predicted work autonomy ten years later, which in turn fostered an increasing sense of competence over time. Similarly, intrinsic, extrinsic, and people-oriented values prior to adult entry to the work force led to the selection of occupational experiences that served to maintain and strengthen these value preferences. Psychological well-being in late adolescence increased the likelihood of marriage, which further heightened subsequent well-being. Alwin, Cohen, and Newcomb's (forthcoming) follow-up study of women who attended Bennington College in the 1930s indicated that the choice of associates and the formation of supportive reference groups—spouses, friends, and children—played a substantial part in maintaining the women's political values.

Elder's longitudinal study of young people growing up during the Great Depression has amassed evidence that successful encounters with problems in adolescence can build confidence and resources that promote effective coping with events later in life, fostering personality continuity

(Elder 1974; Elder, Liker, and Cross 1984). For members of the Oakland cohort, early economic deprivation provided opportunity to help the family in a time of crisis, and the consequent self-efficacy, motivation, and capacity to mobilize effort fostered adult work and family security. Elder and Caspi (1990) similarly found that adolescents with more resilient personalities reacted more positively as young adults to combat in World War II. Negative early events may, however, set in motion processes that accentuate problems. For example, traumatic war experiences in early adulthood can threaten marriage and thereby reinforce a cycle of irritability (Elder and Caspi 1990, p. 235).

Whereas sociologists emphasize the social determination of early adult outcomes, and social psychologists have noted enduring personality and character traits that influence the process of transition to adulthood, it must be recognized that changes in both socioeconomic and personal trajectories do occur, frequently at times of life-course transition. Change can occur as a result of "fortuitous events" that intervene in the developmental process rather than reinforcing patterns of preadult behavior (Elder and Caspi 1988, p. 102). For example, the quality of a first marriage may lead to a change in direction of a previously disorderly or otherwise problematic early life course (Rutter and Quinton 1984).

(SEE ALSO: *Socialization*)

### REFERENCES

Alwin, Duane F., Ronald L. Cohen, and Theodore M. Newcomb (Forthcoming) *Aging, Personality, and Social Change: Attitude Persistence and Change over the Life-Span.* Madison: University of Wisconsin Press.

Aries, Philippe 1962 *Centuries of Childhood: A Social History of Family Life.* New York: Vintage.

Backman, Carl W. 1981 "Attraction in Interpersonal Relationships." In M. Rosenberg and R. H. Turner, eds., *Social Psychology: Sociological Perspectives.* New York: Basic Books.

Baltes, Paul B., Hayne W. Reese, and Lewis P. Lipsitt

1980 "Life-Span Developmental Psychology." *Annual Review of Psychology* 31:65–110.

Blau, Peter M., and Otis Dudley Duncan 1967 *The American Occupational Structure.* New York: Wiley.

Bowles, Samuel, and Herbert Gintis 1976 *Schooling in Capitalist America.* New York: Basic Books.

Buchmann, Marlis 1989 *The Script of Life in Modern Society: Entry into Adulthood in a Changing World.* Chicago: University of Chicago Press.

Clausen, John 1991 "Adolescent Competence and the Shaping of the Life Course." *American Journal of Sociology* 96:805–842.

Coleman, James S., and Torsten Husen 1985 *Becoming Adult in a Changing Society.* Paris: Organization for Economic Co-operation and Development.

Connor, John W., and George A. De Vos 1989 "Cultural Influences on Achievement Motivation and Orientation toward Work in Japanese and American Youth." In D. Stern and D. Eichorn, eds., *Adolescence and Work: Influences of Social Structure, Labor Markets, and Culture.* Hillsdale, N.J.: Lawrence Erlbaum.

Elder, Glen H., Jr. 1974 *Children of the Great Depression.* Chicago: University of Chicago Press.

———, and Avshalom Caspi 1988 "Human Development and Social Change: An Emerging Perspective on the Life Course." In N. Bolger, A. Caspi, G. Downey, and M. Moorehouse, eds., *Persons in Context: Developmental Processes.* New York: Cambridge University Press.

——— 1990 "Studying Lives in a Changing Society: Sociological and Personological Explorations." In A. I. Rabin, R. A. Zucker, and S. Frank, eds., *Studying Persons and Lives.* New York: Springer-Verlag.

Elder, Glen H., Jr., J. K. Liker, and C. E. Cross 1984 "Parent–Child Behavior in the Great Depression: Life Course and Intergenerational Influences." In P. B. Baltes, ed., *Life-Span Development and Behavior.* New York: Academic Press.

Featherman, David L. 1980 "Schooling and Occupational Careers: Constancy and Change in Worldly Success." In O. G. Brim, Jr., and J. Kagan, eds., *Constancy and Change in Human Development.* Cambridge, Mass.: Harvard University Press.

———, and Annemette Sorensen 1983 "Societal Transformation in Norway and Change in the Life Course Transition into Adulthood." *Acta Sociologica* 26:105–126.

———, and Kenneth I. Spenner 1988 "Class and the Socialization of Children: Constancy, Change, or Irrelevance?" In E. Mavis Hetherington, R. M. Lerner, and M. Perlmutter, eds., *Child Development in Perspective.* Hillsdale, N.J.: Lawrence Erlbaum.

Feldman, Kenneth A., and John Weiler 1976 "Changes in Initial Differences among Major-Field Groups: An Exploration of the 'Accentuation Effect.'" In W. H. Sewell, R. M. Hauser, and D. L. Featherman, eds., *Schooling and Achievement in American Society.* New York: Academic Press.

Festinger, Leon 1957 *A Theory of Cognitive Dissonance.* Stanford, Calif.: Stanford University Press.

Finch, Michael D., Michael J. Shanahan, Jeylan T. Mortimer, and Seongryeol Ryu 1990 "Work Experience and Control Orientation in Adolescence." Paper presented at the 1990 American Sociological Association Meeting, Washington, D.C., August.

Foner, Anne, and David Kertzer 1978 "Transitions over the Life Course: Lessons from Age-Set Societies." *American Journal of Sociology* 83:1,081–1,104.

Freeman, Richard B., and David A. Wise 1979 *Youth Unemployment.* Cambridge, Mass.: National Bureau of Economic Research.

Furstenberg, Frank F., Jr., J. Brooks-Gunn, and S. Philip Morgan 1987 *Adolescent Mothers in Later Life.* Cambridge: Cambridge University Press.

Gecas, Viktor 1979 "The Influence of Social Class on Socialization." In W. R. Burr, R. Hill, F. I. Nye, and I. L. Reiss, *Contemporary Theories about the Family.* Vol. 1, *Research-Based Theories.* New York: Free Press.

Glenn, Norval D. 1980 "Values, Attitudes, and Beliefs." In O. G. Brim, Jr., and J. Kagan, eds., *Constancy and Change in Human Development.* Cambridge, Mass.: Harvard University Press.

Granovetter, Mark S. 1974 *Getting a Job.* Cambridge, Mass.: Harvard University Press.

Greenberger, Ellen, and Laurence Steinberg 1986 *When Teenagers Work.* New York: Basic Books.

Grubb, W. Norton 1989 "Preparing Youth for Work: The Dilemmas of Education and Training Programs." In D. Stern and D. Eichorn, eds., *Adolescence and Work: Influences of Social Structure, Labor Markets, and Culture.* Hillsdale, N.J.: Lawrence Erlbaum.

Hall, G. S. 1904 *Adolescence: Its Psychology and Its Relations to Physiology, Anthropology, Sociology, Sex, Crime, Religion, and Education.* New York: Appleton.

Hamilton, Stephen F. 1990 *Apprenticeship for Adulthood. Preparing Youth for the Future.* New York: Free Press.

Hogan, Dennis P., and Nan Marie Astone 1986 "The Transition to Adulthood." *Annual Review of Sociology* 12:109–130.

Jessor, Richard, and Shirley L. Jessor 1977 *Problem*

*Behavior and Psychosocial Development: A Longitudinal Study of Youth.* New York: Academic Press.

Jordaan, Jean Pierre, and Donald E. Super 1974 "The Prediction of Early Adult Vocational Behavior." In D. F. Ricks, A. Thomas, and M. Roff, eds., *Life History Research in Psychopathology.* Minneapolis: University of Minnesota Press.

Keniston, Kenneth 1970 "Youth as a Stage of Life." *American Scholar* 39:631–654.

Kerckhoff, Alan C. 1990 *Getting Started: Transition to Adulthood in Great Britain.* Boulder, Colo.: Westview Press.

Klein, Hugh 1990 "Adolescence, Youth, and Young Adulthood: Rethinking Current Conceptualizations of Life Stage." *Youth and Society* 21:446–471.

Kohn, Melvin L., and Carmi Schooler 1983 *Work and Personality: An Inquiry into the Impact of Social Stratification.* Norwood, N.J.: Ablex Publishing.

———, Kazimierz M. Slomczynski, and Carrie Schoenbach 1986 "Social Stratification and the Transmission of Values in the Family: A Cross-National Assessment." *Sociological Forum* 1:73–102.

Lerner, Richard M., and N. A. Busch-Rossnagel (eds.) 1981 *Individuals as Producers of Their Development: A Life-Span Perspective.* New York: Academic Press.

Lorence, Jon, and Jeylan T. Mortimer 1985 "Job Involvement through the Life Course: A Panel Study of Three Age Groups." *American Sociological Review* 50:618–638.

McLaughlin, Steven D., Barbara D. Melber, John O. G. Billy, Denise M. Zimmerle, Linda D. Winges, and Terry R. Johnson 1988 *The Changing Lives of American Women.* Chapel Hill: University of North Carolina Press.

Mainquist, Sheri, and Dorothy Eichorn 1989 "Competence in Work Settings." In D. Stern and D. Eichorn, eds., *Adolescence and Work: Influences of Social Structure, Labor Markets, and Culture.* Hillsdale, N.J.: Lawrence Erlbaum.

Mannheim, Karl 1952 "The Problem of Generations." In P. Kecskemeti, ed., *Essays in the Sociology of Knowledge.* London: Routledge and Kegan Paul.

Marini, Margaret Mooney 1984a "The Order of Events in the Transition to Adulthood." *Sociology of Education* 57:63–84.

———, 1984b "Age and Sequencing Norms in the Transition to Adulthood." *Social Forces* 63:229–244.

———, 1987 "Measuring the Process of Role Change during the Transition to Adulthood." *Social Science Research* 6:1–38.

———, Hee-Choon Shin, and Jennie Raymond 1989 "Socioeconomic Consequences of the Process of Transition to Adulthood." *Social Science Research* 13:89–135.

Meyer, Robert M., and David A. Wise 1982 "High School Preparation and Early Labor Force Experience." In R. B. Freeman and D. A. Wise, eds., *The Youth Labor Market Problem: Its Nature, Causes, and Consequences.* Chicago: University of Chicago Press.

Modell, John 1980 "Normative Aspects of American Marriage Timing since World War II." *Journal of Family History* 5:210–234.

——— 1989 *Into One's Own: From Youth to Adulthood in the United States, 1920–1975.* Berkeley: University of California Press.

———, Frank Furstenberg, and Theodore Hershberg 1976 "Social Change and Transitions to Adulthood in Historical Perspective." *Journal of Family History* 1:7–32.

Mortimer, Jeylan T., and Michael D. Finch 1986 "The Effects of Part-Time Work on Self-Concept and Achievement." In K. Borman and J. Reisman, eds., *Becoming a Worker.* Norwood, N.J.: Ablex Publishing.

———, Michael D. Finch, and Donald S. Kumka 1982 "Persistence and Change in Development: The Multidimensional Self-Concept." In P. D. Baltes and O. G. Brim, Jr., eds., *Life-Span Development and Behavior.* New York: Academic Press.

———, Michael D. Finch, and Geoffrey Maruyama 1988 "Work Experience and Job Satisfaction: Variation by Age and Gender." In J. T. Mortimer and K. M. Borman, eds., *Work Experience and Psychological Development through the Life Span.* Boulder, Colo.: Westview Press.

———, Michael D. Finch, Michael Shanahan, and Seongryeol Ryu (Forthcoming) "Work Experience, Mental Health, and Behavioral Adjustment in Adolescence." *Journal of Research on Adolescence.*

———, and Donald S. Kumka 1982 "A Further Examination of the 'Occupational Linkage Hypothesis.'" *Sociological Quarterly* 23:3–16.

———, Jon Lorence, and Donald S. Kumka 1986 *Work, Family, and Personality: Transition to Adulthood.* Norwood, N.J.: Ablex Publishing.

———, and Roberta G. Simmons 1978 "Adult Socialization." *Annual Review of Sociology* 4:421–454.

Moss, Howard A., and Elizabeth J. Susman 1980 "Longitudinal Study of Personality Development." In O. G. Brim, Jr., and J. Kagan, eds., *Constancy and Change in Human Development.* Cambridge, Mass.: Harvard University Press.

Neugarten, Bernice L., and Nancy Datan 1973 "Sociological Perspectives on the Life Cycle." In P. B. Baltes and K. Warner Schaie, eds., *Life Span Developmental Psychology: Personality and Socialization.* New York: Academic Press.

Neugarten, Bernice L., Joan W. Moore, and John C. Lowe 1965 "Age Norms, Age Constraints, and Adult Socialization." *American Journal of Sociology* 70:710–717.

Ogbu, John U. 1989 "Cultural Boundaries and Minority Youth Orientation toward Work Preparation." In D. Stern and D. Eichorn, eds., *Adolescence and Work: Influences of Social Structure, Labor Markets, and Culture.* Hillsdale, N.J.: Lawrence Erlbaum.

Osterman, Paul 1980 *Getting Started: The Youth Labor Market.* Cambridge, Mass.: MIT Press.

——— 1989 "The Job Market for Adolescents." In D. Stern and D. Eichorn, eds., *Adolescence and Work: Influences of Social Structure, Labor Markets, and Culture.* Hillsdale, N.J.: Lawrence Erlbaum.

Panel on Youth of the President's Science Advisory Committee 1974 *Youth: Transition to Adulthood.* Chicago: University of Chicago Press.

Phillips, Sarah, and Kent Sandstrom 1990 "Parental Attitudes toward 'Youthwork.'" *Youth and Society* 22:160–183.

Quinton, David 1988 "Longitudinal Approaches to Intergenerational Studies: Definition, Design, and Use." In M. Rutter, ed., *Studies of Psychosocial Risk: The Power of Longitudinal Data.* Cambridge: Cambridge University Press.

———, and Michael Rutter 1988 *Parenting Breakdown: The Making and Breaking of Intergenerational Links.* Aldershot, U.K.: Gower.

Rindfuss, Ronald R., S. Philip Morgan, and Gray Swicegood 1988 *First Births in America: Changes in the Timing of Parenthood.* Berkeley: University of California Press.

Rosenbaum, James 1976 *Making Inequality: The Hidden Curriculum of High School Tracking.* New York: Wiley.

Rosenberg, Morris 1979 *Conceiving the Self.* New York: Basic Books.

Rossi, Alice S. 1980 "Life-Span Theories and Women's Lives." *Signs: Journal of Women in Culture and Society* 6:4–32.

Rutter, Michael, and David Quinton 1984 "Long-Term Follow-Up of Women Institutionalized in Childhood: Factors Promoting Good Functioning in Adult Life." *British Journal of Developmental Psychology* 2:191–204.

Sears, David O. 1981 "Life-Stage Effects on Attitude Change, Especially among the Elderly." In B. Kiesler, J. N. Morgan, and V. Kincade Oppenheimer, eds., *Aging: Social Change.* New York: Academic Press.

Sewell, William H., and Robert M. Hauser 1976 "Causes and Consequences of Higher Education: Models of the Status Attainment Process." In W. H. Sewell, R. M. Hauser, and D. L. Featherman, eds., *Schooling and Achievement in American Society.* New York: Academic Press.

Stern, David, and Yoshi-Fumi Nakata 1989 "Characteristics of High School Students' Paid Jobs, and Employment Experience after Graduation." In D. Stern and D. Eichorn, eds., *Adolescence and Work: Influences of Social Structure, Labor Markets, and Culture.* Hillsdale, N.J.: Lawrence Erlbaum.

Wilson, William Julius 1987 *The Truly Disadvantaged: The Inner City, the Underclass, and Public Policy.* Chicago: University of Chicago Press.

JEYLAN T. MORTIMER

# AFFECT CONTROL THEORY AND IMPRESSION FORMATION

Sociologist Erving Goffman (1967) argued that people conduct themselves so as to generate impressions that maintain the identities, or faces, that they have in social situations. Human action—aside from accomplishing tasks—functions expressively in reflecting actors' social positions and in preserving social understandings. Affect control theory (Heise 1979; Smith-Lovin and Heise 1988; MacKinnon, forthcoming) continues Goffman's thesis, providing a mathematized and empirically grounded model for explaining and predicting expressive aspects of action.

## AFFECTIVE MEANING

Cross-cultural research among people speaking diverse languages in more than twenty-five nations around the world (Osgood, May, and Miron 1975) revealed that any person, behavior, object, setting, or property of persons evokes an affective response consisting of three components. One component consists of approval or disapproval of the entity—an evaluation based on morality (good versus bad), aesthetics (beautiful versus ugly), functionality (useful versus useless), hedonism (pleasant versus unpleasant), or some other criterion. Whatever the primary basis of evaluation, it tends to generalize to other bases, so, for example, something that is useful tends also to seem good, beautiful, and pleasant.

Another component of affective responses is a potency assessment made in terms of physical proportions (large versus small, deep versus shallow), strength (strong versus weak), forcefulness (powerful versus powerless), or other criteria. Again, judgments on the basis of one criterion tend to generalize to other criteria, so, for example, a powerful person seems large, deep (in a metaphorical sense), and strong.

The third component of affective responses—an appraisal of activity—may depend on speed (fast versus slow), perceptual stimulation (noisy versus quiet, bright versus dim), age (young versus old), keenness (sharp versus dull), or other criteria. These criteria also generalize to some degree, so, for example, a young person often seems metaphorically fast, noisy, bright, and sharp.

The evaluation, potency, and activity (EPA) structure in subjective responses is one of the best-documented facts in social science, and an elaborate technology has developed for measuring EPA responses on "semantic differential scales" (Heise 1969). The scales consist of adjectives separated by a number of check positions. For example, a standard scale has Good–Nice at one end and Bad–Awful at the other end, and intervening positions on the scale allow respondents to record the direction and intensity of their evaluations of a stimulus. The middle rating position on such scales represents neutrality.

EPA responses tend to be socially shared within a population (Heise 1966), so a group's average EPA response to an entity indexes the group sentiment about the entity. Sentiments vary across cultures. For example, potent authorities such as an employer are evaluated positively in U.S. and Canadian college populations, but German stu-dents evaluate authorities negatively; small children are evaluated positively in Western nations but neutrally in Japan.

## IMPRESSION FORMATION

Combinations of cognitive elements bring affective meanings together and create outcome impressions through psychological processes that are complex, subtle, and yet highly predictable (Averett and Heise 1987; Anderson 1981).

For example, among U.S. college students (the population of raters for examples henceforth), someone who is rich is evaluatively neutral, very powerful, and a little on the quiet side. Meanwhile, a professor is fairly good, fairly powerful, and a bit quiet. The notion of a "rich professor" combines these sentiments and yields a different outcome. A rich professor is evaluated somewhat negatively, mainly because the personalized power of wealth generates an uneasiness that is not overcome by esteem for academic status. A rich professor seems very powerful because the average potency of wealth and of professors is high, and the mind adds an extra increment of potency because of the personalized power deriving from wealth. A rich professor seems even quieter than the component statuses because activity connotations do not merely average, they add up to some degree.

The processes that are involved in combining a social identity with a status characteristic like "rich" also are involved in combining a social identity with personal traits. Thus, an authoritarian professor evokes an impression roughly similar to a rich professor because the affective association for authoritarian is similar to that for rich.

Another example involving emotion illustrates additional processes involved in combining personal characteristics with social identities (Heise and Thomas 1989). Being outraged implies that one is feeling quite bad, somewhat potent, and somewhat lively. A child is felt to be quite good, quite impotent, and very active. The combination "outraged child," seems fairly bad, partly because the child is flaunting personalized power deriving from an emotion and partly because the mind discounts customary esteem for a person if there is a particular basis for evaluating the person negatively: The child's negative emotion undercuts the regard one usually has for a child. The child's impotency is reduced because of a bad and potent emotional state. And the child's activity is greater than usual because the activity of the emotion and the activity of the identity combine additively.

The above illustrations focus on individual properties combined with social identities. Events are another basis for impression formation. A social event—an actor behaving on an object or person within some setting—amalgamates EPA impressions of the elements composing the event and generates a new impression of each element (Heise 1979; Smith-Lovin 1987a; Smith-Lovin 1987b).

To a degree, the character of a behavior diffuses to the actor who performs the behavior: For example, an admired person who engages in a violent act seems less good, more potent, and more active than usual. Impressions of the actor also are influenced by complex interplays between the nature of the behavior and the nature of the object. For example, violence toward an enemy is not nearly so damaging to an actor as violence toward a child. That is because bad, forceful behaviors toward bad, potent objects seem justified, while such behaviors toward good, weak objects seem ruthless. Moreover, the degree of justification or of ruthlessness depends on how good the actor was in the first place; for example, a person who acts violently toward a child loses more respect if the person was esteemed initially and loses less respect if already stigmatized.

Similar processes of diffusion from one event element to another and of complex interplays between event elements influence impressions of behaviors, objects, and settings. The general principle is that initial affective meanings of event elements combine and thereby produce impressions that reflect the meaning of the event. Those impressions are transient because they, in turn, are the meanings that are transformed by later events.

## IMPRESSION MANAGEMENT

Normal events produce transient impressions that match sentiments, whereas events that generate impressions deviating widely from sentiments seem abnormal or anomalous (Heise and MacKinnon 1987). For example, "a parent assisting a child" creates impressions of parent, child, and assisting; these impressions are close to sentiments provided by our culture, and the event seems normal. On the other hand, "a parent harming a child" seems abnormal because the event produces negative impressions of parent and child, and these impressions are far different from the culturally given notions that parents and children are good.

According to affect control theory, people manage events so as to match transient impressions with sentiments and thereby maintain normality in their experience. Expressive shaping of events occurs along with rational assembly of orderly action, and ordinarily the expressive and the rational components of action complement each other because cultural sentiments incite the very events that are required by the logic of social institutions like the family, law, religion, and so forth.

Having adopted an appropriate identity at a scene and having cast others in complementary identities, a person intuits behaviors that will create normal impressions. For example, if a person in the role of judge is to act on someone who is a proven crook, then she must do something that confirms a judge's power and the badness of a crook, and behaviors like convicting and sentencing produce the right impressions. Fitting behaviors may change in the wake of prior events. For example, a father who is fulfilling his role in a mediocre manner because his child has disobeyed him strives to regain goodness and power by controlling the child or by dramatizing forgiveness. Other people's identities may serve as resources for restoring a compromised identity (Wiggins and Heise 1987); for example, a father shaken by a child's disobedience might recover his poise by supporting and defending mother.

Behaviors that confirm sentiments are the intrinsically motivated behaviors in a situation. Actors sometimes forgo impulses to such behaviors and thereby comply to the demands of others, but compliance also reflects the basic principle because normal behavior in one relationship simultaneously can be abnormal behavior in another relationship. For example, a child acts normally when calling on a playmate though also abnormally if his mother has ordered him not to do so and he disobeys her. The actor maintains the relationship that is most salient.

Sometimes other people produce events that do not confirm sentiments evoked by one's own definition of a situation. Affect control theory suggests several routes for restoring consistency between impressions and sentiments in such cases. First, people may try to reinterpret other's actions so as to optimize expressive coherence. For example, an actor's movement away from another person can be viewed as departing, leaving, escaping, fleeing, or deserting, and one chooses the interpretation that seems most normal, given participants' identities and prior events (Heise 1979). Of course, interpretations of a behavior are bound by determinable facts about the behavior and its consequences, so some behaviors cannot be interpreted in a way that completely normalizes an event.

Another response to disturbing events is construction of new events that transform abnormal impressions back to normality. Restorative events with the self as actor might be feasible and enacted, as in the example of a father controlling a disobedient child. Restorative events that require others to act might be elicited by suggesting what the other should do. For example, after a child has disobeyed his mother, a father might tell the child to apologize.

Intractable disturbances in interaction that cannot be handled by reinterpreting others' actions or by instigating new events lead to more fundamental efforts to achieve expressive coherence, such as attributing character traits to people in order to form complex identities that account for participation in certain kinds of anomalous events. For example, a father who has neglected his child might be viewed as an inconsiderate person.

Changing base identities also can produce the kind of person who would participate in certain events. For example, an employee cheating an employer would be expressively coherent were the employee known to be a lawbreaker, and a cheating incident may instigate work to apply the lawbreaker label and to withdraw the employee identity.

Trait attributions and labels that normalize particular incidents are added to conceptions of people, and thereafter the special identities may be invoked in order to set expectations for a person's behavior in other scenes or to understand other incidents. Everyone who interacts with a person builds up knowledge about the person's capacities in this way, and a person builds up knowledge about the self in this way as well.

## EMOTION

Affect control theory is a central framework in the sociology of emotions (Thoits 1989). According to affect control theory, spontaneous emotion reflects the state a person has reached as a result of events and also how that state compares to the ideal experience of a person with a particular social identity. For example, if events make a person seem neutral on goodness, potency, and activity, then the tendency is to feel emotionally neutral, but someone in the sweetheart role ends up feeling blue because he or she is experiencing so much less than one expects in a romantic relationship.

Because emotions reflect the impressions that events have generated, they are a way of directly sensing the consequences of social interaction. Because emotions simultaneously reflect what kinds of identities people are taking, emotions also are a way of sensing the operative social structure in a situation. Moreover, because displays of emotion broadcast a person's subjective appraisals to others, emotions contribute to intersubjective sharing of views about social matters.

People sometimes mask their emotions or display emotions other than those they feel spontaneously in order to hide their appraisal of events from others or to conceal personal definitions of a situation. Such "emotion work" often occurs when situations intermingle, as when one has an institutional definition of a situation and also a personal definition. Institutional identities invest actors with the responsibility of maintaining the institutional ideology through conduct and through emotional displays, and therefore actors may be obligated to display emotions that are unauthentic by personal definitions.

Emotion work also occurs after abnormal events. For example, an actor caught in misconduct might display guilt and remorse beyond what is felt in order to convince others that he believes his behavior is wrong and that he is not the type who engages in such activity. Heise (1989) showed that this kind of emotion work can be derived from the mathematics of affect control theory.

## CONCLUSION

Overall, affect control theory provides a comprehensive social psychological framework relating to roles, impression formation, behavior, emotion, attribution, labeling, and other issues (Stryker and Statham 1985). Quantitative predictions about EPA outcomes are based on impression-formation equations that have been verified cross-culturally. The model is concrete and precise enough that a computer program (Heise and Lewis 1988) has been built to simulate social interactions—and all of the examples in this report are results from the program. Simulations can be conducted with existing EPA measurements obtained in a variety of nations—the United States, Northern Ireland, Canada, Germany, Japan—and small data sets can be integrated with existing data bases in order to simulate interactions in subcultures (Smith-Lovin and Douglas, forthcoming). Thus, the theory and its instrumentation provide sociologists with useful tools for studying social relations.

(SEE ALSO: *Social Psychology*)

## REFERENCES

Anderson, Norman H. 1981 *Foundations of Information Integration Theory*. New York: Academic Press.

Averett, C. P., and D. R. Heise 1987 "Modified Social Identities: Amalgamations, Attributions, and Emotions." *Journal of Mathematical Sociology* 13:103–132.

Goffman, Erving 1967 *Interaction Ritual: Essays on Face-to-Face Behavior*. Chicago: Aldine.

Heise, David R. 1966 "Social Status, Attitudes, and Word Connotations." *Sociological Inquiry* 36:227–239.

———1969 "Some Methodological Issues in Semantic Differential Research." *Psychological Bulletin* 72:406–422.

———1979 *Understanding Events: Affect and the Construction of Social Action*. New York: Cambridge University Press.

———1989 "Effects of Emotion Displays on Social Identification." *Social Psychology Quarterly* 52:10–21.

Heise, David R., and Elsa Lewis 1988 *Introduction to INTERACT*. Durham, N.C.: National Collegiate Software Clearinghouse, Duke University Press.

Heise, David R., and N. MacKinnon 1987 "Affective Bases of Likelihood judgments." *Journal of Mathematical Sociology* 13:133–151.

Heise, David R., and Lisa Thomas 1989 "Predicting Impressions Created by Combinations of Emotion and Social Identity." *Social Psychology Quarterly* 52:141–148.

MacKinnon, Neil J. (Forthcoming) *Affect Control and Social Interaction: A Cross-Cultural Study*. Albany, N.Y.: State University of New York Press.

Osgood, C. H., W. H. May, and M. S. Miron 1975 *Cross-Cultural Universals of Affective Meaning*. Urbana: University of Illinois Press.

Smith-Lovin, Lynn 1987a "Impressions from Events." *Journal of Mathematical Sociology* 13:35–70.

——— 1987b "The Affective Control of Events within Settings." *Journal of Mathematical Sociology* 13:71–101.

Smith-Lovin, Lynn, and D. R. Heise 1988 *Analyzing Social Interaction: Advances in Affect Control Theory*. New York: Gordon and Breach.

Smith-Lovin, Lynn, and W. Douglas (Forthcoming) "An Affect Control Analysis of Two Religious Subcultures." In V. Gecas and D. Franks, eds., *Social Perspective in Emotions*. Greenwich, Conn.: JAI Press.

Stryker, S., and A. Statham 1985 "Symbolic Interaction and Role Theory." In G. Lindzey and E. Aronson, eds., *Handbook of Social Psychology*, 3rd ed. New York: Random House.

Thoits, P. A. 1989 "The Sociology of Emotions." *Annual Review of Sociology* 15:317–342.

Wiggins, Beverly, and D. R. Heise 1987 "Expectations, Intentions, and Behavior: Some Tests of Affect Control Theory." *Journal of Mathematical Sociology* 13:153–169.

DAVID R. HEISE

**AFFIRMATIVE ACTION** The term *affirmative action* has been used in the United States since the late 1960s to refer to policies that go beyond the simple prohibition of discrimination on grounds of race, national origin, and sex in employment practices and educational programs. These policies require some further action, "affirmative action," to make jobs and promotions and admissions to educational programs available to individuals from groups that have historically suffered from discrimination in gaining these opportunities or are, whether discriminated against or not by formal policies and informal practices, infrequently found in certain occupations or educational institutions and programs.

Affirmative action policies may be policies of governments or governmental units, affecting their own procedures in employment or in granting contracts; or they may be policies of governments, affecting the employment procedures of companies or nonprofit agencies and organizations over whom the governments have power or with whom they deal; or they may be the policies of profit and nonprofit employers, adopted voluntarily or under varying degrees of public or private pressure. Affirmative action policies may include the policies of philanthropic foundations, when they affect the employment policies of their grantees, or educational accrediting agencies, when they affect the employment or admissions policies of the institutions they accredit.

The range of policies that can be called affirmative action is wide, but the term also has a specific legal meaning. It was first used in a legal context in the United States in an executive order of President John F. Kennedy. Subsequent presidential executive orders and other administrative requirements have expanded its scope and meaning, and since 1971 affirmative action so defined has set employment practice standards for contractors of the United States, that is, every company, college, university, hospital, or other institution that has business with the U.S. government. These standards are enforced by an office of the Department of Labor, the Office of Federal Contract Compliance Programs. Because of the wide sweep of the executive order and its reach into the employment practices of almost every large employer, affirmative action policies have become extremely controversial.

Affirmative action, under other names, is also to be found in other countries to help groups, whether majority or minority, that have not fared as well as others in gaining employment in higher status occupations or admissions to advanced educational programs.

Affirmative action has been controversial because it appears to contradict a central objective of traditional liberalism and the U.S. civil rights movement, that is, the treatment of individuals on the basis of their individual talents and not on the basis of their color, race, national origin, or sex. Affirmative action, as it has developed, requires surveys by employers of the race, national origin, and sex of their employees to uncover patterns of "underutilization" and to develop programs to overcome this underutilization and thus to take account of the race, national origin, and sex of applicants for employment and of candidates for promotion. To many advocates of expanded civil rights, this is seen as only the next and a most necessary step in achieving equality for groups that have in the past faced discrimination. To others who deem themselves advocates of civil rights and of the interests of minority groups, affirmative action, in the form in which it has developed, is seen as a violation of the first requirement for a society that promises equal opportunity, that is, to treat individuals as individuals independent of race, national origin, or sex.

This apparent contradiction between civil rights and affirmative action may be glimpsed in the very language of the Civil Rights Act of 1964, the central piece of legislation that banned discrimination in government programs, public facilities, and employment. In the debate over that act, fears were expressed that the prohibition of discrimination in employment, as codified in Title VII, would be implemented by requiring certain numbers of employees to be of a given race. This fear was dealt with by placing language in the act that was understood at the time specifically to forbid the practices that are required under affirmative action since the late 1960s and early 1970s. Title 703 (j) reads:

*Nothing contained in this title shall be interpreted to require any employer . . . to grant preferential treatment to any individual or to any group because of the race, color, religion, sex, or national origin of such individual or group on account of an imbalance which may exist with respect to the total number or percentage of persons of any race, color, religion, sex, or national origin employed by any employer.*

However, federal executive orders governing how the federal government does its business may set their own standards, independent of statutory law. The first executive order using the term *affirmative action* was issued by President John F. Kennedy in 1961. It created a President's Committee on Equal Employment Opportunity to monitor the obligations contractors undertook to extend affirmative action. At this time, the general understanding of affirmative action was that it required such things as giving public notice that the employer did not discriminate, making the availability of positions and promotions widely known, advertising in minority media, and the like. With the Civil Rights Act of 1964—which not only prohibited discrimination on grounds of race, color, and national origin but also on grounds of sex—a new executive order, no. 11,246, was formulated by President Lyndon B. Johnson and came into effect. It replaced the President's Committee on Equal Employment Op-

portunity with an Office of Federal Contract Compliance Programs (which still operates). Subsequent federal regulations of the late 1960s and early 1970s specified what was meant by affirmative action in the executive order, and the meaning of affirmative action was considerably expanded into the full-fledged program that has existed since 1971. Revised order no. 4 of that year, which is part of the *Code of Federal Regulations* and is still in effect, reads in part:

*An affirmative action program is a set of specific and result-oriented procedures to which a contractor commits itself to apply every good effort. The objective of those procedures plus such efforts is equal employment opportunity. Procedures without efforts to make them work are meaningless; and effort, undirected by specific and meaningful procedures, is inadequate. An effective affirmative action program must include an analysis of areas within which the contractor is deficient in the utilization of minority groups and women, and further, goals and timetables to which the contractor's good faith efforts must be directed to correct the deficiencies and, [sic] thus to achieve prompt and full utilization of minorities and women, at all levels and in all segments of its work force where deficiencies exist.* (Code of Federal Regulations 1990, pp. 121–122)

Much of the controversy over affirmative action is over the term *goals and timetables:* Are these "quotas"? Supporters of affirmative action say not—only good faith efforts are required, and if they fail the contractor is not penalized. Further controversy exists over the term *utilization:* What is the basis on which a group is found "underutilized," and to what extent is this evidence of discrimination?

Controversy also arises over the categories of employees that contractors must report on and over whose utilization they must be concerned. The executive order lists four categories: blacks, Spanish-surnamed Americans, American Indians, and Orientals. (These are the terms in the order as of 1971 and are still used in the *Code of Federal Regulations.*) The preferred names of these groups have changed since then to Afro- or African-Americans, Hispanics or Latinos, Native Americans, and Asians. While the original executive order and the Civil Rights Act was a response to the political action of black civil rights groups, and it was the plight of blacks that motivated both the executive order and the Civil Rights Act, it was apparently deemed unwise in the mid-1960s to limit affirmative action requirements to blacks alone. The Civil Rights Act bans discrimination against any person on grounds of race, national origin, and sex and specifies no group in particular for protection; but the Equal Employment Opportunity Commission, set up by the Civil Rights Act to monitor discrimination in employment, from the beginning required reports on the four groups listed above, despite the fact that even in the 1960s it could be argued that discrimination against Asians was far less acute and much less of a problem than discrimination against blacks, that discrimination against American Indians also differed in severity and character from discrimination against blacks, and that discrimination against Spanish-surnamed Americans ranged from the nonexistent or hardly existent (Spaniards from Spain? Cubans? Sephardic Jews?) to the possibly significant. Nevertheless, these four categories set up in the mid-1960s are still the groups that governmental programs of affirmative action target for special attention (Glazer 1987).

Since affirmative action is a governmental program operated by government agencies that grant contracts and is overseen by the Office of Federal Contract Compliance Programs, one major issue of controversy has been over the degree to which these programs are really enforced. It is generally believed that enforcement is more severe under Democratic administrations than under Republican administrations, even though the program was first fully developed under the Republican administration of President Richard Nixon. President Ronald Reagan was an avowed opponent of affirmative action, but despite his eight-year administration no modification of the program took place. Changes were proposed by some parts of the Republican administration but opposed by others. Business, in particular big business, had learned to live with affirmative action and was not eager to upset the apple cart (Belz 1990).

Perhaps the most controversial area in which affirmative action is applied is in the employment and promotion of police, firefighting and sanitation personnel, and teachers and other local government employees. Here strict racial quotas often do apply. They are strongly resented by many employees when new employees are hired by race and even more when promotions are given out by race and layoffs are determined by race. The basis of these quotas is not the presidential executive order but rather consent decrees entered into by local government on the basis of charges of discrimination brought by the federal government. These charges are brought on the basis of the Civil Rights Act; under this act, if discrimination is found, quotas can be required by courts as a remedy. Since local government employment is generally on the basis of tests, one very controversial aspect of such cases is the role of civil service examinations. Blacks and Hispanics characteristically do worse than white applicants. Are these poorer results to be taken as evidence of discrimination? A complex body of law has been built up on the basis of various cases determining when a test should be considered discriminatory. In the Civil Rights Act of 1964, one provision read "it shall not be an unlawful employment practice . . . for an employer to give and act upon the results of any professionally developed ability test provided that such test . . . is not designed, intended, or used to discriminate." But the courts decide whether the test is "designed, intended, or used to discriminate." Because of the frequency with which courts have found tests for the police, fire, or sanitation force discriminatory, and because state and local governments believe they will lose such cases, many have entered into "consent decrees" in which they agree to hire and promote on the basis of racial and sex criteria.

Affirmative action is also used in the granting of government contracts on the basis of either statutes (federal, state, or local) or administrative procedures. Such procedures in granting contracts have also been attacked in the courts. Some have been upheld, while some have been struck down by the Supreme Court. The state of the law will of course change with the composition of the Court, but as of this writing the Court requires some previous showing of discrimination as a basis for establishing preference for minority contractors in getting contracts.

One issue in preferring minority contractors has been that of possible fraud, as various contractors find it to their advantage to take on black partners so as to present themselves as minority contractors and thus to get whatever advantages in bidding that status provides. In this area, as in other areas where advantage might follow from minority status, there have been debates over what groups may be included as minorities. It was unclear, for example, whether Asian Indians—immigrants and American citizens of Indian origin—were to be considered Asian. Asian Indian Americans were divided among themselves on this question, but during the Reagan administration they were reclassified as Asian, presumably in part for the modest political advantage this gave the Republican administration.

Affirmative action also governs the employment practices of colleges and universities, whether public or private, because they all make use of federal grants and loans for their students, and many have government research contracts. Colleges and universities therefore must also survey their faculties and other staffs for underutilization, and they develop elaborate affirmative action programs. Affirmative action applies to women as well as to racial and ethnic minority groups. There has been, perhaps in part because of affirmative action programs, a substantial increase in female faculty. But there has been little increase in black faculty during the 1980s. The numbers of blacks taking doctorates in arts and sciences has been small and has not increased. Possibly the higher rewards of law, business, and medicine have attracted into those fields black students who could prepare themselves for an academic career. Many campuses have been shaken by controversies over the small number of black faculty, with administrators arguing that few were available and protestors, often black students, arguing that greater effort would change the situation.

The term *affirmative action* is also used to describe admissions to undergraduate colleges and graduate and professional programs in which preference is given to black, Hispanic, and Native American students. This kind of affirmative action is not required by government regulations, as in the case of employment, except in the special case of southern public higher education institutions. There parallel and separate black and white institutions existed, and while all of these institutions have been open to both white and black students since at least the early 1970s, an extended lawsuit has charged that they still preserve their identity as traditionally black and traditionally white institutions. As a result of this litigation, many of these institutions accept goals that require them to recruit a certain number of black students. But the major pressure on many other institutions to increase the number of black students has come from goals voluntarily accepted by administrators or as a result of black student demands. (In one case, that of the University of California, the state legislature has called on the institution to mirror in its racial-ethnic composition the graduating classes of California high schools.) Voluntary affirmative action programs for admission of students, targeted on black, Hispanic, and Native American students, became quite popular in the late 1960s and early 1970s, particularly after the death of Martin Luther King. They have led to legal controversies as well as, according to observers, some tension between white and black students (Bunzel 1988).

The first affirmative action cases to reach the Supreme Court challenged such programs of preference for black and other minority students. A rejected Jewish applicant for admission to the University of Washington Law School, which had set a quota to increase the number of its minority students, sued for admission, and his case reached the Supreme Court. It did not rule on it. The Court did rule on a subsequent case, that of Allan Bakke, a rejected applicant to the University of California, Davis, Medical School, which also had set a quota. The Court, splitting into a number of factions, rejected fixed numerical quotas but asserted race was a factor that could be taken into account in admissions decisions for purposes of promoting academic diversity. Most American colleges and universities of any reputation do give such preference to black, Hispanic, and Native American applicants; in the 1970s they may have given such preference to Asian applicants, but this practice ceased in the 1980s as the number of qualified Asian applicants rapidly increased. Indeed, Asian applicants have charged that they now face discrimination (Bunzel and Au 1987).

Since these 1970s cases there have been many Supreme Court cases on many aspects of affirmative action in employment, in the granting of contracts, and in college and university admissions. On the whole, the policies have survived. The Supreme Court has made and continues to make many fine distinctions between legitimate and illegitimate practices. Affirmative action has been a divisive issue in American political life and has sometimes been raised effectively in political campaigns. It has divided former allies on civil rights issues, in particular American Jews, normally liberal, from blacks. Jews oppose quotas in admissions to medical and law schools because they were in the past victims of very low quotas imposed by American universities.

Affirmative action under various names and legal arrangements is found in many countries: in India, to provide opportunities to scheduled castes, scheduled tribes, and other backward classes, where different requirements operate at the national level and within the states and where some degree of preference has existed in some areas and for some purposes as far back as the 1920s (Galanter 1984); in Malaysia, to protect the native Malay population; in Sri Lanka, to benefit the majority Sri Lankan population (Sowell 1990); and in Australia and Canada, where milder forms of affirmative action than those found in the United States operate. The policies called affirmative action in the United States are called "reservations" in India, and "positive discrimination" in other countries.

There is considerable debate as to the effects of affirmative action policies and how weighty these can be as against other factors affecting employment, promotion, and educational achievement (Leonard 1984a; 1984b). A summary judgment is difficult to make. Black leaders generally consider affirmative action an essential foundation for black progress, but some black intellectuals and publicists have been skeptical. Black leaders often denounce opponents of affirmative action as racists, hidden or otherwise, yet it is clear that many opponents simply find the use, required or otherwise, of racial and sexual characteristics to determine job and promotion opportunities and admission to selective college programs in contradiction with the basic liberal principles of treating individuals without regard to race, national origin, color, and sex. Affirmative action has undoubtedly increased the number of blacks who hold good jobs and gain admission to selective programs. But it has also had other costs in the form of increased racial tensions. It has coincided with a period in which a pattern of black advancement occupationally and educationally since World War II has been surprisingly checked. The defenders of affirmative action argue that this is because it has not yet been applied vigorously enough. The opponents argue that the concentration on affirmative action encourages the neglect of the key factors that promote educational and occupational progress, which are basically the acquisition of qualifications for better jobs and superior educational programs.

(SEE ALSO: *Discrimination; Equality of Opportunity*)

## REFERENCES

Belz, Herman 1990 *Equality Transformed: A Quarter-Century of Affirmative Action.* New Brunswick, N.J.: Transaction Books.

Bunzel, John H. 1988 "Affirmative-Action Admissions: How It 'Works' at UC Berkeley." *The Public Interest* 93:111–129.

———, and Jeffrey K. D. Au 1987 "Diversity or Discrimination? Asian Americans in College." *The Public Interest* 87:49–62.

*Code of Federal Regulations* 1990 Title 41, section 60-2.10, pp. 121–122.

Galanter, Marc 1984 *Competing Equalities: Law and the Backward Classes in India.* Berkeley: University of California Press.

Glazer, Nathan 1987 *Affirmative Discrimination: Ethnic Inequality and Public Policy.* Cambridge, Mass.: Harvard University Press. (Originally published 1975 and 1978, New York: Basic Books.)

Leonard, Jonathan 1984a "The Impact of Affirmative Action on Employment." Working Paper No. 1,310. Cambridge, Mass.: National Bureau of Economic Research.

———1984b "What Promises Are Worth: The Impact of Affirmative Action Goals." Working Paper no. 1,346. Cambridge, Mass.: National Bureau of Economic Research. (Also published in *Journal of Human Resources* (1985) 20:3–20.)

Sowell, Thomas 1990 *Preferential Policies: An International Perspective.* New York: William Morrow.

NATHAN GLAZER

**AFRICAN STUDIES** African studies, simply defined, is the systematic, scientific study of African peoples, including their history, institutions, and culture. But such a simple definition fails to adequately encompass the complexity of this important arena for sociological research.

## THE GEOGRAPHY OF AFRICA

In sociology, the definition of one's unit of study is prerequisite to undertaking any research project. Facts of history make the task of defining what encompasses African studies elusive. Geographic or spatial definitions are generally clear-cut, so if one asks "Where is Africa?," a concise answer is expected. However, the answer to this straightforward question is not necessarily definitive. The continent of Africa is easily identifiable in any atlas or on any globe. By association, African studies could be defined as all research falling within the identified geographical boundaries of this landmass, a simple and neat solution, or so it would seem. In reality, even the task of defining the physical boundaries of Africa can be daunting. As a vast continent of rich cultural, linguistic, political, and historical diversity, Africa is subject to considerable geographical disaggregation. Thus, what is one continent is routinely addressed piecemeal in terms of several subcontinents or subregions. Many people, lay and professional alike, are not accustomed to thinking of Egypt and the northern Islamic states (e.g., Algeria, Libya, Morocco) as part of the African continent. Instead, these African states tend to be separated in the scholarly discourse from Africa and African studies, and therefore research on these regions is generally categorized as pertaining to the Middle East or the Mediterranean.

The tendency toward geographic disaggregation in the conceptualization and study of Africa is apparent at levels beyond the "North African" versus "sub-Saharan African" distinction. African studies in the so-called sub-Saharan context is usually divided into four regions: East Africa (e.g., Kenya, Somalia, Tanzania, Uganda); West Africa (e.g., Nigeria, Ghana, Senegal); Central Africa (e.g., Zaire, Congo, Central African Republic), and southern Africa (e.g., South Africa, Zimbabwe, Lesotho). Of all these regions, southern Africa generally, and South Africa in particular, have recently attained the greatest salience in the public mind.

An additional complication in approaching the geography of Africa is represented by the partitioning of the continent, and its various subregions, into arbitrarily imposed nation-states. Our present-day image of Africa became distorted by the continent's division into different spheres of European influence (e.g., English, French, German, Dutch, Portuguese, Italian, and Spanish). Dating back to the period of European conquest and colonization and culminating in the Berlin Conference of 1884–1885, western European powers divided Africa among themselves in order to share in the exploitation of its riches. Since the lines of demarcation were drawn with European, rather than African, interests in mind, these artificially imposed geographic boundaries often dissected cultural and national groups or tribes that had been single entities for centuries.

Beyond the point of geographic disaggregation is the established tendency to misrepresent the scale of Africa in relation to the world's other continents. European cartography successfully established a blatantly distorted view of African topography in the mind of the world's population. The traditional world map portrays Europe's landmass as much larger than its true physical size. The Mercator map scale, the most widely used cartographic scale in the world, has from the 1700s distorted the sizes of continents in favor of the northern hemisphere. While traditional map-making has instilled a picture of North America as equal in size to Africa, in fact the African continent is nearly four times the landmass of North America.

More subtly, the world's geographic view of Africa has evolved into the unidimensional image that consists only of lush, impenetrable, tropical forests. The view of African geography as best personified by the "jungle" fails to do justice to the rich and varied landscape of this vast continent. Tropical rain forests represent only the smallest fraction of Africa's myriad landscape, which ranges from snowcapped mountains to deserts to high plains to hardwood forests, rippling fields of grain, and placid lakes.

Where is Africa? We see that the answer to this, the most essential or rudimentary of originating questions for sociological research can be quite elusive. Facts of history and perception combine to make what should be a simple question quite complicated. Equally elusive, if not more so, is the task of defining who is African.

## THE PEOPLE OF AFRICA

*Who Is African?* On the surface, the answer to the seemingly simple and straightforward question would appear to be obvious. Certainly few people, lay and professional alike, would hesitate very long before answering. More often than not, their responses would conform to the widespread notion of Africans as a race of black people, characterized by dark skin, kinky hair, and broad noses. In fact, the human diversity of Africans matches, and at points surpasses, Africa's vast geographic diversity. Few continents in the world approach or match the breadth of variation of human phenotypes. Africans run the gamut of the human color spectrum. For many centuries Africa has been home not only to blacks but also to Europeans, Asians, Arabs, and the like. Centuries of biological intermingling has produced a genetically diverse people. The human reality defies attempts to categorize race and racial identity neatly.

Traditional conceptions of race fail to ade-

quately embrace the African reality. At best, racial classification is an arbitrary, politically determined, imprecise system that divides the world's population into artificial categories. Ironically, the insidiousness of established systems of racial classification becomes glaringly apparent in the African context. Modern conceptions of race are derived from the European worldview. The lowest status in the racial hierarchy is assigned to Africans, who are equated with blackness, the polar opposite of whiteness or European ancestry. When carefully examined, in either an African or European context, racial identity loses much of its force as a concept. White and black are more political designations than physical ones. Thus, although there are indigenous Africans who are lighter than some indigenous Europeans, the widespread stereotypes of Europe as white and Africa as black still persists.

In general usage, race extends far beyond physical traits. As a socially constructed reality, race attributes inferior and polluting characteristics to subordinated groups. Cultural, intellectual, and economic conditions are erroneously seen as caused by the biological makeup of groups.

Apartheid in South Africa provides the best contemporary example of the politically motivated, exclusionary nature of racial classification systems, an example matched by the historical case of "Jim Crow" segregation in the U.S. South. The assignment of people to categories of White, Coloured, and African (Black) in South Africa, coupled with the subdivision of each racial category into smaller racial groups (e.g., Whites = Afrikaner- and English-speaking; Asians = East Indian and Malaysian; Coloureds = European/African and Asian/African; and Blacks = Zulu, Xhosa) is wholly determined by white efforts as a demographic minority of the population to maintain their historic political, economic, and social dominance.

Apartheid relies on an elaborate system of "racial markers" such as hair texture, skin color, and so on to classify people into certain racial groups. Associated with each racial group are certain privileges and restrictions. Restrictions are greatest and privileges least for Black Africans, the group at the bottom of the South African color hierarchy. Hence, race as an ideology of subjugation exerts overwhelming force in limiting Black and Coloured Africans' access and opportunities. Despite recent gains and government promises, apartheid continues to be a powerful limitation on life chances in South Africa.

Discussions of African racial identity are additionally complicated by the vast global dispersion of people of African ancestry. People of African ancestry are present in sizable numbers in the Americas, Western Europe, and parts of Asia and the South Pacific. In most instances, the dispersion of African people around the world, in Brazil, the United States, the Caribbean, and Britain, is directly traceable to the European conquest and domination of the African continent. Europe installed and operated the system of the African slave trade that eventually displaced millions of Africans and struck a crippling blow to African social and cultural life. America came to institutionalize its own brutal role in the system.

The traffic in slaves was a demographic disaster for the African continent, taking away people in the prime of their reproductive and productive lives. The African slave trade left in its wake destroyed villages, ruined crops, disrupted cultures, and crumbling social institutions. So vast was the devastation of this trade in human lives, and the subsequent colonial exploitation of Africa for natural resources, that four centuries later Africa has yet to recover fully. Europe's successful exploitation of African slave labor fueled the economic, agricultural, and industrial development of the Americas and Europe. The manipulation of race and racial identity was a central feature in this drama.

Dramatic and extensive dispersion of the African diaspora confounded questions of race and racial identity because of the extensive intermingling of Africans with other so-called racial groups. This was particularly true in the Americas, where the pattern of a mixed racial heritage emerged. African ancestry combined with Native American, Asian, and European bloodlines to diversify further the already rich biological heritage of Africans. The extension of the African diaspora to the Americas produced many kinds of African-Americans, a people represented by black Chinese in Mississippi, Jamaica, and Trinidad; black Amerindians in Florida (Seminoles), Oklahoma's black Cherokee, and Surinam's Arawaks; black Irish in Virginia, black English in Barbados, black Portuguese in Brazil; black East Indians in Guyana, black French Canadians in Montreal and black Mexicans in Vera Cruz. A veritable human rainbow resulted from the transplantation of Africans to the New World.

## THE CULTURAL AND SOCIAL INSTITUTIONS OF AFRICA

We have seen the complexity that underlies the seemingly simple questions of where is Africa and who is African. Issues of geography and biology are revealed to be exceedingly complex. The task of defining for sociological study a people who are both geographically and genetically dispersed is extremely challenging. Additional complication results when we ask the next question, "What is African?" Here, we simply raise the logical question of which institutions, customs, values, cultural features, and social forms can be characterized or labeled as distinctively African.

The survival of indigenous African customs, values, and institutions has been complicated by several historical factors. First among these is the historical reality of African conquest and domination by other cultures, most notably those of Europe but also including cultures from the Islamic world. The experience of conquest and domination by external powers left its mark on African civilization. As a result, Africa and people of African ancestry are characterized by an abundance of nonindigenous languages.

The African continent can be divided into European language domains that parallel the geographic regions associated with European domination and partition of Africa (e.g., Anglophone, Francophone). Similarly, members of the dispersed African diaspora have adopted the dominant languages of the cultures and regions in which they found themselves, speaking Arabic,

Portuguese, Spanish, English, French, or Dutch. Strikingly, many recently independent African nations have embarked on programs aimed at the regeneration of indigenous languages, often creating written forms for previously oral languages. Other African nations have substituted indigenous languages for European languages (derived from the country's colonial experience) as the country's "official" language. Language plays a vital role in the process of cultural and personal affirmation. It is not surprising, therefore, that the conquest of Africa and of Africans in the diaspora was commonly associated with systematic attempts by conquerors to suppress or eradicate indigenous language. Stripping Africans of their language was an essential feature of the move to reinforce military and political domination with cultural domination.

There is an essential connection between language, worldview, personal identity, and cultural survival. Thus, Africans, like all other dominated groups, fought to retain their indigenous languages, for their survival as a unique people hinged on successful retention of that language, and the history, cultural values, and self-affirmation embodied by it.

Interesting variations in the retention of African language forms are observable throughout Africa and the African diaspora. At one extreme are societies where indigenous African languages were retained over time; these languages were practiced throughout the colonial experience and were instituted more widely after independence. A related case is provided by places like Bahia in Brazil, where indigenous African languages were successfully transplanted and maintained outside the continent. At the other extreme are societies in which no vestiges of indigenous African language are readily apparent. The most common case across the diaspora, however, synthesizes African syntax with the dominant European language syntax to create a characteristic black dialect (e.g., French Creole, Dutch Papiamento, English Patwa or Nigerian English, West Indian English, and black American Ghulla English).

The pattern of adaptive acculturation or synthesis observed to occur with language also char-

acterizes other sociocultural institutions in Africa and the diaspora. Music and art provide distinctive examples. Artistic products of African people, especially those living in the diaspora, reflect the mixture of cultural influences, partly indigenous and partly nonindigenous, that characterize the African experience. The synthesis contains expressions obviously derived fsom African origins that were integrated with European or Islamic elements. Yet the final melody or picture is truly syncretic, possessing emergent qualities greater than the sum of the two partial influences. Interestingly, it is in the realm of cultural creativity, music, and art where the African influence on the world has been most readily apparent. People of African ancestry have been disproportionately influential in entertainment, in many instances achieving a synthetic merger that joins the indigenous African "authenticity" with nonindigenous traits to create a new form (e.g., rap). In yet other instances, Africans have chosen to embrace, master, and operate within the unmodified European form (e.g., opera).

Religion is another excellent example of a sociocultural institution that challenges us to define what is distinctively African. Forms of indigenous African religion are as diverse as the continent and people themselves. Christianity, Islam, and Judaism all have long histories on the continent. The same is true for traditional, animistic African religions that imbue all features of the environment with spiritual qualities. It is perhaps the long tradition of pantheism, the belief/acceptance of multiple gods, that made Africa and African people so amenable to religion. Religious forms over the African diaspora range from the classical European through the traditional African to the Islamic, with a large variety of syncretic forms interspersed throughout.

The organization of social and community life in Africa and across the African diaspora also runs the spectrum from indigenous to nonindigenous. In a now familiar pattern, there exist places in Africa or in the African diaspora where traditional African forms of family life, dating back centuries, are continued. Similarly, there are places in which family forms are closer to the

European or the Islamic model. The same observations can be offered about education and the organization of schools among Africans in a given society.

Predictably, given Africa's history of subjugation, in realms of international power and influence, economics, government, and the military, its development has been severely restricted. On all indicators of economic development Africa ranks at the bottom. Africa and people of African ancestry have undergone historic economic deprivation. While other people with colonial experiences have managed to advance economically (e.g., those from Singapore or Korea), Africa and the people of the African diaspora continue to be economically dependent. In addition to economic dependence, the continent suffers from ecological devastation, high rates of fertility, unemployment, disease, and educational problems. Africa and those of African ancestry continue to be without adequate power at the centers of international representation, if we judge power by political influence and military might. In each of these aspects, Africa remains the sleeping giant, unable to exert world influence commensurate to its nearly billion people and rich mineral and human resources. The emergence of Africa onto the world stage, like Japan in 1960s and China in 1980s, will have to wait until the twenty-first century or beyond.

## UNIFYING THEMES IN AFRICAN STUDIES

Defining the parameters of African studies can be challenging because there are no simple answers to the basic questions for orienting any scientific, sociological study. Where is Africa? Who are Africans? What is an African cultural or social institution? The history of Africa and its people in the diaspora has been uniquely shaped by experiences of conquest and domination. The experiences of slavery, colonization, and external domination have left in their wake considerable damage and diversity born of accommodation to ensure survival.

Studies of African people and institutions commonly reveal the creative retention of authentic or indigenous traits. Such creative responses have been, in their own way, acts of resistance enabling cultural perpetuation in disguise, from a subordinate position. While these adaptive responses have assured the ultimate survival of many aspects of African culture and institutions, survival has often come at the cost of fundamental change or alteration from the original, indigenous form. This tension, the reconciliation of the old with the new, the indigenous with the nonindigenous, offers African studies its most exciting terrain for future development. The challenge will be to discover a culture and people that have been historically distorted by the twin activities of concealment from below and degradation from above.

## AMERICAN SCHOLARSHIP AND AFRICAN STUDIES

The dismissal of the importance of African studies preceded its acceptance as a scholarly discipline. While clearly diminished today, the white male Eurocentric focus has historically dominated university curriculums. Both grassroots and academic movements pointed to the need for recognition of the African contribution to American culture. Before the incorporation of Afro-American studies into predominantly white colleges, black educators and leaders had stressed the value of Black America's ties to Africa for decades. Notable activists from William Monroe Trotter to Booker T. Washington and Marcus Garvey called for "Back to Africa" movements. The distinguished sociologist W. E. B. DuBois founded the Pan-African Congress in 1921 in order to link the problems of American blacks to those in Africa. Moreover, much of his work over a long and illustrious career focused on Africa.

Within white dominated institutions the value of African studies had some beginnings. Egyptologists and anthropologists gathered information from Africa under the grace of colonial rule. Sociology was both friend and foe. Early sociologists promoted cross-cultural studies as well as research into the social conditions under which blacks lived. However, some sociologists embraced Social Darwinism.

Herbert Spencer, among others, launched the ideology of Social Darwinism, which developed into a popular pseudoscientific justification for the racial hierarchies. Social Darwinism assigned Africans, and thereby African-Americans, to the lowest rung in the evolutionary ladder. A nineteenth-century phenomenon, Social Darwinism persisted well into the twentieth century. Its philosophy may still be heard in the remnants of eugenics and the present-day interest in sociobiology.

Some colleges remained segregated until the 1960s. The inclusion of black studies classes came in response to student protests, which occurred against the backdrop of the push for civil rights and amidst significant racial unrest. The black power movement of this time strongly influenced many African-Americans to reclaim their heritage in everyday life and demand that it be taught in schools and universities. At risk here was the control of knowledge in the society. The black studies movement paved the way for further interest in African studies. Interestingly in today's universities, the field of black (or African-American) studies tends to be dominated by African-Americans while African studies tends to be dominated by European-Americans.

## CONCLUSION

At present, African studies is a woefully under-developed area of research, especially in sociology. Researchers need to mount aggressive programs determined to "ask new questions and question old answers." For this research to be successful, it must be located in a broader context, recognizing the unique historical, economic, social, cultural, political, and academic relationships that determine reality for Africans on the continent and in the diaspora. In each of these areas, relationships are generally structured hierarchically, with African worldviews and concerns subordinated to those of Europeans or whites. Such

distorted structural relations lead inevitably to distortions in research and conclusions. Thoughtful and committed researchers will seek to remedy this disparity in their work.

(SEE ALSO: *Apartheid; Slavery and Involuntary Servitude*)

### REFERENCES

Asante, Molefi 1987 *The Afrocentric Idea.* Philadelphia: Temple University Press.

Chinweizu 1975 *The West and the Rest of Us.* New York: Vintage.

Franklin, John Hope 1980 *From Slavery to Freedom: A History of Negro Americans,* 5th ed. New York: Knopf.

Fyfe, Christopher, ed. 1976 *African Studies Since 1945: A Tribute to Basil Davidson.* London: Longman.

Gromyko, Anatoly, and C. S. Whitaker (eds.) 1990 *Agenda for Action: African-Soviet-U.S. Cooperation.* Boulder, Colo.: L. Rienner.

Jackson, Henry 1984 *From the Congo to Soweto: U.S. Foreign Policy Toward Africa Since 1960.* New York: Quill.

Jones, Ann 1973 *Uncle Tom's Campus.* New York: Praeger.

Mazrui, Ali 1986 *The Africans: A Triple Heritage.* London: BBC Publications.

Mbiti, J. S. 1969 *African Religions and Philosophy.* London: Heinemann.

Nkrumah, Kwame 1965 *Neo-Colonialism: The Last Stage of Imperialism.* New York: International.

Rodney, Walter 1974 *How Europe Underdeveloped Africa.* Washington, D.C.: Howard University Press.

Soyinka, Wole 1976 *Myth, Literature and the African World.* New York: Cambridge University Press.

Sunshine, Catherine 1988 *The Caribbean: Survival, Struggle and Sovereignty.* Boston: South End Press.

Thompson, Vincent 1969 *Africa and Unity: The Evolution of Pan-Africanism.* London: Longman.

WALTER R. ALLEN

**AFRICAN-AMERICAN STUDIES** African-American research has expanded greatly in recent years. This article covers only selected aspects of this research: certain theoretical debates, the sociological interpretation of slavery, the debate on the underclass, and analyses of current discrimination.

## THEORIES OF BLACK–WHITE RELATIONS

Explanatory theories of U.S. racial relations can be classified roughly into "order-deficit" theories and "power-conflict" theories. Order-deficit theories accent the gradual inclusion of an outgroup such as African-Americans into the dominant white society and culture of the United States, and emphasize the internal subcultural barriers to further progress—that is, those that lie within the African-American outgroup—or both. Power-conflict theories, in contrast, emphasize external structural barriers preventing racial integration, such as the huge power and resource imbalance between black and white Americans.

Hirschman has suggested that one major order-deficit viewpoint, the assimilationist perspective, remains the major theoretical framework guiding most sociological research in the field of racial and ethnic relations (Hirschman 1983). One major scholar, Milton Gordon (1964, 1978), distinguishes several types of initial encounters between racial and ethnic groups and an array of subsequent assimilation outcomes ranging from acculturation to intermarriage. In his view immigrants in the United States have adapted by conforming substantially and by giving up much of their heritage for the dominant white Anglo-Saxon Protestant core culture. Gordon applies this scheme to African-Americans, whom he sees as substantially assimilated at the cultural level (for example, in regard to language) yet with some cultural differences remaining because of the "lower class subculture" among blacks. Beyond this acculturation Gordon sees modest integration at the primary-group level and little intermarriage. In more recent work Gordon (1981) has criticized affirmative action programs and adopted some arguments of the underclass perspective (see below). He is optimistic about the full assimilation and integration of the black middle class (see also Glazer 1975).

Power-conflict analysts reject the assimilationist view of eventual African-American inclusion and assimilation and assimilationists' inclination to focus on deficits within African-American subculture as major barriers to further integration. From the power-conflict perspective, the current condition of African-Americans is more oppressive than that of other U.S. immigrant groups because of its roots in the enslavement of Africans and in the subsequent semislavery of low-wage jobs and poor living conditions. Once a system of extreme subordination is established historically, those in the superior position continue to inherit and monopolize disproportionate socioeconomic resources over many generations. One important power-conflict analyst was Oliver C. Cox, who adopted a neo-Marxist approach: From the 1500s onward black–white stratification in North America arose out of the European imperialistic system of profit-oriented capitalism. The African slave trade was in Cox's view "a way of recruiting labor for the purpose of exploiting the great natural resources of America." The color of Africans was not important; they were chosen "simply because they were the best workers to be found for the heavy labor in the mines and plantations across the Atlantic" (Cox 1948, p. 342; see also Willhelm 1983).

Reflecting a power-conflict perspective, Bob Blauner (1972) argues that there are major differences between black Americans and the white immigrant groups at the center of much assimilationist analysis. The Africans brought across the Atlantic Ocean became part of an internal subordinated colony; they were incorporated against their will, providing much hard labor to build the new society—first as slaves, then as sharecroppers and tenant farmers, and later as low-wage urban laborers. As a result of the northward migration accelerating after 1900, African-Americans also became a subordinate part of the urban socioeconomic system.

## SLAVERY

Recent research on slavery has underscored the importance of the power-conflict perspective for understanding the history and conditions of African-Americans. Manning Marable (1985, p. 5) demonstrates that before the African slave trade began, Western Europeans were predisposed to accept slavery. Slavery was accepted by such Western intellectuals as Plato, Aristotle, and Sir Thomas More, and the European words for "black" had long been associated with the devil, barbarians, and slavery. North American enslavement of Africans was facilitated by this European background.

Research by sociologists, social historians, and legal scholars underscores the point that slavery is the foundation of African-American subordination. Legal scholar Patricia Williams has accented the dramatic difference between the oppression faced by the enslaved immigrants and that faced by all white immigrant groups: "The black slave experience was that of lost languages, cultures, tribal ties, kinship bonds, and even of the power to procreate in the image of oneself and not that of an alien master" (Williams, 1987, p. 415). Williams illustrates this last point by relating the story of Austin Miller, her great-great-grandfather, a thirty-five-year-old white lawyer who bought Williams's eleven-year-old black great-great-grandmother, Sophie, and her parents. Miller forced the young Sophie to become the mother of Williams's great-grandmother Mary. Williams's white great-great-grandfather was thus a child molester. African-Americans today constitute the only U.S. racial-ethnic group that is substantially the result of the forced miscegenation of its ancestors with members of the dominant racial group.

This negative impact of slavery did not mean that African-American slaves did not resist. Social historian Eugene Genovese (1974) has demonstrated that the extreme conditions of African-American slaves could produce both servile accommodation and violent rebellion. The slaves also created their own distinctive African-American culture out of African cultural fragments remaining to them and out of their creativity in coping with the immediate oppressiveness of New World culture. Herbert Gutman (1976) has demonstrated the extensive cultural and family resiliency and creativity the slaves possessed.

Recent social science research has made it clear why not only white southerners but also many white northerners were willing to perpetuate African-American slavery. Whites in the North built their society in part on slave labor and in part on white immigrant labor from Europe. By the mid-1600s there were strict slave codes in the North. For example, in 1641, three years after whites brought slaves into Massachusetts, the whites enshrined this slavery in law; and Massachusetts merchants and shippers played crucial roles in the North American slave trade. Not until the 1780s did public opinion and court cases come together to abolish New England slavery (Higginbotham 1978, pp. 63–65). By 1786 slaves made up 7 percent of the New York population. Only in 1799 was a partial emancipation statue passed; not until the 1850s were all slaves freed. Moreover, an intense political and economic subordination of free African-Americans accompanied the emancipation of slaves in the North (Higginbotham 1978, pp. 144–149). As Benjamin Ringer put it, "despite the early emancipation of slaves in the North it [racial subordination] remained there, not merely as fossilized remains but as a deeply engrained coding for the future" (1983, p. 533). This important sociological point helps to explain the extensive system of antiblack discrimination and "Jim Crow" segregation that existed in the northern states before and after the Civil War. The freed slaves and their descendants who migrated from the South to northern cities after 1870 migrated into a socioeconomic system already coded to subordinate African-Americans.

## THE UNDERCLASS

Since the 1980s many social scientists, journalists, and government policy analysts have focused on the black "underclass," usually defined as low-income African-Americans, as the root of contemporary black problems. Many analysts have adopted some version of an order-deficit perspective, one that sees in the values and family structures of the black underclass the barriers to assimilation into middle class society. Recent underclass analysts have rehabilitated a viewpoint developed in a 1965 U.S. government publication, *The Negro Family.* There Daniel P. Moynihan argued that a tangle of pathology characterized much of black America and that "there is considerable evidence that the Negro community is, in fact, dividing between a stable middle class group that is steadily growing stronger and more successful and an increasingly disorganized and disadvantaged lower class group" (Moynihan 1965, pp. 5–6).

Since the late 1970s many white journalists and scholarly analysts have adopted and developed this perspective. For example, Ken Auletta produced an influential series of articles published in the *New Yorker* and later developed into a book entitled *The Underclass* (1982). Auletta discusses the black, white, and Hispanic underclasses but emphasizes black Americans. For Auletta, discrimination plays no significant part in the problems of the underclass, described as those with a lifestyle characterized by poverty and antisocial life patterns including immorality, broken families, and a poorly developed work ethic. About the same time black sociologist William J. Wilson became a major exponent of the underclass perspective. Wilson's 1978 work, *The Declining Significance of Race*, contended that affirmative action programs had widened the gap between the increasingly successful black middle class and the deteriorating underclass (for a thorough analysis of middle class conditions, see Farley 1984; Landry 1987). Most readers interpreted Wilson's book as suggesting that discrimination had little significance for African-Americans moving into the middle class and that class differences were more important than antiblack discrimination in explaining the condition of African-Americans.

In *The Truly Disadvantaged* (1987) Wilson further developed his view of the underclass. There he discusses numerous fallacies in the analysis of order-deficit authors such as Moynihan and Auletta. In *The Truly Disadvantaged* Wilson prefers a structural rather than a value-oriented or subcultural explanation for the plight of the underclass. As he sees it, a central dilemma for the underclass is the departure of middle class families from traditional black areas into better neighborhoods farther away. As a result, not only are there fewer role models for low-income families but there are also fewer supportive institutions, including small stores and churches. Coupled with the resulting social isolation are the concentration effects of having single-parent families, criminals, and the unemployed crowded into one area. Wilson emphasizes joblessness as the important causal factor in the troubles of the underclass: If young black men and women cannot afford to get married, rent an apartment, and live together in a stable economic situation, young black women set up their own households, raise their children, and often depend on welfare benefits.

Other scholars have amplified Wilson's structural critique of order-deficit interpretations of the underclass. Douglas Glasgow (1987) takes issue with the deficit theory's major assumptions: that a value deficiency in the black community created the underclass; that the underclass problem is mainly a female or family problem rather than a racial discrimination problem; and that 1960s poverty programs helped create the underclass. Sidney Willhelm (1983) shows that the restructuring of U.S. capitalism since World War II substantially created the underclass of unemployed and underemployed African-Americans. Those African-Americans who were able to move into better-paying blue-collar jobs during the 1960s and 1970s often faced their industries' decline because of automation and capital flight in the 1980s and 1990s. The movement of jobs from northern cities to Sunbelt cities and overseas is not just part of a routine fluctuation in U.S. history but signals rather that capitalists are moving capital once reinvested in the United States to areas with cheap labor and weak governmental regulation. While the agricultural South and the industrializing cities of the North once needed African-American labor on a significant scale, "today," Willhelm argues, "the economics of corporate capitalism, by turning to automation, makes Black labor unessential" (p. 240). The changing investment strategies of corporate executives, not deficits in black values and family organization, are the major villains in creating an African-American underclass.

## DISCRIMINATION

One additional weakness in most order-deficit arguments is the rejection of racial discrimination as a significant reason for current African-American difficulties. Some, such as Wilson, who criticize the order-deficit interpretation of the underclass problem do not accent continuing racial discrimination. In interviews with rank-and-file whites in the late 1970s and early 1980s, Blauner (1989, p. 197) found that all but one viewed recent decades as an era of great racial progress for black Americans; most viewed racial discrimination as no longer a serious problem in the United States.

Racial discrimination can be defined in social-contextual terms as "practices carried out by members of dominant racial groups which have a differential and negative impact on members of subordinate racial groups" (Eckberg and Feagin 1980; see also Pettigrew 1975). Major dimensions of this discrimination include (a) the motivation for discrimination; (b) the discriminatory action; (c) the effects; (d) the relationship between motivation and action; (e) the relationship between action and effects; (f) the immediate organizational context; and (g) the societal context. Much discrimination research concentrates on (c), the effects of discrimination. A major report by the National Research Council (Jaynes and Williams 1989) summarizes social science evidence on the effects of antiblack discrimination: One in three African-Americans lives in poverty; median African-American family income is 60 percent of median white family income; most African-Americans remain segregated in predominantly minority neighborhoods and schools; and significant inequality remains in political participation.

During recent decades the number of black professional, technical, managerial, and administrative workers has increased significantly. Yet African-Americans in these categories have been disproportionately concentrated in jobs with status lower than those that whites fill. Within the professional and technical categories, African-Americans today are most commonly found in such fields as social and recreational work, elementary school teaching, vocational counseling, personnel, dietetics, and health-care work; they are least often found among lawyers and judges, dentists, writers and artists, engineers, and university teachers. Within the managerial and administrative categories, African-Americans are most commonly found among restaurant and bar managers, health administrators, and government officials; they are least commonly found among top corporate executives, bank and financial managers, and wholesale sales managers (Brimmer 1976; Feagin 1989, p. 226).

Within employment settings black Americans face much subtle and blatant discrimination. One example of subtle discrimination is tokenism. Reluctantly tearing down blatant discriminatory barriers over the last two decades, many white officials and executives have retreated to a second line of defense including tokenism. The tokenist strategy is to hire African-Americans for conspicuous but powerless positions. Kenneth Clark (1980) has noted that well-educated African-Americans moving into nontraditional jobs in corporate America have frequently found themselves tracked into positions in "ghettos" within organizations, positions such as a manager of a department of "community affairs" or "special markets." Clark notes that blacks "are rarely found in line positions concerned with developing or controlling production, supervising the work of large numbers of whites or competing with their white 'peers' for significant positions" (p. 30).

Edward Jones (1985; 1986) has reported on a nationwide survey of black corporate executives, all of whom had graduate-level business degrees. Nearly all (98 percent) felt that black managers had not achieved equal opportunity with white managers in their companies. More than 90 percent felt there was much antiblack hostility in corporations and that black managers had less opportunity than whites to succeed in their firms solely on the basis of ability. Two-thirds felt that many whites in corporations still believe African-Americans are intellectually inferior. Most reported that this adverse racial climate had a negative impact on the evaluations, assignments, and promotions of black executives.

In addition, research on cities reveals high levels of residential segregation and housing discrimination. Using 1980 data, Denton and Massey (1988) found that in twenty metropolitan areas with the largest black populations, blacks at all socioeconomic levels continued to be highly segregated into their own residential areas. There has been some increase in the number of African-Americans living in suburban areas, but researchers have found this is mostly because black residents of central cities have spilled into adjacent, often predominantly black, suburbs. In addition, housing search studies in Dallas, Boston, and Denver have found differential treatment favoring white owners and renters looking for housing; whites were more likely to be shown or told about more housing units than were African-Americans with comparable socioeconomic status (Yinger 1984).

The aforementioned National Research Council report noted that by the mid-1970s "many Americans believed that . . . the Civil Rights Act of 1964 had led to broad-scale elimination of discrimination against Afro-Americans in public accommodations" (Jaynes and Williams 1989, p. 84). Yet recent research (Feagin 1990) based on interviews with middle class African-Americans in fourteen cities found significant discrimination in public accommodations such as restaurants, department stores, and hotels, as well as on the street. African-Americans frequently received poor service in public accommodations and suffered racially motivated hostility from white strangers and white police officers on the street.

Low-income and middle-income African-Americans experience discrimination in a number of different areas. This discrimination has a cumulative impact. Contemporary discrimination for most black Americans entails more than an occasional discriminatory act; it entails, rather, a lifetime of blatant and subtle acts of differential treatment by whites that often cumulate to a severely oppressive psychological and group impact. African-Americans cope with this recurrent discrimination in a variety of ways ranging from repressed rage to angry aggression and retaliation (Cobbs 1988; on response patterns of minorities to discrimination, see Allport 1954). This cumulative and persisting discrimination is a major reason for the periodic resurgence of civil rights organizations and protest movements among African-Americans (see Bloom 1987; Morris 1984). Future research on African-Americans will need to focus more centrally on the significance and impact of cumulative racial discrimination.

(SEE ALSO: *Discrimination; Race; Segregation and Desegregation; Slavery and Involuntary Servitude; Urban Underclass*)

## REFERENCES

Allport, Gordon 1954 *The Nature of Prejudice.* Reading, Mass.: Addison-Wesley.

Auletta, Ken 1982 *The Underclass.* New York: Random House.

Blauner, Bob 1972 *Racial Oppression in America.* New York: Harper and Row.

———1989 *Black Lives, White Lives.* Berkeley: University of California Press.

Bloom, Jack M. 1987 *Class, Race and the Civil Rights Movement.* Bloomington: Indiana University Press.

Brimmer, Andrew F. 1976 *The Economic Position of Black Americans.* Washington, D.C.: National Commission for Manpower Policy.

Clark, Kenneth B. 1980 "The Role of Race." *New York Times Magazine,* October 5, p. 30.

Cobbs, Price M. 1988 "Critical Perspectives on the Psychology of Race." In *The State of Black America: 1988.* New York: National Urban League.

Cox, Oliver C. 1948 *Caste, Class, and Race.* Garden City, N.Y.: Doubleday.

Denton, Nancy A., and Douglas S. Massey 1988 "Residential Segregation of Blacks, Hispanics, and Asians by Socioeconomic Status and Generation." *Social Science Quarterly* 69:797–817.

Eckberg, Douglas, and Joe R. Feagin 1980 "Discrimination: Motivation, Action, Effects, and Context." *Annual Review of Sociology.* 6:1–23.

Farley, Reynolds 1984 *Blacks and Whites: Narrowing the Gap.* Cambridge: Harvard University Press.

Feagin, Joe R. 1989 *Racial and Ethnic Relations,* 3rd ed. Englewood Cliffs, N.J.: Prentice-Hall.

——— 1991 "The Continuing Significance of Race:

The Black Middle Class in Public Places." *American Sociological Review* 56:101–116.

Genovese, Eugene D. 1974 *Roll, Jordan, Roll: The World the Slaves Made.* New York: Pantheon.

Glazer, Nathan 1975 *Affirmative Discrimination.* New York: Basic Books.

Glasgow, Douglas G. 1987 "The Black Underclass in Perspective." In *The State of Black America: 1987.* New York: National Urban League.

Gordon, Milton 1964 *Assimilation in American Life.* New York: Oxford University Press.

—— 1978 *Human Nature, Class and Ethnicity.* New York: Oxford University Press.

—— 1981 "Models of Pluralism." *Annals of the American Academy of Political and Social Science* 454:178–188.

Gutman, Herbert 1976 *The Black Family in Slavery and Freedom, 1790–1925.* New York: Pantheon.

Higginbotham, A. Leon 1978 *In the Matter of Color.* New York: Oxford University Press.

Hirschman, Charles 1983 "America's Melting Pot Reconsidered." *Annual Review of Sociology* 9:397–423.

Jaynes, Gerald D., and Robin Williams, Jr. (eds.) 1989 *A Common Destiny: Blacks and American Society.* Washington, D.C.: National Academy Press.

Jones, Edward 1985 "Beneficiaries or Victims? Progress or Process." Unpublished research report. South Orange, N.J.

—— 1986 "What It's Like to Be a Black Manager." *Harvard Business Review* (May–June):84–93.

Landry, Bart 1987 *The New Black Middle Class.* Berkeley: University of California Press.

Marable, Manning 1985 *Black American Politics.* London: New Left Books, 1985.

Moynihan, Daniel P. 1965 *The Negro Family: The Case for National Action.* Washington, D.C.: U.S. Government Printing Office.

Morris, Aldon D. 1984 *The Origins of the Civil Rights Movement.* New York: Free Press.

Ringer, Benjamin B. 1983 *"We the People" and Others.* New York: Tavistock.

Pettigrew, Thomas 1975 *Racial Discrimination in the United States.* New York: Harper and Row.

Willhelm, Sidney 1983 *Black in a White America.* Cambridge, Mass.: Schenkman.

Williams, Patricia 1987 "Alchemical Notes: Reconstructing Ideals from Deconstructed Rights." *Harvard Civil Rights and Civil Liberties Review* 22: 401–434.

Wilson, William J. 1978 *The Declining Significance of Race.* Chicago: University of Chicago Press.

—— 1987 *The Truly Disadvantaged: The Inner City, the Underclass, and Public Policy.* Chicago: University of Chicago Press.

Yinger, John 1984 "Measuring Racial and Ethnic Discrimination with Fair Housing Audits: A Review of Existing Evidence and Research Methodology." Washington, D.C.: HUD Conference on Fair Housing Testing.

JOE R. FEAGIN

**AGGRESSION**   Perhaps no other construct in social psychology subsumes a broader range of behaviors than does aggression. At a purely descriptive level, swatting a fly, teasing, criticizing, or rendering someone unconscious (either to take a life or to save it) could all be considered aggressive acts. Treating diverse behaviors as indicators of a unitary construct is undoubtedly a reason for many of the empirical inconsistencies observed in research on aggression over the past fifty years. Nonetheless, recent analyses of the various laboratory response measures that have been used to represent aggressive behavior support the notion of a common underlying construct of aggression (Carlson, Marcus-Newhall, and Miller 1989).

Theories put forth to explain aggressive behavior have generally focused on differing aspects of the aggressive act. The ethological/instinctivist approach emphasizes the biological basis of aggressive behavior; frustration-aggression theory emphasizes the antecedent conditions; learning theory looks primarily at the outcomes of the behavior; and the social cognitive perspective focuses on the attributions that people make in social situations. Although there is substantial overlap among them, these approaches differ not only in their primary focus but in their ability to explain the acquisition, persistence, and control of aggressive behavior.

## ETHOLOGICAL/INSTINCTIVE THEORIES

The work of Lorenz (1966) illustrates the ethological approach to the study of aggression. Lorenz views aggression in animals and humans as a "species-preserving instinct" that performs an adaptive function. The energy for aggression is seen as occurring naturally within the organism and is regulated by appropriate stimuli within the environment. Aggression is considered adaptive for several reasons: (1) Territorial aggression serves an ecological function by regulating the dispersion of a species; (2) aggression promotes selection of the fittest for reproduction; and (3) it serves to protect the young. Major drawbacks to the ethological approach concern the minor role allocated to learning principles and the validity of generalizing from infrahumans to humans.

In contrast to the ethological approach, Freud (1927) posited a substantially different type of instinctive, aggressive drive, which he termed *Thanatos* or *the death instinct*. The aim of the death instinct is Nirvana, or the ultimate cessation of all stimulation. Thanatos was invoked to explain sadistic and masochistic behaviors in humans, and aggression was seen as Thanatos turned outward. Although psychoanalytic theory is historically very important in the study of aggression, Freud's notion of a death instinct was highly speculative and never popularly accepted, even among psychoanalysts.

## FRUSTRATION-AGGRESSION THEORY

Frustration-aggression theory can be viewed as a conceptual bridge between the psychoanalytic, instinctive view of aggression and the subsequently emerging behavioristic view. The link between frustration and aggression was formalized by the proposition of Dollard et al. (1939, p. 1) that "the occurrence of aggressive behavior always presupposes the existence of frustration and, contrariwise, that the existence of frustration always leads to some form of aggression." Frustration was defined by Dollard et al. as "an interference with the occurrence of an instigated goal response at its proper time in the behavior sequence" (1939, p. 7); and aggression was defined as a "sequence of behavior, the goal response of which is the injury of the person toward whom it is directed"

(1939, p. 9). According to the theory, the strongest instigation is to aggress against the agent perceived to be responsible for the frustration. If such "direct" aggression is inhibited, "indirect" or "displaced" aggression is expected to occur. Inhibition is presumed to vary directly with the strength of the punishment anticipated for the aggressive act.

Although research has shown that frustration can cause aggression in both animals and humans, it soon became clear that the initial statement of frustration-aggression theory was too restrictive. Miller (1941), in collaboration with the original theorists, acknowledged that frustration could have consequences other than aggression. Subsequent research has also shown that aggression may occur even when there is no apparent frustration, that it can be learned much as any other response, and that it may be instrumental rather than hostile in its intent. Additional research has shown that the presence of aggressive cues (i.e., stimuli associated with aggressive acts in general or with specific characteristics of the frustrating agent) can heighten the probability of aggressive behavior.

Berkowitz (1989) has advanced a reformulation of the frustration-aggression hypothesis in what he has termed a *cognitive-neoassociationistic* model of aggression. This view holds that aversive conditions or events initiate a sequence of responses in which aversive stimulation first gives rise to negative affect (i.e., any feeling that individuals generally seek to avoid). It is this negative affect that, in turn, gives rise to aggression. Thus, frustrations, along with other stimuli such as noxious odors, disgusting scenes, and high temperatures, create an instigation to aggression because they are aversive and lead to negative affect. This negative affect is presumed to activate a variety of expressive-motor reactions, memories, and feeling states that are associated with both fighting and fleeing. A variety of other learned, situational, and dispositional factors then determine the relative strengths of the inclinations toward fleeing and fighting. After these initial, relatively automatic responses have taken place, thinking (cognition) may enter the process to influence subsequent emotional and behavioral reactions. Thus, according to the cognitive-neoassociationistic model, it is only during the later stages of the process that persons make causal attributions about the negative experience and attempt to control their feelings and aggressive actions.

## LEARNING THEORY APPROACHES

All of the major theoretical explanations of aggression allow for the acquisition of aggressive behavior; they differ, however, in the importance of learning as a determinant of aggression. From the learning theory perspective, aggression can be viewed as a learned operant that is reinforced whenever aggression leads to goal attainment. Using this framework, Sears (1958) has argued that the motivation to aggress could also be acquired through a process of secondary reinforcement in which successful goal attainment is consistently paired with the suffering of the victims. For example, when a bully takes candy from another child, the latter's distress is paired with the drive reduction and satisfaction on the part of the bully associated with having the candy for himself. In this manner, distress in others becomes rewarding in itself.

Bandura (1973) has noted that more complicated forms of aggressive behavior (or any behavior for that matter) are unlikely to be emitted as free operants. Similarly, trial and error processes and behavioral shaping techniques are too inefficient to explain the initial occurrence of an aggressive act. Instead, Bandura suggested that aggressive behaviors can be acquired through a four-step process of observational or imitative learning involving (1) attentional processes; (2) memory and retention processes; (3) behavioral acquisition and enactment processes; and (4) reinforcement and motivational processes including self-reinforcement. Self-generated consequences for behavior have important implications for the regulation of aggression. For example, individuals for whom aggressive conduct is a source of pride will experience a sense of satisfaction (i.e., positive self-reinforcement), whereas others may experience a sense of shame.

## SOCIAL COGNITION THEORIES

More recently, a social cognitive approach, developed by Kenneth Dodge and others (e.g., see Dodge and Crick 1990) has built on the work of Bandura, especially with regard to self-regulatory processes. It incorporates developments in a number of social psychological fields including attribution, decision making, and information processing. According to this approach, individuals in social situations proceed through a series of information-processing steps which begin with encoding and interpreting information, and are followed by the consideration, selection, and performance of a behavior. Effective processing at each step will lead to a socially acceptable performance within the situation, whereas deficient processing may result in aggressive behavior.

In the first step of processing, relevant information is encoded. Ineffective processing at this stage, for example the failure to recognize an important facial cue such as a smile by another, may increase the likelihood of an aggressive response. Step 2 is an interpretive step in which the cues encoded in the prior step are given meaning and represented in long-term memory. Thus, a smile may be interpreted to mean that another is "only kidding." Step 3 involves the search of long-term memory for an appropriate response. Some responses will have strong associations with specific mental representations of the relevant cues, and these are most likely to emerge as potential responses within the social situation. The next step in processing involves selecting the most appropriate response. The exact decision strategy that individuals use to select a response is unknown, although idiosyncratic factors are likely to influence the process. The final step is to perform the selected response. An important aspect of behavioral enactment is response monitoring, in which the behavioral response and its effects are observed by the actor. Since this process involves attention to social cues, the five-step process is hypothesized to begin anew.

## CURRENT STATUS OF THEORIES OF AGGRESSION

Each of the theories examined makes a compelling case for focusing on specific aspects of the aggressive response such as the role of biological factors in initiating the response and the role of learning and cognitive processes in maintaining it. Although there has been a greater emphasis on cognitive factors in recent time, it appears that any satisfactory explanation must incorporate the influences of biological, psychological, situational, and cultural factors. As yet, no overarching theory has emerged to integrate these diverse factors.

(SEE ALSO: *Social Psychology*)

### REFERENCES

Bandura, Albert 1973 *Aggression: A Social Learning Analysis.* New York: Holt.

Berkowitz, Leonard 1989 "Frustration-Aggression Hypothesis: Examination and Reformulation." *Psychological Bulletin* 106:59–73.

Carlson, Michael, Amy Marcus-Newhall, and Norman Miller 1989 "Evidence for a General Construct of Aggression." *Personality and Social Psychology Bulletin* 15:377–389.

Dodge, Kenneth, and Nicki Crick 1990 "Social Information-Processing Bases of Aggressive Behavior in Children." *Personality and Social Psychology Bulletin* 16:8–22.

Dollard, John, Leonard Doob, Neal Miller, O. H. Miller, and Robert Sears 1939 *Frustration and Aggression.* New Haven: Yale University Press.

Freud, Sigmund 1927 *Beyond the Pleasure Principle.* New York: Boni and Liveright.

Lorenz, Konrad 1966 *On Aggression.* New York: Harcourt, Brace and World.

Miller, Neal 1941 "The Frustration-Aggression Hypothesis." *Psychological Review* 48:337–342.

Sears, Robert 1958 "Personality Development in the Family." In J. M. Seidman, ed., *The Child.* New York: Rinehart.

KARL KOSLOSKI

**AGING, THE AGED** *See* Cohort Perspectives; Death and Dying; Health and the Life Course; Life Course; Long-Term Care; Nursing Homes; Retirement; Social Gerontology.

**AGRICULTURAL INNOVATION** Getting a new idea adopted can be very difficult. This is all the more frustrating when it seems to the proponents of the new idea that it has very obvious advantages. It can be a challenge to try to introduce new ideas in rural areas, particularly in less developed societies, where people are somewhat set in their ways—ways that have evolved slowly, through trial and error. It's all the more difficult when those introducing new ideas don't understand why people follow traditional practices. Rural sociologists and agricultural extension researchers who have studied the diffusion of agricultural innovations have traditionally been oriented toward speeding up the diffusion process (Rogers 1983). Pro-innovation bias has sometimes led sociologists to forget that "changing people's customs is an even more delicate responsibility than surgery" (Spicer 1952).

Although innovation relies on invention, and although considerable creativity often accompanies the discovery of how to use an invention, innovation and invention are not the same thing. Innovation does, however, involve more than a change from one well-established way of doing things to another well-established practice. As with all innovations, those in agriculture involve a change that requires significant imagination, breaks with established ways of doing things, and creates new production capacity. Of course, these criteria are not exact, and it is often difficult to tell where one innovation stops and another starts. The easiest way out of this is to rely on potential adopters of an innovation to define ideas that they perceive to be new.

Innovations are not all alike. New ways of doing things may be more or less compatible with prevalent norms and values. Some innovations may be perceived as relatively difficult to use and understand (i.e., complex), while others are a good deal simpler. Some can be experimented with in limited trials that reduce the risks of adoption (i.e., divisible). Innovations also vary in the costs and advantages they offer in both economic and social terms (e.g., prestige, convenience, satisfaction). In the economists' terms, innovation introduces a new production function that changes the set of possibilities which define what can be produced (Schumpeter 1950). Rural sociologists have studied the adoption of such agricultural innovations as specially bred crops (e.g., hybrid corn and high-yield wheat and rice); many kinds of machines (e.g., tractors, harvesters, pumps); chemical and biological fertilizers, pesticides, and insecticides; cropping practices (e.g., soil and water conservation); and techniques related to animal husbandry (e.g., new feeds, disease control, breeding). Often they have relied upon government agencies such as the U.S. Department of Agriculture to tell them what the recommended new practices are.

The diffusion of agricultural innovations is a process whereby new ways of doing things are spread within and between agrarian communities. Newness implies a degree of uncertainty both because there are a variable number of alternatives and because there is usually some range of relative probability of outcomes associated with the actions involved. Rogers (1983) stresses that the diffusion of innovations includes the communication of information, by various means, about these sets of alternative actions and their possible outcomes. Information about innovations may come via impersonal channels, such as the mass media, or it may pass through social networks. From an individual's point of view, the process of innovation is usually conceived to start with initial awareness of the innovation and how it functions. It ends with adoption or nonadoption. In between these end points is an interactive, iterative process of attitude formation, decision making, and action. The cumulative frequency of adopters over time describes an S-shaped (logistic) curve. The frequency distribution over time is often bell-shaped and approximately normal.

Individual innovativeness has been character-ized in five ideal-type adopter categories (Rogers 1983). The first 2 to 3 percent to adopt an innovation, the "innovators," are characterized as venturesome. The next 10 to 15 percent, the "early adopters," are characterized as responsible, solid, local opinion leaders. The next 30 to 35 percent are the "early majority," who are seen as being deliberate. They are followed by the "late majority" (30 to 35 percent), who are cautious and skeptical, and innovate under social and economic pressures. Finally, there are the "laggards," who comprise the bottom 15 percent. They are characterized as "traditional," although they are often simply in a precarious economic position.

Earlier adopters are likely to have higher social status and better education, and to be upwardly mobile. They tend to have larger farms, more favorable attitudes toward modern business practices (e.g., credit), and more specialized operations. Earlier adopters are also argued to have greater empathy, rationality, and ability to deal with abstractions. They are less fatalistic and dogmatic, and have both positive attitudes toward change and science, and higher achievement motivation and aspirations. Early adopters report more social participation and network connections, particularly to change agents, and greater exposure to both mass media and interpersonal communication networks.

Although Rogers (1983) provides dozens of such generalizations about the characteristics of early and late adopters, he admits that the evidence on many of these propositions is somewhat mixed (Downs and Mohr 1976). Even the frequently researched proposition that those with higher social status and greater resources are likely to innovate earlier and more often has garnered far less than unanimous support (Cancian 1967, 1979; Gartrell 1977). Cancian argues that this is a result of "upper middle-class conservatism," but subsequent meta-analysis has clearly demonstrated that the relationship between status and innovation is indeed linear (Gartrell and Gartrell 1985; Lewis et al. 1989). If anything, those with very high status or resources show a marked tendency to turn their awareness of innovations into trial at a very high rate (Gartrell and Gartrell 1979).

Ryan and Gross (1942) provide a classic example of diffusion research. Hybrid corn seed, developed by Iowa State and other land-grant university researchers, increased yields 20 percent over those of open-pollinated varieties. Hybrid corn also was more drought-resistant and was better suited to mechanical harvesting. Agricultural extension agents and seed company salesmen promoted it heavily. Its drawback was that it lost its hybrid vigor after only one generation, so farmers could not save the seed from the best-looking plants. (Of course, this was not at all a drawback to the seed companies!)

Based on a retrospective survey of 259 farmers in two small communities, Ryan and Gross found that 10 percent had adopted hybrid corn after five years (by 1933). Between 1933 and 1936 an additional 30 percent adopted, and by the time of the study (1941) only two farmers did not use the hybrid. Early adopters were more cosmopolitan, and had higher social and economic status. The average respondent took nine years to go from first knowledge to adoption, and interpersonal networks and modeling were judged to be critical to adoption. In other cases diffusion time has been much shorter. Beginning in 1944, the average diffusion time for a weed spray (also in Iowa) was between 1.7 years for innovators and 3.1 years for laggards (Beal and Rogers 1960; Rogers 1983, p. 204). Having adopted many innovations, farmers are likely to adopt others more quickly.

Adoption-diffusion research in rural sociology has dominated all research traditions studying innovation. Rural sociology produced 791 (26 percent) of 3,085 studies up to 1981 (Rogers 1983, p. 52). Most of this research relied upon correlational analysis of survey data based on farmers' recall of past behaviors. This kind of study reached its peak in the mid 1960s. By the mid 1970s the farm crisis in the United States and the global depression spurred rural sociologists to begin to reevaluate this tradition. By the 1980s global export markets had shrunk, farm commod-

ity prices had fallen, net farm incomes had declined, and high interest rates had resulted in poor debt-to-asset ratios. What followed was a massive (50 percent) decapitalization of agriculture, particularly in the Midwest and Great Plains.

Criticisms of adoption-diffusion research include (1) pro-innovation bias; (2) a lack of consideration of all the consequences of innovation; (3) an individual bias; (4) methods problems; (5) American ethnocentric biases; (6) the passing of the dominant modernization-development paradigm. The pro-innovation bias of researchers has led them to ignore the negative consequences of innovation (van Es 1983). Indeed, innovativeness itself is positively valued (Downs and Mohr 1976). The agencies that fund research and the commercial organizations (e.g., seed companies) that support it have strong vested interests in promoting diffusion. Furthermore, successful innovations leave visible traces and can be more easily studied using retrospective social surveys, so researchers are more likely to focus on successful innovations.

Since most researchers are well aware of this problem, it can be addressed by deliberately focusing on unsuccessful innovations, and by studying discontinuance and reinvention. It can also be avoided by the use of prospective research designs, including qualitative comparative case studies, that track potential innovation and innovators' perceptions and experiences. This should facilitate the investigation of noncommercial innovations and should result in a better understanding of the reasons why people and organizations decide to use new ideas. Moreover, these methods will likely lead to a better understanding of the system context in which innovations diffuse.

One of the most strident critiques of the pro-innovation bias of the "land-grant college complex" was voiced by Hightower (1972). Agricultural scientists at Davis, California, worked on the development and diffusion of hard tomatoes and mechanized pickers (Friedland and Barton 1975). They ignored the effects of these innovations on small farms and farm labor, except in the sense that they designed both innovations to solve labor problems expected when the U.S. Congress ended the bracero program through which Mexican workers were brought in to harvest the crops. In the six years after that program ended (1964 to 1970) the mechanical harvester took over the industry. About thirty-two thousand former hand pickers were out of work. They were replaced by eighteen thousand workers who rode machines and sorted tomatoes. Of the four thousand farmers who produced tomatoes in California in 1962, only six hundred were still in business in 1971. The tomato industry honored the inventor for saving the tomato for California, and consumers got cheaper, harder tomatoes—even if they preferred softer ones.

Several other classic examples of agricultural innovation illustrate problems that result from not fully considering the consequences of innovation (Fliegel and van Es 1983). Until the late 1970s rural sociologists, among others, studiously ignored Walter Goldschmidt's 1940s study (republished in 1978) of the effects of irrigation on two communities in California's San Joaquin Valley. Dinuba had large family farms, and it also had more local business, greater retail sales, and a greater diversity of social, educational, recreational, and cultural organizations. Arrin was surrounded by large industrial corporate farms supported by irrigation. These farms had absentee owners and Mexican labor. This produced a much lower quality of life that was confirmed three decades later (Buttel et al. 1990, p. 147).

The enforced ban on earlier chemical innovations in agriculture by the U.S. Food and Drug Administration provides another interesting example. Chemical innovations such as DDT insecticide, 2,4-D weed spray, and DES cattle feed revolutionized farm production in the 1950s and 1960s. This revolution provided the basis of Everett Rogers' Ph.D. dissertation in 1954, and of course produced crop surpluses that accumulated in storage bins. Rogers read Rachel Carson's *Silent Spring* (1962) but confessed that he regarded her antichemical arguments as extreme, absurd, and a threat to the progress of American agriculture (Rogers 1983). In 1972, DDT was banned because it constituted a health threat

(Dunlap 1981), and 2,4-D, DES, and similar products were banned soon afterward. Finally, in 1980 the U.S. Department of Agriculture reversed its policy and began to advise farmers and gardeners to consider alternative, organic methods that used fewer chemicals.

The impact of technical changes in U.S. agriculture, particularly the rapid mechanization begun in the Great Depression, put farmers on the "treadmill of technology" (Cochran 1979; LeVeen 1978). Larger farmers who are less risk-aversive adopt early, reap an "innovation rent," reduce their per-unit costs, and increase profits. After the innovation spreads to the early majority, aggregate output increases dramatically. Prices then fall disproportionately, since agricultural products have low elasticity of demand. Lower, declining prices force the late majority to adopt, but they gain little. They have to adopt to stay in business, and some late adopters may be forced out because they cannot compete. This treadmill increases concentration of agricultural production and benefits large farmers, the suppliers of innovations, and consumers. Indeed, it helps to create and to subsidize cheap urban labor. When it comes to environmental practices, however, large farms are not early innovators (Pampel and van Es 1977; Buttel et al. 1990).

The individual bias of adoption-diffusion research is evident in its almost exclusive focus upon individual farmers rather than upon industrial farms or other agribusiness. There is also a tendency to blame the victim if anything goes wrong (Rogers 1983). Change agents are too rarely criticized for providing incomplete or inaccurate information, and governments and corporations are too infrequently criticized for promoting inappropriate or harmful innovations. Empirical surveys of individual farmers also lead to a number of methodological problems. As noted above, if surveys are retrospective, recall relies on fallible memory and renders unsuccessful innovations difficult to study. These surveys are commonly combined with correlational analysis that makes it difficult to address issues of causality. After all, the farmer's attitudes and personality are measured at the time of the interview, and the innovation probably occurred some time before. As we have pointed out, these issues can be addressed by prospective designs that incorporate other methods, such as qualitative case studies and available records data, and focus on the social context of innovation.

To expand this context further, it should be recognized that since World War II, world food markets have been dominated by American interests. Surplus food has been dispensed on a concessionary basis to client states to serve foreign policy goals (Friedmann 1982; Kransner 1986). Adoption-diffusion research fitted quite nicely within the modernization paradigm that dominated American thinking about development before 1970. Diffusion research itself diffused to developing countries with the students who studied in the American universities during the 1960s, then declined in the 1980s. Researchers and planners became aware that trickle-down effects from adoption of innovations really are a trickle, and that the profits of large landowners and multinational agribusiness firms rarely reach the poor. Unless technological innovations are highly divisible and affordable, so that small farmers can use them, and unless innovations create more demand for labor that benefits the lot of the poor, the diffusion of innovations increases inequality (Gartrell 1977; Gartrell and Gartrell 1979).

While it may no longer be as fashionable as it once was, the adoption-diffusion model still has much to offer. Technological change in agriculture is still vitally important throughout the world and, correctly applied, diffusion research can assist in its investigation. As we have stressed above, it is important to consider the consequences of technological change as well as the determinants of adoption of innovation. It is critical to apply the model to environmental practices and other "noncommercial" innovations in agriculture. In-depth case studies over time are needed to further our understanding of how and why individuals and agricultural social collectives adopt technological change. The social contexts that condition the rate of transition from knowl-edge to adoption must be appropriately operationalized. All this provides a basis for continuing to build on a wealth of research materials.

(SEE ALSO: *Diffusion Theories; Rural Sociology*)

## REFERENCES

Buttel, Frederick, Olav Larson, and Gilbert Gillespie, Jr. 1990 *The Sociology of Agriculture.* New York: Greenwood Press.

Cancian, Frank 1967 "Stratification and Risk Taking: A Theory Tested on Agricultural Innovations." *American Sociological Review* 32:912–927.

———— 1979 *The Innovator's Situation: Upper-Middle-Class Conservatism in Agricultural Communities.* Stanford, Calif.: Stanford University Press.

Carson, Rachael 1962 *Silent Spring.* New York: Fawcett/Crest.

Cochran, Willard 1979 *The Development of American Agriculture.* Minneapolis: University of Minnesota Press.

Downs, George, and Lawrence Mohr 1976 "Conceptual Issues in the Study of Innovations." *Administrative Science Quarterly* 21:700–714.

Dunlap, Thomas 1981 *DDT: Scientists, Citizens and Public Policy.* Princeton, N.J.: Princeton University Press.

Fliegel, Frederick, and John van Es 1983 "The Diffusion-Adoption Process in Agriculture: Changes in Technology and Changing Paradigms." In Gene Summers, ed., *Technology and Social Change in Rural Areas.* Boulder, Colo.: Westview Press.

Friedland, William, and Amy Barton 1975 *Destalking the Wily Tomato: A Case Study in Social Consequences in California Agricultural Research.* Research Monograph no. 15. Davis: Department of Applied Behavioral Sciences, University of California.

Friedmann, Harriet 1982 "The Political Economy of Food: The Rise and Fall of the Postwar International Food Order." *American Journal of Sociology* 88 (supp.):S248–S286.

Gartrell, David, and John Gartrell 1985 "Social Status and Agricultural Innovation: A Meta-analysis." *Rural Sociology* 50(1):38–50.

Gartrell, John 1977 "Status, Inequality and Innovation: The Green Revolution in Andhra Pradesh, India." *American Sociological Review* 42:318–337.

————, and David Gartrell 1979 "Status, Knowledge and Innovation." *Rural Sociology* 44:73–94.

Goldschmidt, Walter 1978 *As You Sow.* New York: Harcourt, Brace.

Hightower, James 1972 *Hard Tomatoes, Hard Times: The Failure of America's Land-Grant College Complex.* Cambridge, Mass.: Schenkman.

Kransner, Stephan 1986 *Structural Conflict: The Third World Against Global Liberalism.* Berkeley: University of California Press.

LeVeen, Phillip 1978 "The Prospects for Small-Scale Farming in an Industrial Society: A Critical Appraisal of Small Is Beautiful." In Richard Dorf and Yvonne Hunter, eds., *Appropriate Visions.* San Francisco: Boyd and Fraser.

Lewis, Scott, David Gartrell, and John Gartrell 1989 "Upper-Middle-Class Conservatism in Agricultural Communities: A Meta-analysis." *Rural Sociology* 54, no. 3:409–419.

Pamplel, Fred, and J. C. van Es 1977 "Environmental Quality and Issues of Adoption Research." *Rural Sociology* 42:57–71.

Rogers, Everett 1983 *The Diffusion of Innovations,* 3rd ed. New York: Free Press.

Ryan, Bryce, and Neal Gross 1942 "The Diffusion of Hybrid Corn Seed in Two Iowa Communities." *Rural Sociology* 8:15–24.

Schumpeter, Joseph 1950 *Capitalism, Socialism, and Democracy.* New York: Harper and Row.

Spicer, Edward 1952 *Human Problems in Technological Change.* New York: Russell Sage Foundation.

van Es, J. C. 1983 "The Adoption/Diffusion Tradition Applied to Resource Conservation: Inappropriate Use of Existing Knowledge." *The Rural Sociologist* 3:76–82.

JOHN GARTRELL
DAVID GARTRELL

**ALCOHOL** The sociological study of alcohol in society is concerned with two broad areas. The first area is the study of alcohol behavior, which includes (1) social and other factors in alcohol behavior; (2) the prevalence of drinking in society; and (3) group and individual variations in drinking and alcoholism. The second major area of study has to do with social control of alcohol, which includes (1) the social and legal acceptance or disapproval of alcohol (social norms); (2) the sociolegal regulations and control of alcohol in society; and (3) efforts to change or limit deviant drinking behavior (informal sanctions, law enforcement, treatment, and prevention). Only issues related to the first area of study, sociology of alcohol behavior, will be reviewed here.

## PHYSICAL EFFECTS OF ALCOHOL

Three major forms of beverages containing alcohol (ethanol) are regularly consumed. Wine is made from fermentation of fruits and usually contains up to 14 percent ethanol by volume. Beer is brewed from grains and hops and contains 3 to 6 percent ethanol. Liquor (whisky, gin, vodka, and other distilled spirits) is 40 to 50 percent ethanol (80 to 100 proof). A bottle of beer (12 ounces), a glass of wine (4 ounces), and a cocktail or mixed drink with a shot of liquor in it, therefore, each have about the same absolute alcohol content, one-half to three-fourths of an ounce of ethanol.

Alcohol is a central nervous system depressant, and its physiological effects are a direct function of the percentage of alcohol concentrated in the body's total blood volume (which is determined mainly by the person's body weight). This concentration is usually referred to as the BAC (blood alcohol content) or BAL (blood alcohol level). A 150-pound man can consume one alcoholic drink (about three-fourths of an ounce of ethanol) every hour essentially without physiological effect. The BAC increases with each additional drink during that same time, and the intoxicating effects of alcohol will become noticeable. If a 150-pound man has four drinks in an hour, he will have an alcohol blood content of 0.10 percent, enough for recognizable motor-skills impairment. In almost all states, if he operates a motor vehicle with this BAC (determined by breathalyzer or blood test), he is violating a law and is subject to arrest on a charge of DWI (driving while intoxicated). At 0.25 percent BAC (about ten drinks in an hour) the person is extremely drunk, and at 0.40 percent BAC the person loses consciousness. Excessive drinking of alcohol over time is associated with numerous health problems. Cirrhosis of the liver, hepatitis, heart disease, high blood pressure, brain dysfunction, neurological disorders, sexual and reproductive dysfunction, low blood sugar, and cancer are among the illnesses brought on by alcohol abuse (National Institute of Alcohol Abuse and Alcoholism 1981, 1987; Royce 1989).

## SOCIAL FACTORS IN ALCOHOL BEHAVIOR

Alcohol has direct effects on the brain, affecting motor skills, perception, and eventually consciousness. The way people actually behave while drinking, however, is only partly a function of the direct physical effects of ethanol. Overt behavior while under the influence of alcohol depends also on how individuals have learned to behave in the setting in which they are drinking and with whom they are drinking at the time. Variations in individual experience, group drinking customs, and the social setting produce variations in observable behavior while drinking. Actions reflecting impairment of coordination and perception are direct physical effects of alcohol on the body. These physical factors, however, do not account for "drunken comportment"—the behavior of those who are "drunk" with alcohol before reaching the stage of impaired muscular coordination (MacAndrew and Edgerton 1969). Social, cultural, and psychological factors are more important in overt drinking behavior. Cross-cultural studies (MacAndrew and Edgerton 1969), surveys in the United States (Kantor and Straus 1987), and social psychological experiments (Marlatt and Rohsenow 1981) have shown that both conforming and deviant behavior while "under the influence" are more a function of sociocultural and individual expectations and attitudes than of the physiological effects of alcohol.

Sociological explanations of alcohol behavior emphasize these social, cultural, and social psychological variables not only in understanding the way people act when they are under, or think they are under, the influence of alcohol but also in understanding differences in drinking patterns at both the group and the individual level. Sociologists see all drinking behavior as socially patterned, from abstinence, to moderate drinking, to alcoholism. Within a society persons are subject to different group and cultural influences, depending on the communities in which they reside, their group memberships, and their location in the social structure as defined by their age, sex, class, religion, ethnic, and other statuses in society. Whatever other biological or personality factors and mechanisms may be involved, both conforming and deviant alcohol behavior are explained sociologically as products of the general culture and the more immediate groups and social situations with which individuals are confronted. Differences in rates of drinking and alcoholism across groups in the same society and cross-nationally reflect the varied cultural traditions regarding the functions alcohol serves and the extent to which it is integrated into eating, ceremonial, leisure, and other social contexts.

The more immediate groups within these sociocultural milieux provide social learning environments and social control systems in which the positive and negative sanctions applied to behavior sustain or discourage certain drinking according to group norms. The most significant groups through which the general cultural, religious, and community orientations toward drinking have an impact on the individual are family, peer, and friendship groups, but secondary groups and the media also have an impact. (For a social learning theory of drinking and alcoholism that specifically incorporates these factors in the social and cultural context see Akers 1985; Akers and La Greca, forthcoming. For a review of sociological, psychological, and biological theories of alcohol and drug behavior see Goode 1989.)

## SOCIAL CHARACTERISTICS AND TRENDS IN DRINKING BEHAVIOR

**Age.** Table 1 shows that the percentages of high school seniors who have used alcohol (under the legal age in most states) rival those of young adults and exceed those of older adults. The peak years for drinking are this last year of high school (seventeen to eighteen years of age) and the young adult years of ages eighteen to twenty-five when about eight out of ten are drinkers, two-thirds are

**TABLE 1**
**Percentages of Alcohol Use by Age Group, 1974–1988**

| Age Group | Year | | | |
|---|---|---|---|---|
| | *1974* | *1979* | *1985* | *1988* |
| *12–17* | | | | |
| Ever used | 54 | 70 | 55 | 50 |
| Past year | 51 | 54 | 52 | 45 |
| Past month | 34 | 37 | 31 | 25 |
| *High school seniors* | | | | |
| Ever used | 90* | 93 | 92 | 92 |
| Past year | 85 | 88 | 86 | 85 |
| Past month | 68 | 72 | 66 | 64 |
| *18–25* | | | | |
| Ever used | 81 | 95 | 93 | 90 |
| Past year | 77 | 87 | 87 | 82 |
| Past month | 69 | 76 | 71 | 65 |
| *26+* | | | | |
| Ever used | 73 | 91 | 89 | 87 |
| Past year | 63 | 72 | 74 | 69 |
| Past month | 54 | 61 | 61 | 55 |

SOURCES: National Institute on Drug Abuse 1988; 1989; Johnston, O'Malley, and Bachman 1989.
*Figures in this column for high school seniors are for the year 1975.

current drinkers, and one in twenty are daily drinkers. The many young men and women of this age who are in college are even more likely to drink (Berkowitz and Perkins 1986). For both men and women, the probability that one will drink at all stays relatively high up to about age thirty-five. Heavy or frequent drinking peaks out in later years, somewhat sooner for men than for women. After that the probability for both drinking and heavy drinking declines noticeably, particularly among the elderly. After age sixty, the proportion of both drinkers and of heavy or frequent drinkers decreases. Studies in the general population have found consistently that the elderly are less likely than younger persons to be drinkers, heavy drinkers, and problem drinkers (Cahalan, Cisin, and Crossley 1967; Fitzgerald and Mulford 1981; Meyers et al. 1981–1982; Borgatta, Montgomery, and Borgatta 1982; Holzer et al. 1984).

**Sex.** The difference is not as great as it once was, but more men than women drink, and men have higher rates of problem drinking in all age,

religious, racial, social class, and ethnic groups and in all regions and communities. Teenage boys are more likely to drink and to drink more frequently than teenage girls, but the difference between male and female percentages of current drinkers at this age is less than it is in any older age group. Among adults, men are three to four times more likely than women (among the elderly as much as ten times more likely) to be heavy drinkers and two to three times more likely to report negative personal and social consequences of drinking (National Institute on Alcohol Abuse and Alcoholism 1987).

**Social Class.** The proportion of men and women who drink is higher in the middle class and upper class than in the lower class. The more highly educated and the fully employed are more likely to be current drinkers than the less educated and unemployed. Drinking by elderly adults increases as education increases, but there are either mixed or inconsistent findings regarding the variations in drinking by occupational status, employment status, and income (Holzer 1984; Borgatta, Montgomery, and Borgatta 1982; Akers and La Greca, forthcoming).

**Community and Location.** Rates of drinking are higher in urban and suburban areas than in small towns and rural areas. As the whole country has become more urbanized the regional differences have leveled out so that, while the South continues to have the lowest proportion of drinkers, the most recent studies show no difference in the proportions of teenage and adult drinkers among the other regions. Although there are fewer drinkers in the South, those who do drink tend to drink more per person than drinkers in other regions (National Institute on Alcohol Abuse and Alcoholism 1987).

**Race, Ethnicity, and Religion.** The percent of drinking is higher among both white males and females than among African-American men and women. Drinking among non-Hispanic whites is also higher than among Hispanic whites. The proportion of problem or heavy drinkers is about the same for African-Americans and white Americans (National Institute on Alcohol Abuse and Alcoholism 1981; Fishburne, Abelson, and Cisin 1980; National Institute on Drug Abuse 1988). There may be a tendency for blacks to fall into the two extreme categories, heavy drinkers or abstainers (Brown and Tooley 1989), and black males suffer the highest rate of mortality from cirrhosis of the liver (National Institute on Alcohol Abuse and Alcoholism 1987). American Indians and Alaskan Natives have rates of alcohol abuse and problems several times the rates in the general population (National Institute on Alcohol Abuse and Alcoholism 1987).

Catholics, Lutherans, and Episcopalians have relatively high rates of drinking. Relatively few fundamentalist Protestants, Baptists, and Mormons drink. Jews have low rates of problem drinking, and Catholics have relatively high rates of alcoholism. Irish-Americans have high rates of both drinking and alcoholism. Italian-Americans drink frequently and heavily but apparently do not have high rates of alcoholism (see Cahalan, Cisin, and Crossley 1967; Mulford 1964). Strong religious beliefs and commitment, regardless of denominational affiliation, inhibit both drinking and heavy drinking among teenagers and college students (Cochran and Akers 1989; Berkowitz and Perkins 1986).

**Trends in Prevalence of Drinking.** There has been a century-long decline in the amount of absolute alcohol consumed by the average drinker in the United States. There was a period in the 1970s when the per capita consumption increased (see Table 1), and the proportion of drinkers in the population was generally higher by the end of the 1970s than at the beginning of the decade, although there were yearly fluctuations up and down. The level of drinking among men was already high, and the increases came mainly among youth and women. But in the 1980s the general downward trend resumed (Keller 1958; National Institute on Alcohol Abuse and Alcoholism 1981, 1987). Until the 1980s, this trend was caused mainly by the increased use of lower-content beer and wine and the declining popularity of distilled spirits rather than by a decreasing proportion of the population who are drinkers. In the 1980s the prevalence of drinking alcohol declined for both men and women and all age groups.

In 1979 more than two-thirds of American adolescents (twelve to seventeen years of age) had some experience with alcohol, and nearly four out of ten were current drinkers (drank within the past month). In 1988 these proportions had dropped to one-half and one-fourth, respectively. Lifetime prevalence of alcohol use (ever used) has remained essentially the same for the older age groups in the last decade. Lifetime prevalence is not a sensitive measure of change in the adult population, however, because it can be changed only by the lifetime drinking experience of those newly entering the adult years (since the lifetime prevalence is already fixed for the cohort of adults already sampled in previous surveys). There have been declines in both annual (past year) prevalence of drinking (decreases of 3 to 5 percent) and current (past month) prevalence of drinking (decreases of 7 to 10 percent) among high school seniors, young adults, and older adults. Current use in the general American population twelve years of age and older declined from 59 percent in 1985 to 53 percent in 1988. Among the adult population eighteen years of age and older, current use declined from 71 percent in 1985 to 57 percent in 1988.

The relative size of the reductions in drinking prevalence in recent years has not been great, however, and proportions of drinkers remain high. By the time of high school graduation, two-thirds of adolescents are current drinkers, and the proportion of drinkers in the population remains at this level through the young adult years. Eight out of ten high school seniors and young adults and 70 percent of adults over the age of twenty-five have consumed alcohol in the past year. It should be remembered, however, that most of this is light to moderate consumption; the modal pattern of drinking for all age groups in the United States has long been and continues to be nondeviant, light to moderate social drinking. The moderation in drinking behavior may have become more pronounced in recent years; not only has current drinking declined, there are some indications that frequent (daily) drinking also has moderated. A further indication is that both high school seniors and young adults reported less likelihood of heavy drinking (consumed five or more drinks in a row sometime during the last two weeks) in 1988 than a decade earlier (National Institute on Drug Abuse 1989; Johnston, O'Malley, and Bachman 1989).

**Estimates of Prevalence of Alcoholism.** In spite of these trends in lower levels of drinking, alcoholism remains one of the most serious problems in American society. Alcohol abuse and all of the problems related to it cause enormous personal, social, health, and financial costs in American society. In a 1965 national survey Cahalan, Cisin, and Crossley (1967) characterized 6 percent of the general adult population and 9 percent of the drinkers as "heavy-escape" drinkers, the same figures reported for a 1967 survey (Cahalan 1970). These figures do not seem to have changed very much in the years since. They are similar to findings in national surveys from 1979 to 1988 (National Institute on Alcohol Abuse and Alcoholism 1981; Clark and Midanik 1982; National Institute on Alcohol Abuse and Alcoholism 1987; National Institute on Drug Abuse 1988, 1989), which support an estimate that 6 percent of the general population are problem drinkers and that about 9 percent of those who are drinkers will abuse or fail to control their intake of alcohol. Royce (1989) and Vaillant (1983) both estimate that 4 percent of the general population in the United States are "true" alcoholics. This estimate would mean that there about eight million alcoholics in American society. How many alcoholics or how much alcohol abuse there is in our society is not easily determined because the very concept of alcoholism (and therefore what gets counted in the surveys and estimates) has long been and remains controversial.

## THE CONCEPT OF ALCOHOLISM

The idea of alcoholism as a sickness traces back at least 200 years (Conrad and Schneider 1980). There is no single unified disease concept, but the prevailing concepts of alcoholism today revolve around the one developed by Jellinek (1960) from 1940 to 1960. Jellinek defined alcoholism as a disease entity that is diagnosed by the "loss of control" over one's drinking and that progresses through a series of clear-cut "phases." The final phase of alcoholism means that the disease renders a person powerless to drink in a controlled, moderate, nonproblematic way.

The disease of alcoholism is viewed as a disorder or illness for which the individual is not personally responsible for having contracted. It is viewed as incurable in the sense that alcoholics can never truly control their drinking. That is, sobriety can be achieved only by total abstention: Even if one drink is taken, the alcoholic cannot control how much more he or she will consume. Alcoholism is a "primary" self-contained disease that produces the problems, abuse, and loss of control over drinking associated with the disease. It can be controlled through proper treatment to the point where the alcoholic can be helped to stop drinking so that he or she is in "remission" or is "recovering." "Once an alcoholic, always an alcoholic" is a central tenet of the disease concept.

Thus, one can be a sober alcoholic, which means that one can still suffer from the disease even though one is consuming no alcohol at all. Although the person is not responsible for becoming sick, he or she is viewed as responsible for aiding in the cure by cooperating with the treatment regimen or participation in groups such as Alcoholics Anonymous.

The disease concept is the predominant one in public opinion and discourse on alcohol (according to a 1987 Gallup Poll, 87 percent of the public believes that alcoholism is a disease). It is the principal concept used by the vast majority of the treatment professionals and personnel offering programs for alcohol problems. It receives widespread support among alcohol experts and continues to be vigorously defended by many alcohol researchers (Keller 1976; Vaillant 1983; Royce 1989). Alcoholics Anonymous, the largest single program for alcoholics in the world, defines alcoholism as a disease (Rudy 1986). The concept of alcoholism as a disease is the officially stated position of the American Medical Association and of the federal agency most responsible for alcohol research and treatment, the National Institute on Alcohol Abuse and Alcoholism (1987).

Nonetheless, many sociologists and behavioral scientists remain highly skeptical and critical of the disease concept of alcoholism (Trice 1966; Cahalan and Room 1974; Conrad and Schneider 1980; Rudy 1986; Fingarette 1988; Peele 1989). The concept may do more harm than good by discouraging many heavy drinkers who are having problems with alcohol, but who do not identify themselves as alcoholics or do not want others to view them as sick, from seeking help. The disease concept is a tautological (and therefore untestable) explanation for the behavior of people diagnosed as alcoholic. That is, the diagnosis of the disease is made on the basis of excessive, problematic alcohol behavior that seems to be out of control, and then this diagnosed disease entity is, in turn, used to explain the excessive, problematic, out-of-control behavior.

In so far as claims about alcoholism as a disease can be tested, "almost everything that the American public believes to be the scientific truth about alcoholism is false" (Fingarette 1988, p. 1; see also Peele 1989; Conrad and Schneider 1980). The concept preferred by these authors and by other sociologists is one that refers only to observable behavior and drinking problems. The term *alcoholism* then is nothing more than a label attached to a drinking pattern characterized by personal and social dysfunctions (Mulford and Miller 1960; Conrad and Schneider 1980; Rudy 1986). That is, the drinking is so frequent, heavy, and abusive that it produces or exacerbates financial, familial, occupational, physical, and interpersonal problems for the drinker and those around him. The heavy drinking behavior and its attendant problems are themselves the focus of explanation and treatment. They are not seen as merely symptoms of some underlying disease pathology. When drinking stops or moderate drinking is resumed and drinking does not cause social and personal problems, one is no longer alcoholic. Behavior we label as alcoholic is problem drinking that lies at one extreme of a continuum of drinking behavior, with abstinence at the other end and various other drinking patterns in between (Cahalan, Cisin, and Crossley 1967). From this point of view, alcoholism is a disease only because it has been socially defined as a disease (Conrad and Schneider 1980).

**Genetic Factors in Alcoholism.** Contrary to what is regularly asserted, evidence that there may be genetic, biological factors in alcohol abuse is evidence neither in favor of nor against the disease concept, any more than evidence that there may be genetic variables in criminal behavior demonstrates that crime is a disease. Few serious researchers claim to have found evidence that a specific disease entity is inherited or that there is a genetically programmed and unalterable craving or desire for alcohol. It is genetic susceptibility to alcoholism that interacts with the social environment and the person's drinking experiences, rather than genetic determinism, that is the predominant perspective.

The major evidence for the existence of hereditary factors in alcoholism comes from studies that have found greater "concordance" between the alcoholism of identical twins than between siblings and from studies of adoptees in which offspring of alcoholic fathers were found to have an increased risk of alcoholism even though raised by nonalcoholic adoptive parents (Goodwin 1976; National Institute on Alcohol Abuse and Alcoholism 1982; U.S. Department of Health and Human Services 1987). Some have pointed to serious methodological problems in these studies that limit their support for inherited alcoholism (Lester 1987). Even the studies finding evidence for inherited alcoholism report that only a small minority of those judged to have the inherited traits become alcoholic and an even smaller portion of all alcoholics have indications of hereditary tendencies. Whatever genetic variables there are in alcoholism apparently come into play in a small portion of cases. Depending on the definition of alcoholism used, the research shows that biological inheritance either makes no difference at all or makes a difference for only about one out of ten alcoholics. Social and social psychological factors are the principal variables in alcohol behavior, including that which is socially labeled and diagnosed as alcoholism (Fingarette 1988; Peele 1989).

(SEE ALSO: *Drug Abuse*)

## REFERENCES

Akers, Ronald L. 1985 *Deviant Behavior: A Social Learning Approach.* Belmont, Calif.: Wadsworth.

———, and Anthony J. La Greca (forthcoming) "Alcohol Use among the Elderly: Social Learning, Community Context, and Life Events." In David J. Pittman and Helene White, eds., *Society, Culture, and Drinking Patterns Re-Examined.* New Brunswick, N.J.: Rutgers University Press.

Berkowitz, Alan D., and H. Wesley Perkins 1986 "Problem Drinking among College Students: A Review of Recent Research." *Journal of American College Health* 35:21–28.

Borgatta, Edgar F., Rhonda J. V. Montgomery, and Marie L. Borgatta 1982 "Alcohol Use and Abuse, Life Crisis Events, and the Elderly." *Research on Aging* 4:378–408.

Brown, Frieda, and Joan Tooley 1989 "Alcoholism in the Black Community." In Gary W. Lawson and Ann W. Lawson, eds., *Alcohol and Substance Abuse in Special Populations.* Rockville, Md.: Aspen Publishers.

Cahalan, Don 1970 *Problem Drinkers: A National Survey.* San Francisco: Jossey-Bass.

———, Ira H. Cisin, and Helen M. Crossley 1967 *American Drinking Practices.* Washington, D.C.: George Washington University Press.

———, and Robin Room 1974 *Problem Drinking Among American Men.* New Haven, Conn.: College and University Press.

Clark, Walter B., and Lorraine Midanik 1982 "Alcohol Use and Alcohol Problems Among U.S. Adults: Results of the 1979 Survey." *Alcohol Consumption and Related Problems.* Department of Health and Human Services, No. 82-1190. Washington, D.C.: U. S. Government Printing Office.

Cochran, John K., and Ronald L. Akers 1989 "Beyond Hellfire: An Exploration of the Variable Effects of Religiosity on Adolescent Marijuana and Alcohol Use." *Journal of Research on Crime and Delinquency* 26:198–225.

Conrad, Peter, and Joseph W. Schneider 1980 *Deviance and Medicalization.* St. Louis: C. V. Mosby.

Fingarette, Herbert 1988 *Heavy Drinking: The Myth of Alcoholism as a Disease.* Berkeley: University of California Press.

Fishburne, Patricia, Herbert I. Abelson, and Ira Cisin 1980 *National Survey on Drug Abuse: Main Findings.* Washington, D.C.: U.S. Government Printing Office.

Fitzgerald, J. L., and Harold A. Mulford 1981 "The Prevalence and Extent of Drinking in Iowa, 1979." *Journal of Studies on Alcohol* 42:38–47.

Goode, Erich 1989 *Drugs in American Society,* 3rd ed. New York: Alfred A. Knopf.

Goodwin, Donald 1976 *Is Alcoholism Hereditary?* New York: Oxford University Press.

Holzer, C., Lee Robins, Jerome Meyers, M. Weissman, G. Tischler, P. Leaf, J. Anthony, and P. Bednarski 1984 "Antecedents and Correlates of Alcohol Abuse and Dependence in the Elderly." In George Maddox, Lee Robins, and Nathan Rosenberg, eds., *Nature and Extent of Alcohol Abuse Among the Elderly.* Department of Health and Human Services No. 84-1321. Washington, D.C.: U.S. Government Printing Office.

Jellinek, E. M. 1960 *The Disease Concept of Alcoholism.* New Haven, Conn.: Hillhouse Press.

Johnston, Lloyd D., Patrick M. O'Malley, and Jerald G.

Bachman 1989 *Drug Use, Drinking, and Smoking: National Survey Results from High School, College, and Young Adult Populations, 1975–1988.* Washington, D.C.: U.S. Government Printing Office.

Kantor, Glenda K., and Murray A. Straus 1987 "The 'Drunken Bum' Theory of Wife Beating." *Social Problems* 34:213–230.

Keller, Mark 1958 "Alcoholism: Nature and Extent of the Problem." *Annals of the American Academy of Political and Social Sciences* 315:1–11.

———— 1976 "The Disease Concept of Alcoholism Revisited." *Journal of Studies on Alcohol* 37:1694–1717.

Lester, David 1987 *Genetic Theory: An Assessment of the Heritability of Alcoholism.* New Brunswick, N.J.: Center of Alcohol Studies, Rutgers University.

MacAndrew, Craig, and Robert B. Edgerton 1969 *Drunken Comportment: A Social Explanation.* Chicago: Aldine.

Marlatt, G. Alan, and Damaris J. Rohsenow 1981 "The Think–Drink Effect." *Psychology Today* (Dec.):60–69, 93.

Meyers, A. R., E. Goldman, R. Hingson, N. Scotch, and T. Mangione 1981–1982 "Evidence of Cohort and Generational Differences in Drinking Behavior of Older Adults." *International Journal of Aging and Human Development* 14:31–44.

Mulford, Harold A. 1964 "Drinking and Deviant Drinking, USA, 1963." *Quarterly Journal of Studies on Alcohol* 25:634–650.

————, and Donald Miller 1960 "Drinking in Iowa IV: Preoccupation with Alcohol and Definitions of Alcoholism, Heavy Drinking, and Trouble Due to Drinking." *Quarterly Journal of Studies on Alcohol* 21:279–296.

National Institute on Alcohol Abuse and Alcoholism 1981 *Fourth Special Report to the U.S. Congress on Alcohol and Health.* Washington, D.C.: U.S. Government Printing Office.

———— 1982 *"Researchers Investigating Inherited Alcohol Problems." NIAAA Information and Feature Service* No. 99, August 30. Rockville, Md.: National Institute on Alcohol Abuse and Alcoholism.

———— 1987 *Alcohol and Health: Sixth Special Report to the U. S. Congress from the Secretary of Health and Human Services.* Rockville, Md.: National Institute on Alcohol Abuse and Alcoholism.

National Institute on Drug Abuse 1988 *National Household Survey on Drug Abuse: Main Findings 1985.* Rockville, Md.: National Institute on Drug Abuse.

———— 1989 "Highlights of the 1988 Household Sur-vey on Drug Abuse." *NIDA Capsules*, August. Rockville, Md.: National Institute on Drug Abuse.

Peele, Stanton 1989 *Diseasing of America: Addiction Treatment Out of Control.* Lexington, Mass.: Lexington Books.

Royce, James E. 1989 *Alcohol Problems and Alcoholism,* rev. ed. New York: Free Press.

Rudy, David 1986 *Becoming Alcoholic: Alcoholics Anonymous and the Reality of Alcoholism.* Carbondale: Southern Illinois University Press.

Trice, Harrison 1966 *Alcoholism in America.* New York: McGraw-Hill.

U. S. Department of Health and Human Services 1987 *Sixth Special Report to the U. S. Congress on Alcohol and Health from the Secretary of Health and Human Services.* Rockville, Md.: National Institute on Alcohol Abuse and Alcoholism.

Vaillant, George 1983 *The Natural History of Alcoholism.* Cambridge, Mass.: Harvard University Press.

RONALD L. AKERS

**ALIENATION** Between 1964 and 1974, many commentators were speaking of a crisis of confidence in the United States, a malaise marked by a widespread public belief that major institutions—businesses, labor unions, and especially the government, political parties, and political leaders—were unresponsive, remote, ineffective, and not to be trusted (Lipset and Schneider 1983). The word *alienation* became the catchword for these sentiments and a host of other problems including discontented workers, wayward youth, and militant minority groups. Leaders concerned about the apparent increase in alienation found new relevance in an ongoing discussion among sociologists and other social scientists, who over the years have defined the term *alienation*, used public opinion polls to measure the level of alienation in society, and debated the causes, significance, and consequences of alienation and particularly political alienation.

## DIMENSIONS OF ALIENATION AND POLITICAL ALIENATION

Sociological researchers and theorists have developed different definitions for the word *alienation* (Seeman 1975). Alienation sometimes refers to the isolation of individuals from a community—a detachment from the activities, identifications, and the ties to relatives and friends that a community can provide. In contrast, scholars influenced by the philosophical writings of Karl Marx have used the word to mean self-estrangement and the lack of self-realization (Blauner 1964). Marx argued that although humans by their very nature are capable of creative and intrinsically rewarding work, the Industrial Revolution reduced workers to the unskilled tenders of machines (Braverman 1974). The machinery and other commodities that are produced become part of a system of hierarchies at work and global markets that the worker cannot control. Rather, the system dominates workers as an alienated, "reified" force, apart from the will and interests of workers (Meszaros 1970).

The concept of alienation has included the notion of cultural radicalism, or estrangement from the established values of a society. Ingelhart (1981) has argued that the highly educated generation that came of age in the counterculture of the 1960s has rejected the elders' traditional values of materialism, order, and discipline and instead espouses "postmaterialist" values emphasizing the quality of life, self-realization, and participatory democracy.

Much of the recent discussion of alienation has been on the topic of political alienation and, ironically, has described the politics not of authoritarian regimes but rather of the highly developed democracies of Western Europe and the United States. Sociologists have been particularly interested in measuring the extent to which individuals in political contexts feel powerless (i.e., unable to influence government decisions or secure desired outcomes) and perceive political affairs as meaningless (i.e., too complicated, unclear, or incomprehensible) (Seeman 1975). Sociologists have tried not only to measure political alienation but also to determine its causes and consequences. Powerlessness and meaninglessness may be connected to normlessness, or anomie, which occurs when individuals are no longer guided by the political rules of the game (Lipset and Raab 1978). Thus, social scientists have been concerned

that alienation might lead to nonconventional actions like protest movements and collective violence, while reducing participation through conventional political channels such as voting and interest group activity.

## MEASUREMENT AND CONSEQUENCES OF POLITICAL ALIENATION

Political alienation consists of several specific attitudes whereby citizens evaluate government and politics. Specifically, political alienation is composed of the attitudes of distrust and inefficacy. *Distrust* (also called cynicism) is a generalized negative attitude about governmental outputs: the policies, operations, and conditions produced by government. Compared to the simple dislike of a particular governmental policy or official, distrust is a negative reaction that is broader is scope. Whereas distrust is an evaluation of governmental outputs, *inefficacy* is an expectation about inputs to government, the processes by which groups influence government. People have a sense of inefficacy when they feel they cannot influence government policies or deliberations (Gamson 1971).

Mason, House, and Martin (1985) argue that two specific questions used in opinion polls are the most "internally valid" measures of distrust (i.e., the questions yield answers correlated to only one particular underlying attitude): "How much of the time do you think you can trust the government in Washington to do what is right—just about all of the time, most of the time, or only some of the time?" and "Would you say that the government is pretty much run by a few big interests looking out for themselves or that it is run for the benefit of all people?" Similarly, a person's sense of inefficacy can be measured by asking the person to agree or disagree with statements containing the words "like me": "People like me don't have any say about what the government does" and "I don't think public officials care much what people like me think."

During election years since the 1950s, the Center for Political Studies at the University of Michigan at Ann Arbor has addressed these (and numerous other) questions to national samples of citizens. Those replying that you can trust the government only some of the time or none of the time composed 22 percent in 1964 but 73 percent in 1980. Those disagreeing with the statement that public officials care rose from 25 percent in 1960 to 52 percent in 1980.

Furthermore, polls indicated that in the 1960s and 1970s, increasing numbers of citizens felt that government was less responsive and paid less attention to what the people thought (Lipset and Schneider 1983, pp. 13–29). This feeling, which can be termed *system unresponsiveness,* was measured by asking questions that did not use the words "like me." Responses to the questions thus contained no evaluations of the respondent's own personal power, but rather expressed the respondent's views of the external political system. (Craig 1979 conceptualizes system unresponsiveness as "output inefficacy.")

What are the consequences of the increase in alienated political attitudes among Americans? Social scientists have investigated whether individuals with highly alienated attitudes are more likely to engage in certain types of political actions and behaviors.

Research findings have been complicated by the fact that the same specific attitude of political alienation has been compatible with many different behavioral orientations including withdrawal or the favoring of reform movements or political violence (Schwartz 1973, pp. 162–177).

Social scientists have generally agreed that politically alienated individuals are less likely to participate in conventional political processes. During four presidential elections from 1956 to 1968, citizens with a low sense of efficacy and a low level of trust were less likely to vote, attend political meetings, contribute money, work for candidates, or even pay attention to the mass media coverage of politics. The alienated showed little tendency to support extremist candidates for office. (The only exception was that high-status alienated citizens supported Goldwater's presidential campaign in 1964. See Wright 1976, pp. 227, 251; Herring 1989, p. 98.) Although some studies fail to confirm that those with low *trust* are

likely to be apathetic (Citrin 1974, p. 982), those with low political *efficacy* are indeed likely to be nonvoters, mainly because they are also less educated (Lipset and Schneider 1983, p. 341). In the United States, the percentage of eligible voters who actually cast ballots has declined since 1960, dropping to 53 percent in 1980, while the percentage expressing political inefficacy has risen in the same period; Abramson and Aldrich (1982) estimate that about 27 percent of the former trend is caused by the latter. (See Shaffer 1981 for confirmation but Cassel and Hill 1981 and Miller 1980 for contrary evidence.)

Piven and Cloward (1988) vigorously dispute the notion that the alienated attitudes of individuals are the main cause for the large numbers of nonvoters in the United States. Piven and Cloward construct a historical explanation—that in the early twentieth century, political reformers weakened local party organizations in cities, increased the qualifications for suffrage, and made voting registration procedures more difficult. Legal and institutional changes caused a sharp decrease in voting, which only then led to widespread political alienation. Legal requirements to register in advance of election day and after a change in residence, along with limited locations to register, continue to reduce voting participation, especially among the minority poor in large cities.

Some researchers have found that the politically alienated are more likely to participate in politics using nonconventional tactics such as demonstrations or violence. College students who participated in a march on Washington against the Vietnam War, compared to a matched sample of students from the same classes at the same schools, expressed more alienated attitudes, which in turn stemmed from a sense of inefficacy and system unresponsiveness (Schwartz 1973, pp. 138–142). Paige's (1971) widely influential study drew on Gamson's distinction between trust and efficacy and showed that blacks who participated in the 1967 riot in Newark, New Jersey, had low levels of political trust but high levels of political efficacy (i.e., high capabilities and skills to affect politics, measured indirectly in this instance by the respondent's level of political knowledge). Sigelman and Feldman (1983) attempted to confirm these findings in a study of seven nations. They discovered that those who supported and participated in unconventional forms of politics were only slightly more likely to be both efficacious *and* distrusting. In some nations, however, respondents were more likely to be dissatisfied about specific policies (rather than generally distrusting; see also Citrin 1974, p. 982, and Craig and Maggiotto 1981 for the importance of specific dissatisfactions over policies).

Even though politically alienated individuals may be more likely to participate in social movements, the alienation of individuals is not necessarily a cause of social movements. McCarthy and Zald (1977) have argued that alienation, policy dissatisfactions, and other grievances are quite common in societies. Whether or not a social movement arises depends on the availability of resources and the opportunities for success. The civil rights movement, according to McAdam (1982), succeeded not when blacks believed that the political system was unresponsive but rather when blacks felt that federal authorities were beginning to change the system.

## DISTRIBUTION AND SIGNIFICANCE OF POLITICAL ALIENATION

Social scientists have argued that political alienation is concentrated in different types of groups —first, among those who dislike the administration in Washington; second, in certain socioeconomic classes; and finally, among those dissatisfied with government policy. Each of these findings supports a different assessment of the causes and the importance of political alienation.

**Partisan Bickering?** First of all, high levels of political distrust can be found among those who have a negative view of the performance of the presidential administration then in office. Citrin (1974) concludes that widespread expressions of political distrust (cynicism) merely indicate partisan politics as usual. Cynicism, rather than being an expression of deep discontent, is just rhetoric and ritual. Citrin argues that political distrust is not a threat to the system; even those who intense-ly distrust incumbent politicians are proud of the form of the government in the United States and want to keep it as it is.

**Blue-collar Backlash?** Second, other researchers interested in determining the distribution of political alienation have searched for concentrations not among people with certain attitudes and opinions but rather in demographic groups defined by such variables as age, gender, education, and socioeconomic class. Some studies have found alienation only weakly concentrated among such groups. In the 1960s, inefficacy increased uniformly throughout the entire U.S. population rather than increasing in certain demographic groups such as blacks or youth (House and Mason 1975). Using a 1970 survey, Wright (1976) noted that inefficacy and distrust were somewhat concentrated among the elderly, the poorly educated, and the working class. Still, Wright's conclusion was that the alienated were a diverse group that consisted of both rich and poor, black and white, and old and young, making it very unlikely that the alienated as a group could ever become a unified political force.

Most studies have shown that the politically alienated are indeed concentrated among persons with less education and lower income and occupational status (Wright 1976, p. 136; Lipset and Schneider 1983, pp. 311–315; Finifter 1970; Form and Huber Rytina 1971). Wright argues that even though sizable numbers of such persons express alienated attitudes, these people pose little threat to the stability of regimes because they rarely take political actions and even lack the requisite resources and skills. The alienated have become habituated from an early age to their own lack of power. The alienated are preoccupied with their personal problems and concerns and thus passively give their assent to the regime.

Lipset (1963) has argued that such mass apathy is a virtue because it allows elites in democratic societies to better exert leadership. (For a critique see Wolfe 1977, p. 301.) In fact, for many social scientists in the 1950s, mass apathy was a welcome alternative to the alleged mass activism that had produced the fascist regimes in Germany and Italy. However, Wright (1976, pp. 257–301) counters that since the alienated masses actually pose no threat to the contemporary political system, an increase in mass democratic participation, perhaps the mobilization of workers on the issues of class division, could very well be beneficial, producing more enlightened and humane public policies for the majority in society.

But the class mobilization that Wright envisions might turn out to be a middle-class affair rather than a working-class revolt. Whereas Lipset and Wright have been concerned about the concentration of political alienation in the lower socioeconomic strata, Warren (1976) emphasizes the alienation among "middle American radicals," who believe that they are disfavored by a government that gives its benefits to the poor and the very wealthy. Inefficacy and distrust increased the most, not among the poor or the capitalist class, but rather among the middle strata—private sector managers, middle-income workers, and a "new layer" of public sector professionals (Herring 1989).

Unlike the poor, the middle strata have the resources and capacity to protest and to organize social movements and electoral campaigns, exemplified by the protests against the property tax that culminated with the passage of Proposition 13 in California and Proposition 2½ in Massachusetts. Property tax protesters were middle class homeowners concerned about "taxation without representation." Citizens who felt cut off from political decision making were the most likely to support the tax revolt (Lowery and Sigelman 1981). Protests centered on unresponsive government officials who continued to increase assessments and tax rates without heeding the periodic angry responses of homeowners. Movement activists interpreted their own powerlessness in community and metropolitan politics, thereby shaping the emerging tactics and goals of a grass roots citizen's movement (Lo 1990).

**A Crisis for Democracy?**   Finally, other social scientists, who have found concentrations of political alienation among those with intense dissatisfactions about government policy, reach the more

pessimistic conclusion that political alienation makes effective democratic government almost impossible. Miller (1974) argued that between 1964 and 1970, political distrust (cynicism) increased simultaneously among those favoring withdrawal and those favoring military escalation in the Vietnam War. Distrust increased both among blacks who thought that the civil rights movement was making too little progress and among white segregationists who held the opposite view. The 1960s produced two groups— cynics of the left and cynics of the right, each favoring a set of polarized policy alternatives (see also Lipset and Schneider 1983, p. 332). Cynics of the right, for example, rejected both the Democratic and Republican parties as too liberal. (Herring 1989 has developed a similar "welfare split" thesis: that more social spending has different effects on the distrust of different groups and, overall, raises political distrust.) Miller concludes that increases in cynicism, along with the concomitant extreme positions on issues, make it difficult for political leaders to find compromises and build support for centrist policy options. While agreeing with Wright that the alienated are divided among themselves, Miller argues that this fragmentation does indeed constitute a crisis of legitimacy for American politics.

For some theorists, widespread political alienation not only makes it difficult to choose among polarized policy options, but also is a sign of even deeper political and economic contradictions in American society. Throughout American history, as citizens have fought to extend their democratic freedoms and personal rights, businesses have used the notion of property rights to protect their own interests and stifle reform (Bowles and Gintis 1987). Wolfe (1977) sees political alienation as a symptom of how the democratic aspirations of the citizenry have been frustrated by the state, which has attempted to foster the growth of capitalism while at the same time attempting to maintain popular support. Alienation, once a Marxist concept depicting the economic deprivations of industrial workers, is now a political concept portraying the plight of citizens increasingly subjected to the authority and the bureaucracy of the state in advanced capitalist societies.

(SEE ALSO: *Anomie and Alienation*)

## REFERENCES

Abramson, Paul, and John Aldrich 1982 "Decline of Electoral Participation in America." *American Political Science Review* 76:502–521.

Blauner, Robert 1964 *Alienation and Freedom: The Factory Worker and His Industry.* Chicago: University of Chicago Press.

Bowles, Samuel, and Herbert Gintis 1987 *Democracy and Capitalism: Property, Community, and the Contradictions of Modern Social Thought.* New York: Basic Books.

Braverman, Harry 1974 *Labor and Monopoly Capital.* New York: Monthly Review Press.

Cassel, Carol A., and David B. Hill 1981 "Explanations of Turnout Decline: A Multivariate Test." *American Politics Quarterly* 9:181–195.

Citrin, Jack 1974 "Comment: The Political Relevance of Trust in Government." *American Political Science Review* 68:973–988.

Craig, Stephen C. 1979 "Efficacy, Trust, and Political Behavior: An Attempt to Resolve a Lingering Conceptual Dilemma." *American Politics Quarterly* 7:225–239.

———, and Michael Maggiotto 1981 "Political Discontent and Political Action." *Journal of Politics* 43:514–522.

Finifter, Ada W. 1970 "Dimensions of Political Alienation." *American Political Science Review* 64:389–410.

Form, William H., and Joan Huber Rytina 1971 "Income, Race, and the Ideology of Political Efficacy." *Journal of Politics* 33:659–688.

Gamson, William 1971 "Political Trust and Its Ramifications." In Gilbert Abcarian and John W. Soule, eds., *Social Psychology and Political Behavior: Problems and Prospects.* Columbus, Ohio: Merrill.

Herring, Cedric 1989 *Splitting the Middle: Political Alienation, Acquiescence, and Activism among America's Middle Layers.* New York: Praeger.

House, James, and William Mason 1975 "Political Alienation in America, 1952–1968." *American Sociological Review* 40:123–147.

Ingelhart, Ronald 1981 "Post-Materialism in an Environment of Insecurity." *American Political Science Review* 75:880–900.

Lipset, Seymour Martin, 1963 *Political Man.* Garden City, N.Y.: Anchor.

———, and Earl Raab 1978 *The Politics of Unreason: Right-Wing Extremism in America, 1790–1977.* Chicago: University of Chicago Press.

———and William Schneider 1983 *The Confidence Gap: Business, Labor, and Government in the Public Mind.* New York: Free Press.

Lo, Clarence Y. H. 1990 *Small Property versus Big Government: Social Origins of the Property Tax Revolt.* Berkeley and Los Angeles: University of California Press.

Lowrey, David, and Lee Sigelman 1981 "Understanding the Tax Revolt: Eight Explanations." *American Political Science Review* 75:963–974.

McAdam, Doug 1982 *Political Process and the Development of Black Insurgency.* Chicago: University of Chicago Press.

McCarthy, John D., and Mayer N. Zald 1977 "Resource Mobilization and Social Movements: A Partial Theory." *American Journal of Sociology* 82: 1112–1141.

Mason, William W., James S. House, and Steven S. Martin 1985 "On the Dimensions of Political Alienation in America." In Nancy Brandon Tuma, ed., *Sociological Methodology.* San Francisco. Jossey-Bass.

Meszaros, I. 1970 *Marx's Theory of Alienation.* London: Merlin.

Miller, Arthur 1974 "Political Issues and Trust in Government: 1964–1970." *American Political Science Review* 68:951–972.

Miller, Warren E. 1980 "Disinterest, Disaffection, and Participation in Presidential Politics." *Political Behavior* 2:7–32.

Paige, Jeffery 1971 "Political Orientation and Riot Participation." *American Sociological Review* 36: 801–820.

Piven, Frances Fox, and Richard A. Cloward 1988 *Why Americans Don't Vote.* New York: Pantheon.

Schwartz, David C. 1973 *Political Alienation and Political Behavior.* Chicago: Aldine.

Seeman, Melvin 1975 "Alienation Studies." In Alex Inkeles, James Coleman, and Neil Smelser, eds., *Annual Review of Sociology,* vol. 8. Palo Alto, Calif.: Annual Reviews.

Shaffer, Stephen D. 1981 "A Multivariate Explanation of Decreasing Turnout in Presidential Elections, 1960–1976." *American Journal of Political Science* 25:68–95.

Sigelman, Lee, and Stanley Feldman 1983 "Efficacy, Mistrust, and Political Mobilization: A Cross-

National Analysis." *Comparative Political Studies* 16:118–143.

Warren, Donald I. 1976 *The Radical Center: Middle Americans and the Politics of Alienation.* Notre Dame, Ind.: University of Notre Dame Press.

Wolfe, Alan 1977 *The Limits of Legitimacy: Political Contradictions of Contemporary Capitalism.* New York: Free Press.

Wright, James D. 1976 *The Dissent of the Governed: Alienation and Democracy in America.* New York: Academic Press.

CLARENCE Y. H. LO

## ALTERNATIVE LIFE-STYLES

Considerable concern is voiced from certain segments of the population over the "demise" of the family. The high divorce rate, increased rates of premarital sexuality, cohabitation, and extramarital sex are pointed to as both the culprits and the consequences of the deterioration of family values. This distress, however, is not particularly new; for at least a century American observers and social critics have warned against the negative consequences of changes in the family.

Thanks to books, television, movies, and a variety of other sources, we all know what the family "should" look like. What invariably comes to mind is the white, middle-class, two-parent family in which the father works outside the home and the mother stays at home to take care of the children, at least while they are young. This monolithic model, however, excludes the majority of the population; indeed, a growing number of persons do not desire such a model even if it was attainable. It is based on the false notion of a single and uniform intimate experience that many argue has racist, sexist, and classist connotations.

There are, nonetheless, new reasons for the latest wave of concern of family demise that began to emerge during the 1960s and 1970s. During this period the utility and the structure of many social institutions were seriously questioned, and the family was not exempt. What is the purpose of the family? Is it a useful social institution? Why or why not? How can it be improved? The given cultural milieu of the period exacerbated these questions: the resurgence of the women's movement and the subsequent analysis of gender roles, concern about human rights more generally, and improvements in our reproductive and contraceptive technology. In increasing numbers, individuals began to experiment with alternative ways in which to develop meaningful relationships, including nonmarital sexual relationships, cohabitation, open marriage, and communal living arrangements. A flurry of literature soon abounded among both the academic community and the popular press describing and deliberating on these new life-styles. In 1972 a special issue of *The Family Coordinator* was devoted to the subject of alternative life-styles, with a follow-up issue published in 1975. The subject was firmly entrenched within the field of family sociology by 1980 when the *Journal of Marriage and Family* devoted a chapter to alternative family life-styles in their decade review of research and theory.

Notwithstanding the interest, curiosity, and concern with alternative life-styles, it should be noted that most of the experiments during the 1960s and 1970s attracted only a very small portion of the population, particularly those life-styles considered to be the most "radical" or alien to the traditional family, such as communal living or open marriage. The vast majority of the population, both then and now, prefer to marry, have children, and live in a committed, monogamous relationship. The most profound changes to date have not occurred in alternatives *to* marriage but rather in alternatives *prior* to marriage, and alternative ways in *structuring* marriage itself yet keeping the basic structure and purposes intact. For example, nonmarital sex, delayed marriage, and cohabitation are practiced with increasing frequency, and are tolerated by a larger percentage of the population than ever before. Within marriage itself, certain changes are becoming increasingly popular, such as greater equality between men and women (although gender equality is more an ideal than a reality in most marriages, at least within the United States). The perceived "threats" to the institution of marriage, such as extramarital sex, gay and lesbian relationships, and communal living groups, are not increasing in popularity to the same degree. Generally the public holds these life-styles in greater suspicion because they question the basic values and norms of the traditional family systems: monogamous intimacy and the bearing and socialization of young children. Voluntary childlessness is somewhat unique; while still strongly disapproved of generally, an increasing number of persons are adopting this life-style nonetheless.

## NEVER-MARRIED SINGLES

A small but growing percentage of adult men and women remain single throughout their lives. In the United States, approximately 5 percent never marry. These individuals experience life without the support and obligations of a spouse and, most often, children. While often stereotyped as either "swingers" or "lonely losers," Stein reports that both categorizations are largely incorrect (1981). Instead, singles cannot be easily categorized and do not constitute a single social type. Some have chosen singlehood as a preferred option, perhaps due to career decisions, sexual preference, or other family responsibilities. Others have lived in locations in which demographic imbalances have affected the pool of eligibles for mate selection. And others have been lifelong isolates, have poor social skills, or have significant health impairments that have limited social contacts.

Attitudes toward singlehood have been quite negative historically, especially in the United States, although change has been noted in recent years. Studies report that during the 1950s, remaining single was viewed as a pathology, but by the mid-1970s singlehood was not only tolerated but even viewed by many as an avenue for enhancing one's happiness. Single males are still viewed more favorably than are single females; the former are stereotyped as carefree "bachelors," while single women are characterized as unattractive and unfortunate "spinsters." Oudijk (1983) found that the Dutch population generally affords greater life-style options to women, and only one-quarter of his sample of married and unmarried persons reported that married persons are necessarily happier than are singles.

Shostak (1987) has developed a typology in which to illustrate the divergence among the never-married single population. It is based on two major criteria: the voluntary verses involuntary nature of one's singlehood, and whether their singlehood is viewed as temporary or stable. *Ambivalents* are those who may not at this point be seeking mates but who are open to the idea of marriage at some time in the future. They may be deferring marriage for reasons related to schooling or career, or they may simply enjoy experimenting with a variety of relationships. *Wishfuls* are actively seeking a mate but have been unsuccessful in finding one. They are, generally, dissatisfied with their single state and would prefer to be married. The *resolved* consciously prefer singlehood. They are committed to this life-style for a variety of reasons; career, sexual orientation, or other personal considerations. A study of 482 single Canadians reported that nearly half considered themselves to fall within this category (Austrom and Hanel 1985). They have made a conscious decision to forgo marriage for the sake of a single life-style. A small but important component of this group are priests; nuns; and others who, for religious reasons, choose not to marry. Finally, *regretfuls* are those who would rather marry but who have given up their search for a mate and are resigned to singlehood. They are involuntarily stable singles. Many bright, well-educated, and successful career women are within this category. Because our marital norms decree that men will marry women who are younger or less educated than they, successful older women often find a shortage of men they deem "suitable" mates.

While the diversity and heterogeneity among the never-married population is becoming increasingly apparent, one variable is suspected to be of extreme importance in explaining at least some of the variation: gender. Based on data gathered in numerous treatises, the emerging profiles of male and females singles is in stark contrast. As Bernard (1973) bluntly puts it, the never-married men represent the "bottom of the barrel," while the never-married women are the "cream of the crop." Single women are generally thought to be more intelligent, are better educated, and are more successful in their occupations than are single men, or women who marry. Additionally, research finds that single women report to be happier, less lonely, and have a greater sense of psychological well-being than do their single male counterparts.

Despite the fact that only 2 percent of the population identified singlehood as their preferred choice a decade ago (Roper Organization 1980), social demographers predict that the proportion of singles in our population is likely to increase in the future. As singlehood continues to become a viable and respectable alternative to marriage, more adults may choose to remain single throughout their lives. Others may remain single not out of choice but due to demographic and social trends. The postponement of marriage and the increasing educational level and occupational aspirations of women, coupled with our continued norms of marital homogamy, help to ensure that the number of never-married single persons—women in particular—are likely to increase into the next century. Basing his projections on current patterns, Glick (1984) predicts that 10 percent of males who were between the ages of 25 and 29 in 1980 and 12 percent of females in that age group will never marry.

## CHILD-FREE ADULTS

There is reason to believe that fundamental changes are occurring in the values associated with having children. As economic opportunities for women increase; as birth control, including abortion, becomes more available and reliable; and as tolerance increases for an array of life-styles, having children is likely to become increasing viewed as an option rather than a mandate. Evidence is accumulating to suggest that men and women are reevaluating the costs and benefits of parenthood. This trend is occurring not only in

the United States but in many industrialized countries in Europe as well. The decline in childbearing there has been referred to as the "second demographic transition" (Van de Kaa 1987). Davis (1987) posits that features of industrial societies weaken the individual's desire for children. He lists several interrelated traits of industrialization, including the postponement of marriage, cohabitation, out-of-wedlock births, female labor force participation, and high rates of divorce, claiming that these trends decrease the need for both marriage and childbearing.

Remaining child-free is not a new phenomenon, however. In 1940, for example, 17 percent of married white women between ages thirty-five and thirty-nine were child-free. Some of these women were simply delaying parenthood until their forties; however, in all likelihood most remained child-free. This percentage began to drop considerably after World War II, and by the late 1970s approximately 7 percent of women in the thirty-five to thirty-nine age group remained child-free. Today the figure is rising dramatically. Eighteen percent of women in this age group were without children in 1988. It is predicted that 20 percent to 25 percent of the cohort referred to as "baby-boomers" will remain child-free. This increase is due to a multitude of factors: delayed childbearing, infertility, and voluntary childlessness.

An important distinction to make in the discussion of childlessness is whether the decision was voluntary or involuntary. *Involuntary* childlessness involves those who are infecund or subfecund. They do not have a choice and, unless they adopt or create some other social arrangement, are inevitably committed to this life-style. *Voluntary* childlessness, the focus of this discussion, involves those who choose to remain child-free. Large differences exist within members of this group; *early articulators* have made their decision early in their lives and are committed to their choice. *Postponers*, on the other hand, begin first by delaying their childbearing, but wind up being child-free due to their continual postponement. Early articulators generally exhibit less stereotypical gender roles, are more likely to cohabit, and enjoy the company of children less than do postponers. Seccombe (1990) found that among married persons under age forty who have no children, wives are more likely than their husbands to report a preference for remaining childfree (19 percent and 13 percent, respectively).

Despite increasing rates of voluntary childlessness, most research conducted within the United States documents the pervasiveness of pronatalist sentiment. Those who voluntarily opt to remain child-free are viewed as selfish, immature, lonely, unfulfilled, insensitive, and more likely to have mental problems than are those who choose parenthood. Females, those persons with less education, with large families of their own, Catholics, and those residing in rural areas are most apt to judge the child-free harshly.

Most studies report that those persons who opt to remain child-free are well aware of the sanctions surrounding their decision yet are rarely upset by them (see Houseknecht 1987 for review). In her review of twelve studies, Houseknecht found only three that reported that child-free individuals had trouble dealing with the reaction from others. Sanctions apparently are not strong enough to detract certain persons from what they perceive as the attractiveness of a child-free lifestyle. Houseknecht (1987), in a content analysis of twenty-nine studies reporting the rationales for remaining child-free, identified nine primary motivations. These are, in order of the frequency in which they were found: (1) freedom from child-care responsibilities: greater opportunity for self-fulfillment and spontaneous mobility, (2) more satisfactory marital relationship, (3) female career considerations, (4) monetary advantages, (5) concern about population growth, (6) general dislike of children, (7) negative early socialization experience and doubts about the ability to parent, (8) concern about physical aspects of childbirth and recovery, and (9) concern for children given world conditions. Gender differences were evidenced in a number of areas. Overall, females were more likely to offer altruistic rationales (e.g., concern about population growth, doubts about the ability to parent, concern for children given world condi-

tions). The male samples, conversely, were more apt to offer personal motives (e.g., general dislike of children, monetary advantages).

The consequences of large numbers of persons in industrialized societies forgoing parenthood are far-reaching. For example, the demographic structure in many countries is in the process of radical change; populations are becoming increasingly aged. More persons are reaching old age than ever before, those persons are living longer, and birth rates are low. The cohort age eighty-five or older, in fact, is the fastest-growing cohort in the United States. The question remains: Who will care for the elderly? Some Western European countries provide a variety of services to assist elderly persons in maintaining their independence within the community as long as possible. But social policies in other countries, including the United States, rely heavily on adult children to provide needed care to elderly parents. Formal support services, when available, tend to be uncoordinated and expensive. The question of who will provide that needed care to the large numbers of adults who are predicted to have no children has yet to be answered.

## COMMUNAL LIVING GROUPS

Recent history has witnessed a wide variety of types of communal living groups, including collectives, shared households, experimental communities, and group marriage. Communal living arrangements of these types were more prevalent during the 1960s and 1970s than during any other point in history. It is estimated that within the United States during this period there were approximately 50,000 communal groups with 755,000 participants. These groups coalesce for divergent reasons: simple convenience; political, philosophical, or religious ideologies; sexual variety; economic considerations; or personal growth. Kanter (1972) distinguishes communal living groups during this era as distinctive from previous ones: Communes prior to 1845 generally contained religious themes; after that period economic and political themes were central; and beginning in the 1960s we see that the severe erosion of faith in American institutions was the cornerstone of the formation of communal living groups.

Commune members are a highly divergent group, but certain generalizations can be made. According to the findings of research conducted during the 1970s, most members were young, college-educated, single, and had no children. Approximately three-quarters had never been married, and most were under age thirty. Although most members considered themselves to be politically liberal, commune members resembled the mainstream more so than most people imagine. Most were from middle-class origins, and a higher percentage came from intact families than found among the national average. Many communes had a religious orientation, but even among those that did not, a high number of members reported to have experimented with religious philosophies.

Of the variety of alternative life-styles discussed here, communal living may be the least understood and the most disapproved of. A study conducted in the early 1970s, in the heyday of such living groups, found that only 20 percent of the U.S. population approved of them, and the percentage reporting that they were interested in such living arrangements was much lower still (Yankelovich 1974).

Given the lack of societal support, it is not surprising that communal living groups are unstable. Most arrangements dissolve within a year. The Constantines' study of over a hundred communal living groups in the early 1970s reported that 44 percent of groups lasted for a year or more, 17 percent for three years, and only 7 percent survived for more than five years (Constantine and Constantine 1973).

Today very few persons live in such arrangements. It is estimated that communal living groups contain no more that 250,000 persons in the United States. Other Western countries report similar trends. Studies conducted in the Netherlands and Denmark indicate that not only do very few communal groups exist in these countries, but also they are relatively small, containing only six members per group on average.

## COHABITATION

Cohabitation is generally defined as nonmarried heterosexual persons who share intimacy, sexual relations, and who coreside. Cohabitation is not a recent phenomenon nor a uniquely Western one; many societies today and in the past note within their populations couples who were legally married, and those who reside in the generally less honored state of cohabitation. In Sweden, unlike the United States, cohabitation has become so common that it is considered a social institution in and of itself. It is a variant of marriage rather than of courtship; approximately 20 percent of all couples in Sweden who live together are unmarried.

Cohabitation is becoming increasingly common in the United States, although it has not achieved the same status as in Scandinavia. In 1988 there were 2.6 million couples in the United States, or more than 5 million adults, living together outside of marriage at any given time. National data indicate that the increase since 1970 is almost fivefold. From 1970 to 1980 the percentage of couples who had cohabited prior to marriage, as reported in one specific county in Oregon, rose from 13 percent to 53 percent (Gwartney-Gibbs 1986). Another study, of eighty-seven Canadian couples located through newspaper wedding announcements, reported that 64 percent of the couples had cohabited for some period, 43 percent of these for over three months. Thus cohabitation is now seen as an institutionalized component to the larger progression involving dating, courtship, engagement, and marriage.

Cohabitors tend to differ from noncohabitors in a variety of sociodemographic characteristics. For example, cohabitors tend to see themselves as being more androgynous and more politically liberal, are less apt to be religious, are more experienced sexually, and are younger than married persons. The data on the quality of their home life within their families of orientation is mixed. See Macklin (1987) and Buunk and Van Driel (1989) for two divergent views. Although cohabitors may argue that living together prior to marriage will enhance the latter relationship by increasing their knowledge of their compatibility with day-to-day living prior to legalizing the union, such optimism is generally not supported. While some studies indicate no differences in the quality of marriages among those who first cohabited and those that did not, others indicate that the noncohabitors seem to have the advantage. This may, however, have nothing to do with cohabitation per se but rather may be due to other differences in the personalities and expectations of marriage between the two groups.

A wide variety of personal relationships exist among cohabiting couples. Several typologies have been created to try to capture the diversity found within these relationships. One particularly useful one, articulated by Macklin (1983), is designed to exemplify the diversity in the stability of such relationships. She discusses four types of cohabiting relationships: (1) *temporary or casual* relationships, in which the couple cohabits for convenience or for pragmatic reasons; (2) *going together,* in which the couple is affectionately involved but has no plans for marriage in the future; (3) *transitional,* which serves as a preparation for marriage; and (4) *alternative to marriage,* wherein the couple opposes marriage on ideological or other grounds.

Attitudes toward cohabitation have become increasingly positive, especially among younger persons. However, the majority of persons in the United States still disapprove of living together without the legal ties of marriage. Buunk and Van Driel (1989) remind us that cohabitation in several U.S. states is still a felony, based on a legal code outlawing "crimes against chastity." These laws, however, are rarely if ever enforced. In the Netherlands, or in other countries where cohabitation is institutionalized, the majority of the population sees few distinctions between cohabitation and marriage. Both are viewed as appropriate avenues for intimacy, and the two life-styles resemble one another much more so than in the United States in terms of commitment and stability.

The future of cohabitation, and the subsequent changes in the attitudes toward it, are of considerable interest to sociologists. Many predict that cohabitation will become institutionalized in the United States to a greater degree within the near future, shifting from a pattern of courtship to an alternative to marriage. Whether it will ever achieve the status found within other countries, particularly in Scandinavia, remains to be seen.

## GAY AND LESBIAN RELATIONSHIPS

Not long ago homosexuality was viewed by many professionals as an illness or a perversion. It was only as recently as 1973, for example, that the American Psychiatric Association removed homosexuality from its list of psychiatric disorders. Today, due in large part to the efforts of researchers such as Kinsey and associates (1948, 1953), Masters and Johnson (1979), and to organizations such as the Gay Liberation Front during the late 1960s, homosexuality has generally become to be viewed as a life-style rather than an illness, at least within academic circles. The work of Kinsey and associates illustrated that a sizable minority of the population, particularly males, had experimented with same-sex sexual relationships, although few considered themselves exclusively homosexual. Thirty-seven percent of males, he reported, had experienced at least one homosexual contact to the point of orgasm, although only 4 percent were exclusively homosexual. Among females, 13 percent had a same-sex sexual contact to the point of orgasm, while only 2 percent were exclusively homosexual in their orientation. A recent national probability sample of adult males interviewed by telephone found that 3.7 percent reported to be either homosexual or bisexual (Harry 1990).

Cross-cultural evidence suggests that the majority of cultures recognize the existence of homosexual behavior, particularly in certain age categories such as adolescence, and most are tolerant of homosexual behavior. Culturally speaking, it is rare to find an actual *preference* for same-sex relations; they tend to occur only in societies that define homosexuality and heterosexuality as mutually exclusive, as in many industrial countries.

Among nonacademic circles, attitudes toward homosexuality are less accepting or tolerant. Many states within the United States, particularly those in the South and in the West, still have laws barring homosexual activity among consenting adults. Attitudes among the United States populace parallel such statutes. The results of a recent Gallup poll indicate that 60 percent of adults believe that homosexuals should not be hired as elementary-school teachers (Gallup 1987). According to a statewide study in Alaska, gays and lesbians report that their sexual orientation has caused a variety of problems in securing housing and in the job market. Additionally, almost two-thirds of the respondents reported at least one instance of violence or verbal abuse due to their sexual orientation (Green and Brause 1989). This contrasts sharply with the view toward homosexuality in the Scandinavian countries. Not only are homosexual relations between consenting adults legal, but also the majority of the population considers it to be normal behavior. The AIDS crisis, however, has made the public less tolerant of homosexual behavior in both the United States and Europe.

There is a growing amount of research illuminating various aspects of homosexual relationships, such as gender roles; degree of commitment; quality of relationship; and the couples' interface with other relationships, such as children, ex-spouses, or parents. However, because of unique historical reactions to gays and lesbians, and to the differential socialization of men and women in our society, it is important to explore the nature of lesbian and gay relationships separately. Gender differences emerge in homosexual relations within a variety of contexts; for example, lesbians are more apt to have monogamous, stable relationships than are gay men, although the popular stereotype of gays as sexually "promiscuous" has been exaggerated. The majority of gay men, just like lesbians, are interested in monogamous, long-term relationships. The lack of institutional support for gay and lesbian relationships and the wide variety of obstacles not encountered among heterosexuals, such as prejudice and discriminatory behavior, take their toll on these relationships, however.

The AIDS epidemic has had an enormous impact on the gay subculture. While the impact on lesbians is significantly less, they have not been untouched by the social impact of this devastating medical issue (see Kaplan et al. 1987 for a thorough review of the sociological impact of AIDS). The high mortality rates among AIDS victims has particularly struck San Francisco, New York, Los Angeles, and Miami, and the devastation attributed to this epidemic cannot be ignored, despite the slow response of the world's governments.

## CONCLUDING COMMENTS

There is considerable accumulating evidence to suggest that family life-styles are becoming more varied and that the public is becoming increasingly tolerant of this diversity. The data indicate that marriage itself per se may be less important in sanctioning intimacy. The review by Buunk and Hupka (1986) of seven countries reveals that individualism, as expressed by following one's own personal interests in intimate relationships, was more prevalent in affluent democratic countries such as the United States and in most of Western Europe than in poorer and nondemocratic nations such as the Soviet Union.

This does not mean, however, that people are discarding the institution of marriage. In the United States, as elsewhere, the vast majority of the population continues to endorse marriage and parenthood in general, and for themselves personally. Most still plan to marry and have children, and optimism remains high that theirs will be a lasting union despite high national frequencies of divorce.

Alternative life-styles are not replacing marriage. Instead, they are gaining acceptance because they involve, for some, modifications of the family structure as an adaptation to changing conditions in society. The life-styles discussed here, as well as others such as single-parent families, commuter marriages, sexually open marriages, dual-career families, and stepfamilies, reflect the broader social changes in values, relationships, and even technology that are found within society as a whole. As Macklin notes, the family is not disappearing, but "continuing its age-old process of gradual evolution, maintaining many of its traditional functions and structures while adapting to changing economic circumstances and cultural ideologies" (1987, p. 317). This process has merely accelerated during the past several decades, and these changes have caught the attention of the general public. College classes and their corresponding textbooks within this discipline of sociology are still often titled *Marriage and the Family,* as if there were only one model of intimacy. Yet perhaps a more appropriate title would be Marriages and Families. This would reflect not only the diversity illustrated here but would also acknowledge the tremendous ethnic and class variations that make for rich and meaningful intimate relations.

(SEE ALSO: *American Families; Courtship; Marriage; Mate Selection Theories; Sexual Orientation*)

## REFERENCES

Austrom, Douglas, and Kim Hanel 1985 "Psychological Issues of Single Life in Canada: An Exploratory Study." *International Journal of Women's Studies* 8: 12–23.

Bernard, Jessie 1973 *The Future of Marriage.* New York: Bantam Books.

Buunk, Bram P., and R. B. Hupka 1986 "Autonomy in Close Relationships: A Cross-cultural Study." *Family Perspective* 20:209–221.

———, and Barry Van Driel 1989 Variant Lifestyles and Relationships. Newbury Park, Calif.: Sage Publications.

Constantine L., and J. M. Constantine 1973 *Group Marriage.* New York: Collier Books.

Davis, Kingsley 1987 "Low Fertility in Evolutionary Perspective." In K. Davis, M. S. Bernstam, and R. Ricardo-Campbell, eds., *Below Replacement Fertility in Industrial Societies.* Cambridge: Cambridge University Press.

*Gallup Report* 1987 Report Nos. 244–245:2–9.

Glick, Paul C. 1984 "Marriage, Divorce, and Living Arrangements: Perspective Changes." *Journal of Family Issues* 5:7–26.

Green, Melissa S., and Jay K. Brause 1989 *Identity Reports: Sexual Orientation Bias in Alaska.* Anchorage, Alaska: Identity Inc.

Gwartney-Gibbs, Patricia A. 1986 "The Institutionalization of Premarital Cohabitation: Estimates from Marriage License Applications." *Journal of Marriage and the Family* 48:423–434.

Harry, Joseph 1990 "A Probability Sample of Gay Men." *Journal of Homosexuality* 19:89–104.

Houseknecht, Sharon K. 1987 "Voluntary Childlessness." In M. B. Sussman and S. K. Steinmetz, eds., *Handbook of Marriage and the Family.* New York: Plenum Press.

Kanter, Rosabeth Moss 1972 *Commitment and Community: Communes and Utopias in Sociological Perspective.* Cambridge, Mass.: Harvard University Press.

Kaplan, Howard B., Robert J. Johnson, Carol A. Bailey, and William Simon 1987 "The Sociological Study of AIDS: A Critical Review of the Literature and Suggested Research Agenda." *Journal of Health and Social Behavior* 28:140–157.

Kinsey, Alfred, W. Pomeroy, P. H. Gebhard, and C. E. Martin 1953 *Sexual Behavior in the Human Female.* Philadelphia: W. B. Saunders.

Kinsey, Alfred, W. Pomeroy, and C. E. Martin 1948 *Sexual Behavior in the Human Male.* Philadelphia: W. B. Saunders.

Macklin, Eleanor D. 1983 "Nonmarital Heterosexual Cohabitation: An Overview." In E. D. Macklin and R. H. Rubin, eds., *Contemporary Families and Alternative Lifestyles: Handbook on Research and Theory.* Beverly Hills, Calif.: Sage Publications.

——— 1987 "Nontraditional Family Forms." In M. B. Sussman and S. K. Steinmetz, eds., *Handbook of Marriage and the Family.* New York: Plenum Press.

Masters, William H., and Virginia E. Johnson 1979 *Homosexuality in Perspective.* Boston: Little, Brown.

Oudijk, C. 1983 *Social Atlas of Women* (in Dutch). The Hague: Staatsuitgeverij.

Roper Organization 1980 *The Virginia Slims American Women's Poll.* Storrs, Conn.: Author.

Seccombe, Karen 1990 "Assessing the Costs and Benefits of Children: Gender Comparisons among Childfree Husbands and Wives." *Journal of Marriage and the Family* 53:191–202.

Shostak, Arthur B. 1987 "Singlehood." In M. B. Sussman and S. K. Steinmetz, eds., *Handbook of Marriage and the Family.* New York: Plenum Press.

Stein, Peter J. 1981 *Single Life: Unmarried Adults in Social Context.* New York: St. Martin's Press.

Van de Kaa, Dick J. 1987 "Europe's Second Demographic Transition." *Population Bulletin* 42:1–57.

Yankelovich, Daniel 1974 *The New Morality: Profile of American Youth in the Seventies.* New York: McGraw-Hill.

KAREN SECCOMBE

**ALTRUISM** Helping is variously referred to as prosocial behavior, helping behavior, or altruism. "Prosocial behavior" is the broadest of the three terms and refers to any behavior that can be construed as consistent with the norms of a given society. Thus, murder, when enacted on behalf of one's country on a battlefield, is as prosocial a behavior as intervening to prevent a crime. "Helping behavior" refers simply to any behavior that is intended to provide benefit to its recipient. "Altruism" is the narrowest of the three concepts. Altruism is behavior that not only provides benefits to its recipient but also provides no benefits to the actor and even incurs some costs. Thus, altruism expresses internal motivation to benefit another. If one conceives of psychological rewards as benefits to the actor, this definition of altruism is so narrow that it excludes virtually all human behavior. Hence, many social psychologists maintain simply that altruistic behavior need exclude only the receipt of material benefits by the actor.

## HISTORY

The origins of the contemporary study of altruism have been traced back to August Comte, who explored the development of altruism and "sympathetic instincts." The existence of an altruistic instinct was emphasized in McDougall's *Introduction to Social Psychology* (1908) but argued against by the naturalistic observational research of Lois Murphy (1937). Early symbolic interactionists attributed altruistic behavior to the capacity to take the roles of others (Mead 1934). The developmental study of altruism built on the theoretical work of Piaget (1932), who explored stages in the development of sharing behavior, as well as on the more recent work of Kohlberg (1969) on the development of moral judgment. Hartshorne and May conducted one of the earliest series of empirical studies (1928–30), focusing on honesty and altruism. It is only since the mid-1960s, however, that altruism has been extensively and systematically examined. Most social psychology textbooks attribute this recent interest to the murder of Kitty

Genovese in 1964 and the failure of the thirty-nine witnesses to intervene. The subject of widespread media coverage, this incident motivated Latane and Darley's experimental investigations of why bystanders do not help, published in *The Unresponsive Bystander: Why Doesn't He Help?* (1970). During the 1970s, helping behavior became one of the most popular topics in social psychological research, although this emphasis may have declined somewhat during the 1980s. Virtually all textbooks now have a chapter on altruism and helping behavior, and a number of books on the topic have been published in the past two decades.

## THEORIES OF ALTRUISM AND HELPING BEHAVIOR

Helping behavior has been explained within a variety of theoretical frameworks, among them sociobiology, social learning, and cognitive development. One sociobiological approach maintains that helping behavior has developed through sociobiological evolution, the selective accumulation of behavior transmitted genetically. A second sociobiological theory maintains that helping behavior has developed through sociocultural evolution, the selective accumulation of behavior retained through purely social modes of transmission. (See Krebs and Miller [1985] for an excellent review of this literature.) The cognitive-developmental approach emphasizes transformation of cognitive structures and experiential role-taking opportunities as determinants of the development of helping behavior. Social learning theory explains altruism and helping behavior as learned through interaction with the social environment, mainly through reinforcement and, more commonly, modeling. Reflecting the same behaviorist principles, exchange theory suggests that individuals perform helping acts while guided by the principles of maximizing rewards and minimizing costs. Helping behavior is instrumental in acquiring rewards that may be material, social, or even self-reinforcing. A more explicitly sociological framework suggests that individuals help because they conform to social norms that prescribe helping. Three norms have received special attention: the norm of giving, which prescribes giving for its own sake; the norm of social responsibility, which prescribes helping others who are dependent; and the norm of reciprocity, which prescribes that individuals should help those who have helped them.

Most recently, reflecting the contemporary social psychological emphasis on cognition, several decision-making models of helping behavior have guided research (Latane and Darley 1970; Piliavin et al. 1981; Schwartz and Howard 1981). These models specify sequential decisions that begin with noticing a potential helping situation and end with a decision to help (or not). Recent research has focused on identifying those personality and situational variables that influence this decision-making process and specifying how they do so. There also has begun to be more attention on the social and sociological aspects of helping—to the context in which helping occurs, to the relationship between helper and helped, and to structural factors that may affect these interactions (Gergen and Gergen 1983; Callero 1986).

## RESEARCH ON ALTRUISM AND HELPING BEHAVIOR

**Person Variables.** There has been an extensive and confused debate about the existence of an altruistic personality. Suffice it to say that at best there is some evidence of a pattern of prosocial personality traits that characterize individuals whose behavior is demonstrably altruistic (e.g., community mental health workers; see Krebs and Miller 1985). This correlational evidence is not sufficient to establish the existence of an altruistic personality. Research has demonstrated, however, that a number of person-specific variables do affect whether or not individuals offer help.

Temporary emotional states or moods may affect helping. A series of studies by Isen (1970) and her colleagues demonstrate that the "glow of good will" induces people to perform at least

low-cost helping acts such as helping someone pick up a pile of dropped papers. Internalized values as expressed in personal norms have also been shown to influence helping. Personal norms generate the motivation to help through their implications for self-based costs and benefits; behavior consistent with personal norms creates rewards such as increased self-esteem, whereas behavior that contradicts personal norms generates self-based costs such as shame. This influence has been demonstrated in high-cost helping such as bone marrow donation (Schwartz 1977). Other personality correlates of helping are less directly related to the costs and benefits of the helping act itself. For example, information-processing styles such as cognitive complexity influence helping.

**Situation Variables.** Characteristics of the situation also influence the decision to help. The salience and clarity of a victim's need influence both the initial tendency to notice need and the definition of the perceived need as serious. Salience and clarity of need increase as the physical distance between an observer and a victim decreases; thus, victims of an emergency are more likely to be helped by those physically near by. Situational cues regarding the seriousness of another's need influence whether need is defined as serious enough to warrant action. Bystanders are more likely to offer aid when a victim appears to collapse from a heart attack than from a hurt knee, for example, presumably because of perceived seriousness.

The number of others present in a potential helping situation also influences an individual's decision to help; this process is known as the diffusion of responsibility. Darley and Latane (1968) demonstrated experimentally that the higher the number of others present, the lower the chance of any one individual helping. They reasoned that the higher the number of potential helpers, the more responsibility is diffused among them, thus reducing the perceived responsibility of any given individual. The presence of an individual who may be perceived as having special competence to help also reduces the felt responsibility of others to help. Thus, when someone in a doctor's uniform is present at a medical emergency, others are less likely to help.

**Social Variables.** Research has also demonstrated the influence of social variables on helping. Studies of reactions following natural disasters show that people tend to give aid first to family members, then to friends and neighbors, and last to strangers. Darley and Latane (1968) showed experimentally that people are more likely to provide help in an emergency in the presence of friends rather than in the presence of strangers: They reasoned that responsibility can be shifted more easily to a stranger than to a friend. Thus, preexisting social relationships among bystanders affect helping. Individuals are also more likely to help others who are similar to them, whether in dress style or in political ideology.

The perceived legitimacy of need, a variable defined by social norms, also affects rates of helping. In one ingenious field study of emergency intervention, bystanders were more likely to help a stranger who collapsed in a subway car if the distress was attributed to illness rather than to drunkenness (Piliavin, Rodin, and Piliavin 1969). This study also demonstrates the influence of social statuses. The race of the bystanders did not affect the rate of helping an apparently ill person, but race did influence the rate of helping someone who appeared drunk. In the latter situation, people tended to help only people of their own race.

Other studies of the effect of social statuses on helping indicate, consistent with social categorization theory, that members of one's own group tend to be helped more than outgroup members, particularly members of stigmatized outgroups. Whites are more likely to help whites than blacks, unless the prejudicial treatment is observable (Dovidio 1984). The one exception to this general pattern is that males tend to help females more than they help males, whereas females are equally helpful to females and males (see Piliavin and Unger 1985). This pattern may reflect stereotypic gender roles: Females are stereotyped as dependent and weaker than males.

## THE SOCIOLOGICAL CONTEXT OF HELPING

Gergen and Gergen (1983) call for increased attention to the social structural context of helping and to the interactive history and process of the helping relationship (see also Piliavin and Charng 1990). Social structure is clearly important as a context for helping. Social structure specifies the pool of social roles and meaning systems associated with any interaction (Callero, Howard, and Piliavin 1987). Social structure also influences the distribution of resources that may be necessary for certain helping relationships. One needs money to be able to donate to a charity and medical expertise to be able to help earthquake victims. Social structure also determines the probability of both social and physical interaction among individuals and thus influences the possibility of helping.

Interactive history is also crucial to understanding helping behavior. If a relationship has been positive and mutually supportive, this context suggests that beneficial actions should be defined as helping. If a relationship has been characterized by competition and conflict, this context does not support defining beneficial action as helping. In this case, alternative, more self-serving motivations may underlie helping. Thus the provision of U.S. foreign aid to countries with whom the United States has had conflict is often viewed as a strategic tool, whereas when such aid has been provided to countries with which the United States has had positive relationships, it is viewed generally as genuine helping. Such patterns illustrate this influence of interaction history on the interpretation of helping behavior.

Another sociological approach emphasizes helping as role behavior and is guided by Mead's (1934) conception of roles as patterns of social acts framed by a community and recognized as distinct objects of the social environment. Roles define individual selves and thus also guide individual perception and action. Helping behavior has been shown to express social roles. A study by

Callero, Howard, and Piliavin (1987) demonstrates that role–person merger (when a social role becomes an essential aspect of self) predicts blood donation, one form of helping behavior, independent of the effects of both personal and social norms, and is more strongly associated with a history of blood donation than social or personal norms. This study demonstrates the importance of helping for self-validation and reproduction of the social structure as expressed in roles. This recent attention to concepts such as roles, interaction history, and social structure is evidence of the sociological significance of altruism and helping behavior.

(SEE ALSO: *Social Psychology*)

### REFERENCES

Callero, Peter L. 1986 "Putting the Social in Prosocial Behavior: An Interactionist Approach to Altruism." *Humboldt Journal of Social Relations* 13:15–32.

———, Judith A. Howard, and Jane A. Piliavin 1987 "Helping Behavior as Role Behavior: Disclosing Social Structure and History in the Analysis of Prosocial Action." *Social Psychology Quarterly* 50:247–256.

Darley, John M., and Bibb Latane 1968 "Bystander Intervention in Emergencies: Diffusion of Responsibility." *Journal of Personality and Social Psychology* 8:377–383.

Dovidio, John F. 1984 "Helping Behavior and Altruism: An Empirical and Conceptual Overview." In L. Berkowitz, ed., *Advances in Experimental Social Psychology*, vol. 17. New York: Academic.

Gergen, Kenneth J., and Mary M. Gergen 1983 "Social Construction of Helping Relationships." In J. F. Fisher, A. Nadler, and B. M. DePaulo, eds., *New Directions in Helping*, vol. 1. New York: Academic.

Hartshorne, H., and M. A. May 1928–30 *Studies in the Nature of Character*, vols. 1–3. New York: Macmillan.

Isen, Alice M. 1970 "Success, Failure, Attention and Reaction to Others: The Warm Glow of Success." *Journal of Personality and Social Psychology* 15:294–301.

Kohlberg, Lawrence 1969 "Stage and Sequence: The Cognitive-Developmental Approach to Socialization." In D. Goslin, ed., *Handbook of Socialization Theory and Research*. Chicago: Rand McNally.

Krebs, Dennis L., and Dale T. Miller 1985 "Altruism and Aggression." In G. Lindzey and E. Aronson, eds., *The Handbook of Social Psychology*, 3d ed., vol. 2, Hillsdale, N.J.: Erlbaum.

Latane, Bibb, and John M. Darley 1970 *The Unresponsive Bystander: Why Doesn't He Help?* New York: Appleton-Crofts.

McDougall, William 1908 *Introduction to Social Psychology*. London: Methuen.

Mead, George Herbert 1934 *Mind, Self and Society from the Standpoint of a Social Behaviorist*, edited by C. W. Morris. Chicago: University of Chicago Press.

Murphy, Lois B. 1937 *Social Behavior and Child Personality: An Exploratory Study of Some Roots of Sympathy*. New York: Columbia University Press.

Piaget, Jean 1932 *The Moral Judgment of the Child*. London: Routledge and Kegan Paul.

Piliavin, Irving M., Judith Rodin, and Jane A. Piliavin 1969 "Good Samaritanism: An Underground Phenomenon?" *Journal of Personality and Social Psychology* 13:289–299.

Piliavin, Jane A., and Hong-wn Charng 1990 "Altruism: A Review of Recent Theory and Research." *The Annual Review of Sociology*.

Piliavin, Jane A., John F. Dovidio, Samuel Gaertner, and Russell D. Clark 1981 *Emergency Intervention*. New York: Academic.

Piliavin, Jane A., and Rhoda Kesler Unger 1985 "The Helpful but Helpless Female: Myth or Reality?" In V. E. O'Leary, R. K. Unger, and B. S. Wallston, eds., *Women, Gender, and Social Psychology*. Hillsdale, N.J.: Erlbaum.

Schwartz, Shalom H. 1977 "Normative Influences on Altruism." In L. Berkowitz, ed., *Advances in Experimental Social Psychology*, vol. 10. New York: Academic Press.

———, and Judith A. Howard 1981 "A Normative Decision-Making Model of Altruism." In J. P. Rushton and R. M. Sorrentino, eds., *Altruism and Helping Behavior: Social, Personality, and Developmental Perspectives*. Hillsdale, N.J.: Erlbaum.

JUDITH A. HOWARD

**AMERICAN FAMILIES** Many long-standing assumptions about American families have been challenged in recent years. Among these assumptions is the belief that in colonial times the American family was extended in its structure, with three generations living together under one roof. It has been commonly believed that the nuclear family came about as a result of industrialization, with smaller families better able to meet the demands of an industrialized economy. However, historical data show that the extended family was not typical in the colonial era and that the earliest families arriving from Great Britain and other western European countries were already nuclear in structure (Demos 1970; Laslett and Wall 1972).

More generally, family scholars have successfully challenged the notion of "the American family." As Howe (1972, p. 11) puts it, "the first thing to remember about the American family is that it doesn't exist. Families exist. All kinds of families in all kinds of economic and marital situations." This review will show the great diversity of family patterns that characterize the United States of the past, the present, and the foreseeable future.

## HISTORICAL OVERVIEW

It is unfortunate that textbooks intended for courses on the family rarely include a discussion of Native Americans, for a historical examination of these groups shows a striking range of variation in family patterns. In fact, virtually all the variations in marriage customs, residence patterns, and family structures found the world over could be found in North America alone (Driver 1969). Though some of these traditional family patterns have survived to the present day, others have been disrupted over the course of U.S. history. It is important to note, however, that research has not confirmed the commonly held assumption that Native American societies were placid and unchanging prior to European contact and subsequent subjugation. Important changes were taking place in Native American societies long before the arrival of Europeans (Lurie 1985).

As has been noted, European immigrants to the American colonies came in nuclear rather than extended families (and also came as single persons—for example, as indentured servants). It was long believed that colonial families were very large, with some early writers claiming an average

of ten to twelve children per family. More recently, family scholars have cited evidence showing somewhat lower numbers of children, with an average of eight children born to colonial women (Zinn and Eitzen 1987). Scholars also have distinguished between number of children born per woman and family size at a given point in time. Average family size was somewhat smaller than the average number of children born, due to high infant mortality and because the oldest children often left home prior to the birth of the last child. Evidence suggests an average family size of five to six members during colonial times (Nock 1987). Thus, although the average size of colonial families was somewhat larger than today's families, they are not as large as have been commonly assumed.

To understand the size of colonial households, consideration must also be given to nonrelated persons living in the home. Servants often lived with prosperous colonial families, and other families took in boarders and lodgers when economic conditions required such an arrangement (Zinn and Eitzen 1987). Households might also include apprentices and other employees. The presence of nonfamily members has important implications for family life. Laslett (1973) has argued that the presence of nonkin meant that households offered less privacy to families and hence provided the opportunity for greater scrutiny by "outsiders." Colonial homes also had fewer rooms than most American homes today, which also contributed to the relatively public nature of these households.

Colonial communities placed great importance on marriage, particularly in New England, where sanctions were imposed on those who did not marry (for example, taxes were imposed on single men in some New England colonies). However, historical records indicate that colonists did not marry at especially young ages. The average age at marriage was twenty-four to twenty-five for men and twenty-two to twenty-three for women (Leslie and Korman 1989). Older ages at marriage during this era reflect parental control of sons' labor on the farm (with many sons delaying marriage until their fathers ceded land to them) and also reflect the lower relative numbers of women (Nock 1987). Parents also typically exerted strong influence over the process of mate selection but did not control the decision. Divorce was rare during this period. The low divorce rate cannot be equated with intact marriages, however. Spousal desertion and early widowhood were far more common experiences than they are today.

The population for the American colonies came primarily from Great Britain, other western European countries, and from western Africa. Initially brought to the colonies in 1619 as indentured servants, hundreds of thousands of Africans were enslaved and transported to America during the colonial period (by 1790, the date of the first U.S. census, African-Americans composed almost 20 percent of the population; Zinn and Eitzen 1987). It has been commonly assumed that slavery destroyed the cultural traditions and family life of African-Americans. The reasoning behind this assumption was that slave families often were separated for sale to other masters, males were unable to provide for or protect their families, and slave marriages were not legal. The stereotype of "matriarchal" black families, in which women are the family heads and authorities, usually assumes that slavery produced this family form. Recent research challenges these assumptions. Though slave families lived in constant fear of separation (Genovese 1986), many slave marriages were strong and long-lasting (Gutman 1976). Marriages were legitimized within the slave community (symbolized, for example, by the ritual of "jumping over a broomstick"; Boris and Bardaglio 1987), and two-parent families were common among slaves as well as among free blacks in the North and the South (Gutman 1976). A variety of family structures, including female-headed households, were found in the slave community and attested to the importance placed on kin ties. Rather than the "absent family" assumed to characterize slave life, slaves were connected to one another through extensive kinship networks (Genovese 1986). Extended kin ties continue to be an important aspect of African-American families today.

For decades, the heritage of slavery and its presumed effects on family life has been invoked to explain social problems in poor black communities (e.g., Moynihan 1965). The historical evidence described above does not lend support to this explanation. Most recent writers argue that social problems experienced in poor black communities can more accurately be attributed to the effects of discrimination and the disorganizing effects of mass migration to the urbanized North rather than to the heritage of slavery (e.g., Staples 1986).

Societal changes associated with the Industrial Revolution profoundly affected all types of American families, though the specific nature and extent of these effects varied by social class, race, ethnic origins, and geographic region. Prior to the Industrial Revolution, family members worked together as an economic unit. Their workplace was the home or family farm, with families producing much of what they consumed. Family life and economic life were one and the same, and the boundaries between "private life" in the family and "public life" in the community were blurred. With the development of a commercial economy, the workplace was located away from the family unit. Separation of work and family life created a sharp distinction between the "public" realm of work and the "private" realm of family. Particularly for women's roles, changes initiated by the Industrial Revolution have been long-lasting and far-reaching. Increasingly, women's roles were defined by activities assumed to be noneconomic, in the form of nurturing and caring for family members. This was especially true for middle class women, and married women were excluded from many jobs. Poor and working-class women often participated in wage labor, but this work was generally seen as secondary to their family roles. Men were viewed as having primary responsibility for the economic welfare of their families. No longer an economically interdependent unit, families were transformed such that women and children became economically dependent on the primary wage earner.

Thus, children's roles and family relationships also changed with industrialization. In contrast to earlier times, in which children were viewed as miniature adults and engaged in many of the same tasks they would also perform as adults, childhood came to be seen as a special stage of life characterized by dependence in the home. And although children in working-class homes were more likely to work for pay, the evidence suggests that these families also viewed childhood as a stage of life distinct from adulthood (Zinn and Eitzen 1987). Overall, the family became increasingly defined as a private place specializing in the nurturance of children and the satisfaction of emotional needs, a "haven in a heartless world" (Lasch 1977).

Family structures also changed during the 1800s. Family size declined to an average of four to five members. (Of course, average numbers obscure variation in family sizes across social classes and other important dimensions such as race and ethnicity.) Though the average size of nineteenth-century American families was close to that of today's families, women bore more children during their lifetimes than do American women today. Infant and child mortality was higher and births were spaced further apart, thus decreasing the average size of families at a given point in time. Household size also declined, with fewer households including nonrelated persons such as boarders or apprentices. The average ages at which women and men married were similar to those of colonial times, with an average of twenty-two years for women and twenty-six for men. However, greater life expectancy meant that marriages typically lasted longer than they did during the colonial period (Nock 1987).

From 1830 to 1930 the United States experienced two large waves of immigration. The first wave, from 1830 to 1882, witnessed the arrival of more than ten million immigrants from England, Ireland, Germany, and the Scandinavian countries. During the second wave, from 1882 to 1930, over twenty-two million immigrated to the United States. Peoples from northern and western Europe continued to come to the United States during this second wave, but a large proportion of immigrants came from southern and eastern Europe as well (Zinn and Eitzen 1987). Immigrants' family lives were shaped by their ethnic origins as well as by the diverse social and economic struc-

tures of the cities and communities in which they settled.

Ethnic traditions also helped Mexican-American families adapt to changing circumstances. Annexation of territory from Mexico in 1848 and subsequent immigration from Mexico produced sizable Mexican-American communities in the Southwest. Immigrants from Mexico often reconstructed their original family units within the United States, typically including extended as well as nuclear family members. Extended family households are more common today among Mexican-Americans than among non-Hispanic whites, reflecting Mexican-Americans' strong family orientation (or "familism") as well as their less advantaged economic circumstances (Zinn and Eitzen 1987).

Imbalanced sex ratios among Chinese and Japanese immigrants greatly influenced the family experiences of these groups. First coming to the United States in the early 1900s, Chinese immigrants were predominantly male. The Chinese Exclusion Act of 1882 barred further immigration, and only wealthy Chinese men were able to bring brides to the United States (Boris and Bardaglio 1987). As of 1910, there were 1,413 Chinese men in the United States to every 100 Chinese women. This sex ratio was still skewed in 1940, when there were 258 men to every 100 women. In contrast to the extended family networks typical of traditional Chinese culture, until recent decades many Chinese-American households consisted of single men living alone (Marden and Meyer 1973).

Substantial immigration from Japan took place between 1885 and 1924. Like traditional Chinese families, Japanese families were based on strong extended kin networks. As was true for Chinese immigration, most Japanese immigrants were male. In addition to immigration restrictions, Japanese-American families (especially those on the West Coast) were disrupted by property confiscation and the mass relocations that took place during World War II (Marden and Meyer 1973).

In addition to the "old" immigration of the mid-nineteenth century and the "new" immigration of the late nineteenth and early twentieth centuries, a third wave of large-scale immigration to the United States began in the mid-1960s. In contrast to the earlier waves, when most immigrants came from European countries, most immigration in this third wave has been from Latin America and Asia. However, as has been true of earlier periods of immigration, public controversies surround the economic and social absorption of these new groups (Marger 1991). In addition to occupational and economic challenges facing immigrant families, social challenges include the continuing debate over whether schools should provide bilingual education to non-English-speaking children.

## TRENDS SINCE 1900

The separation of paid work and family life, associated with the transition to an industrialized society, gave rise to profound changes in family life. Over the course of the twentieth century, women's roles have been defined primarily by family responsibilities within the "private sphere" of the home, but women's labor-force participation has risen steadily (except for a brief period following World War II; Andersen 1988). Increases in labor-force participation have been especially great among married women. In 1900, only 6 percent of all married women were in the labor force. By 1984, that figure had risen to 53 percent (Scanzoni and Scanzoni 1988). However, as has been true historically, African-American and other minority women are more likely to work for pay than non-Hispanic white women. As discussed below, women's labor-force participation has important implications for many dimensions of family life.

Though American families have changed in important ways over the past 100 years, examination of historical trends also reveals continuation of some family patterns begun long ago. Notably, the period of the 1950s is commonly thought to mark the end of a golden age of family life. However, historical data show that for a number of family patterns, the 1950s, rather than the 1970s and 1980s, was an unusual period. Lower rates of divorce, lower ages at marriage, and higher rates of childbearing observed during the 1950s have been attributed mainly to greater economic prosperity following the Great Depression and World War II (Cherlin 1981).

**Age at First Marriage.** As of 1986, the average (median) age at first marriage in the United States was twenty-three years for women and almost twenty-six years for men (Scanzoni and Scanzoni 1988). Available evidence suggests somewhat higher ages at first marriage in the future (Sweet and Bumpass 1987). Although some consider the trend toward later marriage a deviation from traditional patterns of family formation, historical data do not support this belief. The timing of marriage today is similar to that observed from the colonial period through the late 1800s (Cherlin 1981; Scanzoni and Scanzoni 1988). Between the early 1900s and the late 1960s, average age at marriage declined to approximately 20.5 years for women and twenty-three years for men. Subsequent to the late 1960s, average age at marriage began to climb once more. Examination of non-Hispanic whites, blacks, and Hispanic whites shows that age at first marriage has climbed more rapidly for blacks than for non-Hispanic whites, with blacks now marrying later than non-Hispanic whites. In contrast, Hispanics marry at younger ages than do other groups. It is difficult to assess whether Hispanics' lower age at marriage reflects long-term trends within the United States due to the large numbers of Mexican-Americans who have immigrated in recent years (Sweet and Bumpass 1987).

Factors promoting later age at marriage in recent decades include greater societal acceptance of singlehood and cohabitation as well as greater emphasis on educational attainment (Zinn and Eitzen 1987). The relationship between age at marriage and level of education is nearly linear for non-Hispanic white men and women, with more education associated with later age at marriage. This relationship is more complex for minority groups, and especially for black and Hispanic men. For these men, later age at marriage is associated *both* with lower and higher educational levels, producing a U-shaped relationship between education and age at marriage. Minority men with low education are likely to have especially poor job prospects, which in turn affect prospects for marriage. Overall, less racial and ethnic diversity in age at marriage is shown for those with higher educational attainment (Sweet and Bumpass 1987).

**Singles.** The size of the unmarried population is increasing, due primarily to later ages at marriage and increases in divorce (to be discussed below). In addition to those who are divorced, separated, or widowed, the single adult population includes persons who have never married. Throughout U.S. history a small but significant proportion of individuals have remained unmarried throughout their lives. In 1980, 5.4 percent of men and 5 percent of women ages fifty-five to sixty-four had never married. Among blacks, 7.9 percent of men and 6.4 percent of women in this age group had never married (Bumpass and Sweet 1987). Due to the continuing stigmatization of homosexuality, it is difficult to ascertain the numbers of single persons who are gay or lesbian. Researchers have estimated that 4 percent of men and 2 percent of women are exclusively homosexual (Collins 1988). Though homosexual marriages are not legally recognized, many gay and lesbian couples form lasting unions.

Diverse factors help to explain the rise in singleness. The pattern of women marrying men several years older than themselves, observed since colonial times, is important to consider. Since 1940, the number of women aged twenty-two (women's "peak marrying year") has been greater than the number of men aged twenty-five (men's peak marrying year). The imbalance of available male partners for women increases with age. Among those ages forty-five to sixty-four, the number of single women is three times greater than the number of single men. The imbalance of available male partners also is greater for black women. The shortage of black men as marital partners for black women has been attributed to various factors, including interracial marriage and black men's greater likelihood of unemployment and incarceration (see Zinn and Eitzen 1987). Women's changing roles have also been linked with the rise in singleness. Women with higher

education and higher personal income are less likely to marry or have children (Andersen 1988). Also, in contrast to earlier eras, there is greater societal tolerance of singlehood, providing greater freedom for both women and men to choose a single life-style.

Though women with greater personal resources are less likely to marry, the proportion of single women who are poor has risen steadily in recent decades. Of those adults whose income fell below the official poverty line in 1983, two out of three were women (Gerstel and Gross 1987). Minority women, older women, and those with children are especially at risk. Both women and men face the potential for economic hardship when they become widowed, divorced, or separated. The economic consequences are greater for women than for men, however (Keith 1986). Among those who divorce, women's subsequent income averages 24 percent of previous family income, while men's is 87 percent (Andersen 1988).

**Childbearing.** Childbearing patterns have varied somewhat over the past 100 years. Women born in 1891 had an average of three children. Women born in 1908, who bore children during the Great Depression, had an average of two children. This figure increased to three children per mother during the 1950s and has since declined to a little less than two per mother today. In addition to fewer numbers of children born, current trends in childbearing include higher age at first childbirth and longer intervals of time between births. These trends are interrelated. Waiting longer to have a first child and spacing births further apart decrease the average number of children born per mother. The timing of childbearing also has important effects on other life experiences, including educational and occupational attainment. Lower rates of childbearing are associated with higher educational levels and higher incomes (Cherlin 1981; Sweet and Bumpass 1987).

Fewer married couples are having their first child in the period immediately following marriage, but there are some important differences by race. In 1960, 54 percent of non-Hispanic white couples had children within twelve to seventeen months of marriage. In 1980 this figure dropped to 36 percent. Little change was shown over this period for black couples, who had children within twelve to seventeen months of marriage. Compared to the total population, black couples are likely to have more children on average and to have a child present at the time of marriage. For whites (Hispanics and non-Hispanics) as well as blacks, nine-tenths of all couples have children within seven to eight years of marriage (Sweet and Bumpass 1987).

Childbearing among single women has increased substantially. For single women ages twenty and over, rates of childbearing rose between 1940 and the 1960s, declined for about ten years, then continued the upward trend. Childbearing among teens ages fifteen to nineteen has increased continuously since the 1940s. In 1960, 5 percent of all births were to single women. In 1985, this figure climbed to 18 percent, or one of every six children born in the United States. Nonmarital childbearing is much higher for blacks than for whites. Among blacks, 55 percent of all children are born to single women, compared to 12 percent among whites. However, childbearing rates among single black women have declined since 1965, while whites' rates have continued to increase. For all races, nonmarital childbearing is highest among those who are poor (Collins 1988; Sweet and Bumpass 1987). Socioeconomic factors can help to explain why blacks, who are disproportionately likely to be poor, have had higher rates of childbearing.

**Divorce.** Divorce rates have been rising in the United States since the Civil War. Over the past century, the proportion of adults currently divorced rose from one in 300 to one in thirteen women and one in eighteen men (Sweet and Bumpass 1987). This long-term trend does not show a smooth and progressive rise, however. Divorce rates have risen more sharply after every major war during this century. Divorce also increased following the Great Depression, apparently reflecting stresses associated with unemployment and economic deprivation. Economic prosperity, as well as greater emphasis on family

life, have been linked to the lower divorce rate observed from 1950 to 1962. Following 1962, dramatic increases in the divorce rate have occurred, with a 100 percent increase between 1963 and 1975 (Cherlin 1981). By the early 1970s, the chance of eventual divorce reached almost 50 percent. The divorce rate has more or less stabilized since that time, such that approximately 50 percent of all marriages begun today are estimated to end in divorce (Collins 1988).

Population trends have been linked with the increased rate of divorce. Among these trends is greater longevity, with an average life expectancy at birth of seventy-eight years for women and seventy-one years for men born in 1985. When they reach the age of sixty-five, women born in 1985 can expect to live an additional nineteen years, while men can expect to live fifteen more years. (These figures are for the total population. Life expectancies are lower for members of racial and ethnic minorities.) In contrast, the life expectancy at birth for those born in 1900 was forty-eight years for women and forty-six years for men (Grambs 1989). Unsatisfactory marriages that formerly may have been terminated by the death of one partner are now more likely to be dissolved by divorce (Uhlenberg 1986). Writers have also noted the apparent connection between women's increasing levels of labor-force participation and the increased rate of divorce in the United States. Studies do show that divorce is more likely to occur in couples where the wife is able to support herself financially (Cherlin 1981).

The risk of divorce also varies with age at marriage, duration of the marriage, education, race, and ethnicity. Age at marriage is one of the most important factors, with the likelihood of divorce twice as great among couples where the wife was seventeen or younger than among couples where the wife was in her early twenties. Further, most divorces take place within the first few years of marriage. The longer a couple has been together, the less likely they will be to get divorced. This pattern also holds among couples in which one or both partners have remarried. Education also seems to be an important factor, with a higher divorce rate observed among high school dropouts than among college graduates. However, the effect of education is due in large part to the fact that college graduates tend to marry at later ages. Looking across racial and ethnic groups, the risk of divorce is greater among African-Americans than among whites, and especially high divorce rates are observed for Hispanics (Puerto Ricans in particular), Native Americans, and Hawaiians. Divorce is less common among Asian-Americans (Sweet and Bumpass 1987).

**Widowhood.** The average age of widowhood has increased with rises in life expectancy. Among women, the median age at widowhood was fifty-one in 1900, compared to fifty-nine in 1964 and sixty-eight in 1979. Median age at widowhood for men was forty-five in 1900, sixty-five in 1964, and seventy-one in 1979. Women today are widowed at younger ages than men and can also expect to live longer in a widowed status due to higher female life expectancy. Of all women over age seventy-five who have been married, two-thirds will be widowed. This figure rises to almost 78 percent for African-American women (Grambs 1989).

**Remarriage.** Most persons who divorce eventually remarry, as do a large proportion of those who are widowed during their prime adult years. Especially for women, remarriage rates are tied closely with age. Among women who divorce prior to age thirty, 75 percent will eventually remarry. In comparison, 50 percent of women who divorce between the ages of thirty and forty will remarry, and 28 percent of women who divorce at forty and older will remarry (Scanzoni and Scanzoni 1988). As is true for rates of marriage and divorce, large race and ethnic differences are observed for remarriage. The proportion of women who remarry in ten years or less following separation is almost three-quarters for non-Hispanic whites, about one-half for Mexican-Americans, and about one-third for blacks. Men are more likely to remarry than women, but similar race and ethnic differences in remarriage rates are observed for both genders (Sweet and Bumpass 1987).

Increased rates of divorce and remarriage are transforming American families. "Blended" families are becoming increasingly common. These

can consist of couples who have previously been married to different partners, the children born in those previous marriages, and the children born to the current marital partners. In 1980 41 percent of all marriages involved one previously married partner. In 1970 this figure was 30 percent (Furstenberg 1980).

**Household Structure.** As defined by the U.S. Census Bureau, "family households" are those containing persons who are related to the household head (the person in whose name the home is owned or rented). "Nonfamily households" consist of one or more unrelated persons. Historically, most American households have been family households, and most of these have included married couples. In 1910 80 percent of all households included married couples. By 1980 this percentage had declined to 61 percent. A breakdown of all U.S. households in 1980 shows that 31 percent were married couples with children under age eighteen; 30 percent were married couples with no children under age eighteen; 7 percent were single parents with children under age eighteen; 6 percent were family households that did not include a married couple or any children of the householder; and 26 percent were "nonfamily." Of the nonfamily households, 86 percent consisted of individuals who were living alone. The proportion of single-person households has risen dramatically over the century. In 1890, only 4 percent of all households were of this type.

Breakdowns of family structure by race and ethnicity show that Americans of Korean, Filipino, Vietnamese, and Mexican heritage are most likely to live in family households (for each group, about 84 percent live in family households). African-Americans and non-Hispanic whites are somewhat less likely to live in family households. Also, compared to other racial and ethnic groups, Puerto Ricans are most likely to live in a household consisting of a mother and one or more children (with 23 percent living in this type of household), followed by African-Americans, Native Americans, and Hawaiians (Sweet and Bumpass 1987).

Type of household is tied closely with economic status. Children are more likely to be poor today as a result of greater poverty among women. Among households headed by women (with no adult male present), almost one-half of all non-Hispanic white children lived in poverty in 1985, compared with 69 percent of all black children and 71 percent of all Hispanic children (Folbre 1987; Sweet and Bumpass 1987).

Likely due to economic as well as cultural factors, racial and ethnic minority groups are more likely than majority whites to live in extended family settings. Groups most likely to do so are of Vietnamese, Filipino, and African heritage. While 35 percent of all Vietnamese-American children live in an extended family setting, only 8 percent of non-Hispanic white children live with relatives in addition to (or other than) one or both parents (Sweet and Bumpass 1987).

## AMERICAN FAMILIES AND THE FUTURE

Traditional distinctions between "family" and "nonfamily" are increasingly challenged. Though still a relatively small proportion of all households (about 4 percent; Scanzoni and Scanzoni 1988), the number of cohabiting heterosexual couples has increased greatly in the past several decades. Marriage between homosexuals is not legally recognized, but some have elected to adopt each other legally, and a growing number are raising children. In addition to the "traditional" nuclear family form of two parents with children, other family types can be expected to continue in the future. These include single parents, blended families resulting from remarriage, and households in which other relatives such as grandparents reside.

Increased longevity has brought about some of the most important changes in American family life over the past century. Children are more likely than ever before to interact with their grandparents. Further, many persons are becoming grandparents while their own parents are still alive (Uhlenberg 1986). Research has documented the prevalence and importance of social interaction, emotional support, financial help, and other assistance between the generations (Horowitz

1985). For all types of American families, indications are that high levels of interaction and assistance between the generations will continue in the future.

(SEE ALSO: *Alternative Life-Styles; Courtship; In-Law Relationships; Marital Adjustment; Marriage; Marriage and Divorce Rates; Mate Selection Theories; Parental Roles; Remarriage*)

## REFERENCES

Andersen, Margaret L. 1988 *Thinking about Women: Sociological Perspectives on Sex and Gender.* 2d ed. New York: Macmillan.

Boris, Eileen, and Peter Bardaglio 1987 "Gender, Race, and Class: The Impact of the State on the Family and the Economy, 1790–1945." In Naomi Gerstel and Harriet Engel Gross, eds., *Families and Work.* Philadelphia: Temple University Press.

Cherlin, Andrew J. 1981 *Marriage, Divorce, Remarriage.* Cambridge, Mass.: Harvard University Press.

Collins, Randall 1988 *Sociology of Marriage and the Family: Gender, Love, and Property.* 2d ed. Chicago: Nelson-Hall.

Demos, John 1970 *A Little Commonwealth.* New York: Oxford University Press.

Driver, Harold E. 1969 *Indians of North America.* 2d ed. Chicago: University of Chicago Press.

Folbre, Nancy 1987 "The Pauperization of Motherhood: Patriarchy and Public Policy in the United States." In N. Gerstel and H. E. Gross, eds., *Families and Work.* Philadelphia: Temple University Press.

Furstenberg, Frank F. Jr. 1980 "Reflections on Remarriage." *Journal of Family Issues* 1:443–453.

Genovese, Eugene D. 1986 "The Myth of the Absent Family." In Robert Staples, ed., *The Black Family: Essays and Studies.* 3d ed. Belmont, Calif.: Wadsworth.

Gerstel, Naomi, and Harriet Engel Gross, eds. 1987 *Families and Work.* Philadelphia: Temple University Press.

Grambs, Jean Dresden 1989 *Women over Forty: Visions and Realities.* New York: Springer.

Gutman, Herbert 1976 *The Black Family in Slavery and Freedom, 1750–1925.* New York: Pantheon.

Horowitz, Amy 1985 "Family Caregiving to the Frail Elderly." In M. P. Lawton and G. L. Maddox, *Annual Review of Gerontology and Geriatrics.* New York: Springer.

Howe, Louise Knapp 1972 *The Future of the Family*. New York: Simon and Schuster.

Keith, Pat M. 1986 "The Social Context and Resources of the Unmarried in Old Age." *International Journal of Aging and Human Development* 23(2): 81–96.

Lasch, Christopher 1977 *Haven in a Heartless World: The Family Besieged*. New York: Basic Books.

Laslett, Barbara 1973 "The Family as a Public and Private Institution: An Historical Perspective." *Journal of Marriage and the Family* 35:480–494.

Laslett, Peter, and Richard A. Wall (eds.) 1972 *Household and Family in Past Time*. New York: Cambridge University Press.

Leslie, Gerald R., and Sheila K. Korman 1989 *The Family in Social Context*. 7th ed. New York: Oxford University Press.

Lurie, Nancy Oestreich 1985 "The American Indian: Historical Background." In N. R. Yetman, ed., *Majority and Minority*. 4th ed. Boston: Allyn and Bacon.

Marden, Charles F., and Gladys Meyer 1973 *Minorities in American Society*. 4th ed. New York: D. Van Nostrand.

Marger, Martin N. 1991 *Race and Ethnic Relations: American and Global Perspectives*. Belmont, Calif.: Wadsworth.

Moynihan, Daniel P. 1965 *The Negro Family: The Case for National Action*. Washington, D.C.: Office of Policy Planning and Research, U.S. Department of Labor.

Nock, Steven L. 1987 *Sociology of the Family*. Englewood Cliffs, N.J.: Prentice-Hall.

Scanzoni, Letha Dawson, and John Scanzoni 1988 *Men, Women, and Change: A Sociology of Marriage and Family*. New York: McGraw-Hill.

Staples, Robert, ed. 1986 *The Black Family: Essays and Studies*. 3d ed. Belmont, Calif.: Wadsworth.

Sweet, James A., and Larry L. Bumpass 1987 *American Families and Households*. New York: Russell Sage.

Uhlenberg, Andrew 1986 "Death and the Family." In A. S. Skolnick and J. H. Skolnick, eds., *Family in Transition*. Boston: Little, Brown.

Zinn, Maxine Baca, and D. Stanley Eitzen 1987 *Diversity in American Families*. New York: Harper and Row.

LAURIE RUSSELL HATCH

## AMERICAN INDIAN STUDIES

American Indian Studies blends many fields in the social sciences and humanities; history and anthropology have been especially prominent, along with education, sociology, psychology, economics, and political science. For convenience, this literature can be grouped into several subject areas: demographic behavior, socioeconomic conditions, political and legal institutions, and culture and religion. Of course, there is a great deal of overlap. To date, this literature deals almost exclusively with aboriginal North Americans and their descendants. As the field has evolved, relatively little attention has been devoted to the natives of South America or the Pacific Islanders.

## DEMOGRAPHY

**Historical Demography.** Historical demography is important for understanding the complexity of indigenous North American societies and for assessing the results of their contacts with Europeans. For example, complex societies require large populations to generate economic surpluses for trade, and large populations often entail highly developed systems of religion, culture, and governance. Because American Indians almost disappeared in the late nineteenth century, large numbers of pre-Columbian Indians would indicate that devastating mortality rates and profound changes in native social organization followed the arrival of Europeans.

No one knows with certainty when populations of *homo sapiens* first appeared in the Western hemisphere. The first immigrants to North America probably followed game from what is now Siberia across the Beringia land bridge, now submerged in the Bering Sea. This land bridge has surfaced during several ice ages, leading to speculation that the first populations arrived as early as 40,000 years ago or as recently as 15,000 years ago—25,000 years ago is a credible estimate (Thornton 1987, p. 9).

In 1918 a Smithsonian anthropologist, James Mooney, published the first systematic estimates of the American Indian population. He reckoned that 1.15 million American Indians were living around 1600. Alfred Kroeber (1934) subsequently reviewed Mooney's early estimates and deemed them correct, though he adjusted the estimate downward to 900,000 (Deneven 1976). The Mooney-Kroeber estimates of approximately one million American Indians in 1600 have been the benchmark for scholars throughout most of this century. These estimates were flawed, however, because they failed to take epidemic disease into account; European pathogens devastated native populations.

Noting the shortcomings of the Mooney-Kroeber figures, Henry Dobyns (1966) revised the estimate for the 1492 precontact population, suggesting that it was as large as twelve million. His article ignited an intense debate that is still not fully resolved. Conservative estimates now number the indigenous 1492 population at approximately three to five million (Snipp 1989). Dobyns's (1983) most recent estimates raise the figure to eighteen million.

Population estimates substantially larger than the Mooney-Kroeber figures are consistent with the archaeological record, which indicates that relatively complex societies occupied the Southwest, the Pacific Northwest, and the Mississippi River valley before the Europeans arrived (Thornton 1987). The effects of European contact were certainly greater than once believed. European diseases, slavery, genocidal practices, and the intensification of conflicts nearly exterminated the native people. Huge population losses undoubtedly caused large-scale amalgamation and reorganization of groups struggling to survive and wrought profound changes in their cultures and social structures.

**Contemporary Demography.** During the twentieth century, the American Indian population grew very quickly, from about 228,000 in 1890 to about 1.4 million in 1980. American Indian fertility is exceedingly high, even higher than that of blacks (Snipp 1989), Indians often have better access to health care (from the Indian Health Service) than other equally impoverished groups, and they are experiencing diminishing infant mortality and increasing longevity (Snipp 1989).

A peculiar characteristic of American Indian population growth, at least since 1970, is that a large share of the increase has resulted from persons switching the racial identification they report to the census from another category (such as black or white) to American Indian (Passell and Berman 1986). The U.S. census, virtually the only comprehensive source of data for American Indians, depends on voluntary racial self-identification. Declining racial discrimination, growing ethnic pride, and a resurgence in tribal organization have been cited as reasons that persons of mixed heritage may choose to report themselves as American Indian (Passell and Berman 1986).

The fluidity of the American Indian population underscores a particularly problematic concern for demographers: namely, defining population boundaries. Definitions abound, and there is no single agreed-upon standard. Some federal agencies and a number of tribes use an arbitrary measure of descent, such as one-fourth blood quantum; standards for tribal membership vary greatly from one-half to one-sixty-fourth Indian blood.

For many other applications, genealogical verification of blood quantum standards is too complex. Agencies such as the Census Bureau thus simply rely on self-identification. By default, most studies of American Indians also rely on self-identification, especially if they use secondary data from federal government sources. To complicate the matter, the Canadian government uses a somewhat different set of standards to define the boundaries of its native Indian population.

Beyond the complexities of counting, studies show that American Indians, more than other minorities, are concentrated in rural areas; slightly less than one-half reside in cities. Most live west of the Mississippi River, primarily because nineteenth-century removal programs were directed at eastern American Indians. A large number of studies document that American Indians are one of the least educated, most often unemployed, poorest, and least healthy groups in American society (see Snipp 1989). Nonetheless, American Indians are more likely than other groups, especially blacks, to live in a large husband-wife household, and about one-third of them speak an Indian language—provisional evidence of the continuing influence of traditional culture in family organization and language use (Sandefur and Sakamoto 1988).

## STUDIES OF SOCIAL AND ECONOMIC STATUS

Most recent studies of the early social and economic status of American Indians focus on the historical development of so-called dependency relations between them and Euro-Americans (White 1983). Dependency theory, a variant of neo-Marxist World Systems Theory, has been widely criticized for its shortcomings, but it has gained some acceptance among scholars of white–Indian relations (Wolf 1982; White 1983; Hall 1989). In this view, economic dependency arose from trade relations in which Euro-Americans enjoyed disproportionate economic advantage stemming from a near monopoly over items such as manufactured goods and rum (Wolf 1982; White 1983). European business practices, such as the use of credit, also fostered dependency.

Dependency relations promoted highly exploitative conditions that were a frequent source of conflict and periodically erupted into serious violence. Unscrupulous traders and a growing commerce in Indian captives, for example, spawned the Yamassee War, which ended Indian slavery in the Southeast (Merrell 1989). Early colonial officials frequently complained about the conflicts created by the unethical practices of frontier traders and sought to curb their abuses, though with little success (Bateman 1989).

Nevertheless, European traders introduced innovations that altered cultures and lifestyles forever. In the Southwest, for example, guns and horses revolutionized relations between nomadic and sedentary groups and allowed the Spanish to exploit their traditional antagonisms (Hall 1989).

The emergence of industrial capitalism, large-scale manufacturing, growing urbanization, and an influx of immigrants from Europe and slaves from Africa changed dramatically the relations between Euro-Americans and indigenous peoples. Trading with Indians subsided in favor of policies and measures designed to remove them from lands desired for development (Jacobsen 1984). Throughout the nineteenth century, American Indians were more or less forcibly induced to cede their lands for the development of agriculture, timber, and water. In the late nineteenth century, U.S. corporations began to develop petroleum, coal, and other minerals on tribal lands (Miner 1976).

Exploitation of Indian lands has continued, prompting some scholars to argue that American Indian tribes have a quasi-colonial status within the U.S. economy (Snipp 1986). Natural resources such as timber, water, and minerals are extracted from reservations and exported to distant urban centers where they are processed. In exchange, manufactured goods are imported for consumption. The value of the imported goods typically exceeds the value of the exported resources. The deficit between imports and exports contributes to the persistent poverty and low levels of economic development on many reservations.

The Meriam Report, published in 1928, furnished the first systematic empirical assessment of the economic status of American Indians. Since its publication, numerous studies have documented the disadvantaged status of American Indians (Levitan and Hetrick 1971). Although many reports have described economic conditions in detail, fewer have attempted to isolate the causes of poverty and unemployment. Clearly, a number of factors can be blamed. American Indians have very little formal education, limiting their access to jobs. Whether racial discrimination limits opportunities is unclear. Some research suggests that discrimination is not a significant disadvantage for American Indians (Sandefur and Scott 1983), but other studies disagree (Gwartney and Long 1978).

Conditions on reservations, where about one-third of all American Indians live, are particularly harsh. Unemployment rates above 50 percent are not unusual. Studies of reservation economies usually blame the isolated locales for many of their woes. Economic development in Indian country is frequently complicated by the collision of traditional native values and the ethics of capitalism (Vinje 1982). In recent years, however, some reservations have enjoyed limited (and in a few instances, spectacular) success in spurring economic development, especially in tourism, gambling, and light manufacturing (Snipp and Summers 1991).

Urban American Indians enjoy a higher standard of living than their counterparts in reservation areas (Sorkin 1978). Even so, there is disagreement about the benefits of rural–urban migration for American Indians; some studies have identified tangible benefits for urban immigrants (Clinton, Chadwick, and Bahr 1975; Sorkin 1978), but other research finds contrary evidence (Gundlach and Roberts 1978; Snipp and Sandefur 1988). Federal programs that encouraged urban immigration for American Indians in the 1950s and 1960s were abandoned amid controversies over their effectiveness and overall results (Fixico 1986).

The economic hardship facing rural and urban American Indians alike have been a major source of other serious distress. Alcoholism, suicide, and homicide are leading causes of death for American Indians (OTA 1986).

## POLITICAL ORGANIZATION AND LEGAL INSTITUTIONS

The political and legal status of American Indians is an extremely complicated subject, tangled in conflicting treaties, formal laws, bureaucratic regulations, and court decisions. Unlike any other racial or ethnic group in U.S. society, American Indians have a distinctive niche in the legal system. As a result of this legal history, a separate agency within the federal government (the Bureau of Indian Affairs [BIA]), a volume of the Code of Federal Regulations, and a multiplicity of other rules exist for dealing with American Indians.

The political status of American Indian tribes is difficult to characterize. In 1831, Chief Justice John Marshall described tribes as "domestic, dependent nations," setting forth the principle that tribes are autonomous political entities that enjoy a quasi-sovereignty yet are subject to the authority of the federal government (Barsh and Henderson 1980). The limits on tribal political autonomy have fluctuated as a result of court decisions and

federal legislation curtailing or extending tribal powers. Since the early 1900s, tribal governments have greatly increased their autonomy (Gross 1989).

One of the most significant political developments in this century for American Indians was the passage of the Wheeler-Howard Indian Reorganization Act (IRA) of 1934. This legislation made it possible for tribes legally to reconstitute themselves for the purpose of limited self-government (Prucha 1984, chap. 37). Subject to the democratic precepts imposed by the federal government, tribes were allowed to have representative governments with judicial, executive, and legislative branches. Other forms of tribal governance—based on the inheritance of authority, for example—were not permitted by the IRA legislation. Today, virtually every reservation has a form of representative government.

Tribal sovereignty is a complex legal doctrine affecting the political autonomy of tribal governments. It is distinct from a closely aligned political principle known as self-determination. The principle of self-determination, unlike tribal sovereignty, is relatively recent in origin and was first posed as a claim for administrative control of reservation affairs. As a political ideology, self-determination developed in response to the unilateral actions of the federal government in implementing policies such as the Termination legislation of the 1950s. In the 1960s, it was a rallying theme for promoting greater tribal involvement in federal policies affecting American Indians. The principle was formally enacted into public law with the passage of the Indian Self-Determination and Educational Assistance Act of 1975. Since its passage, federal agencies have gradually divested control over programs and services such as those once administered by the BIA. For example, many tribal governments have contracts to provide social services similar to the arrangements made with state and local governments.

In recent years, arguments promoting self-determination have developed to the point where self-determination is nearly indistinguishable from tribal sovereignty (Gross 1989). The most influential statement merging the two is a report presented to the Senate by the American Indian Policy Review Commission in 1976. The AIPRC report was a comprehensive though highly controversial evaluation of federal Indian policy. The Reagan and Bush administrations have accepted self-determination only as narrowly defined, and currently there is no indication that the Bush administration is willing to adopt self-determination as promoted by the AIPRC.

The political revitalization of American Indians accelerated with the civil rights movement. Some observers have suggested that Indian political activism in the 1960s was a response to postwar termination policies (Cornell 1988), which tried to dissolve the federal reservation system and liquidate the special status of the tribes. Relocation programs in the 1950s accelerated the urbanization of American Indians and, at the very least, may have contributed to the political mobilization of urban Indians, as well as their reservation counterparts (Fixico 1986). Though often complementary, the political agendas of urban and reservation Indians are not always in strict accord.

The diverse tribal composition of urban Indian populations has meant that it is virtually impossible to organize them around issues affecting only one or a few tribes. In the face of this constraint, the ideology of "pan-Indianism" is particularly appealing to urban Indian groups (Hertzberg 1971). Pan-Indianism is a supratribal ideology committed to broad issues such as economic opportunity and social justice and to cultural events such as intertribal pow-wows.

The roots of modern pan-Indian organizations can be traced first to the Ottawa leader Pontiac and later to the Shawnee leader Tecumseh and Joseph Brant, a Mohawk. These men led pan-Indian movements opposing Euro-American frontier settlement in the late eighteenth and early nineteenth centuries (e.g., Pontiac's Revolt, 1763). In the late nineteenth century, pan-Indian messianic movements known as Ghost Dances swept across the West (Thornton 1986).

Pan-Indian organizations have been active throughout the twentieth century, but urbaniza-

tion hastened their development in the 1950s and 1960s (Cornell 1988). Some, such as the National Congress of American Indians (founded in 1944), have moderate political agendas focused on lobbying; others, such as the American Indian Movement, are highly militant. The latter was involved in the sacking of the Washington, D.C., BIA office in 1972 and in the armed occupation of Wounded Knee, South Dakota, in 1973. Today, most cities with large Indian populations have pan-Indian organizations involved in political organization, cultural events, and social service delivery.

## CULTURE AND RELIGION

The cultures of American Indians are extremely diverse, and the same can be said, in particular, about their religious beliefs. Not much is known about the spiritual life of American Indians before the fifteenth century. Only from archaeological evidence is such knowledge available, and this seldom captures the rich complexity of religious symbol systems. Most of what is known about American Indian religions is based on the later reports of explorers, missionaries, traders, and anthropologists (Brown 1982).

Contemporary spiritual practices reflect several different types of religious observances: Christian, neotraditional, and traditional. Participation in one type does not necessarily preclude participation in another. Furthermore, there is a great deal of tribal variation.

American Indians who are practicing Christians represent the legacy of European missionaries. The Christian affiliation of many, perhaps most, American Indians reflects their tribal membership and the denomination of the missionaries responsible for their tribe's conversion. Numerical estimates are not available, but there are many Catholic Indians in the Southwest, and American Indians in the Midwest are often Lutheran, to mention only two examples.

American Indians who participate in neotraditional religions often belong to a branch of the Native American Church (NAC). NAC is a pan-Indian religion practiced throughout the United States and Canada. It combines elements of Christianity with traditional religious beliefs and practices.

Traditional religions are often practiced in informally organized groups such as sweatlodge or feasting societies. Some of these groups are remnants of older religious movements such as the Ghost Dance. Not much is written about them because they are ordinarily not open to outsiders; the Sun Dance is an exception. It is perhaps best known for the ritual scarification and trances of its participants (Jorgenson 1972).

The secrecy in which many traditional religions are practiced may be due to the intense repression once directed at their observances by the federal government. In 1883, the BIA established Courts of Indian Offenses that prosecuted people for practicing native religions. Among other things, the courts forbade traditional medicines, shaman healers, and all traditional ceremonial observances. Despite their dubious legal foundation, the Courts of Indian Offenses were active until their mandate was rewritten in 1935 (Prucha 1984).

In 1935, the federal government ended its official repression of tribal culture and religion. But the conflicts between government authorities and American Indians trying to practice non-Christian religions did not end. Many Indians regard freedom of religion as an elusive promise. Most controversies involve NAC ceremonies, the preservation of sacred areas, and the repatriation of religious artifacts and skeletal remains in museum collections (Loftin 1989).

NAC ceremonies are controversial because they sometimes involve the use of peyote (a hallucinogen) as a sacrament. Although peyote was once outlawed, the NAC won the right to use it within narrowly defined limits prescribed by the courts. The Supreme Court recently upheld a case in which Oregon banned the use of peyote, however, raising concerns about how the conservative court will interpret freedom of religion cases in the future.

Preservation of sacred areas places Indian groups at odds with land developers, property owners, local governments, and others who would use sites deemed sacred by spiritual leaders. In one case, the Navajo and Hopi in 1983 went to court to petition against the development of a ski resort that intruded on sacred grounds. In this case and several similar ones, the courts ruled against the Indians (Loftin 1989). Similar conflicts have arisen over the repatriation of religious artifacts and skeletal remains in museums. These issues pit academics such as scientists and museum curators against Indian groups. In some instances, remains and artifacts have been returned to tribes; Stanford University returned burial remains to the Ohlone tribe in California, for example. Other institutions have opposed repatriation or are studying the matter. The Smithsonian has developed a complex policy for repatriation, and the University of California appointed a committee to develop a policy. For the foreseeable future, the controversy is likely to linger in the courts, Congress, and academic institutions.

Compared to repatriation, cultural studies are a less controversial though no less important domain of American Indian Studies. Indian religion represents one of the central forms of native culture, but cultural studies also emphasize other elements of Indian lifestyles, values, and symbol systems. Some of these studies focus on the content of tribal culture; other research deals with the consequences of tribal culture.

For decades, studies of American Indians were dominated by ethnologists recording for posterity details about Indian culture, especially material culture, or documenting the ways that European contact influenced the content of tribal culture. The popularity of this type of research has declined significantly, partly because there are few "pristine" cultures left anywhere in the world, much less in North America. Another reason, perhaps more damaging, is the growing realization that studies purporting to document precontact Indian culture were based on secondhand accounts of groups that were not truly pristine. The influence of European diseases and trade goods often arrived far in advance of Europeans (Dobyns 1983).

Many studies of American Indian culture now resemble literary or artistic criticism. Others focus on how European innovations have been incorporated into tribal culture in unique ways; silversmithing and rug weaving are two well-known examples (Highwater 1981). A related set of studies deals with the resurgence of traditional culture, such as the recent increase in the use of American Indian languages (Leap 1988).

The behavioral consequences of culture are perhaps most prominent in a large literature on American Indian mental health, education, and rehabilitation (Bennett and Ames 1985; Foster 1988). Many studies show that education and rehabilitation efforts can be made more effective if they are sensitive to cultural nuances. In fact, many specialists take this idea as a point of departure and focus their research instead on the ways in which Euro-American educational and therapeutic practices can be adapted to the cultural predisposition of American Indian clients.

Like the American Indian population, American Indian Studies is a highly diverse and growing field of inquiry. It is interdisciplinary and eclectic in the perspectives it uses. Once primarily the domain of historians and anthropologists, American Indian Studies has rapidly expanded beyond the bounds of these disciplines with contributions from scholars in a wide variety of fields.

(SEE ALSO: *Discrimination; Race*)

## REFERENCES

Barsh, Russel Lawrence, and James Youngblood Henderson 1980 *The Road: Indian Tribes and Political Liberty.* Berkeley: University of California Press.

Bateman, Rebecca 1989 "The Deerskin Trade in the Southeast." Unpublished manuscript. Baltimore, Md.: Department of Anthropology, Johns Hopkins University.

Bennett, Linda A., and Genevieve M. Ames (eds.) 1985 *The American Experience with Alcohol: Contrasting Cultural Perspectives.* New York: Plenum.

Brown, Joseph Epes 1982 *The Spiritual Legacy of the American Indian.* New York: Crossroad.

Clinton, Lawrence, Bruce A. Chadwick, and Howard M. Bahr 1975. "Urban Relocation Reconsidered: Antecedents of Employment among Indian Males." *Rural Sociology* 40:117–133.

Cornell, Stephen 1988 *The Return of the Native: American Indian Political Resurgence.* New York: Oxford University Press.

Deneven, William M. (ed.) 1976 *The Native Population of the Americas in 1492.* Madison: University of Wisconsin Press.

Dobyns, Henry F. 1966 "Estimating Aboriginal American Population: An Appraisal of Techniques with a New Hemispheric Estimate." *Current Anthropology* 7:395–416.

——— 1983 *Their Number Become Thinned: Native American Population Dynamics in Eastern North America.* Knoxville: University of Tennessee Press.

Fixico, Donald L. 1986 *Termination and Relocation, 1945–1960.* Albuquerque: University of New Mexico Press.

Foster, Daniel V. 1988 "Consideration of Treatment Issues with American Indians in the Federal Bureau of Prisons." *Psychiatric Annals* 18:698–701.

French, Laurence 1987 *Psychocultural Change and the American Indian.* New York: Garland.

Gross, Emma R. 1989 *Contemporary Federal Policy Toward American Indians.* Westport, Conn.: Greenwood Press.

Gundlach, James H., and Alden E. Roberts 1978 "Native American Indian Migration and Relocation: Success or Failure." *Pacific Sociological Review* 21:117–128.

Gwartney, James D., and James E. Long 1978 "The Relative Earnings of Blacks and Other Minorities." *Industrial and Labor Relations Review* 31:336–346.

Hall, Thomas D. 1989 *Social Change in the Southwest, 1350–1880.* Lawrence: University Press of Kansas.

Hertzberg, Hazel W. 1971 *The Search for an American Indian Identity.* Syracuse, N.Y.: Syracuse University Press.

Highwater, Jamake 1981 *The Primal Mind: Vision and Reality in Indian America.* New York: Harper and Row.

Jacobsen, Cardell K. 1984 "Internal Colonialism and Native Americans: Indian Labor in the United States from 1871 to World War II." *Social Science Quarterly* 65:158–171.

Jorgenson, Joseph G. 1972 *The Sun Dance Religion: Power for the Powerless.* Chicago: University of Chicago Press.

Kroeber, Alfred L. 1934 "Native American Population." *American Anthropologist* 36:1–25.

Leap, William L. 1988 "Indian Language Renewal." *Human Organization* 47:283–291.

Levitan, Sar A., and Barbara Hetrick 1971 *Big Brother's*

*Indian Programs: With Reservations.* New York: McGraw-Hill.

Loftin, John D. 1989 "Anglo-American Jurisprudence and the Native American Tribal Quest for Religious Freedom." *American Indian Culture and Research Journal* 13:1–52.

Merrell, James H. 1989 *The Indian's New World: Catawbas and Their Neighbors from European Contact Through the Era of Removal.* Chapel Hill: University of North Carolina Press.

Miner, H. Craig 1976 *The Corporation and the Indian: Tribal Sovereignty and Industrial Civilization in Indian Territory, 1865–1907.* Columbia: University of Missouri Press.

Office of Technology Assessment (OTA) 1986 *Indian Health Care,* OTA-H-290. Washington, D.C.: U.S. Government Printing Office.

Passel, Jeffrey S., and Patricia A. Berman 1986 "Quality of 1980 Census Data for American Indians." *Social Biology* 33:163–182.

Prucha, Francis Paul 1984 *The Great Father: The United States Government and the American Indians.* Lincoln: University of Nebraska Press.

Sandefur, Gary D., and Arthur Sakamoto 1988 "American Indian Household Structure and Income." *Demography* 25:71–80.

Sandefur, Gary D., and Wilbur J. Scott 1983 "Minority Group Status and the Wages of Indian and Black Males." *Social Science Research* 12:44–68.

Snipp, C. Matthew 1986 "The Changing Political and Economic Status of American Indians: From Captive Nations to Internal Colonies." *American Journal of Economics and Sociology* 45:145–157.

———— 1989 *American Indians: The First of This Land.* New York: Russell Sage Foundation.

Snipp, C. Matthew, and Gary D. Sandefur 1988 "Earnings of American Indians and Alaska Natives: The Effects of Residence and Migration." *Social Forces* 66:994–1008.

Snipp, C. Matthew, and Gene F. Summers 1991 "American Indians and Economic Poverty." In Cynthia M. Duncan, ed., *Rural Poverty in America.* Westport, Conn.: Greenwood Press.

Sorkin, Alan L. 1978 *The Urban American Indian.* Lexington, Mass.: D. C. Heath.

————1988 "Health and Economic Development on American Indian Reservations." In C. Matthew Snipp, ed., *Public Policy Impacts on American Indian Economic Development.* Albuquerque: Institute for Native American Development, University of New Mexico.

Thornton, Russell 1986 *We Shall Live Again: The 1870 and 1890 Ghost Dance Movements as Demographic Revitalization.* New York: Cambridge University Press.

————1987 *American Indian Holocaust and Survival: A Population History Since 1492.* Norman: University of Oklahoma Press.

Vinje, David L. 1982 "Cultural Values and Economic Development: U.S. Indian Reservations." *Social Science Journal* 19:87–99.

White, Richard 1983 *The Roots of Dependency: Subsistence, Environment, and Social Change among the Choctaws, Pawnees, and Navajos.* Lincoln: University of Nebraska Press.

Wolf, Eric R. 1982 *Europe and the People Without History.* Berkeley: University of California Press.

C. MATTHEW SNIPP

**AMERICAN SOCIETY** The term *American society* is used here to refer to the society of the United States of America. This conventional usage is brief and convenient and implies no lack of recognition for other societies of North, Central, and South America.

Boundaries of modern national societies are permeable and often socially and culturally fuzzy and changeable. Lines on maps do not take into account the cross-boundary flows and linkages of trade, tourists, information, workers, diseases, military arms and personnel, ethnic or linguistic affiliations, and the like. As a large, heterogeneous country, the United States well illustrates such interdependence and cultural diversity.

Containing less than 6 percent of the world's population, the United States is a polyglot nation of nations that now accepts a greater and more diverse inflow of legal, permanent immigrants than any other country—over four million a decade. It is often called a young nation, but elements of its culture are continuous with the ancient cultures of Europe, Asia, and Africa, and its political system is one of the most long-enduring constitutional democracies. Many writers have alleged that its culture is standardized, but it continues to show great diversity of regions, ethnic groupings, religious orientations, rural–urban contrasts, age groupings, political views, and general life-styles. It is a society in which many people seem convinced that it is undergoing rapid social change, while they hold firmly to many values and social structures inherited from the past. Like all other large-scale societies, in short, it is filled with ambiguities, paradoxes, and contradictions.

This society emerged as a product of the great period of European expansion. From 1790 to the present, the U.S. land area expanded from less than 900,000 square miles to over three million; its population from less than four million to about 250 million. The United States has never been a static social system in fixed equilibrium with its environment. Peopled primarily by history's greatest voluntary intercontinental migration, it has always been a country on the move. The vast growth of metropolitan areas is the most obvious sign of the transformation of a rural-agricultural society into an urban-industrial society. In 1880, the nation had four million farms; in 1980 it had 2.3 million. From 1940 to 1979 the index of output per hour of labor went from about twenty to about 200 (Wittwer 1980, p. 7). The most massive change in the occupational structure, correspondingly, has been the sharply decreasing proportion of workers in agriculture—now about 3 percent of the labor force.

The technological transformations that have accompanied these trends are familiar. The total horsepower of all prime movers in 1940 was 2.8 billion; in 1963 it was 13.4 billion; by 1978 it was over 25 billion. Productive capacities and transportation and communication facilities show similar long-term increases. For example, from 1947 to 1971, the annual per capita energy consumption in the United States went from 230 to 335 million BTUs—an increase of about 50 percent. The American people are dependent to an unprecedented degree on the automobile and the airplane. (As of the late 1980s, the average number of persons per passenger car was 1.8.) Mass transit is only weakly developed. During the single decade of the 1960s there was a 50 percent increase in the number of motor vehicles, and in many cities such vehicles account for 75 percent of the outdoor noise and 80 percent of the air pollution. With about 140 million motor vehicles

in 1986, it is even possible to imagine an ultimate traffic jam—total immobilization from coast to coast (Udall 1972, p. 76).

In short, this is a society of high technology and extremely intensive energy use. It is also a country that has developed a tightly organized and elaborately interdependent economy and social system, accompanied until recently by vast increases in total economic productivity. Thus the real gross national product doubled in just two decades (1959–1979), increasing at an average rate of 4.1 percent per year (Brimmer 1980, p. 98). But beginning with the sharp increases in oil prices after 1973, the society entered a period of economic stagnation and low productivity that was marked in the 1980s by large trade deficits, greatly increased federal budget deficits, and increased problems of international competitiveness. Coming after a long period of sustained growth, the changes of the 1980s resulted in an economy of low savings, high consumption, and low investment—a situation of "living beyond one's means" (Hatsopoulos, Krugman, Summers 1988).

## MAJOR INSTITUTIONS

"Institution" here means a definite set of interrelated norms, beliefs, and values centered on important and recurrent social needs and activities (cf. Williams 1970, chap. 3). Examples are family and kinship, social stratification, economic system, the polity, education, and religion.

**Kinship and Family.** American kinship patterns are essentially adaptations of earlier European forms of monogamous marriage, bilateral descent, neolocal residence, and diffuse extended kinship ties. All these characteristics encourage emphasis on the marriage bond and the nuclear family. In an urbanized society of great geographic and social mobility and of extensive commercialization and occupational instability, kinship units tend to become small and themselves unstable. Since the 1950s, the American family system has continued its long-term changes in the direction of greater instability, smaller family units, lessened kinship ties, greater sexual (gender) equality, lower birth rates, and higher rates of female-headed households. Over one-fifth of households are persons living alone. Marriage rates have decreased, age at marriage has increased, and rates of divorce and separation continue to rise. The percentage of children under eighteen years of age living with both parents declined, in the years between 1960 and 1980, from 92 to 84 among white, and from 69 to 44 among black Americans (Kitagawa 1981, p. 17). As individuals, Americans typically retain a commitment to family life, but the external social and cultural forces are producing severe family stresses.

**Social Stratification.** Stratification refers to structural inequalities in the distribution of such scarce values as income, wealth, power, authority, and prestige. To the extent that such inequalities result in the clustering of similarly situated individuals and families, "strata" emerge, marked by social boundaries and shared styles of life. When succeeding generations inherit positions similar to previous generations, social classes can result.

The American system is basically one of open classes, with relatively high mobility, both within individual lifetimes and across generations. A conspicuous exception has been a caste-like system of racial distinctions, although this has eroded substantially since the civil rights movement of the 1960s (Jaynes and Williams 1989). Although mobility is substantial, inequalities are great (Gilbert and Kahl 1982). The dominant ideology remains individualistic, with an emphasis on equality of opportunity and on individual achievement and success. Although extremes of income, power, and privilege produce strong social tensions, the system has shown remarkable stability.

The history of stratification has included conquest of Native Americans, slavery of African peoples, and extensive discrimination against Asians, Hispanics, and various immigrants of European origin. Assimilation and other processes of societal inclusion have moved the whole society increasingly toward a pluralistic system, but deep cleavages and inequalities continue. A fundamental tension persists between principles of equality of opportunity and individual merit, on the one hand, and practices of ascribed status and group

discrimination, on the other (cf. Myrdal, Sterner, and Rose 1944).

**The Economy.** The American economic system is a complex form of "high capitalism" characterized by large corporations, worldwide interdependence, high levels of private consumption, and close linkages with the state.

Increased specialization leads both to increased complexity and to increased interdependence, two sides of the same coin. In the United States, as in all industrialized countries, the movement from the primary extractive and agricultural industries to manufacturing was followed by growth of the tertiary exchange-facilitating activities, and then to expansion of occupations having to do with control and coordination and those ministering directly to the health, education, recreation, and comfort of the population. As early as 1970, nearly two-thirds of the labor force was in pursuits other than those in "direct production" (primary and secondary industries).

As the economy has thus shifted its focus, the dominance of large corporations has become more and more salient. In manufacturing, the total value added that is accounted for by the 200 largest companies went from 37 percent in 1954 to 43 percent in 1970. Of all employees in manufacturing, the percent working in multi-unit firms increased from 56 percent in 1947 to 75 percent by 1972 (Meyer 1979, pp. 27–28). The top 500 industrial companies account for three-fourths of industrial employment (Wardwell 1978, p. 97). Meanwhile, organized labor has not grown correspondingly; for decades, overall unionization has remained static, increasing only in the service, technical, and quasi-professional occupations. The importance of the great corporations as the primary focus of production and finance continues to increase. Widespread dispersion of income rights in the form of stocks and bonds has made the giant corporation possible, and this same dispersion contributes directly to the concentration of control rights in the hands of salaried management and minority blocs of stockholders. With widened markets for mass production of standardized products, strong incentives were created for effective systems of central control.

Although such tendencies often overreached themselves and led to a measure of later decentralization, the modern corporation, not surprisingly, shows many of the characteristics of the most highly developed forms of bureaucracy.

The interpenetration of what were previously regarded as separate political and economic affairs is a central trend. The interplay takes many different forms. For a long time government has set rules for maintaining or lessening business competition; it has regulated the plane or mode of competition, the conditions of employment, and the place and functioning of labor unions. Pressure groups, based on economic interests, ceaselessly attempt to influence law-making bodies and executive agencies. Governmental fiscal and monetary policies constitute a major factor influencing economic activity. As the economic role of the state has expanded, economic forces increasingly affect government itself and so-called private corporations increasingly have come to be "public bodies" in many ways, rivaling some sovereign states in size and influence.

**Political Institutions.** In ideology and law the American polity is a parliamentary republic, federal in form, marked by a strong central executive but with a tripartite separation of powers. From the highly limited state of the eighteenth century, the actual government has grown in size and scope and has become more complex, centralized, and bureaucratized. Partly because of pervasive involvement in international affairs, since World War II a large permanent military establishment has grown greatly in size and importance. The executive agencies, especially the presidency, are increasingly important relative to the Congress. Among other recent changes, the following appear to be especially consequential:

1. Emergence of the "welfare state," dedicated to maintaining certain minimal safeguards for health and economic welfare;
2. High development of organized interest groups, which propose and "veto" nearly all important legislation. The unorganized general public retains only an episodic and delayed power to ratify or reject whole programs of government action;
3. Decreased cohesion and effectiveness of political parties in aggregating interests, compromising parties in conflicts, and reaching clear public decisions;
4. Increasingly volatile voting and diminished party regularity and party commitment (split-ticket voting, low rates of voting [Wolfinger and Rosenstone 1980], large proportion of the electorate with no firm party preference).

Historically, political parties in the United States have been accommodationist: They have served to articulate and aggregate interests through processes of negotiation and compromise. The resulting "packages" of bargains have converted diverse and diffuse claims into particular electoral decisions. To work well, such parties must be able to plan nominations, arrange for representativeness, and sustain effective competition (Ladd 1979). In the late twentieth century, competitiveness is weakened by volatile elections —for example, landslides and deadlocks with rapidly shifting votes—and by party incoherence. In the nominating process the mass media and direct primaries partly replace party leaders and patronage. Representativeness is reduced by polarization of activists, single-issue voting, and low turnouts in primaries. And the inability of parties to protect legislators seems to increase the influence of single-issue organizations and to enlarge the scope of "symbolic" actions. Hard choices, therefore, tend to be deferred (cf. Fiorina 1980, p. 39).

The existence of an "interest-group" polity is clearly indicated. The political system readily expresses particular interests but finds difficulties in articulating and integrating partly incompatible demands into long-term national programs.

**Education.** In addition to diffuse processes of socialization found in family and community, specialized educational institutions now directly involve one-fifth of the American people as teachers, students, and other participants. In the twentieth century, an unparalleled expansion of mass education has occurred. Nearly 80 percent of the appropriate age group graduate from secondary school, and nearly 40 percent of these attend college.

Historically, the educational system has been radically decentralized, with thousands of school districts and separate educational authorities for each state (Williams 1970, chap. 8). In contrast to countries with strong central control of education and elitist systems of secondary and higher education, the United States for most of its history has had a weak central state and a mass education system. Education was driven by demands for it rather than by state control of standards, facilities, tests, curricula, and so on (cf. Garnier, Hage, and Fuller 1989).

These characteristics partly derive from widespread faith in education as a means of social advancement as well as from commitments to equality of opportunity and to civic unity. Inequalities of access were long enforced by involuntary racial segregation, now somewhat reduced since 1954, when the Supreme Court declared such segregation unconstitutional. Inequalities of access due to social class and related factors, of course, continue (Jencks et al. 1979). Formal educational attainments have come to be so strongly emphasized as a requirement for employment and advancement that some observers speak of the development of a "credential society" (Collins 1979).

**Religious Institutions.** Major characteristics of institutionalized religion include: formal separation of church and state, freedom of religious expression and practice, diversity of faiths and organizations, voluntary support, evangelism, high rates of membership and participation, widespread approval of religion and acceptance of religious beliefs, complex patterns of partial secularization, frequent emergence of new religious groupings, and important linkages between religious affiliations and social class and ethnicity (cf. Williams 1970, chap. 9; Wilson 1978).

Many of these characteristics are causally interrelated. For example, earlier sectarian diversity encouraged separation of church and state and religious toleration, which, in turn, favored further diversity, voluntarism, evangelism, and religious innovations.

Recent changes include growth in membership of evangelical Protestant denominations (now one-fifth of the population) (Hunter 1987), closer ties between religious groupings and political activities, and the rise of many cults and sects.

Among industrialized Western countries, the United States manifests extraordinarily high levels of membership and participation. Thus, although there has been extensive secularization, both of public life and of the practices of religious groups themselves, religious influence remains pervasive and important (Stark and Bainbridge 1985).

## SOCIAL ORGANIZATION

The long-term increase in the importance of large-scale complex formal organizations, salient in the economy and the polity, is evident also in religion, education, and voluntary special-interest associations. Other trends include the reduced autonomy and cohesion of small locality groupings and the increased importance of special-interest formal organizations and of mass publics and mass communication. Local communities and kinship groupings have been penetrated more and more by formal, centralized agencies of control and communication. (Decreasing localism shows itself in many forms. A well-known and striking example is the continuous decrease in the number of public school districts.)

These changes have moved the society in the direction of greater interdependence, centralization, formality, and impersonality.

## VALUES AND BELIEFS

Beliefs are conceptions of realities, of how things are. Values are conceptions of desirability, of how things should be (Williams 1970, chap. 11; 1979). Through shared experience and social interaction, communities, classes, ethnic groupings, or whole societies can come to be characterized by similarities of values and beliefs.

The weight of the evidence for the United States is that the most enduring and widespread value orientations include an emphasis on personal achievement (especially in occupational activity), success, activity and work, stress on moral principles, humanitarianism, efficiency and practicality, science, technology and rationality, progress, material comfort, equality, freedom, democracy, worth of individual personality, conformity, nationalism and patriotism; and, in tension with most other values, values of group superiority and racism.

In contrast to many images projected by the mass media, all systematic national surveys show that most Americans still endorse long-standing beliefs and values: self-reliance, independence, hard work, freedom, personal responsibility, pride in the country and its political system, voluntary civic action, trust in other people, antiauthoritarianism, and equality within limits (Lipset 1968; Williams 1970, chap. 11). And for all their real disaffections and apprehensions, most Americans see no other society they prefer: As late as 1971, surveys in eight countries found that Americans were less likely than persons in any other country to wish to live elsewhere (Campbell, Converse, and Rodgers 1976, pp. 281–285).

(SEE ALSO: *American Families*)

## REFERENCES

Brimmer, Andrew F. 1980 "The Labor Market and the Distribution of Income." In Norman Cousins, ed., *Reflections of America*. Washington, D.C.: U.S. Government Printing Office.

Campbell, Angus, Philip E. Converse, and Willard L. Rodgers 1976 *The Quality of American Life*. New York: Russell Sage Foundation.

Collins, Randall 1979 *The Credential Society: An Historical Sociology of Education and Stratification*. New York: Academic Press.

Fiorina, Morris P. 1980 "The Decline of Collective Responsibility in American Politics." *Daedalus*, Summer: 25–45.

Garnier, Maurice, Jerald Hage, and Bruce Fuller 1989 "The Strong State, Social Class, and Controlled School Expansion in France, 1881–1975." *American Journal of Sociology* 95:279–306.

Gilbert, Dennis, and Joseph A. Kahl 1982 *The American Class Structure: A New Synthesis*. Homewood, Ill.: Dorsey.

Hatsopoulos, George N., Paul R. Krugman, Lawrence H. Summers 1988 "U.S. Competitiveness: Beyond the Trade Deficit." *Science* 241:299–307.

Hunter, James Davidson 1987 *Evangelism: The Coming Generation*. Chicago: University of Chicago Press.

Inkeles, Alex 1979 "Continuity and Change in the American National Character." In Seymour Martin Lipset, ed., *The Third Century: America as a Post-Industrial Society*. Stanford, Calif.: Hoover Institution Press.

Jaynes, Gerald David, and Robin M. Williams, Jr., eds. 1989 *A Common Destiny: Blacks and American Society*. Washington, D.C.: National Academy Press.

Jencks, Christopher, Susan Barlett, Mary Corcoran, James Crouse, David Eaglesfield, Gregory Jackson, Kent McClelland, Peter Mueser, Michael Olneck, Joseph Schwartz, Sherry Ward, and Jill Williams 1979 *Who Gets Ahead: The Determinants of Economic Success in America*. New York: Basic Books.

Kitagawa, Evelyn M. 1981 "New Life Styles: Marriage Patterns, Living Arrangements, and Fertility Outside of Marriage." *The Annals* 453:1–27.

Ladd, Everett Carl 1979 "The American Party System Today." In Seymour Martin Lipset, ed., *The Third Century: America as a Post-Industrial Society*. Stanford, Calif.: Hoover Institution Press.

Lipset, Seymour M. 1968 "Anglo-American Society." In David L. Sills, ed., *Encyclopedia of the Social Sciences*. New York: Macmillan and Free Press.

Meyer, Marshall W. 1979 "Debureaucratization?" *Social Science Quarterly* 60:25–34.

Myrdal, Gunnar, Richard Sterner, and Arnold Rose 1944 *An American Dilemma*. New York: Harper and Row.

Stark, Rodney, and William Sims Bainbridge 1985 *The Future of Religion: Secularization, Revival, and Cult Formation*. Berkeley: University of California Press.

Udall, Stewart 1972 "The Last Traffic Jam." *The Atlantic*, October.

Wardwell, Nancy Needham 1978 "The Corporation." *Daedalus*, Winter: 97–110.

Williams, Robin M., Jr. 1970 *American Society: A Sociological Interpretation*. New York: Knopf.

——— 1979 "Change and Stability in Value Systems: A Sociological Perspective." In Milton Rokeach, ed., *Understanding Human Values*. New York: Free Press.

Wilson, John N. 1978 *Religion in American Society: The*

*Effective Presence.* Englewood Cliffs, N.J.: Prentice-Hall.

Wittwer, Sylvan H. 1980 "Agriculture: America's No. 1 Industry." In Norman Cousins, ed., *Reflections of America.* Washington, D.C.: U.S. Government Printing Office.

Wolfinger, Raymond E., and Steven Rosenstone 1980 *Who Votes?* New Haven, Conn.: Yale University Press.

ROBIN M. WILLIAMS, JR.


# AMERICAN SOCIOLOGICAL ASSOCIATION

"At 3:30 P.M., Wednesday, December 27, 1905, some forty to fifty 'specialists in sociology' from twenty-one educational institutions and a dozen organizations engaged in practical sociological work gathered in McLoy Hall at Johns Hopkins University in Baltimore" (Rhoades 1981). They came together to explore the possibility of forming an organization of sociologists. At this meeting, the American Sociological Society, whose purpose was "the encouragement of sociological research and discussion, and the promotion of intercourse between persons engaged in the scientific study of society," was formed. The society also elected its first president, Lester F. Ward. One year later, at the first annual meeting, the society counted 115 members.

Since it was formed, the American Sociological Society, in addition to a name change in 1959 to the American Sociological Association (ASA), has undergone constitutional, structural, demographic, and other changes in response to changes in the field of sociology and society as a whole. (For a detailed discussion of the history of the American Sociological Association, see Rhoades 1981.)

## ASA MEMBERSHIP TRENDS

An interesting perspective on the association appears through an examination of membership trends. Table 1 shows fairly slow but stable growth up until 1931. During the years of the Great Depression, there were substantial declines. Despite these declines, however, sociologists were becoming very visible in government agencies such as the United States Department of Agriculture and the Census Bureau. Between 1935 and 1953, for example, there were an estimated 140 professional social scientists, the great majority of them sociologists, employed in the Division of Farm Population and Rural Life. This activity reached its peak between 1939 and 1942, when there were approximately sixty professionals working in Washington, D.C., and regional offices.

The years following World War II saw a rapid increase in ASA membership—the number nearly quadrupled between 1944 (1,242) and 1956 (4,682). Between 1957 and 1967, membership more than doubled, from 5,223 to 11,445, and continued upward to 15,000 during the heights of the social protest and anti-Vietnam War movements. However, during the latter half of the 1970s, membership gradually drifted downward and reached a seventeen-year low of 11,223 in 1984.

The growth and decline in the ASA can be accounted for in part by a combination of ideological and demographic factors as well as the gradually changing nature of work in American society, particularly since the end of World War II. For example, the GI bill made it possible for an ordinary veteran to get a college education. The college population jumped from one-half million in 1945 to several million within three years. Gradually, while urban and metropolitan populations grew, the number and percentage of people in the manufacturing sector of the labor force declined, and the farm population declined even more dramatically, while the service sector grew. Within the service sector, information storage, retrieval, and exchange grew in importance with the coming of the computer age. These societal changes helped to stimulate a growth in urban problems involving areas such as family, work, and drugs, and these changes led to a growth of these specialty areas in sociology.

Membership in the ASA rapidly increased in the 1960s and early 1970s, an era of many social protest movements. Sociology was seen as offering a way of understanding the dynamic events that were taking place in this country. Substantive areas within the ASA and sociology were also affected by these social changes. As Randall Col-

**TABLE 1**
**Official Membership Counts of the American Sociological Association, 1906–1990**

| | | | | | |
|------|-------|------|-------|------|--------|
| 1906 | 115   | 1936 | 1,002 | 1964 | 7,789  |
| 1909 | 187   | 1937 | 1,006 | 1965 | 8,892  |
| 1910 | 256   | 1938 | 1,025 | 1966 | 10,069 |
| 1911 | 357   | 1939 | 999   | 1967 | 11,445 |
| 1912 | 403   | 1940 | 1,034 | 1968 | 12,567 |
| 1913 | 621   | 1941 | 1,030 | 1969 | 13,485 |
| 1914 | 597   | 1942 | 1,055 | 1970 | 14,156 |
| 1915 | 751   | 1943 | 1,082 | 1971 | 14,827 |
| 1916 | 808   | 1944 | 1,242 | 1972 | 14,934 |
| 1917 | 817   | 1945 | 1242  | 1973 | 14,398 |
| 1918 | 810   | 1946 | 1,651 | 1974 | 14,654 |
| 1919 | 870   | 1947 | 2,057 | 1975 | 13,798 |
| 1920 | 1,021 | 1948 | 2,450 | 1976 | 13,958 |
| 1921 | 923   | 1949 | 2,673 | 1977 | 13,755 |
| 1922 | 1,031 | 1950 | 3,582 | 1978 | 13,561 |
| 1923 | 1,141 | 1951 | 3,875 | 1979 | 13,208 |
| 1924 | 1,193 | 1952 | 3,960 | 1980 | 12,868 |
| 1925 | 1,086 | 1953 | 4,027 | 1981 | 12,599 |
| 1926 | 1,107 | 1954 | 4,350 | 1982 | 12,439 |
| 1927 | 1,140 | 1955 | 4,450 | 1983 | 11,600 |
| 1928 | 1,352 | 1956 | 4,682 | 1984 | 11,223 |
| 1929 | 1,530 | 1957 | 5,233 | 1985 | 11,485 |
| 1930 | 1,558 | 1958 | 5,675 | 1986 | 11,965 |
| 1931 | 1,567 | 1959 | 6,323 | 1987 | 12,370 |
| 1932 | 1,340 | 1960 | 6,875 | 1988 | 12,382 |
| 1933 | 1,149 | 1961 | 7,306 | 1989 | 12,666 |
| 1934 | 1,202 | 1962 | 7,368 | 1990 | 12,841 |
| 1935 | 1,141 | 1963 | 7,542 |      |        |

SOURCE: American Sociological Association Archives 1990.

lins (1989) points out, the social protest movements of the 1960s and 1970s coincided with the growth within the association of such sections as the Marxist, environmental, population, world systems, collective behavior and social movements, and racial and ethnic minorities sections. In addition, the growing public concerns in the late 1970s and early 1980s about aging and equality for women were reflected within the association by new sections on sex and gender and aging. Similarly, the "me" generation, in the aftermath of the protest movements and the disillusionment that set in after the Vietnam War, may have contributed both to a decline in student enrollments in sociology courses and in ASA membership.

ASA membership trends can also be examined in the context of the availability of research money. Postwar federal support for sociology grew with the development of sponsored research and the growth of research labs and centers on university campuses. Coincident with an increase in ASA membership, research funding from federal agencies during the 1960s and 1970s grew steadily. In the early 1980s, however (particularly 1981 and 1982), cutbacks in research funding for the social sciences were especially noticeable. As we move into the 1990s, major efforts to educate Congress on the importance of social science research have won support for sociology and the other social sciences. The result has been a reversal of the negative trend and a slow but steady improvement in funding, not only for basic research but also in greater amounts for research with applied or policy orientations.

## ASA SECTIONS, PUBLICATIONS, AND PROGRAMS

The increase in the number of sections in the ASA and of membership in them is another sign of growth within the association in recent years. Despite a decline in overall ASA membership in the early 1980s, the number of sections increased from nineteen in 1980 to twenty-six in 1989. Furthermore, this overall increase in sections was not achieved by simply redistributing members already in sections but resulted from an actual growth in section members from 8,000 to 11,000. About half the members belonged to at least one section as the association moved into the 1990s.

The growth of the ASA is also reflected in the growth of the number of journal publications. Since 1936, when the first issue of the *American Sociological Review* was published, ASA publications have expanded to include eight additional journals: *Contemporary Sociology; Journal of Health and Social Behavior; Social Psychology Quarterly; Sociological Methodology; Sociological Theory; Sociology of Education; Teaching Sociology;* and *Sociological Practice Review* (Vol. 1, 1990). These publications attest to the strength of specialty areas such as social psychology and health and to the association's appreciation of the need to provide services to the three major member constituencies: those whose focus is basic research; those who devote most or all of their time to teaching; and those who work in business, government, and nonprofit associations.

In its efforts to establish a scientific basis for the study of society, the association has struggled with the role of applied sociology within the organization. Since the early 1980s, actions have been taken to incorporate the practice of sociology as an integral part of the association's activities. For example, the ASA's new professional development program includes a committee on federal employment of sociologists. A new journal, *Sociological Practice Review,* has been formed, and an award

for a career of distinguished contributions to the practice of sociology has been established to balance the already existing awards for a career of distinguished scholarship and for contributions to teaching.

The teaching of sociology at the elementary, secondary, and university levels has received varying degrees of emphasis over the course of the association's history. In particular, in the late 1970s and early 1980s, when sociology enrollments and membership in the ASA were at a low point, the ASA teaching services program was developed. As of 1989, it had served more than 4,000 sociologists, providing opportunities through seminars and workshops to improve classroom teaching and to examine a wide range of new curricula for almost all sociology courses. The teaching research center in the executive office produces an annual catalogue providing teachers of sociology with a variety of resources, including syllabi sets and publications on topics such as classroom techniques, curriculum, departmental management, and career information.

## THE ASA IN THE YEAR 2000

As the association moves toward the year 2000, a new boomlet appears to be in progress. Membership increased by more than 13 percent from 1984 to 1990, the number of new Ph.D.s is on the rise, and there seem to be more job openings for sociologists, as the number of jobs advertised in the ASA employment bulletin nearly doubled from 444 (1982–1983) to 843 (1988–1989). The ASA is also undergoing a changing demographic profile: In the next decade, we should see an association with at least 50 percent women, 10 to 12 percent minorities, and 15 to 20 percent scholars from foreign countries. The changing profile should also include greater numbers and percentages working for government, business, and the nonprofit sectors so that by the year 2000 fully 25 percent of the members are expected to be employed outside academe.

This changing demographic profile of members attests to the diversity within the American

Sociological Association and reflects the spirit of contemporary sociology, a field covering a broad range of substantive areas with cutting-edge methodology and a variety of theoretical orientations. The challenge for the twenty-first century is to recruit a sufficient number of talented and motivated young people to continue this movement.

(SEE: *Professions; Sociological Organizations*)

### REFERENCES

Collins, Randall 1989 "Future Organizational Trends of the American Sociological Association." *Footnotes.*

Rhoades, Lawrence J. 1981. *A History of the American Sociological Association: 1905–1980.* Washington, D.C.: American Sociological Association.

WILLIAM V. D'ANTONIO
MARIA KRYSAN

**ANALYSIS OF VARIANCE AND COVARIANCE** Analysis of variance and analysis of covariance are statistical techniques most suited for the analysis of data collected using experimental methods. As a result, they have been used more frequently in the fields of psychology and medicine and less frequently in sociological studies, where survey methods predominate. These techniques can be and have been used on survey data, but other forms of data analysis are frequently preferred (specifically, tabular and correlational techniques). Given these techniques' applicability to experimental data, the easiest way to convey their logic and value is first to review the basics of experimental design and the analysis of experimental data. Basic concepts and procedures will then be described, summary measures and assumptions reviewed, and the applicability of these techniques for sociological analysis discussed. General treatments of these techniques can be found in most introductory statistics texts. In particular see texts by Borhnstedt and Knoke (1988) or Blalock (1979). For a more in-depth statistical treatment of these techniques, see Winer (1962) or Scheffe (1959).

## EXPERIMENTAL DESIGN AND ANALYSIS

In a classical experimental design, research subjects are randomly assigned in equal numbers to two or more discrete groups. Each of these groups is then given a different treatment or stimulus and observed to determine whether or not the different treatments or stimuli had predicted effects on some outcome variable. In most cases this outcome variable has continuous values rather than discrete categories. In some experiments there are only two groups—one that receives the stimulus (the experimental group) and one that does not (the control group). In other studies, different levels of a stimulus are administered (e.g., studies testing the effectiveness of different levels of drug dosages), or multiple conditions are created by administering multiple stimuli separately and in combination (e.g., exposure to a violent model and exposure to pacifist literature).

In all experiments, care is taken to eliminate any other confounding influences on subjects' behaviors by randomly assigning subjects to groups (and, therefore, randomly distributing any preexisting differences between subjects, such as age, gender, temperament, experience, etc.). In addition, experiments are conducted in standardized or "physically controlled" situations (e.g., a laboratory). As a result, the researcher is able to make the qualifying statement "Other things being equal . . ." and assert that any differences found between groups on the outcome measure(s) of interest are due solely to the stimuli administered or not administered.

Conceptually, two approaches can be used to determine whether or not one or more experimental stimuli have had an effect on some continuous outcome variable, although only a single analysis procedure—analysis of variance—is necessary. Analysis of covariance, an extension of this technique, includes continuous variables as additional sources of systematic variation in the outcome scores.

First, the outcome scores of individuals in each

group can be summarized by computing group means. These mean scores can then be compared. If the different groups have similar mean scores after one has received the stimulus and the other has not, then it is possible to conclude that the stimulus had little or no effect. If the mean scores are very different, then the only factor that can account for the difference is the effect of the stimulus (since "other things are equal" between the two groups prior to administering the stimulus).

When comparing group means to assess the effects of one or more experimental variables (factors), some criterion is needed to determine how big a difference of means is meaningful. The criterion used by analysis of variance and covariance is the amount of random variation that exists in the scores within each group.

For example, in a three-group comparison, the group mean scores on some outcome measure may be 5, 6, and 7 on a ten-point scale. The meaningfulness of these differences can only be assessed if we know something about the variation of scores in the three groups. If everyone in group one had scores between 4.5 and 5.5, everyone in group two had scores between 5.5 and 6.5, and everyone in group three had scores between 6.5 and 7.5, then in every instance the variation within each group is low. As a result, whenever the outcome score of an individual in one group is compared to the score of an individual in a different group, the scores being compared will be very similar to their respective group mean scores, and the conclusions about who scores higher or lower will be the same. As a result, a great deal of confidence would be placed in the results of the mean comparisons.

If, on the other hand, there were several individuals in each group who scored as low or as high as individuals in other groups—a condition of high variability in scores—then comparisons of these students' scores would lead to a conclusion opposite to that represented by the mean comparisons. As a result, less confidence would be placed in the differences between means.

The second approach is to ask the question,

"How much of the variation in subjects' scores on the outcome measure can be explained or accounted for by knowing what group each subject was in?" This approach is taken by the *general linear model* and is based on the assumption that the variation in outcome scores can be "decomposed" into two elements: variation due to random or chance processes (error variance) and variation due to the fact that individuals in the different groups were exposed to different conditions, experiences, or stimuli (explained variance). Random or chance sources of variation in outcome scores can be such things as measurement error or other causal factors that are randomly distributed across groups through the randomization process. The extent to which variation is due to group differences rather than these chance processes is an indication of the effect of the stimulus on the outcome measure.

## BASIC CONCEPTS AND PROCEDURES

Regardless of what conceptual approach is taken, the underlying concept in analysis of variance and covariance is that of *variance*. Simply put, variance is the amount of difference in scores on some variable across subjects. For example, one might be interested in the effect of different school environments on the self-esteem of seventh graders. To examine this effect, random samples of students from different school environments could be selected and given questionnaires about their self-esteem. The extent to which the students' self-esteem scores differ from each other both within and across groups is an example of the variance.

Variance can be measured in a number of ways. For example, simply stating the range of scores conveys the degree of variation. Statistically, the most useful measures of variation are based on the notion of the *sum of squares*. The sum of squares is obtained by first characterizing a sample or group of scores by calculating an average or mean. The variation of scores is then calculated by subtracting each score from the mean, squaring it, and summing the squared deviations (squaring the deviations before adding them is necessary because the sum of nonsquared deviations from the mean will always be 0). A large sum of squares indicates that the total amount of deviation of scores from a central point in the distribution of scores is large. In other words, there is a great deal of variation in the scores either because of a few scores that are very different from the rest or because of many scores that are slightly different from the rest.

**Decomposing the sum of squares.** The total amount of variation in a sample on some outcome measure is referred to as the *total sum of squares* ($SS_{total}$). In the school study mentioned above, the total sum of squares represents the variation of all students' scores—regardless of school type—from the overall or "grand mean" of scores. The procedure for calculating the total sum of squares is represented by equation 1,

$$SS_{total} = \sum_i \sum_j (Y_{ij} - Y..)^2 \qquad (1)$$

where, $\sum_i \sum_j$ indicates to sum across all individuals ($i$) in all groups ($j$), and $(Y_{ij} - Y..)^2$ is the squared difference of the score of each individual ($Y_{ij}$) from the grand mean of all scores ($Y..$). In terms of explaining variance, this is what the researcher is trying to account for or explain. The total sum of squares can then be "decomposed" or mathematically divided into two components: the *between-groups sum of squares* ($SS_{between}$) and the *within-groups sum of squares* ($SS_{within}$).

The between-groups sum of squares is a measure of how much variation in outcome scores exists between groups. It uses the group mean as the best single representation of how each individual in the group scored on the outcome measure. It essentially assigns the group mean score to every subject in the group and then calculates how much variation there is from the grand mean if there was no variation within the groups and if the only variation comes from cross-group comparisons. The procedure for calculating the between-groups sum of squares is represented by equation 2,

$$SS_{between} = \sum_j N_j(Y._j - Y..)^2 \qquad (2)$$

where, $\sum_j$ indicates to sum across all groups ($j$), and $N_j(Y._j - Y..)^2$ is the number of subjects in each group ($N_j$) times the squared difference between the mean of each group ($Y._j$) and the grand mean ($Y..$).

In terms of the comparison of means, the between-groups sum of squares directly reflects the difference between the group means. If there is no difference between the group means, then the group means will be equal to the grand mean, and the between-groups sum of squares will be 0. If the group means are different from one another, then they will also differ from the grand mean, and the magnitude of this difference will be reflected in the between-groups sum of squares. In terms of explaining variance, the between-groups sum of squares represents only those differences in scores that come about because the individuals in one group are compared to individuals in a different group, that is, the part of the total variance that is "explained" or accounted for by differences in group experiences. (Recall that all individuals within a group were given the same group mean score, resulting in 0 difference of scores within each group.)

The within-group sum of squares is a measure of how much variation exists in the outcome scores within each group. The procedure for calculating the within-group sum of squares is represented by equation 3,

$$\sum_i \sum_j (Y_{ij} - Y._j)^2 L \qquad (3)$$

where $\sum_i \sum_j$ indicates to sum across all individuals ($i$) in all groups ($j$), and $(Y_{ij} - Y._j)^2$ is the squared difference between the individual scores ($Y_{ij}$) and their respective group mean scores ($Y._j$).

Both in terms of comparing means and explaining variance, the within-group sum of squares represents the variance due to "error." It is the degree of variation in scores despite the fact that individuals in a given group were exposed to the same influences or stimuli. If the within-group sum of squares is high relative to the between-groups sum of squares (or the difference between the means), then less confidence can be placed in the conclusion that any group differences are meaningful.

**Adjusting for covariates.** Analysis of variance can be used whenever the predictor variable(s) have a limited number of discrete categories and the outcome variable is continuous. In some cases, however, an additional continuous predictor variable needs to be included in the analysis, or some continuous source of extraneous effect needs to be "controlled for," before the group effects can be assessed. In these cases, analysis of covariance can be used as a simple extension of the analysis of variance model.

In the classic experimental design, the variables being controlled for—the covariates—are frequently some background characteristics or pretest scores on the outcome variable that were not adequately randomized across groups. As a result, group differences in outcome scores may be found and erroneously attributed to the effect of the experimental stimulus or group condition, when in fact the differences between groups existed prior to, or independent of, the presence of the stimulus or group condition.

One example of this situation is provided by Simmons and Blyth (1987). In a study of the effects of different school systems on the changing self-esteem of boys and girls as they make the transition from sixth to seventh grade, these researchers had to account for the fact that boys and girls in these different school systems had different levels of self-esteem in sixth grade. Since those who score high on a measure at one point in time (T1) will have a statistical tendency to score lower at a later time (T2) and vice versa (a negative relationship), these initial differences could lead to erroneous conclusions. In Simmons and Blyth's study, if boys had higher self-esteem than girls in sixth grade, the statistical tendency would be for boys to experience negative change in self-esteem and girls to experience positive change, even though seventh grade girls in certain school systems experience more negative influences on their self-esteem.

The procedure used in adjusting for covariates involves a combination of analysis of variance and correlational techniques. Prior to comparing group means or sources of variation, the outcome scores are adjusted based on the effect of the covariate(s). This is done by computing predicted outcome scores based on equation 4,

$$\hat{Y} = a + b_1 X_1 \qquad (4)$$

where $\hat{Y}$ is the new adjusted outcome score, $a$ is a constant, and $b_1$ is the linear effect of the covariate ($X_1$) on the outcome score ($Y$). The difference between the actual score and the predicted score ($Y - \hat{Y}$) is the residual. These residuals represent that part of the individuals' scores that is not explained by the covariate. These residuals are then analyzed using the analysis of variance techniques described above.

If the effect of the covariate is negative, then those who scored high on the covariate will have their scores adjusted upward. Those who scored lower on the covariate would have their scores adjusted downward. This would counteract the reverse effect that the covariate has had.

## SUMMARY MEASURES

In addition to identifying the sources of variation in some outcome measure, analysis of variance and analysis of covariance procedures produce two summary statistics. The first of these—$ETA^2$—is a measure of how much effect the predictor variable or factor has on the outcome variable. The second statistic—F—tests the *null hypothesis* that there is no difference between group means in the larger population from which the sample data was randomly selected.

**$ETA^2$.** As noted above, a large between-groups sum of squares is indicative of a large difference in the mean scores between groups. The meaningfulness of this difference, however, can be judged only against the overall variation in the scores. If there is a large amount of variation in scores, then larger differences in mean scores can be expected by chance. $ETA^2$ takes into account the difference between means and the total variation in scores. Under conditions where there is the same number of subjects in each of the groups, the equation for computing $ETA^2$ is as shown in equation 5.

$$ETA^2 = \frac{SS_{between}}{SS_{total}} \qquad (5)$$

As can be seen from this equation, ETA² is the proportion of the total sum of squares explained by group differences. When all the variance is explained, ETA² will be equal to 1, indicating a perfect relationship. When there is no difference in the group means, there is no effect and ETA² is equal to 0.

**F Tests.** Even if ETA² indicates that a sizeable proportion of the total variance in the sample scores is explained by group differences, the possibility exists that the sample results do not reflect true differences in the larger population from which the samples were selected. The F statistic tests the null hypothesis that the *population* means are not different. The logic behind this approach is that if each group is an independent random sample of the population, then variation in the sample means should reflect variation within each sample, and both should be unbiased estimates of the population variance. If the sample means vary more than the within-sample variation in scores, then the between-groups variation is said to be biased by the effects of group conditions. That is, the population means will be different.

The F test sounds very similar to ETA². An important difference, however, is that instead of taking the ratio of the between-groups sum of squares to the total sum of squares, the F statistic compares the mean square for mean differences (MS$_{between}$) to the mean square for within-group variation (MS$_{within}$). Under conditions where there is the same number of subjects in each of the groups, the equation for computing F is as shown in equation 6.

$$F = \frac{MS_{between}}{MS_{within}} \qquad (6)$$

The mean square is based on the sum of squares with adjustments made for the *degrees of freedom*. Degrees of freedom reflect the extent to which large variances are possible because of the number of scores being used to calculate them. For example, if there is only one score in a sample, then there is no room for any variation. If, on the other hand, there are 100 scores, a great deal of variation in scores becomes possible.

The degrees of freedom for calculating MS$_{between}$ (df1) is $k - 1$, where $k$ is the number of group means being compared and 1 is subtracted to account for the reduction in possible variation that comes about because the grand mean of scores was used in calculating the sum of squares. The formula for calculating MS$_{between}$ is shown in equation 7.

$$MS_{between} = SS_{between} / (k - 1) \qquad (7)$$

The degrees of freedom for calculating MS$_{within}$ (df2) is $N - k$, where $N$ is the total number of individual scores being compared and $k$ is the number of group means used in calculating the within-group sum of squares. The formula for calculating MS$_{within}$ is shown in equation 8.

$$MS_{within} = SS_{within} / (N - k) \qquad (8)$$

As can be seen in these two equations, when the number of groups is high, the estimate of variation between groups is adjusted downward to account for the greater chance of variation. When the number of cases is high, the estimation of variation within groups is adjusted downward. As a result, the larger the number of cases being analyzed, the higher the F statistic. A high F value reflects greater confidence that any differences in sample means reflect differences in the populations. Using certain assumptions, the possibility that any given F value can be obtained by chance, given the number of groups (df1) and the number of cases (df2), can be calculated and compared to the actual F value. If the chance probability is only 5 percent or less, then the null hypothesis is rejected and the sample mean differences are said to be "significant."

## APPLICABILITY

In sociological studies, the researcher is rarely able to manipulate the stimulus (or independent variable) and tends to be more interested in behavior in natural settings rather than controlled experimental settings. As a result randomization of preexisting differences through random assignment of subjects to experimental and control groups is not possible, and physical control over more immediate outside influences on behavior cannot be attained. In sociological studies, "other things" are rarely equal and must be ruled out as possible alternative explanations for group differences through "statistical control." This statistical control is best accomplished through correlational techniques, although in certain circumstances the analysis of covariance can be used to control statistically for possible extraneous sources of influence.

Where analysis of variance and covariance are more appropriate in sociological studies is: (1) where the independent variable can be manipulated (e.g., field experiments investigating natural reactions to staged incidences or studies of the effectiveness of different modes of intervention or teaching styles); (2) analyses of typologies or global variables that capture a set of unspecified, interrelated causes or stimuli (e.g., comparisons of industrialized versus nonindustrialized countries, differences between white-collar versus blue-collar workers); or (3) where independent (or predictor) variables that have a limited number of discrete categories (e.g., race, gender, religion, country, etc.) are used.

(SEE ALSO: *Correlation and Regression Analysis; Experiments; General Linear Model; Tabular Analysis*)

### REFERENCES

Blalock, Hubert M. 1979 *Social Statistics.* Rev. 2nd ed. New York: McGraw-Hill.

Bohrnstedt, George, and David Knoke 1988 *Statistics for Data Analysis.* 2d ed. Itasca, Ill.: F. E. Peacock Publishers.

Nie, Norman H., C. Hadlai Hull, Jean G. Jenkins, Karin Steinbrenner, and Dale H. Bent 1975 *SPSS: Statistical Package for the Social Sciences.* 2d ed. New York: McGraw-Hill.

Scheffe, H. A. 1959 *The Analysis of Variance.* New York: Wiley.

Simmons, Roberta G., and Dale A. Blyth 1987 *Moving into Adolescence.*

Winer, B. J. 1962 *Statistical Principles in Experimental Design.* New York: McGraw-Hill.

RICHARD A. BULCROFT

**ANDROGYNY** *See* Masculinity/Femininity.

**ANOMIE AND ALIENATION** The concepts *anomie* and *alienation,* while having some important differences, share common roots and quite similar histories. Both concepts were used by early sociologists to describe changes in society produced by the Industrial Revolution. The demise of traditional communities and the disruption of norms, values, and a familiar way of life were major concerns of nineteenth-century philosophers and sociologists. Anomie and alienation are concepts used to describe the major dislocations that were taking place as a result of the Industrial Revolution. For sociologists, *anomie* is most frequently associated with Emile Durkheim, although others used it differently even during his lifetime (Wolff, 1988). *Alienation* is most often associated with Karl Marx, although others have used this term somewhat differently as well (Nisbet 1966).

Durkheim ([1893] 1956) used the French word *anomie,* meaning "without norms," to describe the disruption that societies experienced in the shift from an agrarian, village economy to one based on industry. Marx ([1867] 1977) characterized early capitalism as "alienated," meaning that those under it came to be dominated by an economic system of their own creation. Both anomie and alienation have been used to describe a state of society; they referred to characteristics of the social system, not of individuals, although individuals were affected by these forces. Increasingly, these terms have taken on a more social psychological meaning. This is not to say that they no longer have uses consistent with the initial definitions, but their meanings have been broadened considerably, at times consistent with Durkheim's and Marx's usages, at times at substantial variance with them. Alienation, and to a lesser extent anomie, have even entered into the popular lexicon. In a recent popular song the singer describes "feelings of alienation" resulting from lost love.

There are, no doubt, sociologists who cringe at

any expanded usage of these and other concepts, but the fact of the matter is that we have no more control over their usage than Thomas Kuhn (1970) has over abominable uses of the concept "paradigm," or than computer engineers have over those who say "interface" when they mean "meet with." Although we cannot keep crooners from lamenting alienation when they probably mean "sadness," we can be careful that sociological extensions of anomie and alienation are logically derived from their early uses. While sociology as a discipline can do without unnecessary concept proliferation, when we mean something that is unrelated to anomie or alienation, other words should be used in order to avoid confusion.

## DURKHEIM ON ANOMIE

According to Durkheim, village life based on agriculture had consistent, well-established norms that governed the day-to-day lives of individuals. Norms prescribed patterns of behavior, obligation, and expectations. Durkheim called this pattern of social life mechanical solidarity. Communities characterized by mechanical solidarity were self-contained units in which the family and the village provided for all of the needs of their members. With the emergence of industrial capitalism and the beginnings of population shifts from the hinterland to cities, mechanical solidarity could not successfully structure social life. Durkheim believed that a new, organic solidarity based on a division of labor would emerge, with a regulating normative structure that would be as functional as mechanical solidarity. The emergence of organic solidarity would take time, however. The transitional period, characterized by normative disorganization, Durkheim described as anomic. By this he did not mean to imply literal normlessness but, rather, a state of *relative* normative disorder (Coser 1977). Compared with communities characterized by mechanical solidarity, developing larger towns and cities would have a less regulated, less structured, less ordered pattern of social life.

Release from the restraining influence of norms was not a liberating circumstance, accord-

ing to Durkheim. In this state, without adequate normative direction, people did not know what to expect or how to behave. Many of the social problems that Durkheim witnessed in rapidly changing industrializing Europe, he blamed on inadequate normative regulation. In his classic *Suicide,* Durkheim ([1897] 1951) identifies "anomic suicide" as occurring when the values and norms of the group cease to have meaning— or serve as anchors—for the individual, leading to feelings of isolation, confusion, and personal disorganization.

## MARX ON ALIENATION

Marx's usage of the concept alienation can be traced to the German philosopher Hegel, in whose writings alienation was a key concept. Collins describes Hegel's notion of alienation in this way: ". . . the human individual creates the world by his or her labor, but is then alienated from it because the world, in turn, controls human beings. Alienation means the ironic relationship of being controlled by the products of one's own action" (Collins 1988, p. 102).

In sociology, "alienation" is most often associated with Marx. For him, too, it was a central concept, particularly in his earlier writings. His conception was consistent with Hegel's. Alienation, for Marx, was the subordination of humans to forces of their own creation, in particular the economic order (Coser 1977, p. 50). As was the case with Durkheim's conception of anomie, alienation was seen by Marx as a condition of the social system that affected individuals, rather than as the social psychological consequence of people's lives in an alienated circumstance. While Marx argued that all major institutions in capitalist societies are alienated, it was economic alienation that was central to much of his work. The subordination of workers to the production process and the resultant alienation were key determinants of social patterns and social life. Marx witnessed the replacement of craft shops and guilds, a more controllable, personal production mode, with factories characterized by a more complex division of labor. The new mode, intended to be more efficient and productive to serve people, Marx argued, in the end controls its creators. Men and women end up serving the economic order (capitalism) that was intended to serve them. The society's creation comes to control and determine the pattern of social life.

## CONTEMPORARY USES OF "ANOMIE" AND "ALIENATION"

Both concepts, in particular alienation, continue to be used as defined by Durkheim and Marx. But both have also been extended during the twentieth century. In addition to extensions similar to past uses of these concepts, social psychological conceptions of anomie and alienation have become widespread. Robert Merton's use of "anomie" is very similar to that described by Durkheim. His application (1949) has been the core theoretical statement in one of the twentieth century's major criminological traditions. "Anomia" is a social psychological derivative used to represent a state of disaffection or disconnectedness. "Alienation" is used by Marxists and non-Marxists to describe the state of modern institutions, but increasingly this concept, too, has come to be associated with one of its social psychological by-products: feelings of powerlessness.

**Merton on Anomie.** Merton (1949) used the concept anomie to describe how social structure produced individual deviance. According to Merton, when there existed within a society a disjuncture between the legitimate goals that members of a society are to aspire to and the legitimate means of achieving these goals, then that society was in a state of anomie. For both Durkheim and Merton, frustrated aspirations were an important cause of norm violations, or deviance. They differed in what they saw as the source of aspirations. For Durkheim, it was human nature to have limitless desires, growing from a natural "wellspring" within. Merton argued that desires did not come from within us, but were advanced by a widely held conception of what constitutes "the good life."

Durkheim believed that when a society was characterized by anomie, there were inadequate normative constraints on the desires and expectations of people. Peasants could come to believe, even expect, that they could rise to live like the aristocracy, or become captains of newly developing industry. Part of mechanical solidarity was the norms that constrained these expectations, that ordered the intercourse between social classes, that checked the natural wellsprings of desires and encouraged peasants to be happy with their lot in life. Without these checks, desires exceeded reasonable hope of attainment, producing frustration and potentially deviance.

Merton's conception of anomie placed the society itself in the position of determining both the legitimate goals that people should aspire to and the legitimate means of pursuing these goals. Unfortunately, society frequently caused people to have grandiose expectations without providing all of its members with reasonable opportunities to pursue them legitimately. This circumstance, where the goals and the means were not both universally available to the members of a society, Merton called anomie.

When individuals were faced with anomie, they had to choose whether to forgo the socially advanced goals, their society's shared vision of the good life, or to seek these objectives by means not defined as legitimate. Merton described five choices available to these individuals. With "conformity," the individual uses the socially prescribed means to obtain the goals advanced by that society. "Innovation" is the choice to use illegitimate means to achieve the legitimate goals; much criminal behavior is an example of innovation. When a person goes through the motions of using the legitimate means, fully aware that the socially advanced goals are beyond his reach, this is "ritualism." "Retreatism" is the choice neither to use the legitimate means nor to strive for the legitimate goals of a society. Finally, "rebellion" is rejecting the society's means and goals and replacing them with ones defined by the individual as superior.

A common mistake is interpreting Merton as arguing that an individual chooses to live his or her life as a conformist, or innovator, or retreatist. To the contrary, Merton's position is that we all are constantly making choices when faced with behavioral alternatives. At one point during the day one might choose to act as a conformist, but later, when confronted with another choice, one may choose to innovate. For example, a person who engages in robbery, innovation, is not always an innovator; he or she may also have a job, which indicates conformity. While one of these choices may predominate with some people, they should be seen as alternatives that people choose from in deciding how to act in a particular instance, not identities that they assume.

In applying Merton's perspective to Western nations, sociologists have argued that most of these societies are characterized by some degree of anomie, which manifests itself as a lack of equal opportunity. The extent of anomie, the degree of disjuncture between goals and means in a society, can be used to predict the level of crime and deviance that that society will experience. The high crime rates of the United States can be linked to great inequalities in income, education, and job opportunities (Loftin and Hill 1974). To explain individual propensity to deviate from norms, one must consider the extent to which individuals have accepted the society's conception of "the good life," and the legitimate means individuals can use to attain it (Cloward and Ohlin 1960). As an explanation of crime, this theory has given way in recent decades to newer approaches, but anomie has been absorbed into larger perspectives to explain the relationship between poverty and crime (Messner 1983).

**Twentieth-century Conceptions of Alienation.** According to Robert Nisbet (1966), Marx's conception of alienation, which, as mentioned above, grew out of the Hegelian philosophical tradition, is but one of two major perspectives on alienation. While the Marxist version is the primary source of sociology's connection to the concept, Nisbet argues that "the content of the twentieth-century use of the word 'alienation' comes from the works of Tocqueville, Weber, Durkheim, and Simmel" (Nisbet 1966, pp. 264–265). He further writes: "[T]here are, I suggest, two fundamental and distinguishable perspectives on alienation to be found in nineteenth-century sociological thought. The first rests on an alienat-

ed view of the individual, the second on an alienated view of society" (Nisbet 1966, p. 265). The former perspective has greatly influenced twentieth-century conceptions of alienation.

This conception of alienation describes a situation in which the individual is uprooted, cut loose from the normative moorings of society. This rupture can be a by-product of a particular economic order, but it also may exist outside the context of capitalist modes of production (Collins 1988, p. 452). It is consistent with the second perspective of alienation mentioned above that it has come to be widely used as a social psychological concept.

In the study of organizations this contemporary conception of alienation has frequently been used. The "compliance theory" of Etzioni (1975) seeks to explain how organizations get workers, members, or participants to comply with organization norms and objectives. Three principles, he argues, are used to achieve compliance: (1) coercion, (2) material rewards, and (3) internalized control. For the current discussion, these principles are important because the level of alienation among members of an organization is related to the method used to achieve compliance. Coercion produces the greatest alienation, so it is not surprising that prison inmates, whose very participation in the organization (the prison) is maintained by coercion, are extremely alienated. When organizations use material rewards to produce compliance, far less alienation is produced. In fact, some institutions housing juvenile offenders use "token economies," or reward systems, in an attempt to minimize the degree of alienation produced by incarceration. Companies obviously use material rewards to get those they employ, both on the factory floor and in the corporate suites, to comply with the organization's objectives. Here, too, alienation occurs, but to a lesser extent than when coercion is used. Etzioni's final method of achieving compliance, developing internalized control, is the least alienating and will be most successful with organization members who are least alienated. By internalizing the norms and objectives of the organization, these members come to resemble preindustrial, nineteen-century people whose internalized norms bonded them to the group, guided behavior, and patterned the collective's social life.

**Social Psychological Conceptions of Anomia and Alienation.** Items designed to measure individual feelings of anomia and alienation are now frequently included in surveys such as the General Social Survey, an annual national survey conducted by the National Opinion Research Center (NORC) at the University of Chicago. Examples of these items illustrate the current uses of the concepts, as in the following anomia items from the 1988 NORC survey (respondents were instructed to indicate the extent of their agreement with each statement): "Most public officials (people in public office) are not really interested in the problems of the average man," and "It's hardly fair to bring a child into the world with the way things look for the future" (NORC 1988, pp. 215–216). (Nearly 40 percent of the respondents to the second question agreed, and 68 percent agreed with the first.) Alienation items in the NORC surveys of the late 1970s and early 1980s included "The rich get richer and the poor get poorer," and "Most people with power try to take advantage of people like yourself" (NORC 1988, p. 181). (Seventy-six percent of respondents agreed with the first statement, nearly 60 percent with the second.)

## IN SUMMARY

Anomie and alienation have been and will continue to be mainstay concepts in sociology. Even in the large body of current research that does not focus on them, either the earliest usages of the concepts or their twentieth-century extensions frequently appear in studies on such subjects as deviance (Funk and Wise 1989), the workplace (Molstad 1989; Newman, Rutter and Smith 1989; Yoo 1989), and feelings associated with modern life (Best 1989; Foster 1989; Hodges 1989; Kalekin-Fishman 1989). Papers discussing the meanings and uses of these concepts continue to be written (see, for example, Deflem 1989; Wolff 1988; Hilbert 1989). The basic meanings of the terms anomie and alienation, though—both in

their initial usage as descriptions of society and in their modern extensions—are well established and widely understood within the discipline. Students new to sociology should take care to understand that the definitions of the words may not be as broad for sociologists as for the general public. The utility of the concepts for the study of society is best maintained by extending them in ways that are consistent with their original definitions.

(SEE ALSO: *Alienation*)

## REFERENCES

Best, Steven 1989 "ROBOCOP: In the Detritus of Hi-Technology." *Jump Cut* 34:19–36.

Cloward, Richard A., and Lloyd E. Ohlin 1960 *Delinquency and Opportunity: A Theory of Delinquent Gangs.* New York: Free Press.

Collins, Randall 1988 *Theoretical Sociology.* New York: Harcourt Brace Jovanovich.

Coser, Lewis A. 1977 *Masters of Sociological Thought: Ideas in Historical and Social Context*, 2nd ed. New York: Harcourt Brace Jovanovich.

Deflem, Mathieu 1989 "From Anomie to Anomia and Anomic Depression: A Sociological Critique on the Use of Anomie in Psychiatric Research." *Social Science and Medicine* 29:627–634.

Durkheim, Emile (1897) 1951 *Suicide.* New York: Free Press.

———(1893) 1956 *The Division of Labor in Society.* New York: Free Press.

Etzioni, Amitai 1975 *A Comparative Analysis of Complex Organizations.* New York: Free Press.

Foster, Susan 1989 "Social Alienation and Peer Identification: A Study in the Social Construction of Deafness." *Human Organization* 48:226–235.

Funk, Allie G., and Michael G. Wise 1989 "Anomie, Powerlessness, and Exchange: Parallel Sources of Deviance." *Deviant Behavior* 10 1:53–60.

Hilbert, Richard A. 1989 "Durkheim and Merton on Anomie: An Unexplored Contrast and Its Derivatives." *Social Problems* 36:242–250.

Hodges, Harold M., Jr. 1989 "On Surviving the Day After Tomorrow." *The Humanist* 49:25–29, 40.

Kalekin-Fishman, Devorah 1989 "De-Alienation as an Education Objective." *Humanity and Society* 13:309–326.

Kuhn, Thomas 1970 *The Structure of Scientific Revolutions,* 2nd ed. Chicago: University of Chicago Press.

Loftin, Colin, and Robert H. Hill 1974 "Regional Subculture and Homicide." *American Sociological Review* 39:714–724.

Marx, Karl (1867) 1977 *Capital: A Critique of Political Economy,* vol. 1. New York: Vintage Books.

Merton, Robert K. 1949 *Social Theory and Social Structure: Toward the Codification of Theory and Research.* New York: Free Press.

Messner, Steven F. 1983 "Regional and Racial Effects on the Urban Homicide Rate: The Subculture of Violence Revisited." *American Journal of Sociology* 88:997–1007.

Molstad, Clark 1989 "Coping with Alienation in Industrial Work: An Ethnographic Study of Brewery Workers." Ph.D. diss., University of California at Los Angeles.

National Opinion Research Center 1988 *General Social Surveys, 1972–1988: Cumulative Codebook.* Chicago: National Opinion Research Center, University of Chicago.

Newman, Fred M., Robert A. Rutter, and Marshall S. Smith 1989 "Organization Factors That Affect School Sense of Efficiency, Community, Expectation." *Sociology of Education* 62:221–238.

Nisbet, Robert A. 1966 *The Sociological Tradition.* New York: Basic Books.

Wolff, Kurt H. 1988 "Anomie and the Sociology of Knowledge, in Durkheim and Today." *Philosophy and Social Criticism* 14:53–67.

Yoo, Hong-Joon 1989 "Technology, Organization, and Worker Alienation in Korea." Ph.D. diss., State University of New York—Stony Brook.

ROBERT D. CRUTCHFIELD

**ANTISEMITISM**   *See* Discrimination; Prejudice; Race.

**APARTHEID**   Both similarities and differences exist between the situation of blacks in the United States since about 1940 and the situation of blacks in South Africa (van den Berghe 1967). The differences, however, are critical. The first is that although blacks in the United States have always been a numerical minority, blacks in South Africa have always been a numerical majority. Deracialization in the American context does not pose a major threat to white power, but deracialization in the South African context would very likely lead to the loss of supremacy on the part of whites. Further, given the kind of treatment that blacks have received in South Africa during the last three centuries, some concern exists that if blacks came to power they might "do unto others that which has been done unto them." Consequently, white South Africans have devised a policy of segregation and discrimination called *apartheid,* in an attempt to preserve their dominance and assure the subjugation of the blacks.

As did Southern whites in the United States, the 4.5 million white South Africans, who today constitute only about 17.5 percent of the total population of South Africa, need the labor of the nonwhite population—Indians (2.9 percent), Coloreds (a mix of Hottentots, imported slaves, and early white settlers, 9.4 percent), and indigenous Africans, who constitute the overwhelming majority, some 26 million (70 percent). Although the dominant white South Africans need the labor of these various groups, especially indigenous black Africans, they consider all of them inferior and do not want to share the political and economic resources of the country with them on an egalitarian basis. This lack of egalitarianism is reflected in the legislative and legal history of apartheid, although very recently the South African government has begun to reconsider the usefulness of the various forms of restrictions that have defined this unequal treatment of persons.

As early as the 1760s, pass laws were instituted in South Africa requiring the indigenous black Africans to produce identification cards on demand. These pass laws have remained a feature of South African race relations for more than 200 years, that is, until Prime Minister Botha repealed them and relaxed the control of influx into white areas in South Africa. South African blacks at that time were allowed relatively unencumbered freedom of movement.

South African whites instituted separate schools for indigenous black Africans. The Bantu

Education Act for segregated schools was enacted 1949–1950. Until 1950 black Africans were educated by missionaries, and some of them were becoming educationally and economically competitive. The South African government felt that it could not allow this to happen and therefore decided to exercise control over the education of black Africans, especially the Bantu. In 1954 the government extended its control into higher education and passed the Extension of the University Education Act, which segregated the university system and mandated that all Africans must leave white universities by 1961. Since the unconditional release of black activist Nelson Mandela in 1990, Prime Minister F. W. de Klerk has made plans for desegregating the public school system and possibly integrating the universities.

South Africa has experimented with residential segregation in ways that whites in the United States never considered. In 1945, for example, the Black Urban Area Consolidation Act excluded blacks from white townships and set up a separate system of black urban townships. As a result of this legislation, in 1951, 3.5 million black Africans were forcibly removed from white areas with the passage of the Prevention of Illegal Squatting Act. In the same year the Bantu Authorities Act legalized the development of separate provinces for black Africans. These so-called Homelands, or Bantustans, it was felt, might be the answer for South Africa. It would give indigenous black Africans an opportunity for limited self-government and perhaps allow them to develop a "separate" economy. As a result of the development of the Bantustan structure, 8 million blacks lost their South African citizenship between the years 1976 and 1982. The loss of citizenship resulted from the fact that the Bantustans of Transkei, Bopthuthatswana, Verda, and Ciskei were declared "independent." The new Bantustan citizens, however, were not citizens of independent countries.

Bantustan policy turned out to be a policy of independence in name only, for several reasons. First, each one of the Bantustans was totally dependent on the South African economy for basic subsistence. Second, the lack of attractive-ness of rural areas to Africans who have lived in urban areas for most of their lives meant that the majority of South African blacks continued to live outside the Homelands. Third, the most critical and significant political decisions and bureaucratic functions were either under the control or supervision of whites. Fourth, the extremely high illiteracy rate of Bantustan populations made self-government problematic. For example, many do not even bother to vote. Fifth, one-third of the members of the various Bantustan governing bodies were appointed by the South African government. Sixth, some of the Bantustans border the sea and could, therefore, possibly import armaments for revolutionary purposes from countries (Adam 1971, pp. 60, 85). Consequently, the South African government knew that it must maintain control over the activities of Bantustan officials. Finally, less than half of the African population has chosen to live in the Homelands.

What is likely to happen in South Africa? Urban black townships in South Africa are likely to approximate urban ghettos in the United States, with very high incidences of crime and violence. Many of the residents of these townships are either unmarried or separated from their families. Most residents are very poor. Adam (1971) reports that as of the mid-1960s a subculture of violence was developing among young residents of black townships, and even a gang culture composed of tsotsis groups had begun to evolve. Such groups make violence a way of life. It is also likely that these townships will generate a black middle class that wants nothing more than the opportunity to compete fairly and equally in South Africa. Eventually they will want to eliminate residential segregation and avoid becoming citizens of the Homelands, just as some members of the black middle class in America do not wish to live in black communities. Further, the South African government is increasingly forced by economic necessity to allow larger and larger numbers of blacks outside reserved areas—because white South Africans need their labor.

Under such circumstances racial stratification and industrialization are likely to coexist, but in time, as black workers become more central to the process of production and take on more and more skilled jobs, they may eventually attain both the numbers and the crucially needed industrial expertise to shut down the South African economy with a general strike. Very much aware of this, South Africa is willing to pay the price of inefficiency and accept a slow rate of industrial growth to protect itself from such a possibility. What white South Africa should desire is the development of an African middle class that wants equal opportunity and equal access. Such a middle class would reinforce the already existing system rather than require the creation of a new one. As the barriers to residential integration topple, the black middle class will leave the most disadvantaged segments of the black townships behind. Included in those segments will be "those families that have experienced either long-term poverty and/or welfare dependency, individuals who lack training and skills and have experienced either periods of persistent unemployment or have dropped out of the labor force altogether, and individuals who are frequently involved in street criminal activity" (Wilson 1987, p. 143). This group could become a permanent dependent and destructive underclass, but that would depend on the demand for unskilled labor. If the demand remains high and regular, permanent employment may remain the norm, and if miners for whom there is always work make former black townships their preferred residence, then they might become a leadership cadre, organizing among themselves and including the underclass. Integration usually means that blacks move to white settings, and not the reverse. If that occurs, former black townships may become future seats of revolutionary upheaval.

The Bantustans are likely to experience changes that differ from the black urban townships. This depends on the institutionalization of a democratic system and the working out of many fractional disputes that have grown out of constant episodes of ethnic conflict, usually referred to as tribalism. If the Bantustans can solve these problems, the issue for them will at some point be independence. If the South African government frustrates the desire of the Bantustans for independence, the possibility exists that this would drive the various Homelands together, out of which might grow a common definition of their respective oppressive situations. Under such circumstances the question will be: What role will the Bantustan middle class play? Will they tire of external controls? Will they conclude that the 13 percent of the land that has been reserved for them is inadequate to secure independence and subsequent prosperity? Will the Bantustan middle class, like their earlier anticolonial African predecessors, put aside their differences and become a political class rather than just an economic class? One of the unanticipated consequences of self-rule appears to be the desire to continue to make independent decisions. Will there be a call for revolution? or will the Bantustan middle class become civil servants.

Projecting into the future is one of the tasks not merely of policymakers but also of social scientists, who presumably evaluate the social situation objectively. There are many unknowns, however, as has been demonstrated by the remarkable changes in various parts of the world, especially those following 1989. Thus, the questions raised are not to be set aside lightly. Pursuing them, will South Africa be partitioned into two separate countries, one day, each having a black middle class, but each having a middle class that plays quite different roles? Or, at the other extreme, will South African whites, with the conscious advice, consent, and participation of the black middle classes, maintain control over all parts of South Africa? Indeed, can a white elite, even with the consent of the black middle classes, maintain its power, privilege, and differential status? Further, can the white elite maintain control of a society where they constitute such a small percentage of the total population?

Clearly, apartheid in South Africa represents an issue that is important because of vital concerns with regard to racial, ethnic, and human relations. In addition, it presents a broad opportunity for the application of sociological knowledge and research into the fields of race relations, social change, and political sociology.

(SEE ALSO: *African Studies; Discrimination; Race; Segregation and Desegregation*)

### REFERENCES

Adam, Heribert 1971 *Modernizing Racial Domination: The Dynamics of South African Politics.* Berkeley: University of California Press.

van den Berghe, Pierre L. 1967 *Race and Racism: A Comparative Perspective.* New York: Wiley.

Wilson, William J. 1987 *The Truly Disadvantaged: The Inner City, the Underclass, and Public Policy.* Chicago: University of Chicago Press.

ALBERT N. BLACK, JR.

**APPLIED SOCIOLOGY** Applied sociology is sociology in use. It is policy-oriented, action-directed, and intends to assist people and groups to think reflectively about what it is they do, or how it is that they can create more viable social forms capable of adapting to changing external and internal conditions. The roots of applied sociology in the United States go back to the publication in 1883 of Lester Ward's *Dynamic Sociology: Or Applied Social Science,* a text in which Ward laid the groundwork for distinguishing between an understanding of causal processes and how to intervene in them to foster social progress. Today, applied sociology has blossomed in every arena of sociological endeavor (Olsen and Micklin 1981).

The nature of applied sociology can more easily be grasped by examining those characteristics that distinguish it from basic sociology. Different audiences are involved (Coleman 1972). Basic sociology is oriented toward those who have a concern for the advancement of sociological knowledge. The quality of such work is evaluated in accordance with agreed-upon standards of scientific merit. Applied sociology is oriented more toward those who are making decisions, developing or monitoring programs, or concerned about the accountability of those who are

making decisions and developing programs. The quality of applied work is evaluated in accordance with a dual set of criteria: (1) how useful it is in informing decisions, revealing patterns, improving programs, and increasing accountability; and (2) whether its assumptions and methods are appropriately rigorous for the problems under investigation.

If we were to imagine a continuum between pure research and pure practice, applied sociology would occupy a space in the middle. This space is enlarged along one side when practitioners and applied sociologists collaborate to explain patterns of behavior or give theoretical grounds for predicting the likely impact of different courses of action. It is enlarged on the other side when applied and basic sociologists collaborate in the elaboration of abstract theory so as to make it more useful (Lazarsfeld and Reitz 1975).

The boundaries of applied sociology may also be specified by enumerating the activities that play a central role in what it is that applied sociologists do. Freeman and Rossi (1984) have suggested three activities: (1) mapping and social indicator research; (2) modeling social phenomena; and (3) evaluating purposive action. To this could be added at least one more activity: (4) conceptualizing, studying, and facilitating the adaptability of alternative social forms. Examining these activities also permits considering some of the presumed trade-offs that are commonly thought to distinguish basic from applied sociology.

### MAPPING AND SOCIAL INDICATOR RESEARCH

Such studies are primarily descriptive and designed to provide estimates of the incidence and prevalence of phenomena that are social in nature. There may be interest in how these phenomena are distributed in different social categories (e.g., by ethnic group affiliation, life-styles, or social classes) or are changing over time. For example, corporations may wish to know how consumption patterns for various goods are changing over time for different groups to facilitate the development of marketing strategies. Federal and state agencies may wish to understand how the incidence and prevalence of diseases for different social groups is changing over time to develop more effective prevention and treatment strategies.

It is often assumed that applied sociology is less rigorous than basic sociology. Freeman and Rossi (1984) suggest that it is more appropriate to argue that the norms governing the conduct of basic sociological research are universally rigorous, while the norms governing the conduct of applied sociological research, of which mapping and social indicator research is but one example, have a sliding scale of rigor. For critical decisions, complex phenomena that are either difficult to measure or disentangle, or where precise projections are needed, sophisticated quantitative or qualitative measures may be required, and sophisticated analytic techniques may be needed or may need to be developed. But as time and budget constraints increase, and the need for precision decreases, "quick and dirty" measures might be more appropriate. The level of rigor in applied sociology, in short, is driven by the needs of the client and the situation as well as the nature of the problem under investigation.

## MODELING SOCIAL PHENOMENA

The modeling of social phenomena is an activity that is common to both basic and applied sociology. Sociologists of both persuasions might be interested in modeling the paths by which adolescents develop adaptive or maladaptive coping strategies, or the mechanisms by which social order is maintained in illicit drug networks. The applied sociologist would need to go beyond the development of these causal models. For the adolescents, applied sociologists would need to understand how various interventions might increase the development and maintenance of adaptive strategies. In the case of drug networks, they might need to understand the relative effectiveness of different crime control strategies in reducing the capacity of drug networks to protect themselves.

Just as with mapping and social indicator research, there are rigorous norms to which basic researchers should adhere in the development of causal models, but there is usually a sliding scale of rigor in applied research. There is not a necessary trade-off between doing applied work and levels of rigor. It usually happens, however, that applied problems are relatively more complex and tap into variables that are less easy to quantify. In trying to capture more of the complexity, precision in the specification of variables and elegance of form of the overall model may be sacrificed (Walton 1985).

For both basic and applied work it is imperative that sociologists properly specify the mechanisms by which controllable and uncontrollable variables have an impact on the phenomenon of interest. For basic researchers, it is a matter of properly specifying models so that coefficients are not biased. The clients of applied researchers, however, are not interested in how elegant models are but in how well the implications of these models assist them in reducing the uncertainty associated with decisions that must be made. As time and budget constraints increase, or researchers become more confident in their ability to understand which controllable variables are having the biggest impact, less rigorous techniques may be used to develop and test the models under consideration.

## EVALUATING PURPOSIVE ACTION

Evaluation research is an applied activity in which theories and methods of the social sciences are used to ascertain the extent to which programs are being implemented, services are being delivered, goals are being accomplished, and efforts are being conducted in a cost-effective manner. These may be relatively small-scale efforts with finite and specific research questions in either the public or private sector. A manufacturing company may be interested in evaluating the impact of a new marketing program. A drug rehabilitation center may be interested in evaluating the cost-effectiveness of a new treatment modality.

These programs may not be of national importance, may not have large sums of money contingent on the outcomes, and may not require an understanding of anything but gross effects. It may be necessary to perform such analyses with limited personnel, time, and money. Under such circumstances, relatively unsophisticated methods are going to be used to conduct the evaluations, and reanalysis will not be likely.

On the other hand, programs may involve the lives of many people and deal with critical and complex social issues. The Coleman report on the equality of educational opportunity was presumably intended to establish once and for all that gross differences in school facilities did exist for black and white children in the United States (Coleman et al. 1966). The report, carried out by a team of sophisticated social scientists in a relatively short time, unleashed a storm of reanalyses and critiques (e.g., Mosteller and Moynihan 1972). These reanalyses attempted to apply the most sophisticated theoretical and methodological weapons in the sociological arsenal to the task of evaluating the implications of the Coleman report. Similarly, econometric analyses initially conducted to evaluate the impact of capital punishment on the homicide rate spawned painstaking and sophisticated applied research (e.g., Bowers and Pierce 1975) in an attempt to evaluate the robustness of the conclusions. In these latter two cases, a high level of rigor by any standard was maintained.

## ALTERNATIVE SOCIAL FORMS

A legitimate test of applied sociology is whether it can be used as a basis for designing and implementing better social institutions (Street and Weinstein 1975). Involved here is an element of critical theory that complicates the distinction between basic and applied sociology, for it challenges applied sociologists and their clients to imagine alternative social forms that might be more adaptive in the face of changing social, environmental, and technological trends. At the level of families, this may mean asking what new role relationships could create more adaptive

family structures. At the level of work groups faced with changing technologies and dynamic environments, it is appropriate to ask whether flatter organizational structures and more autonomous work groups might better serve both organizational goals and those of its members (e.g., Myers 1985). At the community level, exploring the viability of alternative interorganizational relationships (e.g., Whyte 1982) or how communities respond to the threat of drug dealing are among a host of legitimate questions.

In applied sociology, problems drive the development of both theory and method. When problems and their dynamics cannot be explained by existing theories, new assumptions are added (Lazersfeld and Reitz 1975), new ways of thinking about concepts like adaptability are developed (e.g., Britt 1988), or more fundamental theoretical shifts take place in a manner described by Kuhn (1961). When problems cannot be studied with existing methodological and statistical techniques, new techniques are developed. For example, the computer was developed under a contract from the Census Bureau so that the 1950 census could be conducted, and advances in area sampling theory were stimulated by the Department of Commerce, which needed to get better unemployment estimates (Rossi 1986).

The continuing pressure on applied sociology to adapt to the needs of clients has had two important second-order effects beyond the development of theory and method. The nature of graduate training for applied sociologists is changing by virtue of the wider repertoire of skills needed by applied sociologists, and the dilemmas faced by sociologists vis-a-vis their clients are being confronted, and norms regarding the appropriateness of various courses of action are being developed.

A universal component of graduate applied education is the internship. Learning by doing, and experiencing the array of problems associated with designing and conducting research under time and budget constraints, while still having supportive ties with the academic program, are very important. The range and depth of coursework in methods and statistics is increasing in applied programs to prepare students for the prospect of needing to employ techniques as varied as structural equations, focus groups, archival analysis, and participant observation in order to deal with the complexity of the problems requiring analysis. There have been corresponding changes in the area of theory, with more emphasis given to moving back and forth from theory to applied problem. And there have been increases in courses designed to train students in the other skills required for successful applied work: networking, problem decomposition, and dealing with client–sociologist dilemmas.

(SEE ALSO: *Evaluation Research*)

### REFERENCES

Bowers, W., and G. Pierce 1975 "The Illusion of Deterrence in Isaac Ehrlich's Research on Capital Punishment." *Yale Law Journal* 85:187–208.

Britt, D. W. 1988 "Analyzing the Shape of Adaptability in Response to Environmental Jolts." *Clinical Sociology Review* 6:59–75.

Coleman, J. S. 1972 *Policy Research in the Social Sciences.* Morristown, N.J.: General Learning Press.

Coleman, J. S., E, Q. Campbell, C. J. Hobson, J. McPartland, A. M. Mood, F. D. Weinfield, and R. L. York 1966 *Equality of Educational Opportunity,* 2 vols. Washington, D.C.: U.S. Government Printing Office.

Freeman, H. E., and P. H. Rossi 1984 "Furthering the Applied Side of Sociology." *American Sociological Review* 49:571–580.

Kuhn, T. S. 1974 *The Structure of Scientific Revolutions,* 2nd ed. Chicago: University of Chicago Press.

Lazarsfeld, P. F., and J. G. Reitz 1975 *An Introduction to Applied Sociology.* New York: Elsevier.

Mosteller, F., and D. P. Moynihan 1972 *On Equality of Educational Opportunity.* New York: Random House.

Myers, J. B. 1985 "Making Organizations Adaptive to Change: Eliminating Bureaucracy at Shenandoah Life." *National Productivity Review* (Spring) 131–139.

Olsen, M. E. and M. Micklin 1981 *Handbook of Applied Sociology.* New York: Praeger.

Rossi, P. H. 1986 "How Applied Sociology Can Save Basic Sociology." *Journal of Applied Sociology* 3:1–6.

Street, D., and E. Weinstein 1975 "Prologue: Problems and Prospects of Applied Sociology." *The American Sociologist* 10:65–72.

Walton, R. 1985 "From Control to Commitment in the Workplace." *Harvard Business Review* 1985:76–84.

Whyte, W. F. 1982 "The Presidential Address: Social Inventions for Solving Human Problems." *American Sociological Review* 47:1–13.

DAVID W. BRITT

**ART AND SOCIETY** There is no consensus as to what art is, nor, until the 1970s, had sociologists expended much energy on its study or on the development of a sociology of the arts. While in Europe art had longer been of interest to sociologists than in the United States, even there it had not developed into an identifiable field with clear and internationally accepted parameters. As recently as 1968 the term *sociology of art* was not indexed in the *International Encyclopaedia of the Social Sciences,* which sought to sum and assess the thinking and accomplishments in the rapidly expanding social sciences of the postwar period. Yet today, as a new century nears, the study of art is moving into the mainstream of sociological theory and rapidly becoming a favored subject for empirical investigation not only in the countries of Central and Western Europe but also in the United States.

Why should art, as a subject for sociological study, have been so neglected as to have virtually disappeared from mention in American textbooks for half a century after World War I? In large part this reflected the inherent tension between sociology and art, which, as noted by Pierre Bourdieu, make an "odd couple." Artists, believing in the uniqueness of the original creator, resent the social scientist's attempt to demystify their achievements by dissecting the role of the artist in society, by questioning to what extent artists are "born" rather than "made," by conceptualizing artistic works as the products of collective rather than individual action, by anthropologically approaching art institutions, by studying the importance of networks in artistic success, and by investigating the economic correlates of artistic productivity. Many scholars in the humanities were also skeptical: For them the appeal of art is a mystery and best left that way; they could hardly relate to the attempts of social scientists to disregard their personal preferences while striving for objectivity, a practice that hardly seems legitimate to aestheticians. Moreover, in their pursuit of a rigorous methodology, many sociologists preferred to study only those problems that could yield readily to statistical analysis, and art did not seem to be one of those. They also preferred to focus on subjects that were important in the solution of social problems, and, in the United States, the arts were not generally regarded as high on this list.

Nonetheless, there has been—especially since the late 1960s—a slow but steady movement toward the development of a sociology of the arts. This is due, in part, to a narrowing of the intellectual gulf between the humanistic and sociological approaches: On the one hand, art historians have legitimated the study of art within its social context, and, on the other, mainstream sociology has become more hospitable to the use of other than purely "scientistic" methodology. In part progress has resulted from the expanded contacts of American sociologists after World War II with their counterparts in other countries where art is regarded as a vital social institution and a public good. And just as art must be understood and studied within its social context, so too the growing sociological interest in the arts reflects the growing importance of the arts within American society and the recognition of their importance by the government. Despite the concerted opposition of those who believe there is no role for government in funding the arts, at every level of government—federal, state, and local—arrangements for the support of grass roots arts have become institutionalized.

A small but dedicated number of scholars can be credited with sparking this postwar advancement of theory and research in the sociology of culture and, more specifically, in the sociology of the arts. The latter term, though not unknown before then, began to surface with some frequency in the 1950s; thus, a session on the sociology of art was listed in the program of the annual meeting of the American Sociological Association in 1954. In 1957 a symposium on the arts and human behavior at the Center for Advanced Study in the Behavioral Sciences served as a catalyst for the production of a book, based partially on papers presented there. In its preface, the editor, Robert N. Wilson, concluded that a sociology of art, though in the early stages of its development, was not yet ripe for formalization. Nonetheless, Wilson's book included a number of articles based on empirical research that attracted attention. In one, Cynthia White, an art historian, and Harrison White, a Harvard sociologist, reported on their investigation into institutional change in the French painting world and how this affected artistic careers. Later expanded and published in book form as *Canvases and Careers* (1965), this research provided a working example of how a changing art form might best be studied and understood within its historical and social context.

Perhaps the most important step toward the development of the field in these postwar years came with the publication of a collection of readings edited by Albrecht, Barnett, and Griff (1970). Clearly titled as to subject matter—*The Sociology of Art and Literature*—it was intended to serve a classroom purpose but also to advance an institutional approach to its study. In one article, originally published in 1968, Albrecht oriented the reader to art as an institution, using *art* as a collective term for a wide variety of aesthetic products, including literature, the visual arts, and music. In another ("The Sociology of Art"), Barnett reprinted his state-of-the-field synthesis as it stood in 1959, and, in still another, Griff published a seminal article on the recruitment and socialization of artists, drawing in some part on his earlier empirical studies of art students in Chicago. Though here, too, the authors spoke of the sociology of art as being still in its infancy, they helped it to take its first steps by including in their reader a large number of empirically grounded articles—by scholars in the humanities as well as the social sciences. Divided into six subjects—forms and styles, artists, distribution and reward systems, tastemakers and publics, methodology, history and theory—it served for many years as an exemplary resource both for those attempting to set up courses on the arts and society and those embarking on research.

Beginning in the 1970s the sociology of art moved toward formalization and began to come into its own. Speeding this development in the new age of television dominance was a growing sociological interest in the mass media, in visual communications, and in the popular arts. The debate about mass versus popular culture was revitalized by new fears about the effects of commercialization, but some scholars began to wonder about the terms in which the debate was being cast. The assumption that art forms could be categorized as "high" or "low" or, put another way, as "mass" or "elite"—an assumption that had fueled the critiques of Adorno and other members of the Frankfurt School—came into question as reputable researchers looked more closely at the empirical evidence (Gans 1974). Becker's conceptualization of art as collective action (1982) did not so much mute the debate as turn attention away from the circumstances surrounding the production of any particular work—that is, what kind of an artist produced work for what kind of audience under what system of rewards—toward the collective (cooperative) nature of the activity whereby works regarded as art are produced as well as to that collective process itself. As attention turned to the production of culture, the arts came to be widely regarded by sociologists as socially constructed entities whose symbolic meanings reside not in the objects themselves but change as circumstances change.

Recent American studies in the sociology of art have taken varied approaches. Some have concentrated on studies of genres that are marginal to established categories of fine art, while others have adopted methodologically unusual approaches to the study of the arts. Both approaches are apparent in Griswold's studies of the social factors influencing the revival of Renaissance plays (1986), in Crane's study of the transformation of art styles in post–World War II New York (1987), in Zolberg's studies of art patronage and new art forms (1990), and in Lang and Lang's study of the building and survival of artistic reputations (1990).

These and numerous studies that have already appeared or are likely to appear within the next decades will make clearer what is meant by a sociology of art. There still may be no consensus as to what art is—nor need there be—but some consensus is shaping up as to the direction in which the field should be moving. Zolberg has cogently stated the case for keeping the arts at the center of theoretical concern by avoiding the narrowness of both social science and aesthetic disciplines, accepting the premise that art should be contextualized in terms of time and place in a general sense as well as a specific sense, that is, in terms of institutional norms, professional training, reward, and patronage or other support. To approach art as a part of society's culture, Zolberg argues, is no more potentially reductionist than to treat it, as aestheticians do, as an activity that only restricted groups with special interests and knowledge can hope to comprehend. Literature in the field is growing at a rapid rate as intellectual barriers between humanistic and social science approaches to the study of art begin to crumble.

## REFERENCES

Adorno, Theodor [1962] 1976 *Introduction to the Sociology of Music.* New York: Seabury Press.

Albrecht, M.C., J.H. Barnett, and M. Griff, eds. 1970 *The Sociology of Art and Literature: A Reader.* New York: Praeger.

Becker, Howard S. 1982 *Art Worlds.* Berkeley: University of California Press.

Bourdieu, Pierre [1979] 1984 *Distinction: A Social Critique of the Judgment of Taste.* Cambridge, Mass.: Harvard University Press.

Crane, Diana 1987 *The Transformation of the Avant-Garde: The New York Art World 1940–85.* Chicago: University of Chicago Press.

Foster, Arnold W., and Judith R. Blau, eds. 1989 *Art and Society: Readings in the Sociology of the Arts.* Albany: State University of New York Press.

Gans, Herbert J. 1974 *Popular Culture and High Culture: An Analysis and Evaluation of Taste.* New York: Basic Books.

Griswold, Wendy 1986 *Renaissance Revivals: City Comedy*

*and Revenge Tragedy in the London Theater, 1576–1980.* Chicago: University of Chicago Press.

Lang, Gladys Engel, and Kurt Lang 1990 *Etched in Memory: The Building and Survival of Artistic Reputation.* Chapel Hill: University of North Carolina Press.

Peterson, Richard A., ed. 1976 *The Production of Culture.* Beverly Hills, Calif.: Sage Publications.

White, Harrison C., and Cynthia A. White 1965 *Canvasses and Careers: Institutional Change in the French Painting World.* New York: Wiley.

Wilson, Robert N., ed. 1964 *The Arts in Society.* Englewood Cliffs, N.J.: Prentice-Hall.

Zolberg, Vera L. 1990 *Constructing a Sociology of the Arts.* New York: Cambridge University Press.

GLADYS ENGEL LANG

## ASIAN-AMERICAN STUDIES

The term *Asian-American* is used in the United States by federal, state, and local governments to designate people of Asian descent, including Pacific Islanders (residents from the Pacific islands that are under U.S. jurisdiction, such as Guam, American Samoa, and the Marshall Islands). Although historically relevant and geographically appropriate, inclusion of the Pacific islands in the generic term *Asian-American* stemmed from administrative convenience for the federal government rather than from race or ethnic identifications.

Historically, in 1917 the Congress of the United States created the Asiatic Barred Zone, which stretched from Japan in the east to India in the west. People from within the zone were banned from immigration. The geographic concept was incorporated into the Immigration Act of 1924 (Oriental Exclusion Act), a law that had a profound impact on the demographic structure of Asian-American communities as well as on U.S. foreign policy. Although it is generally assumed that the term *Asian-American* has a racial basis, particularly from the perspective of U.S. immigration history, the racial overtone is muted by the inclusion in the 1980 census of people from India in the "Asian and Pacific Islander" category; they had been classified as "white" prior to 1980.

### IMMIGRATION AND RESTRICTIONS OF ASIAN-AMERICANS

Asian immigration can be divided into two periods: the old and the new. The old immigration period was marked by nonoverlapping waves of distinct Asian populations who came largely in response to the sociopolitical conditions in their homelands and to the shortage of unskilled labor experienced by special-interest groups in the United States. The new immigration was characterized by the simultaneous arrival of people from the Asia-Pacific Triangle, spurred principally by the 1965 legislative reforms in U.S. immigration policy, shortages of certain skilled and professional labor, the involvement of the United States in Asia, and the sociopolitical situations in Asia.

The year 1848 marked the beginning of Asian immigration to the United States when the coastal Chinese—mostly from Guangdong—responded to failures in the rural economy of China and the gold rush in California, seeking new opportunities on the West Coast. Within less than thirty-five years, the Chinese became the first group in U.S. history to be legally barred from becoming citizens because of race. The 1882 Anti-Chinese Exclusion Act was followed by an influx of immigrants from the southern prefectures of Japan during the last decade of the nineteenth century—until that flow ended abruptly with the Gentlemen's Agreement of 1907–1908. Unlike the termination of Chinese immigration, cessation of entry by Japanese was accomplished through a diplomatic compromise between the two governments rather than through an act of Congress. Without a continuous flow of Japanese farm workers to ease the labor shortage on the Hawaiian plantations, contractors turned to the Philippine Islands—which had been a U.S. possession since 1898—for cheap labor. From 1906 to the independence of the Republic of the Philippines in 1946, over 125,000 (predominantly single) Filipino males, the majority of them from the Ilocos region, labored on Hawaiian sugar plantations.

The exclusions of Asians enacted into the National Origins Act of 1924 essentially remained in effect until 1965. By Act of Congress in 1943, however, 105 Chinese were permitted to immigrate annually, and in 1952, under the 1952 McCarran-Walter Act, a token one hundred persons from each Asian country were allowed entry. The symbolic opening of immigration doors to Asians was attributed to Walter Judd, a congressman from Minnesota who had spent many years in China as a medical missionary. The provision of a quota of one hundred persons seemed to be an important moral victory for those who wanted the elimination of the exclusion act, but it was in fact a restatement of the 1924 national origin quota basis for immigration.

The new stream of Asian immigrants to the United States is the artifact of the 1965 legislative reform that allowed an equal number of persons (20,000) from each country outside the Western Hemisphere to immigrate. Furthermore, family unification and needed skills became the major admission criteria, replacing national origin. Besides China and the Philippines, Korea and the Indian subcontinent became, and continue to be, the major countries of origin of many newly arrived Asian immigrants. Refugees from Vietnam, Cambodia, and Laos began to enter the United States in 1975. By 1990, peoples from Indochina had become the third largest Asian group, following Chinese and Filipinos. In contrast, Japan's immigration to the United States practically ceased from 1945 to 1965, when it resumed at a much lower rate than those reported for other Asian countries.

## SOCIAL CONSEQUENCES OF IMMIGRATION RESTRICTIONS

Several distinct demographic characteristics illustrate most graphically past restrictions and recent reforms in the immigration laws. Earlier immigrants from China and the Philippines were predominantly single males. As a result of racial prejudice that culminated in the passage of anti-miscegenation laws directed primarily against people of color in many western and southwestern states, the majority of these earlier Asian immigrants remained unmarried. The lack of family

life caused unattached immigrants to depend on one another, creating an apparent great solidarity among people of the same ethnic group. Many of the earlier studies of Chinese and Filipino communities depicted themes of social isolation and loneliness, which did not apply to the Japanese community. A well-known portrayal of the extreme social isolation of Chinese laundrymen in Chicago was published by Paul Siu (1952) only as a paper entitled "The Sojourner." Although Siu's work was written under the direction of Robert E. Park and Ernest W. Burgess, it was not included in the Chicago School sociological series published by the University of Chicago Press. Thus, a major piece of Asian-American research, *The Chinese Laundryman: A Study in Social Isolation* (Siu 1987), remained unpublished until after the author's death.

The existence of single-gender communities of Filipinos and Chinese is clearly demonstrated in the U.S. censuses between 1860 and 1970. In 1860, the sex ratio for Chinese was 1,858 men for every 100 women. By 1890, following the peak of Chinese immigration during the previous decade, the ratio was 2,678 males for every 100 females—the highest recorded. Sex ratios for the Chinese population later declined steadily as the result of legislative revisions in 1930 (46 U.S. Stat. 581) and 1931 (46 U.S. Stat. 1511) that enabled women from China to enter the United States.

A second factor that helped to balance the sex ratio in the Chinese community, particularly among the younger age cohorts, was the presence of an American-born generation. In 1900, U.S.-born persons constituted only 10 percent of the Chinese-American population. By 1970, the figure was 53 percent. Nevertheless, in the 1980 census, the sex ratio remained high for some age groups within certain Asian-American subpopulations; among Filipinos, for example, the highest sex ratio was found in those sixty-five and older.

The demographic characteristics of Japanese-Americans present yet another unusual feature. Under the "Gentlemen's Agreement" between Japan and the United States, Japanese women were allowed to land on the West Coast to join their men even though the immigration of male laborers was curtailed. The majority of the women came as picture brides (Glenn 1986, pp. 31–35) within a narrow span of time. Thus, the years following 1910 were the decade of family building for the first (*issei*) generation of Japanese-Americans. Since almost all issei were young and their brides were chosen from a cohort of marriageable applicants of about the same age, it was not surprising that issei began their families at about the same time after marriage. The historical accident of controlled migration of brides resulted in a uniform age cohort of the second-generation Japanese Americans (*nisei*). The relatively homogeneous age group of the nisei generation meant that their children, the third generation (known as *sansei*), were also of about the same age. The fourth generation followed the same pattern. The amazingly nonoverlapping age and generational cohorts among Japanese-Americans is not known to have had parallels in other population groups.

Third, while Asian-Americans in general continue to grow in number as a result of new immigration, the size of the Japanese-American population increases primarily by the addition of new generations of U.S.-born babies. It is generally believed that offspring of Japanese women who marry Caucasians have lost their Japanese identity, even though there are no estimates of the impact of intermarriages upon the shrinkage of the Japanese-American community. Given the fact that Japanese immigrants had lower fertility rates than women in Japan during the period prior to and shortly after World War II, and that the number of new immigrants since the war has remained small, Japanese-American communities have larger percentages of older people than do other ethnic minority populations, including other Asian-Americans. In short, Japanese-Americans will be a much smaller ethnic minority in the future. The plurality ranking for all Asian groups placed the Japanese at the top of the list in 1970; they dropped to third place in 1980, are expected to place fourth in 1990, and to be ranked last by 2000.

One more demographic fact is worthy of note. Hawaii and the West Coast states continue to draw large numbers of new immigrants from Asia. Through a process known as chain migration, relatives are likely to follow the immigrants soon after their arrival. This leads to sudden increases in population within the ethnic enclaves. The post-1965 pattern of population growth in many Chinatowns, for instance, is an example of the renewal and revitalization of ethnic communities —which prior to 1965, were experiencing a decline—as are the formation and expansion of Koreantowns and Filipinotowns. Moreover, the settlement of post-1965 immigrants from Asia is more dispersed than that of the earlier groups, owing to the fact that the need for professional and skilled manpower is widely distributed throughout the country. The emergence of Thai, Malaysian, and Vietnamese communities in major metropolitan areas has added a new dimension to the ethnic composition of Asian-Americans.

Two separate chains of immigration resulted from the new immigration legislation of 1965. One chain, largely found in Chinese and Filipino communities, is kin-selective in that the process of settlement follows the family ties of earlier immigrants. The other process is occupation-selective, based on skills and professional qualifications. These two processes created significantly different immigrant populations, with clearly discerned bimodal distributions of status characteristics. It is therefore common to find recent immigrants from Asia among the high-income groups as well as among the families living below the poverty level; some find their homes in the ethnic enclaves of central cities while others live in posh suburban communities. Any attempt to describe Asian-Americans by using average measures of social status characteristics, such as income, education, and occupation, can produce a distorted profile that fits no particular group except in the combined abstractions of a myth that is of little use to either researchers or planners. A more useful description would be the use of standard errors— to show the polarities or deviations of the immigrant group from the norm of the majority.

In short, the sociodemographic and socioeconomic characteristics of all Asian-American communities since 1850 have been greatly influenced by federal immigration legislation. It is impossible to have a clear grasp of the structure and change of Asian-American communities without an understanding of the history of immigration legislation.

## ASIAN-AMERICAN RESEARCH

Asian-American research may be divided into five periods: (1) the early period before World War II, which was influenced by the Chicago School of thought; (2) the World War II period, which saw a preponderance of Japanese-American studies; (3) the postwar era, with a strong emphasis on culture and personality studies; (4) a shift toward "ethnic studies" as a result of the civil-rights movement; (5) the emergence of a new generation of Asian-American studies in the 1980s.

**The Early Period.** The pioneer sociological studies on the assimilation of immigrants in American urban communities may be attributed to the work of Robert E. Park. Although Park had done little empirical investigation, he had supervised a large number of graduate students and had formulated what was known as the theory of race cycle, which stressed the unidirectional process of competition, accommodation, and assimilation as the basis of race relations in urban America. Park later led a group of researchers to study Chinese and Japanese communities on the Pacific Coast. The results failed to prove the race-cycle theory. In defending his theory, according to Lyman (1977, p. 4), Park employed the Aristotelian doctrine of "obstacles," which suggests that among Chinese and Japanese the assimilation progress in the hypothesized direction was delayed.

Early published sociological research on Asian-Americans included the works of Bogardus (1928, 1930), who attempted to delineate degrees of prejudice against minorities in terms of social distance. There were special topics such as "Oriental crime" in California (Beach 1932); school achievement of Japanese-American children (Bell 1935); and anti-Asian sentiments (Sandmeyer 1939; Ichihashi 1932). A noted pioneer community study of Japanese-Americans conducted by Frank Miyamoto (1939) in Seattle in the late 1930s paved the way for the long and significant

bibliography on Japanese-American studies that followed.

Perhaps the most significant and ambitious piece of work during the prewar era was the study of the social isolation of Chinese immigrants, which took more than a decade to complete. The author, Paul Siu, lived and observed, in extreme poverty, the life of Chinese laundrymen. The product of his research endeavors offers a classic text in the study of "unmeltable" immigrants, from which new sociological concepts were developed (Siu 1952, 1987).

**World War II and Japanese-American Studies.** Large-scale systematic studies on Asian-Americans began shortly after the Japanese attack on Pearl Harbor, when the United States declared war on Japan. The U.S. government stripped Japanese-Americans of their property, relocated them, and housed them in internment camps for several years. Alexander Leighton, a psychiatrist, recruited nisei social-science graduates to assist in his work in the camps, monitoring the morale and loyalty of internees; this perhaps was the pioneer work in assessing their group cohesion and structure. A few of Leighton's nisei assistants completed their doctoral studies after the war, maintaining a close and affectionate relationship with him. All had made their own contributions as social scientists and as Asian-American specialists. Leighton's work on the internment of these civilians (both citizens and noncitizens) resulted in the publication of a classic text on loyalty (Leighton 1945).

Careful documentation of the situation was made by Thomas and Nishimoto (1946), Thomas (1952), and Broom and Kitsuse (1955). U.S. home front conditions had sparked an area of development in social-science research, and it had increased the general knowledge base on Japanese-Americans, including their families, their communities, and their sacrifices and contributions during a time of trial.

**Culture and Personality Studies in the Postwar Era.** During World War II, the U.S. government had the reason and the opportunity to question the suitability of Asians as American citizens in regard to loyalty and civic responsibilities. It was also a time to test the myth that Asian immigrants could not assimilate into American society. Social scientists were intrigued by the way culture shapes the personality. Ruth Benedict's classic work on the Japanese personality and society (Benedict 1946) opened a new vista for research. A cohort of young scholars at the University of Chicago, which included Japanese-American graduate students, became known for their pioneer work in studying Japanese behavioral patterns. It had a profound effect on a generation of interested social scientists and resulted in the publication of many classic works in culture and personality (Caudill 1952; Jacobson and Rainwater 1953; Caudill and DeVos 1956; DeVos 1955; Kitano 1961, 1962, 1964; Caudill and Scarr, 1961; Babcock and Caudill 1958; Meredith 1966; and Vogel 1961). Similar studies on other Asian-American groups are conspicuously absent.

**Ethnic Studies and the Civil-Rights Movement.** In the 1960s, the civil-rights movement, sparked by the death of Martin Luther King, Jr., led, perhaps indirectly, to the passage of an unprecedented immigration-legislation reform. At the time there existed among Asian-Americans a collective search for identity that shared many of the goals and rhetoric of the black movement on the Pacific Coast, principally in California. Research into ethnic (Asian) U.S. communities had added two dimensions. The first was the need to raise consciousness as a part of the social movement. Personal testimonials of experiences as members of an oppressed minority provided insight into the psychology of ethnic minorities. The cathartic as well as the cathectic quality in much of the writings of the postwar era reflected the mood of the period and was perhaps necessary in the absence of an appropriate theoretical model, with empirical data, to argue against the assimilation model in standard texts on racial and ethnic studies. Second, consistent with the radical theme, was the apparent influence of Marxian views on race and ethnic relations, which posited that African-American and other minorities are victims of oppression in a capitalist society.

Expectedly, the civil-rights movement began a renewed interest in research on the experiences of

the earliest Asian-Americans. With time the titles ranged from well-documented academic publication to insightful popular readings for the lay public (Chen 1980; Daniels 1988; Choy 1979; Ichioka 1988; Miller 1969; Nee and de Bary 1973; Saxton 1971; Sung 1971; Takaki 1989; Wilson and Hosokawa 1980).

Asian-American studies was established as an academic discipline at a time when there were only a few major publications as sources of information for undergraduates (see Kitano 1961–1976; Lyman 1974; Petersen 1971). The birth of the specialty was marked by the conspicuous absence of available materials, particularly on Filipinos, Koreans, Vietnamese, and the peoples of India. In response to this void, the Asian-American Studies Center at the University of California at Los Angeles published two collection of papers (*Roots* and *Counterpoint*) and a quarterly journal, *The Amerasian*. On the Atlantic Coast, a group of U.S.-born professionals published an intellectual nonacademic monthly, *The Bridge,* for nearly a decade. For more than a decade, these publications were popular reading materials for college students interested in Asian-American studies.

## NEW GENERATION OF ASIAN-AMERICAN STUDIES AND RESEARCH

Stanley Lyman is generally acknowledged as a pioneer in Asian-American research at the University of California, Berkeley. Through his numerous papers and books, he has demonstrated a combination of theoretical relevance and historical insight into the origin and growth of Asian-American communities, especially those of the Chinese and Japanese. As a social historian, he based his research, by and large, on archival documents (see Lyman 1970b).

In the 1980s, some well-trained sociologists began to emerge, many of them foreign-born and foreign-educated—the "first-generation new immigrants"—scholars who pursued advanced degrees in the United States. Arriving at a time when the United States as a whole had become sensitive to diverse cultures, the new Asian-American researchers are increasingly vocal, questioning traditional sociological theories and concepts based on studies of European-based cultures. Their studies of Asian-American communities have added much to a field that had been underserved by the social sciences. Similarly, they have even questioned neutral and descriptive federal statistics on Asian and Pacific Islander populations, both in terms of inadequate sample design and in terms of their culturally biased instrument design.

Members of the new generation of researchers generally work on specific topical areas that previously had not been systematically scrutinized. The works of Bonacich (1972, 1978, 1980) and her associates (Bonacich, Light, and Wong 1976; Bonacich and Modell 1980) have concentrated on the theory of the split labor market and Asian-American—particularly Korean immigrant—small business in America. Light has begun to build an impressive series of research works on Asian-American small businesses (Light 1972; Light and Wong 1975). Korean communities have become the favorite subject for many publications that have contributed significantly to the literature on new immigrant communities and urban America (S.D. Kim 1975; Hurh and Kim 1984; Kim, Kim, and Hurh 1981; Ilsoo Kim 1981; Yu 1977).

However, a lack of statistics remains a major problem in Asian-American studies. Whereas estimates of the social and economic characteristics of white, African-American, and other groups may be obtained from Current Population Surveys and other special surveys, as well as from the U.S. Bureau of the Census, the only useful and comprehensive source materials for Asian-Americans are census data. However, such information is available for only three major Asian groups from 1940 through 1970 (Chinese, Japanese, Filipino). In 1980, for the first time, the census provided separate counts for three other major Asian groups: Koreans, Asian Indians, and Vietnamese. Through special publications, the Census Bureau has provided excellent data on the socioeconomic status and social mobility of Asian-Americans (Gardner, Robey, and Smith 1985; Hirschman and Wong 1984; Wong 1982), but by and large the

information is rather limited; and it is not always possible to disaggregate the different Asian subgroups from the generic category "Asian-Americans."

The use of averages to represent the social and economic characteristics of diverse groups of Asians in the United States, or the reliance on data from a few older immigrant groups of Asians (such as Japanese, Chinese, and Filipinos) to represent all Asian-Americans, masks the significantly different levels of social attainment experienced by subgroups of Asian-Americans, thereby furthering the myth, popularized in the 1970s, that Asians are a "model minority."

During the 1980s, a number of studies began to counter the myth of Asians as a model minority; they cover a wide spectrum of specific topics that had not been previously published. These include the achievement of Asian-Americans in school (Hsia 1988; Stevenson, Lee, and Stigler 1986; Stevenson et al. 1985; Vernon 1982); health statistics and mental-health issues (Sue and Morishima 1982; Yu et al. 1987, 1989; Liu and Yu 1985, 1986a, 1986b; Liu et al. 1990); families and kinship (Glenn 1986; Liu et al. 1988; Liu 1987; Li 1977; Fernandez and Liu 1988); political participation (Jo 1979); religion (Kim, Kim, and Hurh 1978; Cho 1979); and business and income (Zhou and Logan 1989; Chiswick 1978, 1980).

Though rigorous and systematic studies on Asian America are still in their infancy, a solid beginning was launched in the late 1980s. Asian America as field of academic study and as a research topic became a new section of the American Sociological Association, with more than 300 members in 1990. Nearly all major universities on the Pacific Coast have established Asian-American Studies programs, and new Pacific or Asian Centers have been set up on the East Coast. In addition, many academic programs on Asian-Americans are available as part of broader and undifferentiated ethnic-studies programs throughout the country.

(SEE ALSO: *Discrimination; Race*)

# REFERENCES

Babcock, Charlotte E., and William Caudill 1958 "Personal and Cultural Factors in Treating a Nisei Man." In Georgene Seward, ed., *Social Studies in Culture Conflict*. New York: Ronald Press.

Barth, Gunther 1964 *Bitter Strength: A History of the Chinese in the United States, 1850–1870*. Cambridge, Mass.: Harvard University Press.

Beach, W. C. 1932 *Oriental Crime in California*. Stanford, Calif.: Stanford University Press.

Bell, Richard 1935 *Public School Education of Second Generation Japanese in California*. Stanford, Calif.: Stanford University Press.

Benedict, Ruth 1946 *The Chrysanthemum and the Sword*. Boston: Houghton Mifflin.

Bogardus, Emory S. 1928 *Immigration and Race Attitudes*. Boston: D. C. Heath.

———1930 "A Race Relations Cycle." *American Journal of Sociology* 35.

———1949 "Cultural Pluralism and Acculturation." *Sociolinguistics and Sociology* 34.

Bonacich, Edna 1972 "A Theory of Ethnic Antagonism: The Split Labor Market." *American Sociological Review* 37:549–559.

———1978 "U.S. Capitalism and Korean Immigrant Small Business." Paper read at the Ninth World Congress of Sociology, Uppsala, Sweden, August 14–19.

———1980 "Small Business and Japanese American Ethnic Solidarity." In R. Endo, S. Sue, and N. Wagner, eds., *Asian Americans: Social and Psychological Perspectives*, vol. 2. Palo Alto, Calif.: Science & Behavior Books.

———, Ivan Light, and Charles C. Wong 1976 "Korean Immigrant Small Business in Los Angeles." In R. S. Bryce-Laporte, ed., *Sourcebook on New Immigration*. New Brunswick, N.J.: Transaction Books.

———, and John Modell 1980 *The Economic Base of Ethnic Solidarity: Small Business in the Japanese American Community*. Berkeley: University of California Press.

Broom, Leonard, and John Kitsuse 1956 *The Managed Casualty*. Berkeley: University of California Press.

Brunhouse, Robert L. 1940 "Lascars in Pennsylvania." *Pennsylvania History* 7.

Caudill, William 1952 "Japanese-American Personality & Acculturation." *Genetic Psychology Monographs*.

———, and G. DeVos 1956 "Achievement, Culture, and Personality: The Case of Japanese Americans." *American Anthropologist* 58:1107.

———, and Harry A. Scarr 1961 "Japanese Value Orientations and Cultural Change." *Ethnology* 1:53–91.

Chen, Jack 1980 *The Chinese of America*. New York: Harper and Row.

Chiswick, B. R. 1978 "The Effect of Americanization on the Earnings of Foreign Born Men." *Journal of Population Economy* 86:891–921.

———1980 "Immigrant Earnings Patterns by Sex, Race and Ethnic Groupings." *Monthly Labor Review* pp. 22–25.

Cho, Pill Jay 1979 "The Korean Church in America: A Dahrendorf Model." Paper read at the Asian American Sociological Meeting, Boston, August 28.

Choy, Bong Youn 1979 *Koreans in America*. Chicago: Nelson-Hall.

Daniels, Roger 1962 *The Politics of Prejudice: The Anti-Japanese Movement in California and the Struggle for Japanese Exclusion*. Berkeley: University of California Press.

———1988 *Asian America: Chinese and Japanese in the United States Since 1850*. Seattle: University of Washington Press.

DeVos, George 1955 "A Quantitative Rorschach Assessment of Maladjustment and Rigidity in Acculturating Japanese Americans." *Genetic Psychology Monographs*.

Gardner, R. W., B. Robey, and P. C. Smith 1985 *Asian Americans: Growth, Change and Diversity*. Washington, D.C.: The Population Reference Bureau.

Glenn, Evelyn Nakano 1986 *Issei, Nisei, War Bride*. Philadelphia: Temple University Press.

Hirschman, C., and M. G. Wong 1984 "Socioeconomic Gains of Asian Americans, Blacks and Hispanics: 1960–1976." *American Journal of Sociology* 90:584–607.

Hsia, Jayjia 1988 *Asian Americans in Higher Education and at Work*. Hillsdale, N.J.: Lawrence Erlbaum Associates.

Hurh, Won Moo, and Kwang Chung Kim 1984 *Korean Immigrants in America*. Teaneck, N.J.: Fairleigh Dickinson University Press.

Ichihashi, Y. 1932 *Japanese in the United States*. Stanford, Calif.: Stanford University Press.

Ichioka, Yuji 1988 *The Issei*. New York: The Free Press.

Jacobson, Alan, and Lee Rainwater 1953 "A Study of Management Representative Evaluations of Nisei Workers." *Social Forces* 32:35–41

Kim, David S., and Charles C. Wong 1977 "Business Development in Koreatown, Los Angeles." In Hyung-chan Kim, ed., *The Korean Diaspora.* Santa Barbara, Calif.: ABC-Clio.

Kim, Ilsoo 1981 *New Urban Immigrants: The Korean Community in New York.* Princeton, N.J.: Princeton University Press.

Kim, K. C., H. C. Kim, and W. M. Hurh 1981 "Job Information Deprivation in the United States: A Case Study of Korean Immigrants." *Ethnicity* 8:219–232.

Kim, S. D. 1975 "Findings of National Inquiries on Asian Women of U.S. Servicemen." Paper read at the Methodist Conference, Tacoma, Washington, March 20–21.

Kitano, Harry H. L. 1961 "Differential Child-Rearing Attitudes Between First and Second Generation Japanese in the U.S." *Journal of Social Psychology* 53:13–19.

———1962 "Changing Achievement Patterns of the Japanese in the United States." *Journal of Social Psychology* 58:257–264.

———1964 "Inter-generational Differences in Maternal Attitudes Towards Child-Rearing." *Journal of Social Psychology* 63:215–220.

———1976 *Japanese Americans: The Evolution of a Subculture.* Englewood Cliffs, N.J.: Prentice-Hall.

Lee, Rose Hum 1949 "The Decline of Chinatowns in the United States." *American Journal of Sociology.*

——— 1960 *The Chinese in the United States of America.* Hong Kong: Hong Kong University Press.

Leighton, Alexander 1945 *The Governing of Men.* Princeton, N.J.: Princeton University Press.

Li, Peter 1977 "Fictive Kinship, Conjugal Ties, and Kinship Chain Among Chinese Immigrants in the United States." *Journal of Comparative Family Studies* 8:47–63.

Light, Ivan H. 1972 *Ethnic Enterprise in America.* Berkeley: University of California Press.

———, and C. C. Wong 1975 "Protest or Work." *American Journal of Sociology* 80:1342–1368.

Liu, William T., and Elena Yu 1985 "Ethnicity and Mental Health: An Overview," In L. Maldonaldo and J. Moore, eds., *Urban Ethnicity in U.S.: New Immigrants and Old Minorities.* Beverly Hills, Calif.: Sage.

——— 1986a "Asian/Pacific American Elderly: Mortality Differentials, Health Status, and Use of Health Services." *Journal of Applied Gerontology* 4:35–64.

——— 1986b "Health Services for Asian Elderly." *Research on Aging* 8:156–183.

———, Elena Yu, C. F. Chang, and M. Fernandez 1990 "The Mental Health of Asian American Teenagers." In A. R. Stiffman and L. E. Davis, eds., *Ethnic Issues in Adolescent Mental Health.* Newbury Park, Calif.: Sage.

Lyman, Stanford 1961 "The Structure of Chinese Society in Nineteenth Century America." Ph.D. diss., University of California, Berkeley.

——— 1964 "The Chinese Secret Societies in the Occident: Notes and Suggestions for Research in the Sociology of Secrecy." *Canadian Review of Sociology and Anthropology* 1:2.

——— 1968 "Contrasts in the Community Organization of Chinese and Japanese in North America." *Canadian Review of Sociology and Anthropology* 5:2.

——— 1970a *Asians in the West.* Reno: University of Nevada Press.

——— 1970b *The Asian in North America.* Santa Barbara, Calif.: ABC-Clio.

——— 1974a "Conflict and the Web of Group Affiliation in San Francisco's Chinatown, 1850–1910." *Pacific Historical Review* 43:4.

——— 1974b *Chinese Americans.* New York: Random House.

——— 1977 *The Asian in North America.* Santa Barbara, Calif.: ABC-Clio.

Meredith, Gerald M. 1966 "Amae and Acculturation Among Japanese College Students in Hawaii." *Journal of Social Psychology* 68:171–180.

Miller, Stuart Creighton 1969 *The Unwelcome Immigrant: The American Image of the Chinese, 1775–1882.* Berkeley: University of California Press.

Miyamoto, Frank 1939 "Social Solidarity Among the Japanese in Seattle." *University of Washington Publications in the Social Sciences* 11(2):57–130.

Nee, Victor G., and Brett de Bary 1973 *Longtime Californ: A Documentary Study of an American Chinatown.* New York: Pantheon.

Petersen, William 1971 *Japanese Americans.* New York: Random House.

Reimers, David M. 1985 *Still the Golden Door.* New York: Columbia University Press.

Sandmeyer, Elmer C. 1939 *The Anti-Chinese Movement in California.* Urbana: University of Illinois Press.

Saxton, Alexander 1971 *The Indispensable Enemy: Labor and Anti-Chinese Movement in California.* Berkeley: University of California Press.

Siu, Paul C. P. 1952 "The Sojourner." *American Journal of Sociology.*

———1987 *The Chinese Laundryman: A Study in Social Isolation.* New York: New York University Press.

Stevenson, H. W., S. Y. Lee, and J. W. Stigler 1986 "Mathematics Achievement of Chinese, Japanese and American Children." *Science* 231:693–699.

Stevenson, H. W., et al. 1985 "Cognitive Performance and Academic Achievement of Japanese, Chinese, and American Children." *Child Development* 56: 718–734.

Sue, Stanley, and James Morishima 1982 *The Mental Health of Asian Americans.* San Francisco: Jossey-Bass.

Sung, Betty Lee 1971 *The Story of the Chinese in America.* New York: Collier Books.

Takaki, Ronald 1989 *Strangers from a Different Shore: A History of Asian Americans.* Boston: Little, Brown.

Thomas, Dorothy S. 1952 *The Salvage.* Berkeley: University of California Press.

———, and R. Nishimoto 1946 *The Spoilage.* Berkeley: University of California Press.

Vernon, P. E. 1982 *The Abilities and Achievements of Orientals in North America.* New York: Academic Press.

Vogel, Ezra 1961 "The Go-between in a Developing Society: The Case of the Japanese Marriage Arranger." *Human Organization* 20:112–120.

Wilson, Robert A., and Bill Hosokawa 1980 *East to America: A History of the Japanese in the U.S.* New York: William Morrow.

Wong, Morrison 1982 "The Cost of Being Chinese, Japanese and Filipino in the United States, 1960, 1970, 1976." *Pacific Sociological Review* 25:59–78.

Yu, Elena, and William T. Liu 1987 "The Underutilization of Mental Health Services by Asian Americans: Implication for Manpower Training." In W. T. Liu, ed., *A Decade Review of Mental Health Research, Training, and Services.* Chicago: University of Illinois Press.

Yu, Elena, et al. 1987 "Measurement of Depression in a Chinatown Clinic." In W. T. Liu, ed., *A Decade Review of Mental Health Research, Training, and Services.* Chicago: University of Illinois Press.

———1989 "Suicide Prevention and Intervention Among Asian Youths." In ADAMHA, *Report of the Secretary's Task Force on Youth Suicide,* vol. 3. DHHS Publication no. (ADM)89-1623. Washington, D.C.: U.S. Government Printing Office.

Yu, Eui-Yong 1977 "Koreans in America." *Amerasia Journal* 4:117–131.

Zhou, Min, and John R. Logan 1989 "Returns on Human Capital in Ethnic Enclaves: New York City's Chinatown." *American Sociological Review* 54:809–820.

WILLIAM T. LIU
ELENA S. H. YU

**ASSIMILATION**   *See* Ethnicity.

**ATHEISM**   *See* Religious Orientations.

**ATTITUDES**   *Attitude* "is probably the most distinctive and indispensable concept in contemporary American social psychology" (Allport 1985, p. 35). Hundreds of books and thousands of articles have been published on the topic. A brief review of this literature may be found in McGuire (1985). Despite this popularity, there is considerable disagreement about such basics as terminology. Several terms are frequently used as synonyms for attitude, including *opinion* and *belief.* Contemporary writers often distinguish attitudes from *cognitions,* which is broader and includes attitudes as well as perceptions of one's environment. Most analysts distinguish attitude from *value,* the latter referring to a person's ultimate concerns or preferred modes of conduct.

An attitude is a learned predisposition to respond to a particular object in a generally favorable or unfavorable way. Every attitude is about an object, and the object may be a person, product, idea, or event. Each attitude has three components: (1) a belief, (2) a favorable or unfavorable evaluation, and (3) a behavioral disposition. This definition is used by most contemporary writers. However, a minority define attitude as consisting only of the positive or negative evaluation of an object.

A *stereotype* is one type of attitude. Originally, the term referred to a rigid and simplistic "picture in the head." In current usage, a stereotype is a belief about the characteristics of members of some specified social group. A stereotype may be positive (Asian-Americans are good at math) or negative (women are bad at math). Most stereotypes are resistant to change.

Attitudes link the person to other individuals, groups, and social organizations and institutions. Each person has literally hundreds of attitudes, one for each significant object in the person's physical and social environment. By implication, the individual's attitudes should reflect his or her location in society. Thus, attitudes are influenced by gender, race, religion, education, and social class. Considerable research on the relationship between social position and attitudes has been carried out; this literature is reviewed by Kiecolt (1988).

## ATTITUDE FORMATION

Many attitudes are learned through direct experience with the object. Attitudes toward one's school, job, church, and the groups to which one belongs are examples. Attitudes toward the significant persons in one's life are also learned in this way. More often, attitudes are learned through interactions with others. Socialization by parents, explicit teaching in educational and religious settings, and interactions with friends are important sources of attitudes. Research shows that children's attitudes toward a variety of objects, including gender roles and political issues, are similar to those held by their parents.

Another source of attitudes is the person's observations of the world. A topic of substantial interest since the early 1970s has been the impact of mass media on the attitudes (and behavior) of users. A thorough review of the literature on this topic (Roberts and Maccoby 1985) concludes that television viewing affects both children's and adolescents' attitudes about gender roles. Further, the viewing of programs intentionally designed to teach positive attitudes toward racial or ethnic minorities does increase children's acceptance of such persons. With regard to adults, evidence supports the "agenda setting" hypothesis; the amount and quality of coverage by the media (press, radio, and television) of an issue influences the public's perception of the importance of that issue.

Stereotypes are also learned. A stereotype may arise out of direct experience with a member of the stereotyped group. A person who knows a musically talented black may create a stereotype by overgeneralizing, inferring that all African-Americans are gifted musically. More often, however, stereotypes are learned from those with whom we interact. Other stereotypes may be acquired from books, television, or film. Research indicates that television programming portrays women, the elderly, and members of some ethnic minorities in negative ways and that these portrayals create (or reinforce) misperceptions and negative stereotypes in viewers (McGuire 1985).

Social institutions influence the attitudes one learns in several ways. Adults' ties to particular ethnic, religious, and other institutions influence the attitudes they teach their children. The instruction given in schools reflects the perspectives of the dominant political and economic institutions in society. The amount and quality of media coverage of people and events reflects the interests of particular groups in society. Through these mechanisms, the individual's attitudes reflect the society, institutions, and groups of which she or he is a member.

Each attitude fulfills one or more of four functions for the individual. First, some attitudes serve an instrumental function: An individual develops favorable attitudes toward objects that aid or reward the individual and unfavorable attitudes toward objects that thwart or punish the individual. For example, a person who earns a large salary will have a positive attitude toward the job. Second, attitudes often serve a knowledge function. They provide the person with a meaningful and structured environment. Third, some attitudes express the individual's basic values and reinforce self-image. Whites' attitudes toward black Americans reflect the importance that whites place on the values of freedom and equality. Fourth, some attitudes protect the person from recognizing certain thoughts or feelings that threaten his or her self-image or adjustment.

## ATTITUDE MEASUREMENT

Because attitudes are mental states, they cannot be directly observed. Social scientists have developed a variety of methods for measuring attitudes, some direct and some indirect.

**Direct Methods.** These methods involve asking the person questions and recording the answers. Direct methods include various rating scales and several sophisticated scaling techniques.

The three most frequently used rating scales involve a single item, Likert scales, and the semantic differential. The *single-item scale* usually consists of a direct positive or negative statement about the object, and the respondent indicates whether he or she agrees, disagrees, or is unsure. Such a measure is easy to score, but it is not precise. A *Likert scale* typically involves several statements, and the respondent is asked to indicate the degree to which she or he agrees or disagrees with each. By analyzing differences in the pattern of responses across respondents, the investigator can order individuals from greatest agreement to greatest disagreement. Whereas Likert scales assess the denotative (literal) meaning of an object to a respondent, the *semantic differential* technique assesses the connotative (personal) meaning of the object. Here, an investigator presents the respondent with a series of bipolar adjective scales. Each of these is a scale whose poles are two adjectives having opposite meanings, for example, good–bad, exciting–boring. The respondent rates the attitude object, such as "my job," on each scale. After the data are collected, the researcher can analyze them by various statistical techniques.

A variety of more sophisticated scaling techniques have been developed. These typically involve asking a series of questions about a class of objects, for example, occupations, crimes, or political figures, and then applying various statistical techniques to arrive at a summary measure. These include magnitude techniques (e.g., the Thurstone scale), interlocking techniques (e.g., the Guttman scale), proximity techniques (e.g., small-est space analysis), and the unfolding technique developed by Coombs. None of these has been widely used.

**Indirect Methods.** Direct methods assume that people will report honestly their attitudes toward the object of interest. But when questions deal with sensitive issues, such as attitudes toward members of minority groups or abortion, respondents may not report accurately. In an attempt to avoid such reactivity, investigators have developed various indirect methods.

Some methods involve keeping respondents unaware of what is being measured. The "lost letter" technique involves dropping letters in public areas and observing the behavior of the person who finds it. The researcher can measure attitudes toward abortion by addressing one-half of the letters to a prochoice group and the other half to an antiabortion group. If a greater percentage of letters to the latter group are returned, it suggests people have antiabortion attitudes. Another indirect measure of attitude is pupil dilation, which increases when the person observes an object she or he likes and decreases when the object is disliked.

Some indirect measures involve deceiving respondents. A person may be asked to sort a large number of statements into groups, and the individual's attitude may be inferred from the number or type of categories used. Similarly, a respondent may be asked to write statements characterizing other people's beliefs on an issue, and the content and extremity of the respondent's statements are used to measure his or her own attitude. A third technique is the "bogus pipeline." This involves attaching the person with electrodes to a device and telling the person that the device measures his or her true feelings. The respondent is told that some signal, such as a blinking light, pointer, or buzzer, will indicate the person's real attitude, then the person is asked direct questions.

While these techniques may reduce inaccurate reporting, some of them yield measures whose meaning is not obvious or is of questionable validity. Does mailing a letter reflect one's attitude toward the addressee or the desire to help? There is also evidence that measures based on these techniques are not reliable. Finally, some researchers believe it is unethical to use the techniques that involve deception. Because of the importance of obtaining reliable and valid measures, research has been carried out on how to ask questions about sensitive issues. This research is reviewed by DeLamater (1982). Sudman and Bradburn (1983) provide guidelines for constructing and asking such questions.

For a comprehensive discussion of attitude measurement techniques and issues, see Dawes and Smith (1985).

## ATTITUDE ORGANIZATION AND CHANGE

An individual's attitude toward some object usually is not an isolated psychological unit. It is embedded in a cognitive structure and linked with a variety of other attitudes. Several theories of attitude organization are based on the assumption that individuals prefer consistency among the elements of cognitive structure, that is, among attitudes and perceptions. Two of these are balance theory and dissonance theory.

**Balance Theory.** Balance theory, developed by Heider, is concerned with cognitive systems composed of two or three elements. The elements can be either persons or objects. Consider the statement "I will vote for Mary Sweeney; she supports parental leave legislation." This system contains three elements—the speaker, P; another person (candidate Mary Sweeney), O; and an impersonal object (parental leave legislation), X. According to balance theory, two types of relationships may exist between elements. *Sentiment relations* refer to sentiments or evaluations directed toward objects and people; a sentiment may be either positive (liking, endorsing) or negative (disliking, opposing). *Unit relations* refer to the extent of perceived association between elements. For example, a positive unit relation may result from ownership, a relationship (such as friendship or marriage), or causality. A negative relation indicates dissociation, like that between ex-spouses or members of groups with opposing interests. A null relation exists when there is no association between elements.

Balance theory is concerned with the elements and their interrelations from P's viewpoint. In the example, the speaker favors parental leave legislation, perceives Mary Sweeney as favoring it, and intends to vote for her. This system is balanced. By definition, a *balanced state* is one in which all three relations are positive or in which one is positive and the other two are negative. An *imbalanced state* is one in which two of the relationships between elements are positive and one is negative or in which all three are negative. For example, "I love (+) Jane; Jane loves (+) opera; I hate (−) opera" is imbalanced.

The theory assumes that an imbalanced state is unpleasant and that when one occurs, the person will try to restore balance. There is considerable empirical evidence that people do prefer balanced states and that attitude change often occurs in response to imbalance. Furthermore, people maintain consistency by responding selectively to new information. There is evidence that people accept information consistent with their existing attitudes and reject information inconsistent with their cognitions. This is the major mechanism by which stereotypes are maintained.

**Dissonance Theory.** Dissonance theory assumes that there are three possible relationships between any two cognitions. Cognitions are consistent, or *consonant,* if one naturally or logically follows from the other; they are *dissonant* when one implies the opposite of the other. The logic involved is psycho logic—logic as it appears to the individual, not logic in a formal sense. Two cognitive elements may also be irrelevant; one may have nothing to do with the other.

*Cognitive dissonance* is a state of psychological tension induced by dissonant relationships between cognitive elements. There are three situations in which dissonance commonly occurs. First, dissonance occurs following a decision whenever the decision is dissonant with some cognitive elements. Thus, choice between two (or more) attractive alternatives creates dissonance because knowledge that one chose A is dissonant with the positive features of B. The magnitude of the dissonance experienced is a function of the proportion of elements consonant and dissonant with the choice. Second, if a person engages in a behavior that is dissonant with his or her attitudes, dissonance will be created. Third, when events disconfirm an important belief, dissonance will be created if the person had taken action based on that belief. For example, a person who buys an expensive car in anticipation of a large salary increase will experience dissonance if she or he does not receive the expected raise.

Since dissonance is an unpleasant state, the theory predicts that the person will attempt to reduce it. Usually, dissonance reduction involves changes in the person's attitudes. Thus, following a decision, the person may evaluate the chosen alternative more favorably and the unchosen one more negatively. Following behavior that is dissonant with his or her prior attitude, the person's attitude toward the behavior may become more positive. An alternative mode of dissonance reduction is to change the importance one places on one or more of the attitudes. Following a decision, the person may reduce the importance of the cognitions that are dissonant with the choice; this is the well-known "sour grapes" phenomenon. Following disconfirmation of a belief, one may increase the importance attached to disconfirmed belief. A third way to reduce dissonance is to change behavior. If the dissonance following a choice is great, the person may decide to choose B instead of A. Following disconfirmation, the person may change behaviors that were based on the belief.

Several books and hundreds of articles about dissonance theory have been published since it was introduced by Festinger in 1957. There is a substantial body of research evidence that supports various predictions from and elaborations of the theory. Taken together, this literature has produced a detailed taxonomy of situations that produce dissonance and of preferred modes of dissonance reduction in various types of situations.

Both balance and dissonance theories identify the desire for consistency as a major source of stability and change in attitudes. The desire to maintain consistency leads the individual either to interpret new information as congruent with his or her existing cognitions (assimilation) or to reject it as not relevant (contrast) if it would challenge existing attitudes. At the same time, the desire for consistency will lead to attitude change when imbalance or dissonance occurs. Dissonance theory explicitly considers the link between behavior and attitudes. It predicts that engaging in counterattitudinal behavior may lead to attitude change. This is one mechanism by which social influences on behavior can indirectly affect attitudes. This mechanism may come into play when the person experiences changes in roles and the requirements of the new role are inconsistent with his or her prior attitudes.

## ATTITUDE–BEHAVIOR RELATION

The attitude–behavior relation has been the focus of considerable research since the early 1970s. This research has identified a number of variables that influence the extent to which one can predict a person's behavior from his or her attitudes.

Some of these variables involve the measurement of the attitude and of the behavior. The correspondence of the two measures is one such variable; one can predict behavior more accurately if the two measures are at the same level of specificity. An opinion poll can predict the outcome of an election because there is high correspondence between the attitude ("Which candidate do you prefer for mayor in next month's election?") and the behavior (voting for a candidate in that election). The length of time between the measure of attitude and the occurrence and measure of the behavior is also an important variable. The shorter the time, the stronger the relationship. The longer the elapsed time, the more likely the person's attitude will change, although some attitudes are stable over long periods, for example, twenty years.

The characteristics of the attitude also influence the degree to which one can predict behavior from it. In order for an attitude to influence behavior, it must be activated, that is, brought from memory into conscious awareness. An attitude is usually activated by a person's exposure to the attitude object. Attitudes vary in *accessibility*, the ease with which they are activated. There is evidence that the more accessible an attitude is, the more likely it is to guide future behavior. Another variable is the source of the attitude. Attitudes based on direct experience with the object are more predictive of behavior.

The attitude–behavior relation is also influenced by situational constraints—the social norms governing behavior in a situation. An attitude is more likely to be expressed in behavior when the behavior is consistent with these norms.

An important attempt to specify the relationship between attitude and behavior is the theory of reasoned action, developed by Fishbein and Ajzen. According to this theory, behavior is determined by behavioral intention. Behavioral intention is determined by two factors, attitude and subjective norm. Attitude is one's beliefs about the likely consequences of the behavior and one's evaluation—positive or negative—of each of those outcomes. Subjective norm is the person's belief about other important persons' or groups' reactions to the behavior and the person's motivation to comply with the expectations of each. One of the strengths of the theory is this precise specification of the influences on behavioral intention. It is possible to measure quantitatively each of the four components (likely consequences, evaluations, likely reactions, motivation to comply) and use these to make precise predictions of behavior. A number of empirical studies from the 1980s report results consistent with such predictions. The theory applies primarily to behavior that is under conscious, volitional control; in some situations, behavior may be determined primarily by habit rather than intention.

## ATTITUDE AS INDICATOR

Increasingly, attitudes are employed as indicators. Some researchers use attitude measures as indicators of concepts, while others study changes in attitudes over time as indicators of social change.

**Indicators of Concepts.** Measures of specific attitudes are frequently used as indicators of more general concepts. For example, agreement with the following statement is interpreted as an indicator of powerlessness: "This world is run by the few people in power, and there is not much the little guy can do about it." Powerlessness is considered to be a general orientation toward the social world and is a sense that one has little or no control over events. Feelings of powerlessness may be related to such varied behaviors as vandalism, not voting in elections, and chronic unemployment.

Attitude measures have been used to assess many other concepts used in the analysis of political attitudes and behavior. These include the liberalism–conservatism dimension, political tolerance (of radical or unpopular groups), trust in or disaffection with national institutions, and relative deprivation. (For a review of this literature, see Kinder and Sears 1985.) Attitude measures are used to assess many other characteristics of persons. In the realm of work these include occupational values, job satisfaction, and leadership style.

A major concern when attitudes are employed as indicators is *construct validity*, that is, whether the specific items used are valid measures of the underlying concept. In the powerlessness example, the connection between the content of the item and the concept may seem obvious, but even in cases like this it is important to demonstrate validity. A variety of analytic techniques may be used, including interitem correlations, factor analysis, and LISREL.

**Indicators of Social Change.** Two methodological developments have made it possible to use attitudes to study social change. The first was the development of probability sampling techniques, which allow the investigator to make inferences about the characteristics of a population from the results obtained by surveying a sample of that population. The second is the use of the same attitude measures in surveys of representative samples at two or more points in time.

A major source of such data is the General Social Survey, an annual survey of a probability sample of adults. The GSS repeats a core set of items on a roughly annual basis, making possible the study of changes over a period of twenty years. Many of these items were drawn directly from earlier surveys, making comparisons over a thirty- or forty-year timespan possible. A recently published book describes these items and presents the responses obtained each time the item was used (Niemi, Mueller, and Smith 1989). Other sources of such data include the National Election Studies and the Gallup Polls.

This use of attitude items reflects a general concern with social change at the societal level (Hill 1981). The investigator uses aggregate measures of attitudes in the population as an index of changes in cultural values and social institutions. Two areas of particular interest are attitudes toward race and gender roles. In both areas, efforts have been made to improve access to educational programs, jobs, and professions, increase wages and salaries, and provide greater opportunity for advancement. The availability of responses to the same attitude items over time allows us to assess the consistency between these social changes and attitudes in the population. Consider the question "Do you think civil rights leaders are trying to push too fast, are going too slowly, or are moving at about the right speed?" This question was asked in surveys of national samples every two years from 1964 to 1976 and in 1980. The percentage of whites replying "Too fast" declined from 74 percent in 1964 to 40 percent in 1980 (Bobo 1988), suggesting increased white support for the black movement. In general, research indicates that both racial and gender-role attitudes became more liberal between 1960 and 1985, and this finding is consistent with the social changes in these areas. Other topics that have been studied include attitudes toward abortion, social class identification, and subjective quality of life.

There are several issues involved in this use of attitude items. The first is the problem of "nonattitudes" (Converse 1970). Respondents may answer survey questions or endorse statements even though they have no attitude toward the object. In fact, when respondents are questioned about fictional objects or organizations, some of them will express an opinion. Schuman and Kalton (1985)

discuss this issue in detail and suggest ways to reduce the extent to which nonattitudes are given by respondents.

The second issue involves the interpretation of responses to items. In the example above, the analyst assumes that white respondents who reply "Too fast" feel threatened by the movement. However, there is evidence that small changes in the wording of survey items can produce substantial changes in aggregate response patterns. This evidence and guidelines for writing survey items are discussed in Schuman and Presser (1981) and Sudman and Bradburn (1983).

Finally, there is the problem of equivalence in meaning over time. In order to make meaningful comparisons across time, the items need to be the same or equivalent. Yet over time the meaning of an item may change. Consider the item "Are you in favor of *desegregation,* strict *segregation,* or something in between?" This question was asked of national samples in 1964 and every two years from 1968 to 1978. From 1964 to 1970, the percentage of white, college-educated adults endorsing desegregation increased; from 1970 to 1978, the percentage decreased steadily. Until 1970, desegregation efforts were focused on the South; after 1970, desegregation efforts focused on school integration in northern cities. Evidence suggests that endorsement of desegregation changed because the meaning of the question for white adults changed (Schuman, Steeh, and Bobo 1985).

(SEE ALSO: *Cognitive Consistency Theories; Measurement; Prejudice; Social Indicators; Social Psychology; Survey Research; Value Theory and Research*)

### REFERENCES

Allport, Gordon W. 1985 "The Historical Background of Social Psychology." In G. Lindzey and E. Aronson, eds., *Handbook of Social Psychology,* 3rd ed. New York: Random House.

Bobo, Lawrence 1988 "Attitudes toward the Black Political Movement: Trends, Meaning, and Effects on Racial Policy Preference." *Social Psychology Quarterly* 51:287–302.

Converse, Philip 1970 "Attitudes and Nonattitudes:

Continuation of a Dialogue." In E.R. Tufte, ed., *The Quantitative Analysis of Social Problems.* Reading, Mass.: Addison-Wesley.

Dawes, Robyn M., and Tom L. Smith 1985 "Attitude and Opinion Measurement." In G. Lindzey and E. Aronson, eds., *Handbook of Social Psychology,* 3rd ed. New York: Random House.

DeLamater, John 1982 "Response-Effects of Question Content." In W. Dijkstra and J. van der Zouwen, eds., *Response Behavior in the Survey-Interview.* London: Academic Press.

Festinger, Leon 1957 *A Theory of Cognitive Dissonance.* Stanford, Calif.: Stanford University Press.

Fishbein, Martin, and Icek Ajzen 1975 *Belief, Attitude, Intention, and Behavior.* Reading, Mass.: Addison-Wesley.

Hill, Richard 1981 "Attitudes and Behavior." In M. Rosenberg and R. H. Turner, eds., *Social Psychology: Sociological Perspectives.* New York: Basic Books.

Kiecolt, K. Jill 1988 "Recent Developments in Attitudes and Social Structure." In W. R. Scott and J. Blake, eds., *Annual Review of Sociology,* Vol. 14. Palo Alto, Calif.: Annual Reviews.

Kinder, Donald R., and David O. Sears 1985 "Public Opinion and Political Action." In G. Lindzey and E. Aronson, eds., *Handbook of Social Psychology,* 3rd ed. New York: Random House.

McGuire, William J. 1985 "Attitudes and Attitude Change." In G. Lindzey and E. Aronson, eds., *Handbook of Social Psychology,* 3rd ed. New York: Random House.

Niemi, Richard G., John Mueller, and Tom W. Smith 1989 *Trends in Public Opinion: A Compendium of Survey Data.* New York: Greenwood Press.

Roberts, Donald F., and Nathan Maccoby 1985 "Effects of Mass Communication." In G. Lindzey and E. Aronson, eds., *Handbook of Social Psychology,* 3rd ed. New York: Random House.

Schuman, Howard, and Graham Kalton 1985 "Survey Methods." In G. Lindzey and E. Aronson, eds., *Handbook of Social Psychology,* 3rd ed. New York: Random House.

Schuman, Howard, and Stanley Presser 1981 *Questions and Answers in Attitude Surveys: Experiments on Question Form, Wording, and Context.* New York: Academic Press.

Schuman, Howard, Charlotte Steeh, and Lawrence Bobo 1985 *Racial Attitudes in America.* Cambridge, Mass.: Harvard University Press.

Sudman, Seymour, and Norman R. Bradburn 1983 *Asking Questions: A Practical Guide to Questionnaire Design.* San Francisco: Jossey-Bass.

JOHN D. DeLAMATER

## ATTRIBUTION THEORY

Attribution is a cognitive process that entails linking an event to its causes. Attribution is one of a variety of cognitive inferences that are included within social cognition, which is one of several theoretical models within social psychology. Social cognition has been the most dominant social psychological perspective from the 1960s up to the present time, and this is particularly evident in the popularity of research on attribution. In the mid-1970s as much as 50 percent of the articles in major journals concerned attributional processes, in part because attribution theory is relevant to the study of person perception, event perception, attitude change, the acquisition of self-knowledge, and a host of applied topics including therapeutic interventions, close relationships, legal and medical decision making, and so forth. Although the proportion of published research that focuses on this topic has declined somewhat during the 1980s, attribution remains one of the most popular fields of social psychological research.

### DEFINITION

An attribution is an inference about why an event occurred. More generally, "attribution is a process that begins with social perception, progresses through causal judgment and social inference, and ends with behavioral consequences" (Crittenden 1983, p. 426). Although most theories of and research on attribution focus on causal inference, empirical research has dealt with attributions not only of cause but also of blame and responsibility. Although these types of attributions are closely related, they are not conceptually identical. Furthermore, because personality characteristics constitute a major category of potential causes of behavior, attributions about individuals' traits (both one's own traits and those of others) have received explicit theoretical attention.

## MAJOR THEORIES OF ATTRIBUTION

Even though attribution has been one of the most popular social psychological research topics of the past two decades, only a few theories of attribution exist. The development of theories of attribution began with Fritz Heider's (1958) original attempt to provide a systematic, conceptual explanation of "naive" psychology. Heider maintained that people strive to understand, predict, and control events in their everyday lives in much the same way as scientists do. On the basis of observation, individuals form theories about their social worlds, and new observations then serve to support, refute, or modify these theories. Because people act on the basis of their beliefs, Heider argued that it is important to understand this naive psychology. Although Heider did not develop an explicit theory of attribution, he did assert several principles that have guided all subsequent theorizing on this topic.

Primary among these principles is the notion that people are inclined to attribute actions to stable or enduring causes rather than to transitory factors. Heider also stressed the importance of distinguishing intentional from unintentional behavior, a distinction that has been particularly influential in theories of the attribution of responsibility. He identified environmental and personal factors as two general classes of factors that produce action and hypothesized that an inverse relationship exists between these two sets of causes. He also suggested that the covariational principle is fundamental to attribution: An effect is attributed to a factor that is present when the effect is present and to a factor that is absent when the effect is absent. Heider's early analyses of social perception represent a general conceptual framework about common-sense, implicit theories people use in understanding events in their daily lives. The two most influential theories of attribution are based on Heider's work but go beyond it in the development of more systematic statements about attributional processes.

**Covariational Model.** Harold Kelley's (1967, 1973) covariational model of attribution addresses the question of whether a given behavior is caused by an actor or, alternatively, by an environmental stimulus with which the actor engages. According to this model, the attribution of cause is based on three types of information: consensus, distinctiveness, and consistency. Consensus refers to the similarity between the actor's behavior and the behavior of other people in similar circumstances. Distinctiveness refers to the generality of the actor's behavior: Does she or he behave in this way toward stimuli in general, or is the behavior specific to this stimulus? Consistency refers to the actor's behavior toward this stimulus across time and modality. There are many possible combinations of these three types of information, but Kelley makes explicit predictions about just three. The combination of high consensus, high distinctiveness, and high consistency supports an attribution to the environmental stimulus, whereas a profile of low consensus, low distinctiveness, and high consistency supports an attribution to the actor. When the behavior is inconsistent, an attribution to circumstances is predicted.

Empirical tests of Kelley's model have focused either on the effects of a particular type of information or, more in keeping with his formulation, on the effects of particular patterns of information (McArthur 1972). In a recent and innovative analysis, Hewstone and Jaspars (1987) proposed a different logic (although one consistent with Kelley's model), suggesting that potential attributors consider whether different causal loci are necessary and sufficient conditions for the occurrence of an effect. They conclude that the notion of causality is flexible and thus assert that there may be some advantage to conceiving of situation-specific notions of causality.

**Correspondent Inference.** The theory of correspondent inference (Jones and Davis 1965; Jones and McGillis 1976) addresses the attribution of personality traits to actors on the basis of their behavior and focuses on attributions about persons in greater depth than does Kelley's covariational model. These two theories thus address different questions. Kelley asks: When do we attribute an event to an actor or to some stimulus in the environment? Jones asks: When do we attribute a trait to an actor on the basis of her or his behavior? The theory of correspondent inference focuses more narrowly on the actor but also yields more information about the actor in that it specifies what it is about the actor that caused the behavior. Jones and his co-authors predict that two factors guide attributions: (1) the attributor's prior expectancies for behavior, specifically, expectancies based either on knowledge of earlier behaviors of the actor (target-based) or on the actor's social category memberships (category-based), and (2) the profile of effects that follow from the behavioral choices available to the actor.

Jones and McGillis propose that expectancies determine the degree of confidence with which a particular trait is attributed; the lower the expectancy of behavior, the more confident the attribution. The profile of effects helps the attributor identify what trait might have produced the behavior in question. Noncommon effects—effects that follow from only one of the behavioral options—provide information about the particular disposition. The fewer the noncommon effects, the clearer the attribution. Thus, behavior that contradicts prior expectancies and a profile of behavioral choices with few noncommon effects combine to maximize the possibility of attributing a disposition to the actor (a correspondent inference). Empirical research generally has supported these predictions.

These two models share some attributional principles. Expectancy variables (target-based and category-based) are analogous to Kelley's types of information. Although the predicted effects of consensus information and its analogue, category-based expectancies, are compatible, the predicted effects of consistency and distinctiveness information and their analogue, target-based expectancies, present some incompatibilities. This contradiction has been evaluated both conceptually and empirically (Howard and Allen 1990).

**Attribution in Achievement Situations.** Bernard Weiner (1974) and his colleagues have applied attributional principles in the context of achievement situations. According to this model, people make inferences about an individual's success or failure on the basis of the actor's ability to do the task in question, how much effort is expended, how difficult the task is, and to what extent luck may have influenced the outcome. Other possible causal factors have since been added to this list. More important perhaps is Weiner's development of, first, a structure of causal dimensions in terms of which these causal factors can be described and, second, the implications of the dimensional standing of a given causal factor (Weiner, Russell, and Lerman 1978). The major causal dimensions are locus (internal or external to the actor), stability (stable or unstable), and controllability or intentionality of the factor. Thus, for example, ability is internal, stable, and uncontrollable. The stability of a causal factor primarily affects judgments about expectancies for future behavior, whereas locus and intentionality primarily affect affective responses to behavior. This model has been used extensively in educational research and has guided therapeutic educational efforts such as attribution retraining.

**Attribution Biases.** The theoretical models described above are based on the assumption that social perceivers follow the dictates of logical or rational models in assessing cause. Empirical research has demonstrated, not surprisingly, that there are systematic patterns in what has been variously conceived of as bias or error in the attribution process (Ross 1977). Prominent among these is what has been called the "fundamental attribution error," the tendency of perceivers to overestimate the role of dispositional factors in shaping behavior and to underestimate the impact of situational factors. One variant of this bias has particular relevance for sociologists. This is the general tendency to make inadequate allowance for the role-based nature of much social behavior. That is, perceivers fail to recognize that behavior often derives from role memberships rather than from individual idiosyncrasy. A second systematic pattern is the actor-observer difference; actors tend to attribute their own behavior to situational factors, whereas observers of the same behavior tend to attribute it to the actor's dispositions. A third pattern concerns what have been called self-serving or egocentric biases, that is, attributions that in some way favor the self.

According to the false consensus bias, for example, we tend to see our own behavioral choices and judgments as relatively common and appropriate, whereas those that differ from ours are perceived as uncommon and deviant. There has been heated debate about whether these biases derive from truly egotistical motives or reflect simple cognitive and perceptual errors.

## METHODOLOGICAL AND MEASUREMENT ISSUES

The prevalent methodologies and measurement strategies within attributional research have been vulnerable to many of the criticisms directed more generally at social cognition and to some directed specifically at attribution. The majority of attributional research has used structured response formats to assess attributions. Heider's original distinction between person and environmental cause has had a major influence on the development of these structured measures. Respondents typically are asked to rate the importance of situational and dispositional causes of events. These ratings have been obtained on ipsative scales as well as on independent rating scales. Ipsative measures pose these causes as two poles on one dimension; thus, an attribution of cause to the actor's disposition is also a statement that situational factors are not causal. This assumed inverse relationship between situational and dispositional causality has been rejected on conceptual and empirical grounds. In more recent studies, therefore, respondents assign each type of causality separately. (Ipsative measures are appropriate for answering some questions, however, such as whether the attribution of cause to one actor comes at the expense of attribution to another actor or to society.) In theory, then, both dispositional and situational variables could be identified as causal factors.

The breadth of these two categories has also been recognized as a problem. Dispositional causes may include a wide variety of factors such as stable traits and attitudes, unstable moods and emotions, and intentional choices. Situational cause is perhaps an even broader category. It is quite possible that these categories are so broad as to render a single measure of each virtually meaningless. Thus, researchers often include both general and more specific, narrower responses as possible choices (e.g., choices of attributing blame to an assailant or to the situation might be refined to the assailant's use of a weapon, physical size, and psychological state on the one hand and the location, time of day, and number of people nearby on the other).

Structured measures of attributions are vulnerable to the criticism that the categories of causes presented to respondents are not those they use in their everyday attributions. Recognizing this limitation, a few researchers have used open-ended measures. Comparative studies of the relative utility of several different types of measures of causal attributions conclude that scale methods perform somewhat better in terms of their inter-test validity and reliability, although open-ended measures are preferable when researchers are exploring causal attributions in new situations.

The great majority of attribution studies use stimuli of highly limited social meaning. Generally, the behavior is represented with a brief written vignette, often just a single sentence. Some researchers have shifted to the presentation of visual stimuli, typically with videotaped rather than real behavioral sequences, in order to ensure comparability across experimental conditions. Recognizing the limitations of brief, noncontextualized stimuli, a few researchers have begun to use a greater variety of more extended stimuli including newspaper reports and published short stories. Most of these stimuli, including the videotaped behavioral sequences, rely heavily on language to convey the meaning of behavior. Conceptual attention has turned recently to how attribution relies on language and to the necessity of considering explicitly what that reliance means.

## WHEN DO WE MAKE ATTRIBUTIONS?

Long after attribution had attained its popularity in social psychology, a question that perhaps should have been raised much earlier began to receive attention: When do we make attributions? To what extent are the attributions in this large body of research elicited by the experimental procedures themselves? In one sense this is a question that can be directed to any form of social cognition. It is particularly relevant, however, to attribution; most people, confronted with a form on which they are to answer the question "Why?," do so. There is no way of knowing, within the typical experimental paradigm, whether respondents would make attributions on their own. In a sense there are two questions: Do people make attributions spontaneously, and if they do, under what circumstances do they do so?

In response to the first question, Weiner (1985) has marshaled impressive evidence that people do indeed make attributions spontaneously. Recent years have seen the development of inventive procedures for assessing the presence of attributional processing that was not directly elicited. This line of evidence has dealt almost entirely with causal attributions. Recent research suggests that trait attributions may be made spontaneously much more often than causal attributions. In response to the second question, a variety of studies suggests that people are most likely to make attributions when they encounter unexpected events or events that have negative implications for them.

## SOCIOLOGICAL SIGNIFICANCE OF ATTRIBUTION

Attribution is a cognitive process of individuals; much of the extant research on attribution is, accordingly, highly individualistic. In the 1980s, however, increasing attention has been paid to the sociological relevance of attribution. The process of attribution itself is fundamentally social. Attribution occurs not only within individuals but also at the interpersonal, intergroup, and societal levels. Moreover, the process of attribution may underlie basic sociological phenomena such as labeling and stratification.

**Interpersonal Attribution.** At the interpersonal level, attribution is basic to social interaction. Interpersonal encounters are shaped in

many ways by attributional patterns. Behavioral confirmation, or self-fulfilling prophecies, are examples of the behavioral consequences of attribution in social interaction; attribution of specific characteristics to social actors creates the expectancies that are then confirmed in behavior. Considering attribution at this interpersonal level demonstrates the importance of different social roles and perspectives (actors vs. observers) as well as how attribution is related to evaluation. The self is also important to the attribution process; the evidence for attributional egotism (self-esteem enhancing attributional biases), self-presentation biases, and egocentrism is persuasive. Attributions also affect social interaction through a widespread confirmatory attribution bias that leads perceivers to conclude that their expectancies have been confirmed in social interaction.

The great preponderance of research on social interaction has been based on relationships between strangers in experimental contexts, which may seem to undermine the claim that attribution is significant for interpersonal interaction. The best evidence of this significance, then, is the increasingly large body of research on the role of attribution in the formation, maintenance, and dissolution of close relationships. There is substantial evidence that attributions are linked to relationship satisfaction and behavior in the form of conflict resolution strategies. There is also evidence that distressed and nondistressed couples make differing attributions for significant events in their relationships; these patterns may actually serve to maintain marital distress among distressed couples, thus ultimately influencing marital satisfaction. Attributions also play an important role in relationship dissolution. Attributions are a critical part of the detailed accounts people provide for the dissolution of their relationships, and these accounts go beyond explanation to rationalize and justify the loss of relationships.

Research on interpersonal attribution extends the intrapersonal approach in several ways. When people who interact have substantial knowledge of and feelings about each other, the attribution process involves evaluation as well as cognition.

Issues of communication, and hence potential changes in preexisting attributions for recurrent relationship events, also become salient at the interpersonal level. There is very little research on how attributions change through interaction and relationships, but this is clearly a significant topic. Attributions at the interpersonal level also entail greater concern with accountability for action; causality at this level also raises issues of justification.

**Intergroup Attribution.** Intergroup attribution refers to the ways in which members of different social groups explain the behavior of members of their own and other social groups. At this level, social categorization has a direct impact on attribution. Studies using a variety of subjects from different social groups and often different countries show consistent support for an ingroup-serving attributional pattern, for example, a tendency toward more dispositional attributions for positive than negative behavior for ingroup actors. The evidence for the converse pattern, more dispositional attributions for negative than positive behavior for outgroup actors, is not as strong. (Moreover, these patterns are stronger in dominant than in dominated groups.)

Parallel studies of a group's success and failure show a consistent pattern of ingroup protection. Outgroup failure is attributed more to lack of ability than is ingroup failure. Effects of group membership on attributions about success are not as strong. Interestingly, there is also some evidence of outgroup-favoring and/or ingroup-derogating attributions among widely recognized lower-status, dominated groups such as migrant labor populations (Hewstone 1989).

A third form of evidence of intergroup attribution is provided by studies of attributions about social positions occupied by existing groups. In general, these studies, like those cited above, show higher ratings of ingroup-serving as opposed to outgroup-serving attributions.

**Societal Attribution.** At the societal level, those beliefs shared by the members of a given society form the vocabulary for social attributions. The concept of social representations, which has its origins in Durkheim's concept of "representa-tions collectives," was developed by Moscovici (1976) to represent how knowledge is shared by societal members in the form of common-sense theories about that society. Social representations are intimately connected to the process of attribution. Not only are explanation and accountability part of a system of collective representations, but such representations determine when we seek explanations. Social representations serve as categories that influence the perception and processing of social information; moreover, they underscore the emphasis on shared social beliefs and knowledge. Social representations are useful in interpreting research on laypersons' explanations of societal events such as poverty and wealth, unemployment, and racial inequality. Attributions for poverty are individualistic, for example, but attributions for unemployment are societal.

Cross-cultural research illustrates another aspect of societal attributions. This work compares the extent and type of attributional activity across cultures. Although there has been some support for the applicability of Western models of attribution among non-Western cultures, most of this research has demonstrated in a variety of ways the cultural specificity of particular patterns of attribution (Bond 1988). Miller (1984), for example, provides empirical evidence that the fundamental attribution error, the tendency to attribute cause more to persons than to situations, is characteristic of Western but not non-Western societies.

## SOCIOLOGICAL APPLICATIONS

It may be useful to identify several sociological phenomena to which theories of attribution are relevant. A number of scholars have suggested integrating attribution theory and labeling theory (Crittenden 1983). Attribution occurs within an individual; labels are applied by a group. Howard and Levinson (1985) offer empirical evidence that the process of applying a label is directly analogous to attribution. They report that the relationships between attribution information and jury verdicts are consistent with predictions based on a labeling perspective.

Della Fave (1980) demonstrates the importance

of attribution for understanding a key but neglected aspect of stratification, namely, how it is that stratification systems become legitimated and accepted by those disadvantaged as well as by those advantaged by those systems. He draws heavily on attribution theory in developing a theory of legitimation and in identifying possible sources of delegitimation.

Attribution is a significant social process that ranges widely from cognitive processes to collective beliefs. The field is still imbalanced; there is far more work at the intrapersonal and interpersonal levels. There is evidence for both intergroup and societal attributions, however, and research at these two levels is increasing rapidly (Hewstone 1989). If research continues in this direction, connections will be built across areas as diverse as social cognition, social interaction, intergroup relations, and social representations, and these connections will provide increasing evidence of the importance of attribution for sociological phenomena.

(SEE ALSO: *Social Psychology*)

## REFERENCES

Bond, Michael H. (ed.) 1988 *The Cross-Cultural Challenge to Social Psychology.* Newbury Park, Calif.: Sage.

Crittenden, Kathleen S. 1983 "Sociological Aspects of Attribution," *Annual Review of Sociology* 9:425–446.

Della Fave, L. Richard 1980 "The Meek Shall Not Inherit the Earth: Self-Evaluation and the Legitimacy of Stratification." *American Sociological Review* 45:955–971.

Heider, Fritz 1958 *The Psychology of Interpersonal Relations.* New York: Wiley.

Hewstone, Miles, 1989 *Causal Attribution: From Cognitive Processes to Collective Beliefs.* Oxford: Basil Blackwell.

———, and Jos M. F. Jaspars 1987 "Covariation and Causal Attribution: A Logical Model of the Intuitive Analysis of Variance." *Journal of Personality and Social Psychology* 53:663–672.

Howard, Judith A., and Carolyn Allen 1990 "Making Meaning: Revealing Attributions Through Analyses of Readers' Responses." *Social Psychology Quarterly* 52:280–298.

Howard, Judith A., and Randy Levinson 1985 "The Overdue Courtship of Attribution and Labeling." *Social Psychology Quarterly* 48:191–202.

Jones, Edward E., and Keith E. Davis 1965 "From Acts to Dispositions: The Attribution Process in Person Perception." *Advances in Experimental Social Psychology* 2:219–266.

Jones, Edward E., and Daniel McGillis 1976 "Correspondent Inferences and the Attribution Cube: A Comparative Reappraisal." In J. H. Harvey, W. Ickes, and R. F. Kidd, eds., *New Directions in Attribution Research*, Vol. 1. Hillsdale, N.J.: Erlbaum.

Kelley, Harold H. 1967 "Attribution Theory in Social Psychology." *Nebraska Symposium of Motivation* 15:192–238.

———1973 "The Processes of Causal Attribution." *American Psychologist* 28:107–128.

McArthur, Leslie Z. 1972 "The How and What of Why: Some Determinants and Consequences of Causal Attribution." *Journal of Personality and Social Psychology* 22:171–197.

Miller, Joan G. 1984 "Culture and the Development of Everyday Social Explanation." *Journal of Personality and Social Psychology* 46:961–978.

Moscovici, Serge 1976 *La Psychanalyse: Son image et son public*, 2nd ed. Paris: Presses Universitaires de France.

Ross, Lee 1977 "The Intuitive Psychologist and His Shortcomings: Distortions in the Attribution Process." *Advances in Experimental Social Psychology* 19:174–220.

Weiner, Bernard 1974 *Achievement Motivation and Attribution Theory.* Morristown, N.J.: General Learning Press.

———1985 "'Spontaneous' Causal Thinking." *Psychological Bulletin* 97:74–84.

———, Dan Russell, and David Lerman 1978 "Affective Consequences of Causal Ascription." In J. H. Harvey, W. Ickes, and R. F. Kidd, eds., *New Directions in Attribution Research*, Vol. 3. Hillsdale, N.J.: Erlbaum.

JUDITH A. HOWARD

# B

**BALANCE THEORY** *See* Attitudes; Cognitive Consistency Theories.


**BEHAVIORISM** Behaviorism is the conceptual framework underlying the science of behavior. The science itself is often referred to as the experimental analysis of behavior or behavior analysis. Within the social sciences, the term has referred to the social-learning perspective that emphasizes the importance of rewards and sanctions in regulating individual behavior. Modern behaviorism, however, emphasizes the analysis of conditions that maintain and change behavior as well as the factors that influence the acquisition or learning of behavior. Behaviorists also offer concepts and analyses that go well beyond the common-sense understanding of reward and punishment. Contemporary behaviorism provides an integrated framework for the study of human behavior, society, and culture.

The roots of behaviorism lie in its philosophical debate with introspectionism—the belief that the mind can be revealed from a person's reports of thoughts, feelings, and perceptions. Behaviorists opposed the use of introspective reports as the basic datum of psychology. These researchers argued for a natural-science approach and showed how introspective reports of consciousness were inadequate. Reports of internal states and experiences were said to lack objectivity, were available to only one observer, and were prone to error. Some behaviorists used these arguments and others also to reject cognitive explanations of behavior (Skinner 1974; Pierce and Epling 1984; but see Bandura 1986 for an alternative view).

The natural-science approach of behaviorism emphasizes the search for general laws and principles of behavior. For example, the quantitative law of effect is a mathematical statement of how the rate of response increases with the rate of reinforcement (Herrnstein 1970). Under controlled conditions, this equation allows the scientist to predict precisely and regulate the behavior of organisms. Behavior analysts suggest that this law and others will eventually account for complex human behavior (McDowell 1988).

Contemporary behaviorists usually restrict themselves to the study of observable responses and events. Observable events are those that are directly sensed or are made available to our senses by instruments. The general strategy is to manipulate aspects of the environment and measure well-defined responses. If behavior reliably changes with a manipulated condition, the researcher has established an environment–behavior relationship. Analysis of such relationships has often resulted in behavioral laws and principles. For example, the principle of discrimination states that an organism will respond differently to two situations if its behavior is reinforced in one setting but not in the other. You may talk about politics to one person but not to another, because the first person has been interested in such conversation while the second has not. The principle of discrimination and other behavior principles account for many aspects of human behavior.

Although behaviorism usually has been treated as a uniform and consistent position, a conceptual reconstruction indicates that there are many branches to the behavioral tree (Zuriff 1985). Most behavior analysts share a set of core assumptions; however, there are internal disputes over less central issues. To illustrate, some behaviorists argue against hypothetical constructs (e.g., drive) while others accept such concepts as an important part of theory construction.

Throughout the intellectual history of behaviorism, a variety of assumptions and concepts has been presented to the scientific community. Some of these ideas have flourished when they were found to further the scientific analysis of behavior. Other formulations were interesting variations of behavioristic ideas, but they became extinct when they served no useful function. For instance, one productive assumption is that a person's knowledge of emotional states is due to a special history of verbal conditioning (Bem 1965, 1972; Skinner 1957). Self-perception and attributional approaches to social psychology have built on this assumption, although researchers in this field seldom acknowledge the impact. In contrast, the assumption that thinking is merely subvocal speech was popular at one time but is now replaced by an analysis of problem solving (Skinner 1953, 1974). In this view, thinking is behavior that precedes and guides the final performance of finding a solution. Generally, it is important to recognize that behaviorism continues to evolve as a philosophy of science, a view of human nature, and an ideology that recommends goals for behavioral science and its applications.

## THE STUDY OF BEHAVIOR

Behaviorism requires that a scientist study the behavior of organisms for its own sake. Behaviorists do not study behavior in order to make inferences about mental states or physiological processes. Although most behaviorists emphasize the importance of biology and physiological processes, they focus on the interplay of behavior and environment.

In order to maintain this focus, behaviorists examine the evolutionary history and physiological status of an organism as part of the context for specific environment–behavior interactions. For example, a biological condition that results in blindness may have profound behavioral effects. For a newly sightless individual, visual events, such as watching television or going to a movie no longer support specific interactions, while other sensory events become salient (e.g., reading by braille). The biological condition limits certain kinds of behavioral interactions and, at the same time, augments the regulation of behavior by other aspects of the environment. Contemporary behaviorism therefore emphasizes what organisms are doing, the environmental conditions that regulate their actions, and how biology and evolution constrain or enhance environment–behavior interactions.

Modern behaviorists are interested in voluntary action, and they have developed a way of talking about purpose, volition, and intention within a natural-science approach. They note that the language of intention was pervasive in biology before Darwin's functional analysis of evolution. Although giraffes appear to grow long necks in order to obtain food at the tops of trees, Darwin made it clear that the process of evolution involved no plan, strategy of design, or purpose. Natural variation ensures that giraffes vary in neck size. As vegetation declines at lower heights, animals with longer necks obtain food, survive to adulthood, and reproduce; those with shorter necks starve to death. In this environment (niche), the frequency of long-necked giraffes increases over generations. Such an increase is called natural selection. Contemporary behaviorists insist that selection, as a causal mode, also accounts for the form and frequency of behavior during the lifetime of an individual. A person's current behavior is therefore composed of performances that have been selected in the past (Skinner 1987).

An important class of behavior is selected by its consequences. The term *operant* refers to behavior that operates upon the environment to produce effects, outcomes, or consequences. Operant behavior is said to be emitted because it does not depend on an eliciting stimulus. Examples of operant behavior include manipulation of objects, talking with others, problem solving, drawing, reading, writing, and many other performances. Consequences select this behavior in the sense that specific operants occur at high frequency in a given setting. To illustrate, driving to the store is operant behavior that is likely to occur when there is little food in the house. In this situation, the operant has a high probability if such behavior has previously resulted in obtaining food (i.e., the store is open). Similarly, the conversation of a person also is selected by its social consequences. At the pub, a student shows a high probability of talking to his friends about sports. Presumably, this behavior occurs at high frequency because his friends have previously "shown an interest" in such conversation. The behavior of an individual is therefore adapted to a particular setting by its history of consequences.

A specific operant, such as opening a door, includes many performance variations. The door may be opened by turning the handle, pushing with a foot, or even by asking someone to open it. These variations in performance have a common effect upon the environment in the sense that each one results in the door being opened. Because each variation produces similar consequences, behaviorists talk about an operant as a response class. Operants such as opening a door, talking to others, answering questions, and many other actions are each a response class that includes a multitude of forms, both verbal and nonverbal.

In the laboratory, the study of operant behav-

ior requires a basic measure that is sensitive to changes in the environment. Most behaviorists use an operant's rate of occurrence as the basic datum for analysis. Operant rate is measured as the frequency of an operant (class) over a specified period of time. Although operant rate is not directly observable, a cumulative recorder is an instrument that shows the rate of occurrence as changes in the slope (or rise) of a line on moving paper. When an operant is selected by its consequences, the operant rate increases and the slope becomes steeper. Operants that are not appropriate to the requirements of the environment decrease in rate of occurrence (i.e., decline in slope). Changes in operant rate therefore reflect the basic causal process of "selection by consequences" (Skinner 1969).

Behavior analysts continue to use the cumulative recorder to provide an immediate report on a subject's behavior in an experimental situation. However, most researchers are interested in complex settings where there are many alternatives and multiple operants. Today, microcomputers collect and record a variety of behavioral measures that are later examined by complex numerical analysis. Researchers also use computers to arrange environmental events for individual behavior and provide these events in complex patterns and sequences.

## CONTINGENCIES OF REINFORCEMENT

Behaviorists often focus on the analysis of behavior–environment relationships. The relationship between operant behavior and its consequences defines a contingency of reinforcement. In its simplest form, a two-term contingency of reinforcement may be shown as $R{\rightarrow}Sr$. The symbol $R$ represents the operant class, and $Sr$ stands for the reinforcing stimulus or event. The arrow indicates that "if $R$ occurs, then $Sr$ will follow." In the laboratory, the behavior analyst arranges the environment so that a contingency exists between an operant (e.g., pecking a key) and the occurrence of some event (e.g., appearance of food). If the presentation of the event increases operant behavior, the event is defined as a positive reinforcer. The procedure of repeatedly presenting a positive reinforcer contingent on behavior is called positive reinforcement (Mazur 1986).

A contingency of reinforcement defines the probability that a reinforcing event will follow operant behavior. When a person turns the ignition key of the car (operant), this behavior usually has resulted in the car starting (reinforcement). Turning the key does not guarantee, however, that the car will start; perhaps it is out of gas, the battery is run down, and so on. Thus, the probability of reinforcement is high for this behavior, but reinforcement is not certain. The behavior analyst is interested in how the probability of reinforcement is related to the rate and form of operant behavior. For example, does the person continue to turn the ignition key even though the car doesn't start? Qualities of behavior such as persistence, depression, and elation reflect the probability of reinforcement.

Reinforcement may depend on the number of responses or the passage of time. A schedule of reinforcement is a procedure that states how consequences are arranged for behavior. When reinforcement is delivered after each response, a continuous schedule of reinforcement is in effect. A child who receives payment each time she mows the lawn is on a continuous schedule of reinforcement. Continuous reinforcement produces a very high and steady rate of response, but as any parent knows, the behavior quickly stops if reinforcement no longer occurs.

Continuous reinforcement is a particular form of ratio schedule. Fixed-ratio schedules state the number of responses per reinforcement. These schedules are called *fixed ratio* since a fixed number of responses are required for reinforcement. In a factory, piece rates of payment are examples of fixed-ratio schedules. Thus, a worker may receive $1 for sewing twenty pieces of elastic wristband. When the ratio of responses to reinforcement is high, fixed-ratio schedules produce long pauses following reinforcement: Overall productivity may be low, and plant managers may complain about "slacking off" by the workers. The

problem, however, is the schedule of reinforcement that fixes a high number of responses to payment.

Reinforcement may be arranged on a variable, rather than fixed, basis. The schedule of payoff for a slot machine is a variable-ratio schedule of reinforcement. The operant involves putting in a dollar and pulling the handle, and reinforcement is the jackpot. The jackpot occurs after a variable number of responses. Variable-ratio schedules produce a high rate of response that takes a long time to stop when reinforcement is withdrawn. The gambler may continue to put money in the machine even though the jackpot rarely, if ever, occurs. Behavior on a variable-ratio schedule is said to show "negative utility" since people often invest more than they get back.

Behavior may also be reinforced only after an interval of time has passed. A fixed-interval schedule stipulates that the first response following a specified interval is reinforced. Looking for a bus is behavior that is reinforced after a fixed time set by the bus schedule. If you just missed a bus, the probability of looking for the next one is quite low. As time passes, the rate of response increases with the highest rate occurring just before the bus arrives. Thus, rate of response is initially zero but gradually rises to a peak at the moment of reinforcement. This response pattern is called "scalloping" and is characteristic of fixed-interval reinforcement. In order to eliminate such patterning, a variable-interval schedule may be stipulated. In this case, the first response after a variable amount of time is reinforced. If the bus schedule is irregular, looking for the next bus will occur at a moderate and steady rate because the passage of time no longer signals reinforcement (i.e., arrival of the bus).

The schedules of reinforcement that regulate human behavior are complex combinations of ratio and interval contingencies. An adjusting schedule is one example of a more complex arrangement between behavior and its consequences (Zeiler 1977). When the ratio (or interval) for reinforcement changes on the basis of performance, the schedule is called adjusting. A math teacher who spends more or less time with a student depending on the student's competence (i.e., number of correct solutions) provides reinforcement on an adjusting-ratio basis. When reinforcement is arranged by other people (i.e., social reinforcement), the level of reinforcement is often tied to the level of behavior. This adjustment between behavior and socially arranged consequences may account for the flexibility and variability that characterize adult human behavior.

Human behavior is regulated not only by its consequences. Contingencies of reinforcement also involve the events that precede operant behavior. The preceding event is said to "set the occasion" for behavior and is called a discriminative stimulus or Sd (pronounced es-dē). The ring of a telephone (Sd) may set the occasion for answering it (operant), although the ring does not force one to do so. Similarly, a nudge under the table (Sd) may prompt a new topic of conversation (operant) or cause the person to stop speaking. Discriminative stimuli may be private as well as public events. Thus, a headache may result in taking a pill or calling a physician. A mild headache may be a discriminative stimulus for taking an aspirin, while more severe pain sets the occasion for telephoning a doctor.

Although discriminative stimuli exert a broad range of influences over human behavior, these events do not stand alone. These stimuli regulate behavior because they are an important part of the contingencies of reinforcement. Behaviorism has therefore emphasized a three-term contingency of reinforcement, symbolized as $Sd—R{\rightarrow}Sr$. The notation states that a specific event (Sd) sets the occasion for an operant (R) that produces reinforcement (Sr). The discriminative stimulus regulates behavior only because it signals past consequences. Thus, a sign that states Eat at Joe's may set the occasion for your stopping at Joe's restaurant because of the great meals received in the past. If Joe hires a new cook, and the meals deteriorate in quality, then Joe's sign will gradually loose its influence. Similarly, posted highway speeds regulate driving on the basis of past consequences. The driver who has been caught by a radar trap is more likely to observe the speed limit.

## CONTEXT OF BEHAVIOR

Contingencies of reinforcement, as complex arrangements of discriminative stimuli, operants, and reinforcements, remain a central focus of behavioral research. Contemporary behaviorists are also concerned with the *context of behavior,* and how context affects the regulation of behavior by its consequences (Fantino and Logan 1979). Important aspects of context include the biological and cultural history of an organism, its current physiological status, previous environment–behavior interactions, alternative sources of reinforcement, and a history of deprivation (or satiation) for specific events or stimuli. To illustrate, in the laboratory food is used typically as an effective reinforcer for operant behavior. There are obvious times, however, when food will not function as reinforcement. If a person (or animal) has just had a large meal or has an upset stomach, food has little effect upon behavior.

There are less obvious interrelations between reinforcement and context. Recent research indicates that depriving an organism of one reinforcer may increase the effectiveness of a different behavioral consequence. As deprivation for food increased, animals worked harder to obtain an opportunity to run on a wheel. Additionally, animals who were satiated on wheel running no longer pressed a lever to obtain food. These results imply that eating and running are biologically interrelated. Based on this biological history, the supply or availability of one of these reinforcers alters the effectiveness of the other (Pierce, Epling, and Boer 1986). It is possible that many reinforcers are biologically interrelated. People commonly believe that sex and aggression go together in some unspecified manner. One possibility is that the availability of sexual reinforcement alters the reinforcing effectiveness of an opportunity to inflict harm on others.

## CHOICE AND PREFERENCE

The emphasis on context and reinforcement contingencies has allowed modern behaviorists to explore many aspects of behavior that seem to defy a scientific analysis. Most people believe that choice and preference are basic features of human nature. Our customary way of speaking implies that people make decisions on the basis of their knowledge and dispositions. In contrast, behavioral studies of decision making suggest that we choose an option based on its rate of return compared with alternative sources of reinforcement.

Behaviorists have spent the last thirty years studying choice in the laboratory using concurrent schedules of reinforcement. The word *concurrent* means "operating at the same time." Thus, concurrent schedules are two (or more) schedules operating at the same time, each schedule providing reinforcement independently. The experimental setting is arranged so that an organism is free to alternate between two or more alternatives. Each alternative provides a schedule of reinforcement for choosing it over the other possibilities. A person may choose between two (or more) response buttons that have different rates of monetary payoff. Although the experimental setting is abstract, concurrent schedules of reinforcement provide an analogue of choice in everyday life.

People are often faced with a variety of alternatives, and each alternative has its associated benefits (and costs). When a person puts money in the bank rather than spending it on a new car, television, or refrigerator, we speak of the individual choosing to save rather than spend. In everyday life, choice often involves repeated selection of one alternative (putting money in the bank) over the other alternatives considered as a single option (buying goods and services). Similarly, the criminal chooses to take the property of others rather than the socially acceptable route of working for a living or accepting social assistance. The arrangement of consequences for crime and legitimate ways of making a living is conceptually the same as concurrent schedules of reinforcement (Hamblin and Crosbie 1977).

Behaviorists are interested in the distribution or allocation of behavior when a person is faced with different rates of reinforcement from two (or more) alternatives. The distribution of behavior is measured as the relative rate of response to, or relative time spent on, a specific option. For example, a student may go to school twelve days and skip eight days each month (not counting weekends). The relative rate of response to school is the proportion of the number of days at school to the total number of days, or $12/20 = 0.60$. Expressed as a percentage, the student allocates 60 percent of her behavior to school. In the laboratory, a person may press the left button twelve times and the right button eight times each minute.

The distribution of reinforcement may also be expressed as a percentage. In everyday life, it is difficult to identify and quantify behavioral consequences, but it is easily accomplished in the laboratory. If the reinforcement schedule on the left button produces $30 an hour and the right button yields $20, 60 percent of the reinforcements are on the left. There is a fundamental relationship between relative rate of reinforcement and relative rate of response. This relationship is called the matching law. The law states that the distribution of behavior to two (or more) alternatives matches (equals) the distribution of reinforcement from these alternatives (Herrnstein 1961; de Villiers 1977).

Although it is difficult to identify rates of reinforcement for attending school and skipping, the matching law does suggest some practical solutions (Epling and Pierce 1988). Notice that parents and school may be able to arrange positive consequences when a child goes to school. This means that the rate of reinforcement for going to school has increased, and therefore the relative rate of reinforcement for school has gone up. According to the matching law, a child will now distribute more behavior to the school.

Unfortunately, there is another possibility. A child may receive social reinforcement from friends for skipping, and as the child begins to spend more time at school, friends may increase their rate of reinforcement for cutting classes. Even though the absolute rate of reinforcement for going to school has increased, the relative rate of reinforcement has remained the same or decreased. The overall effect may be no change in school attendance or even further decline. In order to deal with this problem, the matching law implies that interventions must increase reinforcement for attendance and maintain or reduce reinforcement for skipping, possibly by turning up the cost of this behavior (e.g., withdrawal of privileges).

The matching law has been tested with human and nonhuman subjects under controlled conditions. One interesting study assessed human performance in group discussion sessions. Subjects were assigned to groups discussing attitudes toward drug abuse. Each group was composed of three confederates and a subject. Two confederates acted as listeners and reinforced the subject's talk with brief positive words and phrases, provided on the basis of cue lights. Thus, the rate of reinforcement by each listener could be varied depending on the number of signals arranged by the researchers. A third confederate asked questions but did not reinforce talking. Results were analyzed in terms of the relative time subjects spent talking to the two listeners. Speakers matched their distribution of conversation to the distribution of positive comments from the listeners. Apparently, choosing to speak to others is behavior that is regulated by the matching law (Conger and Killeen 1974).

Researchers have found that exact matching does not always hold between relative rate of reinforcement and relative rate of response. A more general theory of behavioral matching has been tested in order to account for the departures from perfect matching. One source of deviation is called response bias. Bias is a systematic preference for an alternative, but the preference is not due to the difference in rate of reinforcement. For example, even though two friends provide similar rates of reinforcement, social characteristics (e.g., status and equity) may affect the distribution of behavior (Sunahara and Pierce 1982). Generalized matching theory is able to address many social factors as sources of bias that affect human choice and preference (Baum 1974; Pierce and Epling 1983; Bradshaw and Szabadi 1988).

A second source of deviation from matching is called sensitivity to differences in reinforcement. Matching implies that an increase of 10 percent (e.g., from 50 to 60 percent) in relative rate of

reinforcement for one alternative results in a similar increase in relative rate of response. In many cases, the increase in relative rate of response is less than expected (e.g., only 5 percent). This failure to discriminate changes in relative rate of reinforcement is incorporated within the theory of generalized matching. To illustrate, low sensitivity to changes in rate of reinforcement may occur when an air-traffic controller rapidly switches between two (or more) radar screens. As relative rate of targets increases on one screen, relative rate of detection may be slow to change. Generalized matching theory allows behaviorists to measure the degree of sensitivity and suggests procedures to modify it (e.g., setting a minimal amount of time on a screen before targets can be detected).

Matching theory is an important contribution of modern behaviorism. In contrast to theories of rational choice proposed by economists and other social scientists, matching theory implies that humans may not try to maximize utility (or reinforcement). People (and animals) do not search for the strategy that yields the greatest overall returns; they equalize their behavior to the obtained rates of reinforcement from alternatives. Research suggests that matching (rather than maximizing) occurs because humans focus on the immediate effectiveness of their behavior. A person may receive a per-hour average of $10 and $5 respectively from the left and right handles of a slot machine. Although the left side generally pays twice as much, there are local periods when the left option actually pays less than the right. People respond to these changes in "local rate of reinforcement" by switching to the lean alternative, even though they lose money overall. The general implication is that human impulsiveness ensures that choice is not a rational process of getting the most in the long run but a behavioral process of doing the best at the moment (Herrnstein 1990).

## BEHAVIORISM AND CULTURAL EVOLUTION

Although the matching law has been a major focus of interest, modern behaviorists are also exploring the interplay of behavior and culture.

Behavior analysts recognize that human behavior is largely a product of the social environment. A social environment is usually referred to as the culture of the group. Culture has been defined in terms of the ideas and values of a community, but a natural-science approach defines culture as all the conditions, events, and stimuli arranged by other people that regulate individual behavior. Thus, a culture is composed of social contingencies of reinforcement. Specification of these contingencies and their behavioral effects involves the fields of behavioral sociology, socialization, and social development (Hamblin and Kunkel 1977; Homans 1974).

The principles and laws of behavior analysis provide an account of how culture regulates individual behavior. A person learns to speak in accord with the verbal practices of the community. Presumably, the community arranges events and consequences to establish and maintain a complex verbal repertoire. From this view, the "rules of language" are descriptive statements about the operating social contingencies set by the cultural practice. A more difficult task is accounting for the practices themselves. The analysis of cultural practices and how they are acquired, maintained, and changed defines the major problem of cultural evolution (Skinner 1953).

In terms of cultural evolution, a practice is the analytical unit at the level of the group, community, or society. A practice involves the interdependent actions of many people, each behaving in accord with common and unique contingencies of reinforcement. The term *interdependent* means that the actions of each individual arrange stimuli and consequences for others involved in the practice.

Cultural practices are functionally similar to the operants at the individual level. Both operants and practices are viewed as behavioral classes with variation among the class members. An operant such as opening the door is composed of various response forms, and the cultural practice of making water jars may also have various forms such as using shells, hollow leaves, or weaving baskets. The form that predominates reflects the basic process of selection by consequences. In terms of selec-

tion, operants are selected by contingencies of reinforcement, and practices are selected by metacontingencies (i.e., contingencies affecting survival of the culture).

Metacontingencies specify the relationship between practices and their effects (Glenn 1988). Behaviorists agree with anthropologists who emphasize the importance of production and reproduction outcomes (i.e., survival) for cultural evolution (Harris 1979, 1977). A cultural practice such as making weapons to kill animals may raise the ratio of calories obtained to calories expended (i.e., efficiency). Based on this consequence, weapon making may increase in frequency over generations. At some point, however, the efficiency of killing becomes so great that the animal populations decline and another mode of production is selected (e.g., agriculture).

Behavior analysts are interested in cultural evolution because cultural changes alter the social system of rewards for individual behavior. Analysis of cultural evolution suggests how the social environment is arranged and rearranged to support specific forms of human behavior. Such an account provides an interpretation of human behavior in the past and allows for prediction of behavior in contemporary society (Holland 1980). Finally, a behavior analysis of cultural evolution allows for the modification of behavioral contingencies at the individual and societal levels. Recently, behavioral technology has been used to manage pollution of the environment, encourage energy conservation, and regulate overpopulation (Glenwick and Jason 1980). Analysis of cultural practices and metacontingencies may eventually allow for large-scale modification of many other societal problems.

## SUMMARY

Modern behaviorism emphasizes the context of behavior and reinforcement. The biological history of an organism favors or constrains specific behavior−environment interactions. This interplay of biology and behavior is a central focus of behavioral research. Another aspect of context concerns alternative sources of reinforcement. An individual selects a specific option based on the relative rate of reinforcement. This means that behavior is regulated not only by its consequences but also by the consequences arranged for alternative actions. Finally, culture is an important part of context. Today, behaviorists are analyzing cultural practices in order to provide a more complete account of human behavior.

(SEE ALSO: *Social Psychology*)

## REFERENCES

Bandura, A. 1986 *Social Foundations of Thought and Action.* Englewood Cliffs, N.J.: Prentice Hall.

Baum, W. M. 1974 "On Two Types of Deviation from the Matching Law: Bias and Undermatching." *Journal of the Experimental Analysis of Behavior* 22:231–242.

Bem, D. J. 1965 "An Experimental Analysis of Self-Persuasion." *Journal of Experimental Social Psychology* 1:199–218.

——— 1972 "Self-Perception Theory." In L. Berkowitz, ed., *Advances in Experimental Social Psychology,* Vol. 6. New York: Academic Press.

Bradshaw, C. M., and E. Szabadi 1988 "Quantitative Analysis of Human Operant Behavior." In G. Davey and C. Cullen, eds., *Human Operant Conditioning and Behavior Modification.* New York: Wiley.

Conger, R., and P. Killeen 1974 "Use of Concurrent Operants in Small Group Research." *Pacific Sociological Review* 17:399–416.

De Villiers, P. A. 1977 "Choice in Concurrent Schedules and a Quantitative Formulation of the Law of Effect." In W. K. Honig and J. E. R. Staddon, eds., *Handbook of Operant Behavior.* Englewood Cliffs, N.J.: Prentice Hall.

Epling, W. F., and W. D. Pierce 1988 "Applied Behavior Analysis: New Directions from the Laboratory." In G. Davey and C. Cullen, eds., *Human Operant Conditioning and Behavior Modification.* New York: Wiley.

Fantino, E., and C. A. Logan 1979 *The Experimental Analysis of Behavior: A Biological Perspective.* San Francisco: W. H. Freeman.

Glenn, S. 1988 "Contingencies and Metacontingencies: Toward a Synthesis of Behavior Analysis and Cultural Materialism." *The Behavior Analyst* 11:161–180.

Glenwick, D., and L. Jason 1980 *Behavioral Community Psychology: Progress and Prospects.* New York: Praeger.

Hamblin, R. L., and P. U. Crosbie 1977 "Anomie and Deviance." In R. L. Hamblin and J. H. Kunkel, eds., *Behavioral Theory in Sociology.* New Brunswick, N.J.: Transaction Books.

Hamblin, R. L., and J. H. Kunkel 1977. *Behavioral Theory in Sociology.* New Brunswick, N.J.: Transaction Books.

Harris, M. H. 1977 *Cannibals and Kings: The Origins of Cultures.* New York: Random House.

——— 1979 *Cultural Materialism.* New York: Random House.

Herrnstein, R. J. 1961 "Relative and Absolute Response Strength as a Function of Frequency of Reinforcement." *Journal of the Experimental Analysis of Behavior* 4:267–272.

——— 1970. "On the Law of Effect." *Journal of the Experimental Analysis of Behavior* 13:243–266.

——— 1990 "Rational Choice Theory: Necessary but Not Sufficient." *American Psychologist* 45:356–367.

Holland, J. 1980 "Alternative Social Systems: An Analysis of Behavior Change in China and Cuba." In D. Glenwick and L. Jason, eds., *Behavioral Community Psychology: Progress and Prospects.* New York: Praeger.

Homans, G. C. 1974 *Social Behavior: Its Elementary Forms,* rev. ed. New York: Harcourt Brace Jovanovich.

Mazur, J. 1986 *Learning and Behavior.* Englewood Cliffs, N.J.: Prentice-Hall.

McDowell, J. J. 1988 "Matching Theory in Natural Human Environments." *The Behavior Analyst* 11:95–109.

Pierce, W. D., and W. F. Epling 1983 "Choice, Matching, and Human Behavior: A Review of the Literature." *The Behavior Analyst* 6:57–76.

——— 1984 "On the Persistence of Cognitive Explanation: Implications for Behavior Analysis." *Behaviorism* 12:15–27.

Pierce, W. D., W. F. Epling, and D. Boer 1986 "Deprivation and Satiation: The Interrelations Between Food and Wheel Running." *Journal of the Experimental Analysis of Behavior* 46:199–210.

Skinner, B. F. 1953 *Science and Human Behavior.* New York: Free Press.

——— 1957 *Verbal Behavior.* New York: Appleton Century Crofts.

——— 1969 *Contingencies of Reinforcement: A Theoretical Analysis.* New York: Appleton Century Crofts.

——— 1974 *About Behaviorism.* New York: Knopf.

——— 1987. "Selection by Consequences." in B. F. Skinner, *Upon Further Reflections.* Englewood Cliffs, N.J.: Prentice-Hall.

Sunahara, D., and W. D. Pierce 1982. "The Matching Law and Bias in a Social Exchange Involving Choice Between Alternatives." *Canadian Journal of Sociology* 7:145–165.

Zeiler, M. 1977 "Schedules of Reinforcement: The Controlling Variables." In W. K. Honig and J. E. R. Staddon, eds., *Handbook of Operant Behavior.* Englewood Cliffs, N.J.: Prentice-Hall.

Zuriff, G. E. 1985 *Behaviorism: A Conceptual Reconstruction.* New York: Columbia University Press.

W. DAVID PIERCE

**BIRTH AND DEATH RATES** Much of the birth and death information published by individual governments and compiled by the United Nations is in absolute numbers. These raw data are difficult to interpret. For example, a comparison of the 11,677 births in Alaska with the 22,425 births in West Virginia in 1987 reveals nothing about the relative levels of fertility because West Virginia has a larger population (National Center for Health Statistics 1989a, p. 21).

To control for the effect of population size, analyses of fertility and mortality usually use rates. A rate measures the number of times an event such as birth occurs in a given period of time divided by the population at risk to that event. The period is usually a year, and the rate is usually expressed per 1,000 people in the population to eliminate the decimal point. Dividing West Virginia's births by the state's population and multiplying by 1,000 yields a birth rate of 12 per 1,000. A similar calculation for Alaska yields 22 per 1,000, evidence that fertility makes a greater contribution to population growth in the younger state.

## BIRTH RATES

The crude birth rate calculated in the preceding example,

Crude birth rate =

$$\frac{\text{Live births in year } x}{\text{Midyear population in year } x} \times 1,000 \qquad (1)$$

is the most common measure of fertility because it requires the least amount of data and measures the impact of fertility on population growth.

Crude birth rates range from over 40 per 1,000 in most African countries and some western and southern Asian countries to less than 18 in the slower growing or declining countries of Europe, North America, Australia, New Zealand, Japan, Taiwan, South Korea, and Hong Kong (Population Reference Bureau 1990).

The crude birth rate is aptly named when used to compare childbearing levels between populations. Its estimate of the population at risk to giving birth includes men, children, and postmenopausal women. If women of childbearing age compose different proportions in the populations under consideration or within the same population in a longitudinal analysis, the crude birth rate is an unreliable indicator of the relative level of childbearing. A small portion of Alaska's 83 percent higher crude birth rate is due to the state's higher proportion of childbearing age women, 25 percent, versus 23 percent in West Virginia (U.S. Bureau of the Census 1988).

Other rates that more precisely specify the population at risk are better comparative measures of childbearing, although only the crude birth rate measures the impact of fertility on population growth. If the number of women in childbearing ages is known, general fertility rates can be used:

General fertility rate =

$$\frac{\text{Live births in year } x}{\text{Women 15–44 in year } x} \times 1,000 \qquad (2)$$

This measure reveals that Alaskan women of childbearing age produce more births, given their number, than their West Virginian counterparts, 89 versus 51 births per 1,000 women between ages 15–44 (National Center for Health Statistics 1989a, p. 21). The 74 percent difference in the two states' general fertility rates is not as great as that indicated by their crude birth rates, which also measure the full impact of age-composition differences.

The general fertility rate is sensitive only to the distribution of childbearing-age women. When women are heavily concentrated in the younger, more fecund ages, such as in the United States in 1980, or in the less fecund older ages, such as in the United States in 2000, the general fertility rate is not the best choice for fertility analysis. It inflates the relative level of fertility in the former population and deflates the estimate in the latter.

Age-specific fertility rates eliminate potential distortions from age compositions. These rates are calculated for five-year age groups beginning with ages 15–19 and ending with ages 45–49:

Age-specific fertility rate =

$$\frac{\text{Live births in year } x \text{ to women age } a}{\text{Women age } a \text{ in year } x} \times 1,000 \quad (3)$$

Age-specific fertility rates also provide a rudimentary measure of the tempo of childbearing. The four countries in Figure 1 have distinct patterns. Honduras, a less developed country with extremely high fertility, has higher rates at all ages. At the other extreme, Japan's low fertility is highly concentrated between the ages of twenty-five and thirty-four, even though these Japanese rates are well below those in Honduras. In contrast, young women in the United States have higher fertility than young women in Japan and most other developed countries, whereas older women in Ireland have unusually high rates.

More detailed analyses of the tempo of childbearing require extensive information about live birth order to make fertility rates for each age group specific for first births, second births, third births, and so forth (Shryock and Siegel 1976,

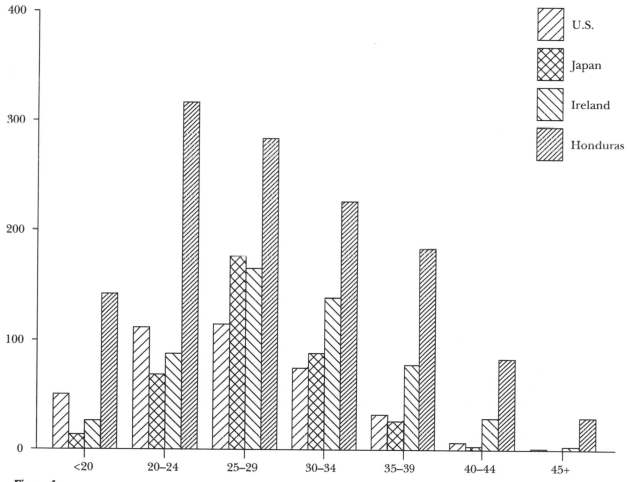

*Figure 1*
*Age-Specific Fertility Rates: Selected Countries, Mid-1980s*
SOURCE: United Nations, *Demographic Yearbook, 1987.*

p. 280). A comparison of these age-order-specific rates in 1976 and 1987 (National Center for Health Statistics 1978, p. 10; 1989a, p. 16) reveals a shift toward later childbearing in the United States. Rates for first and second births increased for women over thirty and first birth rates declined for women ages twenty to twenty-four.

When the tempo of fertility is not of interest, the advantages of age-specific fertility rates are outweighed by the cumbersome task of comparing many rates between more than a few populations. In this case each population's age-specific rates can be condensed in an age-sex adjusted birth rate (Shryock and Siegel 1976, pp. 284–288). The most frequently used age-sex adjusted rate is calculated:

Total fertility rate =

$$\underline{\text{sum (age-specific fertility rates} \times 5),}$$

(4)

if the age-specific fertility rates are for five-year age groups. Single-year age-specific rates are summed without the five-year adjustment. When expressed per single woman, the total fertility rate can be interpreted as the average number of births that a hypothetical group would have at the end of their reproduction if they experienced the age-specific fertility observed in a particular year over the course of their childbearing years.

In reality, age-specific rates in populations that consciously control fertility can be volatile. For example, the fertility rate of American women ages 30–34 fell to 71 per 1,000 in the middle of the Great Depression and climbed back to 119 during the postwar baby boom, only to fall again to 53 in 1975 and rebound to 71 in 1987 (U.S. Bureau of the Census 1975, p. 50; National Center for Health Statistics 1989a, p. 18). Consequently, a total fertility rate calculated from one year's observed age-specific rates is not a good estimate of the eventual completed fertility of childbearing-age women. It is, however, an excellent index of the level of fertility observed in a year that is unaffected by age composition.

The total fertility rate's insensitivity to age composition makes it useful for examining trends in a population with a changing age composition, such as the United States, or between populations with different age compositions, such as whites and nonwhites in this country (Figure 2). After declining since before the turn of the century, American fertility rose sharply after World War II, peaked in the late 1950s, and sank to a historic low in the mid-1970s. Since then, the national rate has crept back to nearly two births per woman. Nonwhites average about one-half a child more than whites. The racial difference narrowed only during the immediate postwar years of the mid-1940s and widened during the peak years of the baby boom, when the economy was expanding rapidly.

The total fertility rate also can be interpreted as an estimate of the reproductivity of a population. Reproductivity is the extent to which a generation exactly replaces its eventual deaths. Theoretically, women would need to average only two births, one of each sex, to maintain a constant population size, if all female newborns survived to the end of their childbearing years. In real populations some females die before menopause. As a result, the total fertility rate must exceed two for a generation to replace all of its deaths. In populations with a low risk of dying before age fifty, such as in the more developed countries of the world, the total fertility rate needs to be only about 2.1 for replacement. Developing countries with higher mortality need a higher total fertility rate for replacement. Nigeria, for example, with an infant mortality rate of 121 per 1,000 live births and a life expectancy of only forty-eight needs a rate of about three births per woman for replacement.

Most developed countries have total fertility rates below replacement (Population Reference Bureau 1990). Many western and southern European countries as well as Japan, Hong Kong, and South Korea have total fertility rates below 1.7 births per woman. Those without net in-migration will decline if their rates do not rebound as they are doing in Finland, Iceland, Sweden, West Germany, and the United States.

In contrast, the total fertility rates of most developing countries far exceed replacement (Population Reference Bureau 1990). The highest

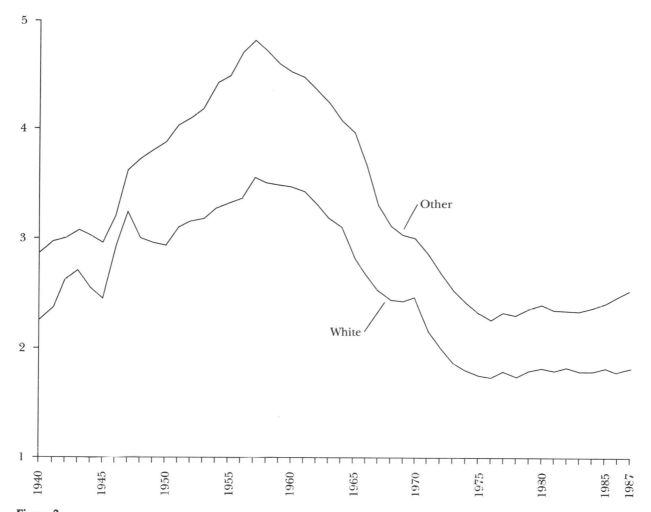

**Figure 2**
*Total Fertility Rates by Race: United States, 1940 to 1987*
SOURCE: National Center for Health Statistics, "Advance Report of Final Natality Statistics, 1987," *Monthly Vital Statistics Report* and U.S. Bureau of the Census, *Historical Statistics of the United States, Colonial Times to 1970*. Part 1.

rates are found in Africa and western Asia, where most countries have rates greater than six births per woman. These populations are growing by more than 2.5 percent per year. A few such as Kenya, Zambia, and Iraq are growing 3.8 percent per year or more. If unchanged, these populations will double in eighteen years, but change is evident. Thailand's rate declined from 4.5 births per woman in 1980 to 2.6 in 1990 (Population Reference Bureau 1980; 1990). A few developing countries, including China, Taiwan, South Korea, Sri Lanka, Cyprus, Barbados, Cuba, Puerto Rico, Jamaica, Chile, and Uruguay, are averaging less than 2.5 births per woman. Others with very high fertility, such as Kenya, India, Bangladesh, and Egypt, have begun to show a decline.

The fertility measures discussed up to this point are period rates. They are based on data for a particular year and represent the behavior of a cross-section of age groups in the population in that year. Fertility also can be measured over the lifetime of birth cohorts. Cumulative fertility rates can be calculated for each birth cohort of women by summing the age-specific fertility rates that prevailed as they passed through each age (Shryock and Siegel 1976, p. 289). This calculation yields a completed fertility rate for birth cohorts that have reached the end of their reproductive years. It is the cohort equivalent of the period total fertility rate.

## DEATH RATES

The measurement of mortality raises many of the same issues discussed with fertility. Rates are more informative than absolute numbers, and those rates that more precisely define the population at risk to dying are more accurate. Unlike fertility, however, the entire population is at risk to dying, and this universal experience happens only once to an individual.

The impact of mortality on population growth can be calculated with a crude death rate:

Crude death rate =

$$\frac{\text{Deaths in year } x}{\text{Midyear population in year } x} \times 1,000 \quad (5)$$

Crude death rates vary from over 20 per 1,000 in some African countries and Afghanistan to as low as 2 or 3 per 1,000. The lowest rates are not in the developed countries of Europe, North America, Oceania, and the Soviet Union, which have rates between 7 and 12 per 1,000 (Population Reference Bureau 1990). Instead, the lowest crude death rates are found in developing countries with high fertility and declining mortality. This anomaly results from the older age composition of developed countries compared to developing countries. The proportion of people age sixty-five and over ranges between 12 and 18 percent in developed countries compared to less than 5 percent in most African, Asian, and Latin American populations. Although the entire population is at risk of dying, the risk rises with age after childhood. Consequently, populations with a higher proportion of elderly have higher crude death rates even when there is no difference in the risk of dying at each age.

To control for the strong influence of age on mortality, age-specific rates can be calculated for five-year age groups:

Age-specific mortality rate =

$$\frac{\text{Deaths in year } x \text{ to the population age } a}{\text{Population age } a \text{ in year } x} \times 1,000 \quad (6)$$

Before age five, the age-specific mortality rate usually is subdivided to capture the higher risk of dying immediately after birth. The rate for one- to four-year olds, like other age-specific rates, is based on the midyear estimate of this population. The conventional infant mortality rate, however, is based on the number of live births:

Infant mortality rate =

$$\frac{\text{Deaths under age 1 in year } x}{\text{Live births in year } x} \times 1,000 \quad (7)$$

The infant mortality rate is often disaggregated into the neonatal mortality rate for the first month of life and the postneonatal rate for the rest of the year:

Neonatal mortality rate =

$$\frac{\text{Deaths under 28 days in year } x}{\text{Live births in year } x} \times 1,000 \quad (8)$$

Postneonatal =

$$\frac{\text{Deaths from 29 days to age 1 in year } x}{\text{Live births in year } x} \times 1,000 \quad (9)$$

Infant mortality varies widely throughout the world. Many African and some Asian countries have 1990 rates that still exceed 100 per 1,000 births, although they have declined (Population Reference Bureau 1990). Latin American infant mortality rates have declined as well. They now range from 12 in Cuba to 122 in Haiti. In contrast, developed countries with market economies have rates at or below 10, led by Japan with under 5 infant deaths per 1,000 live births.

The U.S. infant mortality rate is double that of Japan's, and the downward trend in this rate has slowed (National Center for Health Statistics 1989b, p. 8) as the proportion of premature births has increased (National Center for Health Statistics 1989a, p. 12). The country's largest minority, blacks, have more than double the rates of premature births and infant mortality of whites, but not all minorities have higher infant mortality. Data from eighteen states and the District of Columbia reveal that Hispanic infant mortality is slightly lower than the Anglo rate of 8.4 (National Center for Health Statistics 1989b, p. 9).

Infant mortality also varies by sex in the United States and other countries. The rate for U.S. male newborns is 11 per 1,000 compared to 9 per 1,000 for females (National Center for Health Statistics 1989b, p. 13). This sex difference in mortality is evident at all ages. The greatest gap is among young adults; U.S. males are three times

more likely to die than females between twenty and twenty-four, due largely to motor vehicle fatalities.

Age-specific mortality rates usually are specific for sex as well because of the large differences. This results in thirty-eight rates with the usual age categories, and this can be awkward. When the age pattern of mortality is not of interest, an age-adjusted composite measure is preferable. The most common of these is life expectancy.

Life expectancy is the average number of years that members of an age group would live if they

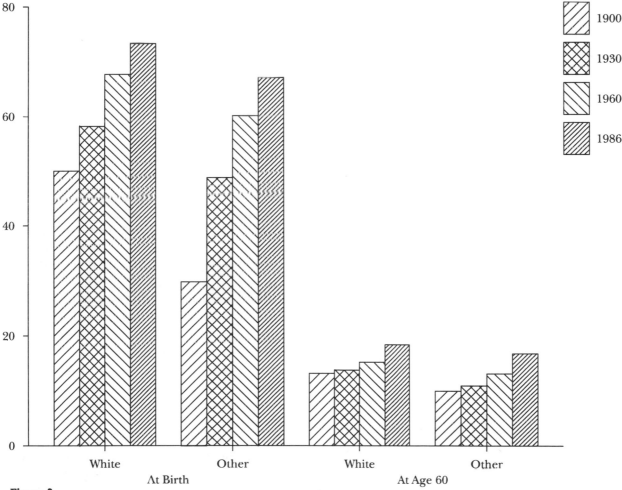

*Figure 3*

*Male Life Expectancy (in Number of Years) at Birth and Age 60 by Race: United States*

SOURCE: National Center for Heatlh Statistics, *1986 Mortality,* Part A and U.S. Bureau of the Census, *Historical Statistics of the United States, Colonial Times to 1970,* Part 1.

NOTE: Life expectancy data for 1900 and 1930 for "Other" indicate blacks only.

were to experience the age-specific death rates prevailing in a given year. It is calculated for each age group in a life table (Shryock and Siegel 1976, pp. 249–68). All developed countries and some developing countries in Asia, Latin America, and Oceania have life expectancies at birth of over seventy (Population Reference Bureau 1990). Japan has the longest, seventy-nine years, due to extremely low infant mortality. African countries, in contrast, with their relatively high infant and child mortality, generally have life expectancies in the forties or fifties.

Declines in infant and child mortality from infectious diseases have been largely responsible for the historical increase in life expectancy in all developed and most developing countries. As a result, life expectancy in the United States has increased far more at birth than at age sixty (Figure 3), and cardiovascular disease and cancer have become the major causes of death (National Center for Health Statistics 1989, p. 6). If cardiovascular mortality continues to decline and the slight reduction in cancer mortality observed in 1986 and 1987 grows, gains in life expectancy at age sixty will accelerate.

(SEE ALSO: *Demography; Infant and Child Mortality; Life Expectancy*)

### REFERENCES

National Center for Health Statistics 1978 "Advance Report of Final Natality Statistics, 1976." *Monthly Vital Statistics Report,* Vol. 26, no. 12, suppl. Hyattsville, Md.: Public Health Service.

——— 1988 *1986 Mortality,* Vol. 2, part A. Washington, D.C.: U.S. Government Printing Office.

——— 1989a "Advance Report of Final Natality Statistics, 1987." *Monthly Vital Statistics Report,* Vol. 38, no. 3, suppl. Hyattsville, Md.: Public Health Service.

——— 1989b "Advance Report of Final Mortality Statistics, 1987." *Monthly Vital Statistics Report,* vol. 38, no. 5, suppl. Hyattsville, Md.: Public Health Service.

Population Reference Bureau 1980 *1980 World Population Data Sheet.* Washington, D.C.: Population Reference Bureau.

——— 1990 *1990 World Population Data Sheet.* Washington, D.C.: Population Reference Bureau.

Shryock, Henry S., and Jacob S. Siegel 1976 *The Methods and Materials of Demography.* San Francisco: Academic Press.

United Nations 1989 *Demographic Yearbook, 1987.* New York: United Nations.

U.S. Bureau of the Census 1975 *Historical Statistics of the United States, Colonial Times to 1970.* Washington D.C.: Government Printing Office.

——— 1988 "Projections of the Population of States by Age, Sex, and Race: 1988–2010." *Current Population Reports,* series P-25, no. 1017. Washington, D.C.: Government Printing Office.

DEBORAH A. SULLIVAN

**BISEXUALITY** *See* Sexual Orientation; Sexually Transmitted Diseases.

**BLACK STUDIES** *See* African-American Studies.

**BRITISH SOCIOLOGY** The roots of sociology in Britain spread wide and deep, extending back into eighteenth-century political economy, philosophy, and political arithmetic. It surfaced as a fashionable intellectual vogue in the nineteenth century but failed to bloom as a fully recognized academic discipline until the 1960s.

The roles of statistician, administrator, reform politician, and social philosopher were already part of the system in the nineteenth century as Abrams has pointed out (1968, p. 5). To these we should add the role of popular educator. Herbert Spencer (1820–1903) dominated general consciousness of sociology until the outbreak of World War I but was shunned by the universities and political establishment. That was in complete contrast to the United States, where Spencer's enormous popular reception was followed by the widespread establishment of sociology in American colleges. In Britain the first chair of sociology was established at the London School of Economics in 1907, and it remained the only chair until after World War II.

If sociology remained for so long outside the

formal institutional structure of education and the professions, there were, nonetheless, many intellectual strands in British culture that contributed to a now characteristic breadth and pluralism in British sociology. Thus, the individualism of British political philosophy and political economy exemplified by Thomas Hobbes or Adam Smith fed through into the thought of Herbert Spencer and to this day into easy reception of the methodological individualism of Max Weber and research into life chances and social mobility. The experience of administering an empire provided an early stimulus for the development of anthropology, which both prepared the ground for sociology and contributes to current debates within it.

The foundations for later expansion were laid at the London School of Economics between 1945 and 1955, when Morris Ginsberg, Tom Marshall, Karl Popper, David Glass, and Edward Shils were teaching there at the same time. Their pupils formed the vanguard of provincial sociology in the 1960s. Chelly Halsey, who was to hold a chair at Oxford, was one of them and has described how they aspired to become professional sociologists with a political outlook colored by British Labour Party Fabian socialism and intent on contributing to the construction of a new postwar social order. Max Weber rather than Karl Marx provided theoretical guidance. At least twelve of them went on to hold chairs, forming "a more or less self-conscious group" (Halsey 1982, p. 151).

The cohesiveness of this group was greatly tested by the developments of the 1960s. In three years in the early part of that decade twenty-four new chairs of sociology were established in Britain, whereas before there had been only five. By 1970 the number of universities at which it was possible for students to take a full degree in sociology had risen from two in 1953 to thirty-seven (Albrow 1989, p. 203).

The impetus came from a coalition of forces: belief in planning and Keynesian economics created a demand for rational social policy and a social research base, and an ideology of equality of opportunity combined with the demographic factor of a maturing postwar baby boom generation to create pressure for new educational opportuni-

ties. Sociology became the fashionable subject to include within the curriculum of the new universities and polytechnics. The state-financed Social Science Research Council (now the Economic and Social Research Council) was established in 1965.

The wave of students and newly appointed young staff of the period brought with them more than the hopes of their sponsors. There was a generational culture, born of steady economic expansion with optimistic beliefs in equality and self-expression. Youthful enthusiasm that challenged the social ameliorism of the older LSE professors embraced a profusion of different theoretical orientations. French Marxism, American symbolic interactionism, and phenomenology were potent attractions producing a many-sided conflict of perspectives.

## PRESENT SITUATION

As a consequence of its takeoff in the 1960s, sociology acquired a public image in Britain as a radical product, expressed and reinforced by an immensely popular fictional representation in the novel *The History Man* (1975) by Malcolm Bradbury, whose antihero gives courses on revolution, is a thorn in the flesh of the town council, and creates havoc in personal relations as well as in his university. Throughout the 1980s sociologists have had to combat political attacks employing this image, which, as the recruits of the 1960s have aged, has become even less a reflection of reality than it was for the earlier period. The reality is that sociology is a well-established academic discipline based in the vast majority of British institutions of higher education, attracting steadily rising numbers of students, and taught by middle-aged lecturers.

The strength of British sociology now undoubtedly derives from its diversity. No single paradigm enjoys majority support, while at the same time a multiplicity of affiliations with other fields and interest groups ensures a relatively stable environment in the face of a diffuse public hostility. That in itself has resulted in an amelioration of the internal hostilities of the 1960s and 1970s, and a "live and let live" atmosphere predominates within the subject.

This pluralism can be illustrated from Oxford where for twenty years John Goldthorpe and Bryan Wilson have worked independently of each other with quite different interests and approaches. The former has become world famous for his development of social mobility methodology and for the definitive study of British mobility (Goldthorpe, Llewellyn, and Payne 1987), while the latter initiated a school of research into sects and new religious movements that is equally world renowned (Wilson 1961).

Quite independently from both of them, Anthony Giddens, who holds the chair in Cambridge, has developed his theory of structuration (Giddens 1984) and through prolific writing has become probably the most widely published theoretician in world sociology since Talcott Parsons. The success of his project depends upon a constructive and open-ended absorption of multiple strands of French, German, and American theory, providing shape and form to the diffuse reception of foreign ideas by the new generation of sociologists. His work marks a secular change in British social thought, from proud insularity to ambitious cosmopolitanism. It is a considerable contribution to the worldwide internationalization of sociology.

One thing Goldthorpe, Giddens, and Wilson have in common is a period spent in their youth at the University of Leicester where Norbert Elias (1978) was introducing British sociologists to a theoretical historical sociology grounded in German traditions. That was a necessary counterweight to the LSE dominance in the provinces, as was John Rex's work in Leeds stimulating renewed interest in Max Weber (Rex 1961).

But the newer forces in postwar Britain outside Oxbridge and London are perhaps best represented by Stuart Hall, who took over the Centre for Contemporary Cultural Studies in Birmingham from Richard Hoggart, whose work (1957) was an inspiration for a whole generation investigating working-class culture. Hall has helped to make the notion of hegemony commonplace through an influential series of studies on deviance and social control (Hall and Jefferson 1976) and now as professor at the Open University, the most important new institution for adult higher education through distance learning in modern Britain.

Research has not been located exclusively within educational institutions. The aspirations to reform society were for some better able to be fulfilled outside those official structures, especially if this meant evaluating the experience of the working classes. Michael (now Lord) Young, Peter Townsend, and Peter Willmott worked in the independent Institute of Community Studies from 1954. Their now classic studies of family and community life (Young and Willmott 1957) and old people (Townsend 1957) continued a long tradition of nonestablishment, problem-oriented social research and acquired a very wide readership and popularity for the newly emerging sociology. Young also captured public imagination with his *The Rise of the Meritocracy* (1958), but in general British sociologists have not been as successful as their American counterparts in writing bestsellers. There has been no one to compare with C. Wright Mills or Vance Packard, and opinion-forming books on British society have tended to be written by historians such as Martin Wiener (1981).

Nor can it be said that sociologists have exercised any substantial influence on public policy except indirectly. Sir Keith Joseph, Conservative Minister for Education in the early 1980s, was impressed with the idea of the cycle of deprivation, and, more recently, policy on community care for the mentally ill has reflected thinking on the dysfunctions of large institutions. Earlier policies on comprehensive school education drew upon the findings of sociologists who pointed to the loss of talent involved in early streaming of school pupils. But it is still extremely rare for sociologists, as compared with economists for instance, to be invited to serve on government committees.

If it is not in best sellers or in public policy that British sociology makes its impact, it has a much more pervasive influence in educational circles. It has even led critics of education at all levels to claim that it is dominated by sociologists, a claim that does not bear examination on any analysis of occupancy of key posts but reflects the fact that sociological perspectives have been absorbed in disciplines such as history and literature and in professional subjects like law and medicine.

Even in the business schools that have developed in the 1980s, much as sociology did in the 1960s, many of the staff have a sociological background that makes it all the easier for concepts such as organizational culture to be received. In all these areas journals exist to promote interdisciplinary debate, and in the general discussion of the relations between academe and society sociologists are prominent in the pages of the influential *Times Higher Education Supplement* and elsewhere. Sociology has often been the voice of the academic establishment in the 1980s, and this has not been an insignificant element in the strained relations between government and education.

Equally, sociology has been the natural study and research destination for all those who are critical of the social order. But feminism has replaced Marxism as the dominant critique. The sociology of women and gender now occupies a prominent position, as exemplified in Anne Oakley's various studies of the division of labor in the household (1989). This focus on women has finally ended the thematic dominance that class, and especially the working class, has exercised over British sociology since the 1950s. It has combined with long-standing research directions in religion and ethnicity to constitute a broad-based orientation to closure and cleavage in British society, which engages directly with the growing diversification of household patterns and life-styles. Painstaking research into everyday coping strategies by individuals and couples faced with the demise of old structures now characterizes much current sociology and is perhaps best exemplified by the work of Ray Pahl (1984).

## INTERNATIONAL CHARACTER

British sociology has always engaged in intensive international intellectual exchange. John Stuart Mill first popularized the ideas of Auguste Comte, while Mill was widely influential outside Britain. The lone professor of sociology in Britain

between the world wars, Morris Ginsberg, was a Russian immigrant who introduced his students to European ideas. A refugee from Nazi Germany, Karl Mannheim, established the most extensive publisher's list in British sociology, Routledge's International Library of Sociology and Social Reconstruction.

But two reservations have to be entered before the conclusion is reached that British sociology is wholly internationalized. The first is that hostility to the subject has arisen at times precisely because of this receptiveness to foreign ideas. Since sociologists claim at least a degree of detachment from their own society for the purposes of scientific study, they have on two counts been prey to the charge of lack of patriotism, and the subject has been thought of as an alien import.

The second point may arise as a compensation for the first in that British sociologists have concentrated on their own society as a field for research. Thus, Christine Delphy, the French feminist, has influenced studies of *British* women; the Spaniard Manuel Castells has become important in the study of *British* urban conditions. It is as if foreign contributions have to be warranted by showing their relevance to Britain.

This has not been a limiting factor for a long line of distinguished foreign scholars who have made their home in Britain, inspired students, and maintained international sociology both theoretically and empirically: Gi Baldamus, Ralf Dahrendorf, Norbert Elias (Germany); Stanislav Andreski, Zygmunt Bauman (Poland); Percy Cohen, John Rex (South Africa); Paul Halmos (Hungary); Viola Klein (Czechoslovakia); Salvador Giner (Spain); Gian Poggi (Italy); Nicos Mouzelis (Greece); Teodor Shanin (Russia); John Westergaard (Denmark). At the same time the world quality of British social theory is demonstrated by the way American universities have enlisted the services of Alasdair Macintyre, John Heritage, John Hall, and Michael Mann.

Those British sociologists who have worked abroad have often also contributed to the institutional framework of international sociology. Tom Bottomore wrote a textbook for students in the Indian subcontinent (1962) and became president of the International Sociological Association as did Margaret Archer, who had become well known for her comparative work on educational systems (1974). She was editor of the ISA's first journal, *Current Sociology,* and was succeeded in turn by James Beckford and William Outhwaite. The ISA's new journal, founded in 1986, *International Sociology,* has also had a British base and been edited by Martin Albrow.

Journals such as *Sociology, The British Journal of Sociology,* and *The Sociological Review* have a worldwide circulation, and the dominance of the English language has been highly advantageous to British sociologists and their publishers. Routledge, Blackwell, Macmillan, Oxford and Cambridge University Presses, Sage, and a newcomer, Polity Press, publish British and other sociology worldwide.

## ORGANIZATION, TRAINING, AND THE FUTURE

Two official reports on sociology in higher education institutions in the late 1980s sought to ascertain the existing provision for teaching and research and to make recommendations (Council for National Academic Awards 1988; University Grants Committee 1989). Their task was made difficult precisely because of the complex way sociology is interwoven with other subjects. Based broadly, however, on their reports and on other information, we can say that there are seventy-five institutions at which students can take a substantial part of their degree in sociology, and in about forty of them it is possible to take it as a main subject for the standard British bachelor degree in which in any one year perhaps 1,150 students are graduating. At the same time about 700 students are working full-time for higher degrees, of whom perhaps 40 percent are from overseas.

Numbers of teachers are equally difficult to assess; there are perhaps 700 with another 200 research staff. They are dispersed relatively evenly across the institutions. The University Grants Committee report found no department with more than 20 lecturing staff and only one with a lecturer under thirty, a reflection of a ten-year

standstill in funding. The new universities founded in the 1960s house the most prominent centers: Essex, Kent, Lancaster, Surrey, and Warwick, but of the older institutions the LSE, Oxford, and Leicester have maintained their standing as have Glasgow and Edinburgh, while Cambridge has set up a new Faculty of Social and Political Sciences in which sociology is central.

The same picture of diversely organized small units applies to research centers associated with perhaps half of the university departments, drawing about half their funds from government contracts and a quarter from research councils. From 1985 to 1988 research income was reported as £27.7 million. Independent research bodies such as the Policy Studies Institute and the government's own Home Office Research Unit and similar units compete with universities for these funds, but it is unlikely that the total available is more than twice this amount.

A long-standing complaint about British sociology has been the inadequate technical training provided. Both the British Sociological Association (with about 2,000 members) and the Social Research Association (with about 700 members) advocate more resources for the training of professional sociologists, but the scarcity of research funding and the virtual cessation of recruitment to teaching in the 1980s have made this no more than a pious expression of hope.

At the beginning of the 1990s, however, there is more than hope; there is excitement in the air. Halsey was already saying (for purely intellectual reasons) in a special journal issue devoted to a survey of British sociology that there was an "exciting unfinished agenda . . . inevitably shaped by passions which are continually renewed in an imperfect, unjust world" (Halsey 1989, p. 371). In the wake of a dramatic global transformation in 1989 has followed the end of an era in national terms. Both a new Conservative government and the Labour opposition have made education the central issue for the 1990s, and the new Prime Minister aspires to a classless society. Higher education is set to double its student intake in a decade.

It may be 1960 over again, but, if it is, sociology

is vastly better prepared to meet the challenge than it was then. The dominance of class analysis has been replaced by cultural analysis and by the desire to probe deeply into the postmodern condition, where cultural pluralism may signify a multicultural mutual incomprehensibility. If there is a danger for British sociology it is that its multiparadigmatic character may already reflect the surrounding culture too closely to be able to offer the coherent detachment and cool appraisal that wins it recognition for independence and guarantees its long-standing identity. In this respect the surest safeguards are the ever-widening links with the international community of sociologists and continuing comparison with their best standards. The American Sociological Association provides a model of professionalism for the British Sociological Association as in the 1990s the key issue facing British sociologists will be how to convert the intellectual esteem they enjoy among their academic peers into a wider public recognition of professional competence. The skills and capacities of practitioners will be as important as the knowledge claims of the discipline they serve.

## REFERENCES

Abrams, Philip 1968 *The Origins of British Sociology.* Chicago and London: University of Chicago Press.

Albrow, Martin 1989 "Sociology in the United Kingdom After the Second World War." In Nikolai Genov, ed., *National Traditions in Sociology.* London: Sage.

Archer, Margaret 1974 *Social Origins of Education Systems.* London: Sage.

Bottomore, Tom B. 1962 *Sociology: A Guide to Problems and Literature.* London: Unwin University Books.

Bradbury, Malcolm 1975 *The History Man.* London: Secker and Warburg.

Bulmer, Martin (ed.) 1985 *Essays on the History of British Sociological Research.* Cambridge: Cambridge University Press.

Council for National Academic Awards 1988 *Review of Sociology: Course and Teaching.* London: Council for National Academic Awards.

Elias, Norbert 1978 *The Civilizing Process: The History of Manners.* Oxford: Basil Blackwell.

Genov, Nikolai (ed.) 1989 *National Traditions in Sociology.* London: Sage.

Giddens, Anthony 1984 *The Constitution of Society.* Cambridge: Polity Press.

Goldthorpe, John H., C. Llewellyn, and C. Payne 1987 *Social Mobility and Class Structure in Britain.* Oxford: Clarendon Press.

Hall, Stuart, and Tony Jefferson (eds.) 1976 *Resistance Through Rituals: Youth Sub-Culture in Great Britain.* London: Hutchinson.

Halsey, A. H. 1982 "Provincials and Professionals: The British Post-War Sociologists." *Archives européennes de sociologie* 23:150–175. (Reprinted in part in Martin Bulmer, ed., *Essays on the History of British Sociology*, 1985, Cambridge: Cambridge University Press.)

——— 1989 "A Turning of the Tide? The Prospects for Sociology in Britain." *British Journal of Sociology* 40:353–373.

Hoggart, Richard 1957 *The Uses of Literacy.* London: Chatto and Windus.

Oakley, Anne 1989 "Women's Studies in British Sociology: To End at Our Beginning?" *British Journal of Sociology* 40:442–470.

Pahl, Ray 1984 *Divisions of Labour.* Oxford: Basil Blackwell.

Rex, John 1961 *Key Problems in Sociological Theory.* London: Routledge.

Townsend, Peter 1957 *The Family Life of Old People.* London: Routledge.

University Grants Committee 1989 *Report of the Review Committee on Sociology.* London: University Grants Committee.

Wiener, Martin J. 1981 *English Culture and the Decline of the Industrial Spirit 1850–1980.* Cambridge: Cambridge University Press.

Wilson, Bryan 1961 *Sects and Society.* London: Heinemann.

Young, Michael 1958 *The Rise of the Meritocracy 1870–2033.* London: Thames and Hudson.

Young, Michael, and Peter Willmott 1957 *Family Life and Kinship in East London.* London: Routledge.

MARTIN ALBROW

**BUREAUCRACY** The origin of the term *bureaucracy* can be traced to eighteenth-century French literature (Albrow 1970). In this early usage, the term referred to the workplace of officials whose activities were routinely determined by fairly explicit rules and regulations. In contradistinction to other forms of administration, modern bureaucracies represent highly formalized and intensely rational systems of administration. As systems of management and supervision, bureaucracies are designed to provide for the rational coordination of duties and responsibilities of officials and employees of organizations. It is important to recognize that this notion of the rational organization of individual behavior pertains to an organizational and not to an individual level of concern. Consequently, bureaucracies represent devices by which the private, idiosyncratic, and uniquely personal interests and actions of individuals are formally orchestrated and constrained in order to achieve specified organizational goals in an efficient way. This orchestration of individual action is accomplished by the use of rules and formal programs of activity (March and Simon 1958) intended to provide a clear outline of mandated duties and responsibilities. With such a delineation of duties and responsibilities, this system of administration tends to ensure that the actions and activities of individuals contribute to the interests of the organizations within which they are employed.

## THE CONTRIBUTION OF MAX WEBER

Interest in bureaucracy, both as a process and as an outcome, has been long standing in sociology. Early concern is evident in the work of Karl Marx ([1852] 1963) and of Alexis de Tocqueville (1877), who were among the first to recognize the relatively recent historical trend toward increasing bureaucratization at the level of distinct organizations, especially military organizations, as well as in Western European society in general. Further understanding of the bureaucratic process was provided by Michels's (1949) analysis of the dynamics of power distribution within bureaucratic organizations and the development of oligarchical tendencies detrimental to democratic principles. However, the emergence of the study of bureaucracy as a major and independent line of sociological inquiry is fundamentally based upon the work of Max Weber (1864–1920). Although Weber

conducted his study immediately prior and subsequent to the turn of the century, his work was not widely recognized by English-speaking theorists until its translation during the late 1940s (Weber 1946, 1947).

Weber's ambitious and richly informative work most notably includes consideration of Chinese, Egyptian, Roman, Prussian, and French administrative systems. In his comparative analysis of this vast array of diverse cultural systems of administration, Weber recognized an inexorable relationship between power and authority, on the one hand, and differing systems of administration on the other. Thus, in Weber's analysis, the bureaucratic form of administration reflects one of three particular ways in which power is legitimated. Consequently, in order to gain a clear appreciation of the unique features of bureaucratic structure and processes, it is necessary briefly to address Weber's notion of the relationship among power, authority, and systems of administration.

*Power,* for Weber, represents the ability or capacity to have other people behave in accordance with certain orders or dictates, irrespective of whether those affected regard its application as rightful or legitimate. *Authority* represents the legitimation of this power by those individuals whose activities are so ordered such that the application of power is perceived to be rightful. In Weber's analysis, three different types of authority are recognized: traditional, charismatic, and rational–legal (Weber 1947, p. 328). Traditional authority represents a system in which the use of power is regarded as legitimate when it is predicated upon belief in the sanctity of time-honored traditions. Charismatic authority has a much more limited focus, in that it is based on intensely personal acts of devotion. Under these circumstances, authority is conferred upon a specific individual who is regarded by devoted followers to exhibit exceptional, sacred, and/or heroic characteristics. Thus, the authority of the charismatic leader is predicated upon the granting of power by these devoted followers. Rational–legal authority derives from the belief in the legitimacy of law, specifically in the legality of rules and the authority of officials and employees to perform certain legally sanctioned and mandated duties that are assigned to them.

Associated with each type of authority are distinctive *systems of administration.* Over the course of premodern social history, traditional authority was the principal means by which social organization was achieved. This type of authority structure resulted in the development of a wide variety of highly stable but nonetheless particularistic systems of administration, in which personal relations of dependence or loyalty provided the underpinning. In general, these systems of administration are most clearly exemplified by patrimonial and feudal systems of administration.

Charismatic authority results in the emergence of highly unstable systems of administration, because the foundation of these systems, the profoundly personal relationships between charismatic leaders and followers, is decisively limited in both time and circumstance. Given the notably conditional foundations of charismatic authority structures, it is not surprising that the systems of administration that arise in such situations encounter difficulties in generating stable administrative practices. In this regard, problems pertaining to the routinization of authority and leadership succession are particularly salient and acute (Weber 1947, pp. 358–373). Thus, systems of administration under the dominion of charismatic authority tend to be inherently transitory and are most likely to arise during periods of crisis or unprecedented change.

Rational–legal authority culminates in the emergence of highly precise and universalistic systems of administration that are most clearly exemplified by the modern rational bureaucracy. Weber clearly regards such bureaucratic practices to be relatively recent in their development: "Bureaucracy . . . is fully developed in political and ecclesiastical communities only in the modern state, and in the private economy only in the most advanced institutions of capitalism" (Weber 1978, p. 956).

## CHARACTERISTICS OF BUREAUCRACIES

Perhaps the most distinguishing feature of modern rational bureaucracies is the fact that individual activity is formally controlled, prescribed, and regulated through the enforcement of rules. Moreover, the intent of enforcing these rules is the efficient achievement of specific organizational goals. In orchestrating individual action, a succinct and unambiguous specification of the official duties and responsibilities is provided, to minimize, if not to eliminate, the influence of personal interests, ambitions, and interests upon the performance of official duties. The official or employee is thus able to concentrate exclusively upon the technical aspects of the work, in particular the efficient and rational completion of assigned tasks. In addition to this attempt to separate individuals' private concerns from their official duties and responsibilities, distinguishing characteristics of bureaucracies include the following:

1. A pervasive hierarchical ordering of authority relations that limits the areas of command and responsibility for subordinate as well as superordinate personnel
2. The recruitment and selective promotion of individuals solely on the basis of technical expertise and competence
3. A structuring of the work environment in ways that ensure continuous and full-time employment, the development and fulfillment of career expectations, and the elimination of other sources of employment competing for the time and attention of officials and employees
4. A clearly defined division of labor in which a high degree of specialization and training is required for the performance of assigned tasks
5. The impersonality and impartiality of relationships involving both organization members and those outside the organization, such as customers or clients
6. An emphasis upon formal and written documentation in the form of "official records."

Bureaucratic organization thus represents an attempt to coordinate individual action on the basis of rational rules, rules that are intended to insulate and contain individual action in ways that promote the technical efficiency of an organization. The distinctive feature of bureaucratic organization is not the use of rules per se but, rather, the type of rules employed within an organization as well as the justification for the use of rules. Rules have been, and continue to be, used in other forms of administration to control individual action; however, the rules used in the other administrative forms (such as rules based on tradition in feudal administration or on dependency in patrimonial bureaucracy) are not necessarily based on technical knowledge and the rational and efficient achievement of specific goals. By contrast, within a modern bureaucracy explicit rules are designed to assure uniformity of performance in accordance with technical requirements. Thus, bureaucracies represent systems of control which attempt to ensure that the technical abilities of individuals are effectively utilized. Factors that would reduce the prospect of an official's or employee's performance being anything other than organizationally focused, affectively neutral, and achievement oriented (Parsons and Shils 1951, pp. 76–91) are thereby systematically excluded.

## THE IDEAL TYPE CONSTRUCT

By underscoring the unique features of modern bureaucratic systems of administration outlined above, Weber implicitly provides an ideal-type characterization of bureaucracies. Despite subsequent confusion as to the value of such a portrayal of bureaucracies, Weber did not intend to provide an accurate description of the reality of bureaucratic processes. As noted in the introduction to one of his edited works, "Situations of such pure type have never existed in history. . . . The ideal types of Weber's sociology are simply mental constructs to serve as categories of thought, the use of which will help us to catch the infinite manifoldness of reality . . ." (Rhinestein 1954, pp. xxix–xxx). Thus, the ideal-type characteriza-

tion is not suggestive of either extreme cases or distinct logical categories of phenomena (Mouzelis 1967). Rather, it provides a simplification and exaggeration of empirical events so that one can appreciate more clearly the features of the phenomena in question. Actual bureaucratic organizations may exhibit only a limited number of these properties or may possess them in varying degrees, a point understood and documented by Weber. In contradistinction to this ideal bureaucratic characterization of organizations are collectivist organizations of the type identified by Rothschild-Whitt (1979). This type of organization, with its explicit rejection of a rational–legal basis for authority, provides an obvious alternative to the bureaucratic model of organization.

## EMPIRICAL ASSESSMENT

Stanley Udy (1959) was among the first to propose that, rather than regarding the specification of bureaucracies to be strictly a matter of definition, we need to ascertain empirically the extent to which bureaucratic characteristics are associated with one another in actual organizations. In the subsequent efforts at empirical assessment of the extent to which organizations exhibit bureaucratic properties, the works of Richard Hall (1963) and the Aston University research group (Pugh et al. 1968) are especially noteworthy. Hall's (1963) findings suggest that among samples of U.S. organizations, bureaucratic features of organizations may vary independently of one another. As is illustrated by the negative relationship between an emphasis on technical qualifications and other bureaucratic features— in particular hierarchy of authority and rule enforcement—Hall's study suggests that bureaucratic systems of organization may be indicative of multidimensional rather than unitary processes.

Similar findings for organizations in Britain were reported by the Aston University research group (Pugh et al. 1968). On the basis of their measurements of the bureaucratic characteristics of organizations specified by Weber, these researchers found four mutually independent dimensions of organizational structure rather than a single overarching bureaucratic dimension. With this finding, the authors concluded that bureaucracy is a multidimensional phenomenon and that it ". . . is not unitary, but that organizations may be bureaucratic in any number of ways" (Pugh et al. 1968, p. 101). However, these findings have not been unchallenged. The contentious nature of inquiry into the precise structure of bureaucratic organization is succinctly reflected in the work of Blau (1970) and of Child (1972), the adoption of a modified position by one of the investigators in the original Aston group (Hickson and McMillan 1981), and the subsequent reply by Pugh (1981).

## THE PARADOX OF BUREAUCRATIC EFFICIENCY: A REVELATION OF UNDERLYING COMPLEXITY

Although bureaucracy existed in imperial Rome and ancient China, as well as in various national monarchies, the complexity of legislative issues in the modern state has caused an enormous growth of administrative function within both government and the private sector. Consequently, with respect to affairs of the state, the power and authority of permanent nonelected officials to control policy within the modern state has, over time, increased appreciably. As Weber noted,

> The bureaucratic structure is everywhere a late product of historical development. The further back we trace our steps, the more typical is the absence of bureaucracy and of officialdom in general. Since bureaucracy has a rational character, with rules, means–ends calculus, and matter-of-factness predominating, its rise and expansion has everywhere had revolutionary results. (1978, p. 1002)

Further, Weber contended that traditional authority structures have been, and will continue to be, replaced by the rational–legal authority structures of modern bureaucracies, given their "purely technical superiority over any other form of organization" (Weber 1946, p. 214). Nevertheless, the increased prominence of bureaucracies in both the public and the private sectors is not

without its problems. The principal concern is that these bureaucracies are often unresponsive to the very public sectors they were designed to serve. To exacerbate the situation still further, few, if any, techniques of control are available to the public to ensure that bureaucracies and their officials become more responsive. As Weber acknowledged, certain negative consequences may be attendant upon the development of bureaucratic systems of administration, including the following:

1. The monopolization of information and the creation of "official secrets"
2. The relative inability to effect change from either inside or outside the bureaucratic structure because of vested incentive and reward systems, as well as the continuing social need for the level of specialization and expertise provided by the bureaucracy.
3. The tendency for bureaucracies to act in an autocratic, self-appointed manner, indifferent to variations not previously articulated within the bureaucracy. (Weber 1947, pp. 224–233)

Hence, on the one hand, bureaucracies are to be regarded as highly efficient and technically superior forms of administration that have proven to be indispensable to large, complex organizations and modern society; however, on the other hand, various practical problems arise within these administrative structures that can result in outcomes at variance with notions of efficiency and technical superiority. These outcomes include implied incompetence, an overly constrained and myopic outlook, the unwarranted application of rules and regulations, the duplication of effort, and a certain unconcerned and even cavalier attitude among officials and employees. As a result, bureaucratic forms of administration may lead to certain paradoxical and dysfunctional developments. As Perrow has noted (1972), criticism of bureaucracies frequently relates to the fact that the actions of officials and employees are not bureaucratic enough.

The classic works of Merton (1940) and of Gouldner (1954) illustrate certain ways in which dysfunctional and unanticipated developments can adversely impact the intended effectiveness of bureaucratic procedures. Merton notes that, commencing with the need for bureaucratic control, individual compliance with rules is enforced, subsequently allowing for the development of routinely prescribed, reliable patterns of activity. However, when this agenda of rule compliance is implemented in a dynamic and fluctuating set of circumstances requiring more spontaneous responses, these prescribed patterns of bureaucratic activity can lead to adverse unintended consequences. Even though the circumstances require a different type of response, prescribed and fixed patterns of response may still be adopted because such responses are legitimated and defensible within the bureaucracy, given the extent to which they enhance individual reliability. Consequently, officials and employees do not accommodate the unique features of the situation, efficiency is undermined, and difficulties with clients and customers ensue.

Eventually, troublesome experiences with customers and clients may contribute to an even greater emphasis on bureaucratically reliable behavior rather than attenuating this encapsulated and counterproductive type of behavior. Thus, as Merton (1940) notes, "Adherence to the rules, originally conceived of as a means, becomes transformed into an end in itself; there occurs the familiar process of displacement of goals whereby an instrumental value becomes a terminal value. . . ." Recognizing that not all behavior within bureaucracies is prescribed by rules and that highly adaptive and flexible behavior also occurs, Merton's model serves as a reminder that, regardless of the type of behavior, various sets of structural constraints operate to promote such behavior (Blau and Meyer 1987; Allinson 1984).

Like Merton, Gouldner (1954) is concerned with possible unintended effects of formal rule enforcement. In Gouldner's model, the implications of the use of general and impersonal rules as a means of enforcing organizational control are investigated. The intended result of the use of such rules is to mask or partially conceal differential power relations between subordinates and their superiors. In societies with egalitarian norms, such as the United States, this serves to enhance the legitimacy of supervisory positions, thereby reducing the prospect of tensions among groups of differing power. However, the use of general and impersonal rules also has the unintended consequence of providing only minimal guidelines as to acceptable organizational behavior. Further, if only minimum standards of performance are specified and if individuals conform only to these standards, then a disparity arises between the stated goals of the organization, which require a level of performance beyond minimally acceptable and specified standards, and the actual level of individual performance. Since a greater level of individual output and performance is required, more personal forms of control are employed, in the form of closer supervision. However, increased closeness of supervision increases the visibility of power relations, an effect contrary to that previously achieved by the use of general and impersonal rules. Thus, Gouldner's study underscores the fact that in actual organizational settings the enforcement of bureaucratic rules does not necessarily represent a "machine-like" procedure in which the actions of individuals and the organizational implications of these actions represent axioms of efficiency.

As further indications that bureaucratic processes may reflect processes other than those dictated by the principle of efficiency, the satirical works of Peter and Hull (1969) and of Parkinson (1957) are suggestive. Peter and Hull contend that even though individual talent and expertise are the formal requisites for recruitment and promotion within a bureaucracy, individuals often are promoted to positions that exceed their level of competence. Instead of being relocated to more suitable positions, the individuals remain in these elevated positions. Consequently, Peter and Hull argue, individuals are promoted to their level of incompetence, a representation at variance with the image of operational efficiency.

As an illustration of the law that bears his name ("Work expands to fill the time available for its completion"), Parkinson (1957) highlights certain correlates of increasing organizational size. In particular, he notes that within the field of public administration, an increase in the number of officials is not necessarily related to the amount of work to be performed. Thus, an increase in the number of officials may be associated with factors other than increasing work demands, which would be the assumption of an efficiency-based assessment of organizational development. Consequently, increases in the number of public officials can be attributed to the opportunity officials have to minimize competition among themselves by creating subordinate positions. In the process of this increase of personnel, previously nonexistent work is created by having to supervise personnel assigned to these new positions.

Besides a valuefree view of bureaucracy that focuses upon the operational efficiency of bureaucratic procedures, an alternative, more "humanistic" approach to the study of bureaucracy is also needed (Kamenka 1989, ch. 5). This alternative approach highlights the situational constraints to which individuals and groups both within and outside bureaucracies are exposed. As Martin Albrow has noted, bureaucracy is "a term of strong emotive overtones and elusive connotations" (1970, p. 13), and as such it represents more than a straightforward technical process. Consequently, comprehensive inquiry into the complexities of bureaucratic processes necessitates a genuinely eclectic perspective.

SEE ALSO: *Complex Organizations; Organizational Effectiveness; Organizational Structure)*

## REFERENCES

Albrow, Martin 1970 *Bureaucracy.* London: Pall Mall Press.

Allinson, Christopher W. 1984 *Bureaucratic Personality and Organization Structure.* Aldershot, England: Gower.

Blau, Peter M. 1970 "Decentralization in Bureaucracies." In Mayer N. Zald, ed., *Power in Organizations.* Nashville, Tenn.: Vanderbilt University Press.

————, and Marshall W. Meyer 1987 *Bureaucracy in Modern Society,* 3rd ed. New York: Random House.

Child, John 1972 "Organization, Structure, and Strategies of Control." *Administrative Science Quarterly* 17:163–177.

Gouldner, Alvin W. 1954 *Patterns of Industrial Bureaucracy.* Glencoe, Ill.: Free Press.

Hall, Richard 1963 "The Concept of Bureaucracy: An Empirical Assessment." *American Journal of Sociology* 69:32–40.

Hickson, David, and C. J. McMillan 1981 *Organization and Nation: The Aston Programme IV.* Westmead, England: Gower.

Kamenka, Eugene 1989 *Bureaucracy.* Oxford: Basil Blackwell.

March, James G., and Herbert A. Simon 1958 *Organizations.* New York: Wiley.

Marx, Karl (1852) 1963 *The Eighteenth Brumaire of Louis Bonaparte.* New York: International Publishing Co.

Merton, Robert K. 1940. "Bureaucratic Structure and Personality." *Social Forces* 18:560–568.

Michels, Robert 1949 *Political Parties: A Sociological Study of the Oligarchial Tendencies of Modern Democracy.* New York: Free Press.

Mouzelis, Nicos P. 1967 *Organization and Bureaucracy.* London: Routledge and Kegan Paul.

Parkinson, C. Northcote 1957 *Parkinson's Law.* Boston: Houghton Mifflin.

Parsons, Talcott, and E. A. Shils 1951 *Toward a General Theory of Action.* Cambridge, Mass: Harvard University Press.

Perrow, Charles 1972 *Complex Organizations: A Critical Essay.* Glenview, Ill.: Scott Foresman.

Peter, Laurence F., and Raymond Hull 1969 *The Peter Principle.* New York: Morrow.

Pugh, D. S. 1981 "The Aston Programme of Research: Retrospect and Prospect." In Andrew H. Van de Ven and W. F. Joyce, eds., *Perspectives on Organization Design and Behavior.* New York: Wiley.

————, et al. 1968 "Dimensions of Organization Structure." *Administrative Science Quarterly* 13:65–105.

Rhinestein, Max 1954 *Max Weber on Law in Economy and Society.* New York: Simon and Schuster.

Rothschild-Whitt, Joyce 1979 "The Collectivist Organization: An Alternative to Rational Bureaucratic Models." *American Sociological Review* 44:509–527.

Tocqueville, Alexis de (1877) 1955 *L'ancien régime and the French Revolution,* J. P. Mayer and A. P. Kerr, eds. Garden City, N.Y.: Doubleday.

Udy, Stanley H. Jr. 1959 "'Bureaucracy' and 'Rationality' in Weber's Organization Theory." *American Sociological Review* 24:591–595.

Weber, Max 1946 *From Max Weber: Essays in Sociology,* H. H. Gerth and C. W. Mills, eds. London: Oxford University Press.

—— 1947 *The Theory of Social and Economic Organization,* A. M. Henderson and T. Parsons, eds. Glencoe, Ill.: Free Press.

—— 1978 *Economy and Society: An Outline of Interpretive Sociology,* Guenther Roth and Claus Wittich, eds. Berkeley: University of California Press.

DAVID G. NICKINOVICH

# C

**CANADIAN SOCIOLOGY** The intellectual roots of sociology in Canada are European, with a greater French and British influence than is typically found in other American countries. U.S. versions of social Darwinism gained little currency in Canada. Instead, French positivism and German rationalism were infused with Fabian socialism and progressive pragmatism to put sociology to use in building a social democratic society. Consequently, early sociology in Canada was identified with social movements such as the agrarian reform movement in the West and the Catholic Action movement in Quebec. By the 1920s, university-level courses in sociology were being offered in a number of disciplines and were included in theology curricula. The Canadian Political Science Association, formed in 1913, accepted sociologists as members. The first academic appointment in sociology in Canada was that of Carl A. Dawson at McGill University in 1922. Honors programs were established at McGill in 1926 and at the University of Toronto in 1932. The minor status of the discipline in universities in Canada reflected its deployment by detached intellectuals and political reformers, and the conservative hegemony of the traditional humanistic disciplines in Canadian universities. The work of S. D. Clark at the University of Toronto during the 1940s was important to the subsequent recognition of sociology as a legitimate academic field.

Significant sociological research in Canada had been ongoing since the 1880s. This included the works of Marius Barbeau, Carl Dawson, Léon Gérin, Diamond Jenness, and Everett Hughes. It focused on Canada's indigenous peoples, urbanization, ethnic settlement in the West, rural social life in Quebec, and, in particular, Francophone–Anglophone relations. By the end of World War II, a substantial body of material on Canada's economic, political, and social development had been accumulated. Historical political economy and human ecology paradigms were predominant, reflecting the British influence at Toronto and that of the Chicago School at McGill.

Francophone sociology in Quebec took its early inspiration from the encyclical *Rerum novarum* (1891). By the 1930s Catholic sociology, perceived as an instrument of national development for Quebec, was taught at Université Laval and Université de Montréal. Father Georges-Henri Lévesque of Laval led a movement to establish a more secularized sociology in Quebec during the 1940s. More quantitative in emphasis, this sociology directed attention away from "la survivance" of traditional French-Canadian culture and toward the industrialization and modernization of Quebec society. By the 1960s a new nationalism emerged in Quebec sociology that supported an ideology of self-determination and sovereignty for Quebec. With the growth of the state system during the 1960s and 1970s, sociologists in Quebec became directly involved in the planning and administration of the new society. As the state instruments of social development took shape and the aim of nationhood for Quebec became institutionalized, the legitimacy of the existing Canadian federation was questioned. Sovereignty became a viable option for Quebec, and captured the attention and support of Quebec sociologists.

The 1960s saw a phenomenal growth in academic sociology in Canada, a consequence of population pressure on the universities, and of a growing demand for empirical knowledge and sociological understanding. In 1960 there were only sixty-one sociologists in Canadian universities. Two decades later, sociology was an established discipline in every academic institution in the country. In 1965 the Canadian Sociology and Anthropology Association was formed and subsequently began publication of the *Canadian Review of Sociology and Anthropology*. Additional scholarly outlets for sociologists in Canada include the *Canadian Journal of Sociology, Recherches sociographiques, Sociologie et sociétés, Cahiers québécois de démographie, Canadian Ethnic Studies, Canadian Journal of Criminology, Canadian Studies in Population, Journal of Canadian Studies, Canadian Women's Studies,* and *Studies in Political Economy.*

Up to 1960, only two doctorates in sociology had been awarded in Canada. Consequently, the demand for university teachers during the 1960s had to be satisfied by recruiting abroad. Many Canadians who had studied in the United Kingdom, France, and the United States returned to academic positions in Canada. The exodus of academics and intellectuals from the United States during the Vietnam war meant that the majority of university posts were filled by U.S. or U.S.-trained teachers. The dominant sociological paradigms, as well as standards of professional performance and publication, of the United States were imported into Canada. Sociology in Canada thus became "mainline." S. D. Clark observed in 1979 that as a result of the concern to dissociate

sociology from social reform and to ensure its scientific credibility, the work of sociologists in Canadian universities had little relevance to Canadian society. The image of Canada as a modern national society, as systemically integrated, as based on a consensus of values, that was being presented to Canadian students did not coincide with the reality of Canadian life. Canada is not a singular nation; its institutional fabric has been state-centered, not based on value consensus; and it has never had an imperial mission or ambition. The dissonance between sociological image and reality, felt throughout academe, led to concerted efforts by the profession and the universities to put Canadian content into the curriculum.

In 1965, John Porter's *The Vertical Mosaic: An Analysis of Social Class and Power in Canada* was published. Described as "*the* sociological study of present day Canada," Porter's book received national and international acclaim, bringing him the McIver Award of the American Sociological Association and a D.Sc. from the University of London. Although he examined Canadian society as a whole, Porter did not presuppose the conditions of a *national* society. His work refutes the conception of Canada as a society based on a consensus of values, and shows how culture, history, and geography have combined in Canada to create a configuration of regional subsocieties subordinated to dominant economic interests and maintained by institutions that ensure a monopoly of power to the central Anglophone elites.

Porter's work became the benchmark for much subsequent Canadian sociology. A generation of sociologists, trained in the tradition of the Carleton School, which bears his intellectual imprint, has extended his analysis, generating debate, dialogue, and criticism within the Canadian academic community. This has produced a distinctive and critical intellectual stance, and has fostered a much broader international intercourse among sociological researchers in Canada. The "new political economy," as this perspective has come to be known, focuses on the social conditions under which Canadian natural resources have been exploited, the class relations these forces have generated, and the dynamics of internal conflicts and transnational linkages. Historical research has superseded static empirical descriptions, and structural, critical, and feminist theories provide conceptual and methodological tools of analysis. A transdisciplinary movement is evident in current sociological work in Canada, reflecting the confluence of the interests of sociologists, social anthropologists, political scientists, feminist scholars, and researchers in cultural studies.

Universities and colleges are the institutional setting for the majority of professional sociologists in Canada. As it has entered into teaching curricula since the 1960s, sociology has come to inform the everyday activities of people and is instrumental in a wide range of occupations. Such applications are less easy to gauge than those resulting from direct deliberations by sociologists on social policy. A number of royal commissions, task forces, and other state-initiated inquiries have been influenced by the perspective and empirical findings of sociological research. The recommendations of the Royal Commission on Health Services (1961–1963) were strongly influenced by sociologists, and effected the establishment of the Canadian health care system. Language and cultural policies were shaped by the recommendations of the Royal Commission on Bilingualism and Biculturalism (1963–1967), the findings of which were greatly influenced by sociological research. Sociologists contributed to the Royal Commission on the Status of Women in Canada (1967–1969). The federal Advisory Council on the Status of Women, recommended by the commission, was established, and its founding chair was a sociologist. Research by sociologists was significant in developing the recommendations of La Commission d'Enquête sur l'Enseignement au Québec (1964–1966), which led to the radical restructuring of Quebec's educational system. Quebec language policy, with its profound implications, was influenced by sociologists working with the Commission d'Enquête sur la Situation de la Langue Française au Québec during the early 1970s. Federal and provincial inquiries into drugs, poverty, aging, aboriginal land claims and sovereignty, criminal justice, and issues of social

and economic development have further drawn sociological work into mainstream thinking and policy formulation in Canada.

Along with Porter's *The Vertical Mosaic*, classic works in Canadian sociology include Léon Gérin's *Le type économique et social des canadiens* (1937); Everett C. Hughes's *French Canada in Transition* (1943); Marcel Giraud's *Le métis canadien* (1947); S. D. Clark's *Church and Sect in Canada* (1948); S. M. Lipset's *Agrarian Socialism* (1950); and Rex Lucas' *Minetown, Milltown, Railtown* (1971).

The role of sociologists as intellectuals and spokespersons on broad national and international issues has been varied in Canada. Early leaders of Canada's social democratic movement and its subsequent political organizations regularly drew on sociological training and insights in formulating their images of Canadian institutions. In Quebec, sociologists have played a seminal role in the constitution of a discourse of sovereignty. In Anglophone Canada, the traditional humanistic disciplines tended to dominate discourse about Canada and its place on the world stage, giving it a more conservative tone by linking current social values to society's traditions. Canada's development in the late twentieth century has rendered many of the older ideologies less salient, and the discipline's links with public inquiries and its focus on broad public issues has drawn it into the field of public discourse and in a generalist direction. This was particularly evident in Anglophone sociology during the nationalist debates of the 1970s. Neoconservatism in the 1980s emphasized economic priorities and muted the voice of social consciousness in both Anglophone and Francophone sociological communities. This generated a more critical interest as well as a broader comparative analytic perspective on Canadian issues. Environmental degradation; issues of gender, race, and ethnic subordination; sovereignty claims by aboriginal peoples; demographic changes occasioned by new immigration patterns; constitutional restructuring; and the resurgent peace movement pose serious and challenging problems for Canada's sociologists. This has produced an incipient resistance to the detachment that professionalization had induced since the 1970s and foreshadows a more active intellectual role for Canadian sociologists in the future.

### REFERENCES

Brym, Robert J., and Bonnie J. Fox 1989 *From Culture to Power: The Sociology of English Canada.* Toronto: Oxford University Press.

Whyte, Donald 1984–1985 "Sociology and the Nationalist Challenge in Canada." *Journal of Canadian Studies* 19, no. 4.

———, and Frank G. Vallee 1987 "Sociology." *The Canadian Encyclopedia*, vol. 3. Edmonton: Hurtig.

DONALD WHYTE

**CAPITALISM** Sociology has no complete, formal consensus on a specific definition of capitalism. The discipline of sociology itself arose as an attempt to understand and explain the emergence and nature of modern capitalist societies. Sociology's founding theorists were very much concerned with the development of capitalism. Émile Durkheim sought to find the bases of new forms of morality and social solidarity in the division of labor, which capitalism both expanded and accelerated (Durkheim 1984). Karl Marx, of course, spent his adult life analyzing and criticizing capitalist society. Marx's project was guided by his hope and expectation that capitalism would be displaced as history moved toward a socialist, and then communist, future. Max Weber, too, devoted considerable attention to the origins of modern capitalism and the historically specific character of Western society under capitalist expansion. Contemporary sociology's treatment of capitalism is grounded in the works of these theorists. The works of Marx and Weber, insofar as they more explicitly focused attention on the dynamics of capitalism, provide a point of departure for discussing modern sociology's approaches to capitalism.

The term *capitalism* is sometimes used to refer to the entire social structure of a capitalist society. Unless otherwise indicated, it is used here with specific reference to a form of economy to which multiple social institutions are effectively bound in relatively compatible ways. Weber used the term *capitalism* in a very general way: "wealth used to gain profit in commerce" (Weber 1976, p. 48). This understanding of capitalism permits the discovery of capitalism in a wide variety of social and historical settings. Weber describes this general form of capitalism in traditional India and China, ancient Babylon, Egypt, and Rome and in medieval and modern Europe. However, Weber also constructs a more specific typology that pertains to the form that capitalism has taken in more contemporary Western society. This form of capitalism is referred to as modern, or Western, capitalism. In *The Protestant Ethic and the Spirit of Capitalism,* Weber (1958 pp. 21–22) contends that this is "a very different form of capitalism which has appeared nowhere else" and that it is unique in its rational "organization of formally free labor." Other important characteristics of modern capitalism, such as the separation of business from the household and rational bookkeeping, derive their significance from this peculiar organization of labor. In this emphasis on the importance of free labor, or the creation of a labor market, Weber's definition of capitalism moves much closer to Marx's use of the term.

For Marx, it is the creation of a market for human labor that is the essence of capitalism. Marx wrote that capitalism can "spring into life only when the owner of the means of production and subsistence meets in the market with the free laborer selling his labor power" (Marx, quoted in Sweezy 1970 pp. 56–57). The emergence of the free laborer represents the destruction of other noncapitalist economic forms. Feudal or slave economies, for example, are not characterized by the recognized right of laborers to sell their own labor power as a commodity. Simple commodity production, or economies in which laborers own their own means of production (tools, equipment, etc.), are not characterized by the need for laborers to sell their labor power as a commodity. In the latter case, Weber concurs with Marx that this freedom is only formal since such laborers are compelled to sell their labor by the "whip of hunger."

The sociological conception of capitalism also varies with particular theoretical understandings of the nature of history. Marxists, guided by an evolutionlike vision of history, tend to see capitalism as a stage in humanity's progressive movement to a communist future. In this manner, Marxist sociology also often refers to various phases of capitalism. Wright (1978 pp. 168–169), for example, describes six stages of capitalist development: primitive accumulation, manufacture, machinofacture, monopoly capital, advanced monopoly capital, and state-directed monopoly capitalism. The implicit assumptions of law-like forces at work in the historical process are evident in the Marxist confidence that capitalism, like all previous socioeconomic orders, will eventually be destroyed by the internal contradictions it generates. References to the current stage of capitalism as "late capitalism" (e.g., Mandel 1978), for instance, reveal a belief in the inevitability of capitalism's demise.

The Weberian tradition, on the other hand, rejects the assumption of history's governance by "iron laws." This leads to a recognition of various types of capitalism but without the presumption that capitalism must eventually be eliminated. The Weberian tradition discovers in the history of Western capitalism a process of rationalization toward depersonalization, improved monetary calculability, increased specialization, and greater technical control over nature as well as over persons (Brubaker 1984). However, while the Weberian tradition can expect the *probability* of continued capitalist rationalization, it does not predict the *inevitability* of such a course for history. It is important to note that, for Weber, a transition from capitalism to socialism would probably only further this rationalization. Such developments were seen as associated with industrial society and bureaucratic forms of domination rather than with capitalism per se.

This background permits a more detailed examination of contemporary sociology's treatment of capitalism. Already, it can be seen that sociology's understanding of capitalism is more specific than popular conceptions of capitalism as simply "free-market" or "free-enterprise" systems. This is especially so insofar as sociology focuses its attention on modern society. It is the emergence of a "free market" in human labor that sociology tends to recognize as the distinguishing characteristic of modern capitalism. For Durkheimian sociology, this market guides the normal division of labor that is the basis of social solidarity. In this view, the absolute freedom of such a market is necessary to generate the conditions of equal opportunity that are required to guarantee norms by which people come to accept capitalism's highly developed division of labor. Under conditions of a truly free labor market, the stratification system is seen as legitimate since individuals attain their position through their own achievement and not by means of some ascribed status (e.g., caste, gender, race, ethnicity, nepotism) or political patronage. For Marxian sociology, it is in this labor market that the two fundamental and opposing classes of capitalism meet: the owners of the means of production or capitalists (bourgeoisie) and the workers (proletariat). In this view, the struggle between these two classes is the dynamic force behind capitalist development. For Weberian sociology, this market for human labor is necessary for the development of the advanced and superior calculability of capitalist economic action. This calculability is, in turn, a fundamental component of the rationalization process in modern Western society.

This transformation of human labor into a commodity is the force behind both capitalism's internal dynamism as well as its outward expansion. On the one hand, capitalism is constantly driven to enhance its productivity. This compulsion of modern capitalism continuously to develop its technical capacity to produce is not driven simply by competition among capitalists but is related to the unique role that human labor plays in capitalist production. Prior to the emergence of a market for human labor, premodern forms of capitalism exhibited no such pressure constantly to revolutionize the technical means of production. Modern capitalism's dependence on human labor as a commodity, however, demands that this cost of production be kept as low as possible. First, technological development can lower the cost of labor as a commodity by vastly increasing the production of mass consumer goods. The subsequent reduction in the cost of items like food and clothing translates into reductions in the cost of wages to sustain laborers and their families. Another means to this end is automation, the creation of technology that can replace or enhance human labor. Such technological development also permits capitalists to circumvent the natural limits of the human body to labor and the tendency of laborers to organize and demand higher wages, especially important spurs to technological development in capitalist societies characterized by a shortage of labor. However, under such conditions the capitalist's demand for profitability may limit the internal expansion of technology as a means of increasing production (i.e., capital-intensive production) in favor of an outward expansion that draws upon new sources of labor. This expansion of capitalism can take two basic forms. On the one hand, there is a drive toward proletarianization, or the inclusion of more and more of society's population segments that have previously escaped the labor market. On the other hand, there is a tendency to reach outside of the society itself toward other societies, thus incorporating ever larger regions of the world into the sphere of capitalism.

In the early development of capitalist societies, peasants are freed from feudal relations and slaves are freed from slave relations to add to the available pool of labor. This transformation is rarely a smooth one. The great revolutions in Western Europe and the U.S. Civil War forced these precapitalist classes to surrender their workers to the capitalist labor market. Another major source of labor for capitalist expansion has been independent laborers or persons who "work for themselves." Farmers who own their own land and equipment and work without hired labor are a good example of the type of self-employed producer that sociologists commonly refer to as simple commodity producers. There are other occupations in this general classification, of course. Highly skilled laborers have at times been able to retain independence from capitalist labor markets. However, capitalism has displayed a powerful capacity to bring these laborers into the sphere of capitalist, wage labor relations. For example, car-

penters, mechanics, butchers, even doctors and lawyers increasingly find themselves working for wages or a salary in a capitalist firm rather than working for themselves. From time to time, the number of self-employed appears actually to rise in certain capitalist societies (Bechhofer and Elliott 1985). This is usually the result of the introduction of some new technology or new service. Sometimes persons who strongly wish to be their "own bosses" are able to take advantage of specific market conditions or are willing to sacrifice potential income to achieve this status. But clearly, if capitalist societies are examined over the course of the last 200 to 300 years, the tendency is strongly toward increased absorption of persons into the capitalist labor market.

In recent times, labor markets in nations like the United States have found another major source of labor power in women. The traditional role of homemaker impeded the inclusion of women in the labor market. That role of women within the home has changed somewhat, but the role played by women in expanding the pool of labor available to capital has increased tremendously. According to Christensen (1987), for example, in 1960 30 percent of American mothers were employed; in 1986, 62 percent were employed. Ethnic minorities have often performed a similar function in expanding the size of the labor market. Succeeding waves of immigrants have frequently played an initially marginal role in the labor market, only to be gradually absorbed into more routine participation as time passes.

Capitalism's inherent expansionary tendencies also push the capitalist society to reach beyond the borders of the nation. This expansion occurs as capitalism seeks markets for its products but also in the search for raw materials and cheaper labor to produce goods for the home market. Eventually, capitalism may simply seek profitable investment outlets outside the nation of origin. Sociology has analyzed capitalism's transnational expansion with two general but conflicting theoretical approaches. Modernization theory views this expansion in a positive way, seeing it as a means by which undeveloped societies are enabled to begin the process of development that the developed societies have already achieved. This theoretical orientation has been especially important in shaping development policies directed at the "third world" by many Western governments, the World Bank, and even the United Nations (Giddens 1987).

Sociology's other basic approach to the emergence of a world-scale capitalist economy involves a more critical interpretation. This view tends to see capitalist expansion as having actually caused underdevelopment. The underdevelopment approach sees the lack of development in less-developed societies (periphery) as a consequence of systematic exploitation of their people and resources by the advanced societies (core). This process of underdevelopment is generally viewed as having occurred in three stages. The first stage, that of merchant capitalism, persisted from the sixteenth century to the late nineteenth century. Merchant capitalism, supported by military force, transferred vast amounts of wealth from the periphery to the European nations to help finance initial industrial development in what are now the advanced capitalist societies. The second stage, colonialism, persisted until about ten to fifteen years after World War II, when many colonial nations were granted formal independence. In the colonial stage, the developed societies organized economic and political institutions in the less-developed nations to serve the needs of industrial capitalism in the advanced nations. In the postcolonial period, formal political independence has been granted, but the persistent economic inequalities between developed and underdeveloped nations strongly favor the more-developed capitalist societies. Even when raw materials and finished products remain in the lesser-developed nation, the profits derived from such production are taken from the periphery and returned to the advanced core societies. Thus, the pattern of underdevelopment continues in the face of formal independence.

Traditionally, much of sociology's attention to international capitalist expansion has focused on relations between nations. Increasingly, sociology is examining these matters with greater attention to relations between classes. This shift of emphasis reflects the increasing importance of the transnational corporation in recent times. The transnational corporation's greater capacity to use several international sites for component production and the shift of much industrial production to underdeveloped regions are generating a process of deindustrialization in the advanced capitalist societies. While capitalism has long been a world system, many sociologists contend that the transnational, or "stateless," corporation has significantly less commitment or loyalty to any specific nation. Capital flows ever more rapidly throughout the world, seeking the cheapest source of labor. Modern computer technology has facilitated this trend. Asian, European, and North American capital markets are increasingly interdependent. Sociology's shift of emphasis reflects this tendency for the U.S. capitalist to have more in common, sociologically, with the Japanese or German capitalist than the U.S. investor has in common with the American worker. Sociology's new attention to the internationalization of capital may present a need for rethinking the usefulness of the nation as the typical boundary of a society. The emergence of the "new Europe" and the demise of state socialism in Eastern Europe and the USSR may also lead to a more flexible notion of what constitutes a society.

The preceding discussion has focused on capitalism as a specific form of economy that is defined by the expansion of a labor market in which propertyless workers sell their labor power for money. Capitalist societies are, of course, far more complex than this. There are a number of distinct economic forms that coexist with capitalism in both complementary and conflictual relations. The capitalist economy itself may be broken down into two basic sectors, one representing big business and one representing small business. Sociologists usually refer to these as the monopoly sector and the competitive sector. This dual economy is reflected in a segmented, or dual, labor market. Monopoly sector workers are more likely to be male, unionized, receive better wages and benefits, have greater job security, and work in a more clearly defined hierarchy of authority based on credentials. Competitive sector workers are less likely to possess strong credentials, more likely to be female, receive lower pay, work under more dangerous conditions, and work without union protection, benefits, or job security.

Noncapitalist economic forms also exist alongside this dual capitalist economy. The self-employed reflect a form distinct from modern capitalism that sociologists commonly refer to as simple commodity producers or petite bourgeoisie. These people produce goods and services (commodities) for sale on the market, but they work for themselves and use only their own labor in production. Most capitalist societies also contain cooperative economic organizations that are distinct from capitalist enterprises. Cooperatives are commercial, nonprofit enterprises, owned and democratically controlled by the members. The nonprofit status and democratic distribution of control (one member, one vote) set cooperatives apart. The cooperative is an especially important form of economic organization for those simple commodity producers, like farmers, described above. All capitalist societies today also contain elements of socialist economy. Key social services, such as health care, and even some commodity production are provided by the state in many societies commonly recognized as capitalist. The United States is perhaps among the most resistant to this movement toward mixed economy. Yet even the United States has, to some extent, socialized education, mail delivery, libraries, police and fire protection, scientific research and technological development, transportation networks (e.g., highways, airports, urban transit), military production, industrial infrastructure provision, and so on. The mixed character of this economy is further indicated by the common practice of the government contracting capitalist firms to produce many goods and services. In a related way, the development of welfare has influenced the nature of capitalist society. The increased intervention of government into the economy has generated the notion of the welfare state. While popular conceptions of the welfare state tend to focus on the role that government plays in alleviating the impacts of poverty on individuals, sociology also recognizes that welfare reduces the cost of reproducing the

commodity—labor. In this sense, welfare functions, in the long run, as a subsidy to capital. Further, many of the socialized sectors of capitalist economies function to ensure a profitable environment for capitalist firms (O'Connor 1973; Offe 1984). In many instances, such subsidization of capital is biased toward the largest corporations.

Some sociologists have contended that the rise of the large capitalist corporation, with its dispersed stock ownership and bureaucratic form of organization, has eroded the power of individual capitalists to control the corporation in which they have invested their capital. Instead, it is argued, bureaucratic managers have gained control over corporate capital. Such managers are thought to be relatively free of the drive to maximize profits and are willing to accept average rates of profit. In this way, the ruthless character of earlier forms of capitalism are seen as giving way to a capitalism that is managed with broader interests in mind. Further, the dispersal of ownership and control is said to eliminate the misuse of capital in the interests of an elite and wealthy minority. This "managerialist" position complements pluralist political theory by providing greater authority for institutions of representative democracy to control the allocation of society's resources.

This view is challenged in a variety of ways. Other sociologists contend that while management may have gained some formal independence, its job requires devotion to profit maximization, and its performance is assessed on this criteria. In this view, the larger companies' executives and owners are able to use interlocking directorates and their common class background (e.g., elite schools, private clubs, policy-planning organizations) to minimize price competition and thus sustain high profit levels. Others argue that those informal ties are of less consequence than their common dependency on banks. In this view, banks, or finance capital, play a disproportionately powerful role in centralizing control over the allocation of capital resources. This position strongly opposes the managerialist arguments and those who envision an independent corporate elite whose power lies in the control of corporate bureaucracies rather than in personal wealth (Glasberg and Schwartz 1983). Further, to the extent that it is valid, this argument is particularly important given the increasing internationalization of capital discussed above, since a great deal of that development has occurred in the sphere of finance capital.

These sorts of arguments reflect an important shift in sociology's understanding of the relationship between capitalism and democracy. Sociology's Enlightenment roots provided a traditional legacy of viewing capitalism and democracy as intertwined in the process of modernization. While this parallel development is certainly recognizable in early forms of modern capitalism, more recent forms of capitalism call into question the extent to which capitalism and democracy are inevitably bound together. Indeed, recent works suggest that capitalism and democracy are now opposed to one another (e.g., Piven and Cloward 1982). This view holds that the tremendous inequality of wealth generated by modern capitalism impedes the possibility of political equality. Even conservative writers (e.g., Huntington 1975) have noted the problematic relationship between contemporary capitalism and democracy, suggesting a retrenchment of democratic forms in defense of capitalism. The future of capitalism will be shaped by this tension with democracy, but that tension itself is located in an increasingly global economy. At the moment, the politics of capitalist society seem to lag behind the economic changes. The individual is increasingly pressured to sell his or her labor as a commodity on a world market, yet at the same time that individual remains a citizen, not of the world, but of the nation. The transnational capitalist enterprise and the flow of capital, on the other hand, are ever more free of such national borders.

(SEE ALSO: *Marxist Sociology; Postindustrial Society*)

### REFERENCES

Bechhofer, F., and B. Elliott 1985 "The Petite Bourgeoisie in Late Capitalism." *Annual Review of Sociology* 11:181–207.

Brubaker, Rogers 1984 *The Limits of Rationality*. London: Allen and Unwin.

Christensen, Kathleen 1987 "Women and Contingent Work." *Social Policy* 17:15–18.

Durkheim, Emile 1984 *The Division of Labor in Society*. New York: Free Press.

Giddens, Anthony 1987 *Sociology: A Brief but Critical Introduction*, 2d ed. New York: Harcourt Brace Jovanovich.

Glasberg, Davita Silfen, and Michael Schwartz 1983 "Ownership and Control of Corporations." *Annual Review of Sociology* 9:311–332.

Huntington, Samuel P. 1975 "The United States." In Michael Crozier, Samuel P. Huntington, and Joji Watanuki, eds., *The Crisis of Democracy: Report on the Governability of Democracies to the Trilateral Commission*. New York: New York University Press.

Mandel, Ernest 1978 *Late Capitalism*. London: Verso.

O'Connor, James 1973 *The Fiscal Crisis of the State*. New York: St. Martin's Press.

Offe, Claus 1984 *Contradictions of the Welfare State*. Cambridge, Mass.: M.I.T. Press.

Piven, Frances Fox, and Richard A. Cloward 1982 *The New Class War*. New York: Pantheon Books.

Sweezy, Paul M. 1970 *The Theory of Capitalist Development*. New York: Monthly Review Press.

Weber, Max 1958 *The Protestant Ethic and the Spirit of Capitalism*. Talcott Parsons, trans. New York: Scribners.

———1976 *The Agrarian Sociology of Ancient Civilizations*. R. I. Frank, trans. London: New Left Books.

Wright, Erik Olin 1978 *Class, Crisis, and the State*. London: New Left Books.

PATRICK H. MOONEY

**CASE STUDIES** Case studies are in-depth analyses of single or a few communities, organizations, or persons' lives. They involve detailed and often subtle understandings of the social organization of everyday life and persons' lived experiences. Because they focus on naturally occurring events and relationships (not laboratory experiments or survey data), case studies are sometimes described as naturalistic. Case studies usually involve extensive interviews about persons' lives and/or direct observation of community or organization members' activities. Social scientists use the understandings developed in case studies to introduce the general public to the unique ways of life and/or problems of communities, test and build theories, and develop clinical and policy interventions concerned with individual and social problems.

The case-study approach is not unique to sociology but is a general approach to social life that is used by social scientists (especially anthropologists and historians), psychotherapists and family therapists, and journalists. All such uses of case studies involve idiographic interpretation that emphasizes how social action and relationships are influenced by their social contexts. Case studies are unique within sociology because they require that researchers immerse themselves in the lives and concerns of the persons, communities, and/or organizations they study. While case studies are based on the general scientific method and are intended to advance the scientific goals of sociology, they are also humanistic because they offer readers insight into the concerns, values, and relationships of persons making up diverse social worlds.

## CASE STUDIES AND THE DEVELOPMENT OF SOCIOLOGY IN THE UNITED STATES

Sociological case studies are most associated with the ethnographic traditions established at the University of Chicago during the first half of the twentieth century. The Chicago school's emphasis on case studies partly reflects the influence of Robert E. Park, who joined the Sociology Department in 1916 and later served as department chair. Park taught his students that case studies should emphasize how persons' lives and the organization of communities are shaped by general social processes and structures. For example, Park analyzed the ways in which cities develop as interrelated territories involving distinctive ways of life and opportunities. He described such territories as "natural areas" and stressed that they emerged based on social and economic competition.

Many of the best-known and most influential sociological case studies done in the United States were conducted in the 1920s and 1930s by students and faculty members at the University of Chicago who were interested in the distinctive ways of life in diverse natural areas (see, e.g., Anderson 1923; Cressey 1932; Shaw 1930, 1931; Thomas 1923; Wirth 1928; and Zorbaugh 1929). Park's approach to case studies has been modified and refined over the years, particularly by Everett C. Hughes (1970), who developed a comparative approach to work groups and settings. The approach involves using case studies to identify and to analyze comparatively generalized aspects of work groups and settings, such as work groups' definitions of "dirty work" and interest in controlling the conditions of their work. Another major contributor to the Chicago school of sociology is Erving Goffman (1959), who used case studies to develop a dramaturgical perspective on social interaction. The perspective treats mundane interactions as quasi-theatrical performances involving scripts, stages, and characters.

Although less influential than the Chicago school, a second source for case studies in American sociology was structural-functionalist theorists who analyzed communities and organizations as stability-seeking social systems. Structural-functional case studies were influenced by anthropological studies of nonindustrial communities and the more abstract theories of Talcott Parsons and Robert Merton. These studies analyze how social systems are maintained and adapt to changing environmental circumstances. For example, structural functionalists have used case studies to analyze the consequences of organizational activities and relationships for maintaining organizational systems (Blau 1955; Gouldner 1954; Sykes 1958).

While many qualitative sociologists continue to work within the Chicago school and structural-functional traditions, several important developments have occurred in qualitative sociology in the past twenty-five years. The changes are associated with sociologists' reconsideration of the purposes of case studies and their importance for the development of sociological theory. Three of the most important changes are the emergence of radical case studies, a focus on reality construction, and concern for the politics and poetics of writing case studies.

## RADICAL CASE STUDIES

While early sociological case studies were sometimes associated with reformist movements, they were seldom intended to advance politically radical causes or build radical social theory. This orientation may be contrasted with that of radical journalists of the same era (such as Upton Sinclair) who used case studies to both highlight social problems and raise questions about the legitimacy of capitalism. In recent years radical sociologists have begun to use case studies to achieve their political and theoretical ends. One source for radical case studies is Marxist sociologists, who are concerned with the ways in which worker–management relations are organized in work settings, how social classes are perpetuated, and how capitalism is justified.

Marxist sociologists use their case studies to challenge more conservative case studies that, from the radicals' standpoint, do not take adequate account of the ways in which persons' everyday lives are shaped by political and economic structures. They are also used to analyze historical changes in capitalism and the consequences of the changes for workers. For Marxist theorists, a major recent change has been the rise of a new kind of society—monopoly capitalism—dominated by multinational corporations. These theorists use case studies of work settings to illustrate and analyze the effects of monopoly capitalism on workers (Burawoy 1970).

Although it is not so well developed in sociology as in anthropology, another focus of radical case studies involves the social and personal consequences of the international division of labor. The studies are concerned with the ways in which multinational corporations internationalize the production process by exporting aspects of production to Third World countries. Recent case studies of this trend show the profound impact of

global economic changes for gender and family roles in Third World countries. Finally, radical sociologists have used the case study method to analyze the ways in which capitalist institutions and relationships are justified and perpetuated by noneconomic institutions such as schools (Willis 1977).

A second recent source for radical case studies is feminist sociology. While it is diverse and includes members who hold many different political philosophies, all forms of feminist sociology are sensitive to the politics of human relationships. A major theme in feminist case studies involves the ways in which women's contributions to social relationships and institutions go unseen and unacknowledged. Feminist sociologists use case studies to call attention to women's contributions to society and analyze the political implications of their invisibility. A related concern involves analyzing relationships and activities that are typically treated as apolitical and private matters as highly political and matters of public concern. One way in which feminist sociologists do so is by treating aspects of their own lives as politically and sociologically significant and making them matters for analysis.

The case-study approach is central to the feminist sociology of Dorothy E. Smith (1987). Smith treats case studies as points of entry for studying general social processes that shape persons' experiences and lives. Her approach to case studies emphasizes how the seemingly unconnected activities of everyday life are related by general social processes (such as market relationships) and how they help to perpetuate the processes. She states, for example,

> when my friend and I sit down over lunch to discuss epistemological issues in the social sciences, we take for granted the social organization of the restaurant producing our meal. We are local participants in it. Our exclusive access to a table and shelter during the period of the eating of the meal, the appropriate behavior vis-à-vis other diners, the elements of a meal, and so forth—these are the locally organized constituents of the extended commodity relations of capitalism (Smith 1987, p. 158).

## CASE STUDIES OF REALITY CONSTRUCTION

Basic to the case-study method and idiographic interpretation is a concern for human values and culture. For example, early sociological case studies emphasized the ways in which diverse urban groups defined social reality, and the consequences of the definitions for group members' actions. Beginning in the 1960s, this concern was refocused on the ways in which social realities are produced in social interactions. The new focus is generally based on the social phenomenology of Alfred Schutz and ethnomethodology that is concerned with the folk methods used by interactants to construct orientations to matters of practical concern. For example, Harold Garfinkel (1967), the founder of ethnomethodology, used a case study of a patient seeking a sex-change operation to analyze how we orient to ourselves and others as men and women.

Case studies of reality construction emphasize how social realities are created, sustained, and changed through language use. The emphasis has given rise to new orientations to traditional areas of sociological research, such as science. Until recently, sociologists of science have treated scientific work as a simple, noninterpretive process centered in scientists' adherence to the rules of the scientific method, which emphasizes how "facts" and "truth" emerge from observations of the "real" world. Viewed this way, scientific facts are not matters of interpretation or social constructions. This view of science has been challenged by recent case studies of scientific work that focus on the ways in which scientific facts are socially produced based on scientists' interpretations of their experiments (Latour and Woolgar 1979).

A major branch of ethnomethodology is conversation analysis, which focuses on the turn-by-turn organization of social interactions (Sacks, Schegloff, and Jefferson 1974). For conversation analysts, social reality is collaboratively constructed within turn-taking sequences, which may be organized around such linguistic practices as questions and answers or charges and rebuttals. A major contribution of conversation-analytic case studies has been to show how IQ and other test results are shaped by the ways in which test-givers and test-takers interact (Marlaire and Maynard 1990). Also, sociologists influenced by conversation analysis theory have considered how power and dominance are interactionally organized and accomplished.

More recently, some qualitative sociologists have extended and reformulated ethnomethodological case studies by analyzing the relationships between the interpretive methods used by interactants in concrete situations and the distinctive meanings they produce in their interactions. This approach to case studies—which Jaber F. Gubrium (1988) calls practical ethnography— focuses on the practical and political uses of meanings in social institutions. Practical ethnographers analyze meanings as rhetorics, which interactants use to persuade others and to assign identities to themselves and others.

For example, Gale Miller (1991) analyzes how staff members in a work-incentive program used various images of attitude and labor market to persuade their clients and supervisors. The approach is also central to Gubrium and James A. Holstein's (1990) analysis of family as a folk concept, which interactants use to organize and make sense of practical issues emergent in everyday life. The folk concept of family is used in a variety of settings to establish social bonds between persons who in other situations may be described as unrelated, and to justify actions that have practical (sometimes fateful) consequences for persons' lives.

## THE POLITICS AND POETICS OF WRITING CASE STUDIES

While some qualitative sociologists focus on the folk methods of description and interpretation used by others in creating realities, other sociologists are reconsidering the reality constructing methods used by sociologists in writing case studies. Their interest centers in this question: How do we do our work? The question raises issues about the relationships between qualitative researchers and the people they study. For example, is it enough that case studies inform the public and sociologists about aspects of contemporary society, or should they also help the persons and communities studied? A related issue involves editorial control over the writing of case studies. That is, should the subjects of case studies have a voice in how they are described and analyzed?

Such questions have given rise to many answers, but most of them involve analyzing case studies as narratives or stories that sociologists tell about themselves and others. For example, John van Maanen (1988) divides ethnographic writing into several types of "tales" involving different orientations to the persons described, readers, and authorship. More sophisticated analyses focus on the various rhetorical devices used by ethnographers to write their case studies; indeed, Severyn Bruyn (1966) raised this issue for sociologists twenty-five years ago. Such rhetorical devices include metaphor, irony, paradox, synecdoche, and metonymy, which ethnographers use both to describe others and to cast their descriptions as objective and authoritative.

Recent developments suggest that qualitative sociologists' interest in writing case studies is part of a larger interdisciplinary movement involving social scientists and humanists. The movement is concerned with analyzing the rhetorics of social scientific inquiry (Nelson et al. 1987) as well as how to write better narratives. The latter issue is basic to recent efforts by British sociologists to develop new forms of writing that better reflect the ways in which their case studies are socially constructed (Woolgar 1988) and other sociologists' interest in developing alternatives to the logico-scientific writing style that better express their theoretical perspectives, political philosophies, and experiences (DeVault 1990; Richardson 1990).

In sum, the case-study method is a dynamic approach to studying social life, which sociologists modify and use to achieve diverse political and theoretical goals. While the popularity of the case-study method waxes and wanes over time, it is likely always to be a major research strategy of humanistically oriented sociologists.

(SEE ALSO: *Ethnomethodology; Field Research Methods; Life Histories; Qualitative Methods*)

## REFERENCES

Anderson, Nels 1923 *The Hobo.* Chicago: University of Chicago Press.

Blau, Peter M. 1955 *The Dynamics of Bureaucracy.* Chicago: University of Chicago Press.

Bruyn, Severyn T. 1966 *The Human Perspective in Sociology.* Englewood Cliffs, N.J.: Prentice-Hall.

Burawoy, Michael 1970 *Manufacturing Consent.* Chicago: University of Chicago Press.

Cressey, Paul 1932 *The Taxi-Dance Hall.* Chicago: University of Chicago Press.

DeVault, Marjorie L. 1990 "Talking and Listening from Women's Standpoint." *Social Problems* 37: 96–116.

Garfinkel, Harold 1967 *Studies in Ethnomethodology.* Englewood Cliffs, N.J.: Prentice-Hall.

Goffman, Erving 1959 *The Presentation of Self in Everyday Life.* Garden City, N.Y.: Doubleday.

Gouldner, Alvin 1954 *Patterns of Industrial Democracy.* New York: Free Press.

Gubrium, Jaber F. 1988 *Analyzing Field Realities.* Newbury Park, Calif.: Sage Publications.

———, and James A. Holstein 1990 *What Is Family?* Mountain View, Calif.: Mayfield.

Hughes, Everett C. 1970 "The Humble and the Proud." *The Sociological Quarterly* 11:147–156.

Latour, Bruno, and Steven Woolgar 1979 *Laboratory Life.* Beverly Hills, Calif.: Sage Publications.

Marlaire, Courtney L., and Douglas W. Maynard 1990 "Standardized Testing as an Interactional Phenomenon." *Sociology of Education* 63:83–101.

Miller, Gale 1991 *Enforcing the Work Ethic.* Albany: State University of New York Press.

Nelson, John S., Allan Megill, and Donald N. McCloskey (eds.) 1987 *The Rhetoric of the Human Sciences.* Madison: University of Wisconsin Press.

Richardson, Laurel 1990 "Narrative and Sociology." *Journal of Contemporary Ethnography* 19:116–135.

Sacks, Harvey, Emmanuel A. Schegloff, and Gail Jefferson 1974 "A Simplest Systematics for the Organization of Turn-Taking for Conversation." *Language* 50:696–735.

Shaw, Clifford 1930 *The Jack-Roller*. Chicago: University of Chicago Press.

——1931 *The Natural History of a Delinquent*. Chicago: University of Chicago Press.

Smith, Dorothy E. 1987 *The Everyday World as Problematic*. Boston: Northeastern University Press.

Sykes, Gresham M. 1958 *The Society of Captives*. Princeton, N.J.: Princeton University Press.

Thomas, W. I. 1923 *The Unadjusted Girl*. Boston: Little, Brown.

Van Maanen, John 1988 *Tales of the Field*. Chicago: University of Chicago Press.

Willis, Paul 1977 *Learning to Labour*. New York: Columbia University Press.

Wirth, Louis 1928 *The Ghetto*. Chicago: University of Chicago Press.

Woolgar, Steven 1988 *Science, the Very Idea*. New York: Tavistock.

Zorbaugh, Harvey 1929 *The Gold Coast and the Slum*. Chicago: University of Chicago Press.

GALE MILLER

**CASTE AND CLASS** The term "caste" is often used to denote large-scale kinship groups that are hierarchically organized within a rigid system of stratification. In such a system a person's social position is determined by birth, and marital connection outside one's caste is prohibited. Sociologists who study stratification frequently contrast caste systems with class systems. In class systems one's opportunities in life, at least in theory, are determined by one's actions, allowing a degree of individual mobility that is not possible in caste systems.

Caste systems are to be found among the Hindus in India and among societies where groups are ranked and closed. Early Hindu literary classics describe a society divided into four *varnas:* Brahman (poet-priest), Kshatriya (warrior-chief), Vaishya (traders), and Shudras (menials, servants). The *varnas* formed ranked categories characterized by differential access to spiritual and material privileges. It excluded the Untouchables, who were despised because they engaged in occupations that were considered unclean and polluting.

The *varna* model of social ranking persisted throughout the Hindu subcontinent for over a millennia. The basis of caste ranking was the sacred concept of purity and pollution with Brahmans, because they were engaged in priestly duties considered ritually pure, while those who engaged in manual labor and with ritually polluting objects were regarded as impure. Usually those who had high ritual status also had economic and political power. Beliefs about pollution generally regulated all relations between castes. Members were not allowed to marry outside their caste; there were strict rules about the kind of food and drink one could accept and from what castes; and there were restrictions on approaching and visiting members of another caste. Violations of these rules entailed purifactory rites and sometimes expulsion from the caste (Ghurye 1969).

The *varna* scheme refers only to broad categories of society, for in reality the small endogamous group or subcaste (*jati*) forms the unit of social organization. In each linguistic area there are about two thousand such subcastes. The status of the subcaste, its cultural traditions, and its numerical strength vary from one region to another, often from village to village.

Field studies of local caste structures revealed that the caste system was more dynamic than the earlier works by social scientists had indicated. For example, at the local level, the position of the middle castes, between the Brahmans and the Untouchables, is often not very clear. This is because castes were often able to change their ritual position after they had acquired economic and political power. A low caste would adopt the Brahminic way of life, such as vegetarianism and teetotalism, and in several generations attain a higher position in the hierarchy. Upward mobility occurred for an entire caste, not for an individual or the family. This process of upward mobility, known as Sanskrtization (Srinivas 1962), did not, however, affect the movement of castes at the extremes. Brahmans in most parts of the country were found at the top, and Untouchables everywhere occupied a degrading status because of their economic dependency and low ritual status.

The operation of this hierarchical society was justified with reference to traditional Hindu religious beliefs about *samsara* (reincarnation) and *karma* (quality of actions). A person's position in this life was determined by his or her actions in previous lives. Persons who were born in a Brahman family must have performed good deeds in their earlier lives. Being born a Shudra or an Untouchable was punishment for the sinful acts committed in previous lives.

Some scholars (Leach 1960; Dumont 1970) saw the caste system as a cooperative, inclusive arrangement where each caste formed an integral part of the local socioeconomic system and had its special privileges. In a *jajmani* system, as this arrangement between castes was known, a village was controlled by a dominant caste, which used its wealth, numerical majority, and high status to dominate the other castes in the village. Most other castes provided services to this caste. Some worked on the land as laborers and tenants. Other castes provided goods and services to the land-owning households and to other castes. A village would thus have a potter, blacksmith, carpenter, tailor, shoemaker, barber, sweeper, and a washerman, with each caste specializing in different occupations. These were hereditary occupations. In return for their services castes would be paid in kind, usually farm produce. These patron-client relationships continued for generations, and it was the religious duty of the *jajman* (patron) to take care of others.

Although the system did provide security for all, it was essentially exploitative and oppressive (Berreman 1981; Beidelman 1959; Freeman 1986), particularly for the Untouchables, who were confined to menial, despised jobs, working as sweepers, gutter and latrine cleaners, scavengers, watchmen, farm laborers, and curers of hides. They were denied access to Hindu temples; were not allowed to read religious Sankrit books and remained illiterate; could not use village wells and tanks; were forced to live in settlements outside the village; and were forbidden to enter the residential areas of the upper castes.

## CHANGES IN THE CASTE SYSTEM

British rule profoundly affected the Indian social order. The ideas of Western culture; the opening of English educational institutions; the legal system, which introduced the principle of equality before the law; and the new economic activities and the kind of employment they generated all brought new opportunities for greater advancement. Although these new developments resulted in greater mobility and opened doors for even the low castes, those castes that benefited most were the ones already in advantageous positions. Thus, Brahmans with a tradition of literacy were the first to avail themselves of English education and occupy administrative positions in the colonial bureaucracy.

The spread of communications enabled local subcastes to link together and form caste associations. These organizations, although initially concerned with raising the caste status in terms of Brahmanical values, later sought educational, economic, and social benefits from the British (Rudolph and Rudolph 1960). When the colonial authorities widened political participation by allowing elections in some provinces, castes organized to make claims for political representation. In some regions, such as the South, the non-Brahman castes were successful in restricting entry of Brahmans in educational institutions and administrative services.

To assuage the fears of communities about upper-caste Hindu rule in independent India and also to weaken the nationalist movement, the British granted special political representation to some groups such as the Untouchables. They had become politically mobilized under the leadership of Dr. B. R. Ambedkar and had learned, like other castes and communities, the use of political means to secure status and power (Zelliot 1970).

After the country became independent from British rule in 1947, the Indian leaders hoped that legislative and legal measures would reorder an entrenched social structure. A new Constitution was adopted, which abolished untouchability and prohibited discrimination in public places. In addition, special places were reserved for Untouchables in higher educational institutions, government services, and in the lower houses of the central and state legislatures.

What progress has the country made toward improving the lives of the Untouchables, who now form nearly 16 percent of the population? Has the traditional caste system disintegrated?

The movement from a traditional to a modern economy—increase in educational facilities; expansion of white-collar jobs, especially in the state sector; expansion of the transportation and communication networks; increase in agricultural production (known as the Green Revolution)—has had a significant impact on the institution of caste. However, political factors have been equally if not more important in producing changes in the caste system. One is the democratic electoral system. The other is the state's impact on intercaste relations through its policy of preferences for selected disadvantaged castes.

The close association between caste and traditional occupation is breaking down because of the expansion of modern education and the urban-industrial sector. In India, an urban middle class has formed whose members are drawn from various caste groups. This has reduced the structural and cultural differences between castes, as divisions based on income, education, and occupation become more important than caste cleavages for social and economic purposes. The reduction, however, is most prominent among the upper socioeconomic strata—the urban, Western-educated, professional, and higher-income groups—whose members share a common life-style (Beteille 1969).

For most Indians, especially those who live in rural areas (73 percent of the Indian population is still rural), caste factors are an integral part of their daily lives. In many parts of the country Scheduled Castes (the common term for Untouchables now) are not allowed inside temples and cannot use village water wells. Marriages are generally arranged between persons of the same caste.

With the support of government scholarships and reservation benefits, a small proportion of Scheduled Castes has managed to gain entry into the middle class—as schoolteachers, clerks, bank tellers, typists, and government officials. Reservation of seats in the legislature has made the political arena somewhat more accessible, although most politicians belonging to the Scheduled Caste community have little say in party matters and government policymaking. The majority of Scheduled Caste members remain landless agricultural laborers, powerless, desperately poor, and illiterate.

Modern economic forces are changing the rural landscape. The increase in cash-crop production, which has made grain payments in exchange for services unprofitable; the introduction of mechanized farming, which has displaced manual labor; the preference for manufactured goods over handmade ones; and the migration to cities and to prosperous agricultural areas for work and better wages have all weakened the traditional patron–client ties and the security it provided. The Scheduled Castes and other low castes have been particularly affected as the other sectors of the economy have not grown fast enough to absorb them.

The rural social structure has been transformed in yet another way. The dominant castes are no longer from the higher castes but belong to the middle and lower peasant castes—the profit-maximizing "bullock capitalists" (Rudolph and Rudolph 1987) who were the chief beneficiaries of land reform and state subsidies to the agricultural sector (Blair 1980; Brass 1985). They have displaced the high-caste absentee landlords, who have moved to cities and taken up modern occupations.

Modern political institutions have also brought about changes in the traditional leadership and power structure of local communities. Relations between castes are now governed by rules of competitive politics, and leaders are selected for their political skills and not because they are members of a particular caste. The role of caste varies at different levels of political action. At the village and district levels caste loyalties are effectively used for political mobilization. But at the state and national levels, caste factors become less important for political parties because one caste rarely commands a majority at these levels.

In recent years there have been numerous instances of confrontations between the middle peasant castes and Scheduled Castes in rural areas. Violence and repression against Scheduled Castes has increased as they have begun to assert themselves. With the support of Communist and Dalit movements (the latter a movement formed of militant Scheduled Castes), they are demanding better wages, the right to till government-granted land, and the use of village wells.

In urban areas, caste conflict has mainly centered around the issue of "reservation." The other backward castes (who belong mainly to the Shudra caste and form approximately 50 percent of the country's population) have demanded from the government benefits similar to those available to Scheduled Castes in government service and educational institutions. Under electoral pressures the state governments have extended these reservation benefits to the other backward castes, leading to discontent among the upper castes.

Extension of preferential treatment from Scheduled Castes to the more numerous and in some states somewhat better-off backward castes has not only created great resentment among the upper castes but also has reduced public support for the policy of special benefits for the Scheduled Castes. In cities they have often been victims during anti-reservation agitations. That this is happening at the very time when the preferential programs have gradually succeeded in improving the educational and economic conditions for Scheduled Castes is not accidental (Sheth 1987).

As education and the meaning of the vote and the ideas of equality and justice spread, the rural and urban areas will witness severe intercaste conflicts. What is significant, however, is that these conflicts are not over caste beliefs and values, but like conflicts elsewhere between ethnic groups,

have to do with control over political and economic resources.

## CASTE IN OTHER SOCIETIES

Do castes exist outside India? Is it a unique social phenomenon distinct from other systems of social stratification? Opinion among scholars is divided over this issue. Castelike systems have been observed in the South Asian subcontinent and beyond (in Japan, Africa, Iran, and Polynesia). Caste has also been used to describe the systems of racial stratification in South Africa and the southern United States.

Whether the term *caste* is applicable to societies outside the South Asian region depends on how the term is defined. Those who focus on its religious foundations argue that caste is a particular species of structural organization found only in the Indian world. Louis Dumont (1970), for example, contends that caste systems are noncomparable to systems of racial stratification because of the differences in ideology—one based on the ideology of hierarchy, the other on an equalitarian ideology.

Others, such as Gerald Berreman (1981) argue, that cultural differences notwithstanding, both systems are alike in their structure and in their effect on the life experiences of those most oppressed. Recently, scholars (Weiner 1983) have shown that similarities also exist in the political consequences of preferential policies that culturally distinct societies such as the United States and India have adopted to reduce group disparities.

(SEE ALSO: *Indian Sociology; Social Stratification*)

## REFERENCES

Beidelman, T. O. 1959 *A Comparative Analysis of the Jajmani System.* Monograph VII of the Association of Asian Studies. Locust Valley, NY: J. J. Augustin.

Berreman, Gerald 1981 *Caste and Other Inequities.* Delhi: Manohar.

Beteille, André 1969 *Caste: Old and New.* Bombay: Asia Publishing House.

Blair, Harry W. 1980 "Rising Kulaks and Backward

Castes in Bihar: Social Change in the Late 1970's." *Economic and Political Weekly,* 12 (Jan.): 64–73.

Brass, Paul R. 1983 *Caste, Faction and Party in Indian Politics: Faction and Party,* vol. 1. Delhi: Chanakya Publications.

———1985 *Caste, Faction and Party in Indian Politics: Election Studies,* vol. 2. Delhi: Chanakya Publications

Breman, Jan 1974 *Patronage and Exploitation.* Berkeley: University of California Press.

Dumont, Louis 1970 *Homo Hierarchicus.* Chicago: University of Chicago Press.

Freeman, James M. 1986 "The Consciousness of Freedom among India's Untouchables." In D. K. Basu and R. Sisson, eds., *Social and Economic Development in India.* Beverly Hills, Calif.: Sage.

Galanter, Marc 1984 *Competing Equalities: Law and the Backward Classes in India.* Berkeley: University of California Press.

Ghurye, G. S. 1969 *Caste and Race in India,* 5th ed. Bombay: Popular Prakashan.

Gould, Harold A. 1987 *The Hindu Caste System: The Sacralization of a Social Order.* Delhi: Chanakya.

Hutton, J. H. 1961 *Caste in India,* 4th ed. Oxford: Oxford University Press.

Kolenda, Pauline 1978 *Caste in Contemporary India: Beyond Organic Solidarity.* Menlo Park, Calif.: Benjamin/Cummings.

Kothari, Rajni 1970 *Caste in Indian Politics.* New Delhi: Orient Longman.

Leach, E. R. (ed.) 1960 *Aspects of Caste in South India, Ceylon, and North-West Pakistan.* Cambridge: Cambridge University Press.

Mahar, J. M. (ed.) 1972 *The Untouchables in Contemporary India.* Tucson: University of Arizona Press.

Rudolph, L. I., and S. H. Rudolph 1960 "The Political Role of India's Caste Associations." *Pacific Affairs* 33(1):5–22.

———1987 *In Pursuit of Laxmi.* Chicago: University of Chicago Press.

Sheth, D. L. 1987 "Reservation Policy Revisited." *Economic and Political Weekly,* vol. 22, Nov. 14.

Srinivas, M. N. 1962 *Caste in Modern India.* London: Asia Publishing House.

———1969 *Social Change in Modern India.* Berkeley: University of California Press.

Weiner, Myron 1983 "The Political Consequences of Preferential Policies: A Comparative Perspective." *Comparative Politics* 16(1):35–52.

Zelliot, Eleanor 1970 "Learning the Uses of Political Means: The Mahars of Maharashtra." In Rajni Kothari, ed., *Caste in Indian Politics.* Delhi: Orient Longman.

RITA JALALI

**CAUSAL INFERENCE MODELS** The notion of causality has been controversial for a very long time, and yet neither scientists, social scientists, nor laypeople have been able to think constructively without using a set of explanatory concepts that, either explicitly or not, have implied causes and effects. Sometimes other words have been substituted, for example, *consequences, results,* or *influences.* Even worse, there are vague terms such as *leads to, reflects, stems from, derives from, articulates with,* or *follows from,* which are often used in sentences that are almost deliberately ambiguous in avoiding causal terminology. Whenever such vague phrases are used throughout a theoretical work, or whenever one merely states that two variables are correlated with one another, it may not be recognized that what purports to be an "explanation" is really not a genuine theoretical explanation at all.

It is, of course, possible to provide a very narrow definition of causation and then to argue that such a notion is totally inadequate in terms of scientific explanations. If, for example, one defines causation in such a way that there can be only a single cause of a given phenomenon, or that a necessary condition, a sufficient condition, or both must be satisfied, or that absolute certainty is required to establish causation, then indeed very few persons would ever be willing to use the term. Indeed, in sociology, causal terminology was almost deliberately avoided before the 1960s, except in reports of experimental research. Since that time, however, the notion of *multivariate causation,* combined with the explicit allowance for impacts of neglected factors, has gradually replaced these more restrictive usages.

There is general agreement that causation can never be proven, and of course in a strict sense *no* statements about the real world can ever be "proven" correct, if only because of indeterminacies produced by measurement errors and the necessity of relying on evidence that has been filtered through imperfect sense organs or fallible measuring instruments. One may accept the fact that, strictly speaking, one is always dealing with causal *models* of real-world processes and that one's inferences concerning the adequacy of such models must inevitably be based on a combination of *empirical evidence* and untested *assumptions,* some of which are about underlying causal processes that can never be subject to empirical verification. This is basically true for all scientific evidence, though the assumptions one may require in making interpretations or explanations of the underlying reality may be more or less plausible in view of supplementary information that may be available. Unfortunately, in the social sciences such supplementary information is likely to be of questionable quality, thereby reducing the degree of faith one has in whatever causal assertions have been made.

In the causal modeling literature, which is basically compatible with the so-called structural equation modeling in econometrics, equation systems are constructed so as to represent as well as possible a presumed real-world situation, given whatever limitations have been imposed in terms of omitted variables that produce unknown biases, possibly incorrect functional forms for one's equations, measurement errors, or in general what are termed *specification errors* in the equations. Since such limitations are always present, any particular equation will contain a disturbance term that is assumed to behave in a certain fashion. One's assumptions about such disturbances are both critical for one's inferences and also (for the most part) inherently untestable with the data at hand. This in turn means that such inferences must always be tentative. One never "finds" effects, for example, but only infers them on the basis of findings about covariances and temporal sequences *and* a set of untested theoretical assumptions. To the degree that such assumptions are hidden from view, both the social scientist and one's readers may therefore be seriously misled to the degree that these assumptions are also incorrect.

In the recursive models commonly in use in sociology, it is assumed that causal influences can be ordered, such that one may designate an $X_1$ that does not depend on any of the remaining variables in the system but, presumably, varies as a result of exogenous causes that have been ignored in the theory. A second variable, $X_2$, may then be found that may depend upon $X_1$ as well as a different set of exogenous factors, but the assumption is that $X_2$ does *not* affect $X_1$, either directly or through any other mechanism. One then builds up the system, equation by equation, by locating an $X_3$ that may depend on either or both of $X_1$ or $X_2$, plus still another set of independent variables (referred to as exogenous factors), but with the assumption that neither of the first two $X$'s is affected by $X_3$. Adding still more variables in this recursive fashion, and for the time being assuming linear and additive relationships, one arrives at the system of equations shown in equation system 1,

$$
\begin{aligned}
X_1 &= \epsilon_1 \\
X_2 &= \beta_{21}X_1 + \epsilon_2 \\
X_3 &= \beta_{31}X_1 + \beta_{32}X_2 + \epsilon_3 \\
&\vdots \\
X_k &= \beta_{k1}X_1 + \beta_{k2}X_2 + \beta_{k3}X_3 + \cdots + \beta_{k,k-1}X_{k-1} + \epsilon_k
\end{aligned}
\tag{1}
$$

in which the disturbance terms are represented by the $\epsilon_i$ and where for the sake of simplicity the constant terms have been omitted.

The essential property of recursive equations that provides a simple causal interpretation is that changes made in any given equation may affect subsequent ones but will *not* affect any of the prior equations. Thus, if a mysterious demon were to change one of the parameters in the equation for $X_3$, this would undoubtedly affect not only $X_3$ but also $X_4$, $X_5$, through $X_k$, but could have no effect on either of the first two equations, which do not depend on $X_3$ or any of the later variables in the system. As will be discussed below, this special property of recursive systems does not hold in the more general setup involving variables that may be reciprocally interrelated. Indeed, it is this recursive property that justifies one's dealing with the equations separately and sequentially as single equations. The assumptions required for such a system are therefore implicit in all data analyses (e.g., log-linear modeling, analysis of variance, or comparisons among means) that are typically discussed in first and second courses in applied statistics.

Assumptions are always critical in causal analyses or—what is often not recognized—in *any* kind of theoretical interpretation of empirical data. Some such assumptions are implied by the forms of one's equations, in this case linearity and additivity. Fortunately, these types of assumptions can be rather simply modified by, for example, introducing second- or higher-degree terms, log functions, or interaction terms. It is a mistake to claim—as some critics have done—that causal modeling requires one to assume such restrictive functional forms.

Far more important are two other kinds of assumptions—those about measurement errors and those concerning the disturbance terms representing the effects of all omitted variables. Simple causal modeling of the type represented by equation system 1 requires the naive assumption that all variables have been perfectly measured, an assumption that is, unfortunately, frequently ignored in many empirical investigations using path analyses based on exactly this same type of causal system. Measurement errors require one to make an auxiliary set of assumptions regarding both the sources of measurement-error bias and the causal connections between so-called true scores and measured indicators. In principle, however, such measurement-error assumptions can be explicitly built into the equation system and empirical estimates obtained, provided there are a sufficient number of multiple indicators to solve for the unknowns produced by these measurement errors, a possibility that will be discussed in the final section.

In many instances, assumptions about one's disturbance terms are even more problematic but equally critical. In verbal statements of theoretical arguments one often comes across the phrase "other things being equal," or the notion that in the ideal experimental design all causes except one must be literally held constant if causal inferences are to be made. Yet both the phrase "other

things being equal" and the restrictive assumption of the perfect experiment beg the question of how one can possibly know that "other things" are in fact equal, that all "relevant" variables have been held constant, or that there are no possible sources of measurement bias. Obviously, an alert critic may always suggest another variable that indeed does vary across settings studied or that has not been held constant in an experiment.

In recursive causal models this highly restrictive notion concerning the constancy of all possible alternative causes is relaxed by allowing for a disturbance term that varies precisely because they are *not* all constant. But if so, can one get by without requiring any other assumptions about their effects? Indeed not. One must assume, essentially, that the omitted variables affecting any one of the $X$'s are uncorrelated with those that affect the others. If so, it can then be shown that the disturbance term in each equation will be uncorrelated with each of the independent variables appearing on the right-hand side, thus justifying the use of ordinary least-squares estimating procedures. In practical terms, this means that if one has had to omit any important causes of a given variable, one must also be willing to assume that they do not systematically affect any of its presumed causes that have been explicitly included in our model. A skeptic may, of course, be able to identify one or more such disturbing influences, in which case a modified model may need to be constructed and tested. For example, if $\epsilon_3$ and $\epsilon_4$ contain a common cause that can be identified and measured, such a variable needs to be introduced explictly into the model as a cause of both $X_3$ and $X_4$.

Perhaps the five-variable model of Figure 1 will help the reader visualize what is involved. To be specific, suppose $X_5$, the ultimate dependent variable, represents some behavior, say, the actual number of delinquent acts a youth has perpetrated. Let $X_3$ and $X_4$, respectively, represent two internal states, say, guilt and self-esteem. Finally, suppose $X_1$ and $X_2$ are two setting variables, parental education and deliquency rates within the youth's neighborhood, with the latter variable

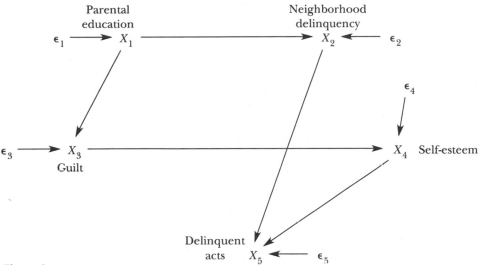

**Figure 1**
*Simple Recursive Model*

being influenced by the former through the parents' ability to select among residential areas.

The fact that the disturbance term arrows are unconnected in Figure 1 represents the assumption that they are mutually uncorrelated, or that the omitted variables affecting any given $X_i$ are uncorrelated with any of its explicitly included causes among the remaining $X$'s. If ordinary least squares is used to estimate the parameters in this model, then the empirically obtained residuals $e_i$ will indeed be uncorrelated with the independent $X$'s in their respective equations, but since this automatically occurs as a property of least-squares estimation, it cannot be used as the basis for a test of our a priori assumptions about the true disturbances.

If one is unwilling to accept these assumptions about the behavior of omitted variables, the only way out of this situation is to reformulate the model and to introduce further complexities in the form of additional measured variables. At some point, however, one must stop and make the (untestable) assumption that the revised causal model is "closed" in the sense that omitted variables do not disturb the patterning of relationships among the included variables.

Assuming such theoretical closure, then, one is in a position to estimate the parameters, attach their numerical values to the diagram, and also evaluate the model in terms of its consistency with the data. In the model of Figure 1, for instance, there are no direct arrows between $X_9$ and $X_3$, between $X_4$ and both $X_1$ and $X_2$, and between $X_5$ and both $X_1$ and $X_3$. This means that with controls for all prior or intervening variables, the respective partial correlations can be predicted to be zero, apart from sampling errors. One arrives at the predictions in equation system 2.

$$r_{23.1} = 0 \qquad r_{14.23} = 0 \qquad r_{24.13} = 0$$
$$r_{15.234} = 0 \qquad r_{35.124} = 0 \qquad (2)$$

Thus, for each omitted arrow one may write out a specific "zero" prediction. Where arrows have been drawn in, it may have been possible to predict the signs of direct links, and these directional predictions may also be used to evaluate the model. Notice a very important property of recursive models. In relating any pair of variables, say, $X_2$ and $X_3$, one expects to control for antecedent or intervening variables, but it is *not* appropriate to introduce as controls any variables that appear as subsequent variables in the model (e.g., $X_4$ or $X_5$). The simple phrase "controlling for all relevant variables" should therefore not be construed to mean variables that are presumed to depend on both of the variables being studied. In an experimental setup, one would presumably be unable to carry out such an absurd operation, but in statistical calculations, which involve pencil-and-paper controlling only, there is nothing to prevent one from doing so.

It is unfortunately the case that controls for dependent variables can sometimes be made inadvertently through one's research design (Blalock 1985). For example, one may select respondents from a list that is based on a dependent variable such as committing a particular crime, entering a given hospital, living in a certain residential area, or being employed in a particular factory. Whenever such improper controls are introduced, whether recognized explicitly or not, our inferences regarding relationships among causally prior variables are likely to be incorrect. If, for example, $X_1$ and $X_2$ are totally uncorrelated, but one controls for their common effect, $X_3$, then even though $r_{12} = 0$, it will turn out that $r_{12.3} \neq 0$.

Recursive models also provide justifications for common-sense rules of thumb regarding the conditions under which it is *not* necessary to control for prior or intervening variables. In the model of Figure 1, for example, it can be shown that although $r_{24.13} = 0$, it would be sufficient to control for *either* $X_1$ or $X_3$ but not both in order for the partial to disappear. Similarly, in relating $X_3$ to $X_5$, the partial will be reduced to zero if one controls for either $X_2$ and $X_4$ or $X_1$ and $X_4$. It is not necessary to control for all three simultaneously. More generally, a number of simplifications become possible, depending on the patterning of omitted arrows, and these simplifications can be used to justify the omission of certain variables if these cannot be measured. If, for example, one could not measure $X_3$, one could draw in a direct arrow from $X_1$ to $X_4$ without altering the remainder of the model. Without such an explicit causal model in front of us, however, the omission of variables must be justified on completely ad hoc grounds. The important point is that pragmatic reasons for such omissions should not be accepted without *theoretical* justifications.

## PATH ANALYSIS AND AN EXAMPLE

Sewall Wright (1934, 1960) introduced a form of causal modeling long before it became fashionable among sociologists. Wright, a population geneticist, worked in terms of standardized variables with unit variances and zero means. Expressing any given equation in terms of what he referred to as path coefficients, which in recursive modeling are equivalent to beta weights, Wright was able to derive a simple formula for decomposing the correlation between any pair of variables $x_i$ and $x_j$. The equation for any given variable can be written as $x_i = p_{i1}x_1 + p_{i2}x_2 + \cdots + p_{ik}x_k + u_i$, where the $p_{ij}$ represent standardized regression coefficients and where the lower-case $x$'s refer to the standardized variables. One may then multiply both sides of the equation by $x_j$, the variable that is to be correlated with $x_i$. Therefore, $x_ix_j = p_{i1}x_1x_j + p_{i2}x_2x_j + \cdots + p_{ik}x_kx_j + u_ix_j$. Summing over all cases and dividing by the number of cases $N$, one has the results in equation system 3.

$$r_{ij} = \frac{\Sigma x_ix_j}{N} = p_{i1}\frac{\Sigma x_1x_j}{N} + p_{i2}\frac{\Sigma x_2x_j}{N} + \cdots + p_{ik}\frac{\Sigma x_kx_j}{N} + \frac{\Sigma u_ix_j}{N}$$

$$= p_{i1}r_{1j} + p_{i2}r_{2j} + \cdots + p_{ik}r_{kj} + 0 = \sum_k p_{ik}r_{kj} \quad (3)$$

The expression in equation system 3 enables one to decompose or partition any total correlation into a sum of terms, each of which consists of a path coefficient multiplied by a correlation coefficient, which itself may be decomposed in a similar way. In Wright's notation the path coefficients are written without any dots that indicate control variables but are indeed merely the (partial) regression coefficients for the standardized variables. Any given path coefficient, say $p_{54}$, can be interpreted as the change that would be imparted in the dependent variable $x_5$, in its standard deviation units, if the other variable $x_4$ were to change by one of its standard deviation units, with the remaining explicitly included independent variables (here $x_1$, $x_2$, and $x_3$) all held constant. In working with standardized variables one is able to simplify these expressions owing to the fact that $r_{ij} = \Sigma x_ix_j/N$, but one must pay the price of then having to work with standard deviation units that may vary across samples or populations. This, in turn, means that two sets of path coefficients for different samples, say men and women, cannot easily be compared since the standard deviations (say, in income earned) may be different.

In the case of the model of Figure 2, which is the same causal diagram as Figure 1, but with the relevant $p_{ij}$ inserted, one may write out expressions for each of the $r_{ij}$ as shown in equation system 4.

$$r_{12} = p_{21}r_{11} = p_{21}(1) = p_{21}$$

$$r_{13} = p_{31}r_{11} = p_{31}$$

$$r_{23} = p_{31}r_{12} = p_{31}p_{21} = r_{13}r_{12} \quad (\text{or } r_{23.1} = 0)$$

$$r_{14} = p_{43}r_{13} = p_{43}p_{31}$$

$$r_{24} = p_{43}r_{23} = p_{43}p_{31}p_{21}$$

$$r_{34} = p_{43}r_{33} = p_{43} \tag{4}$$

$$r_{15} = p_{52}r_{21}+p_{54}r_{41} = p_{52}p_{21}+p_{54}p_{43}p_{31}$$

$$r_{25} = p_{52}r_{22}+p_{54}r_{42} = p_{52}+p_{54}p_{43}p_{31}p_{21}$$

$$r_{35} = p_{52}r_{23}+p_{54}r_{43} = p_{52}p_{31}p_{21}+p_{54}p_{43}$$

$$r_{45} = p_{52}r_{24}+p_{54}r_{44} = p_{52}p_{43}p_{31}p_{21}+p_{54}$$

In decomposing each of the total correlations, one takes the path coefficients for each of the arrows coming into the appropriate dependent variable and multiplies each of these by the total correlation between the variable at the source of the arrow and the "independent" variable in which one is interested. In the case of $r_{12}$, this involves multiplying $p_{21}$ by the correlation of $x_1$ with itself, namely $r_{11} = 1.0$. Therefore one obtains the simple result that $r_{12} = p_{21}$. Similar results obtain for $r_{13}$ and $r_{34}$. The decomposition of $r_{23}$, however, results in the expression $r_{23} = p_{31}r_{12} = p_{31}p_{21} = r_{12}r_{13}$, which also of course implies that $r_{23.1} = 0$.

When one comes to the decomposition of correlations with $x_5$, which has two direct paths into it, the expressions become more complex but also demonstrate the heuristic value of path analysis. For example, in the case of $r_{35}$, this total correlation can be decomposed into two terms, one representing the indirect effects of $x_3$ via the intervening variable $x_4$, namely the product $p_{54}p_{43}$, and the other the spurious association produced by the common cause $x_1$, namely the more complex product $p_{52}p_{31}p_{21}$. In the case of the correlation between $x_4$ and $x_5$ one obtains a similar result except that there is a direct effect term represented by the single coefficient $p_{54}$.

As a numerical substantive example consider the path model of Figure 3, which represents the basic model in Blau and Duncan's classic study, *The American Occupational Structure* (1967, p. 17). Two additional features of the Blau-Duncan model may be noted. A curved, double-headed arrow has been drawn between father's education and

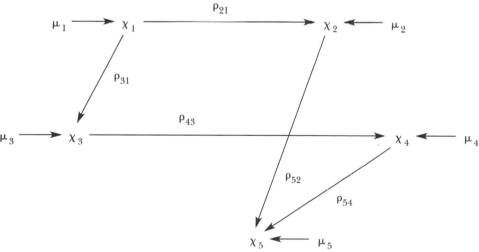

**Figure 2**
*Model of Figure 1, with Path Coefficients and Standardized Variables*

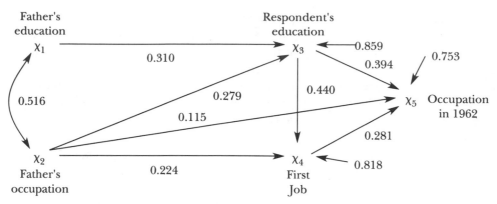

*Figure 3*
*Path Diagram for Blau-Duncan Model*

father's occupation, indicating that the causal paths between these two exogenous or independent variables have not been specified. This means that there is no $p_{21}$ in the model, so that $r_{12}$ cannot be decomposed. Its value of 0.516 has been inserted into the diagram, however. The implication of a failure to commit oneself on the direction of causation between these two variables is that decompositions of subsequent $r_{ij}$ will involve expressions that are sometimes combinations of the relevant $p$'s *and* the unexplained association between father's education and occupation. This, in turn, means that the indirect effects of one of these variables "through" the other cannot be assessed. One can determine the direct effects of, say, father's occupation on respondent's education, or its indirect effects on occupation in 1962 through first job, but not "through" father's education. If one had, instead, committed oneself to the directional flow from father's education to father's occupation, a not unreasonable assumption, then all indirect effects and spurious connections could be evaluated. Sometimes it is indeed necessary to make use of double-headed arrows when the direction of causation among the most causally prior variables cannot be specified, but one then gives up the ability to trace out those indirect effects or spurious associations that involve these unexplained correlations.

The second feature of the Blau-Duncan diagram worth noting involves the small, unattached arrows coming into each of the "dependent" variables in the model. These of course represent

the disturbance terms, which in a correctly specified model are taken to be uncorrelated. But the *magnitudes* of these effects of outside variables are also provided in the diagram to indicate just how much variance remains unexplained by the model. Each of the numerical values of path coefficients coming in from these outside variables, when squared, turns out to be the equivalent of $1 - R^2$, or the variances that remain unexplained by *all* of the included explanatory variables. Thus there is considerable unexplained variance in respondent's education (0.738), first job (0.669), and occupation in 1962 (0.567), indicating, of course, plenty of room for other factors to operate. The challenge then becomes that of locating additional variables to improve the explanatory value of the model. This has, indeed, been an important stimulus to the development of the status attainment literature that the Blau-Duncan study subsequently spawned.

The placement of numerical values in such path diagrams enables the reader to assess, rather easily, the relative magnitudes of the several direct effects. Thus, father's education is inferred to have a moderately strong direct effect on respondent's education, but none on the respondent's occupational status. Father's occupation is estimated to have somewhat weaker direct effects on both respondent's education and first job but a much weaker direct effect on his later occupation. The direct effects of respondent's education on first job are estimated to be only somewhat stronger than those on the subsequent occupation, with first job controlled. In evaluating these numerical values, however, one must keep in mind that all variables have been expressed in standard deviation units rather than some "natural" unit such as years of schooling. This in turn means that if variances for, say, men and women or blacks and whites are not the same, then comparisons across samples should be made in terms of unstandardized, rather than standardized, coefficients.

## SIMULTANEOUS EQUATION MODELS

Recursive modeling requires one to make rather strong assumptions about temporal sequences. This does not, in itself, rule out the possibility of reciprocal causation provided that lag periods can be specified. For example, the actions of party A may affect the later behaviors of party B, which in turn affect still later reactions of the first party. Ideally, if one could watch a dynamic interaction process such as that among family members, and accurately record the temporal sequences, one could specify a recursive model in which the behaviors of the same individual could be represented by distinct variables that have been temporally ordered. Indeed Strotz and Wold (1960) have cogently argued that many simultaneous equation models appearing in the econometric literature have been misspecified precisely because they do not capture such dynamic features, which in causal models should ideally involve specified lag periods. For example, prices and quantities of goods do not simply "seek equilibrium." Instead, there are at least three kinds of autonomous actors—producers, customers, and retailers or wholesalers—who react to one another's behaviors with varying lag periods.

In many instances, however, one cannot collect the kinds of data necessary to ascertain these lag periods. Furthermore, especially in the case of aggregated data, the lag periods for different actors may not coincide, so that macro-level changes are for all practical purposes continuous rather than discrete. Population size, literacy levels, urbanization, industrialization, political alienation, and so forth are all changing at once. How can such situations be modeled and what additional complications do they introduce?

In the general case there will be $k$ mutually interdependent variables $X_i$ that may possibly each directly affect the others. These are referred to as endogenous variables, with the entire set having the property that there is no single dependent variable that does not feed back to affect at least one of the others. Given this situation, it turns out that it is not legitimate to break the equations apart in order to estimate the parameters, one equation at a time, as one does in the case of a recursive setup. Since any given variable may affect the others, this also means that its omitted causes, represented by the disturbance terms $\epsilon_i$, will also directly or indirectly affect the remaining endogenous variables, so that it becomes totally unreasonable to assume these disturbances to be uncorrelated with the "independent" variables in their respective equations. Thus, one of the critical assumptions required to justify the use of ordinary least squares cannot legitimately be made, meaning that a wide variety of single equation techniques discussed in the statistical literature must be modified.

There is an even more serious problem, however, which can be seen more readily if one writes out the set of equations, one for each of the $k$ endogenous variables. To this set are added another set of what are called predetermined variables, $Z_j$, that will play an essential role to be discussed below. Our equation set now becomes as shown in equation system 5.

$$x_1 = \beta_{12}x_2 + \beta_{13}x_3 + \cdots + \beta_{1k}x_k + \gamma_{11}z_1 + \gamma_{12}z_2 + \cdots + \gamma_{1m}z_m + \epsilon_1$$

$$x_2 = \beta_{21}x_1 + \beta_{23}x_3 + \cdots + \beta_{2k}x_k + \gamma_{21}z_1 + \gamma_{22}z_2 + \cdots + \gamma_{2m}z_m + \epsilon_2$$

$$x_3 = \beta_{31}x_1 + \beta_{32}x_2 + \cdots + \beta_{3k}x_k + \gamma_{31}z_1 + \gamma_{32}z_2 + \cdots + \gamma_{3m}z_m + \epsilon_3 \tag{5}$$

$$\vdots$$

$$x_k = \beta_{k1}x_1 + \beta_{k2}x_2 + \cdots + \beta_{k,k-1}x_{k-1} + \gamma_{k1}z_1 + \gamma_{k2}z_2 + \cdots + \gamma_{km}z_m + \epsilon_k$$

The regression coefficients (called "structural parameters") that connect the several endogenous variables in equation system 5 are designated as $\beta_{ij}$ and are distinguished from the $\gamma_{ij}$ representing the direct effects of the predetermined $Z_j$ on the relevant $X_i$. This notational distinction is made because the two kinds of variables play different roles in the model. Although it cannot be assumed that the disturbances $\epsilon_i$ are uncorrelated with the endogenous $X$'s that appear on the right-hand sides of their respective equations, one may make the somewhat less restrictive assumption that these disturbances are uncorrelated with the pre-determined $Z$'s.

Some $Z$'s may be truly exogenous, or distinct independent variables, that are assumed not to be affected by any of the endogenous variables in the model. Others, however, may be lagged endogenous variables, or prior levels of some of the $X$'s. In a sense, the defining characteristic of these predetermined variables is that they be uncorrelated with any of the omitted causes of the endogenous variables. Such an assumption may be difficult to accept in the case of lagged endogenous variables, given the likelihood of autocorrelated disturbances, but we shall not consider this complication further. The basic assumption regarding the truly exogenous variables, however, is that these are uncorrelated with all omitted causes of the $X$'s, though they may of course be correlated with the $X$'s and also possibly each other.

Clearly, there are more unknown parameters than was the case for the original recursive equation system (1). Turning attention back to the simple recursive system represented in equation system 1, one sees that the matrix of betas in that equation system is triangular, with all such coefficients above the main diagonal being set equal to zero on a priori grounds. That is, in equation system 1, half of the possible betas have been set equal to zero, the remainder being estimated using ordinary least squares. It turns out that in the more general equation system 5, there will be too many unknowns unless additional restrictive assumptions are made. In particular, in each of the $k$ equations one will have to make a priori assumptions that at least $k - 1$ coefficients have been set equal to zero or some other known value (which cannot be estimated from the data). This is why one needs the predetermined $Z_i$ and the relevant gammas. If one is willing to assume that, for any given endogenous $X_i$, certain direct arrows are missing, meaning that there are no *direct* effects coming from the relevant $X_j$ or $Z$ variable, then one may indeed estimate the remaining parameters. One does not have to make the very restrictive assumptions required under the recursive setup, namely that if $X_j$ affects $X_i$, then the reverse cannot hold. As long as one assumes that *some* of the coefficients are zero, there is a chance of being able to identify or estimate the others.

It turns out that the *necessary* condition for identification can be easily specified, as implied in the above discussion. For any given equation, one must leave out at least $k - 1$ of the remaining variables. The necessary *and* sufficient condition is far more complicated to state. In many instances, when the necessary condition has been met, so will the sufficient one as well, unless some of the equations contain exactly the same sets of variables (i.e., exactly the same combination of omitted variables). But since this will not always be the case, the reader should consult textbooks in econometrics for more complete treatments.

Returning to the substantive example of delinquency, as represented in Figure 1, one may revise the model somewhat by allowing for a feedback from delinquent behavior to guilt, as well as a reciprocal relationship between the two internal states, guilt and self-esteem. One may also relabel parental education as $Z_1$ and neighborhood delinquency as $Z_2$ because there is no feedback from any of the three endogenous variables to either of these predetermined ones. Renumbering the endogenous variables as $X_1$, $X_2$, and $X_3$, one may represent the revised model as in Figure 4.

In this kind of application one may question whether a behavior can ever influence an internal state. Keeping in mind, however, that the concern is with *repeated* acts of delinquency, it is entirely reasonable to assume that earlier acts feed back to affect subsequent guilt levels, which in turn affect future acts of delinquency. It is precisely this very frequent type of causal process that is ignored

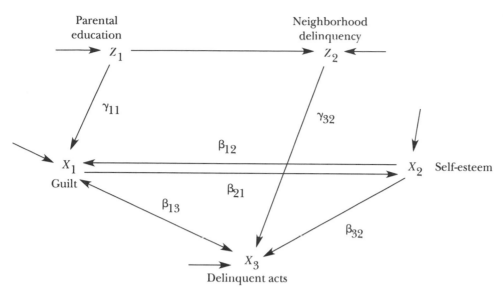

**Figure 4**
*Nonrecursive Modification of Figure 1*

whenever behaviors are taken, rather simply, as "dependent" variables.

Here, $k = 3$, so that at least two variables must be left out of each equation, meaning that their respective coefficients have been set equal to zero. One can rather simply check on the necessary condition by counting arrowheads coming to each variable. In this instance there can be no more than two arrows into each variable, whereas in the case of guilt $X_1$ there are three. The equation for $X_1$ is referred to as being "underidentified," meaning that the situation is empirically hopeless. The coefficients simply cannot be estimated by *any* empirical means. There are exactly two arrows coming into delinquency $X_3$, and one refers to this as a situation in which the equation is "exactly identified." With only a single arrow coming into self-esteem $X_2$, one has an "overidentified" equation for which one actually has an excess of empirical information compared to the number of unknowns to be estimated. It turns out that overidentified equations provide criteria for evaluating goodness of fit, or a test of the model, in much the same way that, for recursive models, one obtains an empirical test of a null hypothesis for each causal arrow that has been deleted.

Since the equation for $X_1$ is underidentified, one must either remove one of the arrows, on a priori grounds, or search for at least one more predetermined variable that does *not* belong in this equation, that is, a predetermined variable that is assumed not to be a direct cause of level of guilt. Perhaps school performance can be introduced as $Z_3$ by making the assumption that $Z_3$ directly affects both self-esteem and delinquency but not guilt level. A check of this revised model indicates that all equations are properly identified, and one may proceed to estimation. Although space does not permit a discussion of alternative estimation methods that enable one to get around the violated assumption required by ordinary least squares, there are various computer programs available to accomplish this task. The simplest such alternative, two-stage least squares (2SLS), will ordinarily be adequate for nearly all sociological applications and turns out to be less sensitive to other kinds of specification errors than many of the more sophisticated alternatives that have been proposed.

## CAUSAL APPROACH TO MEASUREMENT ERRORS

Finally, brief mention should be made of a growing body of literature—closely linked to factor analysis—that has been developed in order to attach measurement-error models to structural-equation approaches that presume perfect measurement. The fundamental philosophical starting point of such models involves the assumption that in many if not most instances, measurement errors can be conceived in causal terms. Most often, the indicator or measured variables are taken as *effects* of underlying or "true" variables, plus additional factors that may produce combinations of random measurement errors, which are unrelated to all other variables in the theoretical system, and systematic biases that are explainable in causal terms. Thus, measures of "true guilt" or "true self-esteem" will consist of responses, usually to paper-and-pencil tests, that may be subject to distortions produced by other variables, including some of the variables in the causal system. Perhaps distortions in the guilt measure may be a function of amount of delinquent behavior or parental education. Similarly, measures of behaviors are likely to overestimate or underestimate true frequencies, with biases dependent on qualities of the observer, inaccuracies in official records, or perhaps the ability of the actor to evade detection.

In all such instances, we may be able to construct an "auxiliary measurement theory" (Blalock 1968; Costner 1969) that is itself a causal model that contains a mixture of measured and unmeasured variables, the latter of which consti-

tute the "true" or underlying variables of theoretical interest. The existence of such unmeasured variables, however, may introduce identification problems by using more unknowns than can be estimated from one's data. If so, the situation will once more be hopeless empirically. But if one has available *several* indicators of each of the imperfectly measured constructs, *and* if one is willing to make a sufficient number of simplifying assumptions strategically placed within the overall model, estimates may be obtainable.

Consider the model of Figure 5 (borrowed from Costner 1969), which contains only two theoretical variables of interest, namely, the unmeasured variables $X$ and $Y$. Suppose one has two indicators each for both $X$ and $Y$ and that one is willing to make the simplifying assumption that $X$ does not affect either of $Y$'s indicators, $Y_1$ and $Y_2$, and that $Y$ does not affect either of $X$'s indicators, $X_1$ and $X_2$. For the time being ignore the variable $W$ as well as the two dashed arrows drawn from it to the indicators $X_2$ and $Y_1$. Without $W$, the nonexistence of other arrows implies that the remaining causes of the four indicators are assumed to be uncorrelated with all other variables in the system, so that one may assume measurement errors to be strictly random.

If one labels the path coefficients (which all connect measured variables to unmeasured ones) by the simple letters $a$, $b$, $c$, $d$, and $e$, then with

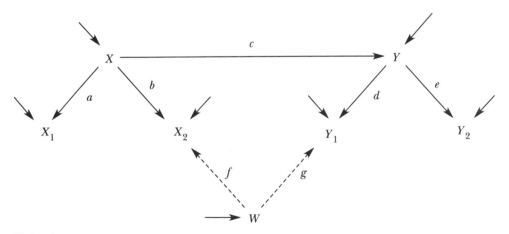

**Figure 5**
*Simple Measurement-Error Model, with Two Unmeasured Variables* X *and* Y, *Two Indicators of Each, and Source of Bias* W

$4(3)/2 = 6$ correlations among the four indicators, there will be six pieces of empirical information (equation system 5) with which to estimate the five unknown path coefficients.

$$
\begin{aligned}
r_{x_1 x_2} &= ab & r_{x_1 y_2} &= ace \\
r_{y_1 y_2} &= de & r_{x_2 y_1} &= bcd \\
r_{x_1 y_1} &= acd & r_{x_2 y_2} &= bce
\end{aligned}
\tag{6}
$$

One may now estimate the correlation or path coefficient $c$ between $X$ and $Y$ by an equation derived from equation system 6.

$$
c^2 = \frac{abc^2 de}{(ab)(de)} = \frac{r_{x_1 y_1} r_{x_2 y_2}}{r_{x_1 x_2} r_{y_1 y_2}} = \frac{r_{x_1 y_2} r_{x_2 y_1}}{r_{x_1 x_2} r_{y_1 y_2}}
\tag{7}
$$

Also notice that there is an excess equation that may be used to check on the consistency of the model with the data, namely the prediction that $r_{x_1 y_1} \, r_{x_2 y_2} = r_{x_1 y_2} \, r_{x_2 y_1} = abc^2 de$.

Suppose next that there is a source of measurement error bias $W$ that is a common cause of one of $X$'s indicators (namely $X_2$) and one of $Y$'s (namely $Y_1$). Perhaps these two items have similar wordings based on a social survey, whereas the remaining two indicators involve very different kinds of measures. There is now a different expression for the correlation between $X_2$ and $Y_1$, namely $r_{x_2 y_1} = bcd + fg$. If one were to use this particular correlation in the estimate of $c^2$, without being aware of the impact of $W$, one would obtain a biased estimate. In this instance one would be able to detect this particular kind of departure from randomness because the consistency criterion would no longer be met. That is, $(acd)(bce) \neq (ace)(bcd + fg)$. Had $W$ been a common cause of the two indicators of either $X$ or $Y$ alone, however, it can be seen that one would have been unable to detect the bias even though it would have been present.

Obviously, most of one's measurement-error models will be far more complex than this, with several (usually unmeasured) sources of bias, possible nonlinearities, and linkages between some of the important variables and indicators of *other* variables in the substantive theory. Also, some indicators may be taken as *causes* of the conceptual variables, as for example often occurs when one is attempting to get at experience variables (e.g., exposure to discrimination) by using simple objective indicators such as race, sex, or age. Furthermore, one's substantive models may involve feedback relationships so that simultaneous equation systems must be joined to one's measurement-error models.

In all such instances, there will undoubtedly be numerous specification errors in one's models, so that it becomes necessary to evaluate alternative models in terms of their goodness of fit to the data. Simple path-analytic methods, although heuristically helpful, will no longer be adequate. Fortunately, there are several highly sophisticated computer programs, such as LISREL, that enable social scientists to carry out sophisticated data analyses designed to evaluate these more complex models and to estimate their parameters once it has been decided that the fit to reality is reasonably close. (See Joreskog and Sorbom 1981; Long 1983; and Herting 1985.)

In closing, what needs to be stressed is that causal modeling tools are highly flexible. They may be modified to handle additional complications such as interactions and nonlinearities. Causal modeling in terms of attribute data has been given a firm theoretical underpinning by Suppes (1970), and even ordinal data may be used in an exploratory fashion, provided that one is willing to assume that dichotomization or categorization has not introduced substantial measurement errors that cannot be modeled.

Like all other approaches, however, causal modeling is heavily dependent on the assumptions one is willing to make. Such assumptions need to be made as explicit as possible—a procedure that is unfortunately often not taken sufficiently seriously in the empirical literature. In short, this set of tools, properly used, has been designed to provide precise meaning to the assertion that neither theory nor data can stand alone and that any interpretations of research findings one wishes to provide must inevitably also be based on a set of assumptions, many of which cannot be tested with the data in hand.

Finally, it should be stressed that causal modeling can be very useful in the process of theory *construction,* even in instances where many of the variables contained in the model will remain unmeasured in any given study. It is certainly a mistake to throw out portions of one's theory merely because data to test it are not currently available. Indeed, without a theory as to how missing variables are assumed to operate, it will be impossible to justify one's assumptions regarding the behavior of disturbance terms that will contain such variables, whether explicitly recognized or not. Causal modeling may thus be an important tool for guiding future research and for providing guidelines as to what kinds of neglected variables need to be measured.

(SEE ALSO: *Correlation and Regression Analysis; Epistemology; Multiple Indicator Models; Scientific Explanation; Tabular Analysis*)

### REFERENCES

Blalock, Hubert M. 1968 "The Measurement Problem: A Gap Between the Languages of Theory and Research." In H. M. Blalock and A. B. Blalock, eds., *Methodology in Social Research.* New York: McGraw-Hill.

————1985 "Inadvertent Manipulations of Dependent Variables in Research Designs." In H. M. Blalock, ed., *Causal Models in Panel and Experimental Designs.* New York: Aldine.

Blau, Peter M., and Otis Dudley Duncan 1967 *The American Occupational Structure.* New York: Wiley.

Costner, Herbert L. 1969 "Theory, Deduction, and Rules of Correspondence." *American Journal of Sociology* 75:245–263.

Herting, Jerald R. 1985 "Multiple Indicator Models Using LISREL." In H. M. Blalock, ed., *Causal Models in the Social Sciences,* 2nd ed. New York: Aldine.

Joreskog, Karl G., and Dag Sorbom 1981 *LISREL V: Analysis of Linear Structural Relationships by the Method of Maximum Likelihood; User's Guide.* Uppsala, Sweden: University of Uppsala Press.

Long, J. Scott 1983 *Confirmatory Factor Analysis: A Preface to LISREL.* Beverly Hills, Calif.: Sage.

Strotz, Robert H., and Herman O. A. Wold 1960 "Recursive Versus Nonrecursive Systems." *Econometrica* 28:417–427.

Suppes, Patrick 1970 *A Probabilistic Theory of Causality.* Amsterdam: North-Holland.

Wright, Sewall 1934 "The Method of Path Coefficients." *Annals of Mathematical Statistics* 5:161–215.

————1960 "Path Coefficients and Path Regressions: Alternative or Complementary Concepts?" *Biometrics* 16:189–202.

HUBERT M. BLALOCK, JR.

**CENSUS** A census is a procedure for establishing the size and characteristics of a total population by attempting to count each of the individuals in the population. A census of a school, church, or other local organization may be quite easy, requiring only a review of membership records and a count of the total number of names. A national census, by contrast, requires attention to an array of definitional issues and the development of elaborate procedures. Planning, execution, and tabulation of the 1990 U.S. Census of Population extended over more than ten years. Hundreds of thousands of people were employed at a cost of nearly three-billion dollars.

A modern national census is "the total process of collecting, compiling, evaluating, analysing and publishing or otherwise disseminating demographic, economic, and social data pertaining, at a specified time, to all persons in a country" (United Nations 1980, p. 2). The United Nations encourages its members to take regular censuses and provides technical assistance. It also publishes an annual demographic yearbook that reports census data and other population information for many countries.

The actual enumeration for a national population census is usually spread over a period of weeks or months, but an attempt is made to record circumstances as of the census day (April 1 for the 1990 U.S. census). In some censuses, persons are recorded in their legal or usual place of residence (a *de jure enumeration*). The Bible reports that a census decree issued by the government in Rome ordered that persons be counted and taxed in their home towns; therefore, for example, Joseph and his pregnant wife, Mary, traveled from Nazareth to Bethlehem. Other censuses record people where they are on the census day (a *de facto enumeration*). Whatever residency rule is followed, a variety of special circumstances must be anticipated and fieldworkers trained to record people appropriately.

A few examples from the 1990 U.S. census illustrate problems that arise in fieldwork and later tallying. On a designated night in March, persons in hotels and rooming houses filled in special census forms indicating their usual place of residence; these forms were later compared to the regular schedules to confirm that these persons were properly reported at their homes. College students, even if they happened to be at home or on spring break when enumerated, were recorded as living in their college residences. Citizens working in another country for the U.S. government, and their families, were included in state population counts for reapportionment purposes but were otherwise reported separately as nonresident population.

The United States conducts many regular censuses, including those on population, housing, business firms, agriculture, and local governments. Each census provides information on the particular population at a specified time. Other parts of the statistical system provide information on the flows of units into and out of the population. For the U.S. population, people are added by birth and immigration and subtracted by death and emigration. Information based on birth and death registrations is of high quality, whereas information on immigration and emigration, both legal and illegal, is grossly deficient.

Some countries keep population registries, continuous records of where their people live and of some of their characteristics. Citizens in the United States are wary of governmental dossiers. The U.S. Census Bureau therefore conducts a series of regular and special sample surveys to provide population information between ten-year censuses.

When a country takes a population census, there is great public interest in the official total. Two very large countries reported new census totals in 1990: for the United States, 249,632,692; for China, 1,133,682,501. The total count is one tiny part of the results of a modern census. Censuses provide information on the population sizes of states, counties, cities, villages, and other administrative units. Censuses also record important characteristics about individuals, such as age, sex, relationship to others living in the same household, educational level, occupation, and so on. The 1990 U.S. census form asked seven questions about each person and twenty-six additional questions of a sample of one of every six persons. Recording and this information for the entire country and for the thousands of cities and other subareas results in the production of hundreds of printed reports and the equivalent of millions of additional pages in computer-readable files.

In the United States, the idea for a regular census emerged during debates about the problems of creating a representative form of government. The U. S. Constitution (Article I, Section 2) directs that membership in the House of Representatives be based on population: "The actual enumeration shall be made within three years after the first meeting of the Congress of the United States, and within every subsequent term of ten years, in such manner as they shall by law direct."

The questions asked in a census reflect political and social issues of the day and often provoke spirited debate. For example, a divisive issue for the Constitutional Convention was how to deal with slavery. The Southern states wanted to increase their representation in Congress by including slaves in the population count. A compromise (Article I, Section 2) provided that: "Representatives . . . shall be apportioned among the several states . . . according to their respective numbers, which shall be determined by adding to the whole number of free persons, excluding Indians not taxed, three-fifths of all other persons."

The 1790 census was modest in scope. Assistants to federal marshals made lists of households, recording for each the number of persons in five categories: free white males over sixteen and under sixteen, free white females, other free persons, and slaves (Anderson 1988, p. 13).

The 1790 census and the next five decennial censuses were conducted with little central organization or statistical expertise. A temporary federal census office was established to conduct the 1850 census. The individual rather than the household became the focus of the enumeration, and the content of the census was expanded to include occupation, country or state of birth, and other items. Experienced statisticians were consulted, and the United States participated in the first International Statistical Congress in 1853.

The conduct of U.S. censuses became increasingly difficult. Population size was growing rapidly and census content was expanding. For the 1890 census, the temporary census office became one of the largest federal agencies, employing 47,000 enumerators and 3,000 clerical workers. To help with the enormous task of tallying the data from the census forms, census officials encouraged the work of a young inventor, Herman Hollerith, who developed an electrical tabulating machine. His punched-card system proved effective in census operations and later contributed to the growth of the IBM company.

A permanent census office was established in 1902, and an increasingly professional staff assumed responsibility for the population censuses and a broad range of other statistical activities. During the early decades of the twentieth century, massive immigrations from Europe were of continuing political interest, and census figures were important evidence in debates over the need for immigration controls.

Deficiencies in the federal statistical systems became apparent during the 1930s as the nation tried to assess the effects of the Great Depression and to analyze an array of new programs and policies. Social scientists in several federal agencies supported expansion of the social and economic content of the 1940 and later population censuses. New questions in 1940 asked about participation in the labor force, earnings, education, migration (place of residence in 1935), and fertility. A housing census was paired with the population census to provide information about housing values and rents, mortgages, condition of dwellings, water supply, and other property issues. Greatly expanded population and housing information was provided for subareas of large cities.

Governmental statistical agencies are often rather set in their ways, concerned with continuity rather than innovation and removed from the higher levels of policymaking. For several decades beginning in the late 1930s, the U.S. Bureau of the Census was extraordinarily creative. Social scientists and statisticians employed by the Bureau were active in research and scholarly publication and played leadership roles in professional organizations. Bureau personnel pioneered in development of the theory and practice of population sampling. To accommodate large increases in content and geographic scope of the 1940 census, the census questionnaire was divided into two parts. A set of basic questions was asked of everyone, while a set of supplementary questions was asked of a one-in-twenty sample. Subsequent U.S. censuses have continued to use sampling, as with the one-in-six long-form version of the 1990 questionnaire. Sampling theory was also applied to the development of periodic sample surveys to provide timely information between censuses.

As they had in 1890, the processing needs of the Bureau led it in 1950 to participate actively in the development and utilization of a new technology, the computer. In later censuses, the schedules were microfilmed and optically scanned for direct input of information (without names and addresses) into a computer for error checking, coding, and tabulating. In the 1960s, the Bureau began issuing special computer-readable files of census data, and these files enabled scholars, policy analysts, and others to conduct their own analyses of population information without relying solely on the Bureau's printed volumes.

Through 1950, census taking in the United States was accomplished almost entirely by personal interview. By 1990, most census questionnaires were distributed and returned to the Bureau by mail, with telephone follow-up replacing many personal visits.

The questions asked in each census have changed more slowly than the procedures. There are three reasons for this. First, keeping the same topics and the same wordings of questions helps the government measure change from one census to the next. This reason appeals more strongly to university researchers and government policy analysts than it does to those policymakers whose attention is focused mainly on current programs and next year's budget. Second, the census is an expensive and visible tool. A lengthy review process confronts any agency that seeks to add, delete, or alter a question. Both the executive branch and the Congress must approve the final census schedule and other aspects of the census process. For example, a question on pet ownership has been regularly proposed but rejected on two grounds: There is no compelling governmental interest in such a question, and, even if there were, separate sample surveys would be more appropriate than the census. A third reason the content of the questionnaire changes little is that citizen cooperation is needed. The Census Bureau thinks that a longer questionnaire would be burdensome and discourage people from completing and returning the forms. The Bureau resists additions to the schedule unless there are compensating cuts. Proponents of new topics and questions must overcome the proponents of topics and questions that were on the previous census. This competition requires extensive lobbying and mobilization of support from federal agencies, congressional committees, lobbyists, and other interest groups.

One domain of growing national policy interest that has an increasing presence on the U.S. census schedules is race and ethnicity. Special tallies were made from the 1950 and 1960 censuses of persons with Spanish surnames, but only for five southwestern states. Beginning in 1970, and with increased elaboration in later censuses, persons were asked if they were of Spanish/Hispanic origin. A contrasting approach was taken by the United Kingdom. Controversy about a proposed ethnic minority question led to its omission from the 1981 census schedule, thus hindering factual analyses of their increasingly diverse population.

Reform of U.S. immigration laws in the mid-1960s led to more immigration and a change in dominant national origins from Europe to several Asian and Latin American countries. The national surge of interest in ethnicity led to a new question asking everyone to report an ancestry or ethnic origin (such as German, Italian, Afro-American,

etc.). Other questions asked year of immigration, language spoken at home, and, for those not using English at home, how well the person spoke English.

The most contentious issue about recent U.S. censuses is not their content but their accuracy. Concern with census undercount arises from the growth in federal, state, and local programs that distribute funds based in part on census information. The recipients of those funds, including states, cities, and many classes of persons represented by interest groups, have become more aware of how they may be affected by inaccuracies in the census. The word *undercount* has acquired symbolic status as an indicator of being shortchanged or deprived of rights.

A second reason for interest in the accuracy of the census is the success of the Bureau in publicizing the census. To encourage citizen cooperation, the Bureau works hard to make each decennial census a mass media event. It has succeeded to the degree that the media report not only the official press releases but also their own investigations of procedural difficulties and interviews with those opposed to or upset by the census.

A third reason for increased concern with undercount is increased knowledge of census accuracy. President George Washington commented about the first census that "our real numbers will exceed, greatly, the official returns of them; because the religious scruples of some would not allow them to give in their lists; the fears of others that it was intended as the foundation of a tax induced them to conceal or diminish theirs; and through the indolence of the people and the negligence of many of the Officers, numbers are omitted" (quoted in Scott 1968, p. 20). Lacking methods for determining "our real numbers," census results, whatever their apparent shortcomings, have remained the agreed-upon basis for legislative reapportionment.

Studies comparing birth certificates and other lists of names to the persons reported in the 1940 census documented a sizable net undercount. To provide more information on census coverage and accuracy, a postenumeration survey was conducted following the 1950 census using specially selected and closely supervised enumerators. One finding from the resurvey was that the undercount of infants in the census did not arise, as had been thought, from a tendency for new parents to forget to mention a new baby to the census enumerator. The problem, rather, was that many young couples and single parents had irregular and difficult-to-find living arrangements, and entire households were missed by census enumerators. Based on this and related findings, much effort has been given in subsequent censuses to precensus and postcensus review of lists of dwelling units.

Improved techniques of demographic analysis have led to new estimates of net undercount, first by demographers outside the Census Bureau and finally by Bureau staff (e.g., Fay, Passel, and Robinson 1988). The infant who was missed in the 1940 census may have been listed in the registry of births during 1939, appeared as a ten-year-old in the 1950 census, been missed as a twenty-year-old in 1960, and been recorded at ages thirty, forty, and fifty in later censuses. Estimates are made by analyzing the numbers of persons of each age, sex, and race in succesive censuses and using plausibly adjusted information on births and deaths by age, sex, and race. Based on demographic analysis, the estimated undercount was about 5.6 percent in 1940, 1.4 percent in 1980 (Fay, Passel, and Robinson 1988, Table 3.2) and 1.8 percent in 1990.

The percentage net undercount understates the total coverage error in the census because omissions of some transients, homeless persons, families doubled up with relatives, and others are accompanied by double counting of persons such as college students counted correctly at a dormitory but also reported improperly as living with parents.

If the net undercount were uniform for all population groups and geographic regions, it would not affect equity in the distribution of congressional seats or public funds. But census errors are not uniform. The estimates for 1980 show net undercounts exceeding 10 percent for adult black males and small net overcounts for some age and race groups.

In 1980, the mayor of Detroit, the City of

Detroit, New York City, and others sued the federal government, alleging violation of their constitutional rights to equal representation and fair distribution of federal funds (Mitroff, Mason, and Barabba 1983). The issue remained alive through the 1980s, and the federal government agreed to analyze early 1990 census results and conduct methodological investigations and then decide whether to produce a set of officially adjusted 1990 results (Robey 1989).

One of the difficulties in the U.S. undercount debates arises from confusion between the ideal of the census as a true count and the reality of the census as a procedure for obtaining a population estimate. There is no feasible method for determining with perfect accuracy the size and characteristics of any large population. A national census is a set of procedures adopted in a political, economic, and social context to produce population figures.

Every nation confronts political and social problems with census taking. Many regularly scheduled censuses have been postponed or abandoned because of international conflict. The United States and the United Kingdom have canceled plans for mid-decade censuses because of national budget constraints. West Germany was unable to take a census for several years because of citizen fears about invasions of privacy (Starr 1987, p. 32). Ethnic conflict has interfered with census taking in India, Lebanon, and many other nations.

The processes by which census procedures are determined, the ways in which census figures are used, and the conflicts that occur about these procedures and numbers are a social process worthy of specific study. The "sociology of official statistics" (Starr 1987) is an area in need of development.

(SEE ALSO: *Demography; Population*)

**REFERENCES**

Anderson, Margo J. 1988 *The American Census: A Social History*. New Haven: Yale University Press.
Fay, Robert E., Jeffrey S. Passel, and J. Gregory Robinson 1988 *The Coverage of Population in the 1980*

*Census*. PHC80-E4. Washington, D.C.: U.S. Government Printing Office.

Mitroff, Ian I., Richard O. Mason, and Vincent P. Barabba 1983 *The 1980 Census: Policymaking amid Turbulence*. Lexington, Mass.: Lexington Books.

Robey, Bryant 1989 "Two Hundred Years and Counting: The 1990 Census." *Population Bulletin* 44, no. 1.

Scott, Ann H. 1968 *Census, USA: Fact Finding for the American People, 1790–1970*. New York: Seabury Press.

Starr, Paul 1987 "The Sociology of Official Statistics." In W. Alonso and P. Starr, eds., *The Politics of Numbers*. New York: Russell Sage Foundation.

United Nations 1980 *Principles and Recommendations for Population and Housing Censuses*. ST/ESA/STAT/SER.M/67. New York: United Nations.

KARL TAEUBER

## CHANGE MEASUREMENT   *See* Experiments; Longitudinal Analysis; Quasi-Experimental Research Designs.

## CHILD ABUSE   *See* Family Violence; Incest; Sexual Violence.

## CHILDBEARING   *See* Family Planning; Family Size; Fertility Determinants.

## CHILDREARING   *See* Parental Roles; Socialization.

## CHINA STUDIES   The sociological study of China has a complex history. It could be argued that Confucian thought embodied a native tradition of sociological thinking about such things as the family, bureaucracy, and deviant behavior. However, modern Chinese sociology initially had foreign origins and inspiration. The appearance of the field in China might be dated from the translation of parts of Herbert Spencer's *The Study of Sociology* into Chinese in 1897. The earliest sociology courses and departments in China were established in private, missionary colleges, and Western sociologists such as D. H. Kulp, J. S. Burgess, and Sidney Gamble played central roles in initiating sociology courses and research programs within China (see Wong 1979.)

The Chinese Sociological Association was established in 1930, and in the following two decades a process of Sinification progressed. Chinese sociologists, trained both at home and in the West, emerged. Sociology courses and departments began to proliferate in government-run, public colleges. Increasingly, texts using material from Chinese towns and villages displaced ones that focused on Chicago gangs and the assimilation of Polish immigrants into America. As this process of setting down domestic roots continued, Chinese sociology developed some distinctive contours. Inspiration for the field came as much from British social anthropology as from sociology. The crisis atmosphere of the 1930s and 1940s fostered a strong emphasis on applied, problem-solving research. As a result of these developments, Chinese sociology in those years came to include what in the United States might be considered social anthropology and social work. Within these broad contours, Chinese sociologists/anthropologists produced some of the finest early ethnographies of "nonprimitive" communities—Chinese peasant villages (see Fei 1939; Yang 1944; Lin 1948).

Although many of the earliest leaders in establishing Chinese sociology were foreigners, by the time of the Chinese communist victory in 1949, its leading practitioners were Chinese. There were only a small number of Western sociologists who concentrated their research on Chinese society (see Lang 1946; Levy 1949), and their methods, problems, and data were not distinctive from those being employed by their Chinese counterparts. Originally a foreign transplant, Chinese sociology had become a thriving enterprise with increasingly strong domestic roots.

When the Chinese Communist Party (CCP) swept to national power in 1949, some Chinese sociologists left the country but most remained. (The development of sociology in the Republic of China on Taiwan after 1949 will not be dealt with here.) Initially, those who remained were optimistic that their skills would be useful to the new government. Experience in community fieldwork and an orientation toward studying social problems seemed to make Chinese sociologists natural allies of those constructing a planned social order. These hopes were dashed in 1952 when the CCP abolished the field of sociology. That decision was motivated by the CCP's desire to follow the Soviet model. Joseph Stalin had earlier denounced sociology as a "bourgeois pseudo-science" and banned the field from Soviet academe. More to the point, there was no room in the People's Republic of China (PRC) for two rival sciences of society, Marxism-Leninism-Maoism and sociology. The CCP argued that it had developed its own methods of "social investigations" during the revolutionary process, with Mao Zedong playing a leading role in this development (see Mao [1927] 1971; Thompson 1990). This approach stressed grass roots investigations designed to further official revolutionary or economic goals of the CCP rather than any sort of attempted value-free search for objective truth. Chinese sociologists, trained in a different tradition and able to use professional claims to raise questions about CCP policies, were seen as a threat to the ideological hegemony of the new regime.

The ban on sociology in China was to last twenty-seven years, until 1979. One major attempt was made by Chinese sociologists in 1956 and 1957 to get the ban lifted. In the more relaxed political atmosphere prevailing at that time, ushered in by the CCP's slogan "let 100 flowers bloom and 100 schools of thought contend" and encouraged by the revival of sociology in the Soviet Union, leading figures such as Fei Xiaotong, Pan Guangdan, Wu Jingchao, and Chen Da wrote articles and made speeches arguing that sociology could be useful to socialist China in the study of social change and social problems—precisely the same rationale used prior to 1952. When the political atmosphere turned harsh again in the latter part of 1957, with the launching of the "anti-rightist campaign," Fei and many of the other leaders of this revival effort were branded "rightist elements" and disappeared from view.

From 1952 to 1979 some of those trained in sociology were assigned to work that had some links to their abolished field. Throughout this period ethnology remained an established discipline, devoted to the study of China's various ethnic minorities. When Fei Xiaotong emerged from his political purgatory in 1972, it was as a leading figure in ethnology. But Fei and others could not do research on the 94 percent of the population that is Han Chinese, and they also had to renounce publicly all their former work and ideas as "bourgeois." Psychology survived better than sociology by becoming defined as a natural, rather than a social, science. Some areas of social psychology (for example, educational psychology) remained at least somewhat active through the 1960s and 1970s (see Chin and Chin 1969). Other components of sociology disappeared in 1952 but reappeared prior to 1979. Demography was established as a separate field in the early 1970s and remains a separate discipline in Chinese academe today. With these partial exceptions, however, Chinese sociology ceased to exist for these twenty-seven years.

While sociology was banned in China, the sociological study of that society developed gradually in the West. Starting in the late 1950s, American foundations and government agencies, and to some extent their European and Japanese counterparts, provided funds for the development of the study of contemporary China—for fellowships, research centers, journals, language training facilities, and other basic infrastucture for the field. Within this developmental effort, sociology was targeted as an underdeveloped discipline (compared to, say, history, literature, and political science) deserving of special priority. Stimulated by this developmental effort, during the 1960s and 1970s the number of Western sociologists active in the study of China increased from a handful to perhaps two dozen.

Prior to the early 1970s, with a few minor exceptions (e.g., Geddes 1963), it was impossible for foreign sociologists to travel to China, much less to do research there. Even when such travel became possible during the 1970s, it was initially restricted to highly superficial "academic tourism." In this highly constrained situation, foreign sociologists studying China developed distinctive research methods.

Much research was based on detailed culling of Chinese mass media reports. Special translation series of Chinese newspapers and magazines and of monitored radio broadcasts developed in the 1950s and became the mainstays of such research. The Chinese media provided fairly clear statements about official policy and social change campaigns. By conveying details about local "positive and negative models" in the implementation of official goals, the media also provided some clues about the difficulties and resistance being encountered in introducing social change. In a few instances the media even yielded apparently "hard" statistical data about social trends. A minor industry developed around scanning local press and radio reports for population totals, and these were pieced together to yield national population estimates (typically plus or minus 100 million).

Some researchers developed elaborate schemes to code and subject to content analysis such media reports (see, for example, Andors 1977; Cell 1977). However, this reliance on media reports to study Chinese social trends had severe limits. Such reports revealed much more about official goals than they did about social reality, and the researcher might erroneously conclude that an effort to produce major changes was actually producing them. The sorts of unanticipated consequences that sociologists love to uncover were for the most part invisible in the highly didactic Chinese media. It was also very difficult to use media reports to analyze variations across individuals and communities, the staple of sociological analysis elsewhere. Studies based on media reports tended to convey an unrealistic impression of uniformity, thus reinforcing the prevailing stereotype of China as a totalitarian society.

Partly in reaction to these limitations, a second primary method of research on China from the outside developed—the refugee interview. Scholars in sociology and related fields spent extended periods of time in Hong Kong interviewing individuals who had left the PRC for the British colony.

Typically, these individuals were used not as respondents in a survey but as ethnographic informants "at a distance" about the corners of the Chinese social world from which they had come. Although the individuals interviewed obviously were not typical of the population remaining in the PRC, for some topics these refugees provided a rich and textured picture of social reality that contrasted with the unidimensional view conveyed by Chinese mass media. Elaborate techniques were developed by researchers to cope with the problems of atypicality and potential bias among refugee informants (see Whyte 1983).

By combining these methods with brief visits to China, sociologists and others produced a large number of useful studies of contemporary mainland society (Whyte, Vogel, and Parish 1977). Even though the arcane methods they used often seemed to nonspecialists akin to Chinese tea-leaf reading, the best of these studies have stood the test of time and have been confirmed by new research made possible by changes in China since 1979. However, the exclusion from meaningful field research in China did have unfortunate effects on the intellectual agendas of researchers. Much energy was focused on examining the "Maoist model" of development and whether or not China was succeeding in becoming a revolutionary new type of social order. Since the reality of Chinese social organizations in the Maoist period was quite different from the slogans and ideals upon which such constructions were based, this effort appears to have been a waste of scarce intellectual resources. Both this unusual intellectual agenda and the distinctive research methods sociologists studying China were forced to use reinforced the isolation of these researchers from "mainstream" work in sociology.

The year 1979 was significant in two ways for the sociological study of China. First, as already noted, that was the year in which China's leaders gave approval for the "rehabilitation" of sociology. After the death of Mao Zedong in 1976, and given the authority crisis that followed in the wake of the Cultural Revolution, the post-Mao leadership reopened many issues. China faced a number of serious social problems that had been ignored previously, and in this situation long-standing arguments about the utility of sociology for the study of social problems could be raised once again.

The second major change that occurred in 1979 was the "normalization" of diplomatic relations between the United States and China. That development led to approval for American and other Western researchers to conduct extended field research in China for the first time since 1949. The days of frustrating confinement to research from outside and academic tourism were over. It also became possible for U.S. sociologists to meet Chinese counterparts and to begin to discuss common research interests and plans for collaboration. Westerners began coming to China to teach sociology courses, Chinese began to be sent abroad for training in sociology, and collaborative conferences and publications were initiated. Leading figures in the West, including Peter Blau, Alex Inkeles, Nan Lin, W. J. Goode, Hubert Blalock, and Jeffrey Alexander, lectured in China and recruited Chinese counterparts for collaborative research and for training in their home institutions. All of the kinds of intellectual interchange between Chinese sociologists and their foreign counterparts that had been impossible for a generation were resumed.

The dangerous political aura surrounding sociology in the Mao era and the lesson of the abortive 1957 attempt to revive the field might have been expected to make it difficult to attract talented people to Chinese sociology after 1979. However, the field revived very rapidly and showed surprising intellectual vigor. A number of surviving pre-1949 sociologists reappeared to play leading roles in the revival, considerable numbers of middle-aged individuals trained in related fields were recruited (or ordered) to become sociologists, and many young people expressed eagerness to be selected for training in the field. The Chinese Sociological Association was formally revived, with Fei Xiaotong as its head. (Fei "unrenounced" his pre-1949 works, weakened his ties with ethnology, and resumed advocacy of the program of Chinese rural development he had championed a generation earlier.) A number of

departments of sociology were established in leading universities, and new sociological journals and a large number of monographs and textbooks began to appear. Institutes of sociology were established within the Chinese Academy of Social Science in Peking as well as in many provincial and city academies. Apparently, the novelty of the field, the chance to make a place for oneself, and perhaps even the chance to study abroad without having to face competition from layers of senior people more than compensated for the checkered political past of sociology. In any case, the speed and vigor with which the field revived surprised the skeptics (see Whyte and Pasternak 1980).

The intellectual focus of the revived sociology was fairly broad. Social problems and the sociology of development were two major foci. Within these and other realms, two sets of issues loomed large. One was the study of the after-effects of the Cultural Revolution and the radical policies pursued under Mao Zedong in the period 1966 to 1976. The other major issue concerned the impact of the opening to the outside world, decollectivization of agriculture, and the market-oriented reforms launched in 1978. A large number of studies began on these and other issues, and by the end of the 1980s the problem facing foreign sociologists studying China was not so much the scarcity of data on their object of study but its abundance. The publication of large amounts of statistical material, the availability of census and survey data dealing with demographic and other matters, and the mushrooming of social science publications threatened to overwhelm those who tried to keep track of Chinese social trends.

In pursuing their new intellectual agendas, Chinese sociologists easily found common ground with Western specialists. The latter were no longer so entranced with the Maoist model and shared a fascination with the social impact of the post-Mao changes. Many Western specialists readily adapted to the chance to conduct research in China and to collaborate with Chinese colleagues. Hong Kong did not die out as a research site and remained vital for some topics, but work from outside China was increasingly seen as supplementary to research conducted within the country. China specialists now had to share the stage with many sociologists who did not have area studies training. With data more readily available and collaboration with Chinese counterparts possible, area studies training and familiarity with the arcane techniques developed in the 1960s and 1970s were no longer so important. Many non-China specialists found the opportunity to study the world's most populous society increasingly attractive. These changes have been beneficial for China specialists within sociology. Given their small numbers and the complexity of Chinese society, there is more than enough "turf" to be shared with sociologists not trained in China studies. And these changes have reduced the intellectual isolation of the specialists, from both colleagues in China and those in their own departments.

As a result of these changes, Chinese sociologists ended their isolation from world sociology, and Western sociologists conducting research on the PRC escaped from a highly constrained environment and began to produce work that was less idiosyncratic. It should be noted, however, that sociological research in China is not without limits, either for foreign researchers or for Chinese. Even in the most liberal phases of the reform decade of 1979 to 1989, some topics remained taboo, some locales were off limits, and bureaucratic approvals and interference were constant facts of life. Nonetheless, even for foreigners it became possible to conduct extended ethnographic studies, carry out probability sample surveys, and gain access for secondary analysis to the raw data from census and survey studies conducted by Chinese, experiences that those who study Soviet society can only envy. The result has been a new spurt of research activity and publication that has enriched our knowledge of Chinese social life immensely. (For a review of Western research since 1979, see Walder 1989. For an overview of developments within Chinese sociology, see Lu 1989.)

However, the political fallout of the 1989 Tiananmen massacre has raised new problems for the sociological study of China. At least some conservatives within the Chinese leadership used the crackdown following the massacre to attack sociology and other newly revived social sciences in terms reminiscent of 1952 and 1957. The field is once again accused of being an ideological Trojan horse designed to spread doubts about socialist orthodoxy. Some sociology departments have not been allowed to enroll new students, while others have had their enrollment targets cut. New restrictions and political interference constrain research topics and international collaboration. As of 1991 it did not appear that the field would suffer abolition once again, but it remained to be seen how much the changed political atmosphere would undermine the impressive progress that had been made in reestablishing Chinese sociology.

## REFERENCES

Andors, Stephen 1977 *China's Industrial Revolution: Politics, Planning, and Management, 1949 to the Present.* New York: Pantheon.

Cell, Charles P. 1977 *Revolution at Work.* New York: Academic Press.

Chin, R., and A. Chin 1969 *Psychological Research in Communist China 1949–1966.* Cambridge, Mass.: MIT Press.

Fei Xiaotong [Fei Hsiao-t'ung] 1939 *Peasant Life in China.* London: G. Routledge.

Geddes, W. R. 1963 *Peasant Life in Communist China.* Ithaca, N.Y.: Society for Applied Anthropology.

Lang, Olga 1946 *Chinese Family and Society.* New Haven, Conn.: Yale University Press.

Levy, Marion J., Jr. 1949 *The Family Revolution in Modern China.* Cambridge, Mass.: Harvard University Press.

Lin Yaohua [Lin Yüeh-hwa] 1948 *The Golden Wing: A Sociological Study of Chinese Familism.* New York: Oxford University Press.

Lu Xueyi 1989 *China Yearbook of Sociology, 1979–1989* (in Chinese). Peking: Chinese Encyclopedia Press.

Mao Zedong (1927) 1971 "Report on an Investigation of the Peasant Movement in Hunan." In Mao Tsetung, *Selected Readings from the Works of Mao Tsetung.* Peking: Foreign Languages Press.

Thompson, Roger 1990 *Mao Zedong: Report from Xunwu.* Stanford, Calif.: Stanford University Press.

Walder, Andrew G. 1989 "Social Change in Post-Revolution China." *Annual Review of Sociology* 15:405–424.

Whyte, Martin K. 1983 "On Studying China at a Distance." In Anne Thurston and Burton Pasternak, eds., *The Social Sciences and Fieldwork in China.* Boulder, Colo.: Westview.

Whyte, Martin K., and Burton Pasternak 1980 "Sociology and Anthropology." In Anne Thurston and Jason Parker, eds., *Humanistic and Social Science Research in China.* New York: Social Science Research Council.

Whyte, Martin K., Ezra F. Vogel, and William L. Parish, Jr. 1977 "Social Structure of World Regions: Mainland China." *Annual Review of Sociology* 3:179–207.

Wong, Siu-lun 1979 *Sociology and Socialism in Contemporary China.* London: Routledge and Kegan Paul.

Yang, C. K. 1944 *A North China Local Market Economy.* New York: Institute of Pacific Relations.

MARTIN KING WHYTE

**CITIES** A city is a relatively large, dense, permanent, heterogeneous, and politically autonomous settlement whose population engages in a range of nonagricultural occupations. Various definitions have been developed for cities and their associated phenomena (Shryock, Siegel, and associates 1976, pp. 83–104). The city is often defined in terms of administrative area, which may be larger than, smaller than, or equal to the area of relatively dense settlement that comprises what is otherwise known as the city proper (Davis 1959). The suburb is a less dense but permanent settlement that is located outside the city proper and contains populations that are socially and economically tied to the city. Urban definitions vary by nation; in the United States the term *urban* refers to populations of 2,500 or more living in towns or cities and to populations living in urbanized areas, including suburbs. *Urbanization* refers to the economic and social changes that accompany population concentration in urban areas and the growth of cities and their surrounding areas.

Cities have always been centers of markets, governments, religion, and culture (Harris and Ullman 1945; Weber 1958, pp. 65–89). The community is a population sharing a physical environment and leading a common and interdependent life. The size, density, and heterogeneity of the urban community have been described as leading to "urbanism as a way of life," which includes organizational, attitudinal, and ecological components different from those of rural areas (Wirth 1938).

## THE CITY IN HISTORY

The development of towns and cities was tied to a technological revolution in agriculture that increased food production, thereby freeing agriculturalists to engage in nonagricultural occupations. This resulted in urban living and led eventually to industrial production (Childe 1950). A contrasting Marxian-related view is that urban development is better explained by the needs of capitalist production for a malleable labor force (Jaret 1983, p. 449). Towns, and then cities, first developed in the fourth to third millennium B.C. in the rich valleys of the Indus River, the delta area of the Tigris and Euphrates rivers, the lower Nile valley, and the east coast of China. Increasing complexity of social organization, environmental adaptation, and technology led to the emergence of cities (Childe 1950; Duncan 1964).

Small agricultural surpluses and limits on transportation meant that the first towns were small and few in number, and contained only a small proportion of the populations of their regions. After the rise of towns in the Middle East, trading centers appeared on the shores and islands of the Mediterranean; some, such as Athens, became city-states. After developing more effective communication and social organization, some city-states expanded and acquired empires, such as those of Alexander the Great and of Rome. Following the decline of Rome, complex city life continued in the West in the Byzantine and Muslim empires while the population of Europe declined and reverted, for the most part, to subsistence agriculture and organized into small territories held together by the Catholic Church (Hawley 1981, pp. 1–35).

Sjoberg (1960) has argued that preindustrial cities were feudal in nature and shared social, ecological, economic, family, class, political, religious, and educational characteristics different from those in modern industrial cities. In the former, the city center, with its government and religious and economic activities, dominated the remainder of the city and was the locale of the upper social classes. Homogeneous residential areas could be differentiated throughout the city, but nonresidential activities were not confined to distinct neighborhoods (Sjoberg 1960).

Beginning in the tenth century, further town development in the West was facilitated by increases in agricultural technology, population, trade, and communication; the rise of an entrepreneurial class; and an expanding web of social norms regarding economic activity. Communication and manufacturing were revived, which led to the growth of towns with local autonomy and public administration, and eventually to networks of cities. Surplus rural populations migrated to cities, which grew because of their specialization and larger markets, becoming focal points of European societies (Hawley 1981, pp. 37–83).

## WESTERN CITIES SINCE THE INDUSTRIAL REVOLUTION

In most countries of the developed world, urbanization and urban growth have occurred at an increasing rate since the beginning of the Industrial Revolution. After 1820, the numbers and sizes of urban areas and cities in the United States increased as a result of employment concentration in construction and manufacturing, so urban areas began to grow more rapidly than rural ones. The population classified as urban by the United States census (based on aggregations of 2,500 or more and including the surrounding densely populated territories) increased from 5 percent in 1790 to 74 percent in 1980. In 1790 the largest urban place in the United States had less than 50,000 inhabitants. As late as 1840, not a single urban place in the United States had more than half a million inhabitants. There were four such places in 1890, fourteen in 1940, and twenty-two in 1980 (U.S. Bureau of the Census 1983, pp. 36–38).

City growth in the United States during the nineteenth century was driven by migration, since

there were sometimes excesses of urban deaths over births in the early part of that century and lower birthrates in the last part of that century. Population concentration facilitated greater divisions of labor within and among families and individuals, as well as increasing numbers of voluntary associations centered on new urban interests and problems. At first, cities were compact, growth was vertical, and workers resided near their workplaces. The outward expansion of the residential population was facilitated in the last part of the century by steam and electric railways, the outward expansion of industry, and the increasing role of the central business district in integrating economic activities (Hawley 1981, pp. 61–145).

The increasing scale of production in the United States led to the development of a system of cities differentiated from each other by their degree of dominance over or subordination to other cities, some of which were engaged in centralized manufacturing, others of which depended on transportation, commercial, administrative, or other functions. According to Hawley (1986), cities may have certain key functions that dominate other cities: that is, integrating, controlling, or coordinating activities with these cities. Examples of key functions are administration, commerce, finance, transportation, and communication (Duncan et al. 1960; Wilson 1984). Since each city exists within its own organizational environment, the expansion of linkages of urban organizations has accompanied the development of urban systems (Turk 1977).

In the United States, the nature of key functions in city systems changed with the expansion of settlements westward, as colonial seaports, river ports, midwestern railway towns, central places on the Great Plains, extractive centers, and government centers were integrated into an urban system. A nationwide manufacturing base was established by 1900, as were commercial and financial centers (Duncan and Lieberson 1970). By 1960 a fully developed system of differentiated urban centers existed within the United States (Duncan and Lieberson 1970).

## METROPOLITAN AREAS

In the United States, metropolitan areas (as of 1990) are defined as being of two kinds. Metropolitan statistical areas (MSAs) are areas including one or more central cities with a population of 50,000 or more, or areas with a less densely populated central city but with a combined urban population of at least 100,000 (75,000 in New England), including surrounding counties or towns. Consolidated metropolitan statistical areas (CMSAs) contain at least one million population and may have subareas called primary metropolitan statistical areas (PMSAs) (Frey 1990, p. 6).

New urban-population-density patterns have appeared with the development of metropolitan areas. Growth has been characterized by increases in population density in central cities, followed by increases in density in the metropolitan ring. Transport and communication technologies have facilitated linkages of diverse neighborhoods into metropolitan communities dominated by more densely populated central cities. These linkages in turn have organized relationships between central cities and less densely populated hinterlands and subcenters. Older metropolitan areas have become the centers of CMSAs, while newer areas have been the frontiers of expansion, growing by natural increase and especially by net migration. Metropolitan sprawl extends beyond many former nonurban functions, as well as more centrally located older features of the cityscape. In the 1970s the redistribution of population within metropolitan areas favored lower-density areas (White 1987, p. 250).

The pattern of population concentration into larger cities and metropolitan areas changed during the 1970s, leading to a population turnaround, as populations in smaller metropolitan areas grew more rapidly than those in larger metropolitan areas and as nonmetropolitan counties grew more rapidly than did metropolitan counties (Frey 1990; Frey and Speare 1988). This change has been described as temporary and unique, representing a shift of growth to new regions, or as one more deconcentration of population (Frey 1987; 1990, pp. 10–11). In the 1980s central cities experienced net out-migration, while suburbs experienced net in-migration.

Intracity and intrametropolitan residential mobility—the individual counterpart of population redistribution processes—is affected by population characteristics and factors influencing mobility decisions. These decisions are tied to socioeconomic and psychological factors pertaining to the family and the family life cycle, housing and the local environment, and occupational and social mobility (Sabagh et al. 1969). For each of these factors, conditions may restrain persons from moving, or push or pull them to new locations. Information concerning new housing opportunities, the state of the housing market, and availability of resources may impede or facilitate moves; subsequent mobility may stem from recent migration or residential turnover in the metropolitan areas (Long 1988, pp. 219–224; Roseman 1971).

## EXPLAINING CITIES

During the nineteenth century the character of the city was seen as different from that of noncity areas. Beginning with the public-health movement and concerns with urban housing, social scientists documented "pathologies" of urban life through the use of social surveys, the purpose of which was to provide policy-relevant findings (Young 1956). But since "urbanism as a way of life" has permeated the United States, many of the social and economic problems of cities have spread into smaller towns and rural areas, thus rendering the notion of unique urban pathologies less valid than when it was formulated.

In the twentieth century, efforts have been made to form theoretical explanations of city development, and disagreements have arisen (Sjoberg 1968, p. 455). Theories based on social Darwinism (Park [1916–1939] 1952) and economics (Burgess 1924) were first used to explain the internal structures of cities. "Subsocial" aspects of social and economic organization—which did not involve direct interpersonal interaction—were viewed as generating population aggregation and expansion. Competitive–cooperative processes—including aggregation–thinning out, expansion–contraction, centralization, displacement, segregation, migration, and mobility—were believed to determine the structures and patterns of urban neighborhoods (Quinn 1950; Hawley 1950). The competition of differing urban populations and activities for optimal locations was described as creating relatively homogeneous communities, labeled "natural areas," which display gradient patterns of decreasing densities of social and economic activities and problems with increasing distance from the city center.

On the basis of competitive–cooperative processes, city growth was assumed to result in characteristic urban shapes. The Burgess hypothesis specifies that in the absence of countervailing factors, the American city takes the form of a series of concentric zones, ranging from the organizing central business district to a commuters' zone (Burgess 1925, pp. 47–52). Other scholars emphasized star-shaped, multiple-nuclei, or cluster patterns of development. These views were descriptive rather than theoretical; assumed a capitalist commercial–industrial city; were distorted by topography, and street and transportation networks; and generally failed to take into account use of land for industrial purposes, which is found in most city zones.

Theodorson (1964, 1982) and Michaelson (1970, pp. 3–32) have described research on American cities as reflecting neo-orthodox, social-area analysis, and sociocultural approaches, each with its own frame of reference and methods.

Neo-orthodox approaches have emphasized the interdependence of components of an ecological system, including population, organization, technology, and environment (Duncan 1964). This view has been applied to larger ecological systems that can extend beyond the urban community. Sustenance organization is an important focus of study (Hawley 1986; Gibbs and Martin 1958). While the neo-orthodox ecologists have not integrated the notion of social Darwinism into their work, the economic aspects of their approach have helped to guide studies of population phenomena, including urban differentiation

(White 1987), residential mobility (Long 1988, pp. 189–251), and segregation (Farley and Allen 1987, pp. 103–159; Lieberson and Waters 1988, pp. 51–93).

Social-area analysis, however, regards modern industrial society as based on increasing scale, which represents "increased rates and intensities of social relation," "increased functional differentiation," and "increased complexity of social organization" (Shevky and Williams 1949; Shevky and Bell 1955). These concepts are related to neighborhood dimensions of social rank, urbanization, and segregation, which are delimited by the factor analysis of neighborhood or census tract measures (Janson 1980; Van Arsdol et al. 1958). The system has been used for classifying census tracts. Janson (1980, p. 454) has argued that factor analysis studies of internal urban social structure, which are associated with social-area analysis and similar approaches, have led to empirical generalizations that are theoretically relevant, but that factorial studies making use of larger urban units lead to less specific generalizations.

Sociocultural ecology has used social values to explain land use in central Boston (Firey 1947) and the movement of Norwegians within greater New York City (Jonassen 1949). While values are relevant to explanations of city phenomena, this perspective had not led to a fully developed line of investigation.

William Michaelson (1970, pp. 17–32) has argued that none of these aforementioned ecological approaches to the city explicitly study the relationship between the physical and the social environment, for the following reasons: (1) their incomplete view of the environment; (2) their focus on population aggregates; (3) their failure to consider contributions of other fields of study; and (4) the newness of the field. Since Michaelson wrote his critique, sociologists are giving more attention to the urban environment.

## RETROSPECT AND PROSPECT

The interior of large Western metropolitan areas represents a merging of urban areas into complex overlapping spatial patterns. The blurring of neighborhood distinctions, facilitated by freeway networks, facilitates interaction among "social circles" of people who are not neighborhood-based. Meanwhile, urban neighborhoods organized around such factors as status, ethnicity, or life-style, may also persist. As the city ages, so does suburban as well as centrally located housing—a delayed consequence of the spread of urban settlement.

Constraints on future city growth include economic decline, shortages of resources and infrastructures, environmental and social problems making cities less attractive, and adoption of growth limitation policies. Sooner or later all cities reach such limits, at which point growth becomes more vertical or new growth centers are established.

Urbanization in developing countries does not necessarily follow the Western pattern. City growth may absorb national population increments and reflect a lack of rural employment, a migration of the rural unemployed to the city, and a lack of urban industrial development. Increasing concentration of population in larger cities may be followed by the emergence of more "Western-style" hierarchies of cities, functions, and interorganizational relationships. Many cities in developing countries experience the environmental hazards of Western cities, a compartmentalization of life, persistent poverty and unemployment, a rapidly worsening housing situation, and other symptoms of Western social disorganization. The juxtaposition of local urbanism and some degree of Western urbanization may vitiate a number of traditional Western solutions to urban problems.

Developing countries are sometimes characterized by primate cities, that is, the largest cities in the country are larger than would be expected on the basis of a "rank-size" rule, which indicates that the rank of a population aggregation times its size equals a constant, thus resulting in an underdeveloped supporting hierarchy of smaller cities (Jefferson 1939; Zipf 1941; Shryock, Siegel, and associates 1976). Primate cities often appear in small countries, and in countries with a dual

economy, but are not as apparent in large countries or those with long urban histories (Berry 1964).

By the year 2000, approximately half of the earth's population will be urban, with the vast majority in developing areas (Population Crisis Committee 1990). While cities in developing nations lack resources when compared with those in developed nations, cities in both types of nations are becoming more responsive to changes in local and worldwide conditions (Friedman and Wolff 1982; Frey 1990, p. 39).

These trends are apparent, for example, in Los Angeles and Mexico City, which ranked eleventh and second in size, respectively, in a recent compilation of data on the world's metropolitan areas (Population Crisis Committee 1990). After World War II and until the 1970s, Los Angeles's industrial and population growth and suburban sprawl made it a prototype for urban development that brought with it many inner-city, energy, suburban, environmental, state-management, ethnic, and capital-accumulation problems.

Since the early 1970s, Los Angeles has become a radically changed giant global city based on reindustrialization, communications, accumulation of global capital, and access to new international markets (Soja, Morales, and Wolff 1983). The reorganization of Los Angeles has greatly affected labor-force demands and the character of both native and immigrant populations. Ivan Light (1987) has emphasized that Los Angeles has a great concentration of industrial technology and great international cultural importance, is dependent on the private automobile, and has air hazards, limited water supplies, housing shortages, serious crime, and uncontrolled intergroup conflicts. Mexico City, while not commanding the same stature as Los Angeles, appears to share many of Los Angeles's problems, including lack of housing and services, expansion of low-income settlements, dependence on the private automobile, lack of sufficient transportation, and air pollution (Schteingart 1987). These consequences suggest that cities at somewhat similar levels of influence within their respective countries share similar characteristics, whether in the developed or in the developing world.

(SEE ALSO: *Suburbanization; Urban Economic Transitions; Urbanization; Urban Sociology; Urban Underclass*)

## REFERENCES

Berry, Brian J. L. 1964 "Cities as Systems Within Systems of Cities." In J. Friedman and W. Alonso, eds., *Regional Development and Planning*. Cambridge, Mass.: MIT Press.

Burgess, Ernest W. 1925 "The Growth of the City, an Introduction to a Research Project." In Robert E. Park, Ernest W. Burgess, and R. D. McKenzie, eds., Chicago: University of Chicago Press.

Childe, V. Gordon 1950 "The Urban Revolution." *Town Planning Review* 21:3–17.

Davis, Kingsley 1959 *The World's Metropolitan Areas*. Berkeley and Los Angeles: University of California Press.

Duncan, Beverly, and Stanley Lieberson 1970 *Metropolis and Region in Transition*. Beverly Hills, Calif.: Sage.

Duncan, Otis D. 1961 "From Social System to Ecosystem." *Sociological Inquiry* 31:140–149.

———1964 "Social Organization and the Ecosystem." In Robert E. L. Faris, ed., *Handbook of Modern Sociology*. Chicago: Rand McNally.

———, William R. Scott, Stanley Lieberson, Beverly Duncan, and Haliman H. Winsborough 1960 *Metropolis and Region*. Baltimore: Johns Hopkins University Press.

Farley, Reynolds, and Walter R. Allen 1987 *The Color Line and the Quality of Life in America*. New York: Russell Sage Foundation.

Firey, Walter 1947 *Land Use in Central Boston*. Cambridge, Mass.: Harvard University Press.

Frey, William, II 1987 "Migration and Depopulation of the Metropolis: Regional Restructuring or Rural Renaissance?" *American Sociological Review* 52: 240–257.

———1990 "Metropolitan America: Beyond the Transition." *Population Bulletin* 45, no. 2:1–53.

———, and Alden Speare, Jr. 1988 *Regional and Metropolitan Growth and Decline in the United States*. New York: Russell Sage Foundation.

Friedmann, John F., and Goetz Wolff 1982 "World City

Formation: An Agenda for Research and Action." *International Journal of Urban and Regional Research* 6:309–344.

Gibbs, Jack P., and Walter T. Martin 1958 "Urbanization and Natural Resources: A Study in Organizational Ecology." *American Sociological Review* 23: 266–277.

Harris, Chauncy D., and Edward L. Ullman 1945 "The Nature of Cities." *Annals of the American Academy of Political and Social Science* 242:7–17.

Hawley, Amos H. 1950 *Human Ecology*. New York: Ronald Press.

———1981 *Urban Society: An Ecological Approach*, 2nd ed. New York: Wiley.

———1986 *Human Ecology: A Theoretical Essay*. Chicago: University of Chicago Press.

Janson, Carl-Gunnar 1980 "Factorial Social Ecology: An Attempt at Summary and Evaluation." In *Annual Review of Sociology*, vol. 6, ed. by A. Inkeles, N. J. Smelser, and R. H. Turner. Palo Alto, Calif.: Annual Reviews.

Jaret, Charles 1983 "Recent Neo Marxist Urban Analysis." In *Annual Review of Sociology*, vol. 9, ed. by Ralph H. Turner and James F. Short, Jr., Palo Alto, Calif.: Annual Reviews.

Jefferson, M. 1939 "The Law of the Primate City." *Geographical Review* 29, no. 7:226–232.

Jonassen, C. T. 1949 "Cultural Variables in the Ecology of an Ethnic Group." *American Sociological Review* 14:32–41.

Lieberson, Stanley, and Mary C. Waters 1988 *From Many Strands: Ethnic and Racial Groups in Contemporary America*. New York: Russell Sage Foundation.

Light, Ivan 1987 "Los Angeles." In M. Dogan and J. D. Kasarda, eds., *The Metropolis Era*, vol. 2, *Mega Cities*. New York: Russell Sage Foundation.

Long, Larry 1988 *Migration and Residential Mobility in the United States*. New York: Russell Sage Foundation.

Michaelson, William 1970 *Man and His Urban Environment: A Sociological Approach*. Reading, Mass.: Addison-Wesley.

Park, R. E. (1916–1939) 1952 "Human Communities: The City and Human Ecology." *Collected Papers*, vol. 2. Glencoe, Ill.: Free Press.

Population Crisis Committee 1990 *Cities: Life in the World's 100 Largest Metropolitan Areas*. Washington, D.C.: Population Crisis Committee.

Quinn, James 1950 *Human Ecology*. New York: Prentice-Hall.

Roseman, Curtis C. 1971 "Migration as a Spatial and

Temporal Process." *Annals of the Association of American Geographers* 61:589–598.

Sabagh, Georges, Maurice D. Van Arsdol, Jr., and Edgar W. Butler 1969 "Determinants of Intrametropolitan Residential Mobility: Conceptual Consideration." *Social Forces* 48, no. 1:88–97.

Schteingart, Martha 1987 "Mexico City." In M. Dogan and J. D. Kasarda, eds., *The Metropolis Era*, vol. 2, *Mega Cities.* New York: Russell Sage Foundation.

Shevky, Eshref, and Wendell Bell 1955 *Social Area Analysis: Theory, Illustrative Applications and Computational Procedures.* Stanford Sociological Series, no. 1. Stanford, Calif.: Stanford University Press.

Shevky, Eshref, and Marilyn Williams 1949 *The Social Areas of Los Angeles: Analysis and Typology.* Berkeley and Los Angeles: University of California Press.

Shryock, Henry S., Jacob S. Siegel, and associates 1976 *The Materials and Methods of Demography,* condensed edition ed. by Edward G. Stockwell. San Diego: Academic Press/Harcourt Brace Jovanovich.

Sjoberg, Gideon 1960 *The Pre-Industrial City: Past and Present.* New York: Free Press.

——1965 "Theory and Research in Urban Sociology." In P. M. Hauser and L. F. Schnore, eds., *The Study of Urbanization.* New York: Wiley.

——1968 "The Modern City." In David L. Sills, ed. *International Encyclopedia of the Social Sciences,* vol. 1. New York: Macmillan and Free Press.

Soja, Edward, Rebecca Morales, and Goetz Wolff 1983 "Urban Restructuring: An Analysis of Social and Spatial Change in Los Angeles." *Economic Geography* 59:195–230.

Theodorson, George A. 1964 *Studies in Human Ecology.* Evanston, Ill.: Row, Peterson.

——1982 *Urban Patterns: Studies in Human Ecology.* University Park: Pennsylvania State University Press.

Turk, Herman 1977 *Organizations in Modern Life: Cities and Other Large Networks.* San Francisco: Jossey-Bass.

U.S. Bureau of the Census 1983 *1980 Characteristics of the Population,* vol. 1. Washington, D.C.: U.S. Government Printing Office.

Van Arsdol, Maurice D., Jr., Santo F. Camilleri, and Calvin F. Schmid 1958 "The Generality of Urban Social Areas Indexes." *American Sociological Review* 23:277–284.

Weber, M. 1958 "The Nature of the City." In Don Martindale and Gertrud Neuwirth, eds., *The City.* New York: Free Press.

White, Michael J. 1987 *American Neighborhoods and Residential Differentiation.* New York: Russell Sage Foundation.

Wilson, Franklin D. 1984 "Urban Ecology: Urbanization and Systems of Cities." In *Annual Review of Sociology,* vol. 10, ed. by Ralph H. Turner and James F. Short, Jr., Palo Alto, Calif.: Annual Reviews.

Wirth, Louis 1938 "Urbanism as a Way of Life." *American Journal of Sociology* 44:1–24.

Young, Pauline V. 1956 *Scientific Social Surveys and Social Research.* New York: Prentice-Hall.

Zipf, G. K. 1941 *National Unity and Disunity.* Bloomington, Ind.: Principia Press.

MAURICE D. VAN ARSDOL, JR.


**CIVIL DISOBEDIENCE** *See* Protest Movements; Student Movements.


**CIVIL-RIGHTS MOVEMENT** *See* Apartheid; Protest Movements; Segregation and Desegregation.


**CLASS** *See* Caste and Class; Marxist Sociology; Social Stratification; Societal Stratification.


**CLASS AND RACE** There is considerable debate in the sociology of race relations over how social inequality based on class and that based on race intertwine or intersect. Are these separate dimensions of inequality that simply coexist? Or are they part of the same reality? A similar question has been raised about gender inequality.

Efforts to develop an understanding of the relationship between class and race have a long history in sociology. In the 1930s and 1940s it was common to conceptualize the issue as "caste and class" (Davis, Gardner, and Gardner 1941; Dollard 1937). Studies were conducted in southern towns of the United States, and a parallel was drawn between the racial order and the Indian caste system. Class differentiation was observed within each of the two racial "castes," but a caste line divided them, severely limiting the social status of upper class African-Americans. This view, while descriptively illuminating, was challenged by Cox (1948), who saw U.S. race relations as only superficially similar to caste and based on a very different dynamic.

Today the relationship between class and race is mainly of concern to Marxist scholars of race and racism. Some authors, particularly those influenced by the New Left of the 1960s (Omi and Winant 1986), assert the independence of race from class and resist the reduction of race to class forces. They see race and racism as having an independent dynamic. They claim that the United States is organized along racial lines from top to bottom and that race is a more primary category than class. (A similar argument is made by some feminist sociologists regarding gender.)

However, for most Marxist sociologists of race relations, class and race cannot be treated as separate dimensions of inequality that somehow intersect. Rather, these Marxist sociologists argue that race and class are both part of the same system and need to be understood through an analysis of that system. Modern race relations are seen as distinctive products of world capitalism. The central question then becomes: How has capitalism, as a system based on class exploitation, shaped the phenomenon of race and racism?

Although ethnic and racial differences have provided a basis for intergroup conflicts for the entire history of humanity, the expansion of Europe, starting in the sixteenth century, set the stage for a new form of intergroup relations. Never before was conquest so widespread and thorough. Nor was it ever associated with such a total ideology of biological and cultural inferiority. Modern racism, with its "scientific" claims of inferiority, is a unique phenomenon.

An understanding of European expansion, and its impact on peoples of color, begins with an analysis of capitalism as it developed in Europe. Capitalism is a system that depends on the private ownership of productive property. In order to earn profits on property, the owners of it depend on the existence of a nonowning class that has no alternative but to sell its labor-power to the owners. The owners accumulate wealth through profit, that is, the surplus they extract from labor. Hence, a class struggle develops between capital-

ists and workers over the rights of capitalists to the surplus.

In Europe, labor came to be "free," that is, people were no longer bound by serfdom or other forms of servitude but were free to sell their labor-power on an open market to the highest bidder. Being free in this sense gave European workers a certain political capacity, even though they were often driven to conditions of misery and poverty.

Capitalism is an expansionary system. Not only does it unleash great economic growth, but it also tends to move beyond national boundaries. The expansive tendencies lie in a need for new markets and raw materials, a search for investment opportunities, and a pursuit of cheaper labor in the face of political advances by national labor forces. European capitalism thus developed into an imperialistic system (Lenin 1939).

European imperialism led to a virtually total conquest of the globe. Europe carved up the entire world into spheres of influence and colonial domination. Since Europeans are "white," the colonial period, which reached its height in the early twentieth century, is a period of "white domination." Europeans, or whites, imposed their political, economic, cultural, and religious rule on the rest of the world, which consisted of peoples of color: "black" Africans, "yellow" Asians, "red" American Indians, and so forth. "White" became associated with a certain form of domination and oppression.

European domination took multiple forms, from unequal treaties, unfair trade relations, conquest, and the establishment of alien rule to annihilation and white settlement in places where once other peoples had thrived. Imperialism received ideological justification in beliefs that non-European cultures were "primitive," "uncivilized," "barbaric," and "savage," and their religions were pagan and superstitious. Europeans were convinced that they had the true religion in Christianity and that all other peoples needed to be "saved." The denigration of other cultures was accompanied by beliefs in "natural," biological inferiority. Dark skin color was a mark of such inferiority, while white skin was viewed as more highly evolved. Africans, in particular, were seen as closer to the apes. These kinds of ideas received "scientific" support in the form of studies of cranial capacity and culturally biased intelligence tests. The totalizing oppression and dehumanization of colonial domination is well captured in Albert Memmi's *The Colonizer and the Colonized* (1967).

European economic domination had many aspects, but a major aspect was the exploitation of colonized workers. Unlike white labor, which was "free," colonial labor was typically subjected to various forms of coercion. As conquered peoples, colonized nations could be denied any political rights and were treated openly as beings whose sole purpose was to enhance white wealth. Throughout the colonial world, various forms of slavery, serfdom, forced migrant labor, indentured servitude, and contract labor were common.

The coercion of colonized workers makes for a vast divide within the working class along color lines. Generally, white labor has been free, with certain political rights, while labor of color has been unfree and denied political rights. The result has been a greater oppression of workers of color as well as secondary conflicts between white workers and workers of color over their different circumstances and needs.

Not only did European imperialists exploit colonized workers in their homelands, but they also moved many people around to other areas of the colonial world where they were needed. The most notorious instance was the African slave trade, under which Africans were brought in bondage to the Caribbean area and sections of North and South America. However, other examples include the movement of contract workers from China and India all over the colonial world. Britain, as the chief imperialist power, moved Indians to southern Africa, Fiji, Trinidad, Mauritius, and other places to serve as laborers in remote parts of the British Empire. These movements created "internal colonies" (Blauner 1972), where workers of color were again subject to special coercion.

Even seemingly free immigrants of color have been subjected to special constraints. For example, Chinese immigrants to the United States in the late nineteenth century were denied naturalization rights, in contrast to European immigrants, and as a result were subjected to special legal disabilities. In the United States, Australia, Canada, and elsewhere, Chinese were singled out for "exclusion" legislation, limiting their access as free immigrants.

The sections of the world with the worst racial conflicts are the "white settler colonies." In the British Empire, these include the United States, South Africa, Zimbabwe (Rhodesia), Canada, Australia, and New Zealand. These societies established large white working classes that came into conflict with colonial capitalists over the use of coerced labor (Harris 1964).

So far we have talked only of the relations between white capital, white labor, and colonized labor. The colonial world was, of course, more complex than this. Not only did colonized people have their own middle or upper classes, but sometimes outside peoples immigrated or were brought in and served as indirect rulers of the colonized.

Middle strata from among the colonized peoples can play a dualistic role in the system. On the one hand, they can help the imperialists exploit more effectively. Examples include labor contractors, police, or small business owners who make use of ethnic ties to exploit members of their own group. In these types of situations, the dominant white group can benefit by having members of the colonized population help to control the workers primarily for the dominant whites while also taking a cut of the surplus for themselves. On the other hand, middle strata can also be the leaders of nationalist movements to rid their people of the colonial yoke.

Outsider middle strata, sometimes known as middleman minorities, can be invaluable to the colonial ruling class. As strangers to the colonized, they have no ambivalence about the aspirations of the colonized for self-determination. They take their cut of profits while not seriously threatening to take over from the Europeans. Because middleman groups tend to serve as the chief interactors with the colonized, they often become a major butt of hostility, deflecting the hostility that would otherwise be directed at the colonial elite.

Thus, the class and race relations resulting from the development of European capitalism and imperialism have been complex and world-shaping. Even though formal colonialism as outright political domination has been successfully challenged by national liberation movements, and even though the most oppressive forms of coerced labor have been legally banned in most of the world, neocolonialism and racial oppression continue in various guises.

For example, African-Americans in the United States remain a relatively disenfranchised and impoverished population. Although illegal, racial discrimination persists in everyday practice, and racist ideology and attitudes pervade the society. Many whites continue to believe that blacks are innately inferior and object to social integration in the schools or through intermarriage. African-Americans are almost totally absent from positions of power in any of the major political, economic, and social institutions of the society. Meanwhile, they suffer from every imaginable social deprivation in such areas as housing, health care, and education.

The capitalist system maintains racism in part because racially oppressed populations are profitable. Racial oppression (along with gender oppression) is a mechanism for obtaining cheap labor. It allows private owners of capital to reduce labor costs and increase their share of the surplus derived from social production. In general, the people of color do the menial work in most white-dominated societies, while a sector of the white population reaps the benefit.

With an increasingly globalized world capitalism, these processes have taken on an international dimension. Not only do capitalists take advantage of oppressed groups in their own nation-states, but they seek them out wherever in the world they can be found. Such people are, once again, of color. Of course, the rise of Japan as a major capitalist power has changed the complexion of the ruling capitalist elite, but the oppressed remain primarily African, Latin American, and Asian.

It is common today for people to assume that prejudice goes both ways and that everyone is equally prejudiced, that African-Americans have just as much animosity toward whites as whites have toward blacks. According to this thinking, whites should not be singled out for special blame because prejudice against those who are different is a universal human trait: We are all equally guilty of prejudice. This view totally disregards the history described above. Europe was never conquered and humiliated by other societies, and its culture and biology were never denigrated. To the extent that peoples of color are antiwhite, it is a reaction to a long history of abuse. Claiming that the antiwhite sentiments of blacks are equally racist and on the same level as white racism is a form of denial of the historically specific basis of white racism.

At the foundation of the problem of race and class oppression lies the value system of capitalism, which asserts that pursuit of self-interest in a competitive marketplace will lead to social enhancement for all and that therefore the social welfare need not be attended to directly. This assumption is patently untrue. The United States, perhaps the worst offender, has let this social philosophy run amok, resulting in the creation of a vast chasm between excessive wealth and grinding poverty, both heavily correlated with color. Without intervention in "free market" processes, the United States is heading toward increased racial polarization and even possible violence.

Societies need to attend to racial issues directly. Their solution lies not only in "affirmative-action" types of programs, where a minority of people of color experience some upward mobility in an otherwise unchanged class system, but rather, the whole system of inequality based on appropriation of surplus wealth by a few, mainly white, private property owners needs to be challenged. Neither class-based nor racial inequality and domination can be attacked alone. They are linked with each other and must be overthrown together.

(SEE ALSO: *African-American Studies; Marxist Sociology*)

## REFERENCES

Blauner, Robert 1972 *Racial Oppression in America*. New York: Harper and Row.

Cox, Oliver Cromwell 1948 *Caste, Class, and Race*. New York: Modern Reader.

Davis, Allison, Burleigh B. Gardner, and Mary R. Gardner 1941 *Deep South*. Chicago: University of Chicago Press.

Dollard, John 1937 *Caste and Class in a Southern Town*. Garden City, N.Y.: Doubleday.

Harris, Marvin 1964 *Patterns of Race in the Americas*. New York: Walker.

Lenin, V. I. 1939 *Imperialism: The Highest Stage of Capitalism*. New York: International.

Memmi, Albert 1967 *The Colonizer and the Colonized*. Boston: Beacon Press.

Omi, Michael, and Howard Winant 1986 *Racial Formation in the United States*. New York: Routledge and Kegan Paul.

EDNA BONACICH

**CLASSIFICATION** *See* Tabular Analysis; Typologies.

**CLUSTER ANALYSIS** *See* Factor Analysis.

**COALITIONS** Originally a word for union or fusion, the term *coalition* came in the eighteenth century to mean a temporary alliance of political parties. In modern social science, the meaning has broadened to include any combination of two or more social actors formed for mutual advantage in contention with other actors in the same social system. In most contemporary theories of coalition formation, it is taken for granted that the principles governing coalition formation are not much affected by the size of the actors, who may be small children or large nations, but *are* significantly affected by the number of actors in the system. In the sociological and social-psychological literature, interest has focused on coalition formation in social systems containing three actors, commonly known as *tri-ads*, and on the factors that influence the formation of coalitions in that configuration. Coalitions in triads have certain properties that are very useful in the analysis of power relationships in and among organizations. Moreover, tetrads, pentads, and higher-order social systems can be viewed for analytical purposes as clusters of linked triads.

The social science perspective on coalitions derives from two major sources: the formal sociology of Georg Simmel (1858–1918) and the *n*-person game theory of John von Neumann (1903–1957). Simmel had the fundamental insight that conflict and cooperation are opposite sides of the same coin so that no functioning social system can be free of internal conflicts or of internal coalitions. Simmel also proposed that the geometry of social relationships is independent of the size of the actors in a social system but heavily influenced by their number; that social systems are held together by internal differentiation; that relationships between superiors and subordinates are intrinsically ambivalent; that groups of three tend to develop coalitions of two against one; and that, in stable social systems, coalitions shift continually from one situation to another.

While the basic ideas are attributable to Simmel, the analytical framework for most of the empirical research on coalitions that has been undertaken so far is that of Von Neumann (and his collaborator Oskar Morgenstern). Any social interaction involving costs and rewards can be described as an *n*-person game. In two-person games, the problem for each player is to find a winning strategy, but in games with three or more players, the formation of a winning coalition is likely to be the major strategic objective. The theory distinguishes between zero-sum games, in which one side loses whatever the other side gains, and non-zero-sum games with more complex payoff schedules. And it provides a mathematical argument for the equal division of gains among coalition partners, the gist of which is that any essential member of a winning coalition who is offered less than an equal share of the joint winnings can be induced to desert the coalition and join an adversary who offers more favorable terms. In the various experimental and real-life

208

settings in which coalitions are studied, this solution has only limited application, but game theory continues to furnish the vocabulary of observation.

Modern empirical work on coalitions falls into two major categories: experimental studies of small groups playing games that have been devised by the experimenter to test hypotheses about the choice of coalition partners and the division of coalition winnings under specified conditions, and observational studies of coalitions in the real world. Stimulated by the publication of divergent theories of coalition formation (Mills 1953; Caplow 1956; Gamson 1961) in the *American Sociological Review*, coalition experiments became part of the standard repertory of social psychology in the 1960s and continue to be so to this day. A great deal has been learned about how the choice of coalition partners and the division of coalition winnings are affected by variations in game rules and player attributes (Miller and Crandall 1980). Much, although by no means all, of this work has focused on three-player games in which the players have unequal resources and any coalition is a winning coalition, the distribution of resources falling into one of three types: (1) $A>B>C$, $A<B+C$; (2) $A=B$, $B>C$, $A<B+C$; (3) $A>B$, $B=C$, $A<B+C$. With respect to the choice of coalition partners, the leading question has been whether subjects will consistently choose the partner with whom they can form the minimum winning coalition, or the stronger partner, or the partner who offers the more favorable terms, or the partner who resembles themselves in attributes or ideology. The general finding is that each of these results can be produced with fair consistency by varying the rules of the experimental game. The division of winnings between coalition partners has attracted even more attention than the choice of partners. The question has been whether winnings will be divided on the principle of *equality*, as suggested by game theory; or of *parity*, proportionate to the contribution of each partner, as suggested by exchange theory; or at an intermediate ratio established by *bargaining*. Although many experimenters have claimed that one or the other of these principles is primary, their collective results seem to show that all three

modes of division occur spontaneously and that subjects may be tilted one way or another by appropriate instructions. Additional nuances of coalition formation have been explored in games having more than three players, variable payoffs, or incomplete information. Non-zero-sum games and sequential games with continually changing weights have been particularly instructive. The findings readily lend themselves to mathematical expression (Kahan and Rapoport 1984).

The explicit application of coalition analysis to real-life situations began with Riker's (1962) study of political coalitions in legislative bodies; he discerned a consistent preference for minimal winning coalitions and emphasized the pivotal role of weak factions. Caplow (1968) showed how the developing theory of coalitions in triads could be used to analyze conflict and competition in nuclear and extended families, organizational hierarchies, revolutionary politics, international relations, and other contexts. The subsequent development of observational studies has been slow and uneven compared with the proliferation of laboratory studies, but there have been some notable achievements, particularly in family dynamics and international relations, where coalition models fit gracefully into earlier lines of investigation. Coalition theory has also been applied, albeit in a more tentative way, to work groups, intra- and interorganizational relationships, litigation and criminal justice, class and ethnic conflict, and military strategy.

Whatever the field of application, the examination of coalition, especially the simple coalition of two against one, provides a key to the social geometry of situations involving conflict, competition, and cooperation. In nearly every conflict, each of the contending parties seeks the support of relevant third parties, and the side that gains that support is likely to prevail. In very many competitive situations, the outcome is eventually decided by the formation of a winning coalition. And any system of cooperation that involves a status order must rely on the routine formation of coalitions of superiors against subordinates and be able to counter coalitions of subordinates against superiors.

All of these situations are susceptible to coalitions of two against one, which tend to transform strength into weakness and weakness into strength. Under many conditions, in the first of the triads mentioned above (A>B>C, A<B+C), both A and B will prefer C as a coalition partner; his initial weakness ensures his inclusion in the winning coalition. When A>B, B=C, A<B+C, B and C will often prefer each other as coalition partners; A's initial strength ensures his exclusion from the winning coalition. When A=B, A>C, C's initial weakness again makes him a likely winner. The first purpose of any hierarchy must be to restrain in one way or another the inherent tendency of subordinates to combine against superiors. Although force and ritual are often deployed for this purpose, the stability of complex status orders depends on certain interactive effects that appear in triads with overlapping membership, called linked triads. In such clusters, the choice of coalition partners in one triad influences the choices made in other triads. The natural rules that seem to govern the formation of coalitions in linked hierarchical triads are that a coalition adversary in one triad may not be chosen as a coalition partner in another triad, and that actors offered a choice between incompatible winning coalitions will choose the one in the higher-ranking triad. The net effect favors conservative coalitions of superiors against subordinates without entirely suppressing revolutionary coalitions of subordinates against superiors.

Cross-cutting the coalition preferences that arise from unequal distributions of power and resources are preferences based on affinity, compatibility, and prior experience with potential partners. These other bases of coalition formation are conspicuous in intimate groups such as the family, where same-sex coalitions alternate with same-generation coalitions.

The study of coalitions in nuclear families is particularly rewarding because the distribution of power in the triad of mother-father-child changes so dramatically as the child grows up, and because same-sex coalitions are differently valued than cross-sex coalitions. The initial distribution of power between husband and wife is always trans-formed by the arrival of children; most cultures encourage certain patterns, such as the Oedipus and Electra complexes described by Sigmund Freud: coalitions of mother and son against father and of father and daughter against mother. Research on the contemporary American family suggests that parental coalitions are quite durable, both mother-daughter and mother-son coalitions against the father are very common, father-daughter coalitions against the mother much less so, and father-son coalitions against the mother comparatively rare. Sibling coalitions are most likely among same-sex siblings adjacent in age. Sibling aggression is endemic in families of this type, especially in the presence of parents. An interesting study by Felson and Russo (1988) suggests that parents usually take side with the weaker child in these incidents, and this leads to more frequent aggression by the excluded child. There are very few family conflicts that cannot be instructively described by a coalition model.

The application of coalition theory to international relations has concentrated on the "strategic triangle" of the United States, China, and the Soviet Union during the Cold War era of 1950–1985. In one of the many studies that have examined the internal dynamics of this triad, Hsiung (1987) concluded that China as the weak player in this triad benefited much more than either of the superpowers from the various coalitional shifts that occurred over time, as would be theoretically expected in a triad of this type (A=B, B>C, A<B+C). A recent study by Caplow (1989) explains the failure of peace planning in 1815, 1919, and 1945, by showing how efforts to put an end to the war system were undermined by the formation of coalitions to prevent the domination of the peacekeeping organization by the strongest of the victorious powers. Many older studies of international balances of power visualize international relations as a game in which the first priority of every major player is to block the domination of the entire system by any other player. Zagare's (1984) analysis of the Geneva Conference on Vietnam in 1954 as a three-person game broadened this approach by comparing the preference schedules of the three players and

showing how they combined to produce the unexpected outcome of the negotiations.

Both family dynamics and international relations in peacetime exemplify situations of continuous conflict, wherein relationships have long histories and are expected to persist indefinitely, and the opposition of interests is qualified by the necessity for cooperation. The choice of coalition partners and the division of winnings is strongly influenced by the past transactions of the parties and by the fact that payoffs are not completely predictable. Continuous conflict triads with $A>B>C$, $A<B+C$ often alternate the three possible coalitions according to circumstances: the *conservative coalition* AB reinforces the existing status order; the *revolutionary coalition* BC challenges it; and the *improper coalition* AC subverts it.

Episodic conflicts, by contrast, involve discrete zero-sum games played under strict rules. The passage of any measure in a legislative body necessarily involves the formation of a coalition. Even when one party has a solid majority, its members will seldom be in complete agreement on an issue. The formation of a coalition for the passage of a specific measure usually involves hard bargaining and payoffs negotiated in advance. Under these conditions, the tendency to minimize costs by forming the minimal winning coalitions is very strong. When $A>B>C$, $A<B+C$, a BC coalition is highly probable. Empirical studies of legislative voting bear this out, although more than minimal coalitions also occur, for various reasons.

The resolution of disputes by civil and criminal litigation is another variety of episodic conflict that has begun to be studied as a coalition process. Black (1989) explores the triad of judge and courtroom adversaries and discovers a clear tendency for judges to favor the litigant to whom they are socially closer, ordinarily the litigant of higher status—a tacit conservative coalition. But in forms of dispute resolution where the third party is less authoritative, the weaker adversary may be favored. Marital counselors, for example, often side with wives against husbands, and ombudsmen and other relatively powerless mediators normally incline toward the weaker party.

In terminal conflicts, the object is the permanent destruction of adversaries, and the formation of coalitions is a delicate matter. In the triad where $A>B>C$, $A<B+C$, a successful BC coalition that destroys A leaves C at the mercy of B. Indeed, any winning coalition is hazardous for the weaker partner. A fragile peace can be maintained if $A>B>C$ and $A=B+C$; the BC coalition forms as a matter of course, creating what is known as a balance of power. This has been the key configuration in European affairs for the past several centuries. The balance breaks down with any significant shift in the relative power of the parties; for example, if A grows stronger than the BC coalition, it will be tempted to conquer them. If B becomes equal to A, an AB coalition may be tempted to attack and partition C. If C grows stronger and the triad assumes the form $A>B$, $B=C$, $B+C>A$, the formation of a BC coalition to overthrow A is likely. In the eighteenth century, the breakdown of a balance of power led to war without delay. Under current conditions, the breakdown of a balance of power among major industrialized states does not involve an automatic resort to arms, but in several regional arenas, such as Southeast Asia and the Middle East, the old mechanism is still intact.

Terminal conflicts occur also within nations as coups, resistance movements, and revolutions. One common pattern is the urban uprising against a dictatorial regime, in which the players are the government, the army, and the populace. If the army continues to support the government and is willing to fire on the populace, the uprising fails. If the army sides with the populace, the government is overthrown. Often the issue is undecided until the moment when the troops confront the demonstrators. At a more fundamental level, successful revolutions require a coalition of formerly separate factions against the ruling group.

Every organization generates both internal and boundary coalitions. Internal coalitions are activated whenever persons or groups of unequal status interact before witnesses. In general, the presence of a high-status witness reinforces the authority of a superior, while the presence of a low-status witness reduces it; examined in detail, these catalytic effects are delicate and precise. Boundary coalitions occur whenever one organization has permanent relations with another. Their respective agents must form a coalition with each other to perform their functions, and that coalition pits them both against their own colleagues, always with interesting consequences.

In a long-term perspective, the two bodies of coalition studies, experimental and observational, exemplify two extremes of scholarly development. The experimental studies have explored nearly every possibility suggested by the available theories, run down every lead, manipulated every variable. Further progress probably waits on a new theoretical framework. The observational studies have scarcely tapped the rich possibilities suggested by the available theories and confirmed by the few empirical studies that have been done thus far. The social psychology of coalitions is well developed; most of the macrosociological work remains to be done.

(SEE ALSO: *Decision-Making Theory and Research*)

### REFERENCES

Adams, Wesley J. 1985 "The Missing Triad: The Case of Two-Child Families." *Family Process* 24:409–413.

Black, Donald 1989 *Sociological Justice.* New York: Oxford University Press.

Bonacich, Phillip, Oscar Grusky, and Mark Peyrot 1985 "Family Coalitions: A New Approach and Method." *Social Psychology Quarterly* 44:42–50.

Caplow, Theodore 1956 "A Theory of Coalitions in the Triad." *American Sociological Review* 21:480–493.

——— 1968 *Two Against One: Coalitions in Triads.* Englewood Cliffs, N.J.: Prentice-Hall.

——— 1989 *Peace Games.* Middletown, Conn.: Wesleyan University Press.

Felson, Richard B., and Natalie Russo 1988 "Parental Punishment and Sibling Aggression." *Social Psychology Quarterly* 51:11–18.

Gamson, William A. 1961 "A Theory of Coalition Formation." *American Sociological Review* 26:565–573.

Hsiung, James C. 1987 "Internal Dynamics in the Sino-Soviet-U.S. Triad." In I. J. Kim, ed., *The Strategic Triangle.* New York: Paragon.

Kahan, James P., and Amnon Rapoport 1984 *Theories of Coalition Formation.* Hillsdale, N.J.: Lawrence Erlbaum Associates.

Komorita, S. S., and Charles E. Miller 1986 "Bargaining Strength as a Function of Coalition Alternatives." *Journal of Personality and Social Psychology* 51:325–332.

Miller, Charles E., and R. Crandall 1980 "Experimental Research on the Social Psychology of Bargaining and Coalition Formation." In R. Paulus, ed., *Psychology of Group Influence,* Hillsdale, N.J.: Lawrence Erlbaum Associates.

Mills, Theodore M. 1953 "Power Relations in Three-Person Groups." *American Sociological Review* 18:351–357.

Murnighan, J. Keith 1978 "Models of Coalition Behavior: Game Theoretic, Social Psychological, and Political Perspectives." *Psychological Bulletin* 85:1130–1153.

Nail, Paul, and Steven G. Cole 1985 "Three Theories of Coalition Behavior: A Probabilistic Extension." *British Journal of Social Psychology* 24:181–190.

Riker, William H. 1962 *The Theory of Political Coalitions.* New Haven, Conn.: Yale University Press.

Rodgers, Joseph Lee, and Vaida D. Thompson 1986 "Towards a General Framework of Family Structure: A Review of Theory-Based Empirical Research." *Population and Environment* 8:143–171.

Rose, Irene Kathryn 1986 "Testing Coalition Theory in the Great Gatsby and the Rabbit Trilogy." Ph.D. diss., University of Oklahoma.

Simmel, Georg 1902 "The Number of Members as Determining the Sociological Form of the Group." *American Journal of Sociology* 8:1–46, 158–196.

——— 1966 *The Social Theory of Georg Simmel,* ed. Nicholas J. Spykman. New York: Atherton.

Von Neumann, John, and Oskar Morgenstern 1944 *Theory of Games and Economic Behavior.* Princeton, N.J.: Princeton University Press.

Zagare, Frank C. 1984 *Game Theory: Concepts and Applications.* Beverly Hills, Calif.: Sage Publications.

THEODORE CAPLOW

## COERCIVE PERSUASION AND ATTITUDE CHANGE

Coercive persuasion and thought reform are alternate names for programs of social influence capable of producing substantial behavior and attitude change through the use of coercive tactics, persuasion, and/or interpersonal and group-based influence manipulations (Schein 1961; Lifton 1961). Such programs have also been labeled "brainwashing" (Hunter 1951), a term more often used in the media than in scientific literature. However identified, these programs are distinguishable from other elaborate attempts to influence behavior and attitudes, to socialize, and to accomplish social control. Their distinguishing features are their totalistic qualities (Lifton 1961), the types of influence procedures they employ, and the organization of these procedures into three distinctive subphases of the overall process (Schein 1961; Ofshe and Singer 1986). The key factors that distinguish coercive persuasion from other training and socialization schemes are (1) the reliance on intense interpersonal and psychological attack to destabilize an individual's sense of self to promote compliance, (2) the use of an organized peer group, (3) applying interpersonal pressure to promote conformity, and (4) the manipulation of the totality of the person's social environment to stabilize behavior once modified.

Thought-reform programs have been employed in attempts to control and indoctrinate individuals, societal groups (e.g., intellectuals), and even entire populations. Systems intended to accomplish these goals can vary considerably in their construction. Even the first systems studied under the label "thought reform" ranged from those in which confinement and physical assault were employed (Schein 1956; Lifton 1954; Lifton 1961 pp. 19–85) to applications that were carried out under nonconfined conditions, in which nonphysical coercion substituted for assault (Lifton 1961, pp. 242–273; Schein 1961, pp. 290–298). The individuals to whom these influence programs were applied were in some cases unwilling subjects (prisoner populations) and in other cases volunteers who sought to participate in what they believed might be a career-beneficial, educational experience (Lifton 1961, p. 248).

Significant differences existed between the social environments and the control mechanisms employed in the two types of programs initially studied. Their similarities, however, are of more importance in understanding their ability to influence behavior and beliefs than are their differences. They shared the utilization of coercive persuasion's key effective-influence mechanisms: a focused attack on the stability of a person's sense of self; reliance on peer group interaction; the development of interpersonal bonds between targets and their controllers and peers; and an ability to control communication among participants. Edgar Schein captured the essential similarity between the types of programs in his definition of the coercive-persuasion phenomenon. Schein noted that even for prisoners, what happened was a subjection to "unusually intense and prolonged persuasion" that they could not avoid; thus, "they were coerced into allowing themselves to be persuaded" (Schein 1961, p. 18).

Programs of both types (confined/assaultive and nonconfined/nonassaultive) cause a range of cognitive and behavioral responses. The reported cognitive responses vary from apparently rare instances, classifiable as internalized belief change (enduring change), to a frequently observed transient alteration in beliefs that appears to be *situationally adaptive* and, finally, to reactions of nothing less than firm intellectual resistance and hostility (Lifton 1961, pp. 117–151, 399–415; Schein 1961, pp. 157–166).

The phrase *situationally adaptive belief change* refers to attitude change that is *not* stable and *is environment dependent*. This type of response to the influence pressures of coercive-persuasion programs is perhaps the most surprising of the responses that have been observed. The combination of psychological assault on the self, interpersonal pressure, and the social organization of the environment creates a situation that can only be coped with by adapting and acting so as to present oneself to others in terms of the ideology supported in the environment (see below for discussion). Eliciting the desired verbal and interactive behavior sets up conditions likely to stimulate the development of attitudes consistent with and that function to rationalize new behavior in which the individual is engaging. Models of attitude change, such as the theory of Cognitive Dissonance (Festinger 1957) or Self-Perception Theory (Bem 1972), explain the tendency for consistent attitudes to develop as a consequence of behavior.

The surprising aspect of the situationally adaptive response is that the attitudes that develop are unstable. They tend to change dramatically once the person is removed from an environment that has totalistic properties and is organized to support the adaptive attitudes. Once removed from such an environment, the person is able to interact with others who permit and encourage the expression of criticisms and doubts, which were previously stifled because of the normative rules of the reform environment (Schein 1961, p. 163; Lifton 1961, pp. 87–116, 399–415; Ofshe and Singer 1986). This pattern of change, first in one direction and then the other, dramatically highlights the profound importance of social support in the explanation of attitude change and stability. This relationship has for decades been one of the principal interests in the field of social psychology.

Statements supportive of the proffered ideology that indicate adaptive attitude change during the period of the target's involvement in the reform environment and immediately following separation should not be taken as mere playacting in reaction to necessity. Targets tend to become genuinely involved in the interaction. The reform experience focuses on genuine vulnerabilities as the method for undermining self-concept: manipulating genuine feelings of guilt about past conduct; inducing the target to make public denunciations of his or her prior life as being unworthy; and carrying this forward through interaction with peers for whom the target develops strong bonds. Involvement developed in these ways prevents the target from maintaining both psychological distance or emotional independence from the experience.

The reaction pattern of persons who display adaptive attitude-change responses is not one of an immediate and easy rejection of the proffered ideology. This response would be expected if they had been faking their reactions as a conscious strategy to defend against the pressures to which they were exposed. Rather, they appear to be conflicted about the sentiments they developed

and their reevaluation of these sentiments. This response has been observed in persons reformed under both confined/assaultive and nonconfined/nonassaultive reform conditions (Schein 1962, pp. 163–165; Lifton 1961, pp. 86–116, 400–401).

Self-concept and belief-related attitude change in response to closely controlled social environments have been observed in other organizational settings that, like reform programs, can be classified as total institutions (Goffman 1957). Thought-reform reactions also appear to be related to, but are far more extreme than, responses to the typically less-identity-assaultive and less-totalistic socialization programs carried out by organizations with central commitments to specifiable ideologies, and which undertake the training of social roles (e.g., in military academies and religious-indoctrination settings (Dornbush 1955; Hulme 1956).

The relatively rare instances in which belief changes are internalized and endure have been analyzed as attributable to the degree to which the acquired belief system and imposed peer relations function to fully resolve the identity crisis that is routinely precipitated during the first phase of the reform process (Schein 1961, p. 164; Lifton 1961, pp. 131–132, 400). Whatever the explanation for why some persons internalize the proffered ideology in response to the reform procedures, this extreme reaction should be recognized as both atypical and probably attributable to an interaction between long-standing personality traits and the mechanisms of influence utilized during the reform process.

Much of the attention to reform programs was stimulated because it was suspected that a predictable and highly effective method for profoundly changing beliefs had been designed, implemented, and was in operation. These suspicions are not supported by fact. Programs identified as though reforming are not very effective at actually changing people's beliefs in any fashion that endures apart from an elaborate supporting social context. Evaluated only on the criterion of their ability to genuinely change beliefs, the programs have to be judged abject failures and massive wastes of effort.

The programs are, however, impressive in their ability to prepare targets for integration into and long-term participation in the organizations that operate them. Rather than assuming that individual belief change is the major goal of these programs, it is perhaps more productive to view the programs as elaborate role-training regimes. That is, as resocialization programs in which targets are being prepared to conduct themselves in a fashion appropriate for the social roles they are expected to occupy following conclusion of the training process.

If identified as training programs, it is clear that the goals of such programs are to reshape behavior and that they are organized around issues of social control important to the organizations that operate the programs. Their objectives then appear to be behavioral training of the target, which result in an ability to present self, values, aspirations, and past history in a style appropriate to the ideology of the controlling organization; to train an ability to reason in terms of the ideology; and to train a willingness to accept direction from those in authority with minimum apparent resistance. Belief changes that follow from successfully coercing or inducing the person to behave in the prescribed manner can be thought of as by-products of the training experience. As attitude-change models would predict, they arise "naturally" as a result of efforts to reshape behavior (Festinger 1957; Bem 1972).

The tactical dimension most clearly distinguishing reform processes from other sorts of training programs is the reliance on psychological coercion: procedures that generate pressure to comply as a means of escaping a punishing experience (e.g., public humiliation, sleep deprivation, guilt manipulation, etc.). Coercion differs from other influencing factors also present in thought reform, such as content-based persuasive attempts (e.g., presentation of new information, reference to authorities, etc.) or reliance on influence variables operative in all interaction (status relations, demeanor, normal assertiveness differentials, etc.). Coercion is principally utilized to gain behavioral compliance at key points and to ensure participation in activities likely to have influencing

effects; that is, to engage the person in the role-training activities and in procedures likely to lead to strong emotional responses, to cognitive confusion, or to attributions to self as the source of beliefs promoted during the process.

Robert Lifton labeled the extraordinarily high degree of social control characteristic of organizations that operate reform programs as their totalistic quality (Lifton 1961). This concept refers to the mobilization of the entirety of the person's social, and often physical, environment in support of the manipulative effort. Lifton identified eight themes or properties of reform environments that contribute to their totalistic quality: (1) control of communication, (2) emotional and behavioral manipulation, (3) demands for absolute conformity to behavior prescriptions derived from the ideology, (4) obsessive demands for confession, (5) agreement that the ideology is faultless, (6) manipulation of language in which clichés substitute for analytic thought, (7) reinterpretation of human experience and emotion in terms of doctrine, and (8) classification of those not sharing the ideology as inferior and not worthy of respect (Lifton 1961, pp. 419–437, 1987).

Schein's analysis of the behavioral sequence underlying coercive persuasion separated the process into three subphases: *unfreezing, change,* and *refreezing* (Schein 1961, pp. 111–139). Phases differ in their principal goals and their admixtures of persuasive, influencing, and coercive tactics. Although others have described the process differently, their analyses are not inconsistent with Schein's three-phase breakdown (Lifton 1961; Farber, Harlow, and West 1956; Meerloo 1956; Sargent 1957; Ofshe and Singer 1986). Although Schein's terminology is adopted here, the descriptions of phase activities have been broadened to reflect later research.

*Unfreezing* is the first step in eliciting behavior and developing a belief system that facilitates the long-term management of a person. It consists of attempting to undercut a person's psychological basis for resisting demands for behavioral compliance to the routines and rituals of the reform program. The goals of unfreezing are to destabilize a person's sense of identity (i.e., to precipitate an identity crisis), to diminish confidence in prior social judgments, and to foster a sense of powerlessness, if not hopelessness. Successful destabilization induces a negative shift in global self-evaluations and increases uncertainty about one's values and position in society. It thereby reduces resistance to the new demands for compliance while increasing suggestibility.

Destabilization of identity is accomplished by bringing into play varying sets of manipulative techniques. The first programs to be studied utilized techniques such as repeatedly demonstrating the person's inability to control his or her own fate, the use of degradation ceremonies, attempts to induce reevaluation of the adequacy and/or propriety of prior conduct, and techniques designed to encourage the reemergence of latent feelings of guilt and emotional turmoil (Hinkle and Wolfe 1956; Lifton 1954, 1961; Schein 1956, 1961; Schein, Cooley, and Singer 1960). Contemporary programs have been observed to utilize far more psychologically sophisticated procedures to accomplish destabilization. These techniques are often adapted from the traditions of psychiatry, psychotherapy, hypnotherapy, and the human-potential movement, as well as from religious practice (Ofshe and Singer 1986; Lifton 1987).

The *change* phase allows the individual an opportunity to escape punishing destabilization procedures by demonstrating that he or she has learned the proffered ideology, can demonstrate an ability to interpret reality in its own terms, and is willing to participate in competition with peers to demonstrate zeal through displays of commitment. In addition to study and/or formal instruction, the techniques used to facilitate learning and the skill basis that can lead to opinion change include scheduling events that have predictable influencing consequences, rewarding certain conduct, and manipulating emotions to create punishing experiences. Some of the practices designed to promote influence might include requiring the target to assume responsibility for the progress of less-advanced "students," to become the responsibility of those further along in the program, to assume the role of a teacher of

the ideology, or to develop ever more refined and detailed confession statements that recast the person's former life in terms of the required ideological position. Group structure is often manipulated by making rewards or punishments for an entire peer group contingent on the performance of the weakest person, requiring the group to utilize a vocabulary appropriate to the ideology, making status and privilege changes commensurate with behavioral compliance, subjecting the target to strong criticism and humiliation from peers for lack of progress, and peer monitoring for expressions of reservations or dissent. If progress is unsatisfactory, the individual can again be subjected to the punishing destabilization procedures used during unfreezing to undermine identity, to humiliate, and to provoke feelings of shame and guilt.

*Refreezing* denotes an attempt to promote and reinforce behavior acceptable to the controlling organization. Satisfactory performance is rewarded with social approval, status gains, and small privileges. Part of the social structure of the environment is the norm of interpreting the target's display of the desired conduct as demonstrating the person's progress in understanding the errors of his or her former life. The combination of reinforcing approved behavior and interpreting its symbolic meaning as demonstrating the emergence of a new individual fosters the development of an environment-specific, supposedly reborn social identity. The person is encouraged to claim this identity and is rewarded for doing so.

Lengthy participation in an appropriately constructed and managed environment fosters peer relations, an interaction history, and other behavior consistent with a public identity that incorporates approved values and opinions. Promoting the development of an interaction history in which persons engage in cooperative activity with peers that is not blatantly coerced and in which they are encouraged but not forced to make verbal claims to "truly understanding the ideology and having been transformed," will tend to lead them to conclude that they hold beliefs consistent with their actions (i.e., to make attributions to self as the source of their behaviors). These reinforcement procedures can result in a significant degree of cognitive confusion and an alteration in what the person takes to be his or her beliefs and attitudes while involved in the controlled environment (Bem 1972; Ofshe et al. 1974).

Continuous use of *refreezing* procedures can sustain the expression of what appears to be significant attitude change for long periods of time. Maintaining compliance with a requirement that the person display behavior signifying unreserved acceptance of an imposed ideology and gaining other forms of long-term behavioral control requires continuous effort. The person must be carefully managed, monitored, and manipulated through peer pressure, the threat or use of punishment (material, social, and emotional) and through the normative rules of the community (e.g., expectations prohibiting careers independent of the organization, prohibiting formation of independent nuclear families, prohibiting accumulation of significant personal economic resources, etc.) (Whyte 1976; Ofshe 1980; Ofshe and Singer 1986).

The rate at which a once-attained level of attitude change deteriorates depends on the type of social support the person receives over time (Schein 1961 pp. 158–166; Lifton pp. 399–415). In keeping with the *refreezing* metaphor, even when the reform process is to some degree successful at shaping behavior and attitudes, the new shape tends to be maintained only as long as temperature is appropriately controlled.

One of the essential components of the reform process in general and of long-term *refreezing* in particular is monitoring and limiting the content of communication among persons in the managed group (Lifton 1961; Schein 1960; Ofshe et al. 1974). If successfully accomplished, communication control eliminates a person's ability to safely express criticisms or to share private doubts and reservations. The result is to confer on the community the quality of being a spy system of the whole, upon the whole.

The typically observed complex of communication-controlling rules requires people to self-report critical thoughts to authorities or to make doubts known only in approved and readily man-

aged settings (e.g., small groups or private counseling sessions). Admitting "negativity" leads to punishment or reindoctrination through procedures sometimes euphemistically termed "education" or "therapy." Individual social isolation is furthered by rules requiring peers to "help" colleagues to progress, by reporting their expressions of doubt. If it is discovered, failure to make a report is punishable, because it reflects on the low level of commitment of the person who did not "help" a colleague to make progress.

Controlling communication effectively blocks individuals from testing the appropriateness of privately held critical perceptions against the views of even their families and most-valued associates. Community norms encourage doubters to interpret lingering reservations as signs of a personal failure to comprehend the truth of the ideology; if involved with religious organizations, to interpret doubt as evidence of sinfulness or the result of demonic influences; if involved with an organization delivering a supposed psychological or medical therapy, as evidence of continuing illness and/or failure to progress in treatment.

The significance of communication control is illustrated by the collapse of a large psychotherapy organization in immediate reaction to the leadership's loss of effective control over interpersonal communication. At a meeting of several hundred of the members of this "therapeutic community" clients were allowed to openly voice privately held reservations about their treatment and exploitation. They had been subjected to abusive practices which included assault, sexual and economic exploitation, extremes of public humiliation, and others. When members discovered the extent to which their sentiments about these practices were shared by their peers they rebelled (Ayalla 1985).

Two widespread myths have developed from misreading the early studies of thought-reforming influence systems (Zablocki 1991). These studies dealt in part with their use to elicit false confessions in the Soviet Union after the 1917 revolution; from American and United Nations forces held as POWs during the Korean War; and from their application to Western missionaries held in China following Mao's revolution.

The first myth concerns the necessity and effectiveness of physical abuse in the reform process. The myth is that physical abuse is not only necessary but is the prime cause of apparent belief change. Reports about the treatment of POWs and foreign prisoners in China documented that physical abuse was present. Studies of the role of assault in the promotion of attitude change and in eliciting false confessions even from U.S. servicemen revealed, however, that it was ineffective. Belief change and compliance was more likely when physical abuse was minimal or absent (Biderman 1960). Both Schein (1961) and Lifton (1961) reported that physical abuse was a minor element in the theoretical understanding of even prison reform programs in China.

In the main, efforts at resocializing China's nationals were conducted under nonconfined/nonassaultive conditions. Millions of China's citizens underwent reform in schools, special-training centers, factories, and neighborhood groups in which physical assault was not used as a coercive technique. One such setting for which many participants actively sought admission, the "Revolutionary University," was classified by Lifton as the "hard core of the entire Chinese thought reform movement" (Lifton 1961, p. 248).

Attribution theories would predict that if there were differences between the power of reform programs to promote belief change in settings that were relatively more or less blatantly coercive and physically threatening, the effect would be greatest in less-coercive programs. Consistent with this expectation, Lifton concluded that reform efforts directed against Chinese citizens were "much more successful" than efforts directed against Westerners (Lifton 1961, p. 400).

A second myth concerns the purported effects of brainwashing. Media reports about thought reform's effects far exceed the findings of scientific studies—which show coercive persuasion's upper limit of impact to be that of inducing personal confusion and significant, but typically transitory, attitude change. Brainwashing was promoted as capable of stripping victims of their *capacity* to assert their wills, thereby rendering them unable to resist the orders of their controllers. People subjected to "brainwashing" were not merely influenced to adopt new attitudes but, according to the myth, suffered essentially an alteration in their psychiatric status from *normal* to *pathological*, while losing their capacity to decide to comply with or resist orders.

This lurid promotion of the power of thought-reforming influence techniques to change a person's capacity to resist direction is entirely without basis in fact: No evidence, scientific or otherwise, supports this proposition. No known mental disorder produces the loss of will that is alleged to be the result of brainwashing. Whatever behavior and attitude changes result from exposure to the process, they are most reasonably classified as the responses of normal individuals to a complex program of influence.

The U.S. Central Intelligence Agency seems to have taken seriously the myth about brainwashing's power to destroy the will. Due, perhaps, to concern that an enemy had perfected a method for dependably overcoming will—or perhaps in hope of being the first to develop such a method—the Agency embarked on a research program, code-named MKULTRA. It became a pathetic and tragic failure. On the one hand, it funded some innocuous and uncontroversial research projects; on the other, it funded or supervised the execution of several far-fetched, unethical, and dangerous experiments that failed completely (Marks 1979; Thomas 1989).

Although no evidence suggests that thought reform is a process capable of stripping a person of the will to resist, a relationship does exist between thought reform and changes in psychiatric status. The stress and pressure of the reform process cause some percentage of *psychological casualties*. To reduce resistence and to motivate behavior change, thought-reform procedures rely on psychological stressors, induction of high degrees of emotional distress, and on other intrinsically dangerous influence techniques (Heide and Borkovec 1983). The process has a potential to cause psychiatric injury, which is sometimes realized. The major early studies (Hinkle and Wolfe 1961; Lifton 1961; Schein 1961) reported that during the *unfreezing* phase individuals were intentionally stressed to a point at which some persons displayed symptoms of being on the brink of psychosis. Managers attempted to reduce psychological pressure when this happened, to avoid serious psychological injury to those obviously near the breaking point.

Contemporary programs speed up the reform process through the use of more psychologically sophisticated and dangerous procedures to accomplish destabilization. In contemporary programs the process is sometimes carried forward on a large group basis, which reduces the ability of managers to detect symptoms of impending psychiatric emergencies. In addition, in some of the "therapeutic" ideologies espoused by thought-reforming organizations, extreme emotional distress is valued positively, as a sign of progress. Studies of contemporary programs have reported on a variety of psychological injuries related to the reform process. Injuries include psychosis, major depressions, manic episodes, and debilitating anxiety (Glass, Kirsch, and Parris 1977, Haaken and Adams 1983, Heide and Borkovec 1983; Higget and Murray 1983; Kirsch and Glass 1977; Yalom and Lieberman 1971; Lieberman 1987; Singer and Ofshe 1990).

Contemporary thought-reform programs are generally far more sophisticated in their selection of both destabilization and influence techniques than were the programs studied during the 1950s (see Ofshe and Singer 1986 for a review). For example, hypnosis was entirely absent from the first programs studied but is often observed in modern programs. In most modern examples in which hypnosis is present, it functions as a remarkably powerful technique for manipulating subjective experience and for intensifying emotional response. It provides a method for influencing people to imagine impossible events such as those that supposedly occurred in their "past lives," the future, or during visits to other planets. If persons so manipulated misidentify the hypnotically induced fantasies, and classify them as previously unavailable memories, their confidence in the content of a particular ideology can be increased (Bainbridge and Stark 1980).

Hypnosis can also be used to lead people to allow themselves to relive actual traumatic life events (e.g., rape, childhood sexual abuse, near-death experiences, etc.) or to fantasize the existence of such events and, thereby, stimulate the experience of extreme emotional distress. When imbedded in a reform program, repeatedly leading the person to experience such events can function simply as punishment, useful for coercing compliance.

Accounts of contemporary programs also describe the use of sophisticated techniques intended to strip away psychological defenses, to induce regression to primitive levels of coping, and to flood targets with powerful emotion (Ayalla 1985; Haaken and Adams 1983; Hockman 1984; Temerlin and Temerlin 1982). In some instances stress and fatigue have been used to promote hallucinatory experiences that are defined as therapeutic (Gerstel 1982). Drugs have been used to facilitate disinhibition and heightened suggestibility (Watkins 1980). Thought-reform subjects have been punished for disobedience by being ordered to self-inflict severe pain, justified by the claim that the result will be therapeutic (Bellack et al. *v.* Murietta Foundation et al.).

Programs of coercive persuasion appear in various forms in contemporary society. They depend on the voluntary initial participation of targets. This is usually accomplished because the target assumes that there is a common goal that unites him or her with the organization or that involvement will confer some benefit (e.g., relief of symptoms, personal growth, spiritual development, etc.). Apparently some programs were developed based on the assumption that they could be used to facilitate desirable changes (e.g., certain rehabilitation or psychotherapy programs). Some religious organizations and social movements utilize them for recruitment purposes. Some commercial organizations utilize them as methods for promoting sales. Under unusual circumstances, modern police-interrogation methods can exhibit some of the properties of a thought-reform program. In some instances, reform programs appear to have been operated for the sole purpose of gaining a high degree of control over individuals to facilitate their exploitation (Ofshe 1986; McGuire and Norton 1988; Watkins 1980).

Virtually any acknowledged expertise or authority can serve as a power base to develop the social structure necessary to carry out thought reform. In the course of developing a new form of rehabilitation, psychotherapy, religious organization, utopian community, school, or sales organization it is not difficult to justify the introduction of thought-reform procedures.

Perhaps the most famous example of a thought-reforming program developed for the ostensible purpose of rehabilitation was Synanon, a drug-treatment program (Sarbin and Adler 1970, Yablonsky 1965; Ofshe et al. 1974). The Synanon environment possessed all of Lifton's eight themes. It used as its principle coercive procedure a highly aggressive encounter/therapy group interaction. In form it resembled "struggle groups" observed in China (Whyte 1976), but it differed in content. Individuals were vilified and humiliated not for past political behavior but for current conduct as well as far more psychologically intimate subjects, such as early childhood experiences, sexual experiences, degrading experiences as adults, etc. The coercive power of the group experience to affect behavior was substantial as was its ability to induce psychological injury (Lieberman, Yalom, and Miles 1973; Ofshe et al. 1974).

Allegedly started as a drug-rehabilitation program, Synanon failed to accomplish significant long-term rehabilitation. Eventually, Synanon's leader, Charles Diederich, promoted the idea that any degree of drug abuse was incurable and that persons so afflicted needed to spend their lives in the Synanon community. Synanon's influence program was successful in convincing many that this was so. Under Diederich's direction, Synanon evolved from an organization that espoused nonviolence into one that was violent. Its soldiers were dispatched to assault and attempt to murder persons identified by Diederich as Synanon's enemies (Mitchell, Mitchell, and Ofshe 1981).

The manipulative techniques of self-styled messiahs, such as People's Temple leader Jim Jones

(Reiterman 1982), and influence programs operated by religious organizations, such as the Unification Church (Taylor 1978) and Scientology (Wallis 1977; Bainbridge and Stark 1980), can be analyzed as thought-reform programs. The most controversial recruitment system operated by a religious organization in recent American history was that of the Northern California branch of the Unification Church (Reverend Moon's organization). The influence program was built directly from procedures of psychological manipulation that were commonplace in the human-potential movement (Bromley and Shupe 1981). The procedures involved various group-based exercises as well as events designed to elicit from participants information about their emotional needs and vulnerabilities. Blended into this program was content intended to slowly introduce the newcomer to the group's ideology. Typically, the program's connection with the Unification Church or any religious mission was denied during the early stages of the reform process. The target was monitored around the clock and prevented from communicating with peers who might reinforce doubt and support a desire to leave. The physical setting was an isolated rural facility far from public transportation.

Initial focus on personal failures, guilt-laden memories, and unfulfilled aspirations shifted to the opportunity to realize infantile desires and idealistic goals, by affiliating with the group and its mission to save the world. The person was encouraged to develop strong affective bonds with current members. They showed unfailing interest, affection, and concern, sometimes to the point of spoon-feeding the person's meals and accompanying the individual everywhere, including to the toilet. If the *unfreezing* and *change* phases of the program succeeded, the individual was told of the group's affiliation with the Unification Church and assigned to another unit of the organization within which *re-freezing* procedures could be carried forward.

Influence procedures now commonly used during modern police interrogation can sometimes inadvertently manipulate innocent persons' beliefs about their own innocence and, thereby, cause them to falsely confess. Confessions resulting from accomplishing the *unfreezing* and *change* phases of thought reform are classified as coerced-internalized false confessions (Kassin and Wrightsman 1985; Gudjonsson and MacKeith 1988). Although they rarely come together simultaneously, the ingredients necessary to elicit a temporarily believed false confession are: erroneous police suspicion, the use of *certain* commonly employed interrogation procedures, and some degree of psychological vulnerability in the suspect. Philip Zimbardo (1971) has reviewed the coercive factors generally present in modern interrogation settings. Richard Ofshe (1989) has identified those influence procedures that if present in a suspect's interrogation contribute to causing *unfreezing* and *change*.

Techniques that contribute to *unfreezing* include falsely telling a suspect that the police have evidence proving the person's guilt (e.g., fingerprints, eyewitness testimony, etc.). Suspects may be given a polygraph examination and then falsely told (due either to error or design) that they failed and the test reveals their unconscious knowledge of guilt. Suspects may be told that their lack of memory of the crime was caused by an alcohol- or drug-induced blackout, was repressed, or is explained because the individual is a multiple personality.

The techniques listed above regularly appear in modern American police interrogations. They are used to lead persons who know that they have committed the crime at issue to decide that the police have sufficient evidence to convict them or to counter typical objections to admitting guilt (e.g., "I can't remember having done that."). In conjunction with the other disorienting and distressing elements of a modern accusatory interrogation, these tactics can sometimes lead innocent suspects to doubt themselves and question their lack of knowledge of the crime. If innocent persons subjected to these sorts of influence techniques do not reject the false evidence and realize that the interrogators are lying to them, they have no choice but to doubt themselves.

Tactics used to *change* the suspect's position and elicit a confession include maneuvers designed to intensify feelings of guilt and emotional distress following from the suspect's assumption of guilt. Suspects may be offered an escape from the emotional distress through confession. It may also be suggested that confession will provide evidence of remorse that will benefit the suspect in court.

Thought reform is not an easy process to study for several reasons. The extraordinary totalistic qualities and hyperorganization of thought-reforming environments, together with the exceptional nature of the influence tactics that appear within them, put the researcher in a position roughly analogous to that of an anthropologist entering into or interviewing someone about a culture that is utterly foreign. The researcher cannot assume that he or she understands or even knows the norms of the new environment. This means that until the researcher is familiar with the constructed environment within which the reform process takes place, it is dangerous to make the routine assumptions about context that underlie research within one's own culture. This problem extends to vocabulary as well as to norms and social structure.

The history of research on the problem has been one in which most of the basic descriptive work has been conducted through post-hoc interviewing of persons exposed to the procedures. The second-most frequently employed method has been that of participant observation. Recently, in connection with work being done on police interrogation methods, it has been possible to analyze contemporaneous recordings of interrogation sessions in which targets' beliefs are actually made to undergo radical change. All this work has contributed to the development of an understanding of the thought-reform phenomenon in several ways.

Studying the reform process demonstrates that it is no more or less difficult to understand than any other complex social process and produces no results to suggest that something new has been discovered. The only aspect of the reform process that one might suggest is new, is the order in which the influence procedures are assembled and the degree to which the target's environment is manipulated in the service of social control. This is at most an unusual arrangement of commonplace bits and pieces.

Work to date has helped establish a dividing line between the lurid fantasies about mysterious methods for stripping one's capacity to resist control and the reality of the power of appropriately designed social environments to influence the behavior and decisions of those engaged by them. Beyond debunking myths, information gathered to date has been used in two ways to further the affirmative understanding of thought reform: It has been possible to develop descriptions of the social structure of thought-reforming environments, of their operations, and to identify the range of influence mechanisms they tend to incorporate; the second use of these data has been to relate the mechanisms of influence present in the reform environment to respondents' accounts of their reactions to these experiences, to increase understanding of both general response tendencies to types of influence mechanisms and the reactions of particular persons to the reform experience.

As it is with all complex, real-world social phenomena that cannot be studied experimentally, understanding information about the thought-reform process proceeds through the application of theories that have been independently developed. Explaining data that describe the type and organization of the influence procedures that constitute a thought-reform process depends on applying established social-psychological theories about the manipulation of behavior and attitude change. Assessing reports about the impact on the experiences of the personalities subjected to intense influence procedures depends on the application of current theories of personality formation and change. Understanding instances in which the reform experience appears related to psychiatric injury requires proceeding as one would ordinarily in evaluating any case history of a stress-related or other type of psychological injury.

(SEE ALSO: *Attitudes; Persuasion; Social Control*)

## REFERENCES

Ayalla, Marybeth 1985 "Insane Therapy: Case Study of the Social Organization of a Psychotherapy Cult." Ph.D. diss., University of California, Berkeley.

Bainbridge, William S., and Rodney Stark 1980 "Scientology, to Be Perfectly Clear." *Sociological Analysis* 41:128–136.

Bellack, Catherine et al. *v.* Murietta Foundation et al. United States District Court, Central District of California. Civil No. 87–08597.

Bem, Darryl 1972 "Self-Perception Theory." In Leonard Berkowitz, ed. *Advances in Experimental Social Psychology,* vol 6. New York: Academic.

Biderman, Albert D. 1960 "Social-Psychological Needs and Involuntary Behavior as Illustrated by Compliance in Interrogation." *Sociometry* 23:120–147.

Bromley, David G., and Anson D. Shupe, Jr. 1981 *Strange Gods.* Boston: Beacon Press.

Dornbush, Sanford M. 1955 "The Military Academy as an Assimilating Institution. *Social Forces* 33:316–321.

Farber, I. E., Harry F. Harlow, and Louis J. West 1956 "Brainwashing, Conditioning and DDD: Debility, Dependency and Dread." *Sociometry* 20:271–285.

Festinger, Leon 1957 *A Theory of Cognitive Dissonance.* Evanston, Ill.: Row Peterson.

Gerstel, David 1982 *Paradise Incorporated: Synanon.* Novato, Calif.: Presidio.

Glass, Leonard L., Michael A. Kirsch, and Frederick A. Parris 1977 "Psychiatric Disturbances Associated with Erhard Seminars Training: I. A Report of Cases." *American Journal of Psychiatry* 134:245–247.

Goffman, Erving 1957 "On the Characteristics of Total Institutions." Proceedings of the Symposium on Preventive and Social Psychiatry. Washington, D.C.: Walter Reed Army Institute of Research.

Gudjonsson, Gisli H., and James A. MacKeith 1988 "Retracted Confessions: Legal, Psychological and Psychiatric Aspects." *Medical Science and Law* 28:187–194.

Haaken, Janice, and Richard Adams 1983 "Pathology as 'Personal Growth': A Participant Observation Study of Lifespring Training." *Psychiatry* 46:270–280.

Heide, F. J., and T. D. Borkovec 1984 "Relaxation Induced Anxiety: Mechanism and Theoretical Implications." *Behavior Research and Therapy* 22:1–12.

Higget, Anna C., and Robin M. Murray 1983 "A

Psychotic Episode Following Erhard Seminars Training." *Acta Psychiatria Scandinavia* 67:436–439.

Hinkle, L. E., and Harold G. Wolfe 1956 "Communist Interrogation and Indoctrination of Enemies of the State." *Archives of Neurology and Psychiatry* 20:271–285.

Hochman, John A. 1984 "Iatrogenic Symptoms Associated with a Therapy Cult: Examination of an Extinct 'New Therapy' with Respect to Psychiatric Deterioration and 'Brainwashing'." *Psychiatry* 47:366–377.

Hulme, Kathryn 1956 *The Nun's Story*. Boston: Little, Brown.

Hunter, Edward 1951 *Brain-washing in China*. New York: Vanguard.

Kassin, Samuel, and Lawrence Wrightsman 1985 "Confession Evidence." In Samuel Kassin and Lawrence Wrightsman, eds., *The Psychology of Evidence and Trial Procedure*. London: Sage.

Kirsch, Michael A., and Leonard L. Glass 1977 "Psychiatric Disturbances Associated with Erhard Seminars Training: II. Additional Cases and Theoretical Considerations." *American Journal of Psychiatry* 134:1254–1258.

Lieberman, Morton A. 1987 "Effect of Large Group Awareness Training on Participants' Psychiatric Status." *American Journal of Psychiatry*, 144:460–464.

Lieberman, Morton A., Irvin D. Yalom, and M. B. Miles 1973 *Encounter Groups: First Facts*. New York: Basic Books.

Lifton, Robert J. 1954 "Home by Ship: Reaction Patterns of American Prisoners of War Repatriated from North Korea." *American Journal of Psychiatry* 110:732–739.

——— 1961 *Thought Reform and the Psychology of Totalism*. New York: Norton.

——— 1986 *The Nazi Doctors*. New York: Basic Books.

——— 1987 "Cults: Totalism and Civil Liberties." In Robert J. Lifton, ed., *The Future of Immortality and Other Essays for a Nuclear Age*. New York: Basic Books.

Mitchell, David V., Catherine Mitchell, and Richard J. Ofshe 1981 *The Light on Synanon*. New York: Seaview.

Marks, John 1979 *The Search for the Manchurian Candidate*. New York: Dell.

McGuire, Christine, and Carla Norton 1988 *Perfect Victim*. New York: Arbor House.

Meerloo, Jorst A. 1956 *The Rape of the Mind: The Psychology of Thought Control, Menticide and Brainwashing*. Cleveland, Ohio: World Publishing.

Ofshe, Richard J. 1980 "The Social Development of the Synanon Cult: The Managerial Strategy of Organizational Transformation." *Sociological Analysis* 41:109–127.

——— 1986 "The Rabbi and the Sex Cult." *Cultic Studies Journal* 3:173–189.

——— 1989 "Coerced Confessions: The Logic of Seemingly Irrational Action." *Cultic Studies Journal* 6:1–15.

———, and Margaret T. Singer 1986 "Attacks on Peripheral Versus Central Elements of Self and the Impact of Thought Reforming Techniques." *Cultic Studies Journal* 3:3–24.

———, Nancy Eisenberg, Richard Coughlin, and Gregory Dolinajec 1974 "Social Structure and Social Control in Synanon." *Voluntary Action Research* 3:67–76.

Reiterman, Timothy, and Dan Jacobs 1982 *The Raven*. New York: Dutton.

Sarbin, Theodore R., and Nathan Adler 1970 "Self-Reconstitution Processes: A Preliminary Report." *Psychoanalytic Review* 4:599–616.

Sargent, William 1957 *Battle for the Mind: How Evangelists, Psychiatrists, and Medicine Men Can Change Your Beliefs and Behavior*. Garden City, N.Y.: Doubleday.

Schein, Edgar W. 1961 *Coercive Persuasion*. New York: Norton.

———, W. E. Cooley, and Margaret T. Singer 1960 *A Psychological Follow-up of Former Prisoners of the Chinese Communists*, Part I, *Results of Interview Study*. Cambridge: MIT.

Shurmann, Franz 1968 *Ideology and Organization in Communist China*. Berkeley: University of California Press.

Singer, Margaret T., and Richard J. Ofshe 1990 "Thought Reform Programs and the Production of Psychiatric Casualties." *Psychiatric Annals* 20:188–193.

Taylor, David 1978 "Social Organization and Recruitment in the Unification Church." Master's diss., University of Montana.

Temerlin, Maurice K., and Jane W. Temerlin 1982 "Psychotherapy Cults: An Iatrogenic Phenomenon." *Psychotherapy Theory, Research Practice* 19:131–41.

Thomas, Gordon 1989 *Journey Into Madness*. New York: Bantam.

Wallis, Roy 1977 *The Road to Total Freedom*. New York: Columbia University Press.

Watkins, Paul 1980 *My Life With Charles Manson*. New York: Bantam.

Whyte, Martin K. 1976 *Small Groups and Political*

*Behavior in China.* Berkeley: University of California Press.

Wright, Stewart 1987 *Leaving Cults: The Dynamics of Defection.* Society of the Scientific Study of Religion, Monograph no. 7, Washington, D.C.

Yablonski, Louis 1965 *The Tunnel Back: Synanon.* New York: Macmillan.

Yalom, Irvin D., and Morton Lieberman 1971 "A Study of Encounter Group Casualties." *Archives of General Psychiatry* 25:16–30.

Zablocki, Benjamin 1991 *The Scientific Investigation of the Brainwashing Conjecture.* American Association for the Advancement of Science, Washington, D.C.

Zimbardo, Philip G. 1971 "Coercion and Compliance." In Charles Perruci and Mark Pilisuk, eds., *The Triple Revolution.* Boston: Little, Brown.

RICHARD J. OFSHE

## COGNITIVE CONSISTENCY THEORIES

Cognitive consistency theories refer to a class of theories that began to emerge in the 1940s and serve as the precursors of contemporary theories of social cognition. The basic premise of all cognitive consistency theories is that persons strive to maintain consistency among their cognitions. That is, people attempt to maintain consistency between their beliefs and their actions and between their views of themselves, their views of others, and their views of objects within the environment.

Cognitions or cognitive elements are seen as existing within a cognitive structure. Depending on the theory, cognitive elements are defined as schemata, attributes, propositions, expectancies, attitudes, knowledge, beliefs, categories, and the like. Cognitive structure refers to the interdependence among the elements, often viewed as a gestalt-like cohesive force governed by principles of perceptual organization (e.g., proximity, continuation, common fate, etc.). Inconsistency among the elements, variously referred to as imbalance, asymmetry, incongruity, and dissonance, is assumed to produce tension or discomfort that motivates the person to reduce it.

There are several major variations on the general notion of cognitive consistency. Specific theories differ in their focus, in their range of application, in the psychological state that results from cognitive inconsistency, and in the steps taken to reduce it. Four of the most influential theories of cognitive consistency are balance theory (Heider 1946), A-B-X theory (Newcomb 1953), congruity theory (Osgood and Tannenbaum 1955), and cognitive dissonance theory (Festinger 1957).

### BALANCE THEORY

Heider (1946) was the first to formalize the concept of balance or consistency by focusing on the pressure toward cognitive consistency in three-element structures. Heider posited two types of relations among cognitive elements in the structure: (1) unit relations, which refer to whether the elements are seen as being connected, and (2) sentiment relations, which involve positive or negative attitudes or feelings toward the elements. Relationships among the three elements can be viewed as having either a positive (+) or negative (−) valence. For example, if person P likes some other person O, and O likes some object X, then there will be a tendency for P to like X also. In general, a balanced state exists if the product of all three signs is positive. Thus, (+ + +) and (+ − −) are balanced, but (+ + −) is not. Balance can be achieved by changing either sentiment relations or unit relations. Cartwright and Harary (1956) extended these principles of balance to cognitive structures of any size.

### THE A-B-X MODEL

Newcomb (1953) extended the balance model to include communicative acts. Newcomb's approach assumes that an important function of communication is to allow people to establish and maintain similar views toward one another and toward relevant issues and objects of joint concern. Communication allows interpersonal relations to operate smoothly by allowing for the development of common interests, by making the behavior of others more predictable, and by providing social validation for one's own views.

There are four basic components of the A-B-X system: (1) person A's attitude toward object X; (2) person B's attitude toward X; (3) person A's attraction to person B; and (4) person B's attraction to person A. These relations can be assessed in terms of both sign and intensity. For example, if person A likes person B and has a positive attitude toward object X, while person B likes A but has an unfavorable opinion toward X, the relations among elements are asymmetrical, and there will be a strain toward symmetry. Symmetry can be achieved by modifying aspects of the system with regard to object X, by modifying aspects of the system with regard to the other person, or tolerating the asymmetry without change.

## THE CONGRUITY THEORY

The congruity theory, put forth by Osgood and Tannenbaum (1955), is a much more restricted form of the consistency model. Congruity theory is basically an extension of an earlier body of research referred to as "prestige suggestion," which focuses on the relationship between attitudes and judgments. The theory is concerned primarily with predicting attitude change that results from the acquisition of new information about cognitions that have different valences.

There are three primary elements affecting congruity: (1) a source; (2) a concept; and (3) an assertion made by the source about the concept. So long as the source and concept are not linked by an assertion, the issue of congruity does not arise. But, for example, when a well-liked politician endorses an unpopular position, incongruity arises, and there is a tendency for the evaluations of both source and object to shift to a new position of equilibrium. Specifically, there is a tendency to evaluate the politician less favorably and the political position more favorably. Both objects do not change equally in evaluation, however. The more polarized object in either positive or negative direction changes proportionally less than the less polarized object. Osgood and Tannenbaum provide precise mathematical estimates of change, along with (1) a correction for incredu-

lity when widely divergent objects are linked, and (2) an assertion constant that is added when predicting attitude change toward the object of an assertion.

## COGNITIVE DISSONANCE THEORY

Another variant on the cognitive consistency theme is cognitive dissonance theory, formulated by Festinger (1957). Cognitive dissonance theory is, undoubtedly, the most important of the cognitive consistency theories for two reasons: (1) it is much broader in scope and application, and (2) it has generated more research and controversy than perhaps any other social psychological theory.

"Dissonance" refers to an inconsistency between two or more cognitive elements. Specifically: "Two elements are in dissonant relation if, considering these two alone, the obverse of one element would follow from the other" (Festinger 1957, p. 13). For example, the two cognitions (1) liking a political candidate and (2) intending to vote for the opposition candidate are in a dissonant relation. In most situations, however, more than two elements are likely to be involved because a single cognition can be related to many others.

Dissonance is presumed to produce a noxious state motivating the individual to restore consonance. The greater the dissonance, the greater the motivation to reduce it. Dissonance reduction generally implies at least one of the following processes: (1) changing behavior; (2) changing cognitions; (3) adding new cognitions; or (4) changing the importance of one or more of the consonant or dissonant cognitions.

Dissonance theory has been put forth to explain a broad range of behavior including postdecision processes, attitudinal change when there is insufficient justification for behavior, the effects of holding contrary or unpopular beliefs, and information seeking and exposure to discrepant information. Certain ambiguities and overgeneralizations in the original formulation of the theory and subsequent research findings have prompted a number of modifications and restrictions to the original theory. For example, Brehm and Cohen (1962) suggested that volition and commitment may be necessary to arouse dissonance. Festinger (1964) conceded the need for commitment and restricted the conditions of post-decision dissonance in his revision of the theory. Deutsch and Krauss (1965) argued for the necessity of justifying one's behavior; Aronson (1968) focused on the implications for one's self-concept; and Wicklund and Brehm (1976) noted the need for personal responsibility for one's actions. More recently, Cooper and Fazio (1984) have argued that the pressure toward attitude change occurs only when the person labels the arousal state negatively and accepts responsibility for an unwanted outcome.

## CURRENT STATUS OF CONSISTENCY THEORIES

Since the 1960s, there has been a substantial drop in the overall importance of cognitive consistency theories. Reasons for the decline vary (e.g., see Berkowitz and Devine 1989; Lord 1989), but emphasis in social cognition research has clearly moved away from dynamic, motivational processes toward more affectively neutral, information-processing models. Recently, however, Markus and Zajonc (1985) have noted that a complete understanding of cognitive processes may be impossible apart from considerations of affective and motivational factors and explicit linkages to overt behavior. Thus, an ultimate return to the concerns of the consistency theories may be inevitable.

(SEE ALSO: *Decision-Making Theory and Research; Social Psychology*)

### REFERENCES

Aronson, Elliot 1968 "Dissonance Theory: Progress and Problems." In Robert Abelson, Elliot Aronson, William McGuire, Theodore Newcomb, Milton Rosenberg, and Percy Tannenbaum, eds., *Theories of Cognitive Consistency: A Source Book.* Skokie, Ill.: Rand McNally.
—— 1989 "Analysis, Synthesis, and Treasuring of the Old." *Personality and Social Psychology Bulletin* 15:508–512.

Berkowitz, Leonard, and Patricia Devine 1989 "Research Traditions, Analysis, and Synthesis in Social Psychological Theories: The Case of Dissonance Theory." *Personality and Social Psychology Bulletin* 15:493–507.

Brehm, Jack, and Arthur Cohen 1962 *Explorations in Cognitive Dissonance.* New York: Wiley.

Cartwright, Dorwin, and Frank Harary 1956 "Structural Balance: A Generalization of Heider's Theory." *Psychological Review* 63:277–293.

Cooper, Joel, and Russell H. Fazio 1984 "A New Look at Dissonance Theory." In L. Berkowitz, ed., *Advances in Experimental Social Psychology.* Vol. 17. New York: Academic Press.

Deutsch, Morton, and Robert Krauss 1965 *Theories in Social Psychology.* New York: Basic Books.

Festinger, Leon 1957 *A Theory of Cognitive Dissonance.* Stanford, Calif.: Stanford University Press.

—— 1964 *Conflict, Decision, and Dissonance.* Stanford, Calif.: Stanford University Press.

Heider, Fritz 1946 "Attitudes and Cognitive Organization." *Journal of Psychology* 21:107–112.

Lord, Charles 1989 "The 'Disappearance' of Dissonance in an Age of Relativism." *Personality and Social Psychology Bulletin* 15:513–518.

Markus, Hazel, and Robert Zajonc 1985 "The Cognitive Perspective in Social Psychology." In Gardner Lindzey and Elliot Aronson, eds., *The Handbook of Social Psychology.* New York: Random House.

Newcomb, Theodore 1953 "An Approach to the Study of Communicative Acts." *Psychological Review* 60:393–404.

Osgood, Charles, and Percy Tannenbaum 1955 "The Principle of Congruity in the Prediction of Attitude Change." *Psychological Review* 62:42–55.

Wicklund, Robert, and Jack Brehm 1976 *Perspectives on Cognitive Dissonance.* Hillsdale, N.J.: Erlbaum.

KARL KOSLOSKI

## COGNITIVE-DISSONANCE THEORY
*See* Cognitive Consistency Theories.


## COHABITATION *See* Alternative Life-Styles; Courtship.

# COHORT ANALYSIS

**COHORT ANALYSIS** Cohort analysis is a format for studying social change. Here its technical aspects are considered; substantive issues are presented elsewhere (see "Cohort Approaches in the Sociological Age"). Principles are exemplified for fertility inquiry, the most common application.

Cohort analysis of the fertility of a set of women requires the birthdate of each woman and the birthdates of her offspring. These identify the passage of personal time in terms of the woman's age, and locate the record in historical time. A birth cohort is the subset of women born during a specified time interval. Observations of temporal change in any parameter of lifetime fertility may be made by two modes of temporal aggregation: the period mode, that is, the behavior across cohorts, period by period; and the cohort mode, that is, the behavior across periods, cohort by cohort (Ryder 1982).

The period mode is characteristic of data originating by event registration; the cohort mode is characteristic of data obtained by census or survey. Demographers systematically relate occurrences to (person-years of) exposure (to risk). In the period mode, one identifies the occurrences and then looks back in time to determine the exposure; in the cohort mode, one identifies the exposure and then looks forward in time to determine the occurrences. Prior to the use of surveys to collect birth histories, a practical consideration favoring the period mode for time series purposes was that registration was annual but enumeration decennial.

The time of observation of an individual ($P$ for period), the time of the individual's birth ($C$ for cohort), and the individual's age ($A$) form an identity: $P = C + A$. When respondent information is classified with interval codes, the common practice is to establish explicit intervals for $P$ and $A$ so that $C$ ends up as an approximate derivation from them. Likewise, it is the common practice to display data for some variable in age rows and period columns (or vice versa), with the implicit consequence that commonality within and differentiation among cohorts must be sought along and across the diagonals. An elementary precept for promoting cohort analysis is accordingly the consideration of alternative coding procedures and tabular arrangements, and description of the findings in terms of all three members of the triad, to preclude neglect of a possibly important direction of interpretation.

A table displaying the values of some variable, such as an age-specific birth rate, over age and time, may be summarized in time series form by calculating some parameter of the total reproductive experience and examining changes in it over time. With the period mode of aggregation, the total fertility rate, for example, is a summation over all ages for a particular period; with the cohort mode, it is a summation of those rates for which the difference between period and age is some fixed value. Ordinarily the time series of period and cohort total fertility rates diverge. It has been shown that the source of divergence is the distribution of cohort fertility by age, and especially the change in the mean age of fertility from cohort to cohort (Ryder 1983). This is a particular instance of a like relation observed over a wide range of isomorphic phenomena, between change in time pattern, and its quantum consequence. For example, a lowering of the age at which a child may enter kindergarten will increase the kindergarten enrollment; a raising of the age at which social security payments may begin without penalty will reduce the disbursements for social security.

Two general points derive from these considerations: (1) An analyst should be sensitive to the possibility of a change in the age pattern of a phenomenon of interest when considering a time series of the incidence of the phenomenon; (2) since there are two different time series resulting from the two modes of temporal aggregation of age-specific data, the analyst is obliged to consider the conceptual basis for one or the other choice. Rationales for the distinctive importance of the three pieces of temporal information—$C$, $P$, and $A$—are readily forthcoming. Many attempts have been made to resist the choice between period and cohort modes of aggregation by purporting to measure the independent role played by each, using an analysis-of-variance format (Mason and Fienberg 1985). All such attempts must confront the identification problem, that is, although one may have convincing arguments for the independent importance of each of the three variables, there is no way to give them separate roles in statistical analysis because each of the three is either the sum or the difference of the other two. Stated most simply, the problem is that one obtains from the evidence two equations in three unknowns. A solution requires a third equation. When different investigators create that equation in different ways, they generate idiosyncratic estimates of the comparative magnitudes of the three effects. Such activities seem otiose (Glenn 1977).

The three proxies, C, P, and A, are generally treated as stimuli of formal equivalence, each of which elicits a response, yet the cohort is a set of actors and the age is their age. The period stands for the context within which the behavior occurs. An alternative view then is that the behavior of actors age by age constitutes a meaningful configuration, with unique location in the stream of history, and showing the stigmata of period-based stimuli.

The source of the identification problem is the resort to primitive proxies for complex determinants. In a statistical sense, the problem vanishes when one or more direct measures of the proposed vector of influence is substituted for at least one of the proxies. The identity, $P = C + A$, is moreover prejudicial to experimental design because it implies imbalance in the data set. Ordinarily data are provided by period by age: The earliest cohorts are represented only in the oldest ages and the latest cohorts only in the youngest ages. In comparing two successive differently censored cohort histories, Hobson's choice is to compare only what is available for both or estimate the missing segment. The former wastes data and begs the question of the comparability of behavior by age. The latter leads to different outcomes with different assumptions. If a cohort has had relatively high fertility up to the last observation, that may signify high fertility thereafter, or it may signify low fertility thereafter. This is the translation problem in another guise.

For the indicated practical reasons, the period mode of temporal aggregation has been preferred. Given a cross section of behavior, age by age, the temptation is almost irresistible to see it as consecutive life. The archetypical example is the conventional life table, the cohort equivalent of which would take more than a century of observations. (Most demographic measurement is in the life table image, including its synthetic cohort construction.) The problem is inherent in the study of a long-lived species experiencing social change.

When data permit, the cohort mode of temporal aggregation is preferable for the analysis of time series of fertility, and inferentially for other forms of social behavior. Consider the contributions to explanation of fertility of a cohort in a period, where "period" is a proxy for the contemporaneous environment, and "cohort" is a proxy for the histories of the actors viewed collectively. Time series of fertility indices show short-term deviations in one and then the other direction. Every cohort displaces fertility in time away from bad years and toward good years; the period consequence is decline or rise in the quantum of fertility. The movement of the period index pinpoints where to look for the source of the disturbance, but the response by the actors is a time-pattern change, requiring examination of the cohort history. Some period-oriented change represents a discontinuous deformation of the environment thereafter, for example, passage of legislation or introduction of technological innovation. Again the period indices locate the source in time, but cohort histories must be considered to gauge the response. It would be difficult to imagine a period stimulus to which the cohorts affected did not respond differently.

Long-term change is the most important subject for time series analysis. Unless there is, fortuitously, observation of its beginning or end, there is no statistical way to attribute its source to the succession of cohorts or the succession of periods. Some analyses modeled variously, to attempt to avoid the identification problem, purport to demonstrate that, in the time series of American fertility, the period "effect" is stronger than the cohort "effect" (Hobcraft, Menken, and Preston 1982). Given that short-term effects are typically period-inspired, and long-term effects are unassignable except by fiat, the finding is unsurprising and unrewarding.

Fertility analyses only begin with a delineation of movements over time. Then fertility is considered with reference to the characteristics of the actors. Typical candidates are demographic data (age, parity, length of interval since last birth) and sociocultural data (education, occupation, rural background, religion). All of these are shorthand summaries of the histories of the actors constituting the cohort. If individuals arrived in each period *tabula rasa*, the focus of the inquiry is properly what the period is a surrogate for. Since that assumption is untenable, the appropriate injunction is to consider the relevance of cumulated experience for response to the environmental stimulus.

Now that demographers have access to detailed survey data, their practice is to shift attention from overt fertility to its proximate determinants. These inquiries into fecundability, contraceptive efficacy, and the like make biologically explicit and precise the concept of exposure to risk, from one pregnancy interval to the next. Without exception, the evidence is in cohort form. One cannot fully exploit the richness of survey data about these instrumental variables to explain fertility if the measures of overt fertility remain cast in the period mode.

Less tractable statistically than the foregoing conventional variables, but no less relevant to the understanding of change in fertility, are the strands of experience that lend integrity to life. The individual actor brings into each successive period mental constructs, such as knowledge and beliefs, established structures of relationship, such as family membership, and long-term commitments, economic and moral. Individuals are disposed to make and execute plans; these establish links between what happens at one time and

what happens at another. Thus, the successive events in an individual history acquire an interpretable configuration. The continuity of individual experience represented by these influential and enduring properties speaks for a cohort mode of temporal aggregation.

Why then has the period mode remained dominant in time series measurement? The first reason is that data are collected period by period: Period indices are convenient to calculate, whereas cohort histories are generally censored. Second, the purposes of data collection ordinarily include administration and policy: The orientation is not to the explanation of the phenomenon so much as to coping with its consequences, and for that the period measures are well suited. In the third place, the period-specific events are dramatic: war, depression, calamity, and Supreme Court rulings on abortion. They make a better story than the relentless creep of the glacier of social change. Analysis of reproductive behavior for successive periods rarely uses indices of the phenomenon more sophisticated than the crude birthrate or the period total fertility rate. The reason is that more sophisticated measures are uninterpretable in the period mode.

To this point, the only cohort mentioned has been the birth cohort, yet, because of individual variability in the tempo of life cycles, this is the lowest common denominator of cohort identification. To study temporal variations in any particular form of life cycle behavior, it may prove advantageous to define successive cohorts by time of occurrence of some relevant change of status prior to the behavior in question. In fertility inquiry, for example, the birth history is often organized in a contingent sequence: The behavior of the birth cohort creates a series of (first) marriage cohorts, each marriage cohort in turn yields a series of parity one cohorts, and so forth. The birth cohort fertility–age function is the epiphenomenon resulting from a sequence of such convolutions. In other areas of inquiry use has been made of graduation cohorts, cohorts of time of entry into the labor force, retirement cohorts, and so forth (Hastings and Berry 1979).

Cohort analysis is a way to study temporal variation in behavior. The general procedure is as follows. For a set of respondents, obtain the record of time of occurrence of a cohort-defining event, generally selected because it represents the beginning of exposure to risk of occurrence of the behavior of interest. Classify the respondents in successive time intervals by reference to the cohort-defining event: Those classes are the aggregates called cohorts. For each respondent, dated observations of the behavior of interest are made and appropriate parameters calculated for each cohort. The cohort analysis consists of explanation of the temporal variations in those parameters using the characteristics of the respective cohorts in interaction with the historically specific environment.

Cohort analysis is similar to the panel study, in which measures are made on the same individuals at successive time points. From this view, the cohort record could be considered as macrobiography, the aggregate analogue of the individual life history. Yet if the purpose of cohort analysis were to explain variance in behavioral histories among individuals, it would properly be considered a blunt, inept, and possibly misleading instrument, showing merely the marginals for the underlying individual-specific data and continually running the risk of perpetrating the ecological fallacy. Cohort analysis is longitudinal in shape, but it is explicitly macroanalytic. For those interested in explanation at the individual level, it may suffice for broad-brush description but little more.

Most research based on fertility surveys is microanalytic. Although coherent accounts can be obtained from individuals to relate their reproductive behavior to their preferences and resources, these have failed to explain why aggregate fertility changes over time. Implicit in these accounts are conditions of compelling relevance for which individuals have neither responsibility nor explanation: not only biological conditions, but also macroeconomic conditions (characteristics of the local, national, and world economy), and sociocultural conditions. To exemplify the last, reproductive decisions cannot be made without consideration of the normatively expected relations between parents and children and between males and females. Change in these normative designs are probably the most influential forces underlying the decline in fertility. They are collective properties of the social system and require explanation in terms of other collective properties (Ryder 1981).

Cohort analysis is peculiarly appropriate for the study of long-term normative change, whether in reproductive institutions or elsewhere in the social structure. Norms governing or at least strongly influencing behavior are acquired in the process of socialization and are reinforced by the process of social control. Because they are internalized within the individual and become part of the self, they are unlikely to be readily supplanted by alternative formulations as these arise in the social setting.

Every social system faces the problem of persistence through time because of the inevitable loss of its individual members. The problem is solved by the admission of new cohorts, year by year. The process is replicated at every level of the system. Each new cohort is simultaneously a threat to social stability and an opportunity for social transformation. It follows that the primary vehicle for normative transformation is the continual and ubiquitous process of cohort succession.

The fundamental element of a population is the birth cohort. Population transformation, as distinct from individual mobility, is manifested by and produced by differences in aggregate life histories from cohort to cohort. A cohort orientation is not simply one of various analytic strategies in demographic inquiry. It is implicit in the basic population model. For the reasons indicated, it is likewise central to the study of normative change and sociocultural transformation.

The cognate procedures of cohort analysis are the parameterization of the life cycle behavior of individuals over personal time, considered in the aggregate, and the study of change in those parameters over historical time. The cohort is a conceptual device for providing a macroanalytic link between movements of individuals from one to another status and movements of the population composition from one period to the next. The congruence of social change and cohort differentiation recommends the measurement of the former by the latter.

(SEE ALSO: *Cohort Perspectives; Longitudinal Research*)

## REFERENCES

Glenn, Norval D. 1977 *Cohort Analysis*. University Papers Series Number 07–005. Beverly Hills, Calif.: Sage Publications.

Hastings, Donald W., and Linda G. Berry, eds. 1979 *Cohort Analysis: A Collection of Interdisciplinary Readings*. Oxford, Ohio: Scripps Foundation for Research in Population Problems.

Hobcraft, John, Jane Menken, and Samuel Preston 1982 "Age, Period, and Cohort Effects in Demography: A Review." *Population Index* 48(1): 4–43.

Mason, William M., and Stephen E. Fienberg, eds. 1985 *Cohort Analysis in Social Research. Beyond the Identification Problem*. New York: Springer-Verlag.

Ryder, Norman B. 1981 "Where Do Babies Come From?" In Hubert M. Blalock, ed., *Sociological Theory and Research*. New York: Free Press.

—— 1982 *Progressive Fertility Analysis*. Technical Bulletin No. 8. London: World Fertility Survey.

———— 1983 "Cohort and Period Measures of Changing Fertility." In Rodolfo A. Bulatao and Ronald D. Lee, eds., *Determinants of Fertility in Developing Countries*. New York: Academic Press.

NORMAN B. RYDER

**COHORT PERSPECTIVES** The birth cohort, or set of people born at approximately the same time, has a dual reference as an analytical tool in sociology: (1) to cohorts of people who are *aging* in particular eras of history and (2) to people from successive cohorts who occupy the age-differentiated *roles and structures* of society at sequential historical periods. The succession of cohorts, as new members enter and ultimately leave the social system, is the universal process that links aging over the life course with social structure and social change. Because society changes, members of successive cohorts age in different ways; and, conversely, when many indivi-

duals in the same cohort are affected by social change in similar ways, the alterations in their collective lives can press for alterations in social structure. Thus, diverse sociological studies use cohort perspectives (i.e., both theoretical and empirical approaches) to investigate varied aspects of the aging process, structural change, and the complex interplay between the two (for a summary, see Riley, Foner, and Waring 1988).

## CONCEPTUAL FRAMEWORK

Figure 1 schematizes the major conceptual elements implicated in these interrelated cohort perspectives (Riley, Johnson, and Foner 1972). The diagram is a social space with two time-related boundaries. The vertical axis is marked off by years of age, calling attention both to the ongoing changes that occur in people's lives as they grow older and to age criteria for entering and leaving roles. The horizontal axis is marked off by dates, calling attention to the changes—economic, political, cultural, and so forth—that occur with the passage of time in societies and their institutions.

**Aging.** The *diagonal bars* represent cohorts of people born at particular time periods who are aging from birth to death—that is, moving across time and upward with age. As they age, they are changing socially and psychologically as well as biologically; moving in and out of age-appropriate roles in school, work, and family; actively participating with role partners; and accumulating knowledge, attitudes, and experiences. The series of diagonal bars denotes how, as successive cohorts of people are continually being born, they grow older through different eras of time and are responsive to unique historical experiences until they eventually die.

**Social Structure.** The *vertical* lines at particular dates identify the people and associated roles composing the age structure of society. A single cross-sectional slice (as in 1980) indicates how people from many coexisting cohorts, who are at different stages of their lives and are involved in different social roles and institutions, are organized roughly in socially recognized age divisions or strata, from the youngest to the oldest. Over time,

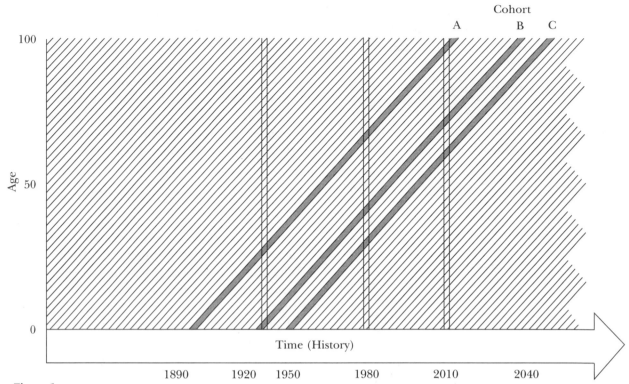

**Figure 1**
*Schematic View of Cohort Perspectives*
SOURCE: Riley, Foner, and Waring 1988 "Sociology of Age." In Neil J. Smelser, ed., *Handbook of Sociology.*
Newbury Park, Calif.: Sage.

as society moves through historical events and changes, this vertical line moves across the space from one period to the next. Over time, the age-related structures of role opportunities and norms are subjected to social and cultural changes, hence may (or may not) be shifting. But the people in particular age strata are no longer the same people; inevitably, they have been replaced by younger entrants from more recent cohorts with more recent life experiences.

This heuristic schematization, though highly oversimplified, aids understanding of sociological work that takes cohort perspectives into account. (For simplicity, the discussion here is limited to cohorts in the larger society, with entry into the system indexed by date of birth. Parallel conceptualization refers also to studies of cohorts entering other systems, such as hospitals, with entry indexed by date of admission, or the community of scientists, with entry indexed by date of the doc-

toral degree—Zuckerman and Merton 1972; here "aging" refers to duration in the particular system.)

## AGING PERSPECTIVES

Cohort perspectives on aging focus on relationships between people's lives and particular characteristics and historical backgrounds of the cohorts to which they belong.

**Intracohort Perspectives.** Many empirical studies and much conceptual work uses the "life-course approach" to trace over time the lives of members of a single cohort (e.g., Clausen 1986). As one familiar example, studies of "status attainment" investigate lifelong trajectories of achievement behaviors, using longitudinal and causal modeling to examine the interconnections among such variables as family background, scholastic achievement, succession of jobs, and employment and unemployment (cf. Featherman 1981). The intracohort perspective is used in many forms—micro and macro level, objective and subjective—in a range of studies on how people as they grow older move through diverse paths in the changing society (Dannefer 1987), how sequences of age roles and role transitions are experienced, and how aging people are articulated with societal role structures through lifelong processes of socialization and allocation.

Longitudinal studies of aging in a single cohort can contribute importantly to causal analysis by establishing the time order of correlated aspects of individual lives and their environing social structures. However, this perspective is vulnerable to possible misinterpretation through the *fallacy of "cohort-centrism,"* that is, erroneously assuming that members of all cohorts will age in exactly the same fashion as members of the cohort under study (Riley 1978). In fact, different cohorts, responding to different periods of history, can age in different ways.

**Intercohort Perspectives.** More powerful than the intracohort focus is a focus on the lives of members of two or more successive cohorts who are growing older under differing historical conditions. Studies of intercohort differences have demonstrated for other sciences what sociologists already knew: the central principle that the process of aging is not immutable or fixed for all time but varies across and within cohorts as society changes (Riley 1978). Thus, such studies have shown that members of cohorts already old differ markedly from those in cohorts not yet old in such respects as standard of living, education, work history, age of menarche, and experience with acute versus chronic diseases. And these cohort differences have pointed to possible linkages with particular social or cultural changes over historical time or with particular "period" events such as epidemics, wars, or depressions (e.g., Elder and Rockwell 1979). These linkages are useful in postulating explanations for changes—or absence of changes—in the process of aging.

Studies of cohort differences, in examining the influences of social and cultural change, focus on aging processes at either the collective or the individual level. At the collective level, the lives of members are aggregated within each cohort to examine alterations in average patterns of aging. At the individual level, cohort membership is treated as a *contextual characteristic* of the individual and then analyzed together with education, religion, and other personal characteristics to investigate how history and other factors affect the heterogeneous ways individuals grow older (e.g., Messeri 1988).

## STRUCTURAL PERSPECTIVES

Complementing sociological work on cohort differences (or similarities) in the aging process are studies of how cohort succession contributes to structural formation and change. Thus, in Figure 1, the vertical lines indicate how cohorts of people and their associated roles fit together to form the age strata of society; and how, as society changes, new cohorts of people are continually aging and entering these strata, replacing the previous incumbents.

**Cross-Sectional Perspectives.** In Figure 1 a single vertical line at a given period (as in 1980) is a cross-sectional slice through all the coexisting cohorts, each with its unique size, composition, earlier life experiences, position in the role structure, and historical background. This familiar cross-sectional view of all the age strata is often denigrated because its misinterpretation is the source of the *life-course fallacy*—that is, the erroneous assumption that cross-sectional age differences refer directly to the process of aging, hence disregarding the cohort differences that may also be implicated (Riley 1973). That people who are differentially located in the age structure of society differ not only in age but also in cohort membership was dramatized early by Karl Mannheim ([1928] 1952) and Norman Ryder (1968); yet persistent failure to comprehend this dual meaning of age has perpetuated numerous false stereotypes (e.g., that intelligence or physical functioning begin inevitable declines at very early ages).

Properly interpreted, of course, a cross-sectional perspective has its special uses: for describing current differences and similarities, social relationships, and interactions among coexisting people who differ in age-cum-cohort membership. Thus, for example, issues of "intergenerational equity" require explication, as a larger share of the federal budget is reportedly spent on cohorts of people now old than on cohorts of children (Duncan, Hill, and Rodgers 1986).

**Social Change Perspectives.** Fuller comprehension of the underlying dynamics requires going beyond the cross-sectional snapshot to a sequence of cross sections (the moving perpendicular line in Figure 1), as successive cohorts interact with historical trends to affect the age-related structures of people and roles (Ryder 1965; Riley 1982). Social change means not only that new cohorts are continually entering the system (through birth or immigration), while others are leaving it (through death or emigration). Social change also means that the members of *all* existing cohorts are simultaneously aging and thus moving from younger to older strata. People at every age are encountering the exigencies of age-related roles, being socialized for new positions, and pressing for allocation to the places held by their predecessors. As Norman Ryder puts it, "Each new cohort is simultaneously a threat to social stability and an opportunity for social transformation" (see "Cohort Analysis").

As successive cohorts move concurrently through the system, they affect the structure in several ways. They can alter the numbers and kinds of people in particular strata, because each cohort starts its life course with a characteristic size, genetic makeup, sex ratio, and other properties that are subsequently modified through migration and mortality (as men tend to die earlier than women, or blacks earlier than whites). The effects of cohort differences in size ("disordered cohort flow," Waring 1975) are forcibly brought to attention as the baby boom cohorts, followed by their smaller successors, first strained the school systems and the labor force and will become the twenty-first-century "senior boom" that will exacerbate the inadequacy of roles for the elderly.

The succession of cohorts can also affect the capacities, attitudes, and actions of people in particular strata as the members of each cohort bring to the social structure their experiences with the social and environmental events spanned by their respective lifetimes. One influence on age structuring is "cohort norm formation" (Riley 1978). As members of the same cohort respond to shared historical experiences, they gradually and subtly develop common patterns of responses, common definitions, and common beliefs that crystallize into common norms and become institutionalized in the social structure. These norms include age criteria as bases for role assignment and role performance. For example, many individual women in the cohorts currently in young adulthood have responded to common social changes by making many millions of separate but similar personal decisions to move in new directions: to go to college, have a career, or structure their family in innovative ways. Such decisions, beginning in one cohort, can gradually pervade entire segments of society, just as the new age norms for married women with children, when brought into the open, have stimulated institutionalization of new role opportunities at work and in the family for people of all ages.

Cohort perspectives are useful, not only in explaining past changes in social structure but also in improving forecasts of future changes. Unlike the more usual straight projections of cross-sectional information, forecasts based on cohorts can be informed by established facts about the past lives of people in each of the cohorts already alive (e.g., Manton 1989). Thus, if cohorts of teenagers today are indeed on the average less healthy, less cared for, or less prepared for life than their parents were at the same age (National Association of State Boards of Education 1990), their lives will, predictably, also differ in the future when both parents and offspring have grown older.

## AGING AND SOCIAL STRUCTURE

Such cohort perspectives disclose the close linkage between the two dynamisms: the aging of people in successive cohorts and cohort contributions to the changing structure of society (e.g.,

Mayer 1988). Their interrelationships are complex. Although the two are distinct and separate processes, they are in continuing interplay: Each influences the other. On the one hand, changes in social structures alter individual aging processes. On the other hand, reciprocal changes in aging cause structural change. Because cohorts differ in size and character, and their members age in new ways, they exert collective pressures for adjustments both in role opportunities throughout the social institutions and in people's age-related ideas, values, and beliefs (e.g., Foner and Kertzer 1978).

**Asynchrony.** While aging and structural change influence each other, they also contain a paradox of timing. A few moments' reflection makes it startlingly apparent that the two dynamisms are marching to different drummers. Aging individuals are moving along the axis of the life course (the diagonal lines in Figure 1). But change in the structures of society (the moving vertical line) proceeds along its own axis of historical time. These two sets of lines are continually crisscrossing each other, hence they can never be perfectly synchronized. And it is this asynchrony that produces a recurring mismatch between them—a lag of one dynamism behind the other.

Most familiar to people in their daily lives is the *lag in aging processes.* While individuals in a particular cohort are aging, the social structure is continually changing around them. Those who are old today first learned the age norms and patterns of behavior prevalent early in the century; they learned from their parents that a few years of schooling would suffice for most jobs and from their grandparents that old age comes early and can be bleak. But now that these people have grown old, social structures have outdistanced them and they must make efforts to "catch up." Similarly, cohorts of people who are young today perceive the occupational ladder as it is now, with little awareness of the fast-breaking technological innovations and accompanying changes in the age structure of the future. These young people will not be old in the same society in which they began. They, too, will be continually attempting to "catch up."

Even more critical at the close of the twentieth century is the problem of *structural lag* (Riley 1988). Aging processes have not merely been "catching up"—in many respects, they are ahead of the structural changes. Cohorts of those who are young today are dissatisfied with traditional norms of personal commitment; those in the middle years are protesting the multiple stresses of combined work and family roles; and those reaching old age are restive in the prolonged "roleless role" of retirement. Cohorts of people now old are more numerous, better educated, and more vigorous than their predecessors were in 1920 or 1950; but few changes have been made in the places for them in society, and they are still generally treated as a disadvantaged minority. Capable people and empty role structures cannot long coexist. Implicit in the asynchrony, then, are perpetual pressures toward structural change.

## A NOTE ON RESEARCH METHODS

When aspects of these broad cohort perspectives are translated into empirical studies, a wide range of research methods is required for specific objectives: from analyses of historical documents and subjective reports, to panel analyses and mathematical modeling, to rigorous tests of specific hypotheses. This brief overview can only hint at the diverse research designs involved in analyses of the multiple factors affecting lives of people in particular cohorts or of the shifting role opportunities for cohort members confronting economic, religious, political, and other social institutions (for one example, see Hendricks and Cutler 1990).

**Cohort Analysis as a Special Case.** The tool most widely used in large-scale studies is cohort analysis, which takes the intercohort aging perspective—in contrast to *period analysis* (Susser 1969), which takes the structural social change perspective. (The difference is illustrated in Figure 1 by comparison of the diagonal cohort lines, in contrast to comparison of a sequence of vertical cross-section slices.) Norman Ryder defines the term as "the parameterization of the life cycle behavior of individuals over personal time, considered in the aggregate, and the study of change in those parameters over historical time" (see "Cohort Analysis"). He also contrasts this "behavior across cohorts, period by period" with the "behavior across periods, cohort by cohort"; and he conceptualizes the cohort as "providing a macroanalytic link between movements of individuals from one to another status, and movements of the population composition from one period to the next." He makes brief reference to his own classic mathematical procedure of "demographic translation" between the cohort and the period "modes of temporal aggregation" (Ryder 1963, 1983).

Also relevant to this method is the identity problem confounding many attempts at cohort analysis. This problem occurs when three concepts used in the interpretation—age, period, and cohort ($A$, $P$, $C$)—are not each measured directly but are indexed by only two variables: date and years of age (Cohn 1972; Rodgers 1982; Riley, Foner, and Waring 1988, pp. 260–261). The confusion, which demands greater conceptual and empirical specification, is inherent in both the similarities and the differences between the dual references of cohorts to (1) people who are *aging* in particular historical eras, and (2) people from successive cohorts who occupy age-related roles in *societal structures* at sequential time periods.

Ryder's exegesis of the strengths and the limitations of this particular method illustrates the utility of the broad conceptualization of cohort perspectives as a heuristic guide. The strengths emphasize the wide significance of cohorts as a macro-analytic vehicle for social change. In the broader cohort perspectives outlined here, many other methods are useful for specific objectives where cohort analysis is inappropriate. Some employ a cross-sectional approach. Others use inter-cohort comparisons to focus on aging processes at the individual as well as the collective levels. Still others complement demographic analyses of populations with examination of the related structures of social roles and institutions.

Thus, despite its signal contributions, neither cohort analysis nor any other single method can comprehend the full power of cohorts as ingredients of aging processes, structural change, and the complex interplay between the two.

(SEE ALSO: *Cohort Analysis; Social Gerontology*)

## REFERENCES

Clausen, John A. 1986 *The Life Course: A Sociological Perspective.* Englewood Cliffs, N.J.: Prentice-Hall.

Cohn, Richard 1972 "On Interpretation of Cohort and Period Analyses: A Mathematical Note." In Matilda White Riley, Marilyn Johnson, and Anne Foner, *Aging and Society,* Vol. 3, *A Sociology of Age Stratification.* New York: Russell Sage Foundation.

Dannefer, Dale 1987 "Aging as Intracohort Differentiation: Accentuation, the Matthew Effect, and the Life Course." *Sociological Forum* 2 (Spring):211–236.

Duncan, Greg J., Martha Hill, and Willard Rodgers 1986 "The Changing Fortunes of Young and Old." *American Demographics* 8:26–34.

Elder, Glenn H., Jr., and R. C. Rockwell 1979 "Economic Depression and Postwar Opportunity in Men's Lives: A Study of Life Patterns and Mental Health." In R. G. Simmons, ed., *Research in Community and Mental Health.* Greenwich, Conn.: JAI Press.

Featherman, David L. 1981 "The Life-Span Perspective." In *The National Science Foundation's Five-Year Outlook on Science and Technology.* Washington, D.C.: U.S. Government Printing Office.

Foner, Anne, and David I. Kertzer 1978 "Transitions over the Life Course: Lessons from Age-Set Societies." *American Journal of Sociology* 83:1081–1104.

Hendricks, Jon, and Stephen J. Cutler 1990 "Leisure and the Structure of our Life Worlds." *Aging and Society* 10:85–94.

Mannheim, Karl (1928) 1952 "The Problem of Generations." In Paul Kecskemeti, ed., *Essays on the Sociology of Knowledge.* London: Routledge and Kegan Paul.

Manton, Kenneth G. 1989 "Life-Style Risk Factors." In Matilda White Riley and John W. Riley, Jr., eds., *The Quality of Aging: Strategies for Interventions.* Special issue of *The Annals* (503). Newbury Park, Calif.: Sage.

Mayer, Karl Ulrich 1988 "German Survivors of World War II: The Impact of the Life Course of the Collective Experiences of Birth Cohorts." In M. W. Riley, B. J. Huber, and B. B. Hess, eds., *Social Structures and Human Lives.* Newbury Park, Calif.: Sage.

Messeri, Peter 1988 "Age, Theory Choice, and the Complexity of Social Structure." In M. W. Riley, B. J. Huber, and B. B. Hess, eds., *Social Structures and Human Lives.* Newbury Park, Calif.: Sage.

National Association of State Boards of Education 1990 *Code Blue: Uniting for Healthier Youth.* Alexandria, Va.: National Association of State Boards of Education.

Riley, Matilda White 1973 "Aging and Cohort Succession: Interpretations and Misinterpretation." *Public Opinion Quarterly* 37:35–49.

—— 1978 "Aging, Social Change, and the Power of Ideas." *Daedalus* 107:39–52.

—— 1982 "Aging and Social Change." In Matilda White Riley, Ronald P. Abeles, and Michael S. Teitelbaum, eds., *Aging from Birth to Death.* Vol. 2, *Sociotemporal Perspectives.* AAAS Selected Symposium 79. Boulder, Colo.: Westview.

—— 1988 "The Aging Society: Problems and Prospects." *Proceedings of the American Philosophical Society* 132:148–153.

Riley, Matilda White, Anne Foner, and Joan Waring 1988 "Sociology of Age." In Neil J. Smelser, ed., *Handbook of Sociology.* Newbury Park, Calif.: Sage.

Riley, Matilda White, Marilyn Johnson, and Anne Foner 1972 *Aging and Society.* Vol. 3: *A Sociology of Age Stratification.* New York: Russell Sage Foundation.

Rodgers, Willard L. 1982 "Estimable Functions of Age, Period, and Cohort Effects." *American Sociological Review* 47:774–787.

Ryder, Norman B. 1963 "The Translation Model of Demographic Change." In Norman B. Ryder, ed., *Emerging Techniques in Population Research.* New York: Milbank Memorial Fund.

—— 1965 "The Cohort as a Concept in the Study of Social Change." *American Sociological Review* 30:843–861.

—— 1968 "Cohort Analysis." In David L. Sills, ed., *International Encyclopedia of the Social Sciences.* New York: Macmillan and Free Press.

—— 1983 "Cohort and Period Measures of Changing Fertility." In Rodolfo A. Bulatao and Ronald D. Lee, eds., *Determinants of Fertility in Developing Countries.* New York: Academic Press.

Susser, Mervyn 1969 "Aging and the Field of Public Health." In M. W. Riley, J. W. Riley, Jr., and M. E. Johnson, eds., *Aging and Society,* Vol. 2, *Aging and the Professions.* New York: Russell Sage Foundation.

Waring, Joan M. 1975 "Social Replenishment and Social Change." *American Behavioral Scientist* 19:237–256.

Zuckerman, Harriet, and Robert K. Merton 1972 "Age, Aging, and Age Structure in Science." In Matilda White Riley, Marilyn Johnson, and Anne Foner, *Aging and Society,* Vol. 3, *A Sociology of Age Stratification.* New York: Russell Sage Foundation.

MATILDA WHITE RILEY

**COLLECTIVE BEHAVIOR** Collective behavior consists of those forms of social behavior in which the usual conventions cease to guide social action and people collectively transcend, bypass, or subvert established institutional patterns and structures. As the name indicates, the behavior is collective rather than individual. Unlike small group behavior, it is not principally coordinated by each-to-each personal relationships, though such relationships do play an important part. Unlike organizational behavior, it is not coordinated by formally established goals, authority, roles, and membership designations, though emergent leadership and an informal role structure are important components. The best-known forms of collective behavior are rumor episodes; spontaneous collective response to crises such as natural disasters; crowds; collective panics; crazes, fads, and fashions; publics; cults; followings; and reform and revolutionary movements. Social movements are sometimes treated as forms of collective behavior but are often viewed as a different order of phenomena because of the degree of organization necessary to sustain social action. This essay will include only those social movement theories that also have relevance for the more elementary forms of collective behavior.

Theories of collective behavior can be classified broadly as focusing on the activity itself (micro level or interactional) or on the larger social and cultural settings within which the activity occurs (macro level or structural). An adequate theory at the micro level must answer three questions, namely: How is it that people come to transcend, bypass, or subvert institutional patterns and structures in their activity; how do people come to translate their attitudes into significant overt action; and how do people come to act collectively rather than singly? Structural theories identify the processes and conditions in culture and social structure that are conducive to the development of collective behavior.

## MICRO-LEVEL CONVERGENCE THEORIES

Micro-level theories can be further divided into *action* theories and *interaction* theories. Action or *convergence* theories assume that when a critical mass of individuals with the same disposition to act in a situation come together, collective action occurs almost automatically. The psychological hypothesis that frustration leads to aggression has been widely applied in this way to explain racial lynchings and riots, rebellion and revolution, and other forms of collective violence. Collective behavior has been conceived as a collective pursuit of meaning and personal identity when strains and imbalances in social institutions have made meaning and identity problematic (Klapp 1972). In order to explain the convergence of a critical mass of people experiencing similar frustrations, investigators posit deprivation shared by members of a social class, ethnic group, gender group, age group, or other social category. Because empirical evidence has shown consistently that the most deprived are not the most likely to engage in collective protest, more sophisticated investigators assume a condition of *relative deprivation* (Gurr 1970), or a discrepancy between expectations and actual conditions. Relative deprivation frequently follows a period of rising expectations brought on by improving conditions, then interrupted by a setback, as in the J-curve hypothesis of revolution (Davies 1962). Early explanations for collective behavior, generally contradicted by empirical evidence and repudiated by serious scholars, characterized much crowd behavior and many social movements as the work of criminals, the mentally disturbed, persons suffering from personal identity problems, and other deviants. In all convergence theories it is assumed that "the individual in the crowd behaves just as he would behave alone, *only more so,*" (Allport 1924, p. 295), meaning that individuals in collective behavior are doing what they wanted to do anyway but could not do or feared to do without the "facilitating" effect of similar behavior by others.

**Rational Decision Theories.** Several recent convergence theories assume that people make rational decisions to participate or not to participate in collective behavior, and that they make these decisions on the basis of self-interest. Two important theories of this sort are those of Richard Berk and Mark Granovetter.

Berk (1974) defines collective behavior as the behavior of people in crowds, which means activity that is transitory, not well planned, and that involves face-to-face contact among participants and considerable cooperation, though he also includes panic as competitive collective behavior. Fundamental to his theory is the assumption that crowd activity involves rational, goal-directed action, in which possible rewards and costs are considered along with the chances of support from others in the crowd. Hence, he looks to decision theory. Rational decision making means reviewing viable options, reviewing events that may occur, arranging information and choices in chronological order, evaluating the consequences of alternative courses of action, judging the chances that uncertain events will occur, and choosing actions with minimax outcomes. Since the best outcome for an individual in collective behavior depends fundamentally on what other people will do, the decision process is analyzed in terms of *game theory*. Participants attempt to advance their own interests by recruiting others and through negotiation. Berk's theory does not explain the origin and nature of the proposals for action that are heard in the crowd but describes the process by which these proposals are sifted as the crowd moves toward collaborative action, usually involving a division of labor. To explain decision making, he offers a simple equation in which the probability of a person beginning to act (e.g., to loot) is a function of the product of the net anticipated personal payoff for acting and the probability of group support in that action.

Granovetter's (1978) application of rational decision theory focuses on the concept of *threshold*. He assumes that each person, in a given situation, has a threshold number or percentage of other people who must already be engaging in a particular action before he or she will join in. Since it can be less risky for the individual to engage in collective behavior (riotous behavior, for example) when many others are doing so than when few are involved, the benefit-to-cost ratio improves as participation increases. Based on the personal importance of the action in question, individual estimation of risk, and a host of other conditions, individual thresholds will vary widely in any situation. Thresholds determine the order in which individuals will join in collective behavior. More interestingly, collective behavior cannot develop without low-threshold individuals to get it started, and development will stop when there is no one with the threshold necessary for the next step in escalation. Collective behavior reaches an equilibrium (which can be ascertained in advance from knowing the distribution of thresholds) when this point is reached. While the mathematical version of the model assigns each additional participant a uniform value of one, Granovetter makes allowance for the possibility that participating friends may count for more than one and that physical dispersion of the participants may modify the threshold effect. Like Berk, Granovetter makes no effort to explain what actions people will value. Furthermore, intuitively appealing as the theory may be, operationalizing and measuring individual thresholds may be, for all practical purposes, impossible.

## MICRO-LEVEL INTERACTION THEORIES

**Contagion Theories.** Early interaction theories, which lay more emphasis on what happens to people in the context of a crowd or other collectivity than on the dispositions people bring to the collectivity, stressed either the emergence of a group mind or processes of imitation, suggestion, or social contagion. While the concept of a group mind is no longer taken seriously, the contagion approach as formulated by Herbert Blumer (1939) has many followers.

Blumer explains that the fitting together of individual actions in most group behavior is based on shared understandings, which are influenced by custom, tradition, conventions, rules, or institutional regulations. In contrast, collective behavior is group behavior that arises spontaneously and not under the guidance of preestablished understandings, traditions, or rules of any kind. If sociology in general studies the social order, collective behavior consists of the processes by which that order comes into existence. While coordination in publics and social movements involves more complex cognitive processes, coordination in the crowd and in other elementary forms of collective behavior is accomplished through a process of *circular reaction*. Circular reaction is a type of interstimulation in which the response by others to one individual's expression of feeling simply reproduces that feeling, thereby reinforcing the first individual's feeling, which in turn reinforces the feelings of the others, setting in motion an escalating spiral of emotion. Circular reaction is contrasted to *interpretative interaction*, which characterizes most human response, including the coordination in publics and social movements. Circular reaction begins with individual restlessness, when people have a blocked impulse to act. When many people share such restlessness and are already sensitized to one another, circular reaction can set in and create a process of *social unrest*, in which the restless state is mutually intensified into a state of milling. In milling, people move or shift their attention aimlessly among each other, thereby becoming preoccupied with each other and decreasingly responsive to ordinary objects and events. In the state of rapport, collective excitement readily takes over, leading to a final stage of *social contagion*, the "relatively rapid, unwitting, and non-rational dissemination of a mood, impulse, or form of conduct" (Blumer 1939, p. 176). Social unrest is also a prelude to the formation of publics and social movements. In the case of the public, the identification of an issue rather than a mood or point of view converts the interaction into discussion rather than circular reaction. Social movements begin with circular reaction, but with persisting concerns they acquire organization and programs, and interpretative interaction prevails.

**Emergent Norm Theory.** Turner and Killian ([1957] 1987) criticized convergence theories for underemphasizing the contribution of interaction processes in the development of collective behavior and found both convergence and contagion theories at fault for assuming that participants in collective behavior become homogeneous in their moods and attitudes. Instead of emotional contagion, it is the emergence of a norm or norms in collective behavior that facilitates coordinated action and creates the illusion of unanimity. The emergent norm is characteristically based on established norms but transforms or applies those norms in ways that would not ordinarily be acceptable. What the emergent norm permits or requires people to believe, feel, and do corresponds to a disposition that is prevalent but not universal among the participants. In contrast to convergence theories, however, it is assumed that participants are usually somewhat ambivalent; people could have felt and acted in quite different ways if the emergent norm had been different. Striking events, symbols, and keynoting—a gesture or symbolic utterance that crystallizes sentiment in an undecided and ambivalent audience—shape the norm and supply the normative power, introducing an element of unpredictability into the development and direction of all collective behavior.

Emergent norm theory differs from contagion theories in at least six important and empirically testable ways. First, the appearance of unanimity in crowds, social movements, and other forms of collective behavior is an illusion, produced by the effect of the emergent norm in silencing dissent. Second, while the collectivity's mood and definition of the situation are spontaneously induced in some of the participants, many participants experience group pressure first and only later, if at all, come to share the collectivity's mood and definition of the situation. Third, unlike collective excitement and contagion, normative pressure is as applicable to quiet states such as dread and sorrow as it is to excited states. Fourth, according to emergent norm theory, a conspicuous component in the symbolic exchange connected with the development of collective behavior should consist of seeking and supplying justifications for the collectivity's definition of the situation and action, whereas there should be no need for justifications if the feelings were spontaneously induced through contagion. Fifth, a norm not only requires or permits certain definitions and behaviors; it also sets acceptable limits, while limits are difficult to explain in terms of a circular reaction spiral. Finally, while contagion theories stress anonymity within the collectivity as facilitating the diffusion of definitions and behavior that deviate from conventional norms, emergent norm theory asserts that familiarity among participants in collective behavior enhances the controlling effect of the emergent norm.

Recently, emergent norm theory has been broadened to make explicit the answers to all three of the key questions micro-level theories must answer. The emergent normative process is the principal answer to the question of why people adopt definitions and behavior that transcend, bypass, or contravene established social norms. Participants translate their attitudes into overt action rather than remaining passive, principally because they see action as feasible and timely. Action is collective rather than individual primarily because of preexisting groupings and networks and because an event or events that challenge conventional understandings impel people to turn to others for help in fashioning a convincing definition of the problematic situation. In addition, the three sets of processes interact and are mutually reinforcing in the development and maintenance of collective behavior. This elaboration of emergent norm theory is presented as equally applicable to elementary forms of collective behavior such as crowds and to highly developed and organized forms such as social movements.

**Other Interaction Theories.** Although all interactional theories presume that collective behavior develops through a cumulative process, Heirich (1971) makes this central to his theory of collective conflict, formulated to explain the 1964–65 year of spiraling conflict between students and the administration at the University of California, Berkeley. Common action occurs when observers perceive a situation as critical, think there is limited time for action, and view the crisis as having a simple cause and being susceptible to influence by simple acts. Heirich specifies determinants of the process by which such common perceptions are created and the process by which successive redefinitions of the situation take place. Under organizational conditions that create unbridged cleavages between groups that must interact regularly, conflict escalates through successive encounters in which cleavages become wider, issues shift, and new participants join the fray, until the conflict becomes focused on the major points of structural strain in the organization.

Also studying collective conflict as a cumulative process, Useem and Kimball (1989) developed a sequence of stages for prison riots, proceeding from preriot conditions to initiation, expansion, siege, and finally termination. While they identify disorganization of the governing body as the key causative factor, they stress that what happens at any one stage is important in determining what happens at the next stage.

Less fully developed as a theory, the *social behaviorist/interactionist* approach of McPhail and Miller (1973) and of Miller (1985) conceives collective behavior as individuals' actions that converge on the basis of explicit instructions or other cues to conduct. Rather than positing an overarching principle such as contagion or norm emergence, this approach uses detailed observation of individual actions and interactions within collectivities and seeks explanations at this level.

## STRUCTURAL THEORIES

Micro-level theories attempt first to understand the internal dynamics of collective behavior, then use that understanding to infer the nature of conditions in the society most likely to give rise to collective behavior. In contrast, structural theories depend primarily on an understanding of the dynamics of society as the basis for developing propositions concerning when and where collective behavior will occur. Historically, most theories of elementary collective behavior have been

micro-level theories, while most theories of social movements have been structural. Neil Smelser's (1963) *value-added* theory is primarily structural but encompasses the full range from panic and crazes to social movements.

Smelser attempted to integrate major elements from the Blumer and Turner-Killian tradition of micro-level theory into an action and structural theory derived from the work of Talcott Parsons. Smelser describes the normal flow of social action as proceeding from values to norms to mobilization into social roles and finally to situational facilities. Values are the more general guides to behavior; norms specify more precisely how values are to be applied. Mobilization into roles is organization for action in terms of the relevant values and norms. Situational facilities are the means and obstacles that facilitate and hinder attainment of concrete goals. The four "components of social action" are placed in a hierarchy: Any redefinition of a component requires adjustment in the components below it but not necessarily in those above. Each of the four components in turn has seven levels of specificity with the same hierachical ordering as the components. Types of collective behavior differ in the level of the action components they aim to restructure. Social movements address either values, in the case of most revolutionary movements, or norms, in the case of most reform movements. Elementary collective behavior is focused at either the mobilization or the situational facilities level. Collective behavior is characterized formally as "an uninstitutionalized mobilization for action in order to modify one or more kinds of strain on the basis of a generalized reconstitution of a component of action" (Smelser 1963, p. 71). The distinguishing feature of this action is that it short-circuits the normal flow of action from the general to the specific, jumping from extremely high levels of generality to specific, concrete situations, without attention to the intervening components and their levels of specificity. Thus, in Smelser's view, collective behavior is intrinsically irrational.

In order for collective behavior to occur, six conditions must be met, each of which is necessary but insufficient without the others. Smelser likens the relationship among the six determinants to the value-added process in economics, with each determinant adding an essential component to the finished product. The first determinant is *structural conduciveness,* meaning that the social structure is organized in a way that makes the particular pattern of action feasible. The second determinant is *structural strain,* consisting of ambiguities, deprivations, conflicts, and discrepancies experienced by particular population segments. Third, and central in Smelser's theorizing, is the growth and spread of a *generalized belief.* The generalized belief identifies and characterizes the supposed source of strain and specifies appropriate responses. The generalized belief incorporates the short-circuiting of the components of action that is a distinctive feature of collective behavior. Fourth are *precipitating factors,* usually a dramatic event or series of events that give the generalized belief concrete and immediate substance and provide a concrete setting toward which collective action can be directed. The fifth determinant is *mobilization of participants for action,* in which leadership behavior is critical. The final determinant is the *operation of social control.* Controls may serve to minimize conduciveness and strain, thus preventing the occurrence of an episode of collective behavior, or they may come into action only after collective behavior has begun to materialize, either dampening or intensifying the action by the way controls are applied. Although these determinants are often read as sequential stages in development of collective behavior, Smelser insists that they need not occur in any particular order.

Addressing a more limited range of phenomena, Waddington, Jones, and Critcher (1989) have formulated a *flashpoint* model to explain public disorders, and this model bears some resemblance to the value-added component of Smelser's theory. Public disorders typically begin when some ostensibly trivial incident becomes a flashpoint. The flashpoint model is a theory of the conditions that give a minor incident such grave significance. Explanatory conditions exist at six levels. At the *structural* level are conflicts inherent in material and ideological differences between social groups, which conflicts are not easily resolvable within the existing social structure, especially the state. At the *political/ideological* level, dissenting groups are unable to express their dissent through established channels, and their declared ends and means are considered illegitimate. At the *cultural* level, the existence of groups with incompatible definitions of the situation, appropriate behavior, or legitimate rights can lead to conflict. At the *contextual* level, a history of past conflicts between a dissenting group and police or other authorities enhances the likelihood that a minor incident will become a flashpoint. At the *situational* level, immediate spatial and social conditions can make public control and effective negotiation difficult. Finally, at the *interactional* level, the dynamics of interaction between police and protesters, as influenced by meanings derived from the other five levels, ultimately determine whether there will or will not be public disorder and how severe it will be. Unlike Smelser, Waddington, Jones, and Critcher make no assumption that all levels of determinants must be operative. Also, they make no explicit assumption that disorderly behavior is irrational, though their goal is to formulate public policy that will minimize the incidence of public disorders.

*Resource mobilization* theories have been advanced as alternatives to Smelser's value-added theory and to most micro-level theories. Although they have generally been formulated to explain social movements and usually disavow continuity between social movements and elementary collective behavior, they have some obvious implications for most forms of collective behavior. Although there are now several versions of resource mobilization theory, certain core assumptions can be identified. Resource mobilization theorists are critical of previous collective behavior and social movement theories for placing too much emphasis on "structural strain," social unrest, or grievances; on "generalized beliefs," values, ideologies, or ideas of any kind; and on grass roots spontaneity in accounting for the development and characteristics of collective behavior. They assume that there is always sufficient grievance and unrest in society to serve as the basis for collective protest (McCarthy and Zald 1977) and that the ideas and beliefs exploited in protest are readily available in the culture (Oberschall 1973). They see collective protest as centrally organized, with the bulk of the participants "mobilized" much as soldiers in an army are mobilized and directed by their commanders. In explaining the rise of collective protest, they emphasize the availability of essential resources, such as money, skills, disposable time, media access, and access to centers of power, and prior organization as the basis for effectively mobilizing the resources. Resource mobilization theorists favor the use of rational decision models to explain the formulation of strategy and tactics and emphasize the role of social movement professionals in directing protest.

In recent years there has been some convergence between resource mobilization theorists and the theorists they criticize. The broadened formulation of emergent norm theory to incorporate resources (under "feasibility") and prior organization as determinants of collective behavior takes account of the resource mobilization contribution without, however, giving primacy to these elements. Similarly, many resource mobilization theorists have incorporated social psychological variables in their models.

Recently introduced to English-speaking audiences, Alberto Melucci (1989) offers a *constructivist* view of collective action, combining macro and micro orientations. Collective action is the product of purposeful negotiations whereby a plurality of perspectives, meanings, and relationships crystallize into a pattern of action. Action is constructed to take account of the goals of action, the means to be utilized, and the environment within which action takes place, all of which remain in a continual state of tension. The critical process is the negotiation of collective identities for the participants. In the current postindustrial era, conflicts leading to collective action develop in those areas of communities and complex organizations in which there is greatest pressure on individuals to conform to the institutions that produce and circulate information and symbolic codes.

(SEE ALSO: *Crowds and Riots; Disaster Research; Social Movements*)

## REFERENCES

Allport, Floyd H. 1924 *Social Psychology*. Boston: Houghton Mifflin.

Berk, Richard A. 1974 "A Gaming Approach to Crowd Behavior." *American Sociological Review* 39:355–373.

Blumer, Herbert 1939 "Collective Behavior." In Robert E. Park, ed., *An Outline of the Principles of Sociology*. New York: Barnes and Noble.

Davies, James C. 1962 "Toward a Theory of Revolution." *American Journal of Sociology* 27:5–19.

Granovetter, Mark 1978 "Threshold Models of Collective Behavior." *American Journal of Sociology* 83: 1420–1443.

Gurr, Ted R. 1970 *Why Men Rebel*. Princeton: Princeton University Press.

Heirich, Max 1971 *The Spiral of Conflict: Berkeley, 1964*. Berkeley: University of California Press.

Klapp, Orrin E. 1972 *Currents of Unrest: An Introduction to Collective Behavior*. New York: Holt, Rinehart, and Winston.

McCarthy, John D., and Mayer N. Zald 1977 "Resource Mobilization and Social Movements: A Partial Theory." *American Journal of Sociology* 82:1212–1241.

McPhail, Clark, and David Miller 1973 "The Assembling Process: A Theoretical and Empirical Examination." *American Sociological Review* 38:721–735.

Melucci, Alberto 1989 *Nomads of the Present: Social Movements and Individual Needs in Contemporary Society*. Philadelphia: Temple University Press.

Miller, David L. 1985 *Introduction to Collective Behavior*. Belmont, Calif.: Wadsworth.

Oberschall, Anthony 1973 *Social Conflicts and Social Movements*. Englewood Cliffs, N.J.: Prentice-Hall.

Smelser, Neil J. 1963 *Theory of Collective Behavior*. New York: Free Press.

Turner, Ralph H., and Lewis M. Killian (1957) 1987 *Collective Behavior*. Englewood Cliffs, N.J.: Prentice-Hall.

Useem, Bert, and Peter Kimball 1989 *States of Siege: U.S. Prison Riots, 1971–1986*. New York: Oxford University Press.

Waddington, David, Karen Jones, and Chas Critcher

1989 *Flashpoints: Studies in Public Disorder*. London: Routledge.

RALPH H. TURNER

**COMMUNES**   *See* Alternative Life-Styles.

**COMMUNISM**   *See* Socialism.

**COMMUNITY**   The sociology of community has been a dominant source of sociological inquiry since the earliest days of the discipline. Each of the three most influential nineteenth century sociologists (Marx, Durkheim, and Weber) regarded the social transformation of community in its various forms as a fundamental problem of sociology and sociological theory. The problem of community has also long been a concern of the social sciences in general. Some fifty years ago sociologist Carle C. Zimmerman observed that the notion of community "has been discussed either directly or incidentally by nearly everyone who has written in the social sciences since Aristotle" (Zimmerman 1938, p. 11). Concerning specifically the emergence of sociology, Bender (1978) suggested that as early social thinkers observed the disruption of the traditional social order and traditional patterns of social life associated with industrialization, urbanization, and the rise of capitalism, significant attention was focused on the social transformation of community and communal life. It should be emphasized that contemporary sociology remains, at its core, a discipline largely concerned with the definition and persistence of community as a form of social organization, social existence, and social experience.

The definition of community in sociology has been problematic for several reasons, not the least of which has been nostalgic attachment to the idealized notion that the existence of community is embodied in the village or small town where human associations are characterized as *Gemeinschaft*—that is, associations that are intimate, familiar, sympathetic, mutually interdependent, and reflective of a shared social consciousness (in contrast to relationships that are *Gesellschaft*—casual, transitory, without emotional investment, and based on self-interest). According to this notion, the requirements of community or communal existence are met only in the context of a certain quality of human association occurring within the confines of limited, shared physical territory.

The classic perspective on community offered by Zimmerman (1938) is consistent with this theme in that the basic four characteristics argued by Zimmerman to define community (social fact, specification, association, and limited area) require a territorial context. Hillary (1955), in a content analysis of ninety-four definitions of community advanced in sociological literature, discovered basic consensus on only three definitional elements: social interaction between people, one or more shared ties, and an area context. An alternative, less restrictive, conception of community that accommodates the recognition of communal experience and the persistence of community in a highly mobile, urbanized society argues that community can be achieved independently of territorial arrangements and attachments where social networks exist sufficient to sustain a *Gemeinschaft* quality of interaction and association (e.g. Lindeman 1930; Bender 1978). Although Zimmerman opposed the notion that the requirements of community could be achieved by social interaction without shared territorial attachments, the findings of Hillary (1955) indicated that of the three unifying elements of community found in the literature (social interaction, common bonds, and area) "area" or "territory" was the least required to achieve a high level of consistency among definitions of community. Although many other definitions of community have been advanced in the decades since Hillary's analysis, the dominant discriminating element and point of debate among definitions remain the role of territorial arrangements.

## MAJOR QUESTIONS

The major questions that concern the sociology of community include the distinguishing characteristics and definition of community; the bases of communal experience and integration; the unique functions and tasks of community; the units of social structure within the community and the relationships and interactions between structural units; the economic and social bases of the community social structure; the relationship and distinction between internal community social structure and macrosocial structures external to the community; the relationship between individual experience and behavior and communal experience and behavior; the causes and processes of transformation from *Gemeinschaft* to *Gesellschaft* states of social existence; and processes of community persistence and adaptation in the face of social change.

Community studies undertaken by sociologists over the past sixty years have to a large extent sought to address some if not all of these issues. The most famous and controversial include Robert Lynd and Helen Lynd's Middletown studies (1929, 1937) and the Yankee City series by W. Lloyd Warner and his associates. The more well-known studies that have focused on the problem of community within large cities have included William Whyte's *Street Corner Society* and Gerald Suttles' *The Social Order of the Slum,* which themselves are aligned with earlier conceptions (associated with Robert Park and Ernest Burgess of the University of Chicago Department of Sociology) of the "natural community" arising within the confines of a seemingly faceless, anonymous, large city (Suttles 1972, pp. 7–9). Descriptive studies that emphasize field work and examine social structure as a spatial phenomenon are the hallmark of the highly influential Chicago School that arose and flourished under Park and Burgess during the 1920s and 1930s.

Robert Lynd and Helen Lynd carried out two studies involving extensive personal field work on the town of Muncie, Indiana, respectively *Middletown* (1929) and *Middletown in Transition* (1937).

In the first Middletown study, the Lynds spent the years 1924 and 1925 participating in and observing the community life of Muncie (population 36,500) and performing extensive survey work. Their objective was to address all aspects of social life and social structure of the community. A fundamental focus of this analysis was the consequences of technological change (industrialization) for the social structure of Muncie, in particular the emergence of social class conflicts subsequent to turn-of-the-century industrialization.

Although the Lynds found distinctions between the living conditions and opportunity structures of business- and working-class families that were consistent with their Marxist expectations (i.e., children of the working class were more likely to drop out of school to help support the family, working-class families worked longer hours for less pay and less financial security, and living conditions in general were more harsh for working-class families), they failed to discover a disparate value structure or alienation among the working class. At all levels of social class the Middletown of 1925 shared a common conservative value structure that entailed a belief in hard work, self-reliance, and faith in the future. The subsequent study, undertaken in 1935 by Robert Lynd and a staff of five assistants, addressed the effects on Muncie of certain events during the period between 1925 and 1935, some of which were economic boom times, a 37-percent population increase, and the emergence of the Great Depression. The Lynds' fundamental questions in the later study addressed the persistence of the social fabric and culture of the community in the face of the "hard times" and other aspects of social change, the stability of community values concerning self-reliance and faith in the future when confronted by structurally induced poverty and dependence, whether the depression promoted a sense of community or undermined community solidarity by introducing new social cleavages, and the outcomes of latent conflicts observed in the mid-1920s (Lynd and Lynd 1937, p. 4). The conclusion reached by the Lynds was that the years of depression did little to diminish or otherwise change the essentially bourgeois value structure and way of life in Middletown, and that in almost all fundamental respects the community culture of Middletown remained much as it did a tumultuous decade earlier: "In the main, a Rip Van Winkle, fallen asleep in 1925 while addressing Rotary or the Central Labor Union, could have awakened in 1935 and gone right on with his interrupted address to the same people with much the same ideas" (Lynd and Lynd 1937, p. 490).

Although this remark seems to reflect some amount of disappointment on the Lynds' part that Middletown's bourgeois value system and class structure remained so unchanged in the face of widespread and unprecedented destitution, the Lynds still remained convinced that the Middletown family was in jeopardy, as evidenced by (among other things) an ever-widening generation gap. The Lynds' apprehensions concerning the survival of the American family were (and are) in keeping with the popular belief concerning the decline of the American family as its socialization functions are assumed by other formal social institutions external to the family. The conclusions of the Middletown III study, undertaken from 1976 to 1978 by Theodore Caplow, Howard M. Bahr, and Bruce A. Chadwick, who attempted to replicate the methodology of the Lynds, firmly reject this point of view. In contrast to the Lynds' foreboding in 1935 and popular sociology since that time, Caplow and his associates contend that Middletown's families of the 1970s have "increased family solidarity, a smaller generation gap, closer marital communication, more religion, and less mobility" (Caplow et al. 1982, p. 323). The conclusions derived from the third Middletown study also reject similar assumptions concerning consistent linear trends in equalization, secularization, bureaucratization, and depersonalization consistent with the relentless *Gemeinschaft*-to-*Gesellschaft* theme (Bahr, Caplow, and Chadwick 1983).

Although many of the Lynds' predictions concerning the social transformation of Middletown failed to come true as history unfolded, their work and remarkable powers of observation remain unparalleled in many respects. Of equal importance, the early Middletown studies helped to inspire such other works as *Street Corner Society* and the Yankee City studies, and remain the standard by which all other community studies are judged.

The largest-scale community study undertaken remains W. Lloyd Warner's Yankee City, published in a five-volume series from 1941 through 1959 (Warner and Lund 1941, 1942; Warner and Srole 1945; Warner and Low 1947; Warner 1959). The Yankee City project was undertaken by Warner and his associates in Newburyport, Massachusetts, during the late 1930s. Warner, an anthropologist whose most recent work prior to the Yankee City project was with Australian aborigines (Vidich, Bensman, and Stein 1964), attempted to obtain a complete ethnographic account of a "representative" American small community with a population range from 10,000 to 20,000. To accomplish this task, Warner's staff (numbering in the thirties) conducted aerial surveys of Newburyport and its surrounding communities, gathered some 17,000 "social personality" cards on every member of the community, gathered data on the professed and de facto reading preferences of its citizens, and even subjected plots of local plays to content analysis (Thernstrom 1964, pp. 227–228). In his criticism of the Yankee City study, Thernstrom (1964) provides the following comment pertaining to the size and scope of Warner's endeavor: "One breathes a sigh of sympathy at the image of a haunted [upper-class citizen] of Warner's Newburyport seeking furtively to pick up his monthly *Esquire* under the cool stare of a Radcliffe graduate student in sociology" (Thernstrom 1964, p. 228).

Warner's conception of Yankee City was that of a stable, rather closed community with a social structure being transformed in very negative ways by the latter stages of industrialization. According to Warner's vision of *Yankee City*, the loss of local economic control over its industries through a factory system controlled by "outsiders" disrupted traditional management—labor relations and communal identification with local leadership. Moreover, the factory system was seen by Warner as promoting an increasingly rigid class structure and decreased opportunities for social mobility. In particular, Warner's discussion of the loss of local economic control through horizontal and vertical affiliation, orientation, and delegation of authority seems to have offered a prophetic glimpse into the future for many American communities.

Although the Yankee City study produced a voluminous ethnographic record of an American city that has remained untouched in scale, Warner found little support for his contention that the ethnographic portrait of Newburyport produced by the Yankee City series could be generalized to other small American communities. Moreover, Warner's contention that social mobility was made more difficult by industrialization was not supported by the quality of his data and is in conflict with social history both before and subsequent to *Yankee City*. The most devastating criticisms of *Yankee City*, however, concerned Warner's ahistorical approach and system of social stratification.

Warner's ahistorical strategy relied almost wholly on original ethnographic information produced by the research team as the principal basis for the formation of their ideas about the community and rejected substantial use of historical record. The rationale for this approach pertained to a wish to escape the ethnocentric biases of previous historical information. However, Thernstrom (1964) suggested that the exclusive reliance on the community's time-bound perspective and beliefs about itself promoted the very biased ethnocentric perceptions Warner wished to avoid. Warner's system of stratification, which rejected economic criteria in favor of six discrete social classes determined through subjective ranking by community informants, provoked the most devastating attacks upon the Yankee City study. The criticisms included the observations that (1) Warner's measure of social class was limited to a measure of social prestige; (2) affixing someone in a particular social class by the representative polling of others was unwieldy and inherently arbitrary; (3) there is difficulty in observing social mobility under a stratification system based on "communal ranking"; and (4) there were refer-

ences by Warner himself in Yankee City that indicated members of the working class ranked people by the simple economic criteria Warner eschewed.

Both Gerald Suttle's *The Social Order of the Slum* (1968) and William Whyte's *Street Corner Society* (1943) provide sociology with unparalleled ethnographic accounts of neighborhood social structure and communal life in urban environs. Suttle's work focused on the territorial relationships, neighborhood social structure, and communal life among Italian, Hispanic, and black slum inhabitants of the Near West Side of Chicago in the 1960s. Whyte's *Street Corner Society*, based on Whyte's residence in a Chicago Italian slum district a generation earlier, provided an understanding of the complex and stable social organization that existed within slum neighborhoods conventionally believed to have epitomized social disorganization. Whyte's observations and keen insights concerning small-group behavior were pioneering contributions to that area of sociology. Both studies, in method, theory, and substance, are classic examples of Chicago School sociology.

## SOCIAL THEORY AND THE TRANSFORMATION OF THE AMERICAN COMMUNITY

The findings of the various community studies have aided enormously in the struggle to refine conceptualization of the social transformation process among American communities. Warren (1978) describes the modern social transformation of community as a change of orientation by the local community units toward the extracommunity systems of which they are a part, with a corresponding decrease in community cohesion and autonomy (Warren 1978, pp. 52–53). In Warren's conception of social transformation, the owner-operated corner cafe is transformed to a franchise with rotating upwardly mobile management personnel and an emphasis on consistency of product over what is unique and local. Warren identifies seven areas through which social transformation can be analyzed: division of labor, differentiation of interests and association, increasing systemic relationships to the larger society, bureaucratization and impersonalization, transfer of functions to profit enterprise and government, urbanization and suburbanization, and changing values. The framework suggested by Warren offers a rich conceptualization of community transformation that goes well beyond an elaboration of the traditional *Gemeinschaft–Gesellschaft* dichotomy.

Like Warren, Bender (1978) speaks the language of social transformation of community rather than disappearance or collapse. Bender proposes that the observations by various community scholars at different points in historical time, each suggesting that theirs is *the* historical tipping point from community to mass society, contradict linear decline or an interpretation of history that stresses the collapse of community. Although Bender acknowledges the ascendance of *Gesellschaft* in American social experience during the period following the Civil War, he suggests that a "bifurcation of social experience" or sharpening of the distinction between *Gemeinschaft* and *Gesellschaft* realms of social interaction is a more accurate interpretation of the historical transformation of community than that provided by the linear *Gemeinschaft*-to-*Gesellschaft* framework.–

## THE DECLINE OF COMMUNITY DEBATE

Ever since nineteenth-century social thinker Ferdinand Tonnies offered sociology *Gemeinschaft* and *Gesellschaft* as contrasting qualities of human association, the fundamental focus of debate within the sociology of community has concerned the hypotheses emphasizing the decline of community. According to this hypothesis and its variations, the intimate, sustained, and mutually interdependent human associations based on shared fate and shared consciousness observed in traditional communal society are relentlessly giving way to the casual, impersonal, transitory, and instrumental relationships based on self-interest that are characteristic of social existence in modern mass society.

Of the many works that derive their perspective from the decline-of-community hypothesis, the most famous is Louis Wirth's "Urbanism as a Way of Life" (1938). Wirth's eloquent essay presents a perspective of urban existence and urban social relationships that managed to capture much sociological thinking about the emergence of a heterogenous urban mass society characterized by a breakdown of informal communal ways of meeting human need and by "human relations which are largely anonymous, superficial, and transitory" (Wirth 1938, p. 1). All other works pertaining to the decline-of-community hypothesis are either a reply to Wirth or an elaboration of Wirth's succinct presentation of the thesis.

Although many of Wirth's observations about the nature of human association, the disruption of a communal social structure, and the rise of formal, impersonal social institutions are difficult to refute, replies to the decline-of-community theme generally offer either (1) an alternative, albeit more limited, communal social structure or (2) evidence that suggests the march from a *Gemeinschaft* to a *Gesellschaft* state of human association has neither been linear nor relentless.

Of the former approach, the most notable is the conception of the "community of limited liability." According to the community-of-limited-liability thesis, networks of human association and interdependence are argued to exist at various levels of social organization, and social status characteristics are identified that are associated with differentiated levels of participation in community life (e.g., family life-cycle phase). The idea of "limited liability" poses the argument that, in a highly mobile society, the attachments to community tend to be based on rationalism rather than on sentiment and that even those "invested" in the community are limited in their sense of personal commitment (Janowitz 1952; Greer 1962).

The approaches that challenge the decline-of-community thesis on the basis of its vision of a linear transformation from a communal *Gemeinschaft* society to an urban mass *Gesellschaft* society do so by offering evidence suggesting that Wirth's vision of the relentless social forces of urbanism is both overly deterministic and blind to the reality that patterns of *Gemeinschaft* and *Gesellschaft* human associations can be found to exist side by side in very complex ways. For example, Bahr, Caplow, and Chadwick (1983) argue that their analysis of Muncie, Indiana (forty years after the Lynds' *Middletown in Transition*), failed to find the singular trends in bureaucratization, secularization, mobility, and depersonalization that would be predicted from a linear decline-of-community hypothesis. Janowitz (1952) suggests that while the *Gemeinschaft*-to-*Gesellschaft* social transformation might be a long-term trend, long-term trends are not useful to the interpretation of contemporary social reality. Redfield (1955), in his reformulation of the folk–urban society contrast, offers an alternative perspective to the Wirth linear transformation of folk *(Gemeinschaft)* society to urban *(Gesellschaft)* society, proposing that both urban ways and folkways can be observed in contemporary communities and cities: "In every isolated little community there is civilization; in every city there is the folk society" (Redfield 1955, p. 146).

While much of the evidence from community studies appears to support Redfield's vision of *Gemeinschaft–Gesellschaft* coexistence in contemporary society, it is left to future sociological investigation to determine where and under what conditions particular patterns of *Gemeinschaft* and *Gesellschaft* social existence emerge.

(SEE ALSO: *Case Studies; Field Research Methods*)

## REFERENCES

Bahr, Howard M., Theodore Caplow, and Bruce Chadwick 1983 "Middletown III: Problems of Replication, Longitudinal Measurement, and Triangulation." *Annual Review of Sociology* 9:249–258.

Bender, Thomas 1978 *Community and Social Change in America*. New Brunswick, N.J.: Rutgers University Press.

Caplow, Theodore, Howard M. Bahr, Bruce A. Chadwick, Reuben Hill, and Margaret Holmes Williamson 1982 *Middletown Families: Fifty Years of Change and Continuity*. Minneapolis: University of Minnesota Press.

Greer, Scott 1962 *The Emerging City: Myth and Reality*. New York: Free Press of Glencoe.

Hillary, George A., Jr. 1955 "Definitions of Community: Areas of Agreement." *Rural Sociology* 20:111–123.

Janowitz, Morris 1952 *The Community Press in an Urban Setting: The Social Elements of Urbanism*. Chicago: University of Chicago Press.

Lindeman, E. C. 1930 "Community." In Edwin R. A. Seligman, ed. *The Encyclopedia of Social Sciences*. New York: Macmillan.

Lynd, Robert, and Helen Lynd 1929 *Middletown: A Study in American Culture*. New York: Harcourt, Brace and Company.

———— 1937 *Middletown in Transition: A Study in Cultural Conflicts*. New York: Harcourt, Brace and Company.

Redfield, Robert 1955 *The Little Community*. Chicago: University of Chicago Press.

————1968 *The Social Order of the Slum: Ethnicity and Territory in the Inner City*. Chicago: University of Chicago Press.

Suttles, Gerald 1972 *The Social Construction of Communities*. Chicago: University of Chicago Press.

Thernstrom, Stephen 1964 *Poverty and Progress*. Cambridge, Mass.: Harvard University Press.

Vidich, Arthur, Joseph Bensman, and Maurice Stein 1964 *Reflections on Community Studies*. New York: Wiley.

Warner, W. Lloyd 1959 *The Living and the Dead: A Study of the Symbolic Life of Americans*. New Haven: Yale University Press.

————, and J. O. Low 1947 *The Social System of the Modern Factory: The Strike, A Social Analysis*. New Haven: Yale University Press.

————, J. O. Low, Paul S. Lund, and Leo Srole 1963 *Yankee City*. New Haven: Yale University Press.

————, and Paul S. Lund 1941 *The Social Life of a Modern Community*. New Haven: Yale University Press.

———— 1942 *The Status System of a Modern Community*. New Haven: Yale University Press.

————, and Leo Srole 1945 *The Social Systems of American Ethnic Groups*. New Haven, Conn.: Yale University Press.

Warren, Roland 1978 *The Community in America*. Chicago: Rand McNally.

Whyte, William Foote 1943 *Street Corner Society: The Social Structure of an Italian Slum*. Chicago: University of Chicago Press.

Wirth, Louis 1938 "Urbanism as a Way of Life." *American Journal of Sociology* 44:1–24.

Zimmerman, Carle C. 1938 *The Changing Community.* New York: Harper and Brothers.

GUNNAR ALMGREN

## COMMUNITY HEALTH

Community health represents an organized community effort to ensure a healthy population. It is both an approach and a discipline. The basic distinction is whether service or science is stressed. As an approach, community health refers to the provision of health services. As a discipline, community health is the science of disease, illness, and health maintenance.

The community health approach includes the institutions and persons that constitute the health care system of a community. Thus, the official public health agencies, the physicians who may practice as community medicine specialists, and all other health practitioners and professionals involved with organized health care delivery in a community are incorporated, as well as a variety of service agencies.

The community health discipline is the population-based study of the causes, control, and prevention of health problems. It uses the science of epidemiology to investigate health and health services.

### COMMUNITY HEALTH SERVICES

Community health services are wide in scope. The services involve (1) official activities of local, state, and federal public health departments, and (2) services delivered by persons or institutions in the private and semipublic sectors. The former are conducted with public funds by agencies designated as official public health departments. The latter are not publicly funded and can include the services of hospitals, long-term care institutions, health education facilities, human service agencies, health administrators, health planners, and staff of community agencies. This last group is

rapidly increasing its community health efforts as society moves away from formal institutional care for long-term and mental health problems to community-based and home care.

The American Public Health Association is also integrally involved in community health efforts. It has a national membership of persons working to improve the health of communities and has recently called for legislation to provide breast and cervical cancer screening, long-term care for the elderly, drug and alcohol treatment centers, a new focus on TB as a health problem, and new policies for the care and education of AIDS patients (Nation's Health 1990).

### PUBLIC HEALTH SERVICES

Public health departments are organized at federal, state, and local levels. They represent a community's official line of defense against disease and injury. Until the middle of the twentieth century public health departments were concerned primarily with the spread of infectious disease. At the present time they concentrate on chronic diseases, with the exception of AIDS and sexually transmitted diseases.

Public health agencies engage in many activities that are prevention-oriented. They attempt to reduce the threat of disease by emphasizing prevention. These activities encompass several areas: providing a safe physical environment; preventing the spread of infectious disease; ensuring maternal and infant health; protecting the public from unintentional injuries; ensuring adequate nutrition; and enhancing the public's knowledge of health maintenance and disease prevention behaviors. Thus, safe disposal of sewage and hazardous waste, monitoring the spread of AIDS and related disorders, providing pregnant women with health care and infant health information, and determining occupational hazards fall within the domain of the public health sector.

Local public health services have existed in the United States since the colonial period (Shonick 1988). Port cities established in the seventeenth century quickly discovered that they had to face the problem of epidemics spread by sailors and new settlers. Local officials began to enforce quarantines on persons or ships to prevent the spread of dread diseases. In the twentieth century major cities typically have a public health department, and counties may also have public health agencies.

Each state has a public health division. The functions of most state public health departments include: maintaining data bases for vital statistics and rates of specific diseases; providing laboratory services to diagnose disease; assessing environmental hazards; and providing aid to expectant mothers and young children. Many states are also involved in health education and nursing service programs and may regulate licensure of health facilities.

Federal legislation governing the health of the public dates from 1796 (Shonick 1988). Early efforts concerned the need to prevent the spread of infectious disease, but the lack of knowledge of the cause and spread of disease hampered these efforts. The U.S. Public Health Service was given its present name in 1912. By 1925, accurate information was available about the methods of transmission of most communicable diseases. Because food, water, insects, and animals were often implicated, federal and local agencies focused their efforts on sanitation, water control, and elimination of pests as disease agents.

At the present time the U.S. Public Health Service conducts a wide range of health activities that include establishing health policies and regulations, enforcement, health education, disease monitoring, and health research. With regard to the latter, the National Institutes of Health sponsor most of the health-related research in this country. These institutes operate under the jurisdiction of the U.S. Public Health Services.

The Center for Disease Control is also an important arm of the U.S. Public Health Service because of its surveillance efforts. This agency collects and circulates a complete set of statistics that detail disease prevalence (rates indicating the presence of specific diseases) and incidence (rates indicating the number of new cases during a particular period, such as a week). It also is involved in major disease-prevention efforts.

## COMMUNITY-BASED HEALTH FACILITIES

Many community agencies are involved in the community health effort. These agencies may include typical health-focused service agencies (e.g., local heart or muscular dystrophy associations, among others). They may also include human and social service agencies (e.g., an aging service agency that institutes a day care center for frail elderly). These agencies may be publicly or privately funded. Their activities can be very diverse.

Community-based agencies may implement health fairs, community-based screening programs, and infant care services or provide health education material. Outreach service programs are often included. They may also mobilize a community to intervene directly. There is renewed interest in the term *empowerment*, which refers to efforts of a community to exert local control over conditions that are troublesome. In some communities persons march to influence officials to remove unsafe housing or clean up dumpsites. Other communities contribute money to clean up lots that can provide safe play areas for children. Still others resort to dubious tactics (such as trying to deny schooling to young AIDS patients) to control the spread of AIDS.

## COMMUNITY MEDICINE

Medical specialties that physicians can pursue on a postgraduate basis now include community medicine. This is a medical practice area directed toward community health. Community medicine had its birth in the 1960s. Health professionals acknowledged that there must be a program responsible for professional development, direction, and coordination of a wide range of ambulatory health care services. Thus, departments of community medicine were established in leading medical schools.

The major premise of community medicine programs is that "the main factors that determine a community's health are to be found within the community itself—in its social, cultural, or biological features, or in its environment, natural and man-made" (Clark 1981, p. 14). At the heart of the statement is the assumption that community health cannot be promoted nor assured without recognizing that resources, circumstances, attitudes, and population characteristics of the community can cause or prevent disease; furthermore, these things determine the medical treatment that ill people can receive.

Community medicine programs acquire and provide information on health and health problems of the community, the health services available, and the planning and management of health care. They also provide the expertise to advise community health and human service agencies on health status concerns. Therefore, persons trained in community medicine programs recognize that the physical and social environments, the behaviors of the citizens, and the way the health care system of the community is organized all govern the health of that community.

## EPIDEMIOLOGY

Community health and health problems are best understood by utilizing a scientific approach. This relies on epidemiological studies. Epidemiology is defined as the study of the determinants and distribution of disease in a population. It is a population-based effort to understand disease and is widely used in community and public health research.

Epidemiological studies investigate (1) the segment of the population at risk for a disease or injury; (2) the biomedical, environmental, and psychosocial factors that influence the onset of the problem; and (3) the factors associated with the course and progression of an illness.

Determining the population at risk for a particular disease or injury is critical if it is to be controlled. Until epidemiological research established that AIDS was primarily confined to hemophiliacs, intravenous drug users, homosexuals, sexual partners of the groups named, and children of infected mothers, it was impossible to plan

intervention strategies. In earlier times, people with dread diseases were isolated because the principle of an at-risk individual was unknown, and it was believed that every person was susceptible. Hence, the diseased citizen was kept from everyone.

The biomedical, environmental, and psychosocial factors that can influence the onset of a disease must be identified before preventive efforts can be successful. Clearly, medical experts could not accurately begin to address lung cancer prevention until sufficient causal linkages of cigarette smoking and lung pathology were established.

Research that identifies factors that exacerbate or ameliorate progression of a disease can provide a major breakthrough. Such research yields important information about slowing the course of a disease or preventing further bodily deterioration. The Framingham Heart Study showed that stress and personality characteristics such as Type A Behavior increase the likelihood of death from a heart attack (Haynes et al. 1978; Haynes, Feinleib, and Kannel 1980). After this epidemiological study, both prevention and treatment efforts began to concentrate on behavioral change and psychosocial phenomena that affect the course of an illness.

## CONCLUSIONS ABOUT COMMUNITY HEALTH

Community health is the approach that addresses health service provision; community health is also the population-based discipline that determines the distribution and causes of health problems in a community. The terms *community health* and *public health* are often used interchangeably, but they are quite different. Public health technically refers to a society's efforts to deal with disease and injury on an official basis, using public funds. Community health, on the other hand is a much broader health effort. It involves many prevention- and treatment-oriented services and includes numerous people and institutions associated with both the public and nonpublic sectors. Preserving health, preventing disease and injury wherever possible, and organizing and providing adequate health care services are ongoing major community health activities.

(SEE ALSO: *Comparative Health-Care Systems; Health Promotion; Medical Sociology*)

### REFERENCES

Clark, Duncan W. 1981 "A Vocabulary for Preventive and Community Medicine." In Duncan W. Clark and Brian MacMahon, eds., *Preventive and Community Medicine*. Boston: Little, Brown.

Haynes, Suzanne G., Manning Feinleib, and William B. Kannel 1980 "The Relationship of Psychosocial Factors to Coronary Heart Disease in the Framingham Study: III. Eight-Year Incidence of Coronary Heart Disease." *American Journal of Epidemiology* 111:37–58.

Haynes, Suzanne G., Manning Feinleib, Sol Levine, Nathan Scotch, and William B. Kannel 1978 "The Relationship of Psychosocial Factors to Coronary Heart Disease in the Framingham Study: II. Prevalence of Coronary Heart Disease." *American Journal of Epidemiology* 107:384–402.

Nation's Health 1990 "Bills Would Fund Breast, Cervical Cancer Screening." *The Nation's Health* 20(4):1, 13.

Shonick, William 1988 "Public Health Services: Background and Present Status." In Stephen J. Williams and Paul R. Torrens, eds., *Introduction to Health Services*, 3rd ed. New York: Wiley.

ROSALIE F. YOUNG

**COMPARABLE WORTH** Comparable worth refers to equal pay for work of equal value. Like affirmative action policies, it has been proposed as a way to remedy the effects of past discrimination and, like affirmative action policies, it is controversial. Comparable worth advocates would extend the right of equal pay for equal work provided by Title VII of the Civil Rights Act of 1964 to a broader concept of equal pay for work requiring comparable levels of effort, skills, and responsibility. A number of legal actions, including one heard in the Supreme Court (Coun-

ty of Washington v. Gunther, 452 U.S. 161 [1981]), have been based on the premise of comparable worth. The Supreme Court ruling in this case removed a major legal obstacle to comparable worth as the basis for equalizing wages. Although it did not endorse the comparable worth approach, it did rule that a man and woman need not do "equal work" in order to establish pay discrimination under Title VII (Heen 1984). Subsequent lower court rulings have not resulted in clear-cut decisions regarding comparable worth, and at present it seems unlikely that court decisions will mandate the comparable worth approach. Nevertheless, the concept remains important in public policy debates.

The issue of comparable worth arose primarily in response to concern over continued wage inequality between men and women. (Although comparable worth policies also have significant implications for minorities, the debate has centered primarily on gender inequalities, and the discussion here focuses on gender.) The concern over the inequality of wages for men and women is not a new one. In the 1922 presidential address to the British Association of Economists, F. Y. Edgeworth (1922) spoke on "Equal Pay to Men and Women for Equal Work." The major issues he outlined are much as they remain: First, that men and women work in different jobs, albeit jobs that often require similar levels of effort and skill; second, that jobs held by women are paid far less than those held by men; and third, whether removing overt discrimination will equalize wages for men and women.

There is considerable evidence demonstrating that men and women work in different occupations. During the 1980s more than half of the workers of one sex would have had to change occupations in order to equalize the distribution of men and women across occupations (Jacobs 1989). Researchers using more specific job titles within firms have found that almost no men and women occupy positions with the same title in the same firm (Bielby and Baron 1986). Comparisons of occupational segregation by sex since 1900 show that levels have remained about the same (Gross 1968; Jacobs 1989).

The difference in wages paid to women relative to men has also changed little during the twentieth century (Marini 1989). In 1986 in the United States, women sixteen years and older working full time brought home about 65 percent of what men earned (U.S. Bureau of the Census 1986). A number of factors account for this wage gap. Some of the difference can be attributed to individual differences in labor-market capital, such as education, training, and experience; however, these differences account for less than half of the difference in wages (U.S. Bureau of the Census 1987). On average, across a number of studies, the concentration of women in low-paying female-dominated occupations accounts for about 25 percent of the gap between men's and women's wages (Sorensen 1986).

A number of skill or work-environment explanations for the lower wages in female-dominated occupations have been proposed. Comparisons of the skill requirements of male- and female-dominated occupations do not support these explanations. Instead, these comparisons have shown that the premium paid for skills in male-dominated occupations is higher. That is, a specific skill requirement in male-dominated occupations increases the wage more than the same skill requirement increases the wage in female-dominated occupations (McLaughlin 1978; Kemp and Beck 1986). Empirical evidence has not supported other possible explanations, such as that female-dominated occupations have greater nonmonetary compensations (Jencks, Perman, and Rainwater 1988) or that they are more accommodating to intermittent careers (England 1982).

The conclusion of J. S. Mill in 1865, as quoted by Edgeworth in 1922—"The remuneration of the peculiar employments of women is always, I believe, greatly below that of employments of equal skill and equal disagreeableness carried on by men"—is similar to the conclusion reached by the Norton-commissioned National Research Council/National Academy of Sciences committee report in 1981:

*[Such] differential earnings patterns have existed for many decades. They may arise in part because women and minority men are paid less than white men for doing the same (or very similar) jobs within the same firm, or in part because the job structure is substantially segregated by sex, race, and ethnicity and the jobs held mainly by women and minority men pay less than the jobs held mainly by non-minority men.* (Treiman and Hartmann 1981, p. 92).

Proponents of comparable worth argue that the lack of improvement in women's wages over past decades demonstrates the need for direct intervention to equalize wage rates. The justification for using comparable worth to adjust wages lies in two basic positions: (1) that the lower wages in historically female jobs represent a form of discrimination, and (2) that job-evaluation systems provide an acceptable remedy to this form of discrimination.

First, certain jobs have been systematically undervalued because the work has been and continues to be done primarily by women and minorities. This process has resulted in wages paid for historically female or minority work being *artificially depressed* relative to wages for jobs historically performed by white males. Thus, past discrimination is embedded in the current wage structure (Remick 1984; Marini 1989). Continued labor-market segregation combined with the systematic undervaluation of jobs held by women and minorities is thereby a principal cause of continued inequality and a form of labor-market discrimination.

Second, job-evaluation techniques provide a viable procedure for identifying and remedying this type of discrimination. The use of job-evaluation plans is neither new nor unusual. Currently, job evaluation is often used to determine pay scales, not only by governments, but also by many businesses.

Job evaluations are used for a variety of reasons; however, they are primarily used when employers cannot rely on the market to establish wages. (See Spilerman 1986, for a discussion of the types of organizations that use nonmarket wage-allocation mechanisms.) Employers must determine wages, for example, when positions are filled entirely from within an organizational unit (e.g., through promotion of an existing work force) or when they fill jobs that are unique to a particular firm. In these cases, "going rates" for all jobs are not always available in local labor markets.

Methods of job evaluation involve the establishment of equivalences for a variety of educational fields and degrees, types of skills, responsibilities, and work environments in order to compare the value to the firm of workers employed in different jobs. In addition to considering the training and work requirements for jobs within the firm, systems of job evaluation often also take into account whatever information is available on prevailing wages for different types of labor.

Actual methods of job evaluation differ, but the usual approach is to start by describing all jobs within a given organization. Next, a list of various requirements that are believed to determine pay differentials is developed and jobs are rated on each requirement. For instance, one requirement could be the use of mathematics. In this case each job would be rated from "low" (e.g., addition and subtraction of whole numbers) to "high" (use of differential equations and the calculus). Most job-evaluation methods have only included technical requirements of the job, such as level of education, skills, level of responsibility, and the environment in which the work is performed. Some job-evaluation methods also include such characteristics of job incumbents as average education, training, and experience. More ambitious job-evaluation models consider how jobs rank with regard to fringe benefits (e.g., sick leave), hours (e.g., shift work), training and promotion opportunities, hazards, autonomy (e.g., employees who may leave work without permission), authority (e.g., supervises others), and organizational setting (e.g., organizational size) as well as the technical and educational requirements of jobs (see Jencks, Perman, and Rainwater 1988). After each job is rated and given a score for each requirement, scores are combined to create an overall score for each job. These composite scores are then used to rank jobs in order to help determine appropriate wages (Blau and Ferber 1986). (Job-evaluation methods are also used in research on stratification and occupational mobility.) The implementation of comparable worth requires an evaluation of the contribution of many different jobs within an organization or firm.

Whereas a number of studies have successfully used this technique (Remick 1984; Steinberg and Cook 1982), there are a number of limitations to these methods in establishing comparable worth. First, while in theory various jobs can be assigned values objectively (i.e., not influenced by the sex and race of the incumbent), existing job-evaluation schemes have been criticized for undervaluing the skills and abilities that are emphasized in female jobs (Beatty and Beatty 1984). Second, job-evaluation methods are designed to be used *within* a particular firm or organization rather than across organizations. This is especially limiting because most organizations are staffed by individuals in a relatively narrow span of occupations. For example, a female occupation, such as nurse, and a male occupation, such as fire fighter, might have similar overall scores—but nurses and fire fighters seldom are incumbents in the same organization. Hence, it is unlikely that job-evaluation methods could be used to equalize wages of nurses and fire fighters. While these limitations prevent the use of job evaluation from being a complete solution to wage inequality arising from the segregation of women into undercompensated occupations, job-evaluation methods are certainly feasible, and a comparable worth strategy could have a substantial impact on reducing this source of inequality.

Although it is unlikely, as noted earlier, that comparable worth will be mandated under Title VII, it may be an important component of changes in the labor-market wage structures. For instance, it may serve as a bargaining chip in union negotiations. Unions in the public sector, especially those in organizations such as universities where public image is important, are particularly likely to pursue the comparable worth agenda (Remick 1984). Therefore, even without a strong legal mandate, comparable worth will likely influence labor-market outcomes.

(SEE ALSO: *Gender; Work and Occupations*)

## REFERENCES

Beatty, R. W., and J. R. Beatty 1984 "Some Problems with Contemporary Job Evaluation Systems." In H. Remick, ed., *Comparable Worth and Wage Discrimination: Technical Possibilities and Political Realities*. Philadelphia: Temple University Press.

Bielby, W. T., and J. N. Baron 1986 "Men and Women at Work: Sex Segregation and Statistical Discrimination." *American Journal of Sociology* 91:759–799.

Blau, F. D., and M. A. Ferber 1986 *The Economics of Women, Men and Work*. New York: Prentice-Hall.

Edgeworth, F. Y. 1922 "Equal Pay to Men and Women for Equal Work." *The Economic Journal* 32:431–456.

England, P. 1982 "The Failure of Human Capital Theory to Explain Occupational Sex Segregation." *Journal of Human Resources* 17:358–370.

Gross, E. 1968 "Plus ça change . . . ? The Sexual Structure of Occupations over Time." *Social Problems* 16:198–208.

Heen, M. 1984 "A Review of Federal Court Decisions Under Title VII of the Civil Rights Act of 1964." In H. Remick, ed., *Comparable Worth and Wage Discrimination: Technical Possibilities and Political Realities*. Philadelphia: Temple University Press.

Jacobs, J. A. 1989 "Long Term Trends in Occupational Segregation by Sex." *American Journal of Sociology* 95:160–173.

Jencks, C., L. Perman, and L. Rainwater 1988 "What Is a Good Job? A New Measure of Labor-Market Success." *American Journal of Sociology* 93:1322–1357.

Kemp, A. A., and E. M. Beck 1986 "Equal Work, Unequal Pay: Gender Discrimination within Work-similar Occupations." *Work and Occupations* 13:324–347.

Marini, M. M. 1989 "Sex Differences in Earnings in the U.S." In W. R. Scott, ed., *Annual Review of Sociology*, vol. 15. Palo Alto, Calif.: Annual Reviews.

McLaughlin, S. 1978 "Occupational Sex Identification and the Assessment of Male and Female Earnings Inequality." *American Sociological Review* 43:909–921.

Remick, H. (ed.) 1984 *Comparable Worth and Wage Discrimination: Technical Possibilities and Political Realities*. Philadelphia: Temple University Press.

Sorensen, E. 1986 "Implementing Comparable Worth: A Survey of Recent Job Evaluation Studies." *American Economic Review* (Papers and Proceedings) 76:364–367.

Spilerman, S. 1986. "Organizational Rules and the Features of Work Careers." *Research in Social Stratification and Mobility* 5:41–102.

Steinberg, Ronnie, and Alice Cook 1982 "Women, Unions and Equal Employment Opportunity" *Working Paper no. 3*. Albany, N.Y.: Center for Women in Government.

Treiman, D. J., and H. I. Hartman 1981 *Woman, Work and Wages: Equal Pay for Jobs of Equal Value*. Washington, D.C.: National Academy Press.

U.S. Bureau of the Census 1986 *Statistical Abstract of the United States: 1987*, 107th ed. Washington, D.C.: U.S. Government Printing Office.

———— 1987 *Male–Female Differences in Work Experience, Occupation and Earnings: 1984*. Current Population Report P-70, No. 10. Washington, D.C.: U.S. Government Printing Office.

NANCY E. DURBIN

## COMPARATIVE HEALTH-CARE SYSTEMS

With increasing pressure expected during the 1990s for restructuring the U.S. health-care system, social scientists as well as political activists have renewed interest in finding successful models abroad. A health-care system can be defined as the set of institutions designed to deliver health services, with mechanisms for financing these services, provisions for assuring access to the services, structures of the division of labor for delivering the services, and the arrangements for training those who provide the services. How these parts are organized and integrated into a system is a key issue in making cross-cultural comparisons. The situation can range from fragmentation, in which potentially there is no system at all, to a tightly interlinked set of structures and procedures.

Light (1986) has noted that the values espoused by a society underlie and partially explain the society's method of delivering health care. He posits four models of a health-care system—the mutual aid, professional, state, and corporatist models. The first of these, the mutual aid model, is not currently typical of any industrialized country and in the past applied chiefly among groups of workers who developed sickness funds. It involves people getting together to provide for their care in sickness and to promote health. It could be argued that this model no longer applies in the modern world, although vestiges remain in such movements as the Boston Women's Health Collective. For comparative purposes applicable to countries as a whole, the other three models are more relevant.

In the professional model, according to Light, the health system is run by medical professionals and is characterized by physician control and autonomy, fee-for-service reimbursement, emphasis on high quality care, and use of advanced technology. The only country that has approached this model is the United States. It does not apply elsewhere, with the possible exception of South Africa, and indeed can be characterized as a nonsystem, a "cottage industry," because of its basis in a market economy and the absence of national planning (Anderson 1989). In understanding the health-care systems in other countries, this model is of limited utility.

In the state model the goal is to keep people healthy at minimum cost in order to maintain the strength of the state. Consequently, the emphasis is on primary care and health promotion, with all planning and coordination centralized. Several countries may fit this model, including Great Britain, the People's Republic of China, and the USSR.

In Light's corporatist model, the interests of consumers, government, and providers are counterbalanced through negotiations that result in jointly agreeable health-care financing and organizational structure. The state may intervene to see that the terms of the agreement are carried out but does not itself run the system. According to Light, examples include Canada, the former West Germany, and Italy.

In reviewing information on health-care systems, it may not always be possible to force them into the state or corporatist mold, but these conceptualizations will be useful in understanding the diversity of organizational forms for providing health services in countries throughout the world, both industrialized (developed) and those still in the process of industrialization (developing). As "ideal types" in the Weberian sense, they are not expected to fit precisely to reality. Roemer (1977)

had specified in more detail the aspects of national systems that should be considered in any analysis, namely economic support, manpower, facilities, delivery patterns, preventive services, regulation, and administration and planning. Again, these may constitute an ideal list since these issues may not all be addressed in reviews of comparative health-care systems. Moreover, Elling (1980, p. 84) complains that this perspective is ahistorical and fails to take into account "the continuing class struggle in a variety of political-economic forms."

Another complexity in comparative research in the health field is the fact that systems are often in flux, in some cases as a result of conscious planning for change, as in Cuba and Ghana, in others as the consequences (perhaps unintended) of changes in the structure of an entire society, as in the case of the People's Republic of China or in the joining of East and West Germany. As a consequence of the fluidity and multiplicity of health-care systems, it is not possible in this brief space to describe them all or indeed with any confidence to use descriptions that date back a decade or more. Thus, the Appendix in Kohn and White (1976), which describes the characteristics of health-services provisions and organization in the six foreign countries used in their WHO comparative study, is chiefly of historical interest, as are Elling's (1980) comparisons of systems in Africa, Asia, Latin America, the Middle East, Europe, Japan, and the USSR. The countries whose systems will be briefly summarized here are Japan, the People's Republic of China, the Soviet Union, Italy, Great Britain, Ghana, and Cuba. In each of these countries relatively recent information is available.

In Japan, based on its cultural beliefs, the physician, who has the title of *sensei* (teacher), is accepted as the leader of the health-care team, in which everyone knows his or her place, and patients accept the hierarchical order as well (Powell and Anesaki 1990). The Health Insurance Law provides for universal compulsory health insurance, but there are diverse insurance carriers and fee coverage rules, producing complex paper work requirements for reimbursement. Most physicians have private practices with open, no-appointment clinics, and also sell medicines.

Recently, the government, in an attempt to cut costs, has mandated that by 1995 each individual will pay 20 percent of medical care costs up to a prescribed ceiling. This has lead to the growth of private insurance, which individuals purchase to cover their 20-percent share, as well as to the merger of some of the health insurance carriers to reduce administrative costs. There is no government evaluation system for quality of services, not even in hospitals, where the average length of stay is the longest in the world, 49.1 days in 1983 (a figure that may be skewed by the inclusion of long-term care for leprosy cases and some elderly). The absence of an evaluation procedure arises, according to Powell and Anesaki (1990, pp. 234–235) from the paternalistic hierarchical system, in which employees and staff monitor themselves in order to gain respect. Among all the models in Light's terminology, Japan's health-care system comes closest to fitting the corporatist. But further change is coming to the system in Japan. Despite the fact that the health status of the Japanese people is very high, the extent to which the state should be more directly involved with the organization, financing, and delivery of health services is open for debate in the last decade of the twentieth century (Steslicke 1989). That Japan will shift to a state model remains a possibility.

In contrast to the island nation of industrialized Japan, the People's Republic of China inhabits a vast land mass and consists mainly of an agricultural population. Its health system from the time of "liberation" in 1949 focused on prevention and the delivery of primary care (Sidel and Sidel 1982). The well-known "barefoot doctor," briefly trained in public health, disease prevention, sanitation, and the care of minor, everyday illness, serves as the first level of health services in the countryside. If necessary, patients are referred to regional health clinics, which in turn may refer patients to hospitals, institutions largely concentrated in the cities (Mechanic and Kleinman 1980). Payments for health services have in the past been made at the commune or production brigade level; this system amounts to a form of mutual aid insurance. Annual membership fees were about 3 percent of family income, but members also had to pay a service fee for clinic visits. If referred to a hospital, the commune fund covered up to 50 percent of the costs, with the balance up to the patient. In urban areas, neighborhood medical workers provided the same services as the barefoot doctors. In all these efforts, integration of traditional Chinese and Western medicine has been a goal.

This description is put in the past tense because in recent years economic reform in China has fostered a market economy that has diminished the role of the commune, particularly in rural areas. As of 1984 only 40 to 45 percent of the rural population was covered by health insurance (Hsiao 1984). The collapse of the rural cooperative system has brought about a drop in the number of barefoot doctors, with some going back into agriculture to increase their income, while others have set up private practices. Some voluntary insurance programs remain in production brigades and farms, but many seriously ill must pay the costs of hospital care. One lesson to be learned, according to Hsaio (1984, p. 935), is that economic structure affects health labor power, service demands, and the organization and financing of health care. In Light's scheme, China appears to have been a state system rooted in a mutual aid format that is breaking apart under conditions of cultural and economic change.

Another country with a large land mass and a widely scattered rural population is the USSR. More industrialized than China, it clearly has had a state system, although what will happen as a result of perestroika remains to be seen. In rural areas in the Soviet Union the *feldsher* is the counterpart of the Chinese barefoot doctor, with similar public health, preventive, and initial primary care responsibilities. Regional or, in the cities, neighborhood polyclinics attend to primary care problems, and there are also polyclinics attached to industrial enterprises. Specialists are located both in these polyclinics and in the hospitals. While Field (1967) is an expert on the Soviet health system, a more recent review (Davis 1989) has pointed out some of the problems. Although qualified medical care is provided free of charge to everyone in need, and the system is run and financed by the state, with the Ministry of Health supposed to carry out central planning and provide uniformity of care, there is considerable diversity depending on the community and the type of facility (Davis 1989, p. 242). There is also a small private sector on a fee-for-service basis.

Several cultural characteristics of the Soviet Union that still apply in the contemporary scene have been identified by Haug (1976). These include the memory of the death and destruction of World War II; the pervasiveness of medical oversight with mandated exercises and checkups in enterprises; neighborhood health supervision; citizens' obligation, enshrined in the legal system, to attend to their health in the interests of the welfare of the state; and the fact that so many primary care physicians are women, creating an ambience of motherly concern and supervision. Another feature of the Soviet system is the extensive patient education program, with posters, pamphlets, and pictorial displays prominent in many polyclinics. Physicians provide approval for compensated time off for illness and for holidays at spas and resorts. Growing demands for medical care have, however, created cost containment problems and shortages of facilities, equipment, and pharmaceuticals. These demands also spawned techniques for circumventing health system regulations, such as the use of "gifts" to secure services and skip queues. Despite these variations, the Soviet example is undoubtedly a prototype of Light's state-run system of health care.

The British health-care system, also a state-run enterprise, has been described in detail by Gill (1980). Like Japan, Britain is an island, is highly industrialized, has a culture steeped in respect for royalty, and has a class-based hierarchy. The National Health Service has a tripartite structure: Primary care is delivered by general practitioners in small dispensaries throughout the country, a medical elite of specialists work in the hospitals

(where general practitioners have no role after their patients are admitted), and a public health sector is responsible for preventive and health promotion programs. The conditions for delivery of services were successfully negotiated between organizations of the medical professions and the state at the initiation of the National Health Service. A national insurance program, based on deductions from wages and salaries, was originally supposed to cover all costs of care, but rising demand for care and increases in its costs later required partial payment for services for some conditions. British general practitioners, as in the USSR, play a gatekeeper role by validating illness pay claims or expediting admission to "council housing" for the elderly (Haug 1976, p. 93). They also play a role in rationing high technology hospital care such as kidney dialysis and organ transplants (Aaron and Schwartz 1984). British rationing is based on hard cost-benefit decisions, which affect the delivery of care to the elderly and the terminally ill.

Reorganizations in the system have attempted to equalize regional differences in services and bring about integration between public health, primary care, and hospital services. During the 1980s a conservative government policy focused on cutting costs. A private sector exists side by side with the National Health Service, particularly in more well-to-do areas and for specialist care. This private sector has grown in recent years because of long waits under the NHS for nonemergency hospital care, and it has spawned a growth in private insurance schemes (Aaron and Schwartz 1984). Thus, although a state system is the basic form of British health care, it coexists with a private enterprise structure as well.

The Italian Health Service serves as an example of a corporatist Western European system. In a country fragmented by regional differences, sometimes in language and frequently by political party ideology (between the Communist party and the Christian Democrats), there has really not been a national health-care system. As described by Krause (1988), Italy has historically had physicians on the public payroll. They are now grouped into *ordini,* the regional organizations to which all persons practicing medicine must belong by law and that have both licensing and disciplinary power. Prior to 1978, there was a proliferation of private health insurance plans covering different population segments—professionals, blue-collar workers, farmers, and civil servants. Although almost everyone was covered for some services, poor primary care facilities meant that treatment for all but minor illnesses required hospitalization. When these insurance schemes went bankrupt, the Italian National Health Service was created in 1978 as a cost-cutting measure. It was given an all-encompassing public fund, which was to be centrally managed but with budgets allocated to regional governments. Doctors were put on full salary. However, the Italian National Health Service is not a health service but a cost-control funding mechanism according to Krause (1988, p. 157), and it is not national but regional. The Italian medical organizations must contract for fees and payment methods with each regional and local government Health Service Administration. Three-year contracts are negotiated for patient panel reimbursements and hospital salaries. The *ordini* became the bargaining agents with the regional governments, who are trying to hold the line in costs. Strike threats could be used as bargaining strategies, and strikes could actually occur. It is the existence of this fragmented system of financing by contracts with medical groups that fits Italy into the category of Light's corporatist model.

An example of the tribulations of a health-care system in a small underdeveloped country in Africa forms a balance to the description of major systems in Asia and Europe. In Ghana, consistent with the WHO goal of health for all by the year 2000, a system of primary health care was adopted before 1980. It was viewed as a first step in developing a comprehensive health-care program. Ghana, like many poor countries, has a high infant and maternal mortality rate, problems of malnutrition, and extensive infective and parasitic diseases, which accounted for a third of all deaths in 1983 (Anyinam 1989). Among reasons for this poor health record has been the poverty of the country, the lack of good drinking water, and, as a hangover from former colonial policies, a tendency to put more funds into hospitals rather than in the system of free regional polyclinics.

In an attempt at cost containment undertaken by a new regime in 1983, "user fees" were introduced in all public health facilities, both primary care and specialist clinics, as well as for hospital inpatient care. These user fees were increased in 1985, with only leprosy and tuberculosis patients completely exempt and hospital care for a specified list of twenty-four diseases partially exempt. A health insurance program has also been instituted, but considering that 60 percent of rural and 45 percent of urban dwellers live below the poverty line, it is likely to be limited in coverage (Anyinam 1989, p. 541). With the help of an International Monetary Fund loan, Ghana has attempted to improve the availability of drugs and equipment. At the same time a decentralization policy has been adopted to make all physicians and hospitals autonomous, whether they are private or public. In the communities, primary health care involves village health workers, not unlike the barefoot doctors in China, supervised by nurses and public health officers. At a district level, a public health and medical team attempts to integrate these activities. But all are plagued by lack of trained staff and the poverty of the people. Ghana's experiences demonstrate the difficulties of implementing a state system when it is not centralized and when the economic context is inadequate to support the needed services.

In sharp contrast to the situation in Ghana is that of another small third world country. Cuba, on the opposite side of the globe, also suffered high infant mortality and was plagued with infectious diseases in the past. In Cuba, the government provides all medical care free; in 1983 this cost 15 percent of the gross national product. Ubell (1983) has described a system run by the Ministry of Public Health, which pays the salaries of all physicians and other health care workers, and runs all the local polyclinics, hospitals, and nursing homes. The polyclinics are the chief sources of ambulatory services, not only primary care but also some specialty care. Teams of physicians and nurses may make house calls, check up on persons at risk, and assess community health and sanitation conditions. Patients are seen by their own doctors, who provide entry into specialist and hospital care. Hospitals, formerly concentrated in Havana, are spread throughout the country, with 60 percent of beds in rural areas and towns. There are national medical institutes for high technology procedures including kidney transplants and heart operations. Sophisticated equipment, including computers and a CAT scan, is available at a major hospital attached to the Havana Medical School; much of this equipment is imported from Japan. Graduates of the medical school, which selects students on the basis of a high grade point average in the equivalent of high school, must perform three years of service in rural areas in community medicine.

Local health policy making is shared to some extent with community organizations, particularly women's groups, but physicians have considerable local authority. In the end, the Ministry of Public Health, which controls the whole system, is responsible for the health advances that have been achieved. According to reports (Ubell 1983), Cuba's success has been comparable to that of the most advanced countries in cutting infant mortality, increasing life expectancy, and eradicating or controlling of infectious diseases. As far back as 1984, Cuba claimed a physician ratio of one for every 750 people, compared to one for every 540 in the United States and one for every 1,750 in Brazil (Ubell 1983, p. 1,472). Part of this success is due to financial aid from the Soviet Union but also to a national commitment to health promotion and health care that is unusual among hardpressed developing countries. Cuba is an example of a successful state system, and it has survived despite a U.S. embargo and many economic problems in the small island nation. What will happen as a result of potential changes in Soviet financial support remains to be seen.

These few examples by no means exhaust the list of varying health-care systems. Partial information, rather than a comprehensive explanation of a total system, often appears in edited books or in journals. A sampling of recent reports of this type include articles about Peru (Andes 1989), Chile (Scarpaci 1985), Nepal (Subedi 1989), Singapore (Quah 1989), the Philippines (de Brun and Elling 1987), South Korea (Cho 1989), Egypt (Abu-Zeid and Daum 1985), New Zealand (Raffel 1989), Australia (Rees and Gibbons 1986), Switzerland (Lehman, Gutzmiller, and Martin 1989), Spain (de Miguel and Guillen 1989), Poland (Sokolowka and Rychard 1989), and Yugoslavia (Parmelee 1989). Besides the occasional book, among the best sources for understanding cross-cultural developments in the health field are the journals *Social Science and Medicine,* published in Great Britain, and the *International Journal of Health Services,* whose editor is located in the United States.

The lessons to be learned in comparing health-care systems cross-culturally concern the importance of historical background, cultural beliefs, economic structure, and even geographic characteristics in accounting for system differences. Yet there are some similarities that emerge, and many will continue in the future. Although there are variations in the structure of service delivery, in the relative importance given to primary care as against high-technology medicine, and in the mechanism of financing, there is one common theme. All health-care systems have to face the tension between the extent of coverage and cost containment. This tension is unlikely to diminish in the face of new technological discoveries, which are usually costly while they extend life or its quality. One additional fact that received little attention in the various reviews of health care systems throughout the world is the rapidly increasing percentage of elderly in both developing and developed countries. Persons of advanced years account for one-third of all health-care costs, at least in industrialized societies. If there is any convergence between systems cross-culturally, it will be not only in problems of coverage and cost but also in finding ways to provide adequate care for the growing numbers of the aged.

(SEE ALSO: *Health-Care Financing; Health Policy Analysis; Medical-Industrial Complex; Medical Sociology*)

## REFERENCES

Aaron, H. J., and W. B. Schwartz 1984 *The Painful Prescription: Rationing Hospital Care.* Washington, D.C.: The Brookings Institution.

Abu-Zeid, H. A., and W. B. Daum, 1985 "Health Services Utilization and Cost in Ismailia, Egypt." *Social Science and Medicine* 21:451–461.

Anderson, O. W. 1989 "Issues in the Health Services of the United States." In M. G. Field, ed., *Success and Crisis in National Health Systems: A Comparative Approach.* New York: Routledge.

Andes, N. 1989 "Socioeconomic, Medical Care, and Public Health Contexts Affecting Infant Mortality: A Study of Community Level Differentiation in Peru." *Journal of Health and Social Behavior* 30:386–397.

Anyinam, C. A. 1989 "The Social Costs of the International Monetary Fund's Adjustment Programs for Poverty: The Case of Health Care Development in Ghana." *International Journal of Health Services* 19:531–547.

Cho, S. 1989 "The Emergence of a Health Insurance System in a Developing Country: The Case of South Korea." *Journal of Health and Social Behavior* 30: 467–471.

Davis, C. M. 1989 "The Soviet Health System: A National Health Service in a Socialist Society." In M. G. Field, ed., *Success and Crisis in National Health Systems: A Comparative Approach.* New York: Routledge.

de Brun, S., and R. H. Elling 1987 "Cuba and the Philippines: Contrasting Cases in World-System Analysis." *International Journal of Health Services* 17:681–701.

de Miguel, J. M., and M. F. Guillen, 1989 "The Health System in Spain." In M. G. Field, ed., *Success and Crisis in National Health Systems: A Comparative Approach.* New York: Routledge.

Elling, R. H. 1980 *Cross-National Study of Health Systems: Political Economies and Health Care.* New Brunswick, N.J.: Transaction Books.

Field, M. G. 1967 *Soviet Socialized Medicine: An Introduction.* New York: Free Press.

Gill, D. G. 1980 *The British National Health Service: A Sociologist's Perspective.* Publication no. 80-2054. Washington, D.C.: U.S. Department of Health and Human Services, National Institute of Health.

Haug, M. R. 1976 "Erosion of Professional Authority: A Cross-Cultural Inquiry in the Case of the Physician." *Milbank Memorial Quarterly* 54:83–106.

Hsiao, W. C. 1984 "Transformation of Health Care in China." *The New England Journal of Medicine* 310:932–936.

Kohn, R., and K. L. White (eds.) 1976 *Health Care: An International Study.* London: Oxford University Press.

Krause, E. A. 1988 "Doctors, Partitocrazia, and the Italian State." *The Milbank Quarterly* 66 (Supp. 2) 148–166.

Lehmann, P., F. Gutzwiller, and J. F. Martin 1989 "The Swiss Health System: The Paradox of Ungovernability and Efficacy." In M. G. Field, ed., *Success and Crisis in National Health Systems: A Comparative Approach.* New York: Routledge.

Light, D. W. 1986 "Comparing Health Care Systems: Lessons from East and West Germany." In P. Conrad and R. Kern, eds., *The Sociology of Health and Illness: Critical Perspectives.* 2d ed. New York: St. Martin's Press.

Mechanic, D., and A. Kleinman 1980 "Ambulatory Medical Care in the People's Republic of China: An Exploratory Study." *American Journal of Public Health* 70:62–66.

Parmelee, D. E. 1989 "Yugoslavia: Health Care under Self-Managing Socialism." In M. G. Field, ed., *Success and Crisis in National Health Systems: A Comparative Approach.* New York: Routledge.

Powell, M., and M. Anesaki 1990 *Health Care in Japan.* New York: Routledge.

Quah, S. R. 1989 "The Social Position and Internal Organization of the Medical Profession in the Third World: The Case of Singapore." *Journal of Health and Social Behavior* 30:450–466.

Raffel, M. W. 1989 "New Zealand Health Services." In M. G. Field, ed., *Success and Crisis in National Health Systems: A Comparative Approach.* New York: Routledge.

Rees, S. J., and L. Gibbons 1986 *The Brutal Game: Patients and the Doctors' Dispute.* North Ryde, NSW Australia: Angus and Robertson Publishers.

Roemer, M. I. 1977 *Comparative National Policies on Health Care.* New York: Marcel Decker.

Scarpaci, J. L. 1985 "Restructuring Health Care Financing in Chile." *Social Science and Medicine* 21: 415–431.

Sidel, R., and V. W. Sidel 1982 *The Health of China.* Boston: Beacon Press.

Sokolowka, M., and A. Rychard 1989 "Alternatives in the Health Area: Poland in Comparative Perspective." In M. L. Kohn, ed., *Cross-National Research in Sociology.* Newbury Park, Calif.: Sage.

Steslicke, W. E. 1989 "Health Care and the Japanese

State." In M. G. Field, ed., *Success and Crisis in National Health Systems: A Comparative Approach.* New York: Routledge.

Subedi, J. 1989 "Modern Health Services and Health Care Behavior: A Survey in Kathmandu, Nepal." *Journal of Health and Social Behavior* 30:412–420.

Ubell, R. N. 1983 "High-Tech Medicine in the Caribbean: Twenty-five years of Cuban Health Care." *The New England Journal of Medicine* 309:1468–1472.

MARIE R. HAUG

# COMPARATIVE-HISTORICAL ANALYSIS

Explicit analytic attention to both time and space as the context, cause, or outcome of fundamental sociological processes distinguishes comparative-historical analysis from other forms of social research. Historical processes occurring in or across large-scale geographic, political, or economic units (e.g., regions, nation-states, or entire world systems) are systemically compared for the purpose of more generally understanding patterns of social stability and social change (Moore 1958; Skocpol 1984a; Tilly 1984). Three very different and influential studies illustrate both the questions addressed and approaches used in comparative-historical analysis.

First is the classic study by Reinhard Bendix ([1956] 1974) on work and authority in industry. Bendix initially observed that all industrial societies must authoritatively coordinate productive activities. Yet by systematically comparing how this was done in four countries—prerevolutionary Russia, postwar East Germany, the United States from the 1870s through the 1930s, and industrializing England—Bendix showed that ideologies of workplace dominance varied from one case to another and that these divergences, in turn, were systematically related to differences in the social structures of the countries studied.

Second is the analysis of the historical origins and development of the modern world system by Immanuel Wallerstein (1974). Wallerstein's unit of analysis was the entire sixteenth-century capitalist world economy. Through comparing instances of the geographic division of labor, and especially the increasing bifurcation of global economic activity into "core" and "peripheral" areas, Wallerstein suggested that the economic interdependence of nation-states likely conditions their developmental trajectories.

Third is the analysis of states and social revolutions by Theda Skocpol (1979). Skocpol compared the historical patterns of revolution in three ancien régime states: pre-1789 France, czarist Russia, and imperial China. One of her objectives was to determine what it was generally about these three cases that accounted for the occurrence of successful social revolutions. She found that revolutionary situations emerged in these states because of the conjuncture of international crises and the adaptive constraints induced by their agrarian class structures and political institutions. Her causal generalizations were then buttressed by a comparison of similar agrarian societies—Meiji Japan, Germany in 1806 and 1848, and England in the seventeenth century—that witnessed failed revolutions.

In each of these influential studies, nonexperimental research methods were combined with theoretical concepts to compare and contrast historical processes occurring within and across a number of geographic cases or instances. By using such research methods, Bendix, Wallerstein, Skocpol, and many others are following in the footsteps of perhaps the most influential founders of sociology. In their attempts to comprehend the sweeping transformations of nineteenth-century Europe, Alexis de Tocqueville, Karl Marx, Emile Durkheim, and Max Weber all employed and contributed to the formulation of this broad analytic frame (Smelser 1976; Abrams 1982). Comparative-historical analysis thus is as old as sociology itself.

## DIFFICULTIES

Rigorous historical comparison immediately suggests the analytic and inferential difficulties induced by, among others, (1) defining and selecting comparable macrosociological units; (2) case interdependence; (3) the nonrepresentativeness of cases; (4) determining conceptual equivalence and measurement reliability and validity across time and space; (5) the paucity of data, especially that which is quantitative, over long periods of time and for newly emerging nations; (6) the accidental or intentional selectivity and general unsoundness of the historical record; and (7) the use of spatially and temporally aggregated data and, more generally, the discrepancy between observational units and inferential units. Thus, while comparative-historical analysis is neither necessarily cross-national or cross-cultural, nor always confronting the same obstacles as narrative history, it does share many of the dilemmas (and their solutions) traditionally associated with both types of data (see, e.g., Bloch [1928] 1969; Carr 1961; Lipset 1968; Hopkins and Wallerstein 1967; Przeworski and Teune 1970; Zelditch 1971; Kohn 1989).

Underlying virtually all of the problems discussed above is the age-old tension between the particular and the general (Weber 1949; Joynt and Rescher 1960) and the implications of this for explanation and interpretation. Can particular historical events be aggregated across space and time and conceptually categorized so that their "general" characteristics can be detected and meaningfully compared and analyzed? How is this possible, and at what violence to the reality under examination? Granting their very real import, these difficulties are nonetheless neither generally intractable nor necessarily intellectually paralyzing. Moreover, they are often offset by the promise and achievement of comparative-historical analysis.

## PURPOSES, PROMISE, ACHIEVEMENTS

The analytic power of comparative-historical strategies stems from the uniquely paradoxical quality of its perspectives, data, and logical and technical tools. On the one hand, historical comparisons have the potential to maximize the amount of known variation in social processes and institutions. Some scholars believe this essential to the development of truly general theory and to transcultural and transhistorical explanation (Przeworski and Teune 1970; Nowak 1989). On the other hand, historical comparisons have the

potential to acknowledge and exploit the "time-space boundedness" of social life and its historical antecedents, specificity, and possibilities of or limits to change. Others view this as equally essential to theoretical development and to concrete, "real world" explanation (Moore 1958; Skocpol 1984b; Tilly 1984). Most comparative-historical analysts capitalize in some fashion on this paradox, finding diversity in the midst of uniformity and producing regularities from differences.

One of the great advantages of historical comparisons is that they reduce analytic and inferential distortions induced by culturally and historically limited analyses and interpretations of the social world. Social structures and processes in the past were generally quite different from those observed today, and specific institutional arrangements and social relations differ substantially across cultures, regions, and states. Patterns of historical change and continuity, moreover, have varied from one country or culture to another. Some scholars, such as Bendix (1963, [1956] 1974), relish this diversity and use historical comparisons to emphasize and interpret the peculiarities of each case. Even seeming uniformities across cases, moreover, may mask important differences in historical processes. So essential is detecting these "false similarities" that Marc Bloch ([1928] 1969) believed it one of the very purposes of historical comparison.

Examination of historical or national differences can also lead to the detection of previously unknown facts that may suggest a research problem or pose a hypothesis amenable to empirical exploration. Bloch (pp. 49–51), for example, tells of how his knowledge of the English land enclosures led him to discover similar events in France. Concept formation and the construction of ideal types, too, are facilitated by comparing histories (Weber 1949; Bendix 1963; Smelser 1976). Weber's ([1904] 1958) conceptualization of "the spirit of capitalism" and Wallerstein's (1974) notion of the "world system," for example, clearly derive from comparative-historical inquiry. Linking apparently disparate phenomena, such as Karl Polanyi ([1944] 1957) does when he relates the gold standard and the one hundred years of relative geopolitical tranquillity in the nineteenth century, is also one of the fruits of comparative-historical analysis (McMichael 1990). New information, conceptual development, and uncovering unlikely commonalities are necessary for the generation, elaboration, and historical grounding of social theory.

The analysis of historical and comparative patterns generally allows for more adequate testing of established theory than does study of a single nation, culture, or time period. Plausible theories of large-scale social change, for example, are intrinsically processual, and historical analysis is therefore crucial for a genuine test or exposition of their hypotheses (Tilly 1984). Historical comparisons can also be used to assess the generality of what is taken to be universal explanations for social structure and social action (e.g., functionalism, Marxism). These "timeless" and "culture-free" propositions are directly confronted through the systematic analysis of "parallel" cases that, theoretically, should display or be subject to the same process (Bonnell 1980; Skocpol and Somers 1980). Successive applications of the parallel-case strategy therefore help determine a theory's generality and specify the scope conditions—the domain of a theory's applicability—necessary to render general theory falsifiable (Griffin et al. 1989; Nowak 1989).

Comparative-historical analysis is sometimes directed toward developing explanations that are "relative" to space and time (Beer 1963, p. 9) or that represent historically or culturally "limited generalizations" (Joynt and Rescher 1960, p. 156). Skocpol's (1979) analysis of social revolutions in France, Russia, and China, for example, resulted in limited causal generalizations deemed valid, but for these three cases only. Exceptions to whatever generality is adduced, moreover, can be conceptualized as "deviant" cases. Their explanation requires modification of the original theory. Werner Sombart ([1906] 1976), for example, posed the question "Why is there no socialism in the United States?" precisely because the United States, when contrasted to the European experience, appeared theoretically and historically

anomalous. When general theoretical questions and historical patterns are comparatively situated, the "inexplicable" residue of the apparent uniqueness of time and place is potentially "explicable" (Sewell 1967). Thus, again, does comparative-historical inquiry establish research problems, generate more inclusive explanation, and develop ever more refined and well-specified social theory.

## ANALYTIC TYPES OF HISTORICAL COMPARISONS

Extant typologies or taxonomies of the purposes, logic, or scope of comparative-historical analysis reveal the very diverse epistemologies and research strategies constituting comparative-historical practice (Bonnell 1980; Skocpol and Somers 1980; Skocpol 1984c; Tilly 1984; Ragin 1987; McMichael 1990). There are at least two basic approaches to analysis, labeled here "analytical formalism" and "interpretive." As will be seen, each type of comparison displays considerable internal diversity and can in principle overlap with the other.

**Analytically Formal Historical Comparison.** Formal comparison conforms generally to conventional scientific practice in that causal explanation is the goal. It is therefore characterized by the development and testing of falsifiable theory, formal logic, and replicable procedures of analysis. Consequently, historical narration and the "unities of time and place" (Skocpol 1984c, p. 383) are deliberately replaced by the language of causal analysis. Criteria for evaluating the merits of analytically formal historical comparisons are widely known or generally accessible. Analytic formal comparison can be used to generalize across time and space, to uncover or produce limited causal regularities among a set of cases, and to establish a theory's scope conditions. There are two major procedural subtypes in this genre: statistical comparisons and formal qualitative comparisons.

1. Statistical analyses of comparative-historical phenomena are logically and inferentially identical to the statistical analyses of any other social phenomena. Thus, they typically use quantitative

counts and rely on statistical controls and inference to assess rigorously the effects of theoretically salient variables, to test the validity of causal arguments, and to develop parsimonious generalizations. Comparative-historical applications of the statistical method vary greatly from one study to another. One tradition uses time-series statistical analyses to chart historical processes in a few countries. These historically based statistical patterns are then compared across countries. In these "comparative time-series" studies, historical variation and change, often over a great length of time (Tilly, Tilly, and Tilly 1975), are the focus of analysis. Studies in this tradition are discussed again briefly in the conclusion of this article.

The second major use of statistical procedures in comparative analysis relies on quantitative data from many nations (or other social units) for only one or a few time points. Emphasis in what is called the "cross-national" tradition (e.g., Chase-Dunn 1979; Jackman 1984) is on detecting causal generalizations that are valid for a large sample or even an entire population of countries. The results of such studies typically resemble a static, cross-sectional snapshot of historical process. This analytic strategy is often necessitated because complete time-series data do not exist for very many nations, especially those in the Third World and now undergoing economic and social development. Cross-national studies tend to be theory-driven and "variable-oriented" in that analytic interest centers on the degree of empirical support that statistical regularities and relationships among variables provide for general theoretical propositions (Ragin 1987). Consequently, the cases from which the quantitative data are drawn are usually not of much intrinsic interest to statistical analysts. One clear indication of this is that the selection of cases often appears to be a function of data availability or the desire to increase the sample size and thus the statistical significance of the results (Ragin 1987).

Cross-national statistical comparisons are a powerful way to assess the empirical consequences of alternative theoretical claims over a large number of cases (Chase-Dunn 1979; Fogel 1983). But critics of the approach charge that they often

falsely homogenize cases and denude them of their historical grounding in the quest for general explanation and statistical significance. The understanding of cases as real social units deserving explanation in their own right sometimes seems lost (Ragin 1987; Tilly 1984; Skocpol 1984b).

**2.** Formal qualitative comparison, by way of contrast, views cases "holistically," as qualitatively distinct and independent units that cannot (or should not) be decomposed into scores on quantitative variables as in statistical analyses. This strategy adopts a "case-oriented" approach that pervades the entire research process (Ragin 1987). The explanation of a few carefully chosen cases, for example, generally is the rationale for and product of the analysis. Explicit and elaborate empirical strategies, moreover, have been designed to select proper instances to be compared and analyzed (Przeworski and Teune 1970; Lijphart 1971).

The logic of formal comparison mimics the experimental method by using case selection to control variation (Frendreis 1983). The actual detection of causal regularities is often inferred through the systematic application of John S. Mill's ([1843] 1967) inductive canons or "methods of agreement" and "method of difference" to comparative data (Skocpol 1984c; Ragin 1987). Using the method of agreement, analysts select cases that have positive outcomes on the phenomenon under study but that differ on putative explanatory conditions. These cases are then compared to see what factor they share. The common element is judged to be causal because it accompanies every positive instance of the outcome. Alternative explanations are eliminated if antecedent conditions representing those claims do not occur in all cases with positive outcomes.

The method of agreement is logically flawed because the imputation of causality is impossible until cases lacking the outcome of interest are analyzed to see if they also lack the causal factor detected by the method of agreement. This is accomplished through the analysis of "negative cases" via the "method of difference." Here analysis is conducted with cases instancing both positive and negative outcomes but that are as similar as possible on the putative causal factors. The objective is to find the one condition that is present in all positive cases and absent in all negative cases. Therefore, the method of difference is essential to guard against making spurious inferences and to reinforce conclusions derived from the method of agreement (Skocpol 1984c; Ragin 1987). Ideally, causal inferences take the form of a series of necessary and sufficient conditions for the presence of the phenomenon.

The use of the methods of agreement and difference presuppose that one causal factor or configuration holds for all cases with positive instances (e.g., Skocpol 1979). This principle of "causal invariance" is why Tilly (1984) labels studies using these methods "universalizing" in their comparative logic. Patterns displaying "causal heterogeneity" or "multiple causal conjunctures"—two or more distinct combinations of causal forces generating the same outcome (Ragin 1987)—are logically ruled out. This serious shortcoming of Mill's canons is due to the excessive weight given negative cases. There are exceptions to almost any general process, and, if used mechanically, the search for and inability to find causal universals that are doubly confirmed by the twin logics of agreement and difference can rule out virtually any nontrivial explanation (Lijphart 1971; Ragin 1987).

Charles Ragin (1987) has developed an alternative comparative logic that allows for the detection of causal heterogeneity in a large number of cases. Called "qualitative comparative analysis" (QCA), this procedure also uses quasi-experimental logic to search for similarities between or among positive instances and to exploit the inferential utility of negative cases. Unlike the methods of agreement and difference, however, it can detect whatever multiple causal generalizations may exist through a data reduction logic rooted in Boolean algebra. Negative or "deviant" cases may be explained by, or give rise to, an alternative causal process, but they are not allowed to invalidate any and all generalizations. Ragin believes the Boolean logic more closely approximates the mode of reasoning—including the use of logically possible "historical hypotheticals" and "historical coun-

terfactuals"—employed by Weber (1949) and Moore (1966, 1978) in their powerful but less formalized comparative studies.

Formal qualitative comparison provides both historically grounded explanation and theoretical generalization. With the advent of QCA, this approach is no longer flawed by the assumption of causal invariance or by the inferential problems induced by the analysis of a small number of cases of unknown representativeness (Ragin 1987; Griffin et al. 1989). Nonetheless, its detractors believe that formal comparison is often fraught with hidden substantive assumptions, unable to exert sufficient control over the multitude of competing historical forces, and compromised by its roots in inductive logic (Burawoy 1989). Moreover, a key assumption of formal comparison—that the historical cases are not systematically interrelated—is seriously challenged by proponents of holistic comparison (Wallerstein 1974; McMichael 1990), discussed below.

**Interpretive Historical Comparison.** "Interpretive" comparisons are most concerned with developing a meaningful understanding of broad cultural or historical patterns (Skocpol 1984c). Two very different comparative logics, "individualizing" and "holistic," are used to construct historical interpretations. Neither logic relies extensively on formal analytic procedures, and neither is geared toward adducing causal inferences from, or in testing theory with, historical comparisons. This is not meant to imply that interpretive comparison is atheoretical or lacking in rigor. Concepts and theories, the latter often of sweeping scope and grandeur, are extensively deployed, but metaphorically, as interpretive and organizing frames, or as lenses through which history is perceived and understood (Bonnell 1980; Skocpol 1984). Critics occasionally find interpretive comparisons compelling and impressive, but sometimes of questionable validity due either to their self-validating logic or to their lack of explicit scientific criteria for evaluating the truth content of the interpretation (Bonnell 1980; Skocpol 1984; Tilly 1984).

1. Holistic comparison is more intimately tied to particular theories than are other kinds of

comparative analytic strategies. It is used when some form of "social whole," such as a world system (Wallerstein 1974), is methodologically posited. Conceptualizing the entire world system as a "spatio-temporal whole" (Bach 1980), for example, suggests that there is but one theoretical unit of analysis, and that unit is the world system. What are considered to be "units of analysis" or "cases" in most comparative-historical strategies are, in the holistic methodological frame, really only interrelated and interdependent historical "moments" or realizations of a singular process or social system. Thus, whether nation-states or cultures, these "moments" are not the discrete and independent units demanded by analytic formalism (Bach 1980; McMichael 1990).

With this methodological postulate, historical comparison proceeds in one of two ways. One way is through a functionalist "encompassing" logic that explains similarities or differences among parts of a whole by the relationship the part has to the whole (Tilly 1984). Thus Wallerstein's (1974) encompassing comparisons explain the differential development of temporally specific and spatially specific economic units in the world system— the core, periphery, and semiperiphery—by their differential positions and role in the world economy. Explanations such as this are often circular in their reasoning and always difficult to test. Theory verification, in fact, is not the purpose of this sort of comparison. Instead, encompassing comparison employs multiple instances of the same process (i.e., the parts of the system) to "illustrate" or interpret (Bonnell 1980) the workings of a social whole or to develop the inner logic of a theory (Skocpol 1984c). Such comparisons are possible only because of what Charles Tilly (1984, p. 325) calls a preexisting "mental map of the whole system and a theory of its operation."

McMichael (1990) suggests "incorporated comparison" as an alternative to purge holistic comparison of its self-validating logic. This strategy posits a kind of social whole that does not preexist and regulate its parts, as does the world system, but that is analytically "reconstituted" by historical comparisons. Through analysis, particular and very different instances are conceptualized as interdependent and interrelated processes that, when cumulated and connected through time and space, "form" the whole as a general but empirically diverse historical process. Thus the very definition and selection of "cases" becomes the object of theorizing and research and not its point of departure (as in encompassing comparisons) or the vehicle conveying data for analysis (as in analytic comparisons). Incorporated comparisons may be especially useful in the development of historically grounded social theory that minimizes the distinction between the general and the particular (McMichael 1990). McMichael identifies Polanyi's (1944/1957) analysis of the emergence and decline of laissez-faire capitalism as a worthy example of this form of holistic comparison.

2. Some interpretive analysts use historical comparison to demonstrate the historical particularity of each individual case. Understanding variation in historical contexts, therefore, motivates these "individualizing" (Tilly 1984) comparisons. The research of Bendix (1956/1974, 1978) is an exemplar of this strategy. Analysts in this tradition choose research questions and cases on the basis of their recurrent moral and historical significance. They are also often sensitive to the culturally embedded meanings in social action and tend self-consciously to eschew general theory (Bonnell 1980; Skocpol 1984c; Tilly 1984). Instead, the argument is sustained by way of the discovery of patterns distilled from rich description and narrative sequencing (Bendix 1963; Tilly 1984) and the use of persuasive concepts that crystallize or resonate with significant social values and themes (Skocpol 1984c). This form of interpretative comparison generally has a distinctly traditional "historicist" tone and appeal (Bonnell 1980).

## THE FUTURE OF COMPARATIVE-HISTORICAL ANALYSIS

The utility of social research rests more on the creative use of good theory than it does on its methodology. But "the creative use" of theory is itself largely a matter of how theory is combined with research strategy. On this dimension, the success of comparative-historical analysis in the near future will hinge on making the most of methodological currents now visible.

One encouraging trend that will likely become more widespread is combining different kinds of comparative logics. Through the cross-national quantitative analysis of a large number of instances, both Jeffrey Paige (1975) and John Stephens (1980), for example, produced statistical generalizations. But Paige also conducted three parallel case studies and found differences in the nature of the general outcome of interest, agrarian revolt. Thus he was engaged in "variation-finding" comparison as well (Tilly 1984). Stephens systematically compared a subset of four cases, showing how the historical processes of welfare state development differed from one nation to another. He was therefore also using an individualizing comparative logic. Combining comparative-historical approaches can yield insights that are otherwise not possible.

Another positive note is the increasing use of statistical techniques developed explicitly to analyze temporal (Tuma and Hannan 1984; Isaac and Griffin 1989; Abbott and Hrycak 1990) and spatial processes (Loftin and Ward 1981). Time-series and spatial analyses of time–space data are not always subject to the same limitations as are cross-national statistical analyses. But even these procedures must be self-consciously grounded in the substantive historical processes studied to contribute fully to comparative-historical research (Moore 1958; Hobsbawm 1981). This requires seriously thinking about time and place and not merely using them as data in formal analysis (Isaac and Griffin 1989; McMichael 1990).

One strategy that could be fruitfully employed more often is multilevel analysis using comparative and historical variation as the two levels of analysis and inference. Comparative time-series analyses can be used to good effect here (Griffin et al. 1989). Charles, Louise, and Richard Tilly (1975) and Douglas Hibbs (1978), for example, use statistical time-series procedures to map and explain historical patterns of collective action within nations. They then qualitatively compare these national patterns to detect and explain differences

or similarities across countries or groups of nations in a second, "higher order" analysis. The Tillys largely individualize, while Hibbs both individualizes and universalizes and develops an insightful empirical typology as well. Again, more is learned than would be possible through analysis of a single level.

What is now lacking is a synthesis of formal analytic and (especially holistic) interpretive comparisons. This clearly is a difficult task because their logical foundations and purposes are so different. It should not be ruled out, however. The compatibility of different approaches is likely heightened if each have designated and noncompeting purposes in the research process (McMichael 1990). But even if these and other differences prove too great to overcome, diversity in methodology and strategy should not be viewed as excessively problematic. It helps prevent complacency and thus stagnation. It promotes innovation and spurs efforts toward analytic synthesis (e.g., Ragin 1987) and even methodological unity. Most important, it provides richly textured, multivoiced portrayals and understandings of perennial questions of fundamental human significance.

(SEE ALSO: *Case Studies; Cross-Cultural Analysis; Field Research Methods; Historical Sociology*)

## REFERENCES

Abbott, A., and A. Hrycak 1990 "Measuring Resemblance in Sequence Data: An Optimal Matching Analysis of Musicians' Careers." *American Journal of Sociology* 96:144–185.

Abrams, P. 1982 *Historical Sociology*. Ithaca, N.Y.: Cornell University Press.

Bach, R. 1980 "On the Holism of a World-System Perspective." In T. Hopkins and I. Wallerstein, eds., *Processes of the World System*. Beverly Hills, Calif.: Sage Publications.

Beer, S. 1963 "Causal Explanation and Imaginative Reenactment." *History and Theory* 3:6–29.

Bendix, R. (1956) 1974 *Work and Authority in Industry: Ideologies of Management in the Course of Industrialization*. Berkeley: University of California Press.

——— 1963 "Concepts and Generalizations in Comparative Sociological Studies." *American Sociological Review* 28:532–539.

——— 1978 *Kings or People? Power and the Mandate to Rule*. Berkeley: University of California Press.

Bloch, M. (1928) 1969 "A Contribution Towards a Comparative History of European Societies." In M. Bloch, *Life and Work in Medieval Europe: Selected Papers of Marc Bloch*. New York: Harper Torchbooks.

——— 1953 *The Historian's Craft*. New York: Alfred A. Knopf.

Bonnell, V. 1980 "The Uses of Theory, Concepts and Comparison in Historical Sociology." *Comparative Studies in Society and History* 22:156–173.

Burawoy, M. 1989 "Two Methods in Search of Science: Skocpol versus Trotsky." *Theory and Society* 18:759–805.

Carr, E. H. 1961 *What Is History?* New York: Vintage.

Chase-Dunn, C. 1979 "Comparative Research on World-System Characteristics." *International Studies Quarterly* 23:601–623.

Fogel, R. 1983 "'Scientific History' and Traditional History." In R. Fogel and G. Elton, *Which Road to the Past?* New Haven, Conn.: Yale University Press.

Frendreis, J. 1983 "Explanation of Variation and Detection of Covariation: The Purpose and Logic of Comparative Analysis." *Comparative Political Studies* 16:255–272.

Griffin, L., P. O'Connell, and H. McCammon 1989 "National Variation in the Context of Struggle: Post-war Class Conflict and Market Distribution in the Capitalist Democracies." *Canadian Review of Sociology and Anthropology* 26:37–68.

Hibbs, D. 1978 "On the Political Economy of Long-run Trends in Strike Activity." *British Journal of Political Science* 8:51–75.

Hobsbawm, E. 1981 "The Contribution of History to Social Science." *International Social Science Journal* 33:624–640.

Hopkins, T., and I. Wallerstein 1967 "The Comparative Study of National Societies." *Social Science Information* 6:25–58.

Isaac, L., and L. Griffin 1989 "Ahistoricism in Time-Series Analyses of Historical Process: Critique, Redirection and Illustrations from U.S. Labor History." *American Sociological Review* 54:873–890.

Jackman, R. 1984 "Cross-National Statistical Research and the Study of Comparative Politics." *American Journal of Political Science* 28:161–182.

Joynt, C., and N. Rescher 1960 "The Problem of Uniqueness in History." *History and Theory* 1:150–162.

Kohn, M. (ed.) 1989 *Cross-National Research in Sociology*. Beverly Hills, Calif.: Sage Publications.

Lijphart, A. 1971 "Comparative Politics and the Comparative Method." *American Political Science Review* 65:682–693.

Lipset, S. M. 1968 "History and Sociology: Some Methodological Considerations." In S. M. Lipset and R. Hofstader, eds., *Sociology and History: Methods*. New York: Basic Books.

Loftin, C., and S. Ward 1981 "Spatial Autocorrelation Models for Galton's Problem." *Behavior Science Research* 16:105–128.

McMichael, P. 1990 "Incorporating Comparison Within a World-Historical Perspective: An Alternative Comparative Method." *American Sociological Review* 55:385–397.

Mill, J. S. (1843) 1967 *A System of Logic: Ratiocinative and Inductive*. Toronto: University of Toronto Press.

Moore, B. 1958 "Strategy in Social Research." In B. Moore, *Political Power and Social Theory*. Cambridge, Mass.: Harvard University Press.

——— 1966 *The Social Origins of Dictatorship and Democracy*. Boston: Beacon Press.

——— 1978 *Injustice: The Social Bases of Obedience and Revolt*. White Plains, N.Y.: M. E. Sharpe.

Nowak, S. 1989 "Comparative Studies and Social Theory." In M. Kohn, ed., *Cross-National Research in Sociology*. Beverly Hills, Calif.: Sage Publications.

Paige, J. 1975 *Agrarian Revolt: Social Movements and Export Agriculture in the Underdeveloped World*. New York: Free Press.

Polanyi, K. (1944) 1957 *The Great Transformation: The Political and Economic Origins of Our Times*. Boston: Beacon Press.

Przeworski, A., and H. Teune 1970 *The Logic of Comparative Social Inquiry*. New York: Wiley.

Ragin, C. 1987 *The Comparative Method*. Berkeley: University of California Press.

Sewell, W. 1967 "Marc Bloch and the Logic of Comparative History." *History and Theory* 6:208–218.

Skocpol, T. 1979 *States & Social Revolutions*. Cambridge: Cambridge University Press.

——— (ed.) 1984a *Vision and Method in Historical Sociology*. New York: Cambridge University Press.

——— 1984b "Sociology's Historical Imagination." In T. Skocpol, ed., *Vision and Method in Historical Sociology*. New York: Cambridge University Press.

——— 1984c "Emerging Agendas and Recurrent Strategies in Historical Sociology." In T. Skocpol, ed., *Vision and Method in Historical Sociology*. New York: Cambridge University Press.

———, and M. Somers 1980 "The Uses of Comparative History in Macrosocial Inquiry." *Comparative Study of Society and History* 22:174–197.

Smelser, N. 1976 *Comparative Methods in the Social Sciences.* Englewood Cliffs, N.J.: Prentice-Hall.

Sombart, W. (1906) 1976 *Why Is There No Socialism in the United States?* White Plains, N.Y.: M. E. Sharpe.

Stephens, J. 1980 *The Transition from Capitalism to Socialism.* Atlantic Highlands, NJ: Humanities Press.

Tilly, Charles 1984 *Big Structures, Large Processes, Huge Comparisons.* New York: Russell Sage Foundation.

———, Louise Tilly, and Richard Tilly 1975 *The Rebellious Century, 1830–1930.* Cambridge, Mass.: Harvard University Press.

Tuma, N., and M. Hannan 1984 *Social Dynamics.* New York: Academic Press.

Wallerstein, I. 1974 *The Modern World System.* New York: Academic Press.

Weber, M. (1904) 1958 *The Protestant Ethic and the Spirit of Capitalism.* New York: Scribners.

——— 1949 *The Methodology of the Social Sciences.* New York: Free Press.

Zelditch, M. 1971 "Intelligible Comparisons." In I. Vallier, ed., *Comparative Methods in Sociology.* Berkeley: University of California Press.

LARRY J. GRIFFIN

**COMPLEMENTARITY** *See* Mate-Selection Theories.

**COMPLEX ORGANIZATIONS** Organizations, as a class, are socially constructed innovations, deliberately designed as solutions to problems. Although some forms of organization, such as churches and armies, have been around for centuries, only since the Industrial Revolution have complex organizations assumed the form people take for granted today. Because they are shaped by the contexts, or environments, in which they are established, contemporary organizations reflect the impact of their historical origins in societies characterized by growing affluence and conflicts over the control and distribution of wealth. Organizations come in a bewildering variety of forms because they have been explicitly created to deal with a wide range of problems and because they have emerged under widely varying environmental conditions.

## DEFINITIONS OF ORGANIZATIONS

What are complex organizations? A simple definition is that organizations are goal-directed, boundary-maintaining, socially constructed systems of human activity. Some definitions add other criteria such as deliberateness of design, existence of status structures, patterned understandings between participants, orientation to an environment, possession of a technical system for accomplishing tasks, and substitutability of personnel (Scott 1987).

Goal orientation and deliberate design of activity systems are distinctive features discriminating between organizations and other collectivities such as families and small groups. Organizations are purposive systems in which members behave as if their organizations have goals, although individual participants may personally feel indifferent toward those goals or even alienated from their organizations. Concerted collective action toward an apparent common purpose also distinguishes organizations from such social units as friendship circles, audiences, and mass publics. Because many organizational forms are now institutionalized in modern societies, people readily turn to them or construct them when a task or objective exceeds their own personal abilities and resources (Meyer and Rowan 1977; Zucker 1988).

Organizations have activity systems, or technologies, for accomplishing work, which can include processing raw materials, information, or people. Activity systems consist of bounded sets of interdependent role behaviors; the nature of the interdependencies is often contingent upon the techniques used.

Other key elements of organizations, such as socially constructed boundaries, are shared with other types of collectivities. The establishment of an "organization" implies a distinction between members and nonmembers, thus marking off organizations from their environments. Maintaining this distinction requires boundary-maintenance activity because boundaries may be permeable, and, thus, some organizations establish an authoritative process to enforce membership distinctions. For example, businesses have human resource management departments that select, socialize, and monitor employees, and voluntary associations have membership committees that perform similar functions. Distinctive symbols of membership may include unique modes of dress and special vocabularies.

Organizations, with few exceptions, are incomplete social systems that depend on interchanges with their environments. Pertinent features of the environment include technical elements directly tied to the accomplishment of work, such as information and other resources, and cultural or institutional elements shared with the wider society such as rules, understandings, and meanings about organizations (Meyer and Scott 1983).

Goal setting by owners or leaders thus must take into account the sometimes contrary preferences of other organizations, as activity systems are fueled by resources obtained from outsiders. For example, participants must be enticed or coerced into contributing to the organization's activities. Businesses pay people to work for them, and nonprofit organizations may offer more intangible benefits such as sociable occasions. Because organizations are not self-sufficient, they are subject to uncertainties and may be vulnerable to exploitation or external control by the outsiders on whom they depend (Pfeffer and Salancik 1978). Contemporary research often focuses on how these external dependencies are managed by organizations.

Within organizations, goal attainment and boundary maintenance manifest themselves as issues of coordination and control, as authorities construct arrangements for allocating resources or integrating work flows. These internal structures affect the perceived meaning and satisfaction of individual participants by, for example, differentially allocating power and affecting the characteristics of jobs. Control structures, which shape the way participants are directed, evaluated, and rewarded, are constrained by participants' multiple external social roles, some complementing, but others conflicting with, organizational

roles. Over the past few decades, organizational sociology has gradually expanded its scope to include more of the external uncertainties associated with organizational life.

## IMPORTANCE OF ORGANIZATIONS

Why are complex organizations important? Organizations, which produce goods, deliver services, maintain order, and challenge the established order, are the fundamental building blocks of modern societies and the basic vehicles through which collective action is undertaken. The prominence of organizations in contemporary society is apparent when we consider some consequences of their actions.

Organizations coordinate the actions of people in pursuit of activities too broad in scope to be accomplished by individuals alone. Railroads were the first large corporations in the United States, arising because the passage of long-distance shipments could not be effectively coordinated by many small, autonomous merchants and traders. In the twentieth century, the production of mass-market consumption goods such as automobiles and electric appliances has been made possible by the rise of large, vertically integrated manufacturing firms. Similarly, in the public sector, the implementation of government social policies has necessitated the development of large government agencies that process thousands of cases on a universalistic, impersonal basis.

The concentration of power in organizations contributes not only to the attainment of large-scale goals in modern societies but also to some major social problems. Hazardous waste contamination in the so-called Love Canal episode in Buffalo, New York, was a result of the careless disposal of unwanted hazardous materials by large chemical manufacturers. Less dramatic, but still illustrative of the capacity of organizations to do harm and good, are accounts of unsafe consumer products and the relative collapse of the savings and loan industry in the late 1980s.

Increasingly, major tasks in society are addressed, not by single organizations, but by sets of interdependent organizations. The National Cooperative Research Act of 1984 allowed businesses that normally compete with each other to establish research-and-development consortia for conducting research on processes or products that benefit an entire industry. Interorganizational arrangements among hospitals, doctors, and university laboratories have been created by the National Cancer Institute to coordinate cancer research and treatment.

## ORGANIZATIONAL DEMOGRAPHICS

The number of organizations in industrial societies is very large. Over five million businesses with at least one employee existed in the United States in 1990, and there were thousands of governmental, nonprofit, membership, and voluntary associations. Social scientists have developed various schemes to describe the diversity of organizations. For example, the Standard Industrial Classification (Office of Management and Budget 1972) sorts establishments by their products and the processes used to make them. Organizations can also be classified according to their goals, the social functions they serve (Parsons 1960), and the prime beneficiaries of organizational actions: owners, members, clients, or the general public (Blau and Scott 1962). Another classification contrasts generalist and specialist organizations and hypothesizes that each type thrives in a different kind of environment (Hannan and Freeman 1989).

Business organizations are highly stratified by size, and large firms have more resources with which to resist and counter environmental pressures. The vast majority of organizations are small, however. Most business establishments employ fewer than one hundred workers, and typical voluntary associations have fewer than fifty members. Thus, most organizations are fairly vulnerable to environmental forces and must adapt to them or disband. A representative sample of organizations would yield predominantly small ones, rather than organizations as large as International Business Machines (IBM), General Motors, or Exxon.

Even though most organizations are small, their numbers are often counterbalanced by the extreme wealth and power of the handful of truly enormous organizations. In the United States, more than 50 percent of the civilian labor force is employed by only 2 percent of employing units, and, in manufacturing, the top 200 firms control about 60 percent of all assets (Useem 1984). About 50 percent of all banking assets are controlled by thirty out of 14,000 banks, and eight out of approximately 1,800 insurance companies hold half of the assets in that industry (Kerbo 1983). Some sociologists have argued that large organizations are so effective at neutralizing competitive forces that their survival is never in jeopardy (Perrow 1986).

Populations of organizations in modern societies are constantly undergoing processes of expansion, contraction, and change. Some organizations are founded in a flash of creative energy and then disbanded almost immediately, whereas others emerge slowly and last for decades. Some organizations adapt readily to every environmental challenge, whereas others succumb to the first traumatic event they face. Sociologists have turned their attention to these vital events surrounding the reproduction and renewal of organizational populations, focusing on three processes: foundings, transformations, and disbandings (Aldrich 1979; Hannan and Freeman 1989).

New organizations are established fairly frequently, although systematic data on founding rates are available only for businesses. Studies in the United States and other Western industrialized nations show that about ten businesses are founded per year for every one hundred businesses active at the start of the year. Explanations for variations in rates of organizational foundings have stressed the characteristics of opportunity structures, organizing capacities of groups, and strategies adopted by entrepreneurs as they take account of opportunities and resources available to them (Aldrich and Wiedenmayer 1991).

Societal demands for special-purpose organizations increased with urbanization and with economic, political, and social differentiation, while the resources required to construct organizations grew more abundant with the development of a money economy and the spread of literacy (Stinchcombe 1965). The spread of facilitative legal, political, and other institutions also played a major role by creating a stable, predictable context within which entrepreneurs could look forward to appropriating the gains from organizational foundings. Occasional periods of political upheaval and revolution stimulate foundings by freeing resources from previous uses, and thus massive changes are likely to occur in the organizational populations of Eastern Europe in the 1990s.

Transformations occur when existing organizations adapt their structures to changing conditions. The issue of how frequently and under what conditions organizations change has provoked some of the most spirited debates in organizational sociology. Strategic choice theorists have argued for managerial autonomy and adaptability, whereas ecological and institutional theorists have tended to stress organizational inertia and dependence. Recent research has moved away from polarizing debates and reframed the question of transformation, asking about the conditions under which organizations change and whether changes occur more frequently in core or peripheral features (Singh and Lumsden 1990).

During the 1980s growing awareness of techniques for performing dynamic analyses produced some useful studies such as those on diversification, top executive changes, and changes in corporate form (Fligstein 1991). These studies tell us that changes *do* occur, although they do not report whether rates of change go up or down over an organization's life cycle. Most of these studies are of the very largest business firms, for which data are publicly available, and not of representative samples.

If all newly founded organizations lived forever, the study of organizational change would be confined to issues of founding, adaptation, and inertia. Research has shown that organizations disband at a fairly high rate, however, and a sizable literature has grown up on organizational mortality (Carroll 1984; Singh 1990). Organizations can cease to exist as separate entities in two ways: by completely dissolving, the process by which the vast majority of organizations disband, or by becoming part of a different entity through merger or acquisition. Between 1963 and 1988, about 75,000 mergers and acquisitions occurred in the United States (Grimm 1989), amounting to less than 1 percent of the incorporated firm population in any given year. In contrast, between 1976 and 1984, the annual rate of dissolution in the business population of the United States was about 10 percent (Small Business Administration 1986).

Age and size are the strongest predictors of how long an organization will survive. Young organizations disband at a substantially higher rate than older ones, a conservative estimate being that only half of new organizations survive more than five years (Birch 1987). Internally, new organizations depend upon the cooperation of strangers, who must be taught new routines, some of which are unique to particular organizations (Stinchcombe 1965). Externally, new organizations must find niches in potentially hostile environments, overcoming competitors and establishing their legitimacy with potential members, customers, suppliers, and others. Survival beyond infancy is easier when an organization adopts a form that has already been institutionalized and is widely regarded as legitimate and proper (Zucker 1988).

## SOURCES OF INTERNAL DIVERSITY AMONG ORGANIZATIONS

All models of organizations as coherent entities can be reduced to two basic views. The systemic view sees organizations as social systems, sustained by the roles allocated to their participants, whereas the associative perspective treats organizations as associations of self-interested parties, sustained by the rewards the participants derive from their association with the organizations (Swanson 1971). These two views each have a venerable heritage in the social sciences. Despite subtle variations, all perspectives on organizations ultimately use one or both of these models.

Institutional, functionalist, and ecological perspectives rely on a systemic model, viewing organizations as relatively coherent, stable entities. Such models emphasize the activity systems in organizations that are deliberately designed to accomplish specific goals. Formal structures of organizations, including division of labor, authority relationships, and prescribed communication channels, are treated as fulfilling a purposeful design. For example, an institutional approach emphasizes member socialization and other processes that make the transmission of shared meanings easier. Ecological models usually treat organizations as units that are being selected for or against by their environments and, thus, assume that organizations cohere as units.

Interpretive and more microanalytic views rely heavily on an associative model, leading to the expectation that organizations are constantly at risk of dissolution (March and Olsen 1976). For example, in the interpretive view, the reproduction of organizational structure depends on participants resubscribing to, or continually negotiating, a shared understanding of what they jointly are doing. Some cultural theories of organization emphasize the different, conflicting views that coexist within one organization (Martin and Meyerson 1988).

Views of organizations as marketplaces of incentives (Dow 1988), bundles of transactions (Williamson 1981), or arenas of class conflict (Clegg 1989) are in harmony with the associative view, insofar as they focus on actors' contributions to sustaining interaction. Indeed, organizational economics views organizations primarily as mechanisms for mediating exchanges among individuals, arguing that they arise only when market-based mechanisms have proven inadequate (Williamson 1981).

These complementary views of organizations, the associative and the systemic, highlight the sources of two fundamental problems of social organization, those of differentiation and integration. Some differentiation occurs through the division of labor among different roles and subunits; for example, employees may be divided into departments such as sales, finance, and manufacturing. Differentiation pressures also arise because participants sometimes bring widely varying

expectations to the same organization. Differentiation is thus a centrifugal force threatening the coherence of social units. Integration, in contrast, refers to procedures for maintaining coherence, as diverse roles are linked and activities coordinated to sustain an organization as a coherent entity. Examples of integrative processes include the holding of weekly departmental meetings or the circulation of interoffice memos.

Differentiation increases organizational complexity because it increases the extent and nature of specialization (Blau 1972). Complexity increases with the number of different components and may be horizontal (tasks spread over many roles or units), vertical (many levels in a hierarchy of authority), or spatial (many operating sites). Complexity also increases when tasks are grouped by product or market (soap, paper products, or foods) or by function (finance, production, or marketing).

There are problems of coordination for any activity system, but especially for a complex one. Many concepts used to describe organizational structure involve alternative processes employed in attempts to achieve integration. One scheme, for example, identified five coordinating mechanisms: direct supervision, formalization, and three forms of standardization (Mintzberg 1983).

With direct supervision, or simple control, decision making is highly centralized: Persons at the top of a hierarchy make decisions that lower-level personnel simply carry out. This coordination pattern was prevalent in preindustrial organizations, and today it is especially likely within small organizations (Edwards 1979).

Formalization, sometimes termed *bureaucratic control,* achieves coordination through rules and procedures. Examples include rules for arriving at work on time, for processing orders, for assembling and packaging products, and for conducting screening interviews for clients. A formalized organization may appear decentralized, since few explicit commands are given and lower-level participants have freedom in making decisions within the rules. The rules may, however, be so restrictive as to leave little room for discretion.

Coordination can also be attained through

standardizing work processes, skills, or outputs to create technical control. With standardized work processes, coordination is built into machinery, as in an assembly line. Most discretion is eliminated by the design of the technical system, and what remains is centralized in the upper echelons.

Standardization of skills involves considerable training and indoctrination of personnel, so that participants carry out organizational policies with minimal oversight. Organizations employing large numbers of professionals are likely to rely on this coordination strategy (Von Glinow 1988). Professionalized participants enjoy considerable autonomy in making decisions, but their prior socialization determines most decision premises for them.

By producing products with standard properties, subunits of an organization are able to work independently of one another; if they use each other's outputs, the standards tell them what to anticipate. For example, large clothing firms produce massive runs of identical garments, and, thus, the various departments within firms know precisely what to expect from one another as they follow daily routines.

## CONCLUSION

Complex organizations are the building blocks of industrial societies, enabling people to accomplish tasks that are otherwise beyond their individual competencies. Organizations also help create and sustain structures of opportunities and constraints that affect nearly all aspects of societies. Sociologists and other social scientists are grappling with a variety of complementary and conflicting perspectives on organizations, ranging from microanalytic interpretive views to macroevolutionary institutional and ecological views. Regardless of perspective, research on organizations has shown its capacity to interest, inform, and provoke us as sociologists investigate these social constructions that figure so prominently in our lives.

(SEE ALSO: *Bureaucracy; Intergroup and Interorganizational Relations; Organizational Effectiveness; Organizational Structure; Voluntary Associations*)

## REFERENCES

Aldrich, Howard E. 1979 *Organizations and Environments.* Englewood Cliffs, N.J.: Prentice-Hall.

———, and Gabriele Wiedenmayer 1991 "From Traits to Rates: An Ecological Perspective on Organizational Foundings." In Jerome Katz and Robert Brockhaus, eds., *Advances in Entrepreneurship, Firm Emergence, and Growth,* vol. 1. Greenwich, Conn.: JAI.

Birch, David 1987 *Job Creation in America.* New York: Free Press.

Blau, Peter M. 1972 "Interdependence and Hierarchy in Organizations." *Social Science Research* 1:1–24.

———, and W. Richard Scott 1962 *Formal Organizations.* San Francisco: Chandler.

Carroll, Glenn R. 1984 "Organizational Ecology" In Ralph H. Turner and James F. Short, Jr., eds., *Annual Review of Sociology,* vol. 10. Palo Alto, Calif.: Annual Reviews.

Clegg, Stewart 1989 "Radical Revisions: Power, Discipline and Organizations." *Organization Studies* 10:97–115.

Dow, Gregory K. 1988 "Configurational and Coactivational Views of Organizational Structure." *Academy of Management Review* 13:53–64.

Edwards, Richard C. 1979 *Contested Terrain: The Transformation of the Workplace in the Twentieth Century.* New York: Basic Books.

Fligstein, Neil 1991 *The Transformation of Corporate Control.* Cambridge, Mass.: Harvard University Press.

Grimm, W. T. 1989 *Mergerstat Review 1988.* Chicago: Grimm.

Hannan, Michael T., and John H. Freeman 1989 *Organizational Ecology.* Cambridge, Mass.: Harvard University Press.

Kerbo, Harold 1983 *Social Stratification and Inequality.* New York: McGraw-Hill.

March, James G., and Johan P. Olsen 1976 *Ambiguity and Choice in Organizations.* Bergen, Norway: Universitetsforlaget.

Martin, Joanne, and Debra Meyerson 1988 "Organizational Cultures and the Denial, Channeling, and Acknowledgment of Ambiguity." In Louis R. Pondy, Richard Boland, Jr., and Howard Thomas, eds., *Managing Ambiguity and Change.* New York: Wiley.

Meyer, John W., and Brian Rowan 1977 "Institutionalized Organizations: Formal Structure as Myth and

Ceremony." *American Journal of Sociology* 83:340–363.

Meyer, John W., and W. Richard Scott 1983 *Organizational Environments: Ritual and Rationality*. Beverly Hills, Calif.: Sage.

Mintzberg, Henry 1983 *Structure in Fives: Designing Effective Organizations*. Englewood Cliffs, N.J.: Prentice-Hall.

Office of Management and Budget, Statistical Policy Division 1972 *Standard Industrial Classification Manual*. Washington, D.C.: U.S. Government Printing Office.

Parsons, Talcott 1960 *Structure and Process in Modern Societies*. New York: Free Press.

Perrow, Charles 1986 *Complex Organizations*. New York: Scott, Foresman.

Pfeffer, Jeffrey, and Gerald R. Salancik 1978 *The External Control of Organizations*. New York: Harper and Row.

Scott, W. Richard 1987 *Organizations: Rational, Natural, and Open Systems*. Englewood Cliffs, N.J.: Prentice-Hall.

Singh, Jitendra (ed.) 1990 *Organizational Evolution*. Beverly Hills, Calif.: Sage.

———, and Charles Lumsden 1990 "Theory and Research in Organizational Ecology." In W. Richard Scott and Judith Blake, eds., *Annual Review of Sociology*, vol. 16. Palo Alto, Calif.: Annual Reviews.

Small Business Administration 1986 *The State of Small Business*. Washington, D.C.: U.S. Government Printing Office.

Stinchcombe, Arthur 1965 "Social Structure and Organizations." In J. G. March, ed., *Handbook of Organizations*. Chicago: Rand McNally.

Swanson, Guy E. 1971 "An Organizational Analysis of Collectivities." *American Sociological Review* 36:607–614.

Useem, Michael 1984 *The Inner Circle*. New York: Oxford University Press.

Von Glinow, Mary Ann 1988 *The New Professionals: Managing Today's High-Tech Employees*. Cambridge, Mass.: Ballinger.

Williamson, Oliver 1981 "The Economics of Organization: The Transaction Cost Approach." *American Journal of Sociology* 87:548–577.

Zucker, Lynne G. (ed.) 1988 *Institutional Patterns and Organizations: Culture and Environment*. Cambridge, Mass.: Ballinger.

HOWARD E. ALDRICH
PETER V. MARSDEN

## COMPLIANCE AND CONFORMITY

Conformity is a change in an individual's behavior or belief toward a group standard as a result of the group's influence on the individual (Kiesler and Kiesler 1976). As this definition indicates, conformity is a type of social influence through which group members come to share similar beliefs and standards of behavior. It includes the processes by which group members converge on given uniformities as well as pressures to uphold developed standards. Compliance is behavioral conformity in order to achieve rewards or avoid punishments (Kelman 1958). Since one can behaviorally adhere to a group standard without personally believing in it, the term *compliance* is often used to indicate conformity that is merely public rather than private as well. Compliance can also refer to behavioral conformity to the demands of authority.

Conformity has a negative connotation in U.S. society. Yet it is a fundamental social process without which people would be unable to organize into groups and take effective action as a collectivity. Simply driving down a street would be nearly impossible if most people did not conform to group norms that organize driving. People must develop and adhere to some standards or regularities of behavior that make each other's actions mutually predictable if they are to coordinate their behavior and work together as a group. Conformity is also the process that establishes boundaries between groups as the members of one group become similar to one another and different from those of another group. Given the pressure of ever-changing circumstances, social groups maintain their distinctive cultural beliefs and moderately stable social structures only through the constant operation of conformity processes.

Although essential, conformity always entails a conflict between a group standard and an alternative belief or behavior (Asch 1951; Cohen and Lee 1975; Moscovici 1985). For their physical and psychological survival, people need and want to belong to social groups. Yet to do so, they must curb the diversity and independence of their beliefs and behavior. Without even being aware of it, people often willingly adopt the group position.

Occasionally, however, individuals believe their alternative to be superior to the group standard and suffer painful conflict when pressured to conform.

Sometimes a nonconforming, deviate alternative is indeed superior to the group standard in that it offers a better response to the group circumstances. Innovation and change is as important to a group's ability to adjust and survive as is conformity. As Janis (1972) pointed out in his analysis of "groupthink," conformity pressures can grow so strong that they strangle a group's ability to analyze critically and respond to the problems it faces. Thus, conformity is a double-edged sword. It enables people to unify for collective endeavors, but it exacts a cost in potential innovation.

## CLASSIC EXPERIMENTS

The social scientific investigation of conformity began with the pioneering experiments of Muzafer Sherif (1936). These experiments beautifully illustrate the easy, almost unconscious way people in groups influence one another to become similar. Sherif made use of the autokinetic effect, which is a visual illusion that makes a stationary pinpoint of light in a dark room appear to move. Sherif asked subjects in his experiments to estimate how far the light moved.

In one condition of the experiment, subjects viewed the light with two or three others, giving their estimates out loud, allowing them to hear each other's judgments. Individual estimates were initially disparate but rapidly converged on a single group estimate. Different groups of subjects settled on different estimates, but each group developed a consensus.

After three sessions together as a group, the group members were split up. When tested alone they continued to use their group standard to guide their personal estimates. This indicates that the group members had not merely induced one another to conform in outward behavior; they had influenced one another's very perception of the light so that they believed the group estimate to be the most accurate judgment of reality.

In another condition, Sherif first tested subjects alone so that they developed personal standards for their estimates. He then put together two or three people with widely divergent personal standards and tested them in a group setting. Over three group sessions, individual estimates merged into a group standard. Thus, even when participants had well-established personal standards for judging, mere exposure to the differing judgments of others influenced them gradually to abandon their divergent points of view for a uniform group standard. This occurred despite the minimal nature of the group setting where the subjects, all strangers, had no power over one another.

The Sherif experiment suggests that conformity pressures in groups are subtle and extremely powerful. But critics quickly noted that the extreme ambiguity of the autokinetic situation might be responsible for his results. In such an ambiguous situation, participants have little to base their personal judgments on, so perhaps it is not surprising that they turn to others to help them decide what to think. Do people conform when the task is clear and unambiguous? Will they yield to a group consensus if it is obvious that the consensus is wrong? These are the questions Asch (1951; 1956) addressed in his classic experiments.

To eliminate ambiguity, Asch employed clear-cut judgment tasks where subjects chose which of three comparison lines was the same length as a standard line. The correct answers were so obvious that individuals working alone reached 98 percent accuracy. Similar to the Sherif experiment, Asch's subjects gave their judgments in the presence of seven to nine of their peers (all male college students). Unknown to the single naive subject in each group, all other group members were confederates of the experimenter. On seven of twelve trials, as the confederates announced their judgments one by one, they unanimously gave the wrong answer. It was arranged so that the naive subject always gave his judgment after the confederates.

The subject here was placed in a position of absolute conflict. Should he abide by what he knows to be true or go along with the unanimous opinion of others? A third of the time subjects violated the evidence of their own senses to agree with the group.

The Asch experiments clearly demonstrated that people feel pressure to conform to group standards even when they know the standards are wrong. It is striking that Asch, like Sherif, obtained these results with a minimal group situation. The group members were strangers who meant little to one another. Yet they exerted substantial influence over one another simply by being in the same situation together. Because of the dramatic way it highlights the conflict between the individual and the group, Asch's experimental design has become the paradigm for studying conformity.

## NORMATIVE AND INFORMATIONAL INFLUENCE

Sherif's and Asch's striking results stimulated an explosion of research to explain how conformity occurs (for reviews see Allen 1965; Kiesler and Kiesler 1976; and Moscovici 1985). It is now clear that two analytically distinct influence processes are involved. Either or both can produce conformity in a given situation. Deutsch and Gerard (1955) labeled these *informational influence* and *normative influence*.

In informational influence, the group defines perceptual reality for the individual. Sherif's experiment is a good illustration of this. The best explanation derives from Festinger's (1954) social comparison theory. According to the theory, people form judgments about ambiguous events by comparing their perceptions with those of similar others and constructing shared, socially validated definitions of the "reality" of the event. These shared definitions constitute the social reality of the situation (Festinger 1950). Because people want the support of others to assure them of the validity of their beliefs, disagreeing with the majority is uncomfortable. People in such situations doubt their judgment. They change to agree with the majority because they assume that the majority view is more likely to be accurate.

As this indicates, conformity as a result of

informational influence is not unwilling compliance with the demands of others. Rather, the individual adopts the group standard as a matter of private belief as well as public behavior. Informational influence is especially powerful in regard to social beliefs, opinions, and events since these are inherently ambiguous and socially constructed.

Normative influence occurs when people go along with the group majority in order to gain rewards or avoid unpleasant costs. Thus, it is normative influence that is behind compliance. Since people depend on others for many valued outcomes, particularly social approval, even strangers have some power to reward and punish one another. Asch's results are a good example. Although a few of Asch's participants actually doubted their judgment (informational influence), most conformed in order to avoid the implicit rejection of being the odd person out. Studies show that fears of rejection for nonconformity are not unfounded. While nonconformists are sometimes admired (Moscovici 1976), they are rarely liked (Sampson and Brandon 1964). Furthermore, they are subject to intense persuasive pressure and criticism from the majority (Schacter 1951; Emerson 1954).

## FACTORS THAT INCREASE CONFORMITY

Anything that increases vulnerability to informational and normative influence increases conformity. Although there may be personality traits that incline people to conform, the evidence for this is conflicting (Crowne and Marlowe 1964; Moscovici 1985). Situational factors seem to be the most important determinants of conformity. Research indicates that conformity is increased by (1) the ambiguity of the task; (2) the similarity of group members; (3) the relative unimportance of the issue to the person; (4) the attractiveness and cohesiveness of the group; (5) the unanimity of the majority; and (6) the necessity of making a public rather than private response (Allen 1965; Kiesler and Kiesler 1976). Each of these factors increases the group's power in the situation to reward and punish the individual and/or to define reality for the individual.

The unanimity of the majority is an especially interesting factor. Asch (1951) found that as long as it was unanimous, a majority of three was as effective in inducing conformity as was a majority of sixteen. Subsequent research generally confirms that the size of a majority past three is not a crucial factor in conformity (Allen 1975). It is unanimity that counts. When Asch (1951) had one confederate give the correct answer to the line task, the naive subjects' conformity to the majority dropped from a third to only 5 percent. One fellow dissenter shows an individual that nonconformity is possible and provides much needed support for an alternate construction of social reality. Interestingly, a dissenter need not agree with an individual to encourage nonconformity (Shaw, Rothschild, and Strickland 1957; Allen 1975). It is only necessary that the dissenter also break with the majority.

Another factor that affects conformity is the sex composition of the group. Although the results of studies are inconsistent, metaanalyses indicate that there is an overall tendency for women to conform somewhat more than men (Becker 1986; Eagly and Wood 1985). Sex differences in conformity are most likely when behavior is under the surveillance of others (Eagly, Wood, and Fishbaugh 1981; Eagly and Chrvala 1986). The evidence suggests two explanations. First, sex carries status value in interaction, causing women to be socially expected to be less competent and influential than men (Berger, Rosenholtz, and Zelditch 1980; Meeker and Weitzel-O'Neill 1977). Second, sex stereotypes pressure men to display independence when they are being observed (see Eagly 1987 for a review).

## CONFORMITY AND STATUS

Research in the Asch and Sherif paradigms focuses on conformity pressures among peers. However, when group members differ in status, this affects the group's tolerance of their nonconformity. Higher status members receive fewer sanctions for nonconformity than lower status members (Gerson 1975). As long as they adhere to central group norms, high status members' nonconformity can actually increase their influence in the group (Berkowitz and Macaulay 1961). Hollander (1958) argues that, because high status members are valued by the group, they are accorded "idiosyncrasy credits" that allow them not to conform and to innovate without penalty as long as they stay within certain bounds. It is middle status members who actually conform the most (Harvey and Consalvi 1960). They have fewer idiosyncrasy credits than do high status members and more investment in the group than do low status members.

Nonconformity can also affect the position of status and influence a person attains in the group. Hollander (1958; 1960) proposed that individuals earn status and idiosyncrasy credits by initially conforming to group norms, but replications of his study do not support this conclusion (Wahrman and Pugh 1972; Ridgeway 1981). Conformity tends to make a person "invisible" in a group and so does little to gain status (Ridgeway 1978). Nonconformity attracts attention and gives the appearance of confidence and competence, both of which can enhance status. But it also appears self-interested, and this detracts from status (Ridgeway 1981). Consequently, moderate levels of nonconformity are most likely to facilitate status attainment.

## COMPLIANCE WITH AUTHORITY

Reacting to the Nazi phenomenon of World War II, studies of compliance to authority have focused on explaining people's obedience even when ordered to engage in extreme or immoral behavior. Compliance in this situation is comparable to conformity in the Asch paradigm in that individuals must go against their own standards of conduct to obey. The power of a legitimate authority to compel obedience was dramatically demonstrated in the Milgram (1963; 1974) experiments. As part of an apparent learning study, a scientist-experimenter ordered subjects to give increasingly strong electric shocks to another person. The shock generator used by the subject labeled increasing levels as "danger-severe shock" and "XXX" (at 450 volts). The victim (a confederate who received no actual shocks) protested, cried out, and complained of heart trouble. Despite this, 65 percent of the subjects complied with the scientist-experimenter and shocked the victim all the way to the 450-volt maximum. It is clear that most of the time, people do as they are told by legitimate authorities.

Uncertainty over their responsibilities in a situation (an issue concerning the definition of social reality) and concern for an authority's ability to punish or reward them seem to be the principle causes for people's compliance in such circumstances. Note the comparability of these factors to informational and normative influence. Situational factors that socially define the individual's responsibility as a duty to obey rather than to disobey increase compliance (Kelman and Hamilton 1989), as do factors that increase the authority's ability to sanction.

Research has demonstrated several such factors. Compliance is increased by the legitimacy of the authority figure and his or her surveillance of the individual's behavior (Milgram 1974; Zelditch and Walker 1984). When others in the situation obey or when the individual's position in the chain of command removes direct contact with the victim, compliance increases (Milgram 1974). On the other hand, when others present resist the authority, compliance drops dramatically. Milgram (1974) found that when two confederates working with the subject refused to obey the experimenter, only 10 percent of subjects complied fully themselves. As with a fellow dissenter from a unanimous majority, other resisters define disobedience as appropriate and provide support for resisting. In an analysis of "crimes of obedience" in many government and military settings, Kelman and Hamilton (1989) review the factors that lead to compliance as well as disobedience to illegal or immoral commands from authority.

After an enormous outpouring of studies following World War II, studies of conformity and compliance have become relatively scarce. Perhaps reflecting a change in social concerns of the times, research has shifted from the impact of the major-

ity on the individual (conformity) to the impact of a nonconforming minority on the majority, called minority influence (Moscovici 1985). Compliance research has turned to studying the legitimation of authority (Zelditch and Walker 1984). Yet conformity and compliance remain fundamental social processes. They demand continued scientific attention.

(SEE ALSO: *Attitudes; Coercive Persuasion and Attitude Change; Interpersonal Power; Persuasion; Social Control*)

## REFERENCES

Allen, Vernon L. 1965 "Situational Factors in Conformity." In L. Berkowitz, ed., *Advances in Experimental Social Psychology*, vol. 2. New York: Academic Press.

——1975 "Social Support for Nonconformity." In L. Berkowitz, ed., *Advances in Experimental Social Psychology*, vol. 8. New York: Academic Press.

Asch, Solomon E. 1951 "Effects of Group Pressure upon the Modification and Distortion of Judgments." In H. Guetzkow, ed., *Groups, Leadership, and Men*. Pittsburgh, Pa.: Carnegie Press.

—— 1956 "Studies of Independence and Conformity: I. A Minority of One against a Unanimous Majority." *Psychological Monographs* 70 (9, whole no. 416):1–70.

Becker, B. J. 1986 "Influence Again: Another Look at Studies of Gender Differences in Social Influence." In Janet Shibley Hyde and Marcia C. Lynn, eds., *The Psychology of Gender: Advances Through Meta-Analysis*. Baltimore: Johns Hopkins University Press.

Berger, Joseph, Susan J. Rosenholtz, and Morris Zelditch, Jr. 1980 "State Organizing Processes." *Annual Review of Sociology* 6:479–508.

Berkowitz, Leonard, and J. R. Macaulay 1961 "Some Effects of Differences in Status Level and Status Stability." *Human Relations* 14:135–147.

Cohen, Bernard P., and Hans Lee 1975 *Conflict, Conformity, and Social Status*. New York: Elsevier.

Crowne, D. P., and D. Marlowe 1964 *The Approval Motive: Studies in Evaluative Dependence*. New York: Wiley.

Deutsch, Morton, and Harold B. Gerard 1955 "A Study of Normative and Informational Influences upon Individual Judgment." *Journal of Abnormal and Social Psychology* 51:629–636.

Eagly, Alice H. 1987 *Sex Differences in Social Behavior: A Social-Role Interpretation.* Hillsdale, N.J.: Erlbaum.

————, and C. Chrvala 1986 "Sex Differences in Conformity: Status and Gender-Role Interpretations." *Psychology of Women Quarterly* 10:203–220.

————, and Wendy Wood 1985 "Gender and Influenceability: Stereotype vs. Behavior." In V. E. O'Leary, R. K. Unger, and B. S. Walson, eds., *Women, Gender, and Social Psychology.* Hillsdale, N.J.: Erlbaum.

————, Wendy Wood, and Linda Fishbaugh 1981 "Sex Differences in Conformity: Surveillance by the Group as a Determinant of Male Nonconformity." *Journal of Personality and Social Psychology* 40:384–394.

Emerson, Richard 1954 "Deviation and Rejection: An Experimental Replication." *American Sociological Review* 19:688–693.

Festinger, Leon 1950 "Informal Social Communication." *Psychological Review* 57:217–282.

———— 1954 "A Theory of Social Comparison Processes." *Human Relations* 7:117–140.

Gerson, Lowell W. 1975 "Punishment and Position: The Sanctioning of Deviants in Small Groups." In P. V. Crosbie, ed., *Interaction in Small Groups.* New York: Macmillan.

Harvey, O. J., and Conrad Consalvi 1960 "Status and Conformity to Pressures in Informal Groups." *Journal of Abnormal and Social Psychology* 60:182–187.

Hollander, Edwin P. 1958 "Conformity, Status, and Idiosyncrasy Credit." *Psychological Review* 65:117–127.

———— 1960 "Competence and Conformity in the Acceptance of Influence." *Journal of Abnormal and Social Psychology* 61:365–369.

Janis, Irving L. 1972 *Victims of Groupthink: A Psychological Study of Foreign-Policy Decisions and Fiascoes.* Boston: Houghton Mifflin.

Kelman, Herbert C. 1958 "Compliance, Identification, and Internalization: Three Processes of Attitude Change." *Journal of Conflict Resolution* 2:51–60.

————, and V. Lee Hamilton 1989 *Crimes of Obedience.* New Haven, Conn.: Yale University Press.

Kiesler, Charles A., and Sara B. Kiesler 1976 *Conformity,* 2nd ed. Reading, Mass.: Addison-Wesley.

Meeker, B. F., and P. A. Weitzel-O'Neill 1977 "Sex Roles and Interpersonal Behavior in Task-Oriented Groups." *American Sociological Review* 42:92–105.

Milgram, Stanley 1963 "Behavioral Study of Obedience." *Journal of Abnormal and Social Psychology* 67:371–378.

———— 1974 *Obedience to Authority: An Experimental View.* New York: Harper and Row.

Moscovici, Serge 1976 *Social Influence and Social Change.* London: Academic Press.

———— 1985 "Social Influence and Conformity." In G. Lindzey and E. Aronson, eds., *The Handbook of Social Psychology.* New York: Random House.

Ridgeway, Cecilia L. 1978 "Conformity, Group-Oriented Motivation, and Status Attainment in Small Groups." *Social Psychology Quarterly* 41:175–188.

———— 1981 "Nonconformity, Competence, and Influence in Groups: A Test of Two Theories." *American Sociological Review* 46:333–347.

Sampson, Edward E., and A. C. Brandon 1964 "The Effects of Role and Opinion Deviation on Small Group Behavior." *Sociometry* 27:261–281.

Schacter, Stanley 1951 "Deviation, Rejection, and Communication." *Journal of Abnormal and Social Psychology* 46:190–207.

Shaw, Marvin E., G. H. Rothschild, and J. F. Strickland 1957 "Decision Processes in Communication Nets." *Journal of Abnormal and Social Psychology* 54:323–330.

Sherif, Muzafer 1936 *The Psychology of Social Norms.* New York: Harper and Row.

Wahrman, Ralph, and Meredith D. Pugh 1972 "Competence and Conformity: Another Look at Hollander's Study." *Sociometry* 35:376–386.

Zelditch, Morris, Jr., and Henry A. Walker 1984 "Legitimacy and the Stability of Authority." In E. Lawler, ed., *Advances in Group Processes,* vol. 1. Greenwich, Conn.: JAI Press.

CECILIA L. RIDGEWAY

**COMPONENT ANALYSIS** *See* Factor Analysis.

**COMPUTER APPLICATIONS TO SOCIAL RESEARCH** The data demands and modeling requirements of social research have united sociologists with computers for the past one hundred years. It was the 1890 U.S. census that inspired Herman Hollerith, a census researcher, to construct the first automated data-processing machinery. Hollerith's punch-card system, while not a true computer by today's definitions, provided the foundation for present-day computer-based data management.

In 1948 the U.S. Bureau of the Census, anticipating the voluminous tabulating requirements of the 1950 census, contracted for the building of Univac I, the first commercially produced electronic computer. The need to count, sort, and analyze the 1950 census data on this milestone computer led to the development of the first high-speed magnetic tape storage system, the first sort-merge software package, and the first statistical package, a set of matrix algebra programs.

Since the early 1960s, sociologists have been developing new ways to use computers in social research. This period saw the publication of the first book of statistical computer programs (Cooley and Lohnes 1962) and the first book devoted entirely to computer applications in social science research (Borko 1962). Not only were social scientists writing about how to apply computers, but they were designing and developing new software. Some of the most popular statistical software packages, for example, SPSS (Nie, Bent, and Hull 1975), were developed by social scientists.

During the thirty years since sociological computing was pioneered, the practice of computing in social research has evolved rapidly. Computers have been applied to practically every research task, including such unlikely ones as field note-taking and interviewing (Brent and Anderson 1990). This transformation of the social sciences dramatically accelerated during the 1980s as affordable microcomputers took on jobs that had been beyond even the biggest mainframe computers of the 1960s. In the United States now it is hard to find a sociologist's office without either a computer or a computer terminal.

As the size of the sociological computing community grew, so did the volume of their scholarly publications. The primary source for articles on social science computer applications is the *Social Science Computer Review,* a quarterly publication of Duke University Press, which also regularly offers book and software reviews. Other relevant software reviews periodically appear in such journals as *Educational and Psychological Measurement, Journal of Marketing Research, The American Statistician,*

and *Simulation and Games.* In addition, JAI Press publishes an annual review on "Computers and the Social Sciences."

In the late 1980s, concurrently with all the professional associations of the social sciences, the American Sociological Association (ASA) formed a "Section on Microcomputing." More than 350 sociologists joined this section in 1990, making it the fastest-growing new section in the history of the ASA. The section publishes a quarterly newsletter and organizes sessions at annual meetings.

Another indicator of growing involvement in computing was the first annual conference, "Advanced Computing for the Social Sciences," held in 1990 at Williamsburg, Virginia. From this conference emerged a new professional association, the Social Science Computing Association. The official journal of this new association is the *Social Science Computer Review.*

The many, diverse uses of computing technology in social research are difficult to categorize because applications overlap and evolve unpredictably. Nonetheless, it is necessary to discuss different categories of applications in order to describe the state of the art of computing in social research. Since 1987, the winter issue of the *Social Science Computer Review* has been devoted to an annual symposium of the "State of the Art of Social Science Computing." The categorization of computer applications in this article reflects that discussion.

First, the major types of applications are summarized in descending order of popularity. Finally, the challenges of computing for social research are highlighted.

## WORD PROCESSING

Once equated with the secretarial pool, word processing now overlaps with a number of critical research functions: literature review of electronic text, preparation of tables, "typesetting" of mathematical equations, and the sizing and resizing of three-dimensional graphs embedded within text. Social researchers are increasingly using such capabilities and are moving rapidly toward workstation environments that obscure the transition between data analysis and manuscript preparation (Steiger and Fouladi 1990).

Not only do researchers use their computing devices for writing papers, but word-processing software plays a central role in the refinement of data-collection instruments, especially questionnaires and codebooks, which allows for rapid production of alternative forms and multiple drafts. A related innovation is software built for designing on-line questionnaires. For example, the Questionnaire Programming Language (QPL), developed by Dooley (1989), allows the researcher to draft a questionnaire with any word processor. From embedded branching commands within the questionnaire document, the QPL software package simultaneously produces two versions of the questionnaire: one for computer administration and the other for interviewer or self-administration. An additional bonus of the program is that it automatically produces data-definition commands for SPSS or SAS to use for data analysis.

Perhaps most profound in their impact are the trends in text processing that blur traditional distinctions between writing and publishing (Lyman 1989). The growing body of articles and books in text form propel social science scholarship toward hypertext—systems that provide for nonsequential reading of text with extensive and perhaps dynamic links across documents (cf. Blank, McCartney, and Brent 1989).

## STATISTICS AND DATA MANAGEMENT

Statistical data analysis often dominates computing in social research. Hundreds of computer programs and articles have been written to address the needs of statistical computing in social research. Prior to the 1980s, all statistical work was performed on large or medium-size mainframe computers. But advances in both hardware and software for microcomputers now make it possible to conduct the statistical data analysis of most small or moderate-size research studies on either microcomputers or mainframes. Consequently, data analysts increasingly work in both

environments, taking advantage of the software procedures available on different systems. This type of flexibility results from networking local, desktop microcomputers with one or more remote, large mainframe computers. A large share of ongoing social data analysis, like the massive census counts, would never get done without computer technology. For example, one use of LISREL, a computer procedure that analyzes linear structural relationships by the method of maximum likelihood, would consume weeks or months without a computer.

Not only does statistical computing save time, but it offers unique views of the patterns in one's data. Without the ability to reorganize data quickly and display it in a variety of graphical forms, social researchers neglect important patterns and subtle relationships within complex data. Some patterns cannot be observed without special software tools. For example, Heise's (1988) computer program called Ethno gives the researcher a framework for conceptualizing, examining, and analyzing data containing event sequences. In addition, several general-purpose statistical packages offer powerful exploratory data analysis capabilities with bidirectionality through dynamic data links (Steiger and Fouladi 1990). One type of bidirectionality puts a graph in one window and frequency distributions in another; when the user adjusts the data in one window, it automatically changes in the other.

## COMPUTER-MEDIATED COMMUNICATION

During the 1980s, networks for "computer-mediated communication" expanded internationally following the traditional logistic diffusion curve (Gurbaxani 1990). With expanding telecommunication networks as well as new forms of data transmission—radio, microwave, and fiber-optic cables—data communications has replaced or supplemented many other forms of social communication. However, the spread of this type of computing among social scientists is sporadic and tends to be concentrated within specific communities of researchers. Ploch (1990) describes the significant variety of resources and knowledge shared within these research networks.

As electronic-mail systems continue to expand, they offer social researchers opportunities for conducting studies using networks. One type of study disseminates on-line survey instruments through networks of potential respondents. Methodological investigations by Kiesler and Sproull (1986) have begun to identify the potential, both positive and negative, of this type of research.

## LITERATURE SEARCHES

Social scientists pioneered computer methods for bibliographic retrieval (Janda 1968). A decade ago students and researchers had to use a library or similar institution to gain access to bibliographic data files; now such services are available in the home or office through terminals or CD-ROM readers. CD-ROM, which stands for "compact disk, read-only memory," uses optical disks produced and read by means of a laser. Each disk can hold a half-billion characters of information. Most indexes to different types of literature are now available on CD-ROM. This includes Sociofile, which contains Sociological Abstracts; PsycLIT, which contains Psychological Abstracts; and a vast amount of data in the form of statistical tables and maps.

## QUALITATIVE COMPUTING

Computer-based content analysis began with Stone and associates (1966) and now plays an important role in the social sciences (Weber 1984). During the past decade this type of computing became much more common as researchers combined content analysis with other tasks associated with qualitative analysis. Several general-purpose programs for qualitative analysis have been widely distributed (Tesch 1989). These tools make the analysis of large amounts of text more accurate and efficient, and potentially direct the focus of attention to analytic procedures. The general tasks of text entry, code assignment, counting, and data organization have been extended to include special routines for improving the quality of coding and code management (Carl-

ey 1988). Hesse-Biber, Dupuis, and Kinder (1989) technically extended this methodology to include the management and analysis of audio and video segments as well as text. And Cropper, Eden, and Ackermann (1990) demonstrate how cognitive-mapping software can be used for improving the analysis of qualitative data.

A survey of 110 qualitative-oriented researchers found that three-fourths regularly used computers (Brent, Scott, and Spencer 1987). While it is not known to what degree qualitative computing has advanced the social sciences, Ragin and Becker (1989, p. 54) persuasively claim that it yields more systematic attention to diversity, for example, by encouraging a "more thorough examination of comparative contrasts among cases."

## SIMULATION, MODELING, AND ARTIFICIAL INTELLIGENCE

Early in the history of sociological computing, Coleman (1962) and McPhee and Glaser (1962) designed computer simulation models and showed how they could be used to identify elusive implications of different theoretical assumptions. Other social scientists followed in their footsteps, but the excitement of the pioneers was lost, and few simulations or formal computer models were developed in the 1970s. During the past decade, with the emergence of artificial intelligence and other modeling methodologies, social researchers demonstrated renewed interest in formal computer-supported models of social processes (cf. Hanneman 1988). New computer simulations for social-policy analysis and for pedagogy or instruction have emerged as well (Brent and Anderson 1990, pp. 188–210).

Neural networks, combined with other techniques of artificial intelligence and expert systems, have excited a number of social scientists (Garson 1990). Neural nets organize computer memory in ways that mimic human brain cells and their ability to process many things in parallel. Systems that use neural nets are especially good when pattern matching is required; however, the computations require high-performance computers such as supercomputers.

## COMPUTER-ASSISTED DATA COLLECTION

Computer-Assisted Telephone Interviewing (CATI) is a computing system with on-line questionnaires or entry screens for telephone interviewers. It has become very common in survey research, although its impact is not fully understood (Groves et al. 1988). It is used on freestanding PCs, networked PCs, or large mainframe computers. These systems generally, but not always, have the following characteristics: centralized facilities for monitoring individual interviewer stations, instantaneous edit-checks with feedback for invalid responses, and automatic branching to different questions depending upon the respondents' answers. Major variations on CATI include (1) Computer-Assisted Personal Interviewing (CAPI), the name used in survey research to refer to face-to-face interviewing assisted with a laptop or hand-held computing device (a technique popular in Europe); (2) Computerized Self-Administered Questionnaires (CSAQ), on-line programs designed for direct input from respondents; and (3) data-entry programs to facilitate entering on the computer data collected manually at a prior time.

## COMPUTER GRAPHICS

Many social researchers have come to rely on computer graphic systems to produce maps, charts summarizing statistical data, and network diagrams. Users of standard presentation graphics software save a great deal of time by not having to draw a graph manually or even to write a program that instructs the computer to draw every line in a specific way. But the integration of these techniques of computer graphics into social research workstations has been slow.

Currently the term *workstation* tends to be reserved for computers more powerful than micros but less so than mainframes, for instance, the IBM-RT, Sun, and Apollo computers. Since these high-speed desktop computer systems have screens capable of very fine detail, they are also called graphics workstations or high-performance workstations. Many of the papers and demonstrations at the 1990 "Advanced Computing for the Social Sciences" conference revealed attempts to solve social science computing problems within this type of computing environment.

## CHALLENGES FOR THE NEXT DECADE

The application of computing to social research is not without problems. Errors in data and software abound, yet rarely do social scientists check their results by running more than one program on the same data. Data and software tend to be very costly, but many impediments inhibit the sharing of these critical resources. Better software is needed, but graduate students often are discouraged from programming new software.

Nonetheless, breakthroughs in computer technology will continue, and major new opportunities will emerge. Many of the advances in social science computing over the next few years undoubtedly will follow the lines of progress already described: hypertext networks; integrated, high-performance, graphic data analysis stations; software for computer-supported cooperative work; and neural networks for complex models of social systems.

Perhaps the most exciting challenge for the future involves a concert of these innovations directed at the problem of modeling and analyzing vast amounts of social data. One solution would incorporate three-dimensional, multicolored, dynamic graphical representations of complex social data structures. But new techniques for analyzing these data will require new models of dynamic social structures as well as parallel social processes. Computer representations of these models will require extremely fast processing, such as that found only in the supercomputers of the early 1990s. Graphics workstations in concert with supercomputer systems may offer major advances in the reduction of vast amounts of demographic data, particularly if they take advantage of color shadings, graphic symbols, and user-controlled animation. The absence of these applications in the social sciences is not so much due to the lack of technology as to the underdevelopment of formal models that can be linked together to represent larger social systems.

Social scientists with computing skills historically have produced many important innovations and advancements for social research. This fact is grounds for optimism, though we cannot predict precisely what new computer-based analytical techniques will fill the social researcher's toolbox.

(SEE ALSO: *Measurement; Statistical Graphics*)

### REFERENCES

Anderson, Ronald E., and Edward Brent 1989 "Computing in Sociology: Promise and Practice." *Social Science Computer Review* 7:487–502.

Bailey, Daniel, 1978 *Computer Science in Social and Behavioral Science Education.* Englewood Cliffs, N.J.: Educational Technology Press.

Blank, Grant, James L. McCartney, and Edward Brent (eds.) 1989 *New Technology in Sociology: Practical Applications in Research and Work.* New Brunswick, N.J.: Transaction.

Borko, Harold (ed.) 1962 *Computer Applications in the Behavioral Sciences.* Santa Monica, Calif.: System Development Corporation.

Brent, Edward, and Ronald E. Anderson 1990 *Computer Applications in the Social Sciences.* New York: McGraw-Hill.

———, James Scott, and John Spencer 1987 "The use of computers by qualitative researchers." *Qualitative Sociology* 10 (3):309–313.

Carley, Kathleen 1988 "Formalizing the Social Expert's Knowledge." *Sociological Methods & Research* 17 (2):165–232.

Coleman, James S. 1962 "Analysis of social structures and simulation of social processes with electronic computers." In Harold Guetzkow, ed., *Simulation in Social Science: Readings.* Englewood Cliffs, N.J.: Prentice-Hall.

Cooley, William, and Paul Lohnes 1962 *Multivariate Procedures for the Behavioral Sciences.* New York: Wiley.

Cropper, Steve, Colin Eden, and Fran Ackermann 1990 "Keeping Sense of Accounts Using Computer-Based Cognitive Maps." *Social Science Computer Review* 8 (3):345–366.

Dooley, Kevin 1989 *QPL Data Collection Program.* Washington, D.C.: Human Resources Division, U.S. General Accounting Office.

Garson, G. David 1990 "Expert Systems: An Overview for Social Scientists." *Social Science Computer Review* 8 (3):387–410.

Groves, Robert M., P. P. Biemer, L. E. Lyberg, J. T. Massey, W. L. Nicholls, and J. Waksberg (eds.) 1988 *Telephone Survey Methodology.* New York: Wiley.

Gurbaxani, Vijay 1990 "Diffusion in Computing Networks: BITNET." *Communications of the ACM* 33 (12):65–75.

Hanneman, Robert A. 1988 *Computer-Assisted Theory Building.* Newbury Park, Calif.: Sage.

Heise, David 1988 "Computer analysis of cultural structures." *Social Science Computer Review* 6:183–196.

Hesse-Biber, Sharlene, Paul Dupuis, and Scott Kinder 1989 "HyperResearch: A computer program for the analysis of qualitative data using the Macintosh." Paper presented at the 1989 annual meeting of the American Sociological Association.

Janda, Kenneth 1962 *Information Retrieval.* Evanston, Ill.: Northwestern University Press.

Kiesler, Sarah, and Lee. S. Sproull 1986 "Response Effects in the Electronic Survey." *Public Opinion Quarterly* 50:402–413.

Lyman, Peter 1989 "The Future of Sociological Literature in an Age of Computerized Texts." In G. Blank, J. L. McCartney, and E. Brent, eds., *New Technology in Sociology: Practical Applications in Research and Work.* New Brunswick, N.J.: Transaction.

McPhee, William N., and William A. Glaser (eds.) 1962 *Public Opinion and Congressional Election.* New York: Free Press.

Nie, Norman, Dale Bent, and Hadley Hull 1975 *Statistical Package for the Social Sciences.* New York: McGraw-Hill.

Ploch, Donald R. 1990 "Computing: Communication and Control." *Social Science Computer Review* 8:614–626.

Ragin, Charles C., and Howard S. Becker 1989 "How the Microcomputer Is Changing Our Analytic Habits." In G. Blank, J. L. McCartney, and E. Brent, eds., *New Technology in Sociology: Practical Applications in Research and Work.* New Brunswick, N.J.: Transaction.

Steiger, James H., and Rachel T. Fouladi 1990 "Some Key Emerging Trends in Statistical and Graphical Software for the Social Scientist." *Social Science Computer Review* 8:627–664.

Stone, Philip, et al. 1966 *The General Inquirer*. Cambridge, Mass.: MIT Press.

Tesch, Renata 1989 "Computer Software and Qualitative Analysis: A Reassessment." In G. Blank, J. L. McCartney, and E. Brent, eds., *New Technology in Sociology: Practical Applications in Research and Work*. New Brunswick, N.J.: Transaction.

Weber, R. P. 1984 "Computer-Aided Content Analysis, A Short Primer." *Qualitative Sociology* 7 (1/2):126–147.

RONALD E. ANDERSON

**CONFIDENCE INTERVALS** *See* Statistical Inference.

**CONFLICT THEORY** Conflict theory explains social structure and changes in it by arguing that actors pursue their interests in conflict with others and according to their resources for social organization. Conflict theory builds upon Marxist analysis of class conflicts, but it is detached from any ideological commitment to socialism. Max Weber generalized conflict to the arenas of power and status as well as economic class, and this multidimensional approach has become widespread since the 1950s.

## WHAT CONSTITUTES A CONFLICT GROUP?

For Marx and Engels, a society's conflicting interests derive from the division between owners and nonowners of property. Dahrendorf (1959) proposed that conflicts are based on power, dividing order-givers, who have an interest in maintaining the status quo, from order-takers, who have an interest in changing it. Property is only one of the bases of power conflict, and conflicts can be expected inside any type of organization, including socialist ones. In the Weberian model there are even more types of conflict, since every cultural group (such as ethnic, religious, or intellectual groups) can also struggle for advantage. In addition, economic conflict takes place in three different types of market relations, pitting employers against workers, producers against consumers, and lenders against borrowers (Wiley 1967). Gender stratification produces yet another dimension of conflict.

## THE PROCESS OF CONFLICT

Conflicting interests remain latent until a group becomes mobilized for active struggle. This occurs when its members are physically concentrated, have material resources for communicating among themselves, and share a similar culture. The higher social classes are typically more mobilized than lower classes, and most struggles over power take place among different factions of the higher classes. Lower classes tend to be fragmented into localized groups and are most easily mobilized when they are a homogeneous ethnic or religious group concentrated in a particular place. The better organized a conflict group is, the longer and more intensely it can struggle; such struggles become routinized, as in the case of entrenched labor unions or political parties. Less organized conflict groups that become temporarily mobilized are more likely to be violent but unable to sustain the conflict.

Overt conflict increases the solidarity of groups on both sides. Coser (1956), elaborating the theory of Georg Simmel, points out that conflict leads to a centralization of power within each group and motivates groups to seek allies. A conflict thus tends to polarize a society into two factions, or a world of warring states into two alliances. This process is limited when there are cross-cutting memberships among groups, for instance, if class, ethnic, and religious categories overlap. In these cases, mobilization of one line of conflict (e.g., class conflict) puts a strain on other dimensions of conflict (e.g., ethnic identity). Thus, cross-cutting conflicts tend to neutralize each other. Conversely, when multiple lines of group membership are superimposed, conflicts are more extreme.

Conflicts escalate as each group retaliates against offenses received from the other. How long this process of escalation continues depends on how much resources a group can draw upon: its numbers of supporters, its weapons, and its economic goods. If one group has many more resources than the other, the conflict ends when the mobilizing capacity of the weaker side is exhausted. When both sides have further resources they have not yet mobilized, escalation continues. This is especially likely when one or both sides have sustained enough damage to outrage and mobilize their supporters but not great enough damage to destroy their organizational resources for struggle.

Deescalation of conflict occurs in two very different ways. If one side has overwhelming superiority over the other, it can destroy opposition by breaking the other group's organizational capacity to fight. The result is not harmony but an uneasy peace, in which the defeated party has been turned back into an unmobilized latent interest. If neither side is able to break up the other's organization, conflict eventually deescalates when resources are eaten up and the prospects of winning become dimmer. Although wars usually arouse popular solidarity at first, costs and casualties reduce enthusiasm and bring most wars to an end within a few years. Civilian uprisings, strikes, and other small-scale conflicts typically have fewer resources to sustain them; these conflicts deescalate more quickly. During a deescalation, the points of contention among the opponents modulate from extreme demands toward compromises and piecemeal negotiation of smaller issues (Kriesberg 1982). Very destructive levels of conflict tend to end more rapidly than moderate conflicts in which resources are continuously replenished.

## COERCIVE POWER AND REVOLUTION

In a highly coercive state, such as a traditional aristocracy or a military dictatorship, power is organized as an enforcement coalition (Collins 1988; Schelling 1962). Members of the ruling organization monitor each other to ensure loyalty. A change in power is possible only when a majority of the enforcers disobey orders simultaneously.

Revolts occur in a rapid "bandwagon effect," during which most members scramble to become part of the winning coalition. The more coercive the state, the more extreme the swings between long periods of tyrannical stability and brief moments of political upheaval.

Since the state claims a monopoly on the instruments of violence, revolutionary changes in power occur through the reorganization of coercive coalitions. Revolts from below are almost always unsuccessful as long as the state's military organization stays intact. For this reason, revolutions typically are preceded by a disintegration of the military, due to defeat in war, depletion of economic resources in previous conflicts, and splits within the ruling group (Skocpol 1979). These breakdowns of military power in turn are determined by geopolitical processes affecting the expansion or contraction of states in the surrounding world (Stinchcombe 1968; Collins 1986).

## WHO WINS WHAT?

Conflict shapes the distribution of power, wealth, and prestige in a society. The victorious side is generally the group that is better mobilized to act in its collective interest. In many cases, the dominant group is well organized, while the opposing interest group remains latent. The result is a stable structure of stratification, in which overt conflict rarely occurs.

Lenski (1966) showed that concentration of wealth throughout world history is determined by the interaction of two factors. The higher the production of economic surplus (beyond what is necessary to keep people alive), the greater the potential for stratification. This surplus in turn is appropriated according to the distribution of power.

Turner (1984) theorizes that the concentration of power is unequal to the extent that there is external military threat to the society or there is a high level of internal conflict among social groups. Both external and internal conflict tend to centralize power, providing that the government wins these conflicts; hence, another condition must also be present, that the society is relatively productive and organizationally well integrated. If the state has high resources relative to its enemies, conflict is the route by which it concentrates power in its own hands.

Prestige is determined by the concentration of power and wealth. Groups that have these resources can invest them in material possessions that make them impressive in social encounters. In addition, they can invest their resources in culture-producing organizations such as education, entertainment, and art, which give them cultural domination. According to Pierre Bourdieu's research (1984), the realm of culture is stratified along the same lines as the stratification of the surrounding society.

## EFFECTS OF CONFLICT GROUPS UPON INDIVIDUALS

The latent lines of conflict in a society divide people into distinctive styles of belief and emotion. Collins (1975) proposed that the differences among stratified groups are due to the microinteractions of daily experience, which can occur along the two dimensions of vertical power and horizontal solidarity. Persons who give orders take the initiative in the interaction rituals described by Goffman (1959). These persons who enact the rituals of power identify with their front-stage selves and with the official symbols of the organizations they control; whereas persons who take orders are alienated from official rituals and identify with their private, backstage selves. Individuals who belong to tightly enclosed, localized groups emphasize conformity to the group's traditions; persons in such positions are suspicious of outsiders and react violently and emotionally against insiders who are disrespectful of the group's symbols. Loosely organized networks have less solidarity and exert less pressure for conformity. Individuals build up emotional energy by microexperiences that give them power or solidarity, and they lose emotional energy when they are subordinated to power or lack experiences of solidarity (Collins 1988). Both emotions and be-

liefs reproduce the stratification of society in everyday life.

(SEE ALSO: *Coalitions; Game Theory and Strategic Interaction; Interpersonal Power*)

### REFERENCES

Bourdieu, Pierre 1984 *Distinction*. Cambridge, Mass.: Harvard University Press.

Collins, Randall 1975 *Conflict Sociology*. New York: Academic Press.

—— 1986 *Weberian Sociological Theory*. Cambridge: Cambridge University Press.

—— 1988 *Theoretical Sociology*. San Diego: Harcourt Brace Jovanovich.

Coser, Lewis A. 1956 *The Functions of Social Conflict*. New York: Free Press.

Dahrendorf, Ralf 1959 *Class and Class Conflict in Industrial Society*. Stanford, Calif.: Stanford University Press.

Goffman, Erving 1959 *The Presentation of Self in Everyday Life*. New York: Doubleday.

Kriesberg, Louis 1982 *Social Conflicts*. Englewood Cliffs, N.J.: Prentice-Hall.

Lenski, Gerhard E. 1966 *Power and Privilege: A Theory of Stratification*. New York: McGraw-Hill.

Schelling, Thomas C. 1962 *The Strategy of Conflict*. Cambridge, Mass.: Harvard University Press.

Skocpol, Theda 1979 *States and Social Revolutions*. New York: Cambridge University Press.

Stinchcombe, Arthur L. 1968 *Constructing Social Theories*. New York: Harcourt.

Turner, Jonathan H. 1984 *Societal Stratification: A Theoretical Analysis*. New York: Columbia University Press.

Wiley, Norbert F. 1967 "America's Unique Class Politics: The Interplay of the Labor, Credit, and Commodity Markets." *American Sociological Review* 32:529–540.

RANDALL COLLINS

**CONTENT ANALYSIS** Content analysis is a set of procedures for making reliable and valid inferences from images, speech, and text. For reasons of economy, this article focuses only on the analysis of text. Content analysis has been used for diverse purposes, including coding open-ended questions in surveys; identifying the intentions of communications; detecting the existence of propaganda; describing attitudinal and behavioral responses to communications; uncovering cultural patterns of groups, organizations, institutions, or societies; revealing the focus of attention; and describing trends in communication content (Weber 1990 p. 9).

People often perform informal content analyses. For example, on reading an editorial in the newspaper, a person may decide that the paper has changed its position on a particular issue. Or, when reading a love letter from an ardent admirer, the reader will try to infer the writer's real intentions. The bases for drawing such inferences may be explicit statements, such as when a president announces new legislation that differs radically from what was promised in the political campaign. Or it may be based on more subtle features of the text, including the specific words used (or not used) and how the writer chooses to sign the love letter.

Content analysis procedures make such inference processes explicit. In developing a content analysis procedure, investigators agree on what words in the text are to be used in drawing an inference. As a scientific procedure, it is somewhat similar to classification rules first developed by Linnaeus in biology. The best measures are those that prove to have reliable utility. Moreover, classification rules should be readily mastered, not esoteric.

What content indicators are best depends on what kinds of inferences are being made. Just as a biologist examines a leaf structure to make inferences about a tree's classification but measures the distances between tree rings to make inferences about climate variations during its life, the content analyst uses some indicators to make some inferences about characteristics of the writer and others to learn about the economic, political, and social climate at the time the materials were produced. For instance, if written materials from the same writer at different times show the same features, then those indicators may be taken to reflect characteristics of the writer. If measures on written materials from different producers covary over time, then the measures are probably valid indicators of climate.

Content analysis investigations are not only carried out by sociologists, but also by anthropologists, political scientists, social psychologists, market researchers, psychiatrists, intelligence experts, and many others. The relevant literature is huge; some of the important works are mentioned in the references. The various textual materials that have been studied include political party platforms, newspaper stories and editorials, letters to stockholders, focus group transcripts, folktales from different cultures, suicide notes, personal letters and diaries, projective test responses, and depth interviews.

Like any scientific procedure, there are advantages to making the content analysis parsimonious and elegant. Simple rules that have the power to make valid, subtle classifications on a wide range of textual materials are usually best. They are less cumbersome to apply and more easily reported. They also can be more convincing. For example, when content analysis was used in a U.S. trial (Loewen v. Turnipseed, Greenville, Miss., 1979) regarding the adoption of a new state history textbook for Mississippi, many contrasts could have been drawn between the proposed new book and the one the state had adopted for years. Rather than giving complicated testimony that may have confused the court, the witness focuses on one criterion laid down by the state textbook adoption commission, namely, that the state history textbook should give the student a sense of identity as being a "Mississippian." To do this, all uses of the word *Mississippians* were retrieved from both texts and the question of whether a young black would find each reference to include his or her ancestors was asked. Obviously, sentences like "Mississippians were disappointed by the United States Supreme Court's school desegregation decision" were not hard to classify, and the resulting fourfold table clearly demonstrated that the current text did not measure up nearly as well as the proposed text in satisfying the state of Mississippi's own criterion.

Universal applicability is also to be preferred, but many measures are only applicable to a limited domain of discourse. One should not expect a measure of folktale structure, for example, to be immediately applicable to today's television commercial. Language changes over time and changes in the nature of a discourse can make comparisons difficult. For instance, the nature of presidential acceptance speeches changed dramatically when Hoover in 1928 first set the pattern of going to the convention and making the acceptance speech on radio. More recently, the discourse of political campaigning has changed markedly to conform to the television "sound byte" (Adatto 1990). Even a more universal content analysis measure such as Philip Tetlock's (1983, 1985) "thought complexity" or the "CAVE" ("Content Analysis of Verbal Explanations") (Zullow et al. 1988) procedure for assessing optimism–pessimism has to be interpreted in reference to the norms of a discourse domain.

Computers have had a major impact on content analysis by taking over much of the routine clerical work and by setting standards regarding a fully specified, objective procedure. If a procedure can be completely specified, then it should be possible to represent it by a set of computer instructions, even if this means providing a large amount of detailed information in order to make valid context-specific scorings. Computers also made it more difficult to produce an acceptable thesis for an advanced degree by just going through the labors of a hand content analysis, just as a hand-calculated factor analysis by itself no longer constituted a thesis.

Computer-aided content analysis first became popular during the 1960s—as a number of social scientists gained competence in programming mainframe computers—at universities including Chicago, Connecticut, Harvard, MIT, Michigan, Minnesota, Northwestern, Stanford, and Yale, as well as several in Europe. Enthused about the potentialities the computer offered and buttressed with research funds available for social science at that time, large amounts of text were converted to "machine-readable" format by being keypunched on IBM cards and processed through complex computer software that was considerably more demanding of computer memory than most statistical packages. The largest continuing use of such computer software, in terms of amount of text processed, is now in market research.

However, as it became convenient to enlist standard statistical packages and other software without having to learn computer programming, the technical competencies needed to do computer-aided content analysis have become less common. Only when the software for conducting content analysis on desktop computers becomes as convenient and easy to use as word-processing or spell-checker programs—and this should be only a matter of time—are many investigators again likely to utilize it in their research. Word-indexing programs for desktop computers, such as *Nota Bene* or *Folio,* are important initial tools for this.

The variety of textual materials already machine-readable has been rapidly growing and should continue to grow immensely. Both the original text and abstracts of many periodicals can be read on a computer screen as well as on paper. The major corporations' annual "letters to stockholders" are now on line as well as in print. Those who watched Iran-Contra hearings could not but notice frequent reference to electronic mail messages—something new compared to the Watergate hearings—showing that the so-called paper trail, at least in some circles, is becoming electronic. When the text is not in machine-readable form, optical character readers often can make the conversion with reasonable accuracy. The greatly reduced cost of optical character reading equipment, using software that runs on a desktop computer, makes such conversions more feasible than a decade ago.

One way to compare different content analysis procedures is in terms of the analysis to be performed. It is useful in this regard to distinguish six kinds of procedures in order of their complexity:

Relatively simple text processing programs allow investigators to begin to look at textual material in ways corresponding to "exploratory data analysis." For instance, some computer programs list all the word types (including all nouns, pronouns, adjectives, verbs, adverbs) occurring in each text in frequency order. Another program might compare these frequencies with the "Zipf curve" norms (Zipf 1932, [1935] 1965; Francis and Kucera 1982) for a language and just print out those words that have a much higher or lower frequency than expected. The actual occurrences in the text of those words that are of interest may then be retrieved and printed out with their surrounding context, using "key-word in context (KWIC)" routines. KWIC lists show how a particular word is being used in the text. Finally, a "type/token" ratio can be calculated for each text, showing the variegation of words used compared to the number of words in the text.

The next level of content analysis programs employs statistical procedures in order to characterize textual materials. Word frequency correlations across documents are used to create a factor analysis, with each document then characterized in terms of its loadings on these factors. The results of any such procedure tend to be heavily based on noun frequencies, for it is likely that some nouns will appear frequently in some documents and not in others. Factors calculated in this manner are often taken to represent underlying categories of meaning on the theory that words that covary will have similar connotations (Weber 1990, pp. 37–38).

A third level of content analysis computer programs utilizes context-sensitive procedures to identify the sense of each word and then uses look-up procedures to classify each word sense as belonging to one or more categories. This classification into categories is especially important for studying values, styles, attitudes, and the like, for people take care to vary their language rather than repeatedly use the same words. An ardent lover had better learn diverse ways to describe her or his love, otherwise the recipient will write off the lover as dull—that is, someone with a low type/token ratio. Any worthwhile computer program to capture such expressions of love had better have some routines to identify word senses and classify alternative forms of expression.

Once the text has been classified into categories, category frequencies can be compared to

category norms in order to flag those frequencies that are much higher or lower than expected. This strategy is used successfully in market research, with investigators then using KWIC retrieval procedures to ply back and forth between flagged category frequencies and the actual occurrences of the words in the text.

Category counts have often been used as the basis for various multivariate statistical procedures such as factor analysis, cluster analysis, and structural equation modeling, including LISREL. In this mode of analysis, factors are assumed to represent themes in the text. The factor loadings show the extent to which variations in category counts are correlated with variations in the occurrence of the underlying theme. The factor scores for each document indicate the extent to which the underlying theme is manifest in the text. Investigators then use excerpts from the text to confirm the interpretation of the theme based on the factor loadings. Once validated, the factor scores can be correlated with indicators of social, political, and economic variables.

Finally, category counts can be used to search for instances of themes. In some cases, the theme can be quite simple. Ramallo (1966) discovered, for example, that successful Peace Corps volunteers, in writing essays describing their work, combined high frequencies on the categories of "thought" and "action." Those who were high on "thought" and low on "action"—or the reverse—were not as successful in the field. Both "thought" and "action" were needed together. A scoring procedure for "need achievement" (Ogilvie, Stone, and Kelly 1980) is somewhat more complex, requiring that the writer identify a need, specify means for fulfilling it, and express an appropriate emotional tone over the success or failure of the outcome.

A content analysis for measuring the presence or absence of a theme often will operate in two stages. First, a check will be made to see if all the necessary ingredients are present in the text being examined—much like a cook might check whether all the ingredients in a recipe are in the pantry before starting to make the item. If all the ingredients are present, then the computer may apply a template, in the form of test rules, to see if the ingredients occur in the right order.

Much of the content analysis research published in the 1970s and 1980s was based on the relative attention paradigm (Namenwirth and Weber 1987) for cultural and social inquiry. Work in this tradition analyzes documents constituting the output of various collective processes, such as party platforms, newspaper editorials, speeches at the opening of the British parliament, and presidential addresses in scientific associations. The relative attention paradigm assumes that the more a particular measure of textual content, such as values, themes, issues, ideologies, disputes, concerns, or categories, is mentioned in the text, the greater the attention devoted to it. Using both computerized and hand-coded content analysis, researchers in this tradition have shown that changes in the attention devoted to various content indicators varies with changes in social, economic, and political variables.

When textual materials span long time periods, investigators may apply time series procedures to identify thematic patterns, sequences, and cycles. Namenwirth and Weber (1987), for instance, showed that changes in concern with parochial, progressive, cosmopolitan, and conservative themes were correlated with long-term fluctuations in economic performance in both America and Great Britain.

Future content analyses may benefit from some developments taking place in artificial intelligence, especially in the domain of natural language understanding. Key problems for computer-aided content analysis, such as pronoun identification, may be at least partly resolved. These capabilities, in turn, will simplify such challenges as extracting attributional statements, as in the CAVE procedure, as well as other types of template matching.

(SEE ALSO: *Sociolinguistics*)

## REFERENCES

Adatto, Kiku 1990 "Sound Byte Demographics." Harvard University, John F. Kennedy School of Government, Research paper #R2.

Allen, James 1987 *Natural Language Understanding.* Menlo Park, Calif.: Benjamin/Cummings.

Francis, W. Nelson, and Henry Kucera 1982 *Frequency Analysis of English Usage: Lexicon and Grammar.* Boston: Houghton Mifflin.

Gerbner, George, Ole R. Holsti, Klaus Krippendorff, William Paisley, and Philip J. Stone, eds. 1969 *The Analysis of Communication Content.* New York: Wiley.

Holsti, Ole R. 1969 *Content Analysis for the Social Sciences and Humanities.* Reading, Mass.: Addison-Wesley.

Kelly, Edward, and Philip J. Stone 1975 *Computer Recognition of English Word Senses.* Amsterdam: North-Holland Press.

Klingemann, Hans-Dieter, Peter Philip Mohler, and Robert Philip Weber 1982 "Cultural Indicators Based on Content Analysis." *Quality and Quantity* 16:1–18.

Markoff, John, Gilbert Shapiro, and Sasha Weitman 1974 "Toward the Integration of Content Analysis and General Methodology." In David R. Heise, ed., *Sociological Methodology 1975.* San Francisco: Jossey-Bass.

Melischek, Gabriele, Karl Erik Rosengren, and James Stappers, eds. 1984 *Cultural Indicators: An International Symposium.* Vienna: Austrian Academy of Sciences.

Namenwirth, J. Zvi, and Robert Philip Weber 1987 *Dynamics of Culture.* Winchester, Mass.: Allen and Unwin.

Ogilvie, Daniel, Philip J. Stone, and Edward F. Kelly 1980 "Computer-Aided Content Analysis." In Robert Smith and P. Manning, eds., *Handbook of Social Science Research Methods.* New York: Irvington.

Ramallo, Luis I. 1966 "The Integration of Subject and Object in the Context of Action." In Philip J. Stone, Dexter J. Dunphy, Daniel M. Ogilvie, and Marshall S. Smith, eds., *The General Inquirer: A Computer Approach to Content Analysis.* Cambridge, Mass.: MIT Press.

Rosengren, Karl Erik, ed. 1981 *Advances in Content Analysis.* Beverly Hills, Calif.:Sage.

Salton, Gerard 1989 *Automated Text Processing.* Reading, Mass.: Addison-Wesley.

Stone, Philip J., Dexter J. Dunphy, Daniel M. Ogilvie, and Marshall S. Smith 1966 *The General Inquirer: A Computer Approach to Content Analysis.* Cambridge, Mass.: MIT Press.

Tetlock, Philip E. 1983 "Accountability and Complexity of Thought." *Journal of Personality and Social Psychology* 45:74–83.

———— 1985 "Integrative Complexity of American and Soviet Foreign Policy Rhetoric: A Time-Series Analysis." *Journal of Personality and Social Psychology* 41, 737–743.

Weber, Robert Philip 1990 *Basic Content Analysis,* 2nd ed. Newbury Park, Calif.: Sage.

Winograd, Terry, and Fernando Flores 1986 *Understanding Computers and Cognition: A New Foundation for Design.* Norwood, N.J.: Ablex.

Zipf, George K. 1932 *Selected Studies of the Principle of Relative Frequency in Language.* Cambridge: Harvard University Press.

————, (1935) 1965 *Psycho-Biology of Language.* Boston: Houghton Mifflin. Cambridge, Mass.: MIT Press.

Zuell, Cornelia, Robert Philip Weber, and Peter Philip Mohler 1989 *Computer-assisted Text Analysis: The General Inquirer III.* Mannheim, Germany: Center for Surveys, Methods, and Analysis (ZUMA).

Zullow, Harold, Gabriele Oettingen, Christopher Peterson, and Martin Seligman 1988 "Pessimistic Explanatory Style in the Historical Record." *American Psychologist* 43:673–682.

PHILIP J. STONE
ROBERT PHILIP WEBER

**CONTINGENCY TABLES** *See* Tabular Analysis.

**CONVERGENCE THEORIES** The idea that societies move toward a condition of similarity—that they converge in one or more respects— is a common feature of various theories of social change. The notion that differences among societies will decrease over time can be found in many works of eighteenth- and nineteenth-century social thinkers, from the prerevolutionary French *philosophes* and the Scottish moral philosophers through de Tocqueville, Toennies, Maine, Marx, Spencer, Weber, and Durkheim (Weinberg 1969; Baum 1974). More recently, the study of "postindustrial" society and the debate over "postmodernism" also reflect to some degree the idea that there is a tendency for broadly similar conditions or attributes to emerge across a range of otherwise distinct societies.

In contemporary sociological discourse, *convergence theory* has a more specific connotation; it refers to the hypothesized link between economic development and concomitant changes in social organization, particularly with regard to work and industrial organization, class structure, demographic patterns, characteristics of the family, education, and the role of government in assuring basic social and economic security. The core notion of convergence theory is that as nations achieve similar levels of economic development they will become more alike in terms of these (and other) aspects of social life. In the 1950s and 1960s, predictions of societal convergence were most closely associated with modernization theories, which held that developing societies will follow a path of economic development similar to that followed by developed societies of the West. In the 1960s, convergence theory was also invoked to account for apparent similarities in industrial organization and patterns of stratification in capitalist and communist nations (Sorokin 1960; Goldthorpe 1964; Galbraith 1967; see Ludz 1972 for a literature review).

## CONVERGENCE THEORY AND MODERNIZATION

The most controversial application of convergence theory has been in the study of modernization, where it is associated with the idea that the experience of developing nations will follow the path charted by Western industrialized nations. Related to this idea is the notion of a relatively fixed pattern of development through which developing nations must pass as they modernize (Rostow 1960). Inkeles (1966), Inkeles and Smith (1974), and Kahl (1968) pursued the idea of convergence at the level of individual attitudes, values, and beliefs, arguing that the emergence of a "modern" psychosocial orientation accompanies national modernization (see Armer and Schnaiberg 1972 for a critique).

*Industrialism and Industrial Man* by Clark Kerr et al. (1960) offers the classic statement of the "logic of industrialism" thesis, which the authors proposed as an alternative to the equation of industrialism with capitalism in Marxian theory. More specifically, Kerr et al. sought to identify the "inherent tendencies and implications of industrialization for the work place," hoping to construct from this a portrait of the "principal features of the new society" (p. 33). The features common to industrial society, they argued, included rapid changes in science, technology, and methods of production; a high degree of occupational mobility, with continual training and retraining of the work force; increasing emphasis on formal education, particularly in the natural sciences, engineering, medicine, managerial training, and administrative law; a work force highly differentiated in terms of occupational titles and job classifications; the increasing importance of urban areas as centers of economic activity; and the increasing role of government in providing expanded public services, orchestrating the varied activities of a large and complex economy, and administering the "web of rules" of industrial society. Importantly, Kerr et al. envisioned these developments as cutting across categories of political ideology and political systems.

Although the "logic of industrialism" argument is often cited as a prime example of convergence theory (see Form 1979; Moore 1979; Goldthorpe 1971), Kerr et al. never explicitly made this claim for their study. Convergence is mentioned at various points in their study, but the authors pay equal attention to important countercurrents leading toward diverse outcomes among industrial societies. The concluding chapter of *Industrialism and Industrial Man* is, in fact, entitled "Pluralistic Industrialism" and addresses the sources of diversity as well as uniformity among industrial societies. Among sources of diversity identified are the persistence of existing national institutions, enduring cultural differences, variations in the timing of industrialization (late versus early), the nature of a nation's dominant industry, and the size and density of population. Counterposed against these factors are various sources of uniformity, such as technological change, exposure

to the industrial world, and a worldwide trend toward increased access to education leading to an attenuation of social and economic inequality.

The critique of convergence theory in the study of modernization recalls critiques of earlier theories of societal evolution advanced under the rubric of social Darwinism in the nineteenth century and structural functionalism in the twentieth century (see, for example, Parsons 1967). The use of convergence theory to analyze modernization has been attacked for its alleged assumptions of unilinearity and determinism (a single path of development that all societies must follow), its teleological or historicist character (Goldthorpe 1971), its Western ideological bias (Portes 1973), and for ignoring the structurally dependent position of less-developed countries in the world economy (Wallerstein 1974). Yet a careful review of the literature suggests that such criticisms have often tended to caricature convergence theory rather than evaluate its application in actual research studies. Since the 1960s few if any researchers have claimed convergence theory, at least in its unreconstructed form, as their own. For example, Wilbert Moore (1979), an exponent of the "conventional" view of modernization, subtitled his *World Modernization* "the limits of convergence" and went to great pains to distance himself from the "model modernized society" position associated with early versions of convergence theory (see pp. 26–28, 150–153). Even some of the theory's early advocates sought to distance themselves from the crude convergence position: in his 1983 study, Kerr pondered whether "convergence or continuing diversity" would mark the future of industrial societies. As Form (1979) observes, convergence theory passed through a cycle typical of social science theories: a burst of initial interest and enthusiasm, followed by intense criticism and controversy, finally giving way to neglect. The major challenge to those wishing to revive convergence theory and rescue it from its critics is to specify its theoretical underpinnings more precisely, to develop appropriate empirical studies, and finally to account for variation as well as similarity among observed cases.

## FORMS OF CONVERGENCE AND DIVERGENCE

In recent years Alex Inkeles (1980, 1981; Inkeles and Sirowy 1983) has made the most systematic attempt to reformulate convergence theory and respecify its core hypotheses and propositions. Inkeles (1981) argues that earlier versions of convergence theory failed to distinguish adequately between different elements of the social system, which is problematic because these elements not only change at different speeds but may move in opposite directions. He proposes dividing the social system into a minimum of five elements for purposes of assessing convergence: modes of production and patterns of resource utilization; institutional arrays and institutional forms; structures or patterns of social relationships; systems of popular attitudes, values, and behavior; and systems of political and economic control. Finally, he specifies the different forms convergence and divergence may take: (1) simple convergence, involving the movement from diversity to uniformity; (2) convergence from different directions, involving movement toward a common point by an increase for some cases and a decrease for others; (3) convergence via the crossing of thresholds rather than changes in absolute differences; (4) divergent paths toward convergence, where short-term fluctuations eventually fall into line or a "deviant" case emerges that eventually defines the norm for other cases (for example, France's move toward small family size in the late eighteenth century); and (5) convergence in the form of parallel change, where nations all moving in the same direction along some dimension of change continue to remain separated by a gap. Although parallel change of this sort does not represent true convergence, it is consistent with the key assumption of convergence theory, namely, that "insofar as they face comparable situations of action . . . nations and individuals will respond in broadly comparable ways" (p. 21).

Inkeles (1981) also describes various forms that divergence may take: (1) simple divergence, the mirror image of simple convergence, in which movement occurs away from a common point toward new points further apart than the original condition; (2) convergence with crossover, where lines intersect and then proceed to spread apart; and (3) convergent trends masking underlying diversity (for example, although the United States, Great Britain, and Sweden all experienced large increases in public-assistance programs from 1950 to the early 1970s, the social groups receiving benefits were quite different among the three nations, as were the political dynamics associated with the spending increases within each nation).

Finally, Inkeles (1981) notes the importance of selecting appropriate units of analysis, levels of analysis, and the time span for which convergence, divergence, or parallel change can be assessed. These comments echo sentiments expressed earlier by Weinberg (1969) and Baum (1974) about how to salvage the useful elements of convergence theory while avoiding the pitfalls of a functionalist-evolutionary approach. Common to these attempts to revive convergence theory is the exhortation to develop more and better empirical research on specific institutional spheres and social processes. As the following sections demonstrate, a good deal of work along these lines is already being done on a wide range of substantive questions and topical concerns involving convergence theory.

## INDUSTRIAL SOCIOLOGY

Despite criticisms of the concept of the logic of industrialism put forward by Kerr et al. (1960), the question of convergent trends in industrial organization has remained the focus of active debate and much research. The large research literature related on this question, reviewed by Form (1979), has produced mixed evidence with respect to convergence. Studies by Shiba (1973, cited in Form 1979), Form (1976), and Form and Kyu Han (1988), covering a range of industrializing and advanced industrial societies, found empirical support for convergence in workers' adaptation to industrial and related social systems, while Gallie's (1977, cited in Form 1979) study of oil refineries in Great Britain and France found consistent differences in workers' attitudes toward systems of authority. On the question of sectoral and occupational shifts, Gibbs and Browning's (1966) twelve-nation study of industrial and occupational division of labor found both similarities —consistent with the convergence hypothesis— and differences. Studies of worker commitment across nations varying in levels of industrial development revealed only "small and unsystematic differences" in worker commitment (Form 1979, p. 9), thus providing some support for the convergence hypothesis. Japan has been regarded as an exceptional case among industrialized nations because of its strong cultural traditions based on mutual obligation between employers and employees. These characteristics led Dore (1973), for example, to argue vigorously against the convergence hypothesis for Japan. A more recent study by Lincoln and Kalleberg (1990) "stands convergence on its head," arguing that patterns of work organization in the United States are being impelled in the direction of the Japanese model. Finally, with respect to women in the labor force, the evidence of convergence is mixed. Some studies found no relationship between female labor-force participation and level of industrialization (Ferber and Lowry 1977; Safilios-Rothchild 1971), though there is strong evidence of a trend toward increasing female participation in nonagricultural employment among advanced industrial societies (Paydarfar 1967; Wilensky 1968) along with the existence of dual labor markets stratified by sex, a pattern found in both communist and capitalist nations (Cooney 1975; Bibb and Form 1977; Lapidus 1976).

## STRATIFICATION

Closely related to the study of industrial organization is the question of converging patterns of stratification and mobility. The attempt to discover common features of the class structure across advanced industrial societies is a central concern for social theorists of many stripes. In recent years the question has inspired intense debate among both neo-Weberian and Marxist sociologists, although the latter tend to eschew the language of convergence theory in analyzing similarities of class structure in advanced capitalist societies (see, e.g., Wright 1989). An early statement of the class-convergence thesis was made by Lipset and Zetterberg (1959), to the effect that observed rates of mobility between social classes tend to be similar from one industrial society to another. Erikson et al. (1983) conducted a detailed test of the class-mobility-convergence hypothesis in England, France, and Sweden, and found little support for it. They concluded that the "process of industrialization is associated with very variable patterns . . . of the social division of labour" (p. 339).

A subcategory of comparative stratification research concerns the evidence of convergence in occupational prestige. A study published in 1956 by Inkeles and Rossi, based on data from six industrialized societies, concluded that the prestige hierarchy of occupations was "relatively invariable" and tended to support the hypothesis that modern industrial systems are "highly coherent . . . relatively impervious to the influence of traditional culture patterns" (p. 329). Although the authors did not specifically mention convergence, their conclusions were fully consistent with the idea. A subsequent study by Treiman (1977) extended the comparison of occupational prestige to some sixty nations, ranging from the least developed to the most developed. The study found that occupational-prestige rankings were markedly similar across all societies, raising the question whether convergence theory or an explanation based on the functional imperatives of social structure of all complex societies, past or present, was most consistent with the empirical results. The conclusion was that both explanations had some merit, since, although all complex societies—whether developed, undeveloped, or developing—showed similar occupational-prestige rankings, there was also evidence that the more similar societies were in terms of levels of industrialization, the more similar their patterns of occupational-prestige evaluation appeared to be.

## DEMOGRAPHIC PATTERNS

The theory of demographic transition provides one of the most straightforward examples of convergence. The essence of the demographic transition concept is that fertility and mortality rates covary over time in a predictable and highly uniform manner. Moreover, these changes are directly linked to broad developmental patterns, such as the move from a rural, agriculturally based economy to an urban-industrial one, increases in per capita income, and adult literacy (Berelson 1978). In the first stage of the demographic transition, both fertility rates and death rates are high, with population remaining fairly constant. In the second stage, death rates drop (as a result of improvements in living conditions and medical care) while fertility rates remain high, and population levels increase rapidly. In the third stage, fertility rates begin to decline, with total size of the population leveling off or even decreasing. This simple model works remarkably well in accounting for demographic patterns observed among all industrialized (and many industrializing) societies during the post-World War II period. A large spread in fertility rates among nations at the beginning of the 1950s gave way to declining rates of fertility, ending with a nearly uniform pattern of zero population growth in the 1970s.

The tendency toward convergence predicted by the theory of demographic transition has not gone unchallenged, however. Freedman (1979), for example, suggests that cultural factors mediate the effects of social structural factors central to transition theory. Coale (1973) and Teitelbaum (1975) note that demographic transition theory has not provided much explanatory or predictive power with regard to the timing of population changes or the regional variations observed within nations undergoing change.

## FAMILY

Inkeles (1980) explored the effects of putative convergent tendencies discussed above for family patterns. While he found evidence of convergence in some aspects of family life, other patterns continue "to be remarkably stable in the face of great variation in their surrounding socio-economic conditions" (p. 34). Aspects of family life that show clear convergent tendencies include the trend toward falling fertility rates, and a shift in relative power and resource control in the direction of increasing autonomy of women and declining authority of parents. Other aspects of the family, such as the age of marriage, present a more complex picture, with short-term fluctuations obscuring long-term changes, and great variation from one culture to another. Still other characteristics of family life seem resistant to change; cited as examples in Inkeles (1980) are cultural patterns such as veneration of elders in Oriental societies, basic human needs for companionship and psychological support, and the role of husbands helping wives with housework. In all, Inkeles estimates that only about half the indicators of family life he examined showed any convergence, and even then not always of a linear nature.

## EDUCATION

Following Inkeles's (1981) reformulation of convergence theory, Inkeles and Sirowy (1983) studied the educational systems of seventy-three rich and poor nations. Among thirty different "patterns of change" in educational systems examined, they found evidence of marked convergence in fourteen, moderate convergence in four, considerable variability in nine, mixed results in two, and divergence in only one. On the basis of these findings, they concluded that the tendency toward convergence on common structures is "pervasive and deep. It is manifested at all levels of the educational system, and affects virtually every major aspect of that system" (p. 326). Also worthy of note is that while the authors take the conventional position that convergence is a response to pressures arising from a complex, technologically advanced social and economic system, they also identified diffusion via integration of networks through which ideas, standards, and practices in education are shared. These networks operate largely through international organizations, such as UNESCO and the OECD; their role as mediating structures in a process leading toward cross-national similarities in education constitutes an important addition to convergence theory, with wide-ranging implications for convergence in other institutions.

## THE WELFARE STATE

The welfare state has been an area of active theoretical debate and empirical research on convergence theory, with researchers divided over the nature and extent of convergence found among nations. On the one hand, there is indisputable evidence that the provision of extensive social security, health-care, and related benefit programs is restricted to nations that have reached a level of economic development where a sufficient surplus exists to support such efforts. Moreover, the development of programs of the welfare state appears to be empirically correlated with distinct bureaucratic and demographic patterns that are in turn grounded in economic development. For example, Wilensky (1975) found that among sixty nations studied, the proportion of the population sixty-five years of age and older and the age of social security programs were the major determinants of levels of total welfare-state spending as a percent of gross national product (GNP). Since levels of economic development and growth of the elderly population both represent areas of convergence among advanced societies, it is reasonable to infer that patterns of welfare-state development will also tend to converge. Indeed, in such respects as the development of large and expensive pension and health-care programs, of which the elderly are the major clientele, this is the case (Coughlin and Armour 1982; Hage et al. 1989). Other empirical studies have found evidence of convergence in public attitudes toward constituent programs of the welfare state (Coughlin 1980), in egalitarian political movements affecting welfare effort across nations (Williamson and Weiss 1979), and in levels of spending (Pryor 1968), normative patterns (Mishra 1976), and social control functions of welfare-state programs

across capitalist and communist nations (Armour and Coughlin 1985).

Other researchers have challenged the idea of convergence in the welfare state. In a historical study of unemployment programs in thirteen Western European nations, Alber (1981) found no evidence that programs had become more alike in eligibility criteria, methods of financing, or generosity of benefits, although he did find some evidence of convergence in duration of unemployment benefits in nations with compulsory systems. A study conducted by O'Connor (1988) testing the convergence hypothesis with respect to trends in welfare spending from 1960 to 1980 concluded that "despite the adoption of apparently similar welfare programmes in economically developed countries there is not only diversity but divergence in welfare effort. Further, the level of divergence is increasing" (p. 295). A much broader challenge to the convergence hypothesis comes from studies focusing on variations in welfare-state development among Western capitalist democracies. Hewitt (1977), Castles (1978, 1982), Stephens (1979), and Korpi (1983), to cite a few leading examples, argue that variations across nations in the strength and reformist character of labor unions and social democratic parties account for large differences in the levels of spending for and redistributive impact of welfare-state programs. However, the disagreement among these studies and scholars arguing for convergence may be simply a function of case selection. For example, in a study of nineteen rich nations, Wilensky (1976, 1981) linked cross-national diversity in the welfare state to differences in "democratic corporatism," and secondarily to the presence of Catholic political parties, thus rejecting the simplistic idea that the convergence observed across many nations at widely different levels of economic development extends to the often divergent policy developments in the relatively small number of advanced capitalist societies.

The debate over convergence in the welfare state is certain to continue. A major obstacle in resolving the question involves disagreement on the selection of nations to be studied, selection and construction of measures (see Uusitalo 1984), and judgments about the time frame appropriate for a definitive test of the convergence hypothesis. Wilensky et al. (1985, pp. 11–12) sum up the mixed status of current research on convergence in welfare-state development as follows:

> Convergence theorists are surely on solid ground when they assert that programs to protect against the seven or eight basic risks of industrial life are primarily responses to economic development. . . . However, showing that societies have adopted the same basic programs . . . is only a partial demonstration of convergence insofar as it does not demonstrate convergence in substantive features of the programs or in the amount of variation among affluent countries compared to poor countries.

## CONCLUSION

The idea of convergence is both powerful and intuitively attractive to sociologists across a broad range (Form 1979). It is difficult to conceive of an acceptable macro theory of social change that does not refer to convergence in one way or another. Despite the controversy over, and subsequent disillusionment with, early versions of convergence theory applied to the study of modernization, and the often mixed results of empirical studies discussed above, it is clear that the concept of societal convergence—as well as the possibilities of divergence and invariance—provides a useful analytical framework within which to conduct cross-national studies of a broad range of social phenomena. Even where the convergence hypothesis ultimately ends up being rejected, the convergence-theory perspective can still offer a useful point of departure for comparative social research. Appropriately reformulated, focused on elements of the social system amenable to empirical study (ideally using longitudinal data to supplement or replace cross-sectional studies), and stripped of the ideological baggage associated with its earlier versions, convergence theory holds promise to advance our understanding of the fundamental processes and laws of social change. Convergence theory has been given a boost by recent developments in Eastern Europe and the Soviet Union, which have revived interest in the idea of large-scale economic and political convergence (see, for example, Lenski et al. 1991, p. 261). Finally, mechanisms other than economic development, narrowly construed, suggest a variety of innovative applications of the convergence hypothesis—for example, that the accelerating pace of globalization of the economy, communications, and culture, which compresses the time and space dimensions of social interaction (Giddens 1990), may lead toward a rapid and more complete diffusion of ideas and patterns of social and economic organization worldwide (cf. Inkeles 1980, p. 32).

(SEE ALSO: *Diffusion Theories; Global Systems Analysis; Postindustrial Society*)

## REFERENCES

Alber, Jens 1981 "Government Responses to the Challenge of Unemployment: The Development of Unemployment Insurance in Western Europe." In Peter Flora and Arnold J. Heidenheimer, eds., *The Development of Welfare States in Europe and America.* New Brunswick, N.J.: Transaction Books.

Armer, Michael, and Allan Schnaiberg 1972 "Measuring Individual Modernity: A Near Myth." *American Sociological Review* 37:301–316.

Armour, Philip K., and Richard M. Coughlin 1985 "Social Control and Social Security: Theory and Research on Capitalist and Communist Nations." *Social Science Quarterly* 66:770–788.

Aron, Raymond 1967 *The Industrial Society.* New York: Simon and Schuster.

Baum, Rainer C. 1974 "Beyond Convergence: Toward Theoretical Relevance in Quantitative Modernization Research." *Sociological Inquiry* 44:225–240.

Bendix, Reinhard 1967 "Tradition and Modernity Reconsidered." *Comparative Studies in Society and History* 9:292–346.

Berelson, B. 1978 "Prospects and Programs for Fertility Reduction: What? Where?" *Population and Development Review* 4:579–616.

Bibb, R., and W. H. Form 1977 "The Effects of Industrial, Occupational, and Sex Stratification in Blue-Collar Markets." *Social Forces* 55:974–996.

Castles, Francis 1978 *The Social Democratic Image of Society.* London: Routledge and Kegan Paul.

—— 1982 "The Impact of Parties on Public Expenditure." In Francis Castles, ed., *The Impact of*

*Parties: Politics and Policies in Democratic Capitalist States.* Beverly Hills, Calif.: Sage.

Coale, Ansley J. 1973 "The Demographic Transition." In *The International Population Conference, Liège.* Liège: International Union for the Scientific Study of Population.

Cooney, R. S. 1975 "Female Professional Work Opportunities: A Cross-National Study." *Demography* 12:107–120.

Coughlin, Richard M. 1980 *Ideology, Public Opinion and Welfare Policy.* Berkeley, Calif.: University of California, Institute of International Studies.

——, and Philip K. Armour 1982 "Sectoral Differentiation in Social Security Spending in the OECD Nations." *Comparative Social Research* 6:175–199.

Dore, Ronald 1973 *British Factory–Japanese Factory.* Berkeley, Calif.: University of California Press.

Erikson, Robert, John H. Goldthorpe, and Lucienne Portocarero 1983 "Intergenerational Class Mobility and the Convergence Thesis: England, France, and Sweden." *British Journal of Sociology* 34:303–343.

Ferber, M., and H. Lowry 1977 "Women's Place: National Differences in the Occupational Mosaic." *Journal of Marketing* 41:23–30.

Form, William 1976 *Blue-Collar Stratification.* Princeton, N.J.: Princeton University Press.

—— 1979 "Comparative Industrial Sociology and the Convergence Hypothesis." *Annual Review of Sociology* 4:1–25.

——, and Bae Kyu Han 1988 "Convergence Theory and the Korean Connection." *Social Forces* 66:618–644.

Fox, William S., and William W. Philliber 1980 "Class Convergence: An Empirical Test." *Sociology and Social Research* 64:236–248.

Freedman, Ronald 1979 "Theories of Fertility Decline: A Reappraisal." *Social Forces* 58:1–17.

Galbraith, John Kenneth 1967 *The New Industrial State.* Boston: Houghton Mifflin.

Gibbs, J. P., and H. L. Browning 1966 "The Division of Labor, Technology, and the Organization of Production in Twelve Countries." *American Sociological Review* 31:81–92.

Giddens, Anthony 1990 *The Consequences of Modernity.* Stanford, Calif.: Stanford University Press.

Goldthorpe, John H. 1964 "Social Stratification in Industrial Society." In P. Halmos, ed., *The Development of Industrial Societies.* Keele, England: University of Keele.

—— 1971 "Theories of Industrial Society: Reflections on the Recrudescence of Historicism and the Future of Futurology." *Archives of European Sociology* 12:263–288.

Hage, Jerald, Robert Hanneman, and Edward T. Gargan 1989 *State Responsiveness and State Activism.* London: Unwin Hyman.

Hewitt, Christopher 1977 "The Effect of Political Democracy and Social Democracy on Equality in Industrial Societies: A Cross-National Comparison." *American Sociological Review* 42:450–464.

Inkeles, Alex 1966 "The Modernization of Man." In M. Weiner, ed., *Modernization.* New York: Basic Books.

—— 1980 "Modernization and Family Patterns: A Test of Convergence Theory." In D. W. Hoover and J. T. A. Koumoulides, eds., *Conspectus of History.* Cambridge: Cambridge University Press.

—— 1981 "Convergence and Divergence in Industrial Societies." In M. O. Attir, B. H. Holzner, and Z. Suda, eds., *Direction of Change: Modernization Theory, Research, and Realities.* Boulder, Colo.: Westview Press.

——, and Peter H. Rossi 1956 "National Comparisons of Occupational Prestige." *American Journal of Sociology* 61:329–339.

——, and Larry Sirowy 1983 "Convergent and Divergent Trends in National Educational Systems." *Social Forces* 62:303–333.

——, and David E. Smith 1974 *Becoming Modern.* Cambridge, Mass.: Harvard University Press.

Kahl, J. A. 1968 *The Measurement of Modernization: A Study of Values in Brazil and Mexico.* Austin, Tex.: University of Texas Press.

Kerr, Clark 1983 *The Future of Industrial Societies.* Cambridge: Harvard University Press.

——, John T. Dunlap, Frederick H. Harbison, and Charles A. Myers 1960 *Industrialism and Industrial Man.* Cambridge, Mass.: Harvard University Press.

Korpi, Walter 1983 *The Democratic Class Struggle.* London: Routledge and Kegan Paul.

Lapidus, Gail W. 1976 "Occupational Segregation and Public Policy: A Comparative Analysis of American and Soviet Patterns." In M. Blaxall and B. Reagan, eds., *Women and the Workplace.* Chicago: University of Chicago Press.

Lenski, Gerhard, Jean Lenski, and Patrick Nolan 1991 *Human Societies,* 6th ed. New York: McGraw-Hill.

Lincoln, James R., and Arne L. Kalleberg 1990 *Culture, Control, and Commitment: A Study of Work Organization and Work Attitudes in the United States and Japan.* Cambridge: Cambridge University Press.

Lipset, Seymour M., and Hans Zetterberg 1959 "Social Mobility in Industrial Societies." In S. M. Lipset and

R. Bendix, eds., *Social Mobility in Industrial Society.* London: Heinemann.

Ludz, Peter C. 1972 "Convergence." In C. D. Kernig, ed., *Marxism, Communism and Western Society,* vol. 2. New York: Herder and Herder.

Mishra, Ramesh 1976 "Convergence Theory and Social Change: The Development of Welfare in Britain and the Soviet Union." *Comparative Studies in Society and History* 18:28–56.

Moore, Wilbert E. 1979 *World Modernization: The Limits of Convergence.* New York: Elsevier.

O'Connor, Julia S. 1988 "Convergence or Divergence? Change in Welfare Effort in OECD Countries 1960–1980." *European Journal of Political Research* 16:277–299.

Parsons, Talcott 1967 *Societies: Evolutionary and Comparative Perspectives.* Englewood Cliffs, N.J.: Prentice Hall.

Paydarfar, A. A. 1967 "Modernization Process and Demographic Changes." *Sociological Review* 15: 141–153.

Portes, Alejandro 1973 "Modernity and Development: A Critique." *Comparative International Development* 8:247–279.

Pryor, Frederick 1968 *Public Expenditure in Capitalist and Communist Nations.* Homewood, Ill.: Irwin.

Rostow, Walt W. 1960 *The Stages of Economic Growth.* Cambridge. Cambridge University Press.

Safilios-Rothchild, C. 1971 "A Cross-Cultural Examination of Women's Marital, Educational and Occupational Aspirations." *Acta Sociologica* 14:96–113.

Sorokin, Pitirim A. 1960 "Mutual Convergence of the United States and the U.S.S.R. to the Mixed Sociocultural Type." *International Journal of Comparative Sociology* 1:143–176.

Stephens, John D. 1979 *The Transition from Capitalism to Socialism.* London: Macmillan.

Teitelbaum, M. S. 1975 "Relevance of Demographic Transition for Developing Countries." *Science* 188:420–425.

Treiman, Donald J. 1977 *Occupational Prestige in Comparative Perspective.* New York: Academic Press.

Uusitalo, Hannu 1984 "Comparative Research on the Determinants of the Welfare State: The State of the Art." *European Journal of Political Research* 12:403–442.

Wallerstein, Immanuel 1974 "The Rise and Future Demise of the World Capitalist System: Concepts for Comparative Analysis." *Comparative Studies in Social History* 16:287–415.

Weed, Frank J. 1979 "Industrialization and Welfare Systems: A Critical Evaluation of the Convergence Hypothesis." *International Journal of Comparative Sociology* 20:282–292.

Weinberg, Ian 1969 "The Problem of the Convergence of Industrial Societies: A Critical Look at the State of the Theory." *Comparative Studies in Society and History* 11:1–15.

Wilensky, Harold L. 1968 "Women's Work: Economic Growth, Ideology, Structure." *Industrial Relations* 7:235–248.

——— 1975 *The Welfare State and Equality.* Berkeley, Calif.: University of California Press.

——— 1976 *The "New Corporatism": Centralization and the Welfare State.* Beverly Hills, Calif.: Sage.

——— 1981 "Leftism, Catholicism, and Democratic Corporatism: The Role of Political Parties in Recent Welfare State Development." In Peter Flora and Arnold J. Heidenheimer, eds., *The Development of Welfare States in Europe and America.* New Brunswick, N.J.: Transaction Books.

———, Gregory M. Luebbert, Susan Reed Hahn, and Adrienne M. Jamieson 1985 *Comparative Social Policy: Theory, Methods, Findings.* Berkeley, Calif.: University of California, Institute of International Studies.

Williamson, John B., and Jeanne J. Fleming 1977 "Convergence Theory and the Social Welfare Sector: A Cross-National Analysis." *International Journal of Comparative Sociology* 18:242–253.

———, and Joseph W. Weiss 1979 "Egalitarian Political Movements, Social Welfare Effort and Convergence Theory: A Cross-National Analysis." *Comparative Social Research* 2:289–302.

Wright, Erik Olin 1989 *The Debate on Classes.* London and New York: Verso.

RICHARD M. COUGHLIN

## CONVERSATION ANALYSIS

Conversation analysis has evolved as a distinct variant of ethnomethodology. Its beginnings can be traced to the mid-1960s, to the doctoral research and the unpublished but widely circulated lectures of Harvey Sacks. Sacks was a University of California sociologist who had studied with Harold Garfinkel, the founder of the ethnomethodological movement, as well as with Erving Goffman. While not an ethnomethodologist, Goffman's proposal that face-to-face interaction could be an analytically independent domain of inquiry certainly helped inspire Sacks's work. Two other key figures whose writings (separately and together with those of Sacks) contributed to the emergence of conversation analysis were Gail Jefferson, one of Sacks's first students, and Emanuel A. Schegloff, another sociologist trained in the University of California system who was decisively influenced by Garfinkel and, in much the same manner as Sacks, by Goffman (Schegloff 1988).

Sacks, like Garfinkel, was preoccupied with discovering the methods or procedures by which humans coordinate and organize their activities and thus with the procedures of practical, common-sense reasoning in and through which "social order" is *locally* constituted (Garfinkel [1967] 1984). In addressing this problem, he devised a remarkably innovative approach. Working with tapes and transcripts of telephone calls to a suicide prevention center (and with recordings of other, somewhat more mundane sorts of conversations), Sacks began examining the talk as an object in its own right, as a fundamental type of social action, rather than primarily as a resource for documenting other social processes. In short, Sacks came to recognize that the talk itself was the action. It was in the details of the talk that we could discover just *how* what was getting done in the activity was accomplished, systematically and procedurally, then and there, by the coparticipants themselves. This appeared to be an especially fruitful way of investigating the local production of social order.

As Schegloff (1989, p. 199) later wrote in a memoir of these first years, Sacks's strategy in his pioneering studies was first to take note of how members of society, in some actual occasion of interaction, achieved some interactional effect—for example, in the suicide center calls, how to exhibit (and have others appreciate) that you have reasonably, accountably, concluded that you have no one to turn to—and then to ask: Was this outcome accomplished methodically? Can we describe it as the product of a method of conduct, such that we can find other enactments of that method, that is, enactments that will yield the accomplishment of the same outcome, the same

recognizable effect? This approach, Sacks suggested, provided an opportunity to develop formal accounts of "members' methods" for conducting social life.

In this way, Sacks sought to address the basic question of (as he put it in one of his early manuscripts) "what it is that sociology can aim to do, and . . . how it can proceed" (Sacks [1964–1968] 1984, p. 21). Sociology, he argued, could be a "natural observational science," concerned with the methodic organization of naturally occurring events, rather than with behavior that was manipulated through experimental techniques or other interventions such as surveys, interviews, and the like. And it could be committed to direct observation of this organization *in situ* rather than dependent upon analytic theorizing and a concomitant reliance on idealized models of action.

Naturalistic observation also met the ethnomethodological mandate that all evidence for the use of members' methods, and for members' orientation to or tacit knowledge of them, was to be derived exclusively from the observed behavior of the coparticipants in an interactional event. As Schegloff and Sacks (1973, p. 290) subsequently summarized the logic of this stance, if the event, the recorded conversational encounter, exhibited a methodically achieved orderliness, it "did so not only to us [the observing analysts], indeed not in the first place for us, but for the co-participants who had produced" it. After all, the task was to discover *members'* methods for coordinating and ordering conversational events, and these could not in any way be determined by analysts' conceptual stipulations or simply deduced from inventive theories.

Finally, Sacks was also making a well-reasoned argument for the importance of studying mundane conversation, directly confronting the belief that sociology's overriding concern should be the study of "big issues," that is, the belief that the search for social order should center on the analysis of large-scale, massive institutions. Social order, he insisted, can be found "at all points," and the close study of what from conventional sociology's point of view seemed like small (and trivial) phenomena—the details of conversation's

304

organization—might actually give us an enormous understanding of the way humans do things and the kinds of methods they use to order their affairs (Sacks [1964–1968] 1984, p. 24).

This last proposition bears special emphasis, for Sacks felt that these details went unnoticed, and perhaps could not even be imagined, by conventional analytic sociology. When had sociologists concerned themselves with the profoundly methodic character of things like how to avoid giving your name without refusing to give it, or how to get help for suicidalness without requesting it? Or, again drawing on tapes of suicide hotline calls, with the specific placement and intricate design features of utterly mundane utterances like "How does this organization work?" or "I'm nothing"? Or with members' methods for things like "doing describing" and "recognizing a description," methods that provide for hearing the first two sentences from a story told by a young child—"The baby cried. The mommy picked it up"—as saying: The mommy who picked up the baby is the baby's mommy, and she picked it up because it was crying. It was by starting with the close study of such actual events, with the study of things whose orderliness may not be currently imaginable and showing that they in fact happened in an endogenously, socially organized manner, that a much sounder basis for studying social life could be established.

It should be evident, then, that the appellation *conversation analysis* does not really capture the enterprise's commitment to addressing the most basic problem for the social sciences: the underlying character and structure of social action. As the title of one of Sacks's first publications, "An Initial Investigation into the Usability of Conversational Data for Doing Sociology," makes clear, the use of recorded conversational materials was more of an opportunistic research strategy than a commitment to studying talk per se (Sacks 1972). Tape recordings of conversations constituted a record of the details of actual, singular events. These recordings could be replayed and studied extensively and would permit other researchers direct access to exactly these same details. Still, for these identical reasons, it is *conversation's* organi-

zation—its detectable, orderly properties—that has remained the concrete object of study for the enterprise since the mid-1960s.

During these years since the "initial investigations," conversation analysis has given rise to a substantial research literature. Pursuing the lines of analysis first identified in the early studies, while simultaneously opening up many new avenues of inquiry, researchers working in this tradition have produced findings that are, in the words of one contemporary practitioner, "strikingly cumulative and interlocking" (Heritage 1987, p. 256). Important collections of papers include Sudnow (1972), Turner (1974), Schenkein (1978), Psathas (1979), Atkinson and Heritage (1984), and Button and Lee (1987). Special issues of *Sociological Inquiry* (1980, vol. 50, nos. 3–4), *Social Psychology Quarterly* (1987, vol. 50, no. 2), *Human Studies* (1986, vol. 19, nos. 2–3), *Social Problems* (1988, vol. 35, no. 4), and the *Western Journal of Speech Communication* (1989, vol. 52, no. 2) have also been devoted to ethnomethodological and conversation-analytic topics.

Three major domains in conversation's organization identified in this literature are the organization of sequences, of turn taking, and of repair. These organizations can be described as systems of naturally organized activity, systems known and used by members as courses of practical action and practical reasoning and designed to resolve generic coordination problems that confront any conversationalist. A sketch of some research findings with respect to the first two of these organizations should serve to illustrate how they function in this fashion as well as the interlocking nature of their domains.

Consider first the organization of sequences. Begin with the fact that even the most cursory inspection of conversational materials reveals that talk-in-interaction has a serial arrangement to it. For example, in a conversation between two parties, party A will talk first, then party B, then A, then B, and so forth. Accordingly, in two-party conversations, turns at talk constitute a series of alternately produced utterances: ABABAB. But overlaying this serial arrangement of utterances are distinctly characterizable conversational sequences, where turns at talk do not simply happen to occur one after the other but rather "belong together" as a socio-organizational unit and where there is thus a methodic relationship between the various turns or parts.

This methodic, structurally linked relationship between sequence parts is central to how sequences work in resolving coordination problems in conversation. This point can be demonstrated by briefly focusing on one of the earliest studies of sequence organization by Schegloff (1968), an investigation into how the initiation of conversational interactions is coordinated. Schegloff directed attention to a frequently occurring initial exchange, which was called a "summons–answer sequence." This sequence is composed, he discovered, of closely linked parts. The production of the first turn in the sequence, the summons, projected a relevant next action, an answer, to be accomplished by the recipient of the summons in the very next turn. Moreover, the occurrence of the expected answer cannot properly be the final turn in the exchange. The summons–answer exchange is therefore nonterminal: Upon production of the answer, the summoner is then expected to speak again, to provide the reason for the summons. This provides for a coordinated entry into conversation and for the possibility of an extended spate of talk.

Observe that a set of mutual obligations is established by the structural relationships between these sequence parts, with each action projecting some "next." In the strongest form of these obligations (sequence classes differ somewhat in this regard), the property of "conditional relevance" holds between the parts of a sequence unit. A summons–answer sequence is but one type of a large class of utterance units, known as "adjacency pairs," that are characterized by this property. Examples here include "greeting–greeting," "question–answer," and "invitation–acceptance/declination." In adjacency pairs, when one utterance or action is conditionally relevant on another, the production of the first provides for the occurrence of the second. It could be said, then, using the example above, that the issuance of a summons is an action that *selects* a

particular next action, an answer, for its recipient. If this action does not occur, its nonoccurrence will be a noticeable event. That is to say, it is not only nonoccurring, it is "notably," "officially" absent; accordingly, this would warrant various inferences and actions. For instance, the summoner might infer that the recipient "didn't hear me," which would provide a relevant reason or grounds for repeating the summons.

The discovery that human activities like conversation were coordinated and organized in a very fundamental way by such methodic relationships between actions, with some current or "first" action projecting and providing for some appropriate "second," led to investigations into the various methods by which the recipient of a first may accomplish a second, or recognizably hold its accomplishment in abeyance until issues relevant to its performance are clarified or resolved, or avoid its accomplishment altogether by undertaking some other activity. Researchers learned, for example, that for some firsts there was not a single appropriate second but rather a range of *alternative* seconds. Note that in the examples of adjacency pair structures listed above, invitations project either an acceptance *or* a declination as a course of action available to the recipient. In this case, and in others like "request–granting/denial" and "compliment–acceptance/rejection," it was found that the alternative second parts are not generally of equal status; rather, some second parts are preferred and others dispreferred, these properties being distinct from the desires or motivations of the coparticipants. "Preference" thus refers to a structural rather than dispositional relationship between alternative but nonequivalent courses of action. Evidence for this includes distributional data across a wide range of speakers and settings and, more important, the fact that preferred and dispreferred alternatives are regularly performed in distinctively different ways. The preference status of an action is therefore exhibited in *how* it is done.

Related to this, conversation-analytic researchers observed that the producers of a first action often dealt in systematic, methodic ways with these properties of preference organization. To take one example, the producer of a request can and often does analyze the recipient silence that follows as displaying or implicating a denial—a denial as yet unstated but nevertheless projected —and seeks to preempt the occurrence of this dispreferred action by issuing a subsequent version of the request, before the recipient starts to speak. Subsequent versions attempt to make the request more acceptable and provide another opportunity for a favorable response (Davidson 1984).

Moreover, members were observed to orient to the properties of preference organization through their performance of actions plainly meant to be understood as preliminary to some first action in an adjacency pair. Such "pre"-type actions are designed to explore the likelihood that producing the first part of some pair will not be responded to in a dispreferred way. For instance, an utterance like "Are you doing anything tonight?" provides, in a methodical way, an opportunity for its producer to determine, without yet having actually to issue the invitation, whether it would most likely be declined. Similarly, this provides an opportunity for the recipient of the "pre" to indicate that a dispreferred action would be forthcoming without ever having to perform that action. Because "pre" actions themselves engender sequences by making some response to them a relevant next action, they constitute the first part of a "pre-sequence."

These interrelated observations on the organization of sequences were generalized outward in conversation-analytic research from the relatively simple adjacency pair organization by the recognition that virtually every utterance occurs at some sequentially relevant, structurally defined place in talk (see especially Heritage and Atkinson 1984, pp. 5–9). Moreover, it is this placement that provides the primary context for an utterance's intelligibility and understanding. Put another way, utterances are in the first place contextually understood by reference to their placement and participation within sequences of action, and it is therefore sequences of action, rather than single utterances or actions, that have become the primary units of analysis for the conversation-analytic enterprise. Accordingly, researchers in this

tradition have not restricted themselves to studying only especially "tight" sequence units but have instead broadened their investigations to (mentioning just a few) the sequencing of laughter, disputes, story and joke telling, political oratory, and the initiation and closing of topics. In addition, the sequential organization of gaze and body movement in relation to turns at talk has been the focus of some truly pathbreaking research using video recordings (see, for example, Goodwin 1981; Heath 1986).

Now let us consider the organization of turn taking, surely a central feature of virtually all talk-in-interaction. Recall that the prior discussion on the organization of sequences frequently made reference to sequence parts as "turns," implicitly trading on the understanding that talk in conversation is produced in and built for turns, with recurring speaker change and a consequent serial ordering of utterances. In conversation, this turn ordering, as well as the size and content of each turn, is neither predetermined nor allocated in advance. Instead, it is locally determined, moment by moment, by the coparticipants in the talk. In fact, this completely local determination of who speaks when, how long they speak, and what they might say or do in their turn is what provides for talk being hearable as a "conversation" rather than as, say, a debate or a ceremony of some kind. But this does not tell us just how speaker change is methodically achieved such that, ordinarily, one party talks at a time and there is little or no silence (or "gap") between turns. Clearly, this requires close coordination among coparticipants in any conversational encounter. The systematic practices by which this is accomplished are analyzed by Sacks, Schegloff, and Jefferson ([1974] 1978) in a paper that remains one of the most important in the literature of conversation analysis.

Basic to the accomplishment of turn taking is the practice of changing speakers at *possible* utterance completion places, what Sacks, Schegloff, and Jefferson term *transition relevance places*. How are such places, where speaker change *may* relevantly occur but is in no way guaranteed or required, discernable by members? A key feature of the units by and through which turns are constructed offers one resource here: For an utterance to be usable as a turn constructional unit, it must have a recognizable completion, and that completion must be recognizable prior to its occurrence (Lerner 1989, p. 168; Sacks, Schegloff, and Jefferson [1974] 1978, p. 12). That is to say, its completion is projectable, and a coparticipant in the conversation who wishes to speak next can therefore begin his or her turn just at the place where the other speaker finishes.

Of course, this does not preclude this coparticipant, or any other, from starting to speak elsewhere in the course of another speaker's turn. (Indeed, what actually constitutes a "turn at talk" is as locally and mutually determined as any other aspect of a conversation's organization, even as the resources for doing so are general ones.) There are various interactional moves that could involve, as one way they might be accomplished, this sort of action. At the same time, however, research on turn taking has revealed that turns beginning elsewhere may well be met with procedures systematically designed to enforce the practice of starting at possible completion places. Further, features of the turn-taking system such as that described just above account for a great deal of the overlapping speech that can occasionally be observed. For instance, a speaker might append a tag question like "you know?" to their turn, while a coparticipant, having no resources available to project such an action, starts to speak just prior to or at the beginning of that appended tag, at the place that was projectably the "first possible completion" of the turn. This would result in overlapping speech, with both parties talking simultaneously. This is just one example; studies of "more than one party at a time" speech have uncovered massive evidence that its occurrence and resolution (the restoration of one party at a time), as well as the solution to the problem of which overlapping action should then be consequential for next action, is methodically organized.

Such findings warrant mention of the entire set of procedures by which errors and violations in turn taking, and various other kinds of "troubles" in the hearing, understanding, or sequencing of talk, are systematically handled and "repaired." Studies of the organization of repair have shown how the turn-taking system incorporates resources and procedures for repair into its fundamental organization and is itself a basic organizational device for the repair of troubles in talk. As Sacks, Schegloff, and Jefferson ([1974] 1978, p. 40) put it, the organization of turn taking and the organization of repair "are thus 'made for each other' in a double sense."

Having described the function of turn constructional practices in turn taking, Sacks, Schegloff, and Jefferson still faced the issue of how coparticipants, at possible completion places, determine just who will be the "next speaker" (note in this regard that conversation can involve more than two parties) or even if there will be a next speaker, given that a current speaker might want to continue talking. They discovered that to deal with this problem, members have available a "turn allocational component" for the system. This component consists of a set of ordered rules that come into play at transition relevance places and that provide for the methodic allocation of the right to produce a next turn or, more accurately, a turn constructional unit. In related research, methods for securing the temporary suspension of turn-taking procedures (to tell an extended story, for example) and for coordinating exit from the system (to end the conversation) have been documented.

The operation of the turn-taking system, when taken together with the practices involved in the organization of sequences and repair, accounts for many of the detectable, orderly features of conversation. And as was the case with the research on sequences and repair, this orderliness was shown to be locally organized and managed, the product of members' methods. It will be useful to make note once again of the research strategy that enabled such findings. Because the data consisted of recordings of naturally occurring activity, a scientific account of the phenomenon under investigation could be empirically grounded in the details of actual occurrences. The investigation began with a set of observable outcomes of these occurrences—that speaker change overwhelmingly recurred; that, overwhelmingly, one party talked at a time; that turn order, size, and content were not fixed but varied; and so on. It was then asked: Could these outcomes be described as products of certain socially organized practices or methods of conduct? At the same time, if members of society did in fact use such formal methods, how were they systematically employed to produce just those outcomes, in just those occurrences, in all their specificity? In addressing the problem in this way, then, conversation analysis was able to discover how a cardinal form of social order—turn taking—was locally constituted.

The research on turn taking in conversation has provided one starting point for more recent studies of interaction in "institutional" settings such as news interviews, doctor–patient and other clinical consultations, courtrooms, plea bargaining sessions, job interviews, human–machine interaction at the work place, and citizen calls to emergency services. In many of these studies, researchers pursued Sacks, Schegloff, and Jefferson's ([1974] 1978, pp. 45–47) suggestion that the practices underlying the management of ordinary conversation are the "base" or primary ones. Other forms of interaction—in this case, so-called institutional forms—are constituted and recognizable through systematic variations from conversational turn taking or through the narrowing and respecification of particular conversational practices involved in the organization of sequences, repair, and other activities.

Take the case of courtroom interaction. The turn-taking system operative in these encounters places restrictions on turn construction and allocation: Coparticipants ordinarily restrict themselves to producing turns that are at least minimally recognizable as "questions" and "answers," and these turn types are pre-allocated to different parties rather than locally determined. The relatively restricted patterns of conduct observable in these settings are, in large part, the product of this form of turn taking. Accordingly, variation in turn taking in such settings has been shown to have a

"pervasive influence both on the range and design of the interactional activities which the different parties routinely undertake and on the detailed management of such encounters" (Heritage 1987, p. 261; Atkinson and Drew 1979).

Note that throughout the above discussion, the term *institutional* has been used with some caution. This was done to emphasize ethnomethodology's preoccupation with the *local* production of social order. From this view, that some activity or encounter is recognizably either an "ordinary conversation" or more "institutional" in nature —for example, is recognizably a "cross-examination," a "call to the police," or a "clinical consultation"—is something that the coparticipants can and do realize, procedurally, at each and every moment of the encounter. The task for the analyst is to demonstrate how they actually do this—how, for example, they construct their conduct, turn by turn, so as progressively to constitute and thus jointly and collaboratively realize the occasion of their encounter, together with their own social roles in it, as having some distinctively institutional sense (Heritage and Greatbatch, forthcoming; also Atkinson 1982; Sharrock and Watson 1989). Conversation-analytic research on "institutional" interaction has therefore undertaken, through its investigations into the methodic practices by which this work gets done, a systematic study of a wide range of human activities. This research, because of its commitment to understanding precisely how any activity becomes what it recognizably and accountably "is"—that is, how it acquires its social facticity—holds enormous scientific promise.

(SEE ALSO: *Ethnomethodology; Field Research Methods; Sociolinguistics*)

## REFERENCES

Atkinson, J. Maxwell 1982 "Understanding Formality: The Categorisation and Production of 'Formal' Interaction." *British Journal of Sociology* 33:86–117.

———, and Paul Drew 1979 *Order in Court: The Organization of Verbal Interaction in Judicial Settings.* London: Macmillan.

———, and John Heritage (eds.) 1984 *Structures of Social Action: Studies in Conversation Analysis*. Cambridge: Cambridge University Press.

Button, Graham, and John R. E. Lee (eds.) 1987 *Talk and Social Organization*. Clevedon, England: Multilingual Matters.

Davidson, Judy 1984 "Subsequent Versions of Invitations, Offers, Requests, and Proposals Dealing with Potential or Actual Rejection." In J. Maxwell Atkinson and John Heritage, eds., *Structures of Social Action: Studies in Conversation Analysis*. Cambridge: Cambridge University Press.

Garfinkel, Harold (1967) 1984 *Studies in Ethnomethodology*. Cambridge: Polity Press.

Goodwin, Charles 1981 *Conversational Organization: Interaction between Speakers and Hearers*. New York: Academic Press.

Heath, Christian C. 1986 *Body Movement and Speech in Medical Interaction*. Cambridge: Cambridge University Press.

Heritage, John 1987 "Ethnomethodology." In Anthony Giddens and Jonathan H. Turner, eds., *Social Theory Today*. Stanford, Calif.: Stanford University Press.

———, and J. Maxwell Atkinson 1984 "Introduction." In Atkinson and Heritage, eds., *Structures of Social Action: Studies in Conversation Analysis*. Cambridge: Cambridge University Press.

———, and David Greatbatch (Forthcoming) "On the Institutional Character of Institutional Talk: The Case of News Interviews." In Deirdre Boden and Don H. Zimmerman, eds., *Talk and Social Structure*. Cambridge: Polity Press.

Lerner, Gene H. 1989 "Notes on Overlap Management in Conversation: The Case of Delayed Completion." *Western Journal of Speech Communication* 53:167–177.

Psathas, George (ed.) 1979 *Everyday Language: Studies in Ethnomethodology*. Boston: Irvington.

Sacks, Harvey 1972 "An Initial Investigation into the Usability of Conversational Data for Doing Sociology." In David Sudnow, ed., *Studies in Social Interaction*. New York: Free Press.

——— (1964–1968) 1984 "Notes on Methodology." In J. Maxwell Atkinson and John Heritage, eds., *Structures of Social Action: Studies in Conversation Analysis*. Cambridge: Cambridge University Press.

Sacks, Harvey, Emanuel A. Schegloff, and Gail Jefferson (1974) 1978. "A Simplest Systematics for the Organization of Turn-Taking for Conversation." In Jim Schenkein, ed., *Studies in the Organization of Conversational Interaction*. New York: Academic Press.

Schegloff, Emanuel A. 1968 "Sequencing in Conversational Openings." *American Anthropologist* 70:1075–1095.

——— 1988 "Goffman and the Analysis of Conversation." In Paul Drew and Anthony Wootton, eds., *Erving Goffman: Exploring the Interaction Order*. Boston: Northeastern University Press.

——— 1989 "Harvey Sacks—Lectures 1964–1965: An Introduction/Memoir." *Human Studies* 12:185–209.

Schegloff, Emanuel A., Gail Jefferson, and Harvey Sacks 1977 "The Preference for Self-Correction in the Organization of Repair in Conversation." *Language* 53:361–382.

Schegloff, Emanuel A., and Harvey Sacks 1973 "Opening Up Closings." *Semiotica* 7:289–327.

Schenkein, Jim (ed.) 1978 *Studies in the Organization of Conversational Interaction*. New York: Academic Press.

Sharrock, W. W., and R. D. Watson 1989 "Talk and Police Work: Notes on the Traffic in Information." In Harold Coleman, ed., *The Language of Work*. The Hague: Mouton.

Sudnow, David (ed.) 1972 *Studies in Social Interaction*. New York: Free Press.

Turner, Roy (ed.) 1974 *Ethnomethodology*. Harmondsworth, England: Penguin.

JACK WHALEN

## COOPERATION AND COMPETITION
*See* Small Groups.

## CORPORATE ORGANIZATIONS
Societies carry out many of their activities through formal organizations. Organizations are units in which offices, or positions, have distinct but interdependent duties. Organizations—hospitals, schools, governments, business firms—share certain features. Usually, at least one of the offices serves as the linchpin: It coordinates the separate duties within the organization. The key office has ultimate authority in that the orders it issues constrain the actions of lower-level offices.

But organizations also differ from one another. In some, the assets belong to particular individuals. In others, ownership resides in a collectivity. The latter represents a corporate organization or *corporation*. Three features describe the modern corporation. First, it has certain legal rights and privileges. By law, a corporation can sue and be sued in the courts, make contracts, and purchase and receive property. Second, it usually exists in perpetuity: It outlasts the individuals who set it up. Ownership rests with stockholders, whose numbers and makeup can change from one time to another. Third, the owners have only a limited responsibility for the obligations the corporation makes.

These features distinguish the corporate organization from two other forms of ownership: the *proprietorship* and the *partnership*. In a proprietorship a particular person owns the property of the organization; in a partnership, two or more persons share it. The right to handle the property and affairs of the organization rests with a designated proprietor or set of partners. Significantly, proprietors and partners bear personal responsibility for the debts of the organization.

The corporation constitutes a social invention. The form evolved to handle problems that arose within religious, political, and other kinds of communities. It holds a place of importance in contemporary Western societies. Because it is the product of social conditions and an influence on them, the corporation represents a topic of substantial interest in sociology.

At present, the corporation appears commonly within the world of business. But when the corporation began to take shape during the Middle Ages, the questions to be resolved lay outside that realm. One of these questions had to do with church ownership. In medieval Germany, landowners often set up churches on their estates and placed a priest in charge of them. As priests gained authority over their charges, they argued that the church and the land surrounding it no longer belonged to the donor. Deciding the true owner proved to be difficult. A given priest could die or be replaced; hence, any particular priest seemed to have no claim to ownership. One practice regarded the owner to be the saint whose name the church bore. Eventually, the idea developed that ownership inhered in the church, and that the church constituted a body independent of its current leaders or members (Coleman 1974; Stone 1975).

Thorny problems also arose as medieval settlements formed into towns. A town required someone to manage its affairs such as collecting tolls and transacting other business. But the laws that prevailed at the time applied only to individuals. Any actions individuals took obligated them personally. By this principle, managers would have to meet any commitments they made on behalf of the town. To eliminate the dilemmas that the principle situation posed, new laws made the town a corporate person. The corporate person would have all the rights and privileges of any human being. This action reduced the risks that public service might otherwise entail. For many of the same reasons that the church and town became corporate persons, the university of the Middle Ages moved towards the corporate form.

The early corporations played rather passive roles. Essentially, they held property for a collective, whose members might change from time to time. Contrastingly, the corporations of the twentieth century constitute spirited forces. They hire multitudes of employees. They produce goods and services and mold ideals and tastes. The decisions their leaders make about where to locate often determine which locales will prosper and which will languish.

The influence that corporations have produces concerns about the control of them. Much of the work on corporations that sociologists have undertaken highlights these concerns. The work on control and corporations covers three topics: the means through which corporations control their employees; the allocation of control between owners and managers; and the extent to which societies control corporations. For all three topics, control implies command over the affairs of and operations within the corporate organization.

## CONTROL OVER EMPLOYEES

The corporate form has a long history, yet it did not typify the early factories that manufacturers established in the United States. Before the early 1900s, most factories operated as small operations under the control of a single entrepreneur. The entrepreneur hired an overseer who might in turn choose a foreman to hire, discipline, and fire workers. Through consolidation and merger, the economic landscape of the 1920s revealed far more large organizations than had the tableau of a half-century earlier.

More changed over the years of the late nineteenth and early twentieth centuries than just the size of organizations. The corporate form spread; the faceless corporation replaced the corporeal entrepreneur. Corporations moved towards professional management. Factories that businessmen once controlled personally now operated through abstract rules and procedures. The people whom the workers now contacted on a regular basis consisted of staff for the corporation and not the corporate owners themselves. Bureaucratic tenets took root.

A bureaucracy constitutes a particular mode that organizations can take. Consistent with all organizations, bureaucratic ones divide up duties. Two features separate a bureaucracy from other modes, however. First, a system of ranks or levels operates. Second, fixed rules and procedures govern actions. The rules define the tasks, responsibilities, and authority for each office and each level.

Few of the factories in nineteenth-century America operated as bureaucracies. Instead, the individuals who made the products decided how the work would be done. A minimum number of levels existed. Supervisors or foremen hired and fired workers, but workers made the rules on the work itself. The workers were craftsmen or artisans, and they contended that only those who possessed the skills that the work demands should decide how or if it should be divided. Gradually, machinery took over the skilled work. Machines and not workers controlled the pace. By the end of the 1920s, neither the laborers nor the machinery shaped the work. Professional managers did. These managers enforced rules and oversaw an organization where specialized tasks and graded authority prevailed (Nelson 1975; Clawson 1980; and Jacoby 1985).

The corporation of the late twentieth century continues to operate as a bureaucracy. Some sources argue that efficiency explains the adoption of the bureaucratic model (see especially Chandler 1980, 1984). Others challenge the emphasis on efficiency, charging it with being overly rational or too apolitical. The first challenge appears most notably in the work on organizations as institutions. This literature regards survival as the premier goal for any organization. The closer an organization approximates an institution—an element taken for granted in the society—the greater its chances for survival.

According to the institutional perspective, organizations adopt practices that appear to be reasonable. Myths develop about which patterns prove most useful and efficient, and any organization that does not adopt a pattern that the myth favors courts failure (Meyer and Rowan 1977; DiMaggio 1988; DiMaggio and Powell 1983; Tolbert and Zucker 1983; also see Scott 1987 for a review of the different branches of institutional theory).

A different argument maintains that the emphasis on efficiency fails to capture the politics of corporations. This perspective treats corporations as systems in which the interests of owners clash with those of workers. Owners, it asserts, seek to reduce uncertainties and to eliminate the vagaries that can plague organizations. From this angle, bureaucracy serves the interests of owners primarily because it reduces the influence that workers exercise and thereby removes a source of uncertainty (Braverman 1974; Edwards 1979).

Workers need not have formal authority in order to affect outcomes within organizations. Studies document the creative ways in which employees enliven monotonous jobs and pursue their own ends (Roy 1952; Mechanic 1962; Burawoy 1979, 1985). Yet, officially, the higher levels have greater power than have the lower levels. This is the consequence of the bureaucratic nature of corporations, not of their pattern of ownership. The bureaucratic mode is not unique to corporations. Proprietorships and partnerships can display the traits of bureaucracy. The diffuseness of ownership that one finds in the corporation possibly makes formal control less obvious than obtains when ownership resides in identifiable persons.

## OWNER VERSUS MANAGERIAL CONTROL

Managers occupy important places in the contemporary organization. One argument regards managers as more powerful than stockholders. Adolph Berle and Gardiner Means offered this argument in the 1930s. As Berle and Means saw the situation, stockholding had become too widely dispersed for any individual holder or even group of holders to command corporations. Managers, they contended, filled the void (Berle and Means 1932). Later discussions echoed the thesis that the expansion of the corporate form had raised the power of corporate managers (Berg and Zald 1978; also see Chandler 1962, 1977).

Critics contend that the thesis overstates the role and power of managers. They base their criticism on studies of the influence that corporate leaders wield. Maurice Zeitlin (1974) helped launch this line of research when he argued that few scholars had tested the Berle and Means thesis and that the handful of extant studies showed owners to be less fractious and fractionated than the thesis supposed. Michael Useem (1984), among others, heeded the call from Zeitlin for research on the networks that link shareholders. Useem concluded from his study on contacts and networks among large shareholders that a corporate community operated, held together by an inner circle whose interests transcended company, region, and industry lines. Beth Mintz and Michael Schwartz (1985) examined the connections between financial institutions and other corporations and decided that control over corporate directions rested disproportionately in the world

of finance. The work from the critics cautions us against the assumption that a multiplicity of owners implies control by managers.

## SOCIAL CONTROL OVER CORPORATIONS

The corporate form constitutes a remarkable innovation. But as the corporation has become ever more active and entrenched, it has generated problems for society. Corporations have at times engaged in criminal behavior (Sutherland 1949; Clinard and Yeager 1980). At other times, their actions have violated no law but have put the well-being of the public at risk. Both situations often show the inadequacy of the mechanisms through which society attempts to control corporations.

Corporations are creatures of the state. Ostensibly, then, they operate only at the indulgence of the state. But myriad corporations now have greater resources than do the states that chartered them. Moreover, the laws that states have at their disposal often fit individuals better than they do corporations. Corporations can be sued for wrongdoing; but a fine that would bankrupt an individual might be a mere pittance for a large corporation. Both James Coleman (1974) and Christopher Stone (1975) have argued that the law can never be the sole means for controlling corporations; a sense of responsibility to the public must prevail within corporations.

Even if the law were shown to be effective in constraining corporations within a state, it might prove rather impotent in the case of multinational organizations. A multinational or transnational corporation holds a charter from one nation-state but transacts business in at least one other. The governmental entity that issues the charter cannot alter the policies the corporation pursues in its other locales. In addition, the very size of many multinationals restricts the pressure that either the home or the host country can impose.

Through various actions corporations demonstrate that they are attentive to the societies they inhabit. Corporate leaders serve on the boards of social service agencies; corporate foundations provide funds for community programs; employees donate their time to local causes. The agenda of corporations long have included these and similar activities. Increasingly, the agenda organize such actions around the idea of corporate social responsibility. Acting responsibly means taking steps to promote the commonweal (Steckmest 1982).

Some corporations strive more consistently to advance social ends than do others. Differences in norms and values apparently explain the contrast. Norms, or maxims for behavior, indicate the culture of the organization (Deal and Kennedy 1982). The culture of some settings gives the highest priority to actions that protect the health, safety, and welfare of citizens and their heirs. Elsewhere, those are not what the culture emphasizes (Clinard 1983; Victor and Cullen 1988).

The large corporation had become such a dominant force by the 1980s that no one envisioned a return to an era of small, diffuse organizations. Yet, during that decade some sectors had started to move from growth to contraction. At times, the shift resulted from legislative action. When the Bell Telephone System divided in 1984, by order of the courts, the change marked a sharp reversal. For more than a century the system had glided toward integration and standardization (Barnett and Carroll 1987; Barnett 1990).

Whether through fiat or choice, corporations contract (Whetten 1987; Hambrick and D'Aveni 1988). Two perspectives associate the rise and fall in the fortunes of corporations to changes in the social context. The first perspective, resource dependence, centers on the idea that organizations must secure their resources from their environs (McCarthy and Zald 1977; Jenkins 1983). When those environs contain a wealth of resources—personnel in the numbers and with the qualifications the organization requires, funds to finance operations—the corporation can thrive. When hard times plague the environs, the corporation escapes that fate only with great difficulty.

The perspective known as population ecology likewise connects the destiny of organizations to conditions in their surroundings. Population ecologists think of organizations as members of a population. Changing social conditions can enrich or impoverish a population. Individual units within it can do little to offset the tide of events that threatens to envelop the entire population. (Hannan and Freeman 1988; Wholey and Brittain 1989; for a critique of the approach see Young 1988).

Neither resource dependency theory nor population ecology theory focuses explicity on the corporate form. But just as analyses of corporations inform the discussions sociologists have undertaken on formal organizations, models drawn from studies of organizations have proved useful as scholars have tracked the progress of corporations.

The corporation clearly constitutes a power to be reckoned with. As with its precursors, the modern corporation serves needs that collectivities develop. In fact, the corporation rests on an assumption that is fundamental in sociology: A collectivity has an identity of its own. But the corporation of the twentieth century touches more than those persons who own its assets or produce its goods. This social instrument of the Middle Ages is now a social fixture.

(SEE ALSO: *Capitalism; Organizational Effectiveness; Organizational Structure; Transnational Corporations*)

## REFERENCES

Barnett, William P. 1990 "The Organizational Ecology of a Technological System." *Administrative Science Quarterly* 35:31–60.

Barnett, William P., and Glenn Carroll 1987 "Competition and Mutualism Among Early Telephone Companies." *Administrative Science Quarterly* 32:400–421.

Berg, Ivar, and Mayer N. Zald 1978 "Business and Society." *Annual Review of Sociology* 4:115–143.

Berle, Adolph A., and Gardiner C. Means 1932 *The Modern Corporation and Private Property*. New York: Macmillan.

Braverman, Harry 1974 *Labor and Monopoly Capital: The Degradation of Work in the Twentieth Century*. New York: Monthly Review.

Burawoy, Michael 1979 *Manufacturing Consent: Changes in the Labor Process under Monopoly Capitalism.* Chicago: University of Chicago Press.

———— 1985 *The Politics of Production: Factory Regimes under Capitalism and Socialism.* London: Verso.

Chandler, Alfred D., Jr. 1962 *Strategy and Structure.* Cambridge, Mass.: MIT Press.

———— 1977 *The Visible Hand.* Cambridge, Mass.: Harvard University Press.

———— 1980 "The United States: Seedbed of Managerial Capitalism." In A. D. Chandler, Jr., and Herman Daems, eds., *Managerial Hierarchies.* Cambridge, Mass.: Harvard University Press.

———— 1984 "The Emergence of Managerial Capitalism." *Business History Review* 58:484–504.

Clawson, Dan 1980 *Bureaucracy and the Labor Process.* New York: Monthly Labor Review.

Clinard, Marshall B. 1983 *Corporate Ethics and Crime.* Beverly Hills, Calif.: Sage.

————, and Peter C. Yeager 1980 *Corporate Crime.* New York: Free Press.

Coleman, James S. 1974 *Power and the Structure of Society.* New York: Norton.

Deal, Terrence, and Allen Kennedy 1982 *Corporate Culture.* Reading, Mass.: Addison-Wesley.

DiMaggio, Paul 1988 "Interest and Agency in Institutional Theory." In Lynne G. Zucker, ed., *Research on Institutional Patterns: Environment and Culture.* Cambridge, Mass.: Ballinger.

————, and Walter Powell 1983 "The Iron Cage Revisited: Institutional Isomorphism and Collective Rationality in Organizational Fields." *American Sociological Review* 48:147–160.

Edwards, Richard 1979 *Contested Terrain: The Transformation of the Workplace in the Twentieth Century.* New York: Basic Books.

Hambrick, Donald C., and Richard A. D'Aveni 1988 "Large Corporate Failures as Downward Spirals." *Administrative Science Quarterly* 33:1–23.

Hannan, Michael, and John Freeman 1988 *Organizational Ecology.* Cambridge, Mass.: Harvard University Press.

Jacoby, Sanford 1985 *Employing Bureaucracy: Managers, Unions and the Transformation of Work in American Industry, 1900–1945.* New York: Columbia University Press.

Jenkins, J. Craig 1983 "Resource Mobilization Theory and the Study of Social Movements." *Annual Review of Sociology* 42:249–268.

McCarthy, John D., and Mayer N. Zald 1977 "Resource Mobilization and Social Movements: A Partial Theory." *American Journal of Sociology* 82:1212–1241.

Mechanic, David 1962 "Sources of Power of Lower Participants in Complex Organizations." *Administrative Science Quarterly* 7:349–364.

Meyer, John, and Brian Rowan 1977 "Institutionalized Organizations: Formal Structure as Myth and Ceremony." *American Sociological Review* 83:340–363.

Mintz, Beth, and Michael Schwartz 1985 *The Power Structure of American Business.* Chicago: University of Chicago Press.

Nelson, Daniel 1975 *Managers and Workers.* Madison: University of Wisconsin Press.

Roy, Donald 1952 "Restriction of Output in a Piecework Machine Shop." Ph.D. diss., University of Chicago, Chicago.

Scott, W. Richard 1987 "The Adolescence of Institutional Theory." *Administrative Science Quarterly* 32:493–511.

Steckmest, Francis W. 1982 *Corporate Performance: The Key to Public Trust.* New York: McGraw-Hill.

Stone, Christopher D. 1975 *Where the Law Ends: The Social Control of Corporate Behavior.* New York: Harper.

Sutherland, Edwin H. 1949 *White Collar Crime.* New York: Holt, Rinehart, and Winston.

Tolbert, Pamela S., and Lynne G. Zucker 1983 "Institutional Sources of Change in the Formal Structure of Organizations: The Diffusion of Civil Service Reform, 1880–1935." *Administrative Science Quarterly* 28:22–39.

Useem, Michael 1984 *The Inner Circle: Large Corporations and the Rise of Political Activity in the U.S. and UK.* New York: Oxford University Press.

Victor, Bart, and John B. Cullen 1988 "The Organizational Bases of Ethical Work Climates." *Administrative Science Quarterly* 33:101–125.

Whetten, David A. 1987 "Organizational Growth and Decline Processes." *Annual Review of Sociology* 13:335–358.

Wholey, Douglas, and Jack Brittain 1989 "Characterizing Environmental Variation." *Academy of Management Journal* 32:867–882.

Young, Ruth 1988 "Is Population Ecology a Useful Paradigm for the Study of Organizations?" *American Journal of Sociology* 94:1–24.

Zeitlin, Maurice 1974 "Corporate Ownership and Control: The Large Corporation and the Capitalist Class." *American Journal of Sociology* 79:1073–1119.

CORA B. MARRETT

**CORRECTIONS SYSTEMS**   *See* Criminal Sanctions; Criminology.

## CORRELATION AND REGRESSION ANALYSIS

In 1885, Francis Galton, a British biologist, published a paper in which he demonstrated with graphs and tables that the children of very tall parents were, on average, shorter than their parents, while the children of very short parents tended to exceed their parents in height (cited in Walker 1929). Galton referred to this as "reversion" or the "law of regression" (i.e., regression to the average height of the species). Galton also saw in his graphs and tables a feature that he named the "co-relation" between variables. The stature of kinsmen are "co-related" variables, Galton stated, meaning, for example, that when the father was taller than average, his son was likely also to be taller than average. Although Galton devised a way of summarizing in a single figure the degree of "co-relation" between two variables, it was Galton's associate Karl Pearson who developed the "coefficient of correlation," as it is now applied. Galton's original interest, the phenomenon of regression toward the mean, is no longer germane to contemporary correlation and regression analysis, but the term "regression" has been retained with a modified meaning.

Although Galton and Pearson originally focused their attention on bivariate (two variables) correlation and regression, in current applications more than two variables are typically incorporated into the analysis to yield partial correlation coefficients, multiple regression analysis, and several related techniques that facilitate the informed interpretation of the linkages between pairs of variables. This summary begins with two variables and then moves to the consideration of more than two variables.

Consider a very large sample of cases, with a measure of some variable, X, and another variable, Y, for each case. To make the illustration more concrete, consider a large number of adults and, for each, a measure of their education (years of school completed = X) and their income (dollars earned over the past twelve months = Y). Subdivide these adults by years of school completed, and for each such subset compute a mean income for a given level of education. Each such mean is called a *conditional mean* and is represented by $\overline{Y}|X$, that is, the mean of Y for a given value of X.

Imagine now an ordered arrangement of the subsets from left to right according to the years of school completed, with zero years of school on the left, followed by one year of school, and so on through the maximum number of years of school completed in this set of cases, as shown in Figure 1. Assume that each of the $\overline{Y}|X$ values (i.e., the mean income for each level of education) falls on a straight line, as in Figure 1. This straight line is the *regression line of Y on X*. Thus the regression line of Y on X is the line that passes through the mean Y for each value of X—for example, the mean income for each educational level.

If this regression line is a straight line, as shown in Figure 1, then the income associated with each additional year of school completed is the same whether that additional year of school represents an increase, for example, from six to seven years of school completed or from twelve to thirteen years. While one can analyze curvilinear regression, a straight regression line greatly simplifies the analysis. Some (but not all) curvilinear regressions can be made into straight-line regressions by a relatively simple transformation of one of the variables (e.g., taking a logarithm). The common assumption that the regression line is a straight line is known as the *assumption of rectilinearity,* or more commonly (even if less precisely) as the *assumption of linearity.*

The slope of the regression line reflects one feature of the relationship between two variables. If the regression line slopes "uphill," as in Figure 1, then Y increases as X increases, and the steeper the slope, the more Y increases for each unit increase in X. In contrast, if the regression line slopes "downhill" as one moves from left to right, Y *decreases* as X increases, and the steeper the slope, the more Y decreases for each unit increase

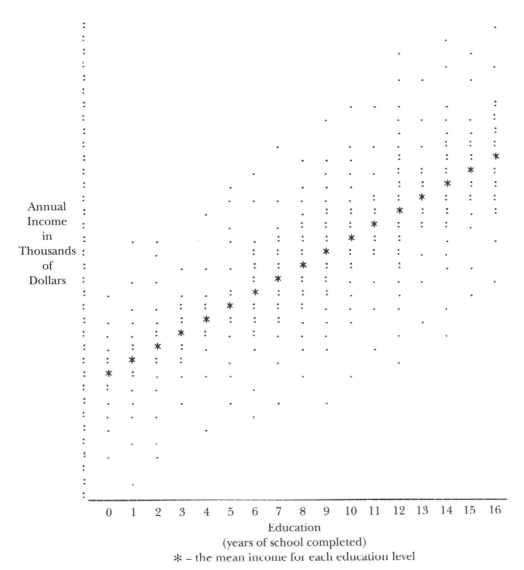

Figure 1 — Education (years of school completed)
* – the mean income for each education level

*Figure 1*
*Hypothetical Regression of Income on Education*
F* = the mean income for each education level

in X. If the regression line doesn't slope at all but is perfectly horizontal, then there is no relationship between the variables. But the slope does not tell how closely the two variables are "co-related" (i.e., how closely the values of Y cluster around the regression line).

A regression line may be represented by a simple mathematical formula for a straight line. Thus:

$$\overline{Y}|X = a_{yx} + b_{yx}X \qquad (1)$$

where $\overline{Y}|X$ = the mean Y for a given value of X, or the regression line values of Y given X; $a_{yx}$ = the Y intercept (i.e., the predicted value of $\overline{Y}|X$ when X = 0); and $b_{yx}$ = the slope of the regression of Y on X (i.e., the amount by which $\overline{Y}|X$ increases or decreases—depending on whether b is positive or negative—for each one-unit increase in X).

Equation 1 is commonly written in a slightly different form:

$$\hat{Y} = a_{yx} + b_{yx}X \qquad (2)$$

where $\hat{Y}$ = the regression prediction for Y for a given value of X, and $a_{yx}$ and $b_{yx}$ are as defined above, with $\hat{Y}$ substituted for $\overline{Y}|X$.

Equations 1 and 2 are theoretically equivalent. Equation 1 highlights the fact that the points on the regression line are assumed to represent conditional means (i.e., the mean Y for a given X). Equation 2 highlights the fact that points on the regression line are not ordinarily found by computing a series of conditional means, but are found by alternative computational procedures.

Typically the number of cases is insufficient to yield a stable estimate of each of a series of conditional means, one for each level of X. Means based on a relatively small number of cases are inaccurate because of sampling variation, and a line connecting such unstable conditional means may not be straight even though the true regression line is. Hence, one assumes that the regression line is a straight line unless there are compelling reasons for assuming otherwise; one can then use the X and Y values for all cases together to estimate the Y intercept, $a_{yx}$, and the slope, $b_{yx}$, of the regression line that is best fit by the *criterion of least squares*. This criterion requires predicted values for Y that will minimize the sum of squared deviations between the predicted values and the observed values. Hence, a "least squares" regression line is the straight line that yields a lower sum of squared deviations between the predicted (regression line) values and the observed values than does any other straight line. One can find the parameters of the "least squares" regression line for a given set of X and Y values by computing

$$b_{yx} = \frac{\Sigma\,(X - \overline{X})\,(Y - \overline{Y})}{\Sigma\,(X - \overline{X})^2} \qquad (3)$$

$$a_{yx} = \overline{Y} - b_{yx}\overline{X} \qquad (4)$$

These parameters (substituted in equation 2) describe the straight regression line that best fits by the criterion of least squares. By substituting the X value for a given case into equation 2, one can then find $\hat{Y}$ for that case. Otherwise stated, once $a_{yx}$ and $b_{yx}$ have been computed, equation 2 will yield a precise predicted income level ($\hat{Y}$) for each education level.

These predicted values may be relatively good or relatively poor predictions, depending on whether the actual values of Y cluster closely around the predicted values on the regression line or spread themselves widely around that line. The *variance* of the Y values (income levels in this illustration) around the regression line will be relatively small if the Y values cluster closely around the predicted values (i.e., when the regression line provides relatively good predictions). On the other hand, the variance of Y values around the regression line will be relatively large if the Y values are spread widely around the predicted values (i.e., when the regression line provides relatively poor predictions). The variance of the Y values around the regression predictions is defined as the mean of the squared deviations between them. The variances around each of the values along the regression line are assumed to be equal. This is known as the assumption of *homoscedasticity* (homogeneous scatter or variance). When the variances of the Y values around the regression predictions are larger for some values of X than for others (i.e., when homoscedasticity is not present), then X serves as a better predictor of Y in one part of its range than in another. The homoscedasticity assumption is usually at least approximately true.

The variance around the regression line is a measure of the accuracy of the regression predictions. But it is not an easily interpreted measure of the degree of correlation because it has not been "normed" to vary within a limited range. Two other measures, closely related to each other, provide such a normed measure. These measures, which are always between zero and one in absolute value (i.e., sign disregarded) are: (a) the correlation coefficient, r, which is the measure devised by Karl Pearson; and (b) the square of that coefficient, $r^2$, which, unlike r, can be interpreted as a percentage.

Pearson's correlation coefficient, r, can be computed using the following formula:

$$r_{yx} = r_{xy} = \frac{\dfrac{\Sigma\,(X - \overline{X})\,(Y - \overline{Y})}{N}}{\sqrt{\left(\dfrac{\Sigma\,(X - \overline{X})^2}{N}\right)\left(\dfrac{\Sigma\,(Y - \overline{Y})^2}{N}\right)}} \qquad (5)$$

The numerator in equation 5 is known as the *covariance* of X and Y. The denominator is the square root of the product of the variances of X and Y. Hence, equation 5 may be rewritten:

$$r_{yx} = r_{xy} = \frac{\text{Covariance (X, Y)}}{\sqrt{[\text{Variance (X)}][\text{Variance (Y)}]}} \quad (6)$$

While equation 5 may serve as a computing guide, neither equation 5 nor equation 6 tells why it describes the degree to which two variables covary. Such understanding may be enhanced by stating that r is the slope of the least squares regression line when both X and Y have been transformed into "standard deviates" or "z measures." Each value in a distribution may be transformed into a "z measure" by finding its deviation from the mean of the distribution and dividing by the standard deviation (the square root of the variance) of that distribution. Thus

$$Z_x = \frac{X - \overline{X}}{\sqrt{\dfrac{\Sigma (X - \overline{X})^2}{N}}} \quad (7)$$

When both the X and Y measures have been thus standardized, $r_{yx} = r_{xy}$ is the slope of the regression of Y on X, and of X on Y. For standard deviates, the Y intercept is necessarily 0, and the following equation holds:

$$\hat{Z}_y = r_{yx} Z_x \quad (8)$$

where $\hat{Z}_y$ = the regression prediction for the "Z measure" of Y, given X; $Z_x$ = the standard deviates of X; and $r_{yx} = r_{xy}$ = the Pearsonian correlation between X and Y.

Like the slope $b_{yx}$, for unstandardized measures, the slope for standardized measures, r, may be positive or negative. But unlike $b_{yx}$, r is always between 0 and 1.0 in absolute value. The correlation coefficient, r, will be 0 when the standardized regression line is horizontal so that the two variables do not covary at all—and, incidentally, when the regression toward the mean, which was Galton's original interest, is complete. On the other hand, r will be 1.0 or −1.0 when all values of $Z_y$ fall precisely on the regression line $rZ_x$. This means that when r = +1.0, for every case $Z_x = Z_y$—that is, each case deviates from the mean on

X by exactly as much and in the same direction as it deviates from the mean on Y, when those deviations are measured in their respective standard deviation units. And when r = −1.0, the deviations from the mean measured in standard deviation units are exactly equal, but they are in opposite directions. (It is also true that when r = 1.0, there is no regression toward the mean, although this is very rarely of any interest in contemporary applications.) More commonly, r will be neither 0 nor 1.0 in absolute value but will fall between these extremes, closer to 1.0 in absolute value when the $Z_y$ values cluster closely around the regression line, which, in this standardized form, implies that the slope will be near 1.0, and closer to 0 when they scatter widely around the regression line.

But while r has a precise meaning—it is the slope of the regression line for standardized measures—that meaning is not intuitively understandable as a measure of the degree to which one variable can be accurately predicted from the other. The square of the correlation coefficient, $r^2$, does have such an intuitive meaning. Briefly stated, $r^2$ indicates the percent of the possible reduction in prediction error (measured by the variance of actual values around predicted values) that is achieved by shifting from (a) $\overline{Y}$ as the prediction, to (b) the regression line values as the prediction. Otherwise stated,

$$r^2 = \frac{\dfrac{\text{Variance of Y values}}{\text{around } \overline{Y}} - \dfrac{\text{Variance of Y values}}{\text{around } \hat{Y}}}{\dfrac{\text{Variance of Y values}}{\text{around } \overline{Y}}} \quad (9)$$

The denominator of Equation 9 is called the *total variance* of Y. It is the sum of two components: (1) the variance of the Y values around $\hat{Y}$, and (2) the variance of the $\hat{Y}$ around $\overline{Y}$. Hence the numerator of equation 9 is equal to the variance of the $\hat{Y}$ values (regression values) around $\overline{Y}$. Therefore

$$r^2 = \frac{\dfrac{\text{Variance of } \hat{Y} \text{ values}}{\text{around } \overline{Y}}}{\dfrac{\text{Variance of Y values}}{\text{around } \overline{Y}}} \quad (10)$$

= proportion of variance explained

Even though it has become common to refer to $r^2$ as the proportion of variance "explained," such terminology should be used with caution. There are several possible reasons for two variables to be correlated, and some of these reasons are inconsistent with the connotations ordinarily attached to terms such as "explanation" or "explained." One possible reason for the correlation between two variables is that X influences Y. This is presumably the reason for the positive correlation between education and income; higher education facilitates earning a higher income, and it is appropriate to refer to a part of the variation in income as being "explained" by variation in education. But there is also the possibility that two variables are correlated because both are measures of the same dimension. For example, among twentieth-century nation-states, there is a high correlation between the energy consumption per capita and the gross national product per capita. These two variables are presumably correlated because both are indicators of the degree of industrial development. Hence, one variable does not "explain" variation in the other, if "explain" has any of its usual meanings. And two variables may be correlated because both are influenced by a common cause, in which case the two variables are "spuriously correlated." For example, among elementary-school children, reading ability is positively correlated with shoe size. This correlation appears not because large feet facilitate learning, and not because both are measures of the same underlying dimension, but because both are influenced by age. As they grow older, schoolchildren learn to read better *and* their feet grow larger. Hence, shoe size and reading ability are "spuriously correlated" because of the dependence of both on age. It would therefore be misleading to conclude from the correlation between shoe size and reading ability that part of the variation in reading ability is "explained" by variation in shoe size, or vice versa.

In the attempt to discover the reasons for the correlation between two variables, it is often useful to include additional variables in the analysis. Several techniques are available for doing so.

## PARTIAL CORRELATION

One may wish to explore the correlation between two variables with a third variable "held constant." The *partial correlation coefficient* may be used for this purpose. If the only reason for the correlation between shoe size and reading ability is because both are influenced by variation in age, then the correlation should disappear when the influence of variation in age is made nil—that is, when age is held constant. Given a sufficiently large number of cases, age could be held constant by considering each age grouping separately—that is, one could examine the correlation between shoe size and reading ability among children who are six years old, among children who are seven years old, eight years old, etc. (And one presumes that there would be no correlation between reading ability and shoe size among children who are homogeneous in age.) But such a procedure requires a relatively large number of children in each age grouping. Lacking such a large sample, one may hold age constant by "statistical adjustment."

To understand the underlying logic of partial correlation, one considers the *regression residuals* (i.e., for each case, the discrepancy between the regression line value and the observed value of the predicted variable). For example, the regression residual of reading ability on age for a given case is the discrepancy between the actual reading ability and the predicted reading ability based on age. Each residual will be either positive or negative (depending on whether the observed reading ability is higher or lower than the regression prediction). Each residual will also have a specific value, indicating how much higher or lower than the age-specific mean (i.e., regression line values) the reading ability is for each person. The complete set of these regression residuals, each being a deviation from the age-specific mean, describes the pattern of variation in reading abilities that would obtain if all of these schoolchildren were identical in age. Similarly, the regression residuals for shoe size on age describe the pattern of variation that would obtain if all of these schoolchildren were identical in age. Hence, the correlation between the two sets of residuals—(1) the regression residuals of shoe size on age and (2) the regression residuals of reading ability on age—is the correlation between shoe size and reading ability, with age "held constant." In practice, it is not necessary to find each regression residual to compute the partial correlation, because shorter computational procedures have been developed. Hence,

$$r_{xy \cdot z} = \frac{r_{xy} - r_{xz}r_{yz}}{\sqrt{(1 - r^2_{xz})(1 - r^2_{yz})}} \qquad (11)$$

where $r_{xy \cdot z}$ = the partial coefficient between X and Y, holding Z constant; $r_{xy}$ = the bivariate correlation coefficient between X and Y; $r_{xz}$ = the bivariate correlation coefficient between X and Z; and $r_{yz}$ = the bivariate correlation coefficient between Y and Z.

It should be evident from equation 11 that if Z is unrelated to both X and Y, controlling for Z will yield a partial correlation that does not differ from the bivariate correlation. If all correlations are positive, each increase in the correlation between the control variable, Z, and each of the focal variables, X and Y, will move the partial, $r_{xy \cdot z}$, closer to 0, and in some circumstances a positive bivariate correlation may become negative after controlling for a third variable. When $r_{xy}$ is positive and the algebraic sign of $r_{yz}$ differs from the sign of $r_{xz}$ (so that their product is negative), the partial will be *larger* than the bivariate correlation, indicating that Z is a *suppressor variable*—that is, a variable that diminishes the correlation between X and Y unless it is controlled. Further discussion of partial correlation and its interpretation will be found in Simon 1954; Mueller, Schuessler, and Costner 1977; and Blalock 1979.

Any correlation between two sets of regression residuals is called a *partial correlation coefficient.* The illustration immediately above is called a *first-order partial,* meaning that one and only one variable has been held constant. A *second-order partial* means that two variables have been held constant. More generally, an *nth-order partial* is

one in which precisely n variables have been "controlled" or held constant by statistical adjustment.

When only one of the variables being correlated is a regression residual (e.g., X is correlated with the residuals of Y on Z), the correlation is called a *part correlation.* Although part correlations are rarely used, they are appropriate when it seems implausible to residualize one variable. Generally, part correlations are smaller in absolute value than the corresponding partial correlation.

## MULTIPLE REGRESSION

Earned income level is influenced not simply by one's education but also by work experience, skills developed outside of school and work, the prevailing compensation for the occupation or profession in which one works, the nature of the regional economy where one is employed, and numerous other factors. Hence it should not be surprising that education alone does not predict income with high accuracy. The deviations between actual income and income predicted on the basis of education are presumably due to the influence of all the other factors that have an effect, great or small, on one's income level. By including some of these other variables as additional predictors, the accuracy of prediction should be increased. Otherwise stated, one expects to predict Y better using both $X_1$ and $X_2$ (assuming both influence Y) than with either of these alone.

A regression equation including more than a single predictor of Y is called a *multiple regression equation.* For two predictors, the multiple regression equation is:

$$\hat{Y} = a_{y.12} + b_{y1.2}X_1 + b_{y2.1}X_2 \qquad (12)$$

where $\hat{Y}$ = the least squares prediction of Y based on $X_1$ and $X_2$; $a_{y.12}$ = the Y intercept (i.e., the predicted value of Y when both $X_1$ and $X_2$ are 0); $b_{y1.2}$ = the (unstandardized) regression slope of Y on $X_1$, holding $X_2$ constant; and $b_{y2.1}$ = the (unstandardized) regression slope of Y on $X_2$, holding $X_1$ constant. In multiple regression analysis, the predicted variable (Y in equation 12) is commonly known as the *criterion variable,* and the X's are called predictors. As in a bivariate regression equation (equation 2), one assumes both rectilinearity and homoscedasticity, and one finds the Y intercept ($a_{y.12}$ in equation 12) and the regression slopes (one for each predictor; they are $b_{y1.2}$ and $b_{y2.1}$ in equation 12) that best fit by the criterion of least squares. The b's or regression slopes are *partial regression coefficients.* The correlation between the resulting regression predictions ($\hat{Y}$) and the observed values of Y is called the *multiple correlation coefficient,* symbolized by R.

In contemporary applications of multiple regression, the partial regression coefficients are typically the primary focus of attention. These coefficients describe the regression of the criterion variable on each predictor, holding constant all other predictors in the equation. The b's in equation 12 are *unstandardized* coefficients. The analogous multiple regression equation for all variables expressed in standardized form is

$$\hat{Z}_y = b^*_{y1.2} Z_1 + b^*_{y2.1} Z_2 \qquad (13)$$

where $\hat{Z}$ = the regression prediction for the "z measure" of Y, given $X_1$ and $X_2$; $Z_1$ = the standard deviate of $X_1$; $Z_2$ = the standard deviate of $X_2$; $b^*_{y1.2}$ = the standardized slope of Y on $X_1$, holding $X_2$ constant; and $b^*_{y2.1}$ = the standardized slope of Y on $X_2$, holding $X_1$ constant.

The standardized regression coefficients in an equation with two predictors may be calculated from the bivariate correlations as follows:

$$b^*_{y1.2} = \frac{r_{y1} - r_{y2}r_{12}}{1 - r^2_{12}} \qquad (14)$$

$$b^*_{y2.1} = \frac{r_{y2} - r_{y1}r_{12}}{1 - r^2_{12}} \qquad (15)$$

where $b^*_{y1.2}$ = the standardized partial regression coefficient of Y on $X_1$, controlling for $X_2$; and $b^*_{y2.1}$ = the standardized partial regression coefficient of Y on $X_2$, controlling for $X_1$.

Standardized partial regression coefficients, here symbolized by b* (read "b star"), are frequently symbolized by the Greek letter beta, and they are commonly referred to as "betas," "beta coefficients," or "beta weights." While this is

common usage, it violates the established practice of using Greek letters to refer to population parameters instead of sample statistics.

A comparison of equation 14, describing the standardized partial regression coefficient, $b^*_{y1.2}$, with equation 11, describing the partial correlation coefficient, $r_{y1.2}$, will make it evident that these two coefficients are closely related. They have identical numerators but different denominators. The similarity can be succinctly expressed by

$$r^2_{y1.2} = b^*_{y1.2}\, b^*_{1y.2} \qquad (16)$$

If any one of the quantities in equation 16 is 0, all are 0, and if the partial correlation is 1.0 in absolute value, both of the standardized partial regression coefficients in equation 16 must also be 1.0 in absolute value. For absolute values between 0 and 1.0, the partial correlation coefficient and the standardized partial regression coefficient will have somewhat different values, although the general interpretation of two corresponding coefficients is the same in the sense that both coefficients represent the relationship between two variables, with one or more other variables held constant. The difference between them is rather subtle and rarely of major substantive import. Briefly stated, the partial correlation coefficient—e.g., $r_{y1.2}$—is the regression of one standardized residual on another standardized residual. The corresponding standardized partial regression coefficient, $b^*_{y1.2}$, is the regression of one residual on another, but the residuals are standard measure discrepancies from standard measure predictions, rather than the residuals themselves having been expressed in the form of standard deviates.

A standardized partial regression coefficient can be transformed into an unstandardized partial regression coefficient by

$$b_{y1.2} = b^*_{y1.2}\, \frac{s_y}{s_1} \qquad (17)$$

$$b_{y2.1} = b^*_{y2.1}\, \frac{s_y}{s_2} \qquad (18)$$

where $b_{y1.2}$ = the unstandardized partial regression coefficient of Y on $X_1$, controlling for $X_2$; $b_{y2.1}$ = the unstandardized partial regression coefficient of Y on $X_2$, controlling for $X_1$; $b^*_{y2.1}$ and

$b^*_{y2.1}$ are standardized partial regression coefficients, as defined above; $s_y$ = the standard deviation of $Y$; $s_1$ — the standard deviation of $X_1$; and $s_2$ = the standard deviation of $X_2$.

Under all but exceptional circumstances, standardized partial regression coefficients fall between $-1.0$ and $+1.0$. The relative magnitude of the *standardized* coefficients in a given regression equation indicates the relative magnitude of the relationship between the criterion variable and the predictor in question, after holding constant all the other predictors in that regression equation. Hence, the *standardized* partial regression coefficients in a given equation can be compared to infer which predictor has the strongest relationship to the criterion, after holding all other variables in that equation constant. The comparison of *unstandardized* partial regression coefficients for different predictors in the same equation does not ordinarily yield useful information because these coefficients are affected by the units of measure. On the other hand, it is frequently useful to compare *unstandardized* partial regression coefficients across equations. For example, in separate regression equations predicting income from education and work experience for the United States and Great Britain, if the unstandardized regression coefficient for education in the equation for Great Britain is greater than the unstandardized regression coefficient for education in the equation for the United States, the implication is that education has a greater influence on income in Great Britain than in the United States. It would be hazardous to draw any such conclusion from the comparison of *standardized* coefficients for Great Britain and the United States because such coefficients are affected by the variances in the two populations.

The multiple correlation coefficient, $R$, is defined as the correlation between the observed values of $Y$ and the values of $Y$ predicted by the multiple regression equation. It would be unnecessarily tedious to calculate the multiple correlation coefficient in that way. The more convenient computational procedure is to compute $R^2$ (for two predictors, and analogously for more than two predictors) by the following:

$$R^2 = b^*_{y1.2}r_{y1} + b^*_{y2.1}r_{y2} \qquad (19)$$

Like $r^2$, $R^2$ varies from 0 to 1.0 and indicates the proportion of variance in the criterion that is "explained" by the predictors. Alternatively stated, $R^2$ is the percent of the possible reduction in prediction error (measured by the variance of actual values around predicted values) that is achieved by shifting from (a) $\overline{Y}$ as the prediction to (b) the multiple regression values, $\hat{Y}$, as the prediction.

## VARIETIES OF MULTIPLE REGRESSION

The basic concept of multiple regression has been adapted to a variety of purposes other than those for which the technique was originally developed. The following paragraphs provide a brief summary of some of these adaptations.

**Dummy Variable Analysis.** As originally conceived, the correlation coefficient was designed to describe the relationship between continuous, normally distributed variables. Dichotomized predictors such as gender (male and female) were introduced early in bivariate regression and correlation, which led to the "point biserial correlation coefficient" (Walker and Lev 1953). For example, if one wishes to examine the correlation between gender and income, one may assign a "0" to each instance of male and a "1" to each instance of female to have numbers representing the two categories of the dichotomy. The unstandardized regression coefficient, computed as specified above in equation 3, is then the difference between the mean income for the two categories of the dichotomous predictor, and the computational formula for $r$ (equation 5), will yield the point biserial correlation coefficient, which can be interpreted much like any other $r$. It was then only a small step to the inclusion of dichotomies as predictors in multiple regression analysis, and then to the creation of a set of dichotomies from a categorical variable with more than two subdivisions—that is, to *dummy variable analysis* (Suits 1957; Cohen 1968; Bohrnstedt and Knoke 1988).

Religious denomination—e.g., Protestant, Catholic, and Jewish—serves as an illustration.

From these three categories, one forms two dichotomies, called "dummy variables." In the first of these, for example, cases are classified as "1" if they are Catholic, and "0" otherwise (i.e., if Protestant or Jewish). In the second of the dichotomies, cases are classified as "1" if they are Jewish, and "0" otherwise (i.e., if Protestant or Catholic). In this illustration, Protestant is the "omitted" or "reference" category (but Protestants can be identified as those who are classified "0" on both of the other dichotomies). The resulting two dichotomized "dummy variables" can serve as the only predictors in a multiple regression equation, or they may be combined with other predictors. When the dummy variables mentioned are the only predictors, the unstandardized regression coefficient for the predictor in which Catholics are classified "1" is the difference between the mean Y for Catholics and Protestants (the "omitted" or "reference" category). Similarly, the unstandardized regression coefficient for the predictor in which Jews are classified "1" is the difference between the mean Y for Jews and Protestants. When the dummy variables are included with other predictors, the unstandardized regression coefficients are the same except that the difference of each mean from the mean of the "reference" category has been statistically adjusted to control for each of the other predictors in the regression equation.

The development of "dummy variable analysis" allowed multiple regression analysis to be linked to the experimental statistics developed by R. A. Fisher, including the analysis of variance and covariance. (See Cohen 1968.)

**Logistic Regression.** Early students of correlation anticipated the need for a measure of correlation when the predicted or dependent variable was dichotomous. Out of this came (a) the phi coefficient, which can be computed by applying the computational formula for r (equation 5) to two dichotomies, each coded "0" or "1," and (b) the tetrachoric correlation coefficient, which uses information in the form of two dichotomies to estimate the Pearsonian correlation for the corresponding continuous variables, assuming the dichotomies result from dividing two continuous

and normally distributed variables by arbitrary cutting points (Kelley 1947; Walker and Lev 1953; Carroll 1961).

These early developments readily suggested use of a dichotomous predicted variable, coded "0" or "1," as the predicted variable in a multiple regression analysis. The predicted value is then the conditional proportion, which is the conditional mean for a dichotomized predicted variable. But this was not completely satisfactory in some circumstances because the regression predictions are, under some conditions, proportions greater than 1 or less than 0. *Logistic regression* (Raftery and Hout 1985) is responsive to this problem. After coding the predicted variable "0" or "1," the predicted variable is transformed to a logistic—that is, the logarithm of the "odds," which is to say the logarithm of the ratio of the number of 1's to the number of 0's. With the logistic as the predicted variable, impossible regression predictions do not result, but the unstandardized logistic regression coefficients, describing changes in the logarithm of the "odds," lack the intuitive meaning of ordinary regression coefficients. An additional computation is required to be able to describe the change in the predicted proportion for a given one-unit change in a predictor, with all other predictors in the equation held constant.

**Path Analysis.** The interpretation of multiple regression coefficients can be difficult or impossible when the predictors include an undifferentiated set of causes, consequences, or spurious correlates of the predicted variable. Path analysis was developed by Sewell Wright (1934) to facilitate the interpretation of multiple regression coefficients by making explicit assumptions about causal structure and including as predictors of a given variable only those variables that precede that given variable in the assumed causal structure. For example, if one assumes that Y is influenced by $X_1$ and $X_2$, and $X_1$ and $X_2$ are, in turn, both influenced by $Z_1$, $Z_2$, and $Z_3$, this specifies the assumed causal structure. One may then proceed to write multiple regression equations to predict $X_1$, $X_2$, and Y, including in each equation only those variables that come prior in the assumed causal order. For example, the Z variables are appropriate predictors in the equation predicting $X_1$ because they are assumed causes of $X_1$. But $X_2$ is not an appropriate predictor of $X_1$ because it is assumed to be a spurious correlate of $X_1$ (i.e., $X_1$ and $X_2$ are presumed to be correlated only because they are both influenced by the Z variables, not because one influences the other). And Y is not an appropriate predictor of $X_1$ because Y is assumed to be an effect of $X_1$, not one of its causes. When the assumptions about the causal structure linking a set of variables have been made explicit, the appropriate predictors for each variable have been identified from this assumed causal structure, and the resulting equations have been estimated by the techniques of regression analysis, the result is a path analysis, and each of the resulting coefficients is said to be a "path coefficient" (if expressed in standardized form) or a "path regression coefficient" (if expressed in unstandardized form).

If the assumed causal structure is correct, a path analysis allows one to "decompose" a correlation between two variables into "direct effects"; "indirect effects"; and, potentially, a "spurious component" as well (Land 1969, Mueller, Schuessler, and Costner 1977; Bohrnstedt and Knoke 1988). For example, we may consider the correlation between the occupational achievement of a set of fathers and the occupational achievement of their sons. Some of this correlation may occur because the father's occupational achievement influences the educational attainment of the son, and the son's educational attainment, in turn, influences his occupational achievement. This is an "indirect effect" of the father's occupational achievement on the son's occupational achievement "through" (or "mediated by") the son's education. A "direct effect," on the other hand, is an effect that is not mediated by any variable included in the analysis. Such mediating variables could probably be found, but if they have not been identified and included in this particular analysis, then the effects mediated through them are grouped together as the "direct effect"—that is, an effect not mediated by variables included in the analysis. If the father's occupational achieve-

ment and the son's occupational achievement are also correlated, in part, because both are influenced by a common cause (e.g., a common hereditary variable), then that part of the correlation that is attributable to that common cause constitutes the "spurious component" of the correlation. If the variables responsible for the "spurious component" of a correlation have been included in the path analysis, the "spurious component" can be estimated; otherwise such a "spurious component" is merged into the "direct effect," which, despite the connotations of the name, absorbs all omitted indirect effects and all omitted spurious components.

**"Stepwise" Regression Analysis.** The interpretation of regression results can sometimes be facilitated without specifying completely the presumed causal structure among a set of predictors. If the purpose of the analysis is to enhance understanding of the variation in a single dependent variable, and if the various predictors presumed to contribute to that variation can be grouped, for example, into proximate causes and distant causes, a *stepwise regression analysis* may be useful. Depending on one's primary interest, one may proceed in two different ways. For example, one may begin by regressing the criterion variable on the distant causes, and then, in a second step, introduce the proximate causes into the regression equation. Comparison of the coefficients at each step will reveal the degree to which the effects of the distant causes are mediated by the proximate causes included in the analysis. Alternatively, one may begin by regressing the criterion variable on the proximate causes, and then introduce the distant causes into the regression equation in a second step. Comparing the coefficients at each step, one can infer the degree to which the first-step regression of the criterion variable on the proximate causes is spurious because of the dependence of both on the distant causes. A stepwise regression analysis may proceed with more than two stages if one wishes to distinguish more than two sets of predictors. One may think of a stepwise regression analysis of this kind as analogous to a path analysis but without a complete specification of the causal structure.

**Nonadditive Effects in Multiple Regression.** In the illustrative regression equations preceding this section, each predictor has appeared only once, and never in a "multiplicative" term. We now consider the following regression equation, which includes such a multiplicative term:

$$\hat{Y} = a_{y.12} + b_{y1.2}X_1 + b_{y2.1}X_2 + b_{y.12}X_1X_2 \qquad (20)$$

In this equation, Y is said to be predicted, not simply by an additive combination of $X_1$ and $X_2$ but also by their product, $X_1X_2$. Although it may not be intuitively evident from the equation itself, the presence of a multiplicative effect (i.e., the regression coefficient for the multiplicative term, $b_{y.12}$, is not 0) implies that the effect of $X_1$ on Y depends on the level of $X_2$, and vice versa. This is commonly called an *interaction effect* (Blalock 1979; Cohen 1968). The inclusion of multiplicative terms in a regression equation is especially appropriate when there are sound reasons for assuming that the effect of one variable differs for different levels of another variable. For example, if one assumes that the "return to education" (i.e., the annual income added by each additional year of schooling) will be greater for men than for women, this assumption can be explored by including all three predictors: education, gender, and the product of gender and education.

When product terms have been included in a regression equation, the interpretation of the resulting partial regression coefficients may become complex. For example, unless all predictors are "ratio variables" (i.e., variables measured in uniform units from an absolute 0), the inclusion of a product term in a regression equation renders the coefficients for the additive terms uninterpretable (see Allison 1977.)

## SAMPLING VARIATION AND TESTS AGAINST THE NULL HYPOTHESIS

Descriptions based on incomplete information will be inaccurate because of "sampling variation." Otherwise stated, different samplings of information will yield different results. This is true of sample regression and correlation coefficients, as it is for other descriptors. Assuming a random selection of observed information, the "shape" of the distribution of such sampling variation is often known by mathematical reasoning, and the magnitude of such variation can be estimated. For example, if the true correlation between X and Y is 0, a series of randomly selected observations will rarely yield a correlation that is precisely 0. Instead, the observed correlation will fluctuate around 0 in the "shape" of a normal distribution, and the standard deviation of that normal sampling distribution—called the *standard error* of r—will be

$$\sigma_r = \frac{1}{\sqrt{N-1}} \qquad (21)$$

where $\sigma_r$ = the standard error of r (i.e. the standard deviation of the sampling distribution of r, given that the true correlation is 0); and N = the sample size (i.e., the number of randomly selected cases used in the calculation of r). For example, if the true correlation were 0, a correlation coefficient based on a random selection of 400 cases will have a standard error of approximately 1/20 or .05. An observed correlation of .15 or greater in absolute value would thus be at least three standard errors away from 0 and hence very unlikely to have appeared simply because of random fluctuations around a true value of 0. This kind of conclusion is commonly expressed by saying that the observed correlation is "significantly different from 0" at a given level of significance (in this instance, the level of significance cited could appropriately be .01). Or the same conclusion may be more simply (but less precisely) stated by saying that the observed correlation is "significant."

The standard error for an unstandardized bivariate regression coefficient, and for an unstandardized partial regression coefficient, may also be estimated, although the formula for doing so is not given here. Other things being equal, the standard error for the regression of the criterion on a given predictor will decrease as (1) the number of observations (N) increases; (2) the variance of observed values around predicted values decreases; (3) the variance of the predictor increases; and (4) the correlation between the predictor and other predictors in the regression equation decreases.

## PROBLEMS IN REGRESSION ANALYSIS

Multiple regression is a special case of a very general and adaptable model of data analysis known as the general linear model (Fennessey 1968; Blalock 1979). Although the assumptions underlying multiple regression seem relatively demanding, the technique has been found to be remarkably "robust," which is to say that the technique yields valid conclusions even when the assumptions are met only roughly (Bohrnstedt and Carter 1971). The two major threats to the validity of conclusions from partial correlation and partial regression coefficients are (1) misspecification of the causal model used in interpreting the coefficients (Blalock 1964; Heise 1969) and (2) errors in the measurement of the variables (Stouffer 1936; Kahneman 1965; Gordon 1968; Bohrnstedt and Carter 1971). Briefly stated, to the degree that measurement error, random or nonrandom, intrudes into the variables, control by statistical adjustment is incomplete and the partial correlation coefficients, regression coefficients, or path coefficients are correspondingly distorted. While these potential sources of error in interpretation suggest appropriate caution, they do not diminish the importance and utility of correlation and regression analysis in social research.

(SEE ALSO: *Analysis of Variance and Covariance; General Linear Model; Measures of Association; Multiple Indicator Models*)

### REFERENCES

Allison, Paul 1977 "Testing for Interaction in Multiple Regression." *American Journal of Sociology* 83:144–153.

Blalock, Hubert M., Jr. 1964 *Causal Inferences in Nonex-*
*perimental Research*. Chapel Hill: University of North Carolina Press.

—— 1979 *Social Statistics*, 2nd ed. New York: Mc-Graw-Hill.

Bohrnstedt, George W., and T. Michael Carter 1971 "Robustness in Regression Analysis." In Herbert L. Costner, ed., *Sociological Methodology 1971*. San Francisco: Jossey-Bass.

——, and David Knoke 1988 *Statistics for Social Data Analysis*, 2nd ed. Itasca, Ill.: F. E. Peacock Publishers.

Carroll, John B. 1961 "The Nature of the Data, or How to Choose a Correlation Coefficient." *Psychometrica* 26:347–372.

Cohen, Jacob 1968 "Multiple Regression as a General Data Analytic System." *Psychological Bulletin* 70:426–443.

Fennessey, James 1968 "The General Linear Model: A New Perspective on Some Familiar Topics." *American Journal of Sociology* 74:1–27.

Gordon, Robert 1968 "Issues in Multiple Regression." *American Journal of Sociology* 73:592–616.

Heise, David R. 1969 "Problems in Path Analysis and Causal Inference." In Edgar Borgatta and George W. Bohrnstedt, eds., *Sociological Methodology 1969*. San Francisco: Jossey-Bass.

Kahneman, D. 1965 "Control of Spurious Association and the Reliability of the Controlled Variable." *Psychological Bulletin* 64:326–329.

Kelley, Truman Lee 1947 *Fundamentals of Statistics*. Cambridge, Mass.: Harvard University Press.

Land, Kenneth C. 1969 "Principles of Path Analysis." In Edgar Borgatta and George W. Bohrnstedt, eds., *Sociological Methodology 1969*. San Francisco: Jossey-Bass.

Mueller, John H., Karl F. Schuessler, and Herbert L. Costner 1977 *Statistical Reasoning in Sociology*, 3rd ed. Boston: Houghton Mifflin.

Raftery, Adrian E., and Michael Hout 1985 "Does Irish Education Approach the Meritocratic Ideal? A Logistic Analysis." *Economic and Social Review* 16:115–140.

Simon, Herbert A. 1954 "Spurious Correlation: A Causal Interpretation." *Journal of the American Statistical Association* 49:467–479.

Stouffer, Samuel A. 1936 "Evaluating the Effects of Inadequately Measured Variables in Partial Correlation Analysis." *Journal of the American Statistical Association* 31:348–360.

Suits, Daniel 1957 "The Use of Dummy Variables in

Regression Equations." *Journal of the American Statistical Association* 52:548–551.

Walker, Helen M. 1929 *Studies in the History of Statistical Method.* Baltimore: Williams and Wilkins.

————, and Joseph Lev 1953 *Statistical Inference.* New York: Holt.

Wright, Sewell 1934 "The Method of Path Coefficients." *The Annals of Mathematical Statistics* 5: 161–215.

HERBERT L. COSTNER


**COUNTERCULTURES**   The enclaves in which people of the modern era live no longer resemble the small, integrated, and homogeneous communities of earlier times; rather, these have been replaced by large societies that are complex and diverse in their composition. The United States, a prime exemplar, is composed of multiple smaller groups holding characteristics, beliefs, customs, and interests that vary from the rest of society. While there are many cultural universals binding such groups to the mainstream, they also exhibit significant cultural diversity. Some of these groups display no clear boundaries demarcating them from the rest of society and fail to achieve any degree of permanence. Yet those that do, and that also share a distinctive set of norms, values, and behavior setting them off from the dominant culture, are considered *subcultures.* Subcultures can be organized around age, ethnicity, occupation, social class, religion, or life-style and usually contain specific knowledge, expressions, ways of dressing, and systems of stratification that serve and guide members. Distinctive subcultures within the United States include jazz musicians, gangs, Chicanos, homosexuals, college athletes, and drug dealers. While it was once hypothesized that these subcultures would merge together in a melting pot incorporating a mix of the remnants of former subcultures, more recent trends suggest that they resist total assimilation and retain their cultural diversity and distinct identity (Irwin 1970).

Some subcultures diverge from the dominant culture without morally rejecting the norms and values with which they differ. Others are more adamant in their condemnation, clearly conflicting with or opposing features of the larger society. Milton Yinger first proposed, in 1960, to call these groups *contracultures,* envisioning them as a subset of all subcultures: those having an element of conflict with dominant norms, values, or both (Yinger 1960). Indeed, the feature he identified as most compelling about a contraculture is its specific organization in opposition to some cultural belief(s) or expression(s). Contracultures often arise, he noted, where there are conflicts of standards or values between subcultural groups and the larger society. Factors strengthening the conflict then strengthen the contracultural response. Contracultural members, especially from such groups as delinquent gangs, may be driven by their experiences of frustration, deprivation, or discrimination within society.

Yinger's conceptualization, although abstract and academic at first, came to enjoy widespread popularity and fruition with the advent of the 1960s and the student movement. Here was the kind of contraculture he had forecast, and his ideas were widely applied to the trends of the time, albeit under another label. Most analysts of contracultures preferred the term *counterculture,* and this soon overtook its predecessor as the predominant expression. In 1969 Theodore Roszak published his *The Making of a Counter Culture,* claiming that a large group of young people (ages fifteen to thirty) had arisen who adamantly rejected the technological and scientific outlook characteristic of Western industrialized culture, replacing this, instead, with a humanistic/mysticist alternative. Keniston (1971) described this counterculture as composed of distinct subgroups (radicals, dropouts, hippies, drug users, communards) rising from the most privileged children of the world's wealthiest nation. Douglas (1970) also discussed the social, political, and economic background to this movement and its roots in members' entrenchment in the welfare state and the existing youth and student cultures. While this movement was clearly political as well, Douglas outlined some of its social dimensions, including its rejection of the workaday world and its idealization of leisure, feeling, openness, and antimaterialism. Flacks (1971) and Davis (1971) followed with descriptions of the counterculture's overarching life-styles, values, political beliefs, and ideologies. Turner (1976), Adler (1972), and Erikson (1968) explored the social psychological implications of this counterculture, positing, respectively, a transformation in the self from "institution" to "impulse," the rise of an antinomian personality, where individuals oppose the obligatoriness of the moral law, and the formation of the "negative identity." Rothchild and Wolf (1976) documented the vast extension of countercultural outposts around the country and their innovations in child rearing. Reich (1970) emphatically stated that this counterculture was being reinforced by merging with nonstudent youth, educated labor, and the women's movement, already effecting a major transformation in Western laws, institutions, and social structure. There was strong belief that this movement would significantly and permanently alter both society and its consciousness (Wuthnow 1976). After researching one commune in depth, Berger (1981) later mused about the survival of the counterculture, acknowledging its failure to meet earlier expectations, yet examining how its ideals and values became incorporated into the mainstream culture (cf. Spates 1976).

Other subcultural analysts noted more broadly that these groups are typically popular among youth, who have the least investment in the existing culture, and that, lacking power within society, they are likely to feel the forces of social control swiftly moving against them, from the mass media to police action. Countercultures were further differentiated from subcultures by the fact that their particular norms and values were not well integrated into the dominant culture, these being generally known only among group members.

Yinger reclaimed theoretical command of the countercultural concept with his reflective expansions on the term in a presidential address for the American Sociological Association (Yinger 1977) and a book that serves as the definitive statement on the topic (1982). He asserted the fundamental import of studying these sharp contradictions to the dominant norms and values of a society as a means of gaining insight into social order. Countercultures, through their oppositional culture (polarity, reversal, inversion, and diametric opposition), attempt to reorganize drastically the normative bases of social order. These alternatives may range from rejecting a norm or value entirely to exaggerating its emphasis in their construction of countervalues. As a result, some countercultures fade rapidly while others are lasting, and some have no significant impact on the larger society while parts of others become incorporated into the broader cultural value system. Examples of countercultural groups would include the 1960s student counterculture (in both its political and social dimensions); youth gangs (especially delinquent groups); motorcycle gangs (such as the Hell's Angels); revolutionary groups (the Weathermen of the Students for a Democratic Society, or the Black Panthers); terrorist organizations (such as the Symbionese Liberation Army); extremist racist groups (the Ku Klux Klan, the skinheads, the Aryan Nation); survivalists; punkers; bohemian Beats, and some extremist religious sects (such as the Amish and the Hare Krishnas).

## VARIETIES OF COUNTERCULTURES

Yinger believed that countercultural groups could take several forms. The *radical activist* counterculture "preaches, creates, or demands new obligations" (Yinger 1977, p. 838). They are intimately involved with the larger culture in their attempts to transform it. Members of the *communitarian utopian* counterculture live as ascetics, withdrawing into an isolated community forged under the guidelines of their new values. *Mystical* countercultures search for the truth and for themselves, turning inward toward consciousness to realize their values. Theirs is more a disregard of society than an effort to change it. These three forms are not necessarily intended to describe particular groups. Rather, they are ideal types, offered to shed insight into characteristics or tendencies groups may combine or approximate in their formation. Hippie communities or bohemian Beat groups combined the mystical and utopian features of countercultures in their withdrawal from conventional society and their search for a higher transcendence. Revolutionary youth gangs, such as the 1960s radicals, the Hell's Angels, and the punkers, fuse the mystical search for new experiences and insights (often through drug use) with an activist attack on the dominant culture and its institutional expressions. Survivalists, Amish, and Hare Krishnas fuse the radical critique of conventional values and life-styles with a withdrawal into an isolated and protected community.

Countercultures can also be differentiated by their primary breaks with the dominant culture. Some take odds with its *epistemology,* or the way society contends that it knows the truth. Hippies and other mystics, for example, have tended to seek insight in homespun wisdom, meditation, sensory deprivation, drugs, or direct experience with the cosmos, rejecting the cold rationality of science and technology. Others assert an alternative system of *ethics,* arguing about the values pursued in defining the good or striving for the good life. Some, like skinheads or KKK members, may be quite conservative in their definition of the good life; others are libertarian, advocating for people to "do their own thing." Third, countercultures offer alternative *aesthetic standards* by which fashion, taste, and beauty are to be judged. Punk or acid rock musical movements, performance or postmodernist art movements, and bohemian or hippie fashion movements were all aesthetic statements that incorporated a radical rejection of the standards of conventional taste and its connection to conventional values. Thus, entire countercultural movements may be based on their advocacy of these competing beliefs.

## COUNTERCULTURES AND SOCIAL CHANGE

Due to their intense opposition to the dominant culture, countercultures are variously regarded as "engines of social change, symbols and effects of change, or mere faddist epiphenomena" (Yinger 1982, p. 285). Examining these in reverse order, countercultures are often considered *mutations* of the normative social order, encompassing such drastic life-style changes that they invoke

deep ambivalence and persecution. Most major countercultural mutations appear in the form of religious movements. Other countercultures arise out of underlying or developing societal stresses: rapid political or economic change; demographic transformations in the population (age, gender, location); a swift influx of new ideas; drastic escalation or diminishment of hopes or aspirations; weakening of ties to primary support circles (families, neighborhoods, work groups); and the erosion of meaning in the deepest symbols and rituals of society. These factors are then augmented by communication among people sharing such experiences or beliefs, leading them to coalesce into normatively and ideologically integrated groups. Countercultures can also precipitate social change if the norms and values they champion are incorporated into the mainstream. In commenting on the 1960s student movement, Chief Justice Warren Burger of the United States Supreme Court stated that "the turbulent American youth, whose disorderly acts [I] once 'resented,' actually had pointed the way to higher spiritual values" (cited in Yinger 1977, p. 848). Lasting influence may not always result from major countercultural movements, as witnessed by the rapid erosion in influence of Mao's cultural revolution after his death, yet it is possible. This occurs through a cultural dialectic, wherein each normative system, containing within it the seeds of its own contradiction, gives rise to the oppositional values of a counterculture that are ultimately incorporated into its future synthesis.

## COUNTERCULTURE CASE STUDIES

While the student movement of the 1960s was undoubtedly the largest and most influential counterculture to arise in the United States, a review of three more contemporary countercultures may yield further insight into the parameters and character of these movements. Let us focus briefly on the Hare Krishnas, punks, and survivalists.

The Hare Krishna movement, also known as the International Society for Krishna Consciousness (ISKCON), is one of the new religious movements that became popular in the United States during the great "cult" period of the 1970s (Judah 1974; Rochford 1985). Its rise after the decline of the 1960s student movement is not coincidental, for many people who were former hippies or who were influenced by or seeking the ideals and values of the 1960s turned toward new religions (Tipton 1982) in search of the same features of community, idealism, antimaterialism, mysticism, transcendence to a higher plane, and "a spiritual way of life, which stands outside the traditional institutions found in America" (Rochford 1985, p. 44). Its primary values conflicting with mainstream culture include the rejection of (1) material success through competitive labor; (2) education to promote that end; (3) possessions for sense gratification; (4) authority favoring the status quo; (5) imperialistic aggression; and (6) the hypocrisy of racial discrimination (Judah 1974, p. 16). After the death of its American spiritual master, Srila Prabhupada, in 1977, however, the movement peaked and became more commercialized, transferring its emphasis from self-expression and uniqueness to survival, thereby becoming more of a mass phenomena.

In contrast to the religious and value components of the Hare Krishnas' rejection of mainstream culture, the punk or punk rock counterculture of the late 1970s and early 1980s was more of a style movement (Hebdige 1981). As Fox (1987, p. 349) has noted, "The punks created a new aesthetic that revealed their lack of hope, cynicism, and rejection of societal norms." This was expressed in both their appearance and their life-style. The punk belief system was antiestablishment and anarchistic, celebrating chaos, cynicism, and distrust of authority. Punks disdained the conventional system, with its bureaucracies, power structures, and competition for scarce goods (Fox 1987). Members lived outside the system, unemployed, in old abandoned houses or with friends, and engaged in heavy use of nihilistic drugs such as heroin and glue. Hard-core commitment was usually associated with semipermanent alteration of members' appearance through tattoos, shaven heads, or Mohawk hairstyles (Brake 1985). The musical scene associated with punks was contrary

to established tastes as well and often involved self-abandonment characterized by "crash dancing" (Street 1986).

In contrast to the hippies, Krishnas, and punks, the survivalist counterculture was grounded in exaggeration of right-wing beliefs and values. While the former groups preached love, survivalists centered themselves on hate. Formed out of extremist coalition splinter groups such as neo-Nazis, Klansmen, John Birchers, fundamentalist Mormon Freemen, the White Aryan Resistance, and tax protesters from Posse Comitatus, survivalists drew on long-standing convictions that an international conspiracy of Jews was taking over everything from banking, real estate, and the press to the Soviet Politburo and that the white race was being "mongrelized" by civil-rights legislation. A cleansing nuclear war or act of God, with "secular" assistance, would soon bring the Armageddon, eradicating the "Beast" in their midst (Coates 1987). Members thus set about producing and distributing survivalist literature, stockpiling machine guns, fuel, food, and medical supplies on remote farms and in underground bunkers, joining survivalist retreat groups, and attending survivalist training courses (Peterson 1984). Within their retreat communities they rejected the rationalization, technologization, secularization, and commodification of society, creating an environment of creative self-expression where an individual could accomplish meaningful work with a few simple tools. In their withdrawn communities and utopian future scenario, men would reclaim their roles as heads of the family; women would regain mastery over crafts and nurturance. Theirs is thus a celebration of fantasy and irrationality (Mitchell 1991, n.d.). Yet while they isolate themselves in countercultures peopled by like-minded individuals, they try to influence mainstream society through activism in radical right-wing politics as well. Their actions and beliefs, although rejecting the directions and trends in contemporary society, arise out of and represent frustrations felt by embattled segments of the moral majority.

Countercultures thus stand on the periphery of culture, spawned by and spawning social trends and changes in their opposition. As Yinger (1977,

p. 850) has noted, "Every society gets the counter-cultures it deserves, for they do not simply contra-dict, they also express the situation from which they emerge. . . . Countercultures borrow from the dominant culture even as they oppose it."

(SEE ALSO: *Alternative Life-Styles; Social Movements; Student Movements*)

## REFERENCES

Adler, Nathan 1972 *The Underground Stream: New Life Styles and the Antinomian Personality.* New York: Harper.

Berger, Bennett 1981 *The Survival of a Counterculture.* Berkeley: University of California Press.

Brake, Michael 1985 *Comparative Youth Culture: The Sociology of Youth Culture and Subcultures in America, Britain, and Canada.* London: Routledge.

Coates, James 1987 *Armed and Dangerous.* New York: Hill and Wang.

Davis, Fred 1971 *On Youth Subcultures: The Hippie Variant.* New York: General Learning Press.

Douglas, Jack D. 1970 *Youth in Turmoil.* Chevy Chase, Md.: National Institute of Mental Health.

Erikson, Erik 1968 *Identity: Youth and Crisis.* New York: W. W. Norton.

Flacks, Richard 1971 *Youth and Social Change.* Chicago: Markham.

Fox, Kathryn J. 1987 "Real Punks and Pretenders: The Social Organization of a Counterculture." *Journal of Contemporary Ethnography* 16:344–370.

Hebdige, Dick 1981 *Subcultures: The Meaning of Style.* New York: Methuen.

Irwin, John 1970 "Notes on the Present Status of the Concept Subculture." In D. O. Arnold, ed., *The Sociology of Subcultures.* Berkeley: Glendessary Press.

Judah, J. Stillson 1974 *Hare Krishna and the Countercul-ture.* New York: Wiley.

Keniston, Kenneth 1971 *Youth and Dissent: The Rise of a New Opposition.* New York: Harcourt Brace Jovanovich.

Mitchell, Richard n.d. "Dancing at Armageddon: Doomsday and Survivalists in America." Unpub-lished paper, Oregon State University.

——— 1991 "Secrecy and Disclosure in Fieldwork." In W. Shaffir and R. Stebbins, eds., *Experiencing Fieldwork.* Newbury Park, Calif.: Sage.

Peterson, Richard G. 1984 "Preparing for Apocalypse: Survivalist Strategies." *Free Inquiry in Creative Sociol-ogy* 12:44–46.

Reich, Charles A. 1970 *The Greening of America.* New York: Random House.

Rochford, E. Burke 1985 *Hare Krishna in America.* New Brunswick, N.J.: Rutgers University Press.

Roszak, Theodore 1969 *The Making of a Counter Cul-ture.* New York: Doubleday.

Rothchild, John, and Susan Berns Wolf 1976 *The Children of the Counter-Culture.* New York: Double-day.

Spates, James L. 1976 "Counterculture and Dominant Culture Values: A Cross-National Analysis of the Underground Press and Dominant Culture Maga-zines." *American Sociological Review* 41:868–883.

Street, J. 1986 *Rebel Rock: The Politics of Popular Music.* Oxford: Basil Blackwell.

Tipton, Steven M. 1982 *Getting Saved from the Sixties.* Berkeley: University of California Press.

Turner, Ralph 1976 "The Real Self: From Institution to Impulse." *American Journal of Sociology* 81:989–1,016.

Wuthnow, Robert 1976 *The Consciousness Revolution.* Berkeley: University of California Press.

Yinger, J. Milton 1960 "Contraculture and Subcul-ture." *American Sociological Review* 25:625–635.

——— 1977 "Countercultures and Social Change." *American Sociological Review* 42:833–853.

——— 1982 *Countercultures.* New York: Free Press.

PATRICIA A. ADLER
PETER ADLER

**COURTSHIP** Given the centrality of the family institution in society, and the role of court-ship in the family formation process, it is not surprising that the study of courtship has received attention from several disciplines. Anthropolo-gists have described practices in primitive and other societies, historians have traced courtship patterns in America from colonial to contempo-rary times, psychologists and social psychologists have examined intra- and interpersonal compo-nents of relationships, and sociologists have developed research-based theories explaining the process of mate selection and have investigated its dynamics. Here, some attention will be given to each of these approaches, along the way selectively noting scholars who have made major contribu-tions.

Historically, according to Rothman, the term

*"courtship* applied to situations where the intention to marry was explicit (if not formally—and mutually—stated). *Courting* was the broader term used to describe socializing between unmarried men and women" (Rothman 1984, p. 23, italics in original).

Scholars have disagreed as to whether dating—a twentieth-century term for a primarily recreational aspect of courting—should be considered a part of courtship since, according to Waller (1938) and others, dating may be merely thrill seeking and exploitative and not marriage-oriented (see Gordon 1981 for an opposing view). However, wooing (that is, seeking favor, affection, love, or any of these) may be integral to courtship but need not result in marriage. For present purposes, then, courtship will be understood in its broadest sense—as a continuum from casual to serious. Thus, "the unattached flirt, the engaged college seniors, the eighth-grade 'steadies,' and the mismatched couple on a blind date are all engaging in courtship" (Bailey 1988, p. 6).

Queen, Habenstein, and Quadagno's (1985) classic text provides much of the basis for the following brief and highly generalized overview of some mate-selection patterns unlike those found in contemporary America. Some of these systems involve little or no courtship. For example, among the ancient Chinese, Hebrews, and Romans, marriage was arranged by male heads of kin groups. Among the ancient Greeks and until recently among the Chinese, many brides and grooms did not meet until their wedding day. Around the turn of the century, infant marriages were the rule among the Toda of south India, and the bride was deflowered at about age ten by a male who was not of her clan and not her husband. In medieval England, contrary to the literature of chivalry, love had little to do with mate selection in any social class because marriages were arranged by lords or parents with primary regard to the acquisition of property.

In societies where romantic love is not a basis for mate choice, such sentiments are seen as dangerous to the formation and stability of desirable marital unions—those that maintain stratification systems (see Goode 1969). Queen, Haben-

stein, and Quadagno (1985) describe still other mate-selection patterns that do involve courtship and some form of love, including the systems found on Israeli kibbutzim at midcentury, among ethnic immigrant groups in the United States, and among American blacks during slavery (see also Ramu 1989). Since the turn of the century, however, and especially since the 1920s, courtship in Western societies has been participant-run and based on romantic love. In the United States today, it is not uncommon for a couple to meet, woo, and wed almost without the knowledge of their respective kin. "Compared with other cultures, ours offers a wide range of choices and a minimum of control" (Queen, Habenstein, and Quadango 1985, pp. 8–9).

In colonial America, practices differed somewhat between the North and South. In the North, mate choice was participant-run, but a suitor's father had control over the timing of marriage because he might delay the release of an adequate section of family land to his son while his labor was needed. Conjugal (not romantic) love was the sine qua non of marriage, and couples came to know and trust one another during often lengthy courtships. In the South, a custom of chivalry developed, closely guarding the purity of (at least upper class) women but condoning promiscuity among men. Parental consent was required for the beginning of courtship and for marriage, and open bargaining about property arrangements was commonplace. Unlike the colonial north, where marriage was considered a civil ceremony, in most parts of the South, Anglican church ministers were required to officiate at weddings. In both regions, banns were published prior to weddings.

During the 1800s, mate choice became more autonomous with the growth of cities and the spread of industrial employment. Choices were affected less by wealth than by personal qualities —especially morality, spirituality, and "character." Wooing was rather formal, with each participant carefully evaluating the qualities of the other. Courtship tended to be exclusive and directed toward marriage.

Then, from about 1900 to World War II, there

was much "playing the field" (casual dating), gradually more exclusive dating (going steady), engagement, and, finally, wedding—a relatively fixed sequence. Following World War II, stages were typically marked by symbols (e.g., wearing a fraternity pin, then an engagement ring), each stage implying increased commitment between the partners. By the 1950s, a separate youth culture had developed. Ages at first marriage declined dramatically, and dating started earlier than ever before. The sexual exploration that had previously been part of the last stage of courtship now occurred earlier, even in very young couples.

During the 1960s, a time of "sexual revolution," nonmarital cohabitation increased in acceptability—not substituting for marriage but perhaps delaying it. In the postwar period and since, among the young especially, demands for both freedom and dependency (e.g., the right to sexual freedom without assuming responsibility for its multifaceted consequences) have been relatively widespread (Queen, Habenstein, and Quadango 1985, p. 271). Concurrently, rates of nonmarital pregnancy rose dramatically.

In general, every society attempts to control sexual activity among unmarried (and married) persons, but the forms of control (e.g., chaperonage) and the degree of enforcement have varied. Virginity, especially in women, is highly prized and guarded in some cultures but has no special value in others. Similarly, all societies attempt to constrain the pool of those eligible to marry, but the precise constraints have differed from society to society and from time to time. Typically, blood kin and relatives by marriage (and in some cases baptismal relatives such as godparents) are delimited to greater or lesser degrees from the eligibility pool.

Where male elders have arranged marriages for their offspring (generally in ascription-based societies), the accumulation of family power and prestige has been of primary concern, with dowries, bride prices, or both figuring importantly in prenuptial arrangements. In participant-run mate selection (generally in achievement-oriented societies), the power and prestige of a dating partner (although defined in terms other than land, cattle, and the like) is still valuable. Good looks in women (however defined), for instance, are a status symbol for men, and conspicuous consumption in men (cars, clothing, and spending habits) provides status for women. Thus, within the field of eligibles is a smaller field of desirables. Unfortunately, the qualities that are valued in dates (from among whom a mate may ultimately be chosen) are not necessarily those one would want in a spouse.

Even in participant-run "free choice" systems, there is a tendency toward homogamy in the selection of courtship partners, whether conscious or not. To the extent that a society becomes more varied in its mix of persons within residential, educational, religious, or work-related clusterings, the tendency toward heterogamy increases—that is, the fields of eligibles and desirables come to be more broadly defined. Heterogeneity leads to a prediction of "universal availability" (Farber 1964) as the salience of social categories declines. For example, interracial relationships, once unthinkable (e.g., in the American colonial South), increased with urbanization, industrialization, and a general movement toward educational and income equality.

Social class endogamy, however, is the general preference, although women are encouraged with varying degrees of subtlety to "marry up," and a dating differential exists such that men tend to court women who are slightly younger, physically smaller, and somewhat less well educated or affluent than themselves.

Contemporary courtship, marked as it is by freedom of choice, has been likened to a market in which the buyer must be wary and in which there is no necessary truth in advertising. Persons compete, given their own assets, for the best marital catch or the most status-conferring date. Waller and Hill (1951) warned about the exploitative potential in both casual and serious courtship, and, indeed, critics of conventional dating have decried it as a sexist bargaining arrangement in which men are exploited for money and women for sexual favors. The superficiality of dating, its commercialization, the deceit involved (given contradictory motives), and the high levels of anxiety produced by fears of rejection (especially in men) are additional drawbacks. Since status differentials still characterize the sexes, dating may also be seen as a contest in which a struggle for power and control between partners is part of the game. Thus, courtship's emphasis on individualism, freedom, commercialism, competitive spirit, and success reflects the larger social system within which it functions. One may well ask whether such a system prepares participants in any sense for marriage, which requires cooperation and compromise for its survival.

Efforts to predict who marries whom and why, to delineate the courtship process itself, or both, have interested a number of scholars. Based on a large body of theoretical and empirical work, Adams (1979) developed a propositional theory to explain how courtship moves from initial acquaintance toward (or away from) marriage in an achievement-oriented society. The propositions, in slightly modified language, are as follows:

1. Proximity, which facilitates contact, is a precondition for courtship and marriage.
2. As time passes, marriage is increasingly more likely to be with a currently propinquitous than with a formerly propinquitous partner.
3. Propinquity increases the likelihood that one will meet, be attracted to, and marry someone of the same social categories as himself or herself.
4. Early attraction is a result of immediate stimuli such as physical attractiveness, valued surface behaviors, and similar interests.
5. The more favorable the reactions of significant others to an early relationship, the more likely the relationship will progress beyond the early attraction stage.
6. The more positive the reaction of the partners to self-disclosures, the better the rapport between the pair.
7. The better the rapport between the pair, the more likely the relationship will be perpetuated beyond the early attraction stage.
8. The greater the value compatibility-consensus between partners, the more likely that the relationship will progress to a deeper level of attraction.

9. The greater the similarity in physical attractiveness between the partners, the more likely that the relationship will progress to a deeper level of attraction.
10. The more the partners' personalities are similar, the more likely that the relationship will progress to a deeper level of attraction.
11. The more salient the categorical homogeneity of the partners, the more likely that the relationship will progress to a deeper level of attraction.
12. The more salient the categorical heterogeneity of the partners, the more likely that the relationship will terminate either before or after reaching a deeper level of attraction.
13. The greater the unfavorable parental intrusion, the more likely that a relationship will terminate either before or after reaching a deeper level of attraction.
14. An alternative attraction to the current partner may arise at any stage of a couple's relationship. The stronger that alternative attraction to either partner, the greater the likelihood that the original couple's relationship will terminate.
15. The greater the role compatibility of couple members, the more likely that the relationship will be perpetuated.
16. The greater the empathy between couple members, the more likely that the relationship will be perpetuated.
17. The more each of the partners defines the other as "right" or "the best I can get," the less likely it is that the relationship will terminate short of marriage.
18. The more a relationship moves to the level of pair communality, the less likely it is that it will terminate short of marriage.
19. The more a relationship moves through a series of formal and informal escalators, the less likely it is to terminate short of marriage. (Adams 1979, pp. 260–267)

Adams (1979) provides some caveats about these propositions. First, some factors (such as a partner's good looks) have greater salience for men than for women, while some (such as a partner's empathic capacity) have greater salience for women than for men. Second, some factors such as parental interference may have different outcomes in the long run compared to the short run. Third, the timing of courtship may bring different considerations into play, e.g., courtship in later life such as following divorce or widowhood, when children from previous marriages must be considered (see Bulcroft and O'Connor 1986). Finally, social class factors may affect the predictive value of the propositions. Bernard (1964) distinguished between parallel and interactional marriages—parallel (or traditional) arrangements are more often found in the working class and among certain ethnic groups, while interactional (or equalitarian) arrangements are more likely to characterize the middle class. Thus, the kind of marriage one anticipates may influence the mate-selection process. (See also Aronson 1972 for specifications of the conditions under which various interpersonal attraction predictors such as propinquity and similar interests operate.)

Further, as courtship has moved away from the fixed-stages sequence of development, it may be best viewed through a circular-causal model (Stephen 1985), in which progress is strongly influenced by communication within the couple, leading to increased (or decreased) movement toward marriage.

The timing of marriage may be influenced by such factors as meaningful employment opportunities for women (which may diminish their motivation to marry), the increasing acceptability of nonmarital cohabitation and adult singlehood (see Stein 1981), and the effects of nonmarital pregnancy or of various intolerable conditions in the family of origin (Adams 1979).

Regarding premarital factors that contribute to later marital adjustment, no scholar has presented evidence to refute Kirkpatrick's ([1955] 1963) conclusions: happiness of parents' marriage; adequate length of courtship; adequate sex information in childhood; a happy childhood including a harmonious relationship with parents; approval of the courtship relationship by significant others; good premarital adjustment of the couple and

strong motivation to marry; homogamy along age, racial-ethnic, and religious lines; and later age (late twenties) at marriage.

In his review of mate-selection scholarship from the 1970s, Murstein (1980) predicted that there would be less focus in the future on such "old standby" variables as race, class, and religion and more on the dynamic aspects of courtship. Murstein was correct. What follows is an attempt to identify some of the major themes that have interested students of courtship phenomena in recent years.

With regard to cohabitation, early studies included efforts to identify its types, both structural and motivational. Later studies focused on the effects of cohabitation on subsequent marital happiness and satisfaction, finding, almost uniformly, that living with someone unmarried has little or no positive effect. Some studies find a negative effect on marital adjustment, partly attributable to the qualities of persons who choose this still nonconventional arrangement (but see Popenoe 1987 for a different view of cohabitation in a setting where it is more normative).

As rates of sexual activity outside of marriage rose, and as sex (especially since the advent of the birth control pill in the 1960s) was disengaged to some extent from procreation, research and theoretical interest focused on changes in sexual behavior and values. (See Schur 1988 for a highly negative view of the "Americanization" of sex.) Also on the negative side of the ledger, there is concern about the spread of sexually transmitted diseases and on factors related to the use (or nonuse) of "safe" sexual practices. Research continues to examine variations in premarital sexual activity rates and their effects.

The study of courtship processes has become part of the broader study of "close" or "intimate" relationships (see Brehm 1985) as practices have changed from stylized conventional dating to the more informal "hanging out" and "partying," and from the-man-always-pays norm to sharing expenses. In part, this follows from a weakening of the normative imperative to marry (Thornton 1989) and in part from a trend toward more egalitarian relationships between the sexes. However, in almost all research, male/female similarities and differences continue to form part of data analysis.

Considerable research interest has been devoted to identifying the components of conventional masculinity and femininity and their effects and on resistance to change in these stereotypes—for example, because of ongoing conventional socialization practices and, as communications experts have documented, because of the effects of various media portrayals supporting the status quo ante. Scholars have also noted the greater likelihood of relational success among androgynous than among conventionally masculine men and feminine women (Cancian 1986).

Barriers to understanding between the sexes have been investigated, including the effects of stereotyping (noted above), and research has extended to the study of "taboo" conversational topics in courtship, degrees and forms of honesty and deception, communication style differences between men and women, and methods of conflict resolution that enhance relationship survival or presage breakup. Interest in failed relationships has attempted to identify factors at both individual and dyadic levels that might have predicted which pairings would last and which would not.

Early-encounter studies have examined the efficacy (or lack of it) of "opening lines," of flirtation patterns leading to meetings, and of "scripts" for early dates and their persistence across social time. In ongoing relationships, scholars have investigated the positive and negative effects of outside influences such as parental and peer pressures, and the parts played by same- and cross-sex friends. Other topics of concern have included barriers to the development of trust and the effects of its loss, the meanings of commitment, and the effects of self-disclosure, self-esteem, self-awareness, and jealousy on close relationships.

Recent years have witnessed a virtual explosion in the study of love—attempts to identify its forms, its properties, its distribution of types across women and men, and the effects of all of these, especially in terms of romantic love. Interestingly, and again on the negative side, a number of studies of courtship violence have shown rela-

tively high rates of this kind of activity but also reveal that a sizeable minority of those who have experienced violence in a close relationship identify it with a loving motive. This seemingly odd justification is readily explained by the practice of parents, when using violence against their children, of indicating that they do it "out of love." Thus, the lesson (or the rationalization) is learned early. Other negative aspects of courtship include the study of "mind games" and other facets of competition between partners, sexual aggression including date rape, and the effects of contrasts between ideal images and courtship realities.

As courtship itself has expanded, researchers have taken interest in an expanded range of relationship types (Buunk and van Driel 1989). For example, the romantic involvements between lesbian women and between gay men have been studied and compared with those between heterosexual partners. A predictable area for future study is the recently legalized status of relationships between same-sex partners.

Other relatively recent innovations such as video- and computer-matching and personal advertisements in print media have also captured researchers' attention. Another fairly recent development is the increased use of prenuptial agreements, and scholars may be expected to pursue the study of their impact on relationships. To a lesser extent, older lines of research have continued to probe the purported decline of or changes in the double standard, the "principle of least interest" (Waller 1938) as related to changes in gender roles, the dimensions of intimacy (including the crucial component of communication), motivators toward marriage and toward single adult status, and on desired traits in partners as these may differ (or not) between dates and mates. Interrelationships between variables have also received wider attention.

As society grows more complex and as the rate of change seems increasingly rapid, confusion over the mate-selection process appears to be rife. A recent study of college student dating shows that these young adults have questions about virtually every aspect of the process and the choices they make (Laner 1989). High divorce rates in recent years have produced a backlash of insecurity as the marriage decision approaches. This is reflected in the frequently voiced question, "How can I be *sure* of making the right choice in a partner?" Sociologists and scholars in related disciplines continue to study a growing set of factors that shed light on the answer.

(SEE ALSO: *Alternative Life-Styles; Love; Mate Selection Theories*)

### REFERENCES

Adams, Bert N. 1979 "Mate Selection in the United States: A Theoretical Summarization." In W. R. Burr, R. Hill, F. I. Nye, and I. L. Reiss, eds., *Contemporary Theories about the Family*. New York: Free Press.

Aronson, Elliot 1972 *The Social Animal*. New York: Viking.

Bailey, Beth L. 1988 *From Front Porch to Back Seat: Courtship in Twentieth-Century America*. Baltimore: Johns Hopkins University Press.

Bernard, Jessie 1964 "The Adjustments of Married Mates." In H. T. Christensen, ed., *The Handbook of Marriage and the Family*. Chicago: Rand McNally.

Brehm, Sharon S. 1985 *Intimate Relationships*. New York: Random House.

Bulcroft, Kris, and Margaret O'Connor 1986 "The Importance of Dating Relationships on Quality of Life for Older Persons." *Family Relations* 35:397–401.

Buunk, Bram P., and Barry van Driel 1989 *Variant Lifestyles and Relationships*. Newbury Park, Calif.: Sage.

Cancian, Francesca 1986 "The Feminization of Love." *Signs* 11:692–709.

Farber, Bernard 1964 *Family Organization and Interaction*. San Francisco: Chandler.

Goode, William J. 1969 "The Theoretical Importance of Love." *American Sociological Review* 34:38–47.

Gordon, Michael 1981 "Was Waller Ever Right? The Rating and Dating Complex Reconsidered." *Journal of Marriage and the Family* 43:67–76.

Kirkpatrick, Clifford [1955] 1963 *The Family as Process and Institution*, 2nd ed. New York: Ronald.

Laner, Mary R. 1989 *Dating: Delights, Discontents, and Dilemmas*. Salem, Wisc.: Sheffield.

Murstein, Bernard I. 1980 "Mate Selection in the 1970s." *Journal of Marriage and the Family* 42:777–792.

Popenoe, David 1987 "Beyond the Nuclear Family: A Statistical Portrait of the Changing Family in Sweden." *Journal of Marriage and the Family* 49:173–183.

Queen, Stuart A., Robert W. Habenstein, and Jill S. Quadagno 1985 *The Family in Various Cultures*, 5th ed. New York: Harper and Row.

Ramu, G. N. 1989 "Patterns of Mate Selection." In K. Ishwaran, ed., *Family and Marriage: Cross-Cultural Perspectives*. Toronto: Wall and Thompson.

Rothman, Ellen K. 1984 *Hands and Hearts: A History of Courtship in America*. New York: Basic Books.

Schur, Edwin M. 1988 *The Americanization of Sex*. Philadelphia: Temple University Press.

Stein, Peter J. (ed.) 1981 *Single Life: Unmarried Adults in Social Context*. New York: St. Martin's.

Stephen, Timothy D. 1985 "Fixed-Sequence and Circular-Causal Models of Relationship Development: Divergent Views on the Role of Communication in Intimacy." *Journal of Marriage and the Family* 47:955–963.

Thornton, Arland 1989 "Changing Attitudes toward Family Issues in the United States." *Journal of Marriage and the Family* 51:873–893.

Waller, Willard 1938 "The Rating and Dating Complex." *American Sociological Review* 2:727–734.

Waller, Willard, and Reuben Hill 1951 *The Family: A Dynamic Interpretation*, rev. ed. New York: Dryden.

MARY RIEGE LANER

## COURT SYSTEMS OF THE UNITED STATES

The American court system is composed of several jurisdictional and hierarchical structures. While these structures are somewhat complex, they delineate the fundamental ways in which courts are organized.

The first and most important distinction is between state and federal courts. All fifty states and the District of Columbia have their own independent court systems for the adjudication of state cases, over which they have jurisdiction. In addition, the United States as a whole has a federal court system, which is completely separate from the state systems in its jurisdictional boundaries and hierarchical structure. Superimposed on this federal–state stratification of courts are still other methods by which courts are organized. Specifically, within both the federal and state systems, there are courts whose subject matter jurisdiction is limited to certain types of cases. For example, there are special bankruptcy courts in the federal system, while many states have courts exclusively for juvenile offenders.

Turning first to the separate hierarchies within the various court systems, it is important to note that each state has a system of lower courts and higher courts (e.g., trial courts and appellate courts), as does the United States. Moreover, the hierarchy may differ within those systems depending on the subject matter of the case. For example, Texas has a separate appellate court for criminal cases; in the federal system, while most courts of appeals are regional, one such court hears appeals from all federal trial courts when the substantive issue at hand is a patent matter. Finally, there is a certain amount of interaction between the state and federal courts. Not only does the jurisdiction of lower state and federal courts sometimes overlap, but the U.S. Supreme Court, under certain circumstances, has the authority to review the ruling of a state supreme court.

## THE FEDERAL SYSTEM

In Article III of the Constitution, the Framers established the U.S. Supreme Court and authorized Congress to create lower federal courts. In the Judiciary Act of 1789, Congress established the federal district courts as the trial courts and the circuit courts of appeal to review the decisions of the lower trial courts. The district courts are the general courts of original jurisdiction in the federal system. Congress has divided the nation into ninety-four federal districts, each with its own district court (28 U.S.C. § 81–131). Every state has at least one federal district within its boundaries; some of the larger states contain as many as four federal districts. The number of federal district court judges appointed to serve in each district depends on the caseload in the district. For example, the district of Wyoming has two district

court judges, while the Southern District of New York has twenty-seven (28 U.S.C. § 133). In 1988, a total of 284,219 cases were commenced in federal district courts nationwide (Administrative Office of the United States Courts 1988, pp. 8, 14).

Continuing up the hierarchy, above the district courts in the federal system are the courts of appeals. In general, cases appealed from the ninety-four federal district courts are reviewed by one of the courts of appeals. Congress has created thirteen circuits, each with its own court of appeals. Twelve of the circuits are territorial; that is, each encompasses one or more of the ninety-four districts. For example, the Seventh Circuit hears appeals from the federal trial courts of Illinois, Indiana, and Wisconsin. Thus, a litigant wishing to challenge a decision of the federal district court for the Southern District of Indiana would appeal to the Court of Appeals for the Seventh Circuit. The thirteenth court of appeals is the Federal Circuit, created in 1982; the Federal Circuit is unique in that it has nationwide appellate jurisdiction over certain specialized areas of federal law including customs, international trade, patent, and trademark cases (28 U.S.C. § 1295).

Whereas cases in the district courts are heard by a single trial judge, cases before the courts of appeals are heard by a panel of three circuit court judges. In 1988, a total of 37,524 appeals were commenced before the thirteen federal courts of appeals (Administrative Office of the United States Courts 1988, p. 2).

The highest court in the federal system is, of course, the U.S. Supreme Court. The Supreme Court reviews decisions of the courts of appeals, and in some cases it reviews the decisions of the district courts. Unlike the federal courts of appeals, the Supreme Court has complete discretion as to which cases it will hear. That is, litigants seeking to challenge a lower court decision have no right to be heard by the Supreme Court. Rather, they must petition the Court for a "writ of certiorari"; their case will be heard only if the Supreme Court decides to grant the petition (28 U.S.C. §§ 1254, 1257). Because of the flood of litigants seeking Supreme Court review, the Court grants only a small percentage of the petitions for writs of certiorari it receives. In 1986, the Supreme Court granted review in only 6.3 percent of the total cases docketed, not counting cases summarily decided without opinion (Bator, Mishkin, Meltzer, and Shapiro 1984, p. 1855). In certain rare cases, the Supreme Court does have original jurisdiction, such as when one state sues another state (Art. III).

In addition to the three levels of federal courts discussed above, there are a number of specialized courts in the federal system. These courts hear cases involving special areas of federal law, cases whose volume or complexity would place too great a burden on the federal district courts. Examples of these courts are the United States Bankruptcy Courts, the United States Tax Court, and the United States Claims Court.

The creation of these specialized courts by Congress brings to light the distinction between so-called constitutional and legislative courts in the federal system. Article III of the Constitution mandates that "the judicial Power of the United States shall be vested in one supreme Court, and in such inferior Courts as the Congress may from time to time ordain and establish." Article III also provides that judges of both the Supreme Court and the lower courts "shall hold their Offices during good Behaviour," which effectively grants them life tenure. In addition, Article III prohibits Congress from diminishing the compensation of these judges while they are in office.

The purpose of these provisions was to ensure that federal judges are insulated from political pressure exercised by the other branches of government as well as the public. In *The Federalist* No. 78, Alexander Hamilton referred to the "good behavior" provision as "the best expedient in any government, to secure a steady, upright and impartial administration of laws" (Wills 1982, p. 393). Indeed, Hamilton considered the permanency of judicial office as "the citadel of the public justice and the public security" (Wills 1982, p. 394). Hamilton went on to note that, besides life tenure, "nothing can contribute more to the independence of the judges than a fixed

provision for their support," because "a power over a man's subsistence amounts to a power over his will" (Wills 1982, p. 400).

Interestingly, in creating the specialized courts delimited above (e.g., the United States Claims Court), Congress decided not to imbue the judges of these courts with the protections of Article III. There are any number of reasons Congress may have wished to avoid creating more Article III judges. By not doing so, Congress retains greater flexibility to adjust its response to whatever problem it seeks to address by creating the court. Importantly, because Congress created these specialized courts under its Article I rather than its Article III authority, these courts are known as "legislative" or "Article I" courts.

The authority of a non-Article III court to exercise judicial power presents a complicated issue of constitutional law. Alexander Hamilton's remarks notwithstanding, Justice Sandra Day O'Connor noted in a recent majority opinion that "an absolute construction of Article III is not possible" and that "the Court has long recognized that Congress is not barred from acting pursuant to its powers under Article I to vest decisionmaking authority in tribunals that lack the attributes of Article III courts" (*Thomas v. Union Carbide Agricultural Products Co.* 1985, p. 583). However, the scope of this congressional authority has never clearly been defined. Several commentators have suggested that current Supreme Court jurisprudence indicates that the validity of laws that give legislative courts the authority to adjudicate cases arising under federal law depends on a balancing of the concerns that prompted Congress to create the court against the Article III values of judicial independence (Bator, Mishkin, Meltzer and Shapiro 1988, p. 470).

## THE STATE SYSTEMS

Turning now to the state court systems, all fifty states and the District of Columbia have their own court systems. Each state has trial courts that serve as the general courts of original jurisdiction for the state. In addition, many states have intermediate appellate courts as well as a supreme court, paralleling the hierarchical structure of the federal system. A number of smaller states (such as Iowa and Rhode Island) have only two levels of courts, with no intermediary review between the lower courts and the highest court. In many states, judges at all levels of the state court system are elected by the public. These judges, much like the legislators and the governor, serve fixed terms. This practice is in striking contrast to the federal system, in which all Article III judges are appointed for life terms. A few states follow the federal model in this regard (New Jersey, for example), but they are the exception rather than the rule.

As in the federal court system, many states additionally have specialized courts that have particular subject matter jurisdiction over particular types of cases. For example, a number of states have special courts for juvenile proceedings, family law matters, and probate cases.

## INTERACTION OF THE FEDERAL AND STATE SYSTEMS

As noted previously, every federal district overlaps geographically with at least one state (if one includes the District of Columbia). Not surprisingly, there is a considerable amount of interaction between the state and federal courts. To understand this interaction, one must first consider the comparative jurisdictions of the two court systems.

The jurisdiction of federal courts can be divided into two broad categories: "federal question" jurisdiction and "diversity" jurisdiction. The first of these two categories is derived from the language of Article III of the Constitution, which states that federal courts may be given jurisdiction over cases "arising under this Constitution, the Laws of the United States, and Treaties made, or which shall be made, under their authority." For the federal court to have jurisdiction, the federal question must be "substantial"; as a result, federal courts lack jurisdiction if the federal claim upon which the plaintiff (the complaining party) bases jurisdiction is obviously frivolous or without merit (Wright, Miller, and Cooper 1984, vol. 13b, p. 68).

Most federal question jurisdiction is based on federal statutory law. Congress does not have the authority to pass whatever laws it pleases; Congress may legislate only according to the specific mandates of authority prescribed in the Constitution. However, these provisions have been read quite liberally, such that federal law now encompasses a very broad range of activity in both the areas of civil and criminal law. To illustrate, the modern federal criminal laws proscribing illegal drug possession and distribution are based on Congress's power to regulate interstate commerce (Abrams 1986, p. 342). Not surprisingly, federal law often regulates the same conduct as does state law. For example, the federal narcotics laws noted above overlap substantially with many state laws. As a result, almost all drug trafficking cases can be prosecuted in either federal or state court. The decision whether to proceed federally or in the state rests with the prosecutor to whom the case is presented.

In many cases, plaintiffs in civil cases will seek to advance both federal and state claims. For example, a plaintiff who feels that her patent has been infringed may couple a federal patent infringement claim with a state unfair competition claim. To accommodate these situations, federal courts have developed a doctrine known as "pendent jurisdiction." Under this doctrine, a federal court may hear a state law claim if it derives from the same "common nucleus of operative fact" as the federal claim (*United Mine Workers v. Gibbs* 1966, p. 725).

The second category of federal court jurisdiction is "diversity" jurisdiction. As with federal question jurisdiction, diversity jurisdiction has its origins in Article III of the Constitution. That provision contains a clause giving Congress the power to vest jurisdiction in the federal courts over cases that involve a dispute between citizens of different states or between a citizen of a state and an alien. Although there is some debate over the intent of the Framers in enshrining federal diversity jurisdiction in the Constitution, the traditional explanation emphasizes a fear that state courts would be prejudiced against out-of-state litigants (Wright, Miller, and Cooper 1984, vol. 13b, p. 338). Under current law, federal courts may hear diversity cases only if the amount in controversy exceeds $50,000 (28 U.S.C. § 1332).

In contrast to this limited federal jurisdiction, state courts have much broader authority to hear disputes. Naturally, state courts have subject matter jurisdiction over all claims based on state law. In addition, state courts have jurisdiction over many federal law claims, except where Congress has given exclusive jurisdiction to the federal courts (bankruptcy, for example).

The subject matter of the lawsuit is not, however, the only consideration in establishing whether a state court has jurisdiction over a dispute. State courts are limited in their ability to exercise personal jurisdiction over litigants who are not in-state residents. In other words, a California court does not automatically have jurisdiction over a defendant who resides in Oklahoma. The United States Supreme Court has held that for a state court to have jurisdiction over individuals (or corporations) who are not residents, the individual must have some "minimum contacts" with that state (*International Shoe Co. v. State of Washington* 1945, p. 316). This requirement will not be satisfied unless the defendant "purposely avails" himself of the "privilege of conducting activities within the forum state" (*Hanson v. Denckla* 1958, p. 253). In other words, there must be evidence of some purposeful act by the defendant, which makes it foreseeable that he could be subject to suit in the forum state (Friedenthal, Kane, and Miller 1985, p. 132).

In the final analysis, federal and state courts often have overlapping original jurisdiction. This interaction extends to the appellate review process, although in a limited manner. The United States Supreme Court is the ultimate arbiter of federal law; similarly, the highest court in a state has the final word as to that state's law. To illustrate, if a litigant loses an appeal on a state law claim in the Virginia Supreme Court, that litigant has no recourse to the United States Supreme Court. On the other hand, if the litigant's claim was based on federal law, he can appeal the Virginia Supreme Court's decision to the United States Supreme Court. The analysis becomes more complex when the litigant's appeal is based on both federal and state law. The established rule provides that if the judgment of the state court is based on a nonfederal ground that is "independent of the federal ground and adequate to support the judgment," the United States Supreme Court has no jurisdiction to hear an appeal of the state court decision (*Fox Film Corp. v. Muller* 1935, p. 210). This "independent and adequate state ground" requirement has proven to be quite difficult in its application (Bator, Mishkin, Meltzer, and Shapiro 1988, p. 536). To elaborate, state courts are often ambiguous as to the grounds for their decisions in cases with both federal and state law issues. In these situations, the U.S. Supreme Court has ruled that unless it is clear from the face of the state court opinion that the decision rests on an independent and adequate state ground, the U.S. Supreme Court has jurisdiction over the case (*Michigan v. Long* 1983, p. 1042).

It is appropriate to examine the different major actors who operate within court systems. As discussed previously, judges in the federal system are appointed for life terms by the President with the advice and consent of the United States Senate; state court judges are generally elected, rather than appointed, for a specific rather than a life term. This distinction holds true for prosecutors. In the federal system, there is a chief prosecutor in each of the federal districts. These prosecutors are known as United States Attorneys; they are appointed by the President, with the advice and consent of the United States Senate. United States Attorneys are in the executive branch of government; as such, they are in a completely distinct hierarchical structure than are federal judges, who are located in the judicial branch. Unlike judges, U.S. Attorneys are under the supervision of the Attorney General of the United States and ultimately the President.

In state systems, the chief prosecutors are almost always elected by the public to fixed terms. They typically are referred to as "district attorneys," and they usually serve a county, local district, or other political subdivision of the state. Similar to the federal system, each state also has an attorney general; unlike the Attorney General for the United States who is appointed by the

President, state attorneys general are usually elected to serve as the chief law enforcement officer in the state.

Private attorneys, both publicly and privately compensated, often practice in both the federal and the state court systems. However, all fifty states and the federal courts regulate separately the attorneys who practice within their respective court systems. As a result, an attorney who wishes to argue a case in a Vermont state court must be admitted to the Vermont bar; attorneys wishing to appear in federal court must be members of the federal bar.

Finally, in both the federal and state systems there are probation officers. Probation officers serve as an arm of the court and play a crucial role in the criminal justice arena. The primary task of probation officers is to monitor the behavior of convicted offenders who are placed on probation or some form of supervised release. In addition, probation officers act as independent fact finders for judges; in this regard they often play a key role at sentencing. This is especially true in the federal system, where probation officers' calculations of the appropriate sentencing range under the new federal guidelines are referred to by judges in determining sentences.

(SEE ALSO: *Criminal Sanctions; Criminology; Law and Legal Systems; Law and Society; Sociology of Law*)

### REFERENCES

#### BOOKS

Abrams, Norman 1986 *Federal Criminal Law and Its Enforcement*. St. Paul, Minn.: West.

Administrative Office of the United States Courts 1988 *Annual Report of the Administrative Office of the United States Courts 1988*. Washington, D.C.: U.S. Government Printing Office.

Bator, Paul M., Paul J. Mishkin, Daniel J. Meltzer, and David L. Shapiro 1984 *Hart and Weschler's The Federal Courts and the Federal System*, 3rd ed. Westbury, N.Y.: Foundation Press.

Friedenthal, Jack H., Mary Kay Kane, and Arthur R. Miller 1985 *Civil Procedure*. St. Paul, Minn.: West.

Wills, Garry (ed.) 1982 *The Federalist Papers*. New York: Bantam Books.

Wright, Charles A., Arthur R. Miller, and Edward H. Cooper 1984 *Federal Practice and Procedure*. 2d ed. Vols. 13, 13b. St. Paul, Minn.: West.

#### CASES

*Fox Film Corp. v. Muller,* 296 U.S. 207 (1935).

*Hanson v. Denckla,* 357 U.S. 235 (1958).

*Michigan v. Long,* 463 U.S. 1032 (1983).

*International Shoe Company v. State of Washington,* 326 U.S. 310 (1945).

*Thomas v. Union Carbide Agricultural Products Co.,* 473 U.S. 568 (1985).

*United Mine Workers v. Gibbs,* 383 U.S. 715 (1966).

#### STATUTES

28 U.S.C.A. §§ 81–131, 133 (West 1968 & Supp. 1990).

28 U.S.C.A. §§ 1254, 1257 (West 1966 & Supp. 1990).

28 U.S.C.A. § 1295 (West 1966 & Supp. 1990).

28 U.S.C.A. § 1332 (West 1966 & Supp. 1990).

ILENE H. NAGEL
NICOLAS D. MANSFIELD

**CRIME DETERRENCE**   Attempts to prevent and control crime have employed three principal techniques, each based on a particular view of the causes of crime and the nature of the criminal. *Incapacitation* seeks to control crime by making it physically impossible for an offender to commit a crime (Cohen 1983). Imprisonment, castration of rapists, and execution are each a form of incapacitation. Policies based on incapacitation assume offenders behave reflexively and impulsively, paying little attention to the consequences of their actions. *Deterrence* attempts to prevent crime by threatening potential offenders with legal punishment. Policies based on deterrence assume offenders are sensitive to incentives and deliberately choose to commit crime because the rewards outweigh the costs (Becker 1968). *Rehabilitation* attempts to control crime through reeducating or resocializing offenders and by treating rather than punishing them (Cullen and Gilbert 1982). Policies based on rehabilitation can be compatible with either of the above conceptions of the offender.

Criminal justice policies of modern societies generally reflect belief in deterrence and view criminals as freely choosing actors. While deterrence had long been a major goal of punishment, in eighteenth-century Europe it came to form the centerpiece of the movement for legal and penal reform. In an age when the death penalty was widely available but relatively infrequently employed, reformers such as Cesare Beccaria and Jeremy Bentham argued that the severity of punishments should vary according to the gravity of the crime; that is, that punishments be both harsh enough to counterbalance the gains from crime and moderate enough that judges, juries, and prosecutors would be prepared to carry them out. Potential offenders would be convinced of the credibility of punishment and thereby be deterred (Beccaria 1977).

The central tenet of deterrence—that the avoidance of pain is a primary motivation for behavior—corresponds to common sense and experience. Many can think of times they have complied with a law only because of the anticipated or actual presence of a police officer. The crime waves that accompany police strikes further illustrate the limits of voluntary conformity (Russell 1975). These are real-world examples of *general deterrence,* or the inhibiting effect of the threat of punishment on potential offenders. Almost any criminal justice system can be said to have some general deterrent effect on crime. However, there have also been questions raised about the extensiveness of deterrence. Most people are aware that many of those punished by the criminal justice system continue to engage in crime. Such high rates of recidivism testify to the limits of *specific deterrence,* or the inhibiting effect of punishment on the punished person's subsequent behavior (Martinson 1974).

Not even the strongest advocates of deterrence argue that *absolute deterrence*—the complete prevention of crime through threatened or actual legal punishment—is possible. Instead, most policies and public debates focus on *partial deterrence,* the reduction in crime from its level were there no punishment, or *marginal deterrence,* the reduction in crime from increasing the punishment by some increment (Zimring and Hawkins 1973). The widely acknowledged limits to absolute deterrence have also shaped the questions addressed by researchers. Rather than asking whether deterrence works, most research examines under what conditions, for what types of persons, behaviors, or both, and through what characteristics of punishment deterrence is likely to work.

Three deterrent characteristics of punishment—its certainty, severity, and celerity (speed)—are generally acknowledged as significant, with certainty considered to be the most important of these (Gibbs 1975). These three aspects of punishment often influence one another and interact to produce complex effects on criminal behavior. For example, even the most horrendous punishment is unlikely to deter if there is almost no probability of its occurrence; that is, extremely high severity accompanied by low certainty limits the deterrent effect of a penalty. Alternatively, when the certainty of punishment is increased—for example, through more efficient policing—the court and penal systems can become overloaded. This may reduce the speed, severity, and hence the deterrent effect of punishments.

Despite the formative role deterrence has played in policies of crime prevention and control, it has been systematically studied only in recent decades. Much has been learned about the potential for controlling crime through the threat of legal punishments, although the complexities associated with answering even basic questions about deterrence have also been highlighted. Perhaps the most common question asked by policy makers and the public is whether a change in a law or its enforcement will affect the crime rate. That is, how much partial, general deterrence will result if sentences for crimes are lengthened or arrest rates are increased?

Research has taken two approaches to answering this question. In one, geographical areas that differ in their legal penalties (e.g., cities, states, countries) are compared to see if these differences are reflected in their crime rates. Some of the earliest research on deterrence used this technique to examine the deterrent effect of the death penalty (Sellin 1959). Since then, a number of such *cross-sectional* studies have used official statistics to study the relationship between punishment and major forms of crime. A second technique involves comparing the crime rates in a single jurisdiction before and after changes in legislation or enforcement practices. This *time-series* approach has been used, for example, to assemble a large body of data on changes in drinking and driving laws and their enforcement (Ross 1984). An important insight from this research is that the deterrent effect of enhanced legal threats may wear off over time.

Both of these techniques are examples of *aggregate-level* analyses, in which group characteristics, rather than perceptions and behaviors of individuals, are studied. Much aggregate-level research has found a deterrent effect for the certainty of punishment by demonstrating, for example, that the higher the likelihood of arrest (or imprisonment) in an area the lower its crime rate (Gibbs 1986). In contrast to the certainty of punishment, the severity of punishment (e.g., prison sentence length) appears to have either weak or no deterrent effects in aggregate-level research.

These conclusions must be interpreted with caution, however. Critics have questioned whether an aggregate approach can accurately estimate deterrent effects for a number of reasons (Blumstein, Cohen, and Nagin 1978). Aggregate-level studies rely on official data on crime and punishment, which can distort estimates of the true incidence of criminal behavior and the true probability of punishment. In addition, it can be difficult to determine whether a relationship between punishment and crime is, in fact, due to the effect of the former on the latter (a deterrent effect). Crime rates may decrease as punishment becomes more certain or severe because more criminals are incapacitated for longer periods of time, not because potential offenders are deterred by threats of punishment. Furthermore, in cross-sectional studies, it may be impossible to rule out the possibility that differences in crime rates lead to differences in the certainty or severity of punishment rather than vice versa. For example, if areas with very low crime rates can expend more

resources on capturing each criminal, low crime rates could raise the certainty of punishment. Finally, in both aggregate cross-sectional and time-series studies, it is unlikely that all of the factors that might influence the rates of both crime and punishment will be taken into account. Unless they are, estimates of the deterrent effect of punishment will be inaccurate.

Other disadvantages of aggregate-level research concern the absence of information on individuals and the situations in which they make decisions about crime. Because aggregate-level research does not examine the perceptions and behaviors of individuals, it ignores the crucial psychological processes in deterrence. There is no way to determine if the people who are most fearful of punishment are those least likely to engage in crime. Aggregate-level research does not reveal whether certain types of people are more likely to be deterred than others or *how* threats of punishment act to deter crime. Is it because people fear the experience of being arrested, tried, convicted, and jailed? Is it because they fear they will lose their friends, family, and job opportunities? Is it because the existence of certain and severe punishments teaches and reaffirms the morality of conforming behavior?

These types of questions, which could be crucial to formulating effective crime control policies, can best be addressed through *individual-level* research. Individual-level research collects information on people's perceptions or experiences of legal punishments and on their criminal behavior. Because it can study both those who have actually experienced punishment and those who have only anticipated it, individual-level research provides insights into both specific and general deterrence. Three types of individual-level research have contributed to our knowledge about deterrence in recent years: *perceptual studies, field experiments,* and *observational studies.*

Perceptual studies ask people to estimate their chances of being punished (certainty) if they committed a crime and the undesirability of the punishment (severity) they would receive. People are also asked either to estimate their chances of engaging in crime or report their actual criminal activity. In addition, they may be asked to indicate what it is they fear about the possibility of punishment. The most valid of these studies interview people first about their perceptions of punishment and then, typically months later, about their criminal activity; this ensures that the perceptions came before the behavior rather than vice versa (Williams and Hawkins 1986).

As in aggregate-level research, evidence from perceptual research is mixed. Among conventional people, the fear of informal consequences of punishment—the loss of family, friends, or reputation—has much more influence on behavior than does the fear of arrest or imprisonment (Tittle 1980). In other words, the perceived threat of legal punishment does appear to have some general deterrent effect, but its effect is largely indirect, rather than directly due to legal reactions. For those who have committed crimes and been punished, their estimates of the likelihood of further punishment appear to matter little for their behavior; instead, they place much more weight on expectations of criminal opportunities and rewards (Piliavin et al. 1986). Hence, perceptual studies provide little evidence of either a general or a specific deterrent effect of legal punishment per se. The more general consequences of legal punishment, however, appear to encourage conformity within the conventional population.

In observational research, people are observed and talked to in their natural surroundings, typically over an extended time. This method is useful for understanding how decisions about crime are made in situations influenced by multiple factors such as peer pressure, group allegiances, and immediate personal needs. These factors appear to affect perceptions of the certainty and severity of punishment and the influence of these perceptions on criminal behavior—though not necessarily as deterrence would predict. For example, legal threats can strengthen the solidarity of a criminal group, and this increased solidarity may increase the likelihood that group members will commit crime. Observational research has shown how

threats of legal punishment influence decisions to commit crime in complex and competing ways, in part depending on informal, interpersonal pressures in the particular situation (Ekland-Olsen, Lieb, and Zurcher 1984).

Because of ethical and practical constraints, field experiments that subject individuals to different types of legal punishments are rare. However, field experiments provide some of the most useful information on deterrence because they examine crime and punishment as they occur in real life. An example is a study of the deterrent effect of arrest on wife abusers (Sherman and Berk 1984). In it, police randomly chose one of three methods of responding when faced with a misdemeanor case of wife assault: They either arrested the suspect, provided advice and mediation, or ordered the suspect to leave for eight hours. The original study found that those who were less likely to abuse their wives again were those who were arrested rather than those subject to the other two treatments. Apparently, then, criminal justice sanctions can have a specific deterrent effect for some types of offenders.

Deterrence will likely remain one of the primary methods of crime prevention and control, despite contradictory evidence on its effectiveness. Clearly, threats of legal punishment can affect criminal decisions in a variety of ways—sometimes directly and indirectly to deter crime, sometimes indirectly to increase the likelihood of crime. Research indicates that potential offenders are not irrational but instead weigh the rewards or costs of crime in predictable, if not always perfectly logical, ways. Finally, it appears that decisions about crime are often influenced by considerations not related to the law—for example, group pressures or moral inhibitions. These considerations may, however, depend on legal prohibitions. All of these have produced new insights into why so many crime prevention and control policies have failed and have suggested ways to make them more effective.

(SEE ALSO: *Criminal Sanctions; Criminology; Social Control*)

## REFERENCES

Beccaria, Cesare 1977 *On Crimes and Punishments,* 6th ed., trans. Henry Paolucci. Indianapolis: Bobbs-Merrill.

Becker, Gary S. 1968 "Crime and Punishment: An Economic Analysis." *Journal of Political Economy* 78:189–217.

Blumstein, Alfred, Jacqueline Cohen, and Daniel Nagin 1978 *Deterrence and Incapacitation: Estimating the Effects of Criminal Sanctions on Crime Rates.* Washington, D.C.: National Academy of Science.

Cohen, Jacqueline 1983 *Incapacitating Criminals: Recent Research Findings.* Washington D.C.: National Institute of Justice.

Cullen, Francis, and Karen Gilbert 1982 *Reaffirming Rehabilitation.* Cincinnati, Ohio: Anderson.

Ekland-Olsen, Sheldon, John Leib, and Louis Zurcher 1984 "The Paradoxical Impact of Criminal Sanctions: Some Microstructural Findings." *Law and Society Review* 18:159–178.

Gibbs, Jack 1975 *Crime, Punishment, and Deterrence.* New York: Elsevier.

——— 1986 "Deterrence Theory and Research." In Gary Melton, ed., *Law as a Behavioral Instrument.* Lincoln: University of Nebraska Press.

Martinson, Robert 1974 "What Works? Questions and Answers About Prison Reform." *Public Interest* 35:22–54.

Piliavin, Irving, Rosemary Gartner, Craig Thornton, and Ross L. Matsueda 1986 "Crime, Deterrence, and Rational Choice." *American Sociological Review* 51:101–119.

Ross, H. Laurence 1984 *Deterring the Drinking Driver: Legal Policy and Social Control.* Lexington, Mass.: Lexington Books.

Russell, Francis 1975 *A City in Terror, 1919: The Boston Police Strike.* New York: Viking.

Sellin, Thorsten 1959 *The Death Penalty.* Philadephia: American Law Institute.

Sherman, Lawrence, and Richard A. Berk 1984 "The Specific Deterrent Effects of Arrest for Domestic Assault." *American Sociological Review* 49:261–272.

Tittle, Charles R. 1980 *Sanctions and Social Deviance.* New York: Praeger.

Williams, Kirk R., and Richard Hawkins 1986 "Perceptual Research on General Deterrence: A Critical Review." *Law and Society Review* 20:545–572.

Zimring, Frank E., and Gordon Hawkins 1973 *Deterrence: The Legal Threat in Crime Control.* Chicago: University of Chicago Press.

ROSEMARY I. GARTNER

**CRIME RATES** In their generic form, crime rates are simple calculations that relate the number of crimes that occur during a given time period in a geographical area to the population base from which the crimes emanate. For instance, equation 1 produces a crude crime rate:

$$\frac{\text{Number of Crimes}}{\text{Population}} \times K = \text{Crude Crime Rate} \quad (1)$$

where $K$ is a constant. When expressing crime rates for large populations (e.g., cities or countries) the constant, $K$, is usually 100,000. The expression indicates the number of crimes committed in a given time period for every 100,000 people living in the geographic area.

If it were possible to generate a number representing all crimes that occur in the United States in a year, that number would be the numerator and the United States population would be the denominator. A crude crime rate is the result of dividing one by the other and multiplying by 100,000. Unfortunately, no number representing all crime that occurs in the United States for any given period of time can be calculated.

The most widely cited number representing crime in the United States is generated from official police reports about crime. "Crime rate" most often refers to the "official crime rate," which is based on police reports of crime. Ultimately these data are compiled by the Federal Bureau of Investigation (FBI) and published in its annual report, *Crime in the United States.*

Accurate crime rates are important because they are used for many purposes: as indicators of the amount of crime in society; as an indicator of trends (increasing or decreasing) of crime in society; by local authorities to allocate law enforcement resources; by politicians to allocate money to law enforcement agencies; and by social scientists to test theories about crime.

## OFFICIAL CRIME RATES

In the 1920s the International Association of Chiefs of Police developed a system for producing uniform police statistics. In 1929 their plan was complete and became the basis for the uniform crime reporting program used in the United States. The object of the system was to produce reliable national statistics about crime. The *Uniform Crime Reporting* (UCR) Program, in place since 1930, remained relatively unchanged through the late 1980s (U.S. Department of Justice 1988a).

One problem in getting national data on crime is that the definition of specific crimes vary in each state. The UCR developed standardized definitions of offenses without reference to local statutes used by local officials to record offenses. No matter which jurisdiction is involved, offenses can be classified in a way that is consistent with UCR definitions (U.S. Department of Justice 1988a).

In its current form the UCR is managed by the FBI and relies on over 16,000 city, county, and state law enforcement agencies voluntarily to report data on crime that comes to their attention. The FBI compiles and publishes these reports and makes available a separate data set for homicide offenses. The original Committee on Uniform Crime Records evaluated various crimes on the basis of their seriousness, frequency of occurrence, pervasiveness in all geographic areas of the country, and likelihood of being reported to law enforcement. On those bases, a compilation of eight "index" crimes is used to gauge fluctuations in overall volume and rate of crime for the country and its regions. The "crime index" includes: murder and nonnegligent manslaughter, forcible rape, robbery, aggravated assault, burglary, larceny-theft, motor vehicle theft. In 1979 arson was added as an index offense and the new list became known as the modified crime index.

Based on records of all reports of crime received from victims, officers who discover infractions, or other sources, law enforcement agencies across the country tabulate the number of crime index offenses during each month and forward that information to the FBI. It is these data that become the national crime statistics. Complaints determined to be false through investigation are eliminated from an agency's count. The number of "actual offenses" (the number of reported offenses minus those eliminated as false) are recorded regardless of whether an arrest is made, stolen property is recovered, or prosecution is undertaken (U.S. Department of Justice 1988a).

Crime rates for the United States are generated by adding together the number of index offenses known to the police in a given year and reported to the FBI, dividing by an estimate of the U.S. population for that year and multiplying by 100,000 (U.S. Department of Justice 1988a). For instance, the index crime rate calculation for 1989 is shown in equation 2.

$$\frac{14,251,400}{248,239,000} \times 100,000 = 5,741 \qquad (2)$$

There were 14,251,400 index crimes recorded by the FBI. The population estimate for 1989 was 248,239,000. For every 100,000 people living in the United States in 1989 there were 5,741 index crimes reported and recorded. This is an increase of 14.6 percent since 1985 but only 6.3 percent more than the 1980 index crime rate (U.S. Department of Justice 1990).

The UCR is meant to gauge fluctuations in crime in the United States by using serious crimes as an indicator of criminal activity. Its success, to some extent, depends on the reportability of the crimes in the index. One of the reasons that the eight crimes designated as index offenses were chosen to represent fluctuations in crime rates is that they are relatively well-reported crimes. But the National Crime Survey and other victimization studies have demonstrated that even for these very serious crimes a high proportion go unreported (the two exceptions being motor vehicle theft and homicide). Crime reporting by the public varies both by seriousness of the event and by the type of crime itself. Forcible rape, one of the most serious crimes against the person, has a relatively low reporting rate due to expected reactions of police, embarrassment, the victim's relation to the offender, and other factors (O'Brien 1985). On the other hand, motor vehicle theft, a much less serious property crime, is highly reported because usually victims can collect their insurance only after they report the crime. With these and a few other exceptions, the more serious the crime, the higher the likelihood of a report being filed. When no report is filed or if the police have not discovered the crime, then for statistical purposes no crime has taken place. There will be no number in the crime index to show that a crime was committed.

Crime also fluctuates by local assignment of police to particular duty (initially raising arrest rates but ultimately lowering arrest rates in the area), and by systematic variations in the way local enforcement agencies record crime, by the degree of professionalism of the force, and by the population to police ratio (O'Brien 1985). Coupled with these issues is the degree of discretion exercised by police. The more discretion exercised, the less likely some crimes are to become statistics. Finally, political pressure to raise or lower the crime rate has at times had an effect on crimes reported at the local level and, in turn, to the FBI. In sum, a variety of variables determines whether or not a criminal event becomes a criminal statistic. Many studies have shown that a large portion of even serious crime does not appear in national criminal statistics. However, the precise impact of local variations in reporting has not been quantitatively assessed and the UCR program does use data quality control measures in an attempt to rectify excessive deviations.

Compounding the problems associated with crimes that do not become known to the police are problems associated with the UCR scoring rules themselves. For instance, when several crimes occur in one incident, only the most serious crime is recorded in the national statistics (the hierarchy rule). In addition, crimes against the person are counted as one crime per victim, while for crimes against property (robbery, burglary, larceny-theft, motor vehicle theft) one offense per distinct operation or attempt is counted. When the two are combined, different units of count have been aggregated.

The UCR is designed to gauge the extent of shifts in serious crimes occurring in the United States. The flaws in the system (under-reporting and the problems associated with the reporting rules) may mean that the program is not accomplishing its goals well. On the other hand, while the results of victimization studies show much more crime, at least some studies have indicated a high correlation with UCR reflections of crime trends.

Despite criticisms levelled at the UCR, the crime index has been used for decades as the basis for policy decisions and comparisons between jurisdictions. In an effort to take advantage of automated law enforcement record keeping, respond to increased demand for refined crime data, rectify some of the program defects and to improve the quality of data generated nationally, the FBI in 1984 began efforts to redesign the UCR. The new version is called the *National Incident-Based Recording System* (NIBRS).

The major differences between the UCR and NIBRS lie in the structure of the data sets generated by the two systems. The new data set allows more sophisticated data manipulations. Most of the general methods for collecting, scoring, and reporting UCR data remain applicable in the NIBRS. Hence, the proportion of all serious crime occurring that become national crime statistics will change only as a result of the change in the hierarchy rule (see below) and changes in police procedures.

In contrast to the UCR summary procedures, NIBRS data are incident based. For each incident the system will attempt to collect information about fifty-two data elements regarding the offense, property characteristics, victim characteristics and offender/arrestee characteristics. Most of the data elements will be new to national crime reporting, and the overall data set will be much richer than the UCR summary information. While the UCR crime index included eight crimes, NIBRS "group A" offenses consist of twenty-two crime categories composed of forty-six offenses. The twenty-two categories include both incidents and arrests and serve as the basis for crime rate calculations (U.S. Department of Justice 1988b).

The following categories make up the list of group A offenses: arson, assault (aggravated, simple, intimidation), bribery, burglary/breaking and entering, counterfeiting/forgery, destruction/damage/vandalism of property, drug/narcotic offenses, embezzlement, extortion/blackmail, fraud offenses, gambling offenses, homicide offenses (murder, nonnegligent homicide, negligent manslaughter, justifiable homicide), kidnapping/abduction, larceny/theft offenses, motor vehicle theft, pornography/obscene material, prostitution offenses, robbery, sex offenses (forcible rape, forcible sodomy, sexual assault with an object, forcible fondling), nonforcible sex offenses (incest, statutory rape), stolen property, and weapon law violations. Other offense data are collected as part of "group B" offenses. These include bad checks, curfew, disorderly conduct, driving under the influence, drunkenness, family offenses (nonviolent), liquor law violations, peeping Tom, runaway, trespass of real property, and all other offenses.

There are no immediate plans to change the crime index as a measure of national fluctuations. For the time being, reports of both the index of crime, "group A" and "group B" criminality will be published.

It is clear that NIBRS represents vast improvements in the types of data collected. The data provide the possibility of constructing victim and offender profiles, of examining victim/offender relationships, and for studying many more demographic correlates of crime. Further, the new system overcomes criticisms of the hierarchy rule (the new system records all incidents) and offense scoring becomes automated.

Group A crimes reflect increases and new interest in particular types of crime. For instance, group A crimes include white collar crimes that are of concern and consequence because of relatively recent awareness of political criminality. The inclusion of drugs reflects the massive problem faced by this country with regard to drug use and importation. On the other hand, group A crimes include many crimes (white collar and drugs included) with dismal reporting histories. Some of the crimes vary substantially by region of the country and valid data will be extremely

difficult to obtain. The inclusion of these crimes may detract from the system's stated purpose of serving as a gauge of crime and criminal behavior in the nation.

While NIBRS addresses some of the criticisms of the old UCR, it does not ensure higher rates of reporting, improve differences in reporting due to differing police practices, or address regional variation due to differences in laws and reporting practices. No doubt the new system, when it is in place, will provide more information, but only time will tell if the quality of data improves along with the quantity.

During the time taken by agencies to obtain data processing and other facilities necessary to join NIBRS, the old UCR will continue. For some time to come the two systems will operate jointly, and data from the new system will be used to create the summary information needed to ensure that national data can be published. The new system began in ten states in 1989. By 1992 more than thirty states should be participating.

Crime rates may seem easy to calculate, but in fact many variables enter into that final number that represents crime in any society. These rates must be used with caution because of the many factors that influence them.

## INTERNATIONAL COMPARISONS

While it is problematic to make comparisons between jurisdictions within the United States, international comparisons are even more difficult. Not only do laws differ substantially, but recording systems often bear no resemblance to one another. Table 1 offers an example of problems in trying to make international comparisons even when the basic information is relatively good. The table presents the best available data about homicide in each country and it is tempting to draw conclusions from the comparative homicide rates. For statistical purposes, however, each country defines homicide slightly differently. In the United States these data include murder, manslaughter (negligent manslaughter and attempted murder and manslaughter *are not* included); in the

**TABLE 1**
**Homicide by Countries, 1986 (Number and Rate per 100,000)**

|        | U.S.A. | U.K. | F.R.G. | France | Canada | Japan | USSR |
|--------|--------|------|--------|--------|--------|-------|------|
| *Number* | 20,613 | 2,160 | 2,728 | 2,413 | 569 | 1,744 | 16,700 |
| *Rate*   | 8.6 | 4.3 | 4.5 | 4.4 | 2.2 | 1.4 | 5.8 |

SOURCES: Ministry of Justice 1989; Statistics Canada 1989; Eklof 1990. Soviet data are for 1989.

United Kingdom the data include murder, attempted murder, threat or conspiracy to murder, manslaughter and infanticide (child destruction is not included); in the Federal Republic of Germany the data are for murder, manslaughter, "murder on demand," and infanticide; France includes murder, manslaughter, parricide (parent killing) infanticide, and poisoning; Japan includes murder, manslaughter, and robbery causing death (attempts *are* included) (Ministry of Justice 1989). Japan's data may also include preparation for commission of a homicide and participation in suicide although it excludes assaults leading to homicide (U.S. Department of Justice 1988c); homicide in Canada is first and second degree murder, manslaughter and infanticide; homicide in the USSR is undefined by the source from which the data were derived. Hence, no two countries' data are the same and some of the differences, particularly the inclusion or exclusion of attempts, involve major substantive differences. Nonetheless, as gross comparisons, these data for homicide are better than for any other crimes. In making international comparisons, probably the best technique is to use multiple sources of data on the same crimes when such information is available. For example, the Department of Justice had some success in comparing various types of crime across nations using World Health Organization, United Nations and Interpol data (U.S. Department of Justice 1988c).

Most international crime comparisons are possible only when one fully grasps the system of reporting, definitions of crime and peculiarities of the systems discussed. A few specific examples complete this introduction to crime rates.

Canada's Uniform Crime Reporting system was modeled on the UCR of the United States but Canada did not start using it until 1962. Because Canada has a single criminal law for the whole country, it has encountered fewer problems of comparability than the U.S. Nonetheless, the Canadian UCR has faced criticisms on virtually identical grounds to those levelled at the U.S. UCR (Silverman, Teevan, and Sacco 1991). Rather than being compiled by a police agency, the Canadian UCR is the responsibility of the Canadian Centre for Justice Statistics, Statistics Canada. Police reporting to that agency is not voluntary; it is mandated by law.

A major element differentiating Canada's UCR from the U.S. UCR is that Canada does not use a crime index to calculate its crime rate. Crime rate is calculated on the basis of all criminal code violations. Hence, overall crime rate cannot be compared with that of the U.S. crime index rate because the Canadian rates take into account much more crime. In 1988 the crime rate for Canada was 9,233 per 100,000 (estimated population, 25,911,800; criminal code violations, 2,392,419).

It is possible to compare crime rates for individual crimes if care is taken to ensure that the categories being used are similar. For instance, it is fairly common to compare Canada's assault rate with that of the United States. The surprising, but incorrect finding is that Canada apparently has a higher assault rate. While the two reporting systems refer to "assault," the U.S. category includes only aggravated assault while the Canadian system counts both aggravated and simple assaults. This example typifies the dangers of international comparisons.

Homicide data are more comparable. The legal

definitions are similar if not identical and the reporting is equally reliable in the two countries. Over many years Canada has consistently had a rate of homicide between one-third and one-fourth that of the United States.

In the early 1990s Canada will switch to an incident based reporting system. Like the U.S. system, it will eliminate many of the problems of the old UCR by expanding the data elements to be included, but it will retain problems associated with initial reporting of crime (coverage). The new Canadian system should be in place by 1992. Because of the uniformity of Canada's criminal law and the attention Canada is giving to implementing the new system, it should generate some of the best official criminal statistics in the world.

In delimiting its crime trends since 1946, Japan reports all offenses including "traffic professional negligence," which the United States would not consider either an index offense or a "group A" offense in NIBRS. Crime rate comparisons with Japan are difficult because of legal definitions and law enforcement emphasis. Given Japan's tendency to include all penal code offenses in calculations, it is, in fact, easier to compare overall Japanese statistics with Canadian statistics. Eliminating the traffic offenses, Japan reports a rate of 1,291 penal offenses per 100,000 for 1987. Hence, Japan's total crime rate is one-fourth the U.S. index rate and one-seventh of the total Canadian rate. The Japanese crime rate declined between the mid-1940s and the mid-1970s (from a high of 2,000 to a low of 1,091). Since that time there has been a slight rise (Ministry of Justice 1989).

While both organized crime gangs and drugs are considered to be major problems in Japan, these issues bear little resemblance in substance or quantity to the same issues in the United States. To understand the absolute rate of crime, crime reporting, and crime trends in Japan, it is necessary to attempt to understand the forces that generate the crime, the informal ways of handling crime, and the law enforcement focus in the country. It has been suggested that the amount of crime that occurs in Japan is far greater than officially recorded crime.

Even in the late 1980s the Soviet Union simply declined to discuss crime. In fact they would argue that their system of government did not generate crime. Crime was a capitalist problem. The only crime of note was political crime, for which dissidents were imprisoned. It is difficult to discern if any really systematic effort was made to keep national criminal statistics. Certainly, no such statistics are published. Even now, when social scientists wish to learn about crimes in the Soviet Union, their best source of information is newspapers, rather than official government publications.

Reports in the Soviet press suggest that street crime, organized crime (Current Digest of the Soviet Press 1990b) and drug use (Moscow News 1990) are rising in the USSR. The press reports that there was 32 percent more crime in 1989 than in 1988 and a further increase of 17 percent in the first three months of 1990 (Current Digest of the Soviet Press 1990a, 1990c). The comparison points are unclear, however. While the crime rate for 1989 is reported to be 866 per 100,000, the source of the data is not specified, nor is the population base (Current Digest of the Soviet Press 1990a).

While there is more information available on crime in the USSR than has been the case in the past, the basis for various types of information is unclear. Comparisons with other nations should be made with extreme caution, if at all. Given rapid changes in the USSR, it is possible that interpretable data from the Soviet Union may become more available in the near future.

International comparisons often require more than looking at the numbers produced by the statistical agencies of the countries. The bases for calculations, counting methods, legal definitions, as well as political motives and cultural differences in dealing with crime all must be taken into account.

(SEE ALSO: *Criminology; Juvenile Delinquency and Juvenile Crime*)

REFERENCES

The Current Digest of the Soviet Press 1989 "State and Law" 41 (2):23–24.

———— 1990a "Fight Crime Don't Fear Statistics." 42 (2):31–32.

———— 1990b "Bakatin Reports on Organized Crime." 42 (8):17–20.

———— 1990c "Bakatin Gives Details on Crime 'Crisis.'" 42 (16):11–12.

Eklof, B. 1990 "Trapped in a Mine Cave-In? The Soviet People Today." *Arts and Sciences* 13:6–10.

Ministry of Justice 1989 *Summary of the White Paper on Crime, 1988*. Tokyo: Research and Training Institute, Government of Japan.

Moscow News 1990 "Narcotics, Narcomania, Narcobusiness." 24:15.

O'Brien, Robert M. 1985. *Crime and Victimization Data*, vol. 4. Law and Criminal Justice Series. Beverly Hills, Calif.: Sage.

Silverman, R. A., J. Teevan, V. Sacco (eds.) 1991 *Crime in Canadian Society*, 4th ed. Toronto: Butterworths.

Statistics Canada 1989 *Canadian Crime Statistics 1988*. Ottawa: Minister of Supply and Services.

U.S. Department of Justice 1988a *Crime in the United States: Uniform Crime Reports, 1987*. Washington, D.C.: U.S. Government Printing Office.

———— 1988b *National Incident-Based Reporting System*, vol. 1, *Data Collection Guidelines*. Washington, D.C.: U.S. Government Printing Office.

———— 1988c *International Crime Statistics*. Bureau of Justice Statistics Special Report. Washington, D.C.: U.S. Department of Justice.

———— 1990 *Crime in the United States: Uniform Crime Reports, 1989*. Washington, D.C.: U.S. Government Printing Office.

ROBERT A. SILVERMAN

**CRIME, THEORIES OF** Most accounts of the rise of criminological inquiry indicate that it had its beginnings in mid-nineteenth-century developments in Europe, including the work of Cesare Lombroso, an Italian prison physician, who argued that many criminals are atavists, that is, biological throwbacks to a human type, *homo delinquens*, that allegedly existed prior to the appearance of *homo sapiens*. Since the time of Lombroso and other early figures in criminology, the field has grown markedly, both in terms of the variety of scholars who have tried to uncover the causes of crime and also in terms of the diverse theories that have been produced by these persons (Vold and Bernard 1986). Currently, criminological theorizing and research is engaged in by legal theorists, psychologists, economists, geographers, and representatives of other scholarly fields as well, but the largest share of work has been carried on by sociologists. Thus, criminology is frequently identified as a subfield of sociology (Gibbons 1979).

Crime and criminal behavior are defined or identified by the criminal laws of nations, states, and local jurisdictions. Acts that are not prohibited or required by the criminal law are not crimes, however much they may offend some members of the community. Also, the reach of the criminal law in modern societies is very broad, involving a wide range of behavioral acts that vary not only in form but in severity as well. The criminal laws of various states and nations prohibit morally repugnant acts such as murder or incest, but they also prohibit less serious offenses such as vandalism, petty theft, and myriad other acts. No wonder, then, that there are a large number of theories of crime, given the varieties of behavior that are defined as criminal and the differing perspectives from which the phenomenon of crime has been addressed.

Persons of all ages violate criminal laws, although a number of forms of criminality are most frequent among persons in their teens or early twenties. Except for "status offense" violations such as running away, truancy, and the like, which apply only to juveniles (usually defined as persons under eighteen years of age), juvenile delinquency and adult criminality are defined by the same body of criminal statutes. However, criminologists have usually constructed theories about delinquency separate from explanations of adult criminality. Although many theories of delinquency closely resemble those dealing with adult crime, some of the former are not paralleled by theories of adult criminality. In the discussion to follow, most attention is upon explanatory arguments about adult lawbreaking, but some mention is also made of causal arguments about juvenile crime.

## CRIMINOLOGICAL QUESTIONS AND CAUSAL THEORIES

There are two basic forms taken by most theories of crime: Some center on the explanation of crime patterns and crime rates, or what might be termed "crime in the aggregate," while others are pitched at the individual level and endeavor to identify factors that account for the involvement or noninvolvement of specific individuals in lawbreaking conduct (Gibbons 1987, pp. 35–38; Sutherland and Cressey 1978, pp. 62–63).

These are related but analytically separate questions about crime causation. As Edwin Sutherland and Donald Cressey (1978, pp. 62–63) have argued, an adequate account of criminality should contain two distinct but consistent aspects: "First, there will be a statement that explains the statistical distribution of criminal behavior in time and space (epidemiology). . . . Second, there will be a statement that identifies the process or processes by which persons come to exhibit criminal behavior."

Statistical distributions of criminal behavior in time and space are usually portrayed in the form of crime rates of one kind or another. One of the most familiar of these is the "index crime rate" reported annually for cities, states, and other jurisdictions by the Federal Bureau of Investigation. The index crime rate involves the number of reported cases of murder, nonnegligent manslaughter, forcible rape, aggravated assault, robbery, larceny, burglary, and auto theft per jurisdiction, expressed as a rate per 100,000 persons in that jurisdiction's population.

Many crime rate patterns are well known, including relatively high rates of violence in the United States compared to other nations, state-by-state variations in forcible rape rates, regional variations in homicide and other crimes within the United States, and so forth. Criminologists have also developed a number of theories or explanations for these crime rate variations. One case in point is Larry Baron and Murray Straus's (1987)

investigation of rape rates for the fifty American states, in which the authors examined the influence of state-to-state variations in gender inequality, social disorganization (high divorce rates, low church attendance, and the like), pornography readership, and "cultural spillover" (authorized paddling of school children, etc.) on forcible rape.

Crime rates are important social indicators that reflect the quality of life in different areas. Additionally, theories such as the one by Baron and Straus, linking various social factors to those rates, provide considerable insight into the causes of lawbreaking. But, it is well to keep in mind that crime rates are the summary expression of illegal acts of individuals. Much of the time, the precise number of offenders who have carried out the reported offenses is unknown because individual law violators engage in varying numbers of crimes per year. But even so, crime rates summarize the illegal actions of individuals. Accordingly, theories of crime must ultimately deal with the processes by which these specific persons come to exhibit criminal behavior.

In practice, criminological theories that focus on crime rates and patterns often have had relatively little to say about the causes of individual behavior. For example, variations in income inequality from one place to another have been identified by criminologists as being related to rates of predatory property crime such as burglary, automobile theft, and larceny. Many of the studies that have reported this finding have had little to say about how income inequality, defined as the unequal distribution of income among an entire population of an area or locale, affects individuals. In short, explanations of crime rate variations often do not indicate how the explanatory variables they identify "get inside the heads of offenders," so to speak.

Although criminological theories about crime rates and crime patterns have often been developed independently of theories relating to the processes by which specific persons come to exhibit criminal conduct, valid theories of these processes should have implications for the task of understanding the realities of criminal conduct. For example, if variations in gender inequality and levels of pornography readership are related to rates of forcible rape, it may be that individuals who carry out sexual assaults also believe that discrimination against women is legitimate and are avid readers of pornography. In the same way, if income inequality bears some consistent relationship to rates of predatory crime, it may also be that individual predators express relatively strong feelings of "relative deprivation," that is, perceptions of economic disadvantage. However, some additional factors may also have to be identified that determine which of the persons who feel relatively deprived become involved in illegal conduct and which do not.

## PERSPECTIVES, THEORIES, AND HYPOTHESES

A number of arguments about crime patterns and the processes through which individuals get involved in lawbreaking are examined below. Before moving to these specific theories, however, two other general observations are in order. First, in criminology, as in sociology more generally, there is considerable disagreement regarding the nature of perspectives, theories, and hypotheses. *Theories* are often described as sets of concepts, along with interconnected propositions that link the concepts together into an "explanatory package"; *perspectives* are identified as broader and less systematically organized arguments; and *hypotheses* are specific research propositions derived from theories. In practice, however, many causal explanations that have been described as theories are incomplete and also conceptually imprecise. Jack Gibbs (1985) has labeled such theories as being in "the discursive mode" rather than as formal theories. According to Gibbs, because most criminological theories are discursive, precise predictions from them are not possible, nor is it possible to subject predictions to empirical test, that is, to validation through research.

Many criminological theories involve vague concepts, faulty underlying logic, and other problems. At the same time, it is possible to identify a number of general theoretical perspectives in criminology and to differentiate these from rela-

tively formalized and precise theories. For example, many criminologists contend that American society is "criminogenic" because it involves social and economic features that appear to contribute heavily to criminality. However, this is a general perspective rather than a theory of crime in that it does not identify the full range of factors that contribute to lawbreaking, and it also lacks a set of explicit and interrelated propositions. By contrast, the income inequality argument more clearly qualifies as a causal theory, as does the formulation that links gender inequality, pornography readership, and certain other influences to forcible rape.

A few other comments are in order on theoretical perspectives in criminology. During most of the developmental history of criminology in the United States, from the early 1900s to the present, sociological criminologists voiced support for the criminogenic culture thesis that directs attention to social-structural factors thought to be responsible for criminality. Thus, this view might also be referred to as "mainstream criminology." Most criminologists have linked lawbreaking to major "rents and tears" in societal structure at the same time that most of them have also assumed that these crime-producing features can be remedied or lessened through social and economic reforms of one kind or another (Gibbons 1979, 1987).

In the 1970s, a markedly different perspective competed for attention. Variously referred to as "radical-Marxist," "critical," or "new" criminology, it asserted that the causes of crime arise out of societal characteristics that are inherent in corporate capitalism (Gibbons 1987, pp. 125–144; Chambliss 1975; Quinney 1974, 1977). According to radical-Marxist criminologists, criminal laws are created to serve the interests of the capitalist ruling class. In turn, the system of corporate capitalism over which the ruling class presides depends for its survival on the exploitation of the resources and people of other countries and the economic oppression of citizens within capitalist nations. These conditions create economic strains for many persons, contribute to the deterioration of family life, and in other ways drive many individuals into desperate acts of lawbreaking.

The radical-Marxist perspective received considerable attention in the 1970s. Those who criticized it claimed that it presented a one-dimensional, oversimplified account of the social sources of criminality. For example, while some criminal laws favor the interests of the owners of capital, many others serve broader social interests. Similarly, while some forms of crime may be related to economic problems, others are not.

A major trend in criminological investigations in recent years has been away from broad mainstream and radical perspectives and toward relatively detailed theories specific to one or another form of crime, such as the argument by Baron and Straus (1987) that links gender inequality, pornography, and social disorganization. Regarding radical-Marxist viewpoints, the delinquency theory of Mark Colvin and John Pauly (1983), centered on serious forms of juvenile misconduct, is another example of the movement away from global formulations to more specific ones. Colvin and Pauly argued that the employer–employee relationships to which lower class workers are subjected are coercive. In turn, the coercive social environment in which workers exist leads to punitive and repressive child-rearing practices on their part, alienating children from their parents. Those youngsters who have poor affectional ties to their parents also become disinterested in activities deemed important to children, activities, for instance, such as doing well in school. Finally, children who are on poor terms with their parents and who are alienated from school become prime candidates for involvement in delinquency, particularly of a serious and repetitive form.

## FORMS OF CRIME AND TYPES OF OFFENDERS

One central problem that quickly comes to the fore when theorizing turns to particular forms of criminality is the classificatory one. The legal codes of the various states and of the federal government include hundreds of specific offenses, but the explanatory task is to develop a relatively small set of theories to make sense of this diverse collection of illegal activities. Accordingly, criminologists have tried to amalgamate these diverse offenses into a smaller number of sociologically meaningful groupings or crime forms (Farr and Gibbons 1990). Some criminologists have singled out crude property crime, consisting of larceny, burglary, robbery, and kindred offenses, as one type of crime; others have placed homicide and assaultive acts into a crime type; while still others have treated forcible rape and other sexual offenses as another broad form of lawbreaking. Then, too, "white-collar" or organizational crime has often been singled out as a crime pattern (Sutherland 1949; Schrager and Short 1978; Coleman 1987). "Organized crime" is still another type that has received a good deal of criminological attention. Some persons have also drawn attention to a collection of offenses that receive little visibility in the media and elsewhere and have termed these "folk crime" (Ross 1960–1961, 1973) or "mundane crime" (Gibbons 1983). Finally, "political crime" has been identified as a major pattern of lawbreaking (Turk 1982).

Although these groupings identify forms of lawbreaking that differ from each other in important ways, it is also true that they are relatively crude in form in that the underlying dimensions or variables on which they are based are not clearly spelled out. Further, there is disagreement among criminologists as to the specific crimes that should be identified as instances of white-collar crime, mundane crime, or some other category.

Criminologists have also developed systems for sorting individual offenders into behavioral types (Gibbons 1965). Although related to crime classification efforts, categorization of lawbreakers into types is a separate form of activity. While it may be possible to identify groupings such as predatory property crime, it may not be true that individual offenders specialize only in that form of criminality, hence it may be incorrect to speak of "predatory offenders" as a type of criminal. Most offender classification systems have been deficient in one respect or another (Gibbons 1985), but the most serious flaw is that these categorizations are oversimplified. Researchers have discovered that many offenders engage in a diverse collection of offenses over their criminal "careers" rather than being crime specialists such as "burglars," "robbers," or "drug dealers" (Chaiken and Chaiken 1982).

## THEORIES OF CRIME

The number of theories regarding particular forms of crime is extensive, thus they cannot all be reviewed here. A sampling of some of the more important ones would include the "routine activities" explanation of predatory property crime. Lawrence E. Cohen and Marcus Felson (1979) have contended that predatory property crime involves three major elements: the supply of motivated offenders, the supply of suitable targets, and the absence of capable guardians. In other words, these crimes are carried out by persons with criminal motives, but the incidence of such offenses also depends upon the number of opportunities to burglarize homes or to rob persons. Also, the number of burglaries from one community to another is influenced by the degree to which residents in local areas act as capable guardians by maintaining surveillance over homes in their neighborhoods or by taking other crime-control steps. This theory contends that crime opportunities have increased in the United States in recent decades at the same time that capable guardianship has declined, due principally to changes in employment patterns. In particular, the number of families in which both adult members work during the day has grown markedly, as has the number of employed, single-parent families. Finally, research evidence lends considerable support to this theory (Cohen and Felson 1979).

Another related theory regarding predatory offenses centers on income inequality, defined as the degree to which the total income of a group, such as the residents of a particular city, is distributed unevenly, with a small portion of the group having control over a large portion of the total income (Braithwaite 1979; Carroll and Jackson 1983).

Research evidence indicates that income inequality is related to predatory property crime. Further, Leo Carroll and Pamela Irving Jackson (1983) have argued that the routine activities and income inequality arguments are interrelated. They have suggested that the labor market trends identified in the former have lead both to increased crime opportunities, declines in guardianship, and heightened levels of income inequality.

## THEORIES OF CRIMINAL BEHAVIOR

While theories about crime patterns and rates have been developed principally by sociological criminologists, representatives of a number of disciplines have endeavored to identify factors and processes that explain the involvement or noninvolvement of specific individuals in lawbreaking. Three basic perspectives can be noted: the biogenic, psychogenic, and sociogenic approaches. *Biogenic views* attribute the genesis or causes of lawbreaking to constitutional and hereditary factors, while *psychogenic perspectives* often contend that lawbreakers exhibit personality problems to which their illegal conduct is a response. By contrast, sociologists have most often advanced *sociogenic theories* arguing that criminal behavior is learned in a socialization process by individuals who are neither biologically nor psychologically flawed. Also, some persons have constructed theories that combine or integrate elements of these three approaches, an important one being James Q. Wilson and Richard J. Herrnstein's (1985) argument that the behavior of criminals has genetic and constitutional roots and that offenders tend to be more mesomorphic in body build, less intelligent, and more burdened with personality defects than their noncriminal peers. Wilson and Herrnstein also contend that various social factors such as unemployment, community influences, and the like play some part in criminality.

Three generalizations can be made about biological theories: First, conclusive evidence supporting these arguments has not yet been produced; second, biological factors cannot be ruled out on the basis of the empirical evidence currently on hand; and third, if biological factors are involved in criminality, they probably are intertwined with social and psychological influences (Trasler 1987; Fishbein 1990).

Edwin H. Sutherland's theory of differential association (Sutherland and Cressey 1978, pp. 80–98) has been the most influential sociological theory about the processes through which persons come to engage in criminality. Sutherland maintained that criminal behavior, including techniques of committing crime and attitudes favorable to lawbreaking activity, is learned in association with other persons. Many of the associations of persons involve face-to-face contact, but criminal conduct definitions can also be acquired indirectly from reference groups, that is, from persons who are important to individuals but with whom they do not directly associate. Sutherland also contended that associations vary in frequency, duration, priority, and intensity. The first three of these conditions are relatively self-evident, while intensity has to do with the personal meaning or significance to individuals of particular social ties.

The core of Sutherland's theory is that before persons engage in lawbreaking, they go through a learning process through which they acquire what he called "definitions favorable to the violation of law," which can be interpreted as motivation to engage in criminality. A radically different theory, directed mainly at explanation of juvenile delinquency, has been put forth by Travis Hirschi (1969). Hirschi has argued that if, through faulty socialization, individuals fail to become bonded to others (that is, if they do not develop positive attachments to adult persons such as parents or teachers), they will then be unlikely to refrain from misbehavior. The emphasis in this theory is on the failure to acquire nondelinquent sentiments rather than on the learning of antisocial ones. In Hirschi's view, delinquency is the result of defective socialization rather than of socialization patterns through which criminal attitudes are learned.

The research evidence that has been produced on delinquents indicates that Hirschi's control theory has merit, particularly as an explanation for relatively petty delinquency and for misconduct on the part of juvenile females (Gibbons and Krohn 1991, pp. 101–105). It is also true, however, that Hirschi's control theory has not been widely adopted as an explanation for adult criminality.

Returning to Sutherland's learning theory and other sociological theories, many of these arguments have asserted or implied that personality differences among individuals are not associated with criminal or delinquent behavior (Sutherland and Cressey 1978). According to Sutherland and Cressey, "No consistent, statistically significant differences between personality traits of delinquents and personality traits of nondelinquents have been found. The explanation of criminal behavior, apparently, must be found in social interaction" (1978, p. 176).

Sutherland and Cressey were not alone in rejecting personality factors as important in lawbreaking. Several reviews of the evidence, particularly findings having to do with the alleged role of personality defects in criminality, have turned up little or no support for this thesis (Schuessler and Cressey 1950; Waldo and Dinitz 1967; Tennebaum 1977). However, some psychologists have argued that even though the theory that criminality is due to marked personality defects on the part of lawbreakers lacks support, it is nonetheless true that individual differences in the form of personality patterns must be incorporated into criminological theories (Andrews and Wormith 1989). And, in the opinion of a number of sociological criminologists, the argument that individual differences make a difference, both in accounting for criminality and conformity, is persuasive (Gibbons 1989). Personality dynamics play a part in the behavior patterns that individuals exhibit, thus such concepts as role and status are often not able entirely to account for the behavior of individuals. It may be that lawbreaking is often related to psychic needs of individuals as well as to economic pressures and the like that play upon them. On this point, Jack Katz (1988) has explored the personal meanings of homicidal acts, shoplifting, and a number of other kinds of criminality to the persons who are engaged in these acts.

A final word: Further theoretical investigation and research probing the interconnections between biological, psychological, and social factors in criminal conduct remain major pieces of unfinished business in the criminological enterprise.

(SEE ALSO: *Criminology; Juvenile Delinquency Theories; Social Control*)

## REFERENCES

Andrews, D. A., and J. Stephen Wormith 1989 "Personality and Crime: Knowledge Destruction and Construction." *Justice Quarterly* 6:289–309.

Baron, Larry, and Murray A. Straus 1987 "Four Theories of Rape: A Macrosociological Analysis." *Social Problems* 34:467–489.

Braithwaite, John 1979 *Inequality, Crime and Public Policy*. London: Routledge and Kegan Paul.

Carroll, Leo, and Pamela Irving Jackson 1983 "Inequality, Opportunity, and Crime Rates in Central Cities." *Criminology* 21:178–194.

Chaiken, Jan, and Marcia Chaiken 1982 *Varieties of Criminal Behavior*. Santa Monica, Calif.: Rand.

Chambliss, William 1975 "Toward a Political Economy of Crime." *Theory and Society* 2:148–155.

Cohen, Lawrence E., and Marcus Felson 1979 "Social Change and Crime Rate Trends: A Routine Activities Approach." *American Sociological Review* 44:588–607.

Coleman, James W. 1987 "Toward an Integrated Theory of White-Collar Crime." *American Journal of Sociology* 93:406–439.

Colvin, Mark, and John Pauly 1983 "A Critique of Criminology: Toward an Integrated Structural-Marxist Theory of Delinquency Production." *American Journal of Sociology* 89:513–551.

Cressey, Donald R. 1972 *Criminal Organization*. New York: Harper and Row.

Farr, Kathryn Ann, and Don C. Gibbons 1990 "Observations on the Development of Crime Categories." *International Journal of Offender Therapy and Comparative Criminology* 34.

Fishbein, Diana H. 1990 "Biological Perspectives in Criminology." *Criminology* 28:27–72.

Gibbons, Don C. 1965 *Changing the Lawbreaker*. Englewood Cliffs, N.J.: Prentice-Hall.

―――― 1979 *The Criminological Enterprise*. Englewood Cliffs, N.J.: Prentice-Hall.

―――― 1983 "Mundane Crime." *Crime and Delinquency* 29:213–227.

―――― 1985 "The Assumption of the Efficacy of Middle-Range Explanations: Typologies." In R. F. Meier, ed., *Theoretical Methods in Criminology*. Beverly Hills, Calif.: Sage.

―――― 1987 *Society, Crime, and Criminal Behavior*, 5th ed. Englewood Cliffs, N.J.: Prentice-Hall.

―――― 1989 "Comment-Personality and Crime: Non-Issues, Real Issues, and a Theory and Research Agenda." *Justice Quarterly* 6:311–323.

――――, and Marvin D. Krohn 1991 *Delinquent Behavior*, 5th ed. Englewood Cliffs, N.J.: Prentice-Hall.

Gibbs, Jack P. 1985 "The Methodology of Theory Construction in Criminology." In R. F. Meier, ed., *Theoretical Methods in Criminology*. Beverly Hills, Calif.: Sage.

Greenberg, David F. 1976 "On One-Dimensional Criminology." *Theory and Society* 3:610–621.

Hirschi, Travis 1969 *Causes of Delinquency*. Berkeley: University of California Press.

Katz, Jack 1988 *Seductions of Crime*. New York: Basic Books.

Quinney, Richard 1974 *Critique of Legal Order*. Boston: Little, Brown.

―――― 1977 *Class, State, and Crime*. New York: McKay.

Ross, H. Laurence 1960–61. "Traffic Law Violation: A Folk Crime." *Social Problems* 9:231–241.

―――― 1973 "Folk Crime Revisited." *Criminology* 11:41–85.

Schrager, Laura Shill, and James F. Short, Jr. 1978 "Toward a Sociology of Organizational Crime." *Social Problems* 25:407–419.

Schuessler, Karl F., and Donald R. Cressey 1950 "Personality Characteristics of Criminals." *American Journal of Sociology* 55:476–484.

Sutherland, Edwin H. 1949 *White Collar Crime*. New York: Dryden.

――――, and Donald R. Cressey 1978 *Criminology*, 10th ed. Philadelphia: Lippincott.

Tennebaum, D. J. 1977 "Personality and Criminality: A Summary and Implications of the Literature." *Journal of Criminal Justice* 5:225–235.

Trasler, Gordon 1987 "Biogenetic Factors." In Herbert C. Quay, ed., *Handbook of Juvenile Delinquency*. New York: Wiley.

Turk, Austin T. 1982 *Political Criminality*. Beverly Hills, Calif.: Sage.

Vold, George B., and Thomas J. Bernard 1986 *Theoretical Criminology*, 3rd ed. New York: Oxford.

Waldo, Gordon P., and Simon Dinitz 1967 "Personality Attributes of the Criminal: An Analysis of Research

Studies, 1950–1965." *Journal of Research in Crime and Delinquency* 4:185–202.

Wilson, James Q., and Richard J. Herrnstein 1985 *Crime and Human Nature.* New York: Simon and Schuster.

DON C. GIBBONS

## CRIMINAL AND DELINQUENT SUB-CULTURES

The notion of a subculture is that it is derivative of, but different from, some larger referential culture. The term is used loosely to denote shared systems of norms, values, or interests that set apart some individuals, groups, or other aggregation of people from larger societies and from broader cultural systems. Common examples include youth subcultures, ethnic subcultures, regional subcultures, subcultures associated with particular occupations, and subcultures that develop among people who share special interests such as bird-watching, stamp collecting, or a criminal or delinquent behavior pattern.

Neither membership in a particular category (age, ethnicity, place of residence, occupation) nor behavior (bird-watching, stamp collecting, crime, or delinquency) is sufficient to define a subculture, however. The critical elements are, rather, (1) the degree to which values, norms, and identities associated with membership in a category or with types of behavior are shared, and (2) the nature of relationships, within some larger cultural system, between those who share these elements and those who do not.

In these terms, criminal or delinquent subcultures denote systems of norms, values, or interests that support criminal or delinquent behavior. The many behaviors specified in law as criminal or delinquent are associated with many criminal and delinquent subcultures. The norms, values, or interests of these subcultures may support particular criminal acts, a limited set of such acts (as, for example, a subculture of pickpockets or safe crackers), or they may be even broader in scope. Donald R. Cressey argues that "subcultural definitions of appropriate behavior pertain to very specific kinds of offenses rather than to crime in general" (1983, p. 587). This is especially true of "professional criminals," who take pride in their craft, organize themselves for the safe and efficient performance of the crimes in which they specialize, and generally avoid other types of criminal involvement that might bring them to the attention of the authorities (see Sutherland 1937). Not all criminal subcultures are this specific, however. Some are more opportunistic, embracing several types of criminal behavior as opportunities arise. So it is with delinquent subcultures, where narrow specialization is rare.

While delinquent subcultures typically are associated with a broad range of illegal behaviors, among delinquent groups and subcultures there is great variation in the nature and strength of group norms, values, and interests. Moreover, the extent to which delinquent behavior is attributable to group norms, values, or special interests is problematic. Much delinquent behavior of highly delinquent gangs, for example, results from the operation of group processes rather than group norms per se (see Short 1990). The normative properties of groups vary greatly, but even the most delinquent gang devotes relatively little of its group life in the pursuit of delinquent behaviors. Further, when gangs do participate in delinquent episodes, some members of the gang typically do not become involved. Why this should be the case is an important feature of delinquent subcultures.

For analytical purposes it is important to distinguish between subcultures and the particular groups and individuals who carry them, that is, the individuals and groups who share the norms, values, and interests of the subculture. While members of a delinquent gang may be the sole carriers of a particular subculture, some subcultures are shared by many gangs. Conflict subcultures, for example, are shared by rival fighting gangs among whom individual and group status involves values related to the defense of "turf" (territory) and "rep" (reputation) and norms supportive of these values. Subcultures oriented to theft and other forms of property crime vary in the extent to which they are associated with particular groups. Some types of property crimes require organization and coordination of activities in order to be successful. Some also necessarily involve the efforts of others, such as "fences," in addition to members of a criminally organized gang (see Klockars 1974). Others, such as mugging and other types of robbery, may be carried out by individual offenders, who nevertheless share a subculture supportive of such behavior. Most drug-using subcultures tend to be less oriented toward particular groups than are conflict subcultures because the subcultural orientation is toward drug consumption, and this orientation can be shared with other drug users in many types of group situations. To the extent that a subculture is oriented to experiences associated with a particular group, however, a drug-using subculture may also be unique to that group.

Cultures, subcultures, and the groups associated with them overlap, often in multiple and complex ways. To speak of youth culture, for example, is to denote a subculture of a larger adult-dominated and institutionally defined culture. Similarly, delinquent subcultures contain elements of both youth and adult cultures. Williams's (1989) lower class, minority "cocaine kids," for example, were entrepreneurial, worked long hours, and maintained self-discipline—all important elements in the achievement ideology of the American Dream. Most saw their involvement in the drug trade as a way to get started in legitimate business or to pursue other conventional goals, and a few succeeded at least temporarily in doing so. The criminal subculture with which they identified shared a symbiotic relationship with their customers (including many middle and upper class persons), who shared subcultural values approving drug use but who were not full participants in the subculture of drug distribution. For these young people drug dealing was a way to "be somebody" and to acquire such things as jewelry, clothing, and cars—the symbols of wealth, power, and respect.

The nature of relationships between delinquent subcultures and larger cultural systems is further illustrated by Mercer Sullivan's study of Brooklyn gangs, among whom the "cultural meaning of crime is constructed in . . . interaction out of materials supplied from two sources: the local area in which they spend their time almost totally unsupervised and undirected by adults, and the consumerist youth culture promoted in the mass media" (1989, p. 249). The research literature on criminal and delinquent subcultures is devoted largely to describing and accounting for these types of varied and complex relationships.

## THEORY AND RESEARCH

Despite efforts to define the concept of subculture—and related concepts—more precisely and to describe and account for the empirical reality represented by these concepts, no general theory of subcultures has emerged (see Yinger 1960; 1977). Instead, research has continued to reveal enormous variation in what are termed subcultures, and theory has proceeded by illustration and analogy, with little progress in measurement or formal theoretical development. Despite this scientifically primitive situation, principles of subcultural formation have been identified, and knowledge of it has advanced.

It is a "fundamental law of sociology and anthropology," notes Daniel Glaser, that "social separation produces cultural differentiation" (1971, p. 90). More formally, and more cautiously, social separation is a necessary but not sufficient condition for the formation of subcultures. To the extent that groups or categories of persons are socially separated from one another, subcultural formation is likely to occur.

Albert Cohen argues that a "crucial" (perhaps "necessary") "condition for the emergence of new cultural forms is the existence, in effective interaction with one another, of a number of actors with similar problems of adjustment" (1955, p. 59). While the notion of "similar problems of adjustment" can be interpreted to include problems faced by quite conventional people with special interests who find themselves "in the same boat" with others who have these same interests (let us say, bird-watchers), this condition seems especially appropriate to subcultures that embrace vandalism, "hell raising," and other types of nonutilitarian delinquent behavior, as Cohen intended. Observing that this type of behavior occurs most frequently among working-class boys, Cohen hypothesized that this type of delinquent subculture was formed in reaction to status problems experienced by working-class boys in middle class institutions such as schools. Many working-class boys are inadequately prepared for either the educational demands or the discipline of formal education, and they are evaluated poorly in terms of this "middle class measuring rod." Working-class girls are less pressured in these terms, Cohen argued, because they are judged according to criteria associated with traditional female roles, and they are subject to closer controls in the family.

The solution to their status problems, for some working-class boys, according to Cohen's theory, is to reject the performance and status criteria of middle class institutions, in effect turning middle class values upside down. The theory thus seeks to account for the highly expressive and hedonistic quality of much delinquency and for the malicious and negativistic quality of vandalism.

Cohen did not attempt to account for the delinquent behavior of particular individuals or for the behavior of all working-class boys. Most of the latter do not become delinquent—at least not seriously so. They choose instead—or are channeled into—alternative adaptations such as the essentially nondelinquent "corner boys" or the high-achieving "college boys" described by William Foote Whyte (1943).

While the forces propelling youngsters into alternative adaptations such as these are not completely understood, many working-class and lower class boys and girls are devalued in middle class institutional contexts. Their marginality sets the stage for subcultural adaptations. Delinquents and criminals occupy even more marginal positions. This is particularly true of persistent delinquents and criminals who commit serious crimes, in contrast to those who only rarely transgress the law and with little consequence. When marginality is reinforced by labeling, stigmatization, or prejudicial treatment in schools and job markets, "problems of adjustment" magnify. The common ecological location of many delinquents, in the inner city slums of large cities, and their coming together in schools, provides the setting for "effective interaction." The result often is the formation of youth gangs, the most common organizational form taken by delinquent subcultures (see Thrasher 1927; Short 1990).

While there is no universally agreed-upon definition of youth gangs, for theoretical purposes it is useful to define them as groups whose members meet together with some regularity over time and whose membership is selected on the basis of group-defined criteria and according to group-defined organizational characteristics. Most importantly, they are not adult-sponsored groups. The nature of relationships between young people and conventional adults is the most critical difference between gangs and other youth groups (see Schwartz 1987). Gang members are less closely tied to conventional institutions and therefore less constrained by institutional controls than are non-gang youth. Group processes of status achievement, allocation, and defense are more likely to result in delinquent behavior among gangs than among adult-sponsored groups.

## HOW DO CRIMINAL AND DELINQUENT SUBCULTURES GET STARTED?

Cressey notes that "delinquent and criminal subcultures have long been present in industrialized societies" (1983, p. 585). Herman and Julia Schwendinger (1985) trace the origins of adolescent subcultures, including delinquent varieties, to social changes associated with the advent of sixteenth-century capitalism in Western Europe. Vast changes in traditional economic and social relationships, which changes were associated with capitalism and the Industrial Revolution, left in their wake large numbers of unemployed persons, disrupting communities, families, and other primordial groups. Cut adrift from traditional crafts and communities, thousands roamed the countryside, subsisting as best they could off the land or by victimizing travelers. The "dangerous classes" eventually settled in cities, again to survive by whatever means were available, including crime.

Criminal subcultures and organizational networks often developed under these circumstances.

The Schwendingers emphasize the importance for criminal subcultural formation of capitalist values and their accompanying norms/and interests—individualism and competitiveness, acquisitiveness and exploitativeness—and the relationship between capitalism and emerging nation-states of the period.

While many of the facts upon which this Marxist interpretation is based are generally accepted, careful historical analysis of economic and political systems and their consequences cautions against any simple or straightforward interpretation (see Chirot 1985). The connection between global phenomena and crime and delinquency always is mediated by historical, cultural, and local circumstances—by the historically concrete (see Tilly 1981).

In contrast to this account of the origins of Western European youth cultures, Ko-lin Chin (1990) traces the development of Chinese youth gangs in the United States to ancient secret society traditions, specifically to more recent Triad societies that formed in the late seventeenth century in China, and their counterpart tongs in the United States. Formed initially as political groups representing "ousted Chinese officials and the alienated poor" (p. 9), these groups initially stressed patriotism, righteousness, and brotherhood as primary values. Their secret nature was conducive to clandestine activities such as gambling, prostitution, and running opium dens. Competition among Triad societies in these areas often led to violence. Failure to achieve political power led to their further transformation into criminal organizations involved in extortion, robbery, drug trafficking, and other serious crimes.

The first Chinese street gangs in the United States did not form until the late 1950s, but their numbers increased dramatically during the following decade, when changed immigration laws permitted more Chinese to enter the country. Conflict between foreign- and American-born youths led to the emergence of several gangs. From the beginning, many Chinese youth gangs have been associated in a variety of ways with established adult secret societies in this country, in Hong Kong and Taiwan, or in all three places. Others, particularly in New York City, emerged from American youth culture in response to conflicts with other racial and ethnic groups. Some evolved into seriously delinquent gangs. Chin attributes this development to alienating problems experienced by immigrant Chinese youth in their families, schools, and communities, in dramatic contrast to their high-achieving, American-born counterparts. The existence of "Triad-influenced" tong organizations has been critical to the types of gangs that have emerged in Chinese communities and to the nature of their criminal activities, however.

While the origins of delinquent subcultures may reside in antiquity, the formation and evolution of modern variations of them thus can be explained in terms of more immediate macro-level developments. Some of these relate primarily to the ongoing activities and interests of gang members rather than to racial or ethnic changes, or to sweeping social changes. The nature of these influences is illustrated by a drug-using group studied by James Short, Fred Strodtbeck, and their associates (Short and Strodtbeck 1965; Short 1990). This gang was observed as it developed its own unique subculture. The subculture of the "Pill Poppers," as they became known to the research team, evolved from their relationship with a larger, conflict-oriented gang of which they had previously been a part. The Pill Poppers' preoccupation with drugs and their refusal to participate in the more bellicose activities of the larger gang led to their withdrawal and increasing isolation, by mutual agreement. The researchers were able to observe the evolution of this subculture, which was characterized by normative approval of drug consumption, a high value on "getting high," and mutual interest in the "crazy" things that happened to them when they were under the influence of drugs. The latter, in particular, became legendary within the group, being told and retold with nostalgia and humor when members of the gang were together. Short and Strodtbeck contrasted the subculture of this gang with that of other gangs that participated in a conflict subculture.

## LEVELS OF EXPLANATION OF CRIMINAL AND DELINQUENT SUBCULTURES

These theories of criminal and delinquent subcultures are macro-level theories. Their purpose is to explain what it is about political, economic, and other social systems that explains the emergence and the social distribution of these phenomena. Other theories at this level focus on the impact of local and broader community opportunities on delinquent subcultures and on youth subcultures generally. Cloward and Ohlin (1960) relate varieties of delinquent subcultures to the availability of legitimate and illegitimate economic opportunities in local communities. Schwartz (1987) stresses the importance of local community youth–adult authority relationships in determining the nature of youth subcultures, including the extent and the nature of delinquent activities associated with them. Sullivan (1989) relates gang adaptations to more global economic developments such as the transfer of manufacturing jobs from the United States to other countries and an increasingly segmented labor market, which has resulted in the concentration of low-wage and surplus labor in inner-city minority communities (see also Hagedorn 1987).

Wilson (1987) argues that an important consequence of these economic changes is the emergence of a permanent underclass of the "truly disadvantaged." Research on delinquent subcultures supports this argument and documents significant changes in gang membership. Because fewer good jobs are available to poor, minority young men, more gang members continue their association with gangs as they enter adulthood. In the past, gang members typically "grew out of" the gang to take jobs, get married, and often to become associated with adult social clubs in stable, ethnically based communities. These options have become less viable among the poor of all races, but minorities have increasingly become the

truly disadvantaged. Gang organization has been affected by this change, as older members assume or continue leadership roles. The result often has been that gang involvement in criminal activities has become more sophisticated and instrumental, and younger members have been exploited in criminal enterprise. Relationships between young people and conventional adults also suffer, as older, stable role models and monitors of youthful behavior are replaced by young adult, often criminal, role models for the young (see Anderson 1990).

Sullivan's study of groups of young males in three Brooklyn communities—black, predominantly Latino, and white—is particularly significant in this regard. The young men in Hamilton Park, the white group, were able to find better jobs than were the others at all ages. More important, because "they had become more familiar with the discipline of the workplace," as they grew older they were able to secure better-quality jobs and to hold on to them, more so than were the minority youth. Familiarity with the discipline of the workplace is a type of human capital that was made possible by an important type of social capital—the superior personal networks that the Hamilton Park youth shared with the adult community (Sullivan 1989, pp. 105, 226). The minority youth were disadvantaged, with respect to both human and social capital, in the family and in other ways (see Coleman 1988).

Human and social capital are individual characteristics determined largely by social experience. All macro-level theories make certain assumptions about the individual level of explanation. The most prominent of these assumptions is that individuals learn subcultural norms, values, and the behaviors they encourage in interaction with others in their environment. The general processes of learning have been well established by research and theory (see Bandura 1986; Eron 1987). The child's most important learning experiences take place in the family, but other influences quickly assert themselves, especially as children associate with age and gender peers. With the beginning of adolescence the latter become especially powerful, as young people experience important biological and social changes. It is at this point that youth subcultures become especially significant.

Subcultures are dynamic and ever changing, influenced by both external and internal forces and processes. Substantial knowledge gaps exist at each level of explanation. Gaps between macro- and individual-level explanations result in large part from the fact that these levels ask different questions and explain different aspects of subcultures and behavior. As noted above, macro-level explanations ask why it is that subcultures and behaviors are distributed as they are in social and cultural systems and why they occur as they do in some times and places. Explanation at this level focuses on differences in rates of subcultural phenomena, while the individual level focuses on individuals—their biological and psychological makeup and their social experiences.

Precisely how these levels of explanation relate to each other is not well understood. Group processes such as those noted above help to inform the nature of the relationship, however. By documenting the ongoing interaction among gang members and between gang members and others, this micro-level explanation reveals group processes that are consistent with what is known at the individual and macro levels of explanation. Both intragang and intergang fighting often serve group purposes, as for example by demonstrating personal qualities that are highly valued by the gang or by reinforcing group solidarity (see Miller, Geertz, and Cutter 1961; Jansyn 1966). Gang conflict often occurs when a gang believes its "rep," its "turf," or its resources (for example, its share of a drug market) are threatened by another gang. Threats to individual or group status often result in violent or other types of criminal behavior (Short 1990).

## CONCLUSION

No general theory of criminal or delinquent subcultures has been entirely successful. The rich research materials that have accumulated suggest two conclusions, however: (1) there is a great variety of such adaptive phenomena and (2) these phenomena are of an ever-changing nature. Because they both effect social change and adapt to it, subcultures—including criminal and delinquent subcultures—continue to be important theoretically, empirically, and practically, that is, as a matter of social policy.

(SEE ALSO: *Crime, Theories of; Criminology; Juvenile Delinquency and Juvenile Crime; Juvenile Delinquency, Theories of*)

## REFERENCES

Anderson, Elijah 1990 *Streetwise: Race, Class, and Change in an Urban Community.* Chicago: University of Chicago Press.

Bandura, Albert 1986 *Social Foundations of Thought and Action: A Social Cognitive Theory.* Englewood Cliffs, N.J.: Prentice-Hall.

Chin, Ko-lin 1990 *Chinese Subculture and Criminality: Nontraditional Crime Groups in America.* Westport, Conn.: Greenwood Press.

Chirot, Daniel 1985 "The Rise of the West." *American Sociological Review* 50:181–195.

Cloward, Richard A., and Lloyd E. Ohlin 1960 *Delinquency and Opportunity: A Theory of Delinquent Gangs.* New York: Free Press.

Cohen, Albert K. 1955 *Delinquent Boys: The Culture of the Gang.* New York: Free Press.

Coleman, James S. 1988 "Social Capital in the Creation of Human Capital." *American Journal of Sociology* 94 (Suppl.): S95–S120.

Cressey, Donald R. 1983 "Delinquent and Criminal Subcultures." In S. E. Kadish, ed., *Encyclopedia of Crime and Justice.* New York: Free Press.

Eron, Leonard D. 1987 "The Development of Aggressive Behavior from the Perspective of a Developing Behaviorism." *American Psychologist* 42:435–442.

Fagan, Jeffrey 1990 "Social Processes of Delinquency and Drug Use among Urban Gangs." In C. Ronald Huff, ed., *Gangs in America.* Newbury Park, Calif.: Sage.

Glaser, Daniel 1971 *Social Deviance.* Chicago: Markham.

Hagedorn, John M., with Perry Macon 1987 *People and Folks: Gangs, Crime, and the Underclass in a Rustbelt City.* Chicago: Lake View Press.

Jansyn, Leon R. 1966 "Solidarity and Delinquency in a Street-Corner Group." *American Sociological Review* 31:600–614.

Johnson, Bruce D., Terry Williams, Kojo A. Dei, and Harry Sanabria 1990 "Drug Abuse in the Inner City: Impact on Hard-Drug Users and the Community." In Michael Tonry and James Q. Wilson, eds., *Drugs and Crime*. Chicago: University of Chicago Press.

Klockars, Carl B. 1974 *The Professional Fence*. New York: Free Press.

Miller, Walter B. 1958 "Lower Class Culture as a Generating Milieu of Gang Delinquency." *Journal of Social Issues* 14:5–19.

Miller, Walter B., Hildred Geertz, Henry S. G. Cutter 1961 "Aggression in a Boys' Street-Corner Group." *Psychiatry* 24:283–298.

Schwartz, Gary 1987 *Beyond Conformity or Rebellion: Youth and Authority in America*. Chicago: University of Chicago Press.

Schwendinger, Herman, and Julia Siegel Schwendinger 1985 *Adolescent Subcultures and Delinquency*. New York: Praeger.

Short, James F. 1990 *Delinquency and Society*. Englewood Cliffs, N.J.: Prentice-Hall.

———, and Fred L. Strodtbeck 1965 *Group Process and Gang Delinquency*. Chicago: University of Chicago Press.

Sullivan, Mercer L. 1989 *"Getting Paid": Youth Crime and Work in the Inner City*. Ithaca, N.Y.: Cornell University Press.

Sutherland, Edwin H. 1937 *The Professional Thief*. Chicago: University of Chicago Press.

Thrasher, Frederic M. 1927 *The Gang: A Study of 1,313 Gangs in Chicago*. Chicago: University of Chicago Press.

Tilly, Charles 1981 *As Sociology Meets History*. New York: Academic Press.

Vigil, James Diego 1988 *Barrio Gangs*. Austin: University of Texas Press.

Whyte, William Foote 1943 *Street Corner Society*. Chicago: University of Chicago Press.

Williams, Terry 1989 *The Cocaine Kids: The Inside Story of a Teenage Drug Ring*. Menlo Park, Calif.: Addison-Wesley.

Wilson, William Julius 1987 *The Truly Disadvantaged: The Inner City, the Underclass, and Public Policy*. Chicago: University of Chicago Press.

Yinger, Milton 1960 "Contraculture and Subculture." *American Sociological Review* 23:625–635.

——— 1977 "Countercultures and Social Change." *American Sociological Review* 42:833–853.

JAMES F. SHORT, JR.

**CRIMINALIZATION OF DEVIANCE** A 1985 household survey dealing with drug abuse revealed that 22 percent of persons eighteen to twenty-five, 17 percent of persons twenty-six to thirty-four, and 2 percent of persons thirty-five years or older had smoked marijuana within the last thirty days (U.S. Department of Health and Human Services 1988). The same survey showed that a majority of persons eighteen to thirty-four had smoked marijuana at least once during their lifetimes. Rather than containing an overwhelming majority who believe that smoking marijuana is wrong and just a sprinkling of individuals who believe that it is legitimate, American society is polarized into first, a large group, probably a majority, who consider smoking marijuana wrong and second, a smaller group (but a substantial proportion of young adults) who consider marijuana harmless and who are indignant at societal interference. A nonconformist is immensely strengthened by having even one ally, as the social psychologist Solomon Asch demonstrated in laboratory experiments (Asch 1955). Unfortunately, contemporary societies, being large and heterogeneous, are likely to provide allies for behavior that the majority condemns.

Yet moral polarization does not characterize American society on every issue. Consensus exists that persons who smell bad and persons who force others to participate unwillingly in sexual relations are reprehensible. Body odor and rape seem an incongruous combination. What they have in common is that both are deviant, which means that they are strongly disapproved by the overwhelming majority of Americans. Where they differ is that only one (rape) is a statutory crime that can result in police arrest, a court trial, and a prison sentence. The other, body odor, although deviant, is not criminalized. When deviance is criminalized, the organized collectivity channels the indignant response of individuals, as the following true story illustrates:

*In March, 1983, a 21-year-old woman, new to a Portuguese neighborhood in New Bedford, Massachusetts, stopped into Big Dan's Tavern for cigarettes and a drink at 9 P.M. on a Sunday evening.*

*She emerged after midnight, screaming for help, bruised, her clothes partially torn off. She told the police that she had been hoisted onto the pool table, held there against her will, and raped repeatedly by a group of men. The patrons of the bar stood watching, taunting her, and cheering on the rapists. A week later 2,500 silent protestors marched through New Bedford carrying lighted candles and banners with the words, "Rape Is Not a Spectator Sport." The march, which drew support from women's groups throughout the Northeast, was covered both by TV and the print media.* (Toby 1988)

In this case, what was alleged to have occurred in the tavern simultaneously aroused both police intervention and widespread public indignation. That indignation was sufficient to pressure the owners of Big Dan's tavern to give up their liquor license and to close down. On the legal level, the rapists were tried, convicted, and sent to prison. Some sociologists argue that when sufficient consensus exists about the wrongfulness of an act, the act gets criminalized. This is usually the case but not always. Despite consensus that failing to bathe for three months is reprehensible, body odor has not been criminalized. And acts *have* become criminalized, for example, patent infringement and other white-collar crimes, but these do not arouse much public indignation. In short, the relationship between what is deviant and what is criminal is complicated.

For a clue to an explanation of how and why deviance gets criminalized, note how difficult it is for members of a society to know with certainty what is deviant. Conceptually, deviance refers to the purposive evasion or defiance of a normative consensus. Defiant deviance is fairly obvious. If Joe, a high school student, is asked a question in class by his English teacher pertaining to the lesson, and he replies, "I won't tell you, asshole," most Americans would probably agree that he is violating the role expectations for high school students in this society. Evasive deviance is less confrontational, albeit more common than defiant deviance, and therefore more ambiguous. If Joe never does the assigned homework or frequently comes late without a good explanation,

many Americans would agree that he is not doing what he is supposed to do, although the point at which he steps over the line into outright deviance is fuzzy. Both evasive and defiant deviance require other members of the society to make a judgment that indignation is the appropriate response to the behavior in question. Such a judgment is difficult to make in a heterogeneous society because members of the society cannot be sure how closely other people share their values.

To be sure, the individual knows from living in a society what sorts of behavior will trigger indignant reactions, but not with great confidence. The issue is blurred by subgroup variation and because norms change with the passage of time. Bathing suits that were entirely proper in 1990 in the United States would have been scandalous in 1920. A survey might find that a large percentage of the population disapproves now of nudity on a public beach. The survey cannot reveal for how long the population will continue to disapprove of public nudity. Nor can the survey help much with the crucial problem of deciding how large a proportion of the population disapproves strongly enough to justify categorizing public nudity as "deviant."

In short, whether a normative consensus has been violated depends, first, on whether a consensus exists at all; to determine this, individual normative judgments must somehow be aggregated, say, by conducting a survey that would enable a representative sample of the population to express reactions to various kinds of behavior. Ideally, these responses differ only by degree, but in a large society there are often qualitatively different conceptions of right and wrong.

In practice, then, in modern society neither the potential perpetrator nor the onlooker can be certain what is deviant. Consequently the social response to an act that is on the borderline between deviance and acceptability is unpredictable. This unpredictability may tempt the individual to engage in behavior he would not engage in if he knew that the response would be widespread disapproval. It may also restrain onlookers from taking action—or at least expressing disapproval—against persons violating the informal rules.

## WHAT CRIME INVOLVES: A COLLECTIVE RESPONSE

Crime is clearer. The ordinary citizen may not know precisely which acts are illegal in a particular jurisdiction. But a definite answer is possible. A lawyer familiar with the criminal code of the State of New Jersey can explain exactly what has to be proved in order to convict a person of drunken driving in New Jersey. The codification of an act as criminal does not depend on its intrinsic danger to the society but on what societal leaders *perceive* as dangerous. For example, Cuba has the following provision in its criminal code:

> *Article 108. (1) There will be a sanction of deprivation of freedom of from one to eight years imposed on anyone who:*
> *(a) incites against the social order, international solidarity or the socialist State by means of oral or written propaganda, or in any other form;*
> *(b) makes, distributes or possesses propaganda of the character mentioned in the preceding clause.*
>
> *(2) Anyone who spreads false news or malicious predictions liable to cause alarm or discontent in the population, or public disorder, is subject to a sanction of from one to four years imprisonment.*
> *(3) If the mass media are used for the execution of the actions described in the previous paragraphs, the sanction will be deprivation of freedom from seven to fifteen years.* (Ripoll 1985, p. 20)

In other words, mere possession of a mimeograph machine in Cuba is a very serious crime because Fidel Castro considers the dissemination of critical ideas a threat to his "socialist State," and in Cuba Castro's opinions are literally law. Hence, possession of a mimeograph machine is a punishable offense. Members of Jehovah's Witnesses who used mimeograph machines to reproduce religious tracts have been given long prison sentences. On the other hand, reproducing religious tracts may not arouse indignation in the Cuban population. If so, it is not deviant.

In California or New Jersey, as in Cuba, a crime is behavior punishable by the state. But the difference is that in the fifty states, as in all democratic societies, the legislators and judges who enact and interpret criminal laws do not simply codify their own moral sentiments; they criminalize behavior in response to influences brought to bear on them by members of their constituencies. True, women, children, members of ethnic and racial minorities, and the poorly educated may not have as much political input as affluent, middle-aged, white male professionals. But *less* influence does not mean they don't count. In a dictatorship, on the other hand, the political process is closed; few people count when it comes to deciding what is a crime.

## WHY DEVIANCE IS CRIMINALIZED

Criminalization solves the problem of predictability of response by transferring the obligation to respond to deviance from the individual members of society to agents of the state (the police). But criminalization creates a new problem: Which members of society are able to persuade the state to enforce *their* moral sentiments? In short, criminalization means that the social control of deviance is politicized. In every society, deviant acts get criminalized in the course of a political process. Generally, the political leadership of a society criminalizes an act when it becomes persuaded that without criminalization the deviant contagion will spread, thereby undermining social order. The leaders may be wrong. Fidel Castro might be able to retain control even if Cubans were allowed access to mimeograph machines and word processors. Nevertheless, leaders decide on crimes based on their perception of what is a threat to the collectivity. According to legal scholars (Packer 1968), the tendency in politically organized societies is to overcriminalize, that is, to involve the state excessively in the punishment of deviance. Political authorities find it difficult to resist the temptation to perceive threats in what may only be harmless diversity and to attempt to stamp it out by state punishment.

Sociology's labeling perspective on deviance (Becker 1963; Lemert 1983) goes further; it suggests that overcriminalization may *increase* deviance by changing the self-concept of the stigmatized individual. Thus, pinning the official label of "criminal" on someone may amplify criminal tendencies. At its most extreme, this point of view denies the desirability of *any* kind of criminalization: "The task [of radical reform] is to create a society in which the facts of human diversity, whether personal, organic, or social, are not subject to the power to criminalize" (Taylor, Walton, and Young 1973, p. 282).

The absence of criminal law—and consequently of state-imposed sanctions for violations—is no threat to small primitive communities: Informal social controls can be counted on to prevent most deviance and to punish what deviance cannot be prevented. In heterogeneous modern societies, however, the lack of some criminalization would make moral unity difficult to achieve. When Emile Durkheim spoke of the collective conscience of a society, he was writing metaphorically; he knew that he was abstracting from the differing consciences of thousands of individuals. Nevertheless, the criminal law serves to resolve these differences and achieve a contrived—and indeed precarious—moral unity. In democratic societies, the unity is achieved by political compromise. In authoritarian or totalitarian societies the power wielders unify the society by imposing their own values on the population at large. In both cases law is a unifying force; large societies could not function without a legal system because universalistic rules, including the rules of the criminal law, meld in this way ethnic, regional, and class versions of what is deviant (Parsons 1977, pp. 138–139).

## THE CONSEQUENCES OF CRIMINALIZATION

The unifying effect of the criminal law has unintended consequences. One major consequence is the development of a large bureaucracy devoted to enforcing criminal laws: police, judges, prosecutors, jailors, probation officers, parole officers, prison guards, and assorted professionals like psychologists and social workers who attempt to rehabilitate convicted offenders. Ideally, these employees of the state should perform their roles dispassionately, not favoring some accused persons or discriminating against others. In practice, however, members of the criminal justice bu-

reaucracy bring to their jobs the parochial sentiments of their social groups as well as a personal interest in financial gain or professional advancement. This helps to explain why police are often more enthusiastic about enforcing some criminal laws than they are about enforcing others.

Another consequence of criminalization is that the criminal law, being universal in its reach, cannot make allowance for subgroup variation in sentiments about what is right and what is wrong. Thus, some people are imprisoned for behavior that neither they nor members of their social group regard as reprehensible, as in Northern Ireland where members of the Irish Republican Army convicted of assassinating British soldiers consider themselves political prisoners. They have gone on hunger strikes—in some cases to the point of death—rather than wear the prison uniform of ordinary criminals.

## CONCLUSION

The more heterogeneous the culture and the more swiftly its norms are changing, the less consensus about right and wrong exists within the society. In the United States, moral values differ to some extent in various regions, occupations, religions, social classes, and ethnic groups. This sociocultural value pluralism means that it is difficult to identify behavior that everyone considers deviant. It is much easier to identify crime, which is codified in politically organized societies. The criminalization of deviance makes it clear when collective reprisals will be taken against those who violate rules.

Deviance exists in smaller social systems, too: in families, universities, corporations. In addition to being subjected to the informal disapproval of other members of these collectivities, the deviant in the family, the university, or the work organization can be subjected to formally organized sanctioning procedures like a disciplinary hearing at a university. However, the worst sanction that these nonsocietal social systems can visit upon deviants is expulsion. A university cannot imprison a student who cheats on a final exam. Even in the larger society, however, not all deviance is criminalized, sometimes for cultural reasons as in American refusal to criminalize the expression of political dissent, but also for pragmatic reasons as in the American failure to criminalize body odor, lying to one's friends, or smoking in church.

(SEE ALSO: *Criminology; Deviance; Deviance Theories*)

### REFERENCES

Asch, Solomon E. 1955 "Opinions and Social Pressure." *Scientific American* 193, November.

Becker, Howard S. 1963 *Outsiders: Studies in the Sociology of Deviance.* New York: Free Press.

Lemert, Edwin M. 1983 "Deviance." In Sanford H. Kadish, ed., *Encyclopedia of Crime and Justice.* New York: Free Press.

Packer, Herbert L. 1968 *The Limits of the Criminal Sanction.* Stanford, Calif.: Stanford University Press.

Parsons, Talcott 1977 *The Evolution of Societies.* Englewood Cliffs, N.J.: Prentice-Hall.

Ripoll, Carlos 1985 *Harnessing the Intellectual: Censoring Writers and Artists in Today's Cuba.* Washington, D.C.: Cuban American National Foundation.

Taylor, Ian, Paul Walton, and Jock Young 1973 *The New Criminology.* London: Routledge and Kegan Paul.

Toby, Jackson 1988 "Should Film Makers Never Choose Myth over Fact?" *Los Angeles Times,* December 18.

U.S. Department of Health and Human Services, National Institute of Drug Abuse 1988 *National Household Survey on Drug Abuse: Main Findings 1985.* Washington, D.C.: U.S. Government Printing Office.

JACKSON TOBY

**CRIMINAL SANCTIONS** Criminal sanctions are the penalties imposed by a legally constituted authority on violators of the criminal laws. These penalties vary widely in form, including corporal and capital punishment, imprisonment, exile, fine, probationary supervision, or community service. Underlying these various forms is a common denominator of stigma, which is not inherent in other deprivations of resources and freedom imposed by the state (Feinberg 1970). This stigma arises from the nature of crime being in principle an offense committed against the community as a whole rather than a wrong committed by one individual against another. Traditionally, this stigma entailed permanent civil disabilities in public employment, child custody, voting, and other rights (Burton, Cullen, and Travis 1987). Because criminal sanctions are so consequential, societies that emphasize the value of individualism tend to elaborate due process in criminal prosecutions more than for any other exercise of state power.

The criminal sanction is a legal category, not a primitive term in social theory. Consequently, instead of developing a general theory of penality, sociology has developed a plurality of inquiries into the social organizational antecedents and consequences of variations in the form and frequency of criminal sanctions. For social theory, the significance of the criminal sanction arises from its position as a critical nexus between the individual and society, exposing the nature of social solidarity (Durkheim [1893] 1950), political power (Foucault 1979), or class relations (Rusche and Kirchheimer [1939] 1968). This article delineates the distinctive agenda of sociological studies of the criminal sanction and then outlines some major lines of empirical study of the criminal sanction's impact on society and the variations in its forms.

### SOCIOLOGICAL PERSPECTIVES ON CRIMINAL SANCTION

Several disciplines examine the relationships between the criminal sanction and social organization. The applied field of *penology* compares the effectiveness of sanction policies, isolating these pragmatic concerns from their political, economic, and social contexts. Alternatively, *moral philosophy* begins with value premises and seeks to evaluate the justification for imposing criminal sanctions. Consider, for instance, the use of the criminal sanction to rehabilitate offenders. Penologists evaluate rehabilitation in terms of the impact alternative treatments produce on the recidivism rate (e.g., Martinson 1974). Moral philosophers assess rehabilitation in light of general principles of social justice (e.g., Fogel 1975).

Sociologists, in contrast, seek to explain variations in the adoption of the rehabilitation rationale for punishment as a function of variations in such aspects of social structure as the nature of class relationships and state power (e.g., Humphries and Greenberg 1981). While policy and moral implications are incorporated in such work, they do not, as in the case of the other two disciplines, constitute the core of the analysis. More central to the sociological enterprise is some form of empirical analysis that tests theoretical generalizations about sanctions and structures. From this perspective sociologists have produced a variety of analyses of the societal consequences and antecedents of variation in criminal sanctions, a sample of which will now be reviewed.

## CONSEQUENCES OF ENFORCING CRIMINAL SANCTIONS

Research on the consequences of enforcing criminal sanctions was initially framed by the utilitarian doctrine of *deterrence:* Crime varies inversely with the certainty, severity, and celerity of the criminal sanction. Several traditions in sociology posit an antithesis to deterrence theory, namely, that criminal sanctions amplify deviance. Amplification may result from imposing on rulebreakers an identity change and opportunity costs (cf. Thomas and Bishop 1984) or, in the case of capital punishment, from reinforcing the social climate of violence (Bowers 1984, pp. 271–335). While several isolated observations support both deterrence and amplification hypotheses, the conditions under which these effects hold remains to be theoretically specified.

Extant empirical research estimates the effects on crime of marginal changes in the severity or certainty of punishment. Much of this work is based on correlations between aggregate rates of crime and punishment using, for example, interstate variations in crime and imprisonment rates. This evidence suggests that (1) the risk of criminal sanctions deters more strongly than severity of

punishment; (2) the effects are neither strong nor consistent; and (3) other social influences create an observed relationship between crime rates and sanction levels. Increasingly sophisticated multivariate research designs have not noticeably reduced the sharpness of debate over the magnitude of deterrence effects (for review of this literature see Beyleveld 1980).

This continuing debate is fed in part by reliance upon aggregate social indicator research beset by various methodological barriers. For example, the deterrence hypothesis predicts that crime rates will decrease as sanction levels increase, but the same correlation will arise from an overloading of the criminal justice system. As the number of cases increase, crime control organizations with fixed budgets can arrest, prosecute, and punish proportionately fewer offenders.

Because the aggregate measures of risk are far removed from individual decision making, researchers have investigated variations in levels of the punishment's publicity (Bailey and Peterson 1989) or the effectiveness of social networks in transmitting information about punishments to potential offenders (Ekland-Olson, Lieb, and Zurcher 1984). Alternatively, survey research may measure more directly the subjective response to the threat of sanctions by having respondents report their perceptions of the risk and severity of sanctions along with confessions of past or intended law breaking. Although these studies often confirm deterrence theory's predictions, the results are open to reservations about the representativeness of samples (Piliavin et al. 1986) and the ability of respondents to report accurately their decision making (Paternoster et al. 1982).

An alternative mode of support for deterrence effects appears in one of the rare field experiments on sanctioning. Sherman and Berk (1984) assigned domestic violence cases randomly to four alternative police responses. Consistent with deterrence theory, they found that arrest produced the greatest reduction in subsequent levels of domestic violence. Questions, particularly about the external validity of these results, have stimulated an ongoing program of replication studies.

While sociologists were once inclined to favor labeling over deterrence theories on a priori moral grounds, current thinking views the issue as open and resolvable only by innovative research designs.

## CONSEQUENCES OF ENACTING CRIMINAL SANCTIONS: LEGAL IMPACT STUDIES

A separate literature examines the related issue of the social impact of imposing criminal sanctions on categories of conduct rather than on individual malefactors. This research is dominated by historical case studies from which investigators seek to extract generalizations about the consequences of criminalization or decriminalization. Unfortunately, such generalizations are not easily excavated from this evidence. For example, Prohibition (1919–1933) is popularly perceived to exemplify the failure of criminalization to change social patterns of drug use. Even assuming this assessment is accurate, the generalization is readily countered by the roughly contemporaneous Harrison Narcotic Act (1914), which appears to have altered dramatically the social class distribution of opiate abuse (Conrad and Schneider 1980, pp. 121–130).

Legal impact research tends to support labeling over deterrence theory; it suggests that if criminal sanctions have any impact at all, it is to exacerbate the problems they are designed to solve at considerable cost in law-enforcement resources. These conflicting conclusions result in part from differences in the crimes studied. Where deterrence research concentrates on common-law crimes of predation and violence, much of the legal impact research has been concerned with "victimless crimes" of abortion, alcohol and drug use, gambling, homosexuality, pornography, and prostitution; all entail strong public demands being regulated by laws resting on contested morality.

Research on the social impact of criminalization tends to be policy relevant, issue specific, and atheoretical. Research has grown primarily through the exploration of new arenas of applica-tion for criminal sanctions, such as pornography (Downs 1989) and drunk driving (Gusfield 1980). Consequently, debates over the consequences of legal change, such as decriminalization of narcotics, rely on precedents and analogies to assess the consequences of legal change, such as decriminalization of narcotics, rely on precedents and analogies to assess the consequences of decriminalization on rates of use and viability of alternative modes of social control (e.g., Nadelmann 1989).

## ANTECEDENTS OF CRIMINAL SANCTION

While the consequences of criminal sanctions are important for both social theory and social policy, sociological research has equally been concerned with understanding the social structural antecedents of criminal sanctions. It is convenient to classify these concerns into issues of qualitative versus quantitative variation.

**Qualitative Variations in Sanctions.** The forms that criminal sanctions take have been extensively investigated. The past two centuries of Western criminal law have been marked by a series of reforms, including the abolition of corporal and capital punishment, the rise of the penitentiary, and probation. Sociological accounts of these developments have emphasized their relationships to concomitant changes in the nature of economic production (Rusche and Kirchheimer [1939] 1968; Humphries and Greenberg 1981), social organization (Erikson 1966), state formation (Hamilton and Sutton 1989), and cultural values (Spierenburg 1984). These varying accounts continue to stimulate a wide range of work concerned with historical origins and subsequent trajectories of the forms of the criminal sanction (for overview, see Garland 1990).

**Quantitative Variations in Sanctions.** Social structure influences not only the form of the criminal sanction but the rate at which it is imposed. Because discretionary decision making plays a key role in selecting lawbreakers for criminal sanctioning, status characteristics may influence the selection of law violators for sanctioning and the nature of the sanction imposed on them. Among the factors that influence discretion, sociological research has given special attention to labor markets. While unemployment may increase crime and thus increase punishment, its effect on sanctions may also be direct. Unemployment levels may lead judges, for example, to impose prison sentences rather than probation because the employed run a lower risk of future lawbreaking (for an overview, see Melossi 1989).

Distinct albeit related factors prominent in the research are race and gender. The research strategy here has been to estimate the effect of extralegal characteristics on sanctions net of crime. This problem corresponds to that in labor-market research on occupational attainment, which attempts to estimate the effects of ascribed characteristics apart from job-related inputs of minorities. Estimates of race and gender effects on sentencing are much more mixed (Wilbanks 1987 offers a comprehensive albeit controversial summary of the work on race; on gender, see Daly 1989). Perhaps the most important development sociologically in this research is a recognition that discrimination itself is a variable with social organizational antecedents. While traditional research sought to document the simple presence of discrimination, the new approach seeks to explain its variability. Closely related is the research concerned with the impact of sentencing reforms designed to reduce discretion in the application of sanctions (Cohen and Tonry 1983). Again, results are mixed, and it may be too soon to obtain a coherent reading of the impact of these reforms.

## FUTURE OF THE CRIMINAL SANCTION

Orwell's nightmare of expanding state repression is well represented in current theory of the "carceral society" (Foucault 1979) and the "maximum security society" (Marx 1988). Forecasting trends in phenomena still only vaguely understood is a risky enterprise. The dramatic expansion of the U.S. prison population in the 1980s may reflect less of a change in the structural propensity to punish than it represents the growth of the age population at risk and changing age-specific propensities to engage in imprisonable offenses.

Observers who point to indicators of increasing state coercion seldom take into account the concomitant expansion in recent years of due process in criminal procedure and the growing body of legal constraints on the treatment of prison inmates (Bottoms 1983). While conservatives have lamented the constraints on crime control created by this expansion of constitutional restraints, the impact of these reforms has yet to be assessed beyond isolated empirical case studies of how particular Supreme Court decisions alter police (mal)practice. Furthermore, some analysts point to the ways in which extension of the criminal sanction into new areas such as juvenile offenses entails expansion of procedural protections (Feld 1984).

The various limitations of the criminal sanction (due-process requirements, level of the burden of proof) may have stimulated the growth of medical controls (Kittrie 1971; Conrad and Schneider 1980) and administrative law and its variants (Freiberg and O'Malley 1984). It is important in thinking about the future of the criminal sanction to extend our vision beyond its familiar forms. These new forms of state control circumvent the constraints that render the criminal sanction especially difficult to apply in victimless, corporate, and organized crimes. By domesticating the criminal sanction, reforms may have stimulated the development for more subtle and pervasive forms of social control.

Such developments are not novel. Indeed, the ambiguities of the legal definition of criminal sanction suggested at the start of this article reflect the extent to which criminal sanctions are the outcome of social organizational processes rather than logical deductions from coherent and consistent principles of law. Some understanding of that process is the promise of sociological investigation of the criminal sanction.

(SEE ALSO: *Crime Deterrence; Probation and Parole; Social Controls*)

## REFERENCES

Bailey, William C., and Ruth D. Peterson 1989 "Murder and Capital Punishment: A Monthly Time-Series Analysis of Execution Publicity." *American Sociological Review* 54:722–743.

Beyleveld, Deryek 1980 *Bibliography on General Deterrence.* Hampshire, England: Saxon House.

Bottoms, Anthony E. 1983 "Neglected Features of Contemporary Penal Systems." In David Garland and Peter Young, eds., *The Power to Punish: Contemporary Penality and Social Analysis.* Atlantic Highlands, N.J.: Humanities Press.

Bowers, William J. 1984 *Legal Homicide: Death as Punishment in America, 1824–1982.* Boston: Northeastern University Press.

Burton, Velmer S., Francis T. Cullen, and Lawrence F. Travis III 1987 "The Collateral Consequences of a Felony Conviction: A National Study of State Statutes." *Federal Probation* 51:52–60.

Cohen, Jacqueline, and Michael Tonry 1983 "Sentencing Reforms and Their Impacts." In Alfred Blumstein, Jacqueline Coyen, Susan E. Martin, and Michael H. Tonry, eds., *Research in Sentencing: The Search for Reform,* vol. 2. Washington, D.C.: National Academy Press.

Conrad, Peter, and Joseph V. Schneider 1980 *Deviance and Medicalization: From Badness to Sickness.* St. Louis: Mosby.

Daly, Kathleen 1989 "Neither Conflict nor Labeling nor Paternalism Will Suffice: Intersections of Race, Ethnicity, Gender, and Family in Criminal Court Decisions." *Crime and Delinquency* 35:136–168.

Downs, Donald A. 1989 *The New Politics of Pornography.* Chicago: University of Chicago Press.

Durkheim, Emile (1893) 1950 *The Rules of Sociological Method.* New York: Free Press.

Ekland-Olson, Sheldon, John Lieb, and Louis Zurcher 1984 "The Paradoxical Impact of Criminal Sanctions: Some Microstructural Findings." *Law and Society Review* 18:159–178.

Erikson, Kai T. 1966 *Wayward Puritans: A Study in the Sociology of Deviance.* New York: Wiley.

Feinberg, Joel 1970 "The Expressive Function of Punishment." In *Doing and Deserving: Essays in the Theory of Responsibility.* Princeton, N.J.: Princeton University Press.

Feld, Barry 1984 "Criminalizing Juvenile Justice: Rules of Procedure for Juvenile Court." *Minnesota Law Review* 69:141–276.

Fogel, David 1975 *We Are the Living Proof: The Justice Model of Corrections.* Cincinnati, Ohio: W. H. Anderson.

Foucault, Michel 1979 *Discipline and Punish.* New York: Vintage.

Freiberg, Arie, and Pat O'Malley 1984 "State Intervention and the Civil Offense." *Law and Society Review* 18:373–394.

Garland, David 1990 *Punishment and Modern Society: A Study in Social Theory.* Chicago: University of Chicago Press.

Gusfield, Joseph 1980 *The Culture of Public Problems: Drunk-Driving and the Symbolic Order.* Chicago: University of Chicago Press.

Hamilton, Gary G., and John R. Sutton 1989 "The Problem of Control in the Weak State: Domination in the United States, 1880–1920." *Theory and Society* 18:1–46.

Humphries, Drew, and David Greenberg 1981 "The Dialectics of Crime Control." In David Greenberg, ed., *Crime and Capitalism.* Palo Alto, Calif.: Mayfield.

Kittrie, Nicholas N. 1971 *The Right to Be Different: Deviance and Enforced Therapy.* Baltimore: Johns Hopkins University Press.

Martinson, Robert 1974 "What Works? Questions and Answers About Prison Reform." *Public Interest* 35: 22–54.

Marx, Gary 1988 *Undercover: Police Surveillance in America.* Berkeley: University of California Press.

Melossi, Dario 1989 "Fifty Years Later: *Punishment and Social Structure* in Comparative Analysis." *Contemporary Crises* 13:311–326.

Nadelmann, Ethan A. 1989 "Drug Prohibition in the United States: Costs, Consequences, and Alternatives." *Science* 245:939–947.

Paternoster, Raymond, Linda Saltzman, Theorodre Chiricos, and Gordon Waldo 1982 "Perceived Risk and Deterrence: Methodological Artifacts in Perceptual Deterrence Research." *Journal of Criminal Law and Criminology* 73:1,238–1258.

Piliavin, Irving, Rosemary Gartner, Craig Thornton, and Ross L. Matsueda 1986 "Crime, Deterrence, and Rational Choice." *American Sociological Review* 51:101–119.

Rusche, Georg, and Otto Kirchheimer (1939) 1968 *Punishment and Social Structure.* New York: Russell and Russell.

Sherman, Lawrence, and Richard A. Berk 1984 "The Specific Deterrent Effect of Arrest for Domestic Assault." *American Sociological Review* 49:261–272.

Spierenburg, Pieter 1984 *The Spectacle of Suffering: Executions and the Evolution of Repression: From a*

*Preindustrial Metropolis to the European Experience.* Cambridge: Cambridge University Press.

Thomas, Charles W., and Donna M. Bishop 1984 "The Effect of Formal and Informal Sanctions on Delinquency: A Longitudinal Comparison of Labeling and Deterrence Theories." *Journal of Criminal Law and Criminology* 75:1222–1245.

Wilbanks, William 1987 *The Myth of a Racist Criminal Justice System.* Monterey, Calif.: Brooks-Cole.

JAMES INVERARITY

**CRIMINOLOGY** Criminology is the scientific study of criminal behavior. Sutherland and Cressey (1978) note that it includes within its purview the processes of making and breaking laws and of reacting toward law breaking. While in the past the discipline of sociology seemed to dominate criminology, other fields such as psychology, political science, economics, and law have contributed greatly to its development. In recent years, biologists and historians have added to criminology by studying physical characteristics of offenders and the evolving definitions of crime. Although there is a heterogeneous nature to criminology, its practitioners share an interest in understanding the true nature of law, crime, and justice.

While criminology has been a constantly evolving field of inquiry over the centuries, its ingredients are unchanging. Significantly, criminology may be thought of as reflecting cyclical change. Indeed the French idiom *Plus ça change, plus c'est la même chose* comes to mind. It appears that down through the centuries a heavy pendulum has been swinging regularly in criminology, between theory and practice, cause and effect, explanation and vengeance, understanding and deterrence. The ghosts of Beccaria, Lombroso, Quetelet, Bentham, and Sutherland seem destined to seek rest in vain. But then, that is the drama, the attraction, the magnetism of the field as it toils among its audience comprised of "liberals" and "conservatives." Paradoxically, one cannot anticipate who the defendents and opponents of the death penalty will be.

Criminology is so complex and yet its pursuits are so simple. Jogging in the park, leaving the front door unlocked, and greeting strangers are not innocent pastimes. They are deadly risks, leading, unfortunately, to sexual assaults, burglary, and murder. Two schools of thought are typically associated with such atrocities: free will and external causation. When the causal process involves motivation or malice, the behavior is likely to be branded *criminal,* and guilt is the more certain conclusion.

Perhaps it is not unfair to observe that, while our causal theories have grown more comprehensive over the centuries, the seriousness, or brutality, of our punishments has waned. But as the scope of our punishments has waned, we have become more protective of capital punishment, which has become more precious as it has become less practiced. More specifically, if we measure the brutality of punishment by the number of crimes designated as capital, it is instructive to note that in England in 1800 there were more than two hundred such crimes; by 1861 there were but three: murder, treason, and piracy. In the United States, the humanizing of the criminal code was led by the Pennsylvania Quakers, resulting in the revised codes of Pennsylvania, which by 1794 had substituted imprisonment for capital punishment and made murder in the first degree the only capital crime. Indeed, today the main debate in the United States is about whether or not the death penalty should ever be used and, if so, the conditions or circumstances of its employment. Ironically, however, the Quaker emphasis on imprisonment may have had an unforeseen consequence. The United States has the highest incarceration rate in the Western world (Moss 1990). Also, the United States is the only Western nation retaining the death penalty for civil homicide. Not surprisingly, there has been a huge recent concentration of concern and research on the "effectiveness," or consequence, of the death sentence.

In addition to deterrence and punishment, we are concerned with the amount of criminal activity and accompanying explanations. The amount of crime found in modern society is usually accompanied by a description of the specific technique employed in measuring it. These different techniques, or methods, involve such diverse tools as self-reports, victim surveys, official police records, adjudications, charges, and sentences. Techniques of analysis must be specified if we are to begin to cope with hidden or secret crime; crime disguised as civil offense; police, bail, and jury biases; prejudicial procedures of justice; and other sources of confusion and argument.

## EXTENT OF AND TRENDS IN CRIMINAL ACTIVITY

Recent data show that violent crime rose in the period 1970–1986 in a number of countries such as Brazil, Denmark, Sweden, and Nigeria. Indeed the homicide rate rose in all four Scandinavian countries (Finland, Norway, Sweden, and Denmark) after 1970, according to the *Yearbook of Nordic Statistics, 1987*. Meanwhile, there was a decline in homicide rates in both the United States and Canada between 1980 and 1987, although Hagan (1989) shows that the homicide rate in the United States was approximately three and one-half times the rate for Canada in 1987. The National Commission on the Causes and Prevention of Violence had reported earlier (Mulvihill et al. 1969) a trend that has continued until today, namely that the United States suffers a homicide rate at least three times higher than the rates sustained by Western European nations. The *Demographic Yearbook* for 1986 (published in 1988) shows the following countries to be among those reporting the highest homicide or other intentional injury rates in the mid-1980s (in no particular order): Venezuela, Mexico, Bahamas, United States, El Salvador, Colombia, and Brazil. Among reporting countries, the following are among those with the lowest homicide rates: Japan, Kuwait, Egypt, Israel, Mauritius, Uruguay, Iceland, Ireland, and Norway. Thus, while Norway has a low homicide rate, its homicide rate rose during the period between 1970 and 1986.

Recently, it should be noted, the homicide rate resumed rising in the United States; 1990, for example, may have been the most murderous year since 1980 (Hackett et al. 1990). With respect to long-term trends (between 1850 and 1980), Gurr (1990) notes that there have been three great waves in American homicide rates, around 1850, 1900, and 1965. While the trend around 1980 was higher than any recorded before that, it was only slightly higher than those of the 1920s. The paucity of data before 1850 in America made it impossible, Gurr notes, to state whether the increases are superimposed on a long-term decline. However, the greater availability of English data made it possible for him to trace a long-term decline there in homicide rates between the fourteenth and twentieth centuries. He noted that the apparently high rate of homicides in twentieth-century London was very low when contrasted with that in medieval London.

While homicide is always at the top of any list of crimes being studied, a number of other crimes of violence were widely studied during the 1970s and 1980s. These include rape, robbery, and aggravated assault. They do not garner as many headlines as homicide for at least two good reasons. First, homicide has been a major concern throughout human history, and, second, official homicide data are the most accurately recorded of all data on interpersonal violence (Gurr 1990).

It has been noted, however, by Weiner and Wolfgang (1990) that the four violent crimes mentioned constitute what the Uniform Crime Reports (prepared by the FBI) designate *index crimes,* a term that implies these are serious crimes and, accordingly, are most likely to be recorded by law-enforcement agencies. Consequently they can serve as a barometer of changing trends in crime. Weiner and Wolfgang note that, although crimes of violence and property crimes were both rising, the former constituted only about 10 percent of all index crimes throughout the period 1969 to 1982. They focus on violent crime because it is the most salient type of crime in the minds of Americans in view of its potential for serious harm. Uniform Crime Report (UCR) data indicate that, between 1969 and 1982, criminal homicide increased by 25 percent, forcible rape by 82 percent, robbery by 56 percent, and aggravated assault by 82 percent. However, a different story emerges from the data collected since 1973 on the victims of violent crimes, excluding criminal homicide, in an annual survey referred to as the National Crime Survey. They show that the rate of forcible rape declined by 10 percent, and the rates of robbery and of aggravated assaults decreased by 7 percent and 8 percent, respectively. Weiner and Wolfgang conclude, however, that, although work needs to be done to bolster the reliability of these two sources of criminal statistics, on balance the rate of violent crime has increased. They find disturbing indications that (1) blacks and young males are disproportionately responsible for acts of murder and criminal violence, (2) disadvantaged persons were most often victims of violent crime, and (3) forcible rape, robbery, and aggravated assault together were predominantly intraracial. It should be emphasized, too, that the UCR data on criminal homicide are not challenged by other data. In connection with these data, criminologists warn us that the concept of race is a complex and unclear term when used as a biological term, and that there is no evidence that African-Americans have a more powerful instinct to kill than whites (Bohannon 1960).

In the study of homicide, race, age, and class have always, it seems, been priority concerns. Recently, however, there has been a rising concern with gender, specifically with females, as both offenders and victims. While there are disputes and resulting uncertainty over whether there is an increase in female offenders, there is no doubt that females are given increasing attention as victims. Thus, in the case of homicide, sex-specific data gathered by the World Health Organization for 118 developed democracies (reported in Gartner 1990), covering the period 1950–1980, show the United States to have the highest homicide rate for females (3.83 per 100,000 persons per year) and Ireland to have the lowest homicide rate for females (.40 per 100,000 per year). Contrary to some predictions, females were not universally found to enjoy a protective advantage over males. Thus, women in the United States were more than four times more likely to be murdered than males in England and Wales, the Netherlands, Switzerland, and Denmark. For all 118 nations, the average homicide rate for females increased by about 50 percent between 1960 and 1980, where-

as for men the increase was 62 percent. In the United States the public is becoming increasingly more aware of the rising tide of violence against women, including rape, battery, and homicide (Salholz et al. 1990). A measure of criminal opportunities (i.e., the convergence of motivated offenders and suitable targets in the absence of capable guardians) is reported to be related to the homicide rate of women. Criminologists, having developed most of their theories of crime causation on the basis of male data, are now increasingly gathering data on women, focusing on attempts to understand both female offenders and assaults on women.

One area of study that permits a focus not only on gender but also on age is the study of the fear of being victimized. This is perhaps the most frequently studied area of criminology today, counting the numerous studies of this topic found in a review of the literature. In a computer-driven review of articles published in 1988, 1989, and 1990, fear analysis was the leading concern of sociologists pursuing criminological studies. Social scientists studied fear among the elderly, the fear of being assaulted or raped, the fear of being robbed, the fear of humiliation by police or courtroom interrogation, the fear of reprisals for reporting crime. Articles on fear of crime are being published in and about a large number of countries. Studies are emerging on the effects of race, gender, locale, and age on the presence of fear. The role of the media in fear arousal is a continuing concern. Contrasted with the effects of such conditions on fear is the study of the effects of fear on attitudes toward capital punishment and deterrence, toward agents of control, toward vigilantism, and toward gun control. These studies of fear and its effects are becoming increasingly sophisticated methodologically, with longitudinal, time series, and experimental approaches on the rise.

**Some Theories.** One does not have to look too far to find various opinions explaining the present preoccupation with fear of crime victimization. First, perhaps, it should be noted that the optimism, in the United States anyway, about the decline in crime and murder during the middle years of the 1980s seems misplaced at worst or short-lived at best. The point has been made here already that 1990 promised to be the year with the highest number of murders in history in the United States. New York, Philadelphia, Boston, Milwaukee, Chicago, Washington, and Los Angeles are among the cities not only reporting an increased homicide rate for 1989, but also appearing to be headed for the highest rates in history, with the nation on track to surpass the record year of 1980, when 23,040 people were slain (Hackett et al. 1990; Hinds 1990). Paired with this report is the ominous news that hate crimes are increasing and that 1990 was the worst year on record for acts of violence motivated by race, religion, and sexual preference in the United States (Tye 1990). Paradoxically, while the elderly generally are the most afraid of being victimized, they were found to be the least often victimized (La Grange and Ferraro 1987; Cohen and Land 1987). The young have been found to be the most frequently victimized. (Along with this, the number of murders by the young is also on the increase). Age, then, is related to victimization risk by virtue of its association with exposure and proximity. It has already been observed that crime against women has increased at an alarming rate. Such crime waves would seem to tally with the increased fears and accompanying studies of fear. But since recent studies of fear must have been triggered by earlier events, the issue of time lag must be considered. The question is, lagged from when? The "popular" answer seems to be that the crime wave of the late 1980s and early 1990s was launched by events in the early 1980s. More specifically, it is suggested that improved medical techniques learned on the battlefields of Vietnam contributed to the decline in homicides in the mid-1980s and that the recent rise is due to an increase in drug disputes, deadlier weapons, and the tendency among more young people to start careers in crime with a gun. Some police experts believe that vigorous gun control would help curb the number of killings, although not immediately.

A different tack is taken by those who attribute the rise in violence in the United States to a Reagan-inspired increase in the economic divide between haves and have-nots. Measured and extensive examinations of this thesis seem to partially support it. Steven Messner, in a study of fifty-two nations (1989), employed indicators of economic discrimination and of homicide to test the hypothesis that nations with intense discrimination exhibit comparatively high levels of homicide and that the effects of discrimination exceed those of income inequality. His results support the hypothesis, but they also suggest that the structuring of economic inequality on the basis of ascribed characteristics is a particularly important source of lethal violence in many contemporary societies. Messner also notes the compatibility of his results with both the macrostructural theory of Blau and classical Durkheimian social thought. Durkheim speculated that solidarity could be achieved in advanced society only to the extent that social inequalities were not rooted in external (i.e., ascribed) characteristics. Such a condition would preclude the development of strong social bonds and (though this inference was not drawn by Durkheim) would generate homicide. Research by Blau and Blau (1982) supported Peter Blau's macrostructural theory (1977) which predicted that discriminatory social practices that generate "consolidated inequality" would promote high levels of homicide by way of pent-up aggression, including aggression against those in similar social positions. The Blaus note that aggressive acts of violence stemmed not from the absolute state of poverty but from the relative deprivation associated with economic inequality. They conclude also that, while racial inequality does have special significance, when economic inequalities are controlled for, poverty and the proportion of African-Americans in a population have greatly reduced influence. This is in large part because economic inequalities also engender violent crime among other ethnic groups.

Such studies of inequality and of discrimination appear to have increased in recent years and to be more efficient and useful than the more static studies of social class and poverty as related to crime. In a sense, social scientists have rediscovered Quetelet's nineteenth-century finding ([1831] 1984) that inequality is superior to poverty in explaining crime. In considering the notion of the relationship of crime to economic discrimination, it should be noted that this relationship probably applies equally to socialist and nonsocialist nations. Economic inequalities, as well as poverty, appear to be emerging as major themes in so-called Eastern or Soviet bloc countries. Doubtless pent-up hostilities will express themselves in rising crime rates as individual liberties increase and as the Iron Curtain falls.

Related to theories of inequality and discrimination is another theory of long-standing interest, Merton's classical theory of crime (1968). Merton's anomie theory focuses on the gulf between the promise of opportunity to achieve and the lack of legitimate access to the means of success in American society, one in which material success is a preeminent goal. Merton's theory of structured strains produced by system irregularities has given rise to numerous theories of strain expressed in terms of educational, vocational, and achievement opportunities. These theories, too numerous to summarize, have appeared in criminological and delinquency writings and in stress theories of social deviance. Albert Cohen (1955) and Richard Cloward and Lloyd Ohlin (1960) are just a few of the theorists who have benefited from Merton's seminal ideas.

Another traditional view of criminological theory appears in Sutherland's theory of differential association. Differential association is a learning theory that asserts that criminal behavior results from normal processes of cultural conditioning. More specifically, definitions of legal codes that favor law violation exist alongside definitions unfavorable to law violation. Sutherland gave the name *differential association* to the process by which persons experience these conflicting definitions about appropriate behavior. Definitions favorable and unfavorable to delinquent or criminal behavior are learned in intimate personal groups. A person becomes criminal because of an excess of definitions favorable to violation of law over definitions unfavorable to violation of law.

Differential association theory is being tested more frequently in current research analysis and remains a viable and attractive explanation of criminal behavior. Donald Cressey, Richard Cloward, and Walter Miller are only a few of the many social scientists who have further developed differential association theory.

A third sociological approach to the explanation of crime is found in control theory. Travis Hirschi (1969) has been one of the strongest advocates of control theories of crime. In contrast to differential association, Hirschi's social control theory denies the existence of normative conflict and the importance of different definitions, assuming instead that the motivation for crime or delinquency is invariant across individuals. The question is not why some people violate the law, since we are all equally motivated to do so, but rather why *more* people don't violate the law. Hirschi's response is that they are deterred by strong bonds to conventional society such as attachment, commitment, involvement, and belief. When a person's bond to society is broken or weakened, he or she is free to engage in crime or delinquency. Ross Matsueda, in his test of two of these theories (1982), somewhat cautiously concludes that differential association theory was supported over control theory. More importantly, he urges that differential association theory can and should be empirically investigated and that the testing of these theories should be continued.

The latter idea is not exactly embraced by some sociologists, who note the continuing failure to support these traditional theoretical approaches. Concern with the reliability and validity of official criminal statistics, with the processes of criminal justice, and with the effects of both stereotyping and discriminatory acts has contributed to the rise of both conflict and labeling theories (Vold and Bernard 1986). Conflict theories, like Marxist philosophy and theories positing the centrality of inequalities, have emphasized the role of power (economic or political) in defining crime, erecting or establishing laws, and enforcing rules. In addition, conflict theorists have, again like Marxists, been influential in and influenced by the study of social class. While many criticisms have been launched against the utopian Marxists, criminologists like Chambliss and Seidman have emphasized the real contributions of Marxist thought to the role of status in the analysis of criminal behavior.

The dynamic stance of conflict theorists has also placed them in alliance with those who focus on the interactionist perspective. The latter school gained new status in the 1970s with the emergence of labeling theory. Labeling theory was used to assess the role of "officials" in defining deviance and also to assess the weight of social reactions in influencing career deviance. This school noted how stereotyping can extend the label of deviance to all members of a group—African-Americans, Hispanics, or Italians, for example. Such labels make persons more likely to be tagged as suspects and to enter the criminal justice system. While labeling theory has been criticized for ignoring the initial criminal behavior that identifies the actor in the first place, it is hard to deny that law enforcement does not treat all people the same way and that the risks of criminalization are much greater for some groups. Societal reaction, especially of official agents of justice, is involved in the ongoing question whether an increase in crime is "real" or is due to the way crimes are reported or treated. This question is also relevant to issues of punishment and deterrence that will be considered shortly.

Phenomenology is a part of the interactionist perspective that is microanalytic and pays particular attention to the views of the individual, who is seen as criminal or deviant, and to whether his intent is truly and clearly understood. As such it may be contrasted with the recent emphasis on victimology, which is concerned with the effects of criminal action on the lives of often-forgotten victims. Indeed, one reason criminal offenses are defined as crimes against the state is that the victim may be unable to speak for herself or himself. Moreover, the state has a vital interest in preventing vigilantism and in discouraging acts of revenge by victims. In doing so, the state must persuade its constituency that wrongdoers will be apprehended and that justice will be served. The school of thought that best defines the need for

swift punishment is the classical school personified by Cesare Beccaria (1738–1794). Before moving to a brief consideration of punishment theory, it is worthwhile to note one similarity, at least, between phenomenology and the classical school of criminology, namely the view that the actor (the deviant or the criminal) acts voluntarily and, therefore, makes the search for external cause unnecessary baggage. More specifically, both schools hold that the actor has free will (choice) and is not coerced by conditions or external sources into the subject behavior.

The views that actors choose to commit crimes, that they do so when opportunities arise, and that the rewards of crime should be eliminated have led to a resurgence of interest not only in the classical school but also in the prevention, deterrence, and punishment of crime.

**Punishment and Deterrence.** As noted, Beccaria was the leader of the so-called classical school. His work, inspired by the need for reform of the criminal justice system, focused on the notion that punishment must fit the crime, be swift, be certain, and follow fair trials. Beccaria also urged that torture be eliminated and that corporal punishment be replaced by imprisonment. An earlier concern with torture and barbaric punishments in Europe had provided an impetus to criminology. The work of Beccaria consolidated these concerns and may be credited with leading to reforms of criminal law in Austria, criminal justice reforms in France and England, and changes in the United States after the Revolution. Perhaps the reader will note that Beccaria's concerns are topical today. Indeed, it seems that classical thinking is more prevalent than causal concerns in the present era. Both the popular press and professional publications are concerned with the punishment of criminal behavior. Thus Barlow (1990), after reviewing Miller's thoughtful 1973 observation on the major ideological positions related to criminal justice, concluded that American public policy on criminal matters is dominated by the ideology of the crime-control model, rather than by the due process model. The crime-control model, of course, disdains sacrificing criminal conviction to due process and focuses instead on the repression of threats to the public order.

If any topic is more written about than the need for new prisons to house the social miscreants, it is the one focusing on the pros and cons of the death penalty. Indeed, in tune with the increase in homicide are the rise in numbers of new prisons and of executions. At the end of 1984 the prison population had increased by 50 percent since 1980, when 300,024 adults were incarcerated, according to the Bureau of Justice Statistics (1985). This was a continuation of a trend that had been in evidence for a number of years. Moreover, by 1990, according to newspaper accounts, the prison population had doubled since 1980, whereas the crime rate had risen by 7.3 percent; and the American Correctional Association has estimated that the prison population will double again by 1995. It appears the search for alternatives to jail or prison has taken a back seat to pressure to legislate mandatory sentencing and to curtail prison furloughs.

With respect to the death penalty, it is more talked about than carried out, although, to be sure, it is being increasingly utilized. Serious debate is taking place as academics, politicians, and laypeople argue about sentencing policies. It is not always clear whether the debate is about punishment or deterrence. Choosing punishment, David Garland recently observed (1990) that, while Foucault sees punishment as an instrument for the rational control of conduct, Durkheim sees punishment as the heart of irrational, unthinking emotion. He states:

*Passion lies at the heart of punishment. The urge to punish is an emotional reaction which flares up at the violation of cherished social sentiments. It is, in Durkheim's view, a direct and powerful expression of the* conscience collective, *relayed through the medium of all the individual consciences who compose it.*

Garland, in short, sees Durkheim and Foucault as complementary, since they are asking different questions about a complex phenomenon. Foucault's control has to be seen as taking place within Durkheim's culture, where sentiments pro-duce solidarity. Perhaps it is this very duality of punishment's role that leads to the protracted debate about differing modes of justice, criminal and civil, for white-collar and blue-collar offenders as well as for white and black offenders. Sutherland's argument that the criminal justice system was discriminatory by status and by race is still a central concern in criminology (Teele 1970). Not surprisingly, perhaps, evidence has been found both in support of and against Sutherland's hypothesis.

With regard to the death penalty, Radelet found (1981) that those accused of murdering whites were more likely to be sentenced to death than those accused of murdering African-Americans when the focus was homicides between strangers. This trend was due primarily to a higher probability for those charged with murdering whites to be indicted for first-degree murder. While Kleck found in his review (1981) that black offender–white victim crimes in the United States are generally punished more severely than crimes involving other racial combinations, he did not find discriminatory sentencing toward African-Americans for murder, except in the South.

In a comprehensive report released in 1990, the General Accounting Office supported the view that race of victims is a major consideration. It found in its evaluation of over 200 studies relating to death penalty sentencing that when the murder victim was white, the criminal justice system was influenced at all stages of the prosecutional process. The GAO's findings were consistent across states and legal jurisdictions.

Parenthetically, one of the hottest arguments, on a par with the death sentence debate, has to do with handgun regulation. It has long been argued by organized gun owners that "guns don't kill, people kill." A sharp retort, however, was fired off recently by *Time* magazine, which noted that 464 Americans were killed in one week by handguns, over half of the killings being homicides. A recently published study comparing crimes of violence in Vancouver, British Columbia, and Seattle, Washington (Sloan et al. 1988) showed that, while there were similar overall rates of criminal activity and assaults in the two cities, the relative risk of death from homicide (adjusted for sex and age) was significantly higher in Seattle than in Vancouver. Virtually all of this excess risk was explained by a fivefold higher probability of being murdered with a handgun in Seattle as compared with Vancouver. Rates of homicide by means other than guns were not substantially different in the two communities. Obviously gun control needs to be taken more seriously in the United States and in other countries where the concealment of weapons is permitted. Indeed, perceptions of the police as overzealous agents of deterrence may stem from the availability, concealment, and increased use of handguns in street crimes. Recent investigations into police brutality in America and Britain have propelled police accountability to the forefront of the criminal-justice debate.

With regard to white-collar crime and punishment, critics of the classical view hold that, for all the post-Watergate concern with white-collar and corporate offenses, the wheels of justice do not mete out equal punishment for such crimes. In what amounts to an eerie 1985 forecasting of the Wall Street stock scandals of the 1988–1989 period, John Hagan and Patricia Parker (1985) revived interest in Sutherland's view of differential social organization and differential power, producing results that, they argue, should interest Marxists and non-Marxists alike by being relevant to both functionalist and structural theories of law. In an analysis of data on persons charged under noncriminal and criminal statues Hagan and Parker observed differential sentencing (among other things) of employers, managers, and workers. They found that, compared with workers, managers were more likely and employers less likely to be charged under the Criminal Code. Employers were, instead, more likely to be charged with Securities Act violations that carried less stigma and lower sentence severity. They note that employers are in positions of power that allow them to be distanced from criminal events and that obscure their involvement. Finally, they state that Sutherland noted an "obfuscation as to responsibility" that accompanies corporate positions of power. Thus, employers face securities charges rather than criminal charges that require a demonstration of malice.

The 1980s opened with the publication of a major account of illegal practices among corporations by Clinard and Yeager (1980) and closed with an apparent decision by the U.S. Justice Department to retract new guidelines calling for stiff mandatory fines for corporations convicted of fraud, dumping toxic wastes, and other serious crimes (*Boston Globe* 1990).

It is apparent that the field of criminology is still a powerfully attractive and important field as sociologists and others deal with the critical questions of crime causation, order, and justice in our society. It will be important for academic criminologists to expand their communication with each other as well as with the various agents of control and justice and with public policymakers. Moreover, the crucial area of comparative study will certainly be a major focus of criminologists the world over as we prepare for the end of the twentieth century and the challenges of a more compact world in the twenty-first century. If criminologists have learned anything in recent years, it is that the phenomenon of crime is not confined by definition and is not restricted by time or place.

(SEE ALSO: *Crime Deterrence; Crime Rates; Crime, Theories of; Criminal and Delinquent Subcultures; Criminalization of Deviance; Criminal Sanctions; Social Control; Violent Crime; White-Collar Crime*)

## REFERENCES

Barlow, Hugh D. 1990 *Introduction to Criminology,* 5th ed. Glenview, Ill.: Scott Foresman/Little, Brown.

Blau, Judith, and Peter Blau 1982 "The Cost of Inequality: Metropolitan Structure and Violent Crime." *American Sociological Review* 47:114–129.

Blau, Peter M. 1977 *Inequality and Heterogeneity.* New York: Free Press.

Bohannon, Paul (ed.) 1960 *African Homicide & Suicide.* Princeton, N.J.: Princeton University Press.

*Boston Globe* 12 May 1990.

Clinard, Marshall B., and Peter C. Yeager 1980 *Corporate Crime.* New York: Free Press.

Cloward, Richard, and Lloyd Ohlin 1960 *Delinquency and Opportunity*. New York: Free Press.

Cohen, Albert 1955 *Delinquent Boys*. New York: Free Press.

Cohen, Lawrence, and Kenneth C. Land 1987 "Age Structure and Crime: Symmetry Versus Asymmetry and the Projection of Crime Rates through the 1990's." *American Sociological Review* 52:170–183.

*Demographic Yearbook, 1986* 1988 New York: United Nations.

Donnelly, Patrick G. 1988 "Individual and Neighborhood Influences on Fear of Crime." *Sociological Focus* 22:69–85.

Garland, David 1990 "Frameworks of Inquiry in the Sociology of Punishment." *British Journal of Sociology* 41:1–15.

Gartner, Rosemary 1990 "The Victims of Homicide: A Temporal and Cross-National Comparison." *American Sociological Review* 55:92–106.

Goode, Erich 1990 "Crime Can Be Fun: The Deviant Experience." *Contemporary Sociology* 19:5–12.

Gurr, Ted R. 1990 "Historical Trends in Violent Crime: A Critical Review of the Evidence." In Neil A. Weiner, Margaret Zahn, and Rita Sagi, eds., *Violence: Patterns, Causes, Public Policy*, pp. 15–24. San Diego: Harcourt Brace Jovanovich.

Hackett, George, et al. 1990 "1990: The Bloodiest Year Yet?" *Newsweek*, 16 July.

Hagan, John 1989 "Comparing Crime and Criminalization in Canada and the U.S.A." *Canadian Journal of Sociology* Summer:361–371.

———, and Patricia Parker 1985 "White Collar Crime and Punishment: The Class Structure and Legal Sanctioning of Securities Violations." *American Sociological Review* 50:302–316.

Hinds, Michael de Courcy 1990 "Number of Killings Soars in Big Cities Across the U.S." *New York Times*, 18 July.

Hirschi, Travis 1969 *Causes of Delinquency*. Berkeley, Calif.: Free Press.

Kleck, Gary 1981 "Racial Discrimination in Criminal Sentencing: A Critical Evaluation of the Evidence with Additional Evidence on the Death Penalty." *American Sociological Review* 46:783–805.

LaGrange, Randy, and Kenneth Ferraro 1987 "The Elderly's Fear of Crime: A Critical Examination of the Research." *Research on Aging* 1987:372–391.

McGahey, Richard 1980 "Dr. Erlich's Magic Bullet: Economic Theory, Econometrics, and the Death Penalty." *Crime and Delinquency* 1980:485–502.

Matsueda, Ross L. 1982 "Testing Control Theory and Differential Association: A Causal Modeling Approach." *American Sociological Review* 47:489–504.

Merton, Robert K. 1968 *Social Theory and Social Structure*. New York: Free Press.

Messner, Steven F. 1989 "Economic Discrimination and Societal Homicide Rates: Further Evidence on the Cost of Inequality." *American Sociological Review* 54:597–611.

Miller, Walter, B. 1973 "Ideology and Criminal Justice Policy: Some Current Issues." *Journal of Criminal Law & Criminology* 64:141–162.

Moss, E. Yvonne 1990 "Critique of Crime and the Administration of Justice." In Wornie Reed, ed., *Assessment of the Status of African-Americans*, Vol. 6. Boston: University of Massachusetts at Boston.

Mulvihill, Donald, Melvin Tumin, and Lynn A. Curtis 1969 *Crimes of Violence* (staff report submitted to the National Commission on the Causes and Prevention of Violence). Washington, D.C.: U.S. Government Printing Office.

Quetelet, Adolph (1831) 1984 *Research on the Propensity for Crime at Different Ages*, trans. F. Sylvester Sawyer. Cincinnati: W. H. Anderson.

Radelet, Michael 1981 "Racial Characteristics and the Imposition of the Death Penalty." *American Sociological Review* 46:918–927.

Salholz, Eloise, et al. 1990 "Women Under Assault." *Newsweek*, 16 July, 23–24.

Shelley, Louise 1980 "The Geography of Soviet Criminality." *American Sociological Review* 45:111–122.

Sloan, John H., et al. 1988 "Handgun Regulations, Crime, Assaults and Homicide: A Tale of Two Cities." *New England Journal of Medicine* 319:1256–1262.

Straus, M. A., R. J. Gelles, and S. K. Steinmetz 1980 *Behind Closed Doors: Violence in the American Family*. New York: Doubleday, Anchor Press.

Sutherland, Edwin H., and Donald R. Cressey 1978 *Criminology*, 10th ed. Philadelphia: Lippincott.

Teele, James E. 1970 "Social Pathology and Stress." In Sol Levine and Norman Scotch, eds., *Social Stress*, pp. 228–256. Chicago: Aldine.

Thio, Alex 1988 *Deviant Behavior*, 3rd ed. New York: Harper and Row.

Tye, Larry 1990 "Hate Crimes on Rise in U.S." *Boston Sunday Globe*, 29 July, 1.

U.S. Department of Justice, Bureau of Justice Statistics 1985 *Prisoners in 1984*. Washington, D.C.: U.S. Department of Justice.

U.S. General Accounting Office 1990 *Death Penalty Sentencing: Report to the Senate and House Committee on the Judiciary.* Washington, D.C.: U.S. General Accounting Office.

Vold, George, and Thomas Bernard 1986 *Criminological Theory,* 3rd ed. New York: Oxford University Press.

Weiner, Neil A., and Marvin Wolfgang 1990 "The Extent and Character of Violent Crime in America, 1969–1982." In Margaret Zahn Weiner and Rita Sagi, eds., *Violence: Patterns, Causes, Public Policy.* San Diego: Harcourt Brace Jovanovich.

Wheeler, Stanton, David Weisburd, and Nancy Bode 1982 "Sentencing the White Collar Offender: Rhetoric and Reality." *American Sociological Review* 47:641–659.

Yablonsky, Lewis 1990 *Criminology, Crime and Criminality.* New York: Harper & Row.

*Yearbook of Nordic Statistics, 1987* 1988 Stockholm: Nordic Council.

JAMES E. TEELE

## CRITICAL THEORY

The term *critical theory* was used originally by members of the Institute for Social Research in Frankfurt, Germany, after they emigrated to the United States in the late 1930s, following the rise of Hitler. The term served as a code word for their version of Marxist social theory and research (Kellner 1990a). The term now refers primarily to Marxist studies done or inspired by this so-called Frankfurt School and its contemporary representatives such as Jurgen Habermas. Critical sociologists working in this tradition share several common tenets including a rejection of sociological positivism and its separation of facts from values; a commitment to the emancipation of humanity from all forms of exploitation, domination, or oppression; and a stress on the importance of human agency in social relations.

### THE FRANKFURT SCHOOL OF CRITICAL THEORY

The Institute for Social Research was founded in 1923 as a center for Marxist studies and was loosely affiliated with the university at Frankfurt, Germany. It remained independent of political party ties. Max Horkheimer became its director in 1931. Theodor Adorno, Erich Fromm, Leo Lowenthal, Herbert Marcuse, and, more distantly, Karl Korsch and Walter Benjamin were among the prominent theorists and researchers associated with the institute (Jay 1973). Initially, institute scholars sought to update Marxist theory by studying new social developments such as the expanding role of the state in social planning and control. The rise of fascism and the collapse of effective opposition by workers' parties, however, prompted them to investigate new sources and forms of authoritarianism in culture, ideology, and personality development and to search for new oppositional forces. By stressing the importance and semiautonomy of culture, consciousness, and activism, they developed an innovative, humanistic, and open-ended version of Marxist theory that avoided the determinism and class reductionism of much of the Marxist theory that characterized their era (Held 1980).

"Immanent critique," a method of description and evaluation derived from Karl Marx and Georg W. F. Hegel, formed the core of the Frankfurt School's interdisciplinary approach to social research (Antonio 1981). As Marxists, members of the Frankfurt School were committed to a revolutionary project of human emancipation. Rather than critique existing social arrangements in terms of a set of ethical values imposed from "outside," however, they sought to judge social institutions by those institutions' own internal (i.e., "immanent") values and self-espoused ideological claims. (An example of the practical application of such an approach is the southern civil rights movement of the 1960s, which judged the South's racial caste system in light of professed American values of democracy, equality, and justice.) Immanent critique thus provided members of the Frankfurt School with a nonarbitrary standpoint for the critical examination of social institutions while it sensitized them to contradictions between social appearances and the deeper levels of social reality.

Immanent critique, or what Adorno (1973) termed "non-identity thinking," is possible because, as Horkheimer (1972, p. 27) put it, there is always "an irreducible tension between concept and being." That is, in any social organization, contradictions inevitably exist between what social practices are called—for example, "democracy" or "freedom" or "workers' parties"—and what, in their full complexity, they really are. This gap between existence and essence or appearance and reality, according to Adorno (1973, p. 5), "indicates the untruth of identity, the fact that the concept does not exhaust the thing conceived." The point of immanent critique is thus to probe empirically whether a given social reality negates its own claims—as, for example, to represent a "just" or "equal" situation—as well as to uncover internal tendencies with a potential for change including new sources of resistance and opposition to repressive institutions.

Frankfurt School theorists found a paradigmatic example of immanent critique in the works of Karl Marx, including both his early writings on alienation and his later analyses of industrial capitalism. Best articulated by Marcuse (1941), their reading of *Capital* interpreted Marx's text as operating on two levels. On one level, *Capital* was read as a historical analysis of social institutions' progressive evolution, which resulted from conflicts between "forces" (such as technology) and "relations" (such as class conflicts) in economic production. Scientistic readings of Marx, however—especially by the generation of Marxist theorists immediately after the death of Marx—essentialized this dimension into a dogma that tended to neglect the role of human agency and stressed economic determinism in social history. But the Frankfurt School also read *Capital* as a "negative" or "immanent" critique of an important form of ideology, the bourgeois pseudo-science of economics. Here, Marx showed that the essence of capitalism as the exploitation of wage slavery contradicts its ideological representation or appearance as being a free exchange among equal parties (e.g., laborers and employers).

Members of the Frankfurt School interpreted the efforts that Marx devoted to the critique of ideology as an indication of his belief that freeing the consciousness of social actors from ideological illusion is an important form of political practice that potentially contributes to the expansion of human agency. Thus, they interpreted Marx's theory of the production and exploitation of economic values as an empirical effort to understand the historically specific "laws of motion" of market-driven, capitalist societies. At the same time, however, it was also interpreted as an effort—motivated by faith in the potential efficacy of active opposition—to see through capitalism's objectified processes that made a humanly created social world appear to be the product of inevitable, autonomous, and "natural" forces and to call for forms of revolutionary activism to defeat such forces of "alienation."

Members of the Frankfurt School attempted to honor both dimensions of the Marxian legacy. On the one hand, they sought to understand diverse social phenomena holistically as parts of an interconnected "totality" structured primarily by such capitalistic principles as the commodity form of exchange relations and bureaucratic rationality. On the other hand, they avoided reducing complex social factors to a predetermined existence as shadowlike reflections of these basic tendencies (Jay 1984). Thus, the methodology of immanent critique propelled a provisional, antifoundationalist, and inductive approach to "truth" that allowed for the open-endedness of social action and referred the ultimate verification of sociological insights to the efficacy of historical struggles rather than to the immediate observation of empirical facts (Horkheimer 1972). In effect, they were saying that social "facts" are never fixed once and for all, as in the world of nature, but rather are subject to constant revisions by both the conscious aims and unintended consequences of collective action.

In their concrete studies, members of the Frankfurt School concentrated on the sources of social conformism that, by the 1930s, had undermined the Left's faith in the revolutionary potential of the working class. They were among the first Marxists to relate Freud's insights into personality development to widespread changes in family and socialization patterns that they believed had weakened the ego boundary between self and society and reduced personal autonomy (Fromm 1941).

After they emigrated to the United States, these studies culminated in a series of survey research efforts, directed by Adorno and carried out by social scientists at the University of California, that investigated the relation between prejudice, especially anti-Semitism, and "the authoritarian personality" (Adorno et al. 1950). Later, in a more radical interpretation of Freud, Marcuse (1955) questioned whether conflicts between social constraints and bodily needs and desires might provide an impetus for revolt against capitalist repression if such conflicts were mediated by progressively oriented politics.

Once in the United States, members of the Frankfurt School emphasized another important source of conformism, the mass media. Holding that the best of "authentic art" contains a critical dimension that negates the status quo by pointing in utopian directions, they argued that commercialized and popular culture, shaped predominantly by market and bureaucratic imperatives, is merely "mimetic" or imitative of the surrounding world of appearances. Making no demands on its audience to think for itself, the highly standardized products of the "culture industry" reinforce conformism by presenting idealized and reified images of contemporary society as the best of all possible worlds (see Kellner 1984–1985).

The most important contribution of the Frankfurt School, however, was its investigation of the "dialectic of enlightenment" (Horkheimer and Adorno [1947] 1972). During the European Enlightenment, scientific reason had played a partisan role in the advance of freedom by challenging religious dogmatism and political absolutism. But according to the Frankfurt School, a particular form of reason, the instrumental rationality of efficiency and technology, has become a source of unfreedom in both capitalist and socialist societies during the modern era. Science and technology no longer play a liberating role in the critique of social institutions but have become new forms of domination. Dogmatic ideologies of scientism and operationalism absolutize the status quo and treat the social world as a "second nature" composed of law-governed facts, subject to manipulation but

not to revolutionary transformation. Thus, under the sway of positivism, social thought becomes increasingly "one-dimensional" (Marcuse 1964). Consequently, the dimension of critique, the rational reflection on societal values and directions, and the ability to see alternative possibilities and new sources of opposition are increasingly suppressed by the hegemony of an eviscerated form of thinking. One-dimensional thinking, as an instrument of the totally "administered society," thus reinforces the conformist tendencies promoted by family socialization and the culture industry and threatens both to close off and absorb dissent.

The Frankfurt School's interpretation of the domination of culture by instrumental reason was indebted to Lukacs's ([1923] 1971) theory of reification and to Max Weber's theory of rationalization. In the case of Lukacs, "reification" was understood to be the principal manifestation of the "commodity form" of social life whereby human activities, such as labor, are bought and sold as objects. Under such circumstances, social actors come to view the world of their own making as an objectified entity beyond their control at the same time that they attribute human powers to things. For Lukacs, however, this form of life was historically unique to the capitalist mode of production and would be abolished with socialism.

In the 1950s, as they grew more pessimistic about the prospects for change, Horkheimer and Adorno, especially, came to accept Weber's belief that rationalization was more fundamental than capitalism as the primary source of human oppression. Thus, they located the roots of instrumental rationality in a drive to dominate nature that they traced back to the origins of Western thought in Greek and Hebrew myths. This historical drive toward destructive domination extended from nature to society and the self. At the same time, Horkheimer and Adorno moved closer to Weber's pessimistic depiction of the modern world as one of no exit from the "iron cage" of rationalization. In the context of this totalizing view of the destructive tendencies of Western culture—the images for which were Auschwitz and Hiroshima—the only acts of defiance that seemed feasible were purely intellectual "negations," or what Marcuse (1964) termed "the great refusal" of intellectuals to go along with the one-dimensional society. Consequently, their interest in empirical sociological investigations, along with their faith in the efficacy of mass political movements, withdrew to a distant horizon of their concerns. Only Marcuse remained something of an optimist, continuing to investigate and support sources of opposition in racial, sexual, and Third World liberation movements.

Even though some of the most prominent founders of the Frankfurt School abandoned radical social research in favor of an immanent critique of philosophy (as in Adorno 1973), the legacy of their sociological thought has inspired a vigorous tradition of empirical research among contemporary American social scientists. In large measure, this trend can be seen as a result of the popularization of Frankfurt School themes in the 1960s, when the New Left stressed liberation and consciousness raising, themes that continue to influence sociological practice. Aronowitz (1973), for example, along with Sennet and Cobb (1973), have rekindled the Frankfurt School's original interests in working-class culture in the context of consumer society. Braverman (1974) has directed attention to processes of reification in work settings by focusing on scientific management and the separation of conception from labor in modern industry. Penetrating analyses also have been made of the impact of commodification and instrumental rationalization on the family and socialization (Lasch 1977), law (Balbus 1977), education (Giroux 1988), advertising culture (Haug 1986), mass media (Kellner 1990b), as well as other institutional areas. Feminist theorists have contributed a "doubled vision" to critical theory by showing the "systematic connectedness" of gender, class, and race relations (Kelly 1979) and by criticizing critical theory itself for its neglect of gender as a fundamental category of social analysis (Benjamin 1978; Fraser 1989). Among the most far-reaching and innovative contemporary studies are those of the contemporary German sociologist and philosopher Jurgen Habermas.

## THE CRITICAL THEORY OF JURGEN HABERMAS

Perhaps no social theorist since Max Weber has combined as comprehensive an understanding of modern social life with as deeply reflective an approach to the implications of theory and methods as Jurgen Habermas. Habermas has attempted to further the emancipatory project of the Frankfurt School by steering critical theory away from the pessimism that characterized the closing decades of Frankfurt School thought. At the same time, he has resumed the dialogue between empirical social science and critical theory to the mutual benefit of both. Further, he has given critical theory a new ethical and empirical grounding by moving its focus away from the relationship between consciousness and society and toward the philosophical and sociological implications of a critical theory of communicative action.

In sharp contrast to the Frankfurt School's increasing pessimism about the "dialectic of enlightenment," Habermas has attempted to defend the liberative potential of reason in the continuing struggle for freedom. While agreeing with the Frankfurt School's assessment of the destruction caused by instrumental rationality's unbridled domination of social life, he nonetheless recognizes the potential benefits of modern science and technology. The solution he offers to one-dimensional thought is thus not to abandon the "project of modernity" but rather to expand rational discourse about the *ends* of modern society. In order to further this goal, he has tried to unite science and ethics (fact and values) by recovering the inherently rational component in symbolic interaction as well as developing an empirical political sociology that helps to critique the political effects of positivism as well as to identify the progressive potential of contemporary social movements.

From the beginning, Habermas (1970) has agreed with the classical Frankfurt School's contention that science and technology have become legitimating rhetorics for domination in modern society. At the same time, he has argued that alternative ways of knowing are mutually legitimate by showing that they have complementary roles to play in human affairs, even though their forms of validity and realms of appropriate application are distinct. That is, plural forms of knowledge represent different but complementary "knowledge interests" (Habermas 1971).

"Instrumental knowledge," based on the ability to predict, represents an interest in the technical control or mastery of nature. "Hermeneutical knowledge" represents an interest in the clarification of intersubjective understanding. Finally, "emancipatory knowledge" is best typified in the self-clarification that occurs freely in the nondirective communicative context provided by psychoanalysis. In the context of a democratic "public sphere," such self-clarification would have a macro-social parallel in the form of ideology critique had this space not been severely eroded by elite domination and technocratic decision making (Habermas 1989). Emancipatory knowledge thus has an interest in overcoming the illusions of reification, whether in the form of neurosis at the level of psychology or ideology at the level of society. In contrast to testable empirical hypotheses about objectified processes, the validity of emancipatory knowledge can be determined only by its beneficiaries. Its validity rests on the extent to which its subjects find themselves increasingly free from compulsion. Thus, a central problem of modern society is the hegemony of instrumental knowledge that, though appropriate in the realm of nature, is used to objectify and manipulate social relations. Instrumental knowledge thus eclipses the interpretive and emancipatory forms of knowledge that are also essential for guiding social life.

When sufficient attention is paid to interpersonal communication, Habermas (1979) contends that every act of speech can be seen as implying a universal demand that interpersonal understanding be based on the free exchange and clarification of meanings. In other words, an immanent critique of language performance (which Habermas terms "universal pragmatics") reveals the presumption that communication not be distorted by differences in power between speakers. Thus, human communication is *implicitly* a demand for

freedom and equality. By this form of immanent critique—consistent with the methodological standards of the Frankfurt School—Habermas attempts to demonstrate the potential validity of emancipatory knowledge so that it can be seen as a compelling challenge to the hegemony of instrumental knowledge. The purpose of Habermas's communication theory is thus highly partisan. By showing that no forms of knowledge are "value free" but always "interested," and that human communication inherently demands to occur freely without distortions caused by social power differentials, Habermas seeks politically to delegitimate conventions that confine social science to investigations of the means rather than the rational ends of social life.

In his subsequent works, Habermas has tried to reformulate this philosophical position in terms of a political sociology. To do so, he has profoundly redirected "historical materialism," the Marxist project to which he remains committed (see Habermas 1979). Habermas contends that Marx gave insufficient attention to communicative action by restricting it to the social class relations of work. This restriction, he argues, inclined the Marxist tradition toward an uncritical attitude toward technological domination as well as towards forms of scientism that contribute to the suppression of critique in regimes legitimated by Marxist ideology. Habermas relates his immanent critique of language performance to historical materialism by showing that sociocultural evolution occurs not only through the increasing rationality of technical control over nature (as Marx recognized) but also through advances in communicative rationality, that is, nondistorted communication. Thus, instrumental rationality and communicative rationality are complementary forms of societal "learning mechanisms." The problem of modernity is not science and technology in and of themselves, because they promise increased control over the environment, but rather the fact that instrumental rationality has eclipsed communicative rationality in social life. In other words, in advanced industrial society, technical forms of control are no longer guided by consensually derived societal values. Democratic decision making is diminished under circumstances in which technical experts manipulate an objectified world, in which citizens are displaced from political decision making, and in which "reason"—identified exclusively with the "value free" prediction of isolated "facts"—is disqualified from reflection about the ends of social life.

More recently, Habermas (1987) has restated this theory sociologically to describe an uneven process of institutional development governed by opposing principles of "system" and "lifeworld." In this formulation, the cultural lifeworld—the source of cultural meanings, social solidarity, and personal identity—is increasingly subject to "colonization" by the objectivistic "steering mechanisms" of the marketplace and bureaucracy. On the levels of culture, society, and personality, such colonization tends to produce political crises resulting from the loss of meaning, increase of anomie, and loss of motivation. At the same time, however, objectivistic steering mechanisms remain indispensable because large-scale social systems cannot be guided by the face-to-face interactions that characterize the lifeworld. Thus, the state becomes a battleground for struggles involving the balance between the structuring principles of systems and lifeworlds. Habermas contends that it is in response to such crises that the forces of conservatism and the "new social movements" such as feminism and ecology are embattled and that it is here that the struggle for human liberation at present is being contested most directly. As formulated by Habermas, a critical theory of society aims at clarifying such struggles in order to contribute to the progressive democratization of modern society.

(SEE ALSO: *Marxist Sociology*)

### REFERENCES

Adorno, Theodor 1973 *Negative Dialectics*. New York: Seabury Press.

———, E. Frenkel-Brunswick, D. Levinson, and R. N. Sanford 1950 *The Authoritarian Personality*. New York: Harper.

Antonio, Robert J. 1981 "Immanent Critique as the Core of Critical Theory." *British Journal of Sociology* 32:330–345.

Aronowitz, Stanley 1973 *False Promises*. New York: McGraw-Hill.

Balbus, Isaac 1977 "Commodity Form and Legal Form: An Essay on 'Relative Autonomy'." *Law and Society Review* 11:571–588.

Benjamin, Jessica 1978 "Authority and the Family Revisited: Or, A World without Fathers?" *New German Critique* 13 (Winter): 35–57.

Braverman, Harry 1974 *Labor and Monopoly Capital*. New York: Monthly Review Press.

Fraser, Nancy 1989 *Unruly Practices: Power, Discourse, and Gender in Contemporary Social Theory*. Minneapolis: University of Minnesota Press.

Fromm, Erich 1941 *Escape from Freedom*. New York: Avon.

Giroux, Henry A. 1988 *Schooling and the Struggle for Public Life*. Minneapolis: University of Minnesota Press.

Habermas, Jurgen 1970 *Toward a Rational Society*. Boston: Beacon Press.

——— 1971 *Knowledge and Human Interests*. Boston: Beacon Press.

——— 1979 *Communication and the Evolution of Society*. Boston: Beacon Press.

——— 1987 *The Theory of Communicative Action II: Lifeworld and System—A Critique of Functionalist Reason*. Boston: Beacon Press.

——— 1989 *The Structural Transformation of the Public Sphere*. Cambridge, Mass.: MIT Press.

Haug, W. F. 1986 *Critique of Commodity Aesthetics*. Minneapolis: University of Minnesota Press.

Held, David 1980 *Introduction to Critical Theory*. Berkeley: University of California Press.

Horkheimer, Max 1972 *Critical Theory: Selected Essays*. New York: Herder and Herder.

———, and Theodor Adorno (1947) 1972 *Dialectic of Enlightenment*. New York: Seabury Press.

Jay, Martin 1973 *The Dialectical Imagination*. Boston: Little, Brown.

——— 1984 *Marxism and Totality*. Berkeley: University of California Press.

Kellner, Douglas 1984–85 "Critical Theory and the Culture Industries: A Reassessment." *Telos* 62:196–209.

——— 1990a "Critical Theory and the Crisis of Social Theory." *Sociological Perspectives* 33:11–33.

——— 1990b *Television and the Crisis of Democracy*. Boulder, Colo.: Westview Press.

Kelly, Joan 1979 "The Doubled Vision of Feminist Theory." *Feminist Studies* 5:216–227.

Lasch, Christopher 1977 *Haven in a Heartless World.* New York: Basic Books.

Lukacs, Georg [1923] 1971 *History and Class Consciousness.* Cambridge, Mass.: MIT Press.

Marcuse, Herbert 1941 *Reason and Revolution.* New York: Oxford University Press.

—— 1955 *Eros and Civilization.* Boston: Beacon Press.

—— 1964 *One-Dimensional Man.* Boston: Beacon Press.

Sennett, Richard, and Jonathan Cobb 1973. *The Hidden Injuries of Class.* New York: Vintage Books.

DWIGHT B. BILLINGS

**CROSS-CULTURAL ANALYSIS** Cross-cultural research has a long history in sociology (Armer and Grimshaw 1973; Kohn 1989). It most generally involves social research across societies or ethnic and subcultural groups within a society. Because a discussion of macro-level comparative historical research appears in another chapter of the encyclopedia, the focus here is on cross-cultural analysis of social psychological processes. These include communicative and interactive processes within social institutions and more generally the relation between the individual and society and its institutions.

Although all sociological research is seen as comparative in nature, comparisons across subcultural or cultural groups have distinct advantages for generating and testing sociological theory. Specifically, cross-cultural research can help "distinguish between those regularities in social behavior that are system specific and those that are universal" (Grimshaw 1973, p. 5). In this way, sociologists can distinguish between generalizations that are true of all cultural groups and those that apply for one group at one point in time. The lack of cross-cultural research has often led to the inappropriate universal application of sociological concepts that imply an intermediate level (one cultural group at one point in time; Bendix 1963).

In addition to documenting universal and system-specific patterns in social behavior, cross-cultural analysis can provide researchers with experimental treatments (independent variables) unavailable in their own culture. Thus, specific propositions that would be impossible to establish in a laboratory in the researcher's own country can be investigated experimentally (Strodtbeck 1964). Finally, cross-cultural analysis is beneficial for theory building in at least two respects. First, the documentation of differences across cultures in social psychological processes is often the first step in the refinement of existing theory and the generation of novel theoretical models. Second, cross-cultural analysis can lead to the discovery of unknown facts (behavioral patterns or interactive processes) that suggest new research problems that are the basis for the refinement and construction of theory.

## INTERPRETIVE AND INFERENTIAL PROBLEMS

Cross-cultural researchers face a number of challenging interpretive and inferential problems that are related to the methodological strategies they employ. For example, Charles Ragin (1989) argues that most cross-cultural research at the macro level involves either intensive studies of one or a small group of representative or theoretically decisive cases or the extensive analysis of a large number of cases. Not surprisingly, extensive studies tend to emphasize statistical regularities, while intensive studies search for generalizations that are interpreted within cultural or historical context. This same pattern also appears in most micro-level cross-cultural research, and it is clearly related to both theoretical orientation and methodological preferences. Some scholars take the position that cultural regularities must always be interpreted in cultural and historical context, while others argue that what appear to be cross-cultural differences may really be explained by lawful regularities at a more general level of analysis. Those in the first group most often employ primarily qualitative research strategies (intensive ethnographic and historical analysis of a few cases), while those in the second usually rely on quantitative techniques (multivariate or other forms of statistical analysis of large data sets).

Using his own cross-cultural work on social structure and personality as an example, Melvin Kohn (1987) maintains that documenting cross-cultural similarities extends the scope of sociological knowledge and that similarities are more readily explained, while cross-cultural differences are much more difficult to interpret. Therefore, he argues that when one finds cross-cultural similarities, explanation should not be focused on the particular historical, cultural, and political features of the groups studied but rather on social structural regularities common to them all. Kohn has quite different recommendations for the interpretation of the discovery of cross-cultural differences. Here one should first seriously consider the possibility that the findings are somehow a methodological artifact. If convinced that such is not the case, then the researcher should interpret the differences in terms of historical, cultural, and political factors (Kohn 1987, pp. 716–722).

Kohn's position has a certain logic. His approach, however, stresses the importance of cross-cultural analysis for theory testing and generalizations while downplaying the importance of such analysis for the generation and refinement of theory. Furthermore, the possibility of methodological artifacts is high in cross-cultural research regardless of whether similarities or differences are discovered.

## METHODOLOGICAL TECHNIQUES AND PROBLEMS

The wide variety of techniques employed in the cross-cultural analysis of social psychological processes reflects the training and disciplinary interests of its practitioners. Anthropologists generally rely on different types of ethnographic tools for data collection, analysis, and reporting. Ethnographic research has the dual task of cultural description and cultural interpretation. The first involves uncovering the "native's point of view" or the criteria the people under study use "to discriminate among things and how they respond to them and assign them meaning, including everything in their physical, behavioral, and social environments" (Goodenough 1980, pp. 31–32); while the second involves "stating, as explicitly as we can manage, what the knowledge thus attained demonstrates about the society in which it is found and, beyond that, about social life as such" (Geertz 1973, p. 27).

Three types of ethnographic approaches and methodological tools are generally employed in cross-cultural research. The first involves long-term participant observation and the thick description of the culture under study in line with Geertz's (1973) interpretive perspective of culture. From this perspective culture is seen as "layered multiple networks of meaning carried by words, acts, conceptions and other symbolic forms" (Marcus and Fisher 1986, p. 29). Thus, the metaphor of culture in the interpretive approach is that of a text to be discovered, described, and interpreted. The second involves methods of ethnoscience, including elicitation tasks and interviews with key informants that yield data amenable to logical and statistical analysis to generate the "organizing principles underlying behavior" (Tyler 1969; also see Werner and Schoepfle 1987). Ethnoscience views these organizing principles as the "grammar of the culture" that is part of the mental competence of members. The final type of ethnographic research is more positivistic and comparative in orientation. In this approach cross-cultural analysis is specifically defined as the use of "data collected by anthropologists concerning the customs and characteristics of various peoples throughout the world to test hypotheses concerning human behavior" (Whiting 1968, p. 693).

All three types of ethnographic research generate data preserved in research monographs or data archives such as the Human Relations Area Files and the *Ethnographic Atlas*. A number of scholars (Barry 1980; Lagacé 1977; Murdock 1967; Whiting 1968) have provided detailed discussions of the contents, coding schemes, and methodological strengths and weaknesses of these archives as well as data analysis strategies.

Although a number of psychologists have recently turned to ethnographic methods in what has been termed "cultural psychology" (Shweder 1990), most cross-cultural research in psychology involves the use of quasi-experimental methods. These include classical experimentation, clinical tests and projective techniques, systematic observation, and unobtrusive methods (see Triandis and Berry 1980). Sociologists most frequently rely on the survey method in cross-cultural research and have contributed to the development of a number of archives of survey data (Kohn 1987; Lane 1990). However, sociologists have also made good use of intensive interviewing (Bertaux 1990) and ethnography (Corsaro 1988; Corsaro and Heise 1990) in cross-cultural analysis.

There are numerous methodological problems in cross-cultural research, including: acquiring the needed linguistic and cultural skills and research funds; gaining access to field sites and data archives; defining and selecting comparable units; ensuring the representativeness of selected cases; and determining conceptual equivalence and measurement reliability and validity. The first two sets of problems are obvious but not easily resolved. Cross-cultural analysis costs much time and money, and it usually demands at least a minimal level (and often much more) of education in the history, language, and culture of groups of people foreign to the researcher. The difficulties of gaining access to and cooperation from individuals and groups in cross-cultural research "are always experienced but rarely acknowledged by comparative researchers" (Armer 1973, pp. 58–59). Specific discussions and development of strategies for gaining access are crucial because research cannot begin without such access. Additionally, casual, insensitive, or ethnocentric presentation of oneself and one's research goals to foreign gatekeepers (officials, scholars, and those individuals directly studied) not only negatively affects the original study but can also cause serious problems for others who plan cross-cultural research (Form 1973; Portes 1973). Given the cultural isolation of most social scientists in

the United States, it is not surprising that these practical problems have contributed to the lack of cross-cultural research in American sociology. However, the internationalization of the social sciences and the globalization of social and environmental issues are contributing to the gradual elimination of many of these practical problems (Sztompka 1988).

For the cross-cultural analysis of social psychological processes the unit of analysis is most often interactive events or individuals that are sampled from whole cultures or subunits such as communities or institutions (e.g., family, school, or workplace). The appropriateness of individuals as the basic unit of analysis has been a hotly debated issue in sociology. The problem is even more acute in cross-cultural analysis, especially in cultures "that lack the individualistic, participatory characteristics of Western societies" (Armer 1973, p. 62). In addition to the special difficulties of representative, theoretical, or random sampling of cases (Elder 1973; Van Meter 1990), cross-cultural researchers must also deal with "Galton's problem." According to the British statistician, Sir Francis Galton, "valid comparison requires mutually independent and isolated cases, and therefore cultural diffusion, cultural contact, culture clash or outright conquest—with their consequent borrowing, imitation, migrations, etc.—invalidates the results of comparative studies" (Sztompka 1988, p. 213). Although several researchers have presented strategies for dealing with Galton's problem for correlational studies of data archives (see Naroll, Michik, and Naroll 1980), the problem of cultural diffusion is often overlooked in many quantitative and qualitative cross-cultural studies.

Undoubtedly, ensuring conceptual equivalence and achieving valid measures are the most challenging methodological problems of cross-cultural research. Central to these problems is the wide variation in language and meaning systems across cultural groups. Anthropologists have attempted to address the problem of conceptual equivalence with the distinction between "emics" and "etics." Emics refer to local (single-culture) meaning, function, and structure, while etics are culture-free (or at least operate in more than one culture) aspects of the world (Pike 1966). A major problem in cross-cultural analysis is the use of emic concepts of one culture to explain characteristics of another culture. In fact, many cross-cultural studies involve the use of "imposed etics," that is Euro-American emics that are "imposed blindly and even ethnocentrically on a set of phenomena which occur in other cultural systems" (Berry 1980, p. 12). A number of procedures have been developed to ensure emic–etic distinctions and to estimate the validity of such measures (Brislin 1980; Naroll, Michik, and Naroll 1980; also see Hazelrigg 1973; Przeworski and Teune 1970).

Addressing conceptual relevance in cross-cultural research does not, of course, ensure valid measures. All forms of data collection and analysis depend on implicit theories of language and communication (Cicourel 1964). As social scientists have come to learn more about communicative systems within and across cultures, there has been a growing awareness that problems related to language in cross-cultural analysis are not easily resolved. There is also a recognition that these problems go beyond the accurate translation of measurement instruments (Brislin 1970; Grimshaw 1973) to the incorporation of findings from studies on communicative competence across cultural groups into cross-cultural research (Briggs 1986; Gumperz 1982).

## THE FUTURE OF CROSS-CULTURAL ANALYSIS

There is a solid basis for optimism regarding the future of cross-cultural analysis of social psychological processes. Over the last twenty years there has been remarkable growth in international organizations and cooperation among international scholars in the social sciences. These developments have not only resulted in an increase in cross-cultural research but also have led to necessary debates about the theoretical and methodological state of cross-cultural analysis (Øyen 1990; Kohn 1989).

Cooperation among international scholars in cross-cultural analysis has also contributed to the

breaking down of disciplinary boundaries. In the area of socialization or child development, for example, there have recently been a number of cross-cultural contributions to what can be termed "development in sociocultural context" by anthropologists (Heath 1989), psychologists (Rogoff 1990), sociologists (Corsaro 1988; Corsaro and Rizzo 1988); and linguists (Ochs 1988).

Despite growing international and multi-discipline cooperation and recognition of the importance of comparative research, it is still fair to say that cross-cultural analysis remains at the periphery of American sociology and social psychology. Although there has been some reversal of the growing trend toward narrow specialization over the last ten years, such specialization is still apparent in the nature of publications and the training of graduate students in these disciplines. There is a clear need to instill in future scholars a healthy skepticism regarding the cultural relativity of a great deal of theory and method in social psychology. Only then will future sociologists and social psychologists come to appreciate fully the potential of cross-cultural analysis.

(SEE ALSO: *Case Studies; Comparative Historical Analysis; Field Research Methods*)

## REFERENCES

Armer, Michael 1973 "Methodological Problems and Possibilities in Comparative Research." In M. Armer and A. Grimshaw, eds., *Comparative Social Research: Methodological Problems and Strategies*. New York: Wiley.

———, and Allen Grimshaw (eds.) 1973 *Comparative Social Research: Methodological Problems and Strategies*. New York: Wiley.

Barry, Herbert 1980 "Description and Uses of the Human Relations Area Files." In H. Triandis and J. Berry, eds., *Handbook of Cross Cultural Methodology*, Vol. 2, *Methodology*. Boston: Allyn and Bacon.

Bendix, Reinhard 1963 "Concepts and Generalizations in Comparative Sociological Studies." *American Sociological Review* 28:532–539.

Berry, J. W. 1980 "Introduction to Methodology." In H. Triandis and J. Berry, eds., *Handbook of Cross Cultural Methodology*, Vol. 2. Boston: Allyn and Bacon.

Bertaux, Daniel 1990 "Oral History Approaches to an International Social Movement." In E. Øyen, ed., *Comparative Methodology: Theory and Practice in International Social Research*. Newbury Park, Calif.: Sage.

Briggs, Charles 1986 *Learning How to Ask*. New York: Cambridge University Press.

Brislin, Richard 1970 "Back-Translation for Cross-Cultural Research. *Journal of Cross-Cultural Psychology* 1:185–216.

——— 1980 "Translation and Content Analysis of Oral and Written Materials." In H. Triandis and J. Berry, eds., *Handbook of Cross Cultural Methodology*, Vol. 2. Boston: Allyn and Bacon.

Cicourel, Aaron 1964 *Method and Measurement in Sociology*. New York: Free Press.

Corsaro, William 1988 "Routines in the Peer Culture of American and Italian Nursery School Children." *Sociology of Education* 61:1–14.

———, and David Heise 1990. "Event Structure Models from Ethnographic Data." In C. Clogg, ed., *Sociological Methodology*. Washington D. C.: American Sociological Association.

———, and Thomas Rizzo 1988 *"Discussione* and Friendship: Socialization Processes in the Peer Culture of Italian Nursery School Children. *American Sociological Review* 53:879–894.

Elder, Joseph 1973 "Problems of Cross-Cultural Methodology: Instrumentation and Interviewing in India." In M. Armer and A. Grimshaw, eds., *Comparative Social Research: Methodological Problems and Strategies*. New York: Wiley.

Form, William 1973 "Field Problems in Comparative Research: The Politics of Distrust." In M. Armer and A. Grimshaw, eds., *Comparative Social Research: Methodological Problems and Strategies*. New York: Wiley.

Geertz, Clifford 1973 *The Interpretation of Cultures*. New York: Basic Books.

Goodenough, Ward 1980 "Ethnographic Field Techniques." In H. Triandis and J. Berry, eds., *Handbook of Cross Cultural Methodology*, Vol. 2. Boston: Allyn and Bacon.

Grimshaw, Allen 1973 "Comparative Sociology: In What Ways Different from Other Sociologies?" In M. Amer and A. Grimshaw, eds., *Comparative Social Research: Methodological Problems and Strategies*. New York: Wiley.

Gumperz, John J. 1982 *Discourse Strategies*. New York: Cambridge University Press.

Hazelrigg, Lawrence 1973 "Aspects of the Measurement of Class Consciousness." In M. Armer and A. Grimshaw, eds., *Comparative Social Research: Methodological Problems and Strategies*. New York: Wiley.

Heath, Shirley 1989 "Oral and Literate Traditions among Black Americans Living in Poverty." *American Psychologist* 44:45–56.

Kohn, Melvin 1987 "Cross-National Research as an Analytic Strategy." *American Sociological Review* 52:713–731.

———(ed.) 1989 *Cross-National Research in Sociology*. Newbury Park: Calif.: Sage.

Lagacé, R. O. ed. 1977 *Sixty Cultures: A Guide to the HRAF Probability Sample Files*. New Haven, Conn: HRAF.

Lane, Jan-Erik 1990 "Data Archives as an Instrument for Comparative Research." In E. Øyen, ed., *Comparative Methodology: Theory and Practice in International Social Research*. Newbury Park, Calif.: Sage.

Marcus, George, and Michael Fischer 1986 *Anthropology as Cultural Critique*. Chicago: University of Chicago Press.

Murdock, G. P. 1967 *Ethnographic Atlas*. Pittsburgh, Pa.: University of Pittsburgh Press.

Naroll, Raoul, Gary Michik, and Frada Naroll 1980 "Holocultural Research." In H. Triandis and J. Berry, eds., *Handbook of Cross Cultural Methodology*, Vol. 2. Boston: Allyn and Bacon.

Ochs, Elinor 1988 *Culture and Language Development: Language Acquisition and Language Socialization in a Samona Village*. New York: Cambridge University Press.

Øyen, Else 1990 "The Imperfection of Comparisons." In E. Øyen, ed., *Comparative Methodology: Theory and Practice in International Social Research*. Newbury Park, Calif.: Sage.

Pike, R. 1966 *Language in Relation to a United Theory of the Structure of Human Behavior*. The Hague: Mouton.

Portes, Alejandro 1973 "Perception of the U.S. Sociologist and Its Impact on Cross-National Research." In M. Amer and A. Grimshaw, eds., *Comparative Social Research: Methodological Problems and Strategies*. New York: Wiley.

Przeworski, Adam, and Henry Teune 1970 *The Logic of Comparative Inquiry*. New York: Wiley.

Ragin, Charles 1989 "New Directions in Comparative Research." In M. Kohn, ed., *Cross-National Research in Sociology*. Newbury Park, Calif.: Sage.

Rogoff, Barbara 1990 *Apprenticeship in Thinking: Cognitive Development in Social Context*. New York: Oxford University Press.

Shweder, Richard 1990 "Cultural Psychology: What Is It?" In J. Stigler, R. Shweder, and G. Herdt, eds., *Cultural Psychology: Essays on Comparative Human Development*. New York: Cambridge University Press.

Strodtbeck, Fred 1964 "Considerations of Meta-Method in Cross-Cultural Studies." *American Anthropologist* 66:223–229.

Sztompka, Piotr 1988 "Conceptual Frameworks in Comparative Inquiry: Divergent or Convergent?" *International Sociology* 3:207–219.

Triandis, Harry, and John Berry 1980 *Handbook of Cross-Cultural Psychology*, Vol. 2, *Methodology*. Boston: Allyn and Bacon.

Tyler, Stephen 1969 "Introduction." In S. Tyler, ed., *Cognitive Anthropology*. New York: Holt, Rinehart, and Winston.

Van Meter, Karl 1990 "Sampling and Cross-Classification Analysis in International Social Research." In E. Øyen, ed., *Comparative Methodology: Theory and Practice in International Social Research*. Newbury Park, Calif.: Sage.

Werner, O., and G. M. Schoepfle 1987 *Systematic Fieldwork: Foundations of Ethnography and Interviewing*. Beverly Hills, Calif.: Sage.

Whiting, John 1968 "Methods and Problems in Cross-Cultural Research." In G. Lindzey and E. Aronson, eds., *Handbook of Social Psychology*, Vol. 2, *Research Methods*. Reading, Mass.: Addison-Wesley.

WILLIAM A. CORSARO

**CROWDS AND RIOTS** Crowds are a ubiquitous feature of everyday life. People have long assembled collectively to observe, to celebrate, and to protest various happenings in their everyday lives, be they natural events, such as a solar eclipse, or the result of human contrivance, such as the introduction of machinery into the production process. The historical record is replete with examples of crowds functioning as important textual markers, helping to shape and define a particular event, as well as strategic precipitants and carriers of the events themselves. The storming of the Bastille and the sit-ins and marches associated with the civil rights movement are examples of crowds functioning as both important markers and carriers of some larger historical happening. Not all crowds function so

significantly, of course. Most are mere sideshows to the flow of history. Nonetheless, the collective assemblages or gatherings called crowds are ongoing features of the social world and, as a consequence, have long been the object of theorizing and inquiry, ranging from the psychologistic renderings of Gustave LeBon (1895) and Sigmund Freud (1921) to the more sociological accounts of Neil Smelser (1963) and Ralph Turner and Lewis Killian (1987) to the highly systematic and empirically grounded observations of Clark McPhail and his associates (1983, 1991).

Crowds have traditionally been analyzed as a variant of the broader category of social phenomena called collective behavior. Broadly conceived, collective behavior refers to group problem-solving behavior that encompasses crowds, mass phenomena, issue-specific publics, and social movements. More narrowly, collective behavior refers to "two or more persons engaged in one or more behaviors (e.g., orientation, locomotion, gesticulation, tactile manipulation, and/or vocalization) that can be judged common or convergent on one or more dimensions (e.g., direction, velocity tempo, and/or substantive content)" (McPhail and Wohlstein 1983, pp. 580–581). Implicit in both conceptions is a continuum on which collective behavior can vary in terms of the extent to which its participants are in close proximity or diffused in time and space. Instances of collective behavior in which individuals are in close physical proximity, such that they can monitor one another by being visible to, or within earshot of, one another, are constitutive of crowds. Examples include protest demonstrations, victory celebrations, riots, and the dispersal processes associated with flight from burning buildings. In contrast are forms of collective behavior that occur among individuals who are not physically proximate but who still share a common focus of attention and engage in some parallel or common behaviors without developing the debate characteristic of the public or the organization of social movements, and who are linked together by social networks, the media, or both. Examples of this form of collective behavior, referred to as diffuse collective behavior

(Turner and Killian 1987) or the mass (Lofland 1981), include fads and crazes, deviant epidemics, mass hysteria, and collective blaming. Although crowds and diffuse collective behavior are not mutually exclusive phenomena, they are analytically distinct and tend to generate somewhat different literatures—thus, the focus on crowds in this selection.

Understanding crowds and the kindred collective phenomenon called "riots" requires consideration of four questions: (1) How do these forms of collective behavior differ from the crowd forms typically associated with everyday behavior, such as audiences and queues? (2) What are the distinctive features of crowds as collective behavior? (3) What are the conditions underlying the emergence of crowds? and (4) What accounts for the coordination of crowd behavior?

## DISTINGUISHING BETWEEN THE CROWDS OF COLLECTIVE BEHAVIOR AND EVERYDAY BEHAVIOR

There has been increasing recognition of the continuity between collective behavior and everyday behavior, yet the existence of collective behavior as an area of sociological analysis rests in part on the assumption of significant differences between collective behavior and everyday institutionalized behavior. In the case of crowds, those commonly associated with everyday life, such as at sports events and holiday parades, tend to be highly conventionalized in at least two or three ways. Such gatherings are recurrent affairs that are scheduled for a definite place at a definite time; they are calendarized both temporally and spatially. Second, associated behaviors and emotional states are typically routinized in the sense that they are normatively regularized and anticipated. And third, they tend to be sponsored and orchestrated by the state, a community, or a societal institution, as in the case of most holiday parades and electoral political rallies. Accordingly, they are typically socially approved affairs that function to reaffirm rather than challenge some institutional arrangement or the larger social order itself.

In contrast, crowds commonly associated with collective behavior, such as protest demonstrations, victory celebrations, and riots, usually challenge or disrupt the existing order. This is due in part to the fact that these crowds are neither temporally nor spatially routinized. Instead, as David Snow and his colleagues (1981) have noted, they are more likely to be unscheduled and staged in spatial areas (streets, parks, malls) or physical structures (office buildings, theaters, lunch counters) that were designed for institutionalized, everyday behavior rather than contentious or celebratory crowds. Such crowd activities are also extrainstitutional, and thus unconventional, in the sense that they are frequently based on normative guidelines that are emergent and ephemeral rather than enduring (Turner and Killian 1987), on the appropriation and redefinition of existing networks or social relationships (Weller and Quarantelli 1973), or on both.

Crowd behavior has long been described as "extraordinary" in the sense that its occurrence indicates that something unusual is happening. Precisely what it is that gives rise to the sense that something "outside the ordinary" is occurring is rarely specified unambiguously, however. John Lofland (1981) suggests that it is increased levels of emotional arousal, but such arousal is not peculiar to crowd episodes. The conceptualization offered here suggests several possibilities: It is the appropriation and use of spatial areas, physical structures, or social networks and relations for purposes other than those for which they were intended or designed that indicates something extraordinary is happening.

## CHARACTERISTIC FEATURES OF CROWDS

Crowds have been portrayed historically and journalistically as if they are monolithic entities characterized by participant and behavioral homogeneity. Turner and Killian (1972) called this image into question, referring to it as "the illusion of unanimity," but not until the recent turn toward more systematic empirical examination of crowds was it firmly established that crowd behaviors are typically quite varied and highly differentiated, and that crowd participants are generally quite heterogeneous in terms of orientation and behavior.

**Variation in Crowd Behaviors.** Based on extensive field observation of crowds, Sam Wright (1978) differentiated between two broad categories of crowd behaviors: crowd activities and task activities. "Crowd activities" refers to the redundant behavior seemingly common to all incidents of crowd behavior, such as assemblage, milling, and divergence. In their overview of empirical research on behaviors within crowds, McPhail and Wohlstein (1983) include collective locomotion, collective orientation, collective gesticulation, and collective vocalization among the types of crowd behaviors "repeatedly observed across a variety of gatherings, demonstrations, and some riots" (p. 595).

Taking these observations together, one can identify the following "crowd activities" (Wright 1978) or "elementary forms" of crowd behavior (McPhail and Wohlstein 1983): assemblage/convergence; milling; collective orientation (e.g., common or convergent gaze, focus, or attention); collective locomotion (e.g., common or convergent movement or surges); collective gesticulation (e.g., common or convergent nonverbal signaling); collective vocalization (e.g., chanting, singing, booing, cheering); and divergence/dispersal. Given the recurrent and seemingly universal character of these basic crowd behaviors, it is clear that they do not distinguish between types of crowds, that is, between demonstrations, celebrations, and riots.

To get at the variation in types of crowds, attention must be turned to what Wright conceptualized as "task activities" (1978). These refer to joint activities that are particular to and necessary for the attainment of a specific goal or the resolution of a specific problem. It is these goal-directed and problem-oriented activities that constitute the primary object of attention and thus help give meaning to the larger collective episode. Examples of task activities include parading or mass marching, mass assembly with speech making, picketing, proselytizing, temporary occupation of

premises, lynching, taunting and harassment, property destruction, looting, and sniping.

Several caveats should be kept in mind with respect to crowd task activities. First, any listing of task activities is unlikely to be exhaustive, because they vary historically and culturally. Charles Tilly's (1978) concept of "repertories of collective action" underscores this variation. Tilly has stressed that, while there are innumerable ways in which people could pursue collective ends, alternatives are in fact limited by sociohistorical forces. His research suggests, for example, that the massed march, mass assembly, and temporary occupation of premises are all collective task activities specific to the twentieth century.

Second, crowd task activities are not mutually exclusive but are typically combined in an interactive fashion during the history of a crowd episode. The mass assembly, for example, is often preceded by the massed march, and property destruction and looting often occur together. Indeed, whether a crowd episode is constitutive of a protest demonstration, a celebration, or a riot depends, in part, on the particular configuration of task activities and, in part, on who or what is the object of protest, celebration, or violence. Both of these points can be illustrated with riots. It is generally agreed that riots involve some level of collective violence against persons or property, but that not all incidents of collective violence are equally likely to be labeled riots. Collective violence against the state or its social control agents is more likely to be labeled riotous, for example, than violence perpetrated by the police against protesting demonstrators. Traditionally, what gets defined as a riot involves interpretive discretion, particularly by the state. But even when there is agreement about what constitutes a riot, distinctions are often made between types of riots, as evidenced by Morris Janowitz's (1979) distinction between communal riots (interracial clashes) and commodity riots (extensive looting), and Gary Marx's (1972) distinction between "protest riots" and "issueless riots."

Following from these observations is a final caveat: The task activities associated with any given crowd episode vary in the degree to which they are the focus of attention. Not all are equally attended to by spectators, social control agents, or the media. Consequently, task activities can be classified according to the amount of attention they receive. One that is the major focus of attention and thus provides the phenomenal basis for defining the episode constitutes "the main task activity," whereas those subordinate to the main task activity are "subordinate or side activities." The major task activity is on center stage. In contrast, the remaining task activities are sideshows, occasioned by and often parasitic to the focal activity. Examples of subordinate task activity include counterdemonstrations, media work, and peace marshaling.

**Variation in Participation Units.** Just as more recent empirical research on crowds has discerned considerable heterogeneity in behavior, so there is corresponding variation in terms of participants. Some are engaged in various task activities, some are observing, and still others are involved in the containment and control of the other participants and their interactions. Indeed, most of the individuals who make up a crowd fall into one of three categories of actors: task performers, spectators or bystanders, and social control agents. Task performers include the individuals performing both main and subordinate tasks. In the case of an antiwar march, for example, the main task performers would include the protesting marchers, with counterdemonstrators, peace marshals, and the press or media constituting the subordinate task performers.

Spectators, who constitute the second set of actors relevant to most instances of crowd behavior, have been differentiated into proximal and distal groupings according to proximity to the collective encounter and the nature of their response. Proximal spectators, who are physically co-present and can thus monitor firsthand the activities of task performers, have generally been treated as relatively passive and nonessential elements of crowd behavior. However, research on a series of victory celebrations shows that some spectators do not merely respond passively to the main task performance and accept the activity as

given, but can actively influence the character of the activity as well (Snow, Zurcher, and Peters 1981). Accordingly, proximal spectators can vary in terms of whether they are passive or animated and aggressive. "Distal spectators" refers to individuals who take note of episodes of crowd behavior even though they are not physically present during the episodes themselves. Also referred to as "bystander publics" (Turner and Killian 1987), they indirectly monitor an instance of crowd behavior and respond to it, either favorably or unfavorably, by registering their respective views with the media, and community officials. Although distal spectators may not affect the course of a single episode of crowd behavior, they can clearly have an impact on the career and character of a series of interconnected crowd episodes.

Social control agents, consisting primarily of police officers and military personnel, constitute the final set of participants relevant to most instances of crowd behavior. Since they are the guardians of public order, their primary aim with respect to crowds is to maintain that order by controlling crowd behavior both spatially and temporally or by suppressing its occurrence. Given this aim, social control agents can clearly have a significant impact on the course and character of crowd behavior. This is evident in most protest demonstrations and victory celebrations, but it is particularly clear in the case of riots, which are often triggered by overzealous police activity and often involve considerable interpersonal violence perpetrated by the police. The urban riots of the 1960s in the United States illustrate both tendencies (Bergesen 1980; Kerner 1968).

Although there is no consensual taxonomy of crowd behaviors and interacting participation units, the foregoing observations indicate that behavioral and participant heterogeneity are characteristic features of most crowd episodes. In turn, the research on which these observations are based lays to rest the traditional image of crowds as monolithic entities composed of like-minded people engaged in undifferentiated behavior.

## CONDITIONS OF EMERGENCE

Under what conditions do individuals come together collectively to engage in crowd task activities constitutive of protest or celebration, and why do these occurrences sometimes turn violent or riotous? Three sets of interacting conditions are discernible in the literature: (1) conditions of conduciveness; (2) situational precipitants or strains; and (3) conditions for mobilization.

**Conditions of Conduciveness.** The concept of conduciveness directs attention to structural and cultural factors that make crowd behavior physically and socially possible (Smelser 1963). Conditions of conduciveness constitute the raw material for crowd behavior and include three sets of factors: ecological, technological, and social control. Ecological factors affect the arrangement and distribution of people in space so as to facilitate interaction and communication. One such factor found to be particularly conducive is the existence of large, spatially concentrated populations. The vast majority of campus protest demonstrations in the 1960s occurred on large universities, for example. Similarly, the urban riots of the 1960s typically occurred in densely populated residential areas, where there were large, easily mobilizable black populations. Seymour Spilerman's (1976) aggregate-level research on ghetto riots found an almost linear relationship between the size of a city's black population and the likelihood and number of disorders experienced, thus suggesting that there was a threshold population size below which riots were unlikely. Taken together, such findings provide strong support for the hypothesis that, all other things being equal, the greater the population density, the greater the likelihood of crowd behavior.

The heightened prospect of interpersonal interaction and communication associated with population concentration can also be facilitated by the diffusion of communication technology, namely telephone, radio, and television. But neither the diffusion of such technology nor population density guarantee the emergence of crowd behavior in the absence of a system of social control that allows for freedom of assembly and speech. It has been found repeatedly that incidence of public protest against the state diminishes considerably in political systems that prohibit and deal harshly with such crowd behavior, whereas the development of a more permissive attitude toward public protest and a corresponding relaxation of measures of social control is frequently conducive to the development of protest behavior. The proliferation of public protest throughout Eastern Europe, including the Soviet Union, in 1989 and 1990 is illustrative of this principle; so is Bert Useem and Peter Kimball's (1989) research on prison riots, which reveals that they are sparked in part by erosion of prison security systems and the increased physical vulnerability of those systems.

**Precipitating Events and Conditions.** However conducive conditions might be for crowd behavior, it will not occur in the absence of some precipitating event or condition. Although the specific precipitants underlying the emergence of crowd behavior may be quite varied, most are variants of two generic conditions: (1) ambiguity; and (2) grievances against the state or some governmental, administrative entity.

Ambiguity is generated by the disruption or breakdown of everyday routines or expectancies, and has long been linked theoretically to the emergence of crowd behavior (Johnson and Feinberg 1990; Turner and Killian 1987). Evidence of its empirical linkage to the emergence of crowd behavior is abundant, as with the materialization of crowds of onlookers at the scene of accidents and fires; the celebrations that sometimes follow high-stakes, unanticipated athletic victories; the collective revelry sometimes associated with disruption of interdependent networks of institutionalized roles, as in the case of power blackouts and police strikes; and prison riots that frequently follow on the heels of unanticipated change in administrative personnel, procedures, and control.

The existence of grievances against the state or some governmental, administrative unit is equally facilitative of crowd behavior, particularly of the protest variety. Such grievances are typically associated with the existence of economic and political inequities that are perceived as unjust or political decisions and policies that are seen as morally bankrupt or advantaging some interests to the exclusion of others. Examples of protest crowds triggered in part by such grievances include the hostile gatherings of hungry citizens and displaced workers in industrializing Europe; the striking crowds of workers associated with the labor movement; and the mass demonstrations (marching, rallying, picketing, vigiling) associated with the civil rights, student, antiwar, and women's movements of the 1960s and 1970s.

Crowd violence—"riotous" task activities such as property destruction, looting, fighting, and sniping—has been an occasional corollary of protest crowds, but it is not peculiar to such crowds. Moreover, the occurrence of crowd violence, whether in association with protest demonstrations or celebrations, is relatively infrequent in comparison to other crowd behaviors (Eisinger 1973; Gamson 1975; Lewis 1982). When it does occur, however, there are two discernible tendencies: Interpersonal violence most often results from the dynamic interaction of protestors and police (Kritzer 1977; MacCannell 1973); and property violence, as in the case of riot looting, tends to be selective and semi-organized rather than random and chaotic (Berk and Aldrich 1972; Quarantelli and Dynes 1968).

**Conditions for Mobilization.** A precipitating condition coupled with a high degree of conduciveness is rarely sufficient to produce an instance of crowd behavior. In addition, people have to be assembled or brought into contact with one another, and attention must be focused on the accomplishment of some task. On some occasions in everyday life the condition of assemblage is already met, as in the case of the pedestrian crowd and conventional audience. More often than not, however, protest crowds, large-scale victory celebrations, and riots do not grow out of conventional gatherings but require the rapid convergence of people in time and space. McPhail and Miller (1973) found this assembling process to be contingent on the receipt of assembling instructions;

ready access, either by foot or by other transportation, to the scene of the action; schedule congruence; and relatively free or discretionary time. It can also be facilitated by life-style circumstances and social networks. Again, the ghetto riots of the 1960s are a case in point. They typically occurred on weekday evenings or weekends in the summer, times when people were at home, were more readily available to receive instructions, and had ample discretionary time (Kerner 1968).

The focusing of attention typically occurs through some "keynoting" or "framing" process whereby the interpretive gesture or utterance of one or more individuals provides a resonant account or stimulus for action. It can occur spontaneously, as when someone yells "Cops!" or "Fire!"; it can be an unintended consequence of media broadcasts; or it can be the product of prior planning, thus implying the operation of a social movement.

## COORDINATION OF CROWD BEHAVIOR

Examination of protest demonstrations, celebratory crowds, and riots reveals in each case that the behaviors in question are patterned and collective rather than random and individualistic. Identification of the sources of coordination has thus been one of the central tasks confronting students of crowd behavior.

Earlier theorists attributed the coordination either to the rapid spread of emotional states and behavior in a contagion-like manner due to the presumably heightened suggestibility of crowd members (LeBon [1895] 1960; Blumer 1951) or to the convergence of individuals who are predisposed to behave in a similar fashion because of common dispositions or background characteristics (Allport 1924; Dollard et al. 1939). Both views are empirically off the mark. They assume a uniformity of action that glosses the existence of various categories of actors, variation in their behaviors, ongoing interaction among them, and the role this interaction plays in determining the direction and character of crowd behavior. These oversights are primarily due to the perceptual trap of taking the behaviors of the most conspicuous element of the episode—the main task performers—as typifying all categories of actors, thus giving rise to the previously mentioned "illusion of unanimity" (Turner and Killian 1987).

A more modern variant of the convergence argument attributes coordination to a rational calculus in which individuals reach parallel assessments regarding the benefits of engaging in a particular task activity (Berk 1974; Granovetter 1978). Blending elements of this logic with strands of theorizing seemingly borrowed from LeBon and Freud, James Coleman (1990) argues that crowd behavior occurs when individuals make a unilateral transfer of control over their actions. Such accounts are no less troublesome than the earlier ones in that they remain highly individualistic and psychologistic, ignoring the extent to which crowd behavior is the product of collective decision making involving the "framing" and "reframing" of probable costs and benefits and the extent to which this collective decision making frequently has a history involving prior negotiation between various sets of crowd participants.

A sociologically more palatable view holds that crowd behavior is coordinated by definition of the situation that functions in normative fashion by encouraging behavior in accordance with the definition. The collective definition may be situationally emergent (Turner and Killian 1987) or preestablished by prior negotiation among the relevant sets of actors (Snow and Anderson 1985). When one or more sets of actors cease to adjust their behaviors to this normative understanding, violence is more likely, especially if the police seek to reestablish normative control, and the episode is likely to be labeled as riotous or moblike.

Today it is generally conceded that most instances of crowd behavior are normatively regulated, but the dynamics underlying the emergence of such regulations are still not well understood empirically. Consequently, there is growing research interest in detailing the interactional dynamics underlying the process by which coordinating understandings emerge and change. Distinctive to this research is the view that social interaction among relevant sets of actors, rather than the background characteristics and cognitive states of individuals, holds the key to understanding the course and character of crowd behavior.

(SEE ALSO: *Collective Behavior*)

## REFERENCES

Allport, Floyd H. 1924 *Social Psychology*. Boston: Houghton Mifflin.

Bergesen, Albert 1980 "Official Violence During the Watts, Newark, and Detroit Race Riots of the 1960s." In Pat Lauderdale, ed., *A Political Analysis of Deviance*. Minneapolis: University of Minnesota Press.

Berk, Richard 1974 "A Gaming Approach to Crowd Behavior." *American Sociological Review* 39:355–373.

———, and Howard Aldrich 1972 "Patterns of Vandalism During Civil Disorders as an Indicator of Selection of Targets." *American Sociological Review* 37:533–547.

Blumer, Herbert 1951 "Collective Behavior." In Alfred McClung Lee, ed., *Principles of Sociology*. New York: Barnes and Noble.

Coleman, James S. 1990 *Foundations of Social Theory*. Cambridge: Harvard University Press.

Dollard, John, Leonard Doob, Neal Miller, Herbert Mowrer, and Robert Sears 1939 *Frustration and Aggression*. New Haven, Conn.: Yale University Press.

Eisinger, Peter 1973 "The Conditions of Protest Behavior in American Cities." *American Political Science Review* 67:11–28.

Freud, Sigmund 1921 *Group Psychology and Analysis of the Ego*. London: International Psychoanalytical Press.

Gamson, William 1975 *The Strategy of Social Protest*. Homewood, Ill.: Dorsey.

Granovetter, Mark 1978 "Threshold Models of Collective Behavior." *American Journal of Sociology* 83: 1420–1443.

Janowitz, Morris 1979 "Collective Racial Violence: A Contemporary History." In Hugh Davis Graham and Ted Gurr, eds., *Violence in America: Historical and Comparative Perspectives*, rev. Beverly Hills, Calif.: Sage.

Johnson, Norris R., and William E. Feinberg 1990 "Ambiguity and Crowds: Results from a Computer Simulation Model." *Research in Social Movements, Conflict and Change* 12:35–66.

Kerner, Otto 1968 *Report of the National Advisory Commission on Civil Disorders*. New York: E. P. Dutton.

Kritzer, Herbert M. 1977 "Political Protest and Political Violence: A Nonrecursive Causal Model." *Social Forces* 55:630–640.

LeBon, Gustave (1895) 1960 *The Crowd: A Study of the Popular Mind*. New York: Viking Press.

Lewis, Jerry 1982 "Fan Violence: An American Social Problem." *Research on Social Problems and Public Policy* 2:175–206.

Lofland, John 1981 "Collective Behavior: The Elementary Forms." In Morris Rosenberg and Ralph Turner, eds., *Social Psychology*. New York: Basic Books.

MacCannell, Dean 1973 "Nonviolent Action as Theater." Nonviolent Action Research Project Series No. 10, Haverford College Center for Nonviolent Conflict Resolution, Haverford, Pa.

Marx, Gary 1972 "Issueless Riots." In James F. Short and Marvin E. Wolfgang, eds., *Collective Violence*. Chicago: Aldine-Atherton.

McPhail, Clark 1991 *The Myth of the Madding Crowd*. New York: Aldine de Gruyter.

McPhail, Clark, and David L. Miller 1973 "The Assembling Process: A Theoretical and Empirical Examination." *American Sociological Review* 38:721–735.

McPhail, Clark, and Ronald T. Wohlstein 1983 "Individual and Collective Behaviors Within Gatherings, Demonstrations, and Riots." *Annual Review of Sociology* 9:579–600.

Quarantelli, Enrico L., and Russell Dynes 1968 "Looting in Civil Disorders: An Index of Social Change." In Louis Masotti and Don R. Bowen, eds., *Riots and Rebellion*. Beverly Hills, Calif.: Sage.

Smelser, Neil 1963 *Theory of Collective Behavior*. New York: Free Press.

Snow, David A., and Leon Anderson 1985 "Field Methods and Conceptual Advances in Crowd Research." Paper presented at Conference on Research Methods in Collective Behavior and Social Movements, Collective Behavior/Social Movements Section of the American Sociological Association, Bowling Green State University.

Snow, David A., Louis A. Zurcher, and Robert Peters 1981 "Victory Celebrations as Theater: A Dramaturgical Approach to Crowd Behavior." *Symbolic Interaction* 4:21–42.

Spilerman, Seymour 1976 "Structural Characteristics of Cities and the Severity of Racial Disorders." *American Sociological Review* 35:627–649.

Tilly, Charles 1978 *From Mobilization to Revolution*. Reading, Mass.: Addison-Wesley.

Turner, Ralph H., and Lewis Killian 1987 *Collective Behavior*. Englewood Cliffs, N.J.: Prentice-Hall.

Useem, Bert, and Peter Kimball 1989 *States of Siege: U.S. Prison Riots 1971–1986*. New York: Oxford University Press.

Weller, Jack, and Enrico L. Quarantelli 1973 "Neglected Characteristics of Collective Behavior." *American Journal of Sociology* 79:665–685.

Wright, Sam 1978 *Crowds and Riots: A Study in Social Organization*. Beverly Hills, Calif.: Sage.

DAVID A. SNOW
RONNELLE PAULSEN

**CULTS** As a sociological term, *cults* has three related but conceptually distinct meanings (Roberts 1984, pp. 241–247). Its oldest meaning developed through attempts to typologize religious groups as churches, denominations, sects, or cults. Howard Becker used the term *cult* to describe a loose association of people who hold eclectic religious views (Becker 1932) and built on Ernst Troeltsch's identification of "mysticism" as a loosely knit association whose participants emphasized the value of "a purely personal and inward experience" (Troeltsch 1911, p. 993; see also Mann 1955). Meredith McGuire refined the typology by distinguishing between organizational characteristics and the religious orientation of members. The organizational characteristics of cults include ideological toleration of other groups despite their own tension with society, and the religious orientation of cult members includes the compartmentalization of religion into particular aspects of life while questing after higher levels of "awareness" (McGuire 1987, pp. 117–125).

The second meaning of the term *cult* specifically depends on whether a new group's theological ideas and related practices have ideational precedent within its culture (Stark and Bainbridge 1985, pp. 26–37). Both sects and cults exist in relatively high tension with society, but sects are schismatic movements that borrow heavily from their parent groups' doctrines and practices, while cults "do not have a prior tie with another established religious body in the society in question" (Stark and Bainbridge 1985, p. 25). Cults, therefore, are cultural innovations, and as such they appear in three forms, differing in their degrees of organization, especially concerning the manner in which leaders relate to members. "Audience cults" have "virtually no aspects of formal organization" concerning either formal membership or the conveyance of ideology, and leaders disseminate their information in loosely structured situations such as lectures or private readings of occult books. "Client cults" often exhibit considerable organization "among those [leaders] offering the cult service," but the partakers of the message are little organized (as is the case with alternative healing organizations [Stark and Bainbridge 1985, p. 26]). Finally, cult movements have formal structures in which followers or members operate under leaders' directives, although the degree of members' participation varies from relatively weak to complete immersion (Stark and Bainbridge 1985, p. 29). Moreover, cult movements offer members the widest degree of general supernatural promises about salvation or deliverance, much like major, traditional religions (Stark and Bainbridge 1985, p. 30).

Third, "cult" carries pejorative connotations as an exploitative group that demands unreasonable obligations from group members, usually under the direction of a manipulative charismatic leader and at the expense of members' former family and friends. "Cults" in this sense appear in the fields of religion, politics, psychotherapy and personal development, health, science, and economics, all of them sharing a fundamental characteristic of ideologies. Their adherents are unable publicly to express doubts about the groups' fundamental assumptions (see Feuer 1975, pp. 104–105). Although few sociologists use "cults" in this manner (partly in reaction to its negative tone), the term has entered popular vocabulary with these inferences.

Cults in this third sense have spurred considerable public debate, especially after the Charles Manson murders (1969), the Patti Hearst kidnapping story (1974), and the Jonestown murder/suicides (1978) (Hall 1987). Numerous "anticult" or "countercult" organizations of varying size, complexity, and activity emerged in the United

States during early 1972 (Shupe and Bromley 1980, p. 90; Shupe and Bromley 1984), followed by similar organizations in other Western countries (see Beckford 1985). These oppositional groups, some of which have evolved into organizations that still are active in the 1990s, initially were comprised largely of relatives with family members involved in various alternative religions, along with some clergy and professionals from the mental health field. Countercult organizations served both as support groups for relatives and former members and as vocal critics of many cult activities and practices. Adopting and later modifying a "brainwashing" and "coercive persuasion" model that initially researchers used to explain ideological reversals among captives in various communist indoctrination programs during the 1950s (Lifton 1961; Ofshe and Singer 1986), many relatives argued that family members had to be removed from the groups (by force if necessary) and "deprogrammed" from their "totalistic" views. Consequently, an intense social debate ensued between the "cults" (or as they preferred to call themselves, the "new religions") and their opponents, with each side attempting to damage the public image of their enemies while at the same time presenting themselves in a favorable light (Kent 1990).

(SEE ALSO: *Religious Organizations*)

## REFERENCES

Becker, Howard 1932 *Systematic Sociology.* New York: Wiley

Beckford, James A. 1985 *Cult Controversies.* London: Tavistock.

Bromley, David G., and Phillip E. Hammond (eds.) 1987 *The Future of New Religious Movements.* Macon, Ga.: Mercer University Press.

Choquette, Diane, comp. 1985 *New Religious Movements in the United States and Canada: A Critical Assessment and Anotated Bibliography.* Westport, Conn.: Greenwood Press.

Feuer, Lewis S. 1975 *Ideology and the Ideologists.* New York: Harper and Row.

Hall, John R. 1987 *Gone from the Promised Land: Jonestown in American Cultural History.* New Brunswick, N.J.: Transaction Books.

Jacobs, Janet 1989 *Divine Disenchantment.* Bloomington and Indianapolis: Indiana University Press.

Kent, Stephen A. 1990 "Deviance Labelling and Normative Strategies in the Canadian 'New Religions/Countercult' Debate." *Canadian Journal of Sociology* 15:393–416.

Lifton, Robert J. 1961 *Thought Reform and the Psychology of Totalism.* New York: W. W. Norton.

McGuire, Meredith B. 1987 *Religion: The Social Context,* 2nd ed. Belmont, Calif.: Wadsworth.

Mann, W. E. 1955 *Sect, Cult and Church in Alberta.* Toronto: University of Toronto Press.

Melton, J. Gordon 1986 *Biographical Dictionary of American Cult and Sect Leaders.* New York: Garland.

——— 1987 *The Encyclopedia of American Religions.* Detroit: Gale Research.

Ofshe, Richard, and Margaret T. Singer 1986 "Attacks on Peripheral Versus Central Elements of Self and the Impact of Thought Reforming Techniques." *The Cultic Studies Journal* 3:3–24.

Robbins, Thomas 1988 *Cults, Converts and Charisma.* Beverly Hills, Calif.: Sage.

Roberts, Keith A. 1984 *Religion in Sociological Perspective.* Homewood, Ill.: Dorsey.

Saliba, John A. 1987 *Psychiatry and the Cults: An Annotated Bibliography.* New York: Garland.

Shupe, Anson D., Jr., and David G. Bromley 1980 *The New Vigilantes: Deprogrammers, Anti-Cultists, and the New Religions.* Beverly Hills, Calif.: Sage.

——— 1984 *The Anti-Cult Movement in America: A Bibliography and Historical Survey.* New York: Garland.

Stark, Rodney, and William Sims Bainbridge 1985 *The Future of Religion.* Berkeley: University of California Press.

Troeltsch, Ernst 1911 *The Social Teachings of the Christian Churches,* 2 vols., trans 1931 by Olive Wyon. London: George Allen and Unwin.

Zald, Mayer N., and John D. McCarthy 1987 "Religious Groups as Crucibles of Social Movements." In *Social Movements in an Organizational Society,* ed. by Mayer N. Zald and John D. McCarthy. New Brunswick, N.J.: Transaction Books.

STEPHEN A. KENT

**CULTURE**  To produce a definition of culture, one can examine the concept in the abstract, that is, explore the concept theoretically from a variety of standpoints and then justify the definition that emerges through deductive logic. Or one can explore how the concept is used in practice, that is, describe how sociologists, both individually and collectively, define culture in the research process and analyze how they inductively construct a shared definition. This article takes the latter collective-inductive approach to defining culture. Such an approach is inherently sociological and does not presume to produce a definition for the field, rather it seeks to document how successful participants in the field have been in producing a shared definition for themselves. To produce such a "working" definition of culture, one starts by examining the social science roots and current status of the sociology of culture.

The focus on culture in sociology has flourished over the past fifteen years, as evidenced by the fact that the Culture Section in the American Sociological Association has become one of the largest and is still one of the fastest-growing sections in the discipline. The growth of interest in culture is also nicely documented by the number of recent review articles (e.g., Peterson 1990, 1989, 1979; Wuthnow and Witten 1988; Blau 1988; Mukerji and Schudson 1986). As is clear from the reviews, interest in cultural analysis has grown significantly. The focus on culture in all spheres of research has increased tremendously, and culture is now readily accepted as a level of explanation in its own right. Even in traditionally materialist-oriented research arenas, such as stratification and Marxist studies, cultural activities and interests are not treated as subordinate to economic explanations in current research (e.g., Bourdieu 1984; Williams 1977, 1981). Cultural studies and analysis have become one of the most fertile areas in sociology.

The rapid growth in the focus on culture and cultural explanations has produced some definitional boundary problems. The term *culture* has been used in contemporary sociological research to describe everything from elite artistic activities (Becker 1982) to the values, styles, and ideology of day-to-day conduct (Swidler 1986). Included among the current "mixed bag" of research that takes place under the auspices of the sociology of culture is work in science (Latour 1987; Star

1989), religion (Neitz 1987), law (Katz 1988), media and popular culture (Gitlin 1985; Chambers 1986), and work organization (Lincoln and Kalleberg 1990). With such an extensive variety in the empirical focus of cultural studies, the question for many participants in the field is how to translate this eclecticism into a coherent research field. This goal has not yet been reached, but while a coherent concept of culture is still evolving and the boundaries of the current sociology of culture research community are still fluid and expanding, it is possible to explore how different types of researchers in the social sciences, both currently and historically, have approached the concept of culture. In this inventory process, a better understanding of the concept of culture will emerge, that is, what different researchers believe the concept of culture includes, what the concept excludes, and how the distinction between categories has been made. This article will provide a historical overview of the two major debates on the appropriate focus and limitations of the definition of culture, and then turn to the contemporary social context in an effort to clarify the issues underlying the current concept of culture.

## THE CULTURE–SOCIAL STRUCTURE DEBATE

From the turn of the century until the 1950s, the definition of culture was embroiled in a dialogue that sought to distinguish the concepts of culture and social structure. This distinction was a major bone of contention among social scientists, most noticeably among anthropologists divided between the cultural and social traditions of anthropology. Researchers in the cultural or ethnological tradition, such as Franz Boas (1896/1940), Bronislaw Malinowski (1927, 1931), Margaret Mead (1928, 1935), Alfred Kroeber (1923/1948, 1952), and Ruth Benedict (1934) felt culture was the central concept in social science. "Culturalists" maintained that culture is primary in guiding all patterns of behavior, including who interacts with whom, and should therefore be given priority in theories about the organization of society. This position was countered by researchers in the structural tradition, such as A. R. Radcliffe-Brown ([1952] 1961) and E. E. Evans-Pritchard (1937, 1940) from the British school of social anthropology, and Claude Levi-Strauss ([1953] 1963) in French structuralism. "Structuralists" contended that social structure was the primary focus of social science and should be given priority in theories about society because social structure (e.g., kinship) determines patterns of social interaction and thought. Both schools had influential and large numbers of adherents.

The culturalists took a holistic approach to the concept of culture. Stemming from Edward Tylor's classic definition, culture was ". . . that complex whole which includes knowledge, belief, art, morals, law, custom, and any other capabilities and habits acquired by man as a member of society" ([1871] 1924, p. 1). This definition leaves little out, but the orientation of the late nineteenth century intended the concept of culture to be as inclusive as possible. Culture is what distinguishes man as a species from other species. Therefore culture consists of all that is produced by human collectivities, that is, all of social life. The focus here stems from the "nature" vs. "nurture" disputes common during this period. Anything that differentiates man's accomplishments from biological and evolutionary origins was relevant to the concept of culture. That includes religion as well as kinship structures, language as well as nation-states.

Following Boas, the study of culture was used to examine different types of society. All societies have cultures, and variations in cultural patterns helped further the argument that culture, not nature, played the most significant role in governing human behavior. In addition, the cultural variances observed in different societies helped break down the nineteenth-century anthropological notions of "the psychic unity of mankind, the unity of human history, and the unity of culture" (Singer 1968, p. 527). The pluralistic and relativistic approaches to culture that followed emphasized a more limited, localized conception. Culture was what produced a distinctive identity for a society, socializing members for greater internal homogeneity and identifying outsiders. Culture is thus treated as differentiating concept, providing recognition factors for internal cohesion and external discrimination.

Although this tradition of ethnographic research on culture tended to be internal and localized, what is termed an "emic" approach in cognitive anthropology (Goodenough 1956), by the 1940s there emerged a strong desire among many anthropologists to develop a comparative "etic" approach to culture, that is, construct a generalized theory of cultural patterns. In the comparison of hundreds of ethnographies written in this period, A. L. Kroeber and Clyde Kluckhohn sought to build such a general definition of culture. They wrote,

> *Culture consists of patterns, explicit and implicit, of and for behavior acquired and transmitted by symbols, constituting the distinctive achievement of human groups, including their embodiments in artifacts; the essential core of culture consists of traditional (i.e., historically derived and selected) ideas and especially their attached values; culture systems may, on the one hand, be considered as products of action, on the other as conditioning elements of further action* ([1952] 1963, p. 181).

Milton Singer (1968) characterized this "pattern theory" definition as a condensation of what most American anthropologists in the 1940s and 1950s called culture. It includes behavior, cultural objects, and cognitive predispositions as part of the concept, thus emphasizing that culture is both a product of social action and a process that guides future action. The pattern theory stated simply that behavior follows a relatively stable routine, from the simplest levels of custom in dress and diet to more complex levels of organization in political, economic, and religious life. The persistence of specific patterns is variable in different arenas and different societies, but larger configurations tend to be more stable, changing incrementally unless redirected by external forces. In addition, the theory emphasized that the culture from any given society can be formally described, that is, it can be placed in formal categories representing different spheres

of social life to facilitate comparison between societies. As such, universal patterns of culture can be constructed.

In comparison, anthropological structuralists in this period conceive of culture less comprehensively. The structuralist concept of culture is made distinct through emphasis on a new concept of social structure. Largely through the efforts of Radcliffe-Brown, a theory emerges that argues social structure is more appropriately represented by a network or system of social relations than a set of norms. The structuralist argument is intended to clarify how actors in a society actively produce and are socially produced by their cultural context. By distinguishing the actors and interaction in a social system from the behavioral norms, structuralists seek to establish a referent for social structure that is analytically independent of the culture and artifacts produced in that system. The production of culture is thus grounded clearly in an interactional framework. Norms of interaction are also produced by interacting participants, but the question of causal primacy between culture and social structure can be considered separately. The initial effort here is simply not to reify the origins of culture.

The exact relationship of culture and social structure, however, becomes the central issue of the structuralist/culturalist debate. For example, how to identify the boundaries of a society one is researching is problematic when the society is not an isolate. Structuralists tend to give social relations, that is, the extent of a network, priority in identifying boundaries, while culturalists focus on the extent of particular types of cultural knowledge or practices. Since both elements are obviously operating interdependently, the efforts to disentangle these concepts make little headway. The arguments to establish causal priority for one concept vis-à-vis the other settle into a fairly predictable exchange. Structuralists base their priority claims on the fact that the interaction of actors in a society is empirically preliminary to the development and application of cultural elements. Culturalists respond that interaction itself is at least partially a cultural phenomenon, and that in most complex societies cultural patterns have been well established prior to ongoing social relationships.

By the late 1950s, the concept of culture is becoming increasingly important to sociologists. To help resolve the now tired debate over cultural and structural foci and precedence, A. L. Kroeber and Talcott Parsons publish a report in the *American Sociological Review* titled "The Concepts of Culture and Social System" (1958), which seeks to establish some ground rules for differentiating the two concepts. At least for sociologists, many of whom identify explicitly with the structural-functional theories of the anthropological structuralists, acknowledgment of a separate social system component that delimits the scope of culture is not difficult. More difficult is ascertaining where the appropriate limits for the concept of culture lie within this domain. Kroeber and Parsons suggest restricting the usage of culture to, "transmitted and created content and patterns of values, ideas, and other symbolic-meaningful systems as factors in the shaping of human behavior and the artifacts produced behavior" (1958, p. 583). This definition emphasizes the predispositional aspect of a cultural referent, limiting the scope of culture to a cognitive perspective, and concentrates on a carefully worded description of "symbolic-meaningful systems" as the appropriate referent for culture. While no longer the omnibus conception of a traditional, Tylor-derived approach, this type of cultural analysis is still potentially applicable to any realm of social activity.

## THE HIGH-MASS CULTURE DEBATE

In the 1950s and early 1960s, the concept of culture becomes enmeshed in a new debate that like the previously documented dialogue has both influential and significant numbers of participants on each side of the dispute. Sociologists, however, are more central to the discussion, pitting those who support a broadly conceived, anthropological interpretation of culture that places both commonplace and elite activities in the same category, against a humanities oriented conception of culture that equates the identification of cultural activity with a value statement. This debate attempts to do two things: to classify different types of cultural activity, and to distinguish a purely descriptive approach to the concept of culture from an axiological approach that defines culture through an evaluative process.

That an axiological approach to culture can be considered legitimate by a "scientific" enterprise is perhaps surprising to contemporary sociologists entrenched in the positivistic interpretation of science, yet a central issue for many sociologists in this period was how and whether to approach questions of moral values. For example, the critical theorist Leo Lowenthal (1950) characterized this period of social science as "applied asceticism" and stated that the moral or aesthetic evaluation of cultural products and activities is not only sociologically possible, but also should be a useful tool in the sociological analysis of cultural differentiation.

These evaluative questions certainly play a part in the analysis of "mass culture," a term that the critic Dwight McDonald explains is used to identify articles of culture that are produced for mass consumption, "like chewing gum" (McDonald 1953, p. 59). A number of commentators, including both sociologists and humanists, observe the growth of mass culture production in the post World War II United States with a mixture of distaste and alarm. The concern of McDonald and critics like him is the decline of intrinsic value in cultural artifacts, a decline in quality that stems from, or is at least attributed to, a combination of economic and social factors associated with the growth of capitalism. For example, mass culture critics argue that the unchecked growth of capitalism in the production and distribution phases of culture industries leads to a "massification" of consumption patterns. Formerly localized, highly differentiated, and competitive markets become dominated by a single corporate actor who merges different sectors of the consumer landscape and monopolizes production resources and distribution outlets. Within these giant culture industry organizations the demand for greater efficiency and the vertical integration of production lead to a bureaucratically focused standardization of output. Both processes function to stamp out cultural difference and create greater homogeneity in moral and aesthetic values, all at the lowest common denominator.

Regardless of the causes of the mass culture phenomenon, the critics of mass culture believe it to be a potentially revolutionary force that will transform the values of society. One critic states that "mass culture is a dynamic, revolutionary force, breaking down the old barriers of class, tradition, taste, and dissolving all cultural distinctions. It mixes and scrambles everything together, producing what might be called homogenized culture, . . . It thus destroys all values, since value judgements imply discrimination" (McDonald 1953, p. 62).

In launching this attack, mass culture opponents see themselves as the saviors of a "true" or "high" culture (e.g., McDonald, Greenberg, Berelson, and Howe; see Rosenberg and White 1957). They argue that the consumption of mass culture undermines the very existence of legitimate high culture, that is, the elite arts and folk cultures. Without the ability to differentiate between increasingly blurred lines of cultural production, the average consumer turns toward mass culture due to its immediate accessibility. Further, simply through its creation, mass culture devalues elite art and folk cultures by borrowing the themes and devices of different cultural traditions and converting them into mechanical, formulaic systems (Greenberg 1946). Thus critics of mass culture argue that it is critical for the health of society to discriminate between types of culture.

Defenders of mass culture, or at least those who feel the attack on mass culture is too extreme, respond that mass culture critics seek to limit the production and appreciation of culture to an elitist minority. They contend that the elitist criticism of culture is ethnocentric and that not only is mass, popular, or public culture more diverse than given credit for (e.g., Lang 1956; Kracauer 1949), but also the benefits of mass cultural participation far outweigh the limitations of a mass media distribution system (White 1956; Seldes 1956). Post-World War II America experienced an economic boom that sent its citizens searching for a variety of new cultural outlets. The increase in cultural participation certainly included what some critics might call "vulgar" activities, but it also included a tremendous increase in audiences for the arts across the board. Essentially, mass culture defenders assert that the argument over the legitimacy of mass culture comes down to a matter of ideology, one that positions the elitist minority vs. the growing democratization of culture.

To extricate themselves from this axiological conundrum, many sociologists of culture retreated from a morally evaluative stance to a normative one. As presented by Gertrude Jaeger and Philip Selznick (1964), the normative sociological approach to culture, while still evaluative, seeks to combine anthropological and humanist conceptions of culture through a diagnostic analysis of cultural experience. The emphasis here is on elaborating the nature of "symbolically meaningful" experiences, the same focus for culture that Kroeber and Parsons (1958) take in their differentiation of culture and social system. To do this, Jaeger and Selznick adopt a pragmatist perspective (Dewey 1958) that accords symbolic status to cultural objects or events through a social signification process. Interacting individuals create symbols through the communication of meaningful experience, using both denotative and connotative processes. By creating symbols, interacting individuals create culture. Thus the definition of culture becomes: "Culture consists of everything that is produced by, and is capable of sustaining, shared symbolic experience" (Jaeger and Selznick 1964, p. 663).

In establishing this sociological definition of culture emphasizing the shared symbolic experience, Jaeger and Selznick also seek to maintain a humanist-oriented capability to distinguish between high and mass culture without marginalizing the focus on high culture. Following Dewey, they argue that the experience of art takes place on a continuum of cultural experience that differs in intensity from ordinary symbolic activities, but has essentially the same basis for the appreciation of meaning. Art or high culture is simply a more "effective" symbol, combining "economy of statement with richness of expression" (Jaeger and Selznick 1964, p. 664). As such, art, like all culture, is identified through the normative evaluation of experience.

In sum, the high culture-mass culture debate shifted the focus on the concept of culture from a question of appropriate scope to a question of appropriate values. From a functionalist point of view, the health of a society's culture is not simply an issue of what type of values are advocated, but of how culture serves a moral and integrative function. Yet the mass culture critique was often unable to distinguish the cultural values of elite intellectuals from the effect of these values on society. To escape from this ethnocentric quagmire, contemporary sociologists have generally turned away from an evaluative position toward culture.

## THE CONTEMPORARY DEBATE ON CULTURE

As mentioned at the beginning, the contemporary approach to culture in sociology is eclectic. Despite the elaborate historical lineage of the concept, there is no current, widely accepted, composite resolution of the definition of culture. Instead, culture is still defined through an extensive variety of perspectives, sanctioning a broad, historically validated range of options. While the omnibus definition from the cultural anthropology tradition has been generally relegated to introductory texts, and the elitist attack on mass culture has been largely replaced by an anti-ethnocentric, relativist position open to a wide spectrum of symbolic arenas and perspectives, many of the elements of these old debates still appear in new cultural analyses.

For example, as categorized by Richard Peterson introducing a recent review of new cultural studies (Peterson 1990), culture tends to be used two ways in sociological research; as a "code of conduct embedded in or constitutive of social life," and as "the symbolic products of group activity" (Peterson 1990, p. 498). The first

approach is clearly indebted to the traditional cultural anthropology approach and indeed is used to characterize social units ranging from whole societies (e.g., Bellah et al. 1985) and extensive youth cohorts (e.g., Hebdige 1979; Willis 1977) to smaller communities organizing collective activities (e.g., see Fine 1987 on Little League baseball; Latour and Woolgar 1979 on science). The second approach takes the more limited focus of culture as symbols and symbol-making and emphasizes the meaning and social effect of specific forms of cultural expression. The range of potential application, however, is as expansive as the general approach and includes the moral discourse on the abortion issue (Luker 1984), the politics and aesthetics of the theater audience (Griswold 1986), and the motivational and ideological context of organizational or work cultures (Burawoy 1979; Fantasia 1988).

From the above array, it is clear that the contemporary concept of culture in sociology does not exclude any particular empirical forms of activity, except perhaps through an emphasis on shared or collective practices, thus discounting purely individual foci. All collective social practices are potentially symbolic and therefore potentially cultural. The question is to what degree the participants in any particular area treat their own or others' activities as symbolic. Certain areas of social practice, such as the arts and religion, are more overtly symbolic than others, such as work and the economy. But an argument could be made that this distinction is merely a matter of emphasis by individual actors and that there is nothing inherently noncultural about utilitarian activities.

Along these lines, recently in order to establish more intelligible parameters in the sociology of culture, some participants in the field have argued that the concept of culture should be centered around traditional substantive foci such as art, science, religion, and popular culture. The centering of the sociology of culture as a substantive focus might serve research coherence, but the expanding application of cultural analysis to non-traditional fields suggests that to many sociologists, culture is more an explanatory perspective than an area of study. As such, future limitations on the focus of culture will likely be conceptual, not empirical. The contemporary emphasis on culture as symbols and symbol-making activity represents such a "working" focus.

In sum, there is a new appreciation of the salience of culture as an explanatory perspective in contemporary sociological research. Whether it involves the convention setting influence of art worlds, the moral authority of organizational cultures, or the facilitation of class privileges through habitus, the concept of culture is used to explain behavior and social structure from a distinct and powerful perspective. The future elaboration of this perspective in sociology looks very promising.

(SEE ALSO: *Diffusion Theories*)

## REFERENCES

Becker, Howard S. 1982 *Art Worlds*. Berkeley: University of California Press.

Bellah, Robert, Richard Madsen, William Sullivan, Ann Swidler, and Steven Tipton 1985 *Habits of the Heart*. Berkeley: University of California Press.

Benedict, Ruth 1934 *Patterns of Culture*. Boston: Houghton Mifflin.

Blau, Judith 1988 "Study of the Arts: A Reappraisal." *Annual Review of Sociology* 14:269–292.

Boas, Franz (1896) 1940 "The Limitations of the Comparative Method of Anthropology." Reprinted in Boas, *Race, Language, and Culture*. New York: Macmillan.

Bourdieu, Pierre 1984 *Distinction*. Cambridge, Mass.: Harvard University Press.

Burawoy, Michael 1979 *Manufacturing Consent*. Chicago: University of Chicago Press.

Chambers, Iain 1986 *Popular Culture*. London: Methuen.

Dewey, John 1958 *Art as Experience*. New York: Capricorn Books.

Evans-Pritchard, E. E. 1937 *Witchcraft, Oracles and Magic Among the Azande*. Oxford: Clarendon Press.
—— 1940. *The Nuer*. London: Oxford University Press.

Fantasia, Rick 1988 *Cultures of Solidarity*. Berkeley: University of California Press.

Fine, Gary 1987 *With the Boys*. Chicago: University of Chicago Press.

Gitlin, Todd 1985 *Inside Prime Time*. New York: Pantheon.

Goodenough, Ward 1956 "Componential Analysis and the Study of Meaning." *Language* 32:22–37.

Greenberg, Clement 1946 "Avant-Garde and Kitsch." *The Partisan Reader* 378–389.

Griswold, Wendy. 1986. *Renaissance Revivals*. Chicago: University of Chicago Press.

Hebdige, Dick 1979 *Subculture: The Meaning of Style*. London: Routledge.

Jaeger, Gertrude, and Philip Selznick 1964 "A Normative Theory of Culture." *American Sociological Review* 29:653–669.

Katz, Jack 1988 *Seductions of Crime: Moral and Sensual Attractions of Doing Evil*. New York: Basic Books.

Kracauer, Siegfried 1949 "National Types as Hollywood Presents Them." *Public Opinion Quarterly* 13:53–72.

Kroeber, Alfred (1923) 1948. *Anthropology*. New York: Harcourt.
—— 1952 *The Nature of Culture*. Chicago: University of Chicago Press.
——, and Clyde Kluckhohn (1952) 1963 *Culture: A Critical Review of Concepts and Definitions*. New York: Vintage Books.
——, and Talcott Parsons 1958 "The Concepts of Culture and Social System." *American Sociological Review* 23:582–583.

Lang, Kurt 1957 "Mass Appeal and Minority Tastes." In Bernard Rosenberg and David Manning White, eds., *Mass Culture*. New York: Free Press.

Latour, Bruno 1987 *Science in Action: How to follow Scientists and Engineers Through Society*. Cambridge, Mass.: Harvard University Press.
——, and Steve Woolgar 1979 *Laboratory Life*. Beverly Hills, Calif.: Sage.

Levi-Strauss, Claude (1953) 1963. *Structural Anthropology*. New York: Basic Books.

Lincoln, James, and Arne Kalleberg 1990 *Culture, Control, and Commitment: A Study of Work Organization and Work Attitudes in the United States and Japan*. Cambridge: Cambridge University Press.

Lowenthal, Leo 1950 "Historical Perspectives of Popular Culture." *American Journal of Sociology* 55:323–332.

Luker, Kristen 1984 *Abortion and the Politics of Motherhood*. Berkeley: University of California Press.

McDonald, Dwight 1953 "A Theory of Mass Culture." *Diogenes* 3:1–17.

Malinowski, Bronislaw 1927 *Sex and Repression in Savage Society*. London: Routledge.

———— 1931 "Culture." *Encyclopedia of the Social Sciences* 4:621–646.

Mead, Margaret 1928 *Coming of Age in Samoa*. New York: Morrow.

———— 1935 *Sex and Temperament in Three Primitive Societies*. New York: Morrow.

Mukerji, Chandra, and Michael Schudson 1986 "Popular Culture." *Annual Review of Sociology* 12:47–66.

Neitz, Mary Jo 1987 *Charisma and Community: A Study of Religious Commitment Within the Charismatic Renewal*. New Brunswick, N.J.: Transaction Books.

Peterson, Richard 1979 "Revitalizing the Culture Concept." *Annual Review of Sociology* 5:137–166.

———— 1989 "La Sociologie de l'art et de la culture aux Etats-Unis." *L'Année sociologique* 39:153–179.

———— 1990 "Symbols and Social Life: The Growth of Cultural Studies." *Contemporary Sociology* 19:498–500.

Radcliffe-Brown, A. R. (1952) 1961 *Structure and Function in Primitive Society: Essays and Addresses*. New York: Free Press.

Rosenberg, Bernard, and David Manning White (eds.) 1957 *Mass Culture*. New York: Free Press.

Seldes, Gilbert 1957 "The Public Arts." In Bernard Rosenberg and David Manning White, eds., *Mass Culture*. New York: Free Press.

Singer, Milton 1968 "Culture: The Concept of Culture." In David L. Sills, ed., *International Encyclopedia of the Social Sciences*. New York: Macmillan and Free Press.

Star, Susan Leigh 1989 *Regions of the Mind: Brain Research and the Quest for Scientific Certainty*. Stanford, Calif.: Stanford University Press.

Swidler, Ann 1986 "Culture in Action." *American Sociological Review* 51:273–286.

Tylor, Edward (1871) 1924 *Primitive Culture*. Gloucester, Mass.: Smith.

White, David M. 1957. "Mass Culture in America: Another Point of View." In Bernard Rosenberg and David Manning White, eds., *Mass Culture*. New York: Free Press.

Williams, Raymond 1977 *Marxism and Literature*. Oxford: Oxford University Press.

———— 1981 *The Sociology of Culture*. New York: Schocken Books.

Willis, Paul 1977 *Learning to Labor*. New York: Columbia University Press.

Wuthnow, Robert, and Marsha Witten 1988 "New Directions in the Study of Culture." *Annual Review of Sociology* 14:49–67.

SAMUEL GILMORE

**DATA BANKS**    *See* Secondary Data Analysis and Data Archives.


**DEATH AND DYING**    In the 1930s a U.S. encyclopedic entry on this topic might well have focused on the economic plight of the bereaved family (Eliot 1932). In the 1950s the focus might have been on the high cost of dying and the commercialization of funerals (Bowman 1959). Twenty years later, it could have shifted to the social implications of relaxing the taboo on death (Riley 1970). This 1990 article will (1) review what sociologists have learned to date and (2) predict that the main focus of sociological interest over the proximate future will be on the process of dying. Two trends make this prediction plausible. Greater longevity dictates that most deaths will continue to occur in the later years of life, and continuing use of life-sustaining technologies dictate that the circumstances of dying will be increasingly controllable and negotiable.

### GENERAL BACKGROUND

There is today no well-developed sociology of "death and dying." The phrase was first celebrated in 1969 in the title of a psychologically oriented best-seller (Kübler-Ross). Sociologists tended to be critical but recognized the appeal of the subject matter. During the subsequent decade a spate of popular literature appeared, but no major sociological work (Charmaz 1986). One sociologist termed the literature of that modern-day "discovery" of death as "a collective bustle" and summarized the ideas as "the happy death movement" (Lofland 1978).

A scattered body of sociological knowledge, however, tells us that death, in all known societies, imposes imperatives. A corpse must be looked after; property must be reallocated; vacated roles must be reassigned; the solidarity of the deceased's group must be reaffirmed (Blauner 1966; Riley 1968). A volume by Kearl (1989) makes notable contributions to the sociological perspective, relating death and dying to politics, the military, religion, war, and popular culture. Throughout this literature death is typically viewed as a transition, as a *rite de passage*.

Several threads running through the research literature also tell us that death and dying can be thought about and talked about quite openly in American society; various "arrangements" are increasingly being negotiated prior to death; dying persons are generally more concerned about their survivors than they are about themselves; dying individuals are able to exercise a significant degree of control over the timing of their deaths;

tensions often exist between the requirements of formal care and the wishes of dying patients; and similar tensions almost always exist between formal and informal caregivers—between hospital bureaucracies and those significant others who are soon to be bereaved (Glaser and Strauss 1965, 1968; Riley 1983; Kalish 1985b).

**No Systematic Sociology.** Despite this background of knowledge and research, death has received surprisingly little systematic attention from sociologists. There are only two indexed references in the 1988 *Handbook of Sociology* (Smelser 1988): one to poverty resulting from death of breadwinners, the other to the role of death in popular religion. The *Encyclopedia of the Social Sciences* (Sills 1968) contains two entries, both on the social meanings of death. Furthermore, sociologists have failed to generate any overarching theory, although there have been many attempts.

Several kernels illustrate the range of these theoretical efforts. Talcott Parsons (1963) related the changing meanings of death to basic social values; Karl Mannheim (1928, 1952) used mortality to explain social change; Renée Fox (1980, 1981) finds that "life and death are coming to be viewed less as absolute . . . entities . . . and more as different points on a meta-spectrum . . . a new theodicity." Dorothy and David Counts (1985) specify the role of death in the various social transformations from preliterate to modern societies; Paul Baker (1990), following Warner (1959) and others, is beginning to elaborate the long-recognized theory that images of the dead exert profound influences on the living; Victor Marshall is engaged in a sustained effort—both theoretical and empirical—to link aging and dying. His basic postulate is that "awareness of finitude" operates as a trigger that permits socialization to death (Marshall 1980; Marshall and Levy 1990).

## TOPICAL SOCIOLOGICAL FINDINGS

A review of the empirical literature tells us that sociological research on death has been largely topical, ranging from a taboo on death to suicide.

**A Taboo on Death.** In contemporary American society, death has, until recently, been viewed as a taboo topic. By the early 1960s, however, a national survey reported that the great majority of Americans (85 percent) are quite realistic and consider it important to "try to make some plans about death" and to talk about it with those closest to them (Riley 1970). Recent studies have shown that bereavement practices, once highly socially structured, are becoming increasingly varied and individually therapeutic; dying is feared primarily because it eliminates the opportunities for self-fulfillment; and active adaptations to death increase as one approaches the end of the life course (the making of wills, leaving instructions, negotiating interpersonal conflicts, etc.).

**Social Organization of Death.** Most deaths in the United States occur in hospitals. Two aspects have been studied sociologically. First, a detailed account of the social organization of death in a public hospital focuses on the corpse. According to the rules, the body must be washed, cataloged, and ticketed. Dignity and bureaucratic efficiency are at odds (Sudnow 1967). A contrasting account of public and private rules governing disposition of the body in contemporary Ireland is even more sociological in emphasis (Prior 1989). Second, the caring issue has been studied more as a social problem. The dying person has often been treated according to rigid rules, and selfhood is put at risk in a hospital setting that is essentially dedicated to efficiency. Changes, however, have been noted, stressing the need for caring attitudes (Kalish 1985b).

**Hospice Care.** The major contemporary response to care of the dying in the United States is found in programs of hospice care, now well over 1,600 in number (Bass 1985). While its definitive sociological significance is still to be documented, several studies have noted that the hospice team "mediates between the families and formal institutions that constitute the social organization of death and dying" (Marshall and Levy 1990; Levy 1982).

**The Funeral.** Sociologists have studied the funeral mainly as a social institution. A massive cross-cultural study attests to its worldwide function in marking a major social transition (Habenstein and Lamers 1963). Although Durkheim had emphasized its ceremonial role in facilitating social regrouping, later sociologists have shown that elaborate and extravagant funeral rites are more reflective of commercial interests than of human grief or mourning (Parsons and Lidz 1967).

**Bereavement.** A now classic study (Eliot 1932) of the bereaved family stimulated a large literature that documents the general proposition that survivors—particularly significant others—require various types of social supports to "get through" the period of intense personal grief and the more publicly expressed mourning. In today's societies, the time devoted to bereavement activities generally becomes shorter (Pratt 1981). This is consistent with Parsons' position that in societies characterized by an "active" orientation, the bereaved are expected to carry out their grief work quickly and privately.

**Widowhood.** It is estimated that by the year 2000 there will be sixty-five men for every 100 women over age sixty-five and that most of the women will be widows. Many studies (e.g., Lopata 1973, 1979) have detailed the negative aspects of widowhood: loneliness, poor health, loss of personal identity, anxiety about the future. A somewhat different picture has emerged from an analysis of data (Hyman 1983) from the General Social Surveys. Samples of widows (who were not interviewed as widows) were compared with control samples of married and divorced women. Although somewhat controversial, this study reported that widowhood does not produce the negative and enduring consequences that the earlier studies had documented.

**Social Stressors and Death.** Sociologists have investigated many social "causes" of death: individually experienced stressors such as retirement and bereavement, and collectively experienced stressors such as economic depressions, wars, and technological revolutions. By and large all such studies have been inconclusive. For example, the hypothesis that a bereaved spouse is at higher risk of death (that death causes death) has been widely investigated but with no conclusive results, although recent and as yet unpublished research

suggests that bereavement may have a negative mortality effect for older spouses. Retirees in some longitudinal studies have been shown to experience excess mortality, whereas other investigations have reported opposite results. (Retirement is a complex process, not a simple or single event.) In an era in which nursing homes play an important role in the lives of many older people, the consequences of residential relocation have come under critical scrutiny. Several studies have reported that the "warehousing" of the frail elderly results in increased mortality, while in other studies feelings of security in the new "home" are reported to enhance both a sense of well-being and lower mortality. (Obviously the nursing home population is far from homogeneous.) Similar caveats apply to macro-level studies that attempt to relate economic and technological change to trends in mortality. Recent advances in mathematical modeling and the increasing availability of relevant data sets make this problem an attractive area for continuing sociological research (Riley 1983).

**Suicide.** Durkheim's studies of suicide spawned a wide, diverse, and sometimes confusing research literature. In most such studies social integration is the operative concept. If the theoretical relationship is believed to be relatively unambiguous, the empirical relationship is far from tidy. For example, war has been found to heighten integration, both economic and political, but it also diminishes the availability of beverage alcohol, which, in turn, reduces suicides triggered by alcohol consumption (Wasserman 1989). Various other types of intervening variables have been studied (e.g., "suggestion") (Phillips 1974).

## FOCUS ON DYING

Apart from suicide, it is a sociological truism that individuals are often socially motivated to try to influence the time of their own deaths. Several studies, for example, have tested the hypothesis of a "death dip"—that social events of significance are preceded by lower than expected mortality (Phillips and Feldman 1973). These studies rest on Durkheim's insight that if some are so detached from society that they commit suicide, others may be so attached to society that they postpone their deaths in order to participate in events in which they are involved (Phillips and Smith 1990). The same hypothesis has been extended to studies of a "birthday dip" in which the event is more personal and local in its significance for death (Phillips 1972). Along similar lines, several sociological investigations have explored the proposition that some people die socially before they die biologically. These studies center on the notion of levels of "awareness" of death (Glaser and Strauss 1965). When both the dying person and his significant others are cognizant of death as a soon-to-be-experienced event, an ensuing "open" awareness may enable them to negotiate various aspects of the final phase of life. Further research on "dying trajectories" involves certainties and uncertainties as to the time of death (Glaser and Strauss 1968).

Recently, this question has been asked: Does the individual, in a society deeply committed to the preservation of life, have a "right" to die? The U.S. Supreme Court has answered this in the affirmative but with limitations. The issue has become one of the most profound, complex, and pressing questions of our time. It involves the "rights" and wishes of the dying person; the "rights" and responsibilities of his or her survivors; the "rights" and obligations of attending physicians; and the "rights" and constraints of the law. And the human side of the issue is producing a tidal wave of public interest: television documentaries, opinion surveys, radio talk shows. The issue is openly debated in leading medical journals, which now carry editorials on euthanasia—an unthinkable topic only a few years ago. It is altering age-old hospital rules in which resuscitation orders were written on blackboards, then quickly erased. A major book proposes rationing medical resources (Callahan 1987). Radical movements have sprung up that advocate active euthanasia. The mounting costs of the last days of life have been dramatized. All this ferment reflects powerful ideas that potentially fuel social change (M. W. Riley 1978).

**New Norms for Dying.** Demography dictates that a substantial proportion of the 5,500 or so deaths that occur each day in the United States will be at the later years of life, but medical technology now offers options as to timing. The period of dying can be lengthened or shortened. Sociology has identified three elements in the process of dying: (1) depending on the "level of awareness," the dying person is able to "negotiate" to some degree both the course of dying and the consequences of death (Glaser and Strauss 1965); (2) depending on "awareness of finitude," dying persons are able to be socialized to death and to prepare themselves for it (Marshall 1980); (3) depending on the quality of care, both the physical pain of dying and the psychosocial pain of separation and loss can be mitigated (Kalish 1985a; Levy forthcoming; Bass 1985).

Today, moreover, the problems and dilemmas inherent in the "management" of death have captured both popular and scientific attention. The reality of the extreme case is starkly clear. Many dying persons have given written or oral instructions that they do not want to go on living under certain conditions, often specified in "living wills." Similarly, many kin of nonsentient or hopelessly ill and suffering persons may not want to have the lives of such patients prolonged. In both instances doctors and lawyers play ambiguous but critical roles. It is, however, the "negotiation" that is of sociological interest. Norms designed to reduce the perplexities in wrenching decisions or to reassure the decision makers (including dying persons) are generally lacking. The need for relevant norms governing "the dying process" has been noted (Riley and Riley 1986), and the main considerations have been specified (Logue 1989). The U.S. Office of Technology Assessment (1987) and the Hastings Center (1987) have issued medical and ethical guidelines, respectively, on the use of life-sustaining procedures. In the 1970s sociologists developed research models for studying the social aspects of heroic operations and the treatment of nonsalvageable terminal patients (Fox and Swazey 1974; Crane 1975). Yet models necessary to the formation of norms capable of handling the "rights" and wishes of the various parties to the process of dying are still clearly needed. Today such models are yet to be developed, although human "rights" are being recognized as basic components in the development of social theory (Coleman 1990).

While a sociology of "dying" is yet to be developed, at least three aspects of norms and "rights" governing the dying process have been identified: timing and level of awareness, socialization to death, and quality of care. These suggest for sociological research a demanding agenda that should carry well into the twenty-first century.

(SEE ALSO: *Long-Term Care; Nursing Homes; Social Gerontology; Widowhood*)

## REFERENCES

Baker, Paul M. 1990 "Socialization After Death: The Might of the Living Dead." In Beth Hess and Elizabeth Markson, eds., *Growing Old in America.* New Brunswick, N.J.: Transaction Books.

Bass, David M. 1985 "The Hospice Ideology and Success of Hospice Care." *Research on Aging* 7:1.

Blauner, Robert 1966 "Death and Social Structure." *Psychiatry* 29:378–394.

Bowman, L. 1959 *The American Funeral: A Study in Guilt, Extravagance, and Sublimity.* Washington, D.C.: Public Affairs Press.

Callahan, Daniel 1987 *Setting Limits: Medical Goals in an Aging Society.* New York: Simon and Schuster.

Charmaz, K. C. 1986 *Social Reality of Death.* Reading, Mass.: Addison-Wesley.

Coleman, James P. 1990 *Foundations of Special Theory.* Cambridge, Mass.: Harvard University Press.

Counts, D. A., and D. C. Counts 1985 *Aging and Its Transformations: Moving Toward Death in Pacific Societies.* Lanham, MD.: University Press of America.

Crane, D. 1975 *The Sanctity of Social Life: Physicians' Treatment of Critically Ill Patients.* New York: Russell Sage Foundation.

Eliot, T. 1932. "The Bereaved Family." Special issue, *The Annals* 160.

Fox, R. C. 1980 "The Social Meaning of Death." *The Annals* 447.

——— 1981 "The Sting of Death in American Society." *Social Service Review* March:42–59.

———, and Swazey, T. P. 1974 *The Courage to Fail: A Social View of Organ Transplantation and Dialysis.* Chicago: University of Chicago Press.

Glaser, B. G., and A. L. Strauss 1965 *Awareness of Dying.* Chicago: Aldine.

——— 1968 *Time for Dying.* Chicago: Aldine.

Habenstein, R. W. 1968 "The Social Organization of Death." In D. L. Sills, ed. *International Encyclopedia of the Social Sciences.* New York: Macmillan and Free Press.

———, and M. W. Lamers 1963 *Funeral Customs the World Over.* Milwaukee, Wisc.: Bulfin.

Hastings Center, The 1987 *Guidelines on the Termination of Life-Sustaining Treatment and the Care of the Dying.* Bloomington: Indiana University Press.

Hyman, H. H. 1983 *Of Time and Widowhood: Nationwide Studies of Enduring Effects.* Durham, N.C.: Duke University Press.

Kalish, R. A. 1985a *Death, Grief and Caring Relationships.* Monterey, Calif.: Brooks/Cole.

——— 1985b "The Social Context of Death and Dying." In R. H. Binstock and E. Shanas, eds., *Handbook of Aging and the Social Sciences.* New York: Van Nostrand Reinhold.

Kearl, Michael C. 1989 *Endings: A Sociology of Death and Dying.* Oxford, Eng.: Oxford University Press.

Kübler-Ross, E. 1969 *On Death and Dying.* New York: Macmillan.

Levine, S., and N. A. Scotch 1970 "Dying as an Emergent Social Problem." In O. G. Brim, Jr., et al., eds., *The Dying Patient.* New York: Russell Sage Foundation.

Levy, Judith A. 1982 "The Staging of Negotiations Between Hospice and Medical Institutions." *Urban Life* 11.

——— Forthcoming "Hospice in an Aging Society." *Journal of Aging Studies.*

Lofland, L. 1978 *The Craft of Dying: The Modern Face of Death.* Beverly Hills, Calif.: Sage Publications.

Logue, B. 1989 *Death Control and the Elderly: The Growing Acceptability of Euthanasia.* Providence, R.I.: Population Studies and Training Center, Brown University.

Lopata, H. Z. 1973 *Widowhood in an American City.* Cambridge, Mass.: Schenkman.

——— 1979 *Women as Widows: Support Systems.* New York: Elvesier.

Mannheim, K. (1928) 1952 "The Problem of Generations." In P. Keeskemeti, ed., *Essays in Sociological Knowledge.* London: Routledge and Kegan Paul.

Marshall, V. W. 1980 *Last Chapters: A Sociology of Aging and Dying*. Belmont, Calif.: Wordsworth.

———, and J. A. Levy 1990 "Aging and Dying." In R. H. Binstock and L. George, eds., *Handbook of Aging and the Social Sciences*, 3rd ed. San Diego, Calif.: Academic Press.

Parsons, T. 1963 "Death in American Society: A Brief Working Paper." *American Behavioral Scientist*.

———, and V. W. Lidz 1967 "Death in American Society." In E. S. Shneidman, ed., *Essays in Self-Destruction*. New York: Science House.

Phillips, D. P. 1972 "Deathday and Birthday: An Unexpected Connection." In J. Tanur, ed., *Statistics: Guide to the Unknown*. San Francisco: Holden-Day.

——— 1974 "The Influence of Suggestion on Suicide: Substantive and Theoretical Implications of the Werther Effect." *American Sociological Review* 39:340–354.

———, and L. L. Carstensen 1986 "Clustering of Teenage Suicides After Television Stories About Suicide." *New England Journal of Medicine* 315 (11).

———, and K. A. Feldman 1973 "A Dip in Deaths Before Ceremonial Occasions: Some New Relationships Between Integration and Mortality." *American Sociological Review* 38:678–696.

———, and D. G. Smith 1990 Postponement of Death Until Symbolically Meaningful Occasions." *Journal of the American Medical Association* 203 (14).

Pratt, L. V. 1981 "Business Temporal Norms and Bereavement Behavior." *American Sociological Review* 4:317–333.

Prior, Lindsay 1989 *The Social Organization of Death: Medical Discourses and Social Practices in Belfast*. New York: St. Martin's Press.

Riley, J. W., Jr. 1968 "Death and Bereavement." In D. L. Sills, ed., *International Encyclopedia of the Social Sciences*. New York: Macmillan and Free Press.

——— 1970 "What People Think About Death." In O. G. Brim, Jr., et al., eds., *The Dying Patient*. New York: Russell Sage Foundation.

——— 1983 "Dying and the Meanings of Death: Sociological Inquiries." *Annual Review of Sociology* 9:191–216.

Riley, M. W. 1978 "Aging, Social Change and the Power of Ideas." *Daedalus* 107:39–52.

———, A. Foner, and J. Waring 1988 "Sociology of Age." In N. J. Smelser, ed., *Handbook of Sociology*. Newbury Park, Calif.: Sage Publications.

———, and J. W. Riley, Jr. 1986 "Longevity and Social Structure: The Added Years," *Daedalus* 115:51–75.

Sills, David L. (ed.) 1968 *International Encyclopedia of the Social Sciences*. New York: Macmillan and Free Press.

Smelser, Neil J. (ed.). 1988 *Handbook of Sociology*. Newbury Park, Calif.: Sage Publications.

Stroebe, W., and M. E. Stroebe 1987 *Bereavement and Health: The Psychological and Physical Consequences of Partner Loss*. Cambridge: Cambridge University Press.

Sudnow, D. 1967 *Passing On: The Social Organization of Dying*. Englewood Cliffs, N.J.: Prentice-Hall.

U.S. Congress, Office of Technology Assessment 1987 *Life-Sustaining Technologies and the Elderly*. Washington, D.C.: U.S. Government Printing Office.

Warner, W. L. 1959 *The Living and the Dead*. New Haven, Conn.: Yale University Press.

Wasserman, I. M. 1989 "The Effects of War and Alcohol Consumption Patterns on Suicide: United States (1910–1953)." *Social Forces* 66:513–533.

JOHN W. RILEY, JR.

## DECISION-MAKING THEORY AND RESEARCH

Theory and research on human judgment and decision making represent a mixture of several distinctive, yet related, approaches. The first approach, often referred to as "normative" or "prescriptive" decision theory, focuses on how rational decisions can and should be made. Normative models specify what decision makers ought to do in order to optimize their outcomes or to remain consistent with their beliefs and values. The second type of decision model is primarily descriptive and focuses on the manner in which information is actually processed and aggregated. Descriptive models attempt to describe what people do rather than what they ought to do. The third approach focuses on hypothesized cognitive mechanisms involved in the decision process, particularly the strategies people use in acquiring and processing information.

Although conceptually useful, these three approaches to organizing research in decision making are not mutually exclusive. For example, a model of decision making can be both prescriptive and descriptive. Moreover, a model need not be descriptive in order to be useful. Where decisions are suboptimal, prescriptive models may be useful in assisting decision makers to maximize their returns.

It is important at the outset to distinguish between decisions made under certainty and those made under risk. Under conditions of certainty, the outcomes associated with specific decisions are known in advance. Under conditions of risk, however, issues of probability become relevant. For example, the ability to order preferences in such a way as one hundred dollars is more attractive than fifty dollars, which is more attractive than zero dollars may explain why a person will select one hundred dollars from among these choices; but it is not sufficient in itself to understand a person's willingness to flip a coin on a fifty-dollar wager. When there is no risk, it is assumed that decision makers try to maximize the utility of their outcomes. Under conditions of risk, however, it is assumed that they will try to maximize their "expected" utility (e.g., Edwards 1954).

## PRESCRIPTIVE THEORIES

Prescriptive models generally contain two important components: (1) differential preferences with respect to potential outcomes, and (2) some estimate of beliefs or expectations concerning the likelihood of these possible outcomes. The expectations about potential outcomes are generally represented as probabilities. Variants of these two components, preferences and expected outcomes, are typically combined linearly in models of the decision process to predict what decision makers will or should do. The underlying assumption is that for risky decisions, decision makers should choose the alternative that maximizes their expected payoff.

Perhaps the earliest model of this form is what is referred to as the expected value (EV) model. It can be expressed as $EV = p_1v_1 + p_2v_2 + \cdots + p_jv_j$, where $p$ is the probability of a particular outcome and $v$ represents the value of that outcome. Rational decision makers would be expected to select the outcome with the greatest expected

value and to be indifferent to outcomes with equal EV.

Research has shown that EV is a very poor model of what people actually do. A classic illustration is the St. Petersburg paradox described by Bernoulli (1738). The situation is one in which a fair coin is tossed until a head appears. A gambler receives $2^n$ dollars if the first head occurs on trial $n$. Because the expected value in this circumstance is infinite—$EV = (.5) (\$2) + (.25) (\$4) + (.125) (\$8) + \cdots + (.5^n) (2^n)$—the EV model predicts that a decision maker should be willing to pay any amount to participate in such a gamble. The paradox is that most people value this infinite EV wager below one hundred dollars, and many even below twenty dollars.

Bernoulli attempted to explain the paradox by suggesting that, rather than maximizing monetary value, decision makers may be maximizing expected utility (EU). He proposed a logarithmic, rather than a linear, function in which the level of utility diminishes with increases in monetary value. The paradox disappears if decisions are based on their expected utility rather than their expected monetary values.

The EU model was formalized by von Neumann and Morgenstern (1944), who added a series of axioms that served to make the model rational (that is, where increasing EU corresponds to increasing preference). The EU model, unlike the EV model, explicitly takes the notion of risk into account. An example is whether to accept a bet of one hundred dollars on the flip of a coin. The expected value of this bet is $.5(\$100) + .5(-\$100) = 0$. The expected value of not betting is also zero. According to the EV model, since the expected values are the same, decision makers should be indifferent to them. Many people would prefer, however, not to bet in this situation. Individuals are said to be "risk averse" when their preference for a bet is less than its expected monetary value.

Although some early support for the EU model was reported, there were also problems. For example, Allais (1953) pointed out that the EU model departs substantially from behavior, especially when the amounts of money are large or when the differences in probabilities are small. In addition, Edwards (1954) found that decision makers prefer certain probabilities over others, independent of utility considerations. Such considerations led to the development of an important variant of the EU model: the subjective expected utility model (SEU). In this approach, clarified and extended by Savage (1954), objective estimates of probability are replaced with subjective ones. A subjective probability is simply the extent to which an individual "thinks" an outcome is likely, at least prior to the initial occurrence of the outcome. Thereafter, subjective estimates about the likelihood of the outcome will be revised according to Bayes's Theorem. This theorem, advanced by Reverend Thomas Bayes (1764), is prescriptive in the sense that it implies an orderly relationship among subjective probabilities and prescribes how decision makers should respond in the light of new information.

The guiding principle of the SEU model is that decision makers choose among risky alternatives so as to maximize SEU where $SEU = S(p_1)U(v_1) + S(p_2)U(v_2) + \cdots + S(p_j)U(v_j)$. Thus, whereas the EV model utilizes objective probabilities and objective utilities, and the EU model uses objective probabilities and subjective utilities, the SEU model accommodates both subjective probabilities and subjective utilities.

Prescriptive decision-making models such as the foregoing illustrations have traditionally been used to choose between risky, unidimensional outcomes such as maximizing monetary gain. Most real-life decisions, however, involve outcomes that are multidimensional. For example, the decision of which car to buy is based not only on purchase cost but also on other factors, such as mileage, reliability, resale value, and aesthetic considerations. Moreover, each of these considerations is, by its nature, assessed in a different metric (for instance, cost is in dollars, mileage is in miles per gallon, and so on). Multiattribute utility theory (MAUT) was developed to make multiple value dimensions comparable by evaluating them on a common scale of value. Variants of this approach have been developed for both risky (e.g., Raiffa 1969) and relatively riskless decisions (e.g.,

Edwards and Newman 1982). MAUT, as an extension of the SEU model, has greatly expanded the application of formal decision theory.

Various methods for estimating relative preferences with multidimensional outcomes have been developed. The characteristic features that these approaches share involve (1) identifying the relevant dimensions, (2) creating measurement scales that are comparable across dimensions, (3) weighing the dimensions according to their relative importance, (4) combining the weighted dimensions (usually in a linear fashion), and (5) selecting the alternative with the largest score.

Prescriptive theories of decision making, by and large, have not been successful in describing what people actually do. They assume that decision makers will choose the "best" alternative in terms of maximizing outcome, and that the decision process can be adequately represented as a mathematical expectation. Extensive research has revealed numerous violations of the normative or prescriptive models (for a review, see Slovic, Fischhoff, and Lichtenstein 1977). Three general types of criticisms have been leveled against prescriptive models: (1) the constraints imposed on such models may be unrealistic; (2) specific models may be applied in inappropriate contexts; and (3) the notion of "prescription" is arbitrary.

With respect to constraints, the axioms on which prescriptive models are based (such as transitivity of preference, consistency, or independence of beliefs and outcomes) have not been universally accepted. But it is only under this set of fairly stringent requirements that it becomes reasonable to attach a single probability and utility to each decision outcome and to expect decision makers to select the one with the highest overall value. With respect to the assumption of consistency, Hogarth (1982) has noted that consistency is not always a desirable property of decision making, especially if it interferes with a search for novel solutions. With respect to environment, it has been shown that decision strategies vary across situations and by demands of the task (Payne 1982). Similarly, Hogarth (1981) makes a distinction between the limited "discrete" environments in which prescriptive models are studied and the natural "continuous" environment for which they may be inappropriate. Finally, with respect to the prescriptive force of such models, the extent to which human decision makers are "rational" is unknown. Perhaps what constitutes "rational" behavior depends upon the individual decision maker. Violations could, in fact, appear more "rational" to any given decision maker than the dictates of the model. Thus, specific prescriptions need not be normative for everyone.

## DESCRIPTIVE THEORIES

Descriptive models of decision making differ from prescriptive models in that they attempt to describe the strategies individuals use in arriving at a decision rather than emphasizing which decision should be made. Prescriptive models of decision making have their roots primarily in economic theory. In contrast, descriptive models have emerged primarily from psychology. Two influential descriptive models are social judgment theory (Hammond, Stewart, Brehmer, and Steinmann 1975) and information integration theory (Anderson 1981).

Social judgment theory (SJT) is an extension of Brunswik's lens model (Brunswik 1956), which describes how individuals function in uncertain environments. According to SJT, individuals attempt to make judgments about uncertain (distal) events (such as the presence of disease states) on the basis of immediately observable (proximal) cues (such as medical symptoms). The nature and difficulty of the judgment depend on five factors: (1) the importance of each cue; (2) the relationship between each cue and outcome (such as linear vs. nonlinear); (3) how the cues should be combined; (4) the unpredictability inherent in the task; and (5) the amount of redundancy in information among the cues. Changes in judgment are brought about by providing the decision maker with feedback that can be either outcome or cognitive. Outcome feedback refers to the accuracy of the judgment (that is, right or wrong). Cognitive feedback is posited to be much more useful and refers to one or more of the relationships between cues and outcome criteria in the environment. The study of decision making, from the perspective of SJT, is thus the study of how judgments are related to environmental variables. Information about cues is provided to research subjects in numerical form, and mathematical models based on multiple regression analyses of the decision makers' judgment "rules" are created.

Information integration theory (IIT) also attempts to make inferences about a decision maker's strategy for combining various types of information from his or her behavior. The approach assumes that any decision can be represented as some algebraic function that combines two parameters: the decision maker's subjective representation of the information on some dimension of judgment (such as a rating scale) and a weight representing the importance of that piece of information for the decision to be made. In this regard, IIT is similar to the prescriptive models examined earlier. It differs in that it attempts to show how people actually combine information rather than how they should combine it.

The IIT process can be modeled in different ways: (1) as an additive process; (2) as an averaging process; or (3) as an interactive (multiplicative) process. The additive model can be described as decision $= x_i + \cdots y_j$, where $x$ and $y$ refer to two separate pieces of information. Although only two variables are illustrated here, the models can be of any size. In the averaging model, decision $= wx_i + (1-w)y_j$, where $w$ is an importance weight for the pieces of information. The averaging model constrains all the weights to sum to 1. Finally, interactions among the pieces of information can be modeled as decision $= (x_i)(y_j)$, where the decision is based on the product of the individual values associated with the separate pieces of information.

Abelson and Levi (1985) noted several important differences between SJT and IIT. First, SJT focuses on the objective cue values available to decision makers, whereas IIT attempts to discover the subjective values of these cues. Moreover, IIT does not necessarily assume a linear relationship between the objective and subjective values. Second, SJT places greater emphasis on task realism and environmental representativeness. In contrast, IIT depends heavily on factorial designs in research situations where subjects judge each possible combination of cue values. Thus, IIT designs produce rather artificial tasks. And third, SJT is concerned with assessing the decision maker's ability to apply a decision strategy consistently and without error. IIT does not share this emphasis on optimality of the decision. Indeed, in most IIT research there is no outcome criterion or standard against which success can be assessed; rather, the focus is on accurately representing the decision maker's strategy.

An important decision-aiding technique that has emerged from the general algebraic modeling approach (particularly SJT) is "bootstrapping." In bootstrapping, the decisions of judges are replaced by algebraic models of their own decision (weighting) policies. Such models consistently perform better than the judges themselves (for a review, see Abelson and Levi 1985). The rationale behind using such an approach is that although decision makers are capable of arriving at valid decision policies, they are not capable of applying them consistently. The success of techniques such as bootstrapping highlights the potential utility of algebraic models of decision processes.

## INFORMATION-PROCESSING APPROACHES TO DECISION MAKING

The prescriptive and descriptive models have focused primarily on input and output—that is, on the information that goes into the decision-making process and on the decision that ultimately "comes out." As a result, the algebraic models that have emerged from this approach contain an "as if" quality (decisions are produced "as if" the decision maker had performed a statistical analysis on the information). An alternative approach to the study of decision making has been the study of the cognitive processes presumed to be central (For a review, see Simon 1979).

At present, there is no general theory to unify the elements of cognitive processing as they affect the decision process. Most reviewers presume the existence of certain sequential processes, such as problem recognition, information search and re-

trieval, information organization, decision strategy, and decision outcome. As Abelson and Levi (1985) note, however, these phases are merely convenient fictions, in that information-processing phases are likely to be iterative and cyclical. (For extensive reviews, see Abelson and Levi 1985; Einhorn and Hogarth 1981; Pitz and Sachs 1984). Two research findings serve to illustrate the relevance of cognitive processes in achieving an understanding of decision making: (1) the apparent limits on the adaptivity of the decision maker, and (2) an understanding of how information is acquired and encoded, particularly the heuristics and biases that decision makers use to simplify decision tasks.

Substantial research has demonstrated that the information-processing capability of a decision maker is not limitless. This feature of the decision-making state has been termed "bounded rationality" (Simon 1955). As a result, decision makers are forced to use techniques that allow them to cope with the complexities of real life within the limits of their "rationality." From this perspective, the optimization assumed by prescriptive models would seem to be an unlikely goal in decision making. Instead of maximizing outcomes, Simon (1957) has suggested that decision makers "satisfice." *Satisficing* refers to selecting the first alternative that is acceptable to the decision maker. For example, a person is likely to purchase a car that is good looking, has an acceptable price, and meets other minimum requirements on relevant dimensions rather than to buy a car that maximizes outcome on all relevant dimensions. Satisficing fits the constraints of the limited information-processing capability of the decision maker and specifies a mechanism that potentially links prescriptive and descriptive models.

An important consequence of bounded rationality is that the search for information cannot be comprehensive but must be selective. Decision makers have been found to employ heuristics or rules of thumb that greatly simplify the demands of information processing but sometimes lead to important biases in decisions. Tversky and Kahneman (1982) describe three commonly used judgmental heuristics that address the way individuals make subjective, probabilistic inferences: (1) representativeness; (2) availability; and (3) anchoring.

*Representativeness* refers to the extent to which an event is representative of the category or population from which it is derived. For example, a man described as "meek and retiring" is selected from a group composed of ninety lawyers and ten librarians, and decision makers are asked to guess to which group the man belongs. People tend to ignore base-rate information and to choose "librarian" because the description fits the stereotype of librarian.

*Availability* describes the case in which a decision maker subjectively estimates the probability of an event based on the ease with which relevant instances come to mind. For example, a decision maker may estimate the risk of failing a driver's test by recalling the number of friends and acquaintances who had failed such a test.

Finally, *anchoring* occurs when decision makers are asked to make judgments by starting from an initial value (anchor point) and then adjusting it to yield an answer. Decision makers are overly influenced by the anchor point and adjustments are generally insufficient. For instance, decision makers were asked to estimate the percentage of African countries in the United Nations. An initial percentage (anchor) was determined by spinning a numbered wheel in the decision makers' presence and then allowing them to adjust that number upward or downward. The median estimate for persons who started at 10 was 25 percent, compared with 45 percent for those who started at 65. Payoffs for accuracy did not reduce the anchoring effect.

Clearly, the study of cognitive processes has important implications for refining models of decision making. As has been shown, prescriptive models generally incorporate subjective probabilities in the quantified expectation of a totally informed decision maker. This view may be useful in a prescriptive sense but is untenable from a descriptive viewpoint. If the goal is to assist decision makers, understanding the limitations in the human decision process is useful. If the goal is to describe human decision making, such understandings are essential.

## DECISION MAKING IN ORGANIZATIONS

In many ways, research into the decision-making processes in organizations parallels that for individuals. Approaches can be grouped into (1) prescriptive and rational choice models; (2) descriptive models; and (3) attention to the constituent or elemental processes hypothesized to occur in organizational decision making. This brief overview of organizational decision making is not comprehensive, but is intended to illustrate the parallels with individual decision-making processes. (For a more comprehensive review of the research literature on organizations, see House and Singh 1987.)

Prescriptive or normative models of decision making generally assume that decisions are made rationally. The characteristics of rationality for organizational behavior are similar to those for individuals. For example, organizations are assumed to have a set of defined alternatives; the consequences of each alternative are understood and can be compared in terms of their utility; there is a consistent preference for the ordering of outcomes; and the organization has a well-defined decision rule (March 1981).

There is, however, substantial evidence indicating that such a normative model does not reflect the way decisions are actually made in organizations. House and Singh (1987) identify three types of criticisms raised against the rational choice approach. First, the theory essentially assumes that time and information are unlimited within the organization. Second, the theory assumes either unanimity among decision makers in organizations or, if there is disagreement, that it can be resolved through coalition building or some other process of agreement building. Empirical studies do not support such an assumption. Third, since assumptions of rationality are largely inappropriate for individual decision makers, they will be inappropriate for individual decision makers within organizations as well. For example, organizational decision makers have been shown to satisfice rather than to maximize (March and Simon 1958).

An alternative approach to understanding decision making within organizations has focused on describing how decision making actually occurs. The most influential "descriptive" model of organizational decision making is what has been labeled the garbage can model (Cohen, March, and Olsen 1972). It is a metaphorical approach in which a choice opportunity is viewed as a garbage can into which various problems and solutions are dumped quite independently of each other. An organization is described as "a collection of choices looking for problems, issues and feelings looking for decision situations in which they might be aired, solutions looking for issues to which they might be the answer, and decision makers looking for work" (Cohen et al. 1972, p. 2). There are four basic parameters to the model: (1) a stream of choices; (2) a stream of problems; (3) a stream of solutions; and (4) a stream of energy from participants. These relatively independent streams are linked by their arrival and departure times, and decisions can be described as the confluence of these streams. Thus, problems are solved when a particular problem, solution, choice opportunity, and decision maker come together.

The major difference between the rational and prescriptive models and the garbage can model is that the latter suspends the sequential requirements of the decision process. The rational decision model views a decision opportunity as a sequential process in which decision alternatives are generated, the consequences of each alternative are evaluated, the consequences of each alternative are compared in terms of objectives, and finally a decision is made. A simulation study (Cohen et al. 1972) showed that problems are rarely resolved in this manner and that the garbage can metaphor is a reasonable model in many circumstances. (See March and Weissinger-Baylon 1986 for additional research on garbage can decision processes.)

Models of organizational decision making are likely to be more complicated than models of individual decision making because they are necessarily more inclusive. That is, all of the variables that enter decision processes at the individual level are likely to affect decisions within organizations, including the biases that influence perception. In addition, House and Singh (1987) identify a number of themes that focus on various elemental features of the decision-making process within organizations. These features include the role of rationalization and justification in decision making, the role of political processes, external constraints, and contextual features. Many, if not all, of these complicating features arise because of the social nature of the decision process. In addition, a number of well-studied social psychological phenomena are relevant to decision making in social contexts, including the role of public commitment (Janis and Mann 1977), the illusion of control (Langer 1975), and groupthink (Janis 1972).

In sum, no all-inclusive models exist that adequately represent decision making at either the individual or the organizational level. Models exist that prescribe how decisions should be made, but they require overly restrictive assumptions. In contrast, models have been put forth to describe how decisions actually occur. Although such descriptive models substantially improve prediction, our understanding of decision processes remains incomplete. Additional research is necessary and, more than likely, will always be necessary. And perhaps this is as it should be. As daily living continues to increase in complexity, so will the decisions that people face.

(SEE ALSO: *Coalitions; Game Theory and Strategic Interaction; Rational Choice Theory; Social Psychology*)

### REFERENCES

Abelson, R., and A. Levi 1985 "Decision Making and Decision Theory." In G. Lindzey and E. Aronson, eds., *The Handbook of Social Psychology.* New York: Random House.

Allais, M. 1953 "Le comportement de l'homme rationnel devant le risque: Critique des postulats et axioms de l'école américaine." *Econometrica* 31:503–546.

Anderson, N. 1981 *Foundations of Information Integration Theory.* New York: Academic Press.

Bayes, T. (1764) 1958 "An Essay Towards Solving a

Problem in the Doctrine of Chances." *Biometrika* 45:296–315.

Bernoulli, D. 1738 "Specimen theoriae novae de mensura sortis." In *Commentarii Academiae scientiarum imperialis petropolitanae*, V. Translated by L. Sommer as "Expositions of a New Theory on the Measurement of Risk." *Econometrica* 22 (1954):23–26.

Brunswik, E. 1956 *Perception and the Representative Design of Psychological Experiments*. Berkeley: University of California Press.

Cohen, M., J. March, and J. Olsen 1972 "A Garbage Can Model of Organizational Choice." *Administrative Science Quarterly* 17:1–25.

Edwards, W. 1954 "The Theory of Decision Making." *Psychological Bulletin* 51:380–417.

———, and J. Newman 1982 *Multiattribute Evaluation*. Beverly Hills, Calif.: Sage.

Einhorn, H., and R. Hogarth 1981 "Behavioral Decision Theory: Processes of Judgment and Choice." *Annual Review of Psychology* 32:53–88.

Hammond, K., T. Stewart, B. Brehmer, and D. Steinmann 1975 "Social Judgment Theory." In M. Kaplan and S. Schwartz, eds., *Human Judgment and Decision Processes*. New York: Academic Press.

Hogarth, R. 1981 "Beyond Discrete Biases: Functional and Dysfunctional Aspects of Judgmental Heuristics." *Psychological Bulletin* 90:197–217.

——— 1982 "On the Surprise and Delight of Inconsistent Responses." In R. M. Hogarth, ed., *New Directions for Methodology of Social and Behavioral Science: The Framing of Questions and the Consistency of Response*. San Francisco: Jossey-Bass.

House, R., and J. Singh 1987 "Organizational Behavior: Some New Directions for I/O Psychology." *Annual Review of Psychology* 38:669–718.

Janis, I. 1972 *Victims of Groupthink: A Psychological Study of Foreign Policy Decisions and Fiascoes*. Boston: Houghton Mifflin.

Janis, I., and L. Mann 1977 *Decision Making: A Psychological Analysis of Conflict, Choice, and Commitment*. New York: Free Press.

Langer, E. 1975 "The Illusion of Control." *Journal of Personality and Social Psychology* 32:311–328.

March, J. 1981 "Decisions in Organizations and Theories of Choice." In A. van de Ven and W. Joyce, eds., *Perspectives on Organization Design and Behavior*. New York: Wiley.

———, and H. Simon 1958 *Organizations*. New York: Wiley.

———, and R. Weissinger-Baylon, eds. 1986 *Ambiguity and Command: Organizational Perspectives on Military Decision Making*. Cambridge, Mass.: Ballinger.

Payne, J. W. 1982 "Contingent Decision Behavior." *Psychological Bulletin* 92:382–402.

Pitz, G., and N. Sachs 1984 "Judgment and Decision: Theory and Application." *Annual Review of Psychology* 35:139–163.

Raiffa, H. 1969 *Decision Analysis*. Reading, Mass.: Addison–Wesley.

Savage, L. 1954 *The Foundations of Statistics*. New York: Wiley.

Simon, H. 1955 "A Behavioral Model of Rational Choice." *Quarterly Journal of Economics* 69:99–118.

——— 1957 *Models of Man: Social and Rational*. New York: Wiley.

——— 1979 "Information Processing Models of Cognition." *Annual Review of Psychology* 30:363–396.

Slovic, P., B. Fischoff, and S. Lichtenstein 1977 "Behavioral Decision Theory." *Annual Review of Psychology* 28:1–39.

Tversky, A., and D. Kahneman 1982 "Judgment Under Uncertainty: Heuristics and Biases." In D. Kahneman, P. Slovic, and A. Tversky, eds., *Judgment Under Uncertainty: Heuristics and Biases*. New York: Cambridge University Press.

Von Neumann, J., and O. Morgenstern 1944 *Theory of Games and Economic Behavior*. Princeton, N.J.: Princeton University Press.

KARL KOSLOSKI

**DECOLONIZATION** Decolonization refers to a polity's movement from a status of political dependence or subordination to a status of formal autonomy or sovereignty. In modern usage, it is generally assumed that the imperial or metropolitan center is physically separated from the dependency and that the two areas are made up of racially distinct populations. The term is almost always used to refer specifically to the disintegration of Western overseas empires and their replacement by sovereign states in the Americas, Asia, and Africa.

There are several routes by which decolonization can take place. Most frequently, the dependency becomes a new sovereign state, a political entity recognized in the international arena as independent of other states and as possessing final jurisdiction over a defined territory and population. Less often, decolonization may occur through the dependency's full incorporation into an existing polity, such that it is no longer separate and subordinate.

It is often unclear when (or whether) decolonization has occurred. Puerto Rico's relation to the United States can be described as one of colonial dependency or as free association. In the 1960s, Portugal claimed to have no colonies, only overseas territories that had been formally incorporated into a unitary Portuguese state (Nogueira 1963). And where political relations are not contested, the absence of overt conflict makes it difficult to know when sovereignty has been achieved. For example, arguments can be made for dating Canadian independence at 1867, 1919, 1926, or 1931.

This article will briefly review the pattern of decolonization in the modern Western experience and outline some central arguments about causes and consequences.

## HISTORICAL OVERVIEW

Virtually all of the decolonization of Western overseas empires occurred in two historical eras (Bergesen and Schoenberg 1980). The major American colonies became independent during the late eighteenth and early nineteenth centuries. The mid-twentieth century witnessed a more rapid and complete wave of decolonization worldwide (Strang 1990). The types of colonies in existence in each period and the nature of the decolonization process vary greatly across the two periods (Fieldhouse 1966).

The first wave of decolonization began with the independence of Britain's thirteen Continental colonies as the United States of America. The French Revolution touched off a slave uprising that led ultimately to the independence of the French colony of Saint Domingue as Haiti. Portuguese Brazil and Spanish Central and South America became independent after the Napoleonic Wars, which had cut Latin America off from the Iberian peninsula.

While the first period of decolonization was limited to the Americas, twentieth-century decolonization was global in scope. It included the independence of most of the Indian subcontinent, Southeast Asia and Australasia, the Middle East, Africa, and the Caribbean. Between the world wars, some of Britain's settler colonies and a number of loosely held protectorates became fully sovereign. Soon after World War II, the major Asian colonies—India, Indonesia, Indochina, and the Philippines—achieved independence. The pace of change rapidly accelerated during the 1960s, which saw the decolonization of nearly all of Africa. By the 1980s nearly all major colonies had become independent or had been fully incorporated into sovereign states.

One fundamental difference between the two eras of decolonization has to do with who sought independence. Early American decolonizations were creole revolutions, as the descendants of European settlers sought political autonomy from the "mother country." The American Revolution and the Spanish Wars for Independence were political but not social revolutions. Slave revolt in Haiti provided the sole instance of destruction of settler rule (to the horror of rebels and loyalists elsewhere).

By contrast, twentieth-century decolonization was generally rooted in indigenous rather than creole movements for independence, as decolonization came to mean freedom from racially alien rule. After World War II, settler minorities generally opposed decolonization, since national independence spelled an end to their privileged economic, political, and social position. Only in South Africa did a racist minority regime survive decolonization.

A second basic difference between the first and second periods of decolonization lies in the degree of violence involved. Early decolonization in the Americas was won through military combat between settler and imperial forces. Wars for independence raged in Britain's thirteen Continental colonies, in Spanish Central and South America, and in Haiti. Only in Portuguese Brazil was independence achieved without a fight, largely because Brazil was several times richer and more populous than Portugal.

During the twentieth century, colonies like Indochina, Indonesia, Algeria, and Angola won their independence after protracted military struggle. But these were the exceptions to the rule. Most colonies became independent with little or no organized violence between the imperial state and colonial nationalists. In much of Africa, imperial powers virtually abandoned colonies at the first sign of popular opposition to the colonial regime. By the mid-1960s, decolonization had become a rather routine activity for many imperial powers, often achieved through institutionalized expressions of popular will (such as plebiscites).

## CAUSES OF DECOLONIZATION

A variety of arguments have been developed about factors contributing to decolonization. While most arguments have dealt with a single dependency or empire, there have been a number of recent efforts to develop explicitly comparative analyses (see Emerson 1960; Grimal 1978; Lang 1975; Smith 1978; Bergesen and Schoenberg 1980; Albertini 1982; Anderson 1983; Holland 1985; Boswell 1989; and Strang 1990).

Decolonization is often seen as the result of structural change in the dependency itself. Settler colonies are thought to undergo a natural process of maturation, well expressed in the physiocratic maxim that colonies are like fruit that fall from the tree when they are ripe. Indigenous populations are also importantly affected by contact with Western economic and political structures.

In both kinds of colonies, the specific condition that seems to precipitate decolonization is the emergence of peripheral nationalism. Settler colonies generally began as economic corporations chartered by European states. Non-Western peoples were generally tribal or segmental societies prior to colonization, and imperial structures were fundamentally dependent on the collaboration of indigenous elites (Robinson 1972). Decolonization required a new vision of the colonial

dependency as a national society (Diamond 1958; Anderson 1983).

Colonial powers contributed unintentionally to the formulation of a national vision. They did so partly by spurring the rise of new social groups—indigenous bourgeois, landless workers, civil servants, teachers—who proved to be the carriers of colonial nationalism and independence. Perhaps most important, contact with the colonial power exposed indigenous groups to the notions and institutions of the Western nation-state while simultaneously denying them participation rights. Settlers, of course, carried notions of these rights with them (see Bailyn 1967 and Greene 1986 on the ideological origins of the American Revolution). Under these conditions, nationalism was a weapon easily turned on its creators (Emerson 1960).

While pressures for decolonization invariably stem from the dependency itself, the response of the metropolitan power plays a crucial role in the outcome. The classic contrast in imperial policy is between British "association" and French "assimilation" (though parallel contrasts between the imperial policies of the United States and Portugal are even more striking). The British empire was administratively structured around indirect rule and local autonomy, which permitted considerable flexibility in the imperial reaction to pressures for decolonization. By contrast, the French aimed at the assimilation of their colonies into a unitary republic, which led to firmer resistance to decolonization.

In some instances, the metropolitan state was simply unable to suppress pressures for decolonization, despite a full-fledged military commitment to do so. Early American decolonization nearly always had this character. In the twentieth century, the major imperial states emerged from World War II as second-rate powers. At critical junctures, these states found themselves unable to project sufficient military power abroad to control events: the British in Suez, the French in Indochina and Algeria, the Dutch in Indonesia.

Finally, several systemic factors or processes may be linked to decolonization. One is the presence of a state that is economically and politically dominant on the world stage. It has been argued that such a "hegemonic" state tends to create a global free-market system rather than paying the overhead costs of empire (Krasner 1976; Bergesen and Schoenberg 1980; Boswell 1989). This argument has much in common with Gallagher and Robinson's (1953) notion of an "imperialism of free trade," which is preferable to direct administration. Both Britain and the United States favored decolonization during their periods of global hegemony.

A second systemic factor is the contagiousness of decolonization. The American Revolution served as a model for insurrection in both Haiti and Latin America. After World War II, the independence of India, Indochina, and Indonesia had a substantial impact on colonized peoples everywhere. The contagiousness of independence is most apparent in the rapidity with which decolonization swept across Africa, where thirty-three colonies became independent between 1957 and 1966.

Finally, the content of global political understandings and discourse plays a critical role in decolonization (Strang 1990). After 1945, the two superpowers were ideologically opposed to colonialism, though each accused the other of imperialism. Even the major imperial powers (Great Britain, France, the Netherlands) found it difficult to reconcile colonial possessions with the political ideas and institutions of the national polity. As a result, the rationale of colonialism crumbled under pressure, with imperialism being formally denounced by the United Nations in 1960.

These understandings lend great political importance to the distinction between a dependency and a territory integrated into the nation-state. A sharp distinction is generally drawn between the overseas empires of European states and "internal colonies" such as Wales, Armenia, or Eritrea. While the empirical basis for such a distinction is shaky, it has real implications. Identification as a colonial dependency greatly increases the chances of mobilizing internal and external support for indigenous nationalism; it also vastly reduces the compulsion that the metropolitan state can legitimately bring to bear.

## CONSEQUENCES OF DECOLONIZATION

The issue that dominates most discussion of decolonization concerns its implications for more general notions of international domination or exploitation. Dependency-world systems theorists view decolonization as producing change in the form but not the content of core–periphery relations (Chase-Dunn and Rubinson 1979). The argument is that contact between more and less developed economies reinforces the differential between them, even in the absence of explicit political controls. Dependence on foreign capital has been argued to slow long-term economic growth (Bornschier, Chase-Dunn, and Rubinson 1978) and more generally to shape the political and economic structure of the dependent society (Amin 1973; Cardoso and Faletto 1979).

On the other hand, it seems clear that decolonization involves a fundamental shift in the structures regulating international exchange, especially in the post–World War II era. Contemporary states are armed with widely accepted rights to control economic activity within their boundaries, including rights to nationalize foreign-owned industries and renegotiate contracts with multinational corporations (Krasner 1978; Lipson 1985). Third-world nations mobilize visibly around these rights (Krasner 1985), and the negative impact of economic dependency seems to decrease when the peripheral state is strong (Delacroix and Ragin 1981).

While notions of dependency and neocolonialism are the subject of vigorous debate, the most straightforward consequence of decolonization is its central role in expanding the originally Western, and now global, interstate system. Most of the present members of the United Nations became sovereign through decolonization. And historically, the political units emerging from decolonization have been strikingly stable. Few ex-dependencies have been recolonized or annexed or have merged or dissolved (Jackson and Rosberg 1982; Strang 1991). Against much expectation, decolonization has produced states that appear to be relatively permanent elements of the international economic and political order.

(SEE ALSO: *Imperialism and Colonialism; Industrialization in Less Developed Countries*)

## REFERENCES

Albertini, Rudolf von 1982 *Decolonization: The Administration and Future of the Colonies 1919–1960.* New York: Holmes and Meier.

Amin, Samir 1973 *Neo-Colonialism in West Africa.* London: Monthly Review Press.

Anderson, Benedict 1983 *Imagined Communities: Reflections on the Origins and Spread of Nationalism.* London: Verso.

Bailyn, Bernard 1967 *The Ideological Origins of the American Revolution.* Cambridge, Mass.: Harvard University Press.

Bergesen, Albert, and Ronald Schoenberg 1980 "The Long Waves of Colonial Expansion and Contraction 1415–1970." In A. Bergesen, ed., *Studies of the Modern World System.* New York: Academic Press.

Bornschier, Volker, Christopher Chase-Dunn, and Richard Rubinson 1978 "Cross-National Evidence of the Effects of Foreign Investment and Aid on Economic Growth and Inequality: A Survey of Findings and a Reanalysis." *American Journal of Sociology* 84:651–683.

Boswell, Terry 1989 "Colonial Empires and the Capitalist World-Economy: A Time Series Analysis of Colonization, 1640–1960." *American Sociological Review* 54:180–196.

Cardoso, Fernando H., and Enzo Faletto 1979 *Dependency and Development in Latin America.* Berkeley: University of California Press.

Chase-Dunn, Christopher, and Richard Rubinson 1979 "Toward a Structural Perspective on the World-System." *Politics and Society* 7:453–476.

Delacroix, Jacques, and Charles C. Ragin 1981 "Structural Blockage: A Cross-National Study of Economic Dependency, State Efficacy, and Underdevelopment." *American Journal of Sociology* 86:1,311–1,347.

Diamond, Sigmund 1958 "From Organization to Society." *American Journal of Sociology* 63:457–475.

Emerson, Rupert 1960 *From Empire to Nation.* Cambridge, Mass.: Harvard University Press.

Fieldhouse, David K. 1966 *The Colonial Empires.* New York: Dell.

Gallagher, John, and Ronald Robinson 1953 "The Imperialism of Free Trade." *Economic History Review,* 2nd. ser., 6:1–15.

Greene, Jack P. 1986 *Peripheries and Center: Constitutional Development in the Extended Polities of the British Empire and the United States 1607–1788.* Athens: University of Georgia Press.

Grimal, Henri 1978 *Decolonization.* London: Routledge and Kegan Paul.

Holland, R. F. 1985 *European Decolonization 1918–1981.* New York: St. Martin's Press.

Jackson, Robert, and Carl Rosberg 1982 "Why Africa's Weak States Persist: The Empirical and the Juridical in Statehood." *World Politics* 35:1–24.

Krasner, Stephen D. 1976 "State Power and the Structure of International Trade." *World Politics* 28:317–343.

—— 1978 *Defending the National Interest.* Princeton, N. J.: Princeton University Press.

—— 1985 *Structural Conflict.* Berkeley: University of California Press.

Lang, James 1975 *Conquest and Commerce: Spain and England in the Americas.* New York: Academic Press.

Lipson, Charles 1985 *Standing Guard: Protecting Foreign Capital in the Nineteenth and Twentieth Centuries.* Berkeley: University of California Press.

Nogueira, Franco 1963 *The United Nations and Portugal: A Study of Anti-Colonialism.* London: Sidgwick and Jackson.

Robinson, Ronald 1972 "Non-European Foundations of European Imperialism: Sketch for a Theory of Collaboration." In R. Owen and B. Sutcliffe, eds., *Studies in the Theory of Imperialism.* Bristol: G. B. Longman.

Smith, Tony 1978 "A Comparative Study of French and British Decolonization." *Comparative Studies in Society and History.* 20:70–102.

Strang, David 1990 "From Dependency to Sovereignty: An Event History Analysis of Decolonization." *American Sociological Review* 55:846–860.

—— 1991 "Anomaly and Commonplace in European Political Expansion: Realist and Institutional Accounts." *International Organization* 45:142–161.

DAVID STRANG

**DEDUCTION/INDUCTION** *See* Scientific Explanation.

**DEMOCRACY** Democracy is one of the most studied and disputed topics in the social sciences. It has drawn such attention because it has come to be a value with considerable legitimacy, shared by many individuals worldwide. As a result, considerable resources have been devoted to understanding the sources, effects, strengths, and weaknesses of democracy. In developing an understanding of this research on democracy it is best to begin by explicitly considering how democracy is defined.

At the core of most discussions of democracy is the common view that democracy is a method of governance or decision making for groups, organizations, or governments in which the members of a group, organization, or polity participate, directly or indirectly, in the decision making of that entity. Further, members participate in decision making to such an extent that they are considered to govern or control that group, organization, or polity. In short, democracy is a system of governance in which members control group decision making.

Yet such a definition leaves considerable room for contention. Two central issues are most often examined: What does, or should, constitute a minimum level of control over decision making by members for a system to be thought of as democratic? Who are, or should, be considered members of the polity? The fact that these issues are matters not only of empirical observation but also of moral and political philosophy makes the analysis of democracy particularly difficult.

Three factors add to the difficulty of approaching democracy as a field of research in the social sciences. First, theoretical and normative definitions are often not fully specified in the analysis of democracy. This in turn can lead to considerable confusion. Democratic systems of governance can be characterized by many attributes—frequency of member participation, the form of member participation, and so forth. Evaluating the extent

to which a particular system of governance is democratic, then, involves making decisions about which attributes are essential to a democratic system. Where a definition is not fully examined, the question of whether a political regime is or is not democratic often leads to conflating theoretical definition and empirical analysis (Macpherson 1962).

A second factor increasing the difficulty of this subject matter is that democracy is a system of governance found in many different kinds of collectivities, including states, formal organizations, and informal groups. It is thus necessary to be cautious in applying models, findings, and relationships that hold in the analysis of democracy for one unit of analysis to other units of analysis. It is not sufficient, for example, to assume that what causes democratic regimes to be effective at a nation-state level also functions in a similar manner in formal organizations.

Finally, democracy is a complex subject because democracy is more than just an outcome variable. Social scientists are interested in democracy not just for its own sake but also because it is thought to be associated with other critical issues, including the efficiency or effectiveness of organizations and nation-states, levels of income inequality and social stratification, and individual liberty.

While the difficulties of this subject can be daunting, much innovative work has been done in this field. It is best to begin in laying out the state of knowledge regarding democracy with the range of theoretical conceptions of democracy that predominate. Sociologists have in this regard relied heavily on ideas and arguments advanced by "democratic theorists," scholars who have concentrated on the moral basis of systems of governance. The first theoretical and definitional issue is: Who is or should be members or citizens of a democratic polity? Most systems commonly thought to be democratic have through the ages excluded some portion of those subject to the will of the democracy from participation in the decision-making process. Such exclusion has occurred on the basis of race, sex, income, relationship to property, criminal status, mental health, religion, age, and other characteristics. While use of many of these categories as a justification for excluding individuals from participation has declined in recent times, others remain, and there is continuing disagreement about the moral and political bases for excluding or including specific groups. Guest workers in Western Europe, for example, are subject to the action of the state on a long-term basis and yet remain excluded from full political participation in those states (Brubaker 1989). At the level of the organization, the movement toward increasing the power of corporate "stakeholders" over decision making by large business corporations is another example. Several theorists have argued that where the lives of individuals are influenced by the decisions of large business corporations, even though those individuals are neither employees, contractors, or shareholders, they should have a say in those key decisions (Nader and Green 1976). This movement is in part motivated and legitimated by democratic claims that value individuals having a say in decisions that affect their lives.

The second and more fundamental definitional issue concerns what should constitute the form of influence and participation that individuals have in decision making in a democratic system. A traditional view has long been that a representative system is appropriate for allowing participation in decision making. Representative democracy is that form of governance in which members of the organization or polity exercise their control over the organization through the regular election of members of a decision-making body. For example, the United States is a representative democracy in which citizens directly elect senators and representatives to the federal Congress, which in turn makes political decisions about the actions of the federal government. Theorists since the Enlightenment have argued that representative democracy is an appropriate means for conveying participation in decision making in large-size organizations, where individuals are thought not to be able to participate in all decisions (Hobbes 1986; Rousseau 1968; Locke 1980; Mill 1958).

Representative democracy has been attacked by critics who argue that in such democracies influence is exercised over the decision-making process

in the government or organization not just through voting but also through the exertion of undue influence in the process of choosing representatives, and through extra-electoral influence over representatives themselves. Hence, these critics argue, it is futile to argue that some government or organization is fully democratic simply because voting is the key procedural element in the decision-making process, when "undue" influence can be exercised, either by swaying votes; through various forms of media or propaganda; or, at the level of the representatives themselves, through postelectoral influence over legislative activity. Such arguments are also raised in the context of democracy in formal organizations, as when larger stockholders or a board of directors and management may be able to influence the decision-making process through control over access to critical information. Indeed, early American legislators sought to reduce this tendency toward oligarchy in business corporations by specifying, in corporate charters, restrictions that limited the maximum number of votes that any single shareholder could control.

A second criticism of representative democracy as a form of governance concerns the problem of oligarchical tendencies on the part of the representatives themselves. First articulated by Mosca, the argument reached its fullest form in the work of Robert Michels (Mosca 1939). The argument is that in any large organization (and hence in any nation-state) a democratic system of governance inevitably leads to the rise of an oligarchy, and worse, to an oligarchy whose leaders have interests that differ from those of the ordinary citizens or members. Oligarchy arises because the organization needs experienced, skilled leaders. Experience in leadership, however, also tends to give leaders access to key organizational resources that are valuable in returning that leadership to office. And as leaders remain in office over an extended time, their interests and attitudes are likely to diverge from those of members, in part because leaders start to have different life chances from the members of organizations. Hence Michels, while arguing that formal organization is necessary for social life, and especially for politics, also believes that democracy in such organization is essentially impossible (Michels 1966).

Joseph Schumpeter and Robert Dahl have defended democratic systems in response to these critiques, and they have done so in part by reconsidering theoretical conceptions of democracy. For them, a key element in determining whether a system is democratic is the extent to which that system remains open to nonelectoral forms of influence by interest groups. The forms of influence and participation that constitute and define the presence of a democratic system are not limited to participation via the immediate electoral system but also include influence and participation external to the electoral system, such as lobbying and mobilization of protest. If a variety of interest groups are able to exercise power and influence in the system through a variety of means, then the system, with all its flaws, can be considered democratic (Schumpeter 1976; Dahl 1961). This view responds to both criticisms of representative government: extra-electoral influence becomes valued, because it is a means of democratic influence open to all interests; and organized extra-electoral influence becomes valued, even if oligarchical, because the multiplicity of interests reduces the costs of oligarchy.

One weakness of the pluralist view of democracy is that not all groups in society may be able effectively to form organizations to defend their interests. Mancur Olson has argued that because of problems associated with the distribution of collective goods, collective actors may not arise to represent groups with large numbers of members. The core of his argument is that if such interest-based organizations representing large numbers of individuals are to be created and maintained, special incentives must be made available to attract members to these groups. Groups representing weak and powerless individuals may be unable to supply such special incentives. Olson's challenge to the likelihood of individuals forming groups under these circumstances is one that sociologists have focused attention on for some time (Olson 1971). Recent work by Pam Oliver and others suggests that social movements are more likely to be formed as interest groups grow

in size (Oliver and Marwell 1988). These criticisms of Olson's analysis of the collective action problem may actually serve to strengthen the pluralist account of democracy.

Yet many theorists remain critical of the pluralist account (Domhoff 1967). As a response to the pluralist arguments, many researchers again returned in the 1970s and 1980s to the question of what democracy should mean. The argument is both that greater participation in decision making is possible than is usually the practice, and that the purpose of democracy as a system of governance has been misconstrued. Rather than just being about democratic control of decision making, theorists such as Finley and Pateman, in examining both the classical Greek case and the neoclassical theory of democracy, argue that democratic systems are also about creating educated members, who are better able to comprehend the decision-making process. As members participate in decision making, they learn more about the criteria that need to be used in effective decision making and thus become even better at evaluating the choice of representatives in a representative democracy (Finley 1985; Pateman 1970). Sociologists also moved to consider empirical examples of organizations more oriented toward participatory management. Burawoy and Kanter, for example, have attempted to show that democratic systems of management are more broadly possible than had previously been expected, although the conditions under which such systems of decision making can be created and maintained remain under debate (Burawoy 1979; Kanter 1984).

These issues, concerning the nature, purposes, and limits of democratic control, form the center of social science treatments of democracy. Yet democracy is also an important topic because it is associated with other issues.

One such central issue has been a focus of research since de Tocqueville and has to do with the relationship between democracy and equality. More recently, research has been centered around this specific question: Does democracy promote or retard income inequality in nation-states? Key research has been performed in this area by Parkin and by Bollen. This is an extremely contentious issue, and is as yet not fully resolved (Parkin 1976; Bollen 1985). A second such question, often raised in the context of formal organizations, is the relationship between democracy and effectiveness. Put more pointedly: Can democratic organizations be effective? This question has been raised for both political organizations and economic organizations (Lenin 1932; Piven and Cloward 1977; Blumberg 1968). As yet there seems to be no definitive answer, and the issue certainly merits more attention. Finally, an important question is: What are the conditions under which democracy arises and fails in nation-states? Also under considerable debate, some of the most interesting work in modern sociology is related to this issue (Moore 1966; Skocpol 1979; Hannan and Carroll 1981).

While these research questions have dominated sociological research about democracy in recent years, other questions deserve attention. For example, the relationship between democracy and individual liberty has not attracted much current sociological attention, yet has been a central concern ever since theorists first turned their attention to the subject (Burke 1987). Further, questions such as those asked above might also be examined more thoroughly at different levels of analysis. For example: What are the sources of democratic governance in formal organizations? And what are the sources of the effectiveness of democratic government in nation-states? These and other questions suggest that considerable research remains to be done on democracy, one of the most important subjects in sociology.

(SEE ALSO: *Capitalism, Individualism in Less Developed Countries*)

## REFERENCES

Blumberg, Paul 1968 *Industrial Democracy: The Sociology of Participation.* New York: Schocken Books.

Bollen, Kenneth A., and Robert W. Jackman 1985 "Political Democracy." *American Sociological Review* 50:438–457.

Brubaker, William Rogers 1989 *Immigration and the Politics of Citizenship in Europe and North America.* Lanham, Md.: University Press of America; German Marshall Fund of the United States.

Burawoy, Michael 1979 *Manufacturing Consent.* Chicago: University of Chicago Press.

Burke, Edmund 1987 *Reflections on the Revolution in France.* Indianapolis: Hackett Publishers.

Dahl, Robert A. 1961 *Who Governs?* New Haven, Conn.: Yale University Press.

—— 1989 *Democracy and Its Critics.* New Haven, Conn.: Yale University Press.

Domhoff, G. William 1967 *Who Rules America?* Englewood Cliffs, N.J.: Prentice-Hall.

Finley, M. I. 1985 *Democracy: Ancient and Modern.* London: Hogarth Press.

Hannan, Michael T., and Glenn R. Carroll 1981 "Dynamics of Formal Political Structure: An Event-History Analysis." *American Sociological Review* 46:19–35.

Hobbes, Thomas 1986 *Leviathan.* Hammondsworth, Eng.: Penguin.

Kanter, Rosabeth M. 1984 *The Change Masters.* New York: Simon and Schuster.

Lenin, V. I. 1932 *State and Revolution.* New York: International Publishers.

Lipset, Seymour Martin, Martin A. Trow, and James S. Coleman 1959 *Union Democracy.* New York: Free Press.

Locke, John 1980 *Second Treatise of Government.* Indianapolis: Hackett Publishers.

Macpherson, C. B. 1962 *The Political Theory of Possessive Individualism: Hobbes to Locke.* Oxford: Clarendon Press.

Michels, Robert 1966 *Political Parties.* New York: The Free Press.

Mill, John Stuart 1958 *Considerations on Representative Government.* New York: Liberal Arts Press.

Moore, Barrington 1966 *The Social Origins of Dictatorship and Democracy.* Boston: Beacon Press.

Mosca, Gaetano 1939 *The Ruling Class (Elementi di Scienze Politica).* New York: McGraw-Hill.

Nader, Ralph, and Mark Green 1976 *Taming the Giant Corporation.* New York: W. W. Norton.

Oliver, Pamela E., and Gerald Marwell 1988 "The Paradox of Group Size in Collective Action." *American Sociological Review* 53:1–8.

Olson, Mancur 1971 *The Logic of Collective Action.* Cambridge, Mass.: Harvard University Press.

Parkin, Frank 1976 *Class Inequality and Political Order.* New York: Praeger Publishers.

Pateman, Carole 1970 *Participation and Democratic Theory.* Cambridge, Eng.: Cambridge University Press.

Piven, Frances Fox, and Richard Cloward 1977 *Poor People's Movements.* New York: Pantheon.

Rothschild-Whitt, Joyce, and A. Whitt 1986 *Work Without Bosses: Conditions and Dilemmas of Organizational Democracy in Grassroots Cooperatives.* New York: Cambridge University Press.

Rousseau, Jean-Jacques 1968 *The Social Contract.* Baltimore: Penguin.

Schumpeter, Joseph A. 1976 *Capitalism, Socialism, and Democracy.* New York: Harper and Row.

Skocpol, Theda 1979 *States and Social Revolution.* Cambridge, Eng.: Cambridge University Press.

Tocqueville, Alexis de 1969 *Democracy in America,* ed. J. P. Jayer. Garden City, N.Y.: Anchor Books.

ANDREW L. CREIGHTON

## DEMOGRAPHIC METHODS

Most fundamentally, demographic methods are used to provide researchers and policymakers with useful information about the size and structure of human populations and the processes that govern population changes. A population, of course, may range in size from a small number of individuals surveyed locally to a large national population enumerated in periodic censuses to even larger aggregated entities.

We use demographic methods not only in purely demographic applications but also in a variety of other fields, among them sociology, economics, anthropology, public health, and business. Demographers, like all researchers, must pay careful attention to the quality of data that enter into an analysis. Some circumstances under which we use these methods are more trying than others. In cases in which the data are viewed to be accurate and complete, the methods we use to analyze them are more straightforward than those that are applied to data of imperfect quality.

### DESCRIPTION OF DATA

First we must develop ways to describe our data in a fashion that allows the most important facts to leap out at us. As one example, let us examine a population's age structure or distribution. Simple descriptive statistics are doubtless helpful in summarizing aspects of population age structure, but demographers often use *age pyramids* to convey to an audience the youthfulness of a population, for example, or even to convey a rough sense of a nation's history.

We might note, for example, that 24 percent of Sweden's population on July 1, 1988, was under the age of fifteen. In contrast, 42 percent of Mexico's population three years earlier fell into this category. But it is perhaps more dramatic to create a visual display of these figures in the form of age pyramids.

An age pyramid is typically constructed as a bar graph, with horizontal bars—one set representing each sex—emanating in both directions from a central vertical age axis. Age increases as one proceeds up the axis, and the unit of the horizontal axis is either the proportion of the total population in each age group or the population size itself.

We see in panel A of figure 1 that Mexico's population is described by a very broad-based pyramid, which reveals a remarkably large proportion of the population not yet having reached adulthood. The median age of this population is about nineteen years. Such a distributional shape is common particularly among high fertility populations. In stark contrast we have the pyramid shown in panel B, representing the population of Sweden. Rather than a pyramid, its age distribution is more rectangular in shape, which is typically seen among countries that have experienced an extended period of low fertility rates. It is easy to see that Sweden's median age (thirty-nine years) is considerably higher than that of Mexico.

As mentioned above, not only can we examine the age structure of populations through the use of pyramids, but we can also gain much insight into a nation's history insofar as that history has either directly or indirectly influenced the size of successive birth cohorts. Note, for example, the age pyramid reflecting the population age structure of France on January 1, 1962 (figure 2). In this figure, several notable events in France's history are apparent. We see (1) the military losses experienced in World War I by male birth cohorts

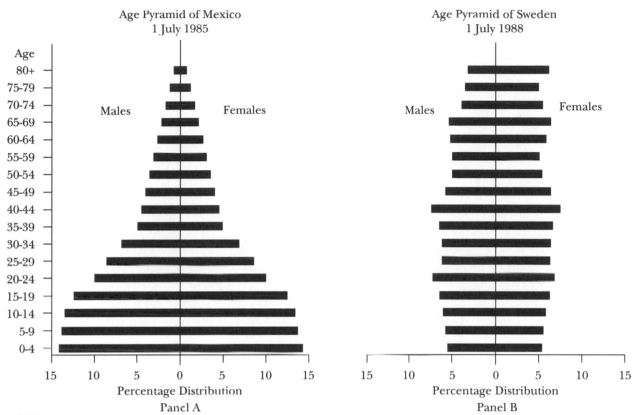

**FIGURE 1**
*Age pyramids for Mexico and Sweden*

of the mid- to late 1890s, (2) the remarkable birth dearth brought about by that war (the cohort aged in their mid-forties or so in 1962), followed by (3) the return of prewar childbearing activity once the war ended (the cohort who in 1962 were in their early forties), and a similar pattern revolving around World War II, during which (4) a substantial decline in births took place (the cohort around age twenty in 1962), succeeded by (5) a dramatic baby boom in the years immediately following (those around age fifteen in 1962).

## COMPARISON OF CRUDE RATES

Much of the work in which social scientists are engaged is comparative in nature. For example, we might seek to contrast the mortality levels of the populations of two countries. Surely, if the two countries in question have accurate vital registra-

tion and census data, this task would appear to be trivial. For each country, we would simply divide the total number of deaths (D) in a given year by the total population (P) at the midpoint of that year. Thus, we would define the crude death rate (CDR) for country A as:

$$\text{CDR}^A = \frac{D^A[t,\, t+1]}{P^A[t+.5]} = \frac{\sum_{x=0,n}^{\omega-n} \left[ {}_nM_x^A \cdot {}_nP_x^A \right]}{\sum_{x=0,n}^{\omega-n} {}_nP_x^A} \quad (1)$$

where $t$ denotes the beginning of the calendar year, $\omega$ is the oldest age attained in the population, ${}_nM_x^A$ is the death rate of individuals aged $x$ to $x+n$, and ${}_nP_x^A$ is the number of individuals in that same age group. ${}_nM_x^A$ and ${}_nP_x^A$ are centered on the midpoint of the calendar year. The rightmost segment of this equation reminds us that the crude death rate is but the sum of the age-specific

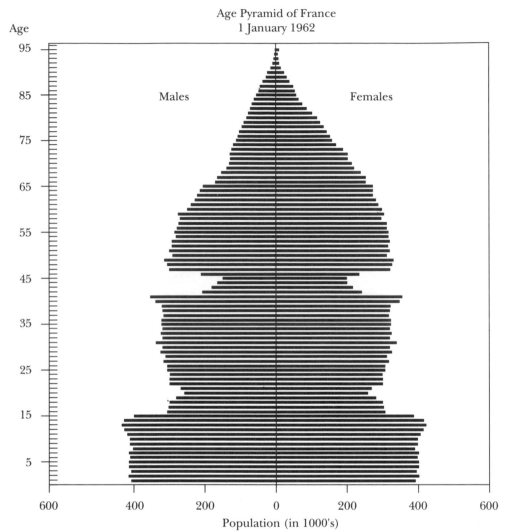

**FIGURE 2**

*Age pyramid of France*

death rates weighted by the number of persons or the proportion of the population at each age.

Unfortunately, comparisons of crude death rates across populations can lead to misleading conclusions. This problem is in fact general to any sort of comparison based on crude rates that do not account for the confounding effects of factors that differentiate the two populations.

Let us examine the death rates of two very different countries, Mexico and Sweden. The crude death rate for males in Mexico in 1985, 5.9 per 1,000, was half that for males in Sweden, 11.9, in 1988. Knowing nothing else about these two countries, we might infer that the health of the

Mexican population was considerably superior to that of the Swedish population. However, once we standardize the crude death rates of the two countries on a common population age structure, we find just the reverse is true.

To accomplish this standarization, instead of applying equation 1 to our data, we use the following:

$$\text{ASCDR}^A = \frac{\sum_{x=0,n}^{\omega-n} \left[ {}_nM_x^A \cdot {}_nP_x^S \right]}{\sum_{x=0,n}^{\omega-n} {}_nP_x^S} \qquad (2)$$

where ASCDR$^A$ is the age-standardized crude death rate of country A, and $_nP_x^S$ is the number of individuals in the standardized population of that same age group. Any age distribution may be chosen as the standard; however, it is common simply to use the average of the two proportionate age distributions (i.e., each normalized to one in order to account for unequal population sizes).

Table 1 gives the death rates and number of persons for each country by five-year age groups (zero through four, five through nine, and so forth through eighty and above). The first fact we

**TABLE 1**
**Standardization using death rates and population distributions from Mexico and Sweden**

| Age group | MEXICO | | | SWEDEN | |
| | Population in 1000s (% distribution) | Death rate (per 1,000) | Standard distribution (%) | Population in 1000s (% distribution) | Death rate (per 1,000) |
|---|---|---|---|---|---|
| 0–4 | 5,748 (14.62) | 8.4 | 10.16 | 237 (5.69) | 1.9 |
| 5–9 | 5,616 (14.29) | 0.7 | 10.10 | 246 (5.91) | 0.2 |
| 10–14 | 5,360 (13.63) | 0.7 | 9.95 | 261 (6.27) | 0.2 |
| 15–19 | 4,578 (11.64) | 1.4 | 9.26 | 286 (6.87) | 0.7 |
| 20–24 | 3,802 (9.67) | 2.4 | 8.64 | 317 (7.61) | 0.9 |
| 25–29 | 3,127 (7.95) | 3.0 | 7.47 | 291 (6.98) | 1.1 |
| 30–34 | 2,525 (6.42) | 3.3 | 6.73 | 293 (7.03) | 1.2 |
| 35–39 | 1,932 (4.91) | 4.7 | 6.14 | 307 (7.36) | 1.5 |
| 40–44 | 1,535 (3.90) | 5.9 | 6.08 | 344 (8.26) | 2.0 |
| 45–49 | 1,277 (3.25) | 7.8 | 4.95 | 277 (6.64) | 3.5 |
| 50–54 | 1,065 (2.71) | 10.1 | 4.02 | 222 (5.34) | 5.9 |
| 55–59 | 819 (2.08) | 14.2 | 3.55 | 209 (5.01) | 9.7 |
| 60–64 | 675 (1.72) | 19.5 | 3.42 | 214 (5.13) | 15.3 |
| 65–69 | 465 (1.18) | 28.1 | 3.22 | 219 (5.25) | 24.5 |
| 70–74 | 360 (0.92) | 41.4 | 2.56 | 175 (4.20) | 41.9 |
| 75–79 | 235 (0.60) | 65.2 | 1.97 | 140 (3.35) | 67.0 |
| 80+ | 195 (0.50) | 163.8 | 1.80 | 129 (3.90) | 135.7 |

glean from the table is that the mortality rates of Swedish males are substantially lower than those of their Mexican counterparts at virtually all ages. We see that almost 40 percent of the Mexican population is concentrated in the three age groups having the lowest death rates (ages five through nineteen). Only 19 percent of the Swedish population is found in that same age range. In contrast, less than 10 percent of the Mexican age distribution is above fifty years of age, an age range with which its highest level of mortality is associated. At the same time, over 30 percent of the Swedish population is fifty or older. Compared with the Mexican crude death rate, then, the Swedish rate is disproportionately weighted toward the relatively high age-specific death rates that exist in the older ages.

Applying the standardization method described by equation 2 to the average of Sweden's and Mexico's proportionate age distribution, we find that the resulting crude death rates are consistent with what we would infer from the two series of age-specific mortality rates. Mexico's age-standardized crude death rate, 10.6 per 1,000 population, is nearly 40 percent greater than that of Sweden, 7.6 per 1,000.

## LIFE TABLES

The life table is a methodological device used by demographers and others to examine the life —either literal or figurative—of a particular duration-dependent phenomenon. The original application of the life table was to the mortality patterns of human populations. Today, the life table technique is applied to such diverse areas as contraceptive efficacy, marital formation and dissolution, and organizational failure. Thus, it is a remarkably general tool for examining the time-dependent survivorship in a given state.

To illustrate the use of the life table method, suppose we use as an example the mortality experience of the United States population in 1987. We might wish to derive the average number of years that an individual would live, subject to the series of age-specific death rates attributed to that population. To find the answer, we could construct a *complete life table,* as in Table 2. It is complete in the sense that it is highly age-detailed, focusing on single years of age. This is in contrast to the *abridged life table,* which is usually constructed using five-year age groups. The abridged life table shown in Table 3 refers also to the total population of the United States in 1987.

Most life tables that we see are called *period* or *current life tables.* They refer to a particular snapshot in time. Although they describe the mortality experience of an actual population, they do not describe the experience of an actual birth cohort —that is, a group of individuals who are born within a specified interval of time. If we wished to portray the mortality history of the birth cohort of 1990, for example, we would have to wait until the last individual of that cohort has died, or beyond the year 2100, before we would be able to calculate all of the values that comprise the life table. In such a life table, called a *generation* or *cohort life table,* we can explicitly obtain the probability of individuals surviving to a given age. As is intuitively clear, however, a generation life table is suitable primarily for historical analyses of cohorts now extinct. Any generation life table that we could calculate would be very much out of date and would in no way approximate the present mortality experience of a population. Thus, we realize the need for the period life table, which treats a population at a given point in time as a *synthetic* or *hypothetical cohort.* The major drawback of the period life table is that, in fact, it refers to no particular cohort of individuals. In an era of declining mortality rates at all ages, such a life table will underestimate true life expectancy for any cohort.

The most fundamental data that underlie the formation of a period life table are the number of deaths attributed to each age group in the population for a particular calendar year ($_nD_x$, where $x$ refers to the exact age at the beginning of the age interval and $n$ is the width of that interval) and the number of individuals living at the midpoint of that year for each of those same age groups ($_nP_x$).

To begin the life table's construction, we take

**TABLE 2**
**Complete life table for the United States, 1987**

| Exact age x | $_1q_x$ | $\ell_x$ | $_1d_x$ | $_1L_x$ | $T_x$ | $e_x$ |
|---|---|---|---|---|---|---|
| 0 | .01011 | 100,000 | 1,011 | 99,135 | 7,497,053 | 75.0 |
| 1 | .00071 | 98,989 | 70 | 98,954 | 7,397,919 | 74.7 |
| 2 | .00055 | 98,919 | 54 | 98,892 | 7,298,965 | 73.8 |
| 3 | .00042 | 98,865 | 42 | 98,844 | 7,200,073 | 72.8 |
| 4 | .00035 | 98,823 | 35 | 98,806 | 7,101,229 | 71.9 |
| 5 | .00030 | 98,788 | 30 | 98,773 | 7,002,423 | 70.9 |
| 6 | .00027 | 98,758 | 27 | 98,745 | 6,903,650 | 69.9 |
| 7 | .00024 | 98,731 | 24 | 98,719 | 6,804,906 | 68.9 |
| 8 | .00021 | 98,707 | 21 | 98,697 | 6,706,187 | 67.9 |
| 9 | .00019 | 98,686 | 19 | 98,677 | 6,607,490 | 67.0 |
| 10 | .00017 | 98,667 | 17 | 98,659 | 6,508,814 | 66.0 |
| ⋮ | ⋮ | ⋮ | ⋮ | ⋮ | ⋮ | ⋮ |
| 80 | .06527 | 45,839 | 2,992 | 44,343 | 374,196 | 8.2 |
| 81 | .07165 | 42,847 | 3,070 | 41,312 | 329,853 | 7.7 |
| 82 | .07886 | 39,777 | 3,137 | 38,209 | 288,541 | 7.3 |
| 83 | .08709 | 36,640 | 3,191 | 35,045 | 250,332 | 6.8 |
| 84 | .09654 | 33,449 | 3,229 | 31,835 | 215,288 | 6.4 |
| 85 | (1.00000) | 30,200 | (30,220) | (183,453) | 183,453 | 6.1 |

**TABLE 3**
**Abridged life table for the United States, 1987**

| Exact age x | $_nD_x$ | $_nP_x$ (in 1,000's) | $_nq_x$ | $\ell_x$ | $_nd_x$ | $_nL_x$ | $T_x$ | $e_x$ |
|---|---|---|---|---|---|---|---|---|
| 0 | 38,408 | 3,771 | .0101 | 100,000 | 1,011 | 99,135 | 7,496,306 | 75.0 |
| 1 | 7,473 | 14,481 | .0020 | 98,989 | 201 | 395,485 | 7,397,171 | 74.7 |
| 5 | 4,301 | 17,661 | .0012 | 98,788 | 121 | 493,611 | 7,001,686 | 70.9 |
| 10 | 4,442 | 16,485 | .0013 | 98,667 | 131 | 493,081 | 6,508,075 | 66.0 |
| 15 | 15,615 | 18,459 | .0042 | 98,536 | 414 | 491,741 | 6,014,994 | 61.0 |
| 20 | 22,408 | 19,793 | .0057 | 98,122 | 555 | 489,250 | 5,523,253 | 56.3 |
| 25 | 26,500 | 21,980 | .0060 | 97,567 | 587 | 486,366 | 5,034,003 | 51.6 |
| 30 | 31,201 | 21,335 | .0073 | 96,980 | 707 | 483,174 | 4,547,637 | 46.9 |
| 35 | 34,902 | 18,738 | .0093 | 96,273 | 900 | 479,243 | 4,064,463 | 42.2 |
| 40 | 38,561 | 15,587 | .0124 | 95,373 | 1,178 | 474,130 | 3,585,220 | 37.6 |
| 45 | 47,613 | 12,350 | .0191 | 94,195 | 1,798 | 466,809 | 3,111,090 | 33.0 |
| 50 | 68,307 | 10,926 | .0307 | 92,397 | 2,841 | 455,329 | 2,644,281 | 28.6 |
| 55 | 107,583 | 11,121 | .0473 | 89,556 | 4,240 | 437,789 | 2,188,952 | 24.4 |
| 60 | 165,741 | 10,899 | .0736 | 85,316 | 6,276 | 411,740 | 1,751,163 | 20.5 |
| 65 | 220,110 | 9,889 | .1059 | 79,040 | 8,368 | 375,183 | 1,339,423 | 16.9 |
| 70 | 265,993 | 7,779 | .1585 | 70,672 | 11,203 | 326,327 | 964,240 | 13.6 |
| 75 | 296,714 | 5,777 | .2292 | 59,469 | 13,630 | 264,101 | 637,913 | 10.7 |
| 80 | 287,621 | 3,524 | .3407 | 45,839 | 15,619 | 190,359 | 373,812 | 8.2 |
| 85 | 439,248 | 2,867 | 1.0000 | 30,220 | 30,220 | 183,453 | 183,453 | 6.1 |

the ratio of these two sets of input data—$_nD_x$ and $_nP_x$—to form a series of age-specific death rates, or $_nM_x$:

$$_nM_x = \frac{_nD_x}{_nP_x} \qquad (3)$$

For each death rate, we compute the corresponding probability of dying within that age interval, given that one has survived to the beginning of the interval. This value, denoted by $_nq_x$, is computed by using the following equation:

$$_nq_x = \frac{n \cdot {_nM_x}}{1 + (n - {_na_x}) \cdot {_nM_x}} \qquad (4)$$

where $_na_x$ is the average number of years lived by those who die within the age interval $x$ to $x+n$. (Except for the first year of life, it is typically assumed that deaths are uniformly distributed within an age interval, implying that $_nan_x = n/2$.) Given the values of $q$ and $a$, we are able to generate the entire life table.

The life table may be thought of as a tracking device by which a cohort of individuals is followed from the moment of their birth until the last surviving individual dies. Under this interpretation, the various remaining columns are defined in the following manner:

$\ell_x$ equals the number of individuals in the life table surviving to exact age $x$. We arbitrarily set the number "born into" the life table, $\ell_0$, which is otherwise known as the *radix*, to some value—most often 100,000. We generate all subsequent $\ell_x$ values by the following equation:

$$\ell_{x+n} = \ell_x \cdot [1 - {_nq_x}]. \qquad (5)$$

$_nd_x$ equals the number of deaths experienced by the life table cohort within the age interval $x$ to $x+n$. It is the product of the number of individuals alive at exact age $x$ and the conditional probability of dying within the age interval:

$$_nd_x = \ell_x \cdot {_nq_x} \qquad (6)$$

The concept of person years is critical to understanding life table construction. Each individual who survives from one birthday to the next contributes one additional person year to those tallied by the cohort to which that person belongs. In the year in which the individual dies, the decedent contributes some fraction of a person year to the overall number for that cohort.

$_nL_x$ equals the total number of person years experienced by a cohort in the age interval $x$ to $x+n$. It is the sum of person years contributed by those who have survived to the end of the interval and those contributed by individuals who die within that interval:

$$_nL_x = [n \cdot \ell_{x+n}] + [_na_x \cdot {_nd_x}]. \qquad (7)$$

$T_x$ equals the number of person years lived beyond exact age $x$:

$$T_x = \sum_{a=x,n}^{\infty} {_nL_a} = T_{x+n} + {_nL_x}. \qquad (8)$$

$e_x$ equals the expected number of years of life remaining for an individual who has already survived to exact age $x$. It is the total number of person years experienced by the cohort above that age divided by the number of individuals starting out at that age:

$$e_x = \frac{T_x}{\ell_x}. \qquad (9)$$

The $_nL_x$ and $T_x$ columns are generated from the oldest age to the youngest. If the last age category is, for example, eighty-five and above (it is typically "open-ended" in this way), we must have an initial value for $T_{85}$ in order to begin the process. This value is obtained in the following fashion: Since for this oldest age group, $\ell_{85} = {_\infty d_{85}}$ (due to the fact that the number of individuals in a cohort who will die at age eighty-five or beyond is simply the number currently alive at age eighty-five) and $T_{85} = {_\infty L_{85}}$, we have:

$$e_{85} = \frac{T_{85}}{\ell_{85}} = \frac{1}{\ell_{85}/T_{85}} = \frac{1}{_\infty d_{85}/_\infty L_{85}} \approx \frac{1}{_\infty M_{85}}. \qquad (10)$$

From the life table, we can obtain mortality information in a variety of ways. In table 2 we see, for example, that the expectation of life at birth, $e_0$, is seventy-five years. If an individual in this population survives to age eighty, then he or she might expect to live 8.2 years longer. We might also note that the probability of surviving from birth to one's tenth birthday is $\ell_{10}/\ell_0$, or 0.98667. Given that one has already lived eighty years, the probability that one survives five additional years is $\ell_{85}/\ell_{80}$, or $30{,}220/45{,}839 = 0.65926$.

## POPULATION PROJECTION

The life table, in addition, is often used to project either total population size or the size of specific age groups. In so doing, we must invoke a different interpretation of the $_nL_x$'s and the $T_x$'s in the life table. We treat them as representing the age distribution of a *stationary population*—that is, one having long been subject to zero growth. Thus, $_5L_{20}$, for example, represents the number of twenty- to twenty-four-year-olds in the life table "population," into which $\ell_0$, or 100,000, individuals are born each year. (One will note by summing the $_nd_x$ column that 100,000 die every year, thus giving rise to stationarity of the life table population.)

If we were to assume that the United States is a *closed population*—that is, a population whose net migration is zero—and, furthermore, that the mortality levels obtaining in 1987 were to remain constant for the following ten years, then we would be able to project the size of any U.S. cohort up to ten years into the future. Thus, if we wished to know the number of fifty- to fifty-four-year-olds in 1997, we would take advantage of the following relation that is assumed to hold approximately:

$$\frac{_nP^{\tau+t}_{x+t}}{_nP^\tau_x} \approx \frac{_tL^\tau_{x+t}}{_nL^\tau_x} \tag{11}$$

where $\tau$ is the base year of the projection (e.g., 1987) and $t$ is the number of years one is projecting the population forward. This equation implies that the fifty- to fifty-four-year-olds in 1997, $_5P^{1997}_{50}$, is simply the number of forty- to forty-four-year-olds ten years earlier, $_5P^{1987}_{40}$, multiplied by the proportion of forty- to forty-four-year-olds in the life table surviving ten years, $_5L_{50}/_5L_{40}$.

In practice, it is appropriate to use the above relation in population projection only if the width of the age interval under consideration, $n$, is sufficiently narrow. If the age interval is very broad—for example, in the extreme case in which we are attempting to project the number of people ages ten and above in 1997 from the number zero and above (i.e., the entire population) in 1987—we cannot be assured that the life table age distribution within that interval resem-

bles closely enough the age distribution of the actual population. In other words, if the actual population's age distribution within a broad age interval is significantly different from that within the corresponding interval of the life table population, then implicitly by using this projection device we are improperly weighing the component parts of the broad interval with respect to survival probabilities.

Parenthetically, if we desired to determine the size of any component of the population under $t$ years old—in this particular example, ten years old—we would have to draw upon fertility as well as mortality information, because at time $\tau$ these individuals had not yet been born.

## HAZARDS MODELS

Suppose we were to examine the correlates of marital dissolution. In a life table analysis, the breakup of the marriage (as measured, e.g., by separation or divorce) would serve as the analogue to death, which is the means of exit in the standard life table analysis.

In the study of many duration-dependent phenomena, it is clear that several factors may affect whether an individual exits from a life table. Certainly, it is well established that a large number of socioeconomic variables simultaneously impinge on the marital dissolution process. In many populations, whether one has given birth premaritally, cohabited premaritally, married at a young age, or had little in the way of formal education, among a whole host of other factors, have been found to be strongly associated with marital instability. In such studies, in which one attempts to disentangle the intricately related influences of several variables on survivorship in a given state, we invoke a hazards model approach. Such an approach may be thought of as a multivariate statistical extension of the simple life table analysis presented above (for theoretical underpinnings, see, e.g., Cox and Oakes 1984; for applications to marital stability, see, e.g., Menken, Trussell, Stempel, and Babakol 1981 and Bennett, Blanc, and Bloom 1988).

In the marital dissolution example, we would

assume that there is a hazard, or risk, of dissolution at each marital duration, $d$, and we allow this duration-specific risk to depend on individual characteristics (such as age at marriage, education, etc.). In the *proportional hazards model*, a set of individual characteristics represented by a vector of covariates shifts the hazard by the same proportional amount at all durations. Thus, for an individual $i$ at duration $d$, with an observed set of characteristics represented by a vector of covariates, $Z_i$, the hazard function, $\mu_i(d)$, is given by

$$\mu_i(d) = \exp[\lambda(d)]\exp[Z_i\beta] \qquad (12)$$

where $\beta$ is a vector of parameters and $\lambda(d)$ is the underlying duration pattern of risk. In this model, then, the underlying risk of dissolution for an individual $i$ with characteristics $Z_i$ is multiplied by a factor equal to $\exp[Z_i\beta]$.

We may also implement a more general set of models to test for departures from some of the restrictive assumptions built into the proportional hazards framework. More specifically, we allow for time-varying covariates (for instance, in this example, the occurrence of a first marital birth) as well as allow for the effects of individual characteristics to vary with duration of first marriage. This model may be written as

$$\mu_i(d) = \exp[\lambda(d)]\exp[Z_i(d)\beta(d)] \qquad (13)$$

where $\lambda(d)$ is defined as in the proportional hazards model, $Z_i(d)$ is the vector of covariates, some of which may be time-varying, and $\beta(d)$ represents a vector of parameters, some of which may give rise to nonproportional effects. The model parameters can be estimated using the method of maximum likelihood. The estimation procedure assumes that the hazard, $\mu_i(d)$, is constant within duration intervals. The interval width chosen by the analyst, of course, should be supported on both substantive and statistical grounds.

## INDIRECT DEMOGRAPHIC ESTIMATION

Unfortunately, many countries around the world have poor or nonexistent data pertaining to a wide array of demographic variables. In the industrialized nations, we typically have access to data from rigorous registration systems that collect data on mortality, marriage, fertility, and other demographic processes. However, when analyzing the demographic situation of less developed nations, we are often confronted with a paucity of available data on these fundamental processes. When such data are in fact collected, they are often sufficiently inadequate to be significantly misleading. For example, in some countries we have learned that as few as half of all actual deaths are recorded. If we mistakenly take the value of the actual number to be the registered number, then we will substantially overestimate life expectancy in these populations. In essence, we will incorrectly infer that people are dying at a slower rate than is truly the case.

## THE STABLE POPULATION MODEL

Much demographic estimation has relied on the notion of stability. A *stable population* is defined as one that is established by a long history of unchanging fertility and mortality patterns. This criterion gives rise to a fixed proportionate age distribution, constant birth and death rates, and a constant rate of population growth (see, e.g., Coale 1972). The basic stable population equation is:

$$c(a) = be^{-ra}p(a) \qquad (14)$$

where $c(a)$ is the proportion of the population exact age $a$, $b$ is the crude birth rate, $r$ is the rate of population growth, and $p(a)$ is the proportion of the population surviving to exact age $a$. Various mathematical relationships have been shown to obtain among the demographic variables in a stable population. This becomes clear when we multiply both sides of the equation by the total population size. Thus, we have:

$$N(a) = Be^{-ra}p(a) \qquad (15)$$

where $N(a)$ is the number of individuals in the population exact age $a$ and $B$ is the current annual number of births. We can see that the number of people aged $a$ this year is simply the product of the number of births entering the population $a$ years ago—namely, the current number of births times a growth rate factor, which discounts the births according to the constant population growth rate $r$ (which also applies to the growth of the number of births over time)—and the proportion of a birth cohort that survives to be aged $a$ today. Note that the constancy over time of the mortality schedule, $p(a)$, and the growth rate, $r$, are crucial to the validity of this interpretation.

When we assume a population is stable, we are imposing structure upon the demographic relationships existing therein. In a country whose data are inadequate, indirect methods allow us—by drawing upon the known structure implied by stability—to piece together sometimes inaccurate information and ultimately derive sensible estimates of the population parameters. The essential strategy in indirect demographic estimation is to infer a value or set of values for a variable whose elements are either unobserved or inaccurate from the relationship among the remaining variables in the above equation (or an equation deriving from the one above). We find that these techniques are robust with respect to moderate departures from stability, as in the case of quasi-stable populations, in which only fertility has been constant and mortality has been gradually changing.

## THE NONSTABLE POPULATION MODEL

Throughout much of the time during which indirect estimation has evolved, there have been many countries whose populations approximated stability. Recently, however, more and more countries have been experiencing rapidly declining mortality or declining or fluctuating fertility and, thus, have undergone a radical departure from stability. Consequently, previously successful indirect methods, grounded in stable population theory, are, with greater frequency, ill-suited to the task for which they were devised. As is often the case, necessity is the mother of invention, and so demographers have sought to adapt their methodology to the changing world.

In recent years, a methodology has been developed that can be applied to populations that

are far from stable (see, e.g., Bennett and Horiuchi 1981; Preston and Coale 1982). Indeed, it is no longer necessary to invoke the assumption of stability, if we rely upon the following equation:

$$c(a) = b \cdot \exp\left[ -\int_0^a r(x)dx \right] \cdot p(a) \qquad (16)$$

where $r(x)$ is the growth rate of the population at exact age $x$. This equation holds true for any closed population. The implied relationships among the age distribution of living persons and deaths, and rates of growth of different age groups, provide the basis for a wide range of indirect demographic methods that allow us to infer accurate estimates of basic demographic parameters that ultimately can be used to better inform policy on a variety of issues.

## MORTALITY MODELING

The field of demography has a long tradition of developing models that are based upon empirical regularities. Typically in demographic modeling, as in all kinds of modeling, we try to adhere to the principle of parsimony—that is, we want to be as efficient as possible with regard to the detail, and therefore the number of parameters, in a model.

Mortality schedules from around the world reveal that death rates follow a common pattern of relatively high rates of infant mortality, rates that decline through early childhood until they bottom out in the age range of five to fifteen or so, then rates that increase slowly through the young and middle adult years, and finally rising more rapidly during the older adult ages beyond the forties or fifties. Various mortality models exploit this regular pattern in the data. Countries differ with respect to the overall level of mortality, as reflected in the expectation of life at birth, and the precise relationship that exists among the different age components of the mortality curve.

Coale and Demeny (1983) examined 192 mortality schedules from different times and regions of the world and found that they could be categorized into four "families" of life tables. Although overall mortality levels might differ, within each family the relationships among the various age components of mortality were shown to be similar. For each family, Coale and Demeny constructed a "model life table" for females that was associated with each of twenty-five expectations of life at birth from twenty through eighty. A comparable set of tables was developed for males. In essence, a researcher can match bits of information that are known to be accurate in a population with the corresponding values in the model life tables and ultimately derive a detailed life table for the population under study. In less developed countries, model life tables are often used to estimate basic mortality parameters, such as $e_0$ or the crude death rate, from other mortality indicators that may be more easily observable.

Other mortality models have been developed, the most notable being that by Brass (1971). Brass noted that one mortality schedule could be related to another by means of a linear transformation of the logits of their respective survivorship probabilities (i.e., the vector of $l_x$ values, given a radix of one). Thus, one may generate a life table by applying the logit system to a "standard" or "reference" life table, given an appropriate pair of parameters that reflect (1) the overall level of mortality in the population under study and (2) the relationship between child and adult mortality.

## MARRIAGE, FERTILITY, AND MIGRATION MODELS

Coale (1971) observed that age distributions of first marriages are structurally similar in different populations. These distributions tend to be smooth, unimodal, and skewed to the right and to have a density close to zero below age fifteen and above age fifty. He also noted that the differences in age-at-marriage distributions across female populations are largely accounted for by differences in their means, standard deviations, and cumulative values at the older ages, for example, at age fifty. As a basis for the application of these observations, Coale constructed a standard schedule of age at first marriage using data from Sweden, covering the period 1865 through 1869.

The model that is applied to marriage data is represented by the following equation:

$$g(a) = \frac{E}{\sigma} 1.2813 \exp\left\{-1.145\left(\frac{a-\mu}{\sigma} + 0.805\right) - \exp\left[-1.896\left(\frac{a-\mu}{\sigma} + 0.805\right)\right]\right\} \tag{17}$$

where $g(a)$ is the proportion marrying at age $a$ in the observed population, and $\mu$, $\sigma$, and E are, respectively, the mean and the standard deviation of age at first marriage (for those who ever marry) and the proportion ever marrying.

The model can be extended to allow for covariate effects by stipulating a functional relationship between the parameters of the model distribution and a set of covariates. This may be specified as follows:

$$\mu_i = X_i'\alpha ,$$
$$\sigma_i = Y_i'\beta , \tag{18}$$
and
$$E_i = Z_i'\gamma ,$$

where $X_i$, $Y_i$, and $Z_i$ are the vector values of characteristics of an individual that determine, respectively, $\mu_i$, $\sigma_i$, and $E_i$, and $\alpha$, $\beta$, and $\gamma$ are the associated parameter vectors to be estimated.

Because the model is parametric, it can be applied to data referring to cohorts who have yet to complete their marriage experience. In this fashion, the model can be used for purposes of projection (see, e.g., Bloom and Bennett 1990). The model has also been found to replicate well the first birth experience of cohorts (see, e.g., Bloom 1982).

Coale and Trussell (1974), recognizing the empirical regularities that exist among age profiles of fertility across time and space and extending the work of Louis Henry, developed a set of model fertility schedules. Their model is based in part on a reference distribution of age-specific marital fertility rates that describes the pattern of fertility in a *natural fertility population*—that is, one that exhibits no sign of deliberate birth control that is "bound to the number of children already born and is modified when the number exceeds the maximum which the couple does not wish to exceed" (Henry 1961, p. 81). When fitted to an observed age pattern of fertility, the model's two parameters describe the overall level of marital fertility in the population and the degree to which their fertility pattern within marriage is affected by some means of control. Perhaps the greatest use of this model has been devoted to comparative analyses, which are facilitated by the two-parameter summary of any age pattern of fertility in question.

Although the application of indirect demographic estimation methods to migration analysis is not yet as mature as that to other demographic processes, strategies similar to those invoked by fertility and mortality researchers have been applied to the development of model migration schedules. Rogers and Castro (1981) found that similar age patterns of migration obtained among many different populations. They have summarized these regularities in a basic eleven-parameter model, and, using Brass and Coale logic, explore ways in which their model can be applied satisfactorily to data of imperfect quality.

The methods described above comprise only a small component of the methodological tools available to demographers and to social scientists in general. Some of these methods are more readily applicable than others to fields outside of demography. It is clear, for example, how we may take advantage of the concept of standardization in a variety of disciplines. So, too, may we apply life table analysis and nonstable population analysis to problems outside the demographic domain. Any analogue to birth and death processes can be investigated productively using these central methods. Even the fundamental concept underlying the above mortality, fertility, marriage, and migration models—that is, exploiting the power to be found in empirical regularities—can be applied fruitfully to other research endeavors.

(SEE ALSO: *Birth and Death Rates; Census; Demography; Segregation Indices, Standardization*)

### REFERENCES

Bennett, Neil G., Ann K. Blanc, and David E. Bloom 1988 "Commitment and the Modern Union: Assessing the Link between Premarital Cohabitation and Subsequent Marital Stability." *American Sociological Review* 53:127–138.

———, and Shiro Horiuchi 1981 "Estimating the Completeness of Death Registration in a Closed Population." *Population Index* 47:207–221.

Bloom, David E. 1982 "What's Happening to the Age at First Birth in the United States? A Study of Recent Cohorts." *Demography* 19:351–370.

———, and Neil G. Bennett 1990 "Modeling American Marriage Patterns." *Journal of the American Statistical Association* 85:1009–1017.

Brass, William 1971 "On the Scale of Mortality." In W. Brass, ed., *The Biological Aspects of Demography*. London: Taylor and Francis.

Coale, Ansley J. 1971 "Age Patterns of Marriage." *Population Studies* 25:193–214.

——— 1972 *The Growth and Structure of Human Populations.* Princeton, N.J.: Princeton University Press.

———, and Paul Demeny 1983 *Regional Model Life Tables and Stable Populations.* 2d ed. New York: Academic Press.

———, and James Trussell 1974 "Model Fertility Schedules: Variations in the Age Structure of Childbearing in Human Populations." *Population Index* 40:185–206.

Cox, D. R., and D. Oakes 1984 *Analysis of Survival Data.* London: Chapman and Hall.

Henry, Louis 1961 "Some Data on Natural Fertility." *Eugenics Quarterly* 8:81–91.

Menken, Jane, James Trussell, Debra Stempel, and Ozer Babakol 1981 "Proportional Hazards Life Table Models: An Illustrative Analysis of Sociodemographic Influences on Marriage Dissolution in the United States." *Demography* 18:181–200.

Preston, Samuel H., and Ansley J. Coale 1982 "Age Structure, Growth, Attrition, and Accession: A New Synthesis." *Population Index* 48:217–259.

Rogers, Andrei, and Luis J. Castro 1981 *Model Migration Schedules.* RR-81-30. Laxenburg, Austria: International Institute for Applied Systems Analysis.

NEIL G. BENNETT

**DEMOGRAPHIC TRANSITION** The human population has maintained its existence at a near equilibrium throughout most of history. This state of near population equilibrium, characterized by oscillation about a very gradual rate of natural increase, was maintained until approximately 10,000 years ago through various combinations of fertility and mortality patterns that yielded a near balance between high rates of birth and high rates of death. Eighteenth-century economist Thomas Malthus, in his *Essay on Population Growth* (1798), observed that population equilibrium could be maintained by either a balance between high rates of birth and death or a balance between low rates of birth and death, with the more desirable state of human existence being achieved by the latter. The demographic transition is the general process through which a population moves from a state of approximate population equilibrium maintained by high rates of birth and death to a state of approximate equilibrium maintained by low rates of birth and death.

According to the broad picture of demographic transition described by demographer Ansley Coale (1974), the process begins with a decline in the death rate introduced by advances in public health and nutrition (though the precedence and domination of either factor is observed to vary by historical and social context), followed at some interval by declines in the birth rate as perceptions change concerning the value of having children. In pre-transition populations the birth rate is constant but the death rate fluctuates, while after transition the death rate is constant but the birth rate fluctuates. A critical feature that distinguishes the population dynamics of post-transition societies from pre-transition societies is the greatly diminished role of mortality in determining the magnitude and direction of population growth.

Under a population equilibrium regime characterized by high rates of birth and high rates of death common to preindustrial societies, average life expectancy is quite short. Life expectancy in Europe prior to the European demographic transition is estimated by Coale (1986) to have ranged from twenty years to thirty-five years, although those surviving the first years of childhood could expect to live much longer than these average life expectancies. Under a population equilibrium regime characterized by low rates of birth and low rates of death that is a general feature of modern industrialized societies, life expectancy at birth is observed to fluctuate around seventy years for males and seventy-eight years for females. Among

contemporary national populations, the shortest life expectancies are observed to occur in underdeveloped countries characterized by preindustrial economies and infrastructures. These conditions are endemic, for example, in the sub-Saharan region of Africa, where United Nations estimates of life expectancy among males in several sub-Saharan Africa nations (Angola, Ethiopia, Nigeria, Somalia, Tanzania, and Uganda) range from a low of thirty-seven to a high of forty-nine years of age (United Nations, 1988).

In a population undergoing demographic transition, because death rates typically fall prior to birth rates, periods of phenomenal population growth occur in the early stages of transition. Population growth then moderates as birth rates also fall, ultimately returning to a zero or near zero growth rate as a balance between low rates of birth and low rates of death is achieved—thus completing the process of demographic transition. In the European experience of demographic transition the entire process generally occurred over a hundred-year period, although there were significant variations in the speed of the demographic transitions observed. The speed of demographic transition is generally spoken of as the lag time between the point at which a significant fall in the death rates of a given population is observed and the fall in birth rates follows. The length of "demographic lag" is related to a variety of cultural, sociological, and economic factors and is a key determinant of the population's final size. Typical of the European demographic transition is Sweden, which had a demographic lag of approximately fifty years between the fall in death rates and the beginning of the fall in birth rates. This lag resulted in the unprecedented population growth and outmigration of surplus population observed in the latter half of the nineteenth century. The overall goal of contemporary population control programs in developing nations undergoing demographic transition can be conceptualized as an effort to reduce the length and consequences of demographic lag.

Because birth and death rates have been observed to fall at different points in a demographic transition for different reasons, demographers do not view demographic transition as a single unified transition but a combination of two entirely different transitions: the mortality (or epidemiological) transition and the fertility transition. Although there seems to be limited evidence of a causal relationship between the mortality transition and the fertility transition, each transition has been observed to have a different causal structure and a varying degree of association with the other under different social contexts. For that reason, it is generally more useful to examine causal explanations of the mortality transition and the fertility transition of a given population separately prior to engaging in conjecture regarding the nature of the underlying association between the two transitions.

## MORTALITY OR EPIDEMIOLOGICAL TRANSITION

Unlike fertility transitions, there are sharp and consistent differences in causal structure and rate of speed between the mortality transitions observed in Europe beginning in the eighteenth century and the mortality transitions that were observed in contemporary lesser developed countries, particularly following World War II. Although there is some amount of dispute among demographers, historians, and others concerning the relative contribution of various factors, the European mortality transition was a gradual one associated with increased industrial and agricultural productivity; improvements in transportation infrastructure, which enabled more efficient food distribution; improvements in medical knowledge and applications in the form of public health measures; and improvements in sanitation and personal hygiene. Most of these advancements are associated with processes of modernization, industrialization, and raised standards of living. Samuel Preston (1975) has outlined several factors that separate the European mortality transition from the more recent mortality transitions that have occurred among the developing nations of Asia, Africa, and Latin America during the twentieth century, particularly over the last forty years. The key general factor relates to the role of industrialized nations in introducing medical technologies and public health strategies that have done much to control infectious diseases. This has enabled contemporary lesser developed countries to achieve substantial gains in life expectancy that are independent of attainments associated with modernization and economic development, most notably gains in per capita income and nutrition. The ability to achieve major gains in life expectancy based upon "imported" medical technology and public health strategies versus attainment of an improved standard of living is what Preston refers to as the exogenous nature of contemporary mortality transitions in lesser developed countries. Reductions in mortality achieved through exogenous factors are also more rapid and generally accessible to contemporary lesser developed countries than global long-term national development strategies. Even relatively weak national governments with limited resources can achieve significant mortality reductions through a range of comparably inexpensive activities like antimalarial campaigns, the training of public health personnel and the distribution of broad spectrum antibiotics. It is estimated by Preston (1975) that such "exogenous" strategies accounted for perhaps as much as 80 percent of gains in life expectancy among lesser developed countries during the thirty-year period between 1930 and 1960.

The speed with which the mortality transition was achieved among contemporary lesser developed countries (substantial gains in life expectancy often taking less than twenty years) has had a profound effect on the magnitude of the population growth that has occurred during the twentieth century. Sweden, used earlier as a model example of the nineteenth-century European demographic transition, peaked at a rate of natural increase of 1.2 percent, a rate of growth that more than doubled its population prior to the achievement of a state of population equilibrium. By comparison, the very rapid mortality declines among many contemporary lesser developed countries have promoted sustained population growth rates commonly exceeding 2 percent or more. Geoffrey McNicoll (1984) utilized United

Nations assumptions regarding the expected speed with which falls in fertility would catch up to contemporary falls in mortality to demonstrate that six- to tenfold increases in the populations of some lesser developed countries might be observed preceding the completion of demographic transition. The contributions of exogenous factors outside of economic development notwithstanding, achievement of "modern" levels of life expectancy comparable to completely industrialized nations still requires minimal levels of national infrastructure and improved standards of living, as well as some education of the population. Preston (1976) observed that among non-Western lesser developed countries, mortality from diarrheal diseases (e.g., cholera) has persisted despite control over other forms of infectious disease due to the close relationship between diarrheal diseases, poverty, and ignorance—and therefore a nation's level of socioeconomic development.

## FERTILITY TRANSITION

Ansley Coale (1973), in an attempt to reconcile the diversity of circumstances under which fertility declines have been observed to occur, identified three major conditions for a major fall in fertility:

1. Fertility must be within the calculus of conscious choice. Parents must consider it an acceptable mode of thought and form of behavior to balance the advantages and disadvantages of having another child.
2. Reduced fertility must be viewed as socially or economically advantageous to couples.
3. Effective techniques of birth control must be available. Procedures to prevent births must be known, and there must be sufficient communication between spouses and mutual sustained will to employ them successfully (Coale 1973).

Beyond the three conditions of major fertility decline identified by Coale as a useful framework for the formulation of theories of fertility decline, efforts over the last forty years by demographers, economists, historians, and others committed to the understanding of human population dynamics have not been successful in achieving consensus on a theory of fertility transition accepted as applicable to a variety of social contexts and suitable as a general model of prediction. Notwithstanding the lack of consensus achieved in the scientific community on any one theory of fertility transition, much of what is known about the process of fertility transition and the first widely accepted theory of fertility transition is based upon the European fertility transition that took place primarily during the twenty-year period between 1890 and 1910. The existence of historical records, the wide variety of social and economic contexts, and the ability to observe completed transitions all have persuaded demographers to use the European experience as a basis for the formulation of fertility transition theory and the development of methodological innovations applicable to the analysis of human fertility worldwide.

In that almost all births in nineteenth-century Europe occurred within marriage, the European model of fertility transition was defined to take place at the point marital fertility was observed to fall by more than 10 percent. Coale and his associates of the Princeton European Fertility Project established a 10 percent fall in marital fertility as the point at which fertility rates were observed to depart from historical fluctuations and embark on an irreversible long-term decline to near parity with mortality rates, thus completing the demographic transition process. Just as important, the scholars of the European Fertility Project identified the existence of varying levels of "natural fertility" (average reproduction in absence of deliberate parity-specific birth control) throughout Europe and European history. Comparative use of "natural fertility" models and measures derived from these models have been of enormous use to demographers in identifying the initiation and progress of fertility transitions in more contemporary contexts.

Theoretical efforts aimed to explain fertility transition preceded the methodological and empirical work of Coale and his associates by several years. Until the findings of the European Fertility Project became known, the most widely accepted view of the causes of fertility transition was the "classic theory" of demographic transition, reviewed by Susan Watkins (1986).

Classic demographic transition theory is the earliest form of a theoretical perspective demographers term "demand" theory. Generally, demand theories incorporate an explicit focus on the economic role of children as a motivation for fertility decisions. The classic description of the causal structure of demographic transition was based upon highly general observations of the European experience and was widely accepted as a universal theory of fertility transition until about the last fifteen years. The essential theme of the classic theory of demographic transition is that a sustained fall in birth rates is consequent to economic and social transformation broadly termed as modernization. As described by Watkins, the classic demographic transition explanation envisions fertility decline as sequential to an emerging urban existence whereby the family functions of production, consumption, recreation, and education are assumed by other social structures. In addition, processes of rationalism and secularism occur whereby traditional normative behavior exerts less influence due to the mobility and anonymity of urban life. Falling death rates both cause a temporary increase in the size of the family and reduce the "replacement" incentive to have many births. Finally, for women, new economic roles and relative freedom from household obligations introduce new conflicts with childbearing (Watkins 1986).

Although classic demographic transition theory has a certain elegance of intuitive appeal, the theory does not hold up well as an unqualified explanation against what has been learned in recent years about the European fertility transition and observations of fertility transition among contemporary developing countries. John Knodel and Etienne van de Walle (1986) have noted two key findings produced by scholars of the European Fertility Project that are at odds with the assumptions implied by classic demographic transition theory:

1. Fertility declines were observed to take place under a variety of social, economic, and demographic conditions.
2. The cultural setting appears to have influenced

the onset and spread of fertility declines independently of socioeconomic conditions.

Other findings from recent analysis of the European experience that undermine the viability of classic demographic transition theory as a complete explanation include the observation that in some instances, reductions in fertility preceded reductions in mortality, and that only weak and statistically nonsignificant relationships existed between fertility and infant mortality (John Cleland and Christopher Wilson 1987). Further, Cleland and Wilson join many demographers and economists in citing the lack of empirical evidence in support of the implicit assumption of classic demographic transition theory and some other "demand" theories that under agrarian labor-intensive economies, children provide a form of "net" productive return to parents. Another problem to classic demographic transition theory is raised by findings among contemporary developing countries indicating that substantial declines in fertility have occurred among countries with very limited socioeconomic advances (Freedman 1979).

Although there are other forms of "demand" theories of fertility decline that appear to have some amount of empirical support in contemporary contexts, at this point fertility transition theories that focus upon normative "innovation" as the critical process by which fertility declines occur are in ascendance among demographers. Essentially, innovation theories of fertility transition argue that the very concept of family limitation is alien to the thinking of pre-transition societies and the "idea" that fertility control is both possible and acceptable as an alternative form of behavior, once introduced, tends to diffuse in a pattern similar to other forms of cultural innovation. In addition to evidence from the European transition that falls in fertility occurred in culturally contiguous regions with vastly different levels of economic development, innovation theory is well supported by significant falls in fertility among contemporary developing countries in East Asia and Latin America that have experienced similar exposure to sociocultural transformation with minimal gains in economic development (Cleland and Wilson 1987).

As a general point in summary of fertility transition theory, it is probably most accurate to say that the evidence appears to support the view that cultural innovation does not replace economic development as a strongly determinant causal factor in fertility decline so much as it enables rapid transition under economically favorable conditions, and further, cultural innovation provides an alternative path through which fertility decline can occur in absence of significant economic development.

## REGIONAL VARIATION IN THE PROGRESS OF DEMOGRAPHIC TRANSITION AMONG DEVELOPING COUNTRIES

Data summarized by Peter Hess (1988) on the status of fertility decline among a sample of fifty-one developing countries, comparative estimates of natural increase and life expectancy provided by the United Nations (1988), and the observations of Coale (1983) on trends in fertility decline are useful as a basis for examining regional variations in the progress of demographic transition. As a general point of reference, nations with estimates of male life expectancy below fifty years of age and rates of natural increase exceeding 2 percent annually are in early or pre-demographic transition states, while nations with male life expectancies exceeding sixty years of age and rates of natural increase below 1.5 percent appear to be approaching the latter stages of demographic transition.

Leaders among developing countries in the process of demographic transition are found in East Asia and Latin America, as well as nations having small populations located elsewhere (Coale 1983). The clear leaders among Asian nations, such as Malaysia, South Korea, and Taiwan, generally have experienced both substantial economic growth and exposure to Western cultural influences. A notable exception is China, which cannot be said to have experienced either Westernization or more than moderate economic development,

with a male life expectancy estimated at sixty-seven years and a rate of natural increase of 1.2 percent (United Nations 1988). Latin American nations that have achieved substantial drops in fertility (exceeding 20 percent) in recent decades with life expectancies surpassing sixty years include Brazil, Chile, Columbia, the Dominican Republic, Jamaica, Mexico, Paraguay, and Venezuela. Transition has proceeded at a more moderate rate (10–20 percent decline in fertility) in much of the remainder of Asia and Latin America, including India, Pakistan, and a substantial part of Central America (Hess 1988; United Nations 1988).

In general, countries of the Middle East and regions of Northern Africa populated by Moslems have been slow to embark on the process of fertility transition. Although many have experienced substantial economic advances and have invited the benefits of Western medical technology in terms of mortality reduction, these countries retain high fertility due to the retention of religious and cultural underpinnings that work to diminish the social status of women and their role in fertility decisions, a factor believed to be strongly associated with fertility (Knodel and van de Walle 1986). As a consequence, developing countries like Algeria, Iran, Iraq, Jordan, Libya, and Morocco have extended the length of demographic lag and have rates of natural increase that range from 2.5 to 3.7 percent.

The region that encompasses countries having the highest rates of natural increase is sub-Saharan Africa. Rates of natural increase generally exceed 2.5 percent, with several countries having rates of natural increase substantially exceeding 3 percent (Kenya has a rate of natural increase estimated to exceed 4 percent). John Caldwell (1976), in a widely respected theory of demographic transition that incorporates elements of both cultural innovation and recognition of the role of children in traditional societies in maintaining net flows of wealth to parents, has speculated that substantial declines in fertility in sub-Saharan Africa are contingent upon a process of cultural transformation to the Western nuclear family model in supplanting the traditional extended kinship family model now predominant in the region.

Taking the long view, the outlook for a completed state of demographic transition for the world population as a whole generally appears positive if not inevitable, although demographers are deeply divided on estimates of the world population at equilibrium, the timing of completed transition, the principal mechanisms at work, and the long-term ecological consequences. Most if not all demographers, however, subscribe to the view expressed by Coale (1974, p. 51) that the entire process of global demographic transition and the phase of phenomenal population growth that has accompanied it will be a transitory (albeit spectacular) episode in human population history.

(SEE ALSO: *Demography; Human Ecology and the Environment; Population*)

### REFERENCES

Caldwell, John 1976 "Toward a Restatement of Demographic Transition Theory." *Population and Development Review* 2:321-366.

Cleland, John, and Christopher Wilson 1987 "Demand Theories of the Fertility Transition: An Iconoclastic View." *Population Studies* 41:5–30.

Coale, Ansley 1973 "The Demographic Transition." *International Population Conference, IUSSP.* Liège, Belgium.

——— 1974 "The History of Human Population." *Scientific American* 23 (3):41–51.

——— 1983 "Recent Trends in Fertility in Less Developed Countries." *Science* 221:828–832.

——— 1986 "The Decline of Fertility in Europe as a Chapter in Human Demographic History." In Ansley Coale and Susan Watkins, eds., *The Decline of Fertility in Europe.* Princeton, N.J.: Princeton University Press.

Freedman, Ronald 1979 "Theories of Fertility Decline: A Reappraisal." *Social Forces* 58:1–17.

Hess, Peter 1988 *Population Growth and Socioeconomic Progress in Less Developed Countries.* New York: Praeger.

Knodel, John, and Etienne van de Walle. 1986. "Lessons from the Past: Policy Implications of Historical Fertility Studies." In Ansley Coale and Susan Watkins, eds., *The Decline of Fertility in Europe.* Princeton, N.J.: Princeton University Press.

McNicoll, Geoffrey 1984 "Consequences of Rapid Population Growth: An Overview and Assessment." *Population and Development Review* 10:177–240.

Preston, Samuel 1975 "The Changing Relationship Between Mortality and Level of Economic Development." *Population Studies* 29:231–248.

——— ed. 1976 *Mortality Patterns in National Populations,* New York: Academic Press.

United Nations 1988 *1986 Demographic Yearbook.* New York: United Nations.

Watkins, Susan 1986 "Conclusions." In Ansley Coale and Susan Watkins, eds., *The Decline of Fertility in Europe.* Princeton, N.J.: Princeton University Press.

GUNNAR ALMGREN

# DEMOGRAPHY

Demography is the study of human populations. It is an important part of sociology and the other social sciences because all persisting social aggregates—societies, states, communities, racial or ethnic groups, professions, formal organizations, kinship groups, and so on—are also populations. The size of the population, its growth or decline, the location and spatial movement of its people, and their changing characteristics are important features of an aggregate without regard to whether one sees it as a culture, an economy, a polity, or a society. As a result some anthropologists, economists, historians, political scientists, and sociologists are also demographers, and most demographers are members of one of the traditional social science disciplines.

A central question for each of the social sciences is this: How does the community, society, or whatever, seen as a culture, an economy, a polity, or whatever, reproduce and renew itself over the years? Formal demography answers this question for aggregates seen as populations. This formal part of demography is fairly independent of the traditional social sciences and has a lengthy history in mathematics and statistics (Smith and Keyfitz 1977). It depends on a definition of age and on the relationship of age to fertility and mortality. Those relationships certainly are socially conditioned, but their major outlines are constrained by biology.

Beyond pursuing formal demography, the task of most social scientist-demographers is detailing the relationships between demographic change and other aspects of social change. Working with concepts, methods, and questions arising from the traditions of each of the social science disciplines as well as those of demography per se, scholars have investigated the relationship between demographic changes and such social changes as those in the nature of families (Davis 1985; Sweet and Bumpass 1987), levels of economic growth (Johnson and Lee 1987), the development of colonialism (McNeill 1990), changes in kinship structures (Dyke and Morrill 1980), and the development of the nation-state (Watkins 1991).

## FORMAL DEMOGRAPHY

At the heart of demography is a body of strong and useful mathematical theory about how populations renew themselves (Keyfitz 1968, 1985; Coale 1972). The theory envisions a succession of female birth cohorts living out their lives subject to a schedule of age-specific mortality chances and age-specific chances of having a female baby. In the simplest form of the model the age-specific rates are presumed constant from year to year.

Each new annual birth cohort is created because the age-specific fertility rates affect women in earlier birth cohorts who have come to a specific age in the year in question. Thus, the mothers of a new cohort of babies are spread among previous cohorts. The size of the new cohort is a weighted average of the age-specific fertility rates. The sizes of preceding cohorts, survived to the year in question, are the weights.

As a cohort of women age through their fertile period, they die and have children in successive years according to the age-specific rates appropriate to those years. Thus the children of a single birth cohort of women are spread over a sequence of succeeding birth cohorts.

The number of girls ever born to a birth cohort, taken as a ratio to the initial size of the cohort, is implicit in the age-specific fertility and mortality rates. This ratio, called the net reproduction rate, describes the growth rate over a

generation that is implicit in the age-specific rates. The length of this generation is also implicit in the age-specific rates as the average age of mothers at the birth of the second-generation daughters. With a rate of increase over a generation and a length of the generation, it is clear that an annual rate of increase is intrinsic to the age-specific rates.

The distribution of the children of a birth cohort over a series of succeeding cohorts has an important effect. If an unusually small or large birth cohort is created, the effects of its largeness or smallness will be distributed among a number of succeeding cohorts. In each of those succeeding cohorts, the effect of the unusual cohort is averaged with that of other birth cohorts to create the new cohort's size. Those new cohort's "inherited" smallness or largeness, now diminished by averaging, will also be spread over succeeding cohorts. In a few generations the smallness or largeness will have averaged out and no reflection of the initial disturbance will be apparent.

Thus, without regard to peculiarities in the initial age distribution, the eventual age distribution of a population experiencing fixed age-specific fertility and mortality will become proportionately constant. As this happens, the population will take on a fixed aggregate birth and death rate and, consequently, a fixed rate of increase. The population so created is called a stable population and its rates, called intrinsic rates, are those implicit in the net reproduction rate and the length of a generation. Such rates, as well as the net reproduction rates, are frequently calculated for the age-specific fertility and mortality rates occurring for a single year as a kind of descriptive, "what if" summary.

This theory is elaborated in a number of ways. In one variant, age-specific rates are not constant but change in a fixed way (Lopez 1961). In another elaboration the population is divided into a number of states with fixed age-specific migration or mobility among the states (Land and Rogers 1982; Schoen 1988). States may be geographic regions, marital circumstances, educational levels, or whatever.

In part, the value of this theory is in the light it

sheds on how populations work. For example, it explains how a population can outlive all of its contemporary members and yet retain its median age, percent in each race, and its regional distribution.

The fruit of the theory lies in its utility for estimation and forecasting. Using aspects of the theory, demographers are able to elaborate rather modest bits and pieces of information about a population to a fairly full description of its trajectory (Coale and Demeny 1983). Combined with this mathematical theory is a body of practical forecasting techniques, statistical estimation procedures, and data-collection wisdom that makes up a core area in demography which is sometimes called formal demography (United Nations 1983; Shryock and Siegel 1976; Pollard, Yusuf, and Pollard 1990).

## DEMOGRAPHIC DATA

Generating the various rates and probabilities used in formal demography requires two different kinds of data. On the one hand are data that count the number of events occurring in the population in a given period of time. How many births, deaths, marriages, divorces, and so on have occurred in the past year? These kinds of data are usually collected through a vital registration system (National Research Council 1981). On the other hand are data that count the number of persons in a given circumstance at a given time. How many never-married women age twenty to twenty-four were there on July 1? These kinds of data are usually collected through a population census or large-scale demographic survey (United Nations 1980; Anderson 1988). From a vital registration system one gets, for example, the number of births to black women age twenty. From a census one collects the number of black women at age twenty. The division of the number of events by the population exposed to the risk of having the event occur to them yields the demographic rate, that is, the fertility rate for black women age twenty. These two data collection systems—vital statistics and census—are remarkably different in their character. To be effective, a vital statistics

system must be ever alert to see that an event is recorded promptly and accurately. A census is more of an emergency. Most countries conduct a census every ten years, trying to enumerate all of the population in a brief time.

If a vital registration system had existed for a long time, were very accurate, and there were no uncounted migrations, one could use past births and deaths to tally up the current population by age. To the degree that such a tallying up does not match a census, one or more of the data collections systems is faulty.

## SOCIAL DEMOGRAPHY

One of the standard definitions of demography is that given by Hauser and Duncan: "Demography is the study of the size, territorial distribution and composition of populations, changes therein, and the components of such change, which may be identified as natality, mortality, territorial movement (migration) and social mobility (change of status)" (1959, p. 2). Each of these parts—size, territorial distribution, and composition—is a major arena in which the relationships between demographic change and social change are investigated by social scientist-demographers. Each part has a somewhat separate literature, tradition, method, and body of substantive theory.

*Population Size.* The issue of population size and change in size is dominated by the shadow of Thomas Malthus (Malthus 1959), who held that while food production can grow only arithmetically because of the limitation of land and other resources, population can grow geometrically and will do so, given the chance. Writing in a time of limited information about birth control and considerable disapproval of its use, and holding little hope that many people would abstain from sexual relations, Malthus believed that populations would naturally grow to the point at which starvation and other deprivations would curtail future expansion. At that point, the average level of living would be barely above the starvation level. Transitory improvements in the supply of food would only lead to increased births and subsequent deaths as the population returned to its equilibrium size. Any permanent improvement in food supplies due to technological advances would, in Malthus's theory, simply lead to a larger population surviving at the previous level of misery.

Although there is good evidence that Malthus understood his contemporary world quite well (Lee 1980), he missed the beginnings of the birth control movement, which were contemporaneous (McLaren 1978). The ability to limit births, albeit at some cost, without limiting sexual activity requires important modifications to the Malthusian model.

Questions of the relationship among population growth, economic growth, and resources persist into the contemporary period. The bulk of the literature is in economics. A good summary of that literature can be found in T. P. Schultz (1981) and in the National Research Council report on population policy (1985). A more polemical treatment, but one that may be more accessible to the noneconomist, is offered by the World Bank (1985).

Sharing the study of population size and its change with Malthusian issues is a body of substantive and empirical work on the demographic revolution or transition (Notestein 1945). The model for this transition is the course of fertility and mortality in Europe during the Industrial Revolution. The transition is thought to occur concurrently with "modernization" in many countries (Coale and Watkins 1986) and to be still in process in many less-developed parts of the world (United Nations 1990).

This transition is a change from (1) a condition of high and stable birthrates combined with high and fluctuating death rates, through (2) a period of initially lowering death rates and subsequently lowering birthrates, to (3) a period of low and fairly constant death rates combined with low and fluctuating birthrates. In the course of part (2) of this transition, the population grows very considerably because the rate of increase, absent migration, is the difference between the birthrate and the death rate.

In large measure because of anxiety that fertility might not fall rapidly enough in developing countries, a good deal of research has focused on the fertility part of the transition. One branch of this research has been a detailed historical investigation of what actually happened in Europe, since that is the base for the analogy about what is thought likely to happen elsewhere (Coale and Watkins 1986). A second branch was the World Fertility Survey, perhaps the largest international social science!research project ever undertaken. This project conducted carefully designed, comparable surveys with 341,300 women in 71 countries to investigate the circumstances of contemporary fertility decline (Cleland and Hobcraft 1985).

Scholars analyzing these two major projects come to a fairly similar assessment of the roots of historical and contemporary fertility decline as centering in an increased secular rationality and growing norms of individual responsibility.

*Territorial Distribution.* Research on the territorial distribution of populations is conducted in sociology, geography, and economics. The history of population distribution appears to be one of population dispersion at the macroscopic level of continents, nations, or regions, and one of population concentration in larger and larger towns and cities at the more microscopic level.

The diffusion of the human population over the globe, begun perhaps as the ice shields retreated in the late Pleistocene, continues to the present (Barraclough 1978). More newly inhabited continents fill up and less habitable land becomes occupied as technical and social change makes it possible to live in previously remote areas. Transportation lines, whether caravan, rail, or superhighway, extend across remote areas to connect distant population centers. Stops along the way become villages and towns specializing in servicing the travelers and the goods in transit. These places are no longer "remote." Exploitation of resources proximate to these places may now become viable because of the access to transportation as well as services newly available in the stopover towns.

As the increasing efficiency of agriculture has released larger and larger fractions of the population from the need to till the soil, it has become possible to sustain increasing numbers of urban people. There is a kind of urban transition more or less concomitant with the demographic transition during which a population's distribution by city size shifts to larger and larger sizes (Kelley and Williamson 1984; Wrigley 1987).

*Population Composition.* The characteristics included as compositional ones in demographic work are not predefined theoretically, with the exception, perhaps, of age and sex. In general, compositional characteristics are those characteristics inquired about on censuses, demographic surveys, and vital registration forms. Such items vary over time as social, economic, and political concerns change. Nonetheless, it is possible to classify most compositional items into one of three classes. First are those items which are close to the reproductive core of a society. They include age, sex, family relationships, and household living arrangements. The second group of items are those characteristics which identify the major, usually fairly endogamous, social groups in the population. They include race, ethnicity, religion, and language. Finally there is a set of socioeconomic characteristics such as education, occupation, industry, earnings, and labor force participation.

Within the first category of characteristics, contemporary research interest has focused on families and households because the period since 1970 has seen such dramatic changes in developed countries (Van de Kaa 1987; Davis 1985). Divorce, previously uncommon, has become a common event. Many couples now live together without record of a civil or religious ceremony having occurred. Generally these unions are not initially for the purposes of procreation, although children are sometimes born into them. Sometimes they appear to be trial marriages and are succeeded by legal marriages. A small but increasing fraction of women in the more developed countries seem to feel that a husband is not a necessary ornament to motherhood. Because of these changes, older models of how marriage comes about and how marriage relates to fertility (Coale

and McNeil 1972; Coale and Trussell 1974) are in need of review as demographers work toward a new demography of the family (Bongaarts 1983; Keyfitz 1987).

Those characteristics which indicate membership in one or another of the major social groupings within a population vary from place to place. Since such social groupings are the basis of inequality, political division, or cultural separation, their demography becomes of interest to social scientists and to policymakers. To the degree that endogamy holds, it is often useful to analyze a social group as a separate population, as is done for the black population in the United States (Farley 1970). Fertility and mortality rates, as well as marital and family arrangements, for blacks in the United States are different from those of the majority population. The relationship between these facts, their implications, and the socioeconomic discrimination and residential segregation experienced by this population is a matter of historic and continuing scholarly work (Farley and Allen 1987; Lieberson 1980).

For other groups, such as religious or ethnic groups in the United States, the issue of endogamy becomes central in assaying the continuing importance of the characteristic for the social life of the larger population (Johnson 1980). Unlike the black population, the ethnic and religious groups seem to be of decreasing appropriateness to analyze as separate populations within the United States, since membership may be a matter of changeable opinion.

The socioeconomic characteristics of a population are analyzed widely by sociologists, economists, and policy-oriented researchers. Other than being involved in the data production for much of this research, the uniquely demographic contributions come in two ways. First is the consideration of the relationship between demographic change and change in these characteristics. The relationships between female labor force participation and changing fertility patterns has been a main topic of the "new home economics" within economic demography (Becker 1960; T. W. Schultz 1974; T. P. Schultz 1981). The relationships between cohort size and earnings is a topic treated by both economists and sociologists (Winsborough 1975; Welch 1979). A system of relationships between cohort size, economic well-being, and fertility has been proposed by Easterlin (1980) in an effort to explain both fertility cycles and long swings in the business cycle.

A second uniquely demographic contribution to the study of socioeconomic characteristics appears to be the notion of a cohort moving through its socioeconomic life course (Duncan and Hodge 1963; Hauser and Featherman 1977; Mare 1980). The process of leaving school, getting a first job, then subsequent jobs, each of which yields income, was initially modeled as a sequence of recursive equations and subsequently in more detailed ways. Early in the history of this project it was pointed out that the process could be modeled as a multistate population (Matras 1967), but early data collected in the project did not lend itself to such modeling and the idea was not pursued.

## POPULATION POLICY

The consideration and analysis of various population policies is often seen as a part of demography. Population policy has two important parts. First is policy related to the population of one's own nation. The United Nations routinely conducts inquiries about the population policies of member nations (United Nations 1990). Most responding governments claim to have official positions about a number of demographic issues, and many have policies to deal with them. It is interesting to note that the odds that a developed country which states that its fertility is too low has a policy to raise the rate is about 7 to 1, while the odds that a less-developed country which states that its fertility is too high has a policy to lower the rate is about 4.6 to 1. The prospect of declining population in the United States has already begun to generate policy proposals (Teitelbaum and Winter 1985).

The second part of population policy is the policy a nation has about the population of other countries. For example, should a country insist on family-planning efforts in a developing country prior to providing economic aid? A selection of opinions and some recommendations are provided in Menken (1986) and in National Research Council (1985) for policy in the United States.

## DEMOGRAPHY AS A PROFESSION

Most demographers in the United States are trained in sociology. Many others have their highest degree in economics, history, or public health. A few are anthropologists, statisticians, or political scientists. Graduate training of demographers in the United States and in much of the rest of the world now occurs primarily in centers. Demography centers are often quasi-departmental organizations that serve the research and training needs of scholars in several departments. In the United States there are about twenty such centers, twelve of which have National Institutes of Health grants. The Ford Foundation has supported similar demography centers at universities in the less-developed parts of the world.

Today, then, most new demographers, without regard for their disciplinary leanings, are trained at a relatively few universities. Most will work as faculty or researchers within universities or at demography centers. Another main source of employment for demographers is government agencies. Census bureaus and vital statistics agencies both provide much of the raw material for demographic work and employ many demographers around the world. There is a small but rapidly growing demand for demographers in the private sector in marketing and strategic planning.

Support for research and training in demography began in the United States in the 1920s with the interest of the Rockefeller Foundation in issues related to population problems. Its support led to the first demography center, the Office of Population Research at Princeton University. The Population Council in New York was established as a separate foundation by the Rockefeller brothers in the 1930s. Substantial additional foundation support for the field has come from the Ford Foundation, the Scripps Foundation, and, more recently, the Hewlett Foundation. Demography was the first of the social sciences to be supported by the newly founded National Science Foundation in the immediate post-World War II era. In the mid 1960s the National Institute of Child Health and Human Development undertook support of demographic research.

(SEE ALSO: *Birth and Death Rates; Census; Demographic Methods; Demographic Transition; Life Expectancy; Population*)

## REFERENCES

Anderson, Margo 1988 *The American Census: A Social History.* New Haven: Yale University Press.

Barraclough, Geoffrey, ed. 1978 *The Times Atlas of World History.* London: Times Books.

Becker, G. S. 1960 "An Economic Analysis of Fertility." In Becker, *Demographic and Economic Change in Developed Countries.* Princeton, N.J.: National Bureau of Economic Research.

Bongaarts, John 1983 "The Formal Demography of Families and Households: An Overview." *IUSSP Newsletter* 17:27–42.

Cleland, John, and John Hobcraft 1985 *Reproductive Change in Developing Countries: Insights from the World Fertility Survey.* London: Oxford University Press.

Coale, Ansley 1972 *The Growth and Structure of Human Populations: A Mathematical Investigation.* Princeton, N.J.: Princeton University Press.

———, and Paul Demeny 1983 *Regional Model Life Tables and Stable Populations.* New York: Academic Press.

———, and D. R. McNeil 1972 "Distribution by Age of Frequency of First Marriage in a Female Cohort." *Journal of the American Statistical Association* 67:743–749.

———, and James Trussell 1974 "Model Fertility Schedules: Measurement and Use in Fertility Models." *Population Index* 40:182–258.

———, and Susan C. Watkins, eds. 1986 *The Decline of Fertility in Europe.* Princeton, N.J.: Princeton University Press.

Davis, Kingsley (ed.) 1985 *Contemporary Marriage.* New York: Russell Sage Foundation.

Duncan, O. D., and William Hodge 1963 "Education and Occupational Mobility." *American Journal of Sociology* 68:629–644.

Dyke, Bennett, and Warren Morrill (eds.) 1980 *Genealogical Demography.* New York: Academic Press.

Easterlin, Richard 1980 *Birth and Fortune: The Impact of Numbers on Personal Welfare.* New York: Basic Books.

Farley, Reynolds 1970 *Growth of the Black Population: A Study of Demographic Trends.* Chicago: Markham.

———, and Walter R. Allen 1987 *The Color Line and the Quality of Life in America.* New York: Russell Sage Foundation.

Hauser, Philip M., and Otis Dudley Duncan 1959 *The Study of Population: An Inventory and Appraisal.* Chicago: University of Chicago Press.

Hauser, Robert M., and David L. Featherman 1977 *The Process of Stratification: Trends and Analyses.* New York: Academic Press.

Johnson, D. Gale, and Ronald D. Lee (eds.) 1987 *Population Growth & Economic Development: Issues and Evidence.* Madison: University of Wisconsin Press.

Johnson, Robert A. 1980 *Religious Assortative Marriage in the United States.* New York: Academic Press.

Kelley, Allen, and Jeffrey Williamson 1984 "Modeling the Urban Transition." *Population and Development Review* 10:419–442.

Keyfitz, Nathan 1968 *Introduction to the Mathematics of Populations.* Reading, Mass.: Addison-Wesley.

——— 1985 *Applied Mathematical Demography.* New York: Springer-Verlag.

——— 1987 "Form and Substance in Family Demography." In J. Bongaarts, T. Burch, and K. Wachter, eds., *Family Demography.* New York: Oxford University Press.

Land, Kenneth C., and Andrei Rogers (eds.) 1982 *Multidimensional Mathematical Demography.* New York: Academic Press.

Lee, Ronald 1980 "An Historical Perspective on Economic Aspects of the Population Explosion: The Case of Preindustrial England." In Richard Easterlin, ed., *Population and Economic Change in Developing Countries.* Chicago: University of Chicago Press.

Lieberson, Stanley 1980 *A Piece of the Pie: Black and White Immigrants Since 1880.* Berkeley: University of California Press.

Lopez, A. 1961 *Some Problems in Stable Population Theory.* Princeton, N.J.: Office of Population Research.

Malthus, Thomas R. 1959 *Population: The First Essay.* Ann Arbor: University of Michigan Press.

Mare, Robert D. 1985 "Social Background and School Continuation Decisions." *Journal of the American Statistical Association* 75:295–305.

Matras, Judah 1967 "Social Mobility and Social Structure: Some Insights from the Linear Model." *American Sociological Review* 33:608–614.

McLaren, Angus 1978 *Birth Control in Nineteenth-Century England*. New York: Holmes & Meier.

McNeill, William H. 1990 *Population and Politics Since 1750*. Charlottesville: University of Virginia Press.

Menken, Jane (ed.) 1986 *World Population & U.S. Policy: The Choices Ahead*. New York: W. W. Norton.

National Research Council 1981 *Collecting Data for the Estimation of Fertility and Mortality*. Report no. 6, Committee on Population and Demography, Assembly of Behavioral and Social Sciences, National Research Council. Washington, D.C.: National Academy Press.

———— Working Group on Population Growth and Economic Development, Committee on Population, Commission on Behavioral and Social Sciences and Education 1985 *Population Growth and Economic Development: Policy Questions*. Washington, D.C.: National Academy Press.

Notestein, Frank W. 1945 "Population—The Long View." In Theodore W. Schultz, ed., *Food for the World*. Chicago: University of Chicago Press.

Pollard, A. H., Farhat Yusuf, and G. N. Pollard 1990 *Demographic Techniques*. Sydney: Pergamon Press.

Schoen, Robert 1988 *Modeling Multigroup Populations*. New York: Plenum Press.

Schultz, T. Paul 1981 *Economics of Population*. Reading, Mass.: Addison-Wesley.

Schultz, T. W. (ed.) 1974 *Economics of the Family*. Chicago: University of Chicago Press.

Shryock, Henry S., and Jacob S. Siegel 1976 *The Methods and Materials of Demography*. New York: Academic Press.

Smith, David P., and Nathan Keyfitz (eds.) 1977 *Mathematical Demography: Selected Essays*. Berlin and New York: Springer-Verlag.

Sweet, James A., and Larry L. Bumpass 1987 *American Families and Households*. New York: Russell Sage Foundation.

Teitelbaum M., and J. Winter 1985 *The Fear of Population Decline*. Orlando, Fla.: Academic Press.

United Nations 1980 *Principles and Recommendations for Population and Housing Censuses*. Statistical Papers, ser. M, no. 67, ST/ESA/STAT/SER.M/68.

United Nations, Department of International Economic and Social Affairs 1983 *Manual X: Indirect Techniques for Demographic Estimation*. Population Studies, no. 81, ST/ESA/SER.A/81.

———— 1990, *World Population at the Turn of the Century*. Population Studies no. 111, ST/ESA/SER.A/111.

Van de Kaa, Dirk 1987 "Europe's Second Demographic Transition." *Population Bulletin* 42:1.

Watkins, Susan C. 1991 *From Provinces into Nations: Demographic Integration in Western Europe, 1870–1960*. Princeton, N.J.: Princeton University Press.

Welch, F. 1979 "Effect of Cohort Size on Earnings: The Baby Boom Babies' Financial Bust." *Journal of Political Economy* 2:565–598.

Winsborough, H. 1975 "Age, Period, Cohort, and Education Effects of Earnings by Race—An Experiment with a Sequence of Cross-Sectional Surveys." In Kenneth Land and Seymour Spilerman, eds., *Social Indicator Models*. New York: Russell Sage Foundation.

World Bank 1985 *Population Change and Economic Development*. New York: Oxford University Press.

Wrigley, E. A. 1987 *People, Cities and Wealth: The Transformation of Traditional Society*. Oxford: Basil Blackwell.

HALLIMAN H. WINSBOROUGH

**DEPENDENCY THEORY** Dependency theory gained prominence in the 1960s as an attempt to analyze contemporary third world underdevelopment as a consequence of asymmetrical contacts with capitalist nations. The thesis is straightforward enough: Once the first wave of modernization occurs, subsequent changes in less-developed countries take place neither inexorably nor in isolation. Rather, these changes are shaped by the nature of a society's contacts with countries, economies, and ideologies that previously experienced social change. Furthermore, interaction between social orders is never a benign form of cultural diffusion. Interaction instead leads to internal reorganization designed to bolster the interests of the more powerful exchange partner without altering the worldwide distribution of affluence.

Widely employed as both a heuristic and empirical framework, dependency theory evolved from neo-Marxist critiques of the failure of significant capital infusion, through the United Nations Economic Commission for Latin America, to change overall quality of life dramatically or provide significant returns to the region. Dependency theory quickly became a vehicle for political commentary as well as an explanatory framework as it couched its arguments in terms of the consequences of substituting cash crops for subsistence farming and replacing local consumer goods with capital goods designed for export. Andre Gunder Frank (1967; 1969), an early proponent, asserts that contemporary underdevelopment is itself an outcome of the international division of labor controlled by capitalist countries. Many others who later refined the model have also argued this.

Frank's contribution was to incorporate the vantage point of those underdeveloped countries where capital infusion occurred into the discussion of the dynamics of economic, social, and political change. In so doing he discounted existing Western and European models of modernization as ethnocentric and apolitical. He asserted that modernization was most frequently conceived of independently of the colonialism that is characteristic of social change in the modern era. However much the first wave of modernization might have been driven by intrinsic, internal factors, all subsequent development has taken place in light of changes external to the individual country. Central to Frank's contention was a differentiation of undeveloped from underdeveloped countries. In the latter, a state of dependency exists as a result of a locality's colonial relationship with "advanced" areas. Frank referred to the "development of underdevelopment" and the domination of development efforts by advanced countries, using a "metropolis–satellite" analogy to denote the powerful center out of which innovations emerge and a dependent hinterland held in its sway. He spoke of the chain of exploitation— or the flow and appropriation of capital through successive metropolis–satellite relationships, each of which participates in the perpetuation of relative inequalities even while experiencing some enrichment. Galtung (1972) characterized this same relationship in terms of "core and periphery," each with something to offer the other, thereby fostering a symbiotic but lopsided relationship. The effect is an intersocietal hierarchy in which the dominant core grows and becomes more complex, while the satellite is subordinated through the transfer of economic surpluses to the core in spite of whatever absolute economic changes may be realized (Hechter 1975).

Dos Santos (1971) amplified Frank's attention to metropolis–satellite relationships. He maintained that what economic or social change does occur takes place for the benefit of the dominant core. This is not to say that the outlying areas are merely plundered or picked clean; to ensure their long-term usefulness, peripheral regions are allowed, indeed encouraged, to develop. Urbanization, industrialization, commercialization of agriculture, and more expedient social, legal, and political organization are all induced. In this way the core not only guarantees a stable supply of raw materials but a ready market for finished goods. With the bulk of economic surplus exported to the core, the less-developed region is unable to disseminate change or innovation across all realms. Dos Santos distinguished colonial, financial-industrial, and technological-industrial forms of dependencies. Moving from what is initially outright control and expropriation of valued resources by absentee decision makers (the colonial form), the financial-industrial form of dependency involves a locally productive economic sector characterized by widespread specialization and focus providing service primarily to the export sector that coexists alongside an indispensable subsistence sector. The latter provides labor and resources and reabsorbs surplus labor but benefits little from economic gains generated by the export sector. In effect two separate economies exist side by side.

In the third form, technological-industrial change takes place in developing regions but is always channeled and shaped by external interests. As the core expands its catchment area, it maximizes its ascendancy by promoting a dispersed, regionalized division of labor in order to maximize its own market potential. International market considerations effect the types of activities local export sectors are permitted to engage in by limiting the influx of capital for specified purposes only. One result is the development of a highly segmented labor market. The international division of labor is reflected in local implementation of capital-intensive technology, improvements in the infrastructure—transportation, public facilities, communications—and, ultimately, even social programming occurring principally in central enclaves or along supply corridors (Hoogvelt 1977; So 1990). Dos Santos maintained that the balance of payments is manipulated, ex parte, not only to bring about desired forms of change but to ensure the outflow of capital accumulation to such an extent that decapitalization of the periphery is inevitable. The price of local export products is established by international capital, which also sets purchase prices of those industrial-technological products essential to the infrastructure of development. While there may be a partial diffusion of technology, since growth in the periphery also enhances profits for the core, it is likely to create unequal pockets of surplus labor in secondary labor markets, thereby further impeding growth of internal markets as well as the quality of life of the general populace (Portes 1976).

Because international capital is able to dictate the terms of the exchange, local political processes have little choice but to comply. As Amin (1976) points out, nearly all development efforts are geared to enhancing productivity and value in the export sector, while relative disadvantages accrue to other sectors. Local and regional inequalities are thereby magnified as those facets of the economy in contact with international concerns become more capital intensive and increasingly affluent while other sectors languish as they shoulder transaction costs for the entire process. One consequence of the social relations of the new production arrangements standing side by side with traditional forms will be a highly visible appearance of obsolescence as status is conferred by and derived from a "narrow primary production structure" (Hoogvelt 1977, p. 96). Legitimation is thus granted to those deemed necessary to primary economic activities. In addition, the debt load remains high, so few opportunities for redistribution occur even if local decision makers were so inclined. Finally, since profit is exported along with products, capital accumulation is not at the source of production but at the core. Despite its variant guises, dependency theory provides global-orienting principles for analyses of international capitalism and its role in domestic development in third world countries.

Baran's (1957) analysis of the relationship between India and Great Britain is frequently cited as an early effort to examine the impact of colonialism. The imperialism of Great Britain was said to exploit India, fostering a one-sided extraction of raw materials and the imposition of impediments to industrialization, except insofar as they were beneficial to Great Britain. Precolonial India was thought to be a locus of other-worldly philosophies and self-supporting subsistence production. Postcolonial India came to be little more than a production satellite in which local elites relished their relative advantages as facilitators of British capitalism. In Baran's view, Indian politics, education, finance, and all other institutional arrangements were restructured to secure further gain to British enterprise. With independence, sweeping changes were undertaken, including many exclusionary practices, as countermeasures to the yoke of colonial rule.

Latin American concerns gave rise to the dependency model, and many of the *dependistas*, as they were originally known, have concentrated on regional case studies to outline the nature of contact with international capitalism. For the most part they have focused less on colonialism per se and more on Dos Santos's (1971) second and third types of dependency. Despite substantial natural resources, countries in the region found themselves burdened with inordinate trade deficits and international debt loads from which they might never emerge (Sweezy and Magdoff 1984). As a consequence, one debt restructuring followed another, in part to benefit recipients but also for the benefit of lenders, as interest payments were thereby continued or, in the worst-case scenarios, bad debts could be written down and tax obligations reduced. In many instances the World Bank and the International Monetary Fund exercised control and supervision, one consequence of this action being promotion of political regimes unlikely to challenge the principal of the loans (So 1990). Chile proved an exception, but one with disastrous and disruptive consequences. In all cases, to default would be to undermine those emoluments and privileges accorded local elites who were more likely to seek further, not fewer, contacts with external capital.

Dos Santos's third form of dependency has also been widely employed. Landsberg (1979) looked to Asia to find empirical support. Through an analysis of manufacturing relationships in Hong Kong, Singapore, Taiwan, and South Korea with the industrial West, he concluded that despite improvements in local circumstances, relative conditions remained unaffected due to the domination of manufacturing and industrial production by multinational corporations. These corporations moved production "off-shore," to Asia or other less-developed regions, in order to limit capitalization and labor costs while selling "on-shore," thereby maximizing profits. Landsberg asserts that because third world industrialization is shaped by external capitalists, it becomes so specialized as to have little recourse when international monopolistic practices become unbearable.

Few more eloquent defenders of the broad dependency perspective have emerged than Cardoso (1973; 1977). He labels his revision a *historical-structural model* to connote the manner in which local traditions, preexisting social patterns, and the time frame of contact serve to color the way in which generalized patterns of dependency are played out. He also coined the phrase *associated-dependent development* to describe the nurturing of some internal prosperity in order to enhance profit realization on investments (Cardoso 1973). He recognized that outright exploitation may generate immediate profit but can only lead to stagnation over the long run. Instead, foreign capital underwrites dynamic developments in those sectors likely to further exports but able also to absorb imports of consumer goods. In the process, internal inequalities are exacerbated in the face of wide-ranging economic dualities.

In his analysis of Brazil, Cardoso broadened the discussion to the political consequences of dependency by including shifts in institutional, ideological, and social parameters in the face of particular modes of foreign capital penetration.

His intent was not to imply that only a finite range of consequences occur but to suggest that local patterns of interaction, entitlements, domination, conflict, and so on have a reciprocal impact on the conditions of dependency. By looking at changes occurring under military rule in Brazil, Cardoso succeeded in demonstrating that foreign capital predominated in essential manufacturing and commercial arenas and that disparities increased as interests supportive of its role grew while the influence of the opposition declined. Wages and other labor-related costs did not keep pace with an expanding economy, thereby resulting in ever larger profit margins. As the military and the bourgeoisie served the interests of multinational corporations, they defined the interests of Brazil to be consonant with their own.

Yet, by the early 1980s the Brazilian economy had stagnated. Evans (1983) examined how what he termed the "triple alliance"—the state, private, and international capital interests—combined to alter the Brazilian economic picture drastically while managing to serve their own vested interests. In an effort to continue the uninterrupted export of profits, international capitalists permitted some local accumulation by a carefully circumscribed local elite, so that each shared in the largess of favorable political decisions and state-sponsored ventures. Still, incongruities abounded; per capita wages fell as GNP increased and consumer goods flourished as necessities became unattainable. At the same time, infant and female mortality remained high and few overall gains in life expectancy were observed. An exacerbation of local inequalities may have contributed to the downswing but so too did international financial shifts, which eventually dictated that the majority of new loans were to be dedicated to servicing old debts.

In the face of these shifts, foreign capital gained concessions, subsidies, and favored-nation accommodations. The contradictions proliferated. Unable to follow through on promises to local capital, the state had little choice but to rescind previous agreements, at the same time incurring the unintended consequence of reducing local market-absorption capabilities. Without new orders and in the face of loan payments, local capital grew disillusioned and moderated its support of state initiatives despite a coercive bureaucracy (O'Donnell, 1988). The value of Evans's work is that it highlights the entanglements imposed on local politics, policies and capitalists by a dependent-development agenda lacking any significant national autonomy. What became apparent was that the state itself legitimated its interests more in terms of multinational interests than in terms of local capital—and certainly more than in terms of local less-privileged groups seeking to leverage a redirection of government of expenditures in their direction. In their own examination of forty-five less-developed countries, Semyonov and Lewin-Epstein (1986) also assert that external influences shaped the growth of productive services most strongly but that internal processes remained capable of filtering the effect these changes have on other sectors.

In his analysis of Peru, Becker (1983) also contends that internal alignments created close allegiances based on mutual interests and that hegemonic control of the alliances in local decision making leads to a devaluing of those who either challenge business as usual or represent the old ways of doing things. Bornschier (1981) also maintains that internal inequalities increase and the rate of economic growth decreases in inverse proportion to the degree of dependency and in light of narrow sectoral targeting of foreign capital's development dollars. These and other researchers customarily assert that internal economic disparities grow unchecked and that tertiary-sector employment eventually becomes the predominant form (Bornschier 1981; Semyonov and Lewin-Epstein 1986; Delacroix and Ragin 1978; Chase-Dunn 1981).

In fact, nearly all advocates of the model contend that many facets of less-developed countries, from structure of the labor force to the form and types of services provided and the role of the state in public welfare programs, are products of the penetration of external capital and the nature of activities in the export sector of the economy (Cardoso 1973; Evans 1979). As capital-intensive production increases, surplus labor is relegated back to agrarian pursuits or to other tertiary employment. It also creates a personal services industry in which marginal employees provide service to local elites but whose own well-being rises or falls with the economic well-being of the elites. Distributional distortions, as embodied by state-sponsored social policies, are also thought to reflect the presence of external capitalism (Kohli, et al. 1984; Clark and Fillinson 1991). Evans is emphatic: the relationship of dependency and internal inequality "is one of the most robust, quantitative, aggregate findings available" (1979, p. 532).

Not everyone is convinced. As investigations of dependency theory proliferated, many investigators failed to find significant effects that could be predicted by the model (Dolan and Tomlin 1980). In fact, Gereffi's (1979) review of quantitative studies of third world development led him to claim that at the time of his review there was little to support the belief that investment of foreign capital had any discernable effect on long-term economic growth. Other critics have said dependency theory is flawed and unable to withstand empirical scrutiny (Becker 1983). Some have even suggested that only about one-third of the variance in inequality among nations is accounted for by penetration of multinational corporations or other forms of foreign investment (Kohli et al. 1984; Bornschier, Chase-Dunn, and Rubinson 1978).

Defenders respond by challenging the measures of operationalization, the way variables are defined, and whether the complex of concepts embraced by the multidimensionality of the notion of dependency can be measured in customary ways or in the absence of a comparative framework juxtaposing third world nations with their industrial counterparts (Ragin 1983; Rubinson and Holtzman 1982). Efforts to isolate commodity concentration and multinational corporate investments have not proven to be reliable indicators, and even use of per capita GNP has its detractors. While important questions on heterogeneity, dispersion, or heteroskedasticity can be addressed by slope differences and recognized estimation techniques (Delacroix and Ragin 1978), proponents of the model are adamant that contextualized historical analysis is not only most appropriate but mandated by the logic of dependency itself (Bach 1977).

Proponents have also turned to sophisticated statistical procedures to elucidate their claims. Rubinson (1976) utilized advanced analytic techniques to examine whether income inequality within countries is related to status in the world economy. His results discerned both the existence of a world economy and its effect on the organization of governmental bureaucracies and a country's internal structural differentiation. London and Robinson (1989) join in asserting that the extent of multinational corporate penetration, and indirectly the latter's effect on income inequality, are associated with incidences of political malaise. Walton and Ragin (1990) concur, maintaining through analyses that the involvement of international interests in domestic political-economic policy combines with the types of "overurbanization" linked to associated dependency and leads to political protest. Boswell and Dixon (1990) carried the analysis a step further. Using regression and path analysis, they examined both economic and military dependency, concluding in the process that both forms contribute to political instability through their effects on domestic class and state structure. They assert that corporate penetration impedes real growth while exacerbating inequalities and the type of class polarization leading to political violence. Interestingly, others (e.g., Bollen 1983) have come to the opposite conclusion, that economic development has significant positive effects on political democracy.

Alternative interpretations of underdevelopment began to gain strength in the early 1970s. The next step was a world systems perspective, which saw a global unity and a division of labor with corresponding political alignments. Wallerstein (1974), Chirot and Hall (1982), and others shifted the focus from spatial definitions of nation-states as the unit of analysis to corporate actors as the most significant players able to shape activities—including the export of capital—according to their own interests. Wallerstein suggested that the most powerful countries of the world constitute a de facto collective core that disperses productive activities so that dependent industrialization is an extension of what had previously been geographically localized divisions of labor. World systems analysts see multinational corporations rather than nation-states as the means by which articulation of global economic arrangements is maintained. So powerful have multinationals become that even the costs of corporate organization are borne by those countries in which the corporations do business, and the costs are calculated according to terms dictated by the multinational corporations. Yet state participation is undeniably necessary as a subsidization of multinational corporate interests and as a means for providing local management that, in addition to facilitating political compliance and other functions, promotes capital concentration for more efficient marketing and the maintenance of demand for existing goods and services. Thus, production, consumption, and political ideologies are transplanted on a global scale, are legitimated, and bring forth a thoroughgoing stratification that, while it cuts across national boundaries, always appears at the local level.

Whatever its shortcomings, dependency theory and its collateral notions have become dispositional concepts utilized by numerous investigations of the effect of dependent development on various dimensions of inequality. Using a liberal interpretation of the model, many investigators have sought to understand how values, types of rationality, definitions of efficiency, and so on influence evaluations of those who do not share those values, views, or competencies. The social organization of the marketplace is thus thought to exert suzerainty over other forms of social relationships (Zeitlin 1972; Hechter 1975). By substituting a figurative, symbolic relationship for a spatial definition, a generalized dependency model evolved through ideas of internal colonialism and has been widely employed as an explanatory framework wherein social and psychological distance from the center of power is seen as a factor in shaping well-being and other aspects of the quality of life.

Gamson's (1968) concept of "stable unrepresentation" is useful for understanding how the politics of inequality are perpetuated by either real or emblematic cores. Internal colonialism and political economic variants have been widely adopted in the analysis of many types of social problems. Blauner's (1970) analysis of American racial problems is illustrative of one such application. So too is Marshall's (1985) analysis of patterns of industrialization, investment debt, and export dependency and their effects on the status of women in sixty less-developed countries. While she was unable to draw firm conclusions relative to the dependency model per se, she does suggest that, with thoughtful specification, gender patterns in employment and education may well yield to dependency-based analyses. Townsend (1981), in a manner similar to Blauner, spoke of "the structured dependency of the elderly" in advanced industrial societies. Hendricks (1982), Neysmith and Edwardth (1984), and others have advocated use of dependency-driven approaches to examine the status of the elderly in the third world and in industrialized societies. Such a perspective casts the situation of the elderly as a consequence of shifts in economic relationships and state policies designed to provide for their needs. In her exposition of the shifting views of dependent populations, Neysmith (1991) maintains that as debts are refinanced in the service of maintenance of investment capital from abroad, domestic policies are rewritten in such a way as to disenfranchise vulnerable populations within those countries. To support her point, Neysmith cites a United Nations finding that human development programs tend to benefit males, households in urban areas, and middle or higher income people, while relatively less is targeted at women, rural residents, or low income persons (United Nations Department of International Economic and Social Affairs 1988).

Variation in the life experiences of subpopulations is one of the enduring themes of sociology. Despite wide disparities, a central focus has been the interconnections of societal arrangements and of political, economic, and individual circumstances. It is through these avenues that assumptions of reciprocity and distributive justice are

shared. As contexts change, so too will norms of what is appropriate. The linkages between political and moral economies is nowhere more apparent than in dependency theory as it facilitates our understanding of the dynamic relationships of individual and structure.

(SEE ALSO: *Global Systems Analysis; Industrialization in Less Developed Countries*)

## REFERENCES

Amin, Samir 1976 *Unequal Development: An Essay on the Social Formation of Peripheral Capitalism.* New York: Monthly Review Press.

Bach, Robert 1977 "Methods of Analysis in the Study of the World Economy: A Comment on Rubinson." *American Sociological Review* 42:811–814.

Baran, Paul 1957 *The Political Economy of Growth.* New York: Monthly Review Press.

Becker, David G. 1983 *The New Bourgeoisie and the Limits of Dependency: Mining, Class, and Power in "Revolutionary" Peru.* Princeton: Princeton University Press.

Blauner, Robert 1970 "Internal Colonialism and Ghetto Revolt." In J. H. Skolnick and E. Currie, eds., *Crisis in American Institutions.* Boston: Little, Brown.

Bollen, Kenneth 1983 "World System Position, Dependency, and Democracy: The Cross-National Evidence." *American Sociological Review* 48:468–479.

Bornschier, Volker 1981 "Dependent Industrialization in the World Economy." *Journal of Conflict Resolution* 25:371–400.

———, C. Chase-Dunn, and R. Rubinson 1978 "Cross-National Evidence of the Effects of Foreign Investment: A Study of Findings and Analysis." *American Journal of Sociology* 84:651–683.

Boswell, Terry, and William J. Dixon 1990 "Dependency and Rebellion: A Cross-National Analysis." *American Sociological Review* 55:540–559.

Cardoso, Fernando H. 1973 "Associated-Dependent Development: Theoretical and Practical Implications." In Alfred Stephen, ed., *Authoritarian Brazil.* New Haven: Yale University Press.

——— 1977 "The Consumption of Dependency Theory in the United States." *Latin American Research Review* 12:7–24.

Chase-Dunn, Christopher 1981 "Instate System and Capitalist World-Economy: One Logic or Two?" *International Studies Quarterly* 25:19–42.

Chirot, Daniel, and Thomas D. Hall 1982 "World

System Theory." *Annual Review of Sociology* 8:81–106.

Clark, Roger, and Rachel Filinson 1991 "Multinational Corporate Penetration, Industrialism, Region, and Social Security Expenditures: A Cross-National Analysis." *International Journal of Aging and Human Development* 32:143–159.

Delacroix, Jacques, and Charles Ragin 1978 "Modernizing Institutions, Mobilization, and Third World Development." *American Journal of Sociology* 84:123–149.

Dolan, M., and B. W. Tomlin 1980 "First World–Third World Linkages: The Effects of External Relations upon Economic Growth, Imbalance, and Inequality in Developing Countries." *International Organization* 34:41–63.

Dos Santos, Theotonio 1971 "The Structure of Dependence." In K. T. Kan and Donald C. Hodges, eds., *Readings in U.S. Imperialism.* Boston: Expanding Horizons.

Evans, Peter 1979 *Dependent Development: The Alliance of Multinational State and Local Capital in Brazil.* Princeton: Princeton University Press.

Frank, Andre Gunder 1967 *Capitalism and Underdevelopment in Latin America.* New York: Monthly Review Press.

——— 1969 *Latin America: Underdevelopment or Revolution.* New York: Monthly Review Press.

Galtung, Johan 1972 "A Structural Theory of Imperialism." *African Review* 1:93–138.

Gamson, William A. 1968 "Stable Unrepresentation in American Society." *American Behavioral Scientist* 12:15–21.

Gereffi, Gary 1979 "A Critical Evaluation of Quantitative, Cross-National Studies of Dependency." Paper presented to International Studies Association Annual Meeting. Toronto, March 1979.

Hechter, Michael 1975 *Internal Colonialism: The Celtic Fringe in British National Development, 1536–1966.* Berkeley: University of California Press.

Hendricks, Jon 1982 "The Elderly in Society: Beyond Modernization." *Social Science History* 6:321–345.

Hoogvelt, A. M. M. 1977 *The Sociology of Developing Societies.* Atlantic Heights, N.J.: Humanities Press.

Kohli, Atul, M. F. Altfeld, S. Lotfian, and R. Mardon 1984 "Inequality in the Third World." *Comparative Political Studies* 17:283–318.

Landsberg, Martin 1979 "Export-Led Industrialization in the Third World: Manufacturing Imperialism." *Review of Radical Political Economics* 11:50–63.

London, Bruce, and Thomas D. Robinson 1989 "The Effects of International Dependence on Income Inequality and Political Violence." *American Sociological Review* 54:305–308.

Marshall, Susan E. 1985 "Development, Dependence, and Gender Inequality in the Third World." *International Studies Quarterly* 29:217–240.

Neysmith, Sheila M. 1991 "Dependency among Third World Elderly: A Need for New Direction in the Nineties." In M. Minkler and C. L. Estes, eds., *Critical Perspectives on Aging: The Political and Moral Economy of Growing Old.* Amityville, N.Y.: Baywood Publishing.

———, and Joey Edwardth 1984 "Economic Dependency in the 1980s: Its Impact on Third World Elderly." *Ageing and Society* 5:21–44.

O'Donnell, Guillermo 1988 *Bureaucratic Authoritarianism: Argentina, 1966–1973, in Comparative Perspective.* Berkeley: University of California Press.

Portes, A. 1976 "On the Sociology of National Development: Theories and Issues." *American Journal of Sociology* 29:339–357.

Ragin, Charles 1983 "Theory and Method in the Study of Dependency and International Inequality." *International Journal of Comparative Sociology* 24:121–136.

Rubinson, Richard 1976 "The World-Economy and the Distribution of Income within States: A Cross-National Study." *American Sociological Review* 41:638–659.

———, and Deborah Holtzman 1982 "Comparative Dependence and Economic Development." *International Journal of Comparative Sociology.* 22:86–101.

Semyonov, Moshe, and Noah Lewin-Epstein 1986 "Economic Development, Investment Dependence, and the Rise of Services in Less Developed Nations." *Social Forces* 64:582–598.

So, Alvin Y. 1990 *Social Change and Development: Modernization, Dependency, and World-System Theories.* Newbury Park, Calif.: Sage.

Sweezy, Paul, and Harry Magdoff 1984 "The Two Faces of Third World Debt: A Fragile Financial Environment and Debt Enslavement." *Monthly Review* 35:1–10.

Townsend, Peter 1981 "The Structured Dependency of the Elderly." *Ageing and Society* 1:5–28.

United Nations Department of International Economic and Social Affairs 1988 *Human Resources Development: A Neglected Dimension of Development Strategy.* New York: United Nations.

Wallerstein, Immanuel 1974 "The Rise and Future Demise of the World Capitalist System: Concepts for

Comparative Analysis." *Comparative Studies in Society and History* 16:387–415.

Walton, John, and Charles Ragin 1990 "Global and National Sources of Political Protest: Third World Responses to the Debt Crisis." *American Sociological Review* 55:876–890.

Zeitlin, I. M. 1972 *Capitalism and Imperialism.* Chicago: Markham.

JON HENDRICKS

## DESCRIPTIVE STATISTICS

The term *descriptive statistics* has generally referred to summary information or characteristics drawn from data collected about groups or populations. Descriptive statistics are usually thought of in contrast to *statistical inference* procedures, the latter being designed to infer from sample characteristics what the characteristics (parameters) are in a real or theoretical population. At least since the early nineteenth century, books labeled "Social Statistics" presented summary information, usually demographic statistics based on enumeration and registration data. Thus, size of population and birth, death, and marriage statistics might be reported, but also other statistics, such as amounts of agricultural products, acres planted, production of manufactured goods, exports, and imports. Emphasis might be on comparison of regions and cities within a nation, and often the summary information would emphasize repeated data collections, such as censuses, providing opportunities for observations of trends.

With the emphasis on counts, summary statistics that were simple to compute and report were rates. Births might be reported as raw counts and then converted to rates to make comparisons understandable. The number of births could be converted to rates based on the total population of the geographical unit being considered, or on the total number of women, or on the total number of women of childbearing ages, or on some other basis. The use of ratios and proportions was also common, such as the proportion of the population that was male, the proportion of the population that was over the age of twenty-one, the ratio of males to females at birth, and so

forth. The point is that a summary piece of information was provided that could be important and useful in describing a city, region, nation, or other entity.

Descriptive statistics may be any summary characteristics based on the data that are available, which may be in the form of numerical values or of counts. Data may be collected as numerical values, such as the ages of persons, which in theory can take all possible values within the viable range (a continuous distribution) or as numerical values representing counts (discrete values). The most simple and direct summary characteristics are the measures of central tendency. The more common measures of central tendency are part of the ordinary language, such as the arithmetic mean or average, the median, and the mode.

The arithmetic mean or average is computed by taking the sum of the values and dividing by the number of values, and as such represents the balance point for the distribution of values. Since the arithmetic mean represents the balance point, extreme values on one end of the distribution may not provide the kind of information on central tendency that is actually required using that indicator. For example, the average for the values 99, 100, and 101 is 100, which intuitively appears to represent a central tendency. However, the average for 0, 0, and 300 is also 100, and this value is not close to either the low values or the high value. There are other types of averages in addition to the arithmetic average or mean, such as the geometric mean, but they rarely are used as descriptive statistics.

The median is the value associated with the middle position in a distribution of values, and in general when the median is sought, there is an implication that the distribution of the values is ordered. Thus, for a set of values such as 1, 2, 3, 4, and 5, the median is 3. The median also has possible limitations in use, since the median may also not provide the information on central tendency that is required. For example, the median of the set of values 50, 51, and 1,000,000 is the same as the median for the very different set of values of 1, 51, 52.

The mode is the value that occurs with the greatest frequency in a distribution. Thus, in the set of values of 1, 2, 2, 3, 3, 3, 4, 4, 5, the value 3 is the mode. However, again, a distribution such as 1, 2, 3, 4, 5, 5, 5 has 5 as the mode, but the distributions represented have quite different shapes.

The distribution of values, thus, may be important to summarize information. Distributions can be arranged by ordering categories, such as a set of categories including values from 0 to 9, 11 to 19, and 20 to 29. However, distributions may also be of other quite different types. So, for example, they may involve allocation of observed entities to geographical or other kinds of categories that are not ordered. It is common for the categorical variables to be described as qualitative. Categorical variables may overlap in definitions, but most often the categories are mutually exclusive and exhaustive, for example, the states.

For ordered categories there is often a notion that the distributions have particular shapes or curves. For example, the distribution may have a symmetric shape, or it can be skewed in one direction or the other. The curve may be one with a high peak, or it may appear to be rather shallow. It may have one peak, or it may have two (bimodal) or more peaks. It may not have a peak in the usual sense, but may have a "J" or other shape. In any event, the categories and the shapes of the distribution of the observed entities in the categories obviously reveal detailed summary information.

Some of the information about distributions may be summarized by measures of dispersion, the simplest of which is the range. The range usually is defined directly from the lowest value to the highest value, for example, from 1 to 100, or as the difference between the highest and the lowest value plus 1, to include the lowest and the highest values. There are variations on the definitions of the range, however, because it also may provide information that is not exactly what is sought. For example, if there is a very extreme value, the range may give the impression of much more dispersion than "effectively" exists. One way to define the "effective" range includes omitting a set number of the lowest and highest values, or a percentage of the lowest and the highest values. The range including the center 90 percent of cases (omitting the lowest and highest 5 percent) may be used to describe the distribution.

The median has been noted above as a measure of central tendency, and it is located as the value associated with the middle position in the distribution. It is possible to divide the distribution in additional ways, such as with two divisions creating thirds, three divisions creating quartiles, four divisions creating quintiles, and so forth. Common to this approach is the use of nine divisions to create deciles and ninety-nine divisions to create percentiles.

Descriptive statistics can be presented in various forms. There is no reason why they cannot be reported as part of a narrative presentation. However, in order to condense and provide summary information in detail, descriptive statistics are frequently presented in tables or in charts and graphs. The variety of methods of presentation is limited only by the ingenuity of the reporter, but clearly some methods are more common than others. Charts are frequently used to present time trend statistics, because it is easy to understand a time trend line, especially if it has a clear pattern. Similarly, bar charts or histograms are used to compare summary statistics for time periods or categories of various types. These types of presentations are common in all forms of reporting, and are ubiquitous in newspapers and magazines.

Even though descriptive statistics tend to use relatively simple summary procedures, they may be quite complex, describing the relationship among variables, causal relationships, and so forth. When information is being gathered for an entire population, only small quantities of information can be collected. For this reason, great emphasis is placed on statistical inference procedures where complex research and analytic questions are examined based on samples, from which inferences within bounds are made to the relevant population. There is a caveat, however, that must be remembered even when dealing directly with a presumed population: Because of fallible procedures or limitations in design, it is rarely possible to have direct access to populations in the broad sense. The Census of the United States does not represent the population of the United States at a given point in time. It is not collected at a single point in time, but during a period in which persons are born, die, and move. Not all persons are included in the census, the errors being introduced for many different reasons, and some of the errors may involve serious biases (e.g., young black males are difficult to locate and may be disproportionately underenumerated.)

The utility of descriptive statistics is not diminished as more sophisticated procedures for statistical inference continue to be developed. The same procedures that are used to describe samples may be used to describe populations, and the breadth of these procedures should be reviewed by referring to central sociological texts in sociology (Knoke and Bohrnstedt 1991; Blalock 1979; Mueller, Schuessler, and Costner 1977).

(SEE ALSO: *Measurement; Statistical Graphics; Statistical Inference*)

### REFERENCES

Blalock, Hubert M. 1979 *Social Statistics,* 2nd ed. New York: McGraw-Hill.

Knoke, David, and George W. Bohrnstedt 1991 *Basic Social Statistics.* Itasca, Ill.: F. E. Peacock Publishers.

Mueller, John H., Karl F. Schuessler, and Herbert L. Costner 1977 *Statistical Reasoning in Sociology.* Boston: Houghton Mifflin.

EDGAR F. BORGATTA

**DESEGREGATION**  *See* Segregation and Desegregation.

**DEVIANCE**  The word *deviance*—today a familiar member of both professional and lay vocabularies—entered the English language only in the early 1940s in *Webster's Ninth Collegiate Dictionary*, quite possibly as an invention of sociologists. What is now known as the study of deviance, a vibrant branch of sociology that attracts large numbers of students and researchers, dates from that period. The background to this linguistic addition reveals much about the modern study of deviant behavior.

There has always been a need in sociology to distinguish crime from the deviance that runs counter to local moral norms but that is not virtually or actually a violation of criminal law. Depending on the community, noncriminal deviance may consist of, among other acts, nudism, homosexuality, mental disorder, religious aberration, living on skid row, certain political belief systems, excessive gambling and consumption of alcohol, and certain sexual and drug use patterns. Where they are not considered criminal or otherwise a significant threat, these acts have in common their tolerance by much of the local population. When they are ostensibly illegal, tolerance is evident in the systematic failure to apply the law, because it is vague, difficult to enforce, or of low police priority (Stebbins 1988, pp. 3–4).

From approximately 1880 to 1940, sociologists held a patently moralistic view of deviance, both criminal and noncriminal, referring to it in such loaded terms as "social pathology," "antisociality," and "social problems" (Lemert 1951, p. 3; Giddings 1896, p. 72). In the 1930s, during the rise of so-called scientific sociology and its value-neutrality, sustaining a censorious outlook on tolerable, noncriminal deviance became increasingly untenable. It is likely, too, that the range of tolerated acts and beliefs had expanded as a result of urbanization (Karp et al. 1977, chap. 5).

Whether by design or by accident, scientific language in the area began to change, moving first to the cold, unemotional notion of statistical deviation from the average. Robert K. Merton (1938), in what is possibly the first exposition of modern deviance theory, discussed "deviate conduct," "deviate behavior," and "deviation from normal behavior." Shortly thereafter, Merl E. Bonney (1941) described and analyzed a variety of "social deviates."

By the end of the 1940s, the statistical model had lost its appeal. Merton (1949), as part of the first revision of his 1938 statement, replaced the earlier terminology with "deviant" and "deviant behavior." Two years later, Edwin M. Lemert (1951) had partially made the same transition, writing both about deviation and about deviants and deviant behavior.

Why this second change? One can only speculate, but it is possible that Merton sensed the inherent inadequacy of the statistical model: Most deviance, whether criminal or noncriminal, is categorical rather than continuous—that is, for sociologists and the lay public alike, being deviant is a matter of identity, of being or not being homeless, alcoholic, mentally disordered, or politically radical. The statistical model assumes a continuum, as found in the measurement of intelligence or eyesight. At any rate, by the early 1950s sociology had arrived at a valid, nonjudgmental conception of what was once known as antisociality or social pathology. The modern speciality of the sociology of deviance had been launched.

## ANOMIE AND LABELING

Although they had important precursors, Merton and Lemert are commonly seen as the fathers of the two main approaches to the study of deviance: anomie and labeling. These two men and their contributions remain prominent to this day. Labeling theory still guides most research and theorizing in this area, whereas anomie is presented in textbooks as an important, albeit partial, explanation of deviance, and one that has engendered little research of late.

Merton's main precursor was Emile Durkheim, who developed (in French) the concept of anomie to help explain his findings on suicide (Durkheim 1951). Merton reworked his ideas into an explanation of deviance in general. We draw here from Merton's second and final revision of his 1938 statement (Merton 1957). The theoretical elaborations made to it by others are mentioned to the extent that they are still regarded as important.

The word *anomie* is conventionally translated into English as "normlessness." Unfortunately, the translation is woefully inadequate and therefore an impediment to understanding Merton's ideas (not to mention those of Durkheim). According to the French dictionary *Le Petit Robert 1*

(1989 update), anomie is the absence of social and legal organization. An anomic society is hardly normless; it is in the course of reorganization, where old norms (values, relations, etc.) no longer apply and new norms (values, relations, etc.) are emerging.

Merton noted that "strain" sometimes develops between the cultural structure and the social structure of the society—that is, there is a discrepancy between the social organization and goals of the society and the capacities of many of its members to reach the goals. Though he believed his theory applied to other culturally accepted goals as well, Merton (1957, p. 181) limited his analysis to the pursuit of success goals of a materialistic nature. This orientation, he said, was particularly characteristic of American society. Although he never clarified what he meant by the "social structure" or "capacity" or "institutionalized means" by which these goals are reached, it is evident that he was referring to occupational roles.

Merton recognized that a disturbance in the equilibrium of society can lead to deviance. He believed that this disturbance stems from the pursuit of goals that lie beyond personal economic means. For those affected in this manner, society is anomic.

Merton suggested that people adapt to anomie in one of five "modes." An adaptation is deviant when it is expressed in behavior that departs from cultural goals or institutional means of reaching those goals or both. Table 1 depicts the five modes of adaptation identified by Merton and how they relate as deviance or conformity to the goals and means. The first of these modes, *conformity*, plays a negligible role in the theory. It is not deviance. It is most prevalent when the society is stable, when there is little or no anomie.

As the strain between cultural structure and social structure increases—as anomie increases—additional (deviant) adaptations are made by some members of the community—that is, most people continue to conform in these circumstances, but the number grows of those who do not. *Innovation* is the deviant adaptation springing from the acceptance of cultural goals and the

**TABLE 1**
**A Typology of Modes of Individual Adaptation**

| Modes of Adaptation | Cultural Goals | Institutionalized Means |
|---|---|---|
| Conformity | + | + |
| Innovation | + | − |
| Ritualism | − | + |
| Retreatism | − | − |
| Rebellion | ± | ± |

+ = acceptance
− = rejection
± = rejection followed by acceptance of new goals and means

SOURCE: Adapted from Merton 1957, p. 140.

rejection of institutionalized means of attaining them. People are most likely to make innovations in a society where success goals are ideally open to all members, but in actuality are restricted or even completely closed to some of them. The incentives for success are provided by the established values of the culture. Yet certain barriers are present, such as educational requirements, monetary resources, and family background, which block achievements. In this situation, says Merton, pressure increases for the use of illegitimate means. This mode of adaptation, when implemented in response to monetary goals, typically manifests itself as crime or vice, particularly among those in the manual labor and lower white-collar occupations.

When an individual scales down or even abandons a culturally approved goal but continues to abide almost compulsively by the means of attaining that goal, he or she has employed *ritualism* as an adaptation to anomie. By diluting achievement goals to manageable size, this person gains security, whereas high ambitions invite possible frustration and failure. The rulebound bureaucrat was the principal example used by Merton. He observed that this sort of adaptation is most likely to occur in lower-middle-class settings where conformity is a strong motive and where social climbing is less likely to be successful than in other parts of the middle class.

Merton believed that *retreatism*, the mode of adaptation where both cultural goals and means

of attainment are rejected, is probably the least common of the five modes. Some of the behavior of psychotics, pariahs, tramps, chronic drunkards, and drug addicts can be interpreted as retreatist. Originally, both the goals and the means were internalized, but these individuals found the way to them blocked. Internalization of conventional values prevents the active innovation of illegitimate means or goals. Instead, the individual only abandons the legitimate means and goals and retreats in a deviant manner. Although such deviants may have contact with others who share their proclivities, Merton held that this adaptation is essentially private. One noteworthy, albeit generally nondeviant, variation of retreatism is found in apathy, indifference, cynicism, and disenchantment.

The final mode of adaptation, *rebellion*, consists of the rejection of established goals and means of the society for those of a new social system. Where the rebellion is small and concentrated among those with little power, subgroups may form that, although isolated from the rest of the community, develop into an integrated society in their own right—for instance, a religious commune. Still, a rebellion involving a substantial number of the members of a society can culminate in a full-scale revolution. The final result here is modification of the established cultural and social structures.

Richard A. Cloward (1959) extended Merton's theory by adding several propositions about the illegitimate opportunities open to those seeking a deviant adaptation to anomie. It was evident to him that there are variations in the availability of illegitimate means, just as Merton had observed a similar variation in legitimate means. This availability of illegitimate means is controlled by the same criteria that control the availability of conventional means. Both are limited and both are differentially open to people in the society according to their positions in the social structure.

Cloward is more specific in his definition of means than Merton. The term "means" implies two things: "First, that there are appropriate environments for the acquisition of the values and skills associated with the performance of a particular role; and second, that the individual has opportunities to discharge the role once he has been prepared. The term, therefore, subsumes both *learning structures and opportunity structures*" (1959, p. 168; emphasis in original). Some people encounter learning and opportunity structures that lead to deviance, whereas others do not. This contingency is partly explained by Edwin H. Sutherland's theory of differential association (Sutherland and Cressey 1978, pp. 80–82)—that is, youth selectively associate with other youth. If they choose to interact with those who are deviant, the first often learn to enjoy the deviance of the second.

Anomie theory offers a causal explanation of deviance, both criminal and noncriminal. Its focus is chiefly on the macrosociological antecedents leading to the initial act or acts of deviance. Thanks to Cloward's insertion of the principle of differential association, the theory now helps explain a variety of forms of deviance at the interactive level as well as at the structural-cultural level.

The enthusiasm for research using the anomie perspective that prevailed in the 1950s and 1960s waned thereafter. Although it had not been empirically rejected, it had also not been supported. Fault lay in part with the abstractness of Merton's formulation, which impeded testing. The most studied area of deviance was juvenile delinquency, which, however, tended to rely on official arrest rates. Such data suggest that crime rates are highest for youth from lower socioeconomic backgrounds, even though it is now evident that similar proportions of youth are delinquent in every social class (Schwendinger and Schwendinger 1985, pp. 181–183). Marshall B. Clinard (1964, pp. 55–56) has compiled a more specific list of weaknesses of anomie theory as it bears on deviance.

## LABELING THEORY

Behind the scenes and out of the spotlight on anomie, labeling theory, or societal reaction theory, was developing quietly, awaiting its ultimate place onstage. Lemert's most immediate precursor was Frank Tannenbaum (1938), who, concerned with crime, observed that the acts of juvenile delinquents are seen as evil in the wider community. This image eventually spreads to the delinquents themselves; they, too, are seen as evil. As the community comes to define delinquents as evil, juvenile delinquents' definitions of themselves change accordingly. The result is a sort of self-fulfilling prophecy: "The process of making the criminal, therefore, is a process of tagging, defining, identifying, segregating, describing, emphasizing, making conscious and self-conscious; it becomes a way of stimulating, suggesting, emphasizing, and evoking the very traits that are complained of" (Tannenbaum 1938, pp. 19–20).

The study of deviance had to wait thirteen years for a more complete statement of this process. At that time Lemert (1951) published his "theory of sociopathic behavior" and later its elaborations (Lemert 1972). Although the complete theory is considerably more detailed and complex, the following summary communicates its essentials:

*People and groups are differentiated in various ways, some of which are deviant and which bring them penalties, rejection, and segregation. Penalties, rejection, and segregation are aspects of a community, or societal reaction against the deviance. This reaction affects the initial process of differentiation by sometimes increasing and other times decreasing the tendency to deviate. Accordingly, deviance can be studied from both a collective perspective (society, community) and an individual perspective* (paraphrased from Lemert 1951, p. 22).

There are three important aspects to this theory that receive a great deal of further elaboration in Lemert's book. The first of these, the process of *differentiation,* refers to the fact that these people differ or deviate from average characteristics of the populations in which they are found and in which they interact. The second is the *societal reaction,* which refers to both the expressive reactions of others (moral indignation) toward deviance and the action directed toward its control. Of course, this depends on the deviant individual or class of individuals being sufficiently visible to react toward. *Individuation,* the third aspect of the theory, refers to the manifestation of the causes of deviance in the individual deviant and to how he or she comes to terms with the deviance.

This framework is then given a more substantive form by being incorporated into a body of postulates:

1. There are modalities in human behavior and clusters of deviations from these modalities that can be identified and described for situations specified in time and space.
2. Behavioral deviations are a function of culture conflict, and such conflict is expressed through social organization.
3. There are societal reactions to deviations ranging from strong approval through indifference to strong disapproval.
4. Sociopathic behavior is deviation that is effectively disapproved.
5. The deviant person is one whose role, status, function, and self-definition are importantly shaped by how much deviation he engages in, by the degree of its social visibility, by the particular exposure he has to the societal reaction, and by the nature and strength of the societal reaction.
6. There are patterns of restriction and freedom in the social participation of deviants that are related directly to their status, role, and self-definitions. The biological strictures upon social participation of deviants are directly significant in comparatively few cases.
7. Deviants are individuated with respect to their vulnerability to the societal reaction because:

(a) the person is a dynamic agent and (b) there is a structuring to each personality that acts as a set of limits within which the societal reaction operates (Lemert 1951, pp. 22–23).

The process of individuation has become the core of modern labeling theory. Individuation can be best understood by looking at the events and processes associated with *primary deviation* and *secondary deviation.* The first of these refers to deviant behavior that is normalized by the deviant person—that is, deviance remains primary or symptomatic and situational as long as it is rationalized or otherwise dealt with as part of a socially accepted role (Lemert 1972). This may be done through normalization, where the deviance is perceived by the individual as a normal variation or merely a minor problem of everyday living. Or it may be done in a way that does not seriously impede the basic accommodation that deviants make to get along with other people.

Secondary deviation refers to the responses that people make to problems created by the societal reaction to their deviance. These problems are those that are generated by social control mechanisms, punishment, stigmatization, segregation, and the like. They are of exceptional importance to the individual in that they alter his or her personality. The secondary deviant is a person whose life and identity are organized around the facts of deviance.

Lemert expresses the relationship between primary and secondary deviation in the following way:

*The sequence of interaction leading to secondary deviation is roughly as follows: (1) primary deviation; (2) social penalties; (3) further primary deviation; (4) stronger penalties and rejections; (5) further deviation, perhaps with hostilities and resentment beginning to focus upon those doing the penalizing; (6) crisis reached in the tolerance quotient, expressed in formal action by the community stigmatizing the deviant; (7) strengthening of the deviant conduct as a reaction to the stigmatizing and penalties; (8) ultimate acceptance of deviant social status and efforts at adjustment on the basis of the associated role* (Lemert 1951, p. 77).

This relationship between primary and secondary deviation can, with little difficulty, be incorporated into the idea of a deviant career.

Howard S. Becker (1963) pioneered the application of concept of career to deviant behavior. A *career*, whether in deviance or an occupation, is the passage of the typical individual through recognized stages in one or more related identities. Careers are further comprised of the adjustments to and interpretations of the contingencies and turning points encountered at each stage.

Objectively, the initial act of deviance launches the individual's deviant career. However, career turning points, including this one, depend on the actor's recognition and interpretation of them before they can be seen by that actor as part of a career. This is usually evident only in retrospect, after he or she has spent a certain amount of time in the identity with which the career is associated. Thus, upon reflection, the first remembered act of homosexuality, the first interest in communist literature, or the first drag on a marijuana cigarette constitutes the inception of the person's deviant career. This may or may not be the initial instance of deviance from a more objective point of view. This act and those further acts of primary deviation that may or may not follow are the results of many factors—social, cultural, psychological, and physiological—and their many combinations. Of course, any discussion of deviance should not overlook the possibility of false accusation of deviant behavior, an event that can also, under certain circumstances, lead to a subsequent deviant career.

Becker (1963, p. 23) identified three types of deviants. There are *secret deviants,* whose behavior is not known beyond themselves and perhaps a few others. The *falsely accused deviants,* whether this attitude is in fact valid or not, believe in their own innocence. These deviants are also discovered deviants in the sense that they have been apprehended for or suspected of deviant behavior. Finally, there are the *pure deviants,* who are also discovered deviants, since they have behaved in an aberrant way, know it, and have been apprehended for or suspected of such activity by the larger community.

Another key idea in labeling theory is Becker's concept of the *moral entrepreneur.* Groups of rule makers, rule enforcers, and ordinary nondeviant members of the community may join hands in this capacity. Such people, be they crusading individuals or change-oriented organizations, create moral norms on their own initiative and subsequently enforce them against those who disapprove of the new rules and deviate from them.

The prototype of the rule creator, says Becker, is the "crusading reformer" whose dissatisfaction with existing rules is acute. This individual campaigns for changes in the moral norms (e.g., to add new laws or procedures, to rescind old ones) or for changes in attitudes; both are designed to produce what he or she considers proper behavior. Society is replete with past and present crusaders. Groups and individuals have tried to eliminate drug abuse, discourage alcohol consumption, reduce the availability of pornography, and stop the exploitation of women in the workplace. Organizations have been formed to stress the need for mental health and for protection against breaking and entering.

It is no accident, then, that the least influential members of society (i.e., the poor, powerless ethnic groups) are most often disproportionately caught in the web of social control and labeled deviant. In other words, deviance is created by society. For moral entrepreneurs the infraction of moral norms constitutes deviance. Moral entrepreneurs also apply these norms to particular people, thereby *labeling* them as deviants of some sort. As Becker (1963, p. 9) points out, "The deviant is one to whom that label has successfully been applied; deviant behavior is behavior that people so label." Lest this statement seem restrictive, it should be added that secret deviants are deviant, too. They have simply not been discovered and publicly labeled as such.

Labeling theory complements anomie theory to the extent that the former focuses on the deviant career and the processes and conditions that commit a person to many years of deviance. The labeling approach offers less insight into why deviants start their careers than into why they continue or fail to continue beyond the initial acts of deviance. Despite Lemert's (1951, pp. 22–23) early interests in differentiation, culture conflict, and social organization and Becker's interest in moral entrepreneurs, labeling theory has developed into a predominantly social psychological explanation of continued deviance.

## OTHER APPROACHES

Labeling theory is not without its problems and hence its critics. According to Barry Glassner (1982), the problems have been analyzed from three principal perspectives: neo-Marxist, empiricalist, and phenomenological. Each critique forms the nucleus of still another approach to the study of deviance.

The principal neo-Marxist objection to labeling theory is that it fails to relate crime and other forms of deviance to the larger society. It fails to account for historical and contemporary political and economic interests. After all, deviant acts and careers do take place within such a context. Neo-Marxists also hold that labeling theorists overlook the division between the powerful and the powerless in explaining deviance. Powerful members of society also violate laws and other norms, even while making some of them in their role as moral entrepreneurs.

The concept of the moral entrepreneur and the categories of secret and falsely accused deviants suggest, however, that labeling theorists have some understanding of the power differences in society. Perhaps the fairest criticism is that they have failed to go as far as they could in linking power to such concepts as labeling, deviant career, and agents of social control. Still, the observation that labeling theory overlooks the larger social context of deviance is apt. It exposes the predominantly social-psychological character of the perspective.

The empiricalists find several research weaknesses in labeling theory and its empirical support. Glassner (1982) discusses three of these. First, labeling theorists are said to examine only, or chiefly, formally labeled deviants—those who have been officially identified as having deviated (charged and convicted or examined and hospital-

ized). It is true that labeling theorists have frequently preferred a narrow conception of the labeling process. Such an approach opens these theorists to the criticism that labeling makes no difference. Yet some deviants—for example, religious fanatics or occultists—are deviant even though they rarely if ever gain official recognition as such.

Second, the empiricalists argue that labeling as a cause of deviance is inadequately conceptualized. This is a misunderstanding. As this article points out, labels are seen by labeling theorists as interpretations rather than causes. The label of deviant is a career contingency, an event, a process, or a situation interpreted by the deviant as having a significant impact on his or her moral career.

Third, the empiricalists claim that labeling theory lacks testable propositions. Consequently, data in this area can be explained in many different ways. Glassner notes that the empiricalists assert that tests by quantitative, statistical means are the only definitive way of confirming propositions. Labeling theorists defend their approach by arguing that qualitative methods, particularly participant observation, are more appropriate for the study of interaction, labeling, career, and self-conception. These phenomena rest on definitions of situations, images of self and others, negotiations of reality, and similar processes that are difficult to measure and therefore hard to quantify. Nevertheless, qualitative research often proceeds from the intense examination of individual groups and cases. Such studies are arduous and time-consuming, with the result that there are relatively few of them. There is only suggestive, yet-to-be confirmed evidence for many of the propositions in labeling theory.

Glassner calls those who follow the writings of Alfred Schutz "phenomenologists." Their chief concern with labeling theory is its tendency to neglect this question: How do people make sense of their social world? The people of interest to phenomenologists are not always deviant, however. Rather, phenomenologists are interested in how agents of social control and ordinary citizens make sense of deviants and deviant acts. Labeling theorists are accused of ignoring the ways in which the conventional world identifies and classifies morally offensive people and behaviors. The important data for the phenomenologists are the clues people use to identify kinds of deviants and deviant acts. People use this knowledge to determine such conclusions as guilt or innocence.

For example, Peter McHugh (1970) observed that for an act to be defined as deviant, it must be seen by ordinary members of the community as one of a set of alternative acts available to the offender—that is, the act, in their view, must not have been coerced, accidental, or miraculous. Moreover, to be deviant it must have been perpetrated by someone who knew what he or she was doing, who knew that he or she was violating a moral rule of the community. David Sudnow (1965) demonstrated how crimes in the American criminal justice system come to be defined as "normal" by the public defender. The category of normal crime enables the public defender to represent the accused person more efficiently than if the crime is exceptional in some significant way and thereby fails to fit established procedure. A crime is normal when it is seen by criminal justice personnel as having, among other characteristics, the following: (1) The focus is on types of offenses rather than on the individual offender. (2) The public defender tries to call attention to aspects of the crime that are familiar to the community at that moment in its history. (3) The act was committed in a geographical location known for this kind of behavior. In short, studying such processes shows how people construct special social realities—the realities of who did what to whom, at what time, and at what place.

To some extent, labeling theorists are guilty as charged. Although there are occasional hints of phenomenological thinking in the literature, there has been, until recently, a tendency to rely heavily on official definitions, or labels of what and who is deviant. But even official definitions and their applications are informed by common sense. They, too, warrant phenomenological analysis.

## CONCLUSION

At present these critiques have done little more than point out weaknesses in the labeling perspective. Andrew T. Scull (1988, pp. 684–685) describes the predicament now faced by the sociology of deviance: None of the new approaches has "succeeded in establishing an alternative orientation to the field that commands wide assent. The study of deviance is thus in a state of profound epistemological and theoretical confusion . . . with few signs that the intellectual crisis will soon be resolved."

(SEE ALSO: *Anomie and Alienation; Criminalization of Deviance; Deviance Theories; Labeling Theories; Legislation of Morality*)

## REFERENCES

Becker, Howard S. 1963 *Outsiders.* New York: Free Press.

Bonney, Merl E. 1941 "Parents as the Makers of Social Deviates." *Social Forces* 20:77–87.

Clinard, Marshall B. 1964 *Anomie and Deviant Behavior.* New York: Free Press.

Cloward, Richard A. 1959 "Illegitimate Means, Anomie, and Deviant Behavior." *American Sociological Review* 24:164–176.

Durkheim, Emile 1951 *Suicide,* trans. John Spaulding and George Simpson; originally published in 1897. New York: Free Press.

Giddings, Franklin 1896 *Principles of Sociology.* New York: Macmillan.

Glassner, Barry 1982 "Labeling Theory." In M. M. Rosenberg, R. A. Stebbins, and A. Turowetz, eds., *The Sociology of Deviance.* New York: St. Martin's Press.

Karp, David A., Gregory P. Stone, and William C. Yoels 1977 *Being Urban.* Lexington, Mass.: D. C. Heath.

Lemert, Edwin M. 1951 *Social Pathology.* New York: McGraw-Hill.

——— 1972 *Human Deviance, Social Problems, and Social Control,* 2nd ed. Englewood Cliffs, N.J.: Prentice-Hall.

McHugh, Peter 1970 "A Common-Sense Conception of Deviance." In Jack D. Douglas, ed., *Deviance and Respectability: The Social Construction of Moral Meanings.* New York: Basic Books.

Merton, Robert K. 1938 "Social Structure and Anomie." *American Sociological Review* 3:672–682.

———— 1949 "Social Structure and Anomie: Revisions
and Extensions." In R. N. Anshen, ed., *The Family.*
New York: Harper & Brothers.

———— 1957 *Social Theory and Social Structure,* rev. ed.
New York: Free Press.

Schwendinger, Herman, and Schwendinger, Julia S.
1985 *Adolescent Subcultures and Delinquency.* New
York: Praeger.

Scull, Andrew T. 1988 "Deviance and Social Control."
In N. J. Smelser, ed., *Handbook of Sociology.* Newbury
Park, Calif.: Sage Publications.

Stebbins, Robert A. 1988 *Deviance: Tolerable Differences.*
Toronto: McGraw-Hill Ryerson.

Sudnow, David 1965 "Normal Crimes: Sociological
Features of the Penal Code in a Public Defender
Office." *Social Problems* 12:255–276.

Sutherland, Edwin H., and David R. Cressey 1978
*Principles of Criminology,* 10th ed. Philadelphia:
Lippincott.

Tannenbaum, Frank 1938 *Crime and the Community.*
New York: Columbia University Press.

ROBERT A. STEBBINS

**DEVIANCE THEORIES** Since its inception as a discipline, sociology has studied the
causes of deviant behavior, examining why some
persons conform to social rules and expectations
and others do not. Typically, sociological theories
of deviance reason that characteristics of individuals and the social areas in which they live assist
in explaining the commission of deviant acts.
These theories are important to understanding
the roots of social problems such as crime, violence, and mental illness and to explaining how
those problems may be remedied. By specifying
the causes of deviance, the theories reveal how
aspects of the social environment influence the
behavior of individuals and groups. Further, the
theories suggest how changes in these influences
may yield changes in problematic behaviors.

Despite their importance, deviance theories
disagree about the precise causes of deviant acts.
Some look to the structure of society and groups
or geographic areas within society, explaining

deviance in terms of broad social conditions in
which deviance is most likely to flourish. Others
explain deviant behavior using the characteristics
of individuals, focusing on those characteristics
that are most highly associated with learning
deviant acts. Other theories view deviance as a
social status conferred by one group or person on
others, a status that is imposed by persons or
groups in power in order to protect their positions
of power. These theories explain deviance in
terms of differentials in power between individuals
or groups.

This article reviews the major sociological theories of deviance. It offers an overview of each
theory, summarizing its explanation of deviant
behavior. Before reviewing the theories, however,
it may prove useful to describe two different
dimensions of theory that will structure our discussion. The first of these, the *level of explanation,*
refers to the scope of the theory and whether it
focuses on the behavior and characteristics of
individuals or on the characteristics of social
aggregates such as neighborhoods, cities, or other
social areas. *Micro-level* theories stress the individual, generally explaining deviant acts in terms of
personal characteristics of individuals or the immediate social context in which deviant acts occur.
In contrast, *macro-level* theories focus on social
aggregates or groups, looking to the structural
characteristics of areas in explaining the origins of
deviance, particularly rates of deviance among
those groups.

Theories of deviance also vary in relation to a
second dimension, *causal focus.* This dimension
divides theories into two groups, those that explain the social origins of norm violations and
those explaining societal reactions to deviance.
*Social origin* theories focus on the causes of norm
violations. Typically, these theories identify aspects of the social environment that trigger norm
violations, social conditions in which the violations are most likely to occur. In contrast, *social
reaction* theories argue that deviance is often a
matter of social construction, a status imposed by
one person or group on others and a status that
ultimately may influence the subsequent behavior

of the designated deviant. Social reaction theories argue that some individuals and groups may be designated or labeled as deviant and that the process of labeling may trap or engulf those individuals or groups in a deviant social role.

These two dimensions offer a fourfold scheme for classifying types of deviance theories. The first type, macro-level origin theories, focuses on the causes of norm violations associated with broad, structural conditions in the society. These theories generally examine the influences of such structural characteristics of populations or communities as the concentration of poverty, levels of community integration, or the density and age distribution of the population on areal rates of deviance.

Second, micro-level origin theories focus on the characteristics of the deviant and his or her immediate social environment. These theories typically examine the relationship between a person's involvement in deviance and such characteristics as the influences of peers and significant others as well as people's emotional stakes in conformity, their beliefs about the propriety of deviance and conformity, and their perceptions of the threat of punishments for deviant acts.

A third type of theories may be termed micro-level reaction theories. These accord importance to those aspects of interpersonal reactions that may seriously stigmatize or label the deviant and thereby reinforce her or his deviant social status. According to these theories, reactions to deviance may have the unintended effect of increasing the likelihood of subsequent deviant behavior.

Finally, macro-level reaction theories emphasize broad structural conditions in society that are associated with the designation of entire groups or segments of the society as deviant. These theories tend to stress the importance of structural characteristics of populations, groups, or geographic areas, such as degrees of economic inequality or concentration of political power within communities or the larger society. According to macro-level reaction theories, powerful groups impose the status of deviant as a mechanism for controlling those groups that represent the greatest political, economic, or social threat to their position of power.

The rest of this article is divided into sections corresponding to each of these "types" of deviance theory. The article concludes with a discussion of new directions for theory—the development of explanations that cut across and integrate different theory types and the elaboration of existing theories through greater specification of the conditions under which those theories apply.

## MACRO-LEVEL ORIGINS OF DEVIANCE

Theories of the macro-level origins of deviance look to the broad, structural characteristics of society, and groups within society, to explain deviant behavior. Typically, these theories examine one of three aspects of social structure. The *first* is the pervasiveness and consequences of poverty in modern American society. Robert Merton's (1938) writing on American social structure and Richard Cloward and Lloyd Ohlin's (1960) subsequent work on urban gangs laid the theoretical foundation for this perspective. Reasoning that pervasive materialism in American culture creates unattainable aspirations for many segments of the population, Merton (1964) and others argued that there exists an environmental state of "strain" among the poor. The limited availability of legitimate opportunities for attaining material wealth forces the poor to adapt through deviance, either by achieving wealth through illegitimate means or by rejecting materialistic aspirations and withdrawing from society altogether.

According to this reasoning, deviance is a by-product of poverty and a mechanism through which the poor may attain wealth, albeit illegitimately. Thus, "strain" theories of deviance interpret behaviors such as illegal drug selling, prostitution, and armed robbery as innovative adaptations to blocked opportunities for legitimate economic or occupational success. Similarly, the theories interpret violent crimes in terms of the frustrations of poverty, as acts of aggression triggered by those frustrations (Blau and Blau 1982). Much of the current research in this tradition is examining the exact mechanisms by which poverty and economic inequality influence rates of deviant behavior.

The second set of macro-level origins theories examine the role of culture in deviant behavior. Although not ignoring structural forces such as poverty in shaping deviance, this class of theories reasons that there may exist cultures within the larger culture that endorse or reinforce deviant values, deviant subcultures that produce higher rates of deviance among those segments of the population sharing subcultural values.

Subcultural explanations have their origin in two distinct sociological traditions. The first is writing on the properties of delinquent gangs that identifies a distinct lower-class culture of gang members that encourages aggression, thrill seeking, and antisocial behavior (e.g., Miller 1958). The second is writing on cultural conflict that recognizes that within complex societies there will occur contradictions between the conduct norms of different groups. Thorsten Sellin (1938) suggested that in heterogeneous societies several different subcultures may emerge, each with its own set of conduct norms. According to Sellin, the laws and norms applied to the entire society do not necessarily reflect cultural consensus but rather the values and beliefs of the dominant social groups.

Subcultural theories emerging from these two traditions argue that deviance is the product of a cohesive set of values and norms that favors deviant behavior and is endorsed by a segment of the general population. Perhaps most prominent among the theories is Marvin Wolfgang and Franco Ferracuti's (1967) writing on subcultures of criminal violence. Wolfgang and Ferracuti reasoned that there may exist a distinct set of beliefs and expectations within the society, a subculture, that promotes and encourages violent interactions. According to Wolfgang and Ferracuti, this violent subculture is pervasive among blacks in the United States and may explain extremely high rates of criminal homicide among young black males.

Although Wolfgang and Ferracuti offer little material specifying the subculture's precise causes, or empirical evidence demonstrating the pervasiveness of subcultural beliefs, other writers have extended the theory, exploring the relationship between beliefs favoring violence and such factors as the structure of poverty in the United States (Curtis 1975; Messner 1983), the history of racial oppression of blacks (Silberman 1980), and ties to the rural South and a southern culture of violence (Gastil 1971; Erlanger 1974). Even these writers, however, offer little empirical evidence of violent subcultures within U.S. society.

A third class of theories about the macro-level origins of deviance began with the work of sociologists at the University of Chicago in 1920s. Unlike strain and subcultural theories, these stress the importance of the social integration of neighborhoods and communities—the degree to which neighborhoods are stable and are characterized by a homogeneous set of beliefs and values—as a force influencing rates of deviant behavior. As levels of integration increase, rates of deviance decrease. Based in the early work of sociologists such as Clifford Shaw and Henry McKay, the theories point to the structure of social controls in neighborhoods, arguing that neighborhoods lacking social controls are "disorganized," that is, areas in which there is a virtual vacuum of social norms. It is in this normative vacuum that deviance flourishes. Therefore, these theories view deviance as a property of areas or locations rather than specific groups of people.

Early writers in the "disorganization" tradition identified industrialization and urbanization as the causes of disorganized communities and neighborhoods. Witnessing immense growth in eastern cities such as Chicago, these writers argued that industrial and urban expansion create zones of disorganization within cities. Property owners move from the residential pockets on the edge of business and industrial areas and allow buildings to deteriorate in anticipation of the expansion of business and industry. This process of natural succession and change in cities disrupts traditional mechanisms of social control in neighborhoods. As property owners leave transitional areas, more mobile and diverse groups enter. But the added mobility and diversity of these groups translate into fewer primary relationships—families and extended kinship and friendship networks. And as the number of primary relationships declines, so will informal social controls in neighborhoods. Hence, rates of deviance will rise.

Recent writing from this perspective looks closely at the mechanisms by which specific places in urban areas become the spawning grounds for deviant acts (Bursik and Webb 1982; Bursik 1984; and others). For example, Rodney Stark (1987) argues that high levels of population density are associated with particularly low levels of supervision of children. With little supervision, children perform poorly in school and are much less likely to develop "stakes in conformity"—that is, emotional and psychological investments in academic achievement and other conforming behaviors. Without such stakes, children and adolescents are much more likely to turn to deviant alternatives. Thus, according to Stark, rates of deviance will be high in densely populated areas because social controls in the form of parental supervision are either weak or entirely absent.

Similarly, Robert Crutchfield (1989) argues that the structure of work opportunities in areas may have the same effect. Areas characterized primarily by secondary sector work opportunities—low pay, few career opportunities, and high employee turnover—may tend to attract and retain persons with few stakes in conventional behavior—a "situation of company" in which deviance is likely to flourish.

In sum, theories of the macro-level origins of deviance argue that many of the causes of deviance may be found in the characteristics of groups within society, or in the characteristics of geographic areas and communities. They offer explanations of group and areal differences in deviance—for example, why some cities have relatively higher rates of crime than others or why blacks have higher rates of serious interpersonal violence than other ethnic groups. These theories make no attempt to explain the behavior of individuals or the occurrence of individual deviant acts. Indeed, they reason that deviance is best understood as a property of an area, community, or group, regardless of the individuals living in the area or community, or the individuals comprising the group.

## MICRO-LEVEL ORIGINS OF DEVIANCE

Many explanations of deviance argue that its causes are rooted in the background or personal circumstances of the individual. Micro-level origins theories have developed over the past fifty years, identifying mechanisms by which ordinarily conforming individuals may become deviant. These theories assume the existence of a homogeneous, pervasive set of norms in society and proceed to explain why persons or entire groups of persons violate the norms. There exist two important traditions within this category of theories. The first tradition involves social learning theories—explanations that focus on the mechanisms through which people learn the techniques and attitudes favorable to committing deviant acts. The second tradition involves social control theories—explanations that emphasize factors in the social environment that regulate the behavior of individuals, thereby preventing the occurrence of deviant acts.

Edwin Sutherland's (1947) theory of differential association laid the foundation for learning theories. At the heart of this theory is the assumption that deviant behavior, like all other behaviors, is learned. Further, this learning occurs within intimate social groups—networks of family members and close friends. Therefore, according to these theories individuals learn deviance from persons closet to them. Sutherland specified a process of *differential association,* reasoning that people become deviant in association with deviant others. People learn from others the techniques of committing deviant acts and attitudes favorable to the commission of those acts. Moreover, Sutherland reasoned that people vary in their degree of association with deviant others; those regularly exposed to close friends and family members who hold beliefs favoring deviance and who commit deviant acts would be much more likely than others to develop those same beliefs and commit deviant acts.

Sutherland's ideas about learning processes have played a lasting role in micro-level deviance theories. Central to his perspective is the view that beliefs and values favoring deviance are a primary cause of deviant behavior. Robert Burgess and Ronald Akers (1966) and subsequently Akers (1985) extended Sutherland's ideas, integrating them with principles of operant conditioning. Reasoning that learning processes may best be understood in terms of the concrete rewards and punishments given for behavior, Burgess and Akers argue that deviance is learned through associations with others and through a system of rewards and punishments, imposed by close friends and relatives, for participation in deviant acts. Subsequent empirical studies offer compelling support for elements of learning theory (Matsueda 1982; Akers et al. 1979; Matsueda and Heimer 1987).

Some examples may be useful at this point. According to the theory of differential association, juveniles develop beliefs favorable to the commission of delinquent acts and knowledge about the techniques of committing deviant acts from their closest friends, typically their peers. Thus, sufficient exposure to peers endorsing beliefs favoring deviance who also have knowledge about the commission of deviant acts will cause the otherwise conforming juvenile to commit such acts. Therefore, if adolescent peer influences encourage smoking, drinking alcohol, and other forms of drug abuse—and exposure to these influences occurs frequently, over a long period of time, and involves relationships that are important to the conforming adolescent—then he or she is likely to develop beliefs and values favorable to committing these acts. Once those beliefs and values develop, he or she is likely to commit the acts.

The second class of micro-level origins theories, control theories, explores the causes of deviance from an altogether different perspective. Control theories take for granted the existence of a cohesive set of norms shared by most persons in the society and reason that most persons want to

and will typically conform to these prevailing social norms. The emphasis in these theories, unlike learning theories, is on the factors that bond individuals to conforming life-styles. The bonds act as social and psychological constraints on the individual, binding persons to normative conformity (Toby 1957; Hirschi 1969). People deviate from norms when these bonds to conventional life-styles are weak, and hence, when they have little restraining influence over the individual. Among control theorists, Travis Hirschi (1969) has made the greatest contributions to our knowledge about bonding processes and deviant behavior. Writing on the causes of delinquency, he argued that four aspects of bonding are especially relevant to control theory: emotional attachments to conforming others, psychological commitments to conformity, involvements in conventional activities, and beliefs consistent with conformity to prevailing norms.

Among the most important of the bonding elements are emotional attachments individuals may have to conforming others and commitments to conformity—psychological investments or stakes people hold in a conforming life-style. Those having weak attachments—that is, people who are insensitive to the opinions of conforming others—and who have few stakes in conformity, in the form of commitments to occupation or career and education, are much more likely than others to deviate (see, e.g., Paternoster et al. 1983; Thornberry and Christenson 1984; Liska and Reed 1985). In effect, these individuals are "free" from the constraints that ordinarily bond people to normative conformity. Conversely, individuals concerned about the opinions of conforming others and who have heavy psychological investments in work or school will see the potential consequences of deviant acts—rejection by friends or loss of a job—as threatening or costly, and consequently will refrain from those acts.

Most recently, Michael Gottfredson, in conjunction with Hirschi, has developed a general theory of crime that builds on and extends the basic assumptions of control theory (Hirschi and Gottfredson 1987; Gottfredson and Hirschi 1990). Arguing that all people are inherently self-interested, pursuing enhancement of personal pleasure and avoiding pain, Gottfredson and Hirschi suggest that most crimes, and for that matter most deviant acts, are the result of choices to maximize pleasure and/or minimize pain. Crimes occur when opportunities to maximize personal pleasure are high and when the certainty of painful consequences is low. Further, people who pursue short-term gratification with little consideration for the long-term consequences of their actions are most prone to criminal behavior. In terms of classical control theory, these are individuals who have weak bonds to conformity or who disregard or ignore the potentially painful consequences of their actions. They are "relatively unable to or unwilling to delay gratification; they are indifferent to punishment and the interests of others" (Hirschi and Gottfredson 1987, pp. 959–960).

A related concern is the role of sanctions in preventing deviant acts. Control theorists like Hirschi reason that most people are utilitarian in their judgments about deviant acts, and thus evaluate carefully the risks associated with each act. Control theories typically maintain that the threat of sanctions actually prevents deviant acts when the risks outweigh the gains. Much of the most recent writing on sanctions and their effects has stressed the importance of perceptual processes in decisions to commit deviant acts (Gibbs 1975, 1977; Tittle 1980; Paternoster et al. 1982, 1983; Piliavin et al 1986; Matsueda, Piliavin, and Gartner 1988). At the heart of this perspective is the reasoning that individuals perceiving the threat of sanctions as high are much more likely to refrain from deviance than those perceiving the threat as low, regardless of the actual level of sanction threat.

In sum, micro-level origins theories look to those aspects of the individual's social environment influencing her or his likelihood of deviance. Learning theories stress the importance of deviant peers and other significant individuals, and their impact on attitudes and behaviors favorable to the commission of deviant acts. These theories assume that the social environment acts as an agent of change, transforming otherwise conforming in-

dividuals into deviants through peer influences. People exposed to deviant others frequently and sufficiently, like persons exposed to a contagious disease who become ill, will become deviant themselves. Control theories avoid this "contagion" model, viewing the social environment as a composite of controls and restraints cementing the individual to a conforming life-style. Deviance occurs when elements of the bond—aspects of social control—are weak or broken, thereby freeing the individual to violate social norms. Sanctions and the threat of sanctions are particularly important to control theories, a central part of the calculus that rational actors use in choosing to commit or refrain from committing deviant acts.

## MICRO-LEVEL REACTIONS TO DEVIANCE

Unlike micro-level origin theories, micro-level reaction theories make no assumptions about the existence of a homogeneous, pervasive set of norms in society. These theories take an altogether different approach to explaining deviant behavior, viewing deviance as a matter of definition, a social status imposed by individuals or groups on others. Most argue that there exists no single pervasive set of norms in society and that deviant behavior may best be understood in terms of norms and their enforcement. These theories typically stress the importance of labeling processes—the mechanisms by which acts become defined or labeled as "deviant"—and the consequences of labeling for the person so labeled. Many of these theories are concerned with the development of deviant life-styles or careers, long-term commitments to deviant action.

One of the most important writers in this tradition is Howard Becker (1963). Becker argues that deviance is not a property inherent in any particular form of behavior but rather a property conferred on those behaviors by audiences witnessing them. Becker (1963, p. 9) notes that "deviance is *not* a quality of the act the person commits, but rather a consequence of the application by others of rules and sanctions to an 'offender.' The deviant is one to whom that label has successfully been applied; deviant behavior is behavior that people so label." Thus, Becker and others in this tradition orient the study of deviance on rules and sanctions, and the application of labels. Their primary concern is the social construction of deviance—that is, how some behaviors and classes of people come to be defined as "deviant" by others observing and judging the behavior.

Equally important is the work of Edwin Lemert (1951). Stressing the importance of labeling to subsequent deviant behavior, he argued that repetitive deviance may arise from social reactions to initial deviant acts. According to Lemert (1951, p. 287), deviance may often involve instances where "a person begins to employ his deviant behavior . . . as a means of defense, attack or adjustment to the . . . problems created by the consequent social reactions to him." Therefore, a cause of deviant careers is negative social labeling: instances where reactions to initial deviant acts are harsh and reinforce a "deviant" self-definition. Such labeling forces the individual into a deviant social role, organizing his or her identity around a pattern of deviance that structures a way of life and perpetuates deviant behavior (Becker 1963; Schur 1971, 1985).

Perhaps the most significant developments in this tradition have contributed to knowledge about the causes of mental illness. Proponents of micro-level reaction theories argue that the label "mentally ill" can be so stigmatizing to those labeled, especially when mental-health professionals impose the label, that they experience difficulty returning to nondeviant social roles. As a result, the labeling process may actually exacerbate mental disorders. Former mental patients may find themselves victims of discrimination at work, in personal relationships, or in other social spheres (Scheff 1966). This discrimination, and the widespread belief that others devalue and discriminate against mental patients, may lead to self-devaluation and fear of social rejection by others (Link 1982, 1987). In some instances, this devaluation and fear may be associated with demoralization of the patient, loss of employment and personal income, and the persistence of mental disorders following treatment (Link 1987).

Hence, micro-level reaction theories reason that deviant behavior is rooted in the process by which persons define and label the behavior of others as deviant. The theories offer explanations of individual differences in deviance, stressing the importance of audience reactions to initial deviant acts. However, these theories make no attempt to explain the origins of the initial acts (Scheff, 1966). Rather, they are concerned primarily with the development and persistence of deviant careers.

## MACRO-LEVEL REACTIONS TO DEVIANCE

The final class of theories looks to the structure of economic and political power in society as a cause of deviant behavior. Macro-level reaction theories—either Marxist or other conflict theories—view deviance as a status imposed by dominant social classes to control and regulate populations that threaten political and economic hegemony. Like micro-level reaction theories, these theories view deviance as a social construction and accord greatest importance to the mechanisms by which society defines and controls entire classes of behavior and people as deviant in order to mediate the threat. However, these theories reason that the institutional control of deviants has integral ties to economic and political order in society.

Marxist theories stress the importance of the economic structure of society and begin with the assumption that the dominant norms in capitalist societies reflect the interests of the powerful economic class, the owners of business. But contemporary Marxist writers (Quinney 1970, 1974, 1980; Spitzer 1975; Young 1983) also argue that modern capitalist societies are characterized by large "problem populations"—people who have become displaced from the work force and alienated from the society. Generally, the problem populations include racial and ethnic minorities, the chronically unemployed, and the extremely impoverished. They are a burden to the society and particularly to the capitalist class because they create a form of social expense that must be carefully controlled if the economic order is to be preserved.

Marxist theories reason that economic elites use institutions such as the legal, mental-health, and welfare systems to control and manage society's problem populations. In effect, these institutions define and process society's problem populations as deviant in order to ensure effective management and control. In societies or communities characterized by rigid economic stratification, elites are likely to impose formal social controls in order to preserve the prevailing economic order.

Conflict theories stress the importance of the political structure of society and focus on the degree of threat to the hegemony of political elites, arguing that elites employ formal social controls to regulate threats to political and social order (Turk 1976; Chambliss 1978; Chambliss and Mankoff 1976). According to these theories, threat varies in relation to the size of the problem population, with large problem populations substantially more threatening to political elites than small populations. Thus, elites in societies and communities in which those problem populations are large and perceived as especially threatening are more likely to process members of the problem populations as deviants than in areas where such populations are small.

Much of the recent writing in this tradition has addressed the differential processing of people defined as deviant. Typically, this writing has taken two forms. The first involves revisionist histories linking the development of prisons, mental asylums, and other institutions of social control to structural changes in U.S. and European societies. These histories demonstrate that those institutions often target the poor and chronically unemployed independent of their involvement in crime and other deviant acts, and thereby protect and serve the interests of dominant economic and political groups (Scull 1978; Rafter 1985).

A second and more extensive literature in-

cludes empirical studies of racial and ethnic disparities in criminal punishments. Among the most important of these studies is Martha Myers and Suzette Talarico's (1987) analysis of the social and structural contexts that foster racial and ethnic disparities in the sentencing of criminal offenders. Myers and Talarico's research, and other studies examining the linkages between community social structure and differential processing (Myers 1987, 1990; Peterson and Hagan 1984; Bridges, Crutchfield, and Simpson 1987; Bridges and Crutchfield 1988), demonstrate the vulnerability of minorities to differential processing during historical periods and in areas in which they are perceived by whites as serious threats to political and social order. In effect, minorities accused of crimes during these periods and in these geographic areas are perceived as threats to white hegemony, and therefore become legitimate targets for social control.

Thus, macro-level reaction theories view deviance as a by-product of inequality in modern society, a social status imposed by powerful groups on those who are less powerful. Unlike micro-level reaction theories, these theories focus on the forms of inequality in society and how entire groups within the society are managed and controlled as deviants by apparatuses of the state. Like those theories, however, macro-level reaction theories make little or no attempt to explain the origins of deviant acts, claiming instead that the status of "deviant" is, in large part, a social construction designed primarily to protect the interests of the most powerful social groups. The primary concern of these theories is explicating the linkages between inequality in society and inequality in the labeling and processing of deviants.

## NEW THEORETICAL DIRECTIONS

A recurring issue in the study of deviance is the contradictory nature of many deviance theories. The theories often begin with significantly different assumptions about the nature of human behavior and end with significantly different conclusions about the causes of deviant acts. Some scholars maintain that the oppositional nature of these theories—the theories are developed and based on systematic rejection of other theories (Hirschi 1989)—tends toward clarity and internal consistency in reasoning about the causes of deviance. However, other scholars argue that this oppositional nature is intellectually divisive—acceptance of one theory precludes acceptance of another—and "has made the field seem fragmented, if not in disarray" (Liska, Krohn, and Messner 1989, p. 1).

A related and equally troublesome problem is the contradictory nature of much of the scientific evidence supporting deviance theories. For each theory, there exists a literature of studies that supports and a literature that refutes major arguments of the theory. And although nearly every theory of deviance may receive empirical confirmation at some level, virtually no theory of deviance is sufficiently comprehensive to withstand empirical falsification at some other level. The difficult task for sociologists is discerning whether and under what circumstances negative findings should be treated as negating a particular theory (Walker and Cohen 1985).

In recent years, these two problems have renewed sociologists' interest in deviance theory and, at the same time, suggested new directions for the development of theory. The oppositional nature of theories has quite recently spawned interest in theoretical integration. Many scholars are dissatisfied with classical theories, arguing that their predictive power is exceedingly low (see Elliott 1985; Liska, Krohn, and Messner 1989). Limited to a few key explanatory variables, any one theory can explain only a limited range and amount of deviant behavior. And because most scholars reason that the causes of deviance are multiple and quite complex, most also contend that it may be "necessary to combine different theories to capture the entire range of causal variables" (Liska, Krohn, and Messner 1989, p. 4).

Because it combines the elements of different theories, the new theory will have greater explanatory power than theories from which it was derived. However, meaningful integration of deviance theories will require much more than the simple combination of variables. Scholars must first reconcile the oppositional aspects of theories, including many of their underlying assumptions about society, the motivations of human behavior, and the causes of deviant acts. For example, learning theories focus heavily on the motivations for deviance, stressing the importance of beliefs and values that "turn" the individual to deviant acts. In contrast, control theories accord little importance to such motivations, examining instead those aspects of the social environment that constrain people from committing deviant acts. Reconciling such differences is never an easy task, and in some instances may be impossible (Hirschi 1979).

The problem of contradictory evidence suggests a related but different direction for deviance theory. Theories may vary significantly in the conditions—termed *scope conditions*—under which they apply (Walker and Cohen 1985; Tittle 1975; Tittle and Curran 1988). Under some scope conditions, theories may find extensive empirical support, and under others virtually none. For instance, macro-level origin theories concerned with the frustrating effects of poverty on deviance may have greater applicability to people living in densely populated urban areas than those living in rural areas. The frustrations of urban poverty may be much more extreme than in rural areas, even though the actual levels of poverty may be the same. As a result, the frustrations of urban poverty may be more likely to cause deviant adaptations in the form of violent crime, drug abuse, and vice than those of rural poverty. In this instance, "urbanness" may constitute a condition that activates strain theories linking poverty to deviance. Obviously, the same theories simply may not apply in rural areas or under other conditions.

Effective development of deviance theory will require much greater attention to the specification of such scope conditions. Rather than combining causal variables from different theories as integrationists would recommend, this approach to theory development encourages scholars to explore more fully the strengths and limitations of their own theories. This approach will require more complete elaboration of extant theory, explicitly specifying those circumstances under which each theory may be meaningfully tested and thus falsified. The result will be a greater specification of each theory's contribution to explanations of deviant behavior.

These two directions have clear and very different implications for the development of deviance theory. Theoretical integration offers overarching models of deviant behavior that cut across classical theories, combining different levels of explanation and causal focuses. If fundamental differences between theories can be reconciled, integration is promising. The specification of scope conditions offers greater clarification of existing theories, identifying those conditions under which each theory most effectively applies. Although this direction promises no general theories of deviance, it offers the hope of more meaningful and useful explanations of deviant behavior.

(SEE ALSO: *Anomie and Alienation; Deviance; Labeling Theory; Legislation of Morality*)

## REFERENCES

Akers, Ronald L. 1985 *Deviant Behavior: A Social Learning Approach.* Belmont, Calif.: Wadsworth.

———, Marvin D. Krohn, Lonn Lanza-Kaduce, and Marcia Radosevich 1979 "Social Learning and Deviant Behavior: A Specific Test of a General Theory." *American Sociological Review* 44:636–655.

Becker, Howard 1963 *The Outsiders.* Chicago: University of Chicago Press.

Blau, Judith, and Peter Blau 1982 "Metropolitan Structure and Violent Crime." *American Sociological Review* 47:114–128.

Bridges, George S., and Robert D. Crutchfield 1988 "Law, Social Standing and Racial Disparities in Imprisonment." *Social Forces* 66:699–724.

———, and Edith Simpson 1987 "Crime, Social Structure and Criminal Punishment." *Social Problems* 34:344–361.

Bursik, Robert J., and J. Webb 1982 "Community Change and Ecological Studies of Delinquency." *American Journal of Sociology* 88:24–42.

Bursik, Robert J. 1984 "Urban Dynamics and Ecological Studies of Delinquency." *Social Forces* 63:393–413.

Burgess, Robert L., and Ronald Akers 1966 "A Differ-

ential Association-Reinforcement Theory of Criminal Behavior." *Social Problems* 14:128–147.

Chambliss, William 1978 *On the Take.* Bloomington: Indiana University Press.

———, and Milton Mankoff 1976 *Whose Law, What Order?* New York: Wiley.

Cloward, Richard 1959 "Illegitimate Means, Anomie and Deviant Behavior." *American Sociological Review* 24:164–176.

———, and Lloyd E. Ohlin 1960 *Delinquency and Opportunity.* New York: Free Press.

Crutchfield, Robert D. 1989 "Labor Stratification and Violent Crime." *Social Forces* 68:489–513.

Curtis, Lynn 1975 *Violence, Race and Culture.* Lexington, Mass.: Heath.

Elliott, Delbert 1985 "The Assumption That Theories Can Be Combined with Increased Explanatory Power: Theoretical Integrations." In Robert F. Meier, ed., *Theoretical Methods in Criminology.* Beverly Hills, Calif.: Sage.

Erlanger, Howard 1974 "The Empirical Status of the Subculture of Violence Thesis." *Social Problems* 22:280–292.

Gastil, Raymond 1971 "Homicide and a Regional Culture of Violence." *American Sociological Review* 36:412–427.

Gibbs, Jack P. 1975 *Crime, Punishment and Deterrence.* New York: Elsevier.

——— 1977 "Social Control, Deterrence, and Perspectives on Social Order." *Social Forces* 62:359–374.

Gottfredson, Michael R., and Travis Hirschi 1990 *A General Theory of Crime.* Palo Alto, Calif.: Stanford University Press.

Hirschi, Travis 1969 *Causes of Delinquency.* Berkeley: University of California Press.

——— 1979 "Separate and Unequal Is Better." *Journal of Research in Crime and Delinquency* 16:34–37.

——— 1989 "Exploring Alternatives to Integrated Theory." In Steven F. Messner, Marvin D. Krohn, and Allen E. Liska, eds., *Theoretical Integration in the Study of Deviance and Crime: Problems and Prospects.* Albany, N.Y.: SUNY Press.

———, and Michael R. Gottfredson 1987 "Causes of White Collar Crime." *Criminology* 25:949–974.

Lemert, Edwin 1951 *Social Pathology.* New York: McGraw-Hill.

Link, Bruce 1982 "Mental Patient Status, Work and Income: An Examination of the Effects of a Psychiatric Label." *American Sociological Review* 47:202–215.

——— 1987 "Understanding Labeling Effects in the Area of Mental Disorders: An Assessment of the Effects of Expectations of Rejection." *American Sociological Review* 52:96–112.

Liska, Allen, and Mark Reed 1985 "Ties to Conventional Institutions and Delinquency." *American Sociological Review* 50:547–560.

Liska, Allen E., Marvin D. Krohn, and Steven F. Messner 1989 "Strategies and Requisites for Theoretical Integration in the Study of Deviance and Crime." In Steven F. Messner, Marvin D. Krohn, and Allen E. Liska, eds., *Theoretical Integration in the Study of Deviance and Crime: Problems and Prospects.* Albany, N.Y.: SUNY Press.

Matsueda, Ross L. 1982 "Testing Control Theory and Differential Association: A Causal Modeling Approach." *American Sociological Review* 47:36–58.

———, and Karen Heimer 1987 "Race, Family Structure and Delinquency: A Test of Differential Association and Social Control Theories." *American Sociological Review* 52:826–840.

———, Irving Piliavin, and Rosemary Gartner 1988 "Ethical Assumptions versus Empirical Research." *American Sociological Review* 53:305–307.

Merton, Robert K. 1938 "Social Structure and Anomie." *American Sociological Review* 3:672–682.

——— 1964 *Social Theory and Social Structure.* New York: Free Press.

Messner, Steven F. 1983 "Regional and Racial Effects on the Urban Homicide Rate: The Subculture of Violence Revisited." *American Journal of Sociology* 88:997–1,007.

Miller, Walter B. 1958 "Lower Class Culture as a Generating Milieu of Gang Delinquency." *Journal of Social Issues* 14:5–19.

Myers, Martha 1987 "Economic Inequality and Discrimination in Sentencing." *Social Forces* 65:746–766.

——— 1990 "Economic Threat and Racial Disparities in Incarceration: The Case of Postbellum Georgia." *Criminology* 28(4):627–656.

———, and Suzette Talarico 1987 *Social Contexts of Criminal Sentencing.* New York: Springer-Verlag.

Paternoster, Raymond L., Linda Saltzman, Gordon P. Waldo, and Theodore Chiricos 1982 "Perceived Risk and Deterrence: Methodological Artifacts in Deterrence Research." *Journal of Criminal Law and Criminology* 73:1,243–1,255.

——— 1983 "Perceived Risk and Social Control." *Journal of Criminal Law and Criminology* 74:457–480.

Peterson, Ruth D., and John Hagan 1984 "Changing Conceptions of Race: Toward an Account of Anomalous Findings of Sentencing Research." *American Sociological Review* 49:56–70.

Piliavin, Irving, Rosemary Gartner, Craig Thornton, and Ross L. Matsueda 1986 "Crime, Deterrence and Rational Choice." *American Sociological Review* 51:101–120.

Quinney, Richard 1970 *The Social Reality of Crime.* Boston: Little, Brown.

——— 1974 *Critique of Legal Order.* Boston: Little, Brown.

——— 1980 *Class, State and Crime.* New York: Longman.

Rafter, Nicole Hahn 1985 *Partial Justice: Women in State Prisons, 1800–1935.* Boston: Northeastern University Press.

Scheff, Thomas 1966 *Being Mentally Ill.* Chicago: Aldine.

Schur, Edwin 1971 *Labelling Deviant Behavior.* New York: Harper and Row.

——— 1985 *Labelling Women Deviant: Gender, Stigma and Social Control.* New York: Harper and Row.

Scull, Andrew T. 1978 *Museums of Madness.* London: Heinemann.

Sellin, Thorsten 1938 *Culture, Conflict and Crime.* New York: Social Science Research Council.

Shaw, Clifford 1930 *The Jack-Roller.* Chicago: University of Chicago Press.

Shaw, Clifford, and Henry McKay 1942 *Juvenile Delinquency and Urban Areas.* Chicago: University of Chicago Press.

Silberman, Charles 1980 *Criminal Justice, Criminal Violence.* New York: Vintage.

Spitzer, Steven 1975 "Toward a Marxian Theory of Deviance." *Social Problems* 22:638–651.

Stark, Rodney 1987 "Deviant Places: A Theory of the Ecology of Crime." *Criminology* 25:893–910.

Sutherland, Edwin H. 1947 *Principles of Criminology,* 4th ed. Philadelphia: Lippincott.

Thornberry, Terence P., and R. L. Christenson 1984 "Unemployment and Criminal Involvement: An Investigation of Reciprocal Causal Structures." *American Sociological Review* 49:398–411.

Tittle, Charles R. 1975 "Deterrents or Labelling?" *Social Forces* 53:399–410.

——— 1980 *Sanctions and Social Deviance.* New York: Praeger.

———, and Barbara A. Curran 1988 "Contingencies for Dispositional Disparities in Juvenile Justice." *Social Forces* 67:23–58.

Toby, Jackson 1957 "Social Disorganization and Stakes in Conformity: Complementary Factors in the Predatory Behavior of Hoodlums." *Journal of Criminal Law and Criminology and Police Science* 48:12–17.

Turk, Austin T. 1976 "Law as a Weapon in Social Conflict." *Social Problems* 23:276–291.

Walker, Howard, and Bernard P. Cohen 1985 "Scope Statements." *American Sociological Review* 50:288–301.

Wolfgang, Marvin E., and Franco Ferracuti 1967 *The Subculture of Violence: Towards an Integrated Theory in Criminology.* London: Tavistock.

Young, Peter 1983 "Sociology, the State and Penal Relations." In David Garland and Peter Young, eds., *The Power to Punish.* London: Heinemann.

GEORGE S. BRIDGES

**DIFFERENTIAL ASSOCIATION** *See* Crime Theories; Deviance Theories.

**DIFFUSION THEORIES** *Diffusion* refers to the spread of dissemination of elements of physical culture, as well as to the spread of social practices and attitudes, through and between populations. Conceptually, diffusion is thus bound with the idea of change and has been so treated throughout the literatures of the social sciences. There is a long history of interest in diffusion by laypersons and social scientists. Indeed, the histories of Herodotus, compiled around 450 B.C., frequently make reference in describing different cultures to borrowed implements and customs (Rawlinson 1880, pp. 318–325). The earliest social scientific use of the term *diffusion* can be traced to Edward Tylor's (1865) treatment of culture change.

The extent to which writings about diffusion have spawned theory in the contemporary understanding of that term may be debated. It is certainly true that there exists no unified, deductive structure through which diffusion can be explained, nor has one been attempted. On the other hand, there are distinct collections of propositions, some well tested over many years, that describe different diffusion phenomena in different arenas. These different arenas form three traditions in diffusion studies. Rogers ([1962] 1983, p. 39) has pointed out that for many years the traditions remained distinct with little overlap and cross-fertilization, but since the late 1970s there has been a greater awareness among them leading to some merging of research and theory. The three traditions are represented by the study of (1) cultural diffusion; (2) diffusion of innovations; and (3) collective behavior.

## CULTURAL DIFFUSION

Early anthropologists focused on an important concern—why different cultures were similar and dissimilar. Tylor's work on culture change first posited the idea of diffusion. By the turn of the twentieth century, diffusion was seen as an alternative to evolution for understanding cultural differentiation and change. While evolutionists emphasized that cultural similarities probably arose through independent invention in different parts of the world, diffusionists stressed that cultural traits and institutions could pass between societies via contact and interaction.

**Historical Development.** The English anthropologists W. J. Perry and Elliot Smith represented the most extreme position on cultural diffusion. These two scholars held that culture originated in Egypt and progressively diffused from that center over the remainder of the earth. In Germany, Fritz Graebner (1911) emphasized the importance of diffusion but did not argue that all civilization flowed from Egypt. Instead, he proposed that certain critical aspects of culture—toolmaking, for example—originated in a small number of isolated societies. This idea became the basis of *culture circles* ("Kulturkreise"), collections of societies sharing similar cultures. Unlike many British scholars who focused on tracing the diffusion of single culture elements, Graebner and others in his tradition focused on the diffusion of collections of elements or cultural complexes.

American anthropologists are generally credited with developing a social scientifically workable view of diffusion. Franz Boas (1896) held that diffusion was a viable mechanism largely among geographically adjacent areas, a view that was later cited as diffusionists moved away from the determinist view of the early British anthropologists. Two of Boas's students, Robert Lowie and Alfred Kroeber, were the principal developers of a "moderate diffusionism" (Lowie 1937, p. 58), which is currently accepted among anthropologists. This view allowed for the coexistence of a variety of mechanisms—independent invention, acculturation, and so forth—in addition to diffusion in accounting for culture change and differentiation (Kroeber 1923, p. 126). Wissler (1929), a contemporary of Kroeber and Lowie, contributed to the empirical basis of diffusion through his research identifying ten culture areas (regions with similar cultural inventories) in North and South America and the Caribbean.

**Theory in Cultural Diffusion.** From a theoretical standpoint, diffusion as the actual movement of a particular social institution or physical implement is distinguished from *stimulus diffusion,* which is seen as the exchange of the principle upon which an institution or implement is based. Many anthropologists have proposed principles and assumptions of cultural diffusion theory. Drawing principally on the research of early twentieth-century American anthropologists, one can identify at least five broadly accepted and empirically supported claims regarding cultural diffusion. First, borrowed elements usually undergo some type of change or adaptation in the new host culture. Second, the act of borrowing hinges on the extent to which the element can be integrated into the belief system of the new culture. Third, elements that are incompatible with the new culture's prevailing normative structure or religious belief system are likely to be rejected. Fourth, acceptance of an element depends on its functional utility to the borrower. Finally, cultures or societies that have a history of past borrowing are more likely to borrow in the future. Each of these propositions can be elaborated and corollaries added (Hayden 1978).

Currently, diffusion is seen as a mechanism for culture change that typically accounts for a large portion of any particular cultural inventory. The deterministic, linear diffusion hypothesis associated with early British anthropologists is discredited. Sociologists concerned with macro-social processes and societal change acknowledge and use the concept of diffusion in much the same way as anthropologists (Lauer 1973).

## DIFFUSION OF INNOVATIONS

Work on the diffusion of innovations has historically focused on the spread of an idea, procedure, or implement within a single social group or organization. Diffusion is defined as the process through which an innovation is communicated within a social system. Also implicit is a time dimension, reflecting the rate of diffusion, and the importance of individuals in the process, reflecting the role of social influence.

**Historical Development.** While some students of the diffusion of innovations claim roots in the work of Tarde (1890), the formative research on the subject began in the United States in the late 1930s. Bowers's (1937) study of the acceptance and use of ham radio sets is commonly cited as the first empirical study of the diffusion of an innovation. For more than two decades following this early research, the study of innovation diffusion took place largely within the context of rural sociology. In part, this grew out of the circumstances of rural sociology itself. Many rural sociologists had close ties to colleges of agriculture at land grant institutions. One of the functions of such colleges was to disseminate knowledge of agricultural innovations to farmers, and a natural role for sociologists was the study of this dissemination or diffusion process (Hightower 1972).

The classic diffusion study in the rural sociology tradition was conducted by Ryan and Gross (1943). The focus of the study was farmers' adoption of an improved hybrid corn seed in two Iowa communities. This study ultimately defined many of the issues that would occupy diffusion researchers for decades to come: the role of social influence, timing of adoptions, the process of adopting innovations, and interactions among adopter characteristics and perceived characteristics of the innovation. During the late 1940s and through the 1950s, rural sociologists continued to develop a large body of empirical studies of the diffusion of various innovations. Most of these innovations remained tied to agriculture and farming. The literature is replete with studies of the diffusion of innovations such as new crop management systems, hybridizations, weed sprays, insect sprays, chemical fertilizers and feeds, and machinery. A common criticism of this era of diffusion research is that the studies seemed to represent copies of each other and the classic Ryan and Gross work, the principal difference among them being the innovation studied. While it is true that many of these studies shared a common methodology and linear conception of the diffusion process, it is also true that they provided a strong foundation of empirical case studies upon which later sophisticated theorizing could be based.

The 1960s marked the beginning of the decline of the central role of rural sociologists in studying the diffusion of innovations. In part this was due to changes in the nature of rural sociology, but it also reflected a substantial growth of involvement by researchers from other disciplinary backgrounds. After more than two decades of intense research on the diffusion of agricultural innovations, rural sociologists—like other social scientists of the period—began to devote more time to examining the consequences of technology and associated social problems. As diffusion studies occupied a smaller proportion of the rural sociology agenda, one more innovation was introduced: A number of rural sociologists moved diffusion research into the international arena. These were principally studies of agricultural innovations in Latin America, Asia, and Africa, and they followed the traditional model of diffusion research. By 1965, even with the international research, rural sociologists no longer dominated research on the diffusion of innovations.

Historically, numerous disciplines have been represented in research on the diffusion of innovations. While rural sociologists were clearly the most prolific researchers operating between 1940 and 1965, studies in education and public health constituted major contributions over the same period. Research on education included examinations of the diffusion of kindergartens and driver education in the early 1950s as well as Carlson's

(1965) study of the diffusion of modern math. The public health area spawned one of the most influential studies in the history of diffusion research. Elihu Katz, Herbert Menzel, and James Coleman studied the diffusion of a new drug, first in a pilot study (Menzel and Katz 1955) and then in studies of four Illinois cities (Coleman, Katz, and Menzel 1957, 1966). The importance of this research rests upon its findings regarding interpersonal diffusion networks, particularly the role of interpersonal influence in adoption. Other studies in the public health arena focused on dissemination of vaccinations, family planning, and new medical technology.

The late 1960s and 1970s saw a substantial increase in the amount of diffusion research from three disciplines in particular: marketing, communication, and geography. Marketing research focused primarily on characteristics of people who adopt new products and the role of opinion leadership. This literature is based almost exclusively on commercial products, from coffee and soap to the touch-tone telephone and personal computer. In contrast, research by scholars trained in communication has been considerably more theoretically oriented. Beginning with a handful of studies of news events in the early 1960s (e.g., the assassination of President Kennedy), this research tradition has branched out to cover a wide variety of specific technological innovations. The emphasis in this tradition, however, has been less on the nature of the innovation itself and more on diffusion theory. In particular, these researchers have focused on communication channels, diffusion networks, interpersonal influence, and the innovation-decision process. Finally, geographers began to conduct diffusion research in the 1970s. The primary focus of geographic research is the role of spatial distance in diffusion processes for technological innovations.

Currently, research on the diffusion of innovations is best characterized as a multidisciplinary endeavor. One of the most important features of the field in the 1980s has been an increasing concern with developing an awareness of the history and range of diffusion research. For years, researchers in the innovation-diffusion arena have tended to be isolated. For example, in the 1970s diffusion researchers began to attend for the first time to the concept of *reinvention* (Eveland 1977), apparently without knowledge of Kroeber's (1923) research on the same phenomenon fifty years before. Katz (1962) acknowledged that at the time he and his colleagues designed the now classic drug diffusion study, they were unaware of the work of Ryan and Gross on hybrid corn diffusion. This concern with the empirical record has also generated a concern with the development of theory.

**Theory in Innovation Diffusion.** Everett Rogers has contributed immensely to the drive for theory in this area. The contribution has been twofold. First, over three decades he has compiled and classified the results of studies of the diffusion of innovations (Rogers and Shoemaker 1971; Rogers 1983). These inventories of findings have contributed to the definition of diffusion research as an area of interdisciplinary study and served as impetus for theory building efforts in the field generally. Second, Rogers ([1962] 1983) has assembled theoretical structures (or models) aimed at explaining principal features of innovation diffusion. These structures elaborate eighty-one generalizations or propositions that have been empirically tested. The theoretical bases of innovation diffusion may be understood in terms of the innovation-decision process, innovation characteristics, and adopter characteristics and opinion leadership.

The innovation-decision process represents the framework on which diffusion research is built. It delineates the process through which a decision maker (individual or organization) chooses to adopt, reinvent (modify), or reject an innovation. The process is generally conceived as consisting of five stages. The first stage, *knowledge,* is when the decision maker learns of the existence of the innovation and its function. The second stage, *persuasion,* represents the stage at which the decision maker forms a positive or negative attitude toward the innovation. The third stage, *decision,* is when a decision maker chooses to accept or to reject the innovation. *Implementation,* the fourth stage, follows a decision to accept and involves putting the innovation into use (in either its accepted form or some modified form). The fifth stage, *confirmation,* is when decision makers assess an adopted innovation, gather information from significant others, and choose to continue to use the innovation, modify it (reinvention), or reject it. While early conceptions of the stage model were criticized as too linear, Rogers ([1962] 1983) has argued that current formulations are flexibly conceived.

It has long been known that different innovations have different probabilities of adoption and, hence, different adoption rates (they travel through the innovation-decision process at different speeds). The literature demonstrates that five attributes of innovations influence the adoption decision. *Compatibility* refers to the congruence between an innovation and the prevailing norms and values and perceived needs of the potential adopter. High levels of perceived compatibility are associated with higher likelihood of adoption. Innovation *complexity,* on the other hand, is negatively associated with adoption. The extent to which use of an innovation is visible to the social group, *observability,* is positively related to adoption. *Relative advantage* refers to the extent to which an innovation is perceived to be better than the idea it replaces. Higher relative advantage increases the likelihood of adoption. Finally, *trial-ability*—the extent to which an innovation may be experimented with—is also positively related to the probability of adoption.

The third component of innovation-diffusion theory centers on adopter characteristics and the concept of opinion leadership. Adopter categories are classifications of individuals based upon how readily they adopt an innovation. Rogers (1983, p. 260) identifies nine socioeconomic variables, twelve personality variables, and ten personal communication characteristics and reviews research on their relationship to adoption choices. In general, the literature holds that early adopters are more likely to be characterized by high socioeconomic status, high tolerance of uncertainty and change, low levels of fatalism and dogmatism, high integration into the social system, high exposure to mass media and interpersonal communication channels, and frequent engagement in information seeking.

Understanding the characteristics of people who adopt innovations raises the question of interpersonal influence and networks (Katz and Lazarsfeld 1955). Three components are important in understanding the role of interpersonal influence in the innovation-decision process: information flow, opinion leadership, and diffusion networks. At different times, information flows have been conceived of in terms of a "hypodermic needle" model, a two-step flow (to opinion leaders then to individuals), and a multistep flow. Currently, communication flows are believed to be multistep and described in terms of homophily and heterophily—the degree to which pairs of interacting individuals are similar or different in terms of adopter attributes. Opinion leadership, evolved in connection with the two-step flow concept, denotes the degree to which one member of a social system can informally influence the attitudes and behavior of other members of the social system. The concept of opinion leadership is more flexibly viewed in terms of spheres of influence, wherein a given person may be a leader or follower depending on the part of the diffusion network being referenced. The diffusion or communication network is the structural stage upon which social influence takes place. Considerable attention has been given to developing analysis strategies and techniques for such networks (Wigand 1988).

## COLLECTIVE BEHAVIOR

While diffusion is not a term common in the literature of collective behavior, the concept of dispersion that it represents is a fundamental part of the area. In collective behavior theory, processes of diffusion are important in connection with two phenomena: crowds and fashion. In both cases, analytic concern focuses on the spread of ideas, attitudes, or styles through a collectivity.

Interestingly, crowd behavior is the only place where all three diffusion theory traditions converge. In discussing the phenomenon of imitation and its meaning for the spread of inventions,

Tarde (1890, pp. 45ff) cited Edward Tylor's use of the concept of cultural diffusion. Subsequently, LeBon (1895) and Tarde (1901) devised approaches to crowd behavior that relied heavily upon the concept of social contagion: rapid dissemination of moods or actions through collectivities. Allport (1924) and Blumer (1939) extended and formalized the contagion approach to collective behavior.

Changes in fashions of dress have also been broadly conceptualized as diffusion processes. Kroeber (1919) examined cycles of fashion change, indicating that there appeared to be order not only in the periodicity of style change but also in the way such changes diffused through civilizations. Katz and Lazarsfeld (1955, pp. 241–270) moved away from a concern with the networks through which fashions move to focus upon the role of social influence in fashion change. Blumer (1969) moved further away from simple diffusion conceptions of fashion by emphasizing the social psychology of collective choice as a mechanism for understanding fashion change. Current theoretical work on fashion continues to emphasize social psychological approaches wherein fashion diffusion questions are peripherial (Davis 1985).

(SEE ALSO: *Collective Behavior; Crowds and Riots; Culture*)

## REFERENCES

Allport, Floyd 1924 *Social Psychology*. Boston: Houghton Mifflin.

Boas, Franz 1896 *The Limitations of the Comparative Method of Anthropology*. New York: Alfred A. Knopf.

Blumer, Herbert 1939 "Collective Behavior." In Robert Park, ed., *Outline of the Principles of Sociology*. New York: Barnes and Noble.

——— 1969 "Fashion." *Sociological Quarterly* 10:275–291.

Bowers, Raymond 1937 "The Direction of Intra-Societal Diffusion." *American Sociological Review* 2:826–836.

Carlson, Richard 1965 *Adoption of Educational Innovations*. Eugene: University of Oregon Center for the Advanced Study of Educational Administration.

Coleman, James, Elihu Katz, and Herbert Menzel 1957

"The Diffusion of an Innovation among Physicians." *Sociometry* 20:253–270.

———— 1966 *Medical Innovation: A Diffusion Study.* New York: Bobbs-Merrill.

Davis, Fred 1985 "Clothing and Fashion as Communication." *Symbolic Interaction* 5:111–126.

Eveland, J. D. 1977 "Issues in Using the Concept of Adoption of Innovation." Paper read at the annual meeting of the American Society for Public Administration, Baltimore, Maryland.

Graebner, Fritz 1911 *Methode der Ethnologie.* Heidelberg, Germany: Carl Winter.

Hayden, Brian 1978 "A General Diffusion Model." In P. G. Duke, ed., *Diffusion and Migration.* Calgary, Alberta: University of Calgary Archeological Association.

Hightower, James 1972 *Hard Tomatoes, Hard Times: The Failure of America's Land-Grant College Complex.* Cambridge, Mass.: Shenkman.

Katz, Elihu 1962 "The Social Itinerary of Technical Change." *Human Organization* 20:70–82.

————, and Paul Lazarsfeld 1955 *Personal Influence.* New York: Free Press.

Kroeber, Alfred 1919 "On the Principle of Order in Civilization as Exemplified by Changes of Fashion." *American Anthropologist* 21:235–263.

———— 1923 *Anthropology.* New York: Harcourt.

Lauer, Robert 1973 *Perspectives on Social Change.* Boston: Allyn Bacon.

LeBon, Gustave 1895 *Psychologie des foules.* Paris: Alcan.

Lowie, Robert 1937 *The History of Ethnological Theory.* New York: Rinehart and Co.

Menzel, Herbert, and Elihu Katz 1955 "Social Relations and Innovation in the Medical Profession." *Public Opinion Quarterly* 19:337–352.

Rawlinson, George, ed. 1880 *History of Herodotus.* London: John Murray.

Rogers, Everett (1962) 1983 *Diffusion of Innovations.* New York: Free Press.

————, and Floyd Shoemaker 1971 *Communication of Innovations.* New York: Free Press.

Ryan, Bryce, and Neal Gross 1943 "The Diffusion of Hybrid Seed Corn in Two Iowa Communities." *Rural Sociology* 8:15–24.

Tarde, Gabriel 1890 *Les Lois de l'imitation.* Paris: Alcan.

———— 1901 *L'opinion et la foule.* Paris: Alcan.

Tylor, Edward 1865 *Early History of Mankind and the Development of Civilisation.* London: John Murray.

Wigand, Rolf 1988 "Communication Network Analysis: History and Overview." In G. Goldhaber and G. Barnett, eds., *Handbook of Organizational Communication.* Norwood, N.J.: Ablex Publishing.

Wissler, Clark 1929 *An Introduction to Social Anthropology.* New York: Henry Holt and Co.

RONALD W. PERRY

**DISASTER RESEARCH** Descriptions of calamities go as far back as the earliest human writings, but systematic empirical studies and theoretical treatises on social aspects of disasters have appeared only in the twentieth century. The first publications in both cases were produced by sociologists. Samuel Prince (1920) wrote a doctoral dissertation in sociology at Columbia University that examined the social change consequences of a munitions ship explosion in the harbor of Halifax, Canada. Two decades later, Pitirim Sorokin (1942) wrote *Man and Society in Calamity*, which mostly speculated on how war, revolution, famine, and pestilence might affect the mental processes, behavior, social organizational, and cultural life of involved populations.

However, there was no building on these pioneering efforts, and it was not until the early 1950s that disaster studies started to show any continuity and the accumulation of a knowledge base. Military interest in possible American civilian reactions to post–World War II threats from nuclear and biological warfare led to support of academic research on peacetime disasters, with the key project being done in 1950–1954 by the National Opinion Research Center (NORC) at the university of Chicago. This project, in intent multidisciplinary, came to be dominated by sociologists, as were other studies at about the same time at the University of Oklahoma, Michigan State University, and the University of Texas. The NORC study not only promoted field research as the major way of studying behavior but also brought sociological ideas from collective behavior and notions of organizational structure and functions into the thinking of disaster researchers (Quarantelli and Dynes 1977; Dynes 1988).

While the military interest quickly waned, research in the area obtained a strategic point of salience and support when the U.S. National Academy of Sciences created the Disaster Research Group (DRG) in the late 1950s. Operationally run by sociologists using the NORC work as a prototype, the DRG supported field research of others in addition to conducting its own studies (Fritz 1961). When DRG was phased out in 1963, the Disaster Research Center (DRC) was established at Ohio State University. DRC helped the field of study to become institutionalized by its continuous existence to the present day (having moved to the University of Delaware in 1985) and by the training of dozens of graduate students, the building of the largest specialized library in the world on social aspects of disasters, the production of over five hundred publications, the continual and conscious opening up to a sociological perspective of new disaster research topics, the setting up of an interactive computer net of researchers in the area, and an intentional effort to help create domestic and international networks and critical masses of disaster researchers (Quarantelli and Dynes 1977; Kreps 1984).

The sociological work in disasters was joined in the late 1960s by geographers with interest in natural hazards, and in the 1980s by risk analysts especially concerned with technological threats (Perrow 1984; Short 1984). The initial focus by sociologists on emergency time behavior also broadened to include studies on mitigation and prevention as well as recovery and reconstruction. More important, in the 1980s disaster research spread around the world and led to the development of a critical mass of researchers that culminated in 1986 in the establishment within the International Sociological Association of the Research Committee on Disasters, with membership in over thirty countries; its own professional journal, *International Journal of Mass Emergencies and Disasters;* and a newsletter, *Unscheduled Events.* Sociologists are particularly prominent in current research in China, Germany, Italy, Japan, the Soviet Union, and Sweden as well as in the United States.

## CONCEPTUALIZATION OF "DISASTER"

Conceptualizations and definitions of "disaster" have slowly evolved from acceptance of everyday usages of the term, through a focus on social aspects, to attempts to set forth more sociological characterizations. The earliest definitions equated disasters with features of physical agents and made distinctions between "acts of God" and "technological" agents. This was followed by notions that disasters were phenomena that resulted in significant disruptions of social life, which, however, might not involve a physical agent of any kind (e.g., a rumor that a dam had burst could evoke the same kind of evacuation behavior, etc., that an actual event would). More recently disasters have been seen not only as social constructions of reality by responders, but also as the political definitions of certain socially disruptive crises in social systems. Other researchers equate disasters with occasions where the demand for emergency actions by community organizations exceeds their capabilities for response. Finally, more recent conceptions of disasters see them as overt manifestations of latent societal vulnerabilities, basically of weaknesses in social structures or systems (Quarantelli 1987; Kreps 1989a; Schorr 1987).

Given these variants about the concept, it is not surprising that no one formulation is totally accepted within the disaster research community. However, there would be considerable agreement that the following would constitute the minimum dimensions involved in using the term "disaster" as a sensitizing concept. Disasters are relatively sudden occasions when, because of perceived threats, the routines of the collective social units involved are seriously disrupted and when unplanned courses of action have to be undertaken to cope with the crisis. The notion of relatively sudden occasions indicates that disasters have unexpected life histories that can be designated in social space and time. Disasters involve perceptions of dangers and risks to valued social objects, especially people and property. The idea of disruption of routines indicates that everyday adjustive social mechanisms cannot cope with the perceived threats. Disasters necessitate the emergence of new behaviors not in the standard repertoire of the endangered collectivity, a community, which is usually the lowest social-level entity accepted by researchers as being able to have a disaster (Kreps 1989b).

In the process of refining the concept, sociologists have almost totally abandoned the distinction between "natural" and "technological" disasters; any disaster is seen as inherently social in nature, whether this be origin, manifestation, or consequences. However, there is lack of consensus on whether social happenings involving intentional, deliberate human actions to produce social disruptions, such as occur in riots, civil disturbances, terrorist attacks, product tampering or sabotage, or wars, should be considered disasters. The majority who oppose their inclusion argue that conflict situations are inherently different in their social intentions and goals. They note that in disaster occasions there is no conscious attempt to bring about negative effects as there is in conflict situations (Quarantelli 1987). However, there is general agreement that both conflict- and consensus-type emergencies are part of a more general category of collective stress situations, as first suggested by Allan Barton (1970).

## MAJOR RESEARCH FINDINGS

While the research efforts have been uneven, much has been learned about the behavior of individuals, organizations, communities, and societies in the pre-, trans-, and postimpact time periods (Kreps 1984, 1985; Drabek 1986).

**Preimpact Behavior.** *Individuals.* Most individuals show little concern about disasters before they happen, even in risk-prone areas. Citizens tend to see disaster planning as primarily a moral rather than a legal responsibility of the government. Exceptions to these passive attitudes occur where there is much recurrent experience of disasters, as occurs in some developing countries, where disaster subcultures (institutionalized expectations) have developed and where potential

disaster settings, such as at hazardous-waste sites, are the focus of attention of citizen groups.

*Organizations.* Except for some disaster-oriented groups such as police and fire departments, there usually is little organizational planning for disasters. Even agencies that plan tend to think of disasters as extensions of everyday emergencies and fail, according to researchers, to recognize the qualitative as well as quantitative differences between routine crises and disaster occasions. These involve the fact that in disasters the involved organizations have to quickly relate to more and different groups than normal, adjust to losing part of their autonomy to overall coordinating groups, apply different performance standards and criteria, operate within a closer-than-usual public and private interface, and function when their own facilities and operations may be directly impacted by the disaster agent.

*Communities.* Usually low priority is given to preparing localities for disasters, and when there is some effort it is almost always independent of general community development and planning. This reflects the reactive rather than the proactive orientation of most politicians and bureaucrats and the fact that the issue of planning very seldom becomes a matter of broad community interests, as would be indicated by mass media focus, discussions in the political arena, or interest groups. Efforts to initiate general overall disaster preparedness often are hindered by prior organizational and community conflicts, cleavages, and disputes.

*Societies.* Generally disaster planning does not rank very high on the agenda of most societies. However, increasingly there are exceptions in developing countries when major recurrent disasters have major impact on the gross national product and on developmental programs. Also, certain catastrophes such as a Bhopal or Chernobyl can become symbolic occasions that lend impetus to instituting preparedness measures for specific disaster agents. Increasingly, too, attention to national-level disaster planning has increased as citizens in recent times have come to expect their governments to provide more security in general for the population.

**Transemergency Period Behavior.** *Individuals.* When disasters occur, individuals generally react very well. They are not paralyzed by a threat but actively seek relevant information and attempt to do what they can in the emergency. Victims, while usually very frightened, not only act positively but also show little deviant behavior; they extremely seldom break in panic flight; they do not act irrationally, especially from their perspective; and they very rarely engage in antisocial activities, although stories of such contrary behavior as looting may circulate very widely. Prosocial behavior especially comes to the fore, with the initial search and rescue being undertaken quickly and mostly by survivors in the immediate area. Most immediate needs, such as emergency housing, are met by family and friends rather than by official relief agencies. Family and household relationships are very important in affecting immediate reactions to disasters, such as whether evacuation will occur or whether warnings will be taken seriously.

*Organizations.* While there are many organizational problems in coping with the emergency time period demands of a disaster, these difficulties are often not the expected ones. Often it is assumed that if there has been organizational disaster planning, there will be successful crisis or emergency management; but apart from the possibility of planning being poor in the first place, planning is not management, and the former does not always translate well into the latter in community disasters. There typically are problems in intra- and interorganizational information flow, and in communication between and to organizations and the general public. Groups initially often have to struggle with major gaps in knowledge about the impact of a disaster. There can be organizational problems in the exercise of authority and decision making. These can stem from losses of higher-echelon personnel because of overwork, conflict regarding authority over new disaster tasks, and clashes over organizational jurisdictional differences. Generally there is much decentralization of organizational response, which in most cases is highly functional. Organizations operating with a command and control model of response do not do well at emergency times. Often, too, problems created by new disaster tasks and by the magnitude of a disaster impact strain organizational relationships.

*Communities.* The greater the disaster, the more there will be the emergence of new and adaptive community structures and functions, especially emergent groups. The greater the disaster, the more organized improvisations of all kinds appear, accompanied by pluralistic decision making. While functional in some ways, the mass convergence of outside personnel and resources on impacted communities creates major coordination problems.

*Societies.* Few societies ignore major disasters, but this does occur, especially in the case of slow and diffuse occurrences such as droughts and famines, and especially if they primarily affect subgroups not in the mainstream of a developing country. In responding to domestic disasters, societies typically provide massive help to impacted areas, even using help from outside enemies. Increasingly, most societies, including governmental officials at all levels, obtain their view of their disasters from mass media accounts; this also affects what is often remembered about the occasions.

**Postimpact Behavior.** *Individuals.* While the experience of a major disaster is a memorable one from a social-psychological point of view, there do not appear to be many lasting negative behavioral consequences. Disasters very seldom produce any new psychoses or severe mental illnesses. They do often, but not always, generate subclinical, short-lived, and self-remitting surface reactions, such as loss of appetite, sleeplessness, and anxiety. More common are many problems in living that stem more from inefficient and ineffective relief and recovery efforts of helping organizations than from the direct physical impact of disasters. In some cases, the experience of undergoing a disaster results in positive self-images and closer social ties among victims. Overall, there is little personal learning as a result of undergoing a single disaster.

*Organizations.* Organizational change, whether for planning for disasters or for other purposes, in the postimpact period is not common and is selective at best. Most modifications are simply accelerations of changes already planned or under way. Much postimpact discussion of how to improve disaster planning seldom gets translated into concrete action (unlike civil disturbances, which at least in American society in the 1960s led to many changes in organizations). However, overall, both in the United States and elsewhere, there has been in recent decades the growth of small, locally based, formal social groups primarily concerned with emergency time disaster planning and management.

*Communities.* There are selective longer-run outcomes and changes in communities that have been impacted by disasters. There can be acceleration of some ongoing and functional community trends (e.g., in local governmental arrangements and power structures), and generation of some limited new patterns (e.g., in providing local mental-health services or some mitigation measures such as regulations for floodproofing). On the other hand, particularly as the result of rehousing and rebuilding patterns, there can be magnifications of preimpact community conflicts as well as generation of new ones; some of the latter is manifested in blame assignation, which, however, tends to deflect attention away from social structural flaws to a mass-media–influenced search for individual scapegoats. It is also being recognized after disasters that changes in technology that create diffuse networks and systems, such as among lifeline organizations, are increasingly creating the need for regional rather than just community-based disaster planning.

*Societies.* In developed societies, there are few long-run negative consequences of disaster losses, whether of people or of property, since such effects are absorbed by the larger system. In developing societies and very small countries, this is not necessarily true. Nevertheless, change or improvement in national disaster planning often does not occur; cases such as after the 1985 Mexico City earthquake, when an unusual set of circumstances existed, including a "political will" to do something, constitute the exception. But increasingly, in the aftermath of major disasters, to the extent that planning is instituted or improved, it is being linked to developmental planning, a move strongly supported by international agencies such as the World Bank.

## THE FUTURE

There is a dialectical process at work: There will be more and worse disasters at the same time that there will be more and better planning. Why more and worse disasters? Risks and threats to human beings and their society are increasing. Traditional natural-disaster agents such as earthquakes and floods will simply have more people on whom to impact as the result of normal population growth and higher, denser concentration of inhabitants in risk-prone localities such as floodplains or hurricane-vulnerable shorelines that otherwise are attractive for human occupancy. There is an escalating increase in certain kinds of technological accidents and mishaps in the chemical, nuclear, and hazardous-waste areas that are new in that they were almost unknown before World War II. Technological advances can create risks and complexities to old threats, such as when fires are prevented in high-rise buildings by constructing them with highly toxic materials, or when removal of hazardous substances from solid sewage waste generates products that contain dangerous viruses and gases. New versions of old threats are also appearing, such as the increasing probability of urban rather than rural droughts, or the potential large-scale collapse of the infrastructure of older metropolitan area lifeline systems. Finally, there is the continual development of newer kinds of risks ranging from the AIDS epidemic to the biological threats inherent in genetic engineering to the crises that will be generated as the world increasingly becomes dependent on computers that are bound to fail at some key point, with drastic consequences for social systems. In addition, the newer threats are frequently dangerous at places and times distant from their initial source or origin, as dramatized by the Chernobyl nuclear radiation fallout and some problems regarding hazardous-waste sites (Quarantelli 1987).

On the other hand, increasing concern and

attention is being paid to disaster planning of all kinds. The future augurs well for more and better planning. Citizens almost everywhere are coming to expect that their governments will take steps to protect them against disasters; this is often actualized in planning for emergency preparedness and response. Whereas two decades ago a number of societies had no preimpact disaster planning of any kind, this is no longer the case. A symbolic manifestation of this trend has been the proclamation by the United Nations of the 1990s as the Decade for Natural-Disaster Reduction. This international attention will undoubtedly accelerate efforts at planning for better prevention of, preparation for, response to, and recovery from disasters; an activity in which there is reason to believe that social scientists, especially sociologists, will have an important role.

## RELATIONSHIP TO SOCIOLOGY

Although this is not true everywhere, sociologists have been increasingly accepted as having an important contribution to make to disaster planning. In part this stems from the fact that in many countries they have played the lead role among social scientists in undertaking disaster studies. While many reasons account for this, probably the crucial factor has been that much in general sociology can be used in doing research in this area.

There has been a close relationship between disaster studies and sociology from the earliest days of work in the area (Killian 1952; Form and Nosow 1958). In part this is because sociologists, being among the leading pioneers and researchers in this area, have tended to use what they could from their discipline. Thus, sociology has contributed to the research techniques used (e.g., field studies and open-ended interviewing), the research methodology utilized (e.g., the "grounded theory" approach and the employment of inductive analytical models), the theoretical ideas utilized (e.g., the notion of emergence from collective-behavior thinking and the idea of informal and formal structures of organizations), and the general perspectives used (e.g., that there can be

latent as well as dysfunctional aspects of any behavior and that societies and communities have a social history that is not easily set aside). In a recent volume entitled *Sociology of Disasters: Contributions of Sociology to Disaster Research* (Dynes, De Marchi, and Pelanda 1987), these and other contributions to disaster theory, disaster research methods, disaster models, and disaster concepts are set forth in considerable detail (see also Wright and Rossi 1981).

The relationship has not been one-sided, since disaster research has also contributed to sociology. The field of collective behavior has probably been most influenced, but there have been significant contributions to the study of formal organizations, social roles, social problems, organizational and social change, mass communications, the urban community, and medical sociology (Dynes and Quarantelli 1968; Dynes 1974; Quarantelli 1978; Wright and Rossi 1981; Kreps 1984; Quarantelli 1989). A recent symposium on social structure and disaster, coattended by disaster researchers and prominent sociological theorists, attempted to examine how disaster studies not only are informed by but also could inform sociological theory; the proceedings have been published in *Social Structure and Disaster* (Kreps 1989b).

(SEE ALSO: *Collective Behavior; Technological Risks and Society*)

## REFERENCES

Barton, Allan 1970 *Communities in Disaster: A Sociological Analysis.* Garden City, N.Y.: Anchor Books.

Drabek, Thomas 1986 *Human System Responses to Disasters: An Inventory of Sociological Findings.* New York: Springer-Verlag.

Dynes, R. R. 1974 *Organized Behavior in Disasters.* Newark, Del.: Disaster Research Center, University of Delaware.

——— (ed.) 1988 "Disaster Classics Special Issue." *International Journal of Mass Emergencies and Disasters* 6:209–395.

———, B. De Marchi, and C. Pelanda (eds.) 1987 *Sociology of Disasters: Contributions of Sociology to Disaster Research.* Milan: Franco Angeli.

————, and E. L. Quarantelli 1968 "Group Behavior Under Stress: A Required Convergence of Organizational and Collective Behavior Perspectives." *Sociology and Social Research* 52:416–429.

Form, William, and Sigmund Nosow 1958 *Community in Disaster.* New York: Harper and Row.

Fritz, Charles 1961 "Disaster." In Robert Merton and Robert Nisbet, eds., *Contemporary Social Problems.* New York: Harcourt, Brace and World.

Killian, Lewis 1952 "The Significance of Multiple Group Membership in Disaster Study." *American Journal of Sociology* 57:309–314.

Kreps, Gary 1984 "Sociological Inquiry and Disaster Research." *Annual Review of Sociology* 10:309–333.

———— 1985 "Disaster and the Social Order." *Sociological Theory* 3:49–65.

———— (ed.) 1989a "The Boundaries of Disaster Research: Taxonomy and Comparative Study Special Issue." *International Journal of Mass Emergencies and Disasters* 7:213–431.

———— 1989b *Social Structure and Disaster.* Newark, Del.: University of Delaware Press.

Perrow, Charles 1984 *Normal Accidents: Living with High-Risk Technologies.* New York: Basic Books.

Prince, Samuel 1920 *Catastrophe and Social Change.* New York: Columbia University Press.

Quarantelli, E. L. (ed.) 1978 *Disasters: Theory and Research.* Beverly Hills, Calif.: Sage Publications.

———— 1987 "What Should We Study? Questions and Suggestions for Researchers About the Concept of Disasters." *International Journal of Mass Emergencies and Disasters* 5:7–32.

———— 1989 "The Social Science Study of Disasters and Mass Communication." In L. Walters, L. Wilkins, and T. Walters, eds., *Bad Tidings: Communication and Catastrophe.* Hillsdale, N. J.: Lawrence Erlbaum.

————, and R. R. Dynes 1977 "Response to Social Crises and Disasters." *Annual Review of Sociology* 3:23–49.

Schorr, J. 1987 "Some Contributions of German *Katastrophensoziologie* to the Sociology of Disaster." *International Journal of Mass Emergencies and Disasters* 5:115–135.

Short, James F. 1984 "The Social Fabric at Risk: Toward the Social Transformation of Risk Analysis." *American Sociological Review* 49:711–725.

Sorokin, Pitirim 1942 *Man and Society in Calamity.* New York: E. P. Dutton.

Wright, James, and Peter Rossi (eds.) 1981 *Social Science and Natural Hazards.* Cambridge, Mass.: Abt Books.

ENRICO L. QUARANTELLI

**DISCRIMINATION** Discrimination, in its sociological meaning, involves highly complex social processes. The term derives from the Latin *discriminatio,* which means to perceive distinctions among phenomena or to be selective in one's judgment. Cognitive psychology retains the first of these meanings, popular usage the second. Individual behavior that limits the opportunities of a particular group is encompassed in many sociological considerations of discrimination. But exclusively individualistic approaches are too narrow for robust sociological treatment. Instead, most sociologists understand discrimination not as isolated individual acts but as "a system of social relations" (Antonovsky 1960, p. 81) that produce intergroup inequities in social outcomes.

This definitional expansion transforms "discrimination" into a truly sociological concept. But in its breadth, the sociological definition leaves room for ambiguity and controversy. Obstacles to consensus on a more precise definition stem from two sources—one empirical, the other ideological and political. First, deficiencies in analysis and evidence limit our ability to trace thoroughly the dynamic web of effects produced by discrimination. Second, because social discrimination is contrary to professed American values and law, a judgment that unequal outcomes reflect discrimination is a call for costly remedies. Variable willingness to bear those social costs contributes to dissension about the extent of discrimination.

The broadest sociological definitions of discrimination assume that racial minorities, women, and other historical targets have no inherent characteristics warranting inferior social outcomes. Thus, all inequality is seen as a legacy of discrimination, whether proximal or distal, and as a social injustice to be remedied.

By contrast, political conservatives favor a far narrower definition, one that limits the concept's scope by including only actions *intended* to restrict a group's chances. For solid conceptual reasons, sociologists have seldom followed suit (but see Burkey 1978, p. 79). First, an intentionality criterion returns the concept to the realm of psychology and deflects attention from restraining social structure. Second, the difficulty in ascertaining intentions creates insuperable obstacles to thorough documentation of discrimination.

Most important, their understanding of intricate societal patterns sensitizes sociologists to the fact that disadvantage accruing from intentional discrimination typically cumulates, extends far beyond the original injury, and long outlives the deliberate perpetration. Many sociologists distinguish between *direct* and *indirect* discrimination (Pettigrew 1985). Direct discrimination occurs at points where inequality is generated, often intentionally. When decisions are based explicitly on race, discrimination is direct. Indirect discrimination is the perpetuation or magnification of the original injury. It occurs when the inequitable results of direct discrimination are used as a basis for later decisions ("past-in-present discrimination") or decisions in linked institutions ("side-effect discrimination"; Feagin and Feagin 1986). In other words, discrimination is indirect when an ostensibly nonracial criterion serves as a *proxy* for race in determining social outcomes.

To illustrate with respect to wages, direct discrimination exists when equally qualified blacks and whites or men and women are paid at different rates for the same work. Indirect discrimination exists when the two groups are paid unequally because prior discrimination in employment, education, or housing created apparent differences in qualifications or channeled the groups into better- and worse-paying jobs. This direct versus indirect distinction resembles the legal distinction between disparate treatment and disparate impact. While intentional direct discrimination may have triggered the causal chain, the original injury is often perpetuated and magnified by unwitting social actors. The application of intentionality criteria would deny that the continuing disadvantage is a legacy of discrimination.

A half-century ago, Williams restricted the concept differently. "Discrimination may be said to exist to the degree that individuals of a given group who are otherwise *formally qualified* are not treated in conformity with these nominally *universal institutionalized codes*" (Williams 1947, p. 39, emphasis added). Antonovsky (1960, p. 81) used a related qualification: Discrimination is "the effective injurious treatment of persons on grounds *rationally irrelevant* to the situation" (emphasis added). Economists use starker terms. For Becker (1968, p. 81), economic discrimination occurs "against members of a group whenever their earnings fall short of the amount '*warranted' by their abilities*" (emphasis added).

Two problems arise with these definitions. First, the assessment of "abilities" and the determination of what treatment is "rationally" relevant or "warranted" is no easy task. Critical examination of common practice has uncovered many instances where formal qualifications and "nominally universal institutionalized codes" proved *not* to provide a logical basis for distinctions. Recent employment testing litigation demonstrates that when hiring criteria once legitimized by tradition or "logic" are put to scientific test, they often fail to predict job performance in the assumed fashion. Analogous fallacies have been identified in the conventional wisdom guiding admission to advanced education. Hence, nominally universalistic standards may provide an imperfect or altogether illogical basis for decision making. If such misguided selection procedures also work to the disadvantage of historical victims of discrimination, these practices should not be protected from the charge of discrimination by their universalistic facade.

The second problem with these definitions is that they ignore another, prevalent form of indirect discrimination. Even where nominally universalistic standards do serve some legitimate social function such as selecting satisfactory workers, adverse impact of these standards on those who bear the cumulated disadvantage of historical discrimination cannot be disregarded.

The intricacy of discrimination and unresolved

issues about its definition impede easy application of social science methods to inform institutional policy. Apparently rigorous quantitative analyses often only camouflage the crucial issues, as critical examination of wage differential decompositions reveals.

Assessments of discrimination, produced by decomposing gross race or gender differences in such social outcomes as wages, are common in sociology (e.g., Corcoran and Duncan 1978; Farley 1984; Featherman and Hauser 1976; Johnson and Sell 1976) as well as economics (e.g., Oaxaca 1973). One segment of the intergroup differential is defined by its empirical linkage to "qualifications" and other factors deemed legitimate determinants of social rewards. The second, residual segment not demonstrably linked to "legitimate" determinants of the outcomes is sometimes labeled the measure of "proximal" or "direct" discrimination but more often is presented simply as *the* estimate of discrimination. However, in the absence of better information than usually available and greater agreement on what constitutes discrimination, no *unique* estimate is possible. Through their choice of control variables to index "legitimate" determinants of social outcomes and their interpretation of findings, researchers consciously or unwittingly shape their own answers: Any appearance of scientific certitude is an illusion. For example, estimates of the proportion of the gender earnings gap caused by discrimination in the United States range from Sanborn's (1969) 10 percent or less to Blinder's (1973) 100 percent. Predictably, each has been challenged (Bergman and Adelman 1973; Rosensweig and Morgan 1976).

A close look at one application of the decompositional approach, a recent analysis of sex differentials in faculty salaries at a large public university, illustrates the difficulty of separating "legitimate" wage differentials from inequity (Taylor 1988). About 90 percent of a $10,000 sex difference in faculty salaries was empirically linked to three factors widely considered legitimate determinants of faculty pay: academic rank, age, and discipline. Women tend to hold lower academic rank, to be younger, and more often than men to be affiliated

with poorly paid disciplines. Insofar as women's lower salaries are linked to rank, age, and discipline, is the salary differential free from any legacy of sex discrimination? Conventional wage differential decompositions imply an unequivocal yes. If a simple answer is given, it surely should be no. But in truth, when policymakers ask for dollar estimates of inequity, or specifically for inequity that the institution is obliged to remedy, the answers are neither unequivocal nor simple.

If the university's promotion system has operated fairly, a sex gap reflecting differences in rank may be warranted. If sex bias has existed in the university's promotion system, depressing the average academic rank of women faculty, the resulting deficit in women's salaries reflects indirect discrimination; attention should then be directed to the offending promotion processes. However, direct salary adjustments may also be in order, because sex bias in promotions makes the link between rank and salary itself look unreasonable. Unlike many embodiments of indirect discrimination, inequitable depression of women's ranks would not necessarily lessen their actual contributions to the faculty, just their status. Application of a universalistic salary determination standard based on rank would then stand as an impediment to the very goal it was intended to promote—the matching of rewards to contributions.

Salary differences tied to the age differential of female and male faculty also raise troublesome questions. If the relative youth of women faculty reflects lower retention and higher turnover as a result of discriminatory review processes or generally inhospitable conditions, salary differentials tied to age differences are again textbook examples of indirect discrimination. The evidence would signal a need for institutional efforts to improve the retention of women faculty. But here it is not clear that salary adjustments are warranted: Because faculty contributions may be a function of experience, application of the universalistic age criterion is arguably reasonable. Any sex gap in salary tied to age differentials could, then, be both a legacy of discrimination and a reasonable conditioning of rewards on contributions. The age-linked salary differential plot grows even thicker when it is recognized that affirmative action efforts often meet with greatest success in recruiting junior candidates. Thus, without supplementary data, it is not even clear whether an age-linked sex gap in salary reflects continuing institutional discrimination or affirmative hiring.

Sex differences in salary associated with discipline present even more complicated interpretational problems. Women and men are distributed across academic disciplines in a fashion that mirrors the sex distribution across occupations. And disciplinary differences in average salary likewise mirror wage differentials across occupations. But are these patterns simply a matter of sex differences in preferences or abilities, with no implication of discrimination? Or are women steered away or outright excluded from lucrative fields, so that sex differentials in salary linked to disciplinary affiliation represent an indirect effect of discrimination in training, recruitment, and hiring? Or does the pattern of occupational wage differentials mirrored in disciplinary differences represent direct discrimination, an influence of sex composition per se on occupational wage structures (England et al. 1988)? In the latter case, assignment of responsibility for remedy presents particular problems. The university, like any other single employer, is simultaneously vulnerable to competitive forces of the wider labor market and a constituent element of that wider market. Defiance of the market by a single organization is costly; adherence by all organizations to the broader occupational wage structure perpetuates sex inequity.

The faculty salary study considered here did not examine the role of scientific "productivity" in relation to salary differentials. But the inclusion of productivity measures among the control variables would raise another difficult issue involving feedback effects and reciprocal causation. There is evidence that on standard "productivity" measures, women faculty average lower scores than men (Fox 1991). Thus, many institutional studies of salary differentials would probably find some segment of the male–female salary gap linked to productivity differences. Fox's research demonstrates, however, that sex differences in scientific

productivity reflect contrasting levels of resources that institutions provide to male and female faculty. Like age and rank, the sex difference in productivity may itself be a product of institutional discrimination; by implication, salary differentials based on these male–female productivity differences represent indirect discrimination. The new ingredient here is that institutional shaping of productivity is subtle. Scientific productivity is ordinarily seen as an outgrowth of talent and effort, not potentially sex-biased institutional resource allocation. Thus, credible documentation of this process of indirect discrimination is a greater challenge for researchers.

Critical reflection on this sample decomposition of a sex differential in faculty salaries has highlighted a set of interrelated points about the complex nature of discrimination and unresolved issues of remedy.

1. In American society today, the injuries of indirect discrimination are often far more extensive than those of direct discrimination.
2. Apparently reasonable universalistic principles may on closer examination be unnecessary or even disfunctional. Scrutiny of employment criteria prompted by the Supreme Court's 1971 *Griggs v. Duke Power Co.* decision has provided useful models for challenging nominally universalistic standards. Where it is possible to substitute standards that do as well or better at screening or evaluation without adversely affecting historical targets of discrimination, there are gains for all involved.
3. When legacies of discrimination take the form of qualifications that may well be reasonable prerequisites for social rewards, as with experience and salary, more extensive remedies are needed. For example, where training deficits impair employability, or inadequate preparation impedes admission to higher education, attention should be given to the earlier schooling processes that generated these deficiencies. This form of remedy aids future generations. In the meantime, compensatory training can reduce the liabilities of those who have already fallen victim to inferior schools.

4. Microcosms cannot escape the discriminatory impact of the societal macrocosm. Just as salary differences across academic disciplines reflect general occupational wage structures, institutions are often both prey to and participant in broader social forces. Narrow, legalistic approaches to the assignment of remedy are inadequate for addressing this dynamic of discrimination.

5. Empirical research on group discrimination must mirror the phenomenon in its variety and complexity. The regression decomposition approach described here has proven useful, but we have noted its limitations. Regression analyses could provide more pertinent information if based on fuller structural equation models that acknowledge reciprocal causation. Most important, if the aim is to guide policy, a framework considerably more complex than the dichotomous discrimination-or-not approach is required. But the sociological arsenal of methods offers other promising approaches. Research that traces the actual processes of institutional discrimination is essential (e.g., Braddock, Crain, and McPartland 1984; Braddock and McPartland 1987; Braddock and McPartland 1989). Also needed is attention to victims' perceptions of discrimination processes and investigation of the changes generated by antidiscrimination efforts.

Finally, a comprehensive understanding of societal discrimination must encompass these two propositions.

1. The long-lasting character of discrimination means that the effects typically outlive the initiators of discriminatory practices. Apart from its importance to the law, this feature of modern discrimination has critical implications for sociological theory. Discrimination is fundamentally normative; its structural web operates in large part independent of the dominant group's present "tastes," attitudes, or awareness. Hence, models based primarily on individual prejudice or "rationality," whether psychological or economic, will uniformly understate and oversimplify the phenomenon.

2. Discrimination is typically cumulative, compounding, and self-perpetuating. For example, an array of research on black Americans has demonstrated that neighborhood racial segregation leads to educational disadvantages, thus to occupational disadvantage, and thus to income deficits (Pettigrew 1979; 1985). To be effective, structural remedies must reverse this "vicious cycle" of discrimination (Myrdal 1944).

Seen in sociological perspective, then, discrimination is considerably more intricate and entrenched than commonly thought. The complexity of discrimination presents major challenges to social scientific attempts to trace its impact. This complexity also makes impossible any one-to-one correspondence between perpetration and responsibility for remedy. Broad social programs will be necessary if the full legacy of discrimination is finally to be erased.

(SEE ALSO: *Affirmative Action; Comparable Worth; Equality of Opportunity; Prejudice; Race; Segregation and Desegregation*)

## REFERENCES

Antonovsky, A. 1960 "The Social Meaning of Discrimination." *Phylon* (11):81–95.

Becker, G. 1968 "Economic Discrimination." In D. L. Sills, ed., *International Encyclopedia of the Social Sciences.* New York: Macmillan.

Bergman, B. R., and I. Adelman 1973 "The 1973 Report of the President's Council of Economic Advisors: The Economic Role of Women." *American Economic Review* (63):509–514.

Blinder, A. S. 1973 "Wage Discrimination: Reduced Form and Structural Estimates." *Journal of Human Resources* (8):463–455.

Braddock, J. H., II, R. L. Crain, and J. M. McPartland 1984 "A Long-Term View of Racial Desegregation: Some Recent Studies of Graduates as Adults." *Phi Delta Kappan* (66):259–264.

Braddock, J. H., II, and J. M. McPartland 1987 "How

Minorities Continue to Be Excluded from Equal Employment Opportunities: Research on Labor Market and Institutional Barriers." *Journal of Social Issues* (43):5–39.

———— 1989 "Social Psychological Processes That Perpetuate Racial Segregation: The Relationship between School and Employment Desegregation." *Journal of Black Studies* (19):267–289.

Burkey, R. 1978 *Ethnic and Racial Groups: The Dynamics of Dominance*. Menlo Park, Calif.: Cummings.

Corcoran, M., and G. J. Duncan 1978 "Work History, Labor Force Attachment, and Earning Differences between Races and Sexes." *Journal of Human Resources* (14):3–20.

England, P., G. Farkas, B. Kilbourne, and T. Dou 1988 "Explaining Occupational Sex Segregation and Wages: Findings from a Model with Fixed Effects." *American Sociological Review* (53):544–558.

Farley, R. 1984 *Blacks and Whites: Narrowing the Gap?* Cambridge, Mass.: Harvard University Press.

Feagin, J. R., and C. B. Feagin 1986 *Discrimination American Style: Institutional Racism and Sexism*. Malabar, Fla.: Krieger.

Featherman, D. L., and R. M. Hauser, 1976 "Changes in the Socioeconomic Stratification of the Races, 1962–1973." *American Journal of Sociology* (82): 621–652.

Fox, M. F. 1991. "Gender, Environmental Milieux, and Productivity in Science." In J. Cole, H. Zuckerman, and J. Bruer, eds., *The Outer Circle: Women in the Scientific Community*. New York: W. W. Norton.

Johnson, M., and R. Sell 1976 "The Cost of Being Black: A 1970 Update." *American Journal of Sociology* (82):183–190.

Myrdal, G. 1944 *An American Dilemma*. New York: Harper and Row.

Oaxaca, R. 1973 "Male–Female Wage Differentials in Urban Labor Markets." *International Economic Review* (14):693–709.

Pettigrew, T. F. 1979 "Racial Change and Social Policy." *Annals of the American Association of Political and Social Science* (441):114–131.

———— 1985 "New Black–White Patterns: How Best to Conceptualize Them?" In R. Turner, ed., *Annual Review of Sociology, 1985*. Palo Alto, Calif.: Annual Reviews.

Rosensweig, M. R., and J. Morgan 1976 "Wage Discrimination: A Comment." *Journal of Human Resources* (11):3–7.

Sanborn, H. 1969 "Pay Differences between Men and Women." *Industrial and Labor Relations Review* (17):534–550.

Taylor, M. C. 1988 "Estimating Race and Sex Inequity in Wages: Substantive Implications of Methodological Choices." Paper presented at the 1989 Research Conference of the Association for Public Policy Analysis and Management, Seattle, Washington, October 29, 1988.

Williams, R. M., Jr. 1947 *The Reduction of Intergroup Tensions*. New York: Social Science Research Council.

THOMAS F. PETTIGREW
MARYLEE C. TAYLOR

**DISENGAGEMENT THEORY** Disengagement theory was an influential early effort to apply an established sociological perspective to the problem of aging. Based on the structural functionalism of Talcott Parsons, Elaine Cumming and William Henry attempted to develop a universal theory of the relationship between aged persons and society. The theory is no longer in wide use and is credited primarily with motivating social gerontologists to develop and test alternative theories to counter it.

Disengagement theory emerged from Cumming and Henry's (1961) analysis of data from a study of 257 healthy and financially independent elderly persons in Kansas City. The theory begins with the observation that elderly people withdraw from social roles. It does not simply assume that this withdrawal occurs because the aged become infirm and disabled and therefore leave social functions and associations. Instead, disengagement theory argues that there is advance preparation for the eventual disengagement brought about by illness and death. The elderly individual begins to disengage *before* it is absolutely necessary.

Why does this occur? It is a tenet of functionalism that society always attempts to keep itself in equilibrium. The death or incapacity of a person who is still performing vitally necessary roles is a great strain on this equilibrium. By gradually phasing elderly people—who are as a class closer to death than the young—out of vitally important roles, it is ensured that infirmity and death will not disrupt the smooth functioning of society.

The process of disengagement has a number of effects on aged persons (Wershow 1981). The individual's life space shrinks, and he or she interacts with fewer people and vacates key work and family roles. In particular, the person's role set comes to exclude those roles that are considered important and powerful by the larger society. Interpersonal contacts are reduced to a small circle of family and closest friends, and the elderly come to interact more exclusively with other aged persons. Since society is less concerned with aged individuals, normative constraints on their behavior are lessened, and more idiosyncratic and eccentric behaviors are permitted.

Cumming and Henry asserted that the disengagement process is mutually satisfying to both society and the individual. In simplest terms, the old person can "die in peace," as he or she has abandoned social ties. Society is content with this arrangement, for it is not disrupted by the death of someone who is not deeply involved in the social process. Cumming and Henry asserted that this pattern of disengagement of the elderly is inevitable and universal, although it might vary somewhat from culture to culture in the precise form it takes.

Criticism of disengagement theory began shortly after its conception, with particularly incisive critiques by Rose (1965) and Hochschild (1975). First, it is held that the theory is too simplistic; quite simply, many elderly persons do not disengage. Further, evidence was provided from other cultures where disengagement was not found. Hochschild (1975) noted that such evidence was dismissed by disengagement theorists, who argued that such still active individuals were either "unsuccessful disengagers," were "off-time" in the disengagement process, or were members of an "elite" that formed a small abnormality in the process. Hochschild thus criticized the theory as unfalsifiable.

Second, activity theorists (Havighurst 1963) provided evidence demonstrating that continued activity, rather than disengagement, was related to high morale for many elderly persons.

Third, critics pointed out that disengagement of the elderly may have more to do with a lack of *opportunity* for the performance of meaningful roles than with a universal functional process. This lack of opportunity is due to society's negative attitudes toward the elderly. In that disengagement theory takes withdrawal from social roles as a given, it does not allow for a critique of society as a *cause* of disengagement nor for proposals to change social forces that pressure elderly persons into disengagement.

With few exceptions, disengagement theory has not been widely used to guide research in aging since the middle 1970s and has been replaced by such more recent developments as age stratification theory (Riley 1985) and continuity theory (Atchley 1989). However, it deserves credit for serving as an early example of the way in which macrosociological theory could be applied to the aging process. Further, the controversy it generated led to the development of additional theories regarding the social aspects of aging.

(SEE ALSO: *Retirement; Social Gerontology*)

## REFERENCES

Atchley, Robert C. 1989 "A Continuity Theory of Normal Aging." *The Gerontologist* 2:183–190.

Cumming, Elaine, and William Henry 1961 *Growing Old: The Process of Disengagement*. New York: Basic Books.

Havighurst, Robert 1963 "Successful Aging." In R. H. Williams, C. Tibbits, and W. Donahue, eds., *Processes of Aging*. New York: Atherton.

Hochschild, Arlie Russell 1975 "Disengagement Theory: A Critique and Proposal." *American Sociological Review* 40:553–569.

Riley, Matilda White 1985 "Age Strata in Social Systems." In R. H. Binstock and E. Shanas, eds., *Handbook of Aging and the Social Sciences*. New York: Van Nostrand Reinhold.

Rose, Arnold 1965 "The Subculture of the Aging." In A. Rose and W. Peterson, eds., *Older People and Their Social World*. Philadelphia: F.A. Davis.

Wershow, Harold J. 1981 "The Theory of Disengage-

—ment." In H. J. Wershow, ed., *Controversial Issues in Gerontology.* New York: Springer.

KARL PILLEMER

## DISTRIBUTION-FREE STATISTICS
*See* Nonparametric Statistics.

## DISTRIBUTIVE JUSTICE *See* Equity Theory.

## DIVORCE
Divorce is of sociological significance for several reasons. To begin, divorce rates are often seen as indicators of the health of the institution of marriage. When divorce rates rise or fall, many sociologists have been inclined to view these changes as indicating something about the aggregate quality of marriages or, alternatively, the stability of social systems.

Viewed from another perspective, divorce interests sociologists as one of several important transitions in the life course of individuals. The adults and children who experience divorce have been studied to understand both the causes and consequences. From this perspective, a divorce is an event in the biography of family members, much as other life course transitions (remarriage, childbirth, retirement).

Sociological interest in divorce also focuses on the macrosocial events associated with it. Divorce figures prominently in any sociological analysis of industrialization, poverty, educational attainment, conflict resolution, or law.

For sociologists, divorce may characterize an individual, a family, a region, a subgroup, a historical period, or an entire social system. It may be studied as either cause or consequence of other phenomena. Still, the overriding concern of almost all research on this topic in the twentieth century has been the increase in divorce over time. This century began with very little divorce. It draws to a close with divorce being as common as its absence in the lives of recently married couples. Although marital instability has not increased

significantly since 1980, present rates are at an all-time high. Recent estimates based on national surveys are that at least one-half, and perhaps as many as two-thirds, of all recent marriages will end in divorce (assuming there is no significant drop in rates of marital disruption; Martin and Bumpass 1989). Understanding the increase in divorce has been the larger sociological endeavor —regardless of the particular sociological perspective employed. A historical account of trends is necessary before considering contemporary issues associated with divorce.

### A BRIEF HISTORICAL RECORD OF DIVORCE IN AMERICA

**The Colonial Period.** Divorce was not legal in any but the New England settlements. The Church of England allowed for legal separations (*a mensa et thoro*) but not for divorce. The New England Puritans who first landed at Plymouth in 1621, however, were disenchanted with this, as well as many other Anglican doctrines. Divorce was permitted on the grounds of adultery or seven-year desertion as early as 1639 in Plymouth. Other New England colonies followed similar guidelines. Divorce governed by rudimentary codified law was effected by legislative decree. Individual petitions for divorce were debated in colonial legislatures and were effected by bills to dissolve a particular marriage. Still, though legal, divorce was very rare. During the seventeenth century, there were fifty-four petitions for divorce in Massachusetts, of which forty-four were successful (Phillips 1988, p. 138). The middle colonies provided annulments or divorces for serious matrimonial offenses such as prolonged absence or bigamy. The southern colonies afforded no provisions for divorce whatsoever.

**Post–Revolutionary War.** Immediately after the Revolutionary War, without British legal impediments to divorce, the states began discussion of laws allowing divorce. In New England and middle states divorce became the province of state courts, while in the more restrictive southern states it was more often a legislative matter. By the turn of the nineteenth century, almost all states had enacted some form of divorce legislation. And by the middle of the century, even southern states were operating within a judicial divorce system.

The shift to judicial divorce is significant. By removing divorce deliberations from legislatures, states were forced to establish grounds that justified a divorce. Such clauses reflected the prevailing sentiments governing normative marriage— they indicated what was expected of marriage at the time. And by investing judges with the authority to interpret and adjudicate, such changes significantly liberalized the availability of divorce. Northern and southern states permitted divorces for specific offenses such as adultery, desertion, bigamy, and, increasingly with time, cruelty. In the newer frontier western states, grounds resembled those of the East plus "any other cause for which the court shall deem it proper that the divorce shall be granted" (Phillips 1988, p. 453).

Throughout the nineteenth century, there was a gradual liberalization of divorce laws in the United States and a corresponding increase in divorce as well. Where divorces totaled a few hundred at the beginning of the nineteenth century, the numbers grew exponentially as the century wore on; 7,380 divorces in 1860, 10,962 in 1870, 19,663 in 1880, 33,461 in 1890, and 55,751 in 1900 (U.S. Bureau of the Census 1975). These figures assume greater significance when growth in population is removed from them. Whereas the divorce rate (number of divorces per 1,000 marriages) was 1.2 in 1869, it had climbed to 4.0 by 1900. In short, the increase in divorce outstripped the increase in population several times.

A number of factors have been identified as causes of such dramatic increases. In part, these can be described as social changes that made marriage less essential. The growth of wage labor in the nineteenth century afforded women an alternative to economic dependence on a husband. In an economy dominated by individuals rather than families, marriage was simply less essential. Life as a single individual gradually lost its stigma (New England settlements had forbidden solitary dwelling, while southern communities had taxed it heavily).

More important, however, were fundamental shifts in the meaning of marriage. Divorce codes reflected the growing belief that marriages should be imbued with heavy doses of affection and equality. Divorce grounds of cruelty or lack of support indicate that marriage was increasingly viewed as a partnership. Where a century earlier men had been granted greater discretion in their personal lives, latter-nineteenth-century morality attacked such double standards. Men were not necessarily less culpable than women for their vices. Victorian morality stressed the highest standards of sexual behavior for *both* husbands and wives. Changing divorce codes coincided with the passage of laws restricting husbands' unilateral control over their wives' property. The passage of married women's property acts throughout the nation in the latter nineteenth century acknowledged married women's claims to property brought to or acquired in marriage. By 1887, thirty-three states and the District of Columbia gave married women control over their property and earnings (Degler 1980, p. 332).

Divorce codes including omnibus grounds such as "cruelty" (which could justify a divorce from a drunkard husband, for example) may be viewed as reflecting a Victorian American belief that women were morally sensitive and fragile and in need of protection (Phillips 1988, p. 500). More particularly, the growing use of offenses against the intimate and emotional aspects of marriage reflected a growing belief that such things constituted matrimonial essentials.

**The Twentieth Century.**   The first half of this century was a continuation of trends established in the late nineteenth century. Gradually increasing divorce rates were interrupted by two world wars and the Great Depression. During each war and during the depression, divorce rates dropped. After each, rates soared before falling to levels somewhat higher than that which preceded these events. Sociological explanations for these trends focus on women's employment opportunities. Women's labor force participation permits the termination of intolerable unions. The separations, hastily timed marriages, and sexual misalliances characteristic of wartime were also undoubtedly factors in the postwar divorce rates. Further, the increases in divorce following these difficult times may be seen, in part, as a delayed reaction. Once the depression or war was over, the reservoir of impending divorces broke. And finally, postwar optimism and affluence may have contributed to an unwillingness to sustain an unhappy marriage.

The second half of the century has witnessed even more dramatic increases in divorce. With the exception of the peculiar 1950s (for an explanation of this anomaly, see Cherlin 1981), the trend for the second half of the 1900s has been a regular and exponential growth in divorce.

Though specific explanations for the increase in divorces during the twentieth century vary, several themes may be noted. First, marriage this century has lost much of its central economic and social significance—especially for women. For example, divorce was undoubtedly inhibited by the fact that prior to the twentieth century, custody of children was uniformly awarded to fathers (since they were legally responsible for financial support). With the acceptance in the early 1900s of Freudian ideas of psychosexual development and similar ideas about intellectual and cognitive growth, the so-called Tender Years Doctrine became accepted practice in courts, which then awarded custody to mothers as regularly as they had once done to fathers. And as it became more commonplace, remarriage began to lose some of its stigma. All these changes made it possible for women to divorce their husbands if they wished. But why did so many wish to obtain divorces?

The simplest explanation is that more divorce is a consequence of higher and higher expectations of marriage. More and more grounds for divorce are developed as there are higher and higher expectations for what a marriage should be. In the nineteenth century, drunkenness, cruelty, and failure to provide were added to more traditional grounds of adultery and desertion. In the early twentieth century, cruelty was continually redefined to include not only physical but mental cruelty as well.

The postwar surges in divorce created sufficient numbers of divorced persons that the practice lost much of its stigma. Add to this the widespread employment of women since the mid 1960s, and increase in divorce becomes more understandable. When women are employed, there is less constraint on them to remain in a marriage. But there is also less constraint on their husbands, who will not be required to support their employed ex-wives after a divorce.

In the last twenty years, divorce has been fundamentally redefined. No-fault divorce laws passed since the early 1970s have defined as unacceptable those marriages in which couples are "incompatible" or have "irreconcilable differences," or those that are "irretrievably broken." The nonadversarial grounds for divorce are now almost entirely based on the failures of emotional essentials. Emotional marital breakdown may have been a feature of large numbers of marriages in earlier historical periods. Only now, however, is such a situation viewed as solely sufficient grounds for terminating the marriage.

## DIVORCE IN THE WEST

Any theory of divorce must be able to account for the broad similarities in trends throughout the Western world during the twentieth century. These similarities exist despite notable differences in national economies, state forms of government, and the role of the church. The trends are well known. There was very little divorce until the end of the nineteenth century, a slow but constant growth in divorce rates through the first half of the twentieth century (interrupted by two world wars and an international economic depression), and significant increases in divorce rates since the 1960s. The twentieth century, in short, is when most significant changes in divorce rates occurred. And the changes noted in America were seen in most other Western nations.

Between World Wars I and II, widespread changes in divorce laws reflected changing beliefs about matrimony and its essentials. The strains of war and the associated problems that produced more divorces made the practice more conspicuous and consequently more acceptible. There is no doubt one cause of divorce is divorce. When obscure, the practice was stigmatized and there was little to counter stereotypes associated with its practice. When divorce became more commonplace, it lost some of its stigma.

Social changes pertaining to women's roles are a large part of the story of divorce during the postwar era. One sign of these changes was the growth, throughout the West, in women's labor force participation. But the most conspicuous symbol of the changing role of women was the passage of suffrage legislation throughout the Western world. Before 1914, women were permitted to vote only in New Zealand, Australia, Finland, Norway, and eleven western U.S. states. In the United States, women were enfranchised in 1920. In Britain, Sweden, Germany, and many other European countries, suffrage passed soon after World War I.

Divorce laws, similarly, were altered between the wars in accordance with changing views of marriage and the role of women. The British Parliament enacted divorce reform in 1937 by significantly extending the grounds for divorce (including "cruelty") and granting women new options for filing for divorce. Scotland reformed its divorce laws in 1938 by extending grounds for divorce to include failures of emotional essentials —cruelty and habitual drunkenness, for example. In 1930, the Canadian Parliament for the first time empowered judicial magistrates to grant divorce rather than requiring legislative decrees. And the Spanish divorce law of 1932 was the most liberal in contemporary Europe—providing divorce by mutual consent (Phillips 1988, p. 539). Even Nazi Germany permitted no-fault divorce by 1938 (though divorce law was aimed at increasing the number of Aryan children born).

Following World War II, divorce rates throughout the Western world stabilized after an initial increase. The low divorce rates, high fertility, and lower age at marriage that characterized all Western nations after World War II are trends that have not been adequately explained. Whether these trends reflected the consequences of war, the effects of having grown up during the worldwide depression, or a short-term rise in social conservatism is now debated. Regardless of the cause, the decade of the 1950s is universally regarded as a temporary aberration in otherwise long-term and continuous twentieth-century trends. Not until the 1960s were there additional significant changes in divorce laws or divorce rates.

The 1960s were years of significant social change in almost all Western nations. The demographic consequences of high fertility during the 1950s became most apparent in the large and vocal youth movements challenging conventional sexual and marital norms, censorship, the war in Vietnam, and educational policies. Challenges to institutional authority were commonplace. Divorce laws were not immune to the general liberalization. "Between 1960 and 1986 divorce policy in almost all the countries of the West was either completely revised or substantially reformed" (Phillips 1988, p. 562). Most such reforms occurred in the late 1960s to the late 1970s. Unlike earlier divorce law reforms, those during the post–World War II era did not extend the grounds for divorce so much as they redefined the jurisdiction over it. The passage of no-fault divorce laws signaled a profound shift in the way divorce was to be handled.

Most significantly, divorce became the prerogative of the married couple with little involvement of the state. No-fault divorce does not require either spouse to be guilty of an offense. Instead, it focuses on the breakdown of the emotional relationship between the spouses. These statutes typically require a period of time during which the spouses do not live together. Beyond that, evidence must be adduced to substantiate one or both spouses' claim that the marriage is irretrievably broken. The significance of no-fault divorce lies entirely in the fact that decisions about divorce are no longer the prerogative of the state or church but rather of the married couple.

The passage of no-fault divorce laws in the West is properly viewed as a response to changing behaviors and attitudes. Indeed, social science research has shown that divorce rates began to increase significantly prior to passage of such laws and did not change any more dramatically afterward (Stetson and Wright 1975).

The changes in divorce law and actual divorce behaviors in the West are a reflection of the redefinition of marriage. The economic constraints that once held spouses together have been replaced by more vulnerable and fragile emotional bonds. The availability of gainful employment for women makes marriage less essential and divorce more possible. Indeed, the significant changes in women's social positions and the corresponding changes in normative expectations (i.e., gender) have been the subject of significant sociological research. These changes are recognized as fundamentally altering almost all social institutions. Marriage is no exception.

The redefinition of marriage in the latter twentieth century throughout the West reflects the profound changes in relationships between men and women that have occurred. No longer an economic institution, marriage is now defined by its emotional significance. Love and companionship are not incidentals of the institution. Rather, they are essentials. Meeting these high expectations may be difficult. But sustaining them is certainly more so.

Taken together, the changes in the second half of this century may be summarized as redefining the meaning of marriage. Children are not economic assets. Spouses are not economic necessities. Marriage is a conjugal arrangement where the primary emphasis is on the relationship between husband and wife. The reasons for divorce are direct consequences of the reasons for marriage. As one changes so does the other. Since it is more difficult to accomplish and sustain matrimonial essentials, it is easier to terminate the legal framework surrounding them. Divorce is less costly (both financially, legally, and reputationally) as marriage is more so (in terms of the investments required to accomplish what is expected of it).

## CORRELATES OF DIVORCE

Sociologists have documented a number of demographic and personal characteristics that correlate with the probability of divorce. These include early age at marriage, premarital births, divorce from a previous marriage, and low educa-

tional attainments. Social class is inversely related to divorce, yet wives' employment significantly increases divorce probabilities (see Huber and Spitze 1988 for a review).

Race correlates with divorce—even after controls are imposed for socioeconomic correlates of race—with black individuals having divorce rates approximately twice those of whites. However, such differences associated with race are recent in origin. Not until the late 1950s did significant differences between blacks and whites emerge in divorce, separation, and other marital statuses. Such recency has been taken to suggest that the differences stem from the contemporary rather than historical circumstances. As Cherlin suggests, the recent changes in black Americans' family situations "represent the response of the poorest, most disadvantaged segment of the black population to the social and economic conditions they have faced in our cities over the past few decades" (Cherlin 1981, p. 108). Such an interpretation is consistent with research showing that marriage plays a less significant role in the transition to adulthood for young American women—especially so for black women (Bennett, Bloom, and Craig 1989).

## CONSEQUENCES OF DIVORCE

**For Children.** A central concern of much of the recent research on divorce is how children fare. The answer to this question depends largely on which aspects of children's lives are studied. When attention is focused on children's personal adjustment (self-control, leadership, responsibility, independence, achievement orientation, aggressiveness, and gender-role orientation), the conclusion from research done over the past ten years seems to be that there is an initial deleterious effect—especially for young boys. However, within two or three years, children who have experienced divorce seem to do as well as those who have not (Demo and Acock 1988). This optimistic conclusion is drawn, almost entirely, from cross-sectional studies, often surveys of individuals.

Longitudinal research is now beginning to offer a decidedly less sanguine view of the consequences of divorce for children. Long-term psychological consequences have been described in dramatic terms for children followed a decade after their parents' marriages ended in divorce:

> The cumulative effect of the failing marriage and divorce rose to a crescendo as each child entered young adulthood. It was here, as these young men and women faced the developmental task of establishing love and intimacy, that they most felt the lack of a template for a loving, enduring, and moral relationship between a man and a woman. It was here that anxiety carried over from divorced family relationships threatened to bar the young people's ability to create new, enduring families of their own. The new families that are formed appear vulnerable to the effects of divorce. (Wallerstein and Blakeslee 1989, pp. 297–298)

Sociological longitudinal research on the intergenerational effects of divorce provides even stronger evidence of the negative consequences of divorce. In their socioeconomic attainments, children who experienced their parents' divorce average one to two fewer years of educational attainment than children from intact homes (Krein and Beller 1988; Hetherington, Camara, and Featherman 1983). Such effects are found even after rigorous controls are imposed for such things as race, sex, years since the divorce, age at time of divorce, parental income, parental education, number of siblings, region of residence, educational materials in the home, or the number of years spent in the single-parent family. There are comparable effects of divorce on occupational prestige, income and earnings, and unemployment (Nock 1988).

White women who spent some childhood time in a single-parent family as a result of divorce are 53 percent more likely to have teenage marriages, 111 percent more likely to have teenage births, 164 percent more likely to have premarital births, and 92 percent more likely to experience marital disruptions than are daughters who grew up in two-parent families. The effects for black women are similar, though smaller. Controls for a wide range of background factors have little effect on the negative consequences of divorce. Further, remarriage does not remove these effects of divorce. And there is no difference between those who lived with their fathers and those who lived with mothers after divorce. Experiencing parents' divorce has the same (statistical) consequences as being born to a never-married mother (McLanahan and Bumpass 1988).

Such large and consistent negative effects have eluded simple explanation. Undoubtedly much of the divorce experience is associated with the altered family structure produced—in 90 percent of all cases a single-mother family. Such a structure is lacking in adult role models, in parental supervision, and in hierarchy. On this last dimension, research has shown that divorced women and their children are closer (less distinguished by generational distinctions) to one another than is true in intact families. Parent and child are drawn together more as peers, both struggling to keep the family going. The excessive demands on single parents force them to depend on their children in ways that parents in intact families do not, leading to a more reciprocal dependency relationship (Weiss 1975, 1976). Single mothers are "likely to rely on their children for emotional support and assistance with the practical problems of daily life" (Hetherington, Camara, and Featherman 1983, p. 218). In matters of discipline, single mothers have been found to rely on restrictive (authoritarian as opposed to authoritative) disciplinary methods—restricting the child's freedom and relying on negative sanctions—a pattern psychologists believe reflects a lack of authority on the part of the parent (Hetherington 1972). Whatever else it implies, the lack of generational boundaries means a less hierarchical family and less authoritative generational distinctions.

The institutional contexts within which achievement occurs, however, are decidedly hierarchical in nature. Education, the economy, and occupations are typically bureaucratic structures in which an individual is categorically subordinate to a superior—an arrangement Goffman described as an "echelon authority structure" (1961, p. 42). The nuclear family has been described as producing in children the skills and attitudes necessary for competition within such echelon authority structures. "There is a significant correspondence between the authority relationships in capitalist production and family childrearing. . . . The hierarchical division of labor (in the economy) is merely reflected in family life" (Bowles and Gintis 1976, pp. 144–147). The relative absence of clear subordinate–superordinate relationships in single-parent families has been argued to socialize children inadequately or place them in a disadvantageous position when and if they find themselves in hierarchical organizations.

**For Adults.** A wide range of psychological problems have been noted among divorcing and recently divorced adults. A divorce occasions changes in most every aspect of adult life—residence, friendship networks, economic situation, and parental roles. Marriage in America makes significant contributions to individual well-being. Thus, regardless of the quality of the marriage that ends, emotional distress is a near-universal experience for those who divorce (Weiss 1979). Anxiety, anger, and fear are dominant psychological themes immediately before and after divorce. At least for a year or two after divorce, men and women report psychosomatic symptoms of headaches, loss of appetite, overeating, drinking too much, trembling, smoking more, sleeping problems, and nervousness (Group for the Advancement of Psychiatry 1980).

The emotional problems occasioned by divorce are accompanied by major changes in economic situations, as well, especially for women. The vast majority of those involved in divorce experience a significant decline in their immediate standard of living. This problem is especially acute for women who—in almost 90 percent of cases—assume custody of children. Immediately after a divorce, women suffer an average 30 to 40 percent decline in their overall standards of living (Peterson 1989). Either in anticipation of or as a consequence of divorce, there is typically an increase in divorced women's labor force participation. Ana-

lyzing national longitudinal data, Peterson estimates that one year before the divorce decree (when most divorcing individuals are separated), women's average standard of living (total family income divided by the poverty threshold for a family of a particular size) is 70 percent of its level in the previous year. As a consequence of increased hours worked, the standard of living increases one year after divorce, and by five or six years after divorce "the standard of living of divorced women is about 85 percent of what it had been before separation" (1989, p. 48). Women who have not been employed during their marriages, however, are particularly hard-hit, the majority ending up in poverty.

Child support from fathers is not a solution to the economic problems for two reasons. First, about one-quarter of women due child support receive none. Another one-quarter receive less than the court-ordered amount. In 1985, the average amount of child support received by divorced mothers was $2,538 per year (U.S. Bureau of the Census 1989b). About 13.5 million or 88 percent of the 15.3 million children in single-parent families in 1988 were living with the mother; their average (mean) family income was $11,989, compared with $34,919 for those in single-father situations and $40,067 for children in households where both parents were present (U.S. Bureau of the Census 1989a). Families headed by single mothers are the most likely to be in poverty. In 1987, one-half of all single-mother families were in poverty (compared to fewer than 8 percent of two-parent families). Analyzing national longitudinal data, Greg Duncan concluded that changes in family status—especially divorce and remarriage—are the most important causes of change in family economic well-being and poverty among women and children (Duncan 1984).

Single-parent families in America have grown dramatically as a result of increasing divorce rates. And even though most divorced persons remarry, Bumpass has shown that the average duration of marital separation experienced by children under age eighteen was 6.3 years for whites and 7.5 years for blacks. In fact, 38 percent of white and 73 percent of black children are still in a single-parent family ten years after the marital disruption—a reflection of blacks' lower propensity to remarry and their longer intervals between divorce and remarriage (Bumpass 1984). The role of divorce in the formation of single-parent families differs by race. Among all single-parent white families, 17 percent are maintained by never-married mothers, 42 percent by divorced mothers. Among blacks, the comparable percentages are 54 and 16. Divorce is the primary route to single parenthood for white mothers, whereas out-of-wedlock childbearing is for black mothers (U.S. Bureau of the Census 1989b, p. 14).

Families headed by single women are the poorest of all major demographic groups regardless of how poverty is measured. Combined with frequent changes in residence and in employment following divorce, children and mothers in such households experience significant instabilities—a fact reflected in the higher rates of mental health problems among such women (Garfinkel and McLanahan 1986, pp. 11–17).

## CONCLUSION

High rates of remarriage following divorce clearly indicate that marital disruption does not signify a rejection of marriage. There is no evidence of widespread abandonment of conjugal life by Americans. Admittedly, marriage rates have dropped in recent years. However, such changes are best seen to be the result of higher educational attainments, occupational commitments, and lower fertility expectations, not a rejection of marriage per se. Rather, increasing divorce rates reflect the fact that marriage is increasingly evaluated as an entirely emotional relationship between two persons. Marital breakdown, or the failure of marriage to fulfill emotional expectations, has come increasingly to be a cause for divorce. Since the 1970s, our laws have explicitly recognized this as justification for terminating a marriage—the best evidence we have that love and emotional closeness are the *sine qua non* of modern American marriage. Contemporary divorce rates thus signal

a growing unwillingness to tolerate an unsatisfying emotional conjugal relationship.

The consequences of divorce for children are difficult to disentangle from the predictable changes in household structure. Whether the long-term consequences are produced by the single-parent situation typically experienced for five to ten years, or from the other circumstances surrounding divorce, is not clear. It is quite apparent, however, that divorce occasions significant instabilities in children's and mothers' lives.

Our knowledge about the consequences of divorce for individuals is limited at this time by the absence of controlled studies that compare the divorced to the nondivorced. Virtually all research done to date follows the lives of divorced individuals without comparing them to a comparable group of individuals who have not divorced. A related concern is whether the consequences of divorce reflect the experience itself or whether they reflect various selection effects. That is, are people who divorce different from others to begin with? Are their experiences the results of their divorce or of antecedent factors?

When half of all marriages are predicted to end in divorce, it is clear that martial disruption is a conspicuous feature of our family and kinship system. Divorce creates new varieties of kin not heretofore incorporated in our dominant institutions. The rights and obligations attached to such kinship positions as that of spouse of the noncustodial father are ambiguous—itself a source of problems. The social institution of the family is redefined continuously as a consequence of divorce. Entering marriage, for example, is less commonly the beginning of adult responsibilities. Ending marriage is less commonly the consequence of death. Parents are not necessarily coresidents with their children. And new categories of "quasi" kin are invented to accommodate the complex connections among previously married spouses and their new spouses and children. In many ways, divorce itself has become a dominant institution in American society. It is, however, significantly less structured by consensual normative beliefs than the family institutions to which it is allied.

(SEE ALSO: *Marriage; Marriage and Divorce Rates; Remarriage*)

## REFERENCES

Bennett, Neil G., David E. Bloom, and Patricia H. Craig 1989 "The Divergence of Black and White Marriage Patterns." *American Journal of Sociology* 95:692–772.

Bowles, Samuel, and Herbert Gintis 1976 *Schooling in Capitalist America*. New York: Basic Books.

Bumpass, Larry L. 1984 "Children and Marital Disruption: A Replication and Update." *Demography* 21:71–82.

Cherlin, Andrew J. 1981 *Marriage, Divorce, and Remarriage*. Cambridge, Mass.: Harvard University Press.

Degler, Carl N. 1980 *At Odds: Women and the Family in America from the Revolution to the Present*. New York: Oxford University Press.

Demo, David H., and Alan C. Acock 1988 "The Impact of Divorce on Children." *Journal of Marriage and the Family* 50:619–648.

Duncan, Greg J. 1984 *Years of Poverty, Years of Plenty*. Ann Arbor: University of Michigan, Institute for Social Research.

Garfinkel, Irwin, and Sara S. McLanahan 1986 *Single Mothers and Their Children*. Washington, D.C.: The Urban Institute Press.

Goffman, Erving 1961 *Asylums*. New York: Anchor.

Group for the Advancement of Psychiatry 1980 *Divorce, Child Custody, and the Family*. San Francisco: Jossey-Bass.

Hetherington, E. Mavis 1972 "Effects of Paternal Absence on Personality Development in Adolescent Daughters." *Developmental Psychology* 7:313–326.

Hetherington, E. M., K. A. Camara, and D. L. Featherman 1983 "Achievement and Intellectual Functioning of Children in One Parent Households." In J. T. Spence, ed., *Achievement and Achievement Motives*. San Francisco: W. H. Freeman.

Huber, Joan, and Glenna Spitze 1988 "Trends in Family Sociology." In N. J. Smelser, ed., *Handbook of Sociology*. Beverly Hills, Calif.: Sage.

Krein, Sheila F., and Andrea H. Beller 1988 "Educational Attainment of Children from Single-Parent Families: Differences by Exposure, Gender, and Race." *Demography* 25:221–234.

Martin, Teresa C., and Larry L. Bumpass 1989 "Recent Trends in Marital Disruption." *Demography* 26:37–51.

McLanahan, Sara S., and Larry Bumpass 1988 "Intergenerational Consequences of Family Disruption." *American Journal of Sociology* 94:130–152.

Nock, Steven L. 1988 "The Family and Hierarchy." *Journal of Marriage and the Family* 50:957–966.

Peterson, Richard R. 1989 *Women, Work, and Divorce*. Albany: State University of New York Press.

Phillips, Roderick 1988 *Putting Asunder: A History of Divorce in Western Society*. New York: Cambridge University Press.

Stetson, Dorothy M., and Gerald C. Wright, Jr. 1975 "The Effects of Law on Divorce in American States." *Journal of Marriage and the Family* 37:537–547.

U.S. Bureau of the Census 1975 *Historical Statistics of the United States: Colonial Times to 1970. Part I*. Washington, D.C.: U.S. Government Printing Office.

——— 1989a "Child Support and Alimony: 1985." *Current Population Reports*. Series P-23, No. 154. Washington, D.C.: U.S. Government Printing Office.

——— 1989b "Studies in Marriage and the Family." Current Population Reports, Series P-23, No. 162. Washington, D.C.: U.S. Government Posting Office.

Wallerstein, Judith S., and Sandra Blakeslee, 1989. *Second Chances: Men, Women, and Children a Decade After Divorce*. 1989. New York: Ticknor and Fields.

Weiss, Robert 1975 *Marital Separation*. New York: Basic Books.

——— 1976 "The Emotional Impact of Marital Separation." *Journal of Social Issues* 32:135–145.

——— 1979 *Going It Alone: The Family Life and Social Situation of the Single Parent*. New York: Basic Books.

STEVEN L. NOCK

**DRAMATURGY** Dramaturgy is a social-psychological perspective used to study social life. Its unique insight is that daily social interaction consists of performances, in which individuals stage or present themselves to others. In this sense, then, everyday life is theater: full of drama, consisting of roles, costuming, rehearsal, staging, and, of course, an audience. More than a metaphor, however, dramaturgy is an analytical tool to advance understanding, a special perspective attempting to answer the Hobbesian question: How is society possible?

Dramaturgical analysis is concerned with everyday life and its taken-for-granted interactions. Although dramaturgy is closely related to two other important social-psychological areas, phenomenology and ethnomethodology, these will not be discussed here. In addition, it is acknowledged that dramaturgy and symbolic interaction are closely related areas, concerned with interactional processes and the creation and maintenance of the self by means of language and symbols. The two are not, however, synonymous. Symbolic interaction is a broad subarea of social psychology that frequently uses dramaturgy as an analytical device. Dramaturgy, therefore, is best viewed as a subarea of symbolic interaction (Hare 1985). Consequently, this essay is confined to an overview of dramaturgy itself that touches briefly on its major concepts and primary contributors.

The historical foundations of dramaturgy come from the pragmatic philosophy of John Dewey (1922) and George Herbert Mead (1932), who shared an impatience with speculative ideas having no practical value for daily life. Both saw a connection between ideas and problem-solving action. Meaning, it was argued, is socially constructed. In fact, the mind itself is a social creation that could not exist if not for shared understanding and communication. Mead also thought that a person's self-concept is a reflection of the opinion of others. Consequently, society provides a looking glass in which people discover who they are. Another contribution of Mead's is the idea that the self contains an "I," or nonreflective, subjective, spontaneous aspect of the self, and a "me," the reflective, objective, evaluative aspect of the self. The two are interdependent parts of the self-concept. The dramaturgist argues that individuals will use various strategies in their interactions with others to preserve and gain support for their self-concept.

The individual most often associated with dramaturgy is Erving Goffman, who used the theater as a metaphor in his book *The Presentation of Self in Everyday Life* (1959). Throughout his career Goffman explored all aspects of the most fundamental, daily interaction, from the attempts by mental patients to "pass" for normal to the backstage behavior of clerks imitating their customers (1961a, 1961b, 1963, 1967, 1974). In a summary of Goffman's contribution, Brisset and Edgley (1990) assert that "Goffman was about guises, semblances, veneers, surfaces, illusions, images, shells, and acts. He was not . . . about substances, things, facts, truths, and depths" (p. 37). Goffman's original work laid out basic concepts that are still being refined and used today. In addition to the self, major concepts to be discussed here include role, definition of the situation, impression management, expressions given, and expressions given off.

Roles are a necessary part of the theatrical metaphor. Yet long before Goffman, both Cooley (1902) and Mead (1932) recognized that an important part of socialization for children is the learning of roles. Dramaturgical researchers try to understand the intricate web of role relationships established through a theatrical (dramatic) process. For example, Haas and Shaffir (1982) examined the process by which individuals learn the role of doctor and, thus, become professionals. How does one become a professional doctor? According to these authors, by learning the vocabulary and convincing others (the patients) of their legitimate right to authority. "Symbolic changes in wardrobe or costume, props, script, and demeanor both affirm the new role and identity and help sustain it. Audiences legitimate the performances and thus help to shape the emerging professional identity and changing conception of self" (Haas and Shaffir 1982, p. 200). A study by Gillespie (1980) analyzed the role of politicians' wives. She describes how wives function as part of the impression management of their husbands' roles as public officials. This study demonstrates the recognition by dramaturgists that people work together (in teams) to protect the image another (a team member) is trying to create, thus, preserving the self that is being created.

These two research examples demonstrate the importance of two major dramaturgical concepts: impression management and definition of the situation. *Impression management* refers to the individual's need to control the impressions others have of him/her. One way to do this is to control the definition of the situation. Thomas (1973) first used the term *definition of the situation* in the early 1920s. He noted that situations demand responses from individuals. First, however, individuals must define the situation, which involves an agreement or working consensus on the part of the individuals involved. For example, both doctor and patient must agree that the situation is a medical examination. The doctor assists in this definition by presenting him/herself as a professional ready to conduct a physical examination. The audience, in this case the patient, can either agree or not agree with the doctor's definition of the situation, on the basis of the credibility of the doctor's performance. The performance is composed of his/her expressions given and expressions given off. Goffman (1959) defines *expressions given* as verbal communication only, while *expressions given off* refers to an extensive category of nonverbal cues (such as a white uniform, medical forms) that the audience can use to judge the individual's presentation.

From the preceding it is clear that the dramaturgist assumes that people are active participants in the creation and presentation of self to others via impression management. Impression management techniques include manipulation of stage props (such as clothing, appearance), the stage or setting, and role performance in order to control both impressions and definitions of the situation. Even other individuals can be important in the presentation of self, as in the case of presidents' wives. These strategies are the essence of impression management (Goffman 1959). This is not to suggest that people consciously seek to manipulate others or to exploit them. Instead, social interactions are an attempt to communicate and to present the self in a way fitting with the individual's definition of the situation. The individual assumes (if the performance is good) that the audience will accept and agree with this definition, and accept the self being presented.

Long before Goffman, dramaturgy was appealing as a metaphor. As his work and the work of others demonstrate, there are many observations to make about social life, using dramaturgy as a qualitative tool. Gross (1986), for example, did a historical analysis of public dramas (for example, pageants such as those depicting the French Revolution). He concluded that such public displays symbolize tradition and loyalty and emphasize solidarity but, more important, demonstrate that power must be presented, via drama, to the public to be legitimated. Consequently, presentation is not confined to the self but can involve larger, community values and ideals.

However, if dramaturgy is to have a future, it must move beyond the analogy, and use its understanding of social life to generate testable hypotheses for those committed to quantitative methods. As Brisset and Edgley (1990) and Stryker (1987) note, dramaturgy is not a theory. Instead, it is descriptive in nature, not explanatory. Nevertheless, a complete description of social life is central to sociology, especially as it leads to what Weber called *verstehen*, sympathetic understanding of everyday life. As Perinbanayagam states, "but for drama, there will not be any communication, and without communication there cannot be interaction; and without interaction there can be no social fact or social structure; and without social facts and social structure, there is no such thing as the sociological argument" (1974, p. 536).

(SEE ALSO: *Symbolic Interaction*)

## REFERENCES

Brisset, D., and C. Edgley (eds.) 1990 *Life as Theater: A Dramaturgical Sourcebook*. New York: Aldine/de Gruyter.

Cooley, C. H. 1902 *Human Nature and the Social Order*. New York: Scribners.

Dewey, J. 1922 "On Motive." In his *Human Nature and Conduct*. New York: Holt.

Gallant, M. J., and S. Kleinman 1983 "Symbolic Interactionism vs. Ethnomethodology." *Symbolic Interaction* 6, no. 1:1–18.

Gillespie, J. B. 1980 "The Phenomenon of the Public Wife: An Exercise in Goffman's Impression Management." *Symbolic Interaction* 3, no. 2:109–125.

Goffman, E. 1959 *The Presentation of Self in Everyday Life*. New York: Doubleday/Anchor.

——— 1961a *Asylums*. Garden City, N.Y.: Doubleday.

——— 1961b *Encounters*. Indianapolis: Bobbs-Merrill.

———— 1963 *Stigma.* Englewood Cliffs, N.J.: Prentice-Hall.

———— 1967 *Interaction Ritual.* Garden City, N.Y.: Anchor.

———— 1974 *Frame Analysis—An Essay on the Organization of Experience.* Cambridge, Mass.: Harvard University Press.

Gross, E. 1986 "The Social Construction of Historical Events through Public Dramas." *Symbolic Interaction* 9, no. 2:179–200.

Haas, J., and W. Shaffir 1982 "Taking on the Role of Doctor: A Dramaturgical Analysis of Professionalization." *Symbolic Interaction* 5, no. 2:187–203.

Hare, A. P. 1985 *Social Interaction as Drama.* Beverly Hills, Calif.: Sage.

Mead, G. H. 1932 *Mind, Self and Society.* Chicago: University of Chicago Press.

Perinbanayagam, R. S. 1974 "The Definition of the Situation: An Analysis of the Ethnomethodological and Dramaturgical View." *The Sociological Quarterly* 15:521–541.

———— 1987 "Drama in Everyday Life." *Studies in Symbolic Interaction* 8:121–141.

Stryker, S. 1987 "The Theatrical Metaphor: Can It Aid Conflict Resolution?" *Contemporary Psychology* 32, no. 7:602–603.

Thomas, William I. 1973 "Life History." Published by P. J. Baker in *American Journal of Sociology* 79, no. 2:243–250.

KATHLEEN A. WARNER

**DRUG ABUSE** Drug abuse is the use of an illicit drug, such as heroin, or the use of a licit substance, such as barbiturates, outside of medical supervision. The substance is taken to modify or maintain a mood and may be potentially harmful to the person or to society. *Abuse* is a term that has been developed and widely used in the United States; *drug dependence* is frequently employed in other countries.

Dependence is defined as a state, psychic and sometimes also physical, characterized by a compulsion to take a drug either continually or periodically, to experience its psychic effects, or to avoid the discomfort of its absence. A person may be dependent on a stimulant (e.g., cocaine), a depressant (e.g., heroin), or a hallucinogen (e.g., LSD). It is more useful to speak of "hard" and "soft" use of drugs than of "hard" or "soft" drugs.

"Addiction" characterizes many people's reactions to opioids, barbiturates, and alcohol. It includes three dimensions: tolerance, or the body's need for increasing doses of the drug; withdrawal, or a predictable physical response when the product is not available; and habituation, or a psychological need for the drug. In some contexts, "addiction" is used to communicate loss of control because of drug use.

There is a perennial debate over whether the drug problem is or ought to be considered a crime or a disease. The U.S. Supreme Court (*Robinson v. California,* 1972) has classified narcotic addiction as a disease that a person cannot control and for which a penalty would represent cruel and unusual punishment. Creation of the National Institute on Drug Abuse in 1973 represented the federal government's formal recognition of drug abuse as a health problem. However, possession or sale of specific substances is handled by the criminal justice system.

The United Nations has a system for coordinating world licit production of opiates, although there has always been illicit production in countries like Turkey, Mexico, and Laos. Most countries, including the United States, subscribe to the 1961 Single Convention on Narcotic Drugs, which deals with opiates, cocaine, and marijuana. In 1971, the Convention on Psychotropic Substances established international controls on amphetamines, barbiturates, and other sedatives and some tranquilizers. The international controls regulate the amount of each medicinally important substance that may be grown or manufactured, in accordance with the world medical requirements for the substance.

There are federal and state laws prohibiting the possession or sale of a wide range of substances and providing prison sentences, fines, or both for violation of the laws. The Drug Enforcement Administration classifies mood-modifying substances into five schedules, with schedule I having the least medical utility and being the most dangerous (e.g., heroin) and schedule V the most medically useful and least subject to abuse (e.g., cold medications that include codeine). Schedule II includes licit substances that may be abused, such as tranquilizers and cocaine. State laws generally are similar to federal laws in terms of the control of mood-modifying substances. Typically, federal agents pursue larger traffickers, and state authorities prosecute lesser distributors and users.

How many drug abusers are there? Each country would answer this question differently, in terms of the substances involved and the frequency of their use. Someone who has only taken a drug once, or is an occasional social-recreational user, is a different kind of user from a person who ingests a substance daily. A person who smokes marijuana is considered differently from one who injects cocaine intravenously. A controlled user who is functioning effectively in a noncriminal setting would be perceived differently from a compulsive user who is heavily involved in a criminal subculture.

The level of drug use is higher in the United States than in any other industrial nation. More than one half of American youth try an illicit drug before they finish high school. An estimated 14.5 million Americans used a drug illicitly in the month prior to a national household survey in 1988. At least one million persons are regular and heavy dysfunctional users of heroin or cocaine. Males are substantially more likely than females to use illegal drugs. Young adults are the age group most likely to use mood-modifying drugs. Drug use is now pervasive in all socioeconomic groups, although cocaine users are most heavily concentrated in urban minority areas.

Overall, drug use has been declining since approximately 1985. The announcement of a national war on drugs, coordinated by a cabinet-level executive in 1989, was typical of previous government responses to a drug problem in that it began after the problem had peaked.

Americans have been taking drugs to modify moods since the Civil War. Until the early twentieth century, many women used opiates that were significant ingredients in patent medicines. When the Harrison Act was passed in 1914, possession of narcotic drugs without a doctor's prescription became illegal. From 1918 through the 1930s, the typical narcotic addict was a white itinerant farm worker in the South.

The modern drug problem began to take shape in the late 1940s, when several large cities reported an epidemic of heroin use among male minority teenagers. This epidemic continued until 1964, when middle class youths became involved. It continued to attract new users steadily until 1974. In the late 1960s, substantial numbers of American military personnel in Vietnam became regular users of the high-quality inexpensive heroin available there. In order to cope with these and other drug problems, President Nixon, in 1971, appointed a Commission on Marijuana and Drug Abuse (1973), the report of which still influences current policy.

Marijuana, which became illegal in 1937, rapidly became a favorite among minorities, musicians, and a number of deviant groups. In the 1960s, it became popular with high school and college students as a symbol of generational conflict, and its use expanded until 1975.

Powdered cocaine had been a moderately popular drug, the use of which was restricted by its high cost, since the 1960s. By 1985, in the form of "crack" crystals, which were smoked in a special pipe, it became the drug of choice among urban minorities, especially young people. As a result of the epidemic of crack use, drug abuse had become the country's most important social problem by 1990.

The amount of crime in which drug abusers engage in order to get money for drugs is a major contributor to the salience of the drug problem. A number of studies have quantified the relationship between crime and drugs. Over an eleven-year period in Baltimore, a sample of 243 male addicts averaged over 2,000 offenses per person. They engaged in six times more criminal activity when addicted than when they were not on drugs. The measure of "crime-days per week at risk" is used to identify a day in which at least one crime is committed (Winick 1983).

Criminal activity by drug abusers has been classified into a variety of "hustles" (Hanson et al. 1985). They may be opportunistic, such as stealing; skilled, such as picking pockets; or drug-related, such as selling drugs. The likelihood that any specific crime of a drug user will result in arrest is very slight. An increase in the price of illegal drugs leads to an increase in the crime rate; a 10 percent increase in illegal drug prices is associated with a 1.1 percent increase in the crime rate.

In order to estimate the proportion of criminals who are drug abusers, a program of urine testing of samples of men and women arrested for all offenses in twenty-one cities has been conducted (National Institute of Justice 1990). The range of positive tests was from 53 to 84 percent for males and 42 to 90 percent for females, with cocaine the most frequently detected drug for both men and women. Thus, the overwhelming majority of arrested persons, at least in recent years, has consisted of users of illegal drugs.

Prior to the 1960s, drug users tended to prefer and use one substance such as marijuana, heroin, or amphetamines. Beginning in the late 1960s, polydependence became the norm. A drug-dependent person might have a specific drug of choice but typically would use other substances, depending on the drug's availability, the individual's access to money, police action, the setting, and similar factors. A large proportion and perhaps even a majority of drug-dependent persons would use alcohol to reinforce or ease the effect of other drugs or instead of other drugs. Polydependent users typically use substances that are chemically analogous to each other or are cross-tolerant, so that a barbiturate user may take alcohol, since the two substances are both depressants.

The drug of choice changes from year to year and from region to region, depending on price, availability, law enforcement efforts, fads, and socioeconomic status of the users. A drug may become less popular but still remain available in a community and reemerge in the future. Thus, heroin was supplanted by cocaine in many urban areas in the mid-1980s but began reemerging as a preferred drug by 1990. Mood-modifying drugs do not vanish completely but enjoy cycles of popularity and unpopularity.

Individuals progress through identifiable developmental stages in the use of licit and illicit drugs from adolescence through young adulthood, when the period of risk for initiation into drugs usually terminates. In men, alcohol precedes marijuana; alcohol and marijuana precede other illicit drugs; alcohol, cigarettes, and marijuana precede prescribed psychoactive drugs. In women, either alcohol or cigarettes precede marijuana; alcohol, cigarettes, and marijuana precede other illicit drugs; alcohol and either cigarettes or marijuana precede prescribed psychoactive drugs (Yamaguchi and Kandel 1984).

A considerable number of drug abusers stop taking drugs, on a permanent basis, often without experiencing treatment. This process of "maturing out," analogous to what happens to delinquents, involves an interaction between individual factors and the environment (Winick 1979). The self-limiting nature of much drug abuse has been a contributor to some sociologists' urging that legislation of drug use be adopted as a national policy. Others argue that legalization or decriminalization pose many problems, but they are less serious than the huge costs and uncertain outcome of current policy, which is to punish and eliminate illegal drug use (Reinarman and Levine 1989).

Recent American policy has been what may be characterized as liberal hard-line. It is liberal in that drug abusers are encouraged to seek treatment, for which there is considerable federal and state funding. It is hard-line in that there is vigorous law enforcement, which receives the bulk of the available funding, and because prevention programs actively discourage young people from beginning or continuing drug use. This policy has been dominant since the report of the President's Commission on Marijuana and Drug Abuse.

American policy views all drugs of abuse as undesirable and is directed at eliminating such use. The policy is based on the concept that any drug can be a gateway to a more dangerous substance so that the use of all such substances is discouraged. Eleven states have decriminalized possession of small quantities of marijuana for personal use, with no significant accompanying increase in the use of other mood-modifying drugs. On the federal level, however, there is consistent opposition to any attempt to liberalize the laws against possession of marijuana.

Community programs to cope with drug abuse typically have three components: interdiction and control of the supply, prevention and education, and treatment. The policy of the federal and local governments has always been to concentrate primarily on control by attempting to interdict supply and arrest sellers and users. Treatment is a secondary priority, and prevention has been a minimal goal. Control programs have never been able to have a significant impact on the problem; treatment approaches are able to engage only a small proportion of abusers and cannot be targeted to specific clients with significant accuracy; and prevention efforts have not been conducted for long enough to have established their efficacy.

There are three major kinds of treatment: pharmacotherapy, therapeutic communities, and outpatient counseling. Most pharmacotherapy consists of methadone maintenance for heroin users, replacing heroin with methadone, a longer-acting opiate that does not give a "high" and enables the patient to function. Therapeutic communities, such as Daytop and Phoenix House, usually require twelve to eighteen months of residence in a total institution with rigid rules of progression through several (usually three or four) stages. Therapeutic communities treat users of all kinds of drugs, and the reasons for their success have been studied by some prominent sociologists (Volkman and Cressey 1963).

Outpatient counseling, also used for all kinds of drug users, probably accounts for approximately three-fifths of all treatment, pharmacotherapy represents approximately three-tenths, and residential programs service one-tenth of the users. Drug dependence is a chronic relapsing condition, so that it is common for a person to revert to drug use after treatment.

During the 1980s, it became clear that acquired immunodeficiency syndrome (AIDS) was transmitted to many people by the use of previously contaminated needles in intravenous injection of various drugs, especially heroin. In cities like New York, two-thirds of AIDS cases result from use of contaminated needles, mostly by heterosexuals. Nationally, approximately one-fourth to one-third of AIDS cases can be attributed to drug abusers' use of contaminated needles.

Sociologists' interest in drug abuse has been increasing because of a growing recognition of the significant role of culture and social structure in the genesis and continuation of drug abuse. Sociologists are actively involved in evaluating the effectiveness of treatment and prevention programs, in estimating the impact and costs of current policies, in conducting cross-cultural investigations, and in conducting surveys and ethnographic studies of epidemiology. Sociologists have also addressed the issue of national policy toward the drug abuse problem (Winick 1974).

(SEE ALSO: *Alcoholism; Criminalization of Deviance*)

## REFERENCES

Commission on Marijuana and Drug Abuse 1973 *Final Report*. Washington, D.C.: U.S. Government Printing Office.

Hanson, B., G. Beschner, J. M. Walters, and E. Bovelle 1985 *Life with Heroin: Voices from the Inner City*. Lexington, Mass.: Lexington Books.

National Institute of Justice 1990 *Drug Use Forecasting*. Washington, D.C.: U.S. Department of Justice.

Reinarman, C., and H. G. Levine 1989 "Crack in Context: Politics and Media in the Making of a Drug Scare." *Contemporary Drug Problems* 18:535–577.

Volkman, R., and D. R. Cressey 1963 "Differential Association and the Rehabilitation of Drug Addicts." *American Journal of Sociology* 69:129–142.

Winick, C. 1979 "The Drug Offender." In H. Toch, ed., *Psychology of Crime and Criminal Justice*. New York: Holt, Rinehart and Winston.

——— 1983 "Addicts and Alcoholics as Victimizers." In D. E. J. MacNamara and A. Karmen, eds., *Deviants: Victims or Victimizers?* Beverly Hills, Calif.: Sage Publications.

——— (ed.) 1974 *Sociological Aspects of Drug Dependence*. Cleveland: CRC Press.

Yamaguchi, K., and D. B. Kandel 1984 "Patterns of Drug Use from Adolescence to Young Adulthood: II. Sequences of Progression." *American Journal of Public Health* 74:668–672.

CHARLES WINICK